CURRENT ISSUES and ENDURING QUESTIONS

A Guide to Critical Thinking
and Argument, with Readings

NINTH EDITION

CURRENT ISSUES and ENDURING QUESTIONS

A Guide to Critical Thinking and Argument, with Readings

SYLVAN BARNET
Professor of English, Tufts University

HUGO BEDAU
Professor of Philosophy, Tufts University

Bedford/St. Martin's   BOSTON ◆ NEW YORK

For Bedford / St. Martin's

Developmental Editor: Adam Whitehurst
Production Editor: Kerri A. Cardone
Assistant Production Manager: Joe Ford
Marketing Manager: Molly Parke
Editorial Assistants: Shannon Walsh and Nicholas McCarthy
Copyeditor: Karen Stocz
Senior Art Director: Anna Palchik
Text Design: Linda M. Robertson
Cover Design: Donna Lee Dennison
Cover Art: © Hitomi Hokada/amanaimages/Corbis
Composition: Glyph International
Printing and Binding: RR Donnelley and Sons

President: Joan E. Feinberg
Editorial Director: Denise B. Wydra
Editor in Chief: Karen S. Henry
Director of Marketing: Karen R. Soeltz
Director of Editing, Design, and Production: Susan W. Brown
Associate Director of Editorial Production: Elise S. Kaiser
Managing Editor: Elizabeth M. Schaaf

Library of Congress Control Number: 2010920484

For information, write: Bedford/St. Martin's, 75 Arlington Street, Boston, MA 02116
(617-399-4000)

ISBN-10: 0–312–54732–3
ISBN-13: 978–0–312–54732–5

Acknowledgments

Edward Abbey, "Eco-Defense," from *One Life at a Time, Please* by Edward Abbey. Copyright © 1988 by Edward Abbey. Reprinted by arrangement with Henry Holt and Company, LLC.
Jean AbiNader, "No, Racial Profiling is Not Acceptable." *CQ Researcher* 12/14/01 Copyright © 2001 CQ Press, a division of SAGE Publications, Inc. Reprinted by permission.
Paul R. Abramson, "Romantic Relationships Between Faculty and Students: Should College Prohibit Them?" *Boston Globe*, September 30, 2007. Copyright © 2007. Reprinted by permission.

Acknowledgments and copyrights are continued at the back of the book on pages 1014–1019, which constitute an extension of the copyright page. It is a violation of the law to reproduce these selections by any means whatsoever without the written permission of the copyright holder.

Preface

This book is a text—a book about reading other people's arguments and writing your own arguments—and it is also an anthology—a collection of more than a hundred selections, ranging from Plato to the present, with a strong emphasis on contemporary arguments. In a moment we will be a little more specific about what sorts of essays we include, but first we want to mention our chief assumptions about the aims of a course that might use *Current Issues and Enduring Questions: A Guide to Critical Thinking and Argument, with Readings.*

Probably most students and instructors would agree that, as **critical readers,** students should be able to

- Summarize accurately an argument they have read;
- Locate the thesis (the claim) of an argument;
- Locate the assumptions, stated and unstated;
- Analyze and evaluate the strength of the evidence and the soundness of the reasoning offered in support of the thesis; and
- Analyze, evaluate, and account for discrepancies among various readings on a topic (for example, explain why certain facts are used, why probable consequences of a proposed action are examined or are ignored, or why two sources might interpret the same facts differently).

Probably, too, students and instructors would agree that, as **thoughtful writers,** students should be able to

- Imagine an audience and write effectively for it (for instance, by using the appropriate tone and providing the appropriate amount of detail);
- Present information in an orderly and coherent way;

- Be aware of their own assumptions;
- Locate sources and incorporate them into their own writing, not simply by quoting extensively or by paraphrasing but also by having digested material so that they can present it in their own words;
- Properly document all borrowings—not merely quotations and paraphrases but also borrowed ideas; and
- Do all these things in the course of developing a thoughtful argument of their own.

In the first edition of this book we quoted Edmund Burke and John Stuart Mill. Burke said,

> He that wrestles with us strengthens our nerves, and sharpens our skill. Our antagonist is our helper.

Mill said,

> He who knows only his own side of the cause knows little.

These two quotations continue to reflect the view of argument that underlies this text: In writing an essay one is engaging in a serious effort to know what one's own ideas are and, having found them, to contribute to a multisided conversation. One is not setting out to trounce an opponent, and that is partly why such terms as *marshaling evidence, attacking an opponent,* and *defending a thesis* are misleading. True, on television talk shows we see right-wingers and left-wingers who have made up their minds and who are concerned only with pushing their own views and brushing aside all others. But in an academic community, and indeed in our daily lives, we learn

- by listening to others and also
- by listening to ourselves.

We draft a response to something we have read, and in the very act of drafting we may find—if we think critically about the words we are putting down on paper—we are changing (perhaps slightly, perhaps radically) our own position. In short, one reason that we write is so that we can improve our ideas. And even if we do not drastically change our views, we and our readers at least come to a better understanding of why we hold the views we do.

FEATURES

The Text

Parts One and Two   Part One, Critical Thinking and Reading (Chapters 1–4), and Part Two, Critical Writing (Chapters 5–7), together offer a short course in methods of thinking about and writing arguments. By "thinking" we mean serious analytic thought, including analysis of one's own assumptions (Chapter 1); by "writing" we mean the use of effective, respectable techniques, not gimmicks (such as the notorious note a politician scribbled in the margin of the text of his speech: "Argument weak; shout here"). For a delightfully wry account of the use of gimmicks, we recommend that you consult "The Art of Controversy" in *The Will to Live* by the nineteenth-century German philosopher Arthur Schopenhauer. Schopenhauer reminds readers that a Greek or Latin quotation (however irrelevant) can be impressive to the uninformed and that one can knock down almost any proposition by loftily saying, "That's all very well in theory, but it won't do in practice."

We offer lots of advice about how to set forth an argument, but we do not offer instruction in one-upmanship. Rather, we discuss responsible ways of arguing persuasively. We know, however, that before one can write a persuasive argument, one must clarify one's own ideas — a process that includes arguing with oneself — to find out what one really thinks about a problem. Therefore, we devote Chapter 1 to critical thinking, Chapters 2, 3, and 4 to critical reading (Chapter 4 is about reading images), and Chapters 5, 6, and 7 to critical writing.

Parts One and Two together contain thirty-six readings (seven are student papers) for analysis and discussion. Some of these essays originated as op-ed newspaper pieces, and we reprint some of the letters to the editor that they generated, so students can easily see several sides to a given issue and in their own responses they can, so to speak, join the conversation. (We have found, by the way, that the format of a letter helps students to frame their ideas, and therefore in later chapters we occasionally suggest writing assignments in the form of a letter to the editor. In Chapter 10 we reprint three letters written by Randy Cohen of the *New York Times Magazine*, and we invite students to write their own responses.)

All of the essays in the book are accompanied by Topics for Critical Thinking and Writing.[1] This is not surprising, given the emphasis we place on asking questions in order to come up with ideas for writing. Among the chief questions that writers should ask, we suggest, are "What is *X*?" and "What is the value of *X*?" (pp. 230–34). By asking such questions — for instance (to look only at these two types of questions), "Is the fetus a person?" or "Is Arthur Miller a better playwright than Tennessee Williams?" — a writer probably will find ideas coming, at least after a few moments of head scratching. The device of developing an argument by identifying issues is, of course, nothing new. Indeed, it goes back to an ancient method of argument used by classical rhetoricians, who identified a *stasis* (an issue) and then asked questions about it: Did *X* do such-and-such? If so, was the

---

[1]With a few exceptions, the paragraphs in the essays are, for ease of reference, numbered in increments of five (5, 10, 15, and so on). The exceptions involve essays in which paragraphs are uncommonly long: In such cases, every paragraph is numbered.

action bad? If bad, how bad? (Finding an issue or *stasis*—a position where one stands—by asking questions is discussed in Chapter 6.)

In keeping with our emphasis on writing as well as reading, we raise issues not only of what can roughly be called the "content" of the essays but also of what can (equally roughly) be called the "style"—that is, the *ways* in which the arguments are set forth. Content and style, of course, cannot finally be kept apart. As Cardinal Newman said, "Thought and meaning are inseparable from each other. . . . *Style is thinking out into language.*" In our Topics for Critical Thinking and Writing we sometimes ask the student

- to evaluate the effectiveness of an essay's opening paragraph,
- to explain a shift in tone from one paragraph to the next, or
- to characterize the persona of the author as revealed in the whole essay.

In short, the book is not designed as an introduction to some power-ful ideas (though in fact it is that, too); it is designed as an aid to *writing* thoughtful, effective arguments on important political, social, scientific, ethical, legal, and religious issues.

The essays reprinted in this book also illustrate different styles of argument that arise, at least in part, from the different disciplinary back-grounds of the various authors. Essays by journalists, lawyers, judges, social scientists, policy analysts, philosophers, critics, activists, and other writers—including first-year undergraduates—will be found in these pages. The authors develop and present their views in arguments that have distinctive features reflecting their special training and concerns. The differences in argumentative styles found in these essays foreshadow the differences students will encounter in the readings assigned in many of their other courses.

Parts One and Two, then, are a preliminary (but we hope substan-tial) discussion of such topics as

- identifying assumptions
- getting ideas by means of invention strategies
- finding, evaluating, and citing printed and electronic sources
- interpreting visual sources
- evaluating kinds of evidence, and
- organizing material

as well as an introduction to some ways of thinking.

Part Three   Part Three, Further Views on Argument, consists of Chapters 8 through 14.

- Chapter 8, A Philosopher's View: The Toulmin Model, is a summary of the philosopher Stephen Toulmin's method for analyzing arguments.

This summary will assist those who wish to apply Toulmin's methods to the readings in our book.

- Chapter 9, A Logician's View: Deduction, Induction, Fallacies, offers a more rigorous analysis of these topics than is usually found in composition courses and reexamines from a logician's point of view material already treated briefly in Chapter 3.

- Chapter 10, A Moralist's View: Ways of Thinking Ethically, consists of a discussion of amoral, immoral, and moral reasoning, A Checklist for Moral Reasoning, two challenging essays, and three short responses to highly specific moral questions.

- Chapter 11, A Lawyer's View: Steps toward Civic Literacy, introduces students to some basic legal concepts such as the distinction between civil and criminal cases, and then gives majority and minority opinions in two cases: burning the flag, searching students for drugs and establishing the right to an abortion. We accompany these judicial opinions with questions that invite the student to participate in these exercises in democracy.

- Chapter 12, A Psychologist's View: Rogerian Argument, with an essay by psychotherapist Carl R. Rogers and an essay by a student, complements the discussion of audience, organization, and tone in Chapter 6.

- Chapter 13, A Literary Critic's View: Arguing about Literature, should help students to see the things literary critics argue about and *how* they argue. Students can apply what they learn not only to the literary readings that appear in the chapter (poems by Robert Frost and Andrew Marvell and a story by Kate Chopin) but also to the readings that appear in Part Six, Enduring Questions: Essays, a Story, Poems, and a Play. Finally, Part Three concludes with

- Chapter 14, A Debater's View: Individual Oral Presentations and Debate, which introduces students to standard presentation strategies and debate format.

The Anthology

Part Four Current Issues: Occasions for Debate (Chapters 15–20), begins with some comments on binary thinking. It then gives a Checklist for Analyzing a Debate and reprints six pairs of arguments — on obesity (who is responsible?), the Equal Rights Amendment (do we need it?), genetic modification of human beings, airport security and racial profiling, romantic relationships between faculty and students, and single-sex classrooms. Here, as elsewhere in the book, many of the selections (drawn from popular journals and newspapers) are very short — scarcely longer than the 500-word essays that students are often asked to write.

Thus, students can easily study the *methods* the writers use, as well as the issues themselves.

Part Five   Current Issues: Casebooks (Chapters 21–31) presents eleven chapters on issues discussed by several writers. For example, the first case-book concerns the nature and purpose of a college education: Is college an ivory tower (Stanley Fish takes this position), or a place where students learn citizenship, or a place for vocational training, or some combination of these?

Part Six   Enduring Questions: Essays, a Story, Poems, and a Play (Chapters 32–34), extends the arguments to three topics: Chapter 32, What Is the Ideal Society? (the eight voices here range from Thomas More, Thomas Jefferson, and Martin Luther King Jr., to literary figures W. H. Auden, Langston Hughes, and Ursula K. Le Guin); Chapter 33, How Free Is the Will of the Individual within Society? (among the authors are Plato, Susan Glaspell, George Orwell, and Stanley Milgram); and Chapter 34, What Is Happiness? (among the nine selections in this chapter are writings by Epictetus, C. S. Lewis, and the Dalai Lama).

WHAT'S NEW IN THE NINTH EDITION

We have made some significant changes in the ninth edition that we believe enrich the book and make the content more accessible:

Fresh and timely new readings. Forty-five of the essays (about one-third of the total) are new, as are a dozen topics such as cyber-bullying, the genetic modification of human beings, student-faculty relationships, the green movement, the call for service, the limits of repro-ductive rights, the gender-pay gap, racial profiling in airport screening procedures, parental spyware, and the morality of eating meat. (In fact, the number of new readings is larger than 45 because some of these new essays were editorials and op-ed pieces that generated letters, some of which we have reprinted.)

New debates and casebook topics. New debates include The Equal Rights Amendment: Is It Still Needed?, Genetic Modification of Human Beings: Is It Acceptable?, Racial Profiling: Should Airports Use It to Screen Passengers?, Romantic Relationships between Faculty and Students: Should Colleges Prohibit Them?, and Single-Sex Classrooms: Do They Offer Advantages? New casebooks include Going Green: What Must Be Done?, Reproductive Rights: What Are the Limits?, and Service: A Duty? A Benefit? Or Both, or Perhaps Neither?

Updated and expanded research features including a new section on synthesis. Chapter 7, Using Sources, features new annotated images of database and Web pages that show students where to find the information they need to confidently evaluate and cite electronic sources.

In addition, a new section on synthesis demonstrates important strategies students can use to frame arguments in their own voices as they join the conversation with the sources they use.

More coverage of strategies for preparing speeches and debates. Chapter 14, A Debater's View: Individual Oral Presentations and Debate, has been expanded to include more coverage of rules and strategies for preparing individual speeches and includes a new checklist, A Checklist for an Oral Presentation.

Idea Prompts model academic writing strategies. Spanning such topics as definition, cartoon analysis, making transitions, and visualizing pros and cons, this new recurring feature helps students choose among different sentence-level rhetorical strategies as they construct arguments by giving them model sentences that show these strategies in action.

In preparing the ninth edition we were greatly aided by suggestions from instructors who were using the eighth edition. There can be no argument about the urgency of the topics that we have retained and have added or about the need to develop civic literacy and visual literacy, but there can be lots of argument about the merits of the positions offered in the selections. That's where the users of the book—students and instructors—come in.

ADDITIONAL RESOURCES

The Companion Web Site

The companion Web site at bedfordstmartins.com/barnetbedau offers students and instructors an extensive set of annotated links on argument and on the controversial topics in the book. Brainteasers allow students to test their understanding of logic and analysis.

Instructor's Edition

The Instructor's Edition includes an appendix, Resources for Teaching, with detailed suggestions about ways to approach the essays and with many additional suggestions for writing.

Two Shorter Editions

For instructors who do not require a text with a large number of essays, a shorter edition of this book, *Critical Thinking, Reading, and Writing: A Brief Guide to Argument,* Seventh Edition, is also available. The shorter version contains Parts One, Two, and Three (Chapters 1–14) of the present book as well as its own Casebook on the State and the Individual, drawn from readings in the longer edition.

A *very* brief version is also available: *From Critical Thinking to Argument,* Third Edition, contains Parts One and Two, plus three Further Views on

Argument: A Philosopher's View (on Toulmin argument); A Logician's View (Deduction, Induction, and Logical Fallacies); and A Psychologist's View (on Rogerian argument). It contains a dozen readings throughout the text.

ACKNOWLEDGMENTS

Finally, it is our pleasant duty to thank those who have strengthened this book by their comments and advice on the eighth edition: Mary Amato, Rider University; Iva Balic, Harrisburg Area Community College; Lise-Pauline Barnett, Harrisburg Area Community College; Laurie E. Buchanan, Clark State Community College; Jeanne Daningburg, Roberts Wesleyan College; Michelle Dowd, Chaffey College; Valerie A. Gray, Harrisburg Area Community College; Debra Hawhee, University of Illinois; Peter Huk, Allan Hancock College; Jay Jordan, University of Utah; Kristin McNamara, Allan Hancock College; John Metzger, Cape Fear Community College; Joyce Marie Miller, Collin College; Sylvia Beaver Perez, Naugatuck Valley Community College; Bonita Startt, Tidewater Community College; Kennette Lawrence Thomas, Surry Community College; Maryann Whitaker, University of Alabama.

We are also grateful to the reviewers who provided comments and advice on the sixth and seventh editions: Martha Bachman, Claudia A. Basha, Debra Taylor Bordeau, Christine Brooks, Mary Cantrell, Paul Carbonaro, Melvin Clark, Gina Claywell, James Cornette, Jennifer Cornette, Marlene Cousens, Mark DiCicco, Bronwen Evans, Lynn Hudson Ezzell, Kristopher Fallon, Teresa Garcia, Kristie Gitnes, Pamela Glindeman, Cathy Gorvine, Patricia Haddix, M. Todd Harper, Sally C. Harris, Janet Hinz, Melanie Jordan, David Kaloustian, Andrew (Michael) Knoll, Robert S. Larson, Mary C. Lawson, Linda Lawliss, Sean Lebofsky, Mary Ann Lee, Sarah Lin, Joe McDade, Eduardo Muroz, Sylvia Newman, Larry Prater, Lesa Schwartz, Larry Severeid, Wayne Shrubsall, Michel Small, Diane S. Thompson, Sandra Valerio, Ryan Wepler, and Holly A. Wheeler.

We'd also like to thank those who reviewed past editions: Alan Ainsworth, Roy M. Anker, Jim Arlandson, Robert Baird, Janet Barnwell, Claudia Basha, Mark Bedau, Frank Beesley, Donavin Bennes, Jack A. Bennett, Laurie J. Bergamini, Jeffrey Berger, B. J. Bowman, Anthony Boyle, Moana Boyle, Beverly M. Braud, Sally J. Bright, Edward Brooks, Duane Bruce, Jacintha Burke, Jim Butterfield, Jenna Call, Mary Cantrell, Janet Carter, Brandon Cesmat, Claire Chantell, Jo Chern, Barbara G. Clark, Denise Clark, Elsie Clark, James Clarke, Lorna Clymer, Sherill Cobb, Bobbie Cohen, Paul Cohen, Daniel F. Collins, Minnie A. Collins, Neil Connelly, Marie Conte, Genevieve Coogan, Michael E. Cooley, Marcia Corcoran, Susan Carolyn Cowan, Jody Cross-Hansen, Linda Daigle, Susan Dalton, Anne D'Arcy, Fara Darland, James M.

Decker, Robert Denham, Kent R. DeVault, Allen DiWederburg, Carl Dockery, Paula Doctor, Mary Lee Donahue, Alberta M. Dougan, Elizabeth Elclepp, Diane El-Rouaiheb, Hal Enger, R. Scott Evans, Lynn H. Ezzell, Dianne Fallon, Amy Farmer, Sandra Feldman, Sister Isabella Ferrell, John Finnegan, Jane Fischer, Robert H. Fleeson, Anne Marie Frank, Amy Freed, George Freund, Tamara Fritze, Stephen Fullmer, Michael J. Galgano, Joseph E. Geist, David Glaub, Sheryl Gobble, Stuart Goodman, Nathanael Gough, Mary Anne F. Grabarek, Tim Gracyk, Becky C. Graham, Rebecca Graham, Richard Grande, Mark A. Graves, Kate Gray, Dr. Laura Gray-Rosendale, Monika E. Gross, Verge Hagopian, Dennis R. Hall, William M. Hamlin, William Hampl, Donald Heidt, Charles Heimler, Janet Ruth Heller, John C. Herold, Edwin L. Hetfield Jr., Katherine Hoffman, Pau-San Hoh, Susan Honeyman, Cathy Hope, Diane W. Howard, Rosemary T. Hunkeler, Barbara Hunter, Joan Hutchison, Dr. Brian D. Ingraffia, Shelly Jaffray, Carol A. Jagielnik, Bonita Nahoum Jaros, Alison Jasper, Heather Bryant Jordan, Janet Juhnke, Diane M. Kammeyer, Priscilla Kelly, Michael Kent, Mary Jane Kinnebrew, Geoffrey Klinger, Bobbie Knable, Prudence Kohl, Catherine W. Kroll, Elaine W. Kromhout, Lita A. Kurth, Dr. Ivonne Lamazares, Brother Christopher Lambert, Richard L. Larson, John Lawing, Erin Lebofsky, J. N. Lee, Charles Lefcourt, Cynthia Lehman-Budd, Mary Lenard, Elizabeth Lewis, L. M. Lewis, Alex Liddie, Miriam Lilley, John Little, Martin Litz, Warren H. Loveless, Christopher Lukasik, Tom Lynch, Carter Lyons, Nelly McFeely, Ted McFerrin, Natalie McKnight, Marcia MacLennan, Kelli Maloy, Ruth E. Manson, Alan P. Marks, Diane Marlett, Brian Massey, Alice Maudsley, James May, Carl E. Meacham, Dan C. Miller, Peggy A. Moore, Richard Moore, Linda Morante, Robin Morris, Mary Munsil, Cris Newport, Melanie Ohler, Leonard Orr, Roswell Park, Scott Payne, Robert Peltier, Nancy P. Pope, Constance Putnam, Jan Rainbird, Sally Lynn Raines, Carol Redmore, Elaine Reed, M. Resnick, Dan Richards, Susan Roberson, Helen M. Robinette, Linda Rosekraus, Barbara E. Roshak, Jennifer O. Rosti, Julie H. Rubio, Rebecca Sabounchi, Christine Sauer, Suzette Schlapkohl, Henry Schwarzschild, Brad Scott, Harsh Sharma, Hassell B. Sledd, Sydney J. Slobodnik, Andrew J. Smyth, Daniel R. Snyder, Lynn Steiner, Skaidrite Stelzer, Elisabeth Stephens, Ed Stieve, Barbara W. Stewart, Steven Strang, Suba Subbarao, Catherine Sutton, Richard C. Taylor, Diane Thompson, Eve Thompson, Linda Toonen, David Tumpleman, Pauline Uchmanowicz, Lynn A. Walkiewicz, Kathleen Walsh, Nancy Weingart, Stephen White, Phyllis C. Whitesoll, Allen D. Widerburg, Marilyn Wienk, Stephen Wilhoit, Josie Williams, Joseph Wilson, James Yard, Michelle L. Zath, Bruce D. Zessin.

We would also like to thank Barbara Fister, who improved our discussion of research, and Susan Doheny, Diane Kraut, and Sandy Schechter, who adeptly managed art research and text permissions.

We are also deeply indebted to the people at Bedford/St. Martin's, especially to our editor, Adam Whitehurst, who is wise, patient, supportive, and unfailingly helpful. Steve Scipione, Maura Shea, and John Sullivan, our editors for all of the preceding editions, have left a lasting impression on us and on the book; without their work on the first six editions, there probably would not be a ninth. Others at Bedford/St. Martin's to whom we are deeply indebted include Charles H. Christensen, Joan E. Feinberg, Elizabeth Schaaf, Kerri Cardone, and Karen Stocz, all of whom have offered countless valuable (and invaluable) suggestions. Intelligent, informed, firm yet courteous, persuasive—all of these folks know how to think and how to argue.

Brief Contents

Contents

asking blacks and other subordinated groups to bear the burden for the good of all."

7 Using Sources   262

29 Service: A Duty? A Benefit? Or Both, or Perhaps Neither? 772

33 How Free Is the Will of the Individual within Society?   902

Thoughts about Free Will   902

34 What Is Happiness? 983

Thoughts About Happiness, Ancient and Modern 983

CURRENT ISSUES and ENDURING QUESTIONS

A Guide to Critical Thinking and Argument, with Readings

PART ONE

CRITICAL THINKING and READING

Critical Thinking

What is the hardest task in the world? To think.

——RALPH WALDO EMERSON

I write entirely to find out what I'm thinking, what I'm looking at, what I see and what it means. What I want and what I fear.

——JOAN DIDION

In all affairs it's a healthy thing now and then to hang a question mark on the things you have long taken for granted.

——BERTRAND RUSSELL

Although Emerson said simply "to think," he pretty clearly was using the word *think* in the sense of *critical thinking*. By itself, *thinking* can mean almost any sort of mental activity, from idle daydreaming ("During the chemistry lecture I kept thinking about how I'd like to go camping") to careful analysis ("I'm thinking about whether I can afford more than one week—say two weeks—of camping in the Rockies," or even "I'm thinking about whether Emerson's comment is true").

In short, when we add the adjective *critical* to the noun *thinking*, we pretty much eliminate reveries, just as we also eliminate snap judgments. We are talking about searching for hidden assumptions, noticing various facets, unraveling different strands, and evaluating what is most significant. The word *critical* comes from a Greek word, *krinein*, meaning "to separate," "to choose"; it implies conscious, deliberate inquiry, and especially it implies adopting a skeptical state of mind. To say that it implies a skeptical state of mind is by no means to say that it implies a self-satisfied fault-finding state of mind. Quite the reverse: Because critical thinkers seek to draw intelligent conclusions, they are sufficiently open-minded that they can adopt a skeptical attitude

- Toward *their own* ideas,
- Toward *their own* assumptions, and
- Toward the evidence *they themselves* tentatively offer,

as well as toward the assumptions and evidence offered by others. When they reread a draft they have written, they read it with a skeptical frame of mind, seeking to improve the thinking that has gone into it.

THINKING ABOUT DRIVERS' LICENSES AND PHOTOGRAPHIC IDENTIFICATION

By way of illustration, let's think about a case that was in the news in 2003. When Sultaana Freeman, an American Muslim woman in Florida, first applied for a driver's license, she refused on religious grounds to unveil her face for the photograph that Florida requires. She was allowed to remain veiled for the photo, with only her eyes showing. Probably in a response to the terrorist attacks of September 11, 2001, she was informed in 2002 that her license would be revoked if she refused to allow the Department of Motor Vehicles to photograph her face. She sued the state of Florida, saying that unveiling would violate her Islamic beliefs. "I'm fighting for the principle and the religious freedom of all people in the country," she said. "It's not about me."

Well, let's think about this—let's think critically, and to do this, we will use a simple aid that is equal to the best word processor, a pencil. Your own experience has already taught you that thinking is largely a matter of association; one thought leads to another, as when you jot down "peanut butter" on a shopping list and then add "bread," and "bread" somehow reminds you—you don't know why—that you also need paper napkins. As the humorist Finley Peter Dunne observed, philosophers and cows have the gift of meditation, but "others don't begin to think till they begin to talk or write." So what are some thoughts that come to mind when we begin to talk or write about this Florida case?

Critical thinking means questioning not only the assumptions of others, but also questioning *your own* assumptions. We will discuss this point at some length later in this chapter, but here we want to say only that when you write an argument, you ought to be *thinking*, evaluating evidence and assumptions, not merely collecting evidence to support a preestablished conclusion.

Back to the Florida case: Here is what we came up with in a few minutes, using a process called *clustering*. (We illustrate clustering again on page 228.)

In the center of a sheet of paper, we jotted down a phrase summarizing the basic issue, and then we began jotting down what must be the most obvious justification for demanding the picture—national safety. (We might equally well have begun with the most obvious justifications for refusing to be photographed—religious belief and perhaps privacy, to think of arguments that Sultaana Freeman—or, more likely,

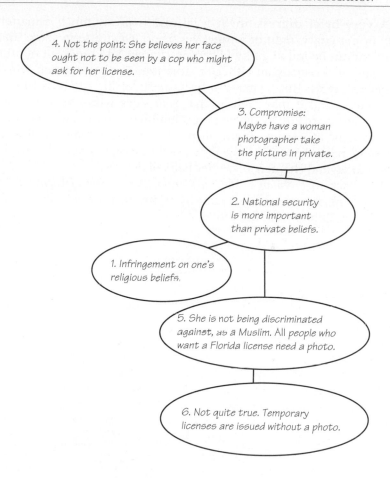

her lawyer—might set forth.) Then we let our minds work, and one thought led to another. Sometimes almost as soon as we jotted down an idea we saw that it wasn't very good, but we made considerable progress.

In the illustration, we have added numbers to the ideas, simply so that you can see how our minds worked, which is to say how we jumped around. Notice, for instance, that our fifth point—our fifth idea—is connected to our second point. When we were rereading our first four jottings, the fifth idea—that she is not being discriminated against as a Muslim—came to mind, and we saw that it should be linked with the second point. Our sixth point—a modification of our fifth, occurred to us even before we finished writing the fifth. The sixth point, that temporary licenses in Florida are issued without photographs, prompted us to start thinking more vigorously about the arguments that Ms. Freeman, or her lawyer, might offer.

A very brief digression: A legal case is pretty much a matter of guilty or not guilty, right or wrong, yes or no. Of course in some trials a defendant can be found guilty of certain charges and innocent of others, but, again, it is usually an either/or situation: The prosecution wins, or the defense wins. But in many other aspects of life, there is room for compromise, and it may well be that *both* sides win—by seeing what ground they share and by developing additional common ground. We go into this topic at greater length on p. 455, where we discuss Rogerian argument (named for Carl Rogers, a psychotherapist) and in our introduction to several chapters that offer pairs of debates.

Now back to *Freeman v. State of Florida, Department of Highway Safety and Motor Vehicles,* where we began by trying to list arguments on one side versus arguments on the other.

4. Not the point: She believes her face ought not to be seen by a cop who might ask for her license.

3. Compromise: Maybe have a woman photographer take the picture in private.

7. Maybe infringement. But the gov't sometimes prohibits beliefs it considers harmful to society. It does not permit the use of drugs in religious ceremonies, or sacrifice.

2. National security is more important than private beliefs.

1. Infringement on one's religious beliefs.

9. But those things are harmful actions that the believer engages in. In the case at issue, the believer is not engaging in harmful action. It's the gov't that is doing the acting—taking a picture.

5. She is not being discriminated against, as a Muslim. All people who want a Florida license need a photo.

6. Not quite true. Temporary licenses are issued without a photo.

8. Some states do not require pictures on licenses.

10. Florida itself issues temporary licenses without photos.

- After making our seventh note, which goes directly back to the central issue (hence we connected it with a line to the central issue) and which turned out to be an argument that the government rather than the plaintiff might make, we decided to keep thinking about government positions, and wrote the eighth note—that some states do not require pictures on drivers' licenses.

- The ninth note—that the government is prohibiting a belief, not a harmful action—in some degree refutes our seventh note, so we connected it to the seventh.

Again, if you think with a pencil and a sheet of paper and let your mind make associations, you will find, perhaps to your surprise, that you have plenty of interesting ideas. Doubtless you will also have some not-so-interesting ones. We confess that we have slightly edited our notes; originally they included two points that we are ashamed we thought of:

- "What is she complaining about? In some strict Islamic countries they don't even let women drive, period."

- "Being deprived of a license isn't a big deal. She can take the bus."

It will take only a moment of reflection to decide that these thoughts can scarcely be offered as serious arguments: What people do in strict

Plaintiff in *Freeman v. State of Florida, Department of Highway Safety and Motor Vehicles.*
(Peter Cosgrove/© AP/Worldwide Photos.)

Islamic countries has nothing to do with what we should do in ours, and that bus service is available is utterly irrelevant to the issue of whether this woman's rights are being infringed. Still, if a fear of making fools of ourselves had prevented us from jotting down ideas, we would not have jotted down any decent ideas, and the page would not have gotten written.

The outcome of the driver's license photo case? Judge Janet C. Thorpe ruled against the plaintiff, explaining that "the State has always had a compelling interest in promoting public safety. That interest is served by having the means to accurately and swiftly determine identities in given circumstances." (You can read Judge Thorpe's entire decision online— sixteen highly readable double-spaced pages—by going to Google and typing in "Sultaana Lakiana.")

> **A RULE FOR WRITERS:** One good way to start writing an essay is to start generating ideas—and at this point don't worry that some of them may be nonsense. Just get ideas down on paper, and evaluate them later.

TOPICS FOR CRITICAL THINKING AND WRITING

1. Think about Judge Thorpe's comment, quoted in the preceding paragraph. Even if we agree that a photograph establishes identity—itself a debatable point—one might raise a question: Given the fact that Florida has not passed a law requiring a photo ID, why should it say that the driver of a vehicle must provide a photo ID? Isn't a driver's license a mere certification of permission to drive?

2. Judge Thorpe wrote the following as part of her explanation for her decision:

   > Although the Court acknowledges that Plaintiff herself most likely poses no threat to national security, there likely are people who would be willing to use a ruling permitting the wearing of fullface cloaks in driver's license photos by pretending to ascribe to religious beliefs in order to carry out activities that would threaten lives.

   Is the judge in effect saying that we should infringe on Sultaana Freeman's religious beliefs because someone else might do something wicked?

3. In England in 2006 a Muslim woman—a British citizen—was removed from her job as a schoolteacher because she wore a veil. The stated reason was that the veil prevented her from effectively communicating with children. What do you think of the view that a woman has a right to wear a veil, but when she enters the marketplace she may rightly be denied certain jobs? What are your reasons?

THINKING ABOUT ANOTHER ISSUE CONCERNING DRIVERS' LICENSES: IMAGINATION, ANALYSIS, EVALUATION

Let's think critically about a law passed in West Virginia in 1989. The law provides that although students may drop out of school at the age of sixteen, no dropout younger than eighteen can hold a driver's license. (Several states now have comparable laws.)

What ought we to think of such a law?

- Is it fair?
- What is its purpose?
- Is it likely to accomplish its purpose?
- Might it unintentionally cause some harm?
- If so, can we weigh the potential harm against the potential good?

Suppose you had been a member of the West Virginia state legislature in 1989: How would you have voted?

In thinking critically about a topic, we try to see it from all sides before we come to our conclusion. We conduct an argument with ourselves, advancing and then questioning opinions:

- What can be said *for* the proposition, and
- What can be said *against* it?

Our first reaction may be quite uncritical, quite unthinking: "What a good idea!" or "That's outrageous!" But critical thinking requires us to reflect further, trying to support our position *and also* trying to see the other side. One can almost say that the heart of critical thinking is a *willingness to face objections to one's own beliefs,* a willingness to adopt a skeptical attitude not only toward authority and toward views opposed to our own but also toward common sense—that is, toward the views that seem obviously right to us. If we assume we have a monopoly on the truth and we dismiss as bigots those who oppose us, or if we say our opponents are acting merely out of self-interest and we do not in fact analyze their views, we are being critical but we are not engaged in critical thinking.

> **A RULE FOR WRITERS:** Early in the process of jotting down your ideas on a topic, stop to ask yourself, "What might reasonably be offered as an *objection* to my view?"

Critical thinking requires us to use our *imaginations,* seeing things from perspectives other than our own and envisioning the likely consequences of our positions. (This sort of imaginative thinking—grasping a perspective other than our own and considering the possible consequences of positions—is, as we have said, very different from daydreaming, an activity of unchecked fantasy.)

Thinking critically involves, along with imagination (so that we can see our own beliefs from another point of view), a twofold activity:

analysis, finding the parts of the problem and then separating them, trying to see how things fit together; and

evaluation, judging the merit of our claims and assumptions and the weight of the evidence in their favor.

If we engage in imaginative, analytic, and evaluative thought, we will have second and third ideas; almost to our surprise we may find ourselves adopting a position that we initially couldn't imagine we would hold. As we think about the West Virginia law, we might find ourselves coming up with a fairly wide variety of ideas, each triggered by the preceding idea but not necessarily carrying it a step further. For instance, we may think X and then immediately think, "No, that's not quite right. In fact, come to think of it, the opposite of X is probably true." We haven't carried X further, but we have progressed in our thinking.

THINKING ABOUT STUDENTS' EVALUATIONS OF THEIR PROFESSORS

Many colleges and universities invite students to evaluate the courses they take, usually by filling out a questionnaire. Customarily the evaluations are made available to instructors after grades have been handed in. At Tufts University, for instance, students are invited to write about each of their courses and also to respond to specific questions by indicating a rating that ranges from 5 to 1 (5 = excellent, 4 = above average, 3 = average, 2 = below average, 1 = poor; na = not applicable). Among the eleven questions about the instructor, students are asked to rate "clarity of presentation" and "tolerance of alternative views"; among the three questions about the course, students are asked to rate "overall organization."

What is the point of such evaluations? Might there be arguments against using questionnaires illustrating negative aspects to their use? Consider the Idea Prompt which lays out the pros and cons (Idea Prompt 1.1).

We have already mentioned that the questionnaires may be used when administrators consider awarding merit increases, and in the last few years a new angle appeared. At Texas A & M, for instance, bonuses ranging from $2,500 to $10,000 are awarded to certain professors who are chosen by a committee of students. (At Texas A & M, tenure and promotion are *not* involved in the program, only money.) The gist of the

IDEA PROMPT 1.1 VISUALIZING PROS AND CONS

	Benefits of evaluations	Arguments against evaluations
Instructors	Learn how they may improve their teaching	May be reluctant to give low grades because of fear of student retaliation
Students	Will benefit in the future because the instructor will do a better job	Are not always qualified to give fair evaluations
Administrators	Receive additional information to help them make decision about promotion, the award of tenure, or salary increases	May rely too heavily on evaluations as evidence of a course's merit

Texas plan, approved by the Faculty Senate, is this: Members of the faculty who wish to compete—this particular practice is voluntary—may invite students in their classes to fill out a questionnaire prepared by a committee created by the Student Government Association. (In preparing the questionnaire, the committee drew on suggestions made by the faculty, students, administrators, and "system officials.") Eleven students examine the questionnaires, and it is these students who decide who gets the bonus money, and how much. At the University of Oklahoma's College of Engineering and College of Business a somewhat comparable program exists, with bonuses ranging from $5,000 to $10,000: In the College of Engineering, for instance, those faculty members who participate and who score in the top 5 percent on the evaluation are each awarded $5,000. Each of those who score in the next 15 percent receives $ 2,500.

The Texas A & M questionnaire has sixteen questions, to which students are asked to respond on a five-point scale, ranging from "strongly agree" to "strongly disagree." Here are two sample questions.

1. My instructor seemed to be very knowledgeable about the subject matter.
2. My instructor seemed to present the course material in an organized manner.

Finalists in the evaluation must then submit a syllabus and a statement of their teaching philosophy, and the head of the department is invited to submit a comment. Students on the committee also may examine the grade distribution curve. The questionnaire, however, is said to be the chief criterion.

TOPICS FOR CRITICAL THINKING AND WRITING

1. Jot down any arguments you think of, not already mentioned, pro and con, for the use of evaluation questionnaires in college classes.

2. Even if you do not favor such questionnaires, jot down three questions that you think might be useful on such a questionnaire.

3. What do you think would be the best way to form a student evaluation committee? Explain the merits of your proposal with respect to possible alternatives.

4. How would you distinguish between a good teacher and a popular teacher?

5. Draft a brief essay, about 500 words, arguing for or against the use of questionnaires in college courses. Be sure to indicate the purpose(s) of the questionnaires. Are the questionnaires to be used by administrators, by students, or both? Should they help to determine promotion, tenure, and compensation?

WRITING AS A WAY OF THINKING

"To learn to write," Robert Frost said, "is to learn to have ideas." But how do you "learn to have ideas"? Often we discover ideas while we are in the process of talking with others. A friend says X about some issue, and we—who have never really thought much about the matter—say,

- "Well, yes, I see what you are saying, but, come to think of it, I'm not of your opinion. I see it differently—*not* X *but* Y." Or maybe we say,
- "*Yes,* X, *sure, and also* a bit of Y too."

Mere chance—the comment of a friend—has led us to an idea that we didn't know we had. This sort of discovery may at first seem something like the discovery we make when we reach under the couch to retrieve a ball that the dog has pushed and we find a ten-dollar bill instead. "How it got there, I'll never know, but I'm glad I found it."

In fact, learning to have ideas is not largely a matter of chance. Or if chance *is* involved, well, as Louis Pasteur put it, "Chance favors the prepared mind." What does this mean? It means that somehow, lurking in the mind, are some bits of information or hints or maybe hunches that in the unexpected circumstance—when talking, or when listening to a lecture or a classroom discussion, or especially when reading—are triggered and result in useful thoughts. A sort of seat-of-the-pants knowledge that, when brought to the surface, when worked on, produces good results.

Consider the famous episode of Archimedes, the ancient Greek mathematician, who discovered a method to determine the volume of an irregularly shaped object. The problem: A king gave a goldsmith a specific weight of gold with which to make a crown in the shape of laurel leaves. When the job was finished the king weighed the crown, found that it was the weight of the gold he had provided, but he nevertheless suspected that the goldsmith might have substituted some silver for the gold. How could Archimedes find out (without melting or in any other way damaging the crown) if the crown was pure gold? Meditating produced no ideas, but when he entered a bathtub Archimedes noticed that the level of water rose as he immersed his body. He suddenly realized that he could thus determine the volume of the crown—by measuring the amount of displaced water. Since silver is less dense than gold, it takes a greater volume of silver to equal a given weight of gold. That is, a given weight of gold will displace less water than the same weight of silver. Archimedes then immersed the given weight of gold, measured the water it displaced, and found that indeed the crown displaced more water than the gold did. In his excitement at hitting upon his idea, Archimedes is said to have leaped out of the tub and run naked through the street, shouting "Eureka" (Greek for "I have found it").

Getting Ideas

Why do we tell this story? Partly because we like it, but chiefly because the word *eureka* comes from the same Greek word that has given our language the word **heuristic** (pronounced hyooRIStik), a method or process of discovering ideas, in short, of thinking. In this method, one thing triggers another. (Note: In computer science *heuristic* has a more specialized meaning.) Now, one of the best ways of getting ideas is to hear what is going on around you—and what is going on around you is talk, in and out of the classroom, and talk in the world of books. You will find, as we said at the beginning of this discussion, that your response may be, "Well, yes, I see what you are saying, but, come to think of it, I don't see it quite that way. I see it differently—not *X* but *Y*." For instance,

> "*Yes*, solar power is a way of conserving energy, *but* do we need to despoil the Mojave Desert and endanger desert life with—literally— fifty thousand solar mirrors, so that folks in Los Angeles can heat their pools? Doesn't it make sense to reduce our use of energy, rather than merely to develop sources of renewable energy that violate the environment? Some sites should be off-limits."

Or maybe your response to the proposal (now at least ten years old) that wind turbines be placed in Cape Cod, Massachusetts, is,

> "*Given our need* for wind power, *how can a reasonable person object* to the proposal that we put 130 wind turbines in Cape Cod, Massachusetts? *Yes*, the view will be changed, *but* in fact the turbines are quite attractive. No one thinks that windmills in Holland spoil the landscape. So the view will be changed, but not spoiled, *and furthermore* wind turbines do not endanger birds or aquatic life.

When you are asked to write about something you have read in this book, if your first response is that you have no ideas, remember the responses that we have mentioned—"No, I don't see it that way," or "Yes, but," or "Yes, and moreover"—and see if one of them helps you to respond to the work—helps you, in short, to get ideas.

A related way of getting ideas practiced by the ancient Greeks and Romans and still regarded as among the best ways, is to consider what the ancients called **topics,** from the Greek word *topos*, meaning "place," as in our word *topography* (a description or representation of a place). For the ancients, certain topics, put into the form of questions, were in effect places where one went to find ideas. Among the classical topics were definition, comparison, relationship, and testimony. By prompting oneself with questions about these topics, one finds oneself moving toward answers (see Idea Prompt 1.2).

If you think you are at a loss for ideas when confronted with an issue (and when confronted with an assignment to write about it), you probably will find ideas coming to you if you turn to the relevant classical topics and begin jotting down your responses. (In classical terminology, you are engaged in the process of invention, from the Latin *invenire*, "to come upon," "to find.") Seeing your ideas on paper—even in the briefest form—will help bring other ideas to mind and will also help you to evaluate them. For instance, after jotting down ideas as they come and responses to them,

IDEA PROMPT 1.2 UNDERSTANDING CLASSICAL TOPICS

Definition	*What is it?*	"The West Virginia law defines a high-school dropout as . . ."
Comparison	*What is it like or unlike?*	"Compared with the national rate of teenagers involved in fatal accidents, teenagers from West Virginia . . ."
Relationship	*What caused it, and what will it cause?*	"The chief cause of teenage fatal driving accidents is alcohol. Admittedly, there are no statistics on whether high school dropouts have a higher rate of alcoholism than teenagers who remain in school, but nevertheless . . ."
Testimony	*What is said about it, for instance, by experts?*	"Judge Smith, in sentencing the youth, said that in all of his long experience . . ."

1. You might go on to organize them into two lists, pro and con;
2. Next, you might delete ideas that, when you come to think about them, strike you as simply wrong or irrelevant; and
3. Then you might develop those ideas that strike you as pretty good.

You probably won't know where you stand until you have gone through some such process. It would be nice if we could make a quick decision, immediately justify it with three excellent reasons, and then give three further reasons showing why the opposing view is inadequate. In fact, however, we almost never can come to a reasoned decision without a good deal of preliminary thinking.

Consider again the West Virginia law we discussed earlier in this chapter. Here is a kind of inner dialogue that you might engage in as you think critically about it:

> The purpose is to give students an incentive to stay in school by making them pay a price if they choose to drop out.
>
> Adolescents will get the message that education really is important.
>
> But come to think of it, *will* they? Maybe they will see this as just another example of adults bullying young people.
>
> According to a newspaper article, the dropout rate in West Virginia decreased by 30 percent in the year after the bill was passed.
>
> Well, that sounds good, but is there any reason to think that kids who are pressured into staying really learn anything? The *assumption* behind the bill is that if would-be dropouts stay in school, they—and society—will gain. But is the assumption sound? Maybe such students will become resentful, will not learn anything, and may even be so disruptive that they will interfere with the learning of other students.

Notice how part of the job is *analytic*, recognizing the elements or complexities of the whole, and part is *evaluative*, judging the adequacy of all of these ideas, one by one. Both tasks require *imagination*.

So far we have jotted down a few thoughts and then immediately given some second thoughts contrary to the first. Of course, the counter-thoughts might not immediately come to mind. For instance, they might not occur until we reread the jottings, or try to explain the law to a friend, or until we sit down and begin drafting an essay aimed at supporting or undermining the law. Most likely, in fact, some good ideas won't occur until a second or third or fourth draft.

Here are some further thoughts on the West Virginia law. We list them more or less as they arose and as we typed them into a computer—not sorted out neatly into two groups, pro and con, or evaluated as you would want to do in further critical thinking of your own. And of course, a later step would be to organize the material into some useful pattern. As you read, you might jot down your own responses in the margin.

Education is *not* optional, something left for the individual to take or not to take — like going to a concert, jogging, getting annual health check-ups, or getting eight hours of sleep each night. Society has determined that it is *for the public good* that citizens have a substantial education, so we require education up to a certain age.

Come to think about it, maybe the criterion of age doesn't make much sense. If we want an educated citizenry, it would make more sense to require people to attend school until they demonstrated competence in certain matters rather than until they reached a certain age. Exceptions, of course, would be made for mentally retarded persons and perhaps for certain other groups.

What is needed is not legal pressure to keep teenagers in school but schools that hold the interest of teenagers.

A sixteen-year-old usually is not mature enough to make a decision of this importance.

Still, a sixteen-year-old who finds school unsatisfying and who therefore drops out may become a perfectly useful citizen.

Denying a sixteen-year-old a driver's license may work in West Virginia, but it would scarcely work in a state with great urban areas, where most high school students rely on public transportation.

We earn a driver's license by demonstrating certain skills. The state has no right to take away such a license unless we have demonstrated that we are unsafe drivers.

To prevent a person of sixteen from having a driver's license prevents that person from holding certain kinds of jobs, and that's unfair.

A law of this sort deceives adults into thinking that they have really done something constructive for teenage education, but it may work *against* improving the schools. It may be *counterproductive:* If we are really serious about educating youngsters, we have to examine the curriculum and the quality of our teachers.

Doubtless there is much that we haven't said, on both sides, but we hope you will agree that the issue deserves thought. In fact, several states now revoke the driver's license of a teenager who drops out of school, and four of these states go even further and revoke the licenses of students whose academic work does not reach a given standard. On the other hand, Louisiana, which for a while had a law like West Virginia's, dropped it in 1997.

✓ A CHECKLIST FOR CRITICAL THINKING

Attitudes

☐ Does my thinking show imaginative open-mindedness and intellectual curiosity?

　☐ Am I willing to examine my assumptions?

　☐ Am I willing to entertain new ideas—both those that I encounter while reading and those that come to mind while writing?

　☐ Am I willing to exert myself—for instance, to do research—to acquire information and to evaluate evidence?

Skills

☐ Can I summarize an argument accurately?

☐ Can I evaluate assumptions, evidence, and inferences?

☐ Can I present my ideas effectively—for instance, by organizing and by writing in a manner appropriate to my imagined audience?

If you were a member of a state legislature voting on this proposal, you would *have* to think about the issue. But just as a thought experiment, try to put into writing your tentative views.

One other point about this issue. If you had to think about the matter *today*, you might also want to know whether the West Virginia legislation of 1989 is considered a success and on what basis. That is, you would want to get answers to such questions as the following:

• What sort of evidence tends to support the law or tends to suggest that the law is a poor idea?

• Did the reduction in the dropout rate continue, or did the reduction occur only in the first year following the passage of the law?

• If indeed students who wanted to drop out did not, was their presence in school a good thing, both for them and for their classmates?

• Have some people emerged as authorities on this topic? What makes them authorities, and what do they have to say?

• Has the constitutionality of the bill been tested? With what results?

Some of these questions require you to do **research** on the topic. The questions raise issues of fact, and some relevant evidence probably is available. If you are to arrive at a conclusion in which you can have confidence, you will have to do some research to find out what the facts are.

Even without doing any research, however, you might want to look over the ideas, pro and con, perhaps adding some totally new thoughts or perhaps modifying or even rejecting (for reasons that you can specify) some of those already given. If you do think a bit further about this issue, and we hope that you will, notice an interesting point about *your own* thinking: It probably is not *linear* (moving in a straight line from *A* to *B* to *C*) but *recursive,* moving from *A* to *C* and back to *B* or starting over at *C* and then back to *A* and *B*. By zigging and zagging almost despite yourself, you'll get to a conclusion that may finally seem correct. In retrospect it seems obvious; *now* you can chart a nice line from *A* to *B* to *C*—but that was not at all evident to you at the start.

A SHORT ESSAY ILLUSTRATING CRITICAL THINKING

When we read an essay, we expect the writer to have thought things through, at least to a considerable degree. We do not want to read every false start, every fuzzy thought, every ill-organized paragraph that the writer knocked off. Yes, writers make false starts, put down fuzzy thoughts, write ill-organized paragraphs, but then they revise and revise yet again, and they end by giving us a readable essay that seems effortlessly written. Still—and here we get to our real point—in argumentative essays, writers need to show their readers that they have made some effort; they need to show us *how* they got to their final (for the moment) views. It is not enough for the writer to say, "I believe *X*"; rather, the writer must in effect say, "I believe *X*—and I hope you will believe it also—because *Y* and *Z*, though attractive, just don't stand up to inquiry as well as *X* does. *Y* is superficially plausible, but . . . , and *Z*, which is an attractive alternative to *Y,* nevertheless fails because . . ."

Notice in the following short essay—on parents putting spyware into the computers of their children—that Harlan Coben frequently brings up objections to his own position; that is, he shows his awareness of other views, and then tries to show why he thinks his position is preferable. Presumably he thus communicates to his readers a sense that he is thoughtful, well-informed, and fair-minded.

Harlan Coben

Harlan Coben (b. 1962) is the author of Hold Tight *(2009). Reprinted here is an essay published in the* New York Times *on March 16, 2008. Following are some letters that were written in response and were later published in the* Times.

The Undercover Parent

Not long ago, friends of mine confessed over dinner that they had put spyware on their fifteen-year-old son's computer so they could monitor all he did online. At first I was repelled at this invasion of privacy. Now, after doing a fair amount of research, I get it.

Make no mistake: If you put spyware on your computer, you have the ability to log every keystroke your child makes and thus a good portion of his or her private world. That's what spyware is—at least the parental monitoring kind. You don't have to be an expert to put it on your computer. You just download the software from a vendor and you will receive reports—weekly, daily, whatever—showing you everything your child is doing on the machine.

Scary. But a good idea. Most parents won't even consider it.

Maybe it's the word: spyware. It brings up associations of Dick Cheney sitting in a dark room, rubbing his hands together and reading your most private thoughts. But this isn't the government we are talking about—this is your family. It's a mistake to confuse the two. Loving parents are doing the surveillance here, not faceless bureaucrats. And most parents already monitor their children, watching over their home environment, their school.

Today's overprotective parents fight their kids' battles on the play- 5 ground, berate coaches about playing time and fill out college applications—yet when it comes to chatting with pedophiles or watching beheadings or gambling away their entire life savings, then . . . then their children deserve independence?

Some will say that you should simply trust your child, that if he is old enough to go on the Internet he is old enough to know the dangers. Trust is one thing, but surrendering parental responsibility to a machine that allows the entire world access to your home borders on negligence.

Some will say that it's better just to use parental blocks that deny access to risky sites. I have found that they don't work. Children know how to get around them. But more than that—and this is where it gets tough—I want to know what's being said in e-mail and instant messages and in chat rooms.

There are two reasons for this. First, we've all read about the young boy unknowingly conversing with a pedophile or the girl who was cyberbullied to the point where she committed suicide. Would a watchful eye have helped? We rely in the real world on teachers and parents to guard against bullies—do we just dismiss bullying on the Internet and all it entails because we are entering difficult ethical ground?

Second, everything your child types can already be seen by the world—teachers, potential employers, friends, neighbors, future dates. Shouldn't he learn now that the Internet is not a haven of privacy?

One of the most popular arguments against spyware is the claim that 10 you are reading your teenager's every thought, that in today's world, a computer is the little key-locked diary of the past. But posting thoughts on the Internet isn't the same thing as hiding them under your mattress. Maybe you should buy your children one of those little key-locked diaries so that they too can understand the difference.

Am I suggesting eavesdropping on every conversation? No. With new technology comes new responsibility. That works both ways. There is a fine line between being responsibly protective and irresponsibly nosy. You shouldn't monitor to find out if your daughter's friend has a crush on Kevin next door or that Mrs. Peterson gives too much homework or what schoolmate snubbed your son. You are there to start conversations and to be a safety net. To borrow from the national intelligence lexicon—and yes, that's uncomfortable—you're listening for dangerous chatter.

Will your teenagers find other ways of communicating to their friends when they realize you may be watching? Yes. But text messages and cellphones don't offer the anonymity and danger of the Internet. They are usually one-on-one with someone you know. It is far easier for a predator to troll chat rooms and MySpace and Facebook.

There will be tough calls. If your sixteen-year-old son, for example, is visiting hardcore pornography sites, what do you do? When I was sixteen, we looked at *Playboy* centerfolds and read *Penthouse Forum*. You may argue that's not the same thing, that Internet pornography makes that stuff seem about as harmful as "SpongeBob."

And you're probably right. But in my day, that's all you could get. If something more graphic had been out there, we probably would have gone for it. Interest in those, um, topics is natural. So start a dialogue based on that knowledge. You should have that talk anyway, but now you can have it with some kind of context.

Parenting has never been for the faint of heart. One friend of mine, 15 using spyware to monitor his college-bound, straight-A daughter, found out that not only was she using drugs but she was sleeping with her dealer. He wisely took a deep breath before confronting her. Then he decided to come clean, to let her know how he had found out, to speak with her about the dangers inherent in her behavior. He'd had these conversations before, of course, but this time he had context. She listened. There was no anger. Things seem better now.

Our knee-jerk reaction as freedom-loving Americans is to be suspicious of anything that hints at invasion of privacy. That's a good and noble thing. But it's not an absolute, particularly in the face of the new and evolving challenges presented by the Internet. And particularly when it comes to our children.

Do you tell your children that the spyware is on the computer? I side with yes, but it might be enough to show them this article, have a discussion about your concerns and let them know the possibility is there.

Overall View of the Essay

Before we comment in some detail on Coben's essay, we need to say that in terms of the length of its paragraphs, this essay is not a model for you to imitate. Material in newspapers customarily is given in very short paragraphs, partly because readers are reading it while eating breakfast or while commuting to work, and partly because the columns are narrow; a paragraph of only two or three sentences may still be an inch or two deep.

The title, "The Undercover Parent" is provocative, attention-getting.

Paragraph 1 contains cues that telegraph the reader that there will be a change ("Not long ago," "At first," and "Now"). These cues set up expectations, and then Coben to some degree fulfills the expectations. We say "to some degree" because the essay still has a number of paragraphs to go.

Paragraph 2 presses the point, almost aggressively ("Make no mistake").

Paragraph 3 pretty much does the same. The writer is clearly reassuring the readers that he knows how most of them feel. The idea is "scary," yes—and then comes a crucial word, "but," signaling to the reader that Coben takes a different view. We then expect him to tell us why. And— who knows?—he may even convince us.

Paragraph 4 reassures us that Coben does have some idea of why the idea is "scary," and it goes on—with another "but"—to clarify the point. We may not agree with Coben, but it is evident that he is *thinking*, inching along from one idea to the next, frequently to an opposing idea.

Paragraph 5 shows that again Coben has a sense of what is going on in the world ("Today's overprotective parents"), or, rather, he has two senses, because he adds "yet," equivalent to "but." In effect he says, "Yes A, but also B."

Paragraph 6 begins "Some will say," another indication that the writer knows what is going on. And we can expect that "some will say" will, sooner or later, lead into another "but" (or other comparable word), indicating that although some say *X*, he says *Y*.

Paragraph 7 again begins "Some will say." *We* will say that again the reader knows Coben's report of what "some" say will lead to a report that what *Coben* says (i.e. thought) is different.

Paragraph 8 begins, "There are two reasons." OK, we as readers know where we will be going: We will hear two reasons. Now, when Coben drafted this paragraph he may—who knows?—have first written "There are three reasons," or "There is one reason." Whatever he wrote as a prompt, it got him moving, got him thinking, and then, in the course of writing, of finding ideas, he revised when he found out exactly how many reasons he could offer. In any case, in the paragraph as we have it, he promises to give two reasons, and in this paragraph he gives the first, nicely labeled "First." Notice too, that he provides *evidence*, and he draws in the reader: "we've all read." In short, he establishes a cozy relationship with his reader.

Paragraph 9 begins, helpfully, "Second." Fine, we know exactly where Coben is taking us: He is giving us the second of the two reasons that he discovered, and that he implicitly promised to give when in the previous paragraph he said, "There are two reasons."

Paragraph 10 begins, "One of the most popular arguments against spying is," and so we know, again, where Coben will be taking us: He will, in effect, be telling us what some folks—but not Coben—say. Very simple, very obvious—Coben will be summarizing one of the most popular arguments against spying—and we are grateful to him for letting us know at the beginning of the paragraph what his intentions are.

Paragraph 11 continues his intimate relation with the reader ("Am I suggesting eavesdropping . . . ?") He thus lets us know that he has a good sense of how the reader probably is responding. As we will say several times in this book, good writers are able to put themselves into their readers' shoes. Because they have a sense of how the reader is responding, they offer whatever the reader needs at the moment, for instance a definition, or an example.

Paragraph 12 begins with a question ("Will your teenagers find other ways of communicating . . . ?"), and this question again indicates that Coben is walking in the shoes of his readers; he knows that this question is on their minds. His answer is twofold, "Yes," and "But." Again the "but" is a sign of critical thinking, a sign that Coben has a clear sense of position *A*, but wants to move his reader from *A* to *B*.

Paragraph 13, beginning "There will be tough calls," is yet another example of Coben's demonstration to his readers that he is aware of their doubts, aware that they may be thinking Coben has simplified things.

Paragraph 14 (beginning "And you're probably right") continues his demonstration that he is aware of how his readers may respond—but it is immediately followed with a "But." Again, he is nudging us from position *A* to his position, Position *B*.

Paragraph 15, like several of the earlier paragraphs, shows Coben is sympathetic to the real-world problems of his readers ("Parenting has never been for the faint of heart"), and it also shows that he is a person of experience. In this paragraph, where he refers to the problem of a friend, he tells us of the happy solution. In short, he tells us that life is tough, but experience shows that there is hope. (The letter-writer, Carol Weston, strongly implies that this bit of experience Coben offers in this paragraph is *not* at all typical.)

Paragraph 16 again indicates the writer's sense of the reader ("Our knee-jerk reaction"), and it again evokes a "But."

Paragraph 17, the final paragraph, pretty directly addresses the reader ("Do you tell your children that the spyware is on the computer?"), and it offers a mixed answer: "I side with yes, but . . . ." Again Coben is showing not only his awareness of the reader, but also his awareness that the problem is complicated: There is something to be said for *A*, but also something to be said for *B*. He ends by suggesting that indeed this article might be discussed by parents with their children, thereby conveying to his readers the suggestion that he is a fair-minded guy, willing to have his ideas put up for discussion.

Following is Carol Weston's response to Coben's essay that the *Times* later published (March 23, 2008).

Letter of Response by Carol Weston

To the Editor:

In "The Undercover Parent" (Op-Ed, March 16), the novelist Harlan Coben writes that putting spyware on a child's computer is a "good idea."

As a mother and advice columnist for girls, I disagree. For most families, spyware is not only unnecessary, but it also sends the unfortunate message, "I don't trust you."

Mr. Coben said a friend of his "using spyware to monitor his college-bound, straight-A daughter, found out that not only was she using drugs but she was sleeping with her dealer." He confronted her about her behavior. "She listened. There was no anger. Things seem better now."

Huh?! No anger? No tears or shouting or slammed doors? C'mon. If only raising teenagers were that simple.

Parenting is both a job and a joy. It does not require spyware, but it does require love, respect, time, trust, money, and being as available as possible 24/7. Luck helps, too.

CAROL WESTON
New York, March 16, 2008

The writer is an advice columnist for Girls' Life *magazine.*

✓ A CHECKLIST FOR EVALUATING LETTERS OF RESPONSE

After reading the letters responding to an editorial or to a previous letter, go back and read each letter. Have you asked yourself the following questions?

□ What assumption(s) does the letter-writer make? Do you share the assumption(s)?

□ What is the writer's claim?

□ What evidence, if any, does the writer offer to support the claim?

□ Is there anything about the style of the letter—the distinctive use of language, the tone—that makes the letter especially engaging or especially annoying?

TOPICS FOR CRITICAL THINKING AND WRITING

1. How important is the distinction (para. 4) between government invasion of privacy and parental invasion of privacy?

2. Complete the following sentence: An invasion of privacy is permissible if and only if . . .

3. Identify the constructive steps a normal parent might consider taking before going so far as to install spyware.

4. Do you agree with Weston's statement that installing spyware translates to "I don't trust you"? Would you feel differently (or not) if you were a parent?

5. Write your own letter to the editor, indicating your reasons for supporting or rejecting Coben's argument.

EXAMINING ASSUMPTIONS

In Chapter 3 we will discuss **assumptions** in some detail, but here we want to introduce the topic by emphasizing the importance of *identifying* and *examining* assumptions—the assumptions you will encounter in the writings of others and the assumptions you will rely on in your own essays.

With this in mind, let's return again to considering the West Virginia driver's license law. What assumptions did the legislature make in enacting this statute? We mentioned earlier one such assumption: If the law helped to keep teenagers from dropping out of school, then that was a good thing for them and for society in general. For all we know, the advocates of this legislation may have made this assumption *explicit* in the course of their argument in favor of the statute. Perhaps they left this assumption *tacit,* believing that the point was obvious and that everyone shared this assumption. The assumption may be obvious, but it was not universally shared; the many teenagers who wanted to drop out of school at sixteen and keep their drivers' licenses did not share it.

Another assumption that the advocates of this legislation may have made is this:

> The provisions of this statute are the most efficient way to keep teenagers in high school.

Defending such an assumption is no easy task because it requires identifying other possible legislative strategies and evaluating their merits against those of the proposed legislation.

Consider now two of the assumptions involved in the Sultaana Freeman case. Thanks to the "clustering" exercise (pp. 4–7), these and other assumptions are already on display. Perhaps the most important and fundamental assumption Ms. Freeman made is this:

> Where private religious beliefs conflict with duly enacted laws, the former should prevail.

This assumption is widely shared in our society and is by no means unique to Muslim women seeking drivers' licenses in Florida after September 11, 2001. Freeman's opponents probably assumed a very different but equally fundamental proposition:

> Private religious practices and beliefs must yield to the demands of national security.

✓ A CHECKLIST FOR EXAMINING ASSUMPTIONS

☐ What assumptions does the writer's argument presuppose?

☐ Are these assumptions explicit or implicit?

☐ Are these assumptions important to the author's argument or only incidental?

☐ Does the author give any evidence of being aware of the hidden assumptions in her or his argument?

☐ Would a critic be likely to share these assumptions, or are they exactly what a critic would challenge?

☐ What sort of evidence would be relevant to supporting or rejecting these assumptions?

☐ Am I willing to grant the author's assumptions?

  ☐ If not, why not?

Obviously these two assumptions were on a collision course and neither side could hope to prevail so long as the key assumptions of the other side were ignored.

Peter Cave

Peter Cave teaches philosophy at the Open University and City University of London. He is the author of Can a Robot be Human?: 33 Perplexing Philosophy Puzzles *(2007) and* What's Wrong with Eating People?: 33 More Perplexing Philosophy Puzzles *(2008). We reprint an essay from this second book.*

Should We Save the Jerboa?

The long-eared jerboa has—er—long ears. It lives in the deserts of Mongolia and China—with its ears. A tiny nocturnal mammal, it is dwarfed by enormous ears. It hops like a kangaroo; and, for mammals, it possesses one of the biggest ear-to-body ratios. That is, it has very big ears for its size. There are little hairs on its feet, almost like snow shoes, which allow the jerboa to jump along the sand. It is said to be cute and comic. It is classified as endangered. Oh, and did I mention the ears?

Why should we care about the jerboa? Our question is about the species, as a kind, or a class of creatures. A species is easily confused in speech with the individual members of the species, not least because our language so easily flips around: 'the jerboa' could designate a particular jerboa, or the species taken to be a group of jerboas, or the species taken to be the type of creature it is. Individual jerboas have two long ears each, but the species, as a collection, does not really have long ears and certainly not merely two, though the species as a type of creature is that type that normally has two long ears. When people are concerned about a species' survival, they usually want to promote the existence of a collection of creatures of a certain type, but not any individuals in particular. Particular individuals die, but the species, the collection with members of a certain type, may persist.

Naturally, we may also care about individual jerboas: probably we do not want any individual jerboa to suffer. We recognize that there is something that counts as going well for an individual jerboa. But the species, as a species, is not the sort of thing that suffers pain. Preserving a species may, in fact, involve culling, killing some members. So our general question is—and a couple of examples are—

Why save a species from extinction?

Why save the jerboa?

Why regret the loss of the dodo?

Some simple quick answers in favour of preservation concern the benefits or possible benefits to humans. Preservation is justified on the grounds of the species' value as an instrument to aid us. Perhaps the different species help maintain Earth's ecological balance. Maybe their genetic information, one day, could aid development of pharmaceuticals. In addition, people gain pleasure from seeing members of different species. For similar reasons, we may regret the loss of the dodo.

Suppose the jerboa lacks such instrumental value with regard to   5 ecology and future genetic researches. Suppose too that the jerboa is so furtive, living in such inhospitable conditions, that people typically will not see a jerboa and so will not gain pleasure from sighting experiences. May the species yet possess value?

Yes. People may value simply knowing that the jerboa exists, knowing that there is such a species and such variety around them. We are identifying a curious instrumental value, curious in that it fails to involve our direct experiences of the jerboa. Once again, though, we are finding value in the jerboa's existence because of its effects on humans, albeit not directly experienced effects. However, may the jerboa, or any species, have an intrinsic value, a value that does not depend for its being a value on something else—that does not depend, for example, on what humans want?

The question does not presuppose that a species cannot have both instrumental value and intrinsic value. This is not an either–or matter. Some items have both. Philosophizing, arguably, is intrinsically valuable, yet may also possess instrumental value in bringing peace and harmony to the universe. Well, okay—maybe that last point is a little fanciful. What is not fanciful is the thought that some things have intrinsic value. Somewhere along the line we stop ourselves from saying 'this is only valuable because it is a means to that . . .' For example, the stopping point is often happiness, usually human happiness: happiness has intrinsic value.

Returning to the jerboa, by pretending that it lacks all instrumental value, we focus on whether there is any other value, an intrinsic value, that applies to the species. Perhaps there is value in the jerboa's existence simply because it is a species of living individuals. Well, it is not obviously the case that 'living' thereby makes something valuable. The smallpox virus, HIV, and malarial mosquitoes are living, yet we question whether they are thereby intrinsically valuable. Our negative attitude, though, may result from their harming us: they could still be intrinsically valuable.

Possibly there is something valuable about nature being left, undisturbed by human beings; however, that certainly does not point to species' conservation. Nature ensures the extinction of vast numbers of species—and it may be in our human nature, quite whatever that means, to destroy species, just as it is to tame parts of nature. The rural landscapes of fields, crops, and national parks would be non-existent, but for human interferences—as would be spectacular bridges, sculptures, and architecturally stunning galleries.

Perhaps we should simply recognize that we value the presence of a 10
variety of species. We value that presence independently of our purposes
and independently of any value for us. We value the jerboa for its own
sake. Note, though, that even here its value may be resting solely on the
fact that we humans value it 'for its own sake'. There is, though, a
stronger suggestion: that the jerboa — or any species — possesses value
independently even of our valuing it. After all, if the species in question
did not possess such value, why should we value it for its own sake?
Why value something unless it is worthy of being valued?

It is difficult, though, to get a grip on 'for its own sake' when applied
to a species. If we do something for an individual jerboa's sake, we have
some idea of how we are acting in its best interests, how its life may go
well. We know that it needs food and shelter. But it is far from clear that
a species, as opposed to particular individuals, has an interest. It is far
from clear how things go well for the species, from the species' viewpoint. After all, a species lacks a viewpoint.

Human beings promote the existence of some things and not of others. We value. We are *valuers*. Perhaps — and perhaps conveniently for
human beings — possessors of intrinsic value include at least those individuals that are themselves valuers, such as we are. We may, though,
wonder why that should be believed. Without valuers, nothing would be
valued; but it neither follows that valuers are valuable nor that items are
only valuable if they happen to be valued.

In our valuing, having preferences, recognizing things as worthy of
desire, perhaps we become aware that there are items that are intrinsically valuable, whose value is other than being experienced by us or even
being experiences. Maybe that is why so many of us, even when godless,
stand in wonder at the different species, seeking to preserve them against
the ravages of both man and impersonal nature. Maybe that is why some
of us see beauty in sunsets, in landscapes, and seascapes, a beauty that is
valuable and would still exist even without humans around to appreciate
that beauty.

In some cases, it may be better not to have human beings around at
all. Just think of those seashores splattered with empty beer cans, cigarette ends, and worse. They offend the eye and detract from beauty; yet,
without the humans around, could there be any offence, any loss or gain
in beauty at all?

Or would the eye of the universe still shed a tear?   15

Topics for Critical Thinking and Writing

1. Is the only or the main reason for preserving the jerboa as a species
   the pleasure or value it gives to members of our species? What is
   Cave's position on this question? Explain your answers in an essay of
   300 words.

2. "A species lacks a viewpoint" (para. 11). So says Cave. What does he mean? What assumptions (if any) does Cave make?

3. How concerned are you that the jerboa be saved? Explain your position, in about 250 words.

4. Cave lists a good number of things that would not exist if it were not for human intervention. Do you think that these interventions outweigh the bad things that exist as a result of human intervention? Do you think the former exceed the latter? Or do the latter outweigh the former? How would you argue the case either way? What assumptions does Cave make in defending his position? Explain your answer.

Five Exercises in Critical Thinking

1. Think further about the 1989 West Virginia law that prohibits high school dropouts younger than eighteen from holding a driver's license. Jot down pros and cons, and then write a balanced dialogue between two imagined speakers who hold opposing views on the merits of the law. You'll doubtless have to revise your dialogue several times, and in revising your drafts you will find that further ideas come to you. Present *both* sides as strongly as possible. (You may want to give the two speakers distinct characters; for instance, one may be a student who has dropped out and the other a concerned teacher, or one a parent— who perhaps argues that he or she needs the youngster to work full-time driving a delivery truck—and one a legislator. But do not write as if the speakers must present the arguments they might be expected to hold. A student might argue *for* the law, and a teacher *against* it.)

2. Take one of the following topics and jot down all the pro and con arguments you can think of in, say, ten minutes. Then, at least an hour or two later, return to your jottings and see whether you can add to them. Finally, as in Exercise 1, write a balanced dialogue, presenting each idea as strongly as possible. (If none of these topics interests you, talk with your instructor about the possibility of choosing a topic of your own.) Suggested topics:

   a. Colleges should not award athletic scholarships.
   b. Bicyclists and motorcyclists should be required by law to wear helmets.
   c. High school teachers should have the right to search students for drugs on school grounds.
   d. Smoking should be prohibited in all parts of all college buildings.
   e. College administrators should take no punitive action against students who use racist language or language that offends any minority.
   f. Students should have the right to drop out of school at any age.
   g. In rape trials, the names of the alleged victims should not be released to the public.
   h. The United States ought to require a national identity card.

3. On the evening of July 31, 2001, after court employees had left the Alabama Judicial Building in Montgomery, Chief Justice Roy S. Moore

of the Alabama Supreme Court and his supporters installed in the lobby of the courthouse a four-foot high, 5,200 pound granite block bearing the text of the Ten Commandments. Moore had not discussed his plan with other justices. Civil liberties groups complained that the monument was an unconstitutional attempt to endorse a specific religion (the First Amendment to the U.S. Constitution says, "Congress shall make no law respecting an establishment of religion"), and in 2002 a federal judge ordered Moore to remove the monument. He refused, saying that the monument is a symbol of the roots of American law. He also said, "To do my duty, I must obey God." His supporters have offered several arguments on his behalf, notably that (a) the Founding Fathers often spoke of God; (b) every courtroom has a Bible to swear in witnesses and jurors; (c) the U.S. Supreme Court has a frieze of lawgivers, including Moses with the Ten Commandments, Hammurabi, Confucius, and Muhammad. In August 2003, Moore was suspended from his position on the court, and the monument was removed from view. Your views?

4. Since 1937, when San Francisco's Golden Gate Bridge opened, some 1,200 people have leaped from it to their deaths. The board of the Golden Gate Bridge, Highway and Transportation District periodically contemplates plans to make it suicide-proof. It discusses the kinds of devices proposed (railings, nets, or a combination), the cost (an estimated $15.25 million, which could be used for other civic purposes), the aesthetic factor (the devices may spoil the appearance of this renowned art deco work), and the engineering uncertainties (some engineers express reservations about the aerodynamic drag the barrier may create). And now consider these additional arguments against altering the bridge: (a) the government has no business paternalistically

interfering with the free will of persons who wish to commit suicide; (b) if the Golden Gate Bridge is made suicide-proof, persons who wish to commit suicide will easily find some other site, such as the nearby Bay Bridge; (c) only 3 percent of the persons who commit suicide in the Bay Area do so by leaping from the bridge.

The assignment: You are on the board of the Golden Gate Bridge. Suicides on the bridge are now averaging two a month, and a proposal to make the bridge suicide-proof has come up. Taking account of the arguments just mentioned, and any others—pro and con—that you can think of, what is your well-reasoned 500-word response?

5. In September 2004, the year of a presidential election, the Bush-Cheney campaign approached Allegheny College (in northwest Pennsylvania), asking to rent for October 13 the college's gymnasium, the largest enclosed space in the area. Because the electoral votes of Pennsylvania were uncertain, Vice President Cheney's appearance at Allegheny was likely to get national attention, at least briefly. The college did *not* have in place a policy against renting space to a political organization, so refusal to rent the gymnasium might seem like discrimination against the Republican Party. Further, the college faculty and administrators involved in making the decision concluded that the event would strengthen town/gown relationships and energize the students to participate in the political process. The gymnasium was therefore rented to the Bush-Cheney campaign, so that the vice president could appear.

The event was a sort of town-hall-style presentation, but tickets were limited: The campaign personnel distributed most of the six hundred tickets to local Republican activists; forty tickets were given to a group called College Republicans, who could distribute the tickets as they saw fit. Obviously the idea was to keep out hecklers and demonstrators, an entirely reasonable plan from the Republican point of view. Why should Republicans rent a hall and stage an event that might get national coverage if the opposing party could use it to get TV attention?

The issue: Should a college—supposedly a site where inquiry is open, where ideas are exchanged freely in robust debate—allow its facilities to be used by those who would stifle debate? Professor Daniel M. Shea, who initially favored the decision to rent the gymnasium, ultimately concluded that he was mistaken. In an essay in the *Chronicle of Higher Education* (August 4, 2006), Shea discusses the affair, and he suggests that colleges and universities ought to band together to "form an open-event alliance." Candidates might have at their disposal half of the available seats, but the other half would be for the college to distribute through some sort of open procedure, perhaps a lottery.

The assignment: Assume that a political party wanted to rent your institution's gymnasium or a large lecture hall. What would your position be? Why? In a letter of about 500 words addressed to the college paper, set forth your views.

2

Critical Reading: Getting Started

Some books are to be tasted, others to be chewed, and some few to be chewed and digested.

— FRANCIS BACON

ACTIVE READING

In the passage that we quote at the top of this page, Bacon makes at least two good points. One is that books are of varying worth; the second is that a taste of some books may be enough.

But even a book (or an essay) that you will chew and digest is one that you first may want to taste. How can you get a taste—that is, how can you get some sense of a piece of writing *before* you sit down to read it carefully?

Previewing

Even before you read a work, you may have some ideas about it, perhaps because you already know something about the **author.** You know, for example, that a work by Martin Luther King Jr. will probably deal with civil rights. You know, too, that it will be serious and eloquent. On the other hand, if you pick up an essay by Woody Allen, you will probably expect it to be amusing. It may be serious—Allen has written earnestly about many topics, especially those concerned with the media—but it's your hunch that the essay will be at least somewhat entertaining and probably will not be terribly difficult to understand. In short, a reader who has some knowledge of the author probably has some idea of what the writing will be like, and so the reader reads it in a certain mood. Admittedly, most of the authors represented in this book are not widely known, but we give biographical notes that may provide you with some sense of what to expect.

The **place of publication** may also tell you something about the essay. For instance, the *National Review* is a conservative journal. If you notice that an essay on affirmative action was published in the *National Review,* you are probably safe in tentatively assuming that the essay will not endorse affirmative action. On the other hand, *Ms. Magazine* is a liberal publication, and an essay on affirmative action published in *Ms.* will probably be an endorsement.

The **title** of an essay, too, may give you an idea of what to expect. Of course, a title may announce only the subject and not the author's thesis or point of view ("On Gun Control," "Should Drugs Be Legal?"), but fairly often it will indicate the thesis too, as in "Give Children the Vote" and "Gay Marriages: Make Them Legal." Knowing more or less what to expect, you can probably take in some of the major points even on a quick reading.

Skimming: Finding the Thesis

Although most of the material in this book is too closely argued to be fully understood by merely skimming, still, skimming can tell you a good deal. Read the first paragraph of an essay carefully because it may announce the author's **thesis** (chief point, major claim), and it may give you some sense of how the argument for that thesis will be conducted. (What we call the *thesis* can also be called the *main idea,* the *point,* or even the *argument,* but in this book we use *argument* to refer not only to the thesis statement but also to the entire development of the thesis in the essay.) Run your eye over the rest, looking for key expressions that indicate the author's conclusions, such as "It follows, then, that . . ." Passages of this sort often occur as the first or last sentence in a paragraph. And of course, pay attention to any headings within the text. Finally, pay special attention to the last paragraph because it probably will offer a summary and a brief restatement of the writer's thesis.

Having skimmed the work, you probably know the author's thesis, and you may detect the author's methods—for instance, whether the author supports the thesis chiefly by personal experience, by statistics, or by ridiculing the opposition. You also have a clear idea of the length and some idea of the difficulty of the piece. You know, then, whether you can read it carefully now before dinner or whether you had better put off a careful reading until you have more time.

Reading with a Pencil: Underlining, Highlighting, Annotating

Once you have a general idea of the work—not only an idea of its topic and thesis but also a sense of the way in which the thesis is argued—you can then go back and start reading it carefully.

As you read, **underline** or **highlight** key passages, and make **annotations** in the margins (but not in library books, please). Because you are reading actively, or interacting with the text, you will not simply let your eye rove across the page.

- You will underline or highlight what seem to be the chief points, so that later when you review the essay you can easily locate the main passages.

- But don't overdo a good thing. If you find yourself underlining or highlighting most of a page, you are probably not thinking carefully enough about what the key points are.

- Similarly, your marginal annotations should be brief and selective. They will probably consist of hints or clues, things like "really?," "doesn't follow," "good," "compare with Jones," and "check this."

- In short, in a paragraph you might underline or highlight a key definition, and in the margin you might write "good," or, "on the other hand," "?" if you think the definition is fuzzy or wrong.

You are interacting with the text and laying the groundwork for eventually writing your own essay on what you have read.

What you annotate will depend largely on your **purpose.** If you are reading an essay in order to see the ways in which the writer organizes an argument, you will annotate one sort of thing. If you are reading in order to challenge the thesis, you will annotate other things. Here is a passage from an essay entitled "On Racist Speech," with a student's rather skeptical, even aggressive annotations. But notice that at least one of the annotations — "Definition of 'fighting words'" — apparently was made chiefly in order to remind the reader of where an important term appears in the essay. The essay, printed in full on page 61, is by Charles R. Lawrence III, a professor of law at Georgetown University. It originally appeared in the *Chronicle of Higher Education* (October 25, 1989), a publication read chiefly by college and university faculty members and administrators.

Example of such a policy?

University officials who have formulated policies to respond to incidents of racial harassment have been characterized in the press as "thought police," but such policies generally do nothing more than impose ⟨sanctions⟩ against intentional face-to-face insults. When *What about* racist speech takes the form of face-to-face insults, catcalls, or other *sexist speech?* assaultive speech aimed at an individual or small group of persons, it falls directly within the "fighting words" exception to First *Definition of* Amendment protection. The Supreme Court has held that words *"fighting* which "by their very utterance inflict injury or tend to incite an *words"* immediate breach of the peace" are not protected by the First Amendment.

?

Example?

If the purpose of the First Amendment is to foster the greatest amount of speech, racial insults disserve that purpose. Assaultive racist speech functions as a preemptive strike. The invective is experienced as a blow, not as a proffered idea, and once the blow is *Really?* struck, it is unlikely that a dialogue will follow. Racial insults are *Probably* particularly undeserving of First Amendment protection because *depends on* the perpetrator's intention is not to discover truth or initiate dia- *the individual.* logue but to injure the victim. In most situations, members *How does he* of minority groups realize that they are likely to lose if they *know?* respond to epithets by fighting and are forced to remain silent and submissive.

Why must speech always seek "to discover truth"?

"This; Therefore, That"

To arrive at a coherent thought or a coherent series of thoughts that will lead to a reasonable conclusion, a writer has to go through a good deal of preliminary effort. On page 12 we talked about patterns of thought that stimulate the generation of specific ideas. The path to sound conclusions involves similar thought patterns that carry forward the arguments presented in the essay:

- While these arguments are convincing, they fail to consider . . .
- While these arguments are convincing, they must also consider . . .
- These arguments, rather than being convincing, instead prove . . .
- While these authors agree, in my opinion . . .
- Although it is often true that . . .

All of these patterns can serve as heuristics or prompts—that is, they can stimulate the creation of ideas.

And if the writer is to convince the reader that the conclusion is sound, the reasoning that led to the conclusion must be set forth in detail, with a good deal of "This; therefore, that"; If this, then that"; and "It might be objected at this point that . . ." The arguments in this book require more comment than President Calvin Coolidge provided when his wife, who hadn't been able to go to church on a Sunday, asked him what the preacher's sermon was about. "Sin," he said. His wife persisted: "What did the preacher say about it?" Coolidge's response: "He was against it."

But, again, when we say that most of the arguments in this book are presented at length and require careful reading, we do not mean that they are obscure; we mean, rather, that the reader has to take the sentences thoughtfully, one by one. And speaking of one by one, we are reminded of an episode in Lewis Carroll's *Through the Looking-Glass:*

> "Can you do Addition?" the White Queen asked. "What's one and one and one and one and one and one and one and one and one and one?"
> "I don't know," said Alice. "I lost count."
> "She can't do Addition," the Red Queen said.

It's easy enough to add one and one and one and so on, and Alice can, of course, do addition, but not at the pace that the White Queen sets. Fortunately, you can set your own pace in reading the cumulative thinking set forth in the essays we reprint. Skimming won't work, but slow reading—and thinking about what you are reading—will.

When you first pick up an essay, you may indeed want to skim it, for some of the reasons mentioned on page 33, but sooner or later you have to settle down to read it and to think about it. The effort will be worthwhile. John Locke, the seventeenth-century English philosopher, said,

Reading furnishes the mind with materials of knowledge; it is *thinking* [that] makes what we read ours. We are of the ruminating kind, and it is not enough to cram ourselves with a great load of collections; unless we chew them over again they will not give us strength and nourishment.

First, Second, and Third Thoughts

Suppose you are reading an argument about pornographic pictures. For the present purpose, it doesn't matter whether the argument favors or opposes censorship. As you read the argument, ask yourself whether *pornography* has been adequately defined. Has the writer taken the trouble to make sure that the reader and the writer are thinking about the same thing? If not, the very topic under discussion has not been adequately fixed; and therefore further debate over the issue may well be so unclear as to be futile. How, then, ought a topic such as this be defined for effective critical thinking?

It goes without saying that pornography can't be defined simply as pictures of nude figures or even of nude figures copulating, for such a definition would include not only photographs taken for medical, socio-logical, and scientific purposes but also some of the world's great art. Nobody seriously thinks that such images should be called pornography.

Is it enough, then, to say that pornography "stirs lustful thoughts" or "appeals to prurient interests"? No, because pictures of shoes probably stir lustful thoughts in shoe fetishists, and pictures of children in ads for underwear probably stir lustful thoughts in pedophiles. Perhaps, then, the definition must be amended to "material that stirs lustful thoughts in the average person." But will this restatement do? First, it may be hard to agree on the characteristics of "the average person." In other matters, the law often does assume that there is such a creature as "the reasonable person," and most people would agree that in a given situa-tion there might be a reasonable response—for almost everyone. But we cannot be so sure that the same is true about the emotional responses of this "average person." In any case, far from stimulating sexual impulses, sadomasochistic pictures of booted men wielding whips on naked women probably turn off "the average person," yet this is the sort of material that most people would agree is pornographic.

Something must be wrong, then, with the definition that pornogra-phy is material that "stirs lustful thoughts in the average person." We began with a definition that was too broad ("pictures of nude figures"), but now we have a definition that is too narrow. We must go back to the drawing board. This is not nitpicking. The label "average person" was found to be inadequate in a pornography case argued before the Supreme Court; because the materials in question were aimed at a homosexual audience, it was agreed that the average person would not find them sexually stimulating.

One difficulty has been that pornography is often defined according to its effect on the viewer ("genital commotion," Father Harold Gardiner, S.J., called it, in *Catholic Viewpoint on Censorship*), but different people, we know, may respond differently. In the first half of the twentieth century, in an effort to distinguish between pornography and art—after all, most people don't want to regard Botticelli's *Venus* or Michelangelo's *David* as "dirty"—it was commonly said that a true work of art does not stimulate in the spectator ideas or desires that the real object might stimulate. But in 1956, Kenneth Clark, probably the most influential English-speaking art critic of the twentieth century, changed all that; in a book called *The Nude* he announced that "no nude, however abstract, should fail to arouse in the spectator some vestige of erotic feeling."

SUMMARIZING AND PARAPHRASING

Perhaps the best approach to a fairly difficult essay is, after first reading, to reread it and simultaneously to take notes on a sheet of paper, perhaps summarizing each paragraph in a sentence or two. Writing a summary will help you to

- Understand the contents and
- See the strengths and weaknesses of the piece.

Don't confuse a summary with a paraphrase. A paraphrase is a word-by-word or phrase-by-phrase rewording of a text, a sort of translation of the author's language into your own. A paraphrase is therefore as long as the original or even longer; a summary is much shorter. A book may be summarized in a page, or even in a paragraph or a sentence. Obviously the summary will leave out all detail, but—if the summary is a true summary—it accurately states the gist, the essential thesis or claim or point of the original.

Why would anyone ever summarize, and why would anyone ever paraphrase? Because, as we have already said, these two activities—in different ways—help readers follow the original author's ideas. But, again, summarizing and paraphrasing are not the same.

- **When you summarize,** you are standing back, saying very briefly what the whole adds up to; you are seeing the forest, not the individual trees.
- **When you paraphrase,** you are inching through the forest, scrutinizing each tree—that is, finding a synonym for almost every word in the original, in an effort to make sure that you know exactly what you are dealing with. (*Caution:* Do not incorporate a summary or a paraphrase into your own essay without acknowledging your source and stating that you are summarizing or paraphrasing.)

Let's examine the distinction between summary and paraphrase in connection with the first two paragraphs of Paul Goodman's essay, "A Proposal to Abolish Grading," which is excerpted from Goodman's book, *Compulsory Miseducation and the Community of Scholars* (1966). The two paragraphs run thus:

> Let half a dozen of the prestigious universities—Chicago, Stanford, the Ivy League—abolish grading, and use testing only and entirely for pedagogic purposes as teachers see fit.
>
> Anyone who knows the frantic temper of the present schools will understand the transvaluation of values that would be effected by this modest innovation. For most of the students, the competitive grade has come to be the essence. The naive teacher points to the beauty of the subject and the ingenuity of the research; the shrewd student asks if he is responsible for that on the final exam.

A **summary** of these two paragraphs might run thus:

> If some top universities used tests only to help students to learn, students would stop worrying about grades and might share the teacher's interest in the beauty of the subject.

We hope we have accurately summarized Goodman's point, though we know we have lost his flavor, his style—for instance, the wry tone in his pointed contrast between "the naive teacher" and "the shrewd student."

Now for a **paraphrase**. Suppose you are not quite sure what Goodman is getting at, maybe because you are uncertain about the meanings of some words (perhaps *pedagogic* and *transvaluation*?), or maybe just because the whole passage is making such a startling point that you want to make sure that you have understood it. In such a case, you may want to move slowly through the sentences, translating them (so to speak) into your own English. For instance, you might turn Goodman's "pedagogic purposes" into "goals in teaching" or "attempts to help students to learn," or some such thing. Here is a paraphrase—not a summary but an extensive rewording—of Goodman's paragraphs:

> Suppose some of the top universities—such as Chicago, Stanford, Harvard, and Yale, and whatever other schools are in the Ivy League—stopped using grades and used tests only in order to help students to learn.
>
> Everyone who is aware of the hysterical mood in schools today will understand the enormous change in views of what is good and bad that would come about by this small change. At present, instructors, unworldly folk, talk about how beautiful their subjects are, but smart students know that grades are what count, so they listen to instructors only if they know that the material the instructor is talking about will be on the exam.

In short, you may want to paraphrase an important text that your imagined reader may find obscure because it is written in specialized, technical language, for instance, the language of psychiatry or of sociology. You want the reader to see the passage itself—you don't want to give just the gist, just a summary—but you know that the full passage will puzzle the reader, so you offer help, giving a paraphrase before going on to make your own point about the author's point.

A second good reason to offer a paraphrase is if there is substantial disagreement about what the text says. The Second Amendment to the U.S. Constitution is a good example of this sort of text:

> A well regulated Militia being necessary to the security of a free
> State, the right of the people to keep and bear Arms shall not be
> infringed.

Exactly what, one might ask, is a "Militia"? And what does it mean for a militia to be "well regulated"? And does "the people" mean each individual, or does it mean—something very different—the citizenry as some sort of unified group? After all, elsewhere in the document, when the Constitution speaks of individuals, it speaks of a "man" or a "person," not "the people." To speak of "the people" is to use a term (some argue) that sounds like a reference to a unified group—perhaps the citizens of each of the thirteen states?—rather than a reference to individuals. On the other hand, if Congress did mean a unified group rather than individuals, why didn't it say "Congress shall not prohibit the states from organizing militias"?

In fact, thousands of pages have been written about this sentence, and if you are going to talk about it, you certainly have to let your reader know exactly what you make out of each word. In short, you almost surely will paraphrase it, going word by word, giving your reader your sense of what each word or phrase says. Here is one paraphrase:

> Because an independent society needs the protection of an armed force
> if it is to remain free, the government may not limit the right of the
> individuals (who may some day form the militia needed to keep the
> society free) to possess weapons.

In this interpretation, the Constitution grants individuals the right to possess weapons, and that is that. Other students of the Constitution, however, offer very different paraphrases, usually along these lines:

> Because each state that is now part of the United States may need to
> protect its freedom [from the new national government], the national
> government may not infringe on the right of each state to form its own
> disciplined militia.

This second paraphrase says that the federal government may not prevent each state from having a militia; it says nothing about every individual person having a right to possess weapons. The first of these two paraphrases, or something like it, is one that might be offered by the National

Rifle Association or any other group that interprets the Constitution as guaranteeing individuals the right to own guns. The second paraphrase, or something like it, might be offered by groups that seek to limit the ownership of guns.

Why paraphrase? Here are two reasons (perhaps the *only* two reasons) why you might paraphrase a passage:

- To help yourself to understand it. In this case, the paraphrase does not appear in your essay.

- To help your reader to understand a passage that is especially important but that for one reason or another is not immediately clear. In this case, you paraphrase the passage to let the reader know exactly what it means. This paraphrase, of course, does appear in your essay.

A Note about Paraphrase and Plagiarism

If you offer a paraphrase, be sure to tell the reader, explicitly, what you are doing and why you are doing it. If you do not explicitly say that you are paraphrasing Jones's material, you are plagiarizing. If you merely cite the author ("As Jones says") and then you give a paraphrase, you are plagiarizing. How, you may ask, can you be accused of plagiarism if you cite your source? Here is how: If you do not explicitly say that you are paraphrasing Jones, the reader assumes you have digested Jones's point and are giving it in a summary form, entirely in your own words; the reader does not think (unless you *say* that you are paraphrasing) that you are merely following Jones's passage phrase by phrase, sentence by sentence, changing some words but not really writing *your own* sentences. In short, when you paraphrase you are translating, not writing. (For a further comment on plagiarism, see page 277.)

> **A RULE FOR WRITERS:** Your essay is *likely to include brief summaries* of points of view that you are agreeing or disagreeing with, but it will *rarely include a paraphrase* unless the original is obscure and you think you need to present a passage at length but in words that are clearer than those of the original. If you do paraphrase, explicitly identify the material as a paraphrase.

Last Words (Almost) about Summarizing

Summarizing each paragraph or each group of closely related paragraphs will help you to follow the thread of the discourse and, when you are finished, will provide you with a useful map of the essay. Then, when you reread the essay yet again, you may want to underline passages that you now understand are the author's key ideas—for instance, definitions, generalizations, summaries—and you may want to jot notes in the margins, questioning the logic, expressing your uncertainty, or calling attention to other writers who see the matter differently. Here is a paragraph from a 1973 decision of the U.S. Supreme Court, written by Chief Justice Warren Burger, setting forth reasons that the government may censor obscene material. We follow it with a sample summary.

> If we accept the unprovable assumption that a complete education requires the reading of certain books, and the well-nigh universal belief that good books, plays, and art lift the spirit, improve the mind, enrich the human personality, and develop character, can we then say that a state legislature may not act on the corollary assumption that commerce in obscene books, or public exhibitions focused on obscene conduct, have a tendency to exert a corrupting and debasing impact leading to antisocial behavior? The sum of experience, including that of the past two decades, affords an ample basis for legislatures to conclude that a sensitive, key relationship of human existence, central to family life, community welfare, and the development of human personality, can be debased and distorted by crass commercial exploitation of sex. Nothing in the Constitution prohibits a State from reaching such a conclusion and acting on it legislatively simply because there is no conclusive empirical data.

Now for a student's summary. Notice that the summary does not include the reader's evaluation or any other sort of comment on the original; it is simply an attempt to condense the original. Notice too that, because its purpose is merely to assist the reader to grasp the ideas of the original by focusing on them, it is written in a sort of shorthand (not every sentence is a complete sentence), though, of course, if this summary were being presented in an essay, it would have to be grammatical.

> Unprovable but acceptable assumption that good books etc. shape character, so that legislature can assume obscene works debase character. Experience lets one conclude that exploitation of sex debases the individual, family, and community. Though "there is no conclusive empirical data" for this view, the Constitution lets states act on it legislatively.

Notice that

- A few words (in the last sentence of the summary) are quoted exactly as in the original. They are enclosed within quotation marks.
- For the most part, the original material is drastically reduced. The first sentence of the original, some eighty words, is reduced in the summary to nineteen words.

Of course, the summary loses much of the detail and flavor of the original: "Good books etc." is not the same as "good books, plays, and art"; and "shape character" is not the same as "lift the spirit, improve the mind, enrich the human personality, and develop character." But the statement in the summary will do as a rough approximation, useful for a quick review. More important, the act of writing a summary forces the reader to go slowly and to think about each sentence of the original. Such thinking may help the reader-writer to see the complexity—or the hollowness—of the original.

The sample summary in the preceding paragraph was just that, a summary; but when writing your own summaries, you will often find it useful to inject your own thoughts ("seems far-fetched," "strong point," "I don't get it"), enclosing them within square brackets or in some other way to keep these responses distinct from your summary of the writer's argument.

Review: If your instructor asks you to hand in a summary,

- It should not contain ideas other than those found in the original piece.
- You can rearrange these, add transitions as needed, and so forth, but the summary should give the reader nothing but a sense of the original piece.
- If the summary includes any of the original wording, these words should be enclosed within quotation marks.
- In your notes, keep a clear distinction between *your* writing and the writing of your *source*. For the most part you will summarize, but if you paraphrase, indicate that the words are a paraphrase, and if you quote directly, indicate that you are quoting.

We don't want to nag you, but we do want to emphasize the need to read with a pencil in hand. If you read slowly and take notes, you will find that what you read will give you the "strength and nourishment" that John Locke spoke of.

> **A RULE FOR WRITERS:** Remember that when you write a summary, you are putting yourself into the author's shoes.

Having insisted that the essays in this book need to be read slowly because the writers build one reason on another, we will now seem to contradict ourselves by presenting an essay that can almost be skimmed. Susan Jacoby's essay originally appeared in the *New York Times*, a thoroughly respectable newspaper but not one that requires its readers to linger over every sentence. Still, compared with most of the news accounts, Jacoby's essay requires close reading. When you read the essay, you will notice that it zigs and zags, not because Jacoby is careless or wants to befuddle her readers but because she wants to build a strong case to support her point of view and must therefore look at some widely held views that she does *not* accept; she must set these forth and then give her reasons for rejecting them.

Susan Jacoby

Susan Jacoby (b. 1946), a journalist since the age of seventeen, is well known for her feminist writings. "A First Amendment Junkie" (our title) appeared in the Hers column in the New York Times *in 1978.*

A First Amendment Junkie

It is no news that many women are defecting from the ranks of civil libertarians on the issue of obscenity. The conviction of Larry Flynt, publisher of *Hustler* magazine—before his metamorphosis into a born-again Christian—was greeted with unabashed feminist approval. Harry Reems, the unknown actor who was convicted by a Memphis jury for conspiring to distribute the movie *Deep Throat*, has carried on his legal battles with almost no support from women who ordinarily regard themselves as supporters of the First Amendment. Feminist writers and scholars have even discussed the possibility of making common cause against pornography with adversaries of the women's movement—including opponents of the equal rights amendment and "right-to-life" forces.

All of this is deeply disturbing to a woman writer who believes, as I always have and still do, in an absolute interpretation of the First Amendment. Nothing in Larry Flynt's garbage convinces me that the late Justice Hugo L. Black was wrong in his opinion that "the Federal Government is without any power whatsoever under the Constitution to put any type of burden on free speech and expression of ideas of any kind (as distinguished from conduct)." Many women I like and respect tell me I am wrong; I cannot remember having become involved in so many heated discussions of a public issue since the end of the Vietnam War. A feminist writer described my views as those of a "First Amendment junkie."

Many feminist arguments for controls on pornography carry the implicit conviction that porn books, magazines, and movies pose a greater threat to women than similarly repulsive exercises of free speech pose to other offended groups. This conviction has, of course, been shared by everyone—regardless of race, creed, or sex—who has ever argued in favor of abridging the First Amendment. It is the argument used by some Jews who have withdrawn their support from the American Civil Liberties Union because it has defended the right of American Nazis to march through a community inhabited by survivors of Hitler's concentration camps.

If feminists want to argue that the protection of the Constitution should not be extended to *any* particularly odious or threatening form of speech, they have a reasonable argument (although I don't agree with it). But it is ridiculous to suggest that the porn shops on 42nd Street are more disgusting to women than a march of neo-Nazis is to survivors of the extermination camps.

The arguments over pornography also blur the vital distinction 5 between expression of ideas and conduct. When I say I believe unreservedly in the First Amendment, someone always comes back at me with the issue of "kiddie porn." But kiddie porn is not a First Amendment issue. It is an issue of the abuse of power—the power adults have over children—and not of obscenity. Parents and promoters have no more right to use their children to make porn movies than they do to send them to work in coal mines. The responsible adults should be prosecuted, just as adults who use children for back-breaking farm labor should be prosecuted.

Susan Brownmiller, in *Against Our Will: Men, Women, and Rape*, has described pornography as "the undiluted essence of antifemale propaganda." I think this is a fair description of some types of pornography, especially of the brutish subspecies that equates sex with death and portrays women primarily as objects of violence.

The equation of sex and violence, personified by some glossy rock record album covers as well as by *Hustler*, has fed the illusion that censorship of pornography can be conducted on a more rational basis than other types of censorship. Are all pictures of naked women obscene? Clearly not, says a friend. A Renoir nude is art, she says, and *Hustler* is trash. "Any reasonable person" knows that.

But what about something between art and trash—something, say, along the lines of *Playboy* or *Penthouse* magazines? I asked five women for their reactions to one picture in *Penthouse* and got responses that ranged from "lovely" and "sensuous" to "revolting" and "demeaning." Feminists, like everyone else, seldom have rational reasons for their preferences in erotica. Like members of juries, they tend to disagree when confronted with something that falls short of 100 percent vulgarity.

In any case, feminists will not be the arbiters of good taste if it becomes easier to harass, prosecute, and convict people on obscenity charges. Most of the people who want to censor girlie magazines are equally opposed to open discussion of issues that are of vital concern to women: rape, abortion, menstruation, contraception, lesbianism—in fact, the entire range of sexual experience from a women's viewpoint.

Feminist writers and editors and filmmakers have limited financial 10 resources: Confronted by a determined prosecutor, Hugh Hefner[1] will fare better than Susan Brownmiller. Would the Memphis jurors who convicted Harry Reems for his role in *Deep Throat* be inclined to take a more positive view of paintings of the female genitalia done by sensitive feminist artists? *Ms.* magazine has printed color reproductions of some of those art works; *Ms.* is already banned from a number of high school libraries because someone considers it threatening and/or obscene.

---

[1]**Hugh Hefner** Founder and longtime publisher of *Playboy* magazine. [Editors' note.]

Feminists who want to censor what they regard as harmful pornography have essentially the same motivation as other would-be censors: They want to use the power of the state to accomplish what they have been unable to achieve in the marketplace of ideas and images. The impulse to censor places no faith in the possibilities of democratic persuasion.

It isn't easy to persuade certain men that they have better uses for $1.95 each month than to spend it on a copy of *Hustler*? Well, then, give the men no choice in the matter.

I believe there is also a connection between the impulse toward censorship on the part of people who used to consider themselves civil libertarians and a more general desire to shift responsibility from individuals to institutions. When I saw the movie *Looking for Mr. Goodbar*, I was stunned by its series of visual images equating sex and violence, coupled with what seems to me the mindless message (a distortion of the fine Judith Rossner novel) that casual sex equals death. When I came out of the movie, I was even more shocked to see parents standing in line with children between the ages of ten and fourteen.

I simply don't know why a parent would take a child to see such a movie, any more than I understand why people feel they can't turn off a television set their child is watching. Whenever I say that, my friends tell me I don't know how it is because I don't have children. True, but I do have parents. When I was a child, they did turn off the TV. They didn't expect the Federal Communications Commission to do their job for them.

I am a First Amendment junkie. You can't OD on the First Amend-   15
ment, because free speech is its own best antidote.

Summarizing Jacoby, Paragraph by Paragraph

Suppose we want to make a rough summary, more or less paragraph by paragraph, of Jacoby's essay. Such a summary might look something like this (the numbers refer to Jacoby's paragraphs):

1. Although feminists usually support the First Amendment, when it comes to pornography, many feminists take pretty much the position of those who oppose ERA and abortion and other causes of the women's movement.
2. Larry Flynt produces garbage, but I think his conviction represents an unconstitutional limitation of freedom of speech.
3, 4. Feminists who want to control (censor) pornography argue that it poses a greater threat to women than similar repulsive speech poses to other groups. If feminists want to say that all offensive speech should be restricted, they can make a case, but it is absurd to say that pornography is a "greater threat" to women than a march of neo-Nazis is to survivors of concentration camps.
5. Trust in the First Amendment is not refuted by kiddie porn; kiddie porn is not a First Amendment issue but an issue of child abuse.

6, 7, 8. Some feminists think censorship of pornography can be more "rational" than other kinds of censorship, but a picture of a nude woman strikes some women as base and others as "lovely." There is no unanimity.

9, 10. If feminists censor girlie magazines, they will find that they are unwittingly helping opponents of the women's movement to censor discussions of rape, abortion, and so on. Some of the art in the feminist magazine *Ms.* would doubtless be censored.

11, 12. Like other would-be censors, feminists want to use the power of the state to achieve what they have not achieved in "the marketplace of ideas." They display a lack of faith in "democratic persuasion."

13, 14. This attempt at censorship reveals a desire to "shift responsibility from individuals to institutions." The responsibility—for instance, to keep young people from equating sex with violence—is properly the parents'.

15. We can't have too much of the First Amendment.

Jacoby's **thesis**, or major claim, or chief proposition—that any form of censorship of pornography is wrong—is clear enough, even as early as the end of her first paragraph, but it gets its life or its force from the **reasons** offered throughout the essay. If we want to reduce our summary even further, we might say that Jacoby supports her thesis by arguing several subsidiary points. We will merely assert them briefly, but Jacoby **argues** them—that is, she gives reasons:

a. Pornography can scarcely be thought of as more offensive than Nazism.

b. Women disagree about which pictures are pornographic.

c. Feminists who want to censor pornography will find that they help antifeminists to censor discussions of issues advocated by the women's movement.

d. Feminists who favor censorship are in effect turning to the government to achieve what they haven't achieved in the free marketplace.

e. One sees this abdication of responsibility in the fact that parents allow their children to watch unsuitable movies and television programs.

If we want to present a brief summary in the form of one coherent paragraph—perhaps as part of our own essay to show the view we are arguing in behalf of or against—we might write something like this summary. (The summary would, of course, be prefaced by a **lead-in** along these lines: "Susan Jacoby, writing in the *New York Times,* offers a forceful argument against censorship of pornography. Jacoby's view, briefly, is . . .".)

When it comes to censorship of pornography, some feminists take a position shared by opponents of the feminist movement. They argue that pornography poses a greater threat to women than other forms of offensive speech offer to other groups, but this interpretation is simply a mistake. Pointing to kiddie porn is also a mistake, for kiddie porn is an issue involving not the First Amendment but child abuse. Feminists who support censorship of pornography will inadvertently aid those who wish to censor discussions of abortion and rape or censor art that is published in magazines such as *Ms.* The solution is not for individuals to turn to institutions (that is, for the government to limit the First Amendment) but for individuals to accept the responsibility for teaching young people not to equate sex with violence.

Whether we agree or disagree with Jacoby's thesis, we must admit that the reasons she sets forth to support it are worth thinking about. Only a reader who closely follows the reasoning with which Jacoby buttresses her thesis is in a position to accept or reject it.

TOPICS FOR CRITICAL THINKING AND WRITING

1. What does Jacoby mean when she says she is a "First Amendment junkie" (para. 15)?

2. The essay is primarily an argument against the desire of some feminists to try to censor pornography of the sort that appeals to some heterosexual adult males, but the next-to-last paragraph is about television and children. Is the paragraph connected to Jacoby's overall argument? If so, how?

3. Evaluate the final paragraph as a final paragraph. (Effective final paragraphs are not, of course, all of one sort. Some, for example, round off the essay by echoing something from the opening; others suggest that the reader, having now seen the problem, should think further about it or even act on it. But a good final paragraph, whatever else it does, should make the reader feel that the essay has come to an end, not just broken off.)

4. This essay originally appeared in the *New York Times.* If you are unfamiliar with this newspaper, consult an issue or two in your library. Next, in a paragraph, try to characterize the readers of the paper—that is, Jacoby's audience.

5. Jacoby claims in paragraph 2 that she "believes . . . in an absolute interpretation of the First Amendment." What does such an interpretation involve? Would it permit shouting "Fire!" in a crowded theater even though the shouter knows there is no fire? Would it permit shouting racist insults at blacks or immigrant Vietnamese? Spreading untruths about someone's past? If the "absolutist" interpretation of the First Amendment does permit these statements, does that argument show that nothing is morally wrong with uttering them? (*Does* the First Amendment, as actually interpreted by the Supreme Court today, permit any or all of these claims? Consult your reference librarian for help in answering this question.)

✓ A CHECKLIST FOR GETTING STARTED

☐ Have I adequately previewed the work?

☐ Can I state the thesis?

☐ If I have jotted down a summary,

  ☐ Is the summary accurate?

  ☐ Does the summary mention all the chief points?

  ☐ If there are inconsistencies, are they in the summary or the original selection?

☐ Will the summary be clear and helpful?

---

6. Jacoby implies that permitting prosecution of persons on obscenity charges will lead eventually to censorship of "open discussion" of important issues such as "rape, abortion, menstruation, contraception, lesbianism" (para. 9). Do you find her fears convincing? Does she give any evidence to support her claim?

Later, in Chapter 5, Writing an Analysis of an Argument, we will go into detail about the business of examining a written argument, but here we can briefly look at the topic.

First, read Anya Kamenetz's essay—it was an op-ed piece in the *New York Times* on February 6, 2008, which is to say it appeared before Obama was elected—and then look at the exercise that follows it.

Anya Kamenetz

Anya Kemenetz (b. 1980), a staff writer for Fast Company, *is the author of* Generation Debt *(2006). We reprint an essay that originally appeared in the* Boston Globe, *February 6, 2008.*

You're 16, You're Beautiful and You're a Voter

The 2008 presidential campaign has made history in many ways, not least being the arrival of a new generation at the polls. Voters under twenty-nine were the first to anoint Barack Obama as their candidate. Reversing a general decline that began in 1972, youth turnout leapt in 2004, and in the early contests in this primary season it was up sharply.

We should hasten the enfranchisement of this generation, born between 1980 and 1995, by lowering the voting age to sixteen.

Age thresholds are meant to bring an impartial data point to bear on insoluble moral questions: who can be legally executed, who can die in

Iraq, who can operate the meat cutter at the local sub shop. But in a time when both youth and age are being extended, these dividing lines are increasingly inadequate.

Legal age requirements should never stand alone. They should be flexible and pragmatic and paired with educational and cognitive requirements for the exercise of legal maturity.

Driving laws provide the best model for combining early beginnings 5 and mandatory education. Many states have had success with a gradual phasing in of driving rights over a year or more, starting with a learner's permit at age sixteen. The most restrictive of these programs are associated with a 38 percent reduction in fatal crashes among the youngest drivers, according to a study conducted by the AAA Foundation for Traffic Safety.

Similarly, sixteen-year-olds who want to start voting should be able to obtain an "early voting permit" from their high schools upon passing a simple civics course similar to the citizenship test. Besides increasing voter registration, this system would reinforce the notion of voting as a privilege and duty as well as a right—without imposing any across-the-board literacy tests for those over eighteen.

And why stop at voting? Sixteen is a good starting point for phasing in adult rights and responsibilities, from voting to drinking to marriage. In reality, this is already when most people have their first jobs, their first drinks, and their sexual initiations. The law ought to empower young people to negotiate these transitions openly, not furtively.

We know driving laws reflect reality; whoever heard of the scourge of under-age driving? On the other hand, studies have shown that three-fourths of high school seniors have drunk alcohol. Surveys show that teenagers who drink at home with their families go on to drink less than those who sneak beers with friends. Imagine sixteen-year-olds receiving a drinking permit upon passage of a mandatory course about alcoholism. The permit would allow a tipple only at family gatherings or school functions for two years—until you graduate or leave home.

The phasing in of credit cards at sixteen could work with firm restrictions. A parental co-signer should be required until young applicants have made a year of on-time payments from their own wages. The most important requirement would be passing a mandatory financial literacy test. The applicant would define "compound interest," correctly decipher the fine print on a credit card agreement and argue with a robotic customer service representative over a mysterious fee. Surely this graduated system would be safer than handing young people a $2,000 line of credit just as they leave home for the first time.

The more we treat teenagers as adults, the more they rise to our 10 expectations. From a developmental and vocational point of view, the late teens are the right starting point for young people to think seriously about their futures. Government can help this process by bestowing rights along with responsibilities.

Tying adult rights to cognitive requirements could also smooth the path to dealing with a much bigger age-related social problem. Demographically, those over eighty-five are our fastest-growing group. By 2020, the entire nation will be about as silver-haired as Florida is today. We need to be able to test Americans of all ages, to make sure they're still qualified to drive and to help them avoid financial scammers. From a public health point of view, the silver tsunami poses more of a threat than marauding teenagers ever did.

Exercise: Creating a Strategies Outline

EXAMINING THE FUNCTIONS OF PARAGRAPHS

Reread the essay, and then, going through it beginning with the title and moving paragraph by paragraph, write a sentence or two about *what* each paragraph does. Note: We are *not* asking you to summarize the content of each paragraph. Rather, we are asking you to examine the author's strategies from start to finish. Thus, we might say:

> The title arouses interest, suspense, because it is so clearly contrary to fact when it asserts that a sixteen-year-old is a voter. The reader wonders how the author will go on to explain the title.

And we might say of the first paragraph:

> By emphasizing the role of young people in the 2008 presidential election, the opening paragraph lays the groundwork for arguing the writer's thesis—that the vote should be given to people as young as sixteen. In short, the opening paragraph does not announce the thesis, but it does remind the reader of an historical fact that prepares the reader to accept the thesis.

The point of the exercise: By looking not only at *what* the writer says but also at *how* she structures her argument, you will increase your sense of ways in which you can structure your own written arguments.

CREATING A STRATEGIES OUTLINE

The second paragraph, a mere single sentence, asserts the thesis. The thesis was more or less implied in the title, but now the writer states it unambiguously. Still, this sentence does not *argue* the point, that is, the sentence does not offer any reasons. With the third paragraph, however, the writer begins to argue in earnest, first by addressing the issue of the "age threshold." She recognizes that this business of establishing an age threshold sometimes literally involves matters of life and death (for instance, "who can be legally executed"), and she claims that the current "dividing lines are increasingly inadequate." She is cautiously working her way toward getting the reader to agree that at least the issue can be debated. That is, readers at this point probably are willing to agree with the writer that the "age threshold" might at least be re-examined. If we are with her on this first point, well, she may be softening us up so that we will agree with her thesis.

And indeed her fourth paragraph is one that probably most readers can agrees with:

Legal age requirements should never stand alone. They should be flexible and pragmatic and paired with educational and cognitive requirements for the exercise of legal maturity.

We probably agree, for instance, that age alone should not be the decisive factor in the matter of who is allowed to drive a vehicle — and this is the very piece of evidence that she introduces in her next paragraph. In short, and to repeat, Kamenetz is slowly gaining our agreement on *related* matters, with the ultimate goal, of course, of getting us to agree with her thesis.

Letters of Response by Betty Agard, Robert Epstein, Delia McQuade Emmons, and Amanda Bergson-Shilcock

To the Editor:

Anya Kamenetz proposes that sixteen-year-olds who can pass a civics test be allowed to vote. I think that we should take it a step further and make everyone take such a test.

We don't expect everyone who is eighteen to know how to drive, so we make them take a test. Age alone is insufficient.

Likewise, every voter should be required to know whom and what they are voting for. A civics test may prevent elections from turning into beauty contests.

BETSY AGARD
Brooklyn, Feb. 6, 2008

To the Editor:

No remarkable abilities emerge suddenly at age sixteen — or, for that matter, at age eighteen or twenty-one. In fact, as I show in a new book on adolescence, human cognitive abilities peak between ages thirteen and fifteen, and American adults are no more competent than American teenagers across a wide range of competencies.

Does this mean we should lower the voting age to thirteen? Absolutely not. Age should simply not be part of the voting equation. It's a stale remnant from eras that restricted voting to twenty-one-year-old male landowners.

What we really need are individual voters who can show themselves to be competent, not who fit our demographic biases: voters who can reason and who know the basics about government, the issues, and the candidates. People of any age, gender, or race who can demonstrate relevant competence should be allowed to vote, and the less competent should be excluded.

Whom would we elect if the electorate were actually competent? And whom would we have never elected?

ROBERT EPSTEIN
San Diego, Feb. 6, 2008

The writer, a visiting scholar at the University of California at San Diego, is former editor-in-chief of Psychology Today.

To the Editor:

Anya Kamenetz proposes that sixteen-year-olds be issued "early voting permits" upon passing a simple civics test similar to the citizenship test.

Her stated reasons? Well, this is the age at which most people have their first job, their first drink, and their sexual initiation.

Two of these three activities reflect bad judgment by teenagers. (It's odd that Ms. Kamenetz doesn't cite increases in reading, math, or SAT scores as reasons to give younger people the vote.)

Anyone who observes sixteen-year-olds close up when they are unaware that they are being watched knows that they still have a lot of growing up to do. Having an out-of-wedlock child won't make adults of them; neither will a voting permit.

DELIA McQUADE EMMONS
North Caldwell, N.J., Feb. 6, 2008

To the Editor:

Here is one more compelling reason for people under eighteen to have the right to vote: taxes.

It's legal in many parts of the country for teenagers to start working at age fourteen. For young people, that means years of having money taken away without a say in its use.

We fought a revolution against taxation without representation. Why should we inflict it on our youth now?

AMANDA BERGSON-SHILCOCK
Fort Washington, Pa., Feb. 6, 2008

TOPICS FOR CRITICAL THINKING AND WRITING

1. What does it mean to describe voting as a "privilege" (para. 6)? Do you agree? Explain yourself in an essay of 100 words.

2. Kamenetz defends the proposition that "Sixteen is a good starting point for phasing in adult rights and responsibilities" without exceptions. What, if any, exceptions would you favor? If you agree with Kamenetz and favor no exceptions, explain.

3. Why do you think that "teenagers who drink at home with their families go on to drink less" than others who don't (para. 8)?

4. Define "compound interest" (para. 9). Why does Kamenetz think it is important to be able to define this term? Can you think of a couple of other terms that a sixteen-year-old teenager ought to be able to define? (How about "date rape"? "plagiarism"? "gay marriage"? Are these important for teenagers to be able to define?)

5. Which of the letters provoked by Kamenetz's essay comes closest to your view? Explain.

Gwen Wilde

This essay was written for a composition course at Tufts University.

Why the Pledge of Allegiance Should Be Revised

(Student Essay)

All Americans are familiar with the Pledge of Allegiance, even if they cannot always recite it perfectly, but probably relatively few know that the *original* Pledge did *not* include the words "under God." The original Pledge of Allegiance, published in the September 8, 1892, issue of the *Youth's Companion*, ran thus:

> I pledge allegiance to my flag, and to the Republic for which it stands:
> one Nation indivisible, with Liberty and justice for all. (Djupe 329)

In 1923, at the first National Flag Conference in Washington, D.C., it was argued that immigrants might be confused by the words "my Flag," and it was proposed that the words be changed to "the Flag of the United States." The following year it was changed again, to "the Flag of the United States of America," and this wording became the official — or, rather, unofficial — wording, unofficial because no wording had ever been nationally adopted (Djupe 329).

In 1942, the United States Congress included the Pledge in the United States Flag Code (4 USC 4, 2006), thus for the first time officially sanctioning the Pledge. In 1954, President Dwight D. Eisenhower approved adding the words "under God." Thus, since 1954 the Pledge reads:

> I pledge allegiance to the flag of the United States of America, and to
> the Republic for which it stands: one nation under God, indivisible,with
> Liberty and Justice for all. (Djupe 329)

In my view, the addition of the words "under God" is inappropriate, and they are needlessly divisive — an odd addition indeed to a Nation that is said to be "indivisible."

Very simply put, the Pledge in its latest form requires all Americans to say something that some Americans do not believe. I say "requires" because although the courts have ruled that students may not be compelled to recite the Pledge, in effect peer pressure does compel all but the bravest to join in the recitation. When President Eisenhower authorized the change, he said,

> In this way we are reaffirming the transcendence of religious faith
> in America's heritage and future; in this way we shall constantly
> strengthen those spiritual weapons which forever will be our country's
> most powerful resource in peace and war. (Sterner)

Exactly what did Eisenhower mean when he spoke of "the transcendence of faith in America's heritage," and when he spoke of "spiritual weapons"? I am not sure what "the transcendence of faith in America's heritage" means. Of course many Americans have been and are deeply religious—no one doubts it—but the phrase certainly goes far beyond saying that many Americans have been devout. In any case, many Americans have *not* been devout, and many Americans have *not* believed in "spiritual weapons," but they have nevertheless been patriotic Americans. Some of them have fought and died to keep America free.

In short, the words "under God" cannot be uttered in good faith by many Americans. True, something like 70 or even 80% of Americans say they are affiliated with some form of Christianity, and approximately another 3% say they are Jewish. I don't have the figures for persons of other faiths, but in any case we can surely all agree that although a majority of Americans say they have a religious affiliation, nevertheless several million Americans do *not* believe in God.

If one remains silent while others are reciting the Pledge, or even if one remains silent only while others are speaking the words "under God," one is open to the charge that one is unpatriotic, is "unwilling to recite the Pledge of Allegiance." In the Pledge, patriotism is connected with religious belief, and it is this connection that makes it divisive and (to be blunt) un-American. Admittedly the belief is not very specific: one is not required to say that one believes in the divinity of Jesus, or in the power of Jehovah, but the fact remains, one is required to express belief in a divine power, and if one doesn't express this belief one is—according to the Pledge—somehow not fully an American, maybe even un-American.

Please notice that I am not arguing that the Pledge is unconstitutional. I understand that the First Amendment to the Constitution says that "Congress shall make no law respecting an establishment of religion, or prohibiting the free exercise thereof." I am not arguing that the words "under God" in the Pledge add up to the "establishment of religion," but they certainly do assert a religious doctrine. Like the words "In God we trust," found on all American money, the words "under God" express an idea that many Americans do not hold, and there is no reason why these Americans—loyal people who may be called upon to defend the country with their lives—should be required to say that America is a nation "under God."

It has been argued, even by members of the Supreme Court, that the words "under God" are not to be taken terribly seriously, not to be taken to say what they seem to say. For instance, Chief Justice Rehnquist wrote,

> To give the parent of such a child a sort of "heckler's veto" over a patriotic ceremony willingly participated in by other students, simply because the Pledge of Allegiance contains the descriptive phrase "under God," is an unwarranted extension of the establishment clause, an extension which would have the unfortunate effect of prohibiting a commendable patriotic observance. (qtd. in Mears)

Chief Justice Rehnquist here calls "under God" a "descriptive phrase," but descriptive of *what*? If a phrase is a "descriptive phrase," it describes something, real or imagined. For many Americans, this phrase does *not* describe a reality. These Americans may perhaps be mistaken—if so, they may learn of their error at Judgment Day—but the fact is, millions of intelligent Americans do not believe in God.

Notice, too, that Chief Justice Rehnquist goes on to say that reciting the Pledge is "a commendable patriotic observance." Exactly. That is my point. It is a *patriotic* observance, and it should not be connected with religion. When we announce that we respect the flag—that we are loyal Americans—we should not also have to announce that we hold a particular religious belief, in this case a belief in monotheism, a belief that there is a God and that God rules.

One other argument defending the words "under God" is often heard: the words "In God We Trust" appear on our money. It is claimed that these words on American money are analogous to the words "under God" in the Pledge. But the situation really is very different. When we hand some coins over, or some paper money, we are concentrating on the business transaction, and we are not making any affirmation about God or our country. But when we recite the Pledge—even if we remain silent at the point when we are supposed to say "under God"—we are very conscious that we are supposed to make this affirmation, an affirmation that many Americans cannot in good faith make, even though they certainly can unthinkingly hand over (or accept) money with the words "In God We Trust."

Because I believe that *reciting* the Pledge is to be taken seriously, with a full awareness of the words that is quite different from when we hand over some money, I cannot understand the recent comment of Supreme Court Justice Souter, who in a case said that the phrase "under God" is "so tepid, so diluted, so far from compulsory prayer, that it should, in effect, be beneath the constitutional radar" (qtd. in "Guide"). I don't follow his reasoning that the phrase should be "beneath the constitutional radar," but in any case I am willing to put aside the issue of constitutionality. I am willing to grant that this phrase does not in any significant sense signify the "establishment of religion" (prohibited by the First Amendment) in the United States. I insist, nevertheless, that the phrase is neither "tepid" nor "diluted." It means what it says—it *must* and *should* mean what it says, to everyone who utters it—and, since millions of loyal Americans cannot say it, it should not be included in a statement in which Americans affirm their loyalty to our great country.

In short, the Pledge, which ought to unite all of us, is divisive; it includes a phrase that many patriotic Americans cannot bring themselves to utter. Yes, they can remain silent when others recite these two words, but, again, why should they have to remain silent? The Pledge of Allegiance should be something that *everyone* can say, say out loud, and say with pride. We hear much talk of returning to the ideas of the Founding Fathers. The Founding Fathers did not create the Pledge of

10

Allegiance, but we do know that they never mentioned God in the Constitution. Indeed the only reference to religion, in the so-called establishment clause of the First Amendment, says, again, that "Congress shall make no law respecting an establishment of religion, or prohibiting the free exercise thereof." Those who wish to exercise religion are indeed free to do so, but the place to do so is not in a pledge that is required of all schoolchildren and of all new citizens.

WORKS CITED

Djupe, Paul A. "Pledge of Allegiance." *Encyclopedia of American Religion and Politics*. Ed. Paul A. Djupe and Laura R. Olson. New York: Facts on File, 2003. Print.
"Guide to Covering 'Under God' Pledge Decision." *ReligionLink*. Religion Newswriters Foundation, 17 Sept. 2005. Web. 9 Feb. 2007.
Mears, Bill. "Court Dismisses Pledge Case." *CNN.com* Cable News Network 15 June Web. 9 Feb. 2007 .
Sterner, Doug. "The Pledge of Allegiance." *Home of Heroes*. N.p., n.d. Web. 9 Feb. 2007.

TOPICS FOR CRITICAL THINKING AND WRITING

1. Summarize the essay in a paragraph.

2. Does the background material about the history of the pledge serve a useful purpose? Should it be deleted? Why, or why not?

3. Does the writer give enough weight to the fact that no one is compelled to recite the pledge? Explain your answer.

4. What arguments does the writer offer in support of her position?

5. Does the writer show an adequate awareness of other counterarguments?

6. Which is the writer's strongest argument? Is any argument notably weak, and, if so, how could it be strengthened? (If you cannot think of how it might be strengthened, should it have been omitted?)

7. What assumptions—tacit or explicit—does the author make? Do you agree or disagree with them? Please explain.

8. What do you take the words "under God" to mean? Do they mean "under God's special protection"? Or "acting in accordance with God's rules"? Or "accountable to God"?

9. Chief Justice Rehnquist wrote that the words "under God" are a "descriptive phrase." What do you think he meant by this?

10. What is the purpose of the Pledge of Allegiance? Does the phrase "under God" promote or defeat that purpose? Explain your answer.

11. What do you think about substituting "with religious freedom" for "under God"? Set forth your response, supported by reasons, in about 250 words.

12. Wilde makes a distinction between the reference to God on U.S. money and the reference to God in the Pledge. Do you agree with her that the two cases are not analogous? Explain.

13. Putting aside your own views on the issue, what grade would you give this essay as a work of argumentative writing? Support your evaluation with reasons.

A CASEBOOK FOR CRITICAL READING:
Should Some Kinds of Speech Be Censored?

Now we present a series of essays that we think are somewhat more difficult than Jacoby and Wilde's but that address in more detail some of the issues of free speech that she raises. We suggest you read each one through to get its gist and then read it a second time, jotting down after each paragraph a sentence or two summarizing the paragraph. Keep in mind the First Amendment to the Constitution, which reads, in its entirety,

> Congress shall make no law respecting an establishment of religion, or prohibiting the free exercise thereof; or abridging the freedom of speech, or of the press; or the right of the people peaceably to assemble, and to petition the government for a redress of grievances.

> For links related to free speech, see the companion Web site **bedfordstmartins.com/barnetbedau.**

Susan Brownmiller

Susan Brownmiller (b. 1935), a graduate of Cornell University, is the founder of Women against Pornography and the author of several books, including Against Our Will: Men, Women, and Rape *(1975). The essay reprinted here is from* Take Back the Night *(1980), a collection of essays edited by Laura Lederer. The book has been called "the manifesto of antipornography feminism."*

Let's Put Pornography Back in the Closet

Free speech is one of the great foundations on which our democracy rests. I am old enough to remember the Hollywood Ten, the screenwriters who went to jail in the late 1940s because they refused to testify before a congressional committee about their political affiliations. They tried to use the First Amendment as a defense, but they went to jail because in those days there were few civil liberties lawyers around who cared to champion the First Amendment right to free speech, when the speech concerned the Communist party.

The Hollywood Ten were correct in claiming the First Amendment. Its high purpose is the protection of unpopular ideas and political dissent. In the dark, cold days of the 1950s, few civil libertarians were willing to declare themselves First Amendment absolutists. But in the brighter, though frantic, days of the 1960s, the principle of protecting unpopular political speech was gradually strengthened.

It is fair to say now that the battle has largely been won. Even the American Nazi party has found itself the beneficiary of the dedicated, tireless work of the American Civil Liberties Union. But—and please notice the quotation marks coming up—"To equate the free and robust exchange of ideas and political debate with commercial exploitation of obscene material demeans the grand conception of the First Amendment and its high purposes in the historic struggle for freedom. It is a misuse of the great guarantees of free speech and free press."

I didn't say that, although I wish I had, for I think the words are thrilling. Chief Justice Warren Burger said it in 1973, in the United States Supreme Court's majority opinion in *Miller v. California.* During the same decades that the right to political free speech was being strengthened in the courts, the nation's obscenity laws also were undergoing extensive revision.

It's amazing to recall that in 1934 the question of whether James 5 Joyce's *Ulysses* should be banned as pornographic actually went before the Court. The battle to protect *Ulysses* as a work of literature with redeeming social value was won. In later decades, Henry Miller's *Tropic* books, *Lady Chatterley's Lover,* and the *Memoirs of Fanny Hill* also were adjudged not obscene. These decisions have been important to me. As the author of *Against Our Will,* a study of the history of rape that does contain explicit sexual material, I shudder to think how my book would have fared if James Joyce, D. H. Lawrence, and Henry Miller hadn't gone before me.

I am not a fan of *Chatterley* or the *Tropic* books, I should quickly mention. They are not to my literary taste, nor do I think they represent female sexuality with any degree of accuracy. But I would hardly suggest that we ban them. Such a suggestion wouldn't get very far anyway. The battle to protect these books is ancient history. Time does march on, quite methodically. What, then, is unlawfully obscene, and what does the First Amendment have to do with it?

In the *Miller* case of 1973 (not Henry Miller, by the way, but a porn distributor who sent unsolicited stuff through the mails), the Court came up with new guidelines that it hoped would strengthen obscenity laws by giving more power to the states. What it did in actuality was throw everything into confusion. It set up a three-part test by which materials can be adjudged obscene. The materials are obscene if they depict patently offensive, hard-core sexual conduct; lack serious scientific, literary, artistic, or political value; and appeal to the prurient interest of an average person—as measured by contemporary community standards.

"Patently offensive," "prurient interest," and "hard-core" are indeed words to conjure with. "Contemporary community standards" are what we're trying to redefine. The feminist objection to pornography is not based on prurience, which the dictionary defines as lustful, itching desire. We are not opposed to sex and desire, with or without the itch, and we certainly believe that explicit sexual material has its place in literature, art, science, and education. Here we part company rather swiftly with old-line conservatives who don't want sex education in the high schools, for example.

No, the feminist objection to pornography is based on our belief that pornography represents hatred of women, that pornography's intent is to humiliate, degrade, and dehumanize the female body for the purpose of erotic stimulation and pleasure. We are unalterably opposed to the presentation of the female body being stripped, bound, raped, tortured, mutilated, and murdered in the name of commercial entertainment and free speech.

These images, which are standard pornographic fare, have nothing to 10 do with the hallowed right of political dissent. They have everything to do with the creation of a cultural climate in which a rapist feels he is merely giving in to a normal urge and a woman is encouraged to believe that sexual masochism is healthy, liberated fun. Justice Potter Stewart once said about hard-core pornography, "You know it when you see it," and that certainly used to be true. In the good old days, pornography looked awful. It was cheap and sleazy, and there was no mistaking it for art.

Nowadays, since the porn industry has become a multimillion dollar business, visual technology has been employed in its service. Pornographic movies are skillfully filmed and edited, pornographic still shots using the newest tenets of good design artfully grace the covers of *Hustler, Penthouse,* and *Playboy,* and the public—and the courts—are sadly confused.

The Supreme Court neglected to define "hard-core" in the *Miller* decision. This was a mistake. If "hard-core" refers only to explicit sexual intercourse, then that isn't good enough. When women or children or men—no matter how artfully—are shown tortured or terrorized in the service of sex, that's obscene. And "patently offensive," I would hope, to our "contemporary community standards."

Justice William O. Douglas wrote in his dissent to the *Miller* case that no one is "compelled to look." This is hardly true. To buy a paper at the corner newsstand is to subject oneself to a forcible immersion in pornography, to be demeaned by an array of dehumanized, chopped-up parts of the female anatomy, packaged like cuts of meat at the supermarket. I happen to like my body and I work hard at the gym to keep it in good shape, but I am embarrassed for my body and for the bodies of all women when I see the fragmented parts of us so frivolously, and so flagrantly, displayed.

Some constitutional theorists (Justice Douglas was one) have maintained that any obscenity law is a serious abridgement of free speech. Others (and Justice Earl Warren was one) have maintained that the First Amendment was never intended to protect obscenity. We live quite compatibly with a host of free-speech abridgements. There are restraints against false and misleading advertising or statements—shouting "fire" without cause in a crowded movie theater, etc.—that do not threaten, but strengthen, our societal values. Restrictions on the public display of pornography belong in this category.

The distinction between permission to publish and permission to display publicly is an essential one and one which I think consonant with First Amendment principles. Justice Burger's words which I quoted above support this without question. We are not saying "Smash the presses" or "Ban the bad ones," but simply "Get the stuff out of our sight." Let the legislatures decide—using realistic and humane contemporary community standards—what can be displayed and what cannot. The courts, after all, will be the final arbiters.

TOPICS FOR CRITICAL THINKING AND WRITING

1. Objecting to Justice Douglas's remark that no one is "'compelled to look'" (para. 13), Brownmiller says, "This is hardly true. To buy a paper at the corner newsstand is to subject oneself to a forcible immersion in pornography, to be demeaned by an array of dehumanized, chopped-up parts of the female anatomy, packaged like cuts of meat at the supermarket." Is this true at your local newsstand, or are the sex magazines kept in one place, relatively remote from the newspapers?

2. When Brownmiller attempts to restate the "three-part test" for obscenity established by the Supreme Court in *Miller v. California*, she writes (para. 7): "The materials are obscene if they depict . . ." and so on. She should have written: "The materials are obscene if and only if they depict . . ." and so on. Explain what is wrong here with her "if," and why "if and only if" is needed.

3. In her next-to-last paragraph, Brownmiller reminds us that we already live quite comfortably with some "free-speech abridgements." The examples she gives are that we may not falsely shout "fire" in a crowded theater and may not issue misleading advertisements. Do you think that these widely accepted restrictions are valid evidence in arguing on behalf of limiting the display of what Brownmiller considers pornography? Why, or why not?

4. Brownmiller insists that defenders of the First Amendment, who will surely oppose laws that interfere with the freedom to publish, need not go on to condemn laws that regulate the freedom to publicly display pornographic publications. Do you agree? Suppose a publisher insists that he cannot sell his product at a profit unless he is permitted to display it to advantage and that restriction on the latter amounts to

interference with his freedom to publish. How might Brownmiller reply?

5. In her last paragraph Brownmiller says that "contemporary community standards" should be decisive. Can it be argued that because standards vary from one community to another and from time to time even in the same place, her recommendation subjects the rights of a minority to the whims of a majority? The Bill of Rights, after all, was supposed to safeguard the constitutional rights of the minority from the possible tyranny of the majority.

6. When Brownmiller accuses "the public . . . and the courts" of being "sadly confused" (para. 11), what does she think they are confused about? The definition of *pornography* or *obscenity*? The effects of such literature on men and women? Or is it something else?

Charles R. Lawrence III

Charles R. Lawrence III (b. 1943), author of numerous articles in law journals and coauthor of We Won't Go Back: Making the Case for Affirmative Action *(1997), teaches law at Georgetown University. This essay originally appeared in the* Chronicle of Higher Education *(October 25, 1989), a publication read chiefly by faculty and administrators at colleges and universities. An amplified version of the essay appeared in* Duke Law Journal *(February 1990).*

On Racist Speech

I have spent the better part of my life as a dissenter. As a high school student, I was threatened with suspension for my refusal to participate in a civil defense drill, and I have been a conspicuous consumer of my First Amendment liberties ever since. There are very strong reasons for protecting even racist speech. Perhaps the most important of these is that such protection reinforces our society's commitment to tolerance as a value, and that by protecting bad speech from government regulation, we will be forced to combat it as a community.

But I also have a deeply felt apprehension about the resurgence of racial violence and the corresponding rise in the incidence of verbal and symbolic assault and harassment to which blacks and other traditionally subjugated and excluded groups are subjected. I am troubled by the way the debate has been framed in response to the recent surge of racist incidents on college and university campuses and in response to some universities' attempts to regulate harassing speech. The problem has been framed as one in which the liberty of free speech is in conflict with the elimination of racism. I believe this has placed the bigot on the moral high ground and fanned the rising flames of racism.

Above all, I am troubled that we have not listened to the real victims, that we have shown so little understanding of their injury, and that we have abandoned those whose race, gender, or sexual preference continues to make them second-class citizens. It seems to me a very sad irony that the first instinct of civil libertarians has been to challenge even the smallest, most narrowly framed efforts by universities to provide black and other minority students with the protection the Constitution guarantees them.

The landmark case of *Brown v. Board of Education* is not a case that we normally think of as a case about speech. But *Brown* can be broadly read as articulating the principle of equal citizenship. *Brown* held that segregated schools were inherently unequal because of the *message* that segregation conveyed—that black children were an untouchable caste, unfit to go to school with white children. If we understand the necessity of eliminating the system of signs and symbols that signal the inferiority of blacks, then we should hesitate before proclaiming that all racist speech that stops short of physical violence must be defended.

University officials who have formulated policies to respond to inci-   5
dents of racial harassment have been characterized in the press as "thought police," but such policies generally do nothing more than impose sanctions against intentional face-to-face insults. When racist speech takes the form of face-to-face insults, catcalls, or other assaultive speech aimed at an individual or small group of persons, it falls directly within the "fighting words" exception to First Amendment protection. The Supreme Court has held that words which "by their very utterance inflict injury or tend to incite an immediate breach of the peace" are not protected by the First Amendment.

If the purpose of the First Amendment is to foster the greatest amount of speech, racial insults disserve that purpose. Assaultive racist speech functions as a preemptive strike. The invective is experienced as a blow, not as a proffered idea, and once the blow is struck, it is unlikely that a dialogue will follow. Racial insults are particularly undeserving of First Amendment protection because the perpetrator's intention is not to discover truth or initiate dialogue but to injure the victim. In most situations, members of minority groups realize that they are likely to lose if they respond to epithets by fighting and are forced to remain silent and submissive.

Courts have held that offensive speech may not be regulated in public forums such as streets where the listener may avoid the speech by moving on, but the regulation of otherwise protected speech has been permitted when the speech invades the privacy of the unwilling listener's home or when the unwilling listener cannot avoid the speech. Racist posters, fliers, and graffiti in dormitories, bathrooms, and other common living spaces would seem to clearly fall within the reasoning of these cases. Minority students should not be required to remain in their rooms in order to avoid racial assault. Minimally, they should find a safe haven in their dorms and in all other common rooms that are a part of their daily routine.

I would also argue that the university's responsibility for ensuring that these students receive an equal educational opportunity provides a compelling justification for regulations that ensure them safe passage in all common areas. A minority student should not have to risk becoming the target of racially assaulting speech every time he or she chooses to walk across campus. Regulating vilifying speech that cannot be anticipated or avoided would not preclude announced speeches and rallies — situations that would give minority-group members and their allies the chance to organize counterdemonstrations or avoid the speech altogether.

The most commonly advanced argument against the regulation of racist speech proceeds something like this: We recognize that minority groups suffer pain and injury as the result of racist speech, but we must allow this hate mongering for the benefit of society as a whole. Freedom of speech is the lifeblood of our democratic system. It is especially important for minorities because often it is their only vehicle for rallying support for the redress of their grievances. It will be impossible to formulate a prohibition so precise that it will prevent the racist speech you want to suppress without catching in the same net all kinds of speech that it would be unconscionable for a democratic society to suppress.

Whenever we make such arguments, we are striking a balance on 10 the one hand between our concern for the continued free flow of ideas and the democratic process dependent on that flow, and, on the other, our desire to further the cause of equality. There can be no meaningful discussion of how we should reconcile our commitment to equality and our commitment to free speech until it is acknowledged that there is real harm inflicted by racist speech and that this harm is far from trivial.

To engage in a debate about the First Amendment and racist speech without a full understanding of the nature and extent of that harm is to risk making the First Amendment an instrument of domination rather than a vehicle of liberation. We have not known the experience of victimization by racist, misogynist, and homophobic speech, nor do we equally share the burden of the societal harm it inflicts. We are often quick to say that we have heard the cry of the victims when we have not.

The *Brown* case is again instructive because it speaks directly to the psychic injury inflicted by racist speech by noting that the symbolic message of segregation affected "the hearts and minds" of Negro children "in a way unlikely ever to be undone." Racial epithets and harassment often cause deep emotional scarring and feelings of anxiety and fear that pervade every aspect of a victim's life.

Brown also recognized that black children did not have an equal opportunity to learn and participate in the school community if they bore the additional burden of being subjected to the humiliation and psychic assault contained in the message of segregation. University students bear an analogous burden when they are forced to live and work in an environment where at any moment they may be subjected to denigrating verbal harassment and assault. The same injury was addressed by the Supreme Court when it held that sexual harassment that creates a hostile or abusive work environment violates the ban on sex discrimination in employment of Title VII of the Civil Rights Act of 1964.

Carefully drafted university regulations would bar the use of words as assault weapons and leave unregulated even the most heinous of ideas when those ideas are presented at times and places and in manners that provide an opportunity for reasoned rebuttal or escape from immediate injury. The history of the development of the right to free speech has been one of carefully evaluating the importance of free expression and its effects on other important societal interests. We have drawn the line between protected and unprotected speech before without dire results. (Courts have, for example, exempted from the protection of the First Amendment obscene speech and speech that disseminates official secrets, that defames or libels another person, or that is used to form a conspiracy or monopoly.)

Blacks and other people of color are skeptical about the argument 15 that even the most injurious speech must remain unregulated because, in an unregulated marketplace of ideas, the best ones will rise to the top and gain acceptance. Our experience tells us quite the opposite. We have seen too many good liberal politicians shy away from the issues that might brand them as being too closely allied with us.

Whenever we decide that racist speech must be tolerated because of the importance of maintaining societal tolerance for all unpopular speech, we are asking blacks and other subordinated groups to bear the burden for the good of all. We must be careful that the ease with which we strike the balance against the regulation of racist speech is in no way influenced by the fact that the cost will be borne by others. We must be certain that those who will pay that price are fairly represented in our deliberations and that they are heard.

At the core of the argument that we should resist all government regulation of speech is the ideal that the best cure for bad speech is good, that ideas that affirm equality and the worth of all individuals will ultimately prevail. This is an empty ideal unless those of us who would fight racism are vigilant and unequivocal in that fight. We must look for ways to offer assistance and support to students whose speech and political participation are chilled in a climate of racial harassment.

Civil rights lawyers might consider suing on behalf of blacks whose right to an equal education is denied by a university's failure to ensure a nondiscriminatory educational climate or conditions of employment. We must embark upon the development of a First Amendment jurisprudence grounded in the reality of our history and our contemporary experience. We must think hard about how best to launch legal attacks against the most indefensible forms of hate speech. Good lawyers can create exceptions and narrow interpretations that limit the harm of hate speech without opening the floodgates of censorship.

Everyone concerned with these issues must find ways to engage actively in actions that resist and counter the racist ideas that we would have the First Amendment protect. If we fail in this, the victims of hate speech must rightly assume that we are on the oppressors' side.

Topics for Critical Thinking and Writing

1. Summarize Lawrence's essay in a paragraph. (You may find it useful first to summarize each paragraph in a sentence and then to revise these summary sentences into a paragraph.)

2. In a sentence state Lawrence's thesis (his main point).

3. Why do you suppose Lawrence included his first paragraph? What does it contribute to his argument?

4. Paragraph 7 argues that "minority students" should not have to endure "racist posters, fliers, and graffiti in dormitories, bathrooms, and other common living spaces." Do you think that Lawrence would also argue that straight white men should not have to endure posters, fliers, or graffiti that speak of "honkies" or "rednecks"? On what do you base your answer?

5. In paragraph 8 Lawrence speaks of "racially assaulting speech" and of "vilifying speech." It is easy to think of words that fit these descriptions, but what about other words? Is *Uncle Tom*, used by an African American about another African American who is eager to please whites, an example of "racially assaulting speech"? Or take the word *gay*. Surely this word is acceptable because it is widely used by homosexuals, but what about *queer* (used by some homosexuals but usually derogatory when used by heterosexuals)? A third example: There can be little doubt that women are demeaned when males speak of them as *chicks* or *babes*, but are these terms "assaulting" and "vilifying"?

6. For a start, you might think about some provisions in the Code of Conduct of Shippensburg University in Pennsylvania. The code says that each student has a "primary" right to be free from harassment, intimidation, physical harm, and emotional abuse, and has a "secondary" right to express personal beliefs in a manner that does not "provoke, harass, demean, intimidate, or harm" another. The code prohibits conduct that "annoys, threatens, or alarms a person or group," such as sexual harassment, "innuendo," "comments, insults," "propositions," "humor/jokes about sex or gender-specific traits," and "suggestive or insulting sounds, leering, whistling, [and] obscene gestures." The president of the university has said (according to the *New York Times*, April 24, 2003, p. A23) that the university encourages free speech as a means to examine ideas and that the university is "committed to the principle that this discussion be conducted appropriately. We do have expectations that our students will conduct themselves in a civil manner that allows them to express their opinions without interfering with the rights of others." Again, you may find that some of this material helps you to generate your own thoughts.

7. Find out if your college or university has a code governing hate speech. If it does, evaluate it. If your college has no such code, imagine that you are Lawrence, and draft one of about 250 words. (See especially his paras. 5, 7, and 14.)

Derek Bok

Derek Bok was born in 1930 in Bryn Mawr, Pennsylvania, and educated at Stanford University and Harvard University, where he received a law degree. From 1971 to 1991 he served as president of Harvard University. The following essay, first published in the Boston Globe *in 1991, was prompted by the display of Confederate flags hung from a window of a Harvard dormitory.*

Protecting Freedom of Expression on the Campus

For several years, universities have been struggling with the problem of trying to reconcile the rights of free speech with the desire to avoid racial tension. In recent weeks, such a controversy has sprung up at Harvard. Two students hung Confederate flags in public view, upsetting students who equate the Confederacy with slavery. A third student tried to protest the flags by displaying a swastika.

These incidents have provoked much discussion and disagreement. Some students have urged that Harvard require the removal of symbols that offend many members of the community. Others reply that such symbols are a form of free speech and should be protected.

Different universities have resolved similar conflicts in different ways. Some have enacted codes to protect their communities from forms of speech that are deemed to be insensitive to the feelings of other groups. Some have refused to impose such restrictions.

It is important to distinguish between the appropriateness of such communications and their status under the First Amendment. The fact that speech is protected by the First Amendment does not necessarily mean that it is right, proper, or civil. I am sure that the vast majority of Harvard students believe that hanging a Confederate flag in public view—or displaying a swastika in response—is insensitive and unwise because any satisfaction it gives to the students who display these symbols is far outweighed by the discomfort it causes to many others.

I share this view and regret that the students involved saw fit to 5
behave in this fashion. Whether or not they merely wished to manifest their pride in the South—or to demonstrate the insensitivity of hanging Confederate flags, by mounting another offensive symbol in return—they must have known that they would upset many fellow students and ignore the decent regard for the feelings of others so essential to building and preserving a strong and harmonious community.

To disapprove of a particular form of communication, however, is not enough to justify prohibiting it. We are faced with a clear example of the conflict between our commitment to free speech and our desire to foster a community founded on mutual respect. Our society has wrestled with this problem for many years. Interpreting the First Amendment, the Supreme Court has clearly struck the balance in favor of free speech.

While communities do have the right to regulate speech in order to uphold aesthetic standards (avoiding defacement of buildings) or to protect the public from disturbing noise, rules of this kind must be applied across the board and cannot be enforced selectively to prohibit certain kinds of messages but not others.

Under the Supreme Court's rulings, as I read them, the display of swastikas or Confederate flags clearly falls within the protection of the free-speech clause of the First Amendment and cannot be forbidden simply because it offends the feelings of many members of the community. These rulings apply to all agencies of government, including public universities.

Although it is unclear to what extent the First Amendment is enforceable against private institutions, I have difficulty understanding why a university such as Harvard should have less free speech than the surrounding society — or than a public university.

One reason why the power of censorship is so dangerous is that it is 10 extremely difficult to decide when a particular communication is offensive enough to warrant prohibition or to weigh the degree of offensiveness against the potential value of the communication. If we begin to forbid flags, it is only a short step to prohibiting offensive speakers.

I suspect that no community will become humane and caring by restricting what its members can say. The worst offenders will simply find other ways to irritate and insult.

In addition, once we start to declare certain things "offensive," with all the excitement and attention that will follow, I fear that much ingenuity will be exerted trying to test the limits, much time will be expended trying to draw tenuous distinctions, and the resulting publicity will eventually attract more attention to the offensive material than would ever have occurred otherwise.

Rather than prohibit such communications, with all the resulting risks, it would be better to ignore them, since students would then have little reason to create such displays and would soon abandon them. If this response is not possible — and one can understand why — the wisest course is to speak with those who perform insensitive acts and try to help them understand the effects of their actions on others.

Appropriate officials and faculty members should take the lead, as the Harvard House Masters have already done in this case. In talking with students, they should seek to educate and persuade, rather than resort to ridicule or intimidation, recognizing that only persuasion is likely to produce a lasting, beneficial effect. Through such effects, I believe that we act in the manner most consistent with our ideals as an educational institution and most calculated to help us create a truly understanding, supportive community.

TOPICS FOR CRITICAL THINKING AND WRITING

1. Bok sketches the following argument (paras. 8 and 9): The First Amendment protects free speech in public universities and colleges; Harvard is not a public university; therefore, Harvard does not enjoy the protection of the First Amendment. This argument is plainly invalid. Bok clearly rejects the conclusion ("I have difficulty understanding why . . . Harvard should have less free speech . . . than a public university"). What would need to be revised in the premises to make the argument valid? Do you think Bok would accept or reject such a revision?

2. Bok objects to censorship that simply prevents students from being "offended." He would not object to the campus police preventing students from being harmed. In an essay of 100 words, explain the difference between conduct that is *harmful* and conduct that is (merely?) *offensive.*

3. Bok advises campus officials (and students) simply to "ignore" offensive words, flags, and so forth (para. 13). Do you agree with this advice? Or do you favor a different kind of response? Write a 250-word essay on the theme "How We Ought to Respond to the Offensive Misconduct of Others."

Andrew Keen

Andrew Keen is the author of The Cult of the Amateur *(2007), a book that is critical of user-based Web sites. We reprint an essay that appeared originally in the* Los Angeles Times, *March 1, 2008.*

Douse the Online Flamers

The cartoon isn't as amusing as it once was. "On the Internet, nobody knows you're a dog," one Web-surfing canine barked to another in that 1993 classic from *The New Yorker*. Back then, of course, at the innocent dawn of the Internet age, the idea that we might all be anonymous on the Web promised infinite intellectual freedom. Unfortunately, however, that promise hasn't been realized. Today, too many anonymous Internet users are posting hateful content about their neighbors, classmates, and coworkers; today, online media is an increasingly shadowy, vertiginous environment in which it is becoming harder and harder to know other people's real identities.

Those of us who have been flamed by faceless critics in online discussion groups are intimately familiar with the problem. This isn't illegal, of course, because online speech—anonymous or otherwise—is protected by both the First Amendment and by the Supreme Court's much-cited 1995 *McIntyre v. Ohio Elections Commission* ruling protecting anonymous speech. But is today's law adequately protecting us? What happens, for example, when anonymous Internet critics go beyond rude and irremediably blacken the reputations of innocent citizens or cause them harm? Should there be legal consequences?

The most notorious case is certainly the cyber-bullying of Megan Meier, a thirteen-year-old girl from a suburb of St. Louis. In 2006, Meier, a troubled, overweight adolescent, became embroiled in an intense, six-week online friendship with "Josh Evans" on MySpace. After "Josh" turned against Megan and posted a comment that "the world would be better place without you," the girl hung herself. Later, when it became clear that the fictitious Josh Evans was actually Lori Drew, a forty-seven-year-old neighbor and mother of a girl with whom Megan Meier had argued, there were calls for a criminal prosecution. But the St. Charles County Sheriff's Department didn't charge Drew; its spokesman said that what she did "might've been rude, it might've been immature, but it wasn't illegal."

Fortunately, the Meier suicide is making officials get more serious about holding anonymous Internet users accountable. In Los Angeles, federal prosecutors were reportedly exploring whether they could charge Drew with defrauding Beverly Hills-based MySpace. In Missouri, the St. Charles County Board of Aldermen passed a law making Internet harassment a misdemeanor punishable by up to a $500 fine and ninety days in jail. And a Missouri state representative introduced legislation that could criminalize online harassment and fraud.

Online free speech fundamentalists would, no doubt, cite the 5 *McIntyre v. Ohio Elections Commission* ruling in any defense. Yet that was a ruling focusing on anonymous "political speech"; Justice John Paul Stevens' opinion for the court cited the example of the Federalist Papers, originally published under pseudonyms, as proof that anonymity represents a "shield from the tyranny of the majority" and is, therefore, vital to a free society. But such a defense doesn't work for cases like the Meier suicide, in which the anonymous speech was anything but political.

The Web 2.0 revolution in self-published content is making the already tangled legal debate around anonymity even harder to unravel. Take, for example, the case of Dr. Lisa Krinsky, president of SFBC International, a Miami-based drug development firm. In 2005, Krinsky's professional and personal reputation was so vilified by anonymous critics on Yahoo message boards that she pursued a lawsuit (*Krinsky v. Doe*) to subpoena the real names of ten of her online tormentors.

Or take the case of a couple of female Yale Law School students whose reputations have been eternally sullied on an online bulletin board called AutoAdmit by "Sleazy Z," "hitlerhitlerhitler," "The Ayatollah of Rock-n-Rollah" and others. Having been publicly accused of lesbianism with the dean of admissions at Yale Law School, possessing "large false breasts" and indulging in exhibitionistic group sex, the two women filed an amended complaint (*Doe v. Ciolli*) in U.S. District Court in Connecticut against the operator of AutoAdmit to reveal the identities of the anonymous critics and take down their libelous posts.

It is troubling that judges in both cases have failed to rule in favor of these victims of anonymous defamation. In the Krinsky case, a California appeals court ruled last month that her accusers had a First Amendment right to speak their minds. Although *Doe v. Ciolli* (filed in June 2007) has yet to be ruled on, the plaintiffs had to drop Anthony Ciolli, the law student in charge of AutoAdmit, from the suit. This is because the law treats Web sites differently than traditional publishers in terms of their liability for libelous content. In Section 230 of the 1996 Communications Decency Act, Congress granted Web sites and Internet service providers immunity from liability for content posted by third parties. So a paper-and-ink newspaper can be sued for publishing a libelous letter from a reader, but, under Section 230, Web bulletin boards like AutoAdmit have no legal responsibility for the published content of their users. Thus the students are now pursuing the identities of their defamers independently of AutoAdmit — a near impossible task given the sophistication of today's software for disguising online identity.

All three of these cases indicate that the U.S. Supreme Court soon might need to rethink the civic value of anonymous speech in the digital age. Today, when cowardly anonymity is souring Internet discourse, it really is hard to understand how anonymous speech is vital to a free society. That *New Yorker* cartoon remains true: On the Internet, nobody knows you're a dog. But it is the responsibility of all of us — parents, citizens and lawmakers — to ensure that contemporary Web users don't behave like antisocial canines. And one way to achieve this is by introducing more legislation to punish anonymous sadists whose online lies are intended to wreck the reputations and mental health of innocent Americans.

Topics for Critical Thinking and Writing

1. Perhaps with some help from a reference librarian, get the text of the Supreme Court's ruling in the 1995 *McIntyre v. Ohio Election Commission* case (para. 2). State and then explain the holding in this case.

2. According to paragraph 3, Drew's malicious actions are not illegal. Does the episode demonstrate that there *should* be a law that would make such behavior illegal? Explain.

3. What do you think is an appropriate punishment (if any) for "anonymous sadists" (para. 8)?

4. Keen says that "it really is hard to understand how anonymous speech is vital to a free society" (para. 9). Spend a few minutes thinking about this issue and see whether you can come up with an example. . . . OK, time has expired: What have you come up with?

Thinking Further about Freedom of Expression, Cyberbullying, and *Facebook*

On February 8, 2009 the *New York Times* reported that a high school senior, Katherine Evans, believed that her English teacher, Sarah Phelps, behaved offensively in two ways: Evans said that the teacher ignored her requests for help with assignments, and, further, that Phelps brusquely reproached her when Evans missed a class because she attended a blood drive. Evans, an honor student, logged into Facebook and wrote about her teacher:

> To those select students who have had the displeasure of having Ms. Sarah Phelps, or simply knowing her and her insane antics: Here is the place to express your feelings of hatred.

The posting drew several responses, including some that criticized the student and supported the teacher. Here is one, written by a former student of Ms. Phelps, quoted by the *Times*:

> Whatever your reasons for hating her are, they're probably very immature.

Ms. Evans removed the posting a few days later but subsequently she was nevertheless reprimanded by the principal and was given a three-day suspension for "cyberbullying." At the time we are writing this, Ms. Evans, now a student at the University of Florida, is suing the principal of the high school. She is not asking for money other than legal fees: She wants the suspension removed from her record. (Additional details are available from various sources on the Web.)

The issue to think about: Was the suspension an attack on Ms. Evans's right to free speech? Or did her comment and her invitation to "express feelings of hatred" constitute a verbal assault that crossed the line of freedom of expression? Howard Simon, executive director of the American Civil Liberties Union of Florida, takes the first position. The *Times* quotes him as saying, "Since when did criticism of a teacher morph into assault? If Katie Evans said what she said over burgers with her friends at the mall, there is no question it would be protected by free speech."

Two Writing Assignments

1. Construct a definition (perhaps two or three sentences) of *cyberbullying*. (If you draw on any sources be sure to cite them.)

2. Given the admittedly scanty information that we have on the Evans case, do you think a suspension was reasonable? If you think it was reasonable, explain why. If you think it was unreasonable, explain why, and indicate whether you think some other (lesser) punishment might have been appropriate. Your essay should be about 250 to 300 words long.

Exercise: Letter to the Editor

Your college newspaper has published a letter that links a hateful attribute to a group and that clearly displays hate for the entire group. (For instance, the letter charges that interracial marriages should be made illegal because "African Americans contain a criminal gene," or that "Jews should not be elected to office because their loyalty is to Israel, not the United States," or that "Muslims should not be allowed to enter the country because they are intent on destroying America.") The letter generates many letters of response; some responses, supporting the editor's decision to publish the letter, make these points:

- The writer of the offending letter is a student in the college, and she has a right to express her views.
- The point of view expressed is probably held only by a few persons, but conceivably it expresses a view held by a significant number of students.
- Editors should not act as censors.
- The First Amendment guarantees freedom of speech.
- Freedom of expression is healthy, i.e., society gains.

On the other hand, among the letters opposing the editor's decision to publish, some make points along these lines:

- Not every view of every nutty student can be printed; editors must make responsible choices.
- The First Amendment, which prohibits the government from controlling the press, has nothing to do with a college newspaper.
- Letters of this sort do not foster healthy discussion; they merely heat things up.

Write a 250- to 500-word letter to the editor, expressing your view of the editor's decision to publish the first letter. (If you wish, you can assume that the letter was on one of the topics we specify in the second sentence of this exercise. But in any case, address the general issue of the editor's decision, not only the specific issue of the charge or charges made in the first letter.)

3

Critical Reading: Getting Deeper into Arguments

He that wrestles with us strengthens our nerves, and sharpens our skill. Our antagonist is our helper.

—EDMUND BURKE

PERSUASION, ARGUMENT, DISPUTE

When we think seriously about an argument (not name calling or mere rationalization), not only do we hear ideas that may be unfamiliar, but we are also forced to examine closely our own cherished opinions, and perhaps for the first time really come to see the strengths and weaknesses of what we believe. As John Stuart Mill put it, "He who knows only his own side of the case knows little."

It is customary, and useful, to distinguish between persuasion and argument. Persuasion has the broader meaning. To **persuade** is to win over—whether

- by giving reasons (that is, by argument),
- by appealing to the emotions, or, for that matter,
- by using torture.

Argument, one form of persuasion, relies on reason; *it offers statements as reasons for other statements.* Rhetoricians often use the Greek word *logos*, which merely means "word" or "reason," to denote this aspect of persuasive writing—the appeal to reason. An appeal to reason may include such things as an appeal to

- Physical evidence;
- The testimony of experts;
- Common sense; and
- Probability.

The appeal to the emotions is known as **pathos.** Strictly speaking, *pathos* is Greek for "feeling," and especially for "suffering," but it now covers all sorts of emotional appeal—for instance, to one's sense of pity or sympathy (Greek for "feeling with") or one's sense of patriotism.

Notice that an argument, in the sense of statements that are offered as reasons for other statements, does not require two speakers or writers who represent opposed positions. The Declaration of Independence is an argument, setting forth the colonists' reasons for declaring their independence. In practice, of course, someone's argument usually advances reasons for a claim in opposition to someone else's position or belief. But even if one is writing only for oneself, trying to clarify one's thinking by setting forth reasons, the result is an argument. **Dispute,** however, is a special kind of argument in which two or more people express views that are at odds.

Most of this book is about argument in the sense of the presentation of reasons in support of claims, but of course, reason is not the whole story. If an argument is to be effective, it must be presented persuasively. For instance, the writer's **tone** (attitude toward self, topic, and audience) must be appropriate if the discourse is to persuade the reader. The careful presentation of the self is not something disreputable, nor is it something that publicity agents or advertising agencies invented. Aristotle (384–22 B.C.) emphasized the importance of impressing on the audience that the speaker is a person of good sense and high moral character. (He called this aspect of persuasion **ethos,** the Greek word for "character," as opposed to *logos*, which we have noted is the word for persuasion by appealing to reason.)

Writers convey their trustworthiness by

- Avoiding vulgar language;
- Showing an awareness of the complexity of the issue (for instance, by granting the goodwill of those offering other points of view and by recognizing that there may be some merit to contrary points of view); and
- Showing attention to detail (for instance, by citing relevant statistics).

In short, writers who are concerned with *ethos* —and all writers should be—employ devices that persuade readers that the writers are trustworthy, are persons in whom the reader can have confidence.

We talk at length about tone, along with other matters such as the organization of an argument, in Chapter 5, Writing an Analysis of an Argument, but here we deal with some of the chief devices used in reasoning, and we glance at emotional appeals.

We should note at once, however, that an argument presupposes a fixed **topic.** Suppose we are arguing about Thomas Jefferson's assertion, in the Declaration of Independence, that "all men are created equal." Jones subscribes to this statement, but Smith says it is nonsense and argues that one has only to look around to see that some people are brighter than others, or healthier, or better coordinated, or whatever. Jones and Smith, if they intend to argue the point, will do well to examine what Jefferson actually wrote:

> We hold these truths to be self-evident, that all men are created equal: that they are endowed by their Creator with certain unalienable rights; and that among these are life, liberty, and the pursuit of happiness.

There is room for debate over what Jefferson really meant and about whether he is right, but clearly he was talking about *equality of rights*. If Smith and Jones wish to argue about Jefferson's view of equality—that is, if they wish to offer their reasons for accepting, rejecting, or modifying it—they will do well first to agree on what Jefferson said or what he probably meant to say. Jones and Smith may still hold different views; they may continue to disagree on whether Jefferson was right and proceed to offer arguments and counterarguments to settle the point. But only if they can agree on *what* they disagree about will their dispute get somewhere.

REASON VERSUS RATIONALIZATION

Reason may not be our only way of finding the truth, but it is a way we often rely on. The subway ran yesterday at 6:00 A.M. and the day before at 6:00 A.M. and the day before, and so I infer from this evidence that it will also run today at 6:00 A.M. (a form of reasoning known as **induction**). Bus drivers require would-be passengers to present the exact change; I do not have the exact change; therefore, I infer I cannot ride on the bus (**deduction**). (The terms *deduction* and *induction* are discussed in more detail on pages 82–88 and 87–88.)

We also know that, if we set our minds to a problem, we can often find reasons (not necessarily sound ones but reasons nevertheless) for almost anything we want to justify. Here is an entertaining example from Benjamin Franklin's *Autobiography:*

> I believe I have omitted mentioning that in my first voyage from Boston, being becalmed off Block Island, our people set about catching cod and hauled up a great many. Hitherto I had stuck to my resolution of not eating animal food, and on this occasion, I considered with my master Tryon the taking of every fish as a kind of unprovoked murder, since none of them had or ever could do us any injury that might justify the slaughter. All this seemed very reasonable. But I had formerly been a great lover of fish, and when this came hot out of the frying pan, it smelt admirably well. I balanced some time between principle and inclination, till I recollected that when the fish were opened I saw smaller fish taken out of their stomachs. Then thought I, if you eat one another, I don't see why we mayn't eat you. So I dined upon cod very

heartily and continued to eat with other people, returning only now and then occasionally to a vegetable diet. So convenient a thing it is to be a *reasonable creature,* since it enables one to find or make a reason for everything one has a mind to do.

Franklin is being playful; he is *not* engaging in critical thinking. He tells us that he loved fish, that this fish "smelt admirably well," and so we are prepared for him to find a reason (here one as weak as "Fish eat fish, therefore people may eat fish") to abandon his vegetarianism. (But think: Fish also eat their own young. May we therefore eat ours?)

Still, Franklin touches on a truth: If necessary, we can find reasons to justify whatever we want. That is, instead of reasoning we may *rationalize* (devise a self-serving but dishonest reason), like the fox in Aesop's fables who, finding the grapes he desired were out of his reach, consoled himself with the thought they were probably sour.

Perhaps we can never be certain that we are not rationalizing, except when, like Franklin, we are being playful—but we can seek to think critically about our own beliefs, scrutinizing our assumptions, looking for counterevidence, and wondering if different conclusions can reasonably be drawn.

SOME PROCEDURES IN ARGUMENT

Definition

Definition, we mentioned in our first chapter, is one of the classical topics, a "place" to which one goes with questions; in answering the questions, one finds ideas. When we define, we are answering the question "What is it?" and in answering this question as precisely as we can, we will find, clarify, and develop ideas.

We have already glanced at an argument over the proposition that "all men are created equal," and we saw that the words needed clarification. *Equal* meant, in the context, not physically or mentally equal but something like "equal in rights," equal politically and legally. (And of course, "men" meant "white men and women.") Words do not always mean exactly what they seem to: There is no lead in a lead pencil, and a standard 2-by-4 is currently $1^5/_8$ inches in thickness and $3^3/_8$ inches in width.

Definition by Synonym   Let's return, for a moment, to *pornography,* a word that, we saw, is not easily defined. One way to define a word is to offer a **synonym.** Thus, pornography can be defined, at least roughly, as "obscenity" (something indecent). But definition by synonym is usually only a start because we find that we will have to define the synonym and, besides, that very few words have exact synonyms. (In fact, *pornography* and *obscenity* are not exact synonyms.)

Definition by Example A second way to define something is to point to an example (this is often called **ostensive definition,** from the Latin *ostendere,* "to show"). This method can be very helpful, ensuring that both writer and reader are talking about the same thing, but it also has its limitations. A few decades ago many people pointed to James Joyce's *Ulysses* and D. H. Lawrence's *Lady Chatterley's Lover* as examples of obscene novels, but today these books are regarded as literary master-pieces. Possibly they can be obscene and also be literary masterpieces. (Joyce's wife is reported to have said of her husband, "He may have been a great writer, but . . . he had a very dirty mind.")

One of the difficulties of using an example, however, is that the example is richer and more complex than the term it is being used to define, and this richness and complexity get in the way of achieving a clear definition. Thus, if one cites Lawrence's *Lady Chatterley's Lover* as an example of pornography, a listener may erroneously think that pornog-raphy has something to do with British novels or with heterosexual rela-tionships outside of marriage. Yet neither of these ideas is part of the concept of pornography.

We are not trying here to formulate a satisfactory definition of *pornography.* Our object is to show that

- An argument will be most fruitful if the participants first agree on what they are talking about;
- One way to secure such agreement is to define the topic osten-sively; and
- Choosing the right example, one that has all the central or typical characteristics, can make a topic not only clear but also vivid.

Definition by Stipulation In arguing, you can legitimately offer a **stipu-lative definition,** saying, perhaps, that by *Native American* you mean any person with any Native American blood; or you might say, "For the purpose of the present discussion, I mean by a *Native American* any per-son who has at least one grandparent of pure Native American blood." A stipulative definition is appropriate where

- No fixed or standard definition is available, and
- Some arbitrary specification is necessary to fix the meaning of a key term in the argument.

Not everyone may be willing to accept your stipulative definition, and alternatives can probably be defended. In any case, when you stipulate a definition, your audience knows what *you* mean by the term thus defined.

It would *not* be reasonable, of course, to stipulate that by *Native American* you mean anyone with a deep interest in North American abo-rigines. That's just too idiosyncratic to be useful. Similarly, an essay on Jews in America will have to rely on some definition of the key idea.

Perhaps the writer will stipulate the definition used in Israel: A Jew is a person who has a Jewish mother or, if not born of a Jewish mother, a person who has formally adopted the Jewish faith. Or perhaps the writer will stipulate another meaning: Jews are people who consider them-selves to be Jews. Some sort of reasonable definition must be offered.

To stipulate, however, that by *Jews* you mean "persons who believe that the area formerly called Palestine rightfully belongs to the Jews" would hopelessly confuse matters. Remember the old riddle and the answer: If you call a dog's tail a leg, how many legs does a dog have? Answer: Four. Calling a tail a leg doesn't make it a leg.

Later in this chapter you will see, in an essay called "When 'Identity' Politics Is Rational," Stanley Fish begin by stipulating a definition. His first paragraph begins thus:

> If there's anything everyone is against in these election times, it's "identity politics," a phrase that covers a multitude of sins. Let me start with a definition. (It may not be yours, but it will at least allow the discussion to be framed.) You're practicing identity politics when you vote for or against someone because of his or her skin color, ethnicity, religion, gender, sexual orientation, or any other marker that leads you to say yes or not independently of a candidates' ideas or policies.

Fish will go on to argue, in later paragraphs, that sometimes identity pol-itics makes very good sense, that it is *not* irrational, is *not* logically inde-fensible, but here we simply want to make two points — one about how a definition helps the writer, the second about how it helps the reader:

- A definition is a good way to get yourself started when you are drafting an essay, a useful stimulus (idea prompt, pattern, tem-plate, heuristic) that will help *you* to think about the issue, a device that will stimulate your further thinking.

- A definition lets readers be certain that they are clear about what the author means by a crucial word.

Readers may disagree with Fish, but at least they know what he means when he speaks of identity politics.

A stipulation may be helpful and legitimate. Here is the opening paragraph of an essay by Richard B. Brandt titled "The Morality and Rationality of Suicide" (from *A Handbook for the Study of Suicide*, edited by Seymour Perlin). Notice that

- The author first stipulates a definition, and

- Then, aware that the definition may strike some readers as too broad and therefore unreasonable or odd, he offers a reason on behalf of his definition:

"Suicide" is conveniently defined, for our purposes, as doing something which results in one's death, either from the intention of ending one's life or the intention to bring about some other state of affairs (such as relief from pain) which one thinks it certain or highly probable can be achieved only by means of death or will produce death. It may seem odd to classify an act of heroic self-sacrifice on the part of a soldier as suicide. It is simpler, however, not to try to define "suicide" so that an act of suicide is always irrational or immoral in some way; if we adopt a neutral definition like the above we can still proceed to ask when an act of suicide in that sense is rational, morally justifiable, and so on, so that all evaluations anyone might wish to make can still be made.

Sometimes a definition that at first seems extremely odd can be made acceptable, if strong reasons are offered in its support. Sometimes, in fact, an odd definition marks a great intellectual step forward. For instance, in 1990 the U.S. Supreme Court recognized that *speech* includes symbolic nonverbal expression such as protesting against a war by wearing armbands or by flying the American flag upside down. Such actions, because they express ideas or emotions, are now protected by the First Amendment. Few people today would disagree that *speech* should include symbolic gestures. (We include an example of controversy over precisely this issue, in Derek Bok's "Protecting Freedom of Expression on the Campus," in Chapter 2, Critical Reading: Getting Started.)

A definition that seems notably eccentric to many readers and thus far has not gained much support is from page 94 of Peter Singer's *Practical Ethics*, in which the author suggests that a nonhuman being can be a *person*. He admits that "it sounds odd to call an animal a person" but says that it seems so only because of our bad habit of sharply separating ourselves from other species. For Singer, *persons* are "rational and self-conscious beings, aware of themselves as distinct entities with a past and a future." Thus, although a newborn infant is a human being, it is not a person; on the other hand, an adult chimpanzee is not a human being but probably is a person. You don't have to agree with Singer to know exactly what he means and where he stands. Moreover, if you read his essay, you may even find that his reasons are plausible and that by means of his unusual definition he has enlarged your thinking.

▷ *The Importance of Definitions* Trying to decide on the best way to define a key idea or a central concept is often difficult as well as controversial. *Death,* for example, has been redefined in recent years. Traditionally, a person was dead when there was no longer any heartbeat. But with advancing medical technology, the medical profession has persuaded legislatures to redefine *death* as cessation of cerebral and cortical functions—so-called brain death.

Some scholars have hoped to bring clarity into the abortion debate by redefining *life*. Traditionally, human life begins at birth or perhaps at viability (the capacity of a fetus to live independently of the uterine environment). However, some have proposed a "brain birth" definition, in the hope of resolving the abortion controversy. A *New York Times* story of November 8, 1990, reported that these thinkers want abortion to be prohibited by law at the point where "integrated brain functioning begins to emerge—about seventy days after conception." Whatever the merits of such a redefinition, the debate is convincing evidence of just how important the definition of certain terms can be.

Last Words about Definition   Since Plato's time, in the fourth century B.C., it has often been argued that the best way to give a definition is to state the *essence* of the thing being defined. Thus, the classic example defines *man* as "a rational animal." (Today, to avoid sexist implications, instead of *man* we would say *human being* or *person*.) That is, the property of *rational animality* is taken to be the essence of every human creature, and so it must be mentioned in the definition of *man*. This statement guarantees that the definition is neither too broad nor too narrow. But philosophers have long criticized this alleged ideal type of definition, on several grounds, one of which is that no one can propose such definitions without assuming that the thing being defined has an essence in the first place—an assumption that is not necessary. Thus, we may want to define *causality,* or *explanation,* or even *definition* itself, but it is doubtful whether it is sound to assume that any of these things has an essence.

A much better way to provide a definition is to offer a set of **sufficient and necessary conditions.** Suppose we want to define the word *circle* and are conscious of the need to keep circles distinct from other geometrical figures such as rectangles and spheres. We might express our definition by citing sufficient and necessary conditions as follows: "Anything is a circle *if and only if* it is a closed plane figure and all points on the circumference are equidistant from the center." Using the connective "if and only if" (called the *biconditional*) between the definition and what is being defined helps to force into our consciousness the need to make the definition neither too exclusive (too narrow) nor too inclusive (too broad). Of course, for most ordinary purposes we don't require such a formally precise and explicit definition. Nevertheless, perhaps the best criterion to keep in mind when assessing a proposed definition is whether it can be stated in the "if and only if " form, and whether, if it is so stated, it is true; that is, if it truly specifies *all and only* the things covered by the word being defined. Idea Prompt 3.1 provides examples.

We are not saying that the four sentences in the table are incontestable. They are arguable. We offer them merely to show ways of defining, and the act of defining is one way of helping you to get your own thoughts going. Notice, too, that the fourth of these examples, a "statement of necessary and sufficient conditions" (indicated by "if and only if") is a bit stiff for ordinary writing. An informal prompt along this line might begin, "Essentially, something can be called *pornography* if it presents. . . ."

IDEA PROMPT 3.1 WAYS TO GIVE DEFINITIONS

Synonym	"Pornography, simply stated, is obscenity."
Example	"Pornography is easily seen in D.H. Lawrence's *Lady Chatterly's Lover* in the scene where . . ."
Stipulation	"For the purposes of this essay, *pornography* refers to . . ."
Statement of necessary and sufficient conditions	"Something can be called *pornography* if and only if it presents sexually stimulating material without offering anything of redeeming social value."

Assumptions

In Chapter 1, Critical Thinking, we discussed the **assumptions** made by the authors of two essays on campus discipline. But we have more to say about assumptions. We have already said that in the form of discourse known as argument certain statements are offered as reasons for other statements. But even the longest and most complex chain of reasoning or proof is fastened to assumptions—one or more *unexamined beliefs.* (Even if such a belief is shared by writer and reader, it is no less an assumption.) Benjamin Franklin argued against paying salaries to the holders of executive offices in the federal government on the grounds that men are moved by ambition (love of power) and by avarice (love of money) and that powerful positions conferring wealth incite men to do their worst. These assumptions he stated, though he felt no need to argue them at length because he assumed that his readers shared them.

An assumption may be unstated. A writer, painstakingly arguing specific points, may choose to keep one or more of the argument's assumptions tacit. Or the writer may be as unaware of some underlying assumption as of the surrounding air. For example, Franklin didn't even bother to state another assumption. He must have assumed that persons of wealth who accept an unpaying job (after all, only persons of wealth could afford to hold unpaid government jobs) will have at heart the interests of all classes of people, not only the interests of their own class. Probably Franklin did not state this assumption because he thought it was perfectly obvious, but if you think critically about the assumption, you may find reasons to doubt it. Surely one reason we pay our legislators is to make certain that the legislature does not consist only of people whose incomes may give them an inadequate view of the needs of others.

An Example: Assumptions in the Argument Permitting Abortion

1. Ours is a pluralistic society, in which we believe that the religious beliefs of one group should not be imposed on others.

2. Personal privacy is a right, and a woman's body is hers, not to be violated by laws that tell her she may not do certain things to her body.

But these (and other) arguments *assume* that a fetus is not—or not yet—a person and therefore is not entitled to the same protection against assaults that we are. Virtually all of us assume that it is usually wrong to kill a human being. Granted, we may find instances in which we believe it is acceptable to take a human life, such as self-defense against a would-be murderer. But even here we find a shared assumption that persons are ordinarily entitled not to be killed.

The argument about abortion, then, usually depends on opposed assumptions: For one group, the fetus is a human being and a potential person—and this potentiality is decisive. But for the other group it is not. Persons arguing one side or the other of the abortion issue ought to be aware that opponents may not share their assumptions.

Premises and Syllogisms

Premises are stated assumptions used as reasons in an argument. (The word comes from a Latin word meaning "to send before" or "to set in front.") A premise thus is a statement set down—assumed—before the argument is begun. The joining of two premises—two statements taken to be true—to produce a conclusion, a third statement, is called a **syllogism** (Greek for "a reckoning together"). The classic example is this:

Major premise: All human beings are mortal.
Minor premise: Socrates is a human being.
Conclusion: Socrates is mortal.

Deduction

The mental process of moving from one statement ("All human beings are mortal") through another ("Socrates is a human being") to yet a further statement ("Socrates is mortal") is called **deduction,** from Latin for "lead down from." In this sense, deductive reasoning does not give us any new knowledge, although it is easy to construct examples that have so many premises, or premises that are so complex, that the conclusion really does come as news to most who examine the argument. Thus, the great detective Sherlock Holmes was credited by his admiring colleague, Dr. Watson, with unusual powers of deduction. Watson meant in part that Holmes could see the logical consequences of apparently disconnected reasons, the number and complexity of which left others at a loss. What is common in all cases of deduction is that the reasons or premises offered are supposed to contain within themselves, so to speak, the conclusion extracted from them.

Often a syllogism is abbreviated. Martin Luther King Jr., defending a protest march, wrote in "Letter from Birmingham Jail":

> You assert that our actions, even though peaceful, must be condemned because they precipitate violence.

Fully expressed, the argument that King attributes to his critics would be stated thus:

> Society must condemn actions (even if peaceful) that precipitate violence.
>
> This action (though peaceful) will precipitate violence.
>
> Therefore, society must condemn this action.

An incomplete or abbreviated syllogism in which one of the premises is left unstated, of the sort found in King's original quotation, is called an **enthymeme** (Greek for "in the mind").

Here is another, more whimsical example of an enthymeme, in which both a premise and the conclusion are left implicit. Henry David Thoreau remarked that "circumstantial evidence can be very strong, as when you find a trout in the milk." The joke, perhaps intelligible only to people born before 1930 or so, depends on the fact that milk used to be sold "in bulk" — that is, ladled out of a big can directly to the customer by the farmer or grocer. This practice was finally prohibited in the 1930s because for centuries the sellers, in order to increase their

profit, were diluting the milk with water. Thoreau's enthymeme can be fully expressed thus:

Trout live only in water.

This milk has a trout in it.

Therefore, this milk has water in it.

These enthymemes have three important properties: Their premises are *true,* the form of their argument is *valid,* and they leave *implicit* either the conclusion or one of the premises.

Sound Arguments

The purpose of a syllogism is to present reasons that establish its conclusion. This is done by making sure that the argument satisfies both of two independent criteria:

- First, all of the premises must be *true.*
- Second, the syllogism must be *valid.*

Once these criteria are satisfied, the conclusion of the syllogism is guaranteed. Any such argument is said to establish or to prove its conclusion, or to use another term, it is said to be **sound.** Here's an example of a sound argument, a syllogism that proves its conclusion:

Extracting oil from the Arctic Wildlife Refuge would adversely affect the local ecology.

Adversely affecting the local ecology is undesirable, unless there is no better alternative fuel source.

Therefore, extracting oil from the Arctic Wildlife Refuge is undesirable, unless there is no better alternative fuel source.

Each premise is **true,** and the syllogism is **valid,** so it establishes its conclusion.

But how do we tell in any given case that an argument is sound? We perform two different tests, one for the truth of each of the premises and another for the validity of the argument.

The basic test for the **truth** of a premise is to determine whether what it asserts corresponds with reality; if it does, then it is true, and if it doesn't, then it is false. Everything depends on the content of the premise—what it asserts—and the evidence for it. (In the preceding syllogism, the truth of the premises can be tested by checking the views of experts and interested parties, such as policymakers, environmental groups, and experts on energy.)

The test for **validity** is quite different. We define a valid argument as one in which the conclusion follows from the premises, so that if all the premises are true then the conclusion *must* be true, too. The general test for validity, then, is this: If one grants the premises, one must also grant the conclusion. Or to put it another way, if one grants the premises but denies the conclusion, is one caught in a self-contradiction? If so, the argument is valid; if not, the argument is invalid.

The preceding syllogism passes this test. If you grant the information given in the premises but deny the conclusion, you have contradicted yourself. Even if the information were in error, the conclusion in this syllogism would still follow from the premises—the hallmark of a valid argument! The conclusion follows because the validity of an argument is a purely formal matter concerning the *relation* between premises and conclusion based on what they mean.

This relationship can be seen more clearly by examining an argument that is valid but that, because one or both of the premises are false, does *not* establish its conclusion. Here is an example of such a syllogism:

> The whale is a large fish.
>
> All large fish have scales.
>
> Therefore, whales have scales.

We know that the premises and the conclusion are false: Whales are mammals, not fish, and not all large fish have scales (sharks have no scales, for instance). But when the validity of the argument is being determined, the truth of the premises and the conclusion is beside the point. Just a little reflection assures us that *if* both of these premises were true, then the conclusion would have to be true as well. That is, anyone who grants the premises of this syllogism and yet denies the conclusion has contradicted herself. So the validity of an argument does not in any way depend on the truth of the premises or the conclusion.

A sound argument, as we said, is an argument that passes both the test of true premises and the test of valid inference. To put it another way, a sound argument

- Passes the test of content (the premises are true, as a matter of fact) and it

- Passes the test of form (its premises and conclusion, by virtue of their very meanings, are so related that it is impossible for the premises to be true and the conclusion false).

Accordingly, an unsound argument, an argument that fails to prove its conclusion, suffers from one or both of two defects.

- First, not all of the premises are true.
- Second, the argument is invalid.

Usually, we have in mind one or both of these defects when we object to someone's argument as "illogical." In evaluating someone's deductive argument, therefore, you must always ask: Is it vulnerable to criticism on the ground that one (or more) of its premises is false? Or is the inference itself vulnerable because even if all the premises are all true, the conclusion still wouldn't follow?

A deductive argument *proves* its conclusion if and only if *two conditions* are satisfied: (1) All the premises are *true,* and (2) it would be *inconsistent to assert the premises and deny the conclusions.*

A Word about False Premises   Suppose that one or more of the premises of a syllogism is false but the syllogism itself is valid. What does that tell us about the truth of the conclusion? Consider this example:

All Americans prefer vanilla ice cream to other flavors.

Tiger Woods is an American.

Therefore, Tiger Woods prefers vanilla ice cream to other flavors.

The first (or major) premise in this syllogism is false. Yet the argument passes our formal test for validity; it is clear that if one grants both premises, then one must accept the conclusion. So we can say that the conclusion *follows from* its premises, even though the premises *do not prove* the conclusion. This is not as paradoxical as it may sound. For all we know, the conclusion of this argument may in fact be true; Tiger Woods may indeed prefer vanilla ice cream, and the odds are that he does because consumption statistics show that a majority of Americans prefer vanilla. Nevertheless, if the conclusion in this syllogism is true, it is not because this argument proved it.

A Word about Invalid Syllogisms   Usually, one can detect a false premise in an argument, especially when the suspect premise appears in someone else's argument. A trickier business is the invalid syllogism. Consider this argument:

All terrorists seek publicity for their violent acts.

John Doe seeks publicity for his violent acts.

Therefore, John Doe is a terrorist.

In the preceding syllogism, let us grant that the first (major) premise is true. Let us also grant that the conclusion may well be true. Finally, the person mentioned in the second (minor) premise could indeed be a terrorist. But it is also possible that the conclusion is false; terrorists are not the only ones who seek publicity for their violent acts; think, for example, of the violence committed against doctors, clinic workers, and patients at clinics where abortions are performed. In short, the truth of the two premises is no guarantee that the conclusion is also true. It is possible to assert both premises and deny the conclusion without self-contradiction.

How do we tell, in general and in particular cases, whether a syllogism is valid? Chemists use litmus paper to enable them to tell instantly whether the liquid in a test tube is an acid or a base. Unfortunately, logic has no litmus test to tell us instantly whether an argument is valid or invalid. Logicians beginning with Aristotle have developed techniques that enable them to test any given argument, no matter how complex or subtle, to determine its validity. But the results of their labors cannot be expressed in a paragraph or even a few pages; not for nothing are semester-long courses devoted to teaching formal deductive logic. Apart from advising you to consult Chapter 9, A Logician's View: Deduction, Induction, Fallacies, all we can do here is repeat two basic points.

First, validity of deductive arguments is a matter of their *form* or *structure*. Even syllogisms like the one on the Arctic Wildlife Refuge on page 84 come in a large variety of forms (256 different ones, to be precise), and only some of these forms are valid. Second, all valid deductive arguments (and only such arguments) pass this test: If one accepts all the premises, then one must accept the conclusion as well. Hence, if it is possible to accept the premises but reject the conclusion (without self-contradiction, of course), then the argument is invalid.

Let us exit from further discussion of this important but difficult subject on a lighter note. Many illogical arguments masquerade as logical. Consider this example: If it takes a horse and carriage four hours to go from Pinsk to Chelm, does it follow that a carriage with two horses will get there in two hours?

Note: In Chapter 9, we discuss at some length other kinds of deductive arguments, as well as **fallacies,** which are kinds of invalid reasoning.

Induction

Whereas deduction takes our beliefs and assumptions and extracts their hidden consequences, **induction** uses information about observed cases to reach a conclusion about unobserved cases. (The word comes from the Latin *in ducere*, "to lead into" or "to lead up to.") If we observe that the bite of a certain snake is poisonous, we may conclude on this evidence that another snake of the same general type is also poisonous. Our inference might be even broader. If we observe that snake after snake of a certain type has a poisonous bite and that these snakes are all rattlesnakes, we are tempted to **generalize** that all rattlesnakes are poisonous.

By far the most common way to test the adequacy of a generalization is to confront it with one or more **counterexamples.** If the counterexamples are genuine and reliable, then the generalization must be false. For example, Ronald Takaki's essay on the "myth" of Asian racial superiority (p. 122) is full of examples that contradict the alleged superiority of Asians; they are counterexamples to that thesis, and they help to expose it as a "myth." What is true of Takaki's reasoning is true generally in argumentative writing. We are constantly testing our generalizations against actual or possible counterexamples.

Unlike deduction, induction gives us conclusions that go beyond the information contained in the premises used in their support. Not surprisingly, the conclusions of inductive reasoning are not always true, even when all the premises are true. On page 75, we gave as an example our observation that on previous days a subway has run at 6:00 A.M. and that therefore we believe that it runs at 6:00 A.M. every day. Suppose, following this reasoning, we arrive at the subway platform just before 6:00 A.M. on a given day and wait an hour without a train. What inference should we draw to explain this? Possibly today is Sunday, and the subway doesn't run before 7:00 A.M. Or possibly there was a breakdown earlier this morning. Whatever the explanation, we relied on a sample that was not large enough (a larger sample might have included some early morning breakdowns) or not representative enough (a more representative sample would have included the later starts on holidays).

A Word about Samples   When we reason inductively, much depends on the size and the quality of the sample. We may interview five members of Alpha Tau Omega and find that all five are Republicans, yet we cannot legitimately conclude that all members of ATO are Republicans. The problem is not always one of failing to interview large numbers. A poll of ten thousand college students tells us very little about "college students" if all ten thousand are white males at the University of Texas. Such a sample, because it leaves out women and minority males, obviously is not sufficiently *representative* of "college students" as a group. Further, though not all of the students at the University of Texas are from Texas or even from the Southwest, it is quite likely that the student body is not fully representative (for instance, in race and in income) of American college students. If this conjecture is correct, even a truly representative sample of University of Texas students would not allow one to draw firm conclusions about American college students.

   In short: An argument that uses samples ought to tell the reader how the samples were chosen. If it does not provide this information, the argument may rightly be treated with suspicion.

Evidence: Experimentation, Examples, Authoritative Testimony, Statistics

Different disciplines use different kinds of evidence:

- In literary studies, the texts are usually the chief evidence.
- In the social sciences, field research (interviews, surveys) usually provides evidence.

In the sciences, reports of experiments are the usual evidence; if an assertion cannot be tested—if an assertion is not capable of being shown to be false—it is a *belief*, an *opinion*, not a scientific hypothesis.

Experimentation   Induction is obviously useful in arguing. If, for example, one is arguing that handguns should be controlled, one will point to specific cases in which handguns caused accidents or were used to commit crimes. If one is arguing that abortion has a traumatic effect on women, one will point to women who testify to that effect. Each instance constitutes **evidence** for the relevant generalization.

In a courtroom, evidence bearing on the guilt of the accused is introduced by the prosecution, and evidence to the contrary is introduced by the defense. Not all evidence is admissible (hearsay, for example, is not, even if it is true), and the law of evidence is a highly developed subject in jurisprudence. In the forum of daily life, the sources of evidence are less disciplined. Daily experience, a particularly memorable observation, an unusual event we witnessed—any or all of these may be used as evidence for (or against) some belief, theory, hypothesis, or explanation. The systematic study of what experience can yield is what science does, and one of the most distinctive features of the evidence that scientists can marshal on behalf of their claims is that it is the result of **experimentation.** Experiments are deliberately contrived situations that are often complex in their technology and designed to yield particular observations. What the ordinary person does with unaided eye and ear, the scientist does, much more carefully and thoroughly, with the help of laboratory instruments.

The variety, extent, and reliability of the evidence obtained in daily life and in the laboratory are quite different. It is hardly a surprise that in our civilization much more weight is attached to the "findings" of scientists than to the corroborative (much less the contrary) experiences of the ordinary person. No one today would seriously argue that the sun really does go around the earth just because it looks that way; nor would we argue that because viruses are invisible to the naked eye they cannot cause symptoms such as swellings and fevers, which are quite plainly visible.

Examples   One form of evidence is the **example.** Suppose that we argue that a candidate is untrustworthy and should not be elected to public office. We point to episodes in his career—his misuse of funds in 1998 and the false charges he made against an opponent in 2002—as examples of his untrustworthiness. Or if we are arguing that President Truman ordered the atom bomb dropped to save American (and, for that matter, Japanese) lives that otherwise would have been lost in a hard-fought invasion of Japan, we point to the stubbornness of the Japanese defenders in battles on the islands of Saipan, Iwo Jima, and Okinawa, where Japanese soldiers fought to the death rather than surrender.

These examples, we say, show us that the Japanese defenders of the main islands would have fought to their deaths without surrendering, even though they knew they would be defeated. Or if we argue that the war was nearly won when Truman dropped the bomb, we can cite secret peace feelers as examples of the Japanese willingness to end the war.

An example is a sample; these two words come from the same Old French word, *essample,* from the Latin *exemplum,* which means "something taken out"—that is, a selection from the group. A Yiddish proverb shrewdly says that "'For example' is no proof," but the evidence of well-chosen examples can go a long way toward helping a writer to convince an audience.

In arguments, three sorts of examples are especially common:

- Real events,
- Invented instances (artificial or hypothetical cases), and
- Analogies.

We will treat each of these briefly.

REAL EVENTS   In referring to Truman's decision to drop the atom bomb, we have already touched on examples drawn from real events — the battles at Saipan and elsewhere. And we have also seen Ben Franklin pointing to an allegedly real happening, a fish that had consumed a smaller fish. The advantage of an example drawn from real life, whether a great historical event or a local incident, is that its reality gives it weight. It can't simply be brushed off.

On the other hand, an example drawn from reality may not provide as clear-cut an instance as could be wished for. Suppose, for instance, that someone cites the Japanese army's behavior on Saipan and on Iwo Jima as evidence that the Japanese later would have fought to the death in an American invasion of Japan and would therefore have inflicted terrible losses on themselves and on the Americans. This example is open to the response that in June and July 1945, Japanese diplomats sent out secret peace feelers, so that in August 1945, when Truman authorized dropping the bomb, the situation was very different.

Similarly, in support of the argument that nations will no longer resort to atomic weapons, some people have offered as evidence the fact that since World War I the great powers have not used poison gas. But the argument needs more support than this fact provides. Poison gas was not decisive or even highly effective in World War I. Moreover, the invention of gas masks made it obsolete.

In short, any *real* event is so entangled in its historical circumstances that it might not be adequate or even relevant evidence in the case being argued. In using a real event as an example (and real events certainly can be used), the writer ordinarily must demonstrate that the event can be taken out of its historical context and be used in the new context of argument. Thus, in an argument against using atomic weapons in warfare, the many deaths and horrible injuries inflicted on the Japanese at Hiroshima and Nagasaki can be cited as effects of nuclear weapons that would invariably occur and did not depend on any special circumstances of their use in Japan in 1945.

INVENTED INSTANCES   **Artificial** or **hypothetical cases — invented instances** — have the great advantage of being protected from objections of the sort just given. Recall Thoreau's trout in the milk; that was a colorful hypothetical case that nicely illustrated his point. An invented instance ("Let's assume that a burglar promises not to shoot a householder if the householder swears not to identify him. Is the house-holder bound by the oath?") is something like a drawing of a flower in a botany textbook or a diagram of the folds of a mountain in a geology textbook. It is admittedly false, but by virtue of its simplifications it sets forth the relevant details very clearly. Thus, in a discussion of rights, the philosopher Charles Frankel says,

> Strictly speaking, when we assert a right for X, we assert that Y has a duty. Strictly speaking, that Y has such a duty presupposes that Y has the capacity to perform this duty. It would be nonsense to say, for example, that a nonswimmer has a moral duty to swim to the help of a drowning man.

This invented example is admirably clear, and it is immune to charges that might muddy the issue if Frankel, instead of referring to a wholly abstract person, Y, talked about some real person, Jones, who did not res-cue a drowning man. For then he would get bogged down over arguing about whether Jones *really* couldn't swim well enough to help, and so on.

Yet invented cases have their drawbacks. First and foremost, they cannot be used as evidence. A purely hypothetical example can illustrate a point or provoke reconsideration of a generalization, but it cannot sub-stitute for actual events as evidence supporting an inductive inference. Sometimes such examples are so fanciful, so remote from life that they fail to carry conviction with the reader. Thus the philosopher Judith Jarvis Thomson, in the course of her argument entitled "A Defense of Abortion," asks you to imagine that you wake up one day and find that against your will a celebrated violinist whose body is not adequately functioning has been hooked up into your body, for life support. Do you have the right to unplug the violinist? Readers of the essays in this book will have to decide for themselves whether the invented cases proposed by various authors are helpful or whether they are so remote that they hinder thought. Readers will have to decide, too, about when they can use invented cases to advance their own arguments.

But we add one point: Even a highly fanciful invented case can have the valuable effect of forcing us to see where we stand. We may say that we are, in all circumstances, against vivisection. But what would we say if we thought that an experiment on one mouse would save the life of someone we love? Or conversely, if one approves of vivisection, would one also approve of sacrificing the last giant panda to save the life of a senile stranger, a person who in any case probably would not live longer than another year? Artificial cases of this sort can help us to see that, well, no, we didn't really mean to say such-and-such when we said so-and-so.

ANALOGIES   The third sort of example, **analogy,** is a kind of com-parison. An analogy asserts that things that are alike in some ways are alike in yet another way. Example: "Before the Roman Empire declined as a world power, it exhibited a decline in morals and in physical stamina;

our culture today shows a decline in morals (look at the high divorce rate, and look at the crime rate) and we also show a decline in physical culture (just read about obesity in children). America, like Rome, will decline as a world power."

Strictly, an analogy is an extended comparison in which different things are shown to be similar in several ways. Thus, if one wants to argue that a head of state should have extraordinary power during wartime, one can argue that the state at such a time is like a ship in a storm: The crew is needed to lend its help, but the decisions are best left to the captain. (Notice that an analogy compares things that are relatively *un*like. Comparing the plight of one ship to another or of one government to another is not an analogy; it is an inductive inference from one case of the same sort to another such case.)

Or take another analogy: We have already glanced at Judith Thomson's hypothetical case in which the reader wakes up to find himself or herself hooked up to a violinist. Thomson uses this situation as an analogy in an argument about abortion. The reader stands for the mother, the violinist for the unwanted fetus. Whether this analogy is close enough to pregnancy to help illuminate our thinking about abortion is something that you may want to think about.

The problem with argument by analogy is this: Two admittedly different things are agreed to be similar in several ways, and the arguer goes on to assert or imply that they are also similar in another way—the point that is being argued. (That is why Thomson argues that if something is true of the reader-hooked-up-to-a-violinist, it is also true of the pregnant mother-hooked-up-to-a-fetus.) But the two things that are said to be analogous and that are indeed similar in characteristics *A, B,* and *C* are also different—let's say in characteristics *D* and *E*. As Bishop Butler is said to have remarked in the early eighteenth century, "Everything is what it is, and not another thing."

Analogies can be convincing, especially because they can make complex issues simple. "Don't change horses in midstream," of course, is not a statement about riding horses across a river but about choosing leaders in critical times. Still, in the end, analogies do not necessarily prove anything. What may be true about riding horses across a stream may not be true about choosing leaders in troubled times or about deciding on a given change of leadership. Riding horses across a stream and choosing leaders are, at bottom, different things, and however much these activities may be said to resemble one another, they remain different, and what is true for one need not be true for the other.

Analogies can be helpful in developing our thoughts. It is sometimes argued, for instance—on the analogy of the doctor-patient or the lawyer-client, or the priest-penitent relationship—that newspaper and television reporters should not be required to reveal their confidential sources. That is worth thinking about: Do the similarities run deep enough, or are there fundamental differences? Or take another example:

Some writers who support abortion argue that the fetus is not a person any more than the acorn is an oak. That is also worth thinking about. But one should also think about this response: A fetus is not a person, just as an acorn is not an oak, but an acorn is a potential oak, and a fetus is a potential person, a potential adult human being. Children, even newborn infants, have rights, and one way to explain this claim is to call attention to their potentiality to become mature adults. And so some people argue that the fetus, by analogy, has the rights of an infant, for the fetus, like the infant, is a potential adult.

Three analogies for consideration: First, let's examine a brief comparison made by Jill Knight, a member of the British Parliament, speaking about abortion:

> Babies are not like bad teeth, to be jerked out because they cause suffering.

Her point is effectively put; it remains for the reader to decide whether or not fetuses are *babies* and if a fetus is not a baby, *why* it can or can't be treated like a bad tooth.

Now, a second bit of analogical reasoning, again about abortion: Thomas Sowell, an economist at the Hoover Institute, grants that women have a legal right to abortion, but he objects to a requirement that the government pay for abortions:

> Because the courts have ruled that women have a legal right to an abortion, some people have jumped to the conclusion that the government has to pay for it. You have a constitutional right to privacy, but the government has no obligation to pay for your window shades. (*Pink and Brown People*, 1981, p. 57)

We leave it to the reader to decide whether the analogy is compelling — that is, if the points of resemblance are sufficiently significant to allow one to conclude that what is true of people wanting window shades should be true of people wanting abortions.

And one more: A common argument on behalf of legalizing gay marriage draws an analogy between gay marriage and interracial marriage, a practice that was banned in sixteen states until 1967, when the Supreme Court declared miscegenation statutes unconstitutional. The gist of the analogy is this: Racism and discrimination against gay and lesbian people are the same. If marriage is a fundamental right—as the Supreme Court held in its 1967 decision when it struck down bans on miscegenation— then it is a fundamental right for gay people as well as heterosexual people.

Authoritative Testimony   Another form of evidence is **testimony,** the citation or quotation of authorities. In daily life we rely heavily on authorities of all sorts: We get a doctor's opinion about our health, we read a book because an intelligent friend recommends it, we see a movie because a critic gave it a good review, and we pay at least a little attention to the weather forecaster.

In setting forth an argument, one often tries to show that one's view is supported by notable figures, perhaps Jefferson, Lincoln, Martin Luther King Jr., or scientists who won the Nobel Prize. You may recall that in the second chapter, in talking about definitions of pornography, we referred to Kenneth Clark. To make certain that you were impressed by his testimony even if you had never heard of him, we described him as "probably the most influential English-speaking art critic of our time." But heed some words of caution:

- Be sure that the authority, however notable, is an authority on the topic in question (a well-known biologist might be an authority on vitamins but not on the justice of a war).

- Be sure that the authority is not biased. A chemist employed by the tobacco industry isn't likely to admit that smoking may be harmful, and a "director of publications" (that means a press agent) for a hockey team isn't likely to admit that watching or even playing ice hockey stimulates violence.

- Beware of nameless authorities: "a thousand doctors," "leading educators," "researchers at a major medical school."

- Be careful when using authorities who indeed were great authorities in their day but who now may be out of date (Adam Smith on economics, Julius Caesar on the art of war, Louis Pasteur on medicine).

- Cite authorities whose opinions your readers will value. William F. Buckley Jr.'s conservative/libertarian opinions mean a good deal to readers of the magazine that he founded, the *National Review*, but probably not to most liberal thinkers. Gloria Steinem's liberal/ feminist opinions carry weight with the readers of the magazines that she cofounded, *New York* and *Ms.* magazine, but probably not to most conservative thinkers. If you are writing for the general reader, your usual audience, cite authorities who are likely to be accepted by the general reader.

One other point: *You* may be an authority. You probably aren't nationally known, but on some topics you perhaps can speak with the authority of personal experience. You may have been injured on a motorcycle while riding without wearing a helmet, or you may have escaped injury because you wore a helmet; you may have dropped out of school and then returned; you may have tutored a student whose native language is not English, or you may be such a student and you may have received tutoring. You may have attended a school with a bilingual education program. In short, your personal testimony on topics relating to these issues may be invaluable, and a reader will probably consider it seriously.

Statistics   The last sort of evidence we discuss here is quantitative or statistical. The maxim "More is better" captures a basic idea of quantitative evidence. Because we know that 90 percent is greater than 75 percent, we are usually ready to grant that any claim supported by experience in 90 percent of the cases is more likely to be true than an alternative claim supported by experience only 75 percent of the time. The greater the difference, the greater our confidence. Consider an example. Honors at graduation from college are often computed on a student's cumulative grade-point average (GPA). The undisputed assumption is that the nearer a student's GPA is to a perfect record (4.0), the better scholar he or she is and therefore the more deserving of highest honors. Consequently, a student with a GPA of 3.9 at the end of her senior year is a stronger candidate for graduating summa cum laude than another student with a GPA of 3.6. When faculty members on the honors committee argue over the relative academic merits of graduating seniors, we know that these quantitative, statistical differences in student GPAs will be the basic (even if not the only) kind of evidence under discussion.

GRAPHS, TABLES, NUMBERS   Statistical information can be marshaled and presented in many forms, but it tends to fall into two main types: the graphic and the numerical. Graphs, tables, and pie charts are familiar ways of presenting quantitative data in an eye-catching manner. (See pages 160–61.) To prepare the graphics, however, one first has to get the numbers themselves under control, and for some purposes it may be acceptable simply to stick with the numbers themselves.

But should the numbers be presented in percentages or in fractions? Should one report, say, that the federal budget underwent a twofold increase over the decade, that it increased by 100 percent, that it doubled, or that the budget at the beginning of the decade was one-half what it was at the end? Taken strictly, these are equivalent ways of saying the same thing. Choice among them, therefore, in an example like this perhaps will rest on whether one's aim is to dramatize the increase (a 100 percent increase looks larger than a doubling) or to play down the size of the increase.

THINKING ABOUT STATISTICAL EVIDENCE   Statistics often get a bad name because it is so easy to misuse them, unintentionally or not, and so difficult to be sure that they have been correctly gathered in the first place. (We remind you of the old saw "There are lies, damned lies, and statistics.") Every branch of social science and natural science needs statistical information, and countless decisions in public and private life are based on quantitative data in statistical form. It is important, therefore, to be sensitive to the sources and reliability of the statistics and to develop a healthy skepticism when confronted with statistics whose parentage is not fully explained.

Consider, for instance, statistics that kept popping up during the baseball strike of 1994. The owners of the clubs said that the average salary of a major-league player was $1.2 million. (The **average** in this case—technically the **mean**—is the result of dividing the total number of salary dollars by the number of players.) The players' union, however, did not talk about the average; rather, the union talked about the **median,** which was less than half of the average, a mere $500,000. (The *median* is the middle value in a distribution. Thus, of the 746 players, 363 earned less than $500,000, 361 earned more, and 22 earned exactly $500,000.) The union said, correctly, that *most* players earned a good deal less than the $1.2 million figure that the owners kept citing; but the $1.2 million average sounded more impressive to the general public, and that is the figure that the guy in the street mentioned when asked for an opinion about the strike.

Consider this statistic: In Smithville in 2005, 1 percent of the victims in fatal automobile accidents were bicyclists. In 2006 the percent of bicyclists killed in automobile accidents was 2 percent. Was the increase 1 percent (not an alarming figure), or was it 100 percent (a staggering figure)? The answer is both, depending on whether we are comparing (a) bicycle deaths in automobile accidents with *all* deaths in automobile accidents (that's an increase of 1 percent), or (b) bicycle deaths in automobile accidents *only with other bicycle deaths* in automobile accidents (an increase of 100 percent). An honest statement would say that bicycle deaths due to automobile accidents doubled in 2006, increasing from 1 to 2 percent. But here's another point: Although every such death is lamentable, if there was one such death in 2009 and two in 2010, the increase from one death to two (an increase of 100 percent!) hardly suggests that there is a growing problem that needs attention. No one would be surprised to learn that in the next year there were no deaths, or only one or even two.

One other example may help to indicate the difficulties of interpreting statistics. According to the San Francisco police department, in 1990 the city received 1,074 citizen complaints against the police. Los Angeles received only half as many complaints in the same period, and Los Angeles has five times the population of San Francisco. Does this mean that the police of San Francisco are much rougher than the police of Los Angeles? Possibly. But some specialists who have studied the statistics not only for these two cities but also for many other cities have concluded that a department with proportionately more complaints against it is not necessarily more abusive than a department with fewer complaints. According to these experts, the more confidence that the citizens have in their police force, the more the citizens will complain about police misconduct. The relatively small number of complaints against the Los Angeles police department thus may indicate that the citizens of Los Angeles are so intimidated and have so little confidence in the system that they are afraid to complain or they do not bother to complain.

If it is sometimes difficult to interpret statistics, it is often at least equally difficult to establish accurate statistics. Consider this example:

> Advertisements are the most prevalent and toxic of the mental pollutants. From the moment your radio alarm sounds in the morning to the wee hours of late-night TV, microjolts of commercial pollution flood into your brain at the rate of about three thousand marketing messages per day. (Kalle Lasn, *Culture Jam*, 1999, pp. 18–19)

Lasn's book includes endnotes as documentation, so, curious about the statistics, we turn to the appropriate page and we find this information concerning the source of his data:

> "three thousand marketing messages per day." Mark Landler, Walecia Konrad, Zachary Schiller, and Lois Therrien, "What Happened to Advertising?" *BusinessWeek*, September 23, 1991, page 66. Leslie Savan in *The Sponsored Life* (Temple University Press, 1994), page 1, estimated that "16,000 ads flicker across an individual's consciousness daily." I did an informal survey in March 1995 and found the number to be closer to 1,500 (this included all marketing messages, corporate images, logos, ads, brand names, on TV, radio, billboards, buildings, signs, clothing, appliances, in cyberspace, etc., over a typical twenty-four hour period in my life). (219)

Well, this endnote is odd. In the earlier passage, you will recall, the author asserted that "about three thousand marketing messages per day" flood into a person's brain. Now, in the documentation, he helpfully cites a source for that statistic, from *BusinessWeek*—though we have not the faintest idea of how the authors of the article in *BusinessWeek* came up with that figure. Oddly, he goes on to offer a very different figure (16,000 ads), and then, to our utter confusion, he offers yet a third figure, 1,500, based on his own "informal survey."

Probably the one thing we can safely say about all three figures is that none of them means very much. Even if the compilers of the statistics told us exactly how they counted—let's say that among countless other criteria they assumed that the average person reads one magazine per day and that the average magazine contains 124 advertisements—it would be hard to take them seriously. After all, in leafing through a magazine, some people may read many ads, some may read none. Some people may read some ads carefully—but perhaps to enjoy their absurdity. Our point: Although the author in his text said, without implying any uncertainty, that "about three thousand marketing messages per day" reach an individual, it is evident (if one checks the endnote) that even he is confused about the figure he gives.

Some last words about the unreliability of some statistical information, stuff that looks impressive but that is, in fact, insubstantial. Marilyn Jager Adams studied the number of hours that families read to their children in

---

✓ A CHECKLIST FOR EVALUATING STATISTICAL EVIDENCE

Regard statistical evidence (like all other evidence) cautiously, and don't accept it until you have thought about these questions:

☐ Was it compiled by a disinterested source? Of course, the name of the source does not always reveal its particular angle (for example, People for the American Way), but sometimes the name lets you know what to expect (National Rifle Association, American Civil Liberties Union).

☐ Is it based on an adequate sample? (A study pointed out that criminals have an average IQ of 91 to 93, whereas the general population has an IQ of 100. The conclusion drawn was that criminals have a lower IQ than the general population. This reading may be accurate, but some doubts have been expressed. For instance, because the entire sample of criminals consisted only of *convicted* criminals, this sample may be biased; possibly the criminals with higher IQs have enough intelligence not to get caught. Or if they are caught, perhaps they are smart enough to hire better lawyers.)

☐ Is the statistical evidence recent enough to be relevant?

☐ How many of the factors likely to be relevant were identified and measured?

☐ Are the figures open to a different and equally plausible interpretation?

☐ If a percent is cited, is it the *average* (or *mean*), or is it the *median*?

---

the five or so years before the children go to school. In her book on the topic, *Beginning to Read: Thinking and Learning about Print* (Massachusetts Institute of Technology Press, 1990), she pointed out that in all those preschool years, poor families read to their children only twenty-five hours, whereas in the same period middle-income families read 1,000 to 1,700 hours. The figures were much quoted in newspapers and by children's advocacy groups. Dr. Adams could not, of course, interview every family in these two groups; she had to rely on samples. What were her samples? For poor families, she selected twenty-four children in twenty families, all in Southern California. One might wonder if families from only one geographic area can provide an adequate sample, but let's think about Dr. Adams's sample of middle-class families. How many families constituted the sample? Exactly one, her own. We leave it to you to decide how much value her findings—again, they were much cited—have.

We are not suggesting that everyone who uses statistics is trying to deceive or even that many who use statistics are unconsciously deceived by them. We mean to suggest only that statistics are open to widely different interpretations and that often those columns of numbers, so precise with their decimal points, are in fact imprecise and possibly even worthless because they may be based on insufficient or biased samples.

Quiz

What is wrong with the following statistical proof that children do not have time for school?

One-third of the time they are sleeping (about 122 days);

One-eighth of the time they are eating (three hours a day, totaling 45 days);

One-fourth of the time is taken up by summer and other vacations (91 days);

Two-sevenths of the year is weekends (104 days).

Total: 362 days — so how can a kid have time for school?

NONRATIONAL APPEALS

Satire, Irony, Sarcasm, Humor

In talking about definition, deduction, and evidence, we have been talking about means of rational persuasion. But as mentioned earlier, there are also other means of persuasion. Take force, for example. If X kicks Y, threatens to destroy Y's means of livelihood, or threatens Y's life, X may persuade Y to cooperate. One form of irrational but sometimes highly effective persuasion is **satire** — that is, witty ridicule. A cartoonist may persuade viewers that a politician's views are unsound by caricaturing (and thus ridiculing) the politician's appearance or by presenting a grotesquely distorted (funny, but unfair) picture of the issue.

Satiric artists often use caricature; satiric writers, also seeking to persuade by means of ridicule, often use **verbal irony.** Irony of this sort contrasts what is said and what is meant. For instance, words of praise may be meant to imply blame (when Shakespeare's Cassius says, "Brutus is an honorable man," he means his hearers to think that Brutus is dishonorable), and words of modesty may be meant to imply superiority ("Of course, I'm too dumb to understand this problem"). Such language, when heavy-handed, is called **sarcasm** ("You're a great guy," said to someone who will not lend the speaker ten dollars). If it is witty — if the jeering is in some degree clever — it is called irony rather than sarcasm.

Although ridicule is not a form of argument (because it is not a form of reasoning), passages of ridicule, especially verbal irony, sometimes appear in essays that are arguments. These passages, like reasons, or for that matter like appeals to the emotions, are efforts to persuade the hearer to accept the speaker's point of view. The great trick in using humor in an argument is, on the one hand, to avoid mere wisecracking, which makes the writer seem like a smart aleck, and, on the other hand, to avoid mere clownishness, which makes the writer seem like a fool. Later in this chapter (p. 104), we print an essay by George F. Will, that is (or seeks to be?) humorous in places. You be the judge.

Emotional Appeals

It is sometimes said that good argumentative writing appeals only to reason, never to emotion, and that any sort of emotional appeal is illegitimate, irrelevant. "Tears are not arguments," the Brazilian writer Machado de Assis said. Logic textbooks may even stigmatize with Latin labels the various sorts of emotional appeal — for instance, *argumentum ad populam* (appeal to the prejudices of the mob, as in "Come on, we all know that schools don't teach anything anymore") and *argumentum ad misericordiam* (appeal to pity, as in "No one ought to blame this poor kid for stabbing a classmate because his mother was often institutionalized for alcoholism and his father beat him").

True, appeals to emotion may get in the way of the facts of the case; they may blind the audience by, in effect, throwing dust in its eyes or by stimulating tears.

Learning from Shakespeare   A classic example is found in Shakespeare's *Julius Caesar*, when Marc Antony addresses the Roman populace after Brutus, Cassius, and others have assassinated Caesar. The real issue is whether Caesar was becoming tyrannical (as the assassins claim) and would therefore curtail the freedom of the people. Antony turns from the evidence and stirs the mob against the assassins by appealing to its emotions. In the ancient Roman biographical writing that Shakespeare drew on, Sir Thomas North's translation of Plutarch's *Lives of the Noble Grecians and Romans*, Plutarch says that Antony,

> perceiving that his words moved the common people to compassion, . . .
> framed his eloquence to make their hearts yearn [that is, grieve] the
> more, and, taking Caesar's gown all bloody in his hand, he laid it open
> to the sight of them all, showing what a number of cuts and holes it had
> upon it. Therewithal the people fell presently into such a rage and
> mutiny that there was no more order kept.

Here are a few extracts from Antony's speeches in Shakespeare's play. Antony begins by asserting that he will speak only briefly:

> Friends, Romans, countrymen, lend me your ears;
> I come to bury Caesar, not to praise him.

After briefly offering some rather insubstantial evidence that Caesar gave no signs of behaving tyrannically (for example, "When that the poor have cried, Caesar hath wept"), Antony begins to play directly on the emotions of his hearers. Descending from the platform so that he may be in closer contact with his audience (like a modern politician, he wants to work the crowd), he calls attention to Caesar's bloody toga:

> If you have tears, prepare to shed them now.
> You all do know this mantle; I remember
> The first time ever Caesar put it on:
> 'Twas on a summer's evening, in his tent,
> That day he overcame the Nervii.
> Look, in this place ran Cassius' dagger through;
> See what a rent the envious Casca made;
> Through this, the well-belovèd Brutus stabbed. . . .

In these few lines Antony

- First prepares the audience by suggesting to them how they should respond ("If you have tears, prepare to shed them now"),
- Then flatters them by implying that they, like Antony, were intimates of Caesar (he credits them with being familiar with Caesar's garment),
- Then evokes a personal memory of a specific time ("a summer's evening")—not just any old specific time but a very important one, the day that Caesar won a battle against the Nervii (a particularly fierce tribe in what is now France).

In fact, Antony was not at the battle, and he did not join Caesar until three years later.

Antony does not mind being free with the facts; his point here is not to set the record straight but to stir the mob against the assassins. He goes on, daringly but successfully, to identify one particular slit in the garment with Cassius's dagger, another with Casca's, and a third with Brutus's. Antony cannot know which slit was made by which dagger, but his rhetorical trick works.

Notice, too, that Antony arranges the three assassins in climactic order, since Brutus (Antony claims) was especially beloved by Caesar:

> Judge, O you gods, how dearly Caesar loved him!
> This was the most unkindest cut of all;
> For when the noble Caesar saw him stab,
> Ingratitude, more strong than traitor's arms,
> Quite vanquished him. Then burst his mighty heart. . . .

Nice. According to Antony, the noble-minded Caesar—Antony's words have erased all thought of the tyrannical Caesar—died not from the wounds inflicted by daggers but from the heartbreaking perception of Brutus's ingratitude. Doubtless there was not a dry eye in the house. We can all hope that if we are ever put on trial, we have a lawyer as skilled in evoking sympathy as Antony.

Are Emotional Appeals Fallacious?   The oration is obviously successful in the play and apparently was successful in real life, but it is the sort of speech that prompts logicians to write disapprovingly of attempts to stir feeling in an audience. (As mentioned earlier in this chapter, the evocation of emotion in an audience is called **pathos,** from the Greek word for "emotion" or "suffering.") There is nothing inherently wrong in stimulating our audience's emotions, but when an emotional appeal confuses the issue that is being argued about or shifts the attention away from the facts of the issue, we can reasonably speak of the fallacy of emotional appeal.

No fallacy is involved, however, when an emotional appeal heightens the facts, bringing them home to the audience rather than masking them. If we are talking about legislation that would govern police actions, it is legitimate to show a photograph of the battered, bloodied face of an alleged victim of police brutality. True, such a photograph cannot tell the whole truth; it cannot tell us if the subject threatened the officer with a gun or repeatedly resisted an order to surrender. But it can tell us that the victim was severely beaten and (like a comparable description in words) evoke in us emotions that may properly enter into our decision about the permissible use of police evidence. Similarly, an animal rights activist who is arguing that calves are cruelly confined might reasonably tell us about the size of the pen in which the beast — unable to turn around or even to lie down — is kept. Others may argue that calves don't much care about turning around or have no right to turn around, but the verbal description, which unquestionably makes an emotional appeal, can hardly be called fallacious or irrelevant.

In appealing to emotions then, the important things are

- Not to falsify (especially by oversimplifying) the issue and
- Not to distract attention from the facts of the case.

Focus on the facts and concentrate on offering reasons (essentially, statements linked with "because"), but you may also legitimately bring the facts home to your readers by seeking to induce in them the appropriate emotions. Your words will be fallacious only if you stimulate emotions that are not rightly connected with the facts of the case.

DOES ALL WRITING CONTAIN ARGUMENTS?

Our answer to the question we have just posed is no — but probably *most* writing *does* contain an argument of sorts. Or put it this way: The writer wants to persuade the reader to see things the way the writer sees them — at least until the end of the essay. After all, even a recipe for a cherry pie in a food magazine — a piece of writing that is primarily expository (how to do it) rather than argumentative (how a reasonable person ought to think about this topic)—probably includes, near the beginning, a sentence with a hint of an argument in it, such as "*Because* [a sign that a *reason* will be offered] this pie can be made quickly and with ingredients (canned cherries) that are always available, give it a try, and it will surely become one of your favorites." Clearly, such a statement cannot stand as a formal argument—a discussion that takes account of possible counterarguments, that relies chiefly on logic and little if at all on emotional appeal, and that draws a conclusion that seems irrefutable.

Still, the statement is something of an argument on behalf of making a pie with canned cherries. In this case, a claim is made (the pie will become a favorite), and two *reasons* are offered in support of this claim:

- It can be made quickly, and
- The chief ingredient—because it is canned—can always be at hand.

✓ A CHECKLIST FOR ANALYZING AN ARGUMENT

☐ What is the writer's claim or thesis? Ask yourself:
  ☐ What claim is being asserted?
  ☐ What assumptions are being made—and are they acceptable?
  ☐ Are important terms satisfactorily defined?
☐ What support (evidence) is offered on behalf of the claim? Ask yourself:
  ☐ Are the examples relevant, and are they convincing?
  ☐ Are the statistics (if any) relevant, accurate, and complete? Do they allow only the interpretation that is offered in the argument?
  ☐ If authorities are cited, are they indeed authorities on this topic, and can they be regarded as impartial?
  ☐ Is the logic—deductive and inductive—valid?
  ☐ If there is an appeal to emotion—for instance, if satire is used to ridicule the opposing view—is this appeal acceptable?
☐ Does the writer seem to you to be fair? Ask yourself:
  ☐ Are counterarguments adequately considered?
  ☐ Is there any evidence of dishonesty or of a discreditable attempt to manipulate the reader?
  ☐ How does the writer establish the image of himself or herself that we sense in the essay? What is the writer's tone, and is it appropriate?

The underlying *assumptions* are

- You don't have a great deal of time to waste in the kitchen, and
- Canned cherries are just as tasty as fresh cherries—and even if they aren't, well, you wouldn't know the difference.

When we read a lead-in to a recipe, then, we won't find a formal argument, but we probably will get a few words that seek to persuade us to keep reading. And most writing does contain such material— sentences that give us a reason to keep reading, that engage our interests, and that make us want to stay with the writer for at least a little longer. If the recipe happens to be difficult and time-consuming, the lead-in may say, "Although this recipe for a cherry pie, using fresh cherries that you will have to pit, is a bit more time-consuming than the usual recipe that calls for canned cherries, once you have tasted it you will never go back to canned cherries." Again, although the logic is scarcely compelling, the persuasive element is evident. The assumption here is that you have a discriminating palate; once you have tasted a pie made with fresh cherries, you will never again enjoy the canned stuff. The writer is not giving us a formal argument, with abundant evidence and with a detailed refutation of counterarguments, but we do know where the writer stands and how the writer wishes us to respond.

AN EXAMPLE: AN ARGUMENT AND A LOOK AT THE WRITER'S STRATEGIES

This essay concerns President George W. Bush's proposal that drilling be allowed in part of the Arctic National Wildlife Refuge (ANWR, pronounced "An-war"). The section of the ANWR that is proposed for drilling is called the "1002 area," as defined by Section 1002 of the Alaska National Interest Lands Conservation Act of 1980. In March 2003, the Senate rejected the Bush proposal, but the issue remains alive.

We follow George F. Will's essay with some comments about the ways in which he constructs his argument.

George F. Will

George F. Will (b. 1941), a syndicated columnist whose writing appears in 460 newspapers, was born in Champaign, Illinois, and educated at Trinity College (Hartford), Oxford University, and Princeton University. Will has served as the Washington, D.C., editor of the National Review *and now writes a regular column for* Newsweek. *His essays have been collected in several books.*

Being Green at Ben and Jerry's

Some Environmental Policies Are Feel-Good Indulgences for an Era of Energy Abundance

If you have an average-size dinner table, four feet by six feet, put a dime on the edge of it. Think of the surface of the table as the Arctic National Wildlife Refuge in Alaska. The dime is larger than the piece of the coastal plain that would have been opened to drilling for oil and natural gas. The House of Representatives voted for drilling, but the Senate voted against access to what Sen. John Kerry, Massachusetts Democrat and presidential aspirant, calls "a few drops of oil." ANWR could produce, for twenty-five years, at least as much oil as America currently imports from Saudi Arabia.

Six weeks of desultory Senate debate about the energy bill reached an almost comic culmination in . . . yet another agriculture subsidy. The subsidy is a requirement that will triple the amount of ethanol, which is made from corn, that must be put in gasoline, ostensibly to clean America's air, actually to buy farmers' votes.

Over the last three decades, energy use has risen about 30 percent. But so has population, which means per capita energy use is unchanged. And per capita GDP has risen substantially, so we are using 40 percent less energy per dollar output. Which is one reason there is no energy crisis, at least none as most Americans understand such things—a shortage of, and therefore high prices of, gasoline for cars, heating oil for furnaces and electricity for air conditioners.

In the absence of a crisis to concentrate the attention of the inattentive American majority, an intense faction—full-time environmentalists—goes to work. Spencer Abraham, the secretary of Energy, says "the previous administration . . . simply drew up a list of fuels it *didn't* like—nuclear energy, coal, hydropower, and oil—which together account for 73 percent of America's energy supply." Well, there are always windmills.

Sometimes lofty environmentalism is a cover for crude politics. The 5 United States has the world's largest proven reserves of coal. But Mike Oliver, a retired physicist and engineer, and John Hospers, professor emeritus of philosophy at USC, note that in 1996 President Clinton put 68 billion tons of America's cleanest-burning coal, located in Utah, off-limits for mining, ostensibly for environmental reasons. If every existing U.S. electric power plant burned coal, the 68 billion tons could fuel them for forty-five years at the current rate of consumption. Now power companies must import clean-burning coal, some from mines owned by Indonesia's Lippo Group, the heavy contributor to Clinton, whose decision about Utah's coal vastly increased the value of Lippo's coal.

The United States has just 2.14 percent of the world's proven reserves of oil, so some people say it is pointless to drill in places like ANWR because "energy independence" is a chimera. Indeed it is. But domestic supplies can provide important insurance against uncertain foreign supplies. And domestic supplies can mean exporting hundreds of billions of dollars less to oil-producing nations, such as Iraq.

Besides, when considering proven reserves, note the adjective. In 1930 the United States had proven reserves of 13 billion barrels. We then fought the Second World War and fueled the most fabulous economic expansion in human history, including the electricity-driven "New Economy." (Manufacturing and running computers consume 15 percent of U.S. electricity. Internet use alone accounts for half of the growth in demand for electricity.) So by 1990 proven reserves were . . . 17 billion barrels, not counting any in Alaska or Hawaii.

In 1975 proven reserves in the Persian Gulf were 74 billion barrels. In 1993 they were 663 billion, a ninefold increase. At the current rate of consumption, today's proven reserves would last 150 years. New discoveries will be made, some by vastly improved techniques of deepwater drilling. But environmental policies will define opportunities. The government estimates that beneath the U.S. outer continental shelf, which the government owns, there are at least 46 billion barrels of oil. But only 2 percent of the shelf has been leased for energy development.

Opponents of increased energy production usually argue for decreased consumption. But they flinch from conservation measures. A new $1 gasoline tax would dampen demand for gasoline, but it would stimulate demands for the heads of the tax increasers. After all, Americans get irritable when impersonal market forces add 25 cents to the cost of a gallon. Tougher fuel-efficiency requirements for vehicles would save a lot of energy. But who would save the legislators who passed those requirements? Beware the wrath of Americans who like to drive, and autoworkers who like to make cars that are large, heavy, and safer than the gasoline-sippers that environmentalists prefer.

Some environmentalism is a feel-good indulgence for an era of   10
energy abundance, which means an era of avoided choices. Or ignored choices—ignored because if acknowledged, they would not make the choosers feel good. Karl Zinsmeister, editor in chief of the *American Enterprise* magazine, imagines an oh-so-green environmentalist enjoying the most politically correct product on the planet— Ben & Jerry's ice cream. Made in a factory that depends on electricity-guzzling refrigeration, a gallon of ice cream requires four gallons of milk. While making that much milk, a cow produces eight gallons of manure, and flatulence with another eight gallons of methane, a potent "greenhouse" gas. And the cow consumes lots of water plus three pounds of grain and hay, which is produced with tractor fuel, chemical fertilizers, herbicides and insecticides, and is transported with truck or train fuel:

"So every time he digs into his Cherry Garcia, the conscientious environmentalist should visualize (in addition to world peace) a pile of grain, water, farm chemicals, and energy inputs much bigger than his ice cream bowl on one side of the table, and, on the other side of the table, a mound of manure eight times the size of his bowl, plus a balloon of methane that would barely fit under the dining room table."

Cherry Garcia. It's a choice. *Bon appêtit.*

George F. Will's Strategies

Now let's look at Will's essay, to see some of the techniques that he uses, techniques that enable him to engage a reader's interest and perhaps enable him to convince the reader, or at least make the reader think, that Will probably is on to something.

We need hardly add that if you think some or all of his techniques—his methods, his strategies—are effective, you will consider adapting them for use in your own essays.

The title, "Being Green at Ben and Jerry's," does not at all prepare the reader for an argument about drilling in the National Arctic Wildlife Refuge, but if you have read any of Will's other columns in *Newsweek*, you probably know that he is conservative and that he will be poking some fun at the green folk—the environmentalists. Will can get away with using a title that is not focused because he has a body of loyal readers—people who will read him because they want to read him, whatever the topic is—but the rest of us writers have to give our readers some idea of what we will be talking about. In short, let your readers know early, perhaps in the title, where you will be taking them.

The subtitle, "Some Environmental Policies Are Feel-Good Indulgences for an Era of Energy Abundance," perhaps added by an editor of the magazine, does suggest that the piece will concern energy, and the words "feel-good indulgence" pretty clearly tell readers that Will believes the environmentalists are indulging themselves.

Paragraph 1 offers a striking comparison. Will wants us to believe that the area proposed for drilling is tiny, so he says that if we imagine the entire Arctic National Wildlife Refuge as a dinner table, the area proposed for drilling is the size of a dime. We think you will agree that this opening seizes a reader's attention. Assuming the truth of the figure—but there seems to be some dispute, since opponents have said that the area would be more like the size of a dinner plate—the image is highly effective. A dime is so small! And is worth so little! Still, one might ask (but probably one doesn't, because Will's figure is so striking) if the tininess of the area really is decisive. One might easily, and apparently with reason, dismiss as absurd the idea that a minuscule tsetse fly could kill a human being, or that the plague is spread by fleas that have bitten rats, because these proposals sound ridiculous—but they are true.

One other point about the first paragraph: Will's voice sounds like a voice you might hear in your living room: "If you have an average-size dinner table," "the dime is larger," "at least as much oil." Don't think that in your own essays you need to adopt a highly formal style. Your reader should think of you as serious but not solemn.

Will goes on to say that Senator John Kerry, an opponent of drilling and therefore on the side that Will opposes, dismisses the oil in the refuge as "a few drops." Will replies that it "could produce, for twenty-five years, at least as much oil as America currently imports from Saudi Arabia." Kerry's "a few drops" is, of course, not to be taken literally; he means, in effect, that the oil is a drop in the bucket. But when one looks into the issue, one finds that estimates by responsible sources vary considerably, from 3.2 billion barrels to 11. 5 billion barrels.

Paragraph 2 dismisses the Senate's debate ("almost comic, actually to buy farmers' votes").

Paragraph 3 offers statistics to make the point that "there is no energy crisis." Here, as in the first paragraph (where he showed his awareness of Kerry's view), Will indicates that he is familiar with views other than his own. In arguing a case, it is important for the writer to let readers know that indeed there are other views—which the writer then goes on to show are less substantial than the writer's. Will is correct in saying that "per capita energy use is unchanged," but those on the other side might say, "Yes, per capita consumption has not increased, but given the population increase, the annual amount has vastly increased, which means that resources are being depleted and that pollution is increasing."

Paragraph 4 asserts again that there is no energy crisis, pokes fun at "fulltime environmentalists" (perhaps there is a suggestion that such people really ought to get a respectable job), and ends with a bit of whimsy: These folks probably think we should go back to using windmills.

Paragraph 5, in support of the assertion that "Sometimes lofty environmentalism is a cover for crude politics," cites an authority (often an effective technique), and, since readers are not likely to recognize the name, it also identifies him ("professor emeritus of philosophy at USC"), and it then offers further statistics (again effective). The paragraph begins by talking about "crude politics" and ends with the assertion that "Now power companies must import clean-burning coal, some from mines owned by Indonesia's Lippo Group, the heavy contributor to Clinton." In short, Will does what he can to suggest that the views of at least some environmentalists are rooted in money and politics.

Paragraph 6 offers another statistic ("The United States has just 2.14 percent of the world's proven reserves of oil"), and he turns it against those who argue that therefore it is pointless for us to drill in Alaska. In effect, Will is replying to people like Senator Kerry who say that the Arctic refuge provides only "a few drops of oil." The point, Will suggests, is not that we can't achieve independence; the point is that "domestic supplies can provide important insurance against uncertain foreign supplies."

Paragraph 7 begins nicely with a transition, "Besides," and then offers additional statistics concerning the large amount of oil that we have. It was, for instance, enough to fuel "the most fabulous economic expansion in human history."

Paragraph 8 offers additional statistics, first about "proven reserves" in the Persian Gulf and then about an estimate—but it is only an estimate—of oil "beneath the U.S. outer continental shelf." We are not certain of Will's point, but in any case the statistics suggest to a reader that the author has done his homework.

Paragraph 9 summarizes the chief position (as Will sees it) of those on the other side: They usually argue for decreased consumption, but they are afraid to argue for the sort of tax on gasoline that might indeed decrease consumption because they know that many Americans want to drive large, heavy cars. Further, the larger, heavier cars that the environmentalists object to are in fact "safer than the gasoline-sippers that environmentalists prefer."

Paragraph 10 uses the term "feel-good indulgence," which is also found in the subtitle of the essay, and now, in the third sentence of the paragraph, we hear again of Ben and Jerry, who have not been in our minds since the title of the essay, "Being Green at Ben and Jerry's." Perhaps we have been wondering all this while why Ben and Jerry are in the title. Almost surely the reader knows that Ben and Jerry are associated with ice cream and therefore with cows and meadows, and probably many readers know, at least vaguely, that Ben and Jerry are somehow associated with environmentalism and with other causes often thought to be on the left. Will (drawing on an article by Karl Zinsmeister, editor of the *American Enterprise*), writes what we consider an extremely amusing paragraph in which he points out that the process of making ice cream "depends on electricity-guzzling refrigeration" and that the cows are, so to speak, supported by fuel that transports fertilizers, herbicides, and insecticides. Further, in the course of producing the four gallons of milk that are required for one gallon of ice cream, the cows themselves—those darlings of environmentalists—contribute "eight gallons of manure, and flatulence with another eight gallons of methane, a potent 'greenhouse' gas." As we see when we read Will's next paragraph, the present paragraph is in large measure a lead-in for the following quotation. Will knows it is is not enough to give a quotation; a writer has to make use of the quotation—has to lead in to it or, after quoting, has to comment on it, or do both.

Paragraph 11 is entirely devoted to quoting Zinsmeister, who imagines an environmentalist digging into a dish of one of Ben and Jerry's most popular flavors, Cherry Garcia. We are invited to see the bowl of ice cream on one side of the table—here Will effectively evokes the table of his first paragraph—and a pile of manure on the other side, "plus a balloon of methane that would barely fit under the dining room table." Vulgar, no doubt, but funny too. George Will knows that humor as well as logic (and statistics and other kinds of evidence) can be among the tools a writer uses in getting an audience to accept or at least to consider an argument.

Paragraph 12 consists of three short sentences, adding up to less than a single line of type: "Cherry Garcia. It's a choice. *Bon appêtit.*" None of the sentences mentions oil or the Arctic Refuge or statistics, and therefore this ending might seem utterly irrelevant to the topic, but we think Will is very effectively saying, "Sure, you have a choice about drilling in the Arctic Refuge; any sensible person will choose the ice cream (drilling) rather than the manure and the gas (not drilling).

TOPICS FOR CRITICAL THINKING AND WRITING

1. What, if anything, makes Will's essay interesting? What, if anything, makes it highly persuasive? How might it be made more persuasive?

2. In paragraph 10, Will clowns a bit about the gas that cows emit, but apparently this gas, which contributes to global warming, is no laughing matter. The government of New Zealand, in an effort to reduce livestock emissions of methane and nitrous oxide, proposed a tax that would subsidize future research on the emissions. The tax would cost the average farmer $300 a year. Imagine that you are a New Zealand farmer. Write a letter to your representative, arguing for or against the tax.

3. Senator Barbara Boxer, campaigning against the proposal to drill in ANWR, spoke of the refuge as "God's gift to us" (*New York Times,* March 20, 2002). How strong an argument is she offering? Some opponents of drilling have said that drilling in ANWR is as unthinkable as drilling in Yosemite or the Grand Canyon. Again, how strong is this argument? Can you imagine circumstances in which you would support drilling in these places? Do we have a moral duty to preserve certain unspoiled areas?

4. The Inupiat (Eskimo) who live in and near ANWR by a large majority favor drilling, seeing it as a source of jobs and a source of funding for schools, hospitals, and police. But the Ketchikan Indians, who speak of themselves as the "Caribou People," see drilling as a threat to the herds that they depend on for food and hides. How does one balance the conflicting needs of these two groups?

5. Opponents of drilling in ANWR argue that over its lifetime of fifty years, the area would produce less than 1 percent of the fuel we need during the period and that therefore we should not risk disturbing the area. Further, they argue that drilling in ANWR is an attempt at a quick fix to U.S. energy needs, whereas what is needed are sustainable solutions, such as the development of renewable energy sources (e.g., wind and sun) and fuel-efficient automobiles. How convincing do you find these arguments?

6. Proponents of drilling include a large majority—something like 75 percent of the people of Alaska, including its governor and its two senators. How much attention should be paid to their voices?

ARGUMENTS FOR ANALYSIS

Stanley Fish

Stanley Fish (b. 1938) established his reputation as a student of English litera-
ture—he has taught literature at the University of California, Berkeley, Johns
Hopkins University, and Duke University—but he has also published on legal
issues. He now teaches at Florida International University's College of Law. This
essay was published in 2008, when Hillary Clinton and Barack Obama were
candidates for the Democratic Party's nomination for president, and inevitably
there was much talk about the candidacy of a woman and an African American.

When "Identity Politics" Is Rational

If there's anything everyone is against in these election times, it's
"identity politics," a phrase that covers a multitude of sins. Let me start
with a definition. (It may not be yours, but it will at least allow the discussion to be framed.) You're practicing identity politics when you vote
for or against someone because of his or her skin color, ethnicity, religion,
gender, sexual orientation, or any other marker that leads you to say yes
or no independently of a candidate's ideas or policies. In essence identity
politics is an affirmation of the tribe against the claims of ideology, and by
ideology I do not mean something bad (a mistake frequently made), but
any agenda informed by a vision of what the world should be like.

An identity politics voter says, in effect, I don't care what views he
holds, or even what bad things he may have done, or what lack of ability
he may display; he's my brother, or he's my kinsman, or he's my landsman,
or he comes from the neighborhood, or he's a Southerner, or (and here the
tribe is really big) my country right or wrong. "My country right or wrong"
is particularly useful in making clear how identity politics differs from politics as many Americans would prefer to see it practiced. Rather than saying
she's right on immigration or he's wrong on the war, the identity-politics
voter says he looks like me or she and I belong to the same church.

Identity politics is illiberal. That is, it is particularist whereas liberalism is universalist. The history of liberalism is a history of extending the
franchise to those who were once excluded from it by their race, gender,
or national origin. Although these marks of identification were retained
(by the census and other forms of governmental classification) and could
still be celebrated in private associations like the church and the social
club, they were not supposed to be the basis of decisions one might
make "as a citizen," decisions about who might best lead the country or
what laws should be enacted or voted down. Deciding as a citizen means
deciding not as a man or a woman or a Jew or an African American or a
Caucasian or a heterosexual, but as a human being.

Stanley Crouch believes that the project of liberal universalizing is
now pretty much complete and that "elements of distinction"—his phrase

for the thinking that was fashionable in "the era of 'identity politics'"—
"have become secondary to the power of human qualities with which
anyone can identify or reject" (*Daily News*, Feb. 11). But his judgment is
belied by almost everything that is going on in this campaign. As I write
this I am watching the returns from the "Potomac Primary" and the news
is being presented entirely in racial, ethnic, and gender terms. Every newspaper or magazine article I read does the same thing. The Obama and
Clinton campaigns accuse each other of playing the race card or the gender card. An Hispanic superdelegate warns that by replacing her Latino
campaign manager with a black one, Senator Clinton risks losing his vote
and the vote of other Hispanic delegates he is in the process of contacting.

Christopher Hitchens looks at the scene and is disgusted by behavior   5
that, in his view, "keeps us anchored in the past." (*Wall Street Journal*,
Jan. 18) He will not, he tells us, vote for Clinton just so that we can have
the "'first woman president'" (I don't remember that one from the past);
and he won't vote for Obama who, he says, "wants us to transcend
something at the same time he implicitly asks us to give that same something as a reason to vote for him." It would seem that we are far from
realizing Ken Connor's dream that we might judge "all of the presidential hopefuls on the basis of the content of their character and their qualifications to serve" (Townhall.com, Jan. 20).

But is it as bad as all that? Is it so irrational and retrograde to base
one's vote on the gender or race or religion or ethnicity of a candidate?
Not necessarily. If the vote is given (or withheld) only because the candidate looks like you or has the same religion, it does seem a shallow and
meretricious act, for it is an act unsupported by reasons. "Because she is
a woman as I am" is of course a reason, but it is not a reason of the relevant kind, a reason that cites goals and programs, and argues for them.
But suppose what was said was something like this: "As a woman I find
government sponsored research skewed in the direction of diseases that
afflict men and inattentive to the medical problems faced by women,
and it is my belief that a woman president will devote resources to the
solution of those problems." That's an identity politics argument which is
thick, not thin; the she's-like-me point is not invoked as sufficient unto
itself, but as it relates to a matter of policy. The calculation may or may
not pan out (successful candidates both disappoint and surprise), but it is
a calculation of the right kind.

One objection to identity politics (Crouch makes it in the same column) is that groups and populations are not monolithic, but display a
diversity of attitudes and positions. Yes they do, but members of a group
who might disagree with each other on any number of things could
nevertheless come together on a matter of shared concern. American
Jews, for example, have widely varying views on many important
issues—tax cuts, tort reform, gay marriage, the Iraq war. Still, the vast
majority believes that it is important to defend the security of Israel.
This is a belief shared even by those American Jews who are strongly

critical of Israel's treatment of the Palestinians. They may deplore Israel's actions and agree with Jimmy Carter when he likens them to apartheid, but if the choice is between a politician who pledges to support Israel and a politician who would withdraw support and leave the Jewish state to fend for itself, most of them would vote for the first candidate every time.

African Americans are no less heterogeneous in their views than Jewish Americans. Yet every African American—conservative or liberal, rich or poor, barely educated or highly educated—meets with obstacles to his or her success and mobility that are all the more frustrating because they are structural (built into the culture's ways of perceiving) rather than official. To the non-African American these obstacles will be more or less invisible, especially in a country where access to opportunity is guaranteed by law. It makes sense, therefore, that an African American voter could come to the conclusion that an African American candidate would be likely to fight for changes that could remove barriers a white candidate might not even see. A vote given for that reason would be a vote based on identity, but it would be more than a mere affirmation of fellowship (he's one of mine and I have to support him); it would be a considered political judgment as to which candidate will move the country in a preferred direction. Identity might be the trigger of the vote, but it would not be the whole of its content.

We should distinguish, I think, between two forms of identity politics. The first I have already named "tribal"; it is the politics based on who a candidate is rather than on what he or she believes or argues for. And that, I agree, is usually a bad idea. (I say "usually" because it is possible to argue that the election of a black or female president, no matter what his or positions happen to be, will be more than a symbolic correction of the errors that have marred the country's history, and an important international statement as well.) The second form of identity politics is what I call "interest" identity politics. It is based on the assumption (itself resting on history and observation) that because of his or her race or ethnicity or gender a candidate might pursue an agenda that would advance the interests a voter is committed to. Not only is there nothing wrong with such a calculation—it is both rational and considered—I don't see that there is an alternative to voting on the basis of interest.

The alternative usually put forward is Crouch's: Vote "for human 10 qualities" rather than sectarian qualities. That is, vote on the basis of reasons everyone, no matter what his or her identity, will acknowledge as worthy. But there are no such reasons and no such human qualities. To be sure, there are words often attached to this chimera—integrity, dedication, honesty, intellect, to name a few. But these qualities, even when they are found, will always be in the service of some set of policies you either favor or reject. It is those policies, not the probity of their proposer, that you will be voting for. (If your candidate is also a good person, that's a nice bonus, but it isn't the essential thing.) You will be voting, in short, for interests, and those who do not have an investment in those interests will be voting for someone else.

What this means is that the ritual deprecation of "special interests" makes no sense. All interests are special interests—proceed from some contestable point of view—and none is "generally human." And that is why identity interests, as long as they are ideological and not merely tribal, constitute a perfectly respectable reason for awarding your vote.

TOPICS FOR CRITICAL THINKING AND WRITING

1. Fish starts out his essay with a formal and explicit definition of "identity politics." What do you think of that definition? Is it too broad? Too narrow? Too vague? Can you think of any ways to improve it?

2. What is the origin of the epigram, "My country right or wrong"? Does Fish endorse it? Do you? Why is it offered as an example of identity politics? Explain your views.

3. Suppose someone said that it is naïve to advocate deciding issues of public concern by appeal to one's status as "a human being" (para. 3). How would you reply? Do so in an essay of 300 words.

4. Fish speaks of two different practices under the rubric of "identity politics." What are they, which if either does Fish prefer, and why? Is either of these related to what Fish in the title of his essay refers to as "rational" politics?

James Carroll

James Carroll, born in Chicago in 1943, was ordained a Roman Catholic priest in 1969. He has published novels, poems, and books on religion and politics. His column appears regularly in the Boston Globe.

If Poison Gas Can Go, Why Not Nukes?

Nuclear abolition is for dreamers. That is the "realist" assessment of the ever-slowing movement to eliminate nuclear weapons from the planet. Despite treaty obligations to the contrary, U.S. planners take for granted the permanent legitimacy of the nuclear arsenal, and, therefore, the necessity of enhancing it with next-generation weapons. This assumption undergirds the determination of other nations either to maintain their nukes, or, if they have none, to acquire them. Here is what keeps the Iran crisis simmering, and ignites future crises with other nuclear wannabes. Only a restoration of the goal of universal nuclear abolition as an achievable program of realpolitik will avert coming catastrophe.

A model for such restoration is right in front of us—the success of the century-old movement to eliminate chemical weapons. That project has evolved so slowly that it is hardly noticed. Yet, with the full abolition of chemical weapons in sight, it should be celebrated as an astonishing triumph of the dream over "realism."

In the beginning, the problem was defined quite simply as "poison." In the early twentieth century, humans already felt as though they were being dragged by new weapons technologies into realms of exile where mere survival could itself seem like treason. They resisted by focusing rejection on "poisonous weapons," and ordered them outlawed with the Hague Convention of 1907. That prohibition did not stop both sides in World War I from using asphyxiating gas (the Germans beginning at Ypres in the spring of 1915, the British at Loos the following fall). Poison gas defined the nightmare of that war, and though relatively few combatants were killed by it (less than 100,000), the grotesque suffering of the many gassed casualties (more than a million) registered powerfully on the European imagination. Perhaps a civilization grown hardened to the sight of spilt blood could not abide the sound of ravaged lungs gasping for air.

Immediately after the war, the movement to ban gas resumed. In 1925, gas was indeed outlawed by the Geneva Convention, but realists always knew better (which explains why the U.S. Senate ratified that treaty only in 1975). "That gas is a legitimate weapon of war," a British commission had concluded in 1919, is beyond a "shadow of doubt . . . for history shows that in no case has a weapon which has proved successful in war been abandoned." Assumptions about the inevitability of weaponized gas prompted Britain, in 1939, both to stockpile the banned substance and to distribute gas masks to its citizens. Yet, for all the barbarities of World War II, gas, including newly developed nerve agents, was hardly used as a weapon in Europe (German use of it in death camps was in its own category and the Japanese used it in Asia, although rarely against Allied forces). Such restraint was grounded more in fear of retaliation than in humanism.

Once nuclear weapons were introduced in 1945, all devils were ⁵ loosed, and both sides in the Cold War accumulated vast stocks of weaponized poison, now designated as "chemical." Though the mushroom cloud dominated nightmares, multiple scenarios for civilization-ending mass destruction became possible. Chemical weapons, having been made morally acceptable by the relatively even more heinous nukes, had come into their own by the time Ronald Reagan and Mikhail Gorbachev tried to call the whole business off. At Geneva and Reykjavik, they set their sights on eliminating nuclear weapons by the year 2000—a purpose that failed. But with chemical weapons they began to succeed. (Saddam Hussein, against both Iran and his own people, was showing that chemical weapons could still actually be used—and to what dread effect.)

In 1990, Gorbachev and George H.W. Bush signed a bilateral treaty agreeing to begin the destruction of chemical weapons stockpiles, and in

1993, the global Chemical Weapons Convention was agreed to—a realization of the dream first articulated at the Hague and Geneva nearly a century before. The 1993 convention, outlawing chemical weapons, has been ratified by almost every nation on Earth. Stockpiles and production facilities remain, but are being reduced and closed. Chemical weapons are being destroyed. Their legitimacy has been entirely removed, their permanence rejected. The poison gas realists of 1919 have been proven wrong. Now to do the same with the nuclear realists of 2008.

Topics for Critical Thinking and Writing

1. What does Carroll hope to accomplish by making a comparison between poison gas and nuclear weapons (para. 5)? How useful do you think the comparison is? Explain.

2. Carroll defends the idea of "universal nuclear abolition" (para. 1). What are the main objections that he faces to creating such a policy?

3. Do you think tear gas should be considered a "weaponized gas" (para. 4)? Explain.

4. Consult a few sources on World War I that expand on Carroll's account (para. 3) of how poison gas was used in that conflict. Based on your reading, compose an essay in which you argue for or against the use of poison gas in warfare.

Gloria Jiménez

Gloria Jiménez married immediately after she graduated from high school, worked briefly, had two children, and then, after her younger child started school, continued her own formal education. This essay, written for a composition course at Tufts University in 2003, is her first publication.

Against the Odds, and Against the Common Good

(Student Essay)

State-run lotteries are now so common—thirty-nine states and Washington, D.C., operate lotteries—that the states probably will never get out of the lottery business. Still, when all is said and done about lotteries bringing a bit of excitement into the lives of many people and bringing a vast amount of money into the lives of a few, the states should not be in the business of urging people to gamble.

And they *do* urge people. Consider a slogan used in Maryland, "Play Today. Cash Tomorrow." If the statement were, "Get a job today and you will have cash tomorrow," it would be true; it would make sense, however small the earnings might be. But "Play Today. Cash Tomorrow" falsely suggests that the way to have money tomorrow is to buy a ticket today. In fact, buying a ticket is an almost sure-fire way of getting nothing for something.

Maryland is not the only state that uses a clever slogan to get its citizens to part with hard-earned money. New York's ads say, "You Can't Win If You Don't Play," and Oregon's ads say, "There Is No Such Thing as a Losing Ticket." This last slogan—which at first glance seems to say that every ticket will benefit the purchaser—is built on the idea that the state's share of the money goes to a worthy cause, usually education or some social service. But no matter how you look at it, this slogan, like the others, urges people to buy a product—a jackpot—that they have almost no chance of receiving.

The chief arguments *in favor* of state-run lotteries seem to be these: (1) people freely choose to participate; (2) funds are used for education or for other important services; (3) if this source of funding disappears, the states will have to compensate by imposing taxes of one sort or another; (4) operation by the government ensures that the lotteries are run honestly; and (5) lotteries create jobs. We can respond briefly to the last two points, and then concentrate on the first three.

It probably is true that the lotteries are run honestly (though I seem to recall reading in the newspaper about one state in which corruption was found in administering the lottery), but that is not the point. If it is wrong to encourage people to gamble, it is hardly relevant to say that the game is run honestly. The other point that can be dismissed briefly is that lotteries create jobs. This argument is usually advanced in connection with the creation of casinos, which surely do create jobs, not only in the casinos but also in nearby restaurants, parking lots, movie theaters, and so forth. But lottery tickets are sold in places where the clerks are already employed. Presumably the only new jobs created by the lottery are the relatively few jobs of the people who dream up the slogans or who are in charge of collecting and processing the receipts.

The three other claims require more attention. The first, that people freely choose to participate, probably is largely true. Although some buyers are compulsive gamblers, people who are addicted and therefore cannot really be said to choose freely, I grant that most people do have a free choice—although, as I have already said, I think that some of the slogans that states use are deceptive, and if this is the case, purchasers who are misled by the ads are not entirely free. Consider a slogan that Illinois used on billboards, especially in poor neighborhoods: "This Could Be Your Ticket Out." Yes, a person might hit the jackpot and get out of poverty, but the chances are one in several million, and to imply that the lottery is a reasonable option to get out of present poverty is to be deceptive. Further, the message is essentially unwholesome. It implies that the way out is luck, rather than education and hard work. Of course, luck plays a part in life, but 99.99 percent of the people who rely on the ticket as the "ticket out" of poverty are going to be terribly disappointed. But again, we can grant that except for gambling addicts, people who buy lottery tickets are freely doing so.

Probably the strongest claim is that the funds are used for important purposes, usually education. This claim apparently is true: The legislators are smart enough to package the lottery bills this way. And the revenue gained seems enormous—$20 billion in 2002, according to the *New York Times* (May 18, 2003, sec. 4, p. 1). On the other hand, this amount is only about 4 percent of the total revenue of the states. That is, this amount *could* be raised by other means, specifically by taxation, but legislators understandably do not want to be associated with increasing taxes. And so, again, advocates of state lotteries emphasize the voluntary nature of the lottery: By buying lottery tickets, they say, people are in effect volunteering to give money to the states, in exchange for the chance (however remote) of getting a ticket out. Buying a ticket, in this view, is paying an optional tax; if you don't want to pay the tax, don't buy the ticket.

I now get to the point in my argument where I may sound condescending, where I may offend decent people. The point is this: Studies show that most of the tickets are bought by people who don't have much money, people who are near the bottom of the economic scale. According to one study, adults whose income was under $10,000 spent nearly three times as much buying lottery tickets as did adults who earned $50,000 or more.[1] I say that this argument is delicate because anyone who advances it is liable to be accused of being snobbish and paternalistic, of saying, in effect, "Poor people don't know how to manage their money, so we ought to remove temptation from their eyes." But such a reply does not get to the central issues: The central issues are (1) that the state should not tempt people, rich or poor, with dreams of an easy buck and (2) that education and social services are immensely important to the whole of society, so they should not be disproportionately financed by the poor and the addicted.

Let me end a bit indirectly. Surely everyone will grant that tobacco is a harmful product. Yes, it is legal, but everyone knows it is harmful. The state puts very heavy taxes on it, presumably not to raise revenue but to discourage the use of tobacco. We agree, surely, that it would be almost criminal if, in an effort to increase its revenues, the state *enticed* people to smoke—for example, by posting billboards showing attractive people smoking or cartoon characters that appealed to children. Would we say, "Oh, well, we need the revenue (from the taxes) to provide services, so let's make smoking as attractive as we can to get people to buy cigarettes"? No, we would say, "People should not smoke, but if they will,

[1]Verna V. Gehring, "The American State Lottery: Sale or Swindle?" *Report from the Institute for Philosophy and Public Policy 20* (Winter/Spring 2000): 15.

well, let's use the revenue from the taxes for two chief purposes: *to dissuade* people from smoking and *to treat* people who have become ill from smoking."

State legislators who genuinely have the interests of their constituents 10 at heart will not pass bills that put the state into the lottery business and that cause the state to engage in an activity that is close to pickpocketing. Rather, they will recognize that, however unpopular taxes are, taxes may have to be raised to support education and social services that the people rightly expect the state to provide. It's against the odds to expect politicians to act this way, but let's hope that some politicians will do the right thing and will vote for the common good.

TOPICS FOR CRITICAL THINKING AND WRITING

1. Jiménez omits at least one important argument that advocates of state-run lotteries sometimes offer: If our state doesn't run a lottery, residents will simply go to nearby states to buy tickets, so we will just be losing revenue that other states pick up; poor people will still be spending money that they can't afford, and our state will in no way benefit. What do you suppose Jiménez might say in reply? And what is your own view of this argument?

2. A bit of humor appears at the end of Jiménez's second paragraph. Is it appropriate? Or is the essay too solemn, too preachy? If you think it is too preachy, cite some sentences, and then revise them to make them more acceptable.

3. What would you say are the strengths and the weaknesses of this essay? What grade would you give it, and why? If you were the instructor in this first-year composition course, what comment (three or four sentences) would you write at the end of the essay?

Anna Lisa Raya

Daughter of a second-generation Mexican American father and a Puerto Rican mother, Anna Lisa Raya grew up in Los Angeles. While an undergraduate at Columbia University in New York, she wrote and published this essay on identity.

It's Hard Enough Being Me

(Student Essay)

When I entered college, I *discovered* I was Latina. Until then, I had never questioned who I was or where I was from: My father is a second-generation Mexican-American, born and raised in Los Angeles, and my mother was born in Puerto Rico and raised in Compton, California. My home is El Sereno, a predominantly Mexican neighborhood in L.A. Every close friend I have back home is Mexican. So I was always just Mexican. Though sometimes I was just Puerto Rican—like when we would visit Mamo (my grandma) or hang out with my Aunt Titi.

Upon arriving in New York as a first-year student, 3,000 miles from home, I not only experienced extreme culture shock, but for the first time I had to define myself according to the broad term "Latina." Although culture shock and identity crisis are common for the newly minted collegian who goes away to school, my experience as a newly minted Latina was, and still is, even more complicating. In El Sereno, I felt like I was part of a majority, whereas at the College I am a minority.

I've discovered that many Latinos like myself have undergone similar experiences. We face discrimination for being a minority in this country while also facing criticism for being "whitewashed" or "sellouts" in the countries of our heritage. But as an ethnic group in college, we are forced to define ourselves according to some vague, generalized Latino experience. This requires us to know our history, our language, our music, and our religion. I can't even be a content "Puerto Mexican" because I have to be a politically-and-socially-aware-Latina-with-a-chip-on-my-shoulder-because-of-how-repressed-I-am-in-this-country.

I am none of the above. I am the quintessential imperfect Latina. I can't dance salsa to save my life, I learned about Montezuma and the Aztecs in sixth grade, and I haven't prayed to the *Virgen de Guadalupe* in years.

Apparently I don't even look Latina. I can't count how many times   5 people have just assumed that I'm white or asked me if I'm Asian. True, my friends back home call me *güera* ("whitey") because I have green eyes and pale skin, but that was as bad as it got. I never thought I would wish my skin were a darker shade or my hair a curlier texture, but since I've been in college, I have—many times.

Another thing: my Spanish is terrible. Every time I call home, I berate my mama for not teaching me Spanish when I was a child. In fact, not knowing how to speak the language of my home countries is the biggest problem that I have encountered, as have many Latinos. In Mexico there is a term, *pocha*, which is used by native Mexicans to ridicule Mexican-Americans. It expresses a deep-rooted antagonism and dislike for those of us who were raised on the other side of the border. Our failed attempts to speak pure, Mexican Spanish are largely responsible for the dislike. Other Latin American natives have this same attitude. No matter how well a Latino speaks Spanish, it can never be good enough.

Yet Latinos can't even speak Spanish in the U.S. without running the risk of being called "spic" or "wetback." That is precisely why my mother refused to teach me Spanish when I was a child. The fact that she spoke Spanish was constantly used against her: It prevented her from getting good jobs, and it would have placed me in bilingual education—a construct of the Los Angeles public school system that has proved to be more of a hindrance to intellectual development than a help.

To be fully Latina in college, however, I *must* know Spanish. I must satisfy the equation: Latina [equals] Spanish-speaking.

So I'm stuck in this black hole of an identity crisis, and college isn't making my life any easier, as I thought it would. In high school, I was being prepared for an adulthood in which I would be an individual, in which I wouldn't have to wear a Catholic school uniform anymore. But though I led an anonymous adolescence, I knew who I was. I knew I was different from white, black, or Asian people. I knew there was a language other than English that I could call my own if I only knew how to speak it better. I knew there were historical reasons why I was in this country, distinct reasons that make my existence here easier or more difficult than other people's existence. Ultimately, I was content.

Now I feel pushed into a corner, always defining, defending, and 10 proving myself to classmates, professors, or employers. Trying to understand who and why I am, while understanding Plato or Homer, is a lot to ask of myself.

A month ago, I heard three Nuyorican (Puerto Ricans born and raised in New York) writers discuss how New York City has influenced their writing. One problem I have faced as a young writer is finding a voice that is true to my community. I was surprised and reassured to discover that as Latinos, these writers had faced similar pressures and conflicts as myself; some weren't even taught Spanish in childhood. I will never forget the advice that one of them gave me that evening: She said that I need to be true to myself. "Because people will always complain about what you are doing — you're a 'gringa' or a 'spic' no matter what," she explained. "So you might as well do things for yourself and not for them."

I don't know why it has taken 20 years to hear this advice, but I'm going to give it a try. *Soy yo* and no one else. *Punto.*[1]

Topics for Critical Thinking and Writing

1. When Raya says she "discovered" she was Latina (para. 1), to what kind of event is she referring? Was she coerced or persuaded to declare herself as Latina, or did it come about in some other way?

2. Is Raya on balance glad or sorry that she did not learn Spanish as a child? What evidence can you point to in her essay one way or the other?

3. What is an "identity crisis" (para. 9)? Does everyone go through such a crisis about the time one enters college? Did you? Or is this an experience that only racial minorities in predominantly white American colleges undergo?

[1]*Soy yo . . . Punto.* I'm me . . . Period (Spanish). [Editors' note.]

Ronald Takaki

Ronald Takaki (1939–2009), the grandson of agricultural laborers who had come from Japan, was a professor of ethnic studies at the University of California at Berkeley. He edited From Different Shores: Perspectives on Race and Ethnicity in America *(1987) and wrote (among other writings)* Strangers from a Different Shore: A History of Asian-Americans *(1989). The essay that we reprint appeared originally in the* New York Times *on June 16, 1990.*

The Harmful Myth of Asian Superiority

Asian Americans have increasingly come to be viewed as a "model minority." But are they as successful as claimed? And for whom are they supposed to be a model?

Asian Americans have been described in the media as "excessively, even provocatively" successful in gaining admission to universities. Asian American shopkeepers have been congratulated, as well as criticized, for their ubiquity and entrepreneurial effectiveness.

If Asian Americans can make it, many politicians and pundits ask, why can't African Americans? Such comparisons pit minorities against each other and generate African American resentment toward Asian Americans. The victims are blamed for their plight, rather than racism and an economy that has made many young African American workers superfluous.

The celebration of Asian Americans has obscured reality. For example, figures on the high earnings of Asian Americans relative to Caucasians are misleading. Most Asian Americans live in California, Hawaii, and New York—states with higher incomes and higher costs of living than the national average.

Even Japanese Americans, often touted for their upward mobility, 5 have not reached equality. While Japanese American men in California earned an average income comparable to Caucasian men in 1980, they did so only by acquiring more education and working more hours.

Comparing family incomes is even more deceptive. Some Asian American groups do have higher family incomes than Caucasians. But they have more workers per family.

The "model minority" image homogenizes Asian Americans and hides their differences. For example, while thousands of Vietnamese American young people attend universities, others are on the streets. They live in motels and hang out in pool halls in places like East Los Angeles; some join gangs.

Twenty-five percent of the people in New York City's Chinatown lived below the poverty level in 1980, compared with 17 percent of the city's population. Some 60 percent of the workers in the Chinatowns of Los Angeles and San Francisco are crowded into low-paying jobs in garment factories and restaurants.

"Most immigrants coming into Chinatown with a language barrier cannot go outside this confined area into the mainstream of American industry," a Chinese immigrant said. "Before, I was a painter in Hong Kong, but I can't do it here. I got no license, no education. I want a living; so it's dishwasher, janitor, or cook."

Hmong and Mien refugees from Laos have unemployment rates that 10 reach as high as 80 percent. A 1987 California study showed that three out of ten Southeast Asian refugee families had been on welfare for four to ten years.

Although college-educated Asian Americans are entering the professions and earning good salaries, many hit the "glass ceiling"—the barrier through which high management positions can be seen but not reached. In 1988, only 8 percent of Asian Americans were "officials" and "managers," compared with 12 percent for all groups.

Finally, the triumph of Korean immigrants has been exaggerated. In 1988, Koreans in the New York metropolitan area earned only 68 percent of the median income of non-Asians. More than three-quarters of Korean greengrocers, those so-called paragons of bootstrap entrepreneurialism, came to America with a college education. Engineers, teachers, or administrators while in Korea, they became shopkeepers after their arrival. For many of them, the greengrocery represents dashed dreams, a step downward in status.

For all their hard work and long hours, most Korean shopkeepers do not actually earn very much: $17,000 to $35,000 a year, usually representing the income from the labor of an entire family.

But most Korean immigrants do not become shopkeepers. Instead, many find themselves trapped as clerks in grocery stores, service workers in restaurants, seamstresses in garment factories, and janitors in hotels.

Most Asian Americans know their "success" is largely a myth. They 15 also see how the celebration of Asian Americans as a "model minority" perpetuates their inequality and exacerbates relations between them and African Americans.

TOPICS FOR CRITICAL THINKING AND WRITING

1. What is the thesis of Takaki's essay? What is the evidence he offers for its truth? Do you find his argument convincing? Explain your answers to these questions in an essay of 500 words.

2. Takaki several times uses statistics to make a point. Do some of the statistics seem more convincing than others? Explain.

3. Consider Takaki's title. To what group(s) is the myth of Asian superiority harmful?

4. Suppose you believed that Asian Americans are economically more successful in America today, relative to white Americans, than African

Americans are. Does Takaki agree or disagree with you? What evidence, if any, does he cite to support or reject the belief?

5. Takaki attacks the "myth" of Asian American success and thus rejects the idea that they are a "model minority" (recall the opening and closing paragraphs). What do you think a genuine model minority would be like? Can you think of any racial or ethnic minority in the United States that can serve as a model? Explain why or why not in an essay of 500 words.

James Q. Wilson

James Q. Wilson (b. 1931) is Collins Professor of Management and Public Policy at the University of California at Los Angeles. Among his books are Thinking about Crime *(1975),* Bureaucracy *(1989),* The Moral Sense *(1993), and* Moral Judgment *(1997). The essay that we reprint appeared originally in the* New York Times Magazine *on March 20, 1994.*

Just Take Away Their Guns

The president wants still tougher gun control legislation and thinks it will work. The public supports more gun control laws but suspects they won't work. The public is right.

Legal restraints on the lawful purchase of guns will have little effect on the illegal use of guns. There are some 200 million guns in private ownership, about one-third of them handguns. Only about 2 percent of the latter are employed to commit crimes. It would take a Draconian, and politically impossible, confiscation of legally purchased guns to make much of a difference in the number used by criminals. Moreover, only about one-sixth of the handguns used by serious criminals are purchased from a gun shop or pawnshop. Most of these handguns are stolen, borrowed, or obtained through private purchases that wouldn't be affected by gun laws.

What is worse, any successful effort to shrink the stock of legally purchased guns (or of ammunition) would reduce the capacity of law-abiding people to defend themselves. Gun control advocates scoff at the importance of self-defense, but they are wrong to do so. Based on a household survey, Gary Kleck, a criminologist at Florida State University, has estimated that every year, guns are used—that is, displayed or fired—for defensive purposes more than a million times, not counting their use by the police. If his estimate is correct, this means that the number of people who defend themselves with a gun exceeds the number of arrests for violent crimes and burglaries.

Our goal should not be the disarming of law-abiding citizens. It should be to reduce the number of people who carry guns unlawfully, especially in places—on streets, in taverns—where the mere presence of a gun can increase the hazards we all face. The most effective way to reduce illegal gun-carrying is to encourage the police to take guns away from people who carry them without a permit. This means encouraging the police to make street frisks.

The Fourth Amendment to the Constitution bans "unreasonable 5 searches and seizures." In 1968 the Supreme Court decided (*Terry v. Ohio*) that a frisk—patting down a person's outer clothing—is proper if the officer has a "reasonable suspicion" that the person is armed and dangerous. If a pat-down reveals an object that might be a gun, the officer can enter the suspect's pocket to remove it. If the gun is being carried illegally, the suspect can be arrested.

The reasonable-suspicion test is much less stringent than the probable-cause standard the police must meet in order to make an arrest. A reasonable suspicion, however, is more than just a hunch; it must be supported by specific facts. The courts have held, not always consistently, that these facts include someone acting in a way that leads an experienced officer to conclude criminal activity may be afoot; someone fleeing at the approach of an officer; a person who fits a drug courier profile; a motorist stopped for a traffic violation who has a suspicious bulge in his pocket; a suspect identified by a reliable informant as carrying a gun. The Supreme Court has also upheld frisking people on probation or parole.

Some police departments frisk a lot of people, but usually the police frisk rather few, at least for the purpose of detecting illegal guns. In 1992 the police arrested about 240,000 people for illegally possessing or carrying a weapon. This is only about one-fourth as many as were arrested for public drunkenness. The average police officer will make *no* weapons arrests and confiscate *no* guns during any given year. Mark Moore, a professor of public policy at Harvard University, found that most weapons arrests were made because a citizen complained, not because the police were out looking for guns.

It is easy to see why. Many cities suffer from a shortage of officers, and even those with ample law-enforcement personnel worry about having their cases thrown out for constitutional reasons or being accused of police harassment. But the risk of violating the Constitution or engaging in actual, as opposed to perceived, harassment can be substantially reduced.

Each patrol officer can be given a list of people on probation or parole who live on that officer's beat and be rewarded for making frequent stops to insure that they are not carrying guns. Officers can be trained to recognize the kinds of actions that the Court will accept as providing the "reasonable suspicion" necessary for a stop and frisk. Membership in a gang known for assaults and drug dealing could be made the basis, by statute or Court precedent, for gun frisks.

The available evidence supports the claim that self-defense is a legiti- 10 mate form of deterrence. People who report to the National Crime Survey that they defended themselves with a weapon were less likely to lose property in a robbery or be injured in an assault than those who did not defend themselves. Statistics have shown that would-be burglars are threatened by gun-wielding victims about as many times a year as they are arrested (and much more often than they are sent to prison) and that the chances of a burglar being shot are about the same as his chances of going to jail. Criminals know these facts even if gun control advocates do not and so are less likely to burgle occupied homes in America than occupied ones in Europe, where the residents rarely have guns.

Some gun control advocates may concede these points but rejoin that the cost of self-defense is self-injury: Handgun owners are more likely to shoot themselves or their loved ones than a criminal. Not quite. Most gun accidents involve rifles and shotguns, not handguns. Moreover, the rate of fatal gun accidents has been declining while the level of gun ownership has been rising. There are fatal gun accidents just as there are fatal car accidents, but in fewer than 2 percent of the gun fatalities was the victim someone mistaken for an intruder.

Those who urge us to forbid or severely restrict the sale of guns ignore these facts. Worse, they adopt a position that is politically absurd. In effect, they say, "Your government, having failed to protect your person and your property from criminal assault, now intends to deprive you of the opportunity to protect yourself."

Opponents of gun control make a different mistake. The National Rifle Association and its allies tell us that "guns don't kill, people kill" and urge the Government to punish more severely people who use guns to commit crimes. Locking up criminals does protect society from future crimes, and the prospect of being locked up may deter criminals. But our experience with meting out tougher sentences is mixed. The tougher the prospective sentence the less likely it is to be imposed, or at least to be imposed swiftly. If the Legislature adds on time for crimes committed with a gun, prosecutors often bargain away the add-ons; even when they do not, the judges in many states are reluctant to impose add-ons.

Worse, the presence of a gun can contribute to the magnitude of the crime even on the part of those who worry about serving a long prison sentence. Many criminals carry guns not to rob stores but to protect themselves from other armed criminals. Gang violence has become more threatening to bystanders as gang members have begun to arm themselves. People may commit crimes, but guns make some crimes worse. Guns often convert spontaneous outbursts of anger into fatal encounters. When some people carry them on the streets, others will want to carry them to protect themselves, and an urban arms race will be underway.

And modern science can be enlisted to help. Metal detectors at airports   15 have reduced the number of airplane bombings and skyjackings to nearly zero. But these detectors only work at very close range. What is needed is a device that will enable the police to detect the presence of a large lump of metal in someone's pocket from a distance of ten or fifteen feet. Receiving such a signal could supply the officer with reasonable grounds for a pat-down. Underemployed nuclear physicists and electronics engineers in the post-cold-war era surely have the talents for designing a better gun detector.

Even if we do all these things, there will still be complaints. Innocent people will be stopped. Young black and Hispanic men will probably be stopped more often than older white Anglo males or women of any race. But if we are serious about reducing drive-by shootings, fatal gang wars and lethal quarrels in public places, we must get illegal guns off the street. We cannot do this by multiplying the forms one fills out at gun shops or by pretending that guns are not a problem until a criminal uses one.

TOPICS FOR CRITICAL THINKING AND WRITING

1. If you had to single out one sentence in Wilson's essay as coming close to stating his thesis, what sentence would that be? Why do you think it states, better than any other sentence, the thesis of the essay?

2. In his third paragraph Wilson reviews some research by a criminologist purporting to show that guns are important for self-defense in American households. Does the research as reported show that displaying or firing guns in self-defense actually prevented crimes? Or wounded aggressors? Suppose you were also told that in households where guns may be used defensively, thousands of innocent people are injured, and hundreds are killed—for instance, children who find a loaded gun and play with it. Would you regard these injuries and deaths as a fair tradeoff? Explain. What does the research presented by Wilson really show?

3. In paragraph 12 Wilson says that people who want to severely restrict the ownership of guns are in effect saying, "'Your government, having failed to protect your person and your property from criminal assault, now intends to deprive you of the opportunity to protect yourself.'" What reply might an advocate of severe restrictions make? (Even if you strongly believe Wilson's summary is accurate, try to put yourself in the shoes of an advocate of gun control, and come up with the best reply that you can.)

4. Wilson reports in paragraph 7 that the police arrest four times as many drunks on the streets as they do people carrying unlicensed firearms. Does this strike you as absurd, reasonable, or mysterious? Does Wilson explain it to your satisfaction?

5. In his final paragraph Wilson grants that his proposal entails a difficulty: "Innocent people will be stopped. Young black and Hispanic men will probably be stopped more often than older white Anglo males or women of any race." Assuming that his predictions are accurate, is Wilson's proposal therefore fatally flawed and worth no further thought, or (to take the other extreme view) do you think that innocent people who fall into certain classifications will just have to put up with frisking for the public good?

6. In an essay of no more than 100 words, explain the difference between the "reasonable-suspicion" test (para. 5) and the "probable-cause standard" (para. 6) that the courts use in deciding whether a street frisk is lawful. (You may want to organize your essay into two paragraphs, one on each topic, or perhaps into three if you want to use a brief introductory paragraph.)

7. Wilson criticizes both gun control advocates and the National Rifle Association for their ill-advised views. In an essay of 500 words, state his criticisms of each side, and explain whether and to what extent you agree.

Sally Satel

Sally Satel, a psychiatrist and resident scholar at the American Enterprise Institute, is a lecturer at the Yale University School of Medicine. Satel is the author of PC, MD: How Political Correctness Is Corrupting Medicine *(2000), and the coauthor of* One Nation under Therapy *(2005). We reprint an op-ed piece that she wrote for the* New York Times *in 2006, and we follow it with several letters written in response.*

Death's Waiting List

March was National Kidney Month. I did my part: I got a new one. My good fortune, alas, does not befall nearly enough people, and the federal government deserves much of the blame.

Today 70,000 Americans are waiting for kidneys, according to the United Network for Organ Sharing, which maintains the national waiting list. Last year, roughly 16,000 people received one (about 40 percent are from living donors, the others from cadavers). More are waiting for livers, hearts, and lungs, which mostly come from deceased donors, bringing the total to about 92,000. In big cities, where the ratio of acceptable organs to needy patients is worst, the wait is five to eight years and is expected to double by 2010. Someone on the organ list dies every ninety seconds. Tick. Tick. Tick.

Until my donor came forward, I was desperate. I had been on the list only for a year and was about to start dialysis. I had joined a Web site, MatchingDonors.com, and found a man willing to give me one of his kidneys, but he fell through. I wished for a Sears organ catalog so I could find a well-matched kidney and send in my check. I wondered about going overseas to become a "transplant tourist," but getting a black market organ seemed too risky.

Paradoxically, our nation's organ policy is governed by a tenet that closes off a large supply of potential organs—the notion that organs from any donor, deceased or living, must be given freely. The 1984 National Organ Transplantation Act makes it illegal for anyone to sell or acquire an organ for "valuable consideration."

In polls, only 30 percent to 40 percent of Americans say they have 5
designated themselves as donors on their driver's licenses or on state-run
donor registries. As for the remainder, the decision to donate will fall to
their families who are as likely as not to deny the hospital's request. In
any event, only a small number of bodies of the recently deceased, perhaps 13,000 a year, possess organs healthy enough for transplanting.

The verdict is in: Relying solely on altruism is not enough. Charities
rely on volunteers to help carry out their good works but they also need
paid staff. If we really want to increase the supply of organs, we need to
try incentives—financial and otherwise.

Many transplant experts recognize this, proposing initiatives that
would allow people to give their organs in exchange for tax breaks,
guaranteed health insurance, college scholarships for their children,
deposits in their retirement accounts, and so on: Ethics committees of
United Network for Organ Sharing, the American Society of Transplant
Surgeons, and the World Transplant Congress, along with the President's
Council on Bioethics and others, have begun discussing the virtues of
such incentives.

Against this backdrop of mounting frustration, the Institute of
Medicine, part of the National Academy of Sciences, this month issued a
report titled, "Organ Donation: Opportunities for Action." Unfortunately,
the report more properly should be subtitled "Recommendations for
Inaction."

Basically, it recommended only one new initiative: expanding donor
eligibility to patients who died of cardiac arrest. (Organs now can be
retrieved only from those who suffer brain death.) This makes sense, as
more people die because their heart stops than because of brain damage.

But even so, this new supply will fall far short of need. At the very 10
least, the report should have shown enthusiasm for other initiatives.
One is the popular and effective European practice of "presumed consent" in which citizens are considered donors at death unless they sign
an anti-donor (or opt-out) card.

Another possibility it could have recommended was pilot studies using
incentives in a regulated market. One model resembles a "futures" market
in cadaver organs. A potential donor could receive compensation—outright payment, a sizable contribution to a charity of his choice, or lifetime health insurance—in installments before death or to his estate
afterwards in exchange for permission to recover his organs at death.

Why so timid? The Institute of Medicine cautioned against treating
the body as if it were "for sale." But that's outdated thinking: we've
accepted markets for human eggs, sperm, and surrogate mothers. A
recent poll by researchers in Pennsylvania found that 59 percent of
respondents favored the general idea of incentives, with 53 percent saying direct payments would be acceptable.

Some critics worry that compensation for kidney donation by the
living would be most attractive to the poor and hence exploit them. But

if it were government-regulated we could ensure that donors would receive education about their choices, undergo careful medical and psychological screening, and receive quality follow-up care. We could even make a donation option that favors the well-off by rewarding donors with a tax credit. Besides, how is it unfair to poor people if compensation enhances their quality of life?

Paying for organs, from the living or deceased, may seem distasteful. But a system with safeguards, begun as a pilot to resolve ethical and practical aspects, is surely preferable to the status quo that allows thousands to die each year. As the International Forum for Transplant Ethics put it: "The well-known shortage of kidneys for transplantation causes much suffering and death. If we are to deny treatment to the suffering and dying, we need better reasons than our own feelings of disgust."

TOPICS FOR CRITICAL THINKING AND WRITING

1. How would you characterize Satel's tone? Businesslike? Wimpy? Or what? Come up with a characterization in a word or two, and then point to two or three sentences to support your view.

2. In a reasoned essay of 250–500 words, set forth your view of "presumed consent" (para. 10).

3. If you have not signed a donor card, explain why you have not. You just haven't gotten around to it? You don't like the idea? Religious reasons?

4. In a reasoned essay of 250–500 words, set forth your view of the proposal that Satel offers in paragraph 11, which involves payment. By the way, do the statistics offered in paragraph 12 play any role in shaping your opinion of the proposal?

5. In 250 words, specify and evaluate the argumentative techniques that Satel uses in her final paragraph.

6. In the United States it is legal and widely acceptable to sell blood, sperm, and eggs. Is there any significant difference between selling such things and selling a kidney? Between selling a kidney and renting a womb? Explain your answer.

7. Suppose that you have a recently signed organ-donor card in your wallet. Then suppose that you die in an accident. On what grounds, if any, would you think it reasonable for a family member to veto your organ donation?

8. Given the great need for organ donors, should the federal government mount a massive (and costly) campaign to alert the public to the need? Give your reasons pro or con, in an essay of 250–500 words.

9. Some doctors and some hospitals make a great deal of money from donated organs. Should doctors and hospitals that receive free organs be required to implant them without charge, or receive, at most, minimal compensation?

Letters of Response by Dorothy H. Hayes, Charles B. Fruit, and Michelle Goodwin

To the Editor:

Re "Death's Waiting List," by Sally Satel (Op-Ed, May 15):

As a kidney donor, I consider cash for organs an obscene proposal. I donated a kidney to a loved one in 2002 and would do it again in a heartbeat. It was a gift to me to offer new life.

But cash for body parts? This option has the potential to promote donor trafficking, and to germinate guilt on a grand scale.

Even in life-and-death situations, some may not be able to risk the pain and their own health for a loved one in need of an organ transplant, no matter how much they love.

But for tax breaks, guaranteed health insurance, college scholarships, and deposits in retirement accounts, as Dr. Satel suggests?

Europe's "presumed consent" is the humane answer and decades overdue.

DOROTHY H. HAYES
Stamford, Conn., May 16, 2006

To the Editor:

Sally Satel and I were both lucky enough to have found donors for kidney transplants that saved our lives. But I disagree with her endorsement of a market-based incentive strategy that would pay organ donors or their family members. That would set a dangerous precedent.

In 2005, a national survey found that 10.8 percent of those polled would be less likely to grant consent for the organs of a deceased family member to be used for transplant if they were offered payment; 68 percent said they would be neither more nor less likely to grant consent.

Thus, there is little data to show that financial incentives would increase donation rates. More likely, "paying for organs" would lead people to view organs as commodities.

The National Kidney Foundation has long maintained that financial incentives for donation would not allow the United States to maintain its values as a society, and that a voluntary system of organ donation, free of commercialization, is the only ethical way transplantation can be practiced in the United States.

The foundation is working to attack the organ shortage through improvement in organ-donation education for families and the establishment of standards to ensure the health and safety of living donors. A wholesale sellout to the law of supply and demand is not the answer.

CHARLES B. FRUIT
Atlanta, May 17, 2006

The writer is chairman of the National Kidney Foundation.

To the Editor:

Sally Satel offers a provocative solution to the American organ transplant system failure: try incentives. She's right.

African-Americans are disproportionately affected by the organ shortage. They represent 40 percent of people on the kidney transplant waiting list, have the longest waits, and experience the highest death rates on lists.

For years, commentators have suggested that African Americans would suffer most under a system with incentives. Their arguments verge on the paternalistic and polemical, and their rationales are outmoded and incendiary.

Such thinking ignores the fact that blacks might benefit from the introduction of incentives into the current transplantation system, because African Americans need kidneys more than any other group.

The consequences of ignoring the possible advantages of cadaveric sales for curing organ deficits and thereby enhancing the health opportunities for all Americans, especially black Americans, are extreme.

MICHELE GOODWIN
Chicago, May 15, 2006

The writer, a professor at DePaul University College of Law, is the author of a book about the supply and demand of body parts.

TOPICS FOR CRITICAL THINKING AND WRITING

1. Hayes says in her second paragraph, "I consider cash for organs an obscene proposal." Do you agree? Why, or why not?

2. Fruit offers statistics concerning financial rewards to the families of the deceased, but he does not address the points Satel raises in paragraph 11 — outright payments to the donor, or to a charity of the donor's choice, or to the donor's estate. Would any of these plans influence you to become a donor after your death? Why, or why not?

3. Goodwin in her third paragraph mentions "paternalistic" arguments, but she doesn't describe them. What do you suppose a paternalistic argument would be?

4. Write a response (250 words, in the form of a letter) to one of the preceding letters.

Heather Rogers

Heather Rogers is a writer and filmmaker. We give an excerpt from her recent book, Gone Tomorrow: The Hidden Life of Garbage *(2005). The message of the book is that our capitalistic society is inherently wasteful — businesses need to create objects that don't last, so they can sell more goods — and that if the planet is not to be destroyed we must create a society that does not need much of what we think we need.*

Hiding in Plain Sight

In the dark chill of early morning, heavy steel garbage trucks chug and creep along neighborhood collection routes. A worker empties the contents of each household's waste bin into the truck's rear compaction unit. Hydraulic compressors scoop up and crush the dross, cramming it into the enclosed hull. When the rig is full, the collector heads to a garbage depot called a "transfer station" to unload. From there the rejectamenta is taken to a recycling center, an incinerator or, most often, to what's called a "sanitary landfill."

Land dumping has long been the favored disposal method in the U.S. thanks to the relative low cost of burial, and North America's abundant supply of unused acreage. Although the great majority of our castoffs go to landfills, they are places the public is not meant to see. Today's garbage graveyards are sequestered, guarded, veiled. They are also high-tech, and, increasingly, located in rural areas that receive much of their rubbish from urban centers that no longer bury their own wastes.

There's a reason landfills are tucked away, on the edge of town, in otherwise untraveled terrain, camouflaged by hydroseeded, neatly tiered slopes. If people saw what happened to their waste, lived with the stench, witnessed the scale of destruction, they might start asking difficult questions. Waste Management Inc., the largest rubbish handling corporation in the world, operates its Geological Reclamation Operations and Waste Systems (GROWS) landfill just outside Morrisville, Pennsylvania—in the docile river valley near where Washington momentously crossed the Delaware leading his troops into Trenton in 1776. Sitting atop the landfill's 300-foot-high butte composed entirely of garbage, the logic of our society's unrestrained consuming and wasting quickly unravels.

Up here is where the dumping takes place; it is referred to as the fill's "working face." Clusters of trailer trucks, yellow earthmovers, compacting machines, steamrollers, and water tankers populate this bizarre, thirty-acre nightmare. Churning in slow motion through the surreal landscape, these machines are remaking the earth in the image of garbage. Scores of seagulls hover overhead then suddenly drop into the rotting piles. The ground underfoot is torn from the metal treads of the equipment. Potato chip wrappers, tattered plastic bags, and old shoes poke through the dirt as if floating to the surface. The smell is sickly and sour.

The aptly named GROWS landfill is part of Waste Management Inc.'s 5 (WMI) 6,000-acre garbage treatment complex, which includes a second landfill, an incinerator and a state-mandated leaf composting lot. GROWS is one of a new breed of waste burial sites referred to as "mega-fills." These high-tech, high-capacity dumps are comprised of a series of earth covered "cells" that can be 10 to 100 acres across and up to hundreds of feet deep—or tall, as is the case at GROWS. (One Virginia whopper has disposal capacity equivalent to the length of one thousand football fields and the height of the Washington Monument.) As of 2002, GROWS was the single largest recipient of New York City's garbage in Pennsylvania, a state that is the country's biggest depository for exported waste.

WMI's Delaware-side operation sits on land that has long served the interests of industry. Overlooking a rambling, mostly decommissioned US Steel factory, WMI now occupies the former grounds of the Warner Company. In the previous century, Warner surface mined the area for gravel and sand, much of which was shipped to its cement factory in Philadelphia. The area has since been converted into a reverse mine of sorts; instead of extraction, workers dump, pack, and fill the earth with almost 40 million pounds of municipal wastes daily.

Back on top of the GROWS landfill, twenty-ton dump trucks gather at the low end of the working face, where they discharge their fetid cargo. Several feet up a dirt bank, a string of large trailers are being detached from semi trucks. In rapid succession each container is tipped almost vertical by a giant hydraulic lift and, within seconds, twenty-four tons of putrescence cascades down into the day's menacing valley of trash. In the middle of the dumping is a "landfill compactor"—which looks like a bulldozer on steroids with mammoth metal spiked wheels— that pitches back and forth, its fifty tons crushing the detritus into the earth. A smaller vehicle called a "track loader" maneuvers on tank treads, channeling the castoffs from kitchens and offices into the compactor's path. The place runs like a well-oiled machine, with only a handful of workers orchestrating the burial.

Get a few hundred yards from the landfill's working face and it's hard to smell the rot or see the debris. The place is kept tidy with the help of thirty-five-foot tall fencing made of "litter netting" that surrounds the perimeter of the site's two landfills. As a backup measure, teams of "paper pickers" constantly patrol the area retrieving discards carried off by the wind. Small misting machines dot fence tops, roads, and hillsides, spraying a fine, invisible chemical-water mixture into the air, which binds with odor molecules and pulls them to the ground.

In new state-of-the-art landfills, the cells that contain the trash are built on top of what is called a "liner." The liner is a giant underground bladder intended to prevent contamination of groundwater by collecting leachate—liquid wastes and the rainwater that seeps through buried trash—and channeling it to nearby water treatment facilities. WMI's two Morrisville landfills leach on average 100,000 gallons daily. If this toxic stew contaminated the site's groundwater it would be devastating.

Once a cell is filled, which might take years, it is closed off or 10 "capped." The capping process entails covering the garbage with several feet of dirt, which gets graded, then packed by steamrollers. After that, layers of clay-embedded fabric, synthetic mesh, and plastic sheeting are

draped across the top of the cell and joined with the bottom liner (which is made of the same materials) to encapsulate all those outmoded appliances, dirty diapers, and discarded wrappers.

Today's landfill regulations, ranging from liner construction to post-capping oversight, mean that disposal areas like WMI's GROWS are potentially less dangerous than the dumps of previous generations. But the fact remains that these systems are short-term solutions to the garbage problem. While they may not seem toxic now, all those underground cells packed with plastics, solvents, paints, batteries, and other hazardous materials will someday have to be treated since the liners won't last forever. Most liners are expected to last somewhere between thirty and fifty years. That time frame just happens to coincide with the post-closure liability private landfill operators are subject to; thirty years after a site is shuttered, its owner is no longer responsible for contamination, the public is.

There is a palpable tension at waste treatment facilities, as though at any minute the visitor will uncover some illegal activity. But what's most striking at these places isn't what they might be hiding; it's what's in plain view. The lavish resources dedicated to destroying used commodities and making that obliteration acceptable, even "green," is what's so astounding. Each landfill (not to mention garbage collection systems, transfer stations, recycling centers and incinerators) is an expensive, complex operation that uses the latest methods developed and perfected at laboratories, universities, and corporate campuses across the globe.

The more state-of-the-art, the more "environmentally responsible" the operation, the more the repressed question pushes to the surface: What if we didn't have so much trash to get rid of?

Topics for Critical Thinking and Writing

1. How does Rogers explain the public's tolerance for waste (para. 3)? Do you think her explanation is the correct one, or not? Explain your position in an essay of 250 words. (Notice that the same kind of explanation is offered on other topics, e.g. the return home of U.S. troops killed or badly wounded fighting in Iraq.)

2. In paragraph 6 Rogers says that Waste Management Inc.'s operation "has long served the interests of industry." Could one argue that it has also long served the interests of ordinary people, such as you? Explain.

3. Rogers writes as if the thirty-year limit on liability for disposal of waste is the result of a plot to protect its creators of this waste from responsibility for its creation (para. 11). Do you think that is a fair interpretation based on the available evidence?

4. Rogers proposes a partial, if not wholly sufficient, solution to the waste disposal problem. What is it? Why isn't it a complete solution to the problem? Do you agree? What progress is being made to adopt her solution nationwide? In your home town? Answer these questions in a 500-word essay.

4

Visual Rhetoric: Images as Arguments

A picture is worth a thousand words.
— CHINESE PROVERB

"What is the use of a book," thought Alice, "without pictures or conversations?"
— LEWIS CARROLL

SOME USES OF IMAGES

Most visual materials that accompany written arguments serve one of two functions—they appeal to the emotions (a photograph of a calf in a pen so narrow that the calf cannot turn, in an essay on animal liberation) or they clarify numerical data (a graph showing five decades of male and female law school enrollments). There are of course additional uses for pictures, for example cartoons may add a welcome touch of humor or satire, but in this chapter we concentrate on appeals to emotion and briefly on graphs and related images.

APPEALS TO THE EYE

We began the preceding chapter by distinguishing between *argument*, which we said relies on reason (*logos*), and *persuasion*, which we said is a broad term that can include appeal to the emotions (*pathos*)—for example, an appeal to pity. Threats, too, can be persuasive. As Al Capone famously said, "You can get a lot more done with a kind word and a gun than with a kind word alone." Indeed, most of the remarks that we can think of link persuasion not with the power of reason but with the power of emotional appeals, of flattery, of threats, and of appeals to self-interest. We have in mind passages spoken not only by the likes of the racketeer Al Capone, but by more significant figures. Consider these two remarks, which both use the word *interest* in the sense of "self-interest":

> Would you persuade, speak of Interest, not Reason.
> —Ben Franklin

> There are two levers for moving men—interest and fear.
> —Napoleon Bonaparte

An appeal to self-interest is obviously at the heart of most advertisements: "Buy *X* automobile, and members of the opposite sex will find you irresistible," "Use *Y* instant soup, and your family will love you more," "Try *Z* cereal and enjoy regularity." We will look at advertisements later in this chapter, but first let's talk a bit more about the use and abuse of visual material in persuasion.

When we discussed the appeal to emotion (p. 100), we quoted from Mark Antony's speech to the Roman populace in Shakespeare's *Julius Caesar.* You will recall that Antony stirred the mob by displaying Caesar's blood-stained mantle, that is, by supplementing his words with visual material:

> Look, in this place ran Cassius' dagger through;
> See what a rent the envious Casca made;
> Through this, the well-belovèd Brutus stabbed. . . .

In courtrooms today, trial lawyers and prosecutors still do this sort of thing when

- They exhibit photos of a bloody corpse, or
- They introduce as witnesses small children who sob as they describe the murder of their parents.

The appeal clearly is not to reason but to the jurors' emotions—and yet, can we confidently say that this sort of visual evidence—this attempt to stir anger at the alleged perpetrator of the crime and pity for the victims —is irrelevant? Why shouldn't jurors vicariously experience the assault?

When we think about it—and it takes only a moment of thinking— the appeal in the courtroom to the eye and then to the heart or mind is evident even in smaller things, such as the clothing that the lawyers wear and the clothing that they advise their clients to wear. To take the most obvious, classic example: The mugger who normally wears jeans, a T-shirt, and a leather jacket appears in court in a three-piece suit, dress shirt, and necktie. Lawyers know that in arguing a case, visuals make statements—perhaps not logical arguments but nevertheless meaningful statements that will attract or repel jurors.

Another sort of visual appeal connected with some arguments should be mentioned briefly—the visual appeal of the specific setting in which

Martin Luther King Jr. delivering his "I Have a Dream" speech on August 28, 1963, from the steps of the Lincoln Memorial. The visual aspects—the setting (the Lincoln Memorial with the Washington Monument and the Capitol in the distance) and King's gestures—are part of the persuasive rhetoric of the speech.

the argument occurs. Martin Luther King Jr.'s great speech of August 28, 1963, "I Have a Dream," still reads very well on the page, but part of its immense appeal when it was first given was due to its setting: King spoke to some 200,000 people in Washington, D.C., as he stood on the steps of the Lincoln Memorial. That setting was part of King's argument.

Pictures — and here we get to our chief subject — are also sometimes used as parts of arguments because pictures make statements. Some pictures, like Edvard Munch's *The Scream* (below), make obvious statements: The swiftly receding diagonal lines of the fence and the walkway, the wavy sky, and the vibrating vertical lines to the right of the figure all convey the great agitation experienced by the figure in the woodcut. Some pictures, like the photographs shown to members of Congress during the debate over whether permission should be given to drill in the Arctic National Wildlife Refuge are a bit less obvious:

- Opponents of drilling showed beautiful pictures of polar bears frolicking, wildflowers in bloom, and caribou on the move.
- Proponents of drilling showed bleak pictures of what they called "barren land" and "a frozen wasteland."

Both sides knew very well that images are powerful persuaders, and they did not hesitate to use images as supplements to words.

We again invite you to think about the appropriateness of using images in arguments. Should argument be entirely a matter of reason, of logic, without appeals to the emotions? Or can images of the sort that we

(Edvard Munch, *The Scream.* © 2007 The Munch Museum/The Munch-Ellingsen Group/Artists Rights Society (ARS), NY. Digital Image ©/The Museum of Modern Art, NY. Licensed by SCALA/Art Resource.)

have already mentioned provide visual (and emotional) support for reasons that are offered? The statement that "the Arctic National Wildlife Refuge is a home for abundant wildlife, notably polar bears, caribou, and wildflowers" may not mean much until it is reinforced with breathtaking images. (And, similarly, the statement that "most of the ANWR land is barren" may not mean much until it is corroborated by images of the vast bleakness.)

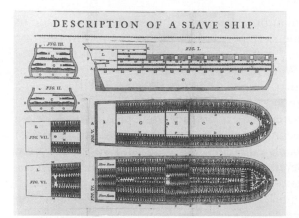

Images played an important role in the activities of the antislavery movement in the nineteenth century. On the top left is a diagram that shows how human cargo was packed into a slave ship; it was distributed with Thomas Clarkson's *Essay on the Slavery and Commerce of the Human Species* (1804). On the top right is Frederick W. Mercer's photograph (April 2, 1863) of Gordon, a "badly lacerated" runaway slave. Images such as the slave ship and Gordon were used against the claims of slaveowners that slavery was a humane institution—claims that also were supported by illustrations, such as the woodcut at the bottom, titled *Attention Paid to a Poor Sick Negro*, from Josiah Priest's *In Defense of Slavery*.

> **A RULE FOR WRITERS:** If you think that pictures will help you to make the point you are arguing, include them with captions explaining sources and relevance.

ARE SOME IMAGES NOT FIT TO BE SHOWN?

Images of suffering—human or, as animal rights activists have made us see, animal—can be immensely persuasive. In the nineteenth century, for instance, the antislavery movement made extremely effective use of images in its campaign. We reproduce two antislavery images here, as well as a counterimage that sought to assure viewers that slavery is a beneficent system. But are there some images not fit to print?

Until recently, many newspapers did not print pictures of lynched African Americans, hanged and burned and maimed. The reasons for not printing such images probably differed in the South and North: Southern papers may have considered the images to be discreditable to whites, while Northern papers may have deemed the images too revolting. Even today, when it is commonplace to see in newspapers and on television

Huynh Cong (Nick) Ut, *The Terror of War: Children on Route 1 near Trang Bang*

Eddie Adams, *Execution of Viet Cong prisoner, Saigon, 1968*

screens pictures of dead victims of war, or famine, or traffic accidents, one rarely sees bodies that are horribly maimed. (For traffic accidents, the body is usually covered, and we see only the smashed car.) The U.S. government has refused to release photographs showing the bodies of American soldiers killed in the war in Iraq, and it has been most reluctant to show pictures of dead Iraqi soldiers and civilians. Only after many Iraqis refused to believe that Saddam Hussein's two sons had been killed did the U.S. government reluctantly release pictures showing the blood-spattered faces of the two men—and some American newspapers and television programs refused to use the images.

There have been notable exceptions to this practice, such as Huynh Cong (Nick) Ut's 1972 photograph of children fleeing a napalm attack in Vietnam (p. 143), which was widely reproduced in the United States and won the photographer a Pulitzer Prize in 1973. The influence of this particular photograph cannot be measured, but it is widely felt to have played a substantial role in increasing public pressure to end the Vietnam War. Another widely reproduced picture of horrifying violence is Eddie Adams's picture (1968) of a South Vietnamese chief of police firing a pistol into the head of a Viet Cong prisoner.

The issue remains: Are some images unacceptable? For instance, although capital punishment is legal in parts of the United States—by methods including lethal injection, hanging, shooting, and electrocution—every state in the Union prohibits the publication of pictures showing a criminal being executed. (On this topic, see Wendy Lesser, *Pictures at an Execution* [1993].)

The most famous recent example of an image widely thought to be unprintable concerns the murder of Daniel Pearl, a Jewish reporter for the *Wall Street Journal.* Pearl was captured and murdered in June 2002 by Islamic terrorists in Pakistan. His killers videotaped Pearl reading a statement denouncing American policy, and being decapitated. The video also shows a man's arm holding Pearl's head. The video ends with the killers making several demands (such as the release of the Muslim prisoners being held by the United States in Guantánamo Bay, Cuba) and asserting that "if our demands are not met, this scene will be repeated again and again."

The chief arguments against reproducing in newspapers material from this video were that

- The video and even still images from it are unbearably gruesome;
- Showing the video would traumatize the Pearl family; and
- The video is propaganda by an enemy.

Those who favored broadcasting the video on television and printing still images from it in newspapers tended to argue that

- The photo will show the world what sort of enemy the United States is fighting;
- Newspapers have published pictures of other terrifying sights (notably, people leaping out of windows of New York's twin towers and endless pictures of the space shuttle *Challenger* exploding); and
- No one was worried about protecting the families of these other victims from seeing painful images.

But ask yourself if the comparison of the Daniel Pearl video to the photos of the twin towers and of the *Challenger* is valid. You may respond that the individuals in the twin towers pictures are not specifically identifiable and that the images of the *Challenger,* though horrifying, are not as visually revolting as the picture of a severed head held up for view.

The *Boston Phoenix,* a weekly newspaper, published some images from the Daniel Pearl video and also put a link to the video (with a warning that the footage is "extremely graphic") on its Web site. The editor of the *Phoenix* justified publication on the three grounds we list. Pearl's wife, Mariane Pearl, was quoted in various newspapers as condemning the "heartless decision to air this despicable video," and a spokeswoman for the Pearl family, when asked for comment, referred reporters to a statement issued earlier, which said that broadcasters who show the video

> fall without shame into the terrorists' plan. . . . Danny believed that journalism was a tool to report the truth and foster understanding—not perpetuate propaganda and sensationalize tragedy. We had hoped that no part of this tape would ever see the light of day. . . . We urge all

networks and news outlets to exercise responsibility and not aid the terrorists in spreading their message of hate and murder.[1]

Although some journalists expressed regret that Pearl's family was distressed, they insisted that journalists have a right to reproduce such material and that the images can serve the valuable purpose of shocking viewers into awareness.

Politics and Pictures

Consider, too, the controversy that erupted in 1991, during the Persian Gulf War, our government decided that newspapers would not be allowed to photograph the coffins returning with the bodies of military personnel killed during the war. In later years the policy was sometimes ignored, but in 2003 the George W. Bush administration decreed that there would be "no arrival ceremony for, or media coverage of, deceased military personnel returning [from Iraq or Afghanistan] . . . to the Dover (Delaware) base." The government enforced the policy strictly.

Members of the news media strongly protested, as did many others, chiefly arguing that

- The administration was trying to sanitize the war, i.e. was depriving the public of important information—images—that showed the real cost of the war. Additional arguments against the ban were

- Grief for the deaths of military personnel is not a matter only for the families of the deceased. The sacrifices were made for the nation, and the nation should be allowed to grieve. Canada and Britain have no such ban, and when the coffins are transported the public lines the streets to pay honor to the fallen warriors. In fact, in Canada a portion of the highway near the Canadian base has been renamed, "Highway of Heroes." Further,

- The coffins at Dover Air Force base are not identified by name, so there is no issue about intruding on the privacy of grieving families.

The chief arguments in defense of the ban are

- Photographs violate the privacy of the families
- If the arrival of the coffins at Dover is given publicity, some grieving families will think they should go to Dover to be present when the bodies arrive, and this may cause a financial hardship on the families. Finally,
- If the families give their consent, the press is *not* barred from individual graveside ceremonies at home-town burials. The ban extends only to the arrival of the coffins at Dover Air Force Base.

---

[1]Quoted in the *Hartford Courant*, June 5, 2002, and reproduced on the Internet by the Freedom of Information Center, under the heading "Boston Paper Creates Controversy."

Coffins at Dover Air Force Base, Delaware

In February 2009, President Obama changed the policy and permitted coverage of the transfer of bodily remains. In his Address to the Joint Session of Congress, February 24, 2009, he said, "For seven years we have been a nation at war. No longer will we hide its price." On February 27, Defense Secretary Robert M. Gates announced that the government ban was lifted, and that families will decide whether

Alexander Gardner, *Home of a Rebel Sharpshooter*

to allow photographs and videos of the "dignified transfer process at Dover."

EXERCISE

In an argumentative essay of about 250 words—perhaps two or three paragraphs—give your view of the matter. In an opening paragraph you may want to explain the issue, and in this same paragraph you may want to summarize the arguments that you reject. The second (and perhaps final) paragraph of a two-paragraph essay may give the reasons you reject those arguments. Additionally, you may want to devote a third paragraph to a more general reflection.

TOPIC FOR CRITICAL THINKING AND WRITING

Marvin Kalb, a distinguished journalist, was quoted as saying that the public has a right to see the tape of Daniel Pearl's murder but that "common sense, decency, [and] humanity would encourage editors . . . to say 'no, it is not necessary to put this out.' There is no urgent demand on the part of the American people to see Daniel Pearl's death." Your view?

Query In June 2006 two American soldiers were captured in Iraq. Later their bodies were found, dismembered and beheaded. Should newspapers have shown photographs of the mutilated bodies? Why, or why not? (In July 2006 insurgents in Iraq posted images on the Internet, showing a soldier's severed head beside his body.)

Another issue concerning the appropriateness or inappropriateness of showing images occurred early in 2006. In September 2005 a Danish newspaper, accused of being afraid to show political cartoons that were hostile to Muslim terrorists, responded by publishing twelve cartoons. One cartoon, for instance, showed the Prophet Muhammad wearing a turban that looked like a bomb. The images at first did not arouse much attention, but when in January 2006 they were reprinted in Norway they attracted worldwide attention and outraged Muslims, most of whom regard any depiction of the Prophet as blasphemous. The upshot is that some Muslims in various Islamic nations burned Danish embassies and engaged in other acts of violence. Most non-Muslims agreed that the images were in bad taste, and apparently in deference to Islamic sensibilities (but possibly also out of fear of reprisals) very few Western newspapers reprinted the cartoons when they covered the news events. Most newspapers (including the *New York Times*) were content merely to describe the images. These papers believed that readers had to be told the news but because the drawings were so offensive to some persons they should be described rather than reprinted. A controversy then arose: Do readers of a newspaper deserve to *see* the evidence for themselves, or can a newspaper adequately fulfill its function by offering only a verbal description?

Persons who argued that the images should be reproduced generally made these points:

- Newspapers should yield neither to the delicate sensibilities of some readers nor to threats of violence.

- Jews for the most part do not believe that God should be depicted (the prohibition against "graven images" is found in Exodus 20.3), but they raise no objections to such Christian images as Michelangelo's painting of God awakening Adam, on the roof of the Sistine Chapel. Further, when Andres Serrano (a Christian) in 1989 exhibited a photograph of a small plastic crucifix submerged in urine, it outraged a wider public—several U.S. senators condemned it because the artist had received federal funds—but virtually all newspapers showed the image, and many even printed its title, *Piss Christ*. That is, the subject was judged to be newsworthy, and the fact that some viewers would regard the image as blasphemous was not considered highly relevant.

- We value freedom of speech, and newspapers should not be intimidated. When certain pictures are a matter of news, the pictures should be shown to readers.

On the other hand, opposing voices were heard:

- Newspapers should—must—recognize deep-seated religious beliefs. They should indeed report the news, but there is no reason to *show* images that some people regard as blasphemous. The images can be adequately *described* in words.

- The Jewish response to Christian images of God and even the tolerant Christian's response to Serrano's image of Christ immersed in urine are simply irrelevant to the issue of whether images of the Prophet Muhammad should be represented in a Western newspaper. Virtually all Muslims regard depictions of the Prophet as blasphemous, and that is what counts.

- Despite all the Western talk about freedom of the press, the press does *not* reproduce all images that become matters of news. For instance, news items about the sale of child pornography do not include images of the pornographic photos.

EXERCISES: THINKING ABOUT IMAGES

1. Does the display of the cartoons constitute an argument? If so, what is the conclusion, and what are the premises? If not, then what sort of statement, if any, does publishing these cartoons constitute?

2. Hugh Hewitt, an evangelical Christian, offered a comparison to the cartoon of Muhammad with a bomblike turban. Suppose, he asked, an abortion clinic had been bombed by someone who said he was an Evangelical Christian. Would newspapers publish "a cartoon of Christ's crown of thorns transformed into sticks of TNT?" Do you think they would? If you were the editor of a paper, would you? Why, or why not?

3. One American newspaper, the *Boston Phoenix,* did not publish any of the cartoons "out of fear of retaliation from the international brotherhood of radical and bloodthirsty Islamists who seek to impose their will on those who do not believe as they do. . . . We could not in good conscience place the men and women who work at the *Phoenix* and its related companies in physical jeopardy." Evaluate this position.

READING ADVERTISEMENTS

Advertising is one of the most common forms of visual persuasion we encounter in everyday life. None of us is so unsophisticated these days as to believe everything we see in an ad, yet the influence of advertising in our culture is pervasive and subtle. Consider, for example, a much-reproduced poster sponsored by Gatorade and featuring Michael Jordan. Such an image costs an enormous amount to produce and disseminate, and nothing in it is left to chance. The photograph of Jordan is typical, his attitude simultaneously strained and graceful, his face exultant, as he performs the feat for which he is so well known and about which most of us could only dream. We are aware of a crowd watching him, but the people in this crowd appear tiny, blurred, and indistinct compared to the huge image in the foreground; the photograph, like the crowd, focuses solely on Jordan. He is a legend, an icon of American culture. He is dressed not in his Chicago Bulls uniform but in a USA jersey, connecting his act of gravity-defying athleticism with the entire nation and with our sense of patriotism. The red, white, and blue of the uniform strengthens this impression in the original color photograph of the advertisement.

What do we make of the verbal message boldly written along the left-hand margin of the poster, "Be like Mike"? We are certainly not foolish enough to believe that drinking Gatorade will enable us to perform like Michael Jordan on the basketball court. But who among us wouldn't like to "Be like Mike" in some small way, to enjoy even a glancing association with his athletic grace and power — to say nothing of his fame, wealth, and sex appeal? Though the makers of Gatorade surely know we will not all rush out to buy their drink to improve our game, they are banking on the expectation that the association of their name with Jordan, and our memory of their logo in association with Jordan's picture, will create a positive impression of their product. If Mike drinks Gatorade — well, why shouldn't I give it a try? The good feelings and impressions created by the ad will, the advertisers hope, travel with us the next time we consider buying a sports drink.

As we discuss the power of advertising, it is appropriate to say a few words about the corporate logos that appear everywhere these days — on billboards, in newspapers and magazines, on television, and on T-shirts. It is useful to think of a logo as a sort of advertisement in shorthand. It is a single, usually simple, image that carries with it a world of associations and impressions. (The makers of Gatorade would certainly hope that we will be reminded of Michael Jordan and his slam dunk when we see their product name superimposed over the orange lightning bolt.)

Let's look at two advertisements — one that combines pictures with verbal text and another that relies almost entirely on a picture accompanied by only three words. The first ad has two head shots, pictures of the sort that show "Ten Most Wanted Men." Both faces are widely known — Martin Luther King Jr. and Charles Manson — and viewers may initially wonder why they are juxtaposed. Then the large type above the pictures captures our attention with its size and a bold statement of fact:

> The man on the left is 75 times more likely to be stopped by the police while driving than the man on the right.

We presume that the statement is true — that is, that dark-skinned people are stopped by police officers seventy-five times more often than whites —

American Civil Liberties Union, *The Man on the Left*

and we probably know why. Almost surely we do *not* conclude that dark people are far more likely than white to speed, go through red lights, or cross lanes. We have heard about racial profiling and racial prejudice, and we may also have heard about the wry offense of which all African Americans are guilty, "driving while black." The small print on this ad goes on to tell us that, every day, "Police stop drivers based on their skin color rather than for the way they are driving," and it supports this assertion with a fact: "For example, in Florida 80% of those stopped and searched were black and Hispanic, while they constituted only 5% of all drivers." We assume that these statistics are true and that most readers find the statement alarming. The poster might have had these very words without the two pictures, but would we then have read the small print?

Incidentally, the American Civil Liberties Union did not print this poster for any reason related to Martin Luther King Jr. or Charles Manson. The poster's purpose appears in very small letters at the end of the caption:

Support the ACLU.

We think that this ad is highly effective, and we invite you to perform a thought experiment. Suppose that the two pictures were omitted and that the text of the large type at the top of the ad was different, something like this:

Persons of color, notably African Americans and non-white Hispanics, are 75 times more likely than white people to be stopped by the police when driving.

And then suppose the rest of the text consisted of the words in the present ad. Do you think this alternate version would make nearly the impact that the ACLU ad makes? The text is essentially the same, the statistics are still shocking, but the impact is gone. When we see the ACLU ad, we are for only a tiny fraction of a second, puzzled: What can the two faces—a civil rights leader and a serial killer—have in common? The large print almost immediately lets us know why these faces are paired, and we are probably hooked by (a) the shocking juxtaposition of faces and (b) the astounding fact that is asserted. So we probably go on to read the small print, though ordinarily we would not bother to read such tiny writing.

Incidentally, the writing beneath the picture could have been as large, or almost as large, as the print above the picture, merely by reducing the blank space at the top and bottom of the page. Why do you suppose the writing beneath the pictures is small? Do you think the ad would have been as compelling if the type above and below were of approximately equal size? Why, or why not?

One other point: The pictures of King and Manson catch the interest of a wide audience, an audience much wider than the group that would normally be targeted as persons who might contribute money or energy to an association chiefly concerned with civil liberties. That is, this ad speaks to almost anyone who may be concerned with fairness or decency.

The second ad, as you can easily see, uses far fewer words than the first. The two lines of text are short and sweet: "Set yourself free" and

"When you're ready to quit smoking, we're here to help." The first of these lines—with "free" in large letters—is re-enforced by the image of free-floating balloons, which in this context almost seem to be giant lungs. The implication is that once the viewer decides to quit smoking, the air will be purer, lungs will fully distend, and there will be a great sense of freedom; one will no longer be tied down in the way that an addiction to tobacco ties one down or restrains one's freedom. The second sentence, beneath the picture—on ground level, so to speak— assures the reader that when the addict is "ready to quit smoking, we're here to help." Who, after all, wouldn't want to be "set . . . free" (especially into the wonderful world of the floating balloons that soar in the

✓ **A CHECKLIST FOR ANALYZING IMAGES (ESPECIALLY ADVERTISEMENTS)**

☐ What is the overall effect of the design? Colorful and busy (suggesting activity)? Quiet and understated (for instance, chiefly white and grays, with lots of empty space)? Old fashioned or cutting edge?

☐ What about the image immediately gets your attention? Size? Position on the page? Beauty of the image? Grotesqueness of the image? Humor?

☐ Who is the audience for the image? Affluent young men? Housewives? Retired persons?

☐ What is the argument?

☐ Does the text make a rational appeal (*logos*) ("Tests at a leading university prove that . . . ," "If you believe X, you should vote 'No' on this referendum")?

☐ Does the image appeal to the emotions, to dearly held values (*pathos*)? Examples: Images of starving children or maltreated animals appeal to our sense of pity; images of military valor may appeal to our patriotism; images of luxury may appeal to our envy; images of sexually attractive people may appeal to our desire to be like them; images of violence or of extraordinary ugliness (as, for instance, in some ads showing a human fetus being destroyed) may seek to shock us.

☐ Does the image make an ethical appeal—that is, does it appeal to our character as a good human being (*ethos*)? Ads by charitable organizations often appeal to our sense of decency, fairness, and pity, but ads that appeal to our sense of prudence (ads for insurance companies or for investment houses) also essentially are making an ethical appeal.

☐ What is the relation of print to image? Does the image do most of the work, or does it serve to attract us and to lead us on to read the text?

tobacco-free air), and who wouldn't want the assurance that, if the experience is a bit risky, someone is there to help?

TOPICS FOR CRITICAL THINKING AND WRITING

1. Imagine that you work for a business that advertises in a publication such as *Time* or *Newsweek*, for instance, a vacation resort, a manufacturer of clothes, or an automaker. Design an advertisement: Describe the picture and write the text, and then, in an essay of 500 words, explain who

your target audience is (college students? young couples about to buy their first home? retired persons?) and explain why you use the sorts of appeals (for instance, to reason, to the emotions, to a sense of humor) that you do.

2. It is often said that colleges, like businesses, are selling a product. Examine a brochure or catalog that is sent to prospective applicants at a college, and analyze the kinds of appeals that some of the images make.

WRITING ABOUT A POLITICAL CARTOON

Most editorial pages print political cartoons as well as editorials. Like the writers of editorials, cartoonists seek to persuade, but they rarely use words to *argue* a point. True, they may use a few words in speech balloons or in captions, but generally the drawing does most of the work. Because their aim usually is to convince the viewer that some person's action or proposal is ridiculous, cartoonists almost always **caricature** their subjects:

- They exaggerate the subject's distinctive features to the point where
- The subject becomes grotesque and ridiculous—absurd, laughable, contemptible.

True, it is scarcely fair to suggest that because, say, the politician who proposes such-and-such is short, fat, and bald his proposal is ridiculous, but that is the way cartoonists work. Further, cartoonists are concerned with producing a striking image, not with exploring an issue, so they almost always oversimplify, implying that there really is no other sane view.

In the course of saying that (a) the figures in the cartoon are ridiculous and *therefore* their ideas are contemptible, and (b) there is only one side to the issue, cartoonists often use **symbolism**, for instance:

- Symbolic figures (Uncle Sam),
- Animals (the Democratic donkey and the Republican elephant),
- Buildings (the White House stands symbolically for the president of the United States),
- Things (a bag with a dollar sign on it usually symbolizes a bribe).

For anyone brought up in our culture, these symbols (like the human figures who are represented) are obvious, and cartoonists assume that viewers will instantly recognize the symbols and figures, will get the joke, will see the absurdity of whatever it is that the cartoonist is seeking to demolish.

In writing about the argument presented in a cartoon, normally you will discuss the ways in which the cartoon makes its point. Caricature, we have said, usually says, "This is ridiculous, as you can plainly see by the absurdity of the figures depicted." "What X's proposal adds up to, despite

---

✓ A CHECKLIST FOR ANALYZING POLITICAL CARTOONS

- ☐ Is a lead-in provided?
- ☐ Is a brief but accurate description of the drawing provided?
- ☐ Is the source of the cartoon cited (and perhaps commented on)?
- ☐ Is a brief report of the event or issue that the cartoon is dealing with, and explanation of all of the symbols included?
- ☐ Is there a statement of the cartoonist's claim (point, thesis)?
- ☐ Is there an analysis of the evidence, if any, that the image offers in support of the claim?
- ☐ Is there an analysis of the ways in which the content and style of the drawing help to convey the message?
- ☐ Is there adequate evaluation of the effectiveness of the drawing?
- ☐ Is there adequate evaluation of the effectiveness of the text (caption or speech balloons) and of the fairness of the cartoon?

---

its apparent complexity, is nothing more than . . ."). As we have already said, this sort of persuasion, chiefly by ridicule, probably is unfair: A funny-looking person *can offer* a thoughtful political proposal, and almost certainly the issue is more complicated than the cartoonist indicates. But this is largely the way cartoons work, by ridicule and by omitting counter-arguments, and we should not reject the possibility that the cartoonist has indeed put his or her finger on the absurdity of the issue.

Probably your essay will include an *evaluation* of the cartoon; indeed, the *thesis* underlying your analytic/argumentative essay may be (for instance) that the cartoon is effective (persuasive) for such-and-such reasons, but it is also unfair for such-and-such reasons.

In analyzing the cartoon—in grasping the attitude of the cartoonist—consider such things as

- The relative size of the figures in the image;
- The quality of the lines—thin and spidery, or thick and seemingly aggressive;
- The amount of empty space in comparison with the amount of heavily inked space (a drawing with lots of inky areas will convey a more oppressive sense than a drawing that is largely open);
- The degree to which text is important, and what the text says—is it witty? Heavy-handed?

Caution: If your instructor lets you choose a cartoon, be sure to choose one with sufficient complexity to make the exercise worthwhile. (See also Idea Prompt 4.1.)

Context	*Who is the artist? Where and when was it published?*	"This cartoon by Walt Handelsman was originally publishing in *Newsday* on September 12, 2009. Handelsman, a Pulitzer-Prize–winning cartoonist, drew this cartoon in response to recent breaches of political decorum."
Description	*What does the cartoon look like?*	"It depicts a group of Washington, D.C. tourists being driven past what the guide calls 'The Museum of Modern American Political Discourse,' a building in the shape of a giant toilet."
Analysis	*How does the cartoon make its point? Is it effective?*	"The toilet as a symbol of the level of political discussion dominates the cartoon, effectively driving home the point that as Americans we are watching our leaders sink to new lows as they debate the future of our nation. Seen on a scale similar to familiar monuments in Washington, Handelsman may be in fact pointing out that today's politicians, rather than being remembered for the great achievements of George Washington or Abraham Lincoln, will instead be remembered for their rudeness and aggression."

Let's look at an example. Jackson Smith wrote this essay in a composition course at Tufts University.

Jackson Smith

Pledging Nothing?

(Student Essay)

Gary Markstein's cartoon about the Pledge of Allegiance is one of dozens that can be retrieved by a search engine. It happens that every one of the cartoons that I retrieved mocked the courts for ruling that schools cannot require students to recite the Pledge of Allegiance in its present form, which includes the words "under God." I personally object to these words, so the cartoons certainly do not speak for me, but I'll try as impartially as possible to analyze the strength of Markstein's cartoon.

Markstein shows us, in the cartoon, four school children reciting the Pledge. Coming out of all four mouths is a speech balloon with the words, "One nation under nothing in particular." The children are facing a furled American flag, and to the right of the flag is a middle-aged female teacher, whose speech balloon is in the form of a cloud, indicating that she is *thinking* rather than saying the words, "God help us."

Certainly the image grabs us: Little kids lined up reciting the Pledge of Allegiance, an American flag, a maternal-looking teacher, and, in fact, if one examines the cartoon closely, one sees an apple on the teacher's desk. It's almost a Norman Rockwell scene, except, of course, it is a cartoon, so the figures are all a bit grotesque — but, still, they are nice folks. What is *not* nice, Markstein says, is what these kids must recite, "One nation under nothing in particular." In fact the cartoon is far from telling the truth. Children who recite the Pledge without the words "under God" will still be saying that they are pledging allegiance to something quite specific — the United States:

> I pledge allegiance to the flag of the United States of America, and to the Republic for which it stands: one nation indivisible, with Liberty and Justice for all.

That's really quite a lot, very far from Markstein's "under nothing in particular." But no one, I suppose, expects fairness in a political cartoon — and of course this cartoon *is* political, because the issue of the Pledge has become a political football, with liberals on the whole wanting the words "under God" removed and conservatives on the whole wanting the words retained.

Let's now look at some of the subtleties of the cartoon. First, although, as I have said, cartoons present grotesque caricatures, the figures here are

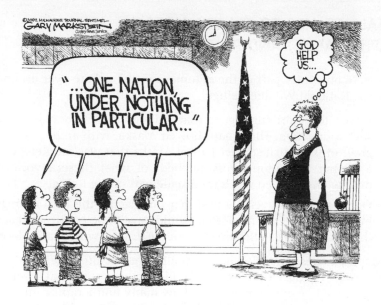

all affectionately presented. None of these figures is menacing. The teacher, with her spectacles and her rather dumpy figure, is clearly a benevolent figure, someone who in the eyes of the cartoonist rightly is disturbed about the fate of these little kids who are not allowed to say the words "under God." (Nothing, of course, prevents the children from speaking about God when they are not in the classroom. Those who believe in God can say grace at mealtime, can go to Sunday School, can go to church regularly, can pray before they go to bed, etc.) Markstein suggests that the absence of these words makes the entire Pledge meaningless ("under nothing in particular"), and in a master stroke he has conveyed this idea of impoverishment by showing a tightly furled flag, a flag that is presented as minimally as possible. After all, the flag could have been shown more fully, perhaps hanging from a pole that extended from a wall into the classroom, or the flag could have been displayed extended against a wall. Instead we get the narrowest of flags, something that is not much more than a furled umbrella, identifiable as the American flag by its stripes and a few stars in the upper third. Markstein thus cleverly suggests that with the loss of the words "under God," the flag itself is reduced to almost nothing.

Fair? No. Effective? Yes, and that's the job of a cartoonist. Readers 5 probably give cartoons no more than three or four seconds, and Markstein has made the most of those few seconds. The reader gets his point, and if the reader already holds this view, he or she probably says, "Hey, here's a great cartoon." I don't hold that view, but I am willing to grant that it is a pretty good cartoon, effectively making a point that I think is wrong-headed.

VISUALS AS AIDS TO CLARITY: MAPS, GRAPHS, TABLES, AND PIE CHARTS

Maps were obviously part of the argument in the debate over drilling in the Arctic National Wildlife Refuge.

- Advocates of drilling argued that drilling would take place only in such a tiny area. Their map showed Alaska, with an indication (in gray) of the much smaller part of Alaska that was the Refuge, and a further indication (cross-hatched) of what these advocates of drilling emphasized was a minuscule part of the Refuge.

- Opponents, however, showed maps indicating the path of migrating caribou and the roads that would have to be constructed across the refuge to get to the area where the drilling would take place.

Graphs, tables, and pie charts usually present quantitative data in visual form, helping writers clarify mind-numbing statistical assertions. For instance, a line graph may tell us how many immigrants came to the United States in each decade of the last century.

A bar graph (the bars can run either horizontally or vertically) offers similar information; we can see at a glance that, say, the second bar is almost double the length of the first, indicating that the number is almost double.

A pie chart is a circle divided into wedges so that we can see—literally see—how a whole is divided into its parts. We can see, for instance, that of the entire pie—which may represent registered voters in a certain state—one-fourth are registered Democrats, one-fifth are registered Republicans, and the remainder do not give a party affiliation.

✓ A CHECKLIST FOR CHARTS AND GRAPHS

☐ Is the source authoritative?

☐ Is the source cited?

☐ Will the chart or graph be intelligible to the imagined audience?

☐ Is the caption, if any, clear and helpful?

A NOTE ON USING VISUALS IN YOUR OWN PAPER

Every paper uses some degree of visual persuasion, merely in its appearance: perhaps a title page, certainly margins (ample—but not so wide that they tell the reader that the writer is unable to write a paper of the assigned length), double-spacing for the convenience of the reader, paragraphing

COMING TO AMERICA . . .

Both the percentage and number of foreign-born people in the United States dropped during much of the twentieth century, but after 1970, the tide was turning again.

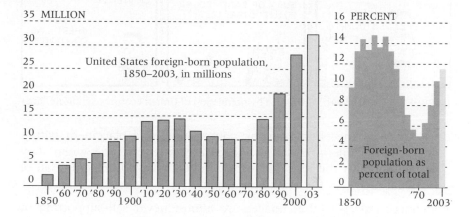

United States foreign-born population, 1850–2003, in millions

Foreign-born population as percent of total

. . . FROM NEAR AND FAR

Central America, Mexico, and Asia contribute most to the foreign-born population.

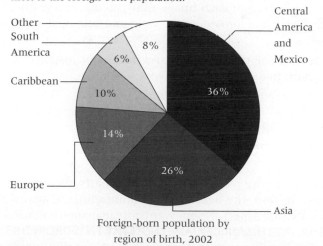

Foreign-born population by region of birth, 2002

*Most recent estimate
Source: United States Census Bureau

(again for the convenience of the reader), and so on. But you may also want to use images—for example, pictures, graphs, or pie charts. Keep a few guidelines in mind as you begin to work with images, "writing" visuals into your own argument with at least as much care as you would read them in others':

- Consider the needs and attitudes of your audience, and select the type of visuals—graphs, drawings, photographs—likely to be most persuasive to that audience.

(DILBERT © Scott Adams. Distributed by permission of United Features Syndicate, Inc.)

- Consider the effect of color, composition, and placement within your document. Because images are most effective when they appear near the text that supplements them, do not group all of your images at the end of the paper.

Remember especially that images are almost never self-supporting or self-explanatory. They may be evidence for your argument (Ut's photograph of napalm victims is *very* compelling evidence of suffering), but they are not arguments themselves.

- Be sure to explain each image that you use, integrating it into the verbal text that provides the logic and principal support of your thesis.
- Be sure to cite the source of any image, for instance, a graph or a pie chart, that you paste into your argument.

A NOTE ON FORMATTING YOUR PAPER: DOCUMENT DESIGN

Even if you do not use pictures or graphs or charts, the format you use — the margins, the font, the headings and subheadings, if any, will still give your paper a visual aspect. NoonewantstoreadapaperthatlookslikethisOR LIKETHIS*ORLIKETHIS*ANDCERTAINLYNOT**LIKETHIS**ORLIKETHIS. For academic papers, margins (one inch on each side), spacing (double-spaced), and font and size (Times New Roman, 12 point) are pretty well standardized, and it is usually agreed that the text should be justified at the left rather than centered (to avoid rivers of white down the page), but you are still in charge of some things, notably headings and bulleted or numbered lists — as well as, of course, the lengths of your paragraphs.

Headings in a long paper (more than five pages) are functional, helping to guide the reader from unit to unit, but the extra white space — a decorative element — is also functional, giving the reader's eye a moment of rest. Longish academic papers often use one, two, or even three levels of headings, normally distinguished by type size, position, and highlighting

("highlighting" includes the use of CAPITALS, **boldface**, and *italic*). Here are examples of three levels:

FIRST-LEVEL HEADING

Second-Level Heading

Third-Level Heading

If you use headings, you must be consistent in the form. For instance, if you use a noun phrase such as "the present system" printed in CAPITAL LETTERS for the first of your first-level headings, you must use noun phrases and caps for the rest of your first-level headings, thus:

THE PRESENT SYSTEM
THE NEED TO CHANGE

But you need not use noun phases and you need not use capitals. You may use, for instance, *-ing* headings (gerund phrases), and you may decide to capitalize only the first letter of each word other than prepositions and articles, thus:

Thinking about Immigration

Reviewing the Past

Thinking about the Future

Reconsidering Legislation

And here are headings that use a single word:

Problems

Answers

Strengths

Weaknesses

Finally, headings that consist of questions can be effective:

What Are We Now Doing?

Why Should We Change?

Caution: Although headings can be useful in a paper of moderate or considerable length, they almost never are useful in a paper of five or fewer pages.

ADDITIONAL IMAGES FOR ANALYSIS

In 1936, photographer Dorothea Lange (1895–1965) took a series of pictures, including the two below, of a migrant mother and her children. Widely reprinted in the nation's newspapers, these photographs helped to dramatize for the American public the poverty of displaced workers during the Great Depression.

TOPICS FOR CRITICAL THINKING AND WRITING

1. Lange drew increasingly near to her subject as she took a series of pictures. Make a list of details gained and lost by framing the mother and children more closely. The final shot in the series (above) became the most famous and most widely reprinted. Do you find it more effective than the other? Why, or why not?

2. Note the expression on the mother's face, the position of her body, and the way she interacts with her children. What sorts of relationships are implied? Why is it significant that she does not look at her children or at the camera? How is the effect of the photographs altered based on how much we can see of the children's faces?

3. As we mentioned earlier in this chapter, these photographs constitute a sort of persuasive "speech." Of what, exactly, might the photographer be trying to persuade her viewers? Try to state the purpose of Lange's photograph by completing this sentence, "Lange would like the viewers of her photographs to . . ." Write a brief essay (250 words) making the same case. Compare your written argument to Lange's visual one. Which form of persuasion do you find more effective? Why?

4. Whom do you think Lange had in mind as her original audience? What assumptions does she make about that audience? What sorts of evidence does she use to reach them?

During World War II, the U.S. government produced a series of posters bearing the legend "This is the enemy." These posters depicted racially stereotyped images of both German and Japanese soldiers, generally engaged in acts of savage violence.

TOPICS FOR CRITICAL THINKING AND WRITING

1. It has been claimed that one role of propaganda is to dehumanize the enemy so that (a) soldiers will feel less remorse about killing opposing soldiers and (b) civilians will continue to support the war effort. What specific features of this poster contribute to this propaganda function?

2. Some would claim that such a racially provocative image of a Japanese soldier should never have been used because of the potential harm to all Asians, including patriotic Asian Americans. (Consisting solely of Japanese American volunteers, the 442nd Regimental Combat Team was by war's end the most decorated unit in U.S. military history for its size and length of service.) Others believe that the ordinary rules do not apply in times of national crisis and that, as the old saying has it, "All's fair in love and war." In an essay of 500 words, argue for one or the other of these propositions. Refer to this poster as one piece of your evidence.

From ancient times until the eighteenth century, when newspapers began to be read widely, public posting was about the only way to reach a large audience. The invention of movable type in the fifteenth century made the dissemination of posted bills and handbills inexpensive, and such bills (along with newspaper

advertisements) were the most common forms of advertising until well into the twentieth century. (Commercial radio broadcasting began only in 1920, and television was not an important medium before 1945.) I Want You *is by James Montgomery Flagg.*

Topics for Critical Thinking and Writing

1. Imagine that this figure of Uncle Sam were in profile, pointing either to the right or left. Would the effect be the same? Why? Imagine the figure as a three-quarter view. Again, would the effect be different? Why? Which of the three versions do you think would be the most effective? Explain your reasons.

2. Approximately what is the date of this poster? What makes you give it this date?

Additional Topics for Critical Thinking and Writing

Gather some of the graphic materials used to promote and reflect your college or university—including a screen shot of its Web site, the college catalog, and the brochures and other materials sent to prospective students.

1. What is the dominant image that your college or university administration seems to be putting forth? Are there different, maybe even competing, images of your school at work? How accurate a story do these materials tell about your campus? Write an essay (250 words) in which you explain to prospective students the ways in which the promotional materials capture, or fail to capture, the true spirit of your campus.

2. Compare the Web site of your institution to one or two from very different institutions—perhaps a community college, a large state university, or an elite private college. How do you account for the similarities and differences among the sites?

Nora Ephron

Nora Ephron, born in 1941, attended Wellesley College. She worked as a reporter for the New York Post *and as a columnist and senior editor for* Esquire. *Ephron has written screenplays and directed films, including* Sleepless in Seattle *(1993), and has continued to write essays on a wide variety of topics. "The Boston Photographs" is from her collection Scribble,* Scribble: Notes on the Media *(1978).*

The Boston Photographs

"I made all kinds of pictures because I thought it would be a good rescue shot over the ladder . . . never dreamed it would be anything

else. . . . I kept having to move around because of the light set. The sky was bright and they were in deep shadow. I was making pictures with a motor drive and he, the fire fighter, was reaching up and, I don't know, everything started falling. I followed the girl down taking pictures. . . . I made three or four frames. I realized what was going on and I completely turned around, because I didn't want to see her hit."

You probably saw the photographs. In most newspapers, there were three of them. The first showed some people on a fire escape — a fireman, a woman, and a child. The fireman had a nice strong jaw and looked very brave. The woman was holding the child. Smoke was pouring from the building behind them. A rescue ladder was approaching, just a few feet away, and the fireman had one arm around the woman and one arm reaching out toward the ladder. The second picture showed the fire escape slipping off the building. The child had fallen on the escape and seemed about to slide off the edge. The woman was grasping desperately at the legs of the fireman, who had managed to grab the ladder. The third picture showed the woman and child in midair, falling to the ground. Their arms and legs were outstretched, horribly distended. A potted plant was falling too. The caption said that the woman, Diana Bryant, nineteen, died in the fall. The child landed on the woman's body and lived.

The pictures were taken by Stanley Forman, thirty, of the *Boston Herald American*. He used a motor-driven Nikon F set at 1/250, f5.6-S. Because of the motor, the camera can click off three frames a second. More than four hundred newspapers in the United States alone carried the photographs: The tear sheets from overseas are still coming in. The

New York Times ran them on the first page of its second section; a paper in south Georgia gave them nineteen columns; the *Chicago Tribune*, the *Washington Post*, and the *Washington Star* filled almost half their front pages, the *Star* under a somewhat redundant headline that read: SENSA-TIONAL PHOTOS OF RESCUE ATTEMPT THAT FAILED.

The photographs are indeed sensational. They are pictures of death in action, of that split second when luck runs out, and it is impossible to look at them without feeling their extraordinary impact and remember-ing, in an almost subconscious way, the morbid fantasy of falling, falling off a building, falling to one's death. Beyond that, the pictures are clas-sics, old-fashioned but perfect examples of photojournalism at its most spectacular. They're throwbacks, really, fire pictures, 1930s tabloid shots; at the same time they're technically superb and thoroughly modern— the sequence could not have been taken at all until the development of the motor-driven camera some sixteen years ago.

Most newspaper editors anticipate some reader reaction to photo-   5 graphs like Forman's; even so, the response around the country was enormous, and almost all of it was negative. I have read hundreds of the letters that were printed in letters-to-the-editor sections, and they repeat the same points. "Invading the privacy of death." "Cheap sensational-ism." "I thought I was reading the *National Enquirer*." "Assigning the agony of a human being in terror of imminent death to the status of a side-show act." "A tawdry way to sell newspapers." The *Seattle Times* received sixty letters and calls; its managing editor even got a couple of them at home. A reader wrote the *Philadelphia Inquirer*: "*Jaws* and *Towering Inferno* are playing downtown; don't take business away from people who pay good money to advertise in your own paper." Another reader wrote the *Chicago Sun-Times*: "I shall try to hide my disappoint-ment that Miss Bryant wasn't wearing a skirt when she fell to her death. You could have had some award-winning photographs of her under-pants as her skirt billowed over her head, you voyeurs." Several news-paper editors wrote columns defending the pictures: Thomas Keevil of the *Costa Mesa* (California) *Daily Pilot* printed a ballot for readers to vote on whether they would have printed the pictures; Marshall L. Stone of Maine's *Bangor Daily News*, which refused to print the famous assassina-tion picture of the Vietcong prisoner in Saigon, claimed that the Boston pictures showed the dangers of fire escapes and raised questions about slumlords. (The burning building was a five-story brick apartment house on Marlborough Street in the Back Bay section of Boston.)

For the last five years, the *Washington Post* has employed various journalists as ombudsmen, whose job is to monitor the paper on behalf of the public. The *Post*'s current ombudsman is Charles Seib, former managing editor of the *Washington Star*; the day the Boston photographs appeared, the paper received over seventy calls in protest. As Seib later wrote in a column about the pictures, it was "the largest reaction to a published item that I have experienced in eight months as the *Post*'s ombudsman. . . .

"In the *Post*'s newsroom, on the other hand, I found no doubts, no second thoughts . . . the question was not whether they should be printed but how they should be displayed. When I talked to editors . . . they used words like 'interesting' and 'riveting' and 'gripping' to describe them. The pictures told of something about life in the ghetto, they said (although the neighborhood where the tragedy occurred is not a ghetto, I am told). They dramatized the need to check on the safety of fire escapes. They dramatically conveyed something that had happened, and that is the business we're in. They were news. . . .

"Was publication of that [third] picture a bow to the same taste for the morbidly sensational that makes gold mines of disaster movies? Most papers will not print the picture of a dead body except in the most unusual circumstances. Does the fact that the final picture was taken a millisecond before the young woman died make a difference? Most papers will not print a picture of a bare female breast. Is that a more inappropriate subject for display than the picture of a human being's last agonized instant of life?" Seib offered no answers to the questions he raised, but he went on to say that although as an editor he would probably have run the pictures, as a reader he was revolted by them.

In conclusion, Seib wrote: "Any editor who decided to print those pictures without giving at least a moment's thought to what purpose they served and what their effect was likely to be on the reader should ask another question: Have I become so preoccupied with manufacturing a product according to professional traditions and standards that I have forgotten about the consumer, the reader?"

It should be clear that the phone calls and letters and Seib's own 10 reaction were occasioned by one factor alone: the death of the woman. Obviously, had she survived the fall, no one would have protested; the pictures would have had a completely different impact. Equally obviously, had the child died as well—or instead—Seib would undoubtedly have received ten times the phone calls he did. In each case, the pictures would have been exactly the same—only the captions, and thus the responses, would have been different.

But the questions Seib raises are worth discussing—though not exactly for the reasons he mentions. For it may be that the real lesson of the Boston photographs is not the danger that editors will be forgetful of reader reaction, but that they will continue to censor pictures of death precisely because of that reaction. The protests Seib fielded were really a variation on an old theme—and we saw plenty of it during the Nixon-Agnew years—the "Why doesn't the press print the good news?" argument. In this case, of course, the objections were all dressed up and cleverly disguised as righteous indignation about the privacy of death. This is a form of puritanism that is often justifiable; just as often it is merely puritanical.

Seib takes it for granted that the widespread though fairly recent newspaper policy against printing pictures of dead bodies is a sound one; I don't know that it makes any sense at all. I recognize that printing pictures of corpses raises all sorts of problems about taste and titillation and sensationalism; the fact is, however, that people die. Death happens to be one of life's main events. And it is irresponsible—and more than that, inaccurate—for newspapers to fail to show it, or to show it only when an astonishing set of photos comes in over the Associated Press wire. Most papers covering fatal automobile accidents will print pictures of mangled cars. But the significance of fatal automobile accidents is not that a great deal of steel is twisted but that people die. Why not show it? That's what accidents are about. Throughout the Vietnam war, editors were reluctant to print atrocity pictures. Why *not* print them? That's what that was about. Murder victims are almost never photographed; they are granted their privacy. But their relatives are relentlessly pictured on their way in and out of hospitals and morgues and funerals.

I'm not advocating that newspapers print these things in order to teach their readers a lesson. The *Post* editors justified their printing of the Boston pictures with several arguments in that direction; every one of them is irrelevant. The pictures don't show anything about slum life; the incident could have happened anywhere, and it did. It is extremely unlikely that anyone who saw them rushed out and had his fire escape strengthened. And the pictures were not news—at least they were not national news. It is not news in Washington, or New York, or Los Angeles that a woman was killed in a Boston fire. The only newsworthy thing about the pictures is that they were taken. They deserve to be printed because they are great pictures, breathtaking pictures of something that happened. That they disturb readers is exactly as it should be: that's why photojournalism is often more powerful than written journalism.

TOPICS FOR CRITICAL THINKING AND WRITING

1. In paragraph 5 Ephron refers to "the famous assassination picture of the Vietcong prisoner in Saigon" (see p. 143). The photo shows the face of a prisoner who is about to be shot in the head at close range. Jot down the reasons why you would or would not approve of printing this photo in a newspaper. Think, too, about this: If the photo on page 142 were not about a war—if it did not include the soldiers and the burning village in the rear but instead showed children fleeing from an abusive parent or from an abusive sibling—would you approve of printing it in a newspaper?

2. In paragraph 9 Ephron quotes a newspaperman as saying that before printing Forman's pictures of the woman and the child falling from the fire escape, editors should have asked themselves "what purpose they served and what their effect was likely to be on the reader." If you were

an editor, what would your answers be? By the way, the pictures were *not* taken in a poor neighborhood, and they did *not* expose slum conditions.

3. In 50 words or so, write a precise description of what you see in the third of the Boston photographs. Do you think readers of your description would be "revolted" by the picture (para. 8), as were many viewers, the *Washington Post*'s ombudsman among them? Why, or why not?

4. Ephron thinks it would be a good thing if more photographs of death and dying were published by newspapers (paras. 11–13). In an essay of 500 words, state her reasons and your evaluation of them.

PART TWO

CRITICAL WRITING

5

Writing an Analysis of an Argument

This is what we can all do to nourish and strengthen one another: listen to one another very hard, ask questions, too, send one another away to work again, and laugh in all the right places.

—NANCY MAIRS

I don't wait for moods. You accomplish nothing if you do that. Your mind must know it has got to get down to work.

—PEARL S. BUCK

Fear not those who argue but those who dodge.

—MARIE VON EBNER-ESCHENBACH

ANALYZING AN ARGUMENT

Examining the Author's Thesis

Most of your writing in other courses will require you to write an analysis of someone else's writing. In a course in political science you may have to analyze, say, an essay first published in *Foreign Affairs,* perhaps reprinted in your textbook, that argues against raising tariff barriers to foreign trade. Or a course in sociology may require you to analyze a report on the correlation between fatal accidents and drunk drivers under the age of twenty-one. Much of your writing, in short, will set forth reasoned responses to your reading as preparation for making an argument of your own.

Obviously you must understand an essay before you can analyze it thoughtfully. You must read it several times—not just skim it—and (the hard part) you must think about it. Again, you'll find that your thinking is stimulated if you take notes and if you ask yourself questions about the material. Notes will help you to keep track of the writer's thoughts and also of your own responses to the writer's thesis. The writer probably *does* have a thesis, a claim, a point, and if so, you must try to locate it. Perhaps the thesis is explicitly stated in the title or in a sentence or two near the beginning of the essay or in a concluding paragraph, but perhaps you will have to infer it from the essay as a whole.

Notice that we said the writer *probably* has a thesis. Much of what you read will indeed be primarily an argument; the writer explicitly or implicitly is trying to support some thesis and to convince you to agree with it. But some of what you read will be relatively neutral, with the argument just faintly discernible — or even with no argument at all. A work may, for instance, chiefly be a report: Here are the data, or here is what *X, Y,* and *Z* said; make of it what you will. A report might simply state how various ethnic groups voted in an election. In a report of this sort, of course, the writer hopes to persuade readers that the facts are correct, but no thesis is advanced, at least not explicitly or perhaps even consciously; the writer is not evidently arguing a point and trying to change our minds. Such a document differs greatly from an essay by a political analyst who presents similar findings to persuade a candidate to sacrifice the votes of this ethnic bloc and thereby get more votes from other blocs.

Examining the Author's Purpose

While reading an argument, try to form a clear idea of the author's **purpose.** Judging from the essay or the book, was the purpose to persuade, or was it to report? An analysis of a pure report (a work apparently without a thesis or argumentative angle) on ethnic voting will deal chiefly with the accuracy of the report. It will, for example, consider whether the sample poll was representative.

Much material that poses as a report really has a thesis built into it, consciously or unconsciously. The best evidence that the prose you are reading is argumentative is the presence of two kinds of key terms: transitions that imply the drawing of a conclusion and verbs that imply proof (see Idea Prompt 5.1). Keep your eye out for such terms, and scrutinize

IDEA PROMPT 5.1 DRAWING CONCLUSIONS AND IMPLYING PROOF

Transitions that imply the drawing of a conclusion	*therefore, because, for the reason that, consequently*
Verbs that imply proof	*confirms, verifies, accounts for, implies, proves, disproves, is (in)consistent with, refutes, it follows that*

their precise role whenever, or whatever they appear. If the essay does not advance a thesis, think of a thesis (a hypothesis) that it might support or some conventional belief that it might undermine.

Examining the Author's Methods

If the essay advances a thesis, you will want to analyze the strategies or methods of argument that allegedly support the thesis.

- Does the writer quote authorities? Are these authorities really competent in this field? Are equally competent authorities who take a different view ignored?

- Does the writer use statistics? If so, are they appropriate to the point being argued? Can they be interpreted differently?

- Does the writer build the argument by using examples or analogies? Are they satisfactory?

- Are the writer's assumptions acceptable?

- Does the writer consider all relevant factors? Has he or she omitted some points that you think should be discussed? For instance, should the author recognize certain opposing positions and perhaps concede something to them?

- Does the writer seek to persuade by means of ridicule? If so, is the ridicule fair: Is it supported also by rational argument?

In writing your analysis, you will want to tell your reader something about the author's purpose and something about the author's **methods.** It is usually a good idea at the start of your analysis—if not in the first paragraph then in the second or third—to let the reader know the purpose (and thesis, if there is one) of the work you are analyzing and then to summarize the work briefly.

Next you will probably find it useful (your reader will certainly find it helpful) to write out *your* thesis (your evaluation or judgment). You might say, for instance, that the essay is impressive but not conclusive, or is undermined by convincing contrary evidence, or relies too much on unsupported generalizations, or is wholly admirable, or whatever. Remember, because your paper is itself an argument, it needs its own thesis.

And then, of course, comes the job of setting forth your analysis and the support for your thesis. There is no one way of going about this work. If, say, your author gives four arguments (for example, an appeal to common sense, the testimony of authorities, the evidence of comparisons, and an appeal to self-interest), you might want to do one of the following:

- Take up these four arguments in sequence.

- Discuss the simplest of the four and then go on to the more difficult ones.

- Discuss the author's two arguments that you think are sound and then turn to the two that you think are not sound (or perhaps the reverse).

- Take one of these approaches and then clinch your case by constructing a fifth argument that is absent from the work under scrutiny but in your view highly important.

In short, the organization of your analysis may or may not follow the organization of the work you are analyzing.

Examining the Author's Persona

You will probably also want to analyze something a bit more elusive than the author's explicit arguments: the author's self-presentation. Does the author seek to persuade readers partly by presenting himself or herself as conscientious, friendly, self-effacing, authoritative, tentative, or in some other light? Most writers do two things:

- They present evidence, and
- They present themselves (or, more precisely, they present the image of themselves that they wish us to behold).

In some persuasive writing this **persona** or **voice** or presentation of the self may be no less important than the presentation of evidence.

In establishing a persona, writers adopt various rhetorical strategies, ranging from the use of characteristic words to the use of a particular form of organization. For instance,

- The writer who speaks of an opponent's "gimmicks" instead of "strategy" is trying to downgrade the opponent and also to convey the self-image of a streetwise person.

- On a larger scale, consider the way in which evidence is presented and the kind of evidence offered. One writer may first bombard the reader with facts and then spend relatively little time drawing conclusions. Another may rely chiefly on generalizations, waiting until the end of the essay to bring the thesis home with a few details. Another may begin with a few facts and spend most of the space reflecting on these. One writer may seem professorial or pedantic, offering examples of an academic sort; another, whose examples are drawn from ordinary life, may seem like a regular guy.

All such devices deserve comment in your analysis.

The writer's persona, then, may color the thesis and help it develop in a distinctive way. If we accept the thesis, it is partly because the writer has won our goodwill by persuading us of his or her good character (*ethos*, in Aristotle's terms). Later we talk more about the appeal to the character of the speaker—the so-called *ethical appeal*, but here we may say that wise writers present themselves not as wise-guys but as decent people whom the reader would like to invite to dinner.

The author of an essay may, for example, seem fair minded and open minded, treating the opposition with great courtesy and expressing interest in hearing other views. Such a tactic is itself a persuasive device. Or take an author who appears to rely on hard evidence such as statistics. This reliance on seemingly objective truths is itself a way of seeking to persuade—a rational way, to be sure, but a mode of persuasion nonetheless.

Especially in analyzing a work in which the author's persona and ideas are blended, you will want to spend some time commenting on the persona. Whether you discuss it near the beginning of your analysis or near the end will depend on your own sense of how you want to construct your essay, and this decision will partly depend on the work you are analyzing. For example, if the author's persona is kept in the background and is thus relatively invisible, you may want to make that point fairly early to get it out of the way and then concentrate on more interesting matters. If, however, the persona is interesting—and perhaps seductive, whether because it seems so scrupulously objective or so engagingly subjective—you may want to hint at this quality early in your essay and then develop the point while you consider the arguments.

Summary

In the last few pages we have tried to persuade you that, in writing an analysis of your reading, you must do the following:

- Read and reread thoughtfully. Writing notes will help you to think about what you are reading.
- Be aware of the purpose of the material to which you are responding.

We have also tried to point out these facts:

- Most of the nonliterary material that you will read is designed to argue, to report, or to do both.
- Most of this material also presents the writer's personality, or voice, and this voice usually merits attention in an analysis. An essay on, say, nuclear war, in a journal devoted to political science, may include a voice that moves from an objective tone to a mildly ironic tone to a hortatory tone, and this voice is worth commenting on.

Possibly all this explanation is obvious. There is yet another point, equally obvious but often neglected by students who begin by writing an analysis and end up by writing only a summary, a shortened version of the work they have read: Although your essay is an analysis of someone else's writing, and you may have to include a summary of the work you are writing about, your essay is *your* essay. The thesis, the organization, and the tone are yours.

- Your thesis, for example, may be that although the author is convinced she has presented a strong case, her case is far from proved.
- Your organization may be deeply indebted to the work you are analyzing, but it need not be. The author may have begun with specific examples and then gone on to make generalizations and to draw conclusions, but you may begin with the conclusions.
- Your tone, similarly, may resemble your subject's (let's say the voice is courteous academic), but it will nevertheless have its own ring, its own tone of, say, urgency, caution, or coolness.

Most of the essays that we have printed thus far are more or less in an academic style, and indeed several are by students and by professors. But

---

✔ A CHECKLIST FOR ANALYZING A TEXT

Have I considered all of the following matters?

- ☐ Who is the author?
- ☐ Is the piece aimed at a particular audience? A neutral audience? Persons who are already sympathetic to the author's point of view? A hostile audience?
- ☐ What is the author's thesis (argument, main point, claim)?
- ☐ What assumptions does the author make? Do I share them? If not, why not?
- ☐ Does the author ever confuse facts with beliefs or opinions?
- ☐ What appeals does the author make? To reason (*logos*), for instance, with statistics, the testimony of authorities, and personal experience? To the emotions (*pathos*), for instance, by an appeal to "our better nature," or to widely shared values? To our sense that the speaker is trustworthy (*ethos*)?
- ☐ How convincing is the evidence?
- ☐ Are significant objections and counterevidence adequately discussed?
- ☐ How is the text organized, and is the organization effective? Are the title, the opening paragraphs, and the concluding paragraphs effective? In what ways?
- ☐ If visual materials such as graphs, pie charts, or pictures are used, how persuasive are they? Do they make a logical appeal? (Charts and graphs presumably make a logical appeal.) Do they make an emotional appeal?
- ☐ What is the author's tone? Is it appropriate?
- ☐ To what extent has the author convinced me? Why?

argumentative writing is not limited to academicians—if it were, your college would not be requiring you to take a course in the subject. The following essay, in a breezy style, comes from a columnist who writes for the *New York Times*.

AN ARGUMENT, ITS ELEMENTS, AND A STUDENT'S ANALYSIS OF THE ARGUMENT

Nicholas D. Kristof

Nicholas D. Kristof (b. 1959) grew up on a farm in Oregon. After graduating from Harvard, he was awarded a Rhodes scholarship to Oxford, where he studied law. In 1984 he joined the New York Times *as a correspondent, and since 2001 he has written as a columnist. He has won two Pulitzer Prizes.*

For Environmental Balance, Pick Up a Rifle

Here's a quick quiz: Which large American mammal kills the most humans each year?

It's not the bear, which kills about two people a year in North America. Nor is it the wolf, which in modern times hasn't killed anyone in this country. It's not the cougar, which kills one person every year or two.

Rather, it's the deer. Unchecked by predators, deer populations are exploding in a way that is profoundly unnatural and that is destroying the ecosystem in many parts of the country. In a wilderness, there might be ten deer per square mile; in parts of New Jersey, there are up to 200 per square mile.

One result is ticks and Lyme disease, but deer also kill people more directly. A study for the insurance industry estimated that deer kill about 150 people a year in car crashes nationwide and cause $1 billion in damage. Granted, deer aren't stalking us, and they come out worse in these collisions—but it's still true that in a typical year, an American is less likely to be killed by Osama bin Laden than by Bambi.

If the symbol of the environment's being out of whack in the 1960s   5 was the Cuyahoga River in Cleveland catching fire, one such symbol today is deer congregating around what they think of as salad bars and what we think of as suburbs.

So what do we do? Let's bring back hunting.

Now, you've probably just spilled your coffee. These days, among the university-educated crowd in the cities, hunting is viewed as barbaric.

The upshot is that towns in New York and New Jersey are talking about using birth control to keep deer populations down. (Liberals presumably support free condoms, while conservatives back abstinence education.) Deer contraception hasn't been very successful, though.

Meanwhile, the same population bomb has spread to bears. A bear hunt has been scheduled for this week in New Jersey—prompting outrage from some animal rights groups (there's also talk of bear contraception: make love, not cubs).

As for deer, partly because hunting is perceived as brutal and vaguely 10 psychopathic, towns are taking out contracts on deer through discreet private companies. Greenwich, Connecticut, budgeted $47,000 this year to pay a company to shoot eighty deer from raised platforms over four nights—as well as $8,000 for deer birth control.

Look, this is ridiculous.

We have an environmental imbalance caused in part by the decline of hunting. Humans first wiped out certain predators—like wolves and cougars—but then expanded their own role as predators to sustain a rough ecological balance. These days, though, hunters are on the decline.

According to "Families Afield: An Initiative for the Future of Hunting," a report by an alliance of shooting organizations, for every hundred hunters who die or stop hunting, only sixty-nine hunters take their place.

I was raised on *Bambi*—but also, as an Oregon farm boy, on venison and elk meat. But deer are not pets, and dead deer are as natural as live deer. To wring one's hands over them, perhaps after polishing off a hamburger, is soggy sentimentality.

What's the alternative to hunting? Is it preferable that deer die of 15 disease and hunger? Or, as the editor of *Adirondack Explorer* magazine suggested, do we introduce wolves into the burbs?

To their credit, many environmentalists agree that hunting can be green. The New Jersey Audubon Society this year advocated deer hunting as an ecological necessity.

There's another reason to encourage hunting: it connects people with the outdoors and creates a broader constituency for wilderness preservation. At a time when America's wilderness is being gobbled away for logging, mining, or oil drilling, that's a huge boon.

Granted, hunting isn't advisable in suburban backyards, and I don't expect many soccer moms to install gun racks in their minivans. But it's an abdication of environmental responsibility to eliminate other predators and then refuse to assume the job ourselves. In that case, the collisions with humans will simply get worse.

In October, for example, Wayne Goldsberry was sitting in a home in northwestern Arkansas when he heard glass breaking in the next room. It was a home invasion—by a buck.

Mr. Goldsberry, who is six feet one inch and weighs two hundred 20 pounds, wrestled with the intruder for forty minutes. Blood spattered the walls before he managed to break the buck's neck.

So it's time to reestablish a balance in the natural world—by accepting the idea that hunting is as natural as bird-watching.

In a moment we will talk at some length about Kristof's essay, but first you may want to think about the following questions.

1. What is Kristof's chief thesis? (State it in one sentence.)
2. Does Kristof make any assumptions—tacit or explicit—with which you disagree? With which you agree?
3. Is the slightly humorous tone of Kristof's essay inappropriate for a discussion of deliberately killing wild animals? Why, or why not?
4. If you are familiar with *Bambi,* does the story make any *argument* against killing deer, or does the story appeal only to our emotions?
5. Do you agree that "hunting is as natural as bird-watching" (para. 21)? In any case, do you think that an appeal to what is "natural" is a good argument for expanding the use of hunting?

OK, time's up. Let's examine Kristof's essay with an eye to identifying those elements we mentioned earlier in this chapter (pp. 177–82) that deserve notice when examining *any* argument: the author's *thesis, purpose, methods,* and *persona.* And while we're at it, let's also notice some other features of Kristof's essay that will help us appreciate its effects and evaluate it. We will thus be in a good position to write an evaluation or an argument that confirms, extends, or even rebuts Kristof's argument.

But first, a caution: Kristof's essay appeared in a newspaper where paragraphs are customarily very short, partly to allow for easy reading and partly because the columns are narrow and even short paragraphs may extend for an inch or two. If his essay were to appear in a book, doubtless the author would join many of the paragraphs, making longer units.

Title   By combining "Environmental Balance" with "Rifle"—terms that don't seem to go together—Kristof starts off with a bang. He gives a hint of his *topic* (something about the environment) and of his thesis (some sort of way of introducing ecological balance). He also conveys something of his persona by introducing a rifle into the environment. He is, the title suggests, a no-nonsense, hard-hitting guy.

Opening Paragraphs   Kristof immediately grabs hold of us ("Here's a quick quiz") and asks a simple question, but one that we probably have not thought much about: "Which large American mammal kills the most humans each year?" In his second paragraph he tells us it is *not* the bear—the answer most readers probably come up with—nor is it the cougar. Not until the third paragraph does Kristof give us the answer, the deer. But remember, Kristof is writing in a newspaper, where paragraphs customarily are very short. It takes us only a few seconds to get to the third paragraph and the answer.

Thesis   What is the basic thesis Kristof is arguing? Somewhat unusually, Kristof does *not* announce it in its full form until his sixth paragraph ("Let's bring back hunting"), but, again, his paragraphs are very short, and if the essay were published in a book, Kristof's first two paragraphs probably would be combined, as would the third and fourth.

Purpose   Kristof's purpose is clear: He wants to *persuade* readers to adopt his view. This amounts to trying to persuade us that his thesis (stated above) is *true*. Kristof, however, does not show that his essay is argumentative or persuasive by using many of the key terms that normally mark argumentative prose. He doesn't call anything his *conclusion*, none of his statements is labeled *my premises*, and he doesn't connect clauses or sentences with *therefore* or *because*. Almost the only traces of the language of argument are "Granted" (para. 18) and "So" (that is, *therefore*) in his final paragraph.

Despite the lack of argumentative language, the argumentative nature of his essay is clear. He has a thesis—one that will strike many readers as highly unusual—and he wants readers to accept it, so he must go on to *support* it; accordingly, after his introductory paragraphs, in which he calls attention to a problem and offers a solution (his thesis), he must offer evidence, and that is what much of the rest of the essay seeks to do.

Methods   Although Kristof will have to offer evidence, he begins by recognizing the folks on the other side, "the university-educated crowd in the cities, [for whom] hunting is viewed as barbaric" (para. 7). He goes on to spoof this "crowd" when, speaking of methods of keeping the deer population down, he says in paragraph 8, "Liberals presumably support free condoms, while conservatives back abstinence education." Ordinarily it is a bad idea to make fun of persons who hold views other than your own—after all, they just may be on to something, they just might know something you don't know, and, in any case, impartial readers rarely want to align themselves with someone who mocks others. In the essay we are looking at, however, Kristof gets away with this smart-guy tone because he (a) has loyal readers and (b) has written the entire essay in a highly informal or playful manner. Think again about the first paragraph, which begins "Here's a quick quiz." The informality is not only in the contraction (*Here's* versus *Here is*), but in the very idea of beginning by grabbing the readers and thrusting a quiz at them. The playfulness is evident throughout: For instance, immediately after Kristof announces his thesis, "Let's bring back hunting," he begins a new paragraph (7) with, "Now, you've probably just spilled your coffee."

Kristof's methods of presenting evidence include providing **statistics** (paras. 3, 4, 10, and 13), giving **examples** (paras. 10, 19–20), and citing **authorities** (paras. 13 and 16).

Persona   Kristof presents himself as a confident, no-nonsense fellow, a persona that not many writers can get away with, but that probably is acceptable in a journalist who regularly writes a newspaper column. His readers know what to expect, and they read him with pleasure. But it probably would be inadvisable for an unknown writer to adopt this persona, unless perhaps he or she were writing for an audience that could be counted on to be friendly (in this instance, an audience of hunters). If this essay appeared in a hunting magazine, doubtless it would please and entertain its audience. It would not convert anybody, but conversion would not be its point if it were published in a magazine read by hunters. In the *New York Times,* where the essay originally appeared, Kristof could count on a moderately sympathetic audience because he has a large number of faithful readers, but one can guess that many of these readers—chiefly city dwellers—read him for entertainment rather than for information about how they should actually behave.

Closing Paragraphs   The first two of the last three paragraphs report an episode (the two hundred pound buck inside the house) that Kristof presumably thinks is pretty conclusive evidence. The final paragraph begins with "So," strongly implying a logical conclusion to the essay.

Let's now turn to a student's analysis of Kristof's essay and then to our analysis of the student's analysis. (We should say that the analysis of Kristof's essay that you have just read is partly indebted to the student's essay that you are about to read.)

Betsy Swinton

Professor Knowles

English 101B

March 12, 2007

Tracking Kristof

Nicholas D. Kristof's "For Environmental Balance, Pick Up a Rifle" is an engaging piece of writing, but whether it is convincing is something I am not sure about. And I am not sure about it for two reasons: (1) I don't know much about the deer problem, and that's my fault; (2) I don't know much about the deer problem, and that's Kristof's fault. The first point needs no explanation, but let me explain the second.

Kristof is making an argument, offering a thesis: Deer are causing destruction, and the best way to reduce the destruction is to hunt deer. For all that I know, he may be correct both in his comment about what deer are doing and also in his comment about what must be done about deer. My ignorance of the situation is regrettable, but I don't think that I am the only reader from Chicago who doesn't know much about the deer problems in New Jersey, Connecticut, and Arkansas, the states that Kristof specifically mentions in connection with the deer problem. He announces his thesis early enough, in his sixth paragraph, and he is entertaining throughout his essay, but does he make a convincing case? To ask "Does he make a convincing case?" is to ask "Does he offer adequate evidence?" and "Does he show that his solution is better than other possible solutions?"

To take the first question: In a short essay Kristof can hardly give overwhelming evidence, but he does convince me that there is a problem. The most convincing evidence he gives appears in paragraph 16, where he says that the New Jersey Audubon Society "advocated deer hunting as an ecological necessity." I don't really know anything about the New Jersey Audubon Society, but I suppose that they are

Swinton 2

people with a deep interest in nature and in conservation, and if even such a group advocates deer hunting, there must be something to this solution.

I am even willing to accept his argument that, in this nation of meat-eaters, "to wring one's hands over them [dead deer], perhaps after polishing off a hamburger, is soggy sentimentality" (para. 14). According to Kristof, the present alternative to hunting deer is that we leave the deer to "die of disease and hunger" (para. 15). But what I am not convinced of is that there is no way to reduce the deer population other than by hunting. I don't think Kristof adequately explains why some sort of birth control is inadequate. In his eighth paragraph he makes a joke about controlling the birth of deer ("Liberals presumably support free condoms, while conservatives back abstinence education"), and the joke is funny, but it isn't an argument, it's just a joke. Why can't food containing some sort of sterilizing medicine be put out for the starving deer, food that will nourish them and yet make them unreproductive? In short, I don't think he has fairly informed his readers of alternatives to his own positions, and because he fails to look at counterproposals, he weakens his own proposal.

Although Kristof occasionally uses a word or phrase that suggests argument, such as "Granted" (para. 18), "So" (final paragraph), and "There's another reason" (para. 17), he relies chiefly on forceful writing rather than on reasoning. And the second of his two reasons for hunting seems utterly unconvincing to me. His first, as we have seen, is that the deer population (and apparently the bear population) is out of control. His second (para. 17) is that hunting "connects people with the outdoors and creates a broader constituency for wilderness preservation." I am not a hunter and I have never been one. Perhaps that's my misfortune, but I don't think I am missing anything. And when I hear Kristof say, in his final sentence—the climactic place in his essay—that "hunting is as natural as bird-watching," I rub my eyes in disbelief. If he had me at least half-convinced by his statistics and his citation of the Audubon Society, he now loses me when he argues that hunting is "natural." One might as well say that war is natural, rape is natural, bribery is natural—all these terrible things occur, but we ought to deplore them and we ought to make every effort to see that they disappear.

In short, I think that Kristof has written an engaging essay, and he may well have an important idea, but I think that in his glib final paragraph, where he tells us that "hunting is as natural as bird-watching," he utterly loses the reader's confidence.

AN ANALYSIS OF THE STUDENT'S ANALYSIS

Swinton's essay seems to us to be excellent, doubtless the product of a good deal of thoughtful revision. She does not cover every possible aspect of Kristof's essay—she concentrates on his reasoning and she says very little about his style—but we think that, given the limits of space (about 500 words), she does a good job. What makes this student's essay effective?

- The essay has a title ("Tracking Kristof") that is of at least a little interest; it picks up Kristof's point about hunting, and it gives a hint of what is to come.

✓ A CHECKLIST FOR WRITING AN ANALYSIS
OF AN ARGUMENT

Have I asked myself the following questions?

☐ Early in my essay have I fairly stated the writer's thesis (claim) and summarized his or her supporting reasons? Have I explained to my reader any disagreement about definitions of important terms?

☐ Have I, again fairly early in my essay, indicated where I will be taking my reader, i.e., have I indicated my general response to the essay I am analyzing?

☐ Have I called attention to the strengths, if any, and the weaknesses, if any, of the essay?

☐ Have I commented not only on the *logos* (logic, reasoning) but also on the *ethos* (character of the writer, as presented in the essay)? For instance, has the author convinced me that he or she is well-informed and is a person of goodwill? Or, on the other hand, does the writer seem to be chiefly concerned with ridiculing those who hold a different view?

☐ If there is an appeal to *pathos* (emotion, originally meaning "pity for suffering," but now interpreted more broadly to include appeals to patriotism, humor, or loyalty to family, for example), is it acceptable? If not, why not?

☐ Have I used occasional brief quotations to let my reader hear the author's tone and to ensure fairness and accuracy?

☐ Is my analysis effectively organized?

☐ Does my essay, perhaps in the concluding paragraphs, indicate my agreement or disagreement with the writer but also my view of the essay as a piece of argumentative writing?

☐ Is my tone appropriate?

- The author promptly identifies her subject (she names the writer and the title of his essay) early.

- Early in the essay she gives us a hint of where she will be going (in her first paragraph she tells us that Kristof's essay is "engaging . . . *but* . . .").

- She uses a few brief quotations, to give us a feel for Kristof's essay and to let us hear the evidence for itself, but she does not pad her essay with long quotations.

- She takes up all of Kristof's main points.

- She gives her essay a reasonable organization, letting us hear Kristof's thesis, letting us know the degree to which she accepts it, and finally letting us know her specific reservations about the essay.

- She concludes without the formality of "in conclusion"; "in short" nicely does the trick.

- Notice, finally, that she sticks closely to Kristof's essay. She does not go off on a tangent about the virtues of vegetarianism or the dreadful politics of the *New York Times,* the newspaper that published Kristof's essay. She was asked to analyze the essay, and she has done so.

EXERCISE

Take one of the essays not yet discussed in class or an essay assigned now by your instructor, and in an essay of 500 words analyze and evaluate it.

ARGUMENTS FOR ANALYSIS

Jeff Jacoby

Jeff Jacoby is a columnist for the Boston Globe, *where this essay was originally published on the op-ed page on February 20, 1997.*

Bring Back Flogging

Boston's Puritan forefathers did not indulge miscreants lightly.

For selling arms and gunpowder to Indians in 1632, Richard Hopkins was sentenced to be "whipt, & branded with a hott iron on one of his cheekes." Joseph Gatchell, convicted of blasphemy in 1684, was ordered "to stand in pillory, have his head and hand put in & have his toung drawne forth out of his mouth, & peirct through with a hott iron." When Hannah Newell pleaded guilty to adultery in 1694, the court ordered "fifteen stripes Severally to be laid on upon her naked back at the Common Whipping post." Her consort, the aptly named Lambert Despair, fared worse: He was sentenced to twenty-five lashes "and that on the next Thursday Immediately after Lecture he stand upon the Pillory for . . . a full hower with Adultery in Capitall letters written upon his brest."

Corporal punishment for criminals did not vanish with the Puritans— Delaware didn't get around to repealing it until 1972—but for all relevant purposes, it has been out of fashion for at least 150 years. The day is long past when the stocks had an honored place on the Boston Common, or when offenders were publicly flogged. Now we practice a more enlightened, more humane way of disciplining wrongdoers: We lock them up in cages.

Imprisonment has become our penalty of choice for almost every offense in the criminal code. Commit murder; go to prison. Sell cocaine; go to prison. Kite checks; go to prison. It is an all-purpose punishment, suitable—or so it would seem—for crimes violent and nonviolent, motivated by hate or by greed, plotted coldly or committed in a fit of passion. If anything, our preference for incarceration is deepening— behold the slew of mandatory minimum sentences for drug crimes and "three-strikes-you're-out" life terms for recidivists. Some 1.6 million Americans are behind bars today. That represents a 250 percent increase since 1980, and the number is climbing.

We cage criminals at a rate unsurpassed in the free world, yet few of   5 us believe that the criminal justice system is a success. Crime is out of control, despite the deluded happy talk by some politicians about how "safe" cities have become. For most wrongdoers, the odds of being arrested, prosecuted, convicted, and incarcerated are reassuringly long. Fifty-eight percent of all murders do *not* result in a prison term. Likewise 98 percent of all burglaries.

Many states have gone on prison-building sprees, yet the penal system is choked to bursting. To ease the pressure, nearly all convicted felons are released early—or not locked up at all. "About three of every four convicted criminals," says John DiIulio, a noted Princeton criminologist, "are on the streets without meaningful probation or parole supervision." And while everyone knows that amateur thugs should be deterred before they become career criminals, it is almost unheard of for judges to send first- or second-time offenders to prison.

Meanwhile, the price of keeping criminals in cages is appalling—a common estimate is $30,000 per inmate per year. (To be sure, the cost to society of turning many inmates loose would be even higher.) For tens of thousands of convicts, prison is a graduate school of criminal studies: They emerge more ruthless and savvy than when they entered. And for many offenders, there is even a certain cachet to doing time—a stint in prison becomes a sign of manhood, a status symbol.

But there would be no cachet in chaining a criminal to an outdoor post and flogging him. If young punks were horsewhipped in public after their first conviction, fewer of them would harden into lifelong felons. A humiliating and painful paddling can be applied to the rear end of a crook for a lot less than $30,000—and prove a lot more educational than ten years' worth of prison meals and lockdowns.

Are we quite certain the Puritans have nothing to teach us about dealing with criminals?

Of course, their crimes are not our crimes: We do not arrest blas-   10 phemers or adulterers, and only gun control fanatics would criminalize the sale of weapons to Indians. (They would criminalize the sale of weapons to anybody.) Nor would the ordeal suffered by poor Joseph Gatchell—the tongue "peirct through" with a hot poker—be regarded today as anything less than torture.

But what is the objection to corporal punishment that doesn't maim or mutilate? Instead of a prison term, why not sentence at least some criminals—say, thieves and drunk drivers—to a public whipping?

"Too degrading," some will say. "Too brutal." But where is it written that being whipped is more degrading than being caged? Why is it more brutal to flog a wrongdoer than to throw him in prison—where the risk of being beaten, raped, or murdered is terrifyingly high?

The *Globe* reported in 1994 that more than two hundred thousand prison inmates are raped each year, usually to the indifference of the guards. "The horrors experienced by many young inmates, particularly those who . . . are convicted of nonviolent offenses," former Supreme Court Justice Harry Blackmun has written, "border on the unimaginable." Are those horrors preferable to the short, sharp shame of corporal punishment?

Perhaps the Puritans were more enlightened than we think, at least on the subject of punishment. Their sanctions were humiliating and painful, but quick and cheap. Maybe we should readopt a few.

TOPICS FOR CRITICAL THINKING AND WRITING

1. When Jacoby says (para. 3) that today we are more "enlightened" than our Puritan forefathers because where they used flogging, "We lock them up in cages," is he being ironic? Explain.

2. Suppose you agree with Jacoby. Explain precisely (a) what you mean by *flogging* (does Jacoby explain what he means?) and (b) how much flogging is appropriate for the crimes of housebreaking, rape, robbery, and murder.

3. In an essay of 250 words, explain why you think that flogging would be more (or less) degrading and brutal than imprisonment.

4. At the end of his essay Jacoby draws to our attention the terrible risk of being raped in prison as an argument in favor of replacing imprisonment

with flogging. Do you think he mentions this point at the end because he believes it is the strongest or most persuasive of all those he mentions? Why, or why not?

5. It is often said that corporal punishment does not have any effect or, if it does, that the effect is the negative one of telling the recipient that violence is an acceptable form of behavior. But suppose it were demonstrated that the infliction of physical pain reduced at least certain kinds of crimes, perhaps shoplifting or unarmed robbery. Should we adopt the practice?

6. Jacoby draws the line (para. 11) at punishment that would "maim or mutilate." Why draw the line here? Some societies punish thieves by amputating a hand. Suppose we knew that this practice really did seriously reduce theft. Should we adopt it? How about adopting castration (surgical or chemical) for rapists? For child molesters?

Gerard Jones

Gerard Jones (b. 1957), author of several works of fiction and nonfiction, has written many comic books for Marvel Comics and other publishers.

Violent Media Is Good for Kids

At thirteen I was alone and afraid. Taught by my well-meaning, progressive, English-teacher parents that violence was wrong, that rage was something to be overcome and cooperation was always better than conflict, I suffocated my deepest fears and desires under a nice-boy persona. Placed in a small, experimental school that was wrong for me, afraid to join my peers in their bumptious rush into adolescent boyhood, I withdrew into passivity and loneliness. My parents, not trusting the violent world of the late 1960s, built a wall between me and the crudest elements of American pop culture.

Then the Incredible Hulk smashed through it.

One of my mother's students convinced her that Marvel Comics, despite their apparent juvenility and violence, were in fact devoted to lofty messages of pacifism and tolerance. My mother borrowed some, thinking they'd be good for me. And so they were. But not because they preached lofty messages of benevolence. They were good for me because they were juvenile. And violent.

The character who caught me, and freed me, was the Hulk: overgendered and undersocialized, half-naked and half-witted, raging against a frightened world that misunderstood and persecuted him. Suddenly I had a fantasy self to carry my stifled rage and buried desire for power. I had a fantasy self who was a self: unafraid of his desires and the world's disapproval, unhesitating and effective in action. "Puny boy follow Hulk!" roared my fantasy self, and I followed.

I followed him to new friends—other sensitive geeks chasing their ⁵ own inner brutes—and I followed him to the arrogant, self-exposing, self-assertive, superheroic decision to become a writer. Eventually, I left him behind, followed more sophisticated heroes, and finally my own lead along a twisting path to a career and an identity. In my thirties, I found myself writing action movies and comic books. I wrote some Hulk stories, and met the geek-geniuses who created him. I saw my own creations turned into action figures, cartoons, and computer games. I talked to the kids who read my stories. Across generations, genders, and ethnicities I kept seeing the same story: people pulling themselves out of emotional traps by immersing themselves in violent stories. People integrating the scariest, most fervently denied fragments of their psyches into fuller senses of selfhood through fantasies of superhuman combat and destruction.

A Scene from Gerard Jones and Gene Ha's comic book "Oktane"

I have watched my son living the same story — transforming himself into a blood-thirsty dinosaur to embolden himself for the plunge into preschool, a Power Ranger to muscle through a social competition in kindergarten. In the first grade, his friends started climbing a tree at school. But he was afraid: of falling, of the centipedes crawling on the trunk, of sharp branches, of his friends' derision. I took my cue from his own fantasies and read him old Tarzan comics, rich in combat and bright with flashing knives. For two weeks he lived in them. Then he put them aside. And he climbed the tree.

But all the while, especially in the wake of the recent burst of school shootings, I heard pop psychologists insisting that violent stories are harmful to kids, heard teachers begging parents to keep their kids away from "junk culture," heard a guilt-stricken friend with a son who loved Pokémon lament, "I've turned into the bad mom who lets her kid eat sugary cereal and watch cartoons!"

That's when I started the research.

"Fear, greed, power-hunger, rage: these are aspects of our selves that we try not to experience in our lives but often want, even need, to experience vicariously through stories of others," writes Melanie Moore, Ph.D., a psychologist who works with urban teens. "Children need violent entertainment in order to explore the inescapable feelings that they've been taught to deny, and to reintegrate those feelings into a more whole, more complex, more resilient selfhood."

Moore consults to public schools and local governments, and is also 10 raising a daughter. For the past three years she and I have been studying the ways in which children use violent stories to meet their emotional and developmental needs—and the ways in which adults can help them use those stories healthily. With her help I developed Power Play, a program for helping young people improve their self-knowledge and sense of potency through heroic, combative storytelling.

We've found that every aspect of even the trashiest pop-culture story can have its own developmental function. Pretending to have superhuman powers helps children conquer the feelings of powerlessness that inevitably come with being so young and small. The dual-identity concept at the heart of many superhero stories helps kids negotiate the conflicts between the inner self and the public self as they work through the early stages of socialization. Identification with a rebellious, even destructive, hero helps children learn to push back against a modern culture that cultivates fear and teaches dependency.

At its most fundamental level, what we call "creative violence"—head-bonking cartoons, bloody videogames, playground karate, toy guns—gives children a tool to master their rage. Children will feel rage. Even the sweetest and most civilized of them, even those whose parents read the better class of literary magazines, will feel rage. The world is uncontrollable and incomprehensible; mastering it is a terrifying, enraging task. Rage can be an energizing emotion, a shot of courage to push us to resist greater threats, take more control, than we ever thought we could. But rage is also the emotion our culture distrusts the most. Most of us are taught early on to fear our own. Through immersion in imaginary combat and identification with a violent protagonist, children engage the rage they've stifled, come to fear it less, and become more capable of utilizing it against life's challenges.

I knew one little girl who went around exploding with fantasies so violent that other moms would draw her mother aside to whisper, "I think you should know something about Emily. . . ." Her parents were separating, and she was small, an only child, a tomboy at an age when her classmates were dividing sharply along gender lines. On the playground she acted out *Sailor Moon* fights, and in the classroom she wrote

The title character of "Oktane" gets nasty

stories about people being stabbed with knives. The more adults tried to control her stories, the more she acted out the roles of her angry heroes: breaking rules, testing limits, roaring threats.

Then her mother and I started helping her tell her stories. She wrote them, performed them, drew them like comics: sometimes bloody, sometimes tender, always blending the images of pop culture with her own most private fantasies. She came out of it just as fiery and strong, but more self-controlled and socially competent: a leader among her peers, the one student in her class who could truly pull boys and girls together.

I worked with an older girl, a middle-class "nice girl," who held herself together through a chaotic family situation and a tumultuous adolescence with gangsta rap. In the mythologized street violence of Ice T, the rage and strutting of his music and lyrics, she found a theater of the mind in which she could be powerful, ruthless, invulnerable. She avoided the heavy drug use that sank many of her peers, and flowered in college as a writer and political activist.   15

I'm not going to argue that violent entertainment is harmless. I think it has helped inspire some people to real-life violence. I am going to argue that it's helped hundreds of people for every one it's hurt, and that it can help far more if we learn to use it well. I am going to argue that our fear of "youth violence" isn't well-founded on reality, and that the fear can do more harm than the reality. We act as though our highest priority is to prevent our children from growing up into murderous thugs—but modern kids are far more likely to grow up too passive, too distrustful of themselves, too easily manipulated.

We send the message to our children in a hundred ways that their craving for imaginary gun battles and symbolic killings is wrong, or at least dangerous. Even when we don't call for censorship or forbid *Mortal Kombat*, we moan to other parents within our kids' earshot about the "awful violence" in the entertainment they love. We tell our kids that it isn't nice to play-fight, or we steer them from some monstrous action figure to a prosocial doll. Even in the most progressive households, where we make such a point of letting children feel what they feel, we rush to substitute an enlightened discussion for the raw material of rageful fantasy. In the process, we risk confusing them about their natural aggression in the same way the Victorians confused their children about their sexuality. When we try to protect our children from their own feelings and fantasies, we shelter them not against violence but against power and selfhood.

TOPICS FOR CRITICAL THINKING AND WRITING

1. In his final paragraph Jones mentions the Victorian treatment of sexuality. Why does he bring this in? Does his use of this point make for an effective ending? Explain.

2. In an essay of 300 words, explain whether you think Jones has made the case for violence in an effective and persuasive way. If so, what is it about his article that makes it effective and persuasive? If it is not, where do the problems lie?

3. What kinds of violence does Jones advocate?

4. Does violence play as large a part in the life of teenaged girls as it does for teenaged boys? Why, or why not?

Sunaura Taylor and Alexander Taylor

Sunaura Taylor (b. 1982) is a writer, artist, and activist in Oakland, California. Alexander Taylor studies philosophy and ethics in Athens, Georgia. This essay appeared in Alternet, *February 18, 2009. (Alternet says that its aim is "to inspire action and advocacy on the environment, human rights and civil liberties, social justice, media, health care issues, and more.")*

Is It Possible to Be a Conscientious Meat Eater?

You may have noticed an onslaught of articles recently on what is being coined as the "new meat movement." The most recent is an article in *Newsweek*, "Head To Hoof: A Butcher Helps Lead a New Carnivore Movement." These articles almost all support the idea that cruelty to animals is wrong and that factory-produced meat is unjustifiably bad for the environment. However, they are not opposed to meat in and of itself, they are simply opposed to industrial meat. These "conscientious omnivores," believe it is possible, and preferable, to eat meat the old-fashioned way—on small, sustainable, and local farms, with farmers who love their animals and perhaps even have pet names for them.

The backlash against industrial meat has been brewing for many reasons. Ever-increasing knowledge of the industry's effect on the environment, human starvation, and animal welfare, is making it harder for even the most ardent omnivore to consume meat without guilt. The much-quoted report by the United Nations Food and Agricultural Organization, "Livestock's Long Shadow—Environmental Issues and Options" (Nov. 29, 2006), did a lot to raise awareness about the animal industry's devastating effects on the planet and global warming. More and more, people are also realizing the troubling connections between human starvation and eating animal products. It takes approximately sixteen pounds of grain and 2,500 gallons of water to produce one pound of meat (thus feeding one or two people on meat versus approximately sixteen people on grain). Much of this grain is grown in developing countries, where a large percentage of their land is used for cattle-raising for export to the United States, instead of being used to grow staple crops, which could feed local people directly. In a world where a child starves to death every two seconds, it seems impossible to justify such waste.

The animal industry is partly responsible for the destruction of the Amazon and other forests, for our world's diminishing water supply, for the release of huge amounts of greenhouse gases, and basically every other environmental problem. People are also more readily accepting that the animals themselves deserve a life free from cruelty and that factory farms give them anything but.

Vegans and vegetarians have been saying many of these things for years, but it seems that people have only started listening now that there is simultaneously a proposed solution to this problem: "happy meat." "Local," "grass-fed," "sustainably produced," "humanely raised," and "free-range" are just a few of the benevolent-sounding phrases that greet conscientious shoppers in the meat department. Animal-rights activists jokingly call these products "happy meat." Many of these products tout pictures of smiling pigs, happy farmers in green pastures, and stickers that say "humane." For many people who care about the environment and animal welfare, choosing to eat "humanely raised" meat seems like an option that honors traditional farmers and diets while also solving the ethical problems of environmental degradation and animal suffering.

But it solves neither of these problems. This meat is high-priced, and 5 its production is an even less-efficient use of land and resources. It is often marketed as luxurious, an indulgence to be lingered over. It is inherently not adaptable to a national or international solution. Local organic meat is for an elite few, and not a practicable alternative to the massive crisis of industrial meat production. For the first time in history, an entire civilization consumes meat as a staple. How can America truly produce enough of this "happy meat" (not too mention happy milk and happy eggs), to feed this country even a fraction of the animal products we currently consume? Truth be told, this meat is a marketing gimmick, an ideological pose, which assuages the ethical compulsions of those who consume it even though it does nothing to kick America's cheap meat habit, and perhaps contributes to the growing international fetishization of meat as a class signifier.

Articles on the "new meat movement" never pose questions like, "could all of America's animal products be grown locally?" And they never mention what the vast majority of Americans who can't afford the prized local animal products will be consuming if all factory farms shut down — they'd be vegan. These farms are described as ethical because of the fact that they are small, sustainable, and have kinder animal-husbandry practices. As many people have pointed out, these farms can individually produce meat in a way that is arguably just as "green" as eating vegan.

However, it is an inherent part of the ethical foundation of these farms that they cannot produce on a massive scale. As we've seen numerous times, the organic farms that do try to do this, very often become virtually no better than factory farms, despite the labels they often still get to keep. For example, many cage-free or free-range chickens still live in devastating conditions — they simply aren't technically kept in cages in the first case, or, in the latter case, are kept in huge, crowded, and perpetually dark buildings, with a single opening leading to a few square yards of bare earth.

The question of methane pollution may also make it hard to raise animals on a massive scale, regardless of whether the farms could be sustainable in other ways. The question is not, "are a few people eating local, sustainable, free-range pork worse environmentally than a few people eating vegan?" The question needs to be, "can we feed the world's entire growing population sustainable animal products?" I have never once seen this question addressed in one of these "new meat" articles. But all of this is in many ways ignoring an even more complex question. Do humans even have the right to make other living beings into objects of production that we can kill even when it is unnecessary to do so, merely for our pleasure? The words "animal rights," "vegetarian," and "vegan" are some of the most mocked and emotionally loaded terms in our language, even in very liberal circles. One has to wonder if a multibillion dollar meat industry hasn't had a part in making these words and the ideals behind them seem so laughable to so many people.

Soy has become the new evil food, and it is often said that vegans and vegetarians are hypocrites because they eat processed foods that are bad for the environment, and their diets are pretentious. In fact, many of the studies that show negative effects of soy are funded by the meat industry, and it is often ignored that the reason soy is so damaging environmentally

is because the vast majority of it is grown to feed factory farm animals —
this is the soy that is destroying the rain forest.

It's flattering that people think that the demands of vegans could be   10
the cause of such huge global effects. However, it is not the small number
of vegans and vegetarians who are misusing soy — it is the meat industry
and the millions of omnivores who eat their products. Eating vegan and
vegetarian does not mean you eat processed food. It also does not mean
you eat soy (many vegans simply do not like soy products or are allergic to
them). There is nothing pretentious, hard, unhealthy, or processed about
eating vegetables, grains, and legumes grown locally. If people could put
aside their biases against these terms, they'd see that the animal-rights
position is based on very rational argument. The concept of equality
itself rests on the ability to feel suffering. There is no other standard by
which to base equality that does not leave out some subset of human
being. If equality is based on intelligence or ability to plan for the future,
then babies and many developmentally disabled people would not be
included.

However, if the concept of equality is based on suffering, then it is
impossible to not include animals in our moral framework. This does not
mean that animals are equal to human beings in every way, it simply
means that we all have an interest in not suffering, and so to cause
unnecessary suffering is unethical. Oddly, this is something that the vast
majority of Americans already agree with — it is wrong to cause unnecessary suffering to animals. Rutgers University Professor Gary Francione
calls this a "moral schizophrenia." We see that unnecessary suffering is
wrong — which is a large part of why there even is a movement of "conscientious omnivores" — and yet we refuse to see meat eating as unnecessary, even though nutritionists agree that the consumption of animal
products is not necessary to our health.

Some people argue that equality should only include human beings,
for no other reason than for that fact that they are human. Historically,
this is very similar to sexist and racist philosophies that argued that only
white men should be treated equally for no other reason than the color of
their skin and their gender. Physiologically and neurochemically, we are
all very similar to the chicken killed at the local farm. We all exhibit similar signs of distress and fear. Chemically, our brains are mostly the same,
obviously with differences in physical scale and complexity. Why not
assume what appears to be pain is pain and that fear is fear? There is no
reason, except for pride, to doubt animals have a rich inner experience.

Many people within this "new meat movement" argue that it is suffering, not killing, that is unethical. Can unnecessary killing ever be
completely separated from suffering? Besides the obvious difficulty in
assuring a life and death free from trauma, there are the FDA regulations, which send all larger meat animals to the same slaughterhouses
that are used for factory-farmed animals — facilities notorious for the
suffering of both the animals and the employees. Even if the animals die

quickly on their home farm, what justifies this killing? Having fore-knowledge of death is not a prerequisite for the right to live, or else killing an infant would not seem unethical. How are we justified in ending a life of happy contentment to satisfy a passing craving?

Meat is deeply American, connected to our culture, tradition, and comfort. Many of these articles on the "new meat movement" emphasize a returning to historical practices. They romanticize the idea of the family farm of 100 years ago. I have even seen many references to getting in touch with your inner caveman through local meat. Culture and tradition are never sufficient justification to continue unethical practices—if they were, we would still have slavery and public torture. Traditions have to adapt with our changing values and ethics, although these changes may be uncomfortable and unwelcome. If we agree that institutions causing animal suffering are wrong, they shouldn't be maintained merely to avoid the potential effects their abolition will have on ranchers, butchers, and small farmers.

"But animals eat other animals. Eating meat is natural," some say.   15
Appealing to nature as a justification for ethical belief is a fallacy, and it has been used historically to justify every conservative power structure. Other animals, with no alternative sustenance, having no language and being isolated in themselves, do not seem to be appropriate role models for our ethical lives. We are animals that have evolved to recognize other beings' subjectivity, to experience empathy, and who have advanced beyond the necessity of violence to supply ourselves with food. We, uniquely, choose what we eat.

Veganism versus vegetarianism is about minimizing suffering. It is impossible to produce eggs and milk without vast amounts of killing. Veganism is about nonviolence. Veganism is more broadly sustainable, less economically divisive, and less cruel than eating local meat and other animal products. There is no truly sustainable and humane way to feed all Americans even a fraction of the amount of animal products they currently consume. An acre of land used for grass-fed beef could feed ten times as many people if used for crops. Animals will always be bad protein converters, and the world's population will continue to grow and be hungry. Veganism recognizes that compassion is not a limited resource. Veganism is not an asceticism. It is not a form of self-denial. Vegans do not claim to be ethically perfect. Agriculture is, and always will be, a messy business—there will most likely always be some level of exploitation and misguided or inefficient methods. Perhaps, as the cynical jibe goes, even the plants feel pain. That is not an argument for the continued exploitation of animals, who demonstrate clear analogs to the states which in humans recognize as indicating suffering. Vegans actively try to stop as much known suffering as possible.

Veganism is humanitarian. Becoming vegan is good for the planet and for hungry people around the globe. It is perhaps the only practicable solution to the global food crisis. It does not indicate a preference for animals over people. It is egalitarian as it does not create a class system of food access. "Conscientious omnivores" may believe that they are eating in a radical and ethical way. However, if one really examines the issues and thinks beyond their taste buds, it has to be agreed that animal products are dangerous for the planet and always cause unnecessary suffering.

What is radical is kindness and nonviolence. We hope most people would agree that these are certainly worthy things to work toward.

TOPICS FOR CRITICAL THINKING AND WRITING

1. If a child starves to death every two seconds (para. 2), how many children die each week? Each year? Does the Taylors' use of statistics impress you? Impress you so much that, if you are a meat-eater, you will stop eating meat, or will at least reduce your consumption of meat? Do the statistics impress you? Why, or why not?

2. Notice the word "onslaught" in the first sentence. How does that sentence compare with, say, "You may have noticed that recently many articles have been published on what is being called the 'new meat movement'"?

3. Paragraph 15 begins with "But." Did you know that a "but" was coming? That is, in reading the earlier paragraphs about "happy meat," did you sense that the writers do *not* favor eating such meat? If so, point out some of the clues the writers provide.

4. In paragraphs 9–10 the authors talk about studies that discuss the "negative effects of soy," and they try to defuse these studies. Are they successful? Why, or why not?

5. In paragraph 10 the authors say, "If people could put aside their biases against these terms ["vegan" and "vegetarian"] they'd see that the animal-rights position is based on very rational argument." First, what is the difference between a vegan and a vegetarian? Second, have the Taylors convinced you that their argument is rational? Why, or why not?

6. Do you agree with the assertion (para. 11) that "to cause unnecessary suffering is unethical"? If so, and if you are a meat-eater and you are pretty sure that animals that are raised for slaughter *do* suffer from extreme confinement, are you content to remain unethical? Explain.

7. The Taylors refer to "the right to live" (para. 13). How do you think the argument should go that we have (or don't have) such a right?

8. In paragraph 15 the authors say (responding to the argument that animals eat animals), "Appealing to nature as a justification for ethical belief is a fallacy." Do you agree? Why, or why not?

9. Is the argument against eating meat essentially the same as the argument against eating baby humans? Explain your answer.

Peter Singer

Peter Singer (b. 1946) is the Ira W. DeCamp Professor of Bioethics at Princeton University. A native of Australia, he is a graduate of the University of Melbourne and Oxford University and the author or editor of more than two dozen books, including Animal Liberation *(1975),* Practical Ethics *(1979),* Rethinking Life and Death *(1995), and* One World: The Ethics of Globalization *(2002). He has written on a variety of ethical issues, but he is especially known for caring about the welfare of animals.*

This essay originally appeared in the New York Review of Books *(April 5, 1973), as a review of* Animals, Men and Morals, *edited by Stanley and Roslind Godlovitch and John Harris.*

Animal Liberation

I

We are familiar with Black Liberation, Gay Liberation, and a variety of other movements. With Women's Liberation some thought we had come to the end of the road. Discrimination on the basis of sex, it has been said, is the last form of discrimination that is universally accepted and practiced without pretense, even in those liberal circles which have long prided themselves on their freedom from racial discrimination. But one should always be wary of talking of "the last remaining form of discrimination." If we have learned anything from the liberation movements, we should have learned how difficult it is to be aware of the ways in which we discriminate until they are forcefully pointed out to us. A liberation movement demands an expansion of our moral horizons, so that practices that were previously regarded as natural and inevitable are now seen as intolerable.

Animals, Men and Morals is a manifesto for an Animal Liberation movement. The contributors to the book may not all see the issue this way. They are a varied group. Philosophers, ranging from professors to graduate students, make up the largest contingent. There are five of them, including the three editors, and there is also an extract from the unjustly neglected German philosopher with an English name, Leonard Nelson, who died in 1927. There are essays by two novelist/critics, Brigid Brophy and Maureen Duffy, and another by Muriel the Lady Dowding, widow of Dowding of Battle of Britain fame and the founder of "Beauty without Cruelty," a movement that campaigns against the use of animals for furs and cosmetics. The other pieces are by a psychologist, a botanist, a sociologist, and Ruth Harrison, who is probably best described as a professional campaigner for animal welfare.

Whether or not these people, as individuals, would all agree that they are launching a liberation movement for animals, the book as a whole amounts to no less. It is a demand for a complete change in our attitudes to nonhumans. It is a demand that we cease to regard the exploitation of other species as natural and inevitable, and that, instead, we see it as a continuing moral outrage. Patrick Corbett, Professor of Philosophy at Sussex University, captures the spirit of the book in his closing words:

> We require now to extend the great principles of liberty, equality, and fraternity over the lives of animals. Let animal slavery join human slavery in the graveyard of the past.

The reader is likely to be skeptical. "Animal Liberation" sounds more like a parody of liberation movements than a serious objective. The reader may think: We support the claims of blacks and women for equality because blacks and women really are equal to whites and males—equal in intelligence and in abilities, capacity for leadership, rationality, and so on. Humans and nonhumans obviously are not equal in these respects. Since justice demands only that we treat equals equally, unequal treatment of humans and nonhumans cannot be an injustice.

This is a tempting reply, but a dangerous one. It commits the non- 5 racist and nonsexist to a dogmatic belief that blacks and women really are just as intelligent, able, etc., as whites and males—and no more. Quite possibly this happens to be the case. Certainly attempts to prove that racial or sexual differences in these respects have a genetic origin have not been conclusive. But do we really want to stake our demand for equality on the assumption that there are no genetic differences of this kind between the different races or sexes? Surely the appropriate response to those who claim to have found evidence for such genetic differences is not to stick to the belief that there are no differences, whatever the evidence to the contrary; rather one should be clear that the claim to equality does not depend on IQ. Moral equality is distinct from factual equality. Otherwise it would be nonsense to talk to the equality of human beings, since humans, as individuals, obviously differ in intelligence and almost any ability one cares to name. If possessing greater intelligence does not entitle one human to exploit another, why should it entitle humans to exploit nonhumans?

Jeremy Bentham expressed the essential basis of equality in his famous formula: "Each to count for one and none for more than one." In other words, the interests of every being that has interests are to be taken into account and treated equally with the like interests of any other being. Other moral philosophers, before and after Bentham, have made the same point in different ways. Our concern for others must not depend on whether they possess certain characteristics, though just what that concern involves may, of course, vary according to such characteristics.

Bentham, incidentally, was well aware that the logic of the demand for racial equality did not stop at the equality of humans. He wrote:

> The day *may* come when the rest of the animal creation may acquire those rights which never could have been withholden from them but

by the hand of tyranny. The French have already discovered that the blackness of the skin is no reason why a human being should be abandoned without redress to the caprice of a tormentor. It may one day come to be recognized that the number of the legs, the villosity of the skin, or the termination of the *os sacrum*, are reasons equally insufficient for abandoning a sensitive being to the same fate. What else is it that should trace the insuperable line? Is it the faculty of reason, or perhaps the faculty of discourse? But a full-grown horse or dog is beyond comparison a more rational, as well as a more conversable animal, than an infant of a day, or a week, or even a month, old. But suppose they were otherwise, what would it avail? The question is not, Can they *reason*? nor Can they *talk*? but, Can they *suffer*?[1]

Surely Bentham was right. If a being suffers, there can be no moral justification for refusing to take that suffering into consideration, and, indeed, to count it equally with the like suffering (if rough comparisons can be made) of any other being.

So the only question is: Do animals other than man suffer? Most people agree unhesitatingly that animals like cats and dogs can and do suffer, and this seems also to be assumed by those laws that prohibit wanton cruelty to such animals. Personally, I have no doubt at all about this and find it hard to take seriously the doubts that a few people apparently do have. The editors and contributors of *Animals, Men and Morals* seem to feel the same way, for although the question is raised more than once, doubts are quickly dismissed each time. Nevertheless, because this is such a fundamental point, it is worth asking what grounds we have for attributing suffering to other animals.

It is best to begin by asking what grounds any individual human has for supposing that other humans feel pain. Since pain is a state of consciousness, a "mental event," it can never be directly observed. No observations, whether behavioral signs such as writhing or screaming or physiological or neurological recordings, are observations of pain itself. Pain is something one feels, and one can only infer that others are feeling it from various external indications. The fact that only philosophers are ever skeptical about whether other humans feel pain shows that we regard such inference as justifiable in the case of humans.

Is there any reason why the same inference should be unjustifiable 10 for other animals? Nearly all the external signs which lead us to infer pain in other humans can be seen in other species, especially "higher" animals such as mammals and birds. Behavioral signs — writhing, yelping, or other forms of calling, attempts to avoid the source of pain, and many others — are present. We know, too, that these animals are biologically similar in the relevant respects, having nervous systems like ours which can be observed to function as ours do.

[1] *The Principles of Morals and Legislation,* ch. XVII, sec. 1, footnote to paragraph 4. [All notes are the author's unless otherwise specified.]

So the grounds for inferring that these animals can feel pain are nearly as good as the grounds for inferring other humans do. Only nearly, for there is one behavioral sign that humans have but nonhumans, with the exception of one or two specially raised chimpanzees, do not have. This, of course, is a developed language. As the quotation from Bentham indicates, this has long been regarded as an important distinction between man and other animals. Other animals may communicate with each other, but not in the way we do. Following Chomsky,[2] many people now mark this distinction by saying that only humans communicate in a form that is governed by rules of syntax. (For the purposes of this argument, linguists allow those chimpanzees who have learned a syntactic sign language to rank as honorary humans.) Nevertheless, as Bentham pointed out, this distinction is not relevant to the question of how animals ought to be treated, unless it can be linked to the issue of whether animals suffer.

This link may be attempted in two ways. First, there is a hazy line of philosophical thought, stemming perhaps from some doctrines associated with Wittgenstein, which maintains that we cannot meaningfully attribute states of consciousness to beings without language. I have not seen this argument made explicit in print, though I have come across it in conversation. This position seems to me very implausible, and I doubt that it would be held at all if it were not thought to be a consequence of a broader view of the significance of language. It may be that the use of a public, rule-governed language is a precondition of conceptual thought. It may even be, although personally I doubt it, that we cannot meaningfully speak of a creature having an intention unless that creature can use a language. But states like pain, surely, are more primitive than either of these, and seem to have nothing to do with language.

Indeed, as Jane Goodall points out in her study of chimpanzees, when it comes to the expression of feelings and emotions, humans tend to fall back on nonlinguistic modes of communication which are often found among apes, such as a cheering pat on the back, an exuberant embrace, a clasp of hands, and so on.[3] Michael Peters makes a similar point in his contribution to *Animals, Men and Morals* when he notes that the basic signals we use to convey pain, fear, sexual arousal, and so on are not specific to our species. So there seems to be no reason at all to believe that a creature without language cannot suffer.

The second, and more easily appreciated way of linking language and the existence of pain is to say that the best evidence that we can have that another creature is in pain is when he tells us that he is. This is a distinct line of argument, for it is not being denied that a non-language-user conceivably could suffer, but only that we could know that he is suffering. Still, this line of argument seems to me to fail, and for reasons similar to

[2]**Chomsky** Noam Chomsky (b. 1928), a professor of linguistics and the author of (among other books) *Language and Mind* (1972). [Editors' note.]
[3]Jane van Lawick-Goodall, *In the Shadow of Man* (Houghton Mifflin, 1971), p. 225.

those just given. "I am in pain" is not the best possible evidence that the speaker is in pain (he might be lying) and it is certainly not the only possible evidence. Behavioral signs and knowledge of the animal's biological similarity to ourselves together provide adequate evidence that animals do suffer. After all, we would not accept linguistic evidence if it contradicted the rest of the evidence. If a man was severely burned, and behaved as if he were in pain, writhing, groaning, being very careful not to let his burned skin touch anything, and so on, but later said he had not been in pain at all, we would be more likely to conclude that he was lying or suffering from amnesia than that he had not been in pain.

Even if there were stronger grounds for refusing to attribute pain to those who do not have a language, the consequences of this refusal might lead us to examine these grounds unusually critically. Human infants, as well as some adults, are unable to use language. Are we to deny that a year-old infant can suffer? If not, how can language be crucial? Of course, most parents can understand the responses of even very young infants better than they understand the responses of other animals, and sometimes infant responses can be understood in the light of later development. 15

This, however, is just a fact about the relative knowledge we have of our own species and other species, and most of this knowledge is simply derived from closer contact. Those who have studied the behavior of other animals soon learn to understand their responses at least as well as we understand those of an infant. (I am not referring to Jane Goodall's and other well-known studies of apes. Consider, for example, the degree of understanding achieved by Tinbergen from watching herring gulls.[4]) Just as we can understand infant human behavior in the light of adult human behavior, so we can understand the behavior of other species in the light of our own behavior (and sometimes we can understand our own behavior better in the light of the behavior of other species).

The grounds we have for believing that other mammals and birds suffer are, then, closely analogous to the grounds we have for believing that other humans suffer. It remains to consider how far down the evolutionary scale this analogy holds. Obviously it becomes poorer when we get further away from man. To be more precise would require a detailed examination of all that we know about other forms of life. With fish, reptiles, and other vertebrates the analogy still seems strong, with molluscs like oysters it is much weaker. Insects are more difficult, and it may be that in our present state of knowledge we must be agnostic about whether they are capable of suffering.

If there is no moral justification for ignoring suffering when it occurs, and it does occur in other species, what are we to say of our attitudes toward these other species? Richard Ryder, one of the contributors to *Animals, Men and Morals*, uses the term "speciesism" to describe the belief that we are entitled to treat members of other species in a way in

[4]N. Tinbergen, *The Herring Gull's World* (Basic Books, 1961).

which it would be wrong to treat members of our own species. The term is not euphonious, but it neatly makes the analogy with racism. The nonracist would do well to bear the analogy in mind when he is inclined to defend human behavior toward nonhumans. "Shouldn't we worry about improving the lot of our own species before we concern ourselves with other species?" he may ask. If we substitute "race" for "species" we shall see that the question is better not asked. "Is a vegetarian diet nutritionally adequate?" resembles the slaveowner's claim that he and the whole economy of the South would be ruined without slave labor. There is even a parallel with skeptical doubts about whether animals suffer, for some defenders of slavery professed to doubt whether blacks really suffer in the way whites do.

I do not want to give the impression, however, that the case for Animal Liberation is based on the analogy with racism and no more. On the contrary, *Animals, Men and Morals* describes the various ways in which humans exploit nonhumans, and several contributors consider the defenses that have been offered, including the defense of meat-eating mentioned in the last paragraph. Sometimes the rebuttals are scornfully dismissive, rather than carefully designed to convince the detached critic. This may be a fault, but it is a fault that is inevitable, given the kind of book this is. The issue is not one on which one can remain detached. As the editors state in their Introduction:

> Once the full force of moral assessment has been made explicit there
> can be no rational excuse left for killing animals, be they killed for
> food, science, or sheer personal indulgence. We have not assembled this
> book to provide the reader with yet another manual on how to make
> brutalities less brutal. Compromise, in the traditional sense of the term,
> is simple unthinking weakness when one considers the actual reasons
> for our crude relationships with the other animals.

The point is that on this issue there are few critics who are genuinely 20 detached. People who eat pieces of slaughtered nonhumans every day find it hard to believe that they are doing wrong; and they also find it hard to imagine what else they could eat. So for those who do not place nonhumans beyond the pale of morality, there comes a stage when further argument seems pointless, a stage at which one can only accuse one's opponent of hypocrisy and reach for the sort of sociological account of our practices and the way we defend them that is attempted by David Wood in his contribution to his book. On the other hand, to those unconvinced by the arguments, and unable to accept that they are merely rationalizing their dietary preferences and their fear of being thought peculiar, such sociological explanations can only seem insultingly arrogant.

II

The logic of speciesism is most apparent in the practice of experimenting on nonhumans in order to benefit humans. This is because the issue is rarely obscured by allegations that nonhumans are so different from humans that we cannot know anything about whether they suffer. The defender of vivisection cannot use this argument because he needs to stress the similarities between man and other animals in order to justify the usefulness to the former of experiments on the latter. The researcher who makes rats choose between starvation and electric shocks to see if they develop ulcers (they do) does so because he knows that the rat has a nervous system very similar to man's, and presumably feels an electric shock in a similar way.

Richard Ryder's restrained account of experiments on animals made me angrier with my fellow men than anything else in this book. Ryder, a clinical psychologist by profession, himself experimented on animals before he came to hold the view he puts forward in his essay. Experimenting on animals is now a large industry, both academic and commercial. In 1969, more than 5 million experiments were performed in Britain, the vast majority without anesthetic (though how many of these involved pain is not known). There are no accurate U.S. figures, since there is no federal law on the subject, and in many cases no state law either. Estimates vary from 20 million to 200 million. Ryder suggests that 80 million may be the best guess. We tend to think that this is all for vital medical research, but of course it is not. Huge numbers of animals are used in university departments from Forestry to Psychology, and even more are used for commercial purposes, to test whether cosmetics can cause skin damage, or shampoos eye damage, or to test food additives or laxatives or sleeping pills or anything else.

A standard test for foodstuffs is the "LD50." The object of this test is to find the dosage level at which 50 percent of the test animals will die. This means that nearly all of them will become very sick before finally succumbing or surviving. When the substance is a harmless one, it may be necessary to force huge doses down the animals, until in some cases sheer volume or concentration causes death.

Ryder gives a selection of experiments, taken from recent scientific journals. I will quote two, not for the sake of indulging in gory details, but in order to give an idea of what normal researchers think they may legitimately do to other species. The point is not that the individual researchers are cruel men, but that they are behaving in a way that is allowed by our speciesist attitudes. As Ryder points out, even if only 1 percent of the experiments involve severe pain, that is 50,000 experiments in Britain each year, or nearly 150 every day (and about fifteen times as many in the United States, if Ryder's guess is right). Here then are two experiments:

O. S. Ray and R. J. Barrett of Pittsburgh gave electric shocks to the feet of 1,042 mice. They then caused convulsions by giving more intense shocks through cup-shaped electrodes applied to the animals' eyes or through pressure spring clips attached to their ears. Unfortunately some of the mice who "successfully completed Day One training were found sick or dead prior to testing on Day Two." [*Journal of Comparative and Physiological Psychology,* 1969, vol. 67, pp. 110–116]

At the National Institute for Medical Research, Mill Hill, London, W. Feldberg and S. L. Sherwood injected chemicals into the brains of cats—"with a number of widely different substances, recurrent patterns of reaction were obtained. Retching, vomiting, defecation, increased salivation and greatly accelerated respiration leading to panting were common features." . . .

The injection into the brain of a large dose of Tubocuraine caused the cat to jump "from the table to the floor and then straight into its cage, where it started calling more and more noisily whilst moving about restlessly and jerkily . . . finally the cat fell with legs and neck flexed, jerking in rapid clonic movements, the condition being that of a major [epileptic] convulsion . . . within a few seconds the cat got up, ran for a few yards at high speed, and fell in another fit. The whole process was repeated several times within the next ten minutes, during which the cat lost faeces and foamed at the mouth."

This animal finally died thirty-five minutes after the brain injection. [*Journal of Physiology,* 1954, vol. 123, pp. 148–167]

There is nothing secret about these experiments. One has only to open any recent volume of a learned journal, such as the *Journal of Comparative and Physiological Psychology,* to find full descriptions of experiments of this sort, together with the results obtained—results that are frequently trivial and obvious. The experiments are often supported by public funds. 25

It is a significant indication of the level of acceptability of these practices that, although these experiments are taking place at this moment on university campuses throughout the country, there has, so far as I know, not been the slightest protest from the student movement. Students have been rightly concerned that their universities should not discriminate on grounds of race or sex, and that they should not serve the purposes of the military or big business. Speciesism continues undisturbed, and many students participate in it. There may be a few qualms at first, but since everyone regards it as normal, and it may even be a required part of a course, the student soon becomes hardened and, dismissing his earlier feelings as "mere sentiment," comes to regard animals as statistics rather than sentient beings with interests that warrant consideration.

Argument about vivisection has often missed the point because it has been put in absolutist terms: Would the abolitionist be prepared to let thousands die if they could be saved by experimenting on a single animal? The way to reply to this purely hypothetical question is to pose another: Would the experimenter be prepared to experiment on a human orphan under six months old, if it were the only way to save many lives? (I say "orphan" to avoid the complication of parental feelings, although in doing so I am being overfair to the experimenter, since the nonhuman subjects of experiments are not orphans.) A negative answer to this question indicates that the experimenter's readiness to use nonhumans is simple discrimination, for adult apes, cats, mice, and other mammals are more conscious of what is happening to them, more self-directing, and, so far as we can tell, just as sensitive to pain as a human infant. There is no characteristic that human infants possess that adult mammals do not have to the same or a higher degree.

(It might be possible to hold that what makes it wrong to experiment on a human infant is that the infant will in time develop into more than the nonhuman, but one would then, to be consistent, have to oppose abortion, and perhaps contraception, too, for the fetus and the egg and sperm have the same potential as the infant. Moreover, one would still have no reason for experimenting on a nonhuman rather than a human with brain damage severe enough to make it impossible for him to rise above infant level.)

The experimenter, then, shows a bias for his own species whenever he carries out an experiment on a nonhuman for a purpose that he would not think justified him in using a human being at an equal or lower level of sentience, awareness, ability to be self-directing, etc. No one familiar with the kind of results yielded by these experiments can have the slightest doubt that if this bias were eliminated the number of experiments performed would be zero or very close to it.

III

If it is vivisection that shows the logic of speciesism most clearly, it is 30 the use of other species for food that is at the heart of our attitudes toward them. Most of *Animals, Men and Morals* is an attack on meat eating—an attack which is based solely on concern for nonhumans, without reference to arguments derived from consideration of ecology, macrobiotics, health, or religion.

The idea that nonhumans are utilities, means to our ends, pervades our thought. Even conservationists who are concerned about the slaughter of wildfowl but not about the vastly greater slaughter of chickens for our tables are thinking in this way—they are worried about what we would lose if there were less wildlife. Stanley Godlovitch, pursuing the Marxist idea that our thinking is formed by the activities we undertake in satisfying our needs, suggests that man's first classification of his environment was into Edibles and Inedibles. Most animals came into the first category, and there they have remained.

Man may always have killed other species for food, but he has never exploited them so ruthlessly as he does today. Farming has succumbed to business methods, the objective being to get the highest possible ratio of output (meat, eggs, milk) to input (fodder, labor costs, etc.). Ruth Harrison's essay "On Factory Farming" gives an account of some aspects of modern methods, and of the unsuccessful British campaigns for effective controls, a campaign which was sparked off by her *Animal Machines* (London: Stuart, 1964).

Her article is in no way a substitute for her earlier book. This is a pity since, as she says, "Farm produce is still associated with mental pictures of animals browsing in the fields . . . of hens having a last forage before going to roost. . . ." Yet neither in her article nor elsewhere in *Animals, Men and Morals* is this false image replaced by a clear idea of the nature and extent of factory farming. We learn of this only indirectly, when we hear of the code of reform proposed by an advisory committee set up by the British government.

Among the proposals, which the government refused to implement on the grounds that they were too idealistic, were: *"Any animal should at least have room to turn around freely."*

Factory farm animals need liberation in the most literal sense. Veal calves are kept in stalls 5 feet by 2 feet. They are usually slaughtered when about four months old, and have been too big to turn in their stalls for at least a month. Intensive beef herds, kept in stalls only proportionately larger for much longer periods, account for a growing percentage of beef production. Sows are often similarly confined when pregnant, which, because of artificial methods of increasing fertility, can be most of the time. Animals confined in this way do not waste food by exercising, nor do they develop unpalatable muscle. 35

"A dry bedded area should be provided for all stock." Intensively kept animals usually have to stand and sleep in slatted floors without straw, because this makes cleaning easier.

"Palatable roughage must be readily available to all calves after one week of age." In order to produce the pale veal housewives are said to prefer, calves are fed on an all-liquid diet until slaughter, even though they are long past the age at which they would normally eat grass. They develop a craving for roughage, evidenced by attempts to gnaw wood from their stalls. (For the same reason, their diet is deficient in iron.)

"Battery cages for poultry should be large enough for a bird to be able to stretch one wing at a time." Under current British practice, a cage for four or five laying hens has a floor area of 20 inches by 18 inches, scarcely larger than a double page of the *New York Review of Books*. In this space, on a sloping wire floor (sloping so the eggs roll down, wire so the dung drips through) the birds live for a year or eighteen months while artificial lighting and temperature conditions combine with drugs in their food to squeeze the maximum number of eggs out of them. Table birds are also sometimes kept in cages. More often they are reared in sheds, no less crowded. Under these conditions all the birds' natural activities are frustrated, and they develop "vices" such as pecking each other to death. To prevent this, beaks are often cut off, and the sheds kept dark.

How many of those who support factory farming by buying its produce know anything about the way it is produced? How many have heard something about it, but are reluctant to check up for fear that it will make them uncomfortable? To nonspeciesists, the typical consumer's mixture of ignorance, reluctance to find out the truth, and vague belief that nothing really bad could be allowed seems analogous to the attitudes of "decent Germans" to the death camps.

There are, of course, some defenders of factory farming. Their argu- 40 ments are considered, though again rather sketchily, by John Harris. Among the most common: "Since they have never known anything else, they don't suffer." This argument will not be put by anyone who knows anything about animal behavior, since he will know that not all behavior has to be learned. Chickens attempt to stretch wings, walk around, scratch, and even dustbathe or build a nest, even though they have never lived under conditions that allowed these activities. Calves can suffer from maternal deprivation no matter at what age they were taken from their mothers. "We need these intensive methods to provide protein for a growing population." As ecologists and famine relief organizations know, we can produce far more protein per acre if we grow the right vegetable crop, soy beans for instance, than if we use the land to grow crops to be converted into protein by animals who use nearly 90 percent of the protein themselves, even when unable to exercise.

There will be many readers of this book who will agree that factory farming involves an unjustifiable degree of exploitation of sentient creatures, and yet will want to say that there is nothing wrong with rearing animals for food, provided it is done "humanely." These people are saying, in effect, that although we should not cause animals to suffer, there is nothing wrong with killing them.

There are two possible replies to this view. One is to attempt to show that this combination of attitudes is absurd. Roslind Godlovitch takes this course in her essay, which is an examination of some common attitudes to animals. She argues that from the combination of "animal suffering is to be avoided" and "there is nothing wrong with killing animals" it follows that all animal life ought to be exterminated (since all sentient creatures will suffer to some degree at some point in their lives). Euthanasia is a contentious issue only because we place some value on living. If we did not, the least amount of suffering would justify it. Accordingly, if we deny that we have a duty to exterminate all animal life, we must concede that we are placing some value on animal life.

This argument seems to me valid, although one could still reply that the value of animal life is to be derived from the pleasures that life can have for them, so that, provided their lives have a balance of pleasure over pain, we are justified in rearing them. But this would imply that we ought to produce animals and let them live as pleasantly as possible, without suffering.

At this point, one can make the second of the two possible replies to the view that rearing and killing animals for food is all right so long as it is done humanely. This second reply is that so long as we think that a nonhuman may be killed simply so that a human can satisfy his taste for meat, we are still thinking of nonhumans as means rather than as ends in themselves. The factory farm is nothing more than the application of technology to this concept. Even traditional methods involve castration, the separation of mothers and their young, the breaking up of herds, branding or earpunching, and of course transportation to the abattoirs and the final moments of terror when the animal smells blood and senses danger. If we were to try rearing animals so that they lived and died without suffering, we should find that to do so on anything like the scale of today's meat industry would be a sheer impossibility. Meat would become the prerogative of the rich.

I have been able to discuss only some of the contributions to this   45 book, saying nothing about, for instance, the essays on killing for furs and for sport. Nor have I considered all the detailed questions that need to be asked once we start thinking about other species in the radically different way presented by this book. What, for instance, are we to do about genuine conflicts of interest like rats biting slum children? I am not sure of the answer, but the essential point is just that we *do* see this as a conflict of interests, that we recognize that rats have interests too. Then we may begin to think about other ways of resolving the conflict—perhaps by leaving out rat baits that sterilize the rats instead of killing them.

I have not discussed such problems because they are side issues compared with the exploitation of other species for food and for experimental purposes. On these central matters, I hope that I have said enough to show that this book, despite its flaws, is a challenge to every human to recognize his attitudes to nonhumans as a form of prejudice no less objectionable than racism or sexism. It is a challenge that demands not just a change of attitudes, but a change in our way of life, for it requires us to become vegetarians.

Can a purely moral demand of this kind succeed? The odds are certainly against it. The book holds out no inducements. It does not tell us that we will become healthier, or enjoy life more, if we cease exploiting animals. Animal Liberation will require greater altruism on the part of mankind than any other liberation movement, since animals are incapable of demanding it for themselves, or of protesting against their exploitation by votes, demonstrations, or bombs. Is man capable of such genuine altruism? Who knows? If this book does have a significant effect, however, it will be a vindication of all those who have believed that man has within himself the potential for more than cruelty and selfishness.

Topics for Critical Thinking and Writing

1. In his fourth paragraph Singer formulates an argument on behalf of the skeptical reader. Examine that argument closely, restate it in your own words, and evaluate it. Which of its premises is most vulnerable to criticism? Why?

2. Singer quotes with approval (para. 7) Bentham's comment, "The question is not, Can they *reason*? nor Can they *talk*? but, Can they *suffer*?" Do

you find this argument persuasive? Can you think of any effective challenge to it?

3. Singer allows that although developed linguistic capacity is not necessary for a creature to have pain, perhaps such a capacity is necessary for "having an intention" (para. 12). Do you think this concession is correct? Have you ever seen animal behavior that you would be willing to describe or explain as evidence that the animal has an intention to do something, despite knowing that the animal cannot talk?

4. Singer thinks that the readiness to experiment on animals argues against believing that animals don't suffer pain (see para. 21). Do you agree with this reasoning?

5. Singer confesses (para. 22) to being made especially angry "with my fellow men" after reading the accounts of animal experimentation. What is it that aroused his anger? Do such feelings, and the acknowledgment that one has them, have any place in a sober discussion about the merits of animal experimentation? Why, or why not?

6. What is "factory farming" (paras. 32–40)? Why is Singer opposed to it?

7. To the claim that there is nothing wrong with "rearing animals for food," provided it is done "humanely" (para. 41), Singer offers two replies (paras. 42–44). In an essay of 250 words summarize them briefly, and then indicate whether either persuades you and why or why not.

8. Suppose someone were to say to Singer: "You claim that capacity to suffer is the relevant factor in deciding whether a creature deserves to be treated as my moral equal. But you're wrong. The relevant factor is whether the creature is *alive*. Being alive is what matters, not being capable of feeling pain." In one or two paragraphs declare what you think would be Singer's reply.

9. Do you think it is worse to kill an animal for its fur than to kill, cook, and eat an animal? Is it worse to kill an animal for sport than to kill it for medical experimentation? What is Singer's view? Explain your view, making use of Singer's if you wish, in an essay of 500 words.

10. Are there any arguments, in your opinion, that show the immorality of eating human flesh (cannibalism) but that do not show a similar objection to eating animal flesh? Write a 500-word essay in which you discuss the issue.

Jonathan Swift

Jonathan Swift (1667–1745) was born in Ireland of English stock. An Anglican clergyman, he became Dean of St. Patrick's in Dublin in 1723, but the post he really wanted, one of high office in England, was never given to him. A prolific pamphleteer on religious and political issues, Swift today is known not as a churchman but as a satirist. His best-known works are Gulliver's Travels *(1726, a serious satire but now popularly thought of as a children's book) and "A Modest Proposal" (1729). In "A Modest Proposal," which was published anonymously, Swift addresses the great suffering that the Irish endured under the British.*

A Modest Proposal

For Preventing the Children of Poor People in Ireland from Being a Burden to Their Parents or Country, and for Making Them Beneficial to the Public

It is a melancholy object to those who walk through this great town or travel in the country, when they see the streets, the roads, and cabin doors, crowded with beggars of the female sex, followed by three, four, or six children, all in rags and importuning every passenger for an alms. These mothers, instead of being able to work for their honest livelihood, are forced to employ all their time in strolling to beg sustenance for their helpless infants: who as they grow up either turn thieves for want of work, or leave their dear native country to fight for the Pretender in Spain, or sell themselves to the Barbadoes.

I think it is agreed by all parties that this prodigious number of children in the arms, or on the backs, or at the heels of their mothers, and frequently of their fathers, is in the present deplorable state of the kingdom a very great additional grievance; and, therefore, whoever could find out a fair, cheap, and easy method of making these children sound, useful members of the commonwealth, would deserve so well of the public as to have his statue set up for a preserver of the nation.

But my intention is very far from being confined to provide only for the children of professed beggars; it is of a much greater extent, and shall take in the whole number of infants at a certain age who are born of parents in effect as little able to support them as those who demand our charity in the streets.

As to my own part, having turned my thoughts for many years upon this important subject, and maturely weighed the several schemes of our projectors,[1] I have always found them grossly mistaken in their computation. It is true, a child just dropped from its dam may be supported by her milk for a solar year, with little other nourishment; at most not above the value of 2s.,[2] which the mother may certainly get, or the value in scraps, by her lawful occupation of begging; and it is exactly at one year old that I propose to provide for them in such a manner as instead of being a charge upon their parents or the parish, or wanting food and raiment for the rest of their lives, they shall on the contrary contribute to the feeding, and partly to the clothing, of many thousands.

[1]**projectors** Persons who devise plans. [All notes are the editors'.]
[2]**2s** Two shillings.

There is likewise another great advantage in my scheme, that it will 5
prevent those voluntary abortions, and that horrid practice of women
murdering their bastard children, alas! too frequent among us! sacrificing the poor innocent babes I doubt more to avoid the expense than the
shame, which would move tears and pity in the most savage and inhuman breast.

The number of souls in this kingdom being usually reckoned one
million and a half, of these I calculate there may be about 200,000
couple whose wives are breeders; from which number I subtract 30,000
couple who are able to maintain their own children (although I appre-
hend there cannot be so many, under the present distress of the kingdom); but this being granted, there will remain 170,000 breeders. I again
subtract 50,000 for those women who miscarry, or whose children die
by accident or disease within the year. There only remain 120,000 children of poor parents annually born. The question therefore is, how this
number shall be reared and provided for? which, as I have already said,
under the present situation of affairs, is utterly impossible by all the
methods hitherto proposed. For we can neither employ them in handi-
craft or agriculture; we neither build houses (I mean in the country) nor
cultivate land; they can very seldom pick up a livelihood by stealing, till
they arrive at six years old, except where they are of towardly parts;
although I confess they learn the rudiments much earlier; during which
time they can, however, be properly looked upon only as probationers;
as I have been informed by a principal gentleman in the county of
Cavan, who protested to me that he never knew above one or two
instances under the age of six, even in a part of the kingdom so
renowned for the quickest proficiency in that art.

I am assured by our merchants, that a boy or a girl before twelve
years old is no salable commodity; and even when they come to this age
they will not yield above 3£. or 3£. 2s. 6d.[3] at most on the exchange;
which cannot turn to account either to the parents or kingdom, the
charge of nutriment and rags having been at least four times that value.

I shall now therefore humbly propose my own thoughts, which I
hope will not be liable to the least objection.

I have been assured by a very knowing American of my acquaintance in London, that a young healthy child well nursed is at a year old
a most delicious, nourishing, and wholesome food, whether stewed,
roasted, baked, or broiled; and I make no doubt that it will equally serve
in a fricassee or a ragout.

I do therefore humbly offer it to public consideration that of the 10
120,000 children already computed, 20,000 may be reserved for breed,
whereof only one-fourth part to be males; which is more than we allow
to sheep, black cattle, or swine; and my reason is, that these children are
seldom the fruits of marriage, a circumstance not much regarded by our

---

[3]**£. . . . d** £ is an abbreviation for "pound sterling" and *d.*, for "pence."

savages; therefore one male will be sufficient to serve four females. That the remaining 100,000 may, at a year old, be offered in sale to the persons of quality and fortune through the kingdom; always advising the mother to let them suck plentifully in the last month, so as to render them plump and fat for a good table. A child will make two dishes at an entertainment for friends; and when the family dines alone, the fore or hind quarter will make a reasonable dish, and seasoned with a little pepper or salt will be very good boiled on the fourth day, especially in winter.

I have reckoned upon a medium that a child just born will weigh twelve pounds, and in a solar year, if tolerably nursed, will increase to twenty-eight pounds.

I grant this food will be somewhat dear, and therefore very proper for landlords, who, as they have already devoured most of the parents, seem to have the best title to the children.

Infant's flesh will be in season throughout the year, but more plentiful in March, and a little before and after: for we are told by a grave author, an eminent French physician, that fish being a prolific diet, there are more children born in Roman Catholic countries about nine months after Lent than at any other season; therefore, reckoning a year after Lent, the markets will be more glutted than usual, because the number of popish infants is at least three to one in this kingdom: and therefore it will have one other collateral advantage, by lessening the number of papists among us.

I have already computed the charge of nursing a beggar's child (in which list I reckon all cottagers, laborers, and four-fifths of the farmers) to be about 2s. per annum, rags included; and I believe no gentleman would repine to give 10s. for the carcass of a good fat child, which, as I have said, will make four dishes of excellent nutritive meat, when he has only some particular friend or his own family to dine with him. Thus the squire will learn to be a good landlord, and grow popular among the tenants; the mother will have 8s. net profit, and be fit for work till she produces another child.

Those who are more thrifty (as I must confess the times require) may flay the carcass; the skin of which artificially dressed will make admirable gloves for ladies, and summer boots for fine gentlemen. 15

As to our city of Dublin, shambles[4] may be appointed for this purpose in the most convenient parts of it, and butchers we may be assured will not be wanting: although I rather recommend buying the children alive, and dressing them hot from the knife as we do roasting pigs.

A very worthy person, a true lover of his country, and whose virtues I highly esteem, was lately pleased in discoursing on this matter to offer a refinement upon my scheme. He said that many gentlemen of this kingdom, having of late destroyed their deer, he conceived that the want of venison might be well supplied by the bodies of young lads and maidens, not exceeding fourteen years of age nor under twelve; so great a

[4]**shambles** Slaughterhouses.

number of both sexes in every country being now ready to starve for want of work and service; and these to be disposed of by their parents, if alive, or otherwise by their nearest relations. But with due deference to so excellent a friend and so deserving a patriot, I cannot be altogether in his sentiments; for as to the males, my American acquaintance assured me from frequent experience that their flesh was generally tough and lean, like that of our schoolboys by continual exercise, and their taste disagreeable; and to fatten them would not answer the charge. Then as to the females, it would, I think, with humble submission be a loss to the public, because they soon would become breeders themselves: and besides, it is not improbable that some scrupulous people might be apt to censure such a practice (although indeed very unjustly), as a little bordering upon cruelty; which, I confess, has always been with me the strongest objection against any project, how well soever intended.

But in order to justify my friend, he confessed that this expedient was put into his head by the famous Psalmanazar[5] a native of the island Formosa, who came from thence to London about twenty years ago: and in conversation told my friend, that in his country when any young person happened to be put to death, the executioner sold the carcass to persons of quality as a prime dainty; and that in his time the body of a plump girl of fifteen, who was crucified for an attempt to poison the emperor, was sold to his imperial majesty's prime minister of state, and other great mandarins of the court, in joints from the gibbet, at 400 crowns. Neither indeed can I deny, that if the same use were made of several plump young girls in this town, who without one single groat to their fortunes cannot stir abroad without a chair, and appear at the playhouse and assemblies in foreign fineries which they never will pay for, the kingdom would not be the worse.

Some persons of a depending spirit are in great concern about the vast number of poor people, who are aged, diseased, or maimed, and I have been desired to employ my thoughts what course may be taken to ease the nation of so grievous an encumbrance. But I am not in the least pain upon that matter, because it is very well known that they are every day dying and rotting by cold and famine, and filth and vermin, as fast as can be reasonably expected. And as to the young laborers, they are now in as hopeful a condition: They cannot get work, and consequently pine away for want of nourishment, to a degree that if at any time they are accidentally hired to common labor, they have not strength to perform it; and thus the country and themselves are happily delivered from the evils to come.

I have too long digressed, and therefore shall return to my subject. I 20 think the advantages by the proposal which I have made are obvious and many, as well as of the highest importance.

---

[5]**Psalmanazar** George Psalmanazar (c. 1679–1763), a Frenchman who claimed to be from Formosa (now Taiwan); he wrote *An Historical and Geographical Description of Formosa* (1704). The hoax was exposed soon after publication.

For first, as I have already observed, It would greatly lessen the number of papists, with whom we are yearly overrun, being the principal breeders of the nation as well as our most dangerous enemies; and who stay at home on purpose to deliver the kingdom to the Pretender, hoping to take their advantage by the absence of so many good Protestants, who have chosen rather to leave their country than stay at home and pay tithes against their conscience to an Episcopal curate.

Secondly, The poor tenants will have something valuable of their own, which by law may be made liable to distress and help to pay their landlord's rent, their corn and cattle being already seized, and money a thing unknown.

Thirdly, Whereas the maintenance of 100,000 children from two years old and upward, cannot be computed at less than 10s. apiece per annum, the nation's stock will be thereby increased £50,000 per annum, beside the profit of a new dish introduced to the tables of all gentlemen of fortune in the kingdom who have any refinement in taste. And the money will circulate among ourselves, the goods being entirely of our own growth and manufacture.

Fourthly, The constant breeders beside the gain of 8s. sterling per annum by the sale of their children, will be rid of the charge of maintaining them after the first year.

Fifthly, This food would likewise bring great custom to taverns, 25 where the vintners will certainly be so prudent as to procure the best receipts for dressing it to perfection, and consequently have their houses frequented by all the fine gentlemen, who justly value themselves upon their knowledge in good eating; and a skilful cook who understands how to oblige his guests, will contrive to make it as expensive as they please.

Sixthly, This would be a great inducement to marriage, which all wise nations have either encouraged by rewards or enforced by laws and penalties. It would increase the care and tenderness of mothers toward their children, when they were sure of a settlement for life to the poor babes, provided in some sort by the public, to their annual profit instead of expense. We should see an honest emulation among the married women, which of them would bring the fattest child to the market. Men would become as fond of their wives during the time of their pregnancy as they are now of their mares in foal, their cows in calf, their sows when they are ready to farrow; nor offer to beat or kick them (as is too frequent a practice) for fear of a miscarriage.

Many other advantages might be enumerated. For instance, the addition of some thousand carcasses in our exportation of barreled beef, the propagation of swine's flesh, and improvement in the art of making good bacon, so much wanted among us by the great destruction of pigs, too frequent at our table; which are no way comparable in taste or magnificence to a well-grown, fat, yearling child, which roasted whole will make a considerable figure at a lord mayor's feast or any other public entertainment. But this and many others I omit, being studious of brevity.

Supposing that 1,000 families in this city would be constant customers for infants' flesh, besides others who might have it at merry-meetings, particularly at weddings and christenings, I compute that Dublin would take off annually about 20,000 carcasses; and the rest of the kingdom (where probably they will be sold somewhat cheaper) the remaining 80,000.

I can think of no one objection that will possibly be raised against this proposal, unless it should be urged that the number of people will be thereby much lessened in the kingdom. This I freely own, and it was indeed one principal design in offering it to the world. I desire the reader will observe, that I calculate my remedy for this one individual kingdom of Ireland and for no other that ever was, is, or I think ever can be upon earth. Therefore let no man talk to me of other expedients: of taxing our absentees at 5s. a pound; of using neither clothes nor household furniture except what is of our own growth and manufacture; of utterly rejecting the materials and instruments that promote foreign luxury; of curing the expensiveness of pride, vanity, idleness, and gaming in our women; of introducing a vein of parsimony, prudence, and temperance; of learning to love our country, in the want of which we differ even from Laplanders and the inhabitants of Topinamboo; of quitting our animosities and factions, nor acting any longer like the Jews, who were murdering one another at the very moment their city was taken; of being a little cautious not to sell our country and conscience for nothing; of teaching landlords to have at least one degree of mercy toward their tenants; lastly, of putting a spirit of honesty, industry, and skill into our shopkeepers; who, if a resolution could now be taken to buy only our native goods, would immediately unite to cheat and exact upon us in the price the measure, and the goodness, nor could ever yet be brought to make one fair proposal of just dealing, though often and earnestly invited to it.

Therefore I repeat, let no man talk to me of these and the like expedients, till he has at least some glimpse of hope that there will be ever some hearty and sincere attempt to put them in practice.   30

But as to myself, having been wearied out for many years with offering vain, idle, visionary thoughts, and at length utterly despairing of success, I fortunately fell upon this proposal; which, as it is wholly new, so it has something solid and real, of no expense and little trouble, full in our own power, and whereby we can incur no danger in disobliging England. For this kind of commodity will not bear exportation, the flesh being of too tender a consistence to admit a long continuance in salt, although perhaps I could name a country which would be glad to eat up our whole nation without it.

After all, I am not so violently bent upon my own opinion as to reject any offer proposed by wise men, which shall be found equally innocent, cheap, easy, and effectual. But before something of that kind shall be advanced in contradiction to my scheme, and offering a better, I desire the author or authors will be pleased maturely to consider two points. First, as things now stand, how they will be able to find food and raiment for 100,000 useless mouths and backs. And secondly, there being a round million of creatures in human figure throughout this kingdom, whose subsistence put into a common stock would leave them in debt 2,000,000£. sterling, adding those who are beggars by profession to the bulk of farmers, cottagers, and laborers, with the wives and children who are beggars in effect; I desire those politicians who dislike my overture, and may perhaps be so bold as to attempt an answer, that they will first ask the parents of these mortals, whether they would not at this day think it a great happiness to have been sold for food at a year old in the manner I prescribe, and thereby have avoided such a perpetual scene of misfortunes as they have since gone through by the oppression of landlords, the impossibility of paying rent without money or trade, the want of common sustenance, with neither house nor clothes to cover them from the inclemencies of the weather, and the most inevitable prospect of entailing the like or greater miseries upon their breed for ever.

I profess, in the sincerity of my heart, that I have not the least personal interest in endeavoring to promote this necessary work, having no other motive than the public good of my country, by advancing our trade, providing for infants, relieving the poor, and giving some pleasure to the rich. I have no children by which I can propose to get a single penny; the youngest being nine years old, and my wife past childbearing.

Topics for Critical Thinking and Writing

1. In paragraph 4 the speaker of the essay mentions proposals set forth by "projectors" — that is, by advocates of other proposals or projects. On the basis of the first two paragraphs of "A Modest Proposal," how would you characterize *this* projector, the speaker of the essay? Write your characterization in one paragraph. Then, in a second paragraph, characterize the projector as you understand him, having read the entire essay. In your second paragraph, indicate what *he thinks he is* and also what the reader sees he really is.

2. The speaker or persona of "A Modest Proposal" is confident that selling children "for a good table" (para. 10) is a better idea than any of the then current methods of disposing of unwanted children, including abortion and infanticide. Can you think of any argument that might favor abortion or infanticide for parents in dire straits, rather than the projector's scheme?

3. In paragraph 29 the speaker considers, but dismisses out of hand, several other solutions to the wretched plight of the Irish poor. Write a 500-word essay in which you explain each of these ideas and their combined merits as an alternative to the solution he favors.

4. What does the projector imply are the causes of the Irish poverty he deplores? Are there possible causes he has omitted? If so, what are they?

5. Imagine yourself as one of the poor parents to whom Swift refers, and write a 250-word essay explaining why you prefer not to sell your infant to the local butcher.

6. The modern version of the problem to which the proposal is addressed is called "population policy." How would you describe our nation's current population policy? Do we have a population policy, in fact? If not, what would you propose? If we do have one, would you propose any changes in it? Why, or why not?

7. It is sometimes suggested that just as persons need to get a license to drive a car, to hunt with a gun, or to marry, a husband and wife ought to be required to get a license to have a child. Would you favor this idea, assuming that it applied to you as a possible parent? Would Swift? Explain your answers in an essay of 500 words.

8. Consider the six arguments advanced in paragraphs 21 to 26, and write a 1,000-word essay criticizing all of them. Or if you find that one or more of the arguments is really unanswerable, explain why you find it so compelling.

9. Write your own "modest proposal," ironically suggesting a solution to a problem. Possible topics: health care or schooling for the children of illegal immigrants, overcrowded jails, children who have committed a serious crime, homeless people.

6

Developing an Argument
of Your Own

The difficult part in an argument is not to defend one's opinion but to know what it is.

— ANDRÉ MAUROIS

Imagine that you enter a parlor. You come late. When you arrive, others have long preceded you, and they are engaged in a heated discussion, a discussion too heated for them to pause and tell you exactly what it is about. In fact, the discussion had already begun long before any of them got there, so that no one present is qualified to retrace for you all the steps that had gone before. You listen for a while, until you decide that you have caught the tenor of the argument; then you put in your oar. Someone answers; you answer him; another comes to your defense; another aligns himself against you, to either the embarrassment or gratification of your opponent, depending upon the quality of your ally's assistance. However, the discussion is interminable. The hour grows late, you must depart. And you do depart, with the discussion still vigorously in progress.

— KENNETH BURKE

No greater misfortune could happen to anyone than that of developing a dislike for argument.

— PLATO

PLANNING, DRAFTING, AND REVISING AN ARGUMENT

First, hear the wisdom of Mark Twain: "When the Lord finished the world, He pronounced it good. That is what I said about my first work, too. But Time, I tell you, Time takes the confidence out of these incautious early opinions."

All of us, teachers and students, have our moments of confidence, but for the most part we know that it takes considerable effort to write clear, thoughtful, seemingly effortless prose. In a conversation we can cover our-selves with such expressions as "Well, I don't know, but I sort of think . . . ," and we can always revise our position ("Oh, well, I didn't mean it that way"), but once we have handed in the final version of our writing, we are helpless. We are (putting it strongly) naked to our enemies.

Getting Ideas

In Chapter 1 we quoted Robert Frost, "To learn to write is to learn to have ideas," and we offered suggestions about getting ideas, a process traditionally called **invention.** A moment ago we said that we often improve our ideas when we try to explain them to someone else. Partly, of course, we are responding to questions or objections raised by our companion in the conversation. But partly we are responding to our-selves: Almost as soon as we hear what we have to say, we may find that it won't do, and, if we are lucky, we may find a better idea surfacing. One of the best ways of getting ideas is to talk things over.

The process of talking things over usually begins with the text that you are reading: Your marginal notes, your summary, and your queries parenthetically incorporated within your summary are a kind of dia-logue between you and the author you are reading. More obviously, when you talk with friends about your topic, you are trying out and developing ideas. Finally, after reading, taking notes, and talking, you may feel that you now have clear ideas and need only put them into writing. And so you take a sheet of blank paper, and perhaps a paralyz-ing thought suddenly strikes: "I have ideas but just can't put them into words."

Despite what many people believe,

- Writing is not only a matter of putting one's ideas into words.
- Just as talking with others is a way of getting ideas, *writing is a way of getting and developing ideas.*

Writing, in short, can be an important part of critical thinking. One big reason we have trouble writing is our fear of putting ourselves on record, but another big reason is our fear that we have no ideas worth putting down. But by jotting down notes—or even free associations— and by writing a draft, however weak, we can help ourselves to think our way toward good ideas.

Freewriting   Writing for five or six minutes, nonstop, without censoring what you produce is one way of getting words down on paper that will help to lead to improved thoughts. Some people who write on a com-puter find it useful to dim the screen so they won't be tempted to look up and fiddle too soon with what they have just written. Later they illu-minate the screen, scroll back, and notice some keywords or passages that can be used later in drafting a paper.

Listing   Jotting down items, just as you do when you make a shopping list, is another way of getting ideas. When you make a shopping list, you write *ketchup,* and the act of writing it reminds you that you also need hamburger rolls—and *that* in turn reminds you (who knows how or why?) that you also need a can of tuna fish. Similarly, when you prepare a list of ideas for a paper, jotting down one item will generate another. Of course, when you look over the list, you will probably drop some of these ideas—the dinner menu will change—but you are making progress.

Diagramming   Sketching some sort of visual representation of an essay is a kind of listing. Three methods of diagramming are especially common:

- **Clustering**   Write, in the middle of a sheet of paper, a word or phrase summarizing your topic (for instance, *health care;* see diagram, below), circle it, and then write down and circle a related word (for example, *gov't-provided*). Perhaps this leads you to write *higher taxes,* and you then circle this phrase and connect it to *gov't-provided.* The next thing that occurs to you is *employer-provided*— and so you write this down and circle it. You will not connect this to *higher taxes,* but you will connect it to *health care* because it is a sort of parallel to *gov't-provided.* The next thing that occurs to you is *unemployed people.* This category does not connect easily with *employer-provided,* so you won't connect these two terms with a line, but you probably will connect *unemployed people* with *health care* and maybe also with *gov't-provided.* Keep going, jotting down ideas, and making connections where possible, indicating relationships.

- **Branching**   Some writers find it useful to build a tree, moving from the central topic to the main branches (chief ideas) and then to the twigs (aspects of the chief ideas).

- **Comparing in columns**   Draw a line down the middle of the page, and then set up two columns showing oppositions. For instance, if you are concerned with health care, you might head one column *gov't-provided* and the other *employer-provided.* Under

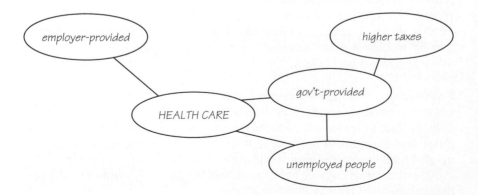

the first column, you might write *covers unemployed,* and under the second column, you might write *omits unemployed.* You might go on to write, under the first column, *higher taxes,* and under the second, *higher prices*—or whatever else relevant comes to mind.

All of these methods can, of course, be executed with pen and paper, but you may also be able to use them on your computer depending on the capabilities of your software.

Whether you are using a computer or a pen, you put down some words and almost immediately see that they need improvement, not simply a little polishing but a substantial overhaul. You write, "Race should be counted in college admissions for two reasons," and as soon as you write these words, a third reason comes to mind. Or perhaps one of those "two reasons" no longer seems very good. As E. M. Forster said, "How can I know what I think till I see what I say?" We have to see what we say, we have to get something down on paper, before we realize that we need to make it better.

Writing, then, is really **rewriting**—that is, **revising**—and a revision is a *re-vision,* a second look. The paper that you hand in should be clear and may even seem effortless to the reader, but in all likelihood the clarity and apparent ease are the result of a struggle with yourself, a struggle during which you greatly improved your first thoughts. You begin by putting down your ideas, such as they are, perhaps even in the random order in which they occurred, but sooner or later comes the job of looking at them critically, developing what is useful in them and chucking out what is not. If you follow this procedure you will be in the company of Picasso, who said that he "advanced by means of destruction."

Whether you advance bit by bit (writing a sentence, revising it, writing the next, and so on) or whether you write an entire first draft and then revise it and revise it again and again is chiefly a matter of temperament. Probably most people combine both approaches, backing up occasionally but trying to get to the end fairly soon so that they can see rather quickly what they know, or think they know, and can then start the real work of thinking, of converting their initial ideas into something substantial.

Asking Questions   Getting ideas, we said when we talked about **topics** and **invention** strategies in Chapter 1 (p. 14) is mostly a matter of asking (and then thinking about) questions. We append questions to the end of each argumentative essay in this book, not to torment you but to help you to think about the arguments—for instance, to turn your attention to especially important matters. If your instructor asks you to write an answer to one of these questions, you are lucky: Examining the question will stimulate your mind to work in a definite direction.

If a topic is not assigned, and you are asked to write an argument, you will find that some ideas (possibly poor ones, at this stage, but that doesn't matter because you will soon revise) will come to mind if you ask yourself questions. You can begin finding where you stand on an issue (**stasis**) by asking the following five basic questions:

1. What is X?
2. What is the value of X?
3. What are the causes (or the consequences) of X?
4. What should (or ought or must) we do about X?
5. What is the evidence for my claims about X?

Let's spend a moment looking at each of these questions.

1. **What is X?** We can hardly argue about the number of people sentenced to death in the United States in 2000—a glance at the appropriate government report will give the answer—but we can argue about whether capital punishment as administered in the United States is discriminatory. Does the evidence, we can ask, support the view that in the United States the death penalty is unfair? Similarly, we can ask whether a human fetus is a human being (in saying what something is, must we take account of its potentiality?), and, even if we agree that a fetus is a human being, we can further ask about whether it is a person. In *Roe v. Wade* the U.S. Supreme Court ruled that even the "viable" unborn human fetus is not a "person" as that term is used in the Fifth and Fourteenth Amendments. Here the question is this: Is the essential fact about the fetus that it is a person?

An argument of this sort makes a claim—that is, it takes a stand, but notice that it does not also have to argue for an action. Thus, it may argue that the death penalty is administered unfairly—that's a big enough issue—but it need not go on to argue that the death penalty should be abolished. After all, another possibility is that the death penalty should be administered fairly. The writer of the essay may be doing enough if he or she establishes the truth of the claim and leaves to others the possible responses.

2. **What is the value of X?** College courses often call for literary judgments. No one can argue with you if you say you prefer the plays of Tennessee Williams to those of Arthur Miller. But academic papers are not mere declarations of preferences. As soon as you say that Williams is a better playwright than Miller, you have based your preference on implicit standards, and it is incumbent on you to support your preference by giving evidence about the relative skill, insight, and accomplishments of Williams and of Miller. Your argument is an evaluation. The question now at issue is the merits of the two authors and the standards appropriate for such an appraisal. (For a discussion of literary evaluations, see pp. 467–98.)

In short, an essay offering an evaluation normally has two purposes:

- To set forth an assessment, and
- To convince the reader that the assessment is reasonable.

In writing an evaluation, you will have to rely on criteria, and these will vary depending on your topic. For instance, if you are comparing the artistic merit of the plays by Williams and by Miller, you may want to talk about the quality of the characterization, the importance of the theme, and so on. But if the topic is "Which playwright is more suitable to be taught in high school?," other criteria may be appropriate, such as

- The difficulty of the author's language,
- The sexual content of some scenes, and
- The presence of obscene words.

Or consider a nonliterary issue: On balance, are college fraternities and sororities good or bad? If good, how good? If bad, how bad? What criteria can we use in making our evaluation? Probably some or all of the following:

- Testimony of authorities (for instance, persons who can offer first-hand testimony about the good or bad effects),
- Inductive evidence (we can collect examples of good or bad effects),
- Appeals to logic ("it follows, therefore, that . . ."), and
- Appeals to emotion (for instance, an appeal to our sense of fairness).

3. **What are the causes (or the consequences) of X?** Why did the rate of auto theft increase during a specific period? If we abolish the death penalty, will that cause the rate of murder to increase? Notice, by the way, that such problems may be complex. The phenomena that people usually argue about — say, such things as inflation, war, suicide, crime — have many causes, and it is therefore often a mistake to speak of *the* cause of X. A writer in *Time* mentioned that the life expectancy of an average American male is about sixty-seven years, a figure that compares unfavorably with the life expectancy of males in Japan and Israel. The *Time* writer suggested that an important cause of the relatively short life span is "the pressure to perform well in business." Perhaps. But the life expectancy of plumbers is no greater than that of managers and executives. Nutrition authority Jean Mayer, in an article in *Life*, attributed the relatively poor longevity of American males to a diet that is "rich in fat and poor in nutrients." Doubtless other authorities propose other causes, and in all likelihood no one cause accounts for the phenomenon.

Or take a second example of discussions of causality, this one concerning the academic performance of girls in single-sex schools, middle schools, and high schools. It is pretty much agreed (based on statistical evidence) that the graduates of these schools do better, as a group, than girls who graduate from co-educational schools. *Why* do girls in single-sex schools tend, as a group, to do better? What is the *cause*? The administrators of girls' schools usually attribute the success to the fact (we are admittedly putting the matter bluntly) that young women flourish better in an atmosphere free from male intimidation: They allegedly gain confidence and become more expressive when they are not threatened by males. And this may be the answer, but skeptics have attributed the success to two other causes:

- Most single-sex schools require parents to pay tuition and it is a documented fact that the children of well-to-do parents do better, academically, than the children of poor parents.

- Further, most single-sex schools are private schools, and they select their students from a pool of candidates. Admissions officers naturally select those candidates who seem to be academically promising — that is, they select students who have *already done well academically.*[1]

In short, the girls who graduate from single-sex schools may owe their later academic success not to the atmosphere inside the schools, but to the fact that even at the time they were admitted to these schools they were academically stronger — we are, again, speaking of a cohort, not of individuals — than the girls who attend co-ed schools.

The lesson? Be cautious in attributing a cause. There may be several causes.

What kinds of support usually accompany claims of cause?

- Factual data, especially statistics;
- Analogies ("The Roman Empire declined because of X and Y," "Our society exhibits X and Y, and therefore . . .");
- Inductive evidence.

4. **What should (or ought or must) we do about X?** Must we always obey the law? Should the law allow eighteen-year-olds to drink alcohol? Should eighteen-year-olds be drafted to do one year of social service? Should pornography be censored? Should steroid use by athletes be banned? Ought there to be Good Samaritan laws, making it a legal duty for a stranger to intervene to save a person from death or great bodily harm, when one might do so with little or no risk to oneself? These questions involve conduct and policy; how we answer them will reveal our values and principles.

An essay answering questions of this sort usually

- Begins by explaining what the issue (the problem) is, then
- States why the reader should care about it, then

---

[1]Until 2004 federal regulations discouraged public schools from separating boys from girls. As of the time of this comment [2009] there are only ninety-five single-sex public schools, twelve of which are in New York City. An article in the *New York Times*, 11 March 2009, page A20, suggests that there is little evidence that girls do better than boys in these schools. Indeed, in California a much-touted program in which six public middle schools and high schools were turned into single-sex academies has been abandoned.

- Offers the proposed solution, then
- Considers alternative solutions, and finally
- Reaffirms the merit of the proposed solution, especially in the light of the audience's interests and needs.

You will recall that throughout this book we have spoken about devices that help a writer to get ideas. If in drafting an essay concerned with policy you begin by jotting down your thoughts on the five bulleted items we have just given, you will almost surely uncover ideas that you didn't know you had.

Support for claims of policy usually include

- Statistics,
- Appeals to common sense and to the reader's moral sense, and
- Testimony of authorities.

5. **What is the evidence for my claims about X?** In commenting on the four previous topics, we have talked about the kinds of support that are commonly offered, but a few additional points can be made.

Critical reading, writing, and thinking depend essentially on identifying and evaluating the evidence for and against the claims one makes and encounters in the writings of others. It is not enough to have an *opinion* or belief one way or the other; you need to be able to support your opinions —the bare fact of your sincere belief in what you say or write is not itself any *evidence* that what you believe is true.

So what are good reasons for opinions, adequate evidence for one's beliefs? The answer, of course, depends on what kind of belief or opinion, assertion or hypothesis, claim or principle, you want to assert. For example, there is good evidence that President John F. Kennedy was assassinated on November 22, 1963, because this is the date for his death reported in standard almanacs. You could further substantiate the date by checking the back issues of the *New York Times*. But a different kind of evidence is needed to support the proposition that the chemical composition of water is H_2O. And you will need still other kinds of evidence to support your beliefs about the likelihood of rain tomorrow, the probability that the Red Sox will win the pennant this year, the twelfth digit in the decimal expansion of pi, the average cumulative grades of the graduating seniors over the past three years in your college, the relative merits of *Hamlet* and *Death of a Salesman*, and the moral dimensions of sexual harassment. None of these issues is merely a matter of opinion; yet on some of them, educated and informed people may disagree over the reasons and the evidence and what they show. Your job as a critical thinker is to be alert to the relevant reasons and evidence and to make the most of them as you present your views.

Again, an argument may take in two or more of these five issues. Someone who argues that pornography should (or should not) be censored

- Will have to mark out the territory of the discussion by defining pornography (our first issue: What is *X*?). The argument probably

- Will also need to examine the consequences of adopting the preferred policy (our third issue) and

- May even have to argue about its value (our second issue). Some people maintain that pornography produces crime, but others maintain that it provides a harmless outlet for impulses that otherwise might vent themselves in criminal behavior.

- Further, someone arguing about the wisdom of censoring pornography might have to face the objection that censorship, however desirable on account of some of its consequences, may be unconstitutional and that even if censorship were constitutional, it would (or might) have undesirable side effects, such as repressing freedom of political opinion.

- And one will always have to keep asking oneself our fifth question, What is the evidence for my claims?

Thinking about one or more of these questions may get you going. For instance, thinking about the first question, What is *X*?, will require you to produce a definition, and as you work at producing a satisfactory definition, you may find new ideas arising. If a question seems relevant, start writing, even if you write only a fragmentary sentence. You'll probably find that one word leads to another and that ideas begin to appear. Even if these ideas seem weak as you write them, don't be discouraged; you have put something on paper, and returning to these words, perhaps in five minutes or perhaps the next day, you will probably find that some are not at all bad and that others will stimulate you to better ones.

It may be useful to record your ideas in a special notebook reserved for the purpose. Such a **journal** can be a valuable resource when it comes time to write your paper. Many students find it easier to focus their thoughts on writing if during the period of gestation they have been jotting down relevant ideas on something more substantial than slips of paper or loose sheets. The very act of designating a notebook as your journal for a course can be the first step in focusing your attention on the eventual need to write a paper.

If what we have just said does not sound convincing, and you know from experience that you often have trouble getting started with your writing, don't despair; first aid is at hand in a sure-fire method that we will now explain.

The Thesis

Let's assume that you are writing an argumentative essay—perhaps an evaluation of an argument in this book—and you have what seems to be a pretty good draft or at least a bunch of notes that are the result of hard thinking. You really do have ideas now, and you want to present them effectively. How will you organize your essay? No one formula works best for every essayist and for every essay, but it is usually advisable to formulate a basic **thesis** (a claim, a central point, a chief position) and to state it early. Every essay that is any good, even a book-length one, has a thesis (a main point), which can be stated briefly, usually in a sentence. Remember Coolidge's remark on the preacher's sermon on sin: "He was against it." Don't confuse the **topic** (sin) with the thesis (sin is bad). The thesis is the argumentative theme, the author's primary claim or contention, the proposition that the rest of the essay will explain and defend. Of course, the thesis may sound commonplace, but the book or essay or sermon ought to develop it interestingly and convincingly.

Here are some sample theses:

- Smoking should be prohibited in all enclosed public places.
- Smoking should be limited to specific parts of enclosed public places and entirely prohibited in small spaces, such as elevators.
- Proprietors of public places such as restaurants and sports arenas should be free to determine whether they wish to prohibit, limit, or impose no limitations on smokers.

✓ A CHECKLIST FOR A THESIS STATEMENT

Consider the following questions:

☐ Does the statement make an arguable assertion rather than (a) merely assert an unarguable fact, (b) merely announce a topic, or (c) declare an unarguable opinion or belief?

☐ Is the statement broad enough to cover the entire argument that I will be presenting, and is it narrow enough for me to be able to cover the topic in the space allotted?

Imagining an Audience

Of course, the questions that you ask yourself to stimulate your thoughts will depend primarily on what you are writing about, but additional questions are always relevant:

- Who are my readers?
- What do they believe?
- What common ground do we share?
- What do I want my readers to believe?
- What do they need to know?
- Why should they care?

These questions require a little comment. The literal answer to the first probably is "my teacher," but (unless you are given instructions to the contrary) you should not write specifically for your teacher. Instead, you should write for an audience that is, generally speaking, like your classmates. In short, your imagined audience is literate, intelligent, and moderately well informed, but it does not know everything that you know, and it does not know your response to the problem that you are addressing.

The essays in this book are from many different sources, each with its own audience. An essay from the *New York Times* is addressed to the educated general reader; an essay from *Ms.* magazine is addressed to readers sympathetic to feminism. An essay from *Commonweal,* a Roman Catholic publication addressed to the nonspecialist, is likely to differ in point of view or tone from one in *Time,* even though both articles may advance approximately the same position. The writer of the article in *Commonweal* may, for example, effectively cite church fathers and distinguished Roman Catholic writers as authorities, whereas the writer of the *Time* article would probably cite few or even none of these figures because a non-Catholic audience might be unfamiliar with them or, even if familiar, might be unimpressed by their views.

The tone as well as the gist of the argument is in some degree shaped by the audience. For instance, popular journals, such as the *National Review* and *Ms.* magazine, are more likely to use ridicule than are journals chiefly addressed to, say, an academic audience.

The Audience as Collaborator

If you imagine an audience and keep asking yourself what this audience needs to be told and what it doesn't need to be told, you will find that material comes to mind, just as it comes to mind when a friend asks you what a film you saw was about, who was in it, and how you liked it.

Your readers do not have to be told that Thomas Jefferson was an American statesman in the early years of this country's history, but they do have to be told that Elizabeth Cady Stanton was a late-nineteenth-century American feminist. Why? You need to identify Stanton because it's your hunch that your classmates never heard of her, or even if they may have heard the name, they can't quite identify it. But what if your class has been assigned an essay by Stanton? In that case your imagined reader knows Stanton's name and knows at least a little about her, so you don't have to identify Stanton as an American of the nineteenth century. But you do still have to remind your reader about relevant aspects of her essay, and you do have to tell your reader about your responses to them.

After all, even if the instructor has assigned an essay by Stanton, you cannot assume that your classmates know the essay inside out. Obviously, you can't say, "Stanton's third reason is also unconvincing," without reminding the reader, by means of a brief summary, of her third reason. Again,

- Think of your classmates—people like you—as your imagined readers; and
- Be sure that your essay does not make unreasonable demands.

If you ask yourself,

- "What do my readers need to know?" and
- "What do I want them to believe?,"

you will find some answers arising, and you will start writing.

We have said that you should imagine your audience as your classmates. But this is not the whole truth. In a sense, your argument is addressed not simply to your classmates but to the world interested in ideas. Even if you can reasonably assume that your classmates have read only one work by Stanton, you will not begin your essay by writing "Stanton's essay is deceptively easy." You will have to name the work; it is possible that a reader has read some other work by Stanton. And by precisely identifying your subject, you help to ease the reader into your essay.

Similarly, you won't begin by writing,

The majority opinion in *Walker v. City of Birmingham* held that . . .

Rather, you'll write something like this:

In *Walker v. City of Birmingham*, the U.S. Supreme Court ruled in 1966 that city authorities acted lawfully when they jailed Martin Luther King Jr. and other clergymen in 1963 for marching in Birmingham without a permit. Justice Potter Stewart delivered the majority opinion, which held that . . .

By the way, if you think you suffer from a writing block, the mere act of writing out such readily available facts will help you to get started. You will find that putting a few words down on paper, perhaps merely copying the essay's title or an interesting quotation from the essay, will stimulate you to jot down thoughts that you didn't know you had in you.

Here, again, are the questions about audience. If you write with a word processor, consider putting these questions into a file. For each assignment, copy (with the Copy command) the questions into the file you are currently working on, and then, as a way of generating ideas, *enter your responses, indented, under each question.*

- Who are my readers?
- What do they believe?
- What common ground do we share?

- What do I want my readers to believe?
- What do they need to know?
- Why should they care?

Thinking about your audience can help you to put some words on paper; even more important, it can help you to get ideas. Our second and third questions about the audience ("What do they believe?" and "How much common ground do we share?") will usually help you get ideas flowing.

- Presumably your imagined audience does not share your views, or at least does not fully share them. But why?
- How can these readers hold a position that to you seems unreasonable?

If you try to put yourself into your readers' shoes—and in your essay you will almost surely summarize the views that you are going to speak against—and if you think about what your audience knows or thinks it knows, you will find yourself getting ideas.

You do not believe (let's assume) that people should be allowed to smoke in enclosed public places, but you know that some people hold a different view. Why do they hold it? Try to state their view *in a way that would be satisfactory to them*. Having done so, you may come to perceive that your conclusions and theirs differ because they are based on different premises, perhaps different ideas about human rights. Examine the opposition's premises carefully, and explain, first to yourself and ultimately to your readers, why you find some premises unacceptable.

Possibly some facts are in dispute, such as whether nonsmokers may be harmed by exposure to tobacco. The thing to do, then, is to check the facts. If you find that harm to nonsmokers has not been proved, but you nevertheless believe that smoking should be prohibited in enclosed public places, of course you can't premise your argument on the wrongfulness of harming the innocent (in this case, the nonsmokers). You will have to develop arguments that take account of the facts, whatever they are.

Among the relevant facts there surely are some that your audience or your opponent will not dispute. The same is true of the values relevant to the discussion; the two of you are very likely to agree, if you stop to think about it, that you share belief in some of the same values (such as the principle mentioned above, that it is wrong to harm the innocent). These areas of shared agreement are crucial to effective persuasion in argument.

> **A RULE FOR WRITERS:** If you wish to persuade, you'll have to begin by finding premises you can share with your audience.

There are two good reasons why you should identify and isolate the areas of agreement:

- There is no point in disputing facts or values on which you and your readers really agree.
- It usually helps to establish goodwill between you and your opponent when you can point to beliefs, assumptions, facts, and values that the two of you share.

In a few moments we will return to the need to share some of the opposition's ideas.

Recall that in writing college papers it is usually best to write for a general audience, an audience rather like your classmates but without the specific knowledge that they all share as students enrolled in one course. If the topic is smoking in public places, the audience presumably consists of smokers and nonsmokers. Thinking about our fifth question on page 235 — "What do [readers] need to know?" — may prompt you to give statistics about the harmful effects of smoking. Or if you are arguing on behalf of smokers, it may prompt you to cite studies claiming that no evidence conclusively demonstrates that cigarette smoking is harmful to nonsmokers. If indeed you are writing for a general audience and you are not advancing a highly unfamiliar view, our second question ("What does the audience believe?") is less important here, but if the audience is specialized, such as an antismoking group, a group of restaurant owners who fear that antismoking regulations will interfere with their business,

---

✓ A CHECKLIST FOR IMAGINING AN AUDIENCE

Have I asked myself the following questions?

☐ Who are my readers?

☐ How much about the topic do they know?

☐ Have I provided necessary background (including definitions of special terms) if the imagined readers probably are not especially familiar with the topic?

☐ Are these imagined readers likely to be neutral? Sympathetic? Hostile?

☐ If they are neutral, have I offered good reasons to persuade them? If they are sympathetic, have I done more than merely reaffirm their present beliefs? That is, have I perhaps enriched their views or encouraged them to act? If they are hostile, have I taken account of their positions, recognized their strengths but also called attention to their limitations, and offered a position that may persuade these hostile readers to modify their position?

or a group of civil libertarians, an effective essay will have to address their special beliefs.

In addressing their beliefs (let's assume that you do not share them or do not share them fully), you must try to establish some common ground. If you advocate requiring restaurants to provide nonsmoking areas, you should at least recognize the possibility that this arrangement will result in inconvenience for the proprietor. But perhaps (the good news) the restaurant will regain some lost customers or will attract some new customers. This thought should prompt you to think of kinds of evidence, perhaps testimony or statistics.

When you formulate a thesis and ask questions about it, such as who the readers are, what do they believe, what do they know, and what do they need to know, you begin to get ideas about how to organize the material or at least to see that some sort of organization will have to be worked out. The thesis may be clear and simple, but the reasons (the argument) may take many pages. The thesis is the point; the argument sets forth the evidence that is offered to support the thesis.

The Title

It's not a bad idea to announce your thesis in your **title.** If you scan the table of contents of this book, you will notice that a fair number of essayists use the title to let the readers know, at least in a very general way, what position will be advocated. Here are a few examples of titles that take a position:

Gay Marriages: Make Them Legal

"Diversity" Is a Smoke Screen for Discrimination

Why Handguns Must Be Outlawed

True, these titles are not especially engaging, but the reader welcomes them because they give some information about the writer's thesis.

Some titles do not announce the thesis, but they at least announce the topic:

CALVIN AND HOBBES. © 1993 Bill Watterson. Reprinted with permission of Universal Press Syndicate. All rights reserved.

Is All Discrimination Unfair?

On Racist Speech

Why Make Divorce Easy?

Although not clever or witty, these titles are informative.

Some titles seek to attract attention or to stimulate the imagination:

A First Amendment Junkie

A Crime of Compassion

Addicted to Health

All of these are effective, but a word of caution is appropriate here. In your effort to engage your reader's attention, be careful not to sound like a wise guy. You want to engage your readers, not turn them off.

Finally, be prepared to rethink your title *after* you have finished the last draft of your paper. A title somewhat different from your working title may be an improvement because the emphasis of your finished paper may have turned out to be rather different from what you expected when you first thought of a title.

The Opening Paragraphs

Opening paragraphs are difficult to write, so don't worry about writing an effective opening when you are drafting. Just get some words down on paper, and keep going. But when you revise your first draft—really a zero draft—you probably should begin to think seriously about the effect of your opening.

A good introduction arouses the reader's interest and helps prepare the reader for the rest of the paper. How? Opening paragraphs usually do at least one (and often all) of the following:

- Attract the reader's interest (often with a bold statement of the thesis or with an interesting statistic, quotation, or anecdote),
- Prepare the reader's mind by giving some idea of the topic and often of the thesis,
- Give the reader an idea of how the essay is organized, and
- Define a key term.

You may not wish to announce your thesis in your title, but if you don't announce it there, you should set it forth early in the argument, in your introductory paragraph or paragraphs. In her title "Human Rights and Foreign Policy," Jeanne J. Kirkpatrick merely announces her topic (subject) as opposed to her thesis (point), but she begins to hint at the thesis in her first paragraph, by deprecating President Jimmy Carter's policy:

In this paper I deal with three broad subjects: first, the content and consequences of the Carter administration's human rights policy;

second, the prerequisites of a more adequate theory of human rights; and third, some characteristics of a more successful human rights policy.

Or consider this opening paragraph from Peter Singer's "Animal Liberation" (p. 205):

> We are familiar with Black Liberation, Gay Liberation, and a variety of other movements. With Women's Liberation some thought we had come to the end of the road. Discrimination on the basis of sex, it has been said, is the last form of discrimination that is universally accepted and practiced without pretense, even in those liberal circles which have long prided themselves on their freedom from racial discrimination. But one should always be wary of talking of "the last remaining form of discrimination." If we have learned anything from the liberation movements, we should have learned how difficult it is to be aware of the ways in which we discriminate until they are forcefully pointed out to us. A liberation movement demands an expansion of our moral horizons, so that practices that were previously regarded as natural and inevitable are now seen as intolerable.

Although Singer's introductory paragraph nowhere mentions animal liberation, in conjunction with its title it gives us a good idea of what Singer is up to and where he is going. Singer knows that his audience will be skeptical, so he reminds them that many of us in previous years were skeptical of reforms that we now take for granted. He adopts a strategy used fairly often by writers who advance unconventional theses: Rather than beginning with a bold announcement of a thesis that may turn off some of his readers because it sounds offensive or absurd, Singer warms up his audience, gaining their interest by cautioning them politely that although they may at first be skeptical of animal liberation, if they stay with his essay they may come to feel that they have expanded their horizons.

Notice, too, that Singer begins by establishing common ground with his readers; he assumes, probably correctly, that they share his view that other forms of discrimination (now seen to be unjust) were once widely practiced and were assumed to be acceptable and natural. In this paragraph, then, Singer is not only showing himself to be fair-minded but is also letting us know that he will advance a daring idea. His opening wins our attention and our goodwill. A writer can hardly hope to do more. (In a few pages we will talk a little more about winning the audience.)

In your introductory paragraphs,

- You may have to give some background information that your readers will need to keep in mind if they are to follow your essay.
- You may wish to define some terms that are unfamiliar or that you use in an unusual sense.

After announcing the topic, giving the necessary background, and stating your position (and perhaps the opposition's) in as engaging a

> **A RULE FOR WRITERS:** In writing or at least in revising these paragraphs, keep in mind this question: What do my readers need to know? Remember, your aim throughout is to write *reader-friendly* prose, and keeping the needs and interests of your audience constantly in mind will help you achieve this goal.

manner as possible, it is usually a good idea to give the reader an idea of *how* you will proceed — that is, what the organization will be. Look on pages 241–42 at Kirkpatrick's opening paragraph for an obvious illustration. She tells us she will deal with three subjects, and she names them. Her approach in the paragraph is concise, obvious, and effective.

Similarly, you may, for instance, want to announce fairly early that there are four common objections to your thesis and that you will take them up one by one, beginning with the weakest (or most widely held, or whatever) and moving to the strongest (or least familiar), after which you will advance your own view in greater detail. Not every argument begins with refuting the other side, though many arguments do. The point to remember is that you usually ought to tell your readers where you will be taking them and by what route.

Organizing and Revising the Body of the Essay

We begin with a wise remark by a newspaper columnist, Robert Cromier: "The beautiful part of writing is that you don't have to get it right the first time — unlike, say, a brain surgeon."

In drafting your essay you will of course begin with an organization that seems to you to make sense, but you may well find, in rereading the draft, that some other organization is better. Here, for a start, is an organization that is common in argumentative essays.

1. Statement of the problem
2. Statement of the structure of the essay
3. Statement of alternative solutions
4. Arguments in support of the proposed solution
5. Arguments answering possible objections
6. A summary, resolution, or conclusion

Let's look at each of these six steps.

1. **Statement of the problem**   Whether the problem is stated briefly or at length depends on the nature of the problem and the writer's audience. If you haven't already defined unfamiliar terms or terms you use in a special way, probably now is the time to do so. In any case, it is advisable here to state the problem objectively (thereby gaining the trust of the reader) and to indicate why the reader should care about the issue.

2. **Statement of the structure of the essay**   After stating the problem at the appropriate length, the writer often briefly indicates the structure of the rest of the essay. The commonest structure is suggested below, in points 3 and 4.

3. **Statement of alternative (but less adequate) solutions**   In addition to stating the alternatives fairly, the writer probably conveys willingness to recognize not only the integrity of the proposals but also the (partial) merit of at least some of the alternative solutions.

The point made in the previous sentence is important and worth amplifying. Because it is important to convey your goodwill—your sense of fairness—to the reader, it is advisable to let your reader see that you are familiar with the opposition and that you recognize the integrity of those who hold that view. This you do by granting its merits as far as you can. (For more about this approach, see the essay by Carl R. Rogers on p. 457.)

The next stage, which constitutes most of the body of the essay, usually is this:

4. **Arguments in support of the proposed solution**   The evidence offered will, of course, depend on the nature of the problem. Relevant statistics, authorities, examples, or analogies may come to mind or be available. This is usually the longest part of the essay.

5. **Arguments answering possible objections**   These arguments may suggest that

   a. The proposal won't work (perhaps it is alleged to be too expensive, to make unrealistic demands on human nature, or to fail to get to the heart of the problem).

   b. The proposed solution will create problems greater than the difficulty to be resolved. (A good example of a proposal that produced dreadful unexpected results is the law mandating a prison term for anyone over eighteen in possession of an illegal drug. Heroin dealers then began to use children as runners, and cocaine importers followed the practice. And while we are on the subject of children, consider this: Five states have statutes that allow the death penalty for adults who molest children. A chief argument *against* this penalty is that the molesters, having nothing further to lose, may kill their victims. A second argument is that victims of sex crimes by family members may be less likely to report the crimes. In your view, how valid are these arguments about unintended consequences?

6. **A summary, resolution, or conclusion**   Here the writer may seek to accommodate the views of the opposition as far as possible but clearly suggest that the writer's own position makes good sense. A conclusion—the word comes from the Latin *claudere*, "to shut"—ought to provide a sense of closure, but it can be much more than a restatement of the writer's thesis. It can,

for instance, make a quiet emotional appeal by suggesting that the issue is important and that the ball is now in the reader's court.

Of course not every essay will follow this six-step pattern, but let's assume that in the introductory paragraphs you have sketched the topic (and have shown or nicely said, or implied, that the reader doubtless is interested in it) and have fairly and courteously set forth the opposition's view, recognizing its merits ("I grant that," "admittedly," "it is true that") and indicating the degree to which you can share part of that view. You now want to set forth your arguments explaining why you differ on some essentials.

In setting forth your own position, you can begin either with your strongest reasons or your weakest. Each method of organization has advantages and disadvantages.

- If you begin with your strongest, the essay may seem to peter out.
- If you begin with the weakest, you build to a climax, but your readers may not still be with you because they may have felt at the start that the essay was frivolous.

The solution to this last possibility is to make sure that even your weakest argument is an argument of some strength. You can, moreover, assure your readers that stronger points will soon be offered and you offer this point first only because you want to show that you are aware of it and that, slight though it is, it deserves some attention. The body of the essay, then, is devoted to arguing a position, which means offering not only supporting reasons but also refutations of possible objections to these reasons.

Doubtless you will sometimes be uncertain, as you draft your essay, whether to present a given point before or after another point. When you write, and certainly when you revise, try to put yourself into your reader's shoes: Which point do you think the reader needs to know first? Which point *leads to* which further point? Your argument should not be a mere list of points, of course; rather, it should clearly integrate one point with another in order to develop an idea. But in all likelihood you won't have a strong sense of the best organization until you have written a draft and have reread it.

A RULE FOR WRITERS: When you revise, make sure that your organization is clear to your readers.

Checking Paragraphs   When you revise your draft, watch out also for short paragraphs. Although a paragraph of only two or three sentences (like some in this chapter) may occasionally be helpful as a transition between complicated points, most short paragraphs are undeveloped paragraphs. (Newspaper editors favor very short paragraphs because they can be read rapidly when printed in the narrow columns typical of newspapers. Many of the essays reprinted in this book originally were published in newspapers, hence they consist of very short paragraphs. There is no reason for you to imitate this style in the argumentative essays you will be writing.)

In revising, when you find a paragraph of only a sentence or two or three, check first to see if it should be joined to the paragraph that precedes or follows. Second, if on rereading you are certain that a given paragraph should not be tied to what comes before or after, think about amplifying the paragraph with supporting detail (this is not the same as mere padding).

Checking Transitions   Make sure, too, in revising, that the reader can move easily from the beginning of a paragraph to the end and from one paragraph to the next. Transitions help the reader to perceive the connections between the units of the argument. For example ("For example" is a transition, of course, indicating that an illustration will follow), they may illustrate, establish a sequence, connect logically, amplify, compare, contrast, summarize, or concede (see Idea Prompt 6.1). Transitions serve as guideposts that enable your reader to move easily through your essay.

When writers revise an early draft, they chiefly

- **Unify** the essay by eliminating irrelevancies;
- **Organize** the essay by keeping in mind an imagined audience;
- **Clarify** the essay by fleshing out thin paragraphs, by making certain that the transitions are adequate, and by making certain that generalizations are adequately supported by concrete details and examples.

We are not talking about polish or elegance; we are talking about fundamental matters. Be especially careful not to abuse the logical connectives (*thus, as a result,* and so on). If you write several sentences followed by *therefore* or a similar word or phrase, be sure that what you write after the *therefore* really *does follow* from what has gone before. Logical connectives are not mere transitional devices used to link disconnected bits of prose. They are supposed to mark a real movement of thought—the essence of an argument.

The Ending

What about concluding paragraphs, in which you try to summarize the main points and reaffirm your position?

If you can look back over your essay and can add something that enriches it and at the same time wraps it up, fine, but don't feel compelled

IDEA PROMPT 6.1 USING TRANSITIONS IN ARGUMENT

Illustrate	*for example, for instance, consider this case*	"Many television crime dramas contain scenes of graphic violence. For example, in the episode of *Law and Order* titled . . ."
Establish a sequence	*a more important objection, a stronger example, the best reason*	"A stronger example of the ways that TV violence is susceptible to being mimicked is . . ."
Connect logically	*thus, as a result, therefore, so, it follows*	"Therefore, the Federal Communications Commission ought to consider more carefully regulating what types of violence they allow on the air."
Amplify	*further, in addition to, moreover*	"Further, fines for networks that violate these regulations should be steeper because . . ."
Compare	*similarly, in a like manner, just as, analogously*	"Just as the FCC regulates language and sexuality on broadcast TV . . ."
Contrast	*on the other hand, in contrast, however, but*	"On the other hands, studies have shown that violent television . . ."
Summarize	*in short, briefly*	"In short, the basic premise of his argument is . . ."
Concede	*admittedly, granted, to be sure*	"Admittedly, there are many points on which the author is correct."

to say, "Thus, in conclusion, I have argued *X, Y,* and *Z,* and I have refuted Jones." After all, *conclusion* can have two meanings: (1) ending, or finish, as the ending of a joke or a novel; or (2) judgment or decision reached after deliberation. Your essay should finish effectively (the first sense), but it need not announce a judgment (the second).

If the essay is fairly short, so that a reader can more or less keep the whole thing in mind, you may not need to restate your view. Just make sure that you have covered the ground and that your last sentence is a good one. Notice that the student essay printed later in this chapter

(p. 259) does not end with a formal conclusion, though it ends conclusively, with a note of finality.

By a note of finality we do *not* mean a triumphant crowing. It's usually far better to end with the suggestion that you hope you have by now indicated why those who hold a different view may want to modify it and accept yours.

If you study the essays in this book, or, for that matter, the editorials and op-ed pieces in a newspaper, you will notice that writers often provide a sense of closure by using one of the following devices:

- A return to something in the introduction,
- A glance at the wider implications of the issue (for example, if smoking is restricted, other liberties are threatened),
- An anecdote that engagingly illustrates the thesis, or
- A brief summary (but this sort of ending may seem unnecessary and even tedious, especially if the paper is short and if the summary merely repeats what has already been said).

A RULE FOR WRITERS: Emulate John Kenneth Galbraith, a distinguished writer on economics. Galbraith said that in his fifth draft he introduced the note of spontaneity for which his writing was famous.

Two Uses of an Outline

The Outline as a Preliminary Guide   Some writers find it useful to sketch an **outline** as soon as they think they know what they want to say, even before they write a first draft. This procedure can be helpful in planning a tentative organization, but remember that in revising a draft new ideas will arise, and the outline may have to be modified. A preliminary outline is chiefly useful as a means of getting going, not as a guide to the final essay.

The Outline as a Way of Checking a Draft   Whether or not you use a preliminary outline, we strongly suggest that after you have written what you hope is your last draft, you make an outline of it; there is no better way of finding out whether the essay is well organized.

Go through the draft and jot down the chief points in the order in which you make them. That is, prepare a table of contents — perhaps a phrase for each paragraph. Next, examine your jottings to see what kind of sequence they reveal in your paper:

- Is the sequence reasonable? Can it be improved?
- Are any passages irrelevant?
- Does something important seem to be missing?

If no coherent structure or reasonable sequence clearly appears in the outline, then the full prose version of your argument probably doesn't have any either. Therefore, produce another draft, moving things around, adding or subtracting paragraphs—cutting and pasting into a new sequence, with transitions as needed—and then make another outline to see if the sequence now is satisfactory.

You are probably familiar with the structure known as a **formal outline.** Major points are indicated by I, II, III; points within major points are indicated by A, B, C; divisions within A, B, C are indicated by 1, 2, 3; and so on. Thus,

I. Arguments for opening all Olympic sports to professionals
   A. Fairness
      1. Some Olympic sports are already open to professionals.
      2. Some athletes who really are not professionals are classified as professionals.
   B. Quality (achievements would be higher)

You may want to outline your draft according to this principle, or it may be enough if you simply jot down a phrase for each paragraph and indent the subdivisions. But keep these points in mind:

- It is not enough for the parts to be ordered reasonably.
- The order must be made clear to the reader, probably by means of transitions such as *for instance, on the other hand, we can now turn to an opposing view,* and so on.

Here is another way of thinking about an outline. For each paragraph, jot down

- What the paragraph *says,* and
- What the paragraph *does.*

An opening paragraph might be outlined thus:

- What the paragraph *says* is that the words "under God" in the Pledge of Allegiance should be omitted.
- What the paragraph *does* is, first, it informs the reader of the thesis, and second, it *provides some necessary background,* for instance, that the words were not in the original wording of the Pledge.

A dual outline of this sort will help you to see whether you have a final draft or a draft that needs refinement.

Tone and the Writer's Persona

Although this book is chiefly about argument in the sense of rational discourse—the presentation of reasons in support of a thesis or conclusion—the appeal to reason is only one form of persuasion. Another form is the appeal to emotion—to pity, for example. Aristotle saw, in addition to the appeal to reason and the appeal to emotion, a third form of persuasion, the appeal to the character of the speaker. He called it the **ethical appeal** (the Greek word for this kind of appeal is **ethos,** "character"). The idea is that effective speakers convey the suggestion that they are

- Informed,
- Intelligent,
- Benevolent, and
- Honest.

Because they are perceived as trustworthy, their words inspire confidence in their listeners. It is, of course, a fact that when we read an argument we are often aware of the *person* or *voice* behind the words, and our assent to the argument depends partly on the extent to which we can share the speaker's assumptions, look at the matter from the speaker's point of view—in short, *identify* with this speaker.

How can a writer inspire the confidence that lets readers identify themselves with the writer? To begin with, the writer should possess the virtues Aristotle specified: intelligence or good sense, honesty, and benevolence or goodwill. As the Roman proverb puts it, "No one gives what he does not have." Still, possession of these qualities is not a guarantee that you will convey them in your writing. Like all other writers, you will have to revise your drafts so that these qualities become apparent, or, stated more moderately, you will have to revise so that nothing in the essay causes a reader to doubt your intelligence, honesty, and goodwill. A blunder in logic, a misleading quotation, a snide remark, even an error in spelling—all such slips can cause readers to withdraw their sympathy from the writer.

But of course all good argumentative essays do not sound exactly alike; they do not all reveal the same speaker. Each writer develops his or her own voice or (as literary critics and teachers call it) **persona.** In fact, one writer will have several voices or personae, depending on the topic and the audience. The president of the United States delivering an address on the State of the Union has one persona; chatting with a reporter at his summer home he has another. This change is not a matter of hypocrisy. Different circumstances call for different language. As a French writer put it, there is a time to speak of "Paris" and a time to speak of "the capital of the nation." When Lincoln spoke at Gettysburg, he didn't say "Eighty-seven years ago," but "Four score and seven years ago." We might say that just as some occasions required him to be the folksy Honest Abe, the occasion of the dedication of hallowed ground required him to be formal and solemn, and so the president of the United States appropriately used biblical language. The election campaigns called for one persona, and the dedication of a military cemetery called for a different persona.

> **A RULE FOR WRITERS:** Present yourself so that your readers see you as knowledgeable, honest, open-minded, and interested in helping them to think about an issue of significance.

When we talk about a writer's persona, we mean the way in which the writer presents his or her attitudes

- Toward *the self,*
- Toward *the audience,* and
- Toward *the subject.*

Thus, if a writer says,

> I have thought long and hard about this subject, and I can say with assurance that . . .

we may feel that we are listening to a self-satisfied ass who probably is simply mouthing other people's opinions. Certainly he is mouthing clichés: "long and hard," "say with assurance."

Let's look at a slightly subtler example of an utterance that reveals an attitude. When we read that

> President Nixon was hounded out of office by journalists,

we hear a respectful attitude toward Nixon ("President Nixon") and a hostile attitude toward the press (they are beasts, curs who "hounded" our elected leader). If the writer's attitudes were reversed, she might have said something like this:

> The press turned the searchlight on Tricky Dick's criminal shenanigans.

"Tricky Dick" and "criminal" are obvious enough, but notice that "shenanigans" also implies the writer's contempt for Nixon, and of course, "turned the searchlight" suggests that the press is a source of illumination, a source of truth. The original version and the opposite version both say that the press was responsible for Nixon's resignation, but the original version ("President Nixon was hounded") conveys indignation toward journalists, whereas the revision conveys contempt for Nixon.

These two versions suggest two speakers who differ not only in their view of Nixon but also in their manner, including the seriousness with which they take themselves. Although the passage is very short, it seems to us that the first speaker conveys righteous indignation ("hounded"), whereas the second conveys amused contempt ("shenanigans"). To our ears the tone, as well as the point, differs in the two versions.

We are talking about **loaded words,** words that convey the writer's attitude and that by their connotations are meant to win the reader to the writer's side. Compare the words in the left-hand column with those in the right:

freedom fighter	terrorist
pro-choice	pro-abortion
pro-life	antichoice
economic refugee	illegal alien
terrorist-surveillance	domestic spying

The words in the left-hand column sound like good things; speakers who use these words are seeking to establish themselves as virtuous people who are supporting worthy causes. The **connotations** (associations, overtones) of these pairs of words differ, even though the **denotations** (explicit meanings, dictionary definitions) are the same, just as the connotations of *mother* and *female parent* differ, although the denotations are the same. Similarly, although Lincoln's "four score and seven" and "eighty-seven" both denote "thirteen less than one hundred," they differ in connotation.

Tone is not only a matter of connotations (*hounded out of office* versus, let's say, *compelled to resign,* or *pro-choice* versus *pro-abortion*); it is also a matter of such things as the selection and type of examples. A writer who offers many examples, especially ones drawn from ordinary life, conveys a persona different from that of a writer who offers no examples or only an occasional invented instance. The first of these probably is, one might say, friendlier, more down-to-earth.

Last Words on Tone   On the whole, when writing an argument, it is advisable to be courteous and respectful of your topic, of your audience, and of people who hold views you are arguing against. It is rarely good for one's own intellectual development to regard as villains or fools persons who hold views different from one's own, especially if some of them are in the audience. Keep in mind the story of the two strangers on a train who, striking up a conversation, found that both were clergymen, though of different faiths. Then one said to the other, "Well, why shouldn't we be friends? After all, we both serve God, you in your way and I in His."

Complacency is all right when telling a joke but not when offering an argument:

- Recognize opposing views.

- Assume they are held in good faith.

- State them fairly (if you don't, you do a disservice not only to the opposition but also to your own position because the perceptive reader will not take you seriously).

- Be temperate in arguing your own position: "If I understand their view correctly . . ."; "It seems reasonable to conclude that . . ."; "Perhaps, then, we can agree that . . ."

We, One, or I?

The use of *we* in the last sentence brings us to another point: May the first-person pronouns *I* and *we* be used? In this book, because two of us are writing, we often use *we* to mean the two authors. And we sometimes use *we* to mean the authors and the readers, as in phrases like the one that ends the previous paragraph. This shifting use of one word can be troublesome, but we hope (clearly the *we* here refers only to the authors) that we have avoided any ambiguity. But can, or should, or must, an individual use *we* instead of *I*? The short answer is no.

If you are simply speaking for yourself, use *I*. Attempts to avoid the first-person singular by saying things like "This writer thinks . . .," and "It is thought that . . .," and "One thinks that . . .," are far more irritating (and wordy) than the use of *I*. The so-called editorial *we* is as odd-sounding in a student's argument as is the royal *we*. Mark Twain said that the only ones who can appropriately say *we* are kings, editors, and people with a tapeworm. And because one *one* leads to another, making the sentence sound (James Thurber's words) "like a trombone solo," it's best to admit that you are the author, and to use *I*. But there is no need to preface every sentence with "I think." The reader knows that the essay is yours; just write it, using *I* when you must, but not needlessly.

Avoiding Sexist Language

Courtesy as well as common sense requires that you respect the feelings of your readers. Many people today find offensive the implicit sexism in the use of male pronouns to denote not only men but also women ("As the reader follows the argument, he will find . . ."). And sometimes the use of the male pronoun to denote all people is ridiculous: "An individual, no matter what his sex, . . ."

In most contexts there is no need to use gender-specific nouns or pronouns. One way to avoid using *he* when you mean any person is to use *he or she* (or *she or he*) instead of *he*, but the result is sometimes a bit cumbersome — although it is superior to the overly conspicuous *he/she* and to *s/he*.

Here are two simple ways to solve the problem:

- *Use the plural* ("As readers follow the argument, they will find . . ."), or
- *Recast the sentence* so that no pronoun is required ("Readers following the argument will find . . .").

Because *man* and *mankind* strike many readers as sexist when used in such expressions as "Man is a rational animal" and "Mankind has not yet solved this problem," consider using such words as *human being, person, people, humanity,* and *we*. (*Examples*: "Human beings are rational animals"; "We have not yet solved this problem.")

✓ A CHECKLIST FOR ATTENDING TO THE NEEDS
OF THE AUDIENCE

☐ Do I have a sense of what the audience probably knows about the issue?

☐ Do I have a sense of what the audience probably thinks about the issue?

☐ Have I stated the thesis clearly and sufficiently early in the essay?

☐ How much common ground do we probably share?

☐ Have I, in the paper, tried to establish common ground and then moved on to advance my position?

☐ Have I supported my arguments with sufficient details?

☐ Have I used the appropriate language (for instance, defined terms that are likely to be unfamiliar)?

☐ Have I indicated *why* my readers should care about the issue and should accept or at least take seriously my views?

☐ Is the organization clear?

☐ Have I used transitions where they are needed?

☐ If visual material (charts, graphs, pictures) will enhance my arguments, have I used them?

☐ Have I presented myself as a person who is (a) fair, (b) informed, and (c) worth listening to?

PEER REVIEW

Your instructor may suggest—or may even require—that you submit an early draft of your essay to a fellow student or small group of students for comment. Such a procedure benefits both author and readers: You get the responses of a reader and the student-reader gets experience in thinking about the problems of developing an argument, especially in thinking about such matters as the degree of detail that a writer needs to offer to a reader and the importance of keeping the organization evident to a reader.

Oral peer reviews allow for the give and take of discussion, but probably most students and most instructors find written peer reviews more helpful because reviewers think more carefully about their responses to the draft, and they help essayists to get beyond a knee-jerk response to criticism. Online reviews on a class Web site or through e-mail are especially helpful precisely because they are not face to face; the peer reviewer gets practice *writing,* and the essayist is not directly challenged.

✓ A PEER REVIEW CHECKLIST FOR A DRAFT
OF AN ARGUMENT

Read the draft through quickly. Then read it again, with the following questions in mind. Remember: You are reading a draft, a work in progress. You are expected to offer suggestions, and it is also expected that you will offer them courteously.

☐ Does the draft show promise of fulfilling the assignment?

☐ Is the writer's tone appropriate?

☐ Looking at the essay as a whole, what thesis (main idea) is advanced?

☐ Are the needs of the audience kept in mind? For instance, do some words need to be defined? Is the evidence (for instance, the examples and the testimony of authorities) clear and effective?

☐ Can I accept the assumptions? If not, why not?

☐ Is any obvious evidence (or counterevidence) overlooked?

☐ Is the writer proposing a solution? If so,

   ☐ Are other equally attractive solutions adequately examined?

   ☐ Has the writer overlooked some unattractive effects of the proposed solution?

☐ Looking at each paragraph separately,

   ☐ What is the basic point?

   ☐ How does each paragraph relate to the essay's main idea or to the previous paragraph?

   ☐ Should some paragraphs be deleted? Be divided into two or more paragraphs? Be combined? Be put elsewhere? (If you outline the essay by jotting down the gist of each paragraph, you will get help in answering these questions.)

   ☐ Is each sentence clearly related to the sentence that precedes and to the sentence that follows?

   ☐ Is each paragraph adequately developed? Are there sufficient details, perhaps brief supporting quotations from the text?

   ☐ Are the introductory and concluding paragraphs effective?

☐ What are the paper's chief strengths?

☐ Make at least two specific suggestions that you think will assist the author to improve the paper.

A STUDENT'S ESSAY, FROM
ROUGH NOTES TO FINAL VERSION

While we were revising this textbook, we asked the students in one of our classes to write a short essay (500–750 words) on some ethical problem that concerned them. Because this assignment was the first writing assignment in the course, we explained that a good way to get ideas is to ask oneself some questions, jot down responses, question those responses, and write freely for ten minutes or so, not worrying about contradictions. We invited our students to hand in their initial jottings along with the finished essay, so that we could get a sense of how they proceeded as writers. Not all of them chose to hand in their jottings, but we were greatly encouraged by those who did. What was encouraging was the confirmation of an old belief, the belief—we call it a fact— that students will hand in a thoughtful essay if before they prepare a final version they nag themselves, ask themselves *why* they think this or that, jot down their responses, and are not afraid to change their minds as they proceed.

Here are the first jottings of a student, Emily Andrews, who elected to write about whether to give money to street beggars. She simply put down ideas, one after the other.

> Help the poor? Why do I (sometimes) do it?
>
> I feel guilty, and think I should help them: poor, cold, hungry (but also some of them are thirsty for liquor, and will spend the money on liquor, not on food).
>
> I also feel annoyed by them—most of them.
>
> Where does the expression "the deserving poor" come from?
>
> And "poor but honest"? Actually, that sounds a bit odd. Wouldn't "rich but honest" make more sense?
>
> Why don't they work? Fellow with red beard, always by bus stop in front of florist's shop, always wants a handout. He is a regular, there all day every day, so I guess he is in a way "reliable," so why doesn't he put the same time in on a job?
>
> Or why don't they get help? Don't they know they need it? They *must* know they need it.
>
> Maybe that guy with the beard is just a con artist. Maybe he makes more money by panhandling than he would by working, and it's a lot easier!

Kinds of poor — how to classify??
> drunks, druggies, etc.
> mentally ill (maybe drunks belong here too)
> decent people who have had terrible luck

Why private charity?

Doesn't it make sense to say we (fortunate individuals) should give some-thing — an occasional handout — to people who have had terrible luck? (I suppose some people might say that there is no need for any of us to give anything — the government takes care of the truly needy — but I *do* believe in giving charity. A month ago a friend of the family passed away, and the woman's children suggested that people might want to make a donation in her name, to a shelter for battered women. I know my parents made a donation.)

BUT how can I tell who is who, which are which? Which of these people asking for "spare change" really need (deserve???) help, and which are phonies? Impossible to tell.

Possibilities:
> Give to no one
> Give to no one but make an annual donation, maybe to United Way
> Give a dollar to each person who asks. This would probably not cost me even a dollar a day
> Occasionally do without something — maybe a CD — or a meal in a restaurant — and give the money I save to people who seem worthy.

WORTHY? What am I saying? How can I, or anyone, tell? The neat-looking guy who says he just lost his job may be a phony, and the dirty bum — probably a drunk — may desperately need food. (OK, so what if he spends the money on liquor instead of food? At least he'll get a little pleasure in life. No! It's not all right if he spends it on drink.)

Other possibilities:
> Do some volunteer work?
> To tell the truth, I don't want to put in the time. I don't feel *that* guilty.

So what's the problem?

Is it, How I can help the very poor (handouts, or through an organiza-tion)? or

How I can feel less guilty about being lucky enough to be able to go to college, and to have a supportive family?

I can't quite bring myself to believe I should help every beggar who approaches, but I also can't bring myself to believe that I should do nothing, on the grounds that:
- a. it's probably their fault
- b. if they are deserving, they can get gov't help. No, I just can't believe that. Maybe some are too proud to look for government help, or don't know that they are entitled to it.

What to do?

On balance, it seems best to
- a. give to United Way
- b. maybe also give to an occasional individual, if I happen to be moved, without worrying about whether he or she is "deserving" (since it's probably impossible to know).

A day after making these notes Emily reviewed them, added a few points, and then made a very brief selection from them to serve as an outline for her first draft:

Opening para.: "poor but honest"? Deserve "spare change"?

Charity: private or through organizations?
>
> pros and cons
> guy at bus
> it wouldn't cost me much, but . . . better to give through
> organizations

Concluding para.: still feel guilty?
>
> maybe mention guy at bus again?

After writing and revising a draft, Emily Andrews submitted her essay to a fellow student for peer review. She then revised her work in light of the suggestions she received and in light of her own further thinking.

On the next page we give the final essay. If after reading the final version you reread the early jottings, you will notice that some of the jottings never made it into the final version. But without the jottings, the essay probably could not have been as interesting as it is. When the writer made the jottings, she was not so much putting down her ideas as *finding* ideas by the process of writing.

Emily Andrews

Professor Barnet

English 102

January 15, 2010

Why I Don't Spare "Spare Change"

"Poor but honest." "The deserving poor." I don't know the origin of these quotations, but they always come to mind when I think of "the poor." But I also think of people who, perhaps through alcohol or drugs, have ruined not only their own lives but also the lives of others in order to indulge in their own pleasure. Perhaps alcoholism and drug addiction really are "diseases," as many people say, but my own feeling — based, of course, not on any serious study — is that most alcoholics and drug addicts can be classified with the "undeserving poor." And that is largely why I don't distribute spare change to panhandlers.

But surely among the street people there are also some who can rightly be called "deserving." Deserving what? My spare change? Or simply the government's assistance? It happens that I have been brought up to believe that it is appropriate to make contributions to charity — let's say a shelter for battered women — but if I give some change to a panhandler, am I making a contribution to charity and thereby helping someone, or, on the contrary, am I perhaps simply encouraging someone not to get help? Or maybe even worse, am I supporting a con artist?

If one believes in the value of private charity, one can give either to needy individuals or to charitable organizations. In giving to a panhandler one may indeed be helping a person who badly needs help, but one cannot be certain that one is giving to a needy individual. In giving to an organization such as the United Way, on the other hand, one can feel that one's money is likely to be used wisely. True, confronted by a beggar one may feel that *this* particular unfortunate individual needs help at *this* moment — a cup of coffee or a sandwich — and the need will not be met unless I put my hand in my pocket right now. But I have come to think that the beggars whom I encounter can get along without my spare change, and indeed perhaps they are actually better off for not having money to buy liquor or drugs.

It happens that in my neighborhood I encounter few panhandlers. There is one fellow who is always by the bus stop where I catch the bus to the college, and I never give him anything precisely because he is always there. He is such a regular that, I think, he ought to be able to hold a regular job. Putting him aside, I probably don't encounter more than three or four beggars in a week. (I'm not counting street musicians. These people seem quite able to work for a living. If they see their "work" as playing or singing, let persons who enjoy their performances pay them. I do not consider myself among their audience.) The truth of the matter is that, since I meet so few beggars, I could give each one a dollar and hardly feel the loss. At most, I might go without seeing a movie some week. But I know nothing about these people, and it's my impression — admittedly based on almost no evidence — that they simply prefer begging to working. I am not generalizing about street people, and certainly I am not talking about street people in the big urban centers. I am talking only about the people whom I actually encounter.

That's why I usually do not give "spare change," and I don't think I will in the future. These people will get along without me. Someone else will come up with money for their coffee or their liquor, or, at worst, they will just have to do without. I will continue to contribute occasionally to a charitable organization, not simply (I hope) to salve my conscience but because I believe that these organizations actually do good work. But I will not attempt to be a mini-charitable organization, distributing (probably to the unworthy) spare change.

THE ESSAY ANALYZED

Finally, here are a few comments about the essay:

The title is informative, alerting the reader to the topic and the author's position. (By the way, the student told us that in her next-to-last draft the title was "Is It Right to Spare 'Spare Change'?" This title, like the revision, introduces the topic but not the author's position. The revised version seems to us to be more striking.)

The opening paragraph holds a reader's interest, partly by alluding to the familiar phrase "the deserving poor" and partly by introducing the *un*familiar phrase "the *un*deserving poor." Notice, too, that this opening paragraph ends by clearly asserting the author's thesis. Of course, writers need not always announce their thesis early, but it is usually advisable to do so. Readers like to know where they are going.

Paragraph two begins by voicing what probably is the reader's somewhat uneasy — perhaps even negative — response to the first paragraph. That is, *the writer has a sense of her audience;* she knows how her reader feels, and she takes account of the feeling.

Paragraph three clearly sets forth the alternatives. A reader may disagree with the writer's attitude, but the alternatives seem to be stated fairly.

Paragraphs four and five are more personal than the earlier paragraphs. The writer, more or less having stated what she takes to be the facts, now is entitled to offer a highly personal response to them.

The final paragraph nicely wraps things up by means of the words "spare change," which go back to the title and to the end of the first paragraph. The reader thus experiences a sensation of completeness. The essayist, of course, has not solved the problem for all of us for all time, but she presents a thoughtful argument and ends the essay effectively.

Exercise

In an essay of 500 words, state a claim and support it with evidence. Choose an issue in which you are genuinely interested and about which you already know something. You may want to interview a few experts and do some reading, but don't try to write a highly researched paper. Sample topics:

1. Students in laboratory courses should not be required to participate in the dissection of animals.
2. Washington, D.C., should be granted statehood.
3. Puerto Rico should be granted statehood.
4. Women should, in wartime, be exempted from serving in combat.
5. The annual Miss America contest is an insult to women.
6. The government should not offer financial support to the arts.
7. The chief fault of the curriculum in high school was . . .
8. Grades should be abolished in college and university courses.
9. No specific courses should be required in colleges or universities.

7

Using Sources

Research is formalized curiosity. It is poking and prying with a purpose.
— ZORA NEALE HURSTON

There is no way of exchanging information that does not involve an act of judgment.
— JACOB BRONOWSKI

For God's sake, stop researching for a while and begin to think.
— WALTER HAMILTON MOBERLY

A problem adequately stated is a problem on its way to being solved.
— R. BUCKMINSTER FULLER

I have yet to see any problem, however complicated, which, when you looked at it in the right way, did not become still more complicated.
— POUL ANDERSON

WHY USE SOURCES?

We have pointed out that one gets ideas by writing. In the exercise of writing a draft, ideas begin to form, and these ideas stimulate further ideas, especially when one questions—when one *thinks* about—what one has written. But of course in writing about complex, serious questions, nobody is expected to invent all the answers. On the contrary, a writer is expected to be familiar with the chief answers already produced by others and to make use of them through selective incorporation and criticism. In short, writers are not expected to reinvent the wheel; rather, they are expected to make good use of it and perhaps round it off a bit or replace a defective spoke. In order to think out your own views in writing, you are expected to do some preliminary research into the views of others.

When you are trying to understand an issue, high-quality sources will inform you of the various approaches others have taken and will help you establish what the facts are. Once you are informed enough to take a position, the sources you present to your readers will inform and

262

persuade them, just as expert witnesses are sometimes brought in to inform and persuade a jury.

Research isn't limited to the world of professors and scientists. In one way or another, everyone does research at some point. If you want to persuade your city council to increase the number of bicycle lanes on city streets, you could bolster your argument with statistics on how much money the city could save if more people rode their bikes to work. If you decide to open your own business, you would do plenty of market research to persuade your bank that you could repay a loan. Sources (whether published information or data you gather yourself through interviews, surveys, or observation) are not only useful for background information; well-chosen and carefully analyzed sources are evidence for your readers that you know what you're talking about and that your interpretation is sound.

Research is often misconstrued as the practice of transcribing information. In fact, it's a process of asking questions and gathering information that helps you come to conclusions about an issue. By using the information you find as evidence, you can develop an effective argument. But don't spend too much time searching, and then waiting until the last minute to start writing. As you begin your search, jot down observations and questions. When you find a useful source, take notes on what you think it means in your own words. This way, you won't find yourself with a pile of printouts and books and no idea what to say about them. What you have to say will flow naturally out of the pre-writing you've already done—and that pre-writing will help guide your search.

The process of research isn't always straightforward and neat. It involves scanning what other people have said about a topic and seeing what kinds of questions have been raised. As you poke and pry, you will learn more about the issue, and that, in turn, will help you develop a question to focus your efforts. Once you have a central idea—a thesis—you can sharpen your search to seek out the evidence that will make your readers sit up and take notice.

Consider arguments about whether athletes should be permitted to take anabolic steroids, drugs that supposedly build up muscle, restore energy, and enhance aggressiveness. A thoughtful argument on this subject will have to take account of information that the writer can gather only by doing some research.

- Do steroids really have the effects commonly attributed to them?
- And are they dangerous?
- If they are dangerous, how dangerous are they?

After all, competitive sports are inherently dangerous, some of them highly so. Many boxers, jockeys, and football players have suffered severe injury, even death, from competing. Does anyone believe that anabolic steroids are more dangerous than the contests themselves?

Obviously, again, a respectable argument about steroids will have to show awareness of what is known about them.

Or take this question:

Why did President Truman order that atomic bombs be dropped on Hiroshima and Nagasaki?

The most obvious answer is to end the war, but some historians believe he had a very different purpose. In their view, Japan's defeat was ensured before the bombs were dropped, and the Japanese were ready to surrender; the bombs were dropped not to save American (or Japanese) lives but to show Russia that the United States would not be pushed around. Scholars who hold this view, such as Gar Alperovitz in *Atomic Diplomacy* (1965), argue that Japanese civilians in Hiroshima and Nagasaki were incinerated not to save the lives of American soldiers who otherwise would have died in an invasion of Japan but to teach Stalin a lesson. Dropping the bombs, it is argued, marked not the end of the Pacific War but the beginning of the cold war.

One must ask: What evidence supports this argument or claim or thesis, which assumes that Truman could not have thought the bomb was needed to defeat the Japanese because the Japanese knew they were defeated and would soon surrender without a hard-fought defense that would cost hundreds of thousands of lives? What about the momentum that had built up to use the bomb? After all, years of effort and $2 billion had been expended to produce a weapon with the intention of using it to end the war against Germany. But Germany had been defeated without the use of the bomb. Meanwhile, the war in the Pacific continued unabated. If the argument we are considering is correct, all this background counted for little or nothing in Truman's decision, a decision purely diplomatic and coolly indifferent to human life. The task for the writer is to evaluate the evidence available and then to argue for or against the view that Truman's purpose in dropping the bomb was to impress the Soviet government.

A student writing on the topic will certainly want to consult the chief books on the subject (Alperovitz's, cited above, Martin Sherwin's *A World Destroyed* [1975], and John Toland's *The Rising Sun* [1970]) and perhaps reviews of them, especially the reviews in journals devoted to political science. (Reading a searching review of a serious scholarly book is a good way to identify quickly some of the book's main contributions and controversial claims.) Truman's letters and statements and books and articles about Truman are also clearly relevant, and doubtless important articles are to be found in recent issues of scholarly journals and electronic sources. In fact, even an essay on such a topic as whether Truman was morally justified in using the atomic bomb for *any* purpose will be a stronger essay if it is well informed about such matters as the estimated loss of life that an invasion would have cost, the international rules governing weapons, and Truman's own statements about the issue.

How does one go about finding the material needed to write a well-informed argument? We will provide help, but first we want to offer a few words about choosing a topic.

CHOOSING A TOPIC

We will be brief. If a topic is not assigned, choose one that

- Interests you and
- Can be researched with reasonable thoroughness in the allotted time.

Topics such as censorship, the environment, and sexual harassment obviously impinge on our lives, and it may well be that one such topic is of especial interest to you. But the scope of these topics makes researching them potentially overwhelming. Type the word *censorship* into an **Internet** search engine, and you will be referred to millions of information sources.

This brings us to our second point—a manageable topic. Any of the previous topics would need to be narrowed substantially before you could begin searching in earnest. Similarly, a topic such as the causes of World War II can hardly be mastered in a few weeks or argued in a ten-page paper. It is simply too big.

You can, however, write a solid paper analyzing, evaluating, and arguing for or against General Eisenhower's views on atomic warfare. What were they, and when did he hold them? (In his books of 1948 and 1963 Eisenhower says that he opposed the use of the bomb before Hiroshima and that he argued with Secretary of War Henry Stimson against dropping it, but what evidence supports these claims? Was Eisenhower attempting to rewrite history in his books?) Eisenhower's own writings and books and other information sources on Eisenhower will, of course, be the major sources for a paper on this topic, but you will also want to look at books and articles about Stimson and at publications that contain information about the views of other generals, so that, for instance, you can compare Eisenhower's view with Marshall's or MacArthur's.

Spend a little time exploring a topic to see if it will be interesting and manageable by taking one or more of these approaches.

- Do a Web search on the topic. Though you may not use any of the sites that turn up, you can quickly put your finger on the pulse of popular approaches to the issue by scanning the first page or two of results to see what issues are getting the most attention.
- Plug the topic into one of the library's article databases. Again, just by scanning titles you can get a sense of what questions are being raised.

- Browse the library shelves where books on the topic are kept. A quick check of the tables of contents of recently published books may give you ideas of how to narrow the topic.

- Ask a librarian to show you where specialized reference books on your topic are found. Instead of general encyclopedias, try sources like these:
  CQ Researcher
  Encyclopedia of Applied Ethics
  Encyclopedia of Bioethics
  Encyclopedia of Crime and Justice
  Encyclopedia of Science, Technology, and Ethics

- Talk to an expert. Members of the faculty who specialize in the area of your topic might be able to spell out some of the most significant controversies around a topic and may point you toward key sources.

FINDING MATERIAL

What strategy you use for finding good sources will depend on your topic. Researching a current issue in politics or popular culture may involve reading recent newspaper articles, scanning information on government Web sites, and locating current statistics. Other topics may be best tackled by seeking out books and scholarly journal articles that are less timely, but more in-depth and analytical. You may want to supplement library and Web sources with your own field work by conducting surveys or interviews.

Critical thinking is crucial to every step of the research process. Whatever strategy you use, remember that you will want to find material that is authoritative, represents a balanced approach to the issues, and is persuasive. As you choose your sources, bear in mind they will be serving as your "expert witnesses" as you make a case to your audience. Their quality and credibility are crucial to your argument.

Finding Quality Information on the Web

The Web is a valuable source of information for many topics and less helpful for others. In general, if you're looking for information on public policy, popular culture, current events, legal affairs, or for any subject of interest to agencies of the federal or state government, the Web is likely to have useful material. If you're looking for literary criticism or scholarly analysis of historical or social issues, you will be better off using library databases, described later in this chapter.

To make good use of the Web, try these strategies.

- Use the most specific terms possible when using a general search engine; put phrases in quotes.

- Use the advanced search option to limit a search to a domain (e.g. *.gov* for government sites) or by date (such as Web sites updated in the past week or month).

- If you're not sure which sites might be good ones for research, try starting with one of the selective directories listed below instead of a general search engine.

- Consider which government agencies and organizations might be interested in your topic and go directly to their Web sites.

- Follow "about" links to see who is behind a Web site and why they put the information on the Web. If there is no "about" link, delete everything after the first slash in the URL to go to the parent site to see if it provides information.

- Use clues in URLs to see where sites originate. For example, URLs containing *.k12* are hosted at elementary and secondary schools, so may be intended for a young audience; those ending in *.gov* are government agencies, so they tend to provide official information.

- Always bear in mind that the sources you choose must be persuasive to your audience. Avoid sites that may be dismissed as unreliable or biased.

Some useful Web sites include the following:

Selective Web Site Directories
   Infomine <http://infomine.ucr.edu/>
   Intute <http://www.intute.ac.uk/>
   Librarian's Internet Index <http://lii.org>

Current News Sources
   Google News <http://news.google.com>
   Kidon Media-Link <http://www.kidon.com/media-link/index.php>

Digital Primary Sources
   American Memory <http://memory.loc.gov>
   Avalon Project <http://avalon.law.yale.edu/default.asp>
   American Rhetoric <http://www.americanrhetoric.com>

Government Information
   GPO Access <http://www.gpoaccess.gov>
   Thomas (federal legislation) <http://thomas.loc.gov>
   University of Michigan Documents Center <http://www.lib.umich.edu/govdocs/>

Scholarly or Scientific Information
   Google Scholar <http://scholar.google.com>
   Scirus <http://www.scirus.com/>

Statistical Information
   American FactFinder <http://factfinder.census.gov>
   Fedstats <http://www.fedstats.gov>
   Pew Global Attitudes Project <http://pewglobal.org>
   U.S. Census Bureau <http://www.census.gov>

A WORD ABOUT WIKIPEDIA

Links to Wikipedia (http://www.wikipedia.org) often rise to the top of Web search results. This vast and decentralized site provides over a million articles on a wide variety of topics. However, anyone can contribute to the online encyclopedia, so the accuracy of articles varies, and, in some cases the coverage of a controversial issue is one-sided or disputed. Even when the articles are accurate, they provide only basic information. Wikipedia's founder, Jimmy Wales, cautions students against using it as a source, except for obtaining general background knowledge: "You're in college; don't cite the encyclopedia."[1]

Finding Articles Using Library Databases

Your library has a wide range of general and specialized databases available through its Web site. Some databases provide references to articles (and perhaps abstracts or summaries) or may provide direct links to the entire text of articles. General and interdisciplinary databases include Academic Search Premier (produced by the EBSCOhost company) and Expanded Academic Index (from InfoTrac).

More specialized databases include PsycINFO (for psychology research) and ERIC (focused on topics in education). Others, such as JSTOR, are full-text digital archives of scholarly journals. You will likely have access to newspaper articles through LexisNexis or Proquest Newsstand, particularly useful for articles that are not available for free on the Web. Look at your library's Web site to see what your options are, or stop by the reference desk for a quick personalized tutorial.

When using databases, first think through your topic using the listing and diagramming techniques described on pages 227–28. List synonyms for your key search terms. As you search, look at words used in titles and descriptors for alternative ideas and make use of the "advanced search" option so that you can easily combine multiple terms. Rarely will you find exactly what you're looking for right away. Try different search terms and different ways to narrow your topic.

Most databases have an advanced search option that offers forms for combining multiple terms. In Figure 7.1, a search on "anabolic steroids" retrieved far too many articles. In this advanced search, three concepts are being combined in a search: anabolic steroids, legal aspects of their use, and use of them by athletes. Related terms are combined with the word "or": *law* or *legal*. The last letters of a word have been replaced with an asterisk so that any ending will be included in the search. Athlet* will search for

---

[1] "Wikipedia Founder Discourages Academic Use of His Creation," *Chronicle of Higher Education: The Wired Campus*, 12 June 2006, 16 Nov. 2006 <http://chronicle.com/wiredcampus/article/1328/wikipedia-founder-discourages-academic-use-of-his-creation>.

FIGURE 7.1   AN ADVANCED WEB SEARCH

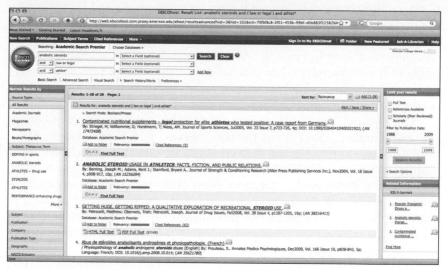

athlete, athletes, or *athletics.* Options on both sides of the list of articles retrieved offer opportunities to refine a search by date of publication or to restrict the results to only academic journals, magazines, or newspapers.

As with a Web search, you'll need to make critical choices about which articles are worth pursuing. In this example, the first article may not be useful because it concerns German law. The second and third look fairly current and potentially useful. Only the third has a full text link, but the others may be available in another database. Many libraries have a program that will check other databases for you at the push of a button; in this case it's indicated by the "Find full text" button.

As you choose sources, keep track of them by selecting choice ones in the list. Then you can print off, save, or e-mail yourself the references you have selected. You may also have an option to export references to citation management program such as RefWorks or EndNote. These programs allow you to create your own personal database of sources in which you can store your references and take notes. Later, when you're ready to create a bibliography, these programs will automatically format your references in MLA, APA, or another style. Ask a librarian if one of these programs is available to students on your campus.

Locating Books

The books that your library owns can be found through its online catalog. Typically, you can search by author or title or, if you don't have a specific book in mind, by keyword or subject. As with databases, think about different search terms to use, keeping an eye out for subject headings used for books that appear relevant. Take advantage of an "advanced search" option. You may, for example, be able to limit a search to books on a particular topic in English published within recent years. In addition to books, the catalog will also list DVDs, sound recordings, and other formats.

Unlike articles, books tend to cover broad topics, so be prepared to broaden your search terms. It may be that a book has a chapter or ten pages that are precisely what you need, but the catalog typically doesn't index the contents of books in detail. Think instead of what kind of book might contain the information you need.

Once you've found some promising books in the catalog, note down the call numbers, find them on the shelves, and then browse. Since books on the same topic are shelved together, you can quickly see what additional books are available by scanning the shelves. As you browse, be sure to look for books that have been published recently enough for your purposes. You do not have to read a book cover-to-cover to use it in your research. Instead, skim the introduction to see if it will be useful, then use its table of contents and index to pinpoint the sections of the book that are the most relevant.

If you have a very specific name or phrase you are searching for, you might try typing it into Google Book Search <http://books.google.com>, which searches the contents of over 7 million scanned books. Though it tends to retrieve too many results for most topics, and you may only be able to see a snippet of context, it can help you locate a particular quote or identify which books might include an unusual name or phrase. There is a "find in a library" link that will help you determine whether the books are available in your library.

INTERVIEWING PEERS AND LOCAL AUTHORITIES

You ought to try to consult experts — for instance, members of the faculty or other local authorities on art, business, law, and so forth. You can also consult interested laypersons. Remember, however, that experts have their biases and that "ordinary" people may have knowledge that experts lack. When interviewing experts, keep in mind Picasso's comment: "You mustn't always believe what I say. Questions tempt you to tell lies, particularly when there is no answer."

If you are interviewing your peers, you will probably want to make an effort to get a representative sample. Of course, even within a group not all members share a single view — many African Americans favor affirmative action but not all do, and many gays favor legalizing gay marriage but, again, some don't. Make an effort to talk to a range of people who might be expected to offer varied opinions. You may learn some unexpected things.

Here we will concentrate, however, on interviews with experts.

1. **Finding subjects for interviews**   If you are looking for expert opinions, you may want to start with a faculty member on your campus. You may already know the instructor, or you may have to scan the catalog to see who teaches courses relevant to your topic. Department

secretaries and college Web sites are good sources of information about the special interests of the faculty and also about lecturers who will be visiting the campus.

2. **Doing preliminary homework**   (1) In requesting the interview, make evident your interest in the topic and in the person. (If you know something about the person, you will be able to indicate why you are asking him or her.) (2) Request the interview, preferably in writing, a week in advance, and ask for ample time—probably half an hour to an hour. Indicate whether the material will be confidential, and (if you want to use a recorder) ask if you may record the interview. (3) If the person accepts the invitation, ask if he or she recommends any preliminary reading, and establish a time and a suitable place, preferably not the cafeteria during lunchtime.

3. **Preparing thoroughly**   (1) If your interviewee recommended any reading or has written on the topic, read the material. (2) Tentatively formulate some questions, keeping in mind that (unless you are simply gathering material for a survey of opinions) you want more than yes or no answers. Questions beginning with *Why* and *How* will usually require the interviewee to go beyond yes and no.

Even if your subject has consented to let you bring a recorder, be prepared to take notes on points that strike you as especially significant; without written notes, you will have nothing if the recorder has malfunctioned. Further, by taking occasional notes you will give the interviewee some time to think and perhaps to rephrase or to amplify a remark.

4. **Conducting the interview**   (1) Begin by engaging in brief conversation, without taking notes. If the interviewee has agreed to let you use a recorder, settle on the place where you will put it. (2) Come prepared with an opening question or two, but as the interview proceeds, don't hesitate to ask questions that you had not anticipated asking. (3) Near the end (you and your subject have probably agreed on the length of the interview) ask the subject if he or she wishes to add anything, perhaps by way of clarifying some earlier comment. (4) Conclude by thanking the interviewee and by offering to provide a copy of the final version of your paper.

5. **Writing up the interview**   (1) As soon as possible—certainly within twenty-four hours after the interview—review your notes and clarify them. At this stage, you can still remember the meaning of your abbreviated notes and shorthand devices (maybe you have been using *n* to stand for *nurses* in clinics where abortions are performed), but if you wait even a whole day you may be puzzled by your own notes. If you have recorded the interview, you may want to transcribe all of it—the laboriousness of this task is one good reason why many interviewers do not use recorders—and you may then want to scan the whole and mark the parts that now strike you as especially significant. If you have taken notes by hand, type them up, along with your own observations, for example, "Jones was very tentative on this matter, but she said she was inclined to believe that . . ." (2) Be especially careful to indicate which words are direct quotations. If in doubt, check with the interviewee.

EVALUATING YOUR SOURCES

Each step of the way, you will be making choices about your sources. As your research proceeds, from selecting promising items in a database search to browsing the book collection, you will want to use the techniques for previewing and skimming detailed on pages 000–00 in order to make your first selection. Ask yourself some basic questions.

- Is this source relevant?
- Is it current enough?
- Does the title and/or abstract suggest it will address an important aspect of my topic?
- Am I choosing sources that represent a range of ideas, not simply ones that support my opinion?

Once you have collected a number of likely sources, you will want to do further filtering. Examine each one with these questions in mind.

- *Is this source credible? Does it include information about the author and his or her credentials that can help me decide whether to rely on it?* In the case of books, you might check a database for book reviews for a second opinion. In the case of Web sites, find out where the site came from and why it has been posted on the Web. Don't use a Web source if you can't determine its authorship or purpose.

- *Will my audience find this source credible and persuasive?* Some publishers are more selective about which books they publish than others. University presses, for instance, have several experts read and comment on manuscripts before they decide which to publish. A story about U.S. politics from the *Washington Post*, whose writers conduct first-hand reporting in the nation's capital, carries more clout than a story from a small-circulation newspaper that is drawing its information from a wire service. A scholarly source may be more impressive than a magazine article.

- *Am I using the best evidence available?* Quoting directly from a government report may be more effective than quoting a news story that summarizes the report. Finding evidence that supports your claims in a president's speeches or letters is more persuasive than drawing your conclusions from a page or two of a history textbook.

- *Am I being fair to all sides?* Make sure you are prepared to address alternate perspectives, even if you ultimately take a position. Avoid sources that clearly promote an agenda in favor of ones that your audience will consider balanced and reliable.

- *Can I corroborate my key claims in more than one source?* Compare your sources to ensure that you aren't relying on facts that can't be confirmed. If you're having trouble confirming a source, check with a librarian.

- *Do I really need this source?* It's tempting to use all the books and articles you have found, but if two sources say essentially the same thing, choose the one that is likely to carry the most weight with your audience.

The information you will look for as you evaluate a Web source is often the same as what you need to record in a citation. You can streamline the process of creating a list of works cited by identifying these elements as you evaluate a source.

In Figure 7.2, the URL includes the ending *.gov*—meaning it is a government Web site, an official document that has been vetted. There is an

FIGURE 7.2   A HOMEPAGE FROM A GOVERNMENT WEB SITE

1. URL—Site has a .gov domain.
2. Sponsor
3. Author
4. Link will explain that this institute is a government agency.
5. Corporate author
6. Web site name
7. Title of page
8. Table of contents
9. Scanning list will give an idea of whether source is reliable and useful.

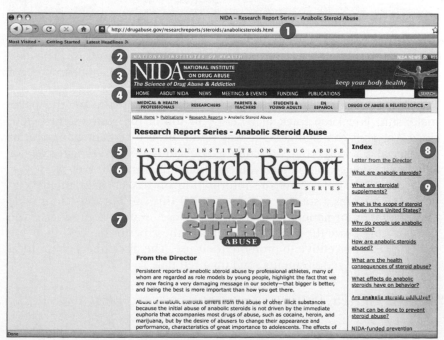

FIGURE 7.3   A HOMEPAGE FROM A COMMERCIAL WEB SITE

This is a .com (commercial) site.

Table of contents looks useful, but . . .   Images seem to promote steriod use.

Disclaimers seem defensive.   Steroids are for sale.

"about" link that will explain the government agency's mission. The date is found at the bottom of the page: "revised 2006." This appears to be a high-quality source of basic information on the issue.

The information you need to cite this report is also on the page; make sure you keep track of where you found the source and when, since Web sites can change. One way to do this is by creating an account at a social bookmarking site such as Delicious *<http://delicious.com>* or Diigo *<http://diigo.com>* where you can store and annotate Web sites.

Figure 7.3 shows how the information on a Web page might lead you to reject it as a source. Clearly, though this site purports to provide educational information, its primary purpose is to sell products. The graphics emphasize the supposed benefits of these performance-enhancing drugs, a visual incentive to promote their use. The disclaimers about legal liability and age requirements send up a red flag.

TAKING NOTES

When it comes to taking notes, all researchers have their own habits that they swear by, and they can't imagine any other way of working. We still

---

✓ A CHECKLIST FOR EVALUATING PRINT SOURCES

For Books:

☐ Is the book recent? If not, is the information I will be using from it likely or unlikely to change over time?

☐ What are the author's credentials?

☐ Is the book titled toward entertainment, or is it in-depth and even-handed?

☐ Is the book broad enough in its focus and written in a style I can understand?

☐ Does the book relate directly to my tentative thesis, or is it of only tangential interest?

☐ Do the arguments in the book seem sound, based on what I have learned about skillful critical reading and writing?

For Articles from Periodicals:

☐ Is the periodical recent?

☐ Is the author's name given? Does he or she seem a credible source?

☐ Does the article treat the topic superficially or in-depth? Does it take sides, or does it offer enough context so that you can make up your own mind?

☐ How directly does the article speak to my topic and tentative thesis?

☐ If the article is from a scholarly journal, am I sure I understand it?

---

prefer to take notes on four- by six-inch index cards, while others use a notebook or a computer for note taking. If you use a citation management program, such as RefWorks or EndNote, you can store your personal notes and commentary with the citations you have saved. Using the program's search function, you can easily pull together related notes and citations, or you can create project folders for your references so that you can easily review what you've collected.

Whatever method you use, the following techniques should help you maintain consistency and keep organized during the research process:

1. If you use a notebook or cards, write in ink (pencil gets smudgy), and write on only one side of the card or paper. (Notes on the backs of cards tend to get lost, and writing on the back of paper will prevent you from later cutting up and rearranging your notes.)
2. Put only one idea in each notebook or computer entry or on each card (though an idea may include several facts).
3. Put a brief heading on each entry or card, such as "Truman's last words on A-bomb."
4. Summarize, for the most part, rather than quote at length.

✔ A CHECKLIST FOR EVALUATING ELECTRONIC SOURCES

An enormous amount of valuable material is available on the World Wide Web—but so is an enormous amount of junk. True, there is also plenty of junk in books and journals, but most printed material has been subjected to a review process: Book publishers and editors of journals send manuscripts to specialized readers who evaluate them and recommend whether the material should or should not be published. Publishing on the Web is quite different. Anyone can publish on the Web with no review process: All that is needed is the right software. Ask yourself:

☐ What person or organization produced the site (a commercial entity, a nonprofit entity, a student, an expert)? Check the electronic address to get a clue about the authorship. If there is a link to the author's homepage, check it out to learn about the author. Does the author have an affiliation with a respectable institution?

☐ What is the purpose of the site? Is the site in effect an infomercial, or is it an attempt to contribute to a thoughtful discussion?

☐ Are the sources of information indicated and verifiable? If possible, check the sources.

☐ Is the site authoritative enough to use? (If it seems to contain review materials or class handouts, you probably don't want to take it too seriously.)

☐ When was the page made available? Is it out of date?

---

5. Quote only passages in which the writing is especially effective, or passages that are in some way crucial.

6. Make sure that all quotations are exact. Enclose quoted words within quotation marks, indicate omissions by ellipses (three spaced periods: . . .), and enclose within square brackets ([]) any insertions or other additions you make.

7. *Never* copy a passage, changing an occasional word. *Either* copy it word for word, with punctuation intact, and enclose it within quotation marks, *or* summarize it drastically. If you copy a passage but change a word here and there, you may later make the mistake of using your note verbatim in your essay, and you will be guilty of plagiarism.

8. Give the page number of your source, whether you summarize or quote. If a quotation you have copied runs in the original from the bottom of page 210 to the top of page 211, in your notes put a diagonal line (/) after the last word on page 210, so that later, if in your paper you quote only the material from page 210, you will know that you must cite 210 and not 210–11.

9. Indicate the source. The author's last name is enough if you have consulted only one work by the author; but if you consult more than one work by an author, you need further identification, such as the author's name and a short title.

10. Add your own comments about the substance of what you are recording. Such comments as "but contrast with Sherwin" or "seems illogical" or "evidence?" will ensure that you are thinking as well as writing and will be of value when you come to transform your notes into a draft. Be sure, however, to enclose such notes within double diagonals (//), or to mark them in some other way, so that later you will know they are yours and not your source's. If you use a computer for note taking, you may wish to write your comments in italics or in a different font.

11. In a separate computer file or notebook page or on separate index cards, write a bibliographic entry for each source. The information in each entry will vary, depending on whether the source is a book, a periodical, an electronic document, and so forth. The kind of information (for example, author and title) needed for each type of source can be found in the sections on MLA Format: The List of Works Cited (p. 295) or APA Format: The List of References (p. 308).

A NOTE ON PLAGIARIZING, PARAPHRASING, AND USING COMMON KNOWLEDGE

Plagiarism is the unacknowledged use of someone else's work. The word comes from a Latin word for "kidnapping," and plagiarism is indeed the stealing of something engendered by someone else. We won't deliver a sermon on the dishonesty (and folly) of plagiarism; we intend only to help you understand exactly what plagiarism is. The first thing to say is that plagiarism is not limited to the unacknowledged quotation of words.

A *paraphrase* is a sort of word-by-word or phrase-by-phrase translation of the author's language into your own language. Unlike a summary, then, a paraphrase is approximately as long as the original. Why would anyone paraphrase something? There are two good reasons:

- You may, as a reader, want to paraphrase a passage in order to make certain that you are thinking carefully about each word in the original;

- You may, as a writer, want to paraphrase a difficult passage in order to help your reader.

Paraphrase thus has its uses, but it is often unnecessarily used, and students who overuse it may find themselves crossing the border into plagiarism. True, if you paraphrase you are using your own words, but

- You are also using someone else's ideas, and, equally important,
- You are using this other person's sequence of thoughts.

Even if you change every third word in your source, you are plagiarizing.

Here is an example of this sort of plagiarism, based on the previous sentence:

> Even if you alter every second or third word that your source gives, you still are plagiarizing.

Further, even if the writer of this paraphrase had cited a source after the paraphrase, he or she would still have been guilty of plagiarism. How, you may ask, can a writer who cites a source be guilty of plagiarism? Easy. Readers assume that only the gist of the idea is the source's, and that the development of the idea—the way it is set forth—is the present writer's work. A paraphrase that runs to several sentences is in no significant way the writer's work: the writer is borrowing not only the idea but the shape of the presentation, the sentence structure. What the writer needs to do is to write something like this:

> Changing an occasional word does not free the writer from the
> obligation to cite a source.

And the source would still need to be cited, if the central idéa were not a commonplace one.

The point that even if you cite a source for your paraphrase you are nevertheless plagiarizing—unless you clearly indicate that the entire passage is a paraphrase of the source—cannot be overemphasized.

You are plagiarizing if, without giving credit, you use someone else's ideas—even if you put these ideas entirely into your own words. When you use another's ideas, you must indicate your indebtedness by saying something like "Alperovitz points out that . . ." or "Secretary of War Stimson, as Martin Sherwin notes, never expressed himself on this point." Alperovitz and Sherwin pointed out something that you had not thought of, and so you must give them credit if you want to use their findings.

Again, even if after a paraphrase you cite your source, you are plagiarizing. How, you may wonder, can you be guilty of plagiarism if you cite a source? Easy. A reader assumes that the citation refers to information or an opinion, *not* to the presentation or development of the idea; and of course, in a paraphrase you are not presenting or developing the material in your own way.

Now consider this question: *Why* paraphrase? Often there is no good answer. Since a paraphrase is as long as the original, you may as well quote the original, if you think that a passage of that length is worth quoting. Probably it is *not* worth quoting in full; probably you should *not* paraphrase but rather should drastically *summarize* most of it, and perhaps quote a particularly effective phrase or two. As we explained on pages 38–43, the chief reason to paraphrase a passage is to clarify it — that is, to make certain that you and your readers understand a passage that — perhaps because it is badly written — is obscure.

Generally, what you should do is

- Take the idea and put it entirely into your own words, perhaps reducing a paragraph of a hundred words to a sentence of ten words, but you must still give credit for the idea.

- If you believe that the original hundred words are so perfectly put that they cannot be transformed without great loss, you'll have to quote them in full and cite your source. You may in this case want to tell the reader *why* you are quoting at such great length.

In short, chiefly you will quote or you will summarize, and only rarely will you paraphrase, but in all cases you will cite your source. There is no point in paraphrasing an author's hundred words into a hundred of your own. Either quote or summarize, but cite the source.

Keep in mind, too, that almost all generalizations about human nature, no matter how common and familiar (for instance, "males are innately more aggressive than females") are not indisputable facts; they are at best hypotheses on which people differ and therefore should

---

✓ A CHECKLIST FOR AVOIDING PLAGIARISM

☐ In my notes did I *always* put quoted material within quotation marks?

☐ In my notes did I summarize *in my own words* and give credit to the source for the idea?

☐ In my notes did I avoid paraphrasing, that is, did I avoid copying, keeping the structure of the source's sentences but using some of my own words? (Paraphrases of this sort, even with a footnote citing the source, are *not* acceptable, since the reader incorrectly assumes that the writing is essentially yours.)

☐ If in my paper I set forth a borrowed idea, do I give credit, even though the words and the shape of the sentences are entirely my own?

☐ If in my paper I quote directly, do I put the words within quotation marks and cite the source?

☐ Do I *not* cite material that can be considered common knowledge (material that can be found in numerous reference works, such as the date of a public figure's birth or the population of San Francisco or the fact that *Hamlet* is regarded as a great tragedy)?

☐ If I have the slightest doubt about whether I should or should not cite a source, have I taken the safe course and cited the source?

either not be asserted at all or should be supported by some cited source or authority. Similarly, because nearly all statistics (whether on the intelligence of criminals or the accuracy of lie detectors) are the result of some particular research and may well have been superseded or challenged by other investigators, it is advisable to cite a source for any statistics you use unless you are convinced they are indisputable, such as the number of registered voters in Memphis in 1988.

On the other hand, there is something called **common knowledge,** and the sources for such information need not be cited. The term does not, however, mean exactly what it seems to. It is common knowledge, of course, that Ronald Reagan was an American president (so you don't cite a source when you make that statement), and under the conventional interpretation of this doctrine, it is also common knowledge that he was born in 1911. In fact, of course, few people other than Reagan's wife and children know this date. Still, information that can be found in many places and that is indisputable belongs to all of us; therefore, a writer need not cite her source when she says that Reagan was born in 1911. Probably she checked a dictionary or an encyclopedia for the date, but the source doesn't matter. Dozens of sources will give exactly the same information, and in fact, no reader wants to be bothered with a citation on such a point.

Some students have a little trouble developing a sense of what is and what is not common knowledge. Although, as we have just said, readers don't want to hear about the sources for information that is indisputable and can be documented in many places, if you are in doubt about whether to cite a source, cite it. Better risk boring the reader a bit than risk being accused of plagiarism.

COMPILING AN ANNOTATED BIBLIOGRAPHY

When several sources have been identified and gathered, many researchers prepare an annotated bibliography. This is a list providing all relevant bibliographic information (just as it will appear in your Works Cited list or References list) as well as a brief descriptive and evaluative summary of each source—perhaps one to three sentences. Your instructor may ask you to provide an annotated bibliography for your research project.

An annotated bibliography serves four main purposes:

- First, constructing such a document helps you to master the material contained in any given source. To find the heart of the argument presented in an article or book, phrase it briefly, and comment on it, you must understand it fully.

- Second, creating an annotated bibliography helps you to think about how each portion of your research fits into the whole of your project, how you will use it, and how it relates to your topic and thesis.

- Third, an annotated bibliography helps your readers: They can quickly see which items may be especially helpful in their own research.

- Fourth, in constructing an annotated bibliography at this early stage, you will get some hands-on practice at bibliographic format, thereby easing the job of creating your final bibliography (the Works Cited list or References list for your paper).

Following are two examples of entries for an annotated bibliography in MLA (Modern Language Association) format for a project on the effect of violence in the media. The first is for a book, the second for an article from a periodical. Notice that each

- Begins with a bibliographic entry—author (last name first), title, and so forth—and then

- Provides information about the content of the work under consideration, suggesting how each may be of use to the final research paper.

Clover, Carol J. *Men, Women, and Chain Saws: Gender in the Modern Horror Film*. Princeton: Princeton UP, 1992. The author focuses on Hollywood horror movies of the 1970s and 1980s. She studies representations of women and girls in these movies and the responses of male viewers to female characters, suggesting that this relationship is more complex and less exploitative than the common wisdom claims.

Winerip, Michael. "Looking for an Eleven O'Clock Fix." *New York Times Magazine* 11 Jan. 1998: 30-40. The article focuses on the rising levels of violence on local television news and highlights a station in Orlando, Florida, that tried to reduce its depictions of violence and lost viewers as a result. Winerip suggests that people only claim to be against media violence, while their actions prove otherwise.

WRITING THE PAPER

Organizing Your Notes

If you have read thoughtfully, taken careful (and, again, thoughtful) notes on your reading, and then (yet again) thought about these notes, you are well on the way to writing a good paper. You have, in fact, already written some of it, in your notes. By now you should clearly have in mind the thesis you intend to argue. But you still have to organize the material, and, doubtless, even as you set about organizing it, you will find points that will require you to do some additional research and much additional thinking.

Divide your notes into clusters, each devoted to one theme or point (for instance, one cluster on the extent of use of steroids, another on evidence that steroids are harmful, yet another on arguments that even if harmful they should be permitted). If your notes are in a computer file, use your word processor's Cut and Paste features to rearrange the notes into appropriate clusters. If you use index cards, simply sort them into packets. If you take notes in a notebook, either mark each note with a number or name indicating the cluster to which it belongs, or cut the notes apart and arrange them as you would cards. Put aside all notes that—however interesting—you now see are irrelevant to your paper.

Next, arrange the clusters or packets into a tentative sequence. In effect, you are preparing a **working outline.** At its simplest, say, you will give three arguments on behalf of *X* and then three counterarguments. (Or you might decide that it is better to alternate material from the two sets of three clusters each, following each argument with an objection. At this stage, you can't be sure of the organization you will finally use, but you can make a tentative decision.)

The First Draft

Draft the essay, without worrying much about an elegant opening paragraph. Just write some sort of adequate opening that states the topic and your thesis. When you revise the whole later, you can put some effort into developing an effective opening. (Most experienced writers find that the opening paragraph in the final version is almost the last thing they write.)

If your notes are on cards or notebook paper, carefully copy into the draft all quotations that you plan to use. If your notes are in a computer, you may simply cut and paste them from one file to another. Do keep in mind, however, that rewriting or retyping quotations will make you think carefully about them and may result in a more focused and thoughtful paper. (In the next section of this chapter we will talk briefly about leading into quotations and about the form of quotations.) Be sure to include citations in your drafts so that if you must check a reference later it will be easy to do so.

Later Drafts

Give the draft, and yourself, a rest—perhaps for a day or two—and then go back to it. Read it over, make necessary revisions, and then **outline** it. That is, on a sheet of paper chart the organization and development, perhaps by jotting down a sentence summarizing each paragraph or each group of closely related paragraphs. Your outline or map may now show you that the paper obviously suffers from poor organization. For instance, it may reveal that you neglected to respond to one argument or that one point is needlessly treated in two places. It may also help you to see that if you gave three arguments and then three counterarguments, you probably should instead have followed each argument with its rebuttal. On the other hand, if you alternated arguments and objections, it may now seem better to use two main groups, all the arguments and then all the criticisms.

No one formula is always right. Much will depend on the complexity of the material. If the arguments are highly complex, it is better to respond to them one by one than to expect a reader to hold three complex arguments in mind before you get around to responding. If, however, the arguments can be stated briefly and clearly, it is effective to state all three and then to go on to the responses. If you write on a word processor, you will find it easy, even fun, to move passages of text around. Even so, you will probably want to print out a hard copy from time to time to review the structure of your paper. Allow enough time to produce several drafts.

A Few More Words about Organization

There is a difference between

- A paper that *has* an organization and
- A paper that helpfully lets the reader know what the organization is.

Write papers of the second sort, but (there is always a "but") take care not to belabor the obvious. Inexperienced writers sometimes either hide the organization so thoroughly that a reader cannot find it, or they so ploddingly lay out the structure ("Eighth, I will show . . .") that the reader becomes impatient. Yet it is better to be overly explicit than to be obscure.

The ideal, of course, is the middle route. Make the overall strategy of your organization evident by occasional explicit signs at the beginning of a paragraph ("We have seen . . . ," "It is time to consider the objections . . . ," "By far the most important . . ."); elsewhere make certain that the implicit structure is evident to the reader. When you reread your draft, if you try to imagine that you are one of your classmates, you will probably be able to sense exactly where explicit signs are needed and where they are not needed. Better still, exchange drafts with a classmate in order to exchange (tactful) advice.

Choosing a Tentative Title

By now a couple of tentative titles for your essay should have crossed your mind. If possible, choose a title that is both interesting and informative. Consider these three titles:

Are Steroids Harmful?

The Fuss over Steroids

Steroids: A Dangerous Game

"Are Steroids Harmful?" is faintly interesting, and it lets the reader know the gist of the subject, but it gives no clue about the writer's thesis, the writer's contention or argument. "The Fuss over Steroids" is somewhat better, for it gives information about the writer's position. "Steroids: A Dangerous Game" is still better; it announces the subject ("steroids") and the thesis ("dangerous"), and it also displays a touch of wit because "game" glances at the world of athletics.

Don't try too hard, however; better a simple, direct, informative title than a strained, puzzling, or overly cute one. And remember to make sure that everything in your essay is relevant to your title. In fact, your title should help you to organize the essay and to delete irrelevant material.

The Final Draft

When at last you have a draft that is for the most part satisfactory, check to make sure that **transitions** from sentence to sentence and from paragraph to paragraph are clear ("Further evidence," "On the other hand," "A weakness, however, is apparent"), and then worry about your opening and your closing paragraphs. Your **opening paragraph** should be clear, interesting, and focused; if neither the title nor the first paragraph announces your thesis, the second paragraph probably should do so.

The **final paragraph** need not say, "In conclusion, I have shown that . . ." It should effectively end the essay, but it need not summarize your conclusions. We have already offered a few words about final paragraphs (p. 246), but the best way to learn how to write such paragraphs is to study the endings of some of the essays in this book and to adopt the strategies that appeal to you.

Be sure that all indebtedness is properly acknowledged. We have talked about plagiarism; now we will turn to the business of introducing quotations effectively.

QUOTING FROM SOURCES

Incorporating Your Reading into Your Thinking: The Art and Science of Synthesis

A much-quoted passage—at least it is much-quoted by teachers of composition and especially by teachers of courses in argument—is by Kenneth Burke (1887–1993), a college dropout who became one of America's most important twentieth-century students of rhetoric. Burke wrote:

> Imagine that you enter a parlor. You come late. When you arrive, others have long preceded you, and they are engaged in a heated discussion, a discussion too heated for them to pause and tell you

exactly what it is about. In fact, the discussion had already begun long before any of them got there, so that no one present is qualified to retrace for you all the steps that had gone before. You listen for a while, until you decide that you have caught the tenor of the argument; then you put in your oar. Someone answers; you answer him; another comes to your defense; another aligns himself against you, to either the embarrassment or gratification of your opponent, depending upon the quality of your ally's assistance. However, the discussion is interminable. The hour grows late, you must depart. And you do depart, with the discussion still vigorously in progress.

> —*The Philosophy of Literary Form* (Baton Rouge:
> Louisiana State University Press, 1941), 110–11.

Why do we quote this passage? Because it is your turn to join the unending conversation.

Notice that Burke says, in this metaphoric discussion of the life of a thoughtful person, "You listen for a while, until you decide that you have caught the tenor of the argument; then you put in your oar." There may be times in your daily life when it is acceptable to make use of Twitter and to shoot off 140 characters, but for serious matters you will want to think about what you are saying before you give it to the world, and you will want to convey your thoughts in more than 140 characters. (We admit that quite a lot can be said in 140 characters, for instance the forceful words in *Brown v. Board of Education of Topeka* that "Separate educational facilities are inherently unequal," or the anonymous insight that "There is no such thing as a free lunch," but most of us lack the genius that will enable us to produce such compressed wisdom.)

During the process of reading, and afterwards, you will want to listen, think, say to yourself something like

- "No, no, I see things very differently; it seems to me that . . . " or
- "Yes, of course, but on one large issue I think I differ," or
- "Yes, sure, I agree, but I would go further and add . . ." or
- "Yes, I agree with your conclusion, but I hold this conclusion for reasons very different from the ones that you offer."

During your composition courses, at least (and we think during your entire life), you will be reading or listening, and will sometimes want to put in your oar—you will sometimes want to respond in writing, for example in the form of a Letter to the Editor, or in a memo at your place of employment. In the course of your response you almost surely will have to summarize very briefly the idea or ideas you are responding to, so that your readers will understand the context of your remarks. These ideas may not come from a single source; you may be responding to several sources. For instance, you may be responding to a report and also to some comments that the report evoked. In any case, you will state these ideas briefly and fairly, and will then set forth your thoughtful responses, thereby giving the reader a statement that you hope represents an advance in the argument, even if only a tiny one. That is, you will **synthesize** sources, combining existing material into something new, drawing nourishment from what has already been said (giving credit, of course), and converting it into something new—a view that you think is worth considering.

Let's pause for a moment and consider this word **synthesis.** You probably are familiar with *photosynthesis*, the chemical process in green plants that produces carbohydrates from carbon dioxide and hydrogen. Synthesis, again, combines pre-existing elements and produces something new. In our use of the word *synthesis*, even a view that you utterly reject becomes a part of your new creation *because it helped to stimulate you to formulate your view*; without the idea that you reject, you might not have developed the view that you now hold. Consider the words of Francis Bacon, Shakespeare's contemporary:

> Some books are to be tasted, others to be swallowed, and some few to be chewed and digested.

Your instructor will expect you to digest the readings—this does not mean you need to accept them, but only that you need to read them thoughtfully—and that, so to speak, you make them your own thoughts by refining them. Your readers will expect you to tell them *what you make out of the assigned readings*, which means that you will go beyond writing a summary and will synthesize the material into your own contribution. *Your* view is what is wanted, and readers expect this view to be thoughtful—not mere summary and not mere tweeting.

A RULE FOR WRITERS: In your final draft *you must give credit to all of your sources.* Let your reader know whether you are quoting (in this case, you will use quotation marks around all material directly quoted), or whether you are summarizing (you will explicitly say so), or whether you are paraphrasing (again, you will explicitly say so).

The Use and Abuse of Quotations

When is it necessary, or appropriate, to quote? Sometimes the reader must see the exact words of your source; the gist won't do. If you are arguing that Z's definition of *rights* is too inclusive, your readers have to know exactly how Z defined *rights*. Your brief summary of the definition may be unfair to Z; in fact, you want to convince your readers that you are being fair, and so you quote Z's definition, word for word. Moreover, if the passage is only a sentence or two long, or even if it runs to a paragraph, it may be so compactly stated that it defies summary. And to attempt to paraphrase it—substituting *natural* for *inalienable,* and so forth—saves no space and only introduces imprecision. There is nothing to do but to quote it, word for word.

Second, you may want to quote a passage that could be summarized but that is so effectively stated that you want your readers to have the pleasure of reading the original. Of course, readers will not give you credit for writing these words, but they will give you credit for your taste and for your effort to make especially pleasant the business of reading your paper.

In short, use (but don't overuse) quotations. Speaking roughly, quotations

- Should occupy no more than 10 to 15 percent of your paper, and
- They may occupy much less.

Most of your paper should set forth your ideas, not other people's ideas.

How to Quote

Long and Short Quotations   **Long quotations** (five or more lines of typed prose or three or more lines of poetry) are set off from your text. To set off material, start on a new line, indent one inch from the left margin, and type the quotation double-spaced. Do not enclose quotations within quotation marks if you are setting them off.

Short quotations are treated differently. They are embedded within the text; they are enclosed within quotation marks, but otherwise they do not stand out.

All quotations, whether set off or embedded, must be exact. If you omit any words, you must indicate the ellipsis by substituting three spaced periods for the omission; if you insert any words or punctuation, you must indicate the addition by enclosing it within square brackets, not to be confused with parentheses.

Leading into a Quotation   Now for a less mechanical matter, the way in which a quotation is introduced. To say that it is "introduced" implies that one leads into it, though on rare occasions a quotation appears without an introduction, perhaps immediately after the title. Normally one leads into a quotation by giving

- The *name of the author* and (no less important)
- *Clues signaling the content of the quotation and the purpose* it serves in the present essay. For example:

William James provides a clear answer to Huxley when he says that ". . ."

The writer has been writing about Huxley and now is signaling readers that they will be getting James's reply. The writer is also signaling (in "a clear answer") that the reply is satisfactory. If the writer believed that James's answer was not really acceptable, the lead-in might have run thus:

> William James attempts to answer Huxley, but his response does not really meet the difficulty Huxley calls attention to. James writes, ". . ."

or thus:

> William James provided what he took to be an answer to Huxley when he said that ". . ."

In this last example, clearly the words "what he took to be an answer" imply that the essayist will show, after the quotation from James, that the answer is in some degree inadequate. Or the essayist may wish to suggest the inadequacy even more strongly:

IDEA PROMPT 7.1 SIGNAL PHRASES

Think of your writing as a conversation between you and your sources. As in conversation, you want to be able to move smoothly between different, sometimes contrary, points of view. You also want to be able to set your thoughts apart from those of yours sources. Signal phrases make it easy for your readers to know where your information came from and why it's trustworthy by including key facts about the source.

> According to psychologist Stephen Ceci . . .

> A report published by the U.S. Bureau of Justice Statistics concludes . . .

> Feminist philosopher Sandra Harding argues . . .

To avoid repetitiveness, vary your sentence structure.

> . . . claims Stephen Ceci.

> . . . according to a report published by the U.S. Bureau of Statistics.

Useful verbs to introduce sources:

acknowledges	contends	points out
argues	denies	recommends
believes	disputes	reports
claims	observes	suggests

Note that papers written using MLA style refer to sources in the present tense. Papers written in APA style use the past tense (acknowledged, argued, believed).

A CHECKLIST FOR USING QUOTATIONS RATHER THAN SUMMARIES

Ask yourself the following questions. If you cannot answer yes to at least one of the questions, consider *summarizing* the material rather than quoting it in full.

☐ Is the quotation given because it is necessary for the reader to see the exact wording of the original?

☐ Is the quotation given because the language is especially engaging?

☐ Is the quotation given because the author is a respected authority and the passage lends weight to my argument?

> William James provided what he took to be an answer to Huxley, but he
> used the word *religion* in a way that Huxley would not have allowed.
> James argues that ". . ."

If after reading something by Huxley the writer had merely given us "William James says . . . ," we wouldn't know whether we were getting confirmation, refutation, or something else. The essayist would have put a needless burden on the readers. Generally speaking, the more difficult the quotation, the more important is the introductory or explanatory lead-in, but even the simplest quotation profits from some sort of brief lead-in, such as "James reaffirms this point when he says . . ."

> **A RULE FOR WRITERS:** In introducing a quotation, it is usually
> advisable to signal the reader *why* you are using the quotation, by
> means of a lead-in consisting of a verb or a verb and adverb, such
> as *claims*, or *convincingly shows*, or *admits*.

DOCUMENTATION

In the course of your essay, you will probably quote or summarize material derived from a source. You must give credit, and although there is no one form of documentation to which all scholarly fields subscribe, you will probably be asked to use one of two. One, established by the Modern Language Association (MLA), is used chiefly in the humanities; the other, established by the American Psychological Association (APA), is used chiefly in the social sciences.

We include two papers that use sources. "Why Trials Should Not Be Televised" (p. 313) uses the MLA format. "The Role of Spirituality and Religion in Mental Health" (p. 327) follows the APA format. (You may notice that various styles are illustrated in other selections we have included.)

A Note on Footnotes (and Endnotes)

Before we discuss these two formats, a few words about footnotes are in order. Before the MLA and the APA developed their rules of style, citations commonly were given in footnotes. Although today footnotes are not so frequently used to give citations, they still may be useful for another purpose. (The MLA suggests endnotes rather than footnotes, but all readers know that, in fact, footnotes are preferable to endnotes. After all, who wants to keep shifting from a page of text to a page of notes at the rear?) If you want to include some material that may seem intrusive in the body of the paper, you may relegate it to a footnote. For example, in a footnote you might translate a quotation given in a foreign language, or you might demote from text to footnote a paragraph explaining why you are not taking account of such-and-such a point. By putting the matter in a footnote you are signaling the reader that it is dispensable; it is something relevant but not essential, something extra that you are, so to speak, tossing in. Don't make a habit of writing this sort of note, but there are times when it is appropriate.

MLA Format: Citations within the Text

Brief citations within the body of the essay give credit, in a highly abbreviated way, to the sources for material you quote, summarize, or make use of in any other way. These *in-text citations* are made clear by a list of sources, titled Works Cited, appended to the essay. Thus, in your essay you may say something like this:

> Commenting on the relative costs of capital punishment and life imprisonment, Ernest van den Haag says that he doubts "that capital punishment really is more expensive" (33).

The **citation,** the number 33 in parentheses, means that the quoted words come from page 33 of a source (listed in the Works Cited) written by van den Haag. Without a Works Cited, a reader would have no way of knowing that you are quoting from page 33 of an article that appeared in the February 8, 1985, issue of the *National Review*.

Usually the parenthetic citation appears at the end of a sentence, as in the example just given, but it can appear elsewhere; its position will depend chiefly on your ear, your eye, and the context. You might, for example, write the sentence thus:

Ernest van den Haag doubts that "capital punishment really is more expensive" than life imprisonment (33), but other writers have presented figures that contradict him.

Five points must be made about these examples:

1. **Quotation marks**   The closing quotation mark appears after the last word of the quotation, *not* after the parenthetic citation. Since the citation is not part of the quotation, the citation is not included within the quotation marks.

2. **Omission of words (ellipsis)**   If you are quoting a complete sentence or only a phrase, as in the examples given, you do not need to indicate (by three spaced periods) that you are omitting material before or after the quotation. But if for some reason you want to omit an interior part of the quotation, you must indicate the omission by inserting an *ellipsis*, the three spaced dots. To take a simple example, if you omit the word "really" from van den Haag's phrase, you must alert the reader to the omission:

Ernest van den Haag doubts that "capital punishment . . . is more expensive" than life imprisonment (33).

Suppose you are quoting a sentence but wish to omit material from the end of the sentence. Suppose, also, that the quotation forms the end of your sentence. Write a lead-in phrase, quote what you need from your source, then type the bracketed ellipses for the omission, close the quotation, give the parenthetic citation, and finally type a fourth period to indicate the end of your sentence.

Here's an example. Suppose you want to quote the first part of a sentence that runs, "We could insist that the cost of capital punishment be reduced so as to diminish the differences." Your sentence would incorporate the desired extract as follows:

Van den Haag says, "We could insist that the cost of capital punishment be reduced . . ." (33).

3. **Punctuation with parenthetic citations**   In the preceding examples, the punctuation (a period or a comma in the examples) *follows* the citation. If, however, the quotation ends with a question mark, include the question mark *within* the quotation, since it is part of the quotation, and put a period *after* the citation:

Van den Haag asks, "Isn't it better—more just and more useful—that criminals, if they do not have the certainty of punishment, at least run the risk of suffering it?" (33).

But if the question mark is your own and not in the source, put it after the citation, thus:

What answer can be given to van den Haag's doubt that "capital punishment really is more expensive" (33)?

4. **Two or more works by an author**   If your list of Works Cited
includes two or more works by an author, you cannot, in your essay,
simply cite a page number because the reader will not know which of
the works you are referring to. You must give additional information.
You can give it in your lead-in, thus:

> In "New Arguments against Capital Punishment," van den Haag expresses
> doubt "that capital punishment really is more expensive" than life impris-
> onment (33).

Or you can give the title, in a shortened form, within the citation:

> Van den Haag expresses doubt that "capital punishment really is more
> expensive" than life imprisonment ("New Arguments" 33).

5. **Citing even when you do not quote**   Even if you don't quote
a source directly, but use its point in a paraphrase or a summary, you will
give a citation:

> Van den Haag thinks that life imprisonment costs more than capital pun-
> ishment (33).

Note that in all of the previous examples, the author's name is given in
the text (rather than within the parenthetic citation). But there are several other ways of giving the citation, and we shall look at them now.
(We have already seen, in the example given under paragraph 4, that
the title and the page number can be given within the citation.)

AUTHOR AND PAGE NUMBER IN PARENTHESES

> It has been argued that life imprisonment is more costly than capital
> punishment (van den Haag 33).

AUTHOR, TITLE, AND PAGE NUMBER IN PARENTHESES

We have seen that if the Works Cited list includes two or more
works by an author, you will have to give the title of the work on which
you are drawing, either in your lead-in phrase or within the parenthetic
citation. Similarly, if you are citing someone who is listed more than
once in the Works Cited, and for some reason you do not mention the
name of the author or the work in your lead-in, you must add the information in your citation:

Doubt has been expressed that capital punishment is as costly as life imprisonment (van den Haag, "New Arguments" 33).

A GOVERNMENT DOCUMENT OR A WORK OF CORPORATE AUTHORSHIP

Treat the issuing body as the author. Thus, you will write something like this:

The Commission on Food Control, in *Food Resources Today*, concludes that there is no danger (37-38).

A WORK BY TWO OR MORE AUTHORS

If a work is by *two or three authors,* give the names of all authors, either in the parenthetic citation (the first example below) or in a lead-in (the second example below):

There is not a single example of the phenomenon (Smith, Dale, and Jones 182-83).

Smith, Dale, and Jones insist there is not a single example of the phenomenon (182-83).

If there are *more than three authors,* give the last name of the first author, followed by *et al.* (an abbreviation for *et alii,* Latin for "and others"), thus:

Gittleman et al. argue (43) that . . .

or

On average, the cost is even higher (Gittleman et al. 43).

PARENTHETIC CITATION OF AN INDIRECT SOURCE (CITATION OF MATERIAL THAT ITSELF WAS QUOTED OR SUMMARIZED IN YOUR SOURCE)

Suppose you are reading a book by Jones in which she quotes Smith and you wish to use Smith's material. Your citation must refer the reader to Jones—the source you are using—but of course, you cannot attribute the words to Jones. You will have to make it clear that you are quoting Smith, and so after a lead-in phrase like "Smith says," followed by the quotation, you will give a parenthetic citation along these lines:

(qtd. in Jones 324-25).

PARENTHETIC CITATION OF TWO OR MORE WORKS

The costs are simply too high (Smith 301; Jones 28).

Notice that a semicolon, followed by a space, separates the two sources.

A WORK IN MORE THAN ONE VOLUME

This is a bit tricky. If you have used only one volume, in the Works Cited you will specify the volume, and so in the parenthetic in-text citation you will not need to specify the volume. All that you need to include in the citation is a page number, as illustrated by most of the examples that we have given.

If you have used more than one volume, your parenthetic citation will have to specify the volume as well as the page, thus:

Jackson points out that fewer than one hundred fifty people fit this description (2: 351).

The reference is to page 351 in volume 2 of a work by Jackson.

If, however, you are citing not a page but an entire volume — let's say volume 2 — your parenthetic citation will look like this:

Jackson exhaustively studies this problem (vol. 2).

or

Jackson (vol. 2) exhaustively studies this problem.

Notice the following points:

- In citing a volume and page, the volume number, like the page number, is given in arabic (not roman) numerals, even if the original used roman numerals to indicate the volume number.
- The volume number is followed by a colon, then a space, then the page number.
- If you cite a volume number without a page number, as in the last example quoted, the abbreviation is *vol.* Otherwise do *not* use such abbreviations as *vol.* and *p.* and *pg.*

AN ANONYMOUS WORK

For an anonymous work, give the title in your lead-in, or give it in a shortened form in your parenthetic citation:

A Prisoner's View of Killing includes a poll taken of the inmates on death row (32).

or

A poll is available (*Prisoner's View* 32).

AN INTERVIEW

Probably you won't need a parenthetic citation because you'll say something like

Vivian Berger, in an interview, said . . .

or

According to Vivian Berger, in an interview . . .

and when your reader turns to the Works Cited, he or she will see that Berger is listed, along with the date of the interview. But if you do not mention the source's name in the lead-in, you will have to give it in the parentheses, thus:

Contrary to popular belief, the death penalty is not reserved for serial killers and depraved murderers (Berger).

AN ELECTRONIC SOURCE

Electronic sources, such as those found on CD-ROMs or the Internet, are generally not divided into pages. Therefore, the in-text citation for such sources cite only the author's name (or, if a work is anonymous, the title):

According to the World Wide Web site for the American Civil Liberties Union . . .

If the source does use pages or breaks down further into paragraphs or screens, insert the appropriate identifier or abbreviation (*p.* or *pp.* for page or pages; *par.* or *pars.* for paragraph or paragraphs; *screen* or *screens*) before the relevant number:

The growth of day care has been called "a crime against posterity" by a spokesman for the Institute for the American Family (Terwilliger, screens 1-2).

MLA Format: The List of Works Cited

As the previous pages explain, parenthetic documentation consists of references that become clear when the reader consults the list titled Works Cited given at the end of an essay.

The list of Works Cited continues the pagination of the essay; if the last page of text is 10, then the Works Cited begins on its own page, in this case page 11. Type the page number in the upper right corner, a half inch from the top of the sheet and flush with the right margin. Next, type the heading Works Cited (*not* enclosed within quotation marks and not italic), centered, one inch from the top, and then double-space and type the first entry.

An Overview   Here are some general guidelines.

FORM ON THE PAGE

- Begin each entry flush with the left margin, but if an entry runs to more than one line, indent a half inch for each succeeding line of the entry. This is known as a hanging indent, and most word processing programs can achieve this effect easily.
- Double-space each entry, and double-space between entries.
- Italicize titles of works published independently—for instance, books, pamphlets, and journals. Enclose within quotation marks a work not published independently—for instance, an article in a journal or a short story.
- If you are citing a book that includes the title of another book, italicize the main title, but do *not* italicize the title mentioned. Example:

    A Study of Mill's On Liberty

- In the sample entries below, pay attention to the use of commas, colons, and the space after punctuation.

ALPHABETIC ORDER

- Arrange the list alphabetically by author, with the author's last name first.
- For information about anonymous works, works with more than one author, and two or more works by one author, see below.

A Closer Look   Here is more detailed advice.

THE AUTHOR'S NAME

Notice that the last name is given first, but otherwise the name is given as on the title page. Do not substitute initials for names written out on the title page.

If your list includes two or more works by an author, do not repeat the author's name for the second title but represent it by three hyphens followed by a period. The sequence of the works is determined by the alphabetic order of the titles. Thus, Smith's book titled *Poverty* would be listed ahead of her book *Welfare*. See the example on page 298, listing two works by Roger Brown.

Anonymous works are listed under the first word of the title or the second word if the first is *A, An,* or *The* or a foreign equivalent. We discuss books by more than one author, government documents, and works of corporate authorship on pages 298 and 299.

THE TITLE

After the period following the author's name, allow one space and then give the title. Take the title from the title page, not from the cover or the spine, but disregard any unusual typography such as the use of all capital letters or the use of the ampersand (&) for *and.* Italicize the title and subtitle (separate them by a colon) but do not italicize the period that concludes this part of the entry.

- Capitalize the first word and the last word.
- Capitalize all nouns, pronouns, verbs, adjectives, adverbs, and subordinating conjunctions (for example, *although, if, because*).
- Do not capitalize (unless it's the first or last word of the title or the first word of the subtitle) articles (*a, an, the*), prepositions (for instance, *in, on, toward, under*), coordinating conjunctions (for instance, *and, but, or, for*), or the *to* in infinitives.

Examples:

The Death Penalty: A New View

On the Death Penalty: Toward a New View

On the Penalty of Death in a Democracy

PLACE OF PUBLICATION, PUBLISHER, DATE, AND MEDIUM OF PUBLICATION

For the place of publication, provide the name of the city; you can usually find it either on the title page or on the reverse of the title page. If a number of cities are listed, provide only the first. If the city is not likely to be known, or if it may be confused with another city of the same name (as is Oxford, Mississippi, with Oxford, England), add the name of the state, abbreviated using the two-letter postal code.

The name of the publisher is abbreviated. Usually the first word is enough (*Random House* becomes *Random*), but if the first word is a first name, such as in *Alfred A. Knopf,* the surname (*Knopf*) is used instead. University presses are abbreviated thus: *Yale UP, U of Chicago P, State U of New York P.*

The date of publication of a book is given when known; if no date appears on the book, write *n.d.* to indicate "no date."

Because you may find your sources in any number of places, each entry should end by indicating the medium of publication for each source ("Print" for books or periodicals, "Web," for sources found on the Internet, and so on).

SAMPLE ENTRIES   Here are some examples, illustrating the points we have covered thus far:

Brown, Roger. *Social Psychology*. New York: Free, 1965. Print.

- - - . *Words and Things*. Glencoe, IL: Free, 1958. Print.

Douglas, Ann. *The Feminization of American Culture*. New York: Knopf, 1977. Print.

Hartman, Chester. *The Transformation of San Francisco*. Totowa, NJ: Rowman, 1984. Print.

Kellerman, Barbara. *The Political Presidency: Practice of Leadership from Kennedy through Reagan*. New York: Oxford UP, 1984. Print.

Notice that a period follows the author's name and another period follows the title. If a subtitle is given, as it is for Kellerman's book, it is separated from the title by a colon and a space. A colon follows the place of publication, a comma follows the publisher, and a period follows the date.

A BOOK BY MORE THAN ONE AUTHOR

The book is alphabetized under the last name of the first author named on the title page. If there are *two or three authors,* the names of these are given (after the first author's name) in the normal order, *first name first:*

Gilbert, Sandra M., and Susan Gubar. *The Madwoman in the Attic: The Woman Writer and the Nineteenth-Century Literary Imagination*. New Haven: Yale UP, 1979. Print.

Notice, again, that although the first author's name is given *last name first,* the second author's name is given in the normal order, first name first. Notice, too, that a comma is put after the first name of the first author, separating the authors.

If there are *more than three authors,* give the name only of the first and then add (but *not* enclosed within quotation marks and not italic) *et al.* (Latin for "and others").

Altshuler, Alan, et al. *The Future of the Automobile*. Cambridge: MIT P, 1984. Print.

GOVERNMENT DOCUMENTS

If the writer is not known, treat the government and the agency as the author. Most federal documents are issued by the Government Printing Office (abbreviated to *GPO*) in Washington, D.C.

United States. Office of Technology Assessment. *Computerized Manufacturing
Automation: Employment, Education, and the Workplace*. Washington:
GPO, 1984. Print.

WORKS OF CORPORATE AUTHORSHIP

Begin the citation with the corporate author, even if the same body
is also the publisher, as in the first example:

American Psychiatric Association. *Psychiatric Glossary*. Washington: American
Psychiatric Association, 1984. Print.

Carnegie Council on Policy Studies in Higher Education. *Giving Youth a
Better Chance: Options for Education, Work, and Service*. San Francisco:
Jossey, 1980. Print.

A REPRINT (FOR INSTANCE, A PAPERBACK VERSION OF AN OLDER CLOTHBOUND BOOK)

After the title, give the date of original publication (it can usually be
found on the reverse of the title page of the reprint you are using), then
a period, and then the place, publisher, and date of the edition you are
using. The example indicates that Gray's book was originally published
in 1970 and that the student is using the Vintage reprint of 1971.

Gray, Francine du Plessix. *Divine Disobedience: Profiles in Catholic
Radicalism*. 1970. New York: Vintage, 1971. Print.

A BOOK IN SEVERAL VOLUMES

If you have used more than one volume, in a citation within your essay
you will (as explained on p. 294) indicate a reference to, say, page 250 of
volume 3 thus: (3: 250).

If, however, you have used only one volume of the set—let's say
volume 3—in your entry in the Works Cited, specify which volume you
used, as in the next example:

Friedel, Frank. *Franklin D. Roosevelt*. Vol. 3. Boston: Little, 1973. Print. 4 vols.

With such an entry in the Works Cited, the parenthetic citation within
your essay would be to the page only, not to the volume and page,
because a reader who consults the Works Cited will understand that you
used only volume 3. In the Works Cited, you may specify volume 3 and
not give the total number of volumes, or you may add the total number
of volumes, as in the preceding example.

ONE BOOK WITH A SEPARATE TITLE IN A SET OF VOLUMES

Sometimes a set with a title makes use also of a separate title for each
book in the set. If you are listing such a book, use the following form:

Churchill, Winston. *The Age of Revolution*. New York: Dodd, 1957. Vol. 3 of
History of the English-Speaking Peoples. Print. 4 vols. 1956-58.

A BOOK WITH AN AUTHOR AND AN EDITOR

Churchill, Winston, and Franklin D. Roosevelt. *The Complete Correspondence*.
Ed. Warren F. Kimball. 3 vols. Princeton: Princeton UP, 1985. Print.

Kant, Immanuel. *The Philosophy of Kant: Immanuel Kant's Moral and
Political Writings*. Ed. Carl J. Friedrich. New York: Modern, 1949. Print.

If you are making use of the editor's introduction or other editorial
material rather than of the author's work, list the book under the name
of the editor rather than of the author, as shown below under An
Introduction, Foreword, or Afterword.

A REVISED EDITION OF A BOOK

Arendt, Hannah. *Eichmann in Jerusalem*. Rev. and enlarged ed. New York:
Viking, 1965. Print.

Honour, Hugh, and John Fleming. *The Visual Arts: A History*. 5th ed.
Englewood Cliffs: Prentice, 1999. Print.

A TRANSLATED BOOK

Franqui, Carlos. *Family Portrait with Fidel: A Memoir*. Trans. Alfred MacAdam.
New York: Random, 1984. Print.

AN INTRODUCTION, FOREWORD, OR AFTERWORD

Goldberg, Arthur J. Foreword. *An Eye for an Eye? The Morality of Punishing by
Death*. By Stephen Nathanson. Totowa, NJ: Rowman, 1987. v-vi. Print.

Usually an introduction or comparable material is listed under the name
of the author of the book (here Nathanson) rather than under the name
of the writer of the foreword (here Goldberg), but if you are referring to
the apparatus rather than to the book itself, use the form just given. The
words *Introduction, Preface, Foreword,* and *Afterword* are neither enclosed
within quotation marks nor underlined.

A BOOK WITH AN EDITOR BUT NO AUTHOR

Let's assume that you have used a book of essays written by various
people but collected by an editor (or editors), whose name(s) appears on
the collection.

LaValley, Albert J., ed. *Focus on Hitchcock*. Englewood Cliffs: Prentice,
1972. Print.

If the book has one editor, the abbreviation is *ed.;* if two or more editors, *eds.*

A WORK WITHIN A VOLUME OF WORKS BY ONE AUTHOR

The following entry indicates that a short work by Susan Sontag, an essay called "The Aesthetics of Silence," appears in a book by Sontag titled *Styles of Radical Will.* Notice that the inclusive page numbers of the short work are cited, not merely page numbers that you may happen to refer to but the page numbers of the entire piece.

Sontag, Susan. "The Aesthetics of Silence." *Styles of Radical Will.* New
York: Farrar, 1969. 3-34. Print.

A BOOK REVIEW

Here is an example, citing Gerstein's review of Walker's book. Gerstein's review was published in a journal called *Ethics.*

Gerstein, Robert S. Rev. of *Punishment, Danger and Stigma: The Morality of
Criminal Justice,* by Nigel Walker. Ethics 93 (1983): 408-10. Print.

If the review has a title, give the title between the period following the reviewer's name and *Rev.*

If a review is anonymous, list it under the first word of the title, or under the second word if the first is *A, An,* or *The.* If an anonymous review has no title, begin the entry with *Rev. of*, and then give the title of the work reviewed; alphabetize the entry under the title of the work reviewed.

AN ARTICLE OR ESSAY (NOT A REPRINT) IN A COLLECTION

A book may consist of a collection (edited by one or more persons) of new essays by several authors. Here is a reference to one essay in such a book. (The essay by Balmforth occupies pages 19 to 35 in a collection edited by Bevan.)

Balmforth, Henry. "Science and Religion." *Steps to Christian Understanding.*
Ed. R. J. W. Bevan. London: Oxford UP, 1958. 19-35. Print.

AN ARTICLE OR ESSAY REPRINTED IN A COLLECTION

The previous example (Balmforth's essay in Bevan's collection) was for an essay written for a collection. But some collections reprint earlier material, such as essays from journals or chapters from books. The following example cites an essay that was originally printed in a book called *The Cinema of Alfred Hitchcock.* This essay has been reprinted in a later collection of essays on Hitchcock, edited by Albert J. LaValley, and it was LaValley's collection that the student used.

Bogdanovich, Peter. "Interviews with Alfred Hitchcock." *The Cinema of
Alfred Hitchcock*. New York: Museum of Modern Art, 1963. 15-18.
Rpt. in *Focus on Hitchcock*. Ed. Albert J. LaValley. Englewood Cliffs:
Prentice, 1972. 28-31. Print.

The student has read Bogdanovich's essay or chapter, but not in
Bogdanovich's book, where it occupied pages 15 to 18. The material was
actually read on pages 28 to 31 in a collection of writings on Hitchcock,
edited by LaValley. Details of the original publication—title, date, page
numbers, and so forth—were found in LaValley's collection. Almost all
editors will include this information, either on the copyright page or at
the foot of the reprinted essay, but sometimes they do not give the original page numbers. In such a case, you need not include the original
numbers in your entry.

Notice that the entry begins with the author and the title of the
work you are citing (here, Bogdanovich's interviews), not with the name
of the editor of the collection or the title of the collection.

AN ENCYCLOPEDIA OR OTHER ALPHABETICALLY ARRANGED REFERENCE WORK

The publisher, place of publication, volume number, and page number do *not* have to be given. For such works, list only the edition (if it is
given) and the date.

For a *signed* article, begin with the author's last name. (If the article is
signed with initials, check elsewhere in the volume for a list of abbreviations, which will inform you who the initials stand for, and use the following form.)

Williams, Donald C. "Free Will and Determinism." *Encyclopedia Americana*.
1987 ed. Print.

For an *unsigned article,* begin with the title of the article:

"Automation." *The Business Reference Book*. 1977 ed. Print.

"Tobacco." *Encyclopaedia Britannica: Macropaedia*. 1988 ed. Print.

A TELEVISION OR RADIO PROGRAM

Be sure to include the title of the episode or segment (in quotation
marks), the title of the show (italicized), the network, the call letters and
city of the station, and the date of broadcast. Other information, such as
performers, narrator, and so forth, may be included if pertinent.

"Back to My Lai." *60 Minutes*. Narr. Mike Wallace. CBS. 29 Mar. 1998.
Television.

"Juvenile Justice." *Talk of the Nation*. Narr. Ray Suarez. Natl. Public Radio.
WBUR, Boston. 15 Apr. 1998. Radio.

AN ARTICLE IN A SCHOLARLY JOURNAL   The title of the article is enclosed within quotation marks, and the title of the journal is italicized.

Some journals are paginated consecutively; the pagination of the second issue begins where the first issue leaves off. Other journals begin each issue with page 1.

A JOURNAL THAT IS PAGINATED CONSECUTIVELY

Vilas, Carlos M. "Popular Insurgency and Social Revolution in Central
America." *Latin American Perspectives* 15.1 (1988): 55-77. Print

Vilas's article occupies pages 55 to 77 in volume 15, which was published in 1988. (Notice that the volume number is followed by a space, then by the year in parentheses, and then by a colon, a space, and the page numbers of the entire article.) When available, give the issue number.

A JOURNAL THAT BEGINS EACH ISSUE WITH PAGE 1

If the journal is, for instance, a quarterly, there will be four page 1's each year, so the issue number must be given. After the volume number, type a period and (without hitting the space bar) the issue number, as in the next example:

Greenberg, Jack. "Civil Rights Enforcement Activity of the Department of
Justice." *Black Law Journal* 8.1 (1983): 60-67. Print

Greenberg's article appeared in the first issue of volume 8 of the *Black Law Journal*.

AN ARTICLE IN A WEEKLY, BIWEEKLY, MONTHLY, OR BIMONTHLY PUBLICATION

Do not include volume or issue numbers, even if given.

Lamar, Jacob V. "The Immigration Mess." *Time* 27 Feb. 1989: 14-15. Print

Markowitz, Laura. "A Different Kind of Queer Marriage." *Utne Reader*
Sept.-Oct. 2000: 24-26. Print

AN ARTICLE IN A NEWSPAPER

Because a newspaper usually consists of several sections, a section number or a capital letter may precede the page number. The example indicates that an article begins on page 1 of section 2 and is continued on a later page.

> Chu, Harry. "Art Thief Defends Action." *New York Times* 8 Feb. 1989, sec.
>   2: 1+. Print

AN UNSIGNED EDITORIAL

> "The Religious Tyranny Amendment." Editorial. *New York Times* 15 Mar.
>   1998, sec. 4: 16. Print.

A LETTER TO THE EDITOR

> Lasken, Douglas. Letter. *New York Times* 15 Mar. 1998, sec. 4: 16. Print.

A PUBLISHED OR BROADCAST INTERVIEW

Give the name of the interview subject and the interviewer, followed by the relevant publication or broadcast information, in the following format:

> Green, Al. Interview with Terry Gross. *Fresh Air*. Natl. Public Radio. WFCR,
>   Amherst, MA. 16 Oct. 2000. Radio.

AN INTERVIEW YOU CONDUCT

> Jevgrafovs, Alexandre L. Personal [or Telephone] interview. 14 Dec. 2003.

PERSONAL CORRESPONDENCE

Add "TS" for a typed letter, "MS" for a handwritten letter, or "E-mail" to the end of the citation.

> Paso, Robert. Letter [or Message, in the case of E-mail] to the author.
>   6 Jan. 2004. TS.

CD-ROM

Books on CD-ROMs are cited very much like their printed counterparts. Add the medium (*CD-ROM*) after the publication information. For articles, to the usual print citation information, add (1) the title of the database, italicized; (2) the medium (*CD-ROM*); (3) the vendor's name; and (4) the date of electronic publication.

> Louisberg, Margaret. *Charlie Brown Meets Godzilla: What Are Our Children
>   Watching?* Urbana: ERIC Clearinghouse on Elementary and Early
>   Childhood Education, 1990. CD-ROM.

> "Pornography." *The Oxford English Dictionary*. 2nd ed. CD-ROM. Oxford:
>   Oxford UP, 1992.

FIGURE 7.4

1 Include the URL only if your Instructor requires it.

2 Sponsor of Web site

3 No author given; start citation with the title

4 Title of Web page

5 Publication date

6 Include the medium (Web) and the date you retrieved it.

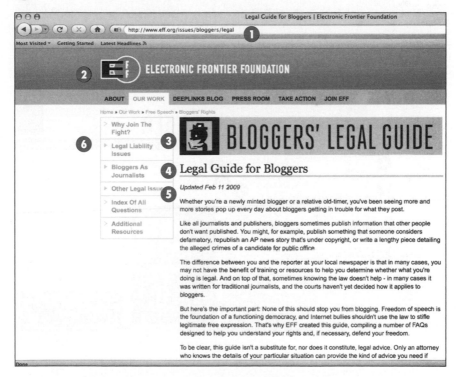

A PERSONAL OR PROFESSIONAL WEB SITE

Include the following elements, separated by periods: the name of the person who created the site (omit if not given, as in Figure 7.4); site title (italicized); name of any sponsoring institution or organization; date of electronic publication or of the latest update (if given); the medium (*Web*); and the date of access.

> *Legal Guide for Bloggers*. Electronic Frontier Foundation. 11 Feb. 2009.
>   Web. 30 May 2009.

AN ARTICLE IN AN ONLINE PERIODICAL

Give the same information as you would for a print article, plus the medium (*Web*) and the date of access. (See Figure 7.5.)

FIGURE 7.5

1 Include the URL only if your Instructor requires it.

2 Title of periodical

3 Title of article

4 Subtitle of article

5 Author

6 Publication date

7 Include the medium (Web) and the date you retrieved it.

Acocella, Joan. "In the Blood: Why Do Vampires Still Thrill?" *New Yorker*.
    16 March 2009. Web. 30 May 2009.

AN ONLINE POSTING

The citation includes the author's name, subject line of posting, description *Online posting*, if the posting has no title, name of the forum, date material was posted, the medium (*Web*), and date of access.

Ricci, Paul. "Global Warming." Global Electronic Science Conference, 10
    June. 1996. Web. 22 Sept. 1997.

A DATABASE SOURCE

Treat material obtained from a computer service, such as Bibliographic Retrieval Service (BRS), like other printed material, but at the end of the entry add (if available) the title of the database (italicized), publication medium (*Web*), name of the computer service if known, and date of access.

Jackson, Morton. "A Look at Profits." *Harvard Business Review* 40 (1962): 106-13. *BRS*. Web. 23 Dec. 2006.

Caution: Although we have covered the most usual kinds of sources, it is entirely possible that you will come across a source that does not fit any of the categories that we have discussed. For approximately two hundred pages of explanations of these matters, covering the proper way to cite all sorts of troublesome and unbelievable (but real) sources, see *MLA Handbook for Writers of Research Papers,* Seventh Edition (New York: Modern Language Association of America, 2009).

APA Format: Citations within the Text

Your paper will conclude with a separate page headed References, in which you list all of your sources. If the last page of your essay is numbered 10, number the first page of the References 11.

The APA style emphasizes the date of publication; the date appears not only in the list of references at the end of the paper but also in the paper itself, when you give a brief parenthetic citation of a source that you have quoted or summarized or in any other way used. Here is an example:

Statistics are readily available (Smith, 1989, p. 20).

The title of Smith's book or article will be given at the end of your paper, in the list titled References. We discuss the form of the material listed in the References after we look at some typical citations within the text of a student's essay.

A SUMMARY OF AN ENTIRE WORK

Smith (1988) holds the same view.

or

Similar views are held widely (Smith, 1988; Jones & Metz, 1990).

A REFERENCE TO A PAGE OR TO PAGES

Smith (1988) argues that "the death penalty is a lottery, and blacks usually are the losers" (p. 17).

A REFERENCE TO AN AUTHOR WHO HAS MORE THAN ONE WORK IN THE LIST OF REFERENCES

If in the References you list two or more works that an author published in the same year, the works are listed in alphabetic order, by the first letter of the title. The first work is labeled *a*, the second *b*, and so on. Here is a reference to the second work that Smith published in 1989:

> Florida presents "a fair example" of how the death penalty is administered (Smith, 1989b, p. 18).

APA Format: The List of References

Your brief parenthetic citations are made clear when the reader consults the list you give in the References. Type this list on a separate page, continuing the pagination of your essay.

An Overview   Here are some general guidelines.

FORM ON THE PAGE

- Begin each entry flush with the left margin, but if an entry runs to more than one line, indent five spaces for each succeeding line of the entry.
- Double-space each entry, and double-space between entries.

ALPHABETIC ORDER

- Arrange the list alphabetically by author.
- Give the author's last name first and then the initial of the first name and of the middle name (if any).
- If there is more than one author, name all of the authors up to seven, again inverting the name (last name first) and giving only initials for first and middle names. (But do not invert the editor's name when the entry begins with the name of an author who has written an article in an edited book.) When there are two or more authors, use an ampersand (&) before the name of the last author. Example (here, of an article in the tenth volume of a journal called *Developmental Psychology*):

> Drabman, R. S., & Thomas, M. H. (1974). Does media violence increase children's tolerance of real-life aggression? *Developmental Psychology*, 10, 418-421.

- For eight or more authors, list the first six followed by three ellipses dots and then the last author. If you list more than one work by an author, do so in the order of publication, the earliest first. If two works by an author were published in the same year, give them in alphabetic order by the first letter of the title, disregarding *A, An,* or *The,* and their foreign equivalent. Designate the first work as *a,* the second as *b.* Repeat the author's name at the start of each entry.

Donnerstein, E. (1980a). Aggressive erotica and violence against women. *Journal of Personality and Social Psychology, 39*, 269-277.

Donnerstein, E. (1980b). Pornography and violence against women. *Annals of the New York Academy of Sciences, 347*, 227-288.

Donnerstein, E. (1983). Erotica and human aggression. In R. Green and E. Donnerstein (Eds.), *Aggression: Theoretical and empirical reviews* (pp. 87-103). New York, NY: Academic Press.

FORM OF TITLE

- In references to books, capitalize only the first letter of the first word of the title (and of the subtitle, if any) and capitalize proper nouns. Italicize the complete title (but not the period at the end).
- In references to articles in periodicals or in edited books, capitalize only the first letter of the first word of the article's title (and subtitle, if any) and all proper nouns. Do not put the title within quotation marks. Type a period after the title of the article. For the title of the journal and the volume and page numbers, see the next instruction.
- In references to periodicals, give the volume number in arabic numerals, and italicize it. Do *not* use *vol.* before the number, and do not use *p.* or *pg.* before the page numbers.

Sample References   Here are some samples to follow.

A BOOK BY ONE AUTHOR

Pavlov, I. P. (1927). *Conditioned reflexes* (G. V. Anrep, Trans.). London, England: Oxford University Press.

A BOOK BY MORE THAN ONE AUTHOR

Belenky, M. F., Clinchy, B. M., Goldberger, N. R., & Torule, J. M. (1986). *Women's ways of knowing: The development of self, voice, and mind.* New York, NY: Basic Books.

A COLLECTION OF ESSAYS

Christ, C. P., & Plaskow, J. (Eds.). (1979). *Woman-spirit rising: A feminist reader in religion.* New York, NY: Harper & Row.

A WORK IN A COLLECTION OF ESSAYS

Fiorenza, E. (1979). Women in the early Christian movement. In C. P. Christ & J. Plaskow (Eds.), *Woman-spirit rising: A feminist reader in religion* (pp. 84-92). New York, NY: Harper & Row.

GOVERNMENT DOCUMENTS

If the writer is not known, treat the government and the agency as the author. Most federal documents are issued by the U.S. Government Printing Office in Washington, D.C. If a document number has been assigned, insert that number in parentheses between the title and the following period.

United States Congress. Office of Technology Assessment. (1984). *Comput-erized manufacturing automation: Employment, education, and the workplace.* Washington, DC: U.S. Government Printing Office.

AN ARTICLE IN A JOURNAL WITH CONTINUOUS PAGINATION

Tversky, A., & Kahneman, D. (1981). The framing of decisions and the psychology of choice. *Science, 211,* 453-458.

AN ARTICLE IN A JOURNAL THAT PAGINATES EACH ISSUE SEPARATELY

Foot, R. J. (1988-89). Nuclear coercion and the ending of the Korean con-flict. *International Security, 13*(4), 92-112.

The reference informs us that the article appeared in issue number 4 of volume 13.:

AN ARTICLE FROM A MONTHLY OR WEEKLY MAGAZINE

Greenwald, J. (1989, February 27). Gimme shelter. *Time, 133,* 50-51.

Maran, S. P. (1988, April). In our backyard, a star explodes. *Smithsonian, 19,* 46-57.

AN ARTICLE IN A NEWSPAPER

Connell, R. (1989, February 6). Career concerns at heart of 1980s' campus protests. *Los Angeles Times*, pp. 1, 3.

(*Note:* If no author is given, simply begin with the title followed by the date in parentheses.)

A BOOK REVIEW

Daniels, N. (1984). Understanding physician power [Review of the book *The social transformation of American medicine*]. *Philosophy and Public Affairs, 13,* 347-356.

Daniels is the reviewer, not the author of the book. The book under review is called *The Social Transformation of American Medicine,* but the review, published in volume 13 of *Philosophy and Public Affairs*, had its own title, "Understanding Physician Power."

If the review does not have a title, retain the square brackets, and use the material within as the title. Proceed as in the example just given.

✓ A CHECKLIST FOR PAPERS USING SOURCES

Ask yourself the following questions:

☐ Are all borrowed words and ideas credited, including those from Internet sources?

☐ Are all summaries and paraphrases acknowledged as such?

☐ Are quotations and summaries not too long?

☐ Are quotations accurate? Are omissions of words indicated by three spaced periods? Are additions of words enclosed within square brackets?

☐ Are quotations provided with helpful lead-ins?

☐ Is documentation in proper form?

And of course, you will also ask yourself the questions that you would ask of a paper that did not use sources, such as:

☐ Is the topic sufficiently narrowed?

☐ Is the thesis (to be advanced or refuted) stated early and clearly, perhaps even in the title?

☐ Is the audience kept in mind? Are opposing views stated fairly and as sympathetically as possible? Are controversial terms defined?

☐ Are assumptions likely to be shared by readers? If not, are they argued rather than merely asserted?

☐ Is the focus clear (evaluation, recommendation of policy)?

☐ Is evidence (examples, testimony, statistics) adequate and sound?

☐ Are inferences valid?

☐ Is the organization clear (effective opening, coherent sequence of arguments, unpretentious ending)?

☐ Is all worthy opposition faced?

☐ Is the tone appropriate?

☐ Has the paper been carefully proofread?

☐ Is the title effective?

☐ Is the opening paragraph effective?

☐ Is the structure reader-friendly?

☐ Is the closing paragraph effective?

A WEB SITE

American Psychological Association. (1995). Lesbian and gay parenting.
    Retrieved June 12, 2000, from http://www.apa.org/pi/parent.html

AN ARTICLE IN AN ONLINE PERIODICAL

Carpenter, S. (2000, October). Biology and social environments jointly
    influence gender development. *Monitor on Psychology 31*. Retrieved
    September 20, 2000, from http://www.apa.org/monitor/oct00/
    maccoby.html

For a full account of the APA method of dealing with all sorts of
unusual citations, see the sixth edition (2009) of the APA manual,
Publication Manual of the American Psychological Association.

AN ANNOTATED STUDENT RESEARCH
PAPER IN MLA FORMAT

The following argument makes good use of sources. Early in the semester the students were asked to choose one topic from a list of ten, and to
write a documented argument of 750 to 1,250 words (three to five pages
of double-spaced typing). The completed paper was due two weeks after
the topics were distributed. The assignment, a prelude to working on a
research paper of 2,500 to 3,000 words, was in part designed to give students practice in finding and in using sources. Citations are given in the
MLA form.

The *MLA Handbook* does not insist on a title page and outline, but many instructors prefer them.

Why Trials Should Not Be Televised

By

Theresa Washington

Title one-third down page

Professor Wilson

English 102

10 December 2009

All lines centered

Small roman
numerals for
page with
outline

Outline

Thesis: The televising of trials is a bad idea because it has several
        negative effects on the First Amendment: It gives viewers a
        deceptive view of particular trials and of the judicial system
        in general, and it degrades the quality of media reporting
        outside the courtroom.

  I. Introduction

     A. Trend toward increasing trial coverage

     B. First Amendment versus Sixth Amendment

 II. Effect of televising trials on First Amendment

     A. Provides deceptive version of truth

Roman numerals
for chief units
(I, II, etc.); capital
letters for chief
units within
these largest
units; for smaller
and smaller
units, arabic
numerals and
lowercase letters

        1. Confidence in verdicts misplaced

           a. William Smith trial

           b. Rodney King trial

        2. Nature of TV as a medium

           a. Distortion in sound bites

           b. Stereotyping trial participants

           c. Misleading camera angles

           d. Commentators and commercials

     B. Confuses viewers about judicial system

        1. Contradicts basic concept "innocent until proven guilty"

        2. Can't explain legal complexities

     C. Contributes to media circus outside of court

        1. Blurs truth and fiction

        2. Affects print media in negative ways

        3. Media makes itself the story

        4. Distracts viewers from other issues

III. Conclusion

Washington 1

Why Trials Should Not Be Televised

Although trials have been televised on and off since the 1950s,[1] in the last few years the availability of trials for a national audience has increased dramatically.[2] Media critics, legal scholars, social scientists, and journalists continue to debate the merits of this trend.

Proponents of cameras in the courtroom argue, falsely, I believe, that confidence in the fairness of our institutions, including the judicial system, depends on a free press, guaranteed by the First Amendment. Keeping trials off television is a form of censorship, they say. It limits the public's ability to understand (1) what is happening in particular trials and (2) how the judicial system operates, which is often confusing to laypeople. Opponents claim that televising trials threatens the defendant's Sixth Amendment rights to a fair trial because it can alter the behavior of the trial participants, including the jury ("Tale"; Thaler).

Regardless of its impact on due process of law,[3] TV in court does not serve the First Amendment well. Consider the first claim, that particular trials are easier to understand when televised. But does watching trials on television really allow the viewer to "see it like it is," to get the full scope and breadth of a trial? Steven Brill, founder of Court TV, would like us to believe so. He points out that most high-profile defendants in televised trials have been acquitted; he names William Kennedy Smith, Jimmy Hoffa, John Connally, and John Delorean as examples (Clark 821). "Imagine if [Smith's trial] had not been shown and he got off. Millions of people would have said the Kennedys fixed the case" (Brill qtd. in "Tale" 29). Polls taken after the trial seem to confirm this claim, since they showed the public by and large agreed with the jury's decision to acquit (Quindlen).

Title is focused and announces the thesis.

Double-space between title and first paragraph — and throughout the essay.

1″ margin on each side and at bottom

Summary of opposing positions

Parenthetic reference to an anonymous source and also to a source with a named author

Superscript numerals indicate endnotes.

Parenthetic reference to author and page

Parenthetic reference to an indirect source (a borrowed quotation)

Washington 2

However, Thaler points out that the public can just as easily disagree with the verdict as agree, and when this happens, the effects can be catastrophic. One example is the Rodney King case. Four white Los Angeles police officers were charged in 1991 with severely beating African American Rodney King, who, according to the officers, had been resisting arrest. At their first trial, all four officers were acquitted. This verdict outraged many African Americans throughout the country; they felt the evidence from watching the trial overwhelmingly showed the defendants to be guilty. The black community of south-central Los Angeles expressed its feelings by rioting for days (Thaler 50-51).

Clearly the black community did not experience the trial the same way the white community and the white jury did. Why? Marty Rosenbaum, an attorney with the New York State Defenders Association, points out that viewers cannot experience a trial the same way trial participants do. "What you see at home 'is not what jurors see'" (qtd. in Thaler 70). The trial process is slow, linear, and methodical, as the defense and prosecution each builds its case, one piece of information at a time (Thaler 11). The process is intended to be thoughtful and reflective, with the jury weighing all the evidence in light of the whole trial (Altheide 299-301). And it emphasizes words — both spoken and written — rather than images (Thaler 11).

Although no words are quoted, the idea is borrowed, and so the source is cited.

In contrast, TV's general strength is in handling visual images that entertain or that provoke strong feelings. News editors and reporters choose footage for its assumed visual and emotional impact on viewers. Words are made to fit the images, not the other way around, and they tend to be short catchy phrases, easy to understand (Thaler 4, 7). As a result, the fifteen- to thirty-second "sound bites" in nightly newscasts often present trial events out of context, emphasizing moments of drama rather than of legal importance (Thaler 7; Zoglin 62).

Clear transition ("In contrast")

Parenthetic citation of two sources

Washington 3

Furthermore, this emphasis on emotional visuals leads to stereotyping the participants, making larger-than-life symbols out of them, especially regarding social issues (Thaler 9): abused children (the Menendez brothers), the battered wife (Hedda Nussbaum), the abusing husband (Joel Steinberg, O. J. Simpson), the jealous lover (Amy Fisher), the serial killer (Jeffrey Dahmer), and date rapist (William Smith). It becomes difficult for viewers to see defendants as ordinary human beings.

One can argue, as Brill has done, that gavel-to-gavel coverage of trials counteracts the distortions in sound-bite journalism (Clark 821). Yet even here a number of editorial assumptions and decisions affect what viewers see. Camera angles and movements reinforce in the viewer differing degrees of intimacy with the trial participant; close-ups are often used for sympathetic witnesses, three-quarter shots for lawyers, and profile shots for defendants (Entner 73–75).[4]

Summary of an opposing view countered with a clear transition ("Yet")

On-air commentators also shape the viewers' experience. Several media critics have noted how much commentators' remarks often have the play-by-play tone of sportscasters informing viewers of what each side (the defense and the prosecution) needs to win (Cole 245; Thaler 71, 151). Continual interruptions for commercials add to the impression of watching a spectacle. "The CNN coverage [of the Smith trial] isn't so much gavel-to-gavel, actually, as gavel-to-commercial-to-gavel, with former CNN Gulf War correspondent Charles Jaco acting more as ringleader than reporter" (Bianculli 60). This encourages a sensationalistic tone to the proceedings that the jury does not experience. In addition, breaking for ads frequently occurs at important points in the trial (Thaler 48).

In-court proponents also believe that watching televised trials will help viewers understand the legal aspects of the judicial system. In June 1991, a month before Court TV went on the air, Vincent Blasi,

Author lets reader hear the opposition by means of a brief quotation

Omitted material indicated by three periods, with a fourth to mark the end of a sentence

a law professor at Columbia University, told *Time* magazine, "Today most of us learn about judicial proceedings from lawyers' sound bites and artists' sketches. . . . Televised proceedings [such as Court TV] ought to dispel some of the myth and mystery that shroud our legal system" (qtd. in Zoglin 62).

But after several years of Court TV and CNN, we can now see this is not so. As a medium, TV is not good at educating the general public, either about concepts fundamental to our judicial system or about the complexities in particular cases.

For example, one basic concept—"innocent until proven guilty"—is contradicted in televised trials in numerous subtle ways: Commentators sometimes make remarks about (or omit comment on) actions of the defense or prosecution that show a bias against the defendant.

Media critic Lewis Cole, watching the trial of Lorena Bobbitt on Court TV in 1994, observed:

Quotation of more than four lines, indented 1″ (ten spaces) from left margin, double-spaced, parenthetic reference set off from quotation

> Court TV commentators rarely challenged the state's characterization of what it was doing, repeating without comment, for instance, the prosecution's claims about protecting the reputation of Lorena Bobbitt and concentrating on the prosecution decision to pursue both cases as a tactical matter, rather than inquiring how the prosecution's view of the incident as a "barroom brawl" had limited its approach to and understanding of the case. (245)

Camera angles play a role also: Watching the defendant day after day in profile, which makes him or her seem either vulnerable or remote, tends to reinforce his or her guilt (Entner 158).

Thaler points out that these editorial effects arise because the goals of the media (print as well as electronic) differ from the goals of

Washington 5

the judicial system. His argument runs as follows: The court is interested in determining only whether the defendant broke the law. The media (especially TV) focus on acts to reinforce social values, whether they're codified into law or not. This can lead viewers to conclude that a defendant is guilty because pretrial publicity or courtroom testimony reveals he or she has transgressed against the community's moral code, even when the legal system later acquits. This happened in the case of Claus von Bulow, who between 1982 and 1985 was tried and acquitted twice for attempting to murder his wife and who clearly had behaved in reprehensible ways in the eyes of the public (35). It also happened in the case of Joel Steinberg, who was charged with murdering his daughter. Extended televised testimony by his former partner, Hedda Nussbaum, helped paint a portrait of "a monster" in the eyes of the public (140-42). Yet the jury chose to convict him on the lesser charge of manslaughter. When many viewers wrote to the prosecutor, Peter Casolaro, asking why the verdict was not first-degree murder, he had to conclude that TV does not effectively teach about due process of law (176).

> Argument supported by specific examples

   In addition to being poor at handling basic judicial concepts, television has difficulty conveying more complex and technical aspects of the law. Sometimes the legal nature of the case makes for a poor translation to the screen. Brill admitted that, despite attempts at hourly summaries, Court TV was unable to convey to its viewers any meaningful understanding of the case of Manuel Noriega (Thaler 61), the Panamanian leader who was convicted by the United States in 1992 of drug trafficking and money laundering ("Former"). In other cases, like the Smith trial, the "civics lesson" gets swamped by its sensational aspects (Thaler 45). In most cases print media are better at exploring and explaining legal issues than is TV (Thaler 4).

Washington 6

Transition
briefly
summarizes
and then
moves to a
new point.

In addition to shaping the viewer's perceptions of trial reality

directly, in-court TV also negatively affects the quality of trial

coverage outside of court, which in turn limits the public's "right to

know." Brill likes to claim that Court TV helps to counteract the

sensationalism of such tabloid TV shows as *A Current Affair* and *Hard

Copy*, which pay trial participants to tell their stories and publish

leaks from the prosecution and defense. "I think cameras in the

courtroom is [*sic*] the best antidote to that garbage" (Brill qtd. in

The author
uses "[*sic*]"
(Latin for
"thus") to
indicate that
the oddity is
in the source
and is not by
the author of
the paper.

Clark 821). However, as founder and editor of Court TV, he obviously

has a vested interest in affirming his network's social and legal worth.

There are several ways that in-court TV, rather than supplying a

sobering contrast, helps to feed the media circus surrounding high-

profile trials (Thaler 43).

One way is by helping to blur the line between reality and

fiction. This is an increasing trend among all media but is especially

true of TV, whose footage can be combined and recombined in so

many ways. An excellent example of this is the trial of Amy Fisher,

who pleaded guilty in September 1992 to shooting her lover's wife

and whose sentencing was televised by Court TV (Thaler 83). Three TV

movies about this love triangle appeared on network TV in the same

week, just one month after she had been sentenced to five to fifteen

years of jail (Thaler 82). Then Geraldo Rivera, the syndicated TV talk-

show host, held a mock grand jury trial of her lover, Joey Buttafuoco;

even though Buttafuoco had not at that point been charged with a

crime, Geraldo felt many viewers thought he ought to have been

(Thaler 83). Then *A Current Affair* had a series that "tried" Fisher for

events and behaviors that never got resolved in the actual trial. The

announcer on the program said, "When Ms. Fisher copped a plea and

went to jail, she robbed the public of a trial, leaving behind many

unanswered questions. Tonight we will try to . . . complete the

unwritten chapter" ("Trial"). Buttafuoco's lawyer from the trial served

Washington 7

as a consultant on this program (Thaler 84). This is also a good
example of how tabloid TV reinforces people's beliefs and plays on
people's feelings. Had her trial not been televised, the excitement
surrounding her case would not have been so high. Tabloid TV played
off the audience's expectation for what a televised trial should and
could reveal. Thus in-court television becomes one more ingredient in
the mix of docudramas, mock trials, talk shows, and tabloid
journalism. This limits the public's "right to know" by making it
difficult to keep fact separate from storytelling.

   In-court TV also affects the quality of print journalism.
Proponents like to claim that "[f]rom the standpoint of the public's
right to know, there is no good reason why TV journalists should be
barred from trials while print reporters are not" (Zoglin 62). But when
TV is present, there is no level playing field among the media. Because
it provides images, sound, movement, and a greater sense of speed
and immediacy, TV can easily outcompete other media for audience
attention and thus for advertising dollars. In attempts to keep pace,
newspapers and magazines offer more and more of the kinds of stories
that once were beneath their standards, such as elaborate focus both
on sensational aspects of the case and on "personalities, analysis, and
prediction" rather than news (Thaler 45). While these attributes have
always been part of TV and the tabloid print press, this trend is
increasingly apparent in supposedly reputable papers like the *New York
Times*. During the Smith trial, for example, the *Times* violated
previously accepted boundaries of propriety by not only identifying
the rape victim but also giving lots of intimate details about her past
(Thaler 45).

   Because the media are, for the most part, commercial, slow
periods — and all trials have them — must always be filled with some
"story." One such story is increasingly the media self-consciously

Useful analysis
of effect of TV

Square brackets
indicate that
the author has
altered text
from a capital
to a lowercase
letter.

Washington 8

No citation is needed for a point that can be considered common knowledge, but the second sentence *is* documented.

watching and analyzing itself, to see how it is handling (or mishandling) coverage of the trial (Thaler 43). At the Smith trial, for example, one group of reporters was covering the trial while another group covered the other reporters (Thaler 44).[5] As bizarre as this "media watching" is, there would be no "story" if the trial itself had not been televised.

Last but not least, televising trials distracts viewers from other important issues. Some of these are abstract and thus hard to understand (like the savings-and-loan scandal in the mid-1980s or the causes of lingering unemployment in the 1990s), while others are painful to contemplate (like overseas wars and famines). Yet we have to stay aware of these issues if we are to function as active citizens in a democracy.

Useful summary of main points

Altogether, televising trials is a bad idea. Not only does it provide deceptive impressions about what's happening in particular trials; it also doesn't reveal much about our judicial system. In addition, televising trials helps to lower the quality of trial coverage outside of court, thus increasingly depriving the public of neutral, fact-based reporting. A healthy free press depends on balance and knowing when to accept limits. Saturating viewers with extended media coverage of sensational trials oversteps those limits. In this case, more is not better.

Realistic appraisal of the current situation and a suggestion of what the reader can do

Yet it is unlikely that TV coverage will be legally removed from the courtroom, now that it is here. Only one state (New York) has ever legislated a return to nontelevised trials (in 1991), and even it changed its mind in 1992 (Thaler 78). Perhaps the best we can do is to educate ourselves about the pitfalls of televising the judicial system, as we struggle to do so with the televised electoral process.

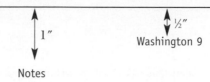

Washington 9

Notes

1. Useful discussions of this history can be found in Clark (829-32) and Thaler (19-31).

2. Cable networks have been showing trial footage to national audiences since at least 1982, when Cable News Network (CNN) covered the trial of Claus von Bulow (Thaler 33). It continues to show trials. In the first week of February 1995, four to five million homes accounted for the top fifteen most-watched shows on cable TV; all were CNN segments of the O. J. Simpson trial ("Cable TV"). In July 1991, Steven Brill founded the Courtroom Television Network, or "Court TV" (Clark 821). Like CNN, it broadcasts around the clock, showing gavel-to-gavel coverage. It now claims over fourteen million cable subscribers (Clark 821) and, as of January 1994, had televised over 280 trials ("In Camera" 27).

3. Thaler's study *The Watchful Eye* is a thoughtful examination of the subtle ways in which TV in court can affect trial participants, inhibiting witnesses from coming forward, provoking grandstanding in attorneys and judges, and pressuring juries to come up with verdicts acceptable to a national audience.

4. Sometimes legal restrictions determine camera angles. For example, in the Steinberg trial (1988), the audience and the jury were not allowed to be televised by New York state law. This required placing the camera so that the judge and witnesses were seen in "full frontal view" (generally a more neutral or positive stance). The lawyers could be seen only from the rear when questioning witnesses, and the defendant was shot in profile (Thaler 110-11). These camera angles, though not chosen for dramatic effect, still resulted in emotionally laden viewpoints not experienced by the jury. George W. Trammell, a Los Angeles Superior Court Judge, has written on how technology can interfere with the fairness of the trial system. He

Double-space between heading and notes and throughout notes.

Superscript number followed by one space

Each note begins with 1/2" indent (five typewriter spaces), but subsequent lines of each note are flush left.

claims that "[t]echnology, well managed, can be a great benefit. Technology poorly managed benefits no one."

5. At the Smith trial a journalist from one German newspaper inadvertently filmed another German reporter from a competing newspaper watching the Smith trial in the pressroom outside the courtroom (Thaler 44).

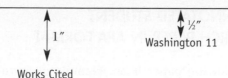

1″

½″

Washington 11

Works Cited

Altheide, David. "TV News and the Social Construction of Justice." *Justice and the Media: Issues and Research*. Ed. Ray Surette. Springfield, IL: Thomas, 1984. 292-304 Print.

Bianculli, David. "Shame on You, CNN." *New York Post* 11 Dec. 1992: 60. Print.

"Cable TV Squeezes High Numbers and Aces Competition." *All Things Considered*. Natl. Public Radio. 9 Feb. 1994. Unedited transcript. Segment 12. NPR Audience Services. Washington. Print.

Clark, Charles S. "Courts and the Media." *CQ Researcher* 23 Sept. 1994: 817-40. Print.

Cole, Lewis. "Court TV." *Nation* 21 Feb. 1994: 243-45. Print.

Entner, Roberta. "Encoding the Image of the American Judiciary Institution: A Semiotic Analysis of Broadcast Trials to Ascertain Its Definition of the Court System." Diss. New York U, 1993. Print.

"Former Panamanian Leader Noriega Sentenced." *Facts on File* 16 July 1992: 526. CD-ROM. *InfoTrac: Magazine Index Plus 1992-Feb. 1995*. Information Access. Feb. 1995.

"In Camera with Court TV." *New Yorker* 24 Jan. 1994: 27-28. Print.

Quindlen, Anna. "The Glass Eye." *New York Times* 18 Dec. 1991: A29. Print.

"A Tale of a Rug." *Economist* 15 Jan. 1994: 28-29. Print.

Thaler, Paul. *The Watchful Eye: American Justice in the Age of the Television Trial*. Westport, CT: Praeger, 1994. Print.

Trammell, George W. "Cirque du O. J." *Court Technology Bulletin*. National Center for State Courts, July-Aug. 1995. Web. 12 Sept. 1996.

"The Trial That Had to Happen: The People versus Amy Fisher." *A Current Affair*. Fox. WFXT, Boston. 1-4 Feb. 1993. Television.

Zoglin, Richard. "Justice Faces a Screen Test." *Time* 17 June 1991: 62. Print.

Alphabetical by author's last name

Hanging indent 1/2″

Transcript of radio program

The title of an unpublished work is not italicized but is enclosed within quotation marks.

CD-ROM source

Anonymous source alphabetized under first word (or second if first is *A, An,* or *The*)

No page reference for this in-text Internet citation

Television program

AN ANNOTATED STUDENT
RESEARCH PAPER IN APA FORMAT

The following paper is an example of a student paper that uses APA format.

The Role of Spirituality and Religion

in Mental Health

Laura DeVeau

English 102

Professor Gardner

April 12, 2010

The APA-style
cover page
gives title,
author, and
course
information.

Short form of
title and page
number as
running head

The Role of Spirituality and Religion

in Mental Health

It has been called "a vestige of the childhood of mankind,"
"the feeling of something true, total and absolute," "an otherworldly
answer as regards the meaning of life" (Jones, 1991, p. 1; Amaro,

Citation of
multiple
works from
references

2000; Kristeva, 1987, p. 27). It has been compared to medicine,
described as a psychological cure for mental illness, and also referred
to as the cause of a dangerous fanaticism. With so many differing
opinions on the impact of religion in people's lives, where would one
begin a search for the truth? Who has the answer: Christians,
humanists, objectivists, atheists, psychoanalysts, Buddhists,
philosophers, cults? This was my dilemma at the advent of my
research into how religion and spirituality affect the mental health of
society as a whole.

In this paper, I explore the claims, widely accepted by
professionals in the field of psychology, that religious and spiritual
practices have a negative impact on mental health. In addition,

Acknowledg-
ment of
opposing
viewpoints

though, I cannot help but reflect on how this exploration has changed
my beliefs as well. Religion is such a personal experience that one
cannot be dispassionate in reporting it. One can, however, subject the
evidence provided by those who have studied the issue to critical
scrutiny. Having done so, I find myself in disagreement with those
who claim religious feelings are incompatible with sound mental
health. There is a nearly limitless number of beliefs regarding
spirituality. Some are organized and involve rituals like mass or
worship. Many are centered around the existence of a higher being,
while others focus on the self. I have attempted to uncover the
perfect set of values that lead to a better lifestyle, but my research
has pointed me in an entirely different direction, where no single
belief seems to be adequate but where spiritual belief in general

Religion in Mental Health 2

should be valued more highly than it is currently in mental health circles.

Thesis explicitly introduced

    I grew up in a moderately devout Catholic family. Like many young people raised in a household where one religion is practiced by both parents, it never occurred to me to question those beliefs. I went through a spiritual cycle, which I believe much of Western society also experiences. I attended religious services because I had to. I possessed a blind, unquestioning acceptance of what I was being taught because the adults I trusted said it was so. Like many adolescents and young adults, though, I stopped going to church when I was old enough to decide because I thought I had better things to do. At this stage, we reach a point when we begin searching for a meaning to our existence. For some, this search is brought on by a major crisis or a feeling of emptiness in their daily lives, while for others it is simply a part of growing up. This is where we begin to make personal choices, but with the barrage of options, where do we turn?

    Beginning with the holistic health movement in the eighties, there has been a mass shift from traditional religions to less structured spiritual practices such as meditation, yoga, the Cabala, and mysticism (Beyerman, 1989). They venture beyond the realm of conventional dogmatism and into the new wave of spirituality. Many of these practices are based on the notion that health of the mind and spirit equals health of the body. Associated with this movement is a proliferation of retreats offering a chance to get in touch with the beauty and silence of nature and seminars where we can take "a break from our everyday environment where our brains are bustling and our bodies are exhausting themselves" ("Psychological benefits," 1999). A major concept of the spiritual new wave is that it focuses inward toward the individual psyche, rather than outward toward another

Author and date cited for summary or paraphrase

Anonymous source cited by title and date

being like a god. Practitioners do not deny the existence of this being, but they believe that to fully love another, we must first understand ourselves. Many find this a preferable alternative to religions where the individual is seen as a walking dispenser of sin who is very fortunate to have a forgiving creator. It is also a relief from the scare tactics like damnation used by traditional religions to make people behave. Many, therefore, praise the potential psychological benefits of such spirituality.

Clear transition refers to previous paragraph

While I believe strongly in the benefits of the new wave, I am not willing to do away with structured religion, for I find that it also has its benefits. Without the existence of churches and temples, it would be harder to expose the public to values beneficial to mental stability. It is much more difficult to hand a child a copy of the Cabala and say "Read this, and then get back to me on it" than it is to bring a child to a service where the ideas are represented with concrete examples. My religious upbringing presented me with a set of useful morals and values, and it does the same for millions of others who are brought up in this manner. Many people, including some followers of the new wave, are bitter toward Christianity because of events in history like the Crusades, the Inquisition, the Salem witch trials, and countless other horrific acts supposedly committed in the name of God. But these events were based not on biblical teachings but on pure human greed and lust for power. We should not reject the benevolent possibilities of organized religion on the basis of historical atrocities any more than we should abandon public education because a few teachers are known to mistreat children.

Another factor contributing to the reluctance concerning religion is the existence of cults that seduce people into following their extreme teachings. The victims are often at vulnerable times in their lives, and the leaders are usually very charming, charismatic, and

Religion in Mental Health 4

sometimes also psychotic or otherwise mentally unstable. Many argue that if we acknowledge these groups as dangerous cults, then we must do the same for traditional religions such as Christianity and Islam, which are likewise founded on the teachings of charismatic leaders. Again, though, critics are too quick to conflate all religious and spiritual practice; we must distinguish between those who pray and attend services and those who commit group suicide because they think that aliens are coming to take over the world. Cults have provided many psychologists, who are eager to discount religion as a factor in improving mental health, with an easy target. Ellis (1993), the founder of rational-emotive therapy, cites many extreme examples of religious commitment, such as cults and antiabortion killings, to show that commitment is hazardous to one's sanity. Anomalies like these should not be used to speak of religion as a whole, though. Religion is clearly the least of these people's mental problems.

> When the author's name appears in text, only the date is cited in parentheses.

Besides Ellis, there are many others in the field of psychology who do not recognize religion as a potential aid for improving the condition of the psyche. Actually, fewer than 45 percent of the members of the American Psychiatric Association even believe in God. The general American public has more than twice that percentage of religious devotees (Larson, 1998). Going back to the days of Freud, many psychologists have held atheist views. The father of psychoanalysis himself called religion a "universal obsessional neurosis." Psychologists have long rejected research that demon-strates the benefits of spirituality by saying that this research is biased. They claim that such studies are out to prove that religion helps because the conductors are religious people who need to justify their beliefs.

While this may be true in some instances, there is also some quite empirical research available to support the claims of those who promote religion and spirituality. The *Journal for the Scientific Study of Religion* has conducted many studies examining the effects of religion on individuals and groups. In one example, the relationship between religious coping methods and positive recovery after major stressful events was observed. The results indicated not only that spirituality was not harmful to the mind but that "the positive religious coping pattern was tied to benevolent outcomes, including fewer symptoms of psychological distress, [and] reports of psychological and spiritual growth as a result of the stressor" (Pargament et al., 1998, p. 721). Clearly, the benefits of piety can, in fact, be examined empirically, and in some cases the results point to a positive correlation between religion and mental health.

Bracketed word in quotation not in original source

Author, date, and page number are cited for a direct quotation.

But let us get away from statistics and studies. If religion is both useless and dangerous, as so many psychologists claim, we must ask why has it remained so vital a part of humanity for so long. Even if it can be reduced to a mere coping method that humans use to justify their existence and explain incomprehensible events, is it futile? I would suggest that this alone represents a clear benefit to society. Should religion, if it cannot be proven as "true," be eliminated and life based on scientific fact alone? Surely many would find this a pointless existence. With all the conflicting knowledge I have gained about spirituality during my personal journey and my research, one idea is clear. It is not the depth of devotion, the time of life when one turns to religion, or even the particular combination of beliefs one chooses to adopt that will improve the quality of life. There is no right or wrong answer when it comes to self-fulfillment. It is whatever works for the individual, even if that means holding no religious or spiritual beliefs at all. But clearly there *are* benefits to be gained, at least for some individuals, and mental health professionals need to begin acknowledging this fact in their daily practice.

Conclusion restates and strengthens thesis

Religion in Mental Health 6

References

Amaro, J. (2000). Psychology, psychoanalysis and religious faith.

   Nielsen's psychology of religion pages. Retrieved March 6, 2000,

   from http://www.psy www.com/psyrelig/amaro.html

Beyerman A. K. (1989). *The holistic health movement*. Tuscaloosa:

   Alabama University Press.

Ellis, A. (1993). Dogmatic devotion doesn't help, it hurts. In B. Slife

   (Ed.), *Taking sides: Clashing views on controversial psychological*

   issues (pp. 297-301). New York, NY: Scribner.

Jones, J. W. (1991). *Contemporary psychoanalysis and religion:*

   Transference and transcendence. New Haven, CT: Yale University

   Press.

Kristeva, J. (1987). *In the beginning was love: Psychoanalysis and*

   faith. New York, NY: Columbia University Press.

Larson, D. (1998). Does religious commitment improve mental health?

   In B. Slife (Ed.), *Taking sides: Clashing views on controversial*

   psychological issues (pp. 292-296). New York, NY: Scribner.

Pargament, K. I., Smith, B. W., Koening, H. G., & Perez, L. (1998).

   Patterns of positive and negative religious coping with major

   life stressors. *Journal for the Scientific Study of Religion, 37*,

   710-724.

"Psychological benefits." (1999). *Walking the labyrinth*. Retrieved April

   3, 2000, from http://www.labyrinthway.com/html/benefits.html

Annotations (right margin):

References begin on a new page.

A World Wide Web source

A book

An article or a chapter in a book

An article in a journal

Anonymous source alphabetized by title

PART THREE

FURTHER VIEWS
on ARGUMENT

8

A Philosopher's View:
The Toulmin Model

All my ideas hold together, but I cannot elaborate them all at once.

— JEAN-JACQUES ROUSSEAU

Clarity has been said to be not enough. But perhaps it will be time to go into that when we are within measurable distance of achieving clarity on some matter.

— J. L. AUSTIN

[Philosophy is] a peculiarly stubborn effort to think clearly.

— WILLIAM JAMES

Philosophy is like trying to open a safe with a combination lock: Each little adjustment of the dials seems to achieve nothing, only when everything is in place does the door open.

— LUDWIG WITTGENSTEIN

In Chapter 3, we explained the contrast between *deductive* and *inductive* arguments to focus on the two main ways in which we reason, either

- Making explicit something concealed in what we already accept (**deduction**) or
- Using what we have observed as a basis for asserting or proposing something new (**induction**).

Both types of reasoning share some structural features, as we also noticed. Thus, all reasoning is aimed at establishing some **thesis** (or conclusion) and does so by means of some **reasons.** These are two basic characteristics that any argument contains.

After a little scrutiny we can in fact point to several features shared by all arguments, deductive and inductive, good and bad alike. We use the vocabulary popularized by Stephen Toulmin, Richard Rieke, and Allan Janik in their book *An Introduction to Reasoning* (1979; second edition 1984) to explore the various elements of argument.

THE CLAIM

Every argument has a purpose, goal, or aim—namely, to establish a **claim** (*conclusion* or *thesis*). Suppose you were arguing in favor of equal rights for women. You might state your thesis or claim as follows:

> Men and women ought to have equal rights.

A more precise formulation of the claim might be

> Men and women ought to have equal legal rights.

A still more precise formulation might be

> Equal legal rights for men and women ought to be protected by our Constitution.

The third version of this claim states what the controversy in the 1970s over the Equal Rights Amendment was all about.

Consequently, in reading or analyzing someone else's argument, your first question should naturally be: What is the argument intended to prove or establish? *What claim is it making*? Has this claim been clearly and precisely formulated, so that it unambiguously asserts what its advocate wants to assert?

GROUNDS

Once we have the argument's purpose or point clearly in mind and thus know what the arguer is claiming to establish, then we can ask for the evidence, reasons, support—in short, for the **grounds**—on which that claim is based. In a deductive argument these grounds are the premises from which the claim is deduced; in an inductive argument the grounds are the evidence—a sample, an observation, or an experiment—that makes the claim plausible or probable.

Not every kind of claim can be supported by every kind of ground, and conversely, not every kind of ground gives equally good support for every kind of claim. Suppose I claim that half the students in the classroom are women. I can ground this claim in any of several ways.

1. I can count all the women and all the men. Suppose the total equals fifty. If the number of women is twenty-five and the number of men is twenty-five, I have vindicated my claim.
2. I can count a sample of, say, ten students and find that in the sample five of the students are women. I thus have inductive—plausible but not conclusive—grounds for my claim.
3. I can point out that the students in the college divide equally into men and women and claim that this class is a representative sample of the whole college.

Obviously, ground 1 is stronger than ground 2, and 2 is far stronger than ground 3.

So far we have merely restated points about premises and conclusions covered in Chapter 3. But now we want to consider four additional features of arguments.

WARRANTS

Once we have the claim or the point of an argument fixed in mind and the evidence or reasons offered in its support, the next question to ask is *why* these reasons support this conclusion. What is the **warrant,** or guarantee, that the reasons proffered do support the claim or lead to the conclusion? In simple deductive arguments, the warrant takes different forms, as we shall see. In the simplest cases, we can point to the way in which the *meanings* of the key terms are really equivalent. Thus, if John is taller than Bill, then Bill must be shorter than John because of the meaning in English of "is shorter than" and "is taller than." In this case, the warrant is something we can state quite literally and explicitly.

In other cases, we may need to be more resourceful. A reliable tactic is to think up a simple *parallel argument*—that is, an argument exactly parallel in form and structure to the argument we are trying to defend. We then point out that if we are ready to accept the simpler argument, then we must accept the more complex argument because both arguments have exactly the same structure. For example, in her much-discussed 1972 essay on the abortion controversy, "A Defense of Abortion," philosopher Judith Thomson argues that a pregnant woman has the right to an abortion to save her life, even if it involves the death of her unborn child. She anticipates that some readers may balk at her reasoning, and so she offers this parallel argument: Suppose you are locked in a tiny room with another human being, which through no fault of its own is growing uncontrollably, with the result that it is slowly crushing you to death. Of course, it would be morally permissible to kill the other person to save your own life. With the reader's presumed agreement on that conclusion, the parallel argument concerning the abortion situation—so Thomson hopes—is obvious and convincing.

In simple inductive arguments, we are likely to point to the way in which observations or sets of data constitute a *representative sample* of a whole (unexamined) population. Here, the warrant is the representativeness of the sample. For instance, in projecting a line on a graph through a set of points, we defend one projection over alternatives on the grounds that it makes the smoothest fit through most of the points. In this case, the warrant is *simplicity* and *inclusiveness*. Or in defending one explanation against competing explanations of a phenomenon, we appeal to the way in which the preferred explanation can be seen as a *special case* of generally accepted physical laws. Examples of such warrants for inductive reasoning will be offered in following pages (see Chapter 9, A Logician's View: Deduction, Induction, Fallacies, pp. 349–92).

Establishing the warrants for our reasoning—that is, explaining why our grounds really support our claims—can quickly become a highly technical and exacting procedure that goes far beyond what we can hope to explain in this book. Only a solid course or two in formal deductive logic and statistical methods can do justice to our current state of knowledge about these warrants. Developing a "feel" for why reasons or grounds are or are not relevant to what they are alleged to support is the most we can hope to do here without recourse to more rigorous techniques.

Even without formal training, however, one can sense that something is wrong with many bad arguments. Here is an example. British professor C. E. M. Joad found himself standing on a station platform, annoyed because he had just missed his train, when another train, making an unscheduled stop, pulled up to the platform in front of him. He decided to jump aboard, only to hear the porter say "I'm afraid you'll have to get off, sir. This train doesn't stop here." "In that case," replied Joad, "don't worry. I'm not on it."

BACKING

The kinds of reasons appropriate to support an amendment to the Constitution are completely different from the kinds appropriate to settle the question of what caused the defeat of Napoleon's invasion of Russia. Arguments for the amendment might be rooted in an appeal to fairness, whereas arguments about the military defeat might be rooted in letters and other documents in the French and Russian archives. The canons of good argument in each case derive from the ways in which the scholarly communities in law and history, respectively, have developed over the years to support, defend, challenge, and undermine a given kind of argument. Thus, the support or **backing** appropriate for one kind of argument might be quite inappropriate for another kind of argument.

Another way of stating this point is to recognize that once you have given reasons for a claim, you are then likely to be challenged to explain why these reasons are good reasons—why, that is, one should believe these reasons rather than regard them skeptically. Why (a simple example) should we accept the testimony of Dr. X when Dr. Y, equally renowned, supports the opposite side? Or why is it safe to rest a prediction on a small though admittedly carefully selected sample? Or why is it legitimate to argue that (1) if I dream I am the King of France, then I must exist, whereas it is illegitimate to argue that (2) if I dream I am the King of France, then the King of France must exist? To answer these kinds of challenges is to *back up* one's reasoning, and no argument is any better than its backing.

MODAL QUALIFIERS

As we have seen, all arguments are made up of assertions or propositions, which can be sorted into four categories:

- The *claim* (conclusion, thesis to be established),
- The *grounds* (explicit reasons advanced),
- The *warrant* (the principle that connects the ground to the claim), and
- The *backing* (implicit assumptions).

All these kinds of propositions have an explicit or tacit **modality** in which they are asserted, indicating the scope and character with which they are believed to hold true. Is the claim, for instance, believed to be *necessary*—or only *probable*? Is the claim believed to be *plausible*—or only *possible*? Of two reasons for a claim, both may be *good*, but one may be *better* than the other. Indicating the modality with which an assertion is advanced is crucial to any argument for or against it.

Empirical generalizations are typically *contingent* on various factors, and it is important to indicate such contingencies to protect the generalization against obvious counterexamples. Thus, consider this empirical generalization:

Students do best on final examinations if they study hard for them.

Are we really to believe that students who study regularly throughout the whole course and so do not need to cram for the final will do less well than students who neglect regular work in favor of several all-nighters at the last minute? Probably not; what is really meant is that *all other things being equal* (in Latin, *ceteris paribus*), concentrated study just before an exam will yield good results. Alluding to the contingencies in this way shows that the writer is aware of possible exceptions and that they are conceded right from the start.

Assertions also have varying **scope,** and indicating their scope is equally crucial to the role that an assertion plays in argument. Thus, suppose you are arguing against smoking, and the ground for your claim is this:

Heavy smokers cut short their life span.

Such an assertion will be clearer, as well as more likely to be true, if it is explicitly **quantified.** Here, there are three obvious alternative quantifications to choose among: *all* smokers cut short their life span, *most* do, or only *some* do. Until the assertion is quantified in one of these ways, we really do not know what is being asserted—and so we do not know what degree and kind of evidence and counterevidence is relevant. Other quantifiers include *few, rarely, many, often, sometimes, perhaps, usually, more or less, regularly, occasionally.*

In sum, sensitivity to the quantifiers and qualifiers appropriate for each of our assertions, whatever their role in an argument, will help prevent you from asserting exaggerations and other misguided generalizations.

REBUTTALS

Very few arguments of any interest are beyond dispute, conclusively knockdown affairs in which the claim of the argument is so rigidly tied to its grounds, warrants, and backing and its quantifiers and qualifiers so precisely orchestrated that it really proves its conclusion beyond any possibility of doubt. On the contrary, most arguments have many counterarguments, and sometimes one of these counterarguments is the most convincing.

Suppose one has taken a sample that appears to be random: An interviewer on your campus accosts the first ten students she encounters, and seven of them happen to be fraternity or sorority members. She is now ready to argue that seven-tenths of enrolled students belong to Greek organizations.

You believe, however, that the Greeks are in the minority and point out that she happens to have conducted her interview around the corner from the Panhellenic Society's office just off Sorority Row. Her random sample is anything but. The ball is now back in her court as you await her response to your rebuttal.

As this example illustrates, it is safe to say that we do not understand our own arguments very well until we have tried to get a grip on the places in which they are vulnerable to criticism, counterattack, or refutation. Edmund Burke (quoted in Chapter 3 but worth repeating) said, "He that wrestles with us strengthens our nerves, and sharpens our skill. Our antagonist is our helper." Therefore, cultivating alertness to such weak spots, girding one's loins to defend at these places, always helps strengthen one's position.

A MODEL ANALYSIS USING
THE TOULMIN METHOD

To see how the Toulmin method can be used, let's apply it to an argument in this book, Susan Jacoby's "A First Amendment Junkie" (p. 43).

The Claim   Jacoby's central thesis or claim is this: Any form of *censorship*—including feminist censorship of pornography in particular—*is wrong*.

Grounds   Jacoby offers six main reasons or grounds for her claim, roughly in this sequence (but arguably not in this order of importance).

First, feminists exaggerate the harm caused by pornography because they confuse expression of offensive ideas with harmful conduct.

Second, letting the government censor the expression of ideas and attitudes is the wrong response to the failure of parents to control the printed materials that get into the hands of their children.

Third, there is no unanimity even among feminists over what is pornography and what isn't.

Fourth, permitting censorship of pornography to please feminists could well lead to censorship on many issues of concern to feminists ("rape, abortion, menstruation, contraception, lesbianism").

Fifth, censorship under law shows a lack of confidence in the democratic process.

Finally, censorship of words and pictures is suppression of self-expression, and that violates the First Amendment.

Warrants   Each of these six grounds needs its own warrant, and the warrants vary considerably in their complexity. Jacoby (like most writers) is not so didactic as to make these warrants explicit. Taking them in order, this is what they look like.

First, since the First Amendment protects speech in the broadest sense, the censorship that the feminist attack on pornography advocates is *inconsistent* with the First Amendment.

Second, if feminists want to be consistent, then they must advocate censorship of *all* offensive self-expression, but such a radical interference with free speech (amounting virtually to repeal of the First Amendment) is indefensible.

Third, if feminists can't agree over what is pornographic, the censorship of pornography they propose is bound to be arbitrary.

Fourth, feminists ought to see that *they risk losing more than they can hope to gain* if they succeed in censoring pornography.

Fifth, the democratic process can be trusted to weed out harmful utterances.

Sixth, if feminists have a legal right to censor pornography, anti-feminists will claim the same right on other issues.

Backing   Why should the reader agree with Jacoby's grounds? She does not appeal to expert authority, the results of experimental tests or other statistical data, or the support of popular opinion. Instead, she relies principally on two things—but without saying so explicitly.

First, she assumes that the reader accepts the propositions that *freedom of self-expression is valuable* and that *censoring self-expression requires the strongest of reasons*. If there is no fundamental agreement on these propositions, several of her reasons cease to support her claim.

Second, she relies on the reader's open-mindedness and willingness to evaluate common sense (untechnical, ordinary, familiar) considerations at each step of the way. She relies also on the reader having had some personal experience with erotica, pornography, and art. Without that open-mindedness and experience, a reader is not likely to be persuaded by her rejection of the feminist demand for censorship.

Modal Qualifiers   Jacoby defends what she calls an "absolute interpretation" of the First Amendment—that is, the view that *all* censorship of words, pictures, and ideas is not only inconsistent with the First Amendment but is also politically unwise and morally objectionable. She allows that *some* pornography is highly offensive (it offends her, she insists); she allows that *some* pornography ("kiddie porn") may even be harmful to *some* viewers. But she also insists that *more* harm than good would result from the censorship of pornography. She points out that *some* paintings of nude women are art, not pornography; she implies that it is *impossible* to draw a sharp line between permissible erotic pornography and impermissible offensive pornography. She clearly believes that *all* Americans ought to understand and defend the First Amendment under the "absolute interpretation" she favors.

Rebuttals   Jacoby mentions several objections to her views, and perhaps the most effective aspect of her entire argument is her skill in identifying possible objections and meeting them effectively. (Notice the diversity of the objections and the various ways in which she replies.)

Objection: Some of her women friends tell her she is wrong.

Rebuttal: She admits she's a "First Amendment junkie," and she doesn't apologize for it.

Objection: "Kiddie porn" is harmful and deserves censorship.

Rebuttal: Such material is *not* protected by the First Amendment because it is an "abuse of power" of adults over children.

Objection: Pornography is a form of violence against women, and therefore it is especially harmful.

Rebuttal: (1) No, it really isn't harmful, but it is disgusting and offensive. (2) In any case, it's surely not as harmful as allowing American neo-Nazis to parade in Jewish neighborhoods. (Jacoby is referring to the march in Skokie, Illinois, in 1977, upheld by the courts as permissible political expression under the First Amendment despite its offensiveness to survivors of the Nazi concentration camps.)

Objection: Censoring pornography advances public respect for women.

Rebuttal: Censoring *Ms.* magazine, which antifeminists have already done, undermines women's freedom and self-expression.

Objection: Reasonable people can tell pornography when they see it, so censoring it poses no problems.

✓ A CHECKLIST FOR USING THE TOULMIN METHOD

Have I asked the following questions?

☐ What claim does the argument make?

☐ What grounds are offered for the claim?

☐ What warrants the inferences from the grounds to the claim?

☐ What backing supports the claim?

☐ With what modalities are the claim and grounds asserted?

☐ To what rebuttals are the claim, grounds, and backing vulnerable?

Rebuttal: Yes, there are clear cases of gross pornography; but there are lots of borderline cases, as women themselves prove when they disagree over whether a photo in *Penthouse* is offensively erotic or "lovely" and "sensuous."

> See the companion Web site
> **bedfordstmartins.com/barnetbedau**
> for links related to the Toulmin model.

PUTTING THE TOULMIN METHOD TO WORK:
Responding to an Argument

Let's look at an argument — it happens to be a proposal concerning illegal immigration — and see how the Toulmin method can be applied.

Michael S. Dukakis and Daniel J. B. Mitchell

Michael S. Dukakis, a professor of political science at Northeastern University, served as the governor of Massachusetts from 1975 to 1979 and from 1983 to 1991. Daniel J. B. Mitchell is a professor of management and public policy at the University of California at Los Angeles. The essay that follows originally appeared in the New York Times *(July 25, 2006).*

Raise Wages, Not Walls

There are two approaches to illegal immigration currently being debated in Congress. One, supported by the House, emphasizes border control and law enforcement, including a wall along the Mexican border and increased border patrols. The other, which is supported by the Bush administration and has been passed by the Senate, relies on employers to police the workplace. Both proposals have serious flaws.

As opponents of the House plan have rightly pointed out, walls rarely work; illegal immigrants will get around them one way or another. Unless we erect something akin to the Berlin Wall, which would cost billions to build and police, a barrier on the border would be monitored by largely symbolic patrols and easily evaded.

The Senate approach is more realistic but it, too, has problems. It creates a temporary worker program but requires employers first to attempt to recruit American workers to fill job openings. It allows for more border fencing, but makes no effort to disguise the basic futility of the enterprise. Instead, it calls on employers to enforce immigration laws in the workplace, a plan that can only succeed through the creation and distribution of a costly national identification card.

A national ID card raises serious questions about civil liberties, but they are not the sole concern. The cost estimates for producing and distributing a counterfeit-proof card for the roughly 150 million people currently in the labor force—and the millions more who will seek work in the near future—extend into the billions of dollars. Employers would have to verify the identity of every American worker, otherwise the program would be as unreliable as the one in place now. Anyone erroneously denied a card in this bureaucratic labyrinth would be unemployable.

There is a simpler alternative. If we are really serious about turning 5 back the tide of illegal immigration, we should start by raising the minimum wage from $5.15 per hour to something closer to $8. The Massachusetts legislature recently voted to raise the state minimum to $8 and California may soon set its minimum even higher. Once the minimum wage has been significantly increased, we can begin vigorously enforcing the wage law and other basic labor standards.

Millions of illegal immigrants work for minimum and even subminimum wages in workplaces that don't come close to meeting health and safety standards. It is nonsense to say, as President Bush did recently, that these jobs are filled by illegal immigrants because Americans won't do them. Before we had mass illegal immigration in this country, hotel beds were made, office floors were cleaned, restaurant dishes were washed and crops were picked—by Americans.

Americans will work at jobs that are risky, dirty, or unpleasant so long as they provide decent wages and working conditions, especially if employers also provide health insurance. Plenty of Americans now work in such jobs, from mining coal to picking up garbage. The difference is they are paid a decent wage and provided benefits for their labor.

However, Americans won't work for peanuts, and these days the national minimum wage is less than peanuts. For full-time work, it doesn't even come close to the poverty line for an individual, let alone provide a family with a living wage. It hasn't been raised since 1997 and isn't enforced even at its currently ridiculous level.

Yet enforcing the minimum wage doesn't require walling off a porous border or trying to distinguish yesterday's illegal immigrant from tomorrow's "guest worker." All it takes is a willingness by the federal government to inspect workplaces to determine which employers obey the law.

Curiously, most members of Congress who take a hard line on immi- 10
gration also strongly oppose increasing the minimum wage, claiming it will hurt businesses and reduce jobs. For some reason, they don't seem eager to acknowledge that many of the jobs they claim to hold dear are held by the same illegal immigrants they are trying to deport.

But if we want to reduce illegal immigration, it makes sense to reduce the abundance of extremely low-paying jobs that fuels it. If we raise the minimum wage, it's possible some low-end jobs may be lost; but more Americans would also be willing to work in such jobs, thereby denying them to people who aren't supposed to be here in the first place. And tough enforcement of wage rules would curtail the growth of an underground economy in which both illegal immigration and employer abuses thrive.

Raising the minimum wage and increasing enforcement would prove far more effective and less costly than either proposal currently under consideration in Congress. If Congress would only remove its blinders about the minimum wage, it may see a plan to deal effectively with illegal immigration, too.

THINKING WITH TOULMIN'S METHOD

At first blush, what we have in this essay is a twelve-paragraph argument divided into two unequal parts. Paragraphs 1–4 offer some proposals for dealing with illegal immigration and reasons why these proposals won't work. This preliminary material is followed by paragraphs 5–12 in which the proposal favored by the authors is introduced, explained, and justified. So much for first impressions.

Let's now deconstruct this essay by identifying each of the six elements that constitute the Toulmin method.

- First and foremost, what is the **claim** being made, the main thesis of the essay? Is it in the title? Is it in paragraph 5? Or is it elsewhere? What kind of claim is it—a claim of fact? A claim of value? In any case, write down the claim for further reference.

- Second, what are the **grounds,** the evidence or reasons advanced in support of the claim? Partly they can be found in what the authors regard as ineffective alternative efforts in paragraphs 1–4. What are these alternatives? Why are they said to be ineffective?

Look also at paragraph 5 and later paragraphs. Write down the sentences you have discovered that are playing this role.

- Third, what are the **warrants** that Dukakis and Mitchell rely on to carry the burden of their argument? In paragraph 5, for example, the authors rely on examples from Massachusetts and California. The evidence they offer amounts to a minimal inductive argument. Could their argument of this sort be stronger? Paragraphs 6 and 7 rely on general knowledge, as do most of the rest of their argument. Is that the best one can do with this issue? Can you think of ways in which the authors' argument can be strengthened? Carefully look through the whole essay for whatever evidence you can find of the mention of and reliance on this or that warrant.

The essence of the Toulmin method lies in these three elements: the claim(s), the ground(s), and the warrant(s). If you have extracted these from the Dukakis-Mitchell essay, you will have identified most of what will suffice for a good grasp of the argument in question.

Of lesser importance are the three other elements of the Toulmin method: the backing, the modal qualifiers, and the rebuttal.

- Fourth, consider the **backing**—the reasons for one's reasons. The authors set out to argue for a claim, which they support on empirical or factual grounds, using warrants appropriate to an argument of that sort. But suppose Dukakis and Mitchell are challenged. How might they back up their reasons with further reasons? They are in effect answering the tacit questions "How do you know . . . ?" and "Why do you believe . . . ?" What might the authors offer in support of their views when confronted with such queries?

- Fifth, there are the **modal qualifiers**—or are there? Can you find any passages in which the authors qualify their assertions ("Perhaps if we tried . . .") ("Most, although not all, illegal immigration . . .")? Look at paragraph 11. There's at least one modal qualifier here—can you spot it?

- Finally, there are the **rebuttals,** the reasons advanced by someone who rejects the authors' claim, or who concedes their claim but rejects the grounds offered in its support, and so forth. Paragraphs 1–4 mention alternatives to the proposals favored by the authors, and the authors reply to these objections. Is their rebuttal convincing? Why, or why not?

9

A Logician's View: Deduction, Induction, Fallacies

Logic is the anatomy of thought.

— JOHN LOCKE

Logic takes care of itself; all we have to do is to look and see how it does it.

— LUDWIG WITTGENSTEIN

In Chapter 3 we introduced the terms *deduction, induction*, and *fallacy*. Here we discuss them in greater detail.

DEDUCTION

The basic aim of deductive reasoning is to start with some assumption or premise and extract from it a conclusion — a logical consequence — that is concealed but implicit in it. Thus, taking the simplest case, if I assert as a premise

    1a. Nuclear power poses more risks of harm to the environment than fossil fuels.

then it is a matter of simple deduction to infer the conclusion that

    1b. Fossil fuels pose fewer risks of harm to the environment than nuclear power.

Anyone who understands English would grant that 1b follows 1a — or equivalently, that 1b can be validly deduced from 1a — because whatever two objects, *A* and *B*, you choose, if *A* does *more things than B*, then *B* must do *fewer things than A*.

    Thus, in this and all other cases of valid deductive reasoning, we can say not only that we are entitled to *infer* the conclusion from the premise —

in this case, infer 1b from 1a—but that the premise *implies* the conclusion. Remember, too, the conclusion (1b) that fossil fuels pose fewer risks than nuclear power—inferred or deduced from the statement (1a) that nuclear power poses more risks—does not depend on the truth of the statement that nuclear power poses more risks. If the speaker (falsely) asserts that nuclear power poses more risks—does not depend on the truth of the statement that nuclear power poses more risks. If the speaker (falsely) asserts that nuclear power poses more risks, then the hearer validly (that is to say, logically) concludes that fossil fuels pose fewer risks. Thus, 1b follows from 1a whether or not 1a is true; consequently, if 1a is true, then so is 1b; but if 1a is false, then 1b must be false also.

Let's take another example—more interesting but comparably simple:

2a. President Truman was underrated by his critics.

Given 2a, a claim amply verified by events of the 1950s, one is entitled to infer

2b. His critics underrated President Truman.

On what basis can we argue that 2a implies 2b? The two propositions are equivalent because a rule of English grammar assures us that we can convert the position of subject and predicate phrases in a sentence by shifting from the passive to the active voice (or vice versa) without any change in the conditions that make the proposition true (or false).

Both pairs of examples illustrate that in deductive reasoning, our aim is to transform, reformulate, or restate in our conclusion some (or, as in the two examples above, all) of the information contained in our premises.

Remember, even though a proposition or statement follows from a previous proposition or statement, the statements need not be true. We can see why if we consider another example. Suppose someone asserts or claims that

3a. The Gettysburg Address is longer than the Declaration of Independence.

As every student of American history knows, 3a is false. But false or not, we can validly deduce from it that

3b. The Declaration of Independence is shorter than the Gettysburg Address.

This inference is valid (even though the conclusion is untrue) because the conclusion follows logically (more precisely, deductively) from 3a: In English, as we know, the meaning of "*A* is shorter than *B*," which appears in 3b, is simply the converse of "*B* is longer than *A*," which appears in 3a.

The deductive relation between 3a and 3b reminds us again that the idea of validity, which is so crucial to deduction, is not the same as the idea of truth. False propositions have implications—logical consequences—too, just as true propositions do.

In the three pairs of examples so far, what can we point to as the warrant for our claims? Well, look at the reasoning in each case; the arguments rely on rules of ordinary English, on the accepted meanings of words like on, under, and underrated.

In many cases, of course, the deductive inference or pattern of reasoning is much more complex than that which we have seen in the examples so far. When we introduced the idea of deduction in Chapter 3, we gave as our primary example the *syllogism*. Here is another example:

> 4. Texas is larger than California; California is larger than Arizona; therefore, Texas is larger than Arizona.

The conclusion in this syllogism is derivable from the two premises; that is, anyone who asserts the two premises is committed to accepting the conclusion as well, whether or not one thinks of it.

Notice again that the *truth* of the conclusion is not established merely by validity of the inference. The conclusion in this syllogism happens to be true. And the premises of this syllogism imply the conclusion. But the argument establishes the conclusion only because both of the premises on which the conclusion depends are true. Even a Californian admits that Texas is larger than California, which in turn is larger than Arizona. In other words, argument 4 is a *sound* argument because (as we explained in Chapter 3) it is valid and all its premises are true. All—and only—arguments that *prove* their conclusions have these two traits.

How might we present the warrant for the argument in 4? Short of a crash course in formal logic, either of two strategies might suffice. One is to argue from the fact that the validity of the inference depends on the meaning of a key concept, *being larger than*. This concept has the property of *transitivity*, a property that many concepts share (for example, *is equal to, is to the right of, is smarter than*—all are transitive concepts). Consequently, whatever *A, B,* and *C* are, if *A* is larger than *B,* and *B* is larger than *C,* then *A* will be larger than *C.* The final step is to substitute "Texas," "California," and "Arizona" for *A, B,* and *C,* respectively.

A second strategy, less abstract and more graphic, is to think of representing Texas, California, and Arizona by nested circles. Thus, the first premise in argument 4 would look like this:

The second premise would look like this:

The conclusion would look like this:

We can see that this conclusion follows from the premises because it amounts to nothing more than what one gets by superimposing the two premises on each other. Thus, the whole argument can be represented like this:

The so-called middle term in the argument—California—disappears from the conclusion; its role is confined to be the link between the other two terms, Texas and Arizona, in the premises. (This is an adaptation of the technique used in elementary formal logic known as Venn diagrams.) In this manner one can give graphic display to the important fact that the conclusion follows from the premises because one can literally *see* the conclusion represented by nothing more than a representation of the premises.

Both of these strategies bring out the fact that validity of deductive inference is a purely *formal* property of argument. Each strategy abstracts the form from the content of the propositions involved to show how the concepts in the premises are related to the concepts in the conclusion.

For the sake of illustration, here is another syllogistic argument with the same logical features as argument 4. (A nice exercise is to restate argument 5 using diagrams in the manner of argument 4.)

5. African American slaves were treated worse than white indentured servants. Indentured white servants were treated worse than free white labor. Therefore, African American slaves were treated worse than free white labor.

Not all deductive reasoning occurs in syllogisms, however, or at least not in syllogisms like the ones in 4 and 5. (The term *syllogism* is sometimes used to refer to any deductive argument of whatever form, provided only that it has two premises.) In fact, syllogisms such as 4 are not the commonest form of our deductive reasoning at all. Nor are they the simplest (and of course, not the most complex). For an argument that is even simpler, consider this:

6. If a youth is an African American slave, he is probably treated worse than a youth in indentured service. This youth is an African American slave. Therefore, he is probably treated worse than if he had been an indentured servant.

Here the pattern of reasoning has the form: If *A*, then *B*; *A*; there-fore, *B*. Notice that the content of the assertions represented by *A* and *B* do not matter; any set of expressions having the same form or structure will do equally well, including assertions built out of meaningless terms, as in this example:

7. If the slithy toves, then the gyres gimble. The slithy toves. Therefore, the gyres gimble.

Argument 7 has the form: If *A*, then *B*; *A*; therefore *B*. As a piece of deductive inference it is every bit as good. Unlike 6, however, 7 is of no interest to us because none of its assertions make any sense (unless you are a reader of Lewis Carroll's "Jabberwocky," and even then the sense of 7 is doubtful). You cannot, in short, use a valid deductive argument to prove anything unless the premises and the conclusion are *true*, but they can't be true unless they *mean* something in the first place.

This parallel between arguments 6 and 7 shows once again that deductive validity in an argument rests on the *form* or structure of the argument, and not on its content or meaning. If all one can say about an argument is that it is valid—that is, its conclusion follows from the premises—one has not given a sufficient reason for accepting the argument's conclusion. It has been said that the Devil can quote Scripture; similarly, an argument can be deductively valid and of no further interest or value whatever because valid (but false) conclusions can be drawn from false or even meaningless assumptions. For example,

8. New York's Metropolitan Museum of Art has the finest collection of abstract impressionist painting in the world. The finest collec-tion of abstract impressionist paintings includes dozens of can-vases by Winslow Homer. Therefore, the Metropolitan Museum of Art has dozens of paintings by Winslow Homer.

Here, the conclusion follows validly from the premises, even though all three propositions are false. Nevertheless, although validity by itself is not enough, it is a necessary condition of any deductive argument that purports to establish its conclusion.

Now let us consider another argument with the same form as 8, only more interesting.

9. If President Truman knew the Japanese were about to surrender, then it was immoral of him to order that atom bombs be dropped on Hiroshima and Nagasaki. Truman knew the Japanese were about to surrender. Therefore, it was immoral of him to order dropping those bombs.

As in the two previous examples, anyone who assents to the premises in argument 9 must assent to the conclusion; the form of arguments 8 and 9 is identical. But do the premises of argument 9 *prove* the conclusion? That depends on whether both premises are true. Well, are they? This turns on a number of considerations, and it is worthwhile pausing to examine this argument closely to illustrate the kinds of things that are involved in answering this question.

Let us begin by examining the second (minor) premise. Its truth is controversial even to this day. Autobiography, memoranda, other documentary evidence—all are needed to assemble the evidence to back up the grounds for the thesis or claim made in the conclusion of this valid argument. Evaluating this material effectively will probably involve not only further deductions, but inductive reasoning as well.

Now consider the first (major) premise in argument 9. Its truth doesn't depend on what history shows but on the moral principles one accepts. The major premise has the form of a hypothetical proposition ("if . . . then . . .") and asserts a connection between two very different kinds of things. The antecedent of the hypothetical (the clause following "if") mentions facts about Truman's *knowledge,* and the consequent of the hypothetical (the clause following "then") mentions facts about the *morality* of his conduct in light of such knowledge. The major premise as a whole can thus be seen as expressing *a principle of moral responsibility.*

Such principles can, of course, be controversial. In this case, for instance, is the principle peculiarly relevant to the knowledge and conduct of a president of the United States? Probably not; it is far more likely that this principle is merely a special case of a more general proposition about anyone's moral responsibility. (After all, we know a great deal more about the conditions of our own moral responsibility than we do about those of high government officials.) We might express this more general principle in this way: If we have knowledge that would make our violent conduct unnecessary, then we are immoral if we deliberately act violently anyway. Thus, accepting this general principle can serve as a basis for defending the major premise of argument 9.

We have examined this argument in some detail because it illustrates the kinds of considerations needed to test whether a given argument is not only valid but whether its premises are true—that is, whether its premises really prove the conclusion.

The great value of the form of argument known as hypothetical syllogism, exemplified by arguments 6 and 7, is that the structure of the argument is so simple and so universally applicable in reasoning that it is often both easy and worthwhile to formulate one's claims so that they can be grounded by an argument of this sort.

Before leaving the subject of deductive inference, consider three other forms of argument, each of which can be found in actual use elsewhere in the readings in this volume. The simplest of these is **disjunctive syllogism,** so called because its major premise is a **disjunction.** For example,

10. Either censorship of television shows is overdue, or our society is indifferent to the education of its youth. Our society is not

indifferent to the education of its youth. Therefore, censorship of television is overdue.

Notice, by the way, that the validity of an argument, as in this case, does not turn on pedantic repetition of every word or phrase as the argument moves along; nonessential elements can be dropped, or equivalent expressions substituted for variety without adverse effect on the reasoning. Thus, in conversation or in writing, the argument in 10 might actually be presented like this:

11. Either censorship of television is overdue, or our society is indifferent to the education of its youth. But, of course, we aren't indifferent; it's censorship that's overdue.

The key feature of disjunctive syllogism, as example 11 suggests, is that the conclusion is whichever of the disjuncts is left over after the others have been negated in the minor premise. Thus, we could easily have a very complex disjunctive syllogism, with a dozen disjuncts in the major premise, and seven of them denied in the minor premise, leaving a conclusion of the remaining five. Usually, however, a disjunctive argument is formulated in this manner: Assert a disjunction with two or more disjuncts in the major premise; then *deny all but one* in the minor premise; and infer validly the remaining disjunct as the conclusion. That was the form of argument 11.

Another type of argument, especially favored by orators and rhetoricians, is the **dilemma.** Ordinarily we use the term *dilemma* in the sense of an awkward predicament, as when we say, "His dilemma was that he didn't have enough money to pay the waiter." But when logicians refer to a dilemma, they mean a forced choice between two or more equally unattractive alternatives. For example, the predicament of the U.S. government during the mid-1980s as it faced the crisis brought on by terrorist attacks on American civilian targets, which were believed, during that time, to be inspired and supported by the Libyan government, can be formulated in a dilemma:

12. If the United States bombs targets in Libya, innocent people will be killed, and the Arab world will be angered. If the United States doesn't bomb Libyan targets, then terrorists will go unpunished, and the United States will lose respect among other governments. Either the United States bombs Libyan targets, or it doesn't. Therefore, in either case unattractive consequences will follow: The innocent will be killed, or terrorists will go unpunished.

Notice first the structure of the argument: two conditional propositions asserted as premises, followed by another premise that states a **necessary truth.** (The premise, "Either we bomb the Libyans, or we don't," is a disjunction; since its two alternatives are exhaustive, one of the two alternatives must be true. Such a statement is often called analytically true, or a *tautology*.) No doubt the conclusion of this dilemma follows from its premises.

But does the argument prove, as it purports to do, that whatever the U.S. government does, it will suffer "unattractive consequences"? It is customary to speak of "the horns of the dilemma," as though the challenge posed by the dilemma were like a bull ready to gore you whichever direction you turn. But if the two conditional premises failed to exhaust the possibilities, then one can escape from the dilemma by going "between the horns"; that is, by finding a third alternative. If (as in this case) that is not possible, one can still ask whether both of the main premises are true. (In this argument, it should be clear that neither of these main premises spells out all or even most of the consequences that could be foreseen.) Even so, in cases where both these conditional premises are true, it may be that the consequences of one alternative are nowhere nearly so bad as those of the other. If that is true, but our reasoning stops before evaluating that fact, we may be guilty of failing to distinguish between the greater and the lesser of two admitted evils. The logic of the dilemma itself cannot decide this choice for us. Instead, we must bring to bear empirical inquiry and imagination to the evaluation of the grounds of the dilemma itself.

Writers commonly use the term *dilemma* without explicitly formulating the dilemma to which they refer, leaving it for the readers to do. And sometimes, what is called a dilemma really isn't one. (Remember the dog's tail? Calling it a leg doesn't make it a leg.) As an example, consider the plight of Sophie in William Styron's novel, *Sophie's Choice*. The scene is Birkenau, the main Nazi extermination camp during World War II. Among the thousands arriving at the prison gates are Sophie and her two children, Jan and Eva. On the train platform they are confronted by a Nazi SS medical officer. He will decide which are the lucky ones; they will live to work in the camp. The rest will go to their death in the gas chambers. When Sophie insists she is Polish but not Jewish, the officer says she may choose one of her children to be saved. Which of the two ought to be saved? On what basis ought Sophie resolve her dilemma? It looks as if she has only two alternatives, each of which presents her with an agonizing outcome. Or is there a third way out?

Finally, one of the most powerful and dramatic forms of argument is **reductio ad absurdum** (from the Latin, meaning "reduction to absurdity"). The idea of a reductio argument is to disprove a proposition by showing the absurdity of its inevitable conclusion. It is used, of course, to refute your opponent's position and prove your own. For example, in Plato's *Republic*, Socrates asks an old gentleman, Cephalus, to define what right conduct is. Cephalus says that it consists of paying your debts and keeping your word. Socrates rejects this answer by showing that it leads to a contradiction. He argues that Cephalus cannot have given the correct answer because if we believe that he did, we will be quickly led into contradictions; in some cases when you keep your word you will nonetheless be doing the wrong thing. For suppose, says Socrates, that you borrowed a weapon from a man, promising to return it when he asks for it. One day he comes to your door, demanding his weapon and swearing angrily that he intends to murder a neighbor. Keeping your word under those circumstances is absurd, Socrates implies, and the reader of the dialogue is left to infer that Cephalus's definition, which led to this result, is refuted.

Let's take a closer look at another example. Suppose you are opposed to any form of gun control, whereas I am in favor of gun control. I might try to refute your position by attacking it with a reductio argument. To do that, I start out by assuming the very opposite of what I believe or favor and try to establish a contradiction that results from following out the consequences of this initial assumption. My argument might look like this:

13. Let's assume your position—namely, that there ought to be no legal restrictions whatever on the sale and ownership of guns. That means that you'd permit having every neighborhood hardware store sell pistols and rifles to whoever walks in the door. But that's not all. You apparently also would permit selling machine guns to children, antitank weapons to lunatics, small-bore cannons to the nearsighted, as well as guns and the ammunition to go with them to anyone with a criminal record. But this is utterly preposterous. No one could favor such a dangerous policy. So the only question worth debating is what kind of gun control is necessary.

Now in this example, my reductio of your position on gun control is not based on claiming to show that you have strictly contradicted yourself, for there is no purely logical contradiction in opposing all forms of gun control. Instead, what I have tried to do is to show that there is a contradiction between what you profess—no gun controls whatever—and what you probably really believe, if only you will stop to think about it—no lunatic should be allowed to buy a loaded machine gun.

My refutation of your position rests on whether I succeed in establishing an inconsistency among your own beliefs. If it turns out that you really believe lunatics should be free to purchase guns and ammunition, then my attempted refutation fails.

In explaining reductio ad absurdum, we have had to rely on another idea fundamental to logic, that of **contradiction,** or inconsistency. (We used this idea, remember, to define validity in Chapter 3. A deductive argument is valid if and only if affirming the premises and denying the conclusion results in a contradiction.) The opposite of contradiction is **consistency,** a notion of hardly less importance to good reasoning than validity. These concepts deserve a few words of further explanation and illustration. Consider this pair of assertions:

14. Abortion is homicide.
15. Racism is unfair.

No one would plausibly claim that we can infer or deduce 15 from 14, or, for that matter, 14 from 15. This almost goes without saying, because there is no evident connection between these two assertions. They are unrelated assertions; logically speaking, they are *independent* of each other. In such cases the two assertions are mutually *consistent;* that is, both could be true — or both could be false. But now consider another proposition:

16. Euthanasia is not murder.

Could a person assert 14 (*Abortion is homicide*) and also assert 16 (*Euthanasia is not murder*) and be consistent? This question is equivalent to asking whether one could assert the **conjunction** of these two propositions — namely,

17. Abortion is homicide, and euthanasia is not murder.

It is not so easy to say whether 17 is consistent or inconsistent. The kinds of moral scruples that might lead a person to assert one of these conjuncts (that is, one of the two initial propositions, *Abortion is homicide* and *Euthanasia is not murder*) might lead to the belief that the other one must be false and thus to the conclusion that 17 is inconsistent. (Notice that if 14 were the assertion that *Abortion is murder,* instead of *Abortion is homicide,* the problem of asserting consistently both 14 and 15 would be more acute.) Yet if we think again, we might imagine someone being convinced that there is no inconsistency in asserting that *Abortion is homicide,* say, and that *Euthanasia is not murder,* or even the reverse. (For instance, suppose you believed that the unborn deserve a chance to live and that putting elderly persons to death in a painless manner and with their consent confers a benefit on them.)

Let us generalize: We can say of any set of propositions that they are *consistent* if and only if *all could be true together.* (Notice that it follows from this definition that propositions that mutually imply each other, as do *Seabiscuit was America's fastest racehorse* and *America's fastest racehorse was Seabiscuit.* Remember that, once again, the truth of the assertions in question does not matter. Two propositions can be consistent or not, quite apart from whether they are true. Not so with falsehood: It follows from our definition of consistency that an *inconsistent* proposition must be *false.* (We have relied on this idea in explaining how a reductio ad absurdum works.)

Assertions or claims that are not consistent can take either of two forms. Suppose you assert proposition 14, that abortion is homicide, early in an essay you are writing, but later you assert that

18. Abortion is harmless.

You have now asserted a position on abortion that is strictly contrary to the one with which you began; contrary in the sense that both assertions 14 and 18 cannot be true. It is simply not true that if an abortion involves killing a human being (which is what *homicide* strictly means), then it causes no one any harm (killing a person always causes harm— even if it is excusable, justifiable, not wrong, the best thing to do in the circumstances, and so on). Notice that although 14 and 18 cannot both be true, they can both be false. In fact, many people who are perplexed about the morality of abortion believe precisely this. They concede that abortion does harm the fetus, so 18 must be false; but they also believe that abortion doesn't kill a person, so 14 must also be false.

Or consider another, simpler case. If you describe the glass as half empty and I describe it as half full, both of us can be right; the two assertions are consistent, even though they sound vaguely incompatible. (This is the reason that disputing over whether the glass is half full or half empty has become the popular paradigm of a futile, purely *verbal disagreement*.) But if I describe the glass as half empty whereas you insist that it is two-thirds empty, then we have a real disagreement; your description and mine are strictly contrary, in that both cannot be true—although both can be false. (Both are false if the glass is only one-quarter full.)

This, by the way, enables us to define the difference between a pair of **contradictory** propositions and a pair of **contrary** propositions. Two propositions are contrary if and only if both cannot be true (though both can be false); two propositions are contradictory if and only if they are such that if one is true the other must be false, and vice versa. Thus, if Jack says that Alice Walker's *The Color Purple* is a better novel than Mark Twain's *Huckleberry Finn*, and Jill says, "No, *Huckleberry Finn* is better than *The Color Purple*," she is contradicting Jack. If what either one of them says is true, then what the other says must be false.

A more subtle case of contradiction arises when two or more of one's own beliefs implicitly contradict each other. We may find ourselves saying "Travel is broadening," and saying an hour later, "People don't really change." Just beneath the surface of these two beliefs lies a self-contradiction: How can travel broaden us unless it influences—and changes—our beliefs, values, and outlook? But if we can't really change ourselves, then traveling to new places won't change us, either. (Indeed, there is a Roman saying to the effect that travelers change the skies above them, not their hearts.) "Travel is broadening" and "People don't change" collide with each other; something has to give.

Our point, of course, is not that you must never say today something that contradicts something you said yesterday. Far from it; if you think you were mistaken yesterday, of course you will take a different position today. But what you want to avoid is what George Orwell called *doublethink* in his novel *1984*: "*Doublethink* means the power of holding two contradictory beliefs in one's mind simultaneously, and accepting them both."

Genuine contradiction, and not merely contrary assertion, is the situation we should expect to find in some disputes. Someone advances a thesis—such as the assertion in 14, *Abortion is homicide*—and someone else flatly contradicts it by the simple expedient of negating it, thus:

19. Abortion is not homicide.

If we can trust public opinion polls, many of us are not sure whether to agree with 14 or with 19. But we should agree that whichever is true, *both* cannot be true, and *both* cannot be false. The two assertions, between them, exclude all other possibilities; they pose a forced choice for our belief. (Again, we have met this idea, too, in a reductio ad absurdum.)

Now it is one thing for Jack and Jill in a dispute or argument to contradict each other. It is quite another matter for Jack to contradict himself. One wants (or should want) to avoid self-contradiction because of the embarrassing position in which one then finds oneself. Once I have contradicted myself, what are others to believe I really believe? What, indeed, *do* I believe, for that matter?

It may be, as Emerson observed, that a "foolish consistency is the hobgoblin of little minds"—that is, it may be shortsighted to purchase a consistency in one's beliefs at the expense of flying in the face of common sense. But making an effort to avoid a foolish inconsistency is the hallmark of serious thinking.

While we are speaking of inconsistency, we should spend a moment on **paradox.** The word refers to two different things:

- An assertion that is essentially self-contradictory and therefore cannot be true and

- A seemingly contradictory assertion that nevertheless may be true.

An example of the first might be, "Evaluations concerning quality in literature are all a matter of personal judgment, but Shakespeare is the world's greatest writer." It is hard to make any sense out of this assertion. Contrast it with a paradox of the second sort, a *seeming* contradiction that may make sense, such as "The longest way round is the shortest way home," or "Work is more fun than fun," or "The best way to find happiness is not to look for it." Here we have assertions that are striking because as soon as we hear them we realize that although they seem inconsistent and self-defeating, they contain (or may contain) profound truths. Paradoxes of this second sort are especially common in religious texts, where they may imply a mysterious reality concealed by a world of contradictory appearances. Examples are "Some who are last shall be first, and some who are first shall be last" (Jesus, quoted in Luke 13:30), and "Death, thou shalt die" (the poet John Donne, alluding to the idea that the person who has faith in Jesus dies to this world but lives eternally). If you use the word *paradox* in your own writing—for instance, to characterize an argument that you are reading—be sure that your reader will understand in which sense you are using the word. (And, of course, you will not want to write paradoxes of the first, self-contradictory sort.)

INDUCTION

Deduction involves logical thinking that applies to any assertion or claim whatever—because every possible statement, true or false, has its deductive logical consequences. Induction is relevant to one kind of assertion only; namely, to **empirical** or *factual* claims. Other kinds of assertions (such as definitions, mathematical equations, and moral or legal norms) simply are not the product of inductive reasoning and cannot serve as a basis for further inductive thinking.

And so, in studying the methods of induction, we are exploring tactics and strategies useful in gathering and then using **evidence**—empirical, observational, experimental—in support of a belief as its ground. Modern scientific knowledge is the product of these methods, and they differ somewhat from one science to another because they depend on the theories and technology appropriate to each of the sciences. Here, all we can do is discuss generally the more abstract features common to inductive inquiry generally. For fuller details, you must eventually consult your local physicist, chemist, geologist, or their colleagues and counterparts in other scientific fields.

Observation and Inference

Let us begin with a simple example. Suppose we have evidence (actually we don't, but that will not matter for our purposes) in support of the claim that

1. In a sample of 500 smokers, 230 persons observed have cardio-vascular disease.

The basis for asserting 1—the evidence or ground—would be, presumably, straightforward physical examination of the 500 persons in the sample, one by one.

With this claim in hand, we can think of the purpose and methods of induction as being pointed in both of two opposite directions: toward establishing the basis or ground of the very empirical proposition with which we start (in this example the observation stated in 1) or toward understanding what that observation indicates or suggests as a more general, inclusive, or fundamental fact of nature.

In each case, we start from something we *do* know (or take for granted and treat as a sound starting point)—some fact of nature, perhaps a striking or commonplace event that we have observed and recorded—and then go on to something we do *not* fully know and perhaps cannot directly observe. In example 1, only the second of these two orientations is of any interest, and so let us concentrate exclusively on it. Let us also generously treat as a *method* of induction any regular pattern or style of nondeductive reasoning that we could use to support a claim such as that in 1.

Anyone truly interested in the observed fact that *230 of 500 smokers have cardiovascular disease* is likely to start speculating about, and thus be interested in finding out, whether any or all of several other propositions are also true. For example, one might wonder whether

2. *All* smokers have cardiovascular disease or will develop it during their lifetimes.

This claim is a straightforward generalization of the original observation as reported in claim 1. When we think inductively about the linkage between 1 and 2, we are reasoning from an observed sample (some smokers—that is, 230 of the 500 *observed*) to the entire membership of a more inclusive class (*all* smokers, whether observed or not). The fundamental question raised by reasoning from the narrower claim 1 to the broader claim 2 is whether we have any ground for believing that what is true of *some* members of a class is true of them *all*. So the difference between 1 and 2 is that of *quantity* or scope.

We can also think inductively about the *relation* between the factors mentioned in 1. Having observed data as reported in 1, we may be tempted to assert a different and profounder kind of claim:

3. Smoking *causes* cardiovascular disease.

Here our interest is not merely in generalizing from a sample to a whole class; it is the far more important one of *explaining* the observation with which we began in claim 1. Certainly the preferred, even if not the only, mode of explanation for a natural phenomenon is a *causal* explanation. In proposition 3, we propose to explain the presence of one phenomenon (cardiovascular disease) by the prior occurrence of an independent phenomenon (smoking). The observation reported in 1 is now being used as evidence or support for this new conjecture stated in 3.

Our original claim in 1 asserted no causal relation between anything and anything else; whatever the cause of cardiovascular disease may be, that cause is not observed, mentioned, or assumed in assertion 1. Similarly, the observation asserted in claim 1 is consistent with many explanations. For example, the explanation of 1 might not be 3, but some other, undetected, carcinogenic factor unrelated to smoking—for instance, exposure to high levels of radon. The question one now faces is what can be added to 1, or teased out of it, to produce an adequate ground for claiming 3. (We shall return to this example for closer scrutiny.)

But there is a third way to go beyond 1. Instead of a straightforward generalization, as we had in 2, or a pronouncement on the cause of a phenomenon, as in 3, we might have a somewhat more complex and cautious further claim in mind, such as this:

4. Smoking is a factor in the causation of cardiovascular disease in some persons.

This proposition, like 3, advances a claim about causation. But 4 is obviously a weaker claim than 3. That is, other observations, theories, or evidence that would require us to reject 3 might be consistent with 4; evidence that would support 4 could easily fail to be enough to support 3. Consequently, it is even possible that 4 is true although 3 is false, because 4 allows for other (unmentioned) factors in the causation of cardiovascular disease (genetic or dietary factors, for example) which may not be found in all smokers.

Propositions 2, 3, and 4 differ from proposition 1 in an important respect. We began by assuming that 1 states an empirical fact based on direct observation, whereas these others do not. Instead, they state empirical *hypotheses* or conjectures—tentative generalizations not fully confirmed—each of which goes beyond the observed facts asserted in 1. Each of 2, 3, and 4 can be regarded as an *inductive inference* from 1. We can also say that 2, 3, and 4 are hypotheses relative to 1, even if relative to some other starting point (such as all the information that scientists today really have about smoking and cardiovascular disease) they are not.

Probability

Another way of formulating the last point is to say that whereas proposition 1, a statement of observed fact (*230 out of 500 smokers have cardiovascular disease*), has a **probability** of 1.0—that is, it is absolutely certain—the probability of each of the hypotheses stated in 2, 3, and 4, *relative* to 1 is smaller than 1.0. (We need not worry here about how much smaller than 1.0 the probabilities are, nor about how to calculate these probabilities precisely.) Relative to some starting point other than 1, however, the probability of these same three hypotheses might be quite different. Of course, it still would not be 1.0, absolute certainty. But it takes only a moment's reflection to realize that, whatever may be the probability of 2 or 3 or 4 relative to 1, those probabilities in each case will be quite different relative to different information, such as this:

5. Ten persons observed in a sample of 500 smokers have cardiovascular disease.

The idea that a *given proposition can have different probabilities* relative to different bases is fundamental to all inductive reasoning. It can be convincingly illustrated by the following example. Suppose we want to consider the probability of this proposition being true:

6. Susanne Smith will live to be eighty.

Taken as an abstract question of fact, we cannot even guess what the probability is with any assurance. But we can do better than guess; we can in fact even calculate the answer, if we are given some further information. Thus, suppose we are told that

7. Susanne Smith is seventy-nine.

Our original question then becomes one of determining the probability that 6 is true given 7; that is, relative to the evidence contained in proposition 7. No doubt, if Susanne Smith really is seventy-nine, then the probability that she will live to be eighty is greater than if we know only that

8. Susanne Smith is more than nine years old.

Obviously, a lot can happen to Susanne in the seventy years between nine and seventy-nine that is not very likely to happen to her in the one year between seventy-nine and eighty. And so, proposition 6 is more probable relative to proposition 7 than it is relative to proposition 8.

Let us disregard 7 and instead further suppose for the sake of the argument that the following is true:

9. Ninety percent of the women alive at seventy-nine live to be eighty.

Given this additional information, we now have a basis for answering our original question about proposition 6 with some precision. But suppose, in addition to 8, we are also told that

10. Susanne Smith is suffering from inoperable cancer.

and also that

11. The survival rate for women suffering from inoperable cancer is 0.6 years (that is, the average life span for women after a diagnosis of inoperable cancer is about seven months).

With this new information, the probability that 6 will be true has dropped significantly, all because we can now estimate the probability in relation to a new body of evidence.

The probability of an event, thus, is not a fixed number but one that varies because it is always relative to some evidence — and given different evidence, one and the same event can have different probabilities. In other words, the probability of any event is always relative to how much is known (assumed, believed), and because different persons may know different things about a given event, or the same person may know different things at different times, one and the same event can have two or more probabilities. This conclusion is not a paradox but a logical consequence of the concept of what it is for an event to have (that is, to be assigned) a probability.

If we shift to the *calculation* of probabilities, we find that generally we have two ways to calculate them. One way to proceed is by the method of **a priori** or **equal probabilities** — that is, by reference to the relevant possibilities taken abstractly and apart from any other information.

Thus, in an election contest with only two candidates, Smith and Jones, each of the candidates has a fifty-fifty chance of winning (whereas in a three-candidate race, each candidate would have one chance in three of winning). Therefore, the probability that Smith will win is 0.5, and the probability that Jones will win is also 0.5. (The sum of the probabilities of all possible independent outcomes must always equal 1.0, which is obvious enough if you think about it.)

But in politics the probabilities are not reasonably calculated so abstractly. We know that many empirical factors affect the outcome of an election and that a calculation of probabilities in ignorance of those factors is likely to be drastically misleading. In our example of the two-candidate election, suppose Smith has strong party support and is the incumbent, whereas Jones represents a party long out of power and is further handicapped by being relatively unknown. No one who knows anything about electoral politics would give Jones the same chance of winning as Smith. The two events are not equiprobable in relation to all the information available.

Not only that, a given event can have more than one probability. This happens whenever we calculate a probability by relying on different bodies of data that report how often the event in question has been observed to happen. Probabilities calculated in this way are **relative frequencies.** Our earlier hypothetical example of Susanne Smith provides an illustration. If she is a smoker and we have observed that 100 out of a random set of 500 smokers are observed to have cardiovascular disease, we have a basis for claiming that she has a probability of 100 in 500, or 0.2 (one-fifth), of having this disease. However, if we had other data showing that 250 out of 500 women smokers aged eighty or older have cardiovascular disease, we have a basis for believing that there is a probability of 250 in 500, or 0.5 (one-half), that she has this disease. Notice, of course, that in both calculations we assume that Susanne Smith is not among the persons we have examined. In both cases we infer the probability with which she has this disease from observing its frequency in populations that exclude her.

Both methods of calculating probabilities are legitimate; in each case the calculation is relative to observed circumstances. But as the examples show, it is most reasonable to have recourse to the method of equiprobabilities only when few or no other factors affecting possible outcomes are known.

Mill's Methods

Let us return to our earlier discussion of smoking and cardiovascular disease and consider in greater detail the question of a causal connection between the two phenomena. We began thus:

1. In a sample of 500 smokers, 230 persons observed have cardiovascular disease.

We regarded 1 as an observed fact, though in truth, of course, it is mere supposition. Our question now is, how might we augment this information so as to strengthen our confidence that

3. Smoking *causes* cardiovascular disease.

or at least

4. Smoking is a factor in the causation of cardiovascular disease in some persons.

Suppose further examination showed that

12. In the sample of 230 smokers with cardiovascular disease, no other suspected factor (such as genetic predisposition, lack of physical exercise, age over fifty) was also observed.

Such an observation would encourage us to believe 3 or 4 is true. Why? We are encouraged to believe it because we are inclined to believe also that whatever the cause of a phenomenon is, it must *always* be present when its effect is present. Thus, the inference from 1 to 3 or 4 is supported by 12, using **Mill's Method of Agreement,** named after the British philosopher, John Stuart Mill (1806–1873), who first formulated it. It is called a method of agreement because of the way in which the inference relies on *agreement* among the observed phenomena where a presumed cause is thought to be *present.*

Let us now suppose that in our search for evidence to support 3 or 4 we conduct additional research and discover that

13. In a sample of 500 nonsmokers, selected to be representative of both sexes, different ages, dietary habits, exercise patterns, and so on, none is observed to have cardiovascular disease.

This observation would further encourage us to believe that we had obtained significant additional confirmation of 3 or 4. Why? Because we now know that factors present (such as male sex, lack of exercise, family history of cardiovascular disease) in cases where the effect is absent (no cardiovascular disease observed) cannot be the cause. This is an example of **Mill's Method of Difference,** so called because the cause or causal factor of an effect must be *different* from whatever the factors are that are present when the effect is *absent.*

Suppose now that, increasingly confident we have found the cause of cardiovascular disease, we study our first sample of 230 smokers ill with the disease, and discover this:

14. Those who smoke two or more packs of cigarettes daily for ten or more years have cardiovascular disease either much younger or much more severely than those who smoke less.

This is an application of **Mill's Method of Concomitant Variation,** perhaps the most convincing of the three methods. Here we deal not merely with the presence of the conjectured cause (smoking) or the absence of the effect we are studying (cardiovascular disease), as we were previously, but with the more interesting and subtler matter of the *degree and regularity of the correlation* of the supposed cause and effect. According to the observations reported in 14, it strongly appears that the more we have of the "cause" (smoking), the sooner or the more intense the onset of the "effect" (cardiovascular disease).

Notice, however, what happens to our confirmation of 3 and 4 if, instead of the observation reported in 14, we had observed

15. In a representative sample of 500 nonsmokers, cardiovascular disease was observed in 34 cases.

(Let us not pause here to explain what makes a sample more or less representative of a population, although the representativeness of samples is vital to all statistical reasoning.) Such an observation would lead us almost immediately to suspect some other or additional causal factor: Smoking might indeed be *a* factor in causing cardiovascular disease, but it can hardly be *the* cause because (using Mill's Method of Difference) we cannot have the effect, as we do in the observed sample reported in 15, unless we also have the cause.

An observation such as the one in 15, however, is likely to lead us to think our hypothesis that *smoking causes cardiovascular disease* has been disconfirmed. But we have a fallback position ready; we can still defend a weaker hypothesis, namely 4, *Smoking is a factor in the causation of cardiovascular disease in some persons.* Even if 3 stumbles over the evidence in 15, 4 does not. It is still quite possible that smoking is a factor in causing this disease, even if it is not the *only* factor—and if it is, then 4 is true.

Confirmation, Mechanism, and Theory

Notice that in the discussion so far, we have spoken of the *confirmation* of a hypothesis, such as our causal claim in 4, but not of its *verification*. (Similarly, we have imagined very different evidence, such as that stated in 15, leading us to speak of the *dis*confirmation of 3, though not of its *falsi*fication.) Confirmation (getting some evidence for) is weaker than verification (getting sufficient evidence to regard as true); and our (imaginary) evidence so far in favor of 4 falls well short of conclusive support. Further research—the study of more representative or much larger samples, for example—might yield very different observations. It might lead us to conclude that although initial research had confirmed our hypothesis about smoking as the cause of cardiovascular disease, the additional information obtained subsequently disconfirmed the hypothesis. For most interesting hypotheses, both in detective stories and in modern science, there is both confirming and disconfirming evidence simultaneously. The challenge is to evaluate the hypothesis by considering such conflicting evidence.

As long as we confine our observations to *correlations* of the sort reported in our several (imaginary) observations, such as proposition 1, *230 smokers in a group of 500 have cardiovascular disease*, or 12, *230 smokers with the disease share no other suspected factors*, such as lack of exercise, any defense of a *causal* hypothesis such as claim 3, *Smoking causes cardiovascular disease*, or claim 4, *Smoking is a factor in causing the disease*, is not likely to convince the skeptic or lead those with beliefs alternative to 3 and 4 to abandon them and agree with us. Why is that? It is because a causal hypothesis without any account of the *underlying mechanism* by means of which the (alleged) cause produces the effect will seem superficial. Only when we can specify in detail *how* the (alleged) cause produces the effect will the causal hypothesis be convincing.

In other cases, in which no mechanism can be found, we seek instead to embed the causal hypothesis in a larger *theory*, one that rules out as incompatible any causal hypothesis except the favored one. (That is, we appeal to the test of consistency and thereby bring deductive reasoning to bear on our problem.) Thus, perhaps we cannot specify any mechanism — any underlying structure that generates a regular sequence of events, one of which is the effect we are studying — to explain why, for example, the gravitational mass of a body causes it to attract other bodies. But we can embed this claim in a larger body of physical theory that rules out as inconsistent any alternative causal explanation. To do that convincingly in regard to any given causal hypothesis, as this example suggests, requires detailed knowledge of the current state of the relevant body of scientific theory, something far beyond our aim or need to consider in further detail here.

FALLACIES

The straight road on which sound reasoning proceeds gives little latitude for cruising about. Irrationality, carelessness, passionate attachment to one's unexamined beliefs, and the sheer complexity of some issues, not to mention original sin, occasionally spoil the reasoning of even the best of us. Although in this book we reprint many varied voices and arguments, we hope we have reprinted no readings that exhibit the most flagrant errors or commit the graver abuses against the canons of good reasoning. Nevertheless, an inventory of those abuses and their close examination can be an instructive (as well as an amusing) exercise — instructive because the diagnosis and repair of error helps to fix more clearly the principles of sound reasoning on which such remedial labors depend; amusing because we are so constituted that our perception of the nonsense of others can stimulate our mind, warm our heart, and give us comforting feelings of superiority.

The discussion that follows, then, is a quick tour through the twisting lanes, mudflats, forests, and quicksands of the faults that one sometimes encounters in reading arguments that stray from the highway of clear thinking.

We can and do apply the term *fallacy* to many types of errors, mistakes, and confusions in oral and written discourse, in which our reasoning has gone awry. For convenience, we can group the fallacies by referring to the six aspects of reasoning identified in the Toulmin Method, described earlier (p. 337). Or, following the suggestion of S. Morris Engel in his book, *Without Good Reason* (2000), we can group fallacies according to whether they involve a crucial *ambiguity*, an *erroneous presumption*, or an *irrelevance*.

We ought not, however, take these categories too rigidly because it is often the case that a piece of fallacious thinking involves two or more fallacies. That is, it is possible (as we shall see) to find traces of faulty reasoning of several varieties, in which case we classify it under one rather than another of the headings above because we have chosen what in our judgment amounts to the dominant or most prominent of the fallacious features on display. Thus, most of the fallacies exhibit an irrelevant consideration. (Red herring is a good example. Is it best described as a fallacy of false presumption or as a fallacy of irrelevance? Same with erroneous presupposition.) In the end, classifying the fallacies under this or that system of headings is not very important. What is important is being able to spot the fallacious thinking no matter what it is called.

Fallacies of Ambiguity

Ambiguity   Near the center of the town of Concord, Massachusetts, is an empty field with a sign reading "Old Calf Pasture." Hmm. A pasture in former times in which calves grazed? A pasture now in use for old calves? An erstwhile pasture for old calves? These alternative readings arise because of **ambiguity;** brevity in the sign has produced a group of words that give rise to more than one possible interpretation, confusing the reader and (presumably) frustrating the sign writer's intentions.

Consider a more complex example. Suppose someone asserts *People have equal rights* and also *Everyone has a right to property.* Many people believe both these claims, but their combination involves an ambiguity. On one interpretation, the two claims entail that everyone has an *equal right* to property. (That is, you and I each have an equal right to whatever property we have.) But the two claims can also be interpreted to mean that everyone has a *right to equal property.* (That is, whatever property you have a right to, I have a right to the same, or at least equivalent, property.) The latter interpretation is radically revolutionary, whereas the former is not. Arguments over equal rights often involve this ambiguity.

Division   In the Bible, we are told that the apostles of Jesus were twelve and that Matthew was an apostle. Does it follow that Matthew was twelve? No. To argue in this way from a property of a group to a property of a member of that group is to commit the **fallacy of division.** The example of the apostles may not be a very tempting instance of this error; here is a classic version that is a bit more interesting. If it is true that the average American family has 1.8 children, does it follow that your brother and sister-in-law are likely to have 1.8 children? If you think it does, you have committed the fallacy of division.

Composition   Could an all-star team of professional basketball players beat the Boston Celtics in their heyday—say, the team of 1985 to 1986? Perhaps in one game or two, but probably not in seven out of a dozen games in a row. As students of the game know, teamwork is an indispensable part of outstanding performance, and the 1985 to 1986 Celtics were famous for their self-sacrificing style of play.

The **fallacy of composition** can be convincingly illustrated, therefore, in this argument: *A team of five NBA all-stars is the best team in basketball if each of the five players is the best at his position.* The fallacy is called composition because the reasoning commits the error of arguing from the true premise that each member of a group has a certain property to the not necessarily true conclusion that the group (the composition) itself has the property. (That is, because *A* is the best player at forward, *B* is the best center, and so on, therefore, the team of *A, B, . . .* is the best team.)

Equivocation   In a delightful passage in Lewis Carroll's *Through the Looking-Glass*, the king asks his messenger, "Who did you pass on the road?" and the messenger replies, "Nobody." This prompts the king to observe, "Of course, Nobody walks slower than you," provoking the messenger's sullen response: "I do my best. I'm sure nobody walks much faster than I do." At this the king remarks with surprise, "He can't do that or else he'd have been here first!" (This, by the way, is the classic predecessor of the famous comic dialogue "Who's on First?" between the comedians Bud Abbott and Lou Costello.) The king and the messenger are equivocating on the term *nobody*. The messenger uses it in the normal way as an indefinite pronoun equivalent to "not anyone." But the king uses the word as though it were a proper noun, *Nobody*, the rather odd name of some person. No wonder the king and the messenger talk right past each other.

Equivocation (from the Latin for "equal voice"— that is, giving utterance to two meanings at the same time in one word or phrase) can ruin otherwise good reasoning, as in this example: *Euthanasia is a good death; one dies a good death when one dies peacefully in old age; therefore, euthanasia is dying peacefully in old age.* The etymology of *euthanasia* is literally "a good death," and so the first premise is true. And the second premise is certainly plausible. But the conclusion of this syllogism is false. Euthanasia cannot be defined as a peaceful death in one's old age, for two reasons. First, euthanasia requires the intervention of another person who kills someone (or lets the person die); second, even a very young person can be euthanized. The problem arises because "a good death" is used in the second premise in a manner that does not apply to euthanasia. Both meanings of "a good death" are legitimate, but when used together, they constitute an equivocation that spoils the argument.

The fallacy of equivocation takes us from the discussion of confusions in individual claims or grounds to the more troublesome fallacies that infect the linkages between the claims we make and the grounds (or reasons) for them. These are the fallacies that occur in statements that, following the vocabulary of the Toulmin Method, are called the *warrant* of reasoning. Each fallacy is an example of reasoning that involves a **non sequitur** (Latin for "It does not follow"). That is, the *claim* (the conclusion) does not follow from the *grounds* (the premises).

For a start, here is an obvious non sequitur: "He went to the movies on three consecutive nights, so he must love movies." Why doesn't the claim ("He must love movies") follow from the grounds ("He went to the movies on three consecutive nights")? Perhaps the person was just fulfilling an assignment in a film course (maybe he even hated movies so much that he had postponed three assignments to see films and now had to see them all in quick succession), or maybe he went with a girlfriend who was a movie buff, or maybe . . . —well, one can think of any number of other possible reasons.

Fallacies of Presumption

Distorting the Facts   Facts can be distorted either intentionally (to deceive or mislead) or unintentionally, and in either case usually (but not invariably) to the benefit of whoever is doing the distortion. Consider this not entirely hypothetical case. A pharmaceutical company spends millions of dollars to develop a new drug that will help pregnant women avoid spontaneous abortion. The company reports its findings, but it does not also report that it has learned from its researchers of a serious downside for this drug in many cases, resulting in deformed limbs in the neonate. Had the company informed the public of this fact, the drug would not have been certified for use.

Here is another case. Half a century ago the surgeon general reported that smoking cigarettes increased the likelihood that smokers would eventually suffer from lung cancer. The cigarette manufacturers vigorously protested that the surgeon general relied on inconclusive research and was badly misleading the public about the health risks of smoking. It later turned out that the tobacco companies knew that smoking increased the risk of lung cancer—a fact established by the company's own laboratories but concealed from the public. Today, thanks to public access to all the facts, it is commonplace knowledge that inhaled smoke—including secondhand smoke—is a risk factor for many illnesses.

Post Hoc, Ergo Propter Hoc   One of the most tempting errors in reasoning is to ground a claim about causation on an observed temporal sequence; that is, to argue "after this, therefore because of this" (which is what the phrase **post hoc, ergo propter hoc** means in Latin). Nearly forty years ago, when the medical community first announced that smoking tobacco caused lung cancer, advocates for the tobacco industry replied that doctors were guilty of this fallacy.

These industry advocates argued that medical researchers had merely noticed that in some people, lung cancer developed *after* considerable smoking, indeed, years after; but (they insisted) this correlation was not at all the same as a causal relation between smoking and lung cancer. True enough. The claim that *A causes B* is not the same as the claim that *B* comes after *A*. After all, it was possible that smokers as a group had some other common trait and that this factor was the true cause of their cancer.

As the long controversy over the truth about the causation of lung cancer shows, to avoid the appearance of fallacious *post hoc* reasoning one needs to find some way to link the observed phenomena (the correlation of smoking and the onset of lung cancer). This step requires some further theory and preferably some experimental evidence for the exact sequence or physical mechanism, in full detail, of how ingestion of tobacco smoke is a crucial factor—and is not merely an accidental or happenstance prior event—in the subsequent development of the cancer.

Many Questions   The old saw, "When did you stop beating your wife?" illustrates the **fallacy of many questions.** This question, as one can readily see, is unanswerable unless all three of its implicit presuppositions are true. The questioner presupposes that (1) the addressee has or had a wife, (2) he has beaten her, and (3) he has stopped beating her. If any of these presuppositions is false, then the question is pointless; it cannot be answered strictly and simply with a date.

Hasty Generalization   From a logical point of view, **hasty generalization** is the precipitous move from true assertions about *one* or a *few* instances to dubious or even false assertions about *all*. For example, while it may be true, based on your personal experience, that the only native Hungarians you personally know do not speak English very well, that is no basis for asserting that Hungarians do not speak English very well. Or if the clothes you recently ordered online turn out not to fit very well, it doesn't follow that *all* online clothes turn out to be too large or too small. A hasty generalization usually lies behind a **stereotype**— that is, a person or event treated as typical of a whole class. Thus, in 1914, after the German invasion of Belgium, during which some atrocities were committed by the invaders, the German troops were quickly stereotyped by the Allies as brutal savages who skewered helpless babies on their bayonets.

The Slippery Slope   One of the most familiar arguments against any type of government regulation is that if it is allowed, then it will be just the first step down the path that leads to ruinous interference, overregulation, and totalitarian control. Fairly often we encounter this mode of argument in the public debates over handgun control, the censorship of pornography, and physician-assisted suicide. The argument is called the **slippery slope argument** (or the **wedge argument,** from the way we use the thin end of a wedge to split solid things apart; it is also called, rather colorfully, "letting the camel's nose under the tent"). The fallacy here is in implying that the first step necessarily leads to the second, and so on down the slope to disaster, when in fact there is no necessary slide from the first step to the second. (Would handgun registration lead to a police state? Well, it hasn't in Switzerland.) Sometimes the argument takes the form of claiming that a seemingly innocent or even attractive principle that is being applied in a given case (censorship of pornography, to avoid promoting sexual violence) requires one for the sake of consistency to apply the same principle in other cases, only with absurd and catastrophic results (censorship of everything in print, to avoid hurting anyone's feelings).

Here's an extreme example of this fallacy in action:

> Automobiles cause more deaths than handguns do. If you oppose handguns on the ground that doing so would save lives of the innocent, you'll soon find yourself wanting to outlaw the automobile.

Does opposition to handguns have this consequence? Not necessarily. Most people accept without dispute the right of society to regulate the operation of motor vehicles by requiring drivers to have a license, a greater restriction than many states impose on gun ownership. Besides, a gun is a lethal weapon designed to kill, whereas an automobile or truck is a vehicle designed for transportation. Private ownership and use in both cases entail risks of death to the innocent. But there is no inconsistency in a society's refusal to tolerate this risk in the case of guns and its willingness to do so in the case of automobiles.

Closely related to the slippery slope is what lawyers call a **parade of horrors,** an array of examples of terrible consequences that will or might follow if we travel down a certain path. A good example appears in Justice William Brennan's opinion for the Supreme Court in *Texas v. Johnson* (1989), concerned with a Texas law against burning the American flag in political protest. If this law is allowed to stand, Brennan suggests, we may next find laws against burning the presidential seal, state flags, and the Constitution.

False Analogy   Argument by analogy, as we point out in Chapter 3 and as many of the selections in this book show, is a familiar and even indispensable mode of argument. But it can be treacherous because it runs the risk of the **fallacy of false analogy.** Unfortunately, we have no simple or foolproof way of distinguishing between the useful, legitimate analogies and the others. The key question to ask yourself is this: Do the two things put into analogy differ in any essential and relevant respect, or are they different only in unimportant and irrelevant aspects?

In a famous example from his discussion in support of suicide, philosopher David Hume rhetorically asked: "It would be no crime in me to divert the Nile or Danube from its course, were I able to effect such purposes. Where then is the crime of turning a few ounces of blood from their natural channel?" This is a striking analogy, except that it rests on a false assumption. No one has the right to divert the Nile or the Danube or any other major international watercourse; it would be a catastrophic crime to do so without the full consent of people living in the region, their government, and so forth. Therefore, arguing by analogy, one might well say that no one has the right to take his or her own life, either. Thus, Hume's own analogy can be used to argue against his thesis that suicide is no crime. But let us ignore the way in which his example can be turned against him. The analogy is a terrible one in any case. Isn't it obvious that the Nile, whatever its exact course, would continue to nourish Egypt and the Sudan, whereas the blood flowing out of someone's veins will soon leave that person dead? The fact that the blood is the same blood, whether in one's body or in a pool on the floor (just as the water of the Nile is the same body of water whatever path it follows to the sea) is, of course, irrelevant to the question of whether one has the right to commit suicide.

Let us look at a more complex example. During the 1960s, when the United States was convulsed over the purpose and scope of its military involvement in Southeast Asia, advocates of more vigorous U.S. military participation appealed to the so-called domino effect, supposedly inspired by a passing remark from President Eisenhower in the 1950s. The analogy refers to the way in which a row of standing dominoes will collapse, one after the other, if the first one is pushed. If Vietnam turns Communist, according to this analogy, so too will its neighbors, Laos and Cambodia, followed by Thailand and then Burma, until the whole region is as communist as China to the north. The domino analogy (or metaphor) provided, no doubt, a vivid illustration and effectively portrayed the worry of many anti-Communists. But did it really shed any light on the likely pattern of political and military developments in the region? The history of events there during the 1970s and 1980s did not bear out the domino analogy.

Straw Man   It is often tempting to reframe or report your opponent's thesis to make it easier to attack and perhaps refute it. If you do this in the course of an argument, you are creating a straw man, a thing of no substance and easily blown away. The straw man you've constructed is usually a radically conservative or extremely liberal thesis, which few if any would want to defend. That is why it is easier to refute than the view your opponent actually holds. "So you defend the death penalty—and all the horrible things done in its name. No one in his right mind would hold such a view." It's highly unlikely that your friend supports *everything* that has been done in the name of capital punishment—crucifixion and beheading, for example, or execution of the children of the guilty offender.

Special Pleading   We all have our favorites—relatives, friends, and neighbors—and we are all too likely to show that favoritism in unacceptable ways. How about this: "Yes, I know Billy hit Sally first, but he's my son. He's a good boy, and I know he must have had a good reason." Or this: "True, she's late for work again—the third time this week!—but her uncle's my friend, and it will be embarrassing to me if she is fired, so we'll just ignore it." Special pleading inevitably leads to unmerited advantages, as illustrated above.

Begging the Question   The argument over whether the death penalty is a deterrent illustrates another fallacy. From the fact that you live in a death-penalty state and were not murdered yesterday, we cannot infer that the death penalty was a deterrent. Yet it is tempting to make this inference, perhaps because—all unawares—we are relying on the **fallacy of begging the question.** If someone tacitly assumes from the start that the death penalty is an effective deterrent, then the fact that you weren't murdered yesterday certainly looks like evidence for the truth of that assumption. But it isn't, so long as there are competing but unexamined alternative explanations, as in this case. (The fallacy is called "begging the question," *petitio principii* in Latin, because the conclusion of the argument is hidden among its assumptions—and so the conclusion, not surprisingly, follows from the premises.)

Of course, the fact that you weren't murdered is *consistent* with the claim that the death penalty is an effective deterrent, just as someone else's being murdered is also consistent with that claim (for an effective deterrent need not be a *perfect* deterrent). In general, from the fact that two propositions are consistent with each other, we cannot infer that either is evidence for the other.

Note: The term "begging the question" is often wrongly used to mean "raises the question," as in "His action of burning the flag begs the question, What drove him to do such a thing?"

False Dichotomy   Sometimes oversimplification takes a more complex form, in which contrary possibilities are wrongly presented as though they were exhaustive and exclusive. "Either we get tough with drug users, or we must surrender and legalize all drugs." Really? What about doing neither and instead offering education and counseling, detoxification programs, and incentives to "Say no"? A favorite of debaters, **either/or** reasoning always runs the risk of ignoring a third (or fourth) possibility. Some disjunctions are indeed exhaustive: "Either we get tough with drug users, or we do not." This proposition, though vague (what does "get tough" really mean?), is a tautology; it cannot be false, and there is no third alternative.

But most disjunctions do not express a pair of *contradictory* alternatives: They offer only a pair of *contrary* alternatives, and mere contraries do not exhaust the possibilities (recall our discussion of contraries versus contradictories on p. 359).

An example of **false dichotomy** can be found in the essay by Jeff Jacoby on flogging (p. 192). His entire discussion is built on the relative superiority of whipping over imprisonment, as though there was no alternative punishment worth considering. But of course, there is, notably community service (especially for white-collar offenders, juveniles, and many first offenders).

Oversimplification   "Poverty causes crime," "Taxation is unfair," "Truth is stranger than fiction"—these are examples of generalizations that exaggerate and therefore oversimplify the truth. Poverty as such can't be the sole cause of crime because many poor people do not break the law. Some taxes may be unfairly high, others unfairly low—but there is no reason to believe that *every* tax is unfair to all those who have to pay it. Some true stories do amaze us as much or more than some fictional stories, but the reverse is true, too. (In the language of the Toulmin Method, **oversimplification** is the result of a failure to use suitable modal qualifiers in formulating one's claims or grounds or backing.)

Red Herring   The fallacy of **red herring,** less colorfully named irrelevant thesis, occurs when one tries to distract one's audience by invoking a consideration that is irrelevant to the topic under discussion. (This fallacy probably gets its name from the fact that a rotten herring, or a cured herring, which is reddish, will throw pursuing hounds off the right track.) Consider this case. Some critics, seeking to defend our government's refusal to sign the Kyoto accords to reduce global warming, argue that signing is supported mainly by left-leaning scientists. This argument supposedly shows that global warming—if there is such a thing—is not a serious, urgent issue. But claiming that the supporters of these accords are left-inclined is a red herring, an irrelevant thesis. By raising doubts about the political views of the advocates of signing, it distracts attention from the scientific question (Is there global warming?) and also from the separate political question (Ought the United States sign these accords?). The refusal of a government to sign these accords does not show there is no such thing as global warming. And even if all of the advocates of signing were left-leaning (they aren't), this fact (if it were a fact, but it isn't) would not show that worries about global warming are exaggerated.

Fallacies of Relevance

Tu Quoque   The Romans had a word for it: *Tu quoque* means "you, too." Consider this: "You're a fine one, trying to persuade me to give up smoking when you indulge yourself with a pipe and a cigar from time to time.

Maybe I should quit, but then so should you. As things stand now, how-ever, it's hypocritical of you to complain about my smoking when you persist in the same habit." The fallacy is this: The merit of a person's argument has nothing to do with the person's character or behavior. Here, the assertion that smoking is bad for one's health is *not* weakened by the fact that a smoker offers the argument.

The Genetic Fallacy   A member of the family of fallacies that includes poisoning the well and ad hominem is the **genetic fallacy.** Here the error takes the form of arguing against some claim by pointing out that its origin (genesis) is tainted or that it was invented by someone deserv-ing our contempt. Thus, one might attack the ideas of the Declaration of Independence by pointing out that its principal author, Thomas Jefferson, was a slaveholder. Assuming that it is not anachronistic and inappropriate to criticize a public figure of two centuries ago for practicing slavery, and conceding that slavery is morally outrageous, it is nonetheless fallacious to attack the ideas or even the sincerity of the Declaration by attempting to impeach the credentials of its author. Jefferson's moral faults do not by themselves falsify, make improbable, or constitute counterevidence to the truth or other merits of the claims made in his writings. At most, one's faults cast doubt on one's integrity or sincerity if one makes claims at odds with one's practice.

The genetic fallacy can take other forms less closely allied to ad hominem argument. For example, an opponent of the death penalty might argue,

> Capital punishment arose in barbarous times; but we claim to be civi-lized; therefore, we should discard this relic of the past.

Such reasoning shouldn't be persuasive because the question of the death penalty for our society must be decided by the degree to which it serves our purposes—justice and defense against crime, presumably— to which its historic origins are irrelevant. The practices of beer- and wine-making are as old as human civilization, but their origin in antiq-uity is no reason to outlaw them in our time. The curious circumstances in which something originates usually play no role whatever in its valid-ity. Anyone who would argue that nothing good could possibly come from molds and fungi is refuted by Sir Alexander Fleming's discovery of penicillin in 1928.

Poisoning the Well   During the 1970s some critics of the Equal Rights Amendment (ERA) argued against it by pointing out that Marx and Engels, in their *Communist Manifesto*, favored equality of women and men—and therefore the ERA was immoral, undesirable, and perhaps even a Communist plot. This kind of reasoning is an attempt to **poison the well;** that is, an attempt to shift attention from the merits of the argument—the validity of the reasoning, the truth of the claims—to the source or origin of the argument. Such criticism deflects attention from the real issue; namely, whether the view in question is true and what the quality of evidence is in its support. The mere fact that Marx (or Hitler, for that matter) believed something does not show that the belief is false or immoral; just because some scoundrel believes the world is round, that is no reason for you to believe it is flat.

Appeal to Ignorance   In the controversy over the death penalty, the issues of deterrence and executing the innocent are bound to be raised. Because no one knows how many innocent persons have been convicted for murder and wrongfully executed, it is tempting for abolitionists to argue that the death penalty is too risky. It is equally tempting for the proponent of the death penalty to argue that since no one knows how many people have been deterred from murder by the threat of execution, we abolish it at our peril.

Each of these arguments suffers from the same flaw: the **fallacy of appeal to ignorance.** Each argument invites the audience to draw an inference from a premise that is unquestionably true—but what is that premise? It asserts that there is something "we don't know." But what we *don't* know cannot be *evidence* for (or against) anything. Our ignorance is no reason for believing anything, except perhaps that we ought to try to undertake an appropriate investigation in order to reduce our ignorance and replace it with reliable information.

Ad Hominem   Closely allied to poisoning the well is another fallacy, **ad hominem** argument (from the Latin for "against the person"). A critic can easily yield to the temptation to attack an argument or theory by trying to impeach or undercut the credentials of its advocates.

Example: Jones is arguing that prayer should not be permitted in public schools, and Smith responds by pointing out that Jones has twice been convicted of assaulting members of the clergy. Jones's behavior doubtless is reprehensible, but the issue is not Jones, it is prayer in school, and what must be scrutinized is Jones's argument, not his police record or his character.

Appeal to Authority   The example of Jefferson given to illustrate the genetic fallacy can be turned around to illustrate another fallacy. One might easily imagine someone from the South in 1860 defending the slave-owning society of that day by appealing to the fact that no less a person than Jefferson—a brilliant public figure, thinker, and leader by any measure—owned slaves. Or today one might defend capital punishment on the ground that Abraham Lincoln, surely one of the nation's greatest presidents, signed many death warrants during the Civil War, authorizing the execution of Union soldiers. No doubt the esteem in which such figures as Jefferson and Lincoln are deservedly held amounts to impressive endorsement for whatever acts and practices, policies and institutions, they supported. But the **authority** of these figures in itself is not evidence for the truth of their views, and so their authority cannot be a reason for anyone to agree with them. Obviously, Jefferson and Lincoln themselves could not support their beliefs by pointing to the fact that they held them. Because their own authority is no reason for them to believe what they believe, it is no reason for anyone else, either.

Sometimes the appeal to authority is fallacious because the authoritative person is not an expert on the issue in dispute. The fact that a high-energy physicist has won the Nobel Prize is no reason for attaching any special weight to her views on the causes of cancer, the reduction of traffic accidents, or the legalization of marijuana. On the other hand, one would be well advised to attend to her views on the advisability of ballistic missile-defense systems, for there may be a connection between the kind of research for which she received the prize and the defense research projects.

All of us depend heavily on the knowledge of various experts and authorities, and so we tend not to ignore their views. Conversely, we should resist the temptation to accord their views on diverse subjects the same respect that we grant them in the area of their expertise.

Appeal to Fear   The Romans called this fallacy *ad baculum*, "resorting to violence" (*baculum* means "stick," or "club"). Trying to persuade people to agree with you by threatening them with painful consequences is obviously an appeal that no rational person would contemplate. The violence need not be physical; if you threaten someone with the loss of a job, for instance, you are still using a stick. Violence or the threat of harmful consequences in the course of an argument is beyond reason and always shows the haste or impatience of those who appeal to it. It is also an indication that the argument on its merits would be unpersuasive, inconclusive, or worse. President Teddy Roosevelt's epigrammatic doctrine for the kind of foreign policy he favored—"Speak softly but carry a big stick"—illustrates an attempt to have it both ways, an appeal to reason for starters, but a recourse to coercion, or the threat of coercion, as a backup if needed.

Finally, we add two fallacies, not easily embraced by Engel's three categories that have served us well thus far (ambiguity, erroneous presumption, and irrelevance): death by a thousand qualifications and protecting the hypothesis.

Death by a Thousand Qualifications   In a letter of recommendation, sent in support of an applicant for a job on your newspaper, you find this sentence: "Young Smith was the best student I've ever taught in an English course." Pretty strong endorsement, you think, except that you do not know, because you have not been told, the letter writer is a very junior faculty member, has been teaching for only two years, is an instructor in the history department, taught a section of freshman English as a courtesy for a sick colleague, and had only eight students enrolled in the course. Thanks to these implicit qualifications, the letter writer did not lie or exaggerate in his praise; but the effect of his sentence on you, the unwitting reader, is quite misleading. The explicit claim in the letter, and its impact on you, is quite different from the tacitly qualified claim in the mind of the writer.

Death by a thousand qualifications gets its name from the ancient torture of death by a thousand small cuts. Thus, a bold assertion can be virtually killed, its true content reduced to nothing, bit by bit, as all the appropriate or necessary qualifications are added to it. Consider another example. Suppose you hear a politician describing another country (let's call it Ruritania so as not to offend anyone) as a "democracy"—except it turns out that Ruritania doesn't have regular elections, lacks a written constitution, has no independent judiciary, prohibits religious worship except of the state-designated deity, and so forth. So what is left of the original claim that Ruritania is a democracy is little or nothing. The qualifications have taken all the content out of the original description.

Protecting the Hypothesis   In Chapter 3, we contrasted *reasoning* and *rationalization* (or the finding of bad reasons for what one intends to believe anyway). Rationalization can take subtle forms, as the following example indicates. Suppose you're standing with a friend on the shore or on a pier, and you watch as a ship heads out to sea. As it reaches the horizon, it slowly disappears—first the hull, then the upper decks, and finally the tip of the mast. Because the ship (you both assume) isn't sinking, it occurs to you that you have in this sequence of observations convincing evidence that the earth's surface is curved. Nonsense, says your companion. Light waves sag, or bend down, over distances of a few miles, and so a flat surface (such as the ocean) can intercept them. Hence the ship, which appears to be going "over" the horizon, really isn't: It's just moving steadily farther and farther away in a straight line. Your friend, you discover to your amazement, is a card-carrying member of the Flat Earth Society (yes, there really is such an organization). Now most of us would regard the idea that light rays bend down in the manner required by the Flat Earther's argument as a rationalization whose sole purpose is to protect the flat-earth doctrine against counterevidence. We would be convinced it was a rationalization, and not a very good one at that, if the Flat Earther held to it despite a patient and thorough explanation from a physicist that showed modern optical theory to be quite incompatible with the view that light waves sag.

This example illustrates two important points about the *backing* of arguments. First, it is always possible to protect a hypothesis by abandoning adjacent or connected hypotheses; this is the tactic our Flat Earth friend has used. This maneuver is possible, however, only because—and this is the second point—whenever we test a hypothesis, we do so by taking for granted (usually quite unconsciously) many other hypotheses

---

✓ A CHECKLIST FOR EVALUATING AN ARGUMENT
FROM A LOGICAL POINT OF VIEW

☐ Is the argument purely deductive, purely inductive, or a mixture of the two?

☐ If it is deductive, is it valid?

☐ If it is valid, are all its premises and assumptions true?

☐ If it is not valid, what fallacy does it commit?

☐ If it is not valid, are the claims at least consistent with each other?

☐ If it is not valid, can you think of additional plausible assumptions that would make it valid?

☐ If the argument is inductive, on what observations is it based?

☐ If the argument is inductive, how probable are its premises and its conclusion?

☐ In any case, can you think of evidence that would further confirm the conclusion? Disconfirm the conclusion?

---

as well. So the evidence for the hypothesis we think we are confirming is impossible to separate entirely from the adequacy of the connected hypotheses. As long as we have no reason to doubt that light rays travel in straight lines (at least over distances of a few miles), our Flat Earth friend's argument is unconvincing. But once that hypothesis is itself put in doubt, the idea that looked at first to be a pathetic rationalization takes on an even more troublesome character.

There are, then, not one but two fallacies exposed by this example. The first and perhaps graver is in rigging your hypothesis so that *no matter what* observations are brought against it, you will count nothing as falsifying it. The second and subtler is in thinking that as you test one hypothesis, all of your other background beliefs are left safely to one side, immaculate and uninvolved. On the contrary, our beliefs form a corporate structure, intertwined and connected to each other with great complexity, and no one of them can ever be singled out for unique and isolated application, confirmation, or disconfirmation, to the world around us.

EXERCISE: FALLACIES — OR NOT?

Here, for diversion and practice, are some fallacies in action. Some of these statements, however, are not fallacies. Can you tell which is which? Can you detect *what* has gone wrong in the cases where something has gone wrong? Please explain your reasoning.

    1. Abortion is murder—and it doesn't matter whether we're talking about killing a human embryo or a human fetus.

2. Euthanasia is not a good thing, it's murder—and it doesn't matter how painful one's dying may be.

3. Never loan a tool to a friend. I did once and never got it back.

4. If the neighbors don't like our loud music, that's just too bad. After all, we have a right to listen to the music we like when and where we want to play it.

5. The Good Samaritan in the Bible was pretty foolish; he was taking grave risks with no benefits for him in sight.

6. "Shoot first and ask questions afterward" is a good epigram for the kind of foreign policy we need.

7. "You can fool some of the people all of the time, and you can fool all the people some of the time, but you can't fool all the people all of the time." That's what Abraham Lincoln said, and he was right.

8. It doesn't matter whether Shakespeare wrote the plays attributed to him. What matters is whether the plays are any good.

9. The Golden Gate Bridge in San Francisco ought to be closed down. After all, just look at all the suicides that have occurred there.

10. Reparations for African Americans are way overdue; it's just another version of the reparations eventually paid to the Japanese Americans who were wrongly interned in 1942 during World War II.

11. Animals don't have rights any more than do trees or stones. They don't have desires, either. What they have are feelings and needs.

12. The average American family is said to have 2.1 children. This is absurd—did you ever meet 2.1 children?

13. My marriage was a failure, which just proves my point: Don't ever get married in the first place.

14. The Red Queen in *Alice in Wonderland* was right: Verdict first, evidence later.

15. Not until astronauts sailed through space around the moon and could see its back side for themselves did we have adequate reason to believe that the moon even had a back side.

16. If you start out with a bottle of beer a day and then go on to a glass or two of wine on the weekends, you're well on your way to becoming a hopeless drunk.

17. Two Indians are sitting on a fence. The small Indian is the son of the big Indian, but the big Indian is not the small Indian's father. How is that possible?

18. If you toss a coin five times and each time it come up heads, it is more likely than not that on the sixth throw you'll come up heads again—or is it more likely that you'll come up tails? Or is neither more likely?

19. Going to church on a regular basis is bad for your health. Instead of sitting in a pew for an hour each Sunday you'd be better off taking an hour's brisk walk.

20. You can't trust anything he says. When he was young he was an avid Communist.

21. Since 9/11 we've tried and convicted few terrorists, so our defense systems must be working.

22. We can trust the White House in its press releases because it's a reliable source of information.

23. Intelligent design must be true because the theory of evolution can't explain how life began.

24. Andreas Serrano's notorious photograph called *Piss Christ* (1989), show-ing a small plastic crucifix submerged in a glass of urine, never should have been put on public display, let alone financed by public funds.

25. Doubting Thomas was right—you need more than somebody's say-so to support a claim of resurrection.

26. You are a professional baseball player and you have a good-luck charm. When you wear it the team wins. When you don't wear it the team loses. What do you infer?

27. Resolve the following dilemma: When it rains you can't fix the hole in the roof. When it's not raining there is no need to mend the roof. Conclusion: Leave the roof as it is.

28. You are at the beach and you watch a ship steaming toward the horizon. Bit by bit it disappears from view—first the masts, then the upper deck, then the main deck, then the stern, and then it's gone. Why would it be wrong to infer that the ship is sinking?

29. How can it be true that "it's the exception that proves the rule"? If any-thing, isn't it the exception that *dis*proves the rule?

30. How come herbivores don't eat herbs?

31. In the 1930s it was commonplace to see ads announcing "More Doctors Smoke Camels." What do you make of such an ad?

32. Suppose the only way you could save five innocent people was by killing one of them. Would you do it? Suppose the only way you could save one innocent person was by killing five others. Would you do it?

Max Shulman

Having read about proper and improper arguments, you are now well equipped to read a short story on the topic.

Max Shulman (1919–1988) began his career as a writer when he was a journalism student at the University of Minnesota. Later he wrote humorous nov-els, stories, and plays. One of his novels, Barefoot Boy with Cheek *(1943), was made into a musical, and another,* Rally Round the Flag, Boys! *(1957), was made into a film starring Paul Newman and Joanne Woodward.* The Tender Trap *(1954), a play he wrote with Robert Paul Smith, still retains its popularity with theater groups.*

"Love Is a Fallacy" was first published in 1951, when demeaning stereotypes about women and minorities were widely accepted in the marketplace as well as the home. Thus, jokes about domineering mothers-in-law or about dumb blondes routinely met with no objection.

Love Is a Fallacy

Cool was I and logical. Keen, calculating, perspicacious, acute, and astute—I was all of these. My brain was as powerful as a dynamo, as precise as a chemist's scales, as penetrating as a scalpel. And—think of it!—I was only eighteen.

It is not often that one so young has such a giant intellect. Take, for example, Petey Bellows, my roommate at the university. Same age, same background, but dumb as an ox. A nice enough fellow, you understand, but nothing upstairs. Emotional type. Unstable. Impressionable. Worst of all, a faddist. Fads, I submit, are the very negation of reason. To be swept up in every new craze that comes along, to surrender yourself to idiocy just because everybody else is doing it—this, to me, is the acme of mindlessness. Not, however, to Petey.

One afternoon I found Petey lying on his bed with an expression of such distress on his face that I immediately diagnosed appendicitis. "Don't move," I said. "Don't take a laxative. I'll call a doctor."

"Raccoon," he mumbled thickly.

"Raccoon?" I said, pausing in my flight.   5

"I want a raccoon coat," he wailed.

I perceived that his trouble was not physical, but mental. "Why do you want a raccoon coat?"

"I should have known it," he cried, pounding his temples. "I should have known they'd come back when the Charleston came back. Like a fool I spent all my money for textbooks, and now I can't get a raccoon coat."

"Can you mean," I said incredulously, "that people are actually wearing raccoon coats again?"

"All the Big Men on Campus are wearing them. Where've you   10 been?"

"In the library," I said, naming a place not frequented by Big Men on Campus.

He leaped from the bed and paced the room. "I've got to have a raccoon coat," he said passionately. "I've got to!"

"Petey, why? Look at it rationally. Raccoon coats are unsanitary. They shed. They smell bad. They weigh too much. They're unsightly. They——"

"You don't understand," he interrupted impatiently. "It's the thing to do. Don't you want to be in the swim?"

"No," I said truthfully.   15

"Well, I do," he declared. "I'd give anything for a raccoon coat. Anything!"

My brain, that precision instrument, slipped into high gear. "Anything?" I asked, looking at him narrowly.

"Anything," he affirmed in ringing tones.

I stroked my chin thoughtfully. It so happened that I knew where to get my hands on a raccoon coat. My father had had one in his undergraduate days; it lay now in a trunk in the attic back home. It also happened that Petey had something I wanted. He didn't *have* it exactly, but at least he had first rights on it. I refer to his girl, Polly Espy.

I had long coveted Polly Espy. Let me emphasize that my desire for   20 this young woman was not emotional in nature. She was, to be sure, a girl who excited the emotions, but I was not one to let my heart rule my head. I wanted Polly for a shrewdly calculated, entirely cerebral reason.

I was a freshman in law school. In a few years I would be out in practice. I was well aware of the importance of the right kind of wife in furthering a lawyer's career. The successful lawyers I had observed were, almost without exception, married to beautiful, gracious, intelligent women. With one omission, Polly fitted these specifications perfectly.

Beautiful she was. She was not yet of pin-up proportions, but I felt sure that time would supply the lack. She already had the makings.

Gracious she was. By gracious I mean full of graces. She had an erectness of carriage, an ease of bearing, a poise that clearly indicated the best of breeding. At table her manners were exquisite. I had seen her at the Kozy Kampus Korner eating the specialty of the house—a sandwich that contained scraps of pot roast, gravy, chopped nuts, and a dipper of sauerkraut—without even getting her fingers moist.

Intelligent she was not. In fact, she veered in the opposite direction. But I believed that under my guidance she would smarten up. At any rate, it was worth a try. It is, after all, easier to make a beautiful dumb girl smart than to make an ugly smart girl beautiful.

"Petey," I said, "are you in love with Polly Espy?"   25

"I think she's a keen kid," he replied, "but I don't know if you'd call it love. Why?"

"Do you," I asked, "have any kind of formal arrangement with her? I mean are you going steady or anything like that?"

"No. We see each other quite a bit, but we both have other dates. Why?"

"Is there," I asked, "any other man for whom she has a particular fondness?"

"Not that I know of. Why?"   30

I nodded with satisfaction. "In other words, if you were out of the picture, the field would be open. Is that right?"

"I guess so. What are you getting at?"

"Nothing, nothing," I said innocently, and took my suitcase out of the closet.

"Where you going?" asked Petey.

"Home for the week end." I threw a few things into the bag.   35

"Listen," he said, clutching my arm eagerly, "while you're home, you couldn't get some money from your old man, could you, and lend it to me so I can buy a raccoon coat?"

"I may do better than that," I said with a mysterious wink and closed my bag and left.

"Look," I said to Petey when I got back Monday morning. I threw open the suitcase and revealed the huge, hairy, gamy object that my father had worn in his Stutz Bearcat in 1925.

"Holy Toledo!" said Petey reverently. He plunged his hands into the raccoon coat and then his face. "Holy Toledo!" he repeated fifteen or twenty times.

"Would you like it?" I asked.   40

"Oh yes!" he cried, clutching the greasy pelt to him. Then a canny look came into his eyes. "What do you want for it?"

"Your girl," I said, mincing no words.

"Polly?" he said in a horrified whisper. "You want Polly?"

"That's right."

He flung the coat from him. "Never," he said stoutly.   45

I shrugged. "Okay. If you don't want to be in the swim, I guess it's your business."

I sat down in a chair and pretended to read a book, but out of the corner of my eye I kept watching Petey. He was a torn man. First he looked at the coat with the expression of a waif at a bakery window. Then he turned away and set his jaw resolutely. Then he looked back at the coat, with even more longing in his face. Then he turned away, but with not so much resolution this time. Back and forth his head swiveled, desire waxing, resolution waning. Finally he didn't turn away at all; he just stood and stared with mad lust at the coat.

"It isn't as though I was in love with Polly," he said thickly. "Or going steady or anything like that."

"That's right," I murmured.

"What's Polly to me, or me to Polly?"   50

"Not a thing," said I.

"It's just been a casual kick — just a few laughs, that's all."

"Try on the coat," said I.

He complied. The coat bunched high over his ears and dropped all the way down to his shoe tops. He looked like a mound of dead raccoons. "Fits fine," he said happily.

I rose from my chair. "Is it a deal?" I asked, extending my hand.   55

He swallowed. "It's a deal," he said and shook my hand.

I had my first date with Polly the following evening. This was in the nature of a survey; I wanted to find out just how much work I had to do to get her mind up to the standard I required. I took her first to dinner. "Gee, that was a delish dinner," she said as we left the restaurant. Then I took her to a movie. "Gee, that was a marvy movie," she said as we left the theater. And then I took her home. "Gee, I had a sensaysh time," she said as she bade me good night.

I went back to my room with a heavy heart. I had gravely underestimated the size of my task. This girl's lack of information was terrifying. Nor would it be enough merely to supply her with information. First she had to be taught to *think*. This loomed as a project of no small dimensions, and at first I was tempted to give her back to Petey. But then I got to thinking about her abundant physical charms and about the way she entered a room and the way she handled a knife and fork, and I decided to make an effort.

I went about it, as in all things, systematically. I gave her a course in logic. It happened that I, as a law student, was taking a course in logic myself, so I had all the facts at my fingertips. "Polly," I said to her when I picked her up on our next date, "tonight we are going over to the Knoll and talk."

"Oo, terrif," she replied. One thing I will say for this girl: You would go far to find another so agreeable. 60

We went to the Knoll, the campus trysting place, and we sat down under an old oak, and she looked at me expectantly: "What are we going to talk about?" she asked.

"Logic."

She thought this over for a minute and decided she liked it. "Magnif," she said.

"Logic," I said, clearing my throat, "is the science of thinking. Before we can think correctly, we must first learn to recognize the common fallacies of logic. These we will take up tonight."

"Wow-dow!" she cried, clapping her hands delightedly. 65

I winced, but went bravely on. "First let us examine the fallacy called Dicto Simpliciter."

"By all means," she urged, batting her lashes eagerly.

"Dicto Simpliciter means an argument based on an unqualified generalization. For example: Exercise is good. Therefore everybody should exercise."

"I agree," said Polly earnestly. "I mean exercise is wonderful. I mean it builds the body and everything."

"Polly," I said gently, "the argument is a fallacy. *Exercise is good* is an 70 unqualified generalization. For instance, if you have heart disease, exercise is bad, not good. Many people are ordered by their doctors *not* to exercise. You must *qualify* the generalization. You must say exercise is *usually* good, or exercise is good *for most people.* Otherwise you have committed a Dicto Simpliciter. Do you see?"

"No," she confessed. "But this is marvy. Do more! Do more!"

"It will be better if you stop tugging at my sleeve," I told her, and when she desisted, I continued. "Next we take up a fallacy called Hasty Generalization. Listen carefully: You can't speak French. I can't speak French. Petey Bellows can't speak French. I must therefore conclude that nobody at the University of Minnesota can speak French."

"Really?" said Polly, amazed. "*Nobody?*"

I hid my exasperation. "Polly, it's a fallacy. The generalization is reached too hastily. There are too few instances to support such a conclusion."

"Know any more fallacies?" she asked breathlessly. "This is more fun 75 than dancing even."

I fought off a wave of despair. I was getting nowhere with this girl, absolutely nowhere. Still, I am nothing if not persistent. I continued. "Next comes Post Hoc. Listen to this: Let's not take Bill on our picnic. Every time we take him out with us, it rains."

"I know somebody just like that," she exclaimed. "A girl back home—Eula Becker, her name is. It never fails. Every single time we take her on a picnic——"

"Polly," I said sharply, "it's a fallacy. Eula Becker doesn't *cause* the rain. She has no connection with the rain. You are guilty of Post Hoc if you blame Eula Becker."

"I'll never do it again," she promised contritely. "Are you mad at me?"

I sighed. "No, Polly, I'm not mad."   80

"Then tell me some more fallacies."

"All right. Let's try Contradictory Premises."

"Yes, let's," she chirped, blinking her eyes happily.

I frowned, but plunged ahead. "Here's an example of Contradictory Premises: If God can do anything, can He make a stone so heavy that He won't be able to lift it?"

"Of course," she replied promptly.   85

"But if He can do anything, He can lift the stone," I pointed out.

"Yeah," she said thoughtfully. "Well, then I guess He can't make the stone."

"But He can do anything," I reminded her.

She scratched her pretty, empty head. "I'm all confused," she admitted.

"Of course you are. Because when the premises of an argument con-   90
tradict each other, there can be no argument. If there is an irresistible force, there can be no immovable object. If there is an immovable object, there can be no irresistible force. Get it?"

"Tell me some more of this keen stuff," she said eagerly.

I consulted my watch. "I think we'd better call it a night. I'll take you home now, and you go over all the things you've learned. We'll have another session tomorrow night."

I deposited her at the girls' dormitory, where she assured me that she had had a perfectly terrif evening, and I went glumly home to my room. Petey lay snoring in his bed, the raccoon coat huddled like a great hairy beast at his feet. For a moment I considered waking him and telling him that he could have his girl back. It seemed clear that my project was doomed to failure. The girl simply had a logic-proof head.

But then I reconsidered. I had wasted one evening; I might as well waste another. Who knew? Maybe somewhere in the extinct crater of her mind a few embers still smoldered. Maybe somehow I could fan them into flame. Admittedly it was not a prospect fraught with hope, but I decided to give it one more try.

Seated under the oak the next evening I said, "Our first fallacy 95
tonight is called Ad Misericordiam."

She quivered with delight.

"Listen closely," I said. "A man applies for a job. When the boss asks him what his qualifications are, he replies that he has a wife and six chil-dren at home, the wife is a helpless cripple, the children have nothing to eat, no clothes to wear, no shoes on their feet, there are no beds in the house, no coal in the cellar, and winter is coming."

A tear rolled down each of Polly's pink cheeks. "Oh, this is awful, awful," she sobbed.

"Yes, it's awful," I agreed, "but it's no argument. The man never answered the boss's question about his qualifications. Instead he appealed to the boss's sympathy. He committed the fallacy of Ad Misericordiam. Do you understand?"

"Have you got a handkerchief?" she blubbered.   100

I handed her a handkerchief and tried to keep from screaming while she wiped her eyes. "Next," I said in a carefully controlled tone, "we will discuss False Analogy. Here is an example: Students should be allowed to look at their textbooks during examinations. After all, surgeons have X rays to guide them during an operation, lawyers have briefs to guide them during a trial, carpenters have blueprints to guide them when they are building a house. Why, then, shouldn't students be allowed to look at their textbooks during an examination?"

"There now," she said enthusiastically, "is the most marvy idea I've heard in years."

"Polly," I said testily, "the argument is all wrong. Doctors, lawyers, and carpenters aren't taking a test to see how much they have learned, but students are. The situations are altogether different, and you can't make an analogy between them."

"I still think it's a good idea," said Polly.

"Nuts," I muttered. Doggedly I pressed on. "Next we'll try Hypothesis   105
Contrary to Fact."

"Sounds yummy," was Polly's reaction.

"Listen: If Madame Curie had not happened to leave a photographic plate in a drawer with a chunk of pitchblende, the world today would not know about radium."

"True, true," said Polly, nodding her head. "Did you see the movie? Oh, it just knocked me out. That Walter Pidgeon is so dreamy. I mean he fractures me."

"If you can forget Mr. Pidgeon for a moment," I said coldly, "I would like to point out that the statement is a fallacy. Maybe Madame Curie would have discovered radium at some later date. Maybe somebody else would have discovered it. Maybe any number of things would have happened. You can't start with a hypothesis that is not true and then draw any supportable conclusions from it."

"They ought to put Walter Pidgeon in more pictures," said Polly. "I   110
hardly ever see him any more."

One more chance, I decided. But just one more. There is a limit to what flesh and blood can bear. "The next fallacy is called Poisoning the Well."

"How cute!" she gurgled.

"Two men are having a debate. The first one gets up and says, 'My opponent is a notorious liar. You can't believe a word that he is going to say.' . . . Now, Polly, think. Think hard. What's wrong?"

I watched her closely as she knit her creamy brow in concentration. Suddenly a glimmer of intelligence — the first I had seen — came into her eyes. "It's not fair," she said with indignation. "It's not a bit fair. What chance has the second man got if the first man calls him a liar before he even begins talking?"

"Right!" I cried exultantly. "One hundred percent right. It's not fair. 115 The first man has *poisoned the well* before anybody could drink from it. He has hamstrung his opponent before he could even start. . . . Polly, I'm proud of you."

"Pshaw," she murmured, blushing with pleasure.

"You see, my dear, these things aren't so hard. All you have to do is concentrate. Think—examine—evaluate. Come now, let's review everything we have learned."

"Fire away," she said with an airy wave of her hand.

Heartened by the knowledge that Polly was not altogether a cretin, I began a long, patient review of all I had told her. Over and over and over again I cited instances, pointed out flaws, kept hammering away without letup. It was like digging a tunnel. At first everything was work, sweat, and darkness. I had no idea when I would reach the light, or even *if* I would. But I persisted. I pounded and clawed and scraped, and finally I was rewarded. I saw a chink of light. And then the chink got bigger and the sun came pouring in and all was bright.

Five grueling nights this took, but it was worth it. I had made a logi- 120 cian out of Polly; I had taught her to think. My job was done. She was worthy of me at last. She was a fit wife for me, a proper hostess for my many mansions, a suitable mother for my well-heeled children.

It must not be thought that I was without love for this girl. Quite the contrary. Just as Pygmalion loved the perfect woman he had fashioned, so I loved mine. I decided to acquaint her with my feelings at our very next meeting. The time had come to change our relationship from academic to romantic.

"Polly," I said when next we sat beneath our oak, "tonight we will not discuss fallacies."

"Aw, gee," she said, disappointed.

"My dear," I said, favoring her with a smile, "we have now spent five evenings together. We have gotten along splendidly. It is clear that we are well matched."

"Hasty Generalization," said Polly brightly.   125

"I beg your pardon," said I.

"Hasty Generalization," she repeated. "How can you say that we are well matched on the basis of only five dates?"

I chuckled with amusement. The dear child had learned her lessons well. "My dear," I said, patting her hand in a tolerant manner, "five dates is plenty. After all, you don't have to eat a whole cake to know that it's good."

"False Analogy," said Polly promptly. "I'm not a cake. I'm a girl."

I chuckled with somewhat less amusement. The dear child had 130 learned her lesson perhaps too well. I decided to change tactics. Obviously

the best approach was a simple, strong, direct declaration of love. I
paused for a moment while my massive brain chose the proper words.
Then I began:

"Polly, I love you. You are the whole world to me, and the moon and
the stars and the constellations of outer space. Please, my darling, say
that you will go steady with me, for if you will not, life will be meaningless. I will languish. I will refuse my meals. I will wander the face of the
earth, a shambling, hollow-eyed hulk."

There, I thought, folding my arms, that ought to do it.

"Ad Misericordiam," said Polly.

I ground my teeth. I was not Pygmalion; I was Frankenstein, and my
monster had me by the throat. Frantically I fought back the tide of panic
surging through me. At all costs I had to keep cool.

"Well, Polly," I said, forcing a smile, "you certainly have learned   135
your fallacies."

"You're darn right," she said with a vigorous nod.

"And who taught them to you, Polly?"

"You did."

"That's right. So you do owe me something, don't you, my dear? If I
hadn't come along you never would have learned about fallacies."

"Hypothesis Contrary to Fact," she said instantly.   140

I dashed perspiration from my brow. "Polly," I croaked, "You mustn't
take all these things so literally. I mean this is just classroom stuff. You
know that the things you learn in school don't have anything to do with
life."

"Dicto Simpliciter," she said, wagging her finger at me playfully.

That did it. I leaped to my feet, bellowing like a bull. "Will you or
will you not go steady with me?"

"I will not," she replied.

"Why not?" I demanded.   145

"Because this afternoon I promised Petey Bellows that I would go
steady with him."

I reeled back, overcome with the infamy of it. After he promised,
after he made a deal, after he shook my hand! "That rat!" I shrieked,
kicking up great chunks of turf. "You can't go with him, Polly. He's a liar.
He's a cheat. He's a rat."

"Poisoning the Well," said Polly, "and stop shouting. I think shouting
must be a fallacy too."

With an immense effort of will, I modulated my voice. "All right,"
I said. "You're a logician. Let's look at this thing logically. How could
you choose Petey Bellows over me? Look at me—a brilliant student, a
tremendous intellectual, a man with an assured future. Look at Petey—
a knothead, a jitterbug, a guy who'll never know where his next meal is
coming from. Can you give me one logical reason why you should go
steady with Petey Bellows?"

"I certainly can," declared Polly. "He's got a raccoon coat."   150

Topic for Critical Thinking and Writing

After you have finished reading "Love Is a Fallacy," you may want to write an argumentative essay of 500 to 750 words on one of the following topics: (1) the story, rightly understood, is not antiwoman; (2) if the story is antiwoman, it is equally antiman; (3) the story is antiwoman but nevertheless belongs in this book; or (4) the story is antiwoman and does not belong in the book.

See the companion Web site
bedfordstmartins.com/barnetbedau
for a series of brain teasers and links related to
the logical point of view in argument.

10

A Moralist's View:
Ways of Thinking Ethically

About morals, I know only that what is moral is what you feel good after and what is immoral is what you feel bad after.

— ERNEST HEMINGWAY

Our whole life is startlingly moral. There is never an instant's truth between virtue and vice.

— HENRY DAVID THOREAU

Elsewhere in this book we explain *deductive reasoning* (p. 349), *inductive reasoning* (p. 361), and *legal reasoning* (p. 428). More familiar and probably more important is **moral reasoning.** If truth be told, virtually every essay reprinted in this book is an example of more or less self-conscious moral reasoning. (In passing, at the outset we note that we do not draw any distinction between morals and ethics or between moral reasoning and ethical reasoning. Apart from insignificant connotations, the terms *moral* and *ethical* differ mainly in their origins, *ethical* deriving from the Greek *ethos,* meaning "custom" or "manners," and *moral* deriving from the Latin *moralis,* meaning "moral" or "ethical.")

Moral reasoning has various purposes, particularly guidance for conduct—for what someone actually does or fails to do. In this light, consider the parable Jesus tells of the Good Samaritan (Luke 10:30–37). On a journey from Jerusalem to Jericho, a man is robbed by thieves, beaten, and left nearly dead. First a priest came along, "looked on him, and passed by on the other side." Then a Levite (an assistant to a temple priest) does the same thing. (Implied in the story is that both the priest and the Levite are fellow countrymen of the victim and so might well be expected to come to the man's aid.) "But a certain Samaritan . . . came where he was and when he saw him, he had compassion on him." The Samaritan bound up his wounds, took him to an inn, and paid for his lodging.

Jesus tells this story to answer the question, Who is my neighbor? In context, this amounts to the question, Which of the three passersby acts toward the beaten man in a truly neighborly manner? The answer, of course, is that only the Samaritan—a person from a different culture—does.

Most of the moral reasoning in this parable is left implicit by the Gospel writer. To understand the indifference of the priest and Levite to the plight of the victim, we might imagine them thinking as follows: "Nothing I have done or failed to do caused the victim to be robbed and assaulted, so I have no responsibility to interrupt my travels to care for him. Nothing binds him to me as kinship would; he and I are not neighbors in the ordinary sense of that term (persons who live nearby, in the same neighborhood), so I do not owe him assistance as I would to my kin and my immediate neighbors. His need gives him no claim on my attention. Finally, why put myself at uncertain risk in trying to help him? Perhaps the thieves are still in the vicinity, just waiting to pounce on anyone foolish enough to stop and give aid."

Clearly, Jesus implies that none of these reasons is adequate. His parable is intended in part to stretch our ordinary notion of what it means to be someone's neighbor. Jesus is in effect telling us that the beaten stranger ought to elicit the same concern and care that we would give to an assaulted family member, close friend, or immediate neighbor.

What makes Jesus' parable a story told from the moral point of view is that his implicit evaluation of the conduct of the three passersby depends on an unspoken moral principle that he believes but that he knows is not widely shared: *We ought to help the needy even at some cost or risk to ourselves.*

As a next step in the effort to deepen our grasp of moral reasoning, it is useful to be clear about what it *isn't.* To do that we need to think about two kinds of reasoning sharply contrasted to moral reasoning: *amoral* reasoning and *immoral* reasoning.

AMORAL REASONING

Amorality consists of conduct of no moral significance—that is, conduct not to be evaluated by reference to moral considerations. For example, suppose you are in the market for a used car. You want a two-door car and have narrowed your choices to three: a 2005 Honda, a 2006 Subaru, and a 2007 Toyota. No moral consideration enters your deliberation over which car to choose; morality is silent on your choice. Daily life is filled with examples of this sort, situations in which nothing of moral relevance seems to be involved, and so our decisions and choices can be made without worry over their morality or immorality. In short, for most of us, morality just does not control or pervade everything we do in life. And when we judge moral considerations to be irrelevant, we are dealing with what we regard as amoral matters.

Let us examine another example in greater detail. You are about to dine with a friend at a nice restaurant. The waiter brings you the menu, and you look it over, pondering whether to have an appetizer, order a bottle of white or red wine, choose fish or poultry for the main dish, and top it all off with dessert and coffee. Since the restaurant is noted for its cuisine, you are trying to design a meal for yourself worthy of the occasion. There is nothing particularly moral or immoral in your deliberations as you study the menu and make your choices. By eating in this restaurant, you are not depriving anyone else of their dinner, much less depriving them unfairly. You are not coercing others to turn over their food to you. You have not stolen the money to pay for your food. You are not breaking a promise to anyone to avoid this restaurant or to avoid rich and expensive restaurant food. You have no intention of leaving without paying the bill. Thus, various standard and familiar ways of acting immorally can be seen to play no role in your dinner deliberations.

On the other hand, there is no moral requirement that you dine in this restaurant or that you order this rather than that from the menu. You have no moral duty to have a feast, no obligation to anyone to have an expensive dinner. You have not promised anyone to dine in this restaurant. Your failure to dine there would flout no moral rule or principle.

Situations such as this, which call for reasoning and decision but where no moral principle or rule is involved, are without moral significance whichever way they are decided. To put this another way, in cases such as this, moral reasoning tells us we are *permitted* (neither prohibited nor required by morality) to go ahead with our restaurant meal as planned, and in this regard we may do whatever we like.

So the first of several questions that capture the idea of moral reasoning can be put this way:

- Is your (or someone else's) conduct prohibited or required by a moral rule or principle? If not, then it is probably not morally wrong: Morality permits you to act as you please.

Two kinds of considerations raised by this example deserve a closer look. First, if you are on a diet that forbids rich food, you are at risk in doing yourself some harm unless you read the menu carefully and order accordingly (no steak or other red meat, for example, and no fatty custards or sauces). The best way to treat yourself, we can probably agree, dictates caution in what you select to eat. But suppose you fail to act cautiously. Well, you are not acting immorally—although your behavior is imprudent, ill advised, and contrary to your best interests. We break no moral rule when we choose not to act in our own rational self-interest. The rule "Act always to promote your own rational self-interest" is not a moral rule.

Unless, of course, one's morality does consist of some form of self-interest, as in, for example, the views of the novelist-turned-philosopher Ayn Rand in her widely read book *The Virtue of Selfishness* (1965). Her defense of selfishness is exceptional and somewhat misleading— exceptional because very few moralists agree with her, and somewhat misleading because her main thesis—*everyone would do better if each of us*

"Which entrée raises the fewest ethical issues?"

pursued only our own rational self-interest—is obviously contestable. Most moralists would insist that all of us do *not* do better if each of us acts without ever taking into account the needs of others except where they impinge on our own welfare. (For another version of a morality of selfishness, see the essay by Garrett Hardin, p. 414.) Of course, any given moral code or moral principle is subject to criticism on moral grounds. Not all moralities—sets of moral principles that a person or a society holds—are equally reasonable, fair, or free of some other moral defect.

Second, if, for example, you are concerned about animal rights, you may see the choice between a meatless salad and a chef's salad as a moral issue. That is not the only way the choice of a meal may turn out to conceal a moral issue. The more expensive the dinner, the more you may feel uneasy about such self-indulgence when you could eat an adequate dinner elsewhere at one-third the cost and donate the difference to Oxfam or UNESCO. Many moralists would insist that we who are well fed in fact have a responsibility to see to it that the starving are fed. Some influential moral thinkers in recent years have gone even further, arguing that the best moral principles, preeminently the utilitarian principle that one always ought to act so as to maximize the net benefits among the available choices, require those of us in affluent nations to reduce radically our standard of living to improve the standard of living of people in the poorest nations. (See the essay by Peter Singer, p. 402.) This example nicely illustrates how something as seemingly harmless and amoral as having an expensive meal in a nice restaurant can turn out, after all, to pose a moral choice—because one's moral principles turn out to be applicable to the case in question, even if the moral principles acknowledged by others are not.

IMMORAL REASONING

The most obvious reasoning to be contrasted with moral reasoning is *immoral* reasoning. Immorality, defined abstractly, is conduct contrary to what morality requires or prohibits. Hence a person is reasoning immorally whenever he or she is contemplating judgment or conduct that violates or disregards some relevant moral rule or principle.

We are acting immorally when we use *force or fraud* in our dealings with other people and when we treat them *unfairly.* Typically we act in these ways toward others when our motives are *selfish*—that is, when we act in ways intended to gain advantage for ourselves without regard to the effects that advantage will have on others. For example,

Suppose you are short of cash and try to borrow some from a friend. You don't expect your friend simply to give you the money, so

You know you will have to promise to repay her as soon as you can, say, in a week.

But you know you really have no intention of keeping your promise to pay her back.

Nonetheless, you make the promise—well, you utter words such as "Sure, you can rely on me; I'll pay you back in a few days"—and she loans you the money. Weeks go by. Eventually your paths cross and she reminds you that you haven't yet paid her back.

What to say? Some of your options:

Laugh in her face for being so naive as to loan you the money in the first place?

Make up some phony excuse, and hope she'll accept it?

Renew your promise to pay her back but without any change in your intention not to do so?

Act tough, and threaten her if she doesn't lay off?

Each of these is an immoral tactic, and deliberating among them to choose the most effective is immoral reasoning. Why? Because each of them violates a familiar moral principle (albeit rarely formulated expressly in words). First, *promises are fraudulent if they are made with no intention to keep them.* (Underlying that principle is another one: Fraud is morally wrong.) Second, *promises ought to be kept.* Whatever else morality is, it is a constraint on acting purely out of self-interest and in a manner heedless of the consequences for others. Making fraudulent promises and unfairly breaking genuine promises are actions usually done out of selfish intentions and are likely to cause harm to others.

The discussion so far yields this important generalization:

- If the reasons for your proposed judgment and conduct are purely selfish, they are not moral reasons.

Of course, there are exceptions to the two principles mentioned in the previous paragraph. Neither principle is a rigid moral rule. Why? Because on some occasions making a fraudulent promise or breaking a sincere promise can be *excused,* and on other occasions such conduct can be *justified.* (Or so most of us in our society think when we reflect on the matter.) Both invoking a legitimate excuse or justification for breaking a moral rule and rejecting illegitimate excuses or justifications, are crucial features of everyday moral reasoning. For example, you ought to be excused for breaking a sincere promise—say, a promise to meet a friend for lunch at a certain time and place—if your car gets a flat tire on the way. On the other hand, you would be justified in breaking your promise if, for example, while driving on the way to your lunch date you are late because you stopped to help a stranded motorist change his flat tire. In general,

- We *excuse* violating a moral rule when we argue that we know breaking it was wrong but it couldn't be helped, whereas
- We *justify* violating a moral rule when we argue that doing so was the right or the best thing to do in the circumstances.

We have now identified two more questions to keep in mind as you try to assess the morality of your own or someone else's reasoning. The first is this:

- Are the reasons you offer an attempt to excuse wrongful conduct? If so, is the excuse a legitimate one?

Typical excuses include these: "It was an *accident;* he *couldn't help* it; she *didn't know it was wrong;* they did it *by mistake;* we were *forced* to do it; I was *provoked.*" The legitimacy of an excuse in any given case depends on the facts of the matter. Claiming that the harm you caused, for example, was an accident doesn't *make* it an accident. (Children are quick to learn these excuses and can be quite adept at misusing them to their own advantage.)

The second question to ask is this:

- Are the reasons you offer an attempt to justify breaking a moral rule knowingly? If so, is the proposed justification really convincing?

Typical justifications include these: "It was the *best* thing to do in the circumstances; the *sacrifice* was necessary to protect something else of greater value; *little or no harm to others will be done* if the rule is ignored; *superior orders* required me to do what I did." A justification is convincing in a given case just to the extent that it invokes a moral rule or principle of greater weight or scope than the rule or principle being violated.

MORAL REASONING: A CLOSER LOOK

What does this brief excursion into amoral and immoral reasoning teach us about *moral* reasoning? Just this: Moral reasoning involves (1) reasoning from *moral* rules, principles, or standards and (2) resolving conflicts among them, thereby placing limits on what one may do with a clear conscience.

This point can be restated as follows:

- Do the reasons you propose for your conduct violate any of the relevant moral rules you accept? If not, then your morality raises no objection to your conduct.

Morality and moral reasoning can be conveniently subdivided into several narrower areas. We are sexual beings, and our pursuit of sexual experience will inevitably raise questions about the morality of our conduct. Hence we often have occasion to think about *sexual* morality—our own and that of others. *Sexual* morality can be defined as the moral rules, principles, and standards relevant to judgment and conduct in which someone's sexual behavior is at issue. Similarly, *political* morality concerns the moral rules, principles, and standards with which people ought to conduct and evaluate political activities, practices, and institutions. *Professional* ethics all involve special rules, norms, and principles relevant to judgment and conduct, and these rules are often stated in the form of a *code* of ethics suitable to the judgments and conduct more or less unique to each profession (such as business, medicine, journalism, law). What is common to all such codes are prohibitions against coercion and misrepresentation, unfair advantage, and the failure to obtain informed voluntary consent from one's clients, patients, witnesses, and employees.

Second, the rules, principles, and standards that constitute a morality differ in different religions and cultures, just as they differ historically. The morality of ancient Greece was not the morality of feudal Europe or contemporary America; the morality of the Trobriand Islanders is not the same as the morality of the Kwakiutl Indians. This does not imply *moral relativism*—that is, the view that there is no rational ground on which to choose among alternative moralities. (The purely descriptive thesis that *different cultures endorse different moral codes* does not imply the evaluative thesis that *one moral code is as good as another*.) The fact that different cultures endorse different moral codes does, however, imply that there may be a need for tolerance of moral standards other than one's own.

Third, in the morality most widely shared in our society, moral rules are not rigid; they permit exceptions (as we have seen above), and they are of different importance and weight. For example, few would deny that it is more important to help a stranded motorist than to keep a lunch date. Unlike the ancient Hebrews, however, who were guided by the Ten Commandments, most of us have no book or engraved tablet where our moral principles are listed for all to study at their leisure and violate at their peril. Where, then, do a society's moral rules come from? How do we learn these rules? They come from the collective experience of peoples and cultures in their search for stability, continuity, and harmony among persons of diverse interests, talents, and preferences. And we learn them in our youth (unless we have the misfortune to be neglected by our parents and teachers) in the daily processes of socialization.

What gives these rules authority over our conduct and judgment? Indeed, what makes a rule, principle, or standard a *moral* rule, standard, or principle? These are serious philosophical questions that we cannot adequately discuss and answer here. Suffice it to say that a person's *principles* guide that person's conduct and judgment; a rule or principle counts as a *moral* rule or principle when it gives guidance regarding rational constraints on self-interested conduct. A rule or principle gives such guidance when it takes into account the legitimate and relevant interests of people generally—not just one's own interests, those of one's friends and relatives, clan, or tribe, or those of one's fellow citizens but the interests of persons generally—and does so in a manner neither deliberately nor negligently indifferent to the interests of others.

This constraining function of moral rules is most evident in the best-known Western moral code, the Ten Commandments. Apart from the first three of the Commandments, which concern people's behavior toward God, the rest—Honor thy father and thy mother, Do not kill, Do not covet thy neighbor's property, and so on—clearly amount to constraints on the pursuit of self-interest regardless of its cost to others. The immoralist flouts all such constraints; the amoralist believes that most of his and our conduct involves no moral considerations one way or the other. The rest of us, however, recognize that there are constraints on our conduct. The *moral skeptic* needs to be reminded of certain indisputable facts: Does anyone seriously believe that lying and cheating are never wrong? Or that murder, rape, assault, arson, and kidnapping are wrong only because they are against the law? Or that it is merely a matter of personal opinion or taste that we ought to help the needy and ought not to take unfair advantage of others?

To be sure, honesty requires us to admit that we do not always comply with the constraints we acknowledge—we are not saints—hence the familiar experience of feeling guilty over having knowingly done the wrong thing to somebody who deserved better of us. If morality involves constraints on the pursuit of self-interest, moral reasoning involves identifying and weighing those constraints and being prepared to explain, when appropriate, why one has not complied with them.

CRITERIA FOR MORAL RULES

Philosophers and moralists over the centuries have developed various tests or criteria against which to measure the adequacy of a moral rule. Presupposed by all these criteria is the answer to this question:

- What is the rule, principle, or standard on which you propose to act?

If you can't formulate such a rule, then the rationality of your proposed action is in doubt. (In the excerpts later in this chapter, we identify some relevant moral principles and show how they are used in practice.)

Among the questions worth asking in the evaluation of someone's conduct and the rule or rules on which it relies is this:

- Would you be willing to argue for the general adoption of whatever rules you profess?

This principle is a version of the Categorical Imperative proposed by Immanuel Kant (1724–1804): Always act so that the principle of your action could be the principle on which everyone else acts in similar situations. Could a society of utterly selfish persons accept such a principle? Surely, a general practice of fraudulent promise-making could never pass this test.

Here's another criterion:

- Would you be willing to argue openly for the general adoption of whatever reasons you accept?

Here's yet another criterion:

- Do the reasons for your proposed conduct take into account the greatest good for the greatest number?

This is a version of the utilitarian principle (for an alternative version, see p. 397; for an application, see the essay by Peter Singer, p. 402).

Still other criteria include the following:

- Do the reasons for your proposed conduct take into account the relevant moral rights of others?
- Would an unbiased observer, fully informed of what you regard as all the relevant facts, approve of your reasons for your proposed conduct?

Which one of these criteria is the best? Or do they all come to the same thing in practice? Answering such questions involves reasoning *about* moral principles, whereas up to now we have been discussing only reasoning *with* such principles. Reasoning about moral principles arises naturally out of reflection on reasoning with such principles. *Meta-ethics*—thinking about the nature of moral concepts, values, and norms—has been a matter of immense philosophical interest since Socrates and Plato. We must leave further development of these issues to their heirs.

✓ A CHECKLIST FOR MORAL REASONING

☐ Is my (or someone else's) conduct prohibited or required by a moral rule or principle? If not, then it is probably not morally right or wrong: Morality permits me to act as I please.

☐ If the reasons for my proposed judgment or conduct are purely selfish, they are not moral reasons.

☐ Are my reasons an attempt to excuse wrongful conduct? If so, is the excuse a legitimate one?

☐ Are my reasons an attempt to justify breaking a moral rule knowingly? If so, is the proposed justification convincing?

☐ Do the reasons I propose for my conduct violate any of the relevant moral rules I accept? If not, then my morality raises no objection to your conduct.

☐ What is the rule, principle, or standard on which I propose to act?

☐ Would I be willing to argue openly for the general adoption of whatever rules I accept?

☐ Would I be willing to argue openly for the general adoption of whatever reasons I accept?

☐ Do the reasons for my proposed conduct take into account the greatest good for the greatest number?

☐ Do the reasons for my proposed conduct take into account the relevant moral rights of others?

☐ Would an unbiased observer, fully informed of what I regard as all the relevant facts, approve of my reasons for my proposed conduct?

Peter Singer

Peter Singer is the Ira W. DeCamp Professor of Bioethics at Princeton University. A native of Australia, he is a graduate of the University of Melbourne and Oxford University and the author or editor of more than two dozen books, including Animal Liberation *(1975),* Practical Ethics *(1979),* Rethinking Life and Death *(1995), and* One World: The Ethics of Globalization *(2002). His views on several life-and-death issues have been the source of much public and scholarly controversy. This essay originally appeared in* Philosophy and Public Affairs *(Spring 1972).*

Famine, Affluence, and Morality

As I write this, in November 1971, people are dying in East Bengal from lack of food, shelter, and medical care. The suffering and death that are occurring there now are not inevitable, not unavoidable in any fatalistic sense of the term. Constant poverty, a cyclone, and a civil war have turned at least nine million people into destitute refugees; nevertheless, it is not beyond the capacity of the richer nations to give enough assistance to reduce any further suffering to very small proportions. The decisions and actions of human beings can prevent this kind of suffering. Unfortunately, human beings have not made the necessary decisions. At the individual level, people have, with very few exceptions, not responded to the situation in any significant way. Generally speaking, people have not given large sums to relief funds; they have not written to their parliamentary representatives demanding increased government assistance; they have not demonstrated in the streets, held symbolic fasts, or done anything else directed toward providing the refugees with the means to satisfy their essential needs. At the government level, no government has given the sort of massive aid that would enable the refugees to survive for more than a few days. Britain, for instance, has given rather more than most countries. It has, to date, given £14,750,000. For comparative purposes, Britain's share of the nonrecoverable development costs of the Anglo-French Concorde project is already in excess of £275,000,000, and on present estimates will reach £440,000,000. The implication is that the British government values a supersonic transport more than thirty times as highly as it values the lives of the 9 million refugees. Australia is another country which, on a per capita basis, is well up in the "aid to Bengal" table. Australia's aid, however, amounts to less than one-twelfth of the cost of Sydney's new opera house. The total amount given, from all sources, now stands at about £65,000,000. The estimated cost of keeping the refugees alive for one year is £464,000,000. Most of the refugees have now been in the camps for more than six months. The World Bank has said that India needs a minimum of £300,000,000 in assistance from other countries before the end of the year. It seems obvious that assistance on this scale will not be forthcoming. India will be forced to choose between letting the refugees starve or diverting funds from her own development program, which will mean that more of her own people will starve in the future.[1]

These are the essential facts about the present situation in Bengal. So far as it concerns us here, there is nothing unique about this situation except its magnitude. The Bengal emergency is just the latest and most acute of a series of major emergencies in various parts of the world, arising both from natural and from man-made causes. There are also many parts of the world in which people die from malnutrition and lack of food independent of any special emergency. I take Bengal as my example only because it is the present concern, and because the size of the problem has ensured that it has been given adequate publicity. Neither individuals nor governments can claim to be unaware of what is happening there.

[1]There was also a third possibility: that India would go to war to enable the refugees to return to their lands. Since I wrote this paper, India has taken this way out. The situation is no longer that described above, but this does not affect my argument, as the next paragraph indicates. [All notes are Singer's.]

What are the moral implications of a situation like this? In what follows, I shall argue that the way people in relatively affluent countries react to a situation like that in Bengal cannot be justified; indeed, the whole way we look at moral issues—our moral conceptual scheme—needs to be altered, and with it, the way of life that has come to be taken for granted in our society.

In arguing for this conclusion I will not, of course, claim to be morally neutral. I shall, however, try to argue for the moral position that I take, so that anyone who accepts certain assumptions, to be made explicit, will, I hope, accept my conclusion.

I begin with the assumption that suffering and death from lack of food, shelter, and medical care are bad. I think most people will agree about this, although one may reach the same view by different routes. I shall not argue for this view. People can hold all sorts of eccentric positions, and perhaps from some of them it would not follow that death by starvation is in itself bad. It is difficult, perhaps impossible, to refute such positions, and so for brevity I will henceforth take this assumption as accepted. Those who disagree need read no further.

My next point is this: If it is in our power to prevent something bad from happening, without thereby sacrificing anything of comparable moral importance, we ought, morally, to do it. By "without sacrificing anything of comparable moral importance" I mean without causing anything else comparably bad to happen, or doing something that is wrong in itself, or failing to promote some moral good, comparable in significance to the bad thing that we can prevent. This principle seems almost as uncontroversial as the last one. It requires us only to prevent what is bad, and not to promote what is good, and it requires this of us only when we can do it without sacrificing anything that is, from the moral point of view, comparably important. I could even, as far as the application of my argument to the Bengal emergency is concerned, qualify the point so as to make it: If it is in our power to prevent something very bad from happening, without thereby sacrificing anything morally significant, we ought, morally, to do it. An application of this principle would be as follows: If I am walking past a shallow pond and see a child drowning in it, I ought to wade in and pull the child out. This will mean getting my clothes muddy, but this is insignificant, while the death of the child would presumably be a very bad thing.

The uncontroversial appearance of the principle just stated is deceptive. If it were acted upon, even in its qualified form, our lives, our society, and our world would be fundamentally changed. For the principle takes, firstly, no account of proximity or distance. It makes no moral difference whether the person I can help is a neighbor's child ten yards from me or a Bengali whose name I shall never know, ten thousand miles away. Secondly, the principle makes no distinction between cases in which I am the only person who could possibly do anything and cases in which I am just one among millions in the same position.

distance doesn't matter

I do not think I need to say much in defense of the refusal to take proximity and distance into account. The fact that a person is physically near to us, so that we have personal contact with him, may make it more likely that we *shall* assist him, but this does not show that we *ought* to help him rather than another who happens to be further away. If we accept any principle of impartiality, universalizability, equality, or whatever, we cannot discriminate against someone merely because he is far away from us (or we are far away from him). Admittedly, it is possible that we are in a better position to judge what needs to be done to help a person near to us than one far away, and perhaps also to provide the assistance we judge to be necessary. If this were the case, it would be a reason for helping those near to us first. This may once have been a justification for being more concerned with the poor in one's own town than with famine victims in India. Unfortunately for those who like to keep their moral responsibilities limited, instant communication and swift transportation have changed the situation. From the moral point of view, the development of the world into a "global village" has made an important, though still unrecognized, difference to our moral situation. Expert observers and supervisors, sent out by famine relief organizations or permanently stationed in famine-prone areas, can direct our aid to a refugee in Bengal almost as effectively as we could get it to someone in our own block. There would seem, therefore, to be no possible justification for discriminating on geographical grounds.

There may be a greater need to defend the second implication of my principle—that the fact that there are millions of other people in the same position, in respect to the Bengali refugees, as I am, does not make the situation significantly different from a situation in which I am the only person who can prevent something very bad from occurring. Again, of course, I admit that there is a psychological difference between the cases; one feels less guilty about doing nothing if one can point to others, similarly placed, who have also done nothing. Yet this can make no real difference to our moral obligations.[2] Should I consider that I am less obliged to pull the drowning child out of the pond if on looking around I see other people, no further away than I am, who have also noticed the child but are doing nothing? One has only to ask this question to see the absurdity of the view that numbers lessen obligation. It is a view that is an ideal excuse for inactivity; unfortunately most of the major evils— poverty, overpopulation, pollution—are problems in which everyone is almost equally involved.

[2]In view of the special sense philosophers often give to the term, I should say that I use "obligation" simply as the abstract noun derived from "ought," so that "I have an obligation to" means no more, and no less, than "I ought to." This usage is in accordance with the definition of "ought" given by the *Shorter Oxford English Dictionary*: "the general verb to express duty or obligation." I do not think any issue of substance hangs on the way the term is used; sentences in which I use "obligation" could all be rewritten, although somewhat clumsily, as sentences in which a clause containing "ought" replaces the term "obligation."

easy, equal

The view that numbers do make a difference can be made plausible if 10 stated in this way: If everyone in circumstances like mine gave £5 to the Bengal Relief Fund, there would be enough to provide food, shelter, and medical care for the refugees; there is no reason why I should give more than anyone else in the same circumstances as I am; therefore I have no obligation to give more than £5. Each premise in this argument is true, and the argument looks sound. It may convince us, unless we notice that it is based on a hypothetical premise, although the conclusion is not stated hypothetically. The argument would be sound if the conclusion were: If everyone in circumstances like mine were to give £5, I would have no obligation to give more than £5. If the conclusion were so stated, however, it would be obvious that the argument has no bearing on a situation in which it is not the case that everyone else gives £5. This, of course, is the actual situation. It is more or less certain that not everyone in circumstances like mine will give £5. So there will not be enough to provide the needed food, shelter, and medical care. Therefore by giving more than £5 I will prevent more suffering than I would if I gave just £5.

It might be thought that this argument has an absurd consequence. Since the situation appears to be that very few people are likely to give substantial amounts, it follows that I and everyone else in similar circumstances ought to give as much as possible, that is, at least up to the point at which by giving more one would begin to cause serious suffering for oneself and one's dependents—perhaps even beyond this point to the point of marginal utility, at which by giving more one would cause oneself and one's dependents as much suffering as one would prevent in Bengal. If everyone does this, however, there will be more than can be used for the benefit of the refugees, and some of the sacrifice will have been unnecessary. Thus, if everyone does what he ought to do, the result will not be as good as it would be if everyone did a little less than he ought to do, or if only some do all that they ought to do.

The paradox here arises only if we assume that the actions in question—sending money to the relief funds—are performed more or less simultaneously, and are also unexpected. For if it is to be expected that everyone is going to contribute something, then clearly each is not obliged to give as much as he would have been obliged to had others not been giving too. And if everyone is not acting more or less simultaneously, then those giving later will know how much more is needed, and will have no obligation to give more than is necessary to reach this amount. To say this is not to deny the principle that people in the same circumstances have the same obligations, but to point out that the fact that others have given, or may be expected to give, is a relevant circumstance: Those giving after it has become known that many others are giving and those giving before are not in the same circumstances. So the seemingly absurd consequence of the principle I have put forward can occur only if people are in error about the actual circumstances—that is, if they think they are giving when others are not, but in fact they are giving when others are. The result of everyone doing what he really ought to do cannot be worse than the result of everyone doing less than he ought to do, although the result of everyone doing what he reasonably believes he ought to do could be.

If my argument so far has been sound, neither our distance from a preventable evil nor the number of other people who, in respect to that evil, are in the same situation as we are, lessens our obligation to mitigate or prevent that evil. I shall therefore take as established the principle I asserted earlier. As I have already said, I need to assert it only in its qualified form: If it is in our power to prevent something very bad from happening, without thereby sacrificing anything else morally significant, we ought, morally, to do it.

The outcome of this argument is that our traditional moral categories are upset. The traditional distinction between duty and charity cannot be drawn, or at least, not in the place we normally draw it. Giving money to the Bengal Relief Fund is regarded as an act of charity in our society. The bodies which collect money are known as "charities." These organizations see themselves in this way—if you send them a check, you will be thanked for your "generosity." Because giving money is regarded as an act of charity, it is not thought that there is anything wrong with not giving. The charitable man may be praised, but the man who is not charitable is not condemned. People do not feel in any way ashamed or guilty about spending money on new clothes or a new car instead of giving it to famine relief. (Indeed, the alternative does not occur to them.) This way of looking at the matter cannot be justified. When we buy new clothes not to keep ourselves warm but to look "well-dressed" we are not providing for any important need. We would not be sacrificing anything significant if we were to continue to wear our old clothes, and give the money to famine relief. By doing so, we would be preventing another person from starving. It follows from what I have said earlier that we ought to give money away, rather than spend it on clothes which we do not need to keep us warm. To do so is not charitable, or generous. Nor is it the kind of act which philosophers and theologians have called "supererogatory"—an act which it would be good to do, but not wrong not to do. On the contrary, we ought to give the money away, and it is wrong not to do so.

I am not maintaining that there are no acts which are charitable, or   15
that there are no acts which it would be good to do but not wrong not to do. It may be possible to redraw the distinction between duty and charity in some other place. All I am arguing here is that the present way of drawing the distinction, which makes it an act of charity for a man living at the level of affluence which most people in the "developed nations" enjoy to give money to save someone else from starvation, cannot be supported. It is beyond the scope of my argument to consider whether the distinction should be redrawn or abolished altogether. There would

be many other possible ways of drawing the distinction—for instance, one might decide that it is good to make other people as happy as possible, but not wrong not to do so.

Despite the limited nature of the revision in our moral conceptual scheme which I am proposing, the revision would, given the extent of both affluence and famine in the world today, have radical implications. These implications may lead to further objections, distinct from those I have already considered. I shall discuss two of these.

One objection to the position I have taken might be simply that it is too drastic a revision of our moral scheme. People do not ordinarily judge in the way I have suggested they should. Most people reserve their moral condemnation for those who violate some moral norm, such as the norm against taking another person's property. They do not condemn those who indulge in luxury instead of giving to famine relief. But given that I did not set out to present a morally neutral description of the way people make moral judgments, the way people do in fact judge has nothing to do with the validity of my conclusion. My conclusion follows from the principle which I advanced earlier, and unless that principle is rejected, or the arguments shown to be unsound, I think the conclusion must stand, however strange it appears.

It might, nevertheless, be interesting to consider why our society, and most other societies, do judge differently from the way I have suggested they should. In a well-known article, J. O. Urmson suggests that the imperatives of duty, which tell us what we must do, as distinct from what it would be good to do but not wrong not to do, function so as to prohibit behavior that is intolerable if men are to live together in society.[3] This may explain the origin and continued existence of the present division between acts of duty and acts of charity. Moral attitudes are shaped by the needs of society, and no doubt society needs people who will observe the rules that make social existence tolerable. From the point of view of a particular society, it is essential to prevent violations of norms against killing, stealing, and so on. It is quite inessential, however, to help people outside one's own society.

If this is an explanation of our common distinction between duty and supererogation, however, it is not a justification of it. The moral point of view requires us to look beyond the interests of our own society. Previously, as I have already mentioned, this may hardly have been feasible, but it is quite feasible now. From the moral point of view, the prevention of the starvation of millions of people outside our society must be considered at least as pressing as the upholding of property norms within our society.

It has been argued by some writers, among them Sidgwick and Urmson, that we need to have a basic moral code which is not too far

---

[3] J. O. Urmson, "Saints and Heroes," in Essays in *Moral Philosophy*, ed. Abraham I. Melden (Seattle and London, 1958), p. 214. For a related but significantly different view see also Henry Sidgwick, *The Methods of Ethics*, 7th ed. (London, 1907), pp. 220–21, 492–93.

beyond the capacities of the ordinary man, for otherwise there will be a general breakdown of compliance with the moral code. Crudely stated, this argument suggests that if we tell people that they ought to refrain from murder and give everything they do not really need to famine relief, they will do neither, whereas if we tell them that they ought to refrain from murder and that it is good to give to famine relief but not wrong not to do so, they will at least refrain from murder. The issue here is: Where should we draw the line between conduct that is required and conduct that is good although not required, so as to get the best possible result? This would seem to be an empirical question, although a very difficult one. One objection to the Sidgwick-Urmson line of argument is that it takes insufficient account of the effect that moral standards can have on the decisions we make. Given a society in which a wealthy man who gives 5 percent of his income to famine relief is regarded as most generous, it is not surprising that a proposal that we all ought to give away half our incomes will be thought to be absurdly unrealistic. In a society which held that no man should have more than enough while others have less than they need, such a pro-posal might seem narrow-minded. What it is possible for a man to do and what he is likely to do are both, I think, very greatly influenced by what people around him are doing and expecting him to do. In any case, the possibility that by spreading the idea that we ought to be doing very much more than we are to relieve famine we shall bring about a general breakdown of moral behavior seems remote. If the stakes are an end to widespread starvation, it is worth the risk. Finally, it should be emphasized that these considerations are relevant only to the issue of what we should require from others, and not to what we ourselves ought to do.

The second objection to my attack on the present distinction between duty and charity is one which has from time to time been made against utilitarianism. It follows from some forms of utilitarian theory that we all ought, morally, to be working full time to increase the balance of happi-ness over misery. The position I have taken here would not lead to this conclusion in all circumstances, for if there were no bad occurrences that we could prevent without sacrificing something of comparable moral importance, my argument would have no application. Given the present conditions in many parts of the world, however, it does follow from my argument that we ought, morally, to be working full time to relieve great suffering of the sort that occurs as a result of famine or other disasters. Of course, mitigating circumstances can be adduced—for instance, that if we wear ourselves out through overwork, we shall be less effective than we would otherwise have been. Nevertheless, when all considerations of this sort have been taken into account, the conclusion remains: We ought to be preventing as much suffering as we can without sacrificing something else of comparable moral importance. This conclusion is one which we may be reluctant to face. I cannot see, though, why it should be regarded as a criticism of the position for which I have argued, rather than a criticism of our ordinary standards of behavior. Since most people are self-interested to some degree, very few of us are likely to do everything that we ought to do. It would, however, hardly be honest to take this as evidence that it is not the case that we ought to do it.

It may still be thought that my conclusions are so wildly out of line with what everyone else thinks and has always thought that there must be something wrong with the argument somewhere. In order to show that my conclusions, while certainly contrary to contemporary Western moral standards, would not have seemed so extraordinary at other times and in other places, I would like to quote a passage from a writer not normally thought of as a way-out radical, Thomas Aquinas.

> Now, according to the natural order instituted by divine providence, material goods are provided for the satisfaction of human needs. Therefore the division and appropriation of property, which proceeds from human law, must not hinder the satisfaction of man's necessity from such goods. Equally, whatever a man has in superabundance is owed, of natural right, to the poor for their sustenance. So Ambrosius says, and it is also to be found in the *Decretum Gratiani:* "The bread which you withhold belongs to the hungry; the clothing you shut away, to the naked; and the money you bury in the earth is the redemption and freedom of the penniless."[4]

I now want to consider a number of points, more practical than philosophical, which are relevant to the application of the moral conclusion we have reached. These points challenge not the idea that we ought to be doing all we can to prevent starvation, but the idea that giving away a great deal of money is the best means to this end.

It is sometimes said that overseas aid should be a government responsibility, and that therefore one ought not to give to privately run charities. Giving privately, it is said, allows the government and the non-contributing members of society to escape their responsibilities.

This argument seems to assume that the more people there are who 25 give to privately organized famine relief funds, the less likely it is that the government will take over full responsibility for such aid. This assumption is unsupported, and does not strike me as at all plausible. The opposite view—that if no one gives voluntarily, a government will assume that its citizens are uninterested in famine relief and would not wish to be forced into giving aid—seems more plausible. In any case, unless there were a definite probability that by refusing to give one would be helping to bring about massive government assistance, people who do refuse to make voluntary contributions are refusing to prevent a certain amount of suffering without being able to point to any tangible

---

[4]*Summa Theologica*, II–II, Question 66, Article 7, in *Aquinas, Selected Political Writings*, ed. A. P. d'Entreves, trans. J. G. Dawson (Oxford, 1948), p. 171.

beneficial consequence of their refusal. So the onus of showing how their refusal will bring about government action is on those who refuse to give.

I do not, of course, want to dispute the contention that governments of affluent nations should be giving many times the amount of genuine, no-strings-attached aid that they are giving now. I agree, too, that giving privately is not enough, and that we ought to be campaigning actively for entirely new standards for both public and private contributions to famine relief. Indeed, I would sympathize with someone who thought that campaigning was more important than giving oneself, although I doubt whether preaching what one does not practice would be very effective. Unfortunately, for many people the idea that "it's the government's responsibility" is a reason for not giving which does not appear to entail any political action either.

Another, more serious reason for not giving to famine relief funds is that until there is effective population control, relieving famine merely postpones starvation. If we save the Bengal refugees now, others, perhaps the children of these refugees, will face starvation in a few years' time. In support of this, one may cite the now well-known facts about the population explosion and the relatively limited scope for expanded production.

This point, like the previous one, is an argument against relieving suffering that is happening now, because of a belief about what might happen in the future; it is unlike the previous point in that very good evidence can be adduced in support of this belief about the future. I will not go into the evidence here. I accept that the earth cannot support indefinitely a population rising at the present rate. This certainly poses a problem for anyone who thinks it important to prevent famine. Again, however, one could accept the argument without drawing the conclusion that it absolves one from any obligation to do anything to prevent famine. The conclusion that should be drawn is that the best means of preventing famine, in the long run, is population control. It would then follow from the position reached earlier that one ought to be doing all one can to promote population control (unless one held that all forms of population control were wrong in themselves, or would have significantly bad consequences). Since there are organizations working specifically for population control, one would then support them rather than more orthodox methods of preventing famine.

A third point raised by the conclusion reached earlier relates to the question of just how much we all ought to be giving away. One possibility, which has already been mentioned, is that we ought to give until we reach the level of marginal utility—that is, the level at which, by giving more, I would cause as much suffering to myself or my dependents as I would relieve by my gift. This would mean, of course, that one would reduce oneself to very near the material circumstances of a Bengali refugee. It will be recalled that earlier I put forward both a strong and a moderate version of the principle of preventing bad occurrences. The strong version, which required us to prevent bad things from happening unless in doing so we would be sacrificing something of comparable moral significance, does seem to require reducing ourselves to the level of marginal utility. I should also say that the strong version seems to me to be the correct one. I proposed the more moderate version—that we should prevent bad occurrences unless, to do so, we had to sacrifice something morally significant—only in order to show that even on this surely undeniable principle a great change in our way of life is required. On the more moderate principle, it may not follow that we ought to reduce ourselves to the level of marginal utility, for one might hold that to reduce oneself and one's family to this level is to cause something significantly bad to happen. Whether this is so I shall not discuss, since, as I have said, I can see no good reason for holding the moderate version of the principle rather than the strong version. Even if we accepted the principle only in its moderate form, however, it should be clear that we would have to give away enough to ensure that the consumer society, dependent as it is on people spending on trivia rather than giving to famine relief, would slow down and perhaps disappear entirely. There are several reasons why this would be desirable in itself. The value and necessity of economic growth are now being questioned not only by conservationists, but by economists as well.[5] There is no doubt, too, that the consumer society has had a distorting effect on the goals and purposes of its members. Yet looking at the matter purely from the point of view of overseas aid, there must be a limit to the extent to which we should deliberately slow down our economy; for it might be the case that if we gave away, say, 40 percent of our Gross National Product, we would slow down the economy so much that in absolute terms we would be giving less than if we gave 25 percent of the much larger GNP that we would have if we limited our contribution to this smaller percentage.

I mention this only as an indication of the sort of factor that one would have to take into account in working out an ideal. Since Western societies generally consider 1 percent of the GNP an acceptable level for overseas aid, the matter is entirely academic. Nor does it affect the question of how much an individual should give in a society in which very few are giving substantial amounts.

It is sometimes said, though less often now than it used to be, that philosophers have no special role to play in public affairs, since most public issues depend primarily on an assessment of facts. On questions of fact, it is said, philosophers as such have no special expertise, and so it has been possible to engage in philosophy without committing oneself to any position on major public issues. No doubt there are some issues of

[5]See, for instance, John Kenneth Galbraith, *The New Industrial State* (Boston, 1967); and E. J. Mishan, *The Costs of Economic Growth* (London, 1967).

social policy and foreign policy about which it can truly be said that a really expert assessment of the facts is required before taking sides or acting, but the issue of famine is surely not one of these. The facts about the existence of suffering are beyond dispute. Nor, I think, is it disputed that we can do something about it, either through orthodox methods of famine relief or through population control or both. This is therefore an issue on which philosophers are competent to take a position. The issue is one which faces everyone who has more money than he needs to support himself and his dependents, or who is in a position to take some sort of political action. These categories must include practically every teacher and student of philosophy in the universities of the Western world. If philosophy is to deal with matters that are relevant to both teachers and students, this is an issue that philosophers should discuss.

Discussion, though, is not enough. What is the point of relating philosophy to public (and personal) affairs if we do not take our conclusions seriously? In this instance, taking our conclusion seriously means acting upon it. The philosopher will not find it any easier than anyone else to alter his attitudes and way of life to the extent that, if I am right, is involved in doing everything that we ought to be doing. At the very least, though, one can make a start. The philosopher who does so will have to sacrifice some of the benefits of the consumer society, but he can find compensation in the satisfaction of a way of life in which theory and practice, if not yet in harmony, are at least coming together.

TOPICS FOR CRITICAL THINKING AND WRITING

1. How does Singer tell when one thing we might do is more or less "morally significant" (para. 6) than something else we might do? Do you agree with him on this point?

2. Explain whether you agree with Singer that, morally speaking, there is no difference between my coming to the aid of someone I know and love (say, my child or my parent) and coming to the aid of a stranger thousands of miles away, someone "whose name I shall never know" (para. 7)—perhaps someone whom I would thoroughly dislike if I did know him or her?

3. What is the view that "numbers lessen obligation" (para. 9), and why does Singer refer to it as an "absurdity"?

4. What does Singer mean by the affluent giving money or other resources to the needy up to the point or level of "marginal utility" (paras. 11 and 29)?

5. What does Singer mean by "the traditional distinction between duty and charity" (para. 14)? Why does he think this distinction collapses? Does he in fact contradict himself on this point in paragraph 15?

6. Suppose that a gift of large-scale resources by the affluent to the currently starving in some nation reduces what can be given to their successors, the

next generation, when the next famine hits that nation (see paras. 27 and 28). Would Singer favor giving those resources to the currently starving or to their descendants?

7. Singer considers two objections to his position (paras. 16–21). What are they, and how does he respond to them? In an essay of 1,000 words, state concisely those objections, his replies, and your evaluation.

8. Singer refers to "the principle which I advanced earlier" (para. 17). State in a sentence what that principle is. (Hint: A version is found in para. 21.)

9. Suppose someone were to object to Singer that the plight of starving people in Africa, Asia, or elsewhere in the world is to a large extent their own fault, a result of uncontrolled overpopulation, leading to their destruction of their physical habitat and aggravated by corrupt self-government. How might Singer reply?

10. What is Singer's answer to the question of "how much we all ought to be giving away" (para. 29)?

Garrett Hardin

Garrett Hardin (1915–2003) was Emeritus Professor of Human Ecology at the University of California, Santa Barbara. Born in Dallas, Texas, he received his Ph.D. in biology from Stanford in 1941 and is the author of several books, including The Limits of Altruism *(1977),* Managing the Commons *(1977),* Filters Against Folly *(1988), and* The Ostrich Factor *(1998). The essay reprinted here originally appeared in* Psychology Today *(September 1974).*

Lifeboat Ethics:
The Case against Helping the Poor

Environmentalists use the metaphor of the earth as a "spaceship" in trying to persuade countries, industries, and people to stop wasting and polluting our natural resources. Since we all share life on this planet, they argue, no single person or institution has the right to destroy, waste, or use more than a fair share of its resources.

But does everyone on earth have an equal right to an equal share of its resources? The spaceship metaphor can be dangerous when used by misguided idealists to justify suicidal policies for sharing our resources through uncontrolled immigration and foreign aid. In their enthusiastic but unrealistic generosity, they confuse the ethics of a spaceship with those of a lifeboat.

A true spaceship would have to be under the control of a captain, since no ship could possibly survive if its course were determined by committee. Spaceship Earth certainly has no captain; the United Nations is merely a toothless tiger, with little power to enforce any policy upon its bickering members.

If we divide the world crudely into rich nations and poor nations, two thirds of them are desperately poor, and only one third comparatively rich, with the United States the wealthiest of all. Metaphorically each nation can be seen as a lifeboat full of comparatively rich people. In the ocean outside each lifeboat swim the poor of the world, who would like to get in, or at least to share some of the wealth. What should the lifeboat passengers do?

First, we must recognize the limited capacity of any lifeboat. For 5 example, a nation's land has a limited capacity to support a population and as the current energy crisis has shown us, in some ways we have already exceeded the carrying capacity of our land.

ADRIFT IN A MORAL SEA

So here we sit, say fifty people in our lifeboat. To be generous, let us assume it has room for ten more, making a total capacity of sixty. Suppose the fifty of us in the lifeboat see 100 others swimming in the water outside, begging for admission to our boat or for handouts. We have several options: We may be tempted to try to live by the Christian ideal of being "our brother's keeper," or by the Marxist ideal of "to each according to his needs." Since the needs of all in the water are the same, and since they can all be seen as "our brothers," we could take them all into our boat, making a total of 150 in a boat designed for sixty. The boat swamps, everyone drowns. Complete justice, complete catastrophe.

Since the boat has an unused excess capacity of ten more passengers, we could admit just ten more to it. But which ten do we let in? How do we choose? Do we pick the best ten, the neediest ten, "first come, first served"? And what do we say to the ninety we exclude? If we do let an extra ten into our lifeboat, we will have lost our "safety factor," an engineering principle of critical importance. For example, if we don't leave room for excess capacity as a safety factor in our country's agriculture, a new plant disease or a bad change in the weather could have disastrous consequences.

Suppose we decide to preserve our small safety factor and admit no more to the lifeboat. Our survival is then possible, although we shall have to be constantly on guard against boarding parties.

While this last solution clearly offers the only means of our survival, it is morally abhorrent to many people. Some say they feel guilty about their good luck. My reply is simple: "Get out and yield your place to others." This may solve the problem of the guilt-ridden person's conscience, but it does not change the ethics of the lifeboat. The needy person to whom the guilt-ridden person yields his place will not himself feel guilty about his good luck. If he did, he would not climb aboard. The net result of conscience-stricken people giving up their unjustly held seats is the elimination of that sort of conscience from the lifeboat.

This is the basic metaphor within which we must work out our 10
solutions. Let us now enrich the image, step by step, with substantive
additions from the real world, a world that must solve real and pressing
problems of overpopulation and hunger.

The harsh ethics of the lifeboat become even harsher when we
consider the reproductive differences between the rich nations and the
poor nations. The people inside the lifeboats are doubling in numbers every eighty-seven years; those swimming around outside are
doubling, on the average, every thirty-five years, more than twice as
fast as the rich. And since the world's resources are dwindling, the difference in prosperity between the rich and the poor can only increase.

As of 1973, the United States had a population of 210 million people,
who were increasing by 0.8 percent per year. Outside our lifeboat, let us
imagine another 210 million people (say the combined populations of
Colombia, Ecuador, Venezuela, Morocco, Pakistan, Thailand, and the
Philippines), who are increasing at a rate of 3.3 percent year. Put differently, the doubling time for this aggregate population is twenty-one
years, compared to eighty-seven years for the United States.

MULTIPLYING THE RICH AND THE POOR

Now suppose the United States agreed to pool its resources with
those seven countries, with everyone receiving an equal share. Initially
the ratio of Americans to non-Americans in this model would be one-
to-one. But consider what the ratio would be after eighty-seven years,
by which time the Americans would have doubled to a population of
420 million. By then, doubling every twenty-one years, the other
group would have swollen to 354 billion. Each American would have
to share the available resource with more than eight people.

But, one could argue, this discussion assumes that current population trends will continue, and they may not. Quite so. Most likely the
rate of population increase will decline much faster in the United
States than it will in the other countries, and there does not seem to be
much we can do about it. In sharing with "each according to his
needs," we must recognize that needs are determined by population
size, which is determined by the rate of reproduction, which at present
is regarded as a sovereign right of every nation, poor or not. This being
so, the philanthropic load created by the sharing ethic of the spaceship
can only increase.

THE TRAGEDY OF THE COMMONS

The fundamental error of spaceship ethics, and the sharing it 15
requires, is that it leads to what I call "the tragedy of the commons."
Under a system of private property, the men who own property recognize
their responsibility to care for it, for if they don't they will eventually

suffer. A farmer, for instance, will allow no more cattle in a pasture than its carrying capacity justifies. If he overloads it, erosion sets in, weeds take over, and he loses the use of the pasture.

If a pasture becomes a commons open to all, the right of each to use it may not be matched by a corresponding responsibility to protect it. Asking everyone to use it with discretion will hardly do, for the considerate herdsman who refrains from overloading the commons suffers more than a selfish one who says his needs are greater. If everyone would restrain himself, all would be well; but it takes only one less than everyone to ruin a system of voluntary restraint. In a crowded world of less than perfect human beings, mutual ruin is inevitable if there are no controls. This is the tragedy of the commons.

One of the major tasks of education today should be the creation of such an acute awareness of the dangers of the commons that people will recognize its many varieties. For example, the air and water have become polluted because they are treated as commons. Further growth in the population or per-capita conversion of natural resources into pollutants will only make the problem worse. The same holds true for the fish of the oceans. Fishing fleets have nearly disappeared in many parts of the world, technological improvements in the art of fishing are hastening the day of complete ruin. Only the replacement of the system of the commons with a responsible system of control will save the land, air, water, and oceanic fisheries.

THE WORLD FOOD BANK

In recent years there has been a push to create a new commons called a World Food Bank, an international depository of food reserves to which nations would contribute according to their abilities and from which they would draw according to their needs. This humanitarian proposal has received support from many liberal international groups, and from such prominent citizens as Margaret Mead, U.N. Secretary General Kurt Waldheim, and Senators Edward Kennedy and George McGovern.

A world food bank appeals powerfully to our humanitarian impulses. But before we rush ahead with such a plan, let us recognize where the greatest political push comes from, lest we be disillusioned later. Our experience with the "Food for Peace program," or Public Law 480, gives us the answer. This program moved billions of dollars' worth of U.S. surplus grain to food-short, population-long countries during the past two decades. But when PL 480 first became law, a headline in the business magazine *Forbes* revealed the real power behind it: "Feeding the World's Hungry Millions: How It Will Mean Billions for U.S. Business."

And indeed it did. In the years 1960 to 1970, U.S. taxpayers spent a total of $7.9 billion on the Food for Peace program. Between 1948 and 1970, they also paid an additional $50 billion for other economic-aid 20 programs, some of which went for food and food-producing machinery and technology. Though all U.S. taxpayers were forced to contribute to the cost of PL 480, certain special interest groups gained handsomely under the program. Farmers did not have to contribute the grain; the government, or rather the taxpayers, bought it from them at full market prices. The increased demand raised prices of farm products generally. The manufacturers of farm machinery, fertilizers, and pesticides benefited by the farmers' extra efforts to grow more food. Grain elevators profited from storing the surplus until it could be shipped. Railroads made money hauling it to ports, and shipping lines profited from carrying it overseas. The implementation of PL 480 required the creation of a vast government bureaucracy, which then acquired its own vested interest in continuing the program regardless of its merits.

EXTRACTING DOLLARS

Those who proposed and defended the Food for Peace program in public rarely mentioned its importance to any of these special interests. The public emphasis was always on its humanitarian effects. The combination of silent selfish interests and highly vocal humanitarian apologists made a powerful and successful lobby for extracting money from taxpayers. We can expect the same lobby to push now for the creation of a World Food Bank.

However great the potential benefit to selfish interests, it should not be a decisive argument against a truly humanitarian program. We must ask if such a program would actually do more good than harm, not only momentarily but also in the long run. Those who propose the food bank usually refer to a current "emergency" or "crisis" in terms of world food supply. But what is an emergency? Although they may be infrequent and sudden, everyone knows that emergencies will occur from time to time. A well-run family, company, organization, or country prepares for the likelihood of accidents and emergencies. It expects them, it budgets for them, it saves for them.

LEARNING THE HARD WAY

What happens if some organizations or countries budget for accidents and others do not? If each country is solely responsible for its own well-being, poorly managed ones will suffer. But they can learn from experience. They may mend their ways, and learn to budget for infrequent but certain emergencies. For example, the weather varies from year to year, and periodic crop failures are certain. A wise and competent government saves out of the production of the good years in anticipation of bad years to come. Joseph taught this policy to Pharaoh in Egypt more than 2,000 years ago. Yet the great majority of the governments in the world today do not follow such a policy. They lack either the wisdom or the competence, or both. Should those nations that do manage to put something aside be forced to come to the rescue each time an emergency occurs among the poor nations?

"But it isn't their fault!" some kindhearted liberals argue. "How can we blame the poor people who are caught in an emergency? Why must they suffer for the sins of their governments?" The concept of blame is simply not relevant here. The real question is, what are the operational consequences of establishing a world food bank? If it is open to every country every time a need develops, slovenly rulers will not be motivated to take Joseph's advice. Someone will always come to their aid. Some countries will deposit food in the world food bank, and others will withdraw it. There will be almost no overlap. As a result of such solutions to food shortage emergencies, the poor countries will not learn to mend their ways, and will suffer progressively greater emergencies as their populations grow.

POPULATION CONTROL THE CRUDE WAY

On the average, poor countries undergo a 2.5 percent increase in 25 population each year; rich countries, about 0.8 percent. Only rich countries have anything in the way of food reserves set aside, and even they do not have as much as they should. Poor countries have none. If poor countries received no food from the outside, the rate of their population growth would be periodically checked by crop failures and famines. But if they can always draw on a world food bank in time of need, their populations can continue to grow unchecked, and so will their "need" for aid. In the short run, a world food bank may diminish that need, but in the long run it actually increases the need without limit.

Without some system of worldwide food sharing, the proportion of people in the rich and poor nations might eventually stabilize. The overpopulated poor countries would decrease in numbers, while the rich countries that had room for more people would increase. But with a well-meaning system of sharing, such as a world food bank, the growth differential between the rich and the poor countries will not only persist, it will increase. Because of the higher rate of population growth in the poor countries of the world, 88 percent of today's children are born poor, and only 12 percent rich. Year by year the ratio becomes worse, as the fast-reproducing poor outnumber the slow-reproducing rich.

A world food bank is thus a commons in disguise. People will have more motivation to draw from it than to add to any common store. The less provident and less able will multiply at the expense of the abler and more provident, bringing eventual ruin upon all who share in the commons. Besides, any system of "sharing" that amounts to foreign aid from the rich nations to the poor nations will carry the taint of charity, which will contribute little to the world peace so devoutly desired by those who support the idea of a world food bank.

As past U.S. foreign-aid programs have amply and depressingly demonstrated, international charity frequently inspires mistrust and antagonism rather than gratitude on the part of the recipient nation.

CHINESE FISH AND MIRACLE RICE

The modern approach to foreign aid stresses the export of technology and advice, rather than money and food. As an ancient Chinese proverb goes: "Give a man a fish and he will eat for a day; teach him how to fish and he will eat for the rest of his days." Acting on this advice, the Rockefeller and Ford foundations have financed a number of programs for improving agriculture in the hungry nations. Known as the "Green Revolution," these programs have led to the development of "miracle rice" and "miracle wheat," new strains that offer bigger harvests and greater resistance to crop damage. Norman Borlaug, the Nobel Prize–winning agronomist who, supported by the Rockefeller Foundation, developed "miracle wheat," is one of the most prominent advocates of a world food bank.

Whether or not the Green Revolution can increase food production   30 as much as its champions claim is a debatable but possibly irrelevant point. Those who support this well-intended humanitarian effort should first consider some of the fundamentals of human ecology. Ironically, one man who did was the late Alan Gregg, a vice president of the Rockefeller Foundation. Two decades ago he expressed strong doubts about the wisdom of such attempts to increase food production. He likened the growth and spread of humanity over the surface of the earth to the spread of cancer in the human body, remarking that "cancerous growths demand food; but, as far as I know, they have never been cured by getting it."

OVERLOADING THE ENVIRONMENT

Every human born constitutes a draft on all aspects of the environment: food, air, water, forests, beaches, wildlife, scenery, and solitude. Food can, perhaps, be significantly increased to meet a growing demand. But what about clean beaches, unspoiled forests, and solitude? If we satisfy a growing population's need for food, we necessarily decrease its per-capita supply of the other resources needed by men.

India, for example, now has a population of 600 million, which increases by 15 million each year. This population already puts a huge load on a relatively impoverished environment. The country's forests are now only a small fraction of what they were three centuries ago, and floods and erosion continually destroy the insufficient farmland that remains. Every one of the 15 million new lives added to India's population puts an additional burden on the environment, and increases the economic and social costs of crowding. However humanitarian our intent, every Indian life saved through medical or nutritional assistance from abroad diminishes the quality of life for those who remain, and for subsequent generations. If rich countries make it possible, through foreign aid, for 600 million Indians to swell to 1.2 billion in a mere twenty-eight years, as their current growth rate threatens, will future generations of Indians thank us for hastening the destruction of their environment? Will our good intentions be sufficient excuse for the consequences of our actions?

My final example of a commons in action is one for which the public has the least desire for rational discussion — immigration. Anyone who publicly questions the wisdom of current U.S. immigration policy is promptly charged with bigotry, prejudice, ethnocentrism, chauvinism, isolationism, or selfishness. Rather than encounter such accusations, one would rather talk about other matters, leaving immigration policy to wallow in the crosscurrents of special interests that take no account of the good of the whole, or the interest of posterity.

Perhaps we still feel guilty about things we said in the past. Two generations ago the popular press frequently referred to Dagos, Wops, Polacks, Chinks, and Krauts, in articles about how America was being "overrun" by foreigners of supposedly inferior genetic stock. But because the implied inferiority of foreigners was used then as justification for keeping them out, people now assume that restrictive policies could only be based on such misguided notions. There are no other grounds.

A NATION OF IMMIGRANTS

Just consider the numbers involved. Our government acknowledges   35
a net inflow of 400,000 immigrants a year. While we have no hard data on the extent of illegal entries, educated guesses put the figure at about 600,000 a year. Since the natural increase (excess of births over deaths) of the resident population now runs about 1.7 million per year, the yearly gain from immigration amounts to at least 19 percent of the total annual increase, and may be as much as 37 percent if we include the estimate for illegal immigrants. Considering the growing use of birth-control devices, the potential effect of educational campaigns by such organizations as Planned Parenthood Federation of America and Zero Population Growth, and the influence of inflation and the housing shortage, the fertility rate of American women may decline so much that immigration could account for all the yearly increase in population. Should we not at least ask if that is what we want?

For the sake of those who worry about whether the "quality" of the average immigrant compares favorably with the quality of the average resident, let us assume that immigrants and native-born citizens are of exactly equal quality, however one defines that term. We will focus here only on quantity; and since our conclusions will depend on nothing else, all charges of bigotry and chauvinism become irrelevant.

IMMIGRATION VS. FOOD SUPPLY

World food banks *move food to the people,* hastening the exhaustion of
the environment of the poor countries. Unrestricted immigration, on the
other hand, *moves people to the food,* thus speeding up the destruction of
the environment of the rich countries. We can easily understand why
poor people should want to make this latter transfer, but why should
rich hosts encourage it?

As in the case of foreign-aid programs, immigration receives support
from selfish interests and humanitarian impulses. The primary selfish
interest in unimpeded immigration is the desire of employers for cheap
labor, particularly in industries and trades that offer degrading work. In
the past, one wave of foreigners after another was brought into the
United States to work at wretched jobs for wretched wages. In recent
years, the Cubans, Puerto Ricans, and Mexicans have had this dubious
honor. The interests of the employers of cheap labor mesh well with the
guilty silence of the country's liberal intelligentsia. White Anglo-Saxon
Protestants are particularly reluctant to call for a closing of the doors to
immigration for fear of being called bigots.

But not all countries have such reluctant leadership. Most educated
Hawaiians, for example, are keenly aware of the limits of their environment, particularly in terms of population growth. There is only so much
room on the islands, and the islanders know it. To Hawaiians, immigrants from the other forty-nine states present as great a threat as those
from other nations. At a recent meeting of Hawaiian government officials in Honolulu, I had the ironic delight of hearing a speaker, who like
most of his audience was of Japanese ancestry, ask how the country
might practically and constitutionally close its doors to further immigration. One member of the audience countered: "How can we shut the
doors now? We have many friends and relatives in Japan that we'd like
to bring here some day so that they can enjoy Hawaii too." The Japanese-
American speaker smiled sympathetically and answered: "Yes, but we
have children now, and someday we'll have grandchildren too. We can
bring more people here from Japan only by giving away some of the
land that we hope to pass on to our grandchildren some day. What right
do we have to do that?"

At this point, I can hear U.S. liberals asking: "How can you justify   40
slamming the door once you're inside? You say that immigrants should
be kept out. But aren't we all immigrants, or the descendants of immigrants? If we insist on staying, must we not admit all others?" Our craving for intellectual order leads us to seek and prefer symmetrical rules
and morals: a single rule for me and everybody else; the same rule yesterday, today, and tomorrow. Justice, we feel, should not change with
time and place.

We Americans of non-Indian ancestry can look upon ourselves as
the descendants of thieves who are guilty morally, if not legally, of stealing

this land from its Indian owners. Should we then give back the land to the now living American descendants of those Indians? However morally or logically sound this proposal may be, I, for one, am unwilling to live by it and I know no one else who is. Besides, the logical consequence would be absurd. Suppose that, intoxicated with a sense of pure justice, we should decide to turn our land over to the Indians. Since all our wealth has also been derived from the land, wouldn't we be morally obliged to give that back to the Indians too?

PURE JUSTICE VS. REALITY

Clearly, the concept of pure justice produces an infinite regression to absurdity. Centuries ago, wise men invented statutes of limitations to justify the rejection of such pure justice, in the interest of preventing continual disorder. The law zealously defends property rights, but only relatively recent property rights. Drawing a line after an arbitrary time has elapsed may be unjust, but the alternatives are worse.

We are all descendants of thieves, and the world's resources are inequitably distributed. But we must begin the journey to tomorrow from the point where we are today. We cannot remake the past. We cannot safely divide the wealth equitably among all peoples so long as people reproduce at different rates. To do so would guarantee that our grandchildren, and everyone else's grandchildren, would have only a ruined world to inhabit.

To be generous with one's own possessions is quite different from being generous with those of posterity. We should call this point to the attention of those who, from a commendable love of justice and equality, would institute a system of the commons, either in the form of a world food bank, or of unrestricted immigration. We must convince them if we wish to save at least some parts of the world from environmental ruin.

Without a true world government to control reproduction and the 45 use of available resources, the sharing ethic of the spaceship is impossible. For the foreseeable future, our survival demands that we govern our actions by the ethics of a lifeboat, harsh though they may be. Posterity will be satisfied with nothing less.

TOPICS FOR CRITICAL THINKING AND WRITING

1. Hardin says that "in some ways we have already exceeded the carrying capacity of our land" (para. 5). Does he tell us later what some of those ways are? Can you think of others?

2. The central analogy on which Hardin's argument rests is that human life on planet Earth is like living in an overcrowded lifeboat. Evaluate this analogy.

3. What does Hardin mean by "ethics" in the title of his essay? What, if any, ethical principle does Hardin believe should guide our conduct in lifeboat Earth?

4. What is "the tragedy" and what is "the commons" in what Hardin calls "the tragedy of the commons" (paras. 15–17)?

5. What does Hardin mean by "a truly humanitarian program" (para. 22) to alleviate future problems of hunger and starvation? Why does he think a World Food Bank would aggravate, rather than alleviate, the problem?

6. How do you react to the analogy that compares the growth of the human race over the earth to "the spread of cancer in the human body" (para. 30)?

7. Hardin's view of the relationship between population growth and available resources can be described (though he doesn't) as a zero-sum game. Do you agree with such a description? Why, or why not?

8. Hardin refers to an organization named Zero Population Growth (para. 35). In your public or college library find out about this organization, and then write a 250-word essay describing its origin and aims.

9. Hardin offers a reductio ad absurdum argument (see pp. 414–23) against large-scale restitution by the current nonnative American population to the surviving native Americans (para. 41). Evaluate this argument in an essay of 250 words.

10. Hardin refers frequently (for example, para. 42) and unsympathetically to what he calls "pure justice." To what principle, exactly, is he referring by this phrase? Would you agree that this principle is, indeed, well described as "pure justice"? Why, or why not?

11. Suppose someone, after reading Hardin's essay, described it as nothing more than selfishness on a national scale. Would Hardin agree? Would he consider this a serious criticism of his analysis and proposals?

Randy Cohen

Since 1999, the New York Times Magazine *has been publishing a column called "The Ethicist," in which Randy Cohen or occasionally a guest writer responds to a reader's letter that poses an ethical question. Some of these letters and responses have been collected in a book called* The Good, the Bad, and the Difference *(2002). The letters have posed such questions as these:*

1. *I am a lesbian who will become a freshman college student in the autumn. Should I inform my roommates?*
2. *On the subway I saw a mother slap her child for crying. Should I have spoken up?*
3. *As a police officer, I handle phone inquiries about persons who have just been arrested. When a wife asks about her husband, who has been arrested for soliciting prostitution, can I withhold the truth?*

Following, we give three letters on other topics, with Cohen's responses.

Three Letters (to an Ethicist)

DYING WISH

Recently at the hospice where I work, the family of an African-American patient requested an African-American nursing assistant rather than the Latino we had planned to assign. I feel uncomfortable when a white patient requests a white care provider, but this seems different. After all, the requests of female patients for female nursing assistants seem reasonable on the basis of modesty. What should I do here?—Anonymous

Your proclivity to accede to any request of a dying patient does you credit. Yet, though your intentions are benign, you should not assign jobs simply on the basis of race. If the former segregationist Strom Thurmond demanded a white nurse's aide, few hospices would comply. And while the victims of racism confront different circumstances than its beneficiaries do, that is not sufficient reason to establish a race-based jobs policy. To do so would be to discriminate against members of your staff, and that rejected Latino aide would have grounds to complain if you did.

You could honor a request for a particular aide: I want Rosa. She's capable and kind, and I love beating her at gin. And going further, a hospice can consider race as one of many factors—age, experience, geographic background, temperament, sense of humor—when deciding which aide would be a great match for a particular patient. Indeed, given America's history, how could race not be a factor in such decisions? This is akin to what some university admissions officers do, treating race as one of many factors that inform them about prospective students. Thus, after considering all criteria, you may well decide to grant the request of your African-American patient.

As for sex and health care, here too we meet some demands but not others. Most of us would consent to a woman's request for a female gynecologist, deferring to her sense of sexual modesty. But few would honor her request for a female heart surgeon. And while a nurse's aide does perform intimate tasks—bathing a patient, for example—the analogy of race and sex has only limited application here, given the essential similarity of all human bodies.

Follow up: Anonymous later learned that an episode in the patient's past had instilled in her a fear of white faces. This new information makes assigning her an African-American aide not racism but compassion, an honorable response to her individual circumstances.

SUFFER THE LITTLE CHILDREN

I am a university researcher using magnetic resonance imaging to study how children learn to speak and read. All such work is monitored by a review board to

assess its safety. Our board has given me permission to study children as young as 7. There is as yet no evidence at all that M.R.I. is harmful, but I worry about later discoveries, and so I may not let my own 7-year-old participate. Can I run other children in this study if I wouldn't run my own?—Anonymous

Different people accept different levels of risk. That this study entails more than you find palatable does not mean others will concur. Some let their kids drive dirt bikes; others don't. (Although few would allow their 7-year-old to drive a motorcycle through an M.R.I.) Forbidding your child to be a research subject does not make you a hypocrite. Your duty as a researcher is to be a responsible scientist, not a model father.

It is your obligation to make sure that potential participants understand the current risks as well as the dangers that might be confirmed in the future—not just statistical possibilities, but information meaningful to a lay person. You must be alert to the deference we civilians sometimes show doctors and scientists, which inhibits us from asking pertinent questions. And your volunteers must be truly that: you must avoid offering, for example, the sort of payments to participants that exploit the desperation of the financially hard pressed.

After that, it is up to other parents to decide. If anyone asks if you'd allow your child to participate, you must of course answer calmly and honestly. That is, you should not shriek, unprompted: "I'd never let my kid within 50 feet of an M.R.I. Those things could blow sky high!" By appealing to parents' emotions rather than to their reasoned judgment, by manipulating their regard for you as an authority figure, you would undermine not only this valuable research but your respect for science itself.

COLLEGE PARKING

At the public university where I used to work, it was first-arrive, first-park. (The later you came to work, the more likely you had to park in the satellite lot and ride the shuttle.) Recently, just before I left, a number of closer spots were reserved for particular deans and vice presidents. I then had fewer spots to choose from, even when I arrived before them. Is it ethical for them to get preferred parking?—Andrew Feldman, Long Island

Sure, rank has its privileges. I've even heard of cases in which some high-ranking people make more money than we hoi polloi—and talk about scarce resources.

But while this policy is not unethical, it is unwise. To elevate administrators to a privileged class is contrary to the American ideal of an egalitarian society. Why bestow parking perks on a dean rather than a math professor or a grad student or, for that matter, a cafeteria worker? What's more—or perhaps less—it will not improve a dean's ability to do his job if his experience of campus life has little in common with the people who work and study there.

However, if your university is eager to create a petty aristocracy, it could instead force students with lower than a C average to carry administrators around the campus in sedan chairs, providing both an incentive to excel academically and a public display of the university's values.

Topics for Critical Thinking and Writing

The following letters were *not* sent to Randy Cohen, but the problems they raise are real. Choose one letter, and write your response.

1. Assume that *you* hold Cohen's job. Write a response to one letter. Or, alternatively, write a response to one of Cohen's letters.

2. Following my instructor's advice, I submitted the draft of an essay to my roommate for peer review. She corrected numerous spelling errors, pointed out some wordy sentences, and gave me some ideas that I think are really better than my own. Is it enough if in a note I merely thank her for "reading the draft and making suggestions"?

3. In my high school course in biology, we are required to dissect frogs. I think this is cruel and pointless. Whatever we learn about a frog's anatomy can be learned from a book. My teacher says that I must dissect the frog.

4. My high school requires that we dissect frogs. I am a vegetarian because I believe in reverence for life, but the teacher says that I cannot be exempted. What should I do?

5. My high school requires that we dissect frogs. I am a Buddhist, and we Buddhists have a reverence for all living creatures. I do not even swat mosquitos. My teacher says that I must do the work to pass the course. What should I do?

6. My friend was a sperm donor in the days when donors were assured of anonymity. I happen to know the young woman—she is sixteen—who was born from this sperm, and she now is deeply concerned with finding her biological father. Should I tell the father? Should I tell the daughter? Should I at least let the mother know that I know? Or should I keep my mouth shut?

11

A Lawyer's View:
Steps toward Civic Literacy

The law is reason free from passion.

— ARISTOTLE

Hard cases make bad law.

— PROVERBIAL SAYING

We are in bondage to the law so that we might be free.

— CICERO

The business of the law is to make sense of the confusion of what we call human life — to reduce it to order but at the same time to give it possibility, scope, even dignity.

— ARCHIBALD MACLEISH

When John Adams in 1774 said that ours is "a government of law, and not of men," he meant that much of public conduct is regulated, rightly, by principles of law that by general agreement ought to be enforced and that can be altered only by our duly elected representatives, whose power is derived from our consent. In a democracy, laws, not individuals (for instance, kings or tyrants), govern. Adams and other early Americans rejected the view attributed to Louis XIV, "I am the state" (*L'état c'est moi*).

But what exactly the law in a given situation is often causes hot debate (as we know from watching the TV news). Whether we are ever personally called on to decide the law — as are legislators, judges, jurors, or lawyers — all of us find our daily lives constantly affected by the law. It is fitting, therefore, and even necessary that we develop **civic literacy,** the ability to understand the principles by which our government and its courts operate so that we can act appropriately. (In today's global community, our civic literacy must also include a knowledge of the ways our and others' governments function.)

428

From the time of Plato's *Apology*, reporting Socrates' trial before the Athenian assembly in 399 B.C. on charges of corrupting the young and preaching false gods, courtroom argument has been a staple of dramatic verbal cut-and-thrust. (Think of popular television shows such as *Boston Legal* and *Law and Order*.) Probably no profession prides itself more on the ability of its members to argue than does the legal profession. The uninitiated are easily intimidated by the skill with which a lawyer can marshal relevant considerations to support a client's interests. But legal argument is, after all, *argument*, and so its main features are those already discussed in Chapter 3 (such as definition, assumption, premise, deduction, conclusion, evidence, validity). What is distinctive about legal reasoning is fairly straightforward in all but the most unusual cases.

CIVIL AND CRIMINAL CASES

Legal cases are divided into civil and criminal. In a *civil* case one party (the plaintiff) brings suit against another party (the defendant), claiming that he or she has suffered some wrong at the hands of the defendant and deserves some remedy (for instance, due to a dispute over a property boundary or over fault in a multicar accident). The judge or jury decides for or against the plaintiff based on the evidence and the relevant law. All crimes are wrongs, but not all wrongs are crimes. For instance, an automobile accident that involves negligence on the part of one of the drivers and results in harm to another is surely a wrong, but the driver responsible for the accident, even if found guilty, does not face a prison sentence (that could happen only if the accident were in fact the result of driving with gross recklessness or driving while intoxicated or were no "accident" at all). Why? Because the harm inflicted was not criminal; that is, it was not intentional, deliberate, malicious, or premeditated.

Criminal cases involve someone (the defendant) charged either with a *felony* (a serious crime like assault or battery) or with a *misdemeanor* (a less serious crime). In criminal cases the state, through its prosecutor, seeks to convict the defendant as charged; the defendant, through his or her attorney, seeks an acquittal or, at worst, a conviction on a lesser charge (manslaughter instead of murder) and a milder punishment. The decision to convict or acquit on the basis of the facts submitted in evidence and the relevant law is the duty of the jury (or the judge, if there is no jury). The prosecutor and defense lawyer present what they believe are the relevant facts. Defining the relevant law is the responsibility of the trial judge. Public interest in criminal cases is often high, especially when the crime is particularly heinous. (Think of the 1995 trial of O. J. Simpson, charged with the murder of his wife and one of her friends, and the 1997 trial of Timothy McVeigh for the Oklahoma City federal building bombing.)

As you begin reading a legal case, therefore, you will want to be sure you can answer this question:

- Is the court trying to decide whether someone accused of a crime is guilty as charged, or is the court trying to resolve some non-criminal (civil) dispute?

TRIAL AND APPEAL

Most cases (civil or criminal) never go to *trial* at all. Most civil cases are settled out of court, and most criminal cases are settled with a plea bargain in which the prosecutor and the defense attorney persuade the judge to accept the defendant's guilty plea in exchange for a less severe sentence. Of the cases that are settled by trial, the losing party usually does not try to reopen, or *appeal*, the case. If, however, the losing party believes that he or she should have won, the case may be appealed for review by a higher appellate court (provided, of course, the loser can finance the appeal). The party bringing the appeal (the appellant) typically argues that because the relevant law was misstated or misapplied during the trial, the decision must be reversed and a new trial ordered. On rare occasion the issue in dispute is appealed all the way to the highest court in the nation—the U.S. Supreme Court—for a final decision. (The cases we reprint for discussion in this chapter are all cases decided by the Supreme Court.)

A pair of useful questions to answer as you work your way through a reported case are these:

- What events gave rise to the legal controversy in this case?
- What intermediate steps did the case go through before reaching the final court of appeal?

DECISION AND OPINION

With rare exceptions, only cases decided by the appellate courts are *reported*—that is, published. A reported case consists of two very different elements: (1) the court's decision, or *holding*, and (2) the court's *opinion* in support of its decision. Typically, a court's decision can be stated in a sentence; it amounts to the conclusion of the court's argument. The opinion, however, is more complex and lengthy; as with most arguments, the premises of judicial reasoning and their linkages with each other involve several steps.

To illustrate, in *Texas v. Johnson*, the U.S. Supreme Court considered a Texas statute that made it a crime to burn the American flag in political protest. The Court decided that the statute was an unconstitutional interference with freedom of speech. (The decision, as you see, can be stated concisely.)

The Court's opinion, however, runs to several pages. The gist is this: The purpose of the First Amendment prohibiting abridgment of speech by the government is to protect personal expression, especially where there is a political intention or significance to the speech. Previous decisions of the Court interpreting the amendment have established that the protection of "speech" applies also to nonverbal acts; flag burning in political protest is such an act. Under certain conditions the state may regulate "speech," but in no case may the state prohibit "speech" because of its content or meaning. The Texas statute did not merely regulate the circumstances of "speech"; rather, it regulated the content or meaning of the "speech." Therefore, the statute is unconstitutional.

Thus, in reading the report of a decided case, you will want to be able to answer these two questions:

- What did the court decide?
- What reasons did the court offer to justify its decision?

MAJORITY, CONCURRING, AND DISSENTING OPINIONS

Not all appellate court decisions are unanimous ones. A court's *majority opinion* contains the ruling and reasoning of a majority of its judges. In *Texas v. Johnson*, for example, Justice William Brennan wrote the majority opinion in which four of his colleagues joined. Occasionally one or more of the judges in the majority files a *concurring opinion*; in such cases the judge agrees with the majority's decision but disagrees with its reasoning. Justice John Paul Stevens wrote a concurring opinion in *Johnson*.

In any appellate court decision, at least one judge is likely to dissent from the majority opinion and file a *dissenting opinion* explaining why. (Throughout this book we make the point that intelligent, honorable people may differ on issues of importance.) In the *Johnson* case, four judges dissented but joined in one dissenting opinion. Minority opinions have much to offer for reflection, and in many instances today's dissenting opinion becomes tomorrow's law. The most famous example is Justice John Marshall Harlan's solitary dissent in *Plessy v. Ferguson* (1896), the case that upheld "separate but equal" racial segregation; Harlan's dissent was eventually vindicated by a unanimous vote of the Supreme Court in *Brown v. Board of Education* (1954).

Thus, where there are majority, concurring, and minority opinions, you will want to think about these questions:

- On what issues do the majority and concurring opinions agree?
- On what issues do they disagree?

- Where does the minority in its dissenting opinion(s) disagree with the majority?
- Which opinion is more convincing, the majority or the minority?

FACTS AND LAW

Every court's decision is based on the relevant facts and the relevant law. What the relevant facts are is often in dispute at the trial but not on appeal; appellate court judges rarely reexamine the facts as decided by the trial court. The appellate court, however, usually restates the relevant facts in the opening paragraphs of its opinion. An old joke told among lawyers is appropriate here: "Argue the facts if the facts are on your side, argue the law if the law is on your side; if neither the law nor the facts are on your side, pound the table!"

Unfortunately, a sharp distinction between facts and law cannot always be maintained. For example, if we describe the defendant's conduct as "careless," is that a matter of fact? Or is it in part a matter of law because "careless" conduct may also be judged "negligent" conduct, and the law defines what counts as negligence?

As you read through the reported case, keep in mind these two questions:

- What are the relevant facts in the case, insofar as they can be determined by what the appellate court reported?
- Are there issues of fact omitted or ignored by the appellate court that, had they been addressed, might have shed light on the decision?

For instance, consider a case in which a cattle rancher finds one of her cows dead after it collided with a railroad train. She decides to sue for negligence and wins, and the defendant (the railroad company) appeals. Why did she sue the railroad in the first place, rather than the engineer of the train that killed her cow? Suppose the appellate court's opinion fails to mention whether there was a fence at the edge of the field to keep her cattle off the tracks; wouldn't that be relevant to deciding whether she was partly at fault for the accident? (Ought the railroad to have erected a fence on its property parallel to the track?) Information about such facts could well shed light on the strength and correctness of the court's opinion and decision.

Appellate court judges are almost entirely preoccupied with what they believe is the relevant law to deciding the case at hand. The law can come in any of several different forms: *common law principles* ("No one may enlist the courts to assist him in profiting from his own wrong"), *statutes* enacted by a legislature ("As of January 1, 2004, income taxes shall be levied according to the following formula . . ."), *ordinances* enacted by a town council ("Dogs must be leashed in public places"), a *precedent* found in a prior case decided by some appellate court ("The decision in the case before us is governed by the Supreme Court's earlier holding in . . ."), *executive orders* ("All persons of Japanese extraction currently resident in California shall be removed inland to a relocation center"), *administrative regulations* ("Milk shipped interstate must have a butterfat content not less than . . ."), as well as *constitutional interpretations* ("Statements critical of a public official but not malicious or uttered by one who knows they are false are not libelous and are permitted under the First Amendment"). Not all laws are of equal weight; a state statute inconsistent with the federal Bill of Rights will be nullified, not the other way around.

Appellate court judges devote much of their attention to **interpretation,** trying to decide exactly what the relevant statute, regulation, or prior decision really means and whether it applies to the case before the court. For example, does a local ordinance prohibiting "four-wheeled vehicles" in the park apply to a nanny pushing a baby carriage? The answer often turns on what was the *purpose* of the law or the *intention* of the lawmaker.

It is not easy to decide what the lawmakers' **intention** was; lawmakers are rarely available to state for the courts what their intention was. Can we confidently infer what a legislature's intention was from the legislative history left behind in the form of debates or hearings? From what the relevant committee chairperson says it was? What if (as is typically true) the legislature never declared its intentions when it enacted a law? When a legislature creates a statute, do all those who vote for it act with the same intention? If not, which of the many intentions involved should dominate? How do we find out what those intentions were? What counts as relevant evidence for ascribing this rather than that as someone's intention?

Accordingly, as you read a reported legal case, your study of the court's opinion should lead you to ask these questions:

- Exactly what law or laws is the court trying to interpret?
- What evidence does the court cite in favor of its interpretation?

BALANCING INTERESTS

In U.S. Supreme Court cases, the decision often turns on how competing interests are to be *balanced* or weighed. This pattern of reasoning is especially relevant when one of the conflicting interests is apparently protected by the Constitution. The majority opinion in *New Jersey v. T.L.O.* (1985) (p. 435) is a good example of such balancing; there, the privacy interests of high school students are weighed (metaphorically speaking, of course—no one can literally "weigh" or "balance" anyone's interests) against the competing interest of school officials responsible for maintaining an orderly environment for teaching. The Court decided that the latter ought to prevail and concluded that "reasonable" searches are not forbidden under the Fourth Amendment's prohibition of "unreasonable searches and seizures."

This leads directly to several other questions you will want to try to answer in the legal cases you study:

- In a constitutional case, what are the conflicting interests?
- How does the Supreme Court propose to balance them?
- Why does it strike the balance one way rather than the other?

A WORD OF CAUTION

Lawyers are both officers of the court and champions for their clients' causes. In the first role they share with judges and other officials the duty to seek justice by honorable means. But in the second role lawyers often see their job as one in which they ought to bend every rule as far as they can in pursuit of their clients' interests (after all, it is the client who pays the bills). This attitude is nicely conveyed in the title of a book, *How to Argue and Win Every Time* (1995), by Gerry Spence, one of the nation's leading trial lawyers. And it is reinforced by a comment from defense attorney Alan Dershowitz: "All sides in a trial want to hide at least some of the truth."

Yet it would be wrong to see lawyers as motivated only by a ruthless desire to win at any cost. Lawyers have a civic duty to present their clients' cases in the most favorable light and to challenge whatever evidence and testimony is offered in court against them. (If you were hiring a lawyer to defend you, would you settle for anything less?) In a society such as ours—a society of law rather than of powerful individuals—it is right that accused persons be found guilty as charged only after the strongest defenses have been mounted.

To be sure, everyone concerned to argue on behalf of any claim, whether in or out of court, whether as a lawyer or in some other capacity, ought to take the challenge seriously. But it is too much to hope to "win every time"—and in fact winning is not the only, much less the highest, goal. Sometimes the other side does have the better argument, and in such cases we should be willing, indeed eager, to see the merits and to enlarge our minds.

In any case, in this book we think of argument not as a weapon for use in mortal combat but as a device for exploring the controversy or dispute under discussion, a tool for isolating the issues in contention and for helping in the evaluation of different possible outcomes. We expect you will use argument to persuade your audience to accept your views, just as a lawyer typically does; but we hope you will use argument sometimes—even often—to clarify your ideas *for yourself;* when you develop arguments for effective presentation to your colleagues and associates, you will probably improve the quality of your ideas.

✓ A CHECKLIST FOR ANALYZING LEGAL ARGUMENTS

☐ Is the court trying to decide whether someone accused of a crime is guilty as charged, or is the court trying to resolve some noncriminal (civil) dispute?

☐ What events gave rise to the legal controversy in this case?

☐ What intermediate steps did the case go through before reaching the final court of appeal?

☐ What did the court decide?

☐ What reasons did the court offer to justify its decision?

☐ On what issues do the majority and concurring opinions agree?

☐ On what issues do they disagree?

☐ Where does the minority in its dissenting opinion(s) disagree with the majority?

☐ Which opinion is more convincing, the majority or the minority?

☐ What are the relevant facts in the case, insofar as they can be determined by what the appellate court reported?

☐ Are there issues of fact omitted or ignored by the appellate court that, had they been addressed, might have shed light on the decision?

☐ Exactly what law or laws is the court trying to interpret?

☐ What evidence does the court cite in favor of its interpretation?

☐ In constitutional cases, what are the conflicting interests?

☐ How does the Supreme Court propose to balance them?

☐ Why does it strike the balance one way rather than the other?

A CASEBOOK ON THE LAW AND SOCIETY:
What Rights Do the Constitution and the Bill of Rights Protect?

Byron R. White and John Paul Stevens

In January 1985, a majority of the U.S. Supreme Court, in a case called New Jersey v. T.L.O. *(a student's initials), ruled six to three that a school official's search of a student who was suspected of disobeying a school regulation does not violate the Fourth Amendment's protection against unreasonable searches and seizures.*

The case originated thus: An assistant principal in a New Jersey high school opened the purse of a fourteen-year-old girl who had been caught violating school rules by smoking in the lavatory. The girl denied that she ever smoked, and the assistant principal thought that the contents of her purse would show whether she was lying. The purse was found to contain cigarettes, marijuana, and some notes that seemed to indicate that she sold marijuana to other students. The school then called the police.

The case went through three lower courts; almost five years after the event occurred, the case reached the Supreme Court. Associate Justice Byron R. White wrote the majority opinion, joined by Chief Justice Warren E. Burger and by Associate Justices Lewis F. Powell Jr., William H. Rehnquist, and Sandra Day O'Connor. Associate Justice Harry A. Blackmun concurred in a separate opinion. Associate Justices William J. Brennan Jr., John Paul Stevens, and Thurgood Marshall dissented in part. In the excerpt that follows, legal citations have been omitted.

New Jersey v. T.L.O.

Justice White delivered the opinion of the Court.

In determining whether the search at issue in this case violated the Fourth Amendment, we are faced initially with the question whether that amendment's prohibition on unreasonable searches and seizures applies to searches conducted by public school officials. We hold that it does.

It is now beyond dispute that "the Federal Constitution, by virtue of the Fourteenth Amendment, prohibits unreasonable searches and seizures by state officers." Equally indisputable is the proposition that the Fourteenth Amendment protects the rights of students against encroachment by public school officials.

On reargument, however, the State of New Jersey has argued that the history of the Fourth Amendment indicates that the amendment was intended to regulate only searches and seizures carried out by law enforcement officers; accordingly, although public school officials are concededly state agents for purposes of the Fourteenth Amendment, the Fourth Amendment creates no rights enforceable against them.

But this Court has never limited the amendment's prohibition on unreasonable searches and seizures to operations conducted by the police. Rather, the Court has long spoken of the Fourth Amendment's strictures as restraints imposed upon "governmental action"—that is, "upon the activities of sovereign authority." Accordingly, we have held the Fourth Amendment applicable to the activities of civil as well as criminal authorities: building inspectors, OSHA inspectors, and even firemen entering privately owned premises to battle a fire, are all subject to the restraints imposed by the Fourth Amendment.

Notwithstanding the general applicability of the Fourth Amendment to the activities of civil authorities, a few courts have concluded that school officials are exempt from the dictates of the Fourth Amendment by virtue of the special nature of their authority over schoolchildren. Teachers and school administrators, it is said, act *in loco parentis* [that is, in place of a parent] in their dealings with students: Their authority is that of the parent, not the state, and is therefore not subject to the limits of the Fourth Amendment.

Such reasoning is in tension with contemporary reality and the teachings of this Court. We have held school officials subject to the commands of the First Amendment, and the Due Process Clause of the Fourteenth Amendment. If school authorities are state actors for purposes of the constitutional guarantees of freedom of expression and due process, it is difficult to understand why they should be deemed to be exercising parental rather than public authority when conducting searches of their students.

In carrying out searches and other disciplinary functions pursuant to such policies, school officials act as representatives of the state, not merely as surrogates for the parents, and they cannot claim the parents' immunity from the strictures of the Fourth Amendment.

To hold that the Fourth Amendment applies to searches conducted by school authorities is only to begin the inquiry into the standards governing such searches. Although the underlying command of the Fourth Amendment is always that searches and seizures be reasonable, what is reasonable depends on the context within which a search takes place.

STANDARD OF REASONABLENESS

The determination of the standard of reasonableness governing any   10 specific class of searches requires balancing the need to search against the invasion which the search entails. On one side of the balance are arrayed the individual's legitimate expectations of privacy and personal security; on the other, the government's need for effective methods to deal with breaches of public order.

We have recognized that even a limited search of the person is a substantial invasion of privacy. A search of a child's person or of a closed purse or other bag carried on her person, no less than a similar search carried out on an adult, is undoubtedly a severe violation of subjective expectations of privacy.

Of course, the Fourth Amendment does not protect subjective expectations of privacy that are unreasonable or otherwise "illegitimate." The State of New Jersey has argued that because of the pervasive supervision to which children in the schools are necessarily subject, a child has virtually no legitimate expectation of privacy in articles of personal property "unnecessarily" carried into a school. This argument has two factual premises: (1) the fundamental incompatibility of expectations of privacy with the maintenance of a sound educational environment; and (2) the minimal interest of the child in bringing any items of personal property into the school. Both premises are severely flawed.

Although this Court may take notice of the difficulty of maintaining discipline in the public schools today, the situation is not so dire that students in the schools may claim no legitimate expectations of privacy.

PRIVACY AND DISCIPLINE

Against the child's interest in privacy must be set the substantial interest of teachers and administrators in maintaining discipline in the classroom and on school grounds. Maintaining order in the classroom has never been easy, but in recent years, school disorder has often taken particularly ugly forms; drug use and violent crime in the schools have become major social problems. Accordingly, we have recognized that maintaining security and order in the schools requires a certain degree of flexibility in school disciplinary procedures, and we have respected the value of preserving the informality of the student-teacher relationship.

How, then, should we strike the balance between the schoolchild's 15 legitimate expectations of privacy and the school's equally legitimate need to maintain an environment in which learning can take place? It is evident that the school setting requires some easing of the restrictions to which searches by public authorities are ordinarily subject. The warrant requirement, in particular, is unsuited to the school environment; requiring a teacher to obtain a warrant before searching a child suspected of an infraction of school rules (or of the criminal law) would unduly interfere with the maintenance of the swift and informal disciplinary procedures needed in the schools. We hold today that school officials need not obtain a warrant before searching a student who is under their authority.

The school setting also requires some modification of the level of suspicion of illicit activity needed to justify a search. Ordinarily, a search— even one that may permissibly be carried out without a warrant—must be based upon "probable cause" to believe that a violation of the law has occurred. However, "probable cause" is not an irreducible requirement of a valid search.

BALANCING OF INTERESTS

The fundamental command of the Fourth Amendment is that searches and seizures be reasonable, and although "both the concept of probable cause and the requirement of a warrant bear on the reasonableness of a search, . . . in certain limited circumstances neither is required." Thus, we have in a number of cases recognized the legality of searches and seizures based on suspicions that, although "reasonable," do not rise to the level of probable cause. Where a careful balancing of governmental and private interests suggests that the public interest is best served by a Fourth Amendment standard of reasonableness that stops short of probable cause, we have not hesitated to adopt such a standard.

We join the majority of courts that have examined this issue in concluding that the accommodation of the privacy interests of school-children with the substantial need of teachers and administrators for freedom to maintain order in the schools does not require strict adherence to the requirement that searches be based on probable cause to believe that the subject of the search has violated or is violating the law.

Rather, the legality of a search of a student should depend simply on the reasonableness, under all the circumstances, of the search. Determining the reasonableness of any search involves a twofold inquiry; first, one must consider "whether the . . . action was justified at its inception," second, one must determine whether the search as actually conducted "was reasonably related in scope to the circumstances which justified the interference in the first place."

Under ordinary circumstances, a search of a student by a teacher or 20 other school official will be "justified at its inception" when there are reasonable grounds for suspecting that the search will turn up evidence that the student has violated or is violating either the law or the rules of the school. Such a search will be permissible in its scope when the measures adopted are reasonably related to the objectives of the search and not excessively intrusive in light of the age and sex of the student and the nature of the infraction.

This standard will, we trust, neither unduly burden the efforts of school authorities to maintain order in their schools nor authorize unrestrained intrusions upon the privacy of schoolchildren. By focusing attention on the question of reasonableness, the standard will spare teachers and school administrators the necessity of schooling themselves in the niceties of probable cause and permit them to regulate their conduct according to the dictates of reason and common sense. At the same time, the reasonableness standard should insure that the interests of students will be invaded no more than is necessary to achieve the legitimate end of preserving order in the schools.

There remains the question of the legality of the search in this case. We recognize that the "reasonable grounds" standard applied by the New Jersey Supreme Court in its consideration of this question is not substantially different from the standard that we have adopted today. Nonetheless, we believe that the New Jersey court's application of that standard to strike down the search of T.L.O.'s purse reflects a somewhat crabbed notion of reasonableness. Our review of the facts surrounding the search leads us to conclude that the search was in no sense unreasonable for Fourth Amendment purposes.

Justice Stevens, dissenting.

The majority holds that "a search of a student by a teacher or other school official will be `justified at its inception' when there are reasonable grounds for suspecting that the search will turn up evidence *that the student has violated or is violating either the law or the rules of the school."*

This standard will permit teachers and school administrators to search 25
students when they suspect that the search will reveal evidence of [viola-
tion of] even the most trivial school regulation or precatory guideline for
students' behavior. For the Court, a search for curlers and sunglasses in
order to enforce the school dress code is apparently just as important as a
search for evidence of heroin addiction or violent gang activity.

A standard better attuned to this concern would permit teachers and
school administrators to search a student when they have reason to
believe that the search will uncover *evidence that the student is violating the
law or engaging in conduct that is seriously disruptive of school order, or the educational process.*

A standard that varies the extent of the permissible intrusion with
the gravity of the suspected offense is also more consistent with common-
law experience and this Court's precedent. Criminal law has traditionally recognized a distinction between essentially regulatory offenses and
serious violations of the peace, and graduated the response of the criminal justice system depending on the character of the violation.

Topics for Critical Thinking and Writing

1. In the majority opinion Justice White says that "it is evident that the
   school setting requires some easing of the restrictions to which searches
   by public authorities are ordinarily subject" (para. 15). Does White offer
   evidence supporting what he says is "evident"? List any evidence that
   White gives or any that you can think of.

2. What argument does White give to show that the Fourth Amendment
   prohibition against "unreasonable searches and seizures" (para. 3)
   applies to the behavior of school officials? Do you think his argument is
   reasonable? Explain.

3. On what ground does White argue that school students have "legitimate
   expectations of privacy" (para. 15) and so New Jersey is wrong in arguing the contrary?

4. What are the conflicting interests involved in the case, according to
   White? How does the Supreme Court resolve this conflict?

5. Why does White argue (para. 16) that school authorities may search
   students without first obtaining a search warrant? (By the way, who
   issues a search warrant? Who seeks one?) What does he mean when he
   says that the requirement of "probable cause" is "not an irreducible
   requirement of a valid search" (para. 16)?

6. Could a search undertaken on the principle enunciated by the Court's
   majority mean that whenever authorities perceive what they choose to
   call "disorder" — perhaps in the activity of an assembly of protesters in
   the streets of a big city — they may justify otherwise unlawful searches
   and seizures?

7. Some forty years before this case, Justice Robert H. Jackson argued that the schools have a special responsibility for adhering to the Constitution: "That they are educating the young for citizenship is reason for scrupulous protection of constitutional freedoms of the individual, if we are not to strangle the free mind at its source and teach youth to discount important principles of our government as mere platitudes." Similarly, in 1967 in an analogous case involving another female pupil, Justice Brennan argued that "schools cannot expect their students to learn the lessons of good citizenship when the school authorities themselves disregard the fundamental principles underpinning our constitutional freedoms." Do you find these arguments compelling? Why, or why not?

8. Let's admit that maintaining order in schools may be extremely difficult. In your opinion, does the difficulty justify diminishing the rights of citizens? Smoking is not an illegal activity, yet in this instance a student suspected of smoking—that is, merely of violating a school rule—was searched. In an essay of 250 words, consider whether the maintenance of school discipline in such a matter justifies a search.

9. White relies on a standard of "reasonableness." Do you think this criterion is too subjective to be a proper standard to distinguish between permissible and impermissible searches? Write a 500-word essay on the standard of reasonable searches and seizures, giving a hypothetical but plausible example of a reasonable search and seizure and then of an unreasonable search and seizure.

Harry Blackmun and William H. Rehnquist

The first important case in which the U.S. Supreme Court decided a controversy by appeal to our "right of privacy" was in 1965 in Griswold v. Connecticut. *Plaintiffs argued that the state statute forbidding the sale of birth control devices, as well as birth control information from a licensed physician, was an unconstitutional invasion of privacy. The Court ruled in their favor, a controversial ruling because there is no explicit "right of privacy" in the Bill of Rights or elsewhere in the Constitution. The seven Justices in the majority divided over the best way to locate this right in the interstices of prior rulings, and they invoked the "penumbra" of recognized constitutional provisions as the locus of this protection.*

The storm aroused by the Court's ruling in Griswold *was as nothing compared to the raging protest eight years later caused by the Court's ruling (again, by a vote of seven to two) supporting a woman's right to choose whether to carry her pregnancy to completion or, instead, to arrange to terminate her pregnancy by abortion under the direction of a licensed physician. In 1973, when* Roe v. Wade *was decided, abortion (except in special cases) was illegal in most states in the nation; the decision in* Roe *effectively nullified all such statutes. Justice Harry Blackmun, who wrote the opinion for the Court majority, proposed dividing pregnancy into three trimesters of equal length. During the first trimester, a woman's right to have an abortion was virtually absolute; not so in the second and third trimesters.*

The decision provoked a sharp and deep division between those who embraced it because it recognized a woman's autonomy and the finality of her choice and those who deplored the decision as a violation of the unborn's right to life. The struggle between "right-to-life" advocates (who would, typically, limit abortion to those rare cases where it is medically necessary to save the life of the mother) and the advocates of a "right to choose" (who favor leaving all questions of pregnancy and its termination to the decision of the pregnant woman) rages unabated. Now, more than three decades later, it can be said that Roe v. Wade *ranks as the most controversial decision by the Supreme Court in the past century. While it is not likely to be overturned in any future ruling by the Court, influential political forces are manifestly at work to limit its scope. Many observers have noted that, were* Roe v. Wade *up for decision today before a more conservative Supreme Court, it would be decided differently.*

Roe v. Wade

Mr. Justice Blackmun delivered the opinion of the Court. . . .

We forthwith acknowledge our awareness of the sensitive and emotional nature of the abortion controversy, of the vigorous opposing views, even among physicians, and of the deep and seemingly absolute convictions that the subject inspires. One's philosophy, one's experiences, one's exposure to the raw edges of human existence, one's religious training, one's attitudes toward life and family and their values, and the moral standards one establishes and seeks to observe, are all likely to influence and to color one's thinking and conclusions about abortion.

In addition, population growth, pollution, poverty, and racial overtones tend to complicate and not to simplify the problem.

Our task, of course, is to resolve the issue by constitutional measurement, free of emotion and of predilection. We seek earnestly to do this, and, because we do, we have inquired into, and in this opinion place some emphasis upon, medical and medical-legal history and what that history reveals about man's attitudes toward the abortion procedure over the centuries. . . .

The Texas statutes that concern us here are Articles 1191–1194 and   5
1196 of the State's Penal Code. These make it a crime to "procure an abortion," as therein defined, or to attempt one, except with respect to "an abortion procured or attempted by medical advice for the purpose of saving the life of the mother." Similar statutes are in existence in a majority of the states. . . .

The principal thrust of appellant's attack on the Texas statutes is that they improperly invade a right, said to be possessed by the pregnant woman, to choose to terminate her pregnancy. Appellant would discover this right in the concept of personal "liberty" embodied in the Fourteenth

Amendment's Due Process Clause; or in personal, marital, familial, and sexual privacy said to be protected by the Bill of Rights or its penumbras, see *Griswold v. Connecticut,* 381 U.S. 479 (1965); *Eisenstadt v. Baird,* 405 U.S. 438 (1972); id., at 460 (White, J., concurring in result); or among those rights reserved to the people by the Ninth Amendment, *Griswold v. Connecticut,* 381 U.S., at 486 (Goldberg, J., concurring). Before addressing this claim, we feel it desirable briefly to survey, in several aspects, the history of abortion, for such insight as that history may afford us, and then to examine the state purposes and interests behind the criminal abortion laws.

It perhaps is not generally appreciated that the restrictive criminal abortion laws in effect in a majority of states today are of relatively recent vintage. Those laws, generally proscribing abortion or its attempt at any time during pregnancy except when necessary to preserve the pregnant woman's life, are not of ancient or even of common-law origin. Instead, they derive from statutory changes effected, for the most part, in the latter half of the nineteenth century. . . .

THE AMERICAN LAW

In this country, the law in effect in all but a few states until mid-nineteenth century was the pre-existing English common law. Connecticut, the first state to enact abortion legislation, adopted in 1821 that part of Lord Ellenborough's Act [in England] that related to a woman "quick with child." The death penalty was not imposed. Abortion before quickening was made a crime in that state only in 1860. In 1828, New York enacted legislation that, in two respects, was to serve as a model for early anti-abortion statutes. First, while barring destruction of an unquickened fetus as well as a quick fetus, it made the former only a misdemeanor, but the latter second-degree manslaughter. Second, it incorporated a concept of therapeutic abortion by providing that an abortion was excused if it "shall have been necessary to preserve the life of such mother, or shall have been advised by two physicians to be necessary for such purpose." By 1840, when Texas had received the common law, only eight American states had statutes dealing with abortion. It was not until after the War Between the States that legislation began generally to replace the common law. Most of these initial statutes dealt severely with abortion after quickening but were lenient with it before quickening. Most punished attempts equally with completed abortions. While many statutes included the exception for an abortion thought by one or more physicians to be necessary to save the mother's life, that provision soon disappeared and the typical law required that the procedure actually be necessary for that purpose.

Gradually, in the middle and late nineteenth century the quickening distinction disappeared from the statutory law of most states and the degree of the offense and the penalties were increased. By the end of the

1950s, a large majority of the jurisdictions banned abortion, however and whenever performed, unless done to save or preserve the life of the mother. The exceptions, Alabama and the District of Columbia, permitted abortion to preserve the mother's health. Three states permitted abortions that were not "unlawfully" performed or that were not "without lawful justification," leaving interpretation of those standards to the courts. In the past several years, however, a trend toward liberalization of abortion statutes has resulted in adoption, by about one-third of the states, of less stringent laws, most of them patterned after the ALI Model Penal Code, §230.3. . . .

It is thus apparent that at common law, at the time of the adoption 10 of our Constitution, and throughout the major portion of the nineteenth century, abortion was viewed with less disfavor than under most American statutes currently in effect. Phrasing it another way, a woman enjoyed a substantially broader right to terminate a pregnancy than she does in most states today. At least with respect to the early stage of pregnancy, and very possibly without such a limitation, the opportunity to make this choice was present in this country well into the nineteenth century. Even later, the law continued for some time to treat less punitively an abortion procured in early pregnancy.

THE POSITION OF THE AMERICAN MEDICAL ASSOCIATION

The anti-abortion mood prevalent in this country in the late nineteenth century was shared by the medical profession. Indeed, the attitude of the profession may have played a significant role in the enactment of stringent criminal abortion legislation during that period. . . .

In 1970, after the introduction of a variety of proposed resolutions, and of a report from its Board of Trustees, a reference committee noted "polarization of the medical profession on this controversial issue"; division among those who had testified; a difference of opinion among AMA councils and committees; "the remarkable shift in testimony" in six months, felt to be influenced "by the rapid changes in state laws and by the judicial decisions which tend to make abortion more freely available;" and a feeling "that this trend will continue." On June 25, 1970, the House of Delegates adopted preambles and most of the resolutions proposed by the reference committee. The preambles emphasized "the best interests of the patient," "sound clinical judgment," and "informed patient consent," in contrast to "mere acquiescence to the patient's demand." The resolutions asserted that abortion is a medical procedure that should be performed by a licensed physician in an accredited hospital only after consultation with two other physicians and in conformity with state law, and that no party to the procedure should be required to violate personally held moral principles. Proceedings of the AMA House of Delegates 200 (June 1970). The AMA Judicial Council rendered a complementary opinion.

THE POSITION OF THE AMERICAN
PUBLIC HEALTH ASSOCIATION

In October 1970, the Executive Board of the APHA adopted Standards for Abortion Services. These were five in number:

a. Rapid and simple abortion referral must be readily available through state and local public health departments, medical societies, or other nonprofit organizations.
b. An important function of counseling should be to simplify and expedite the provision of abortion services; it should not delay the obtaining of these services.
c. Psychiatric consultation should not be mandatory. As in the case of other specialized medical services, psychiatric consultation should be sought for definite indications and not on a routine basis.
d. A wide range of individuals from appropriately trained, sympathetic volunteers to highly skilled physicians may qualify as abortion counselors.
e. Contraception and/or sterilization should be discussed with each abortion patient.

Among factors pertinent to life and health risks associated with abortion were three that "are recognized as important":

a. the skill of the physician,
b. the environment in which the abortion is performed, and above all
c. the duration of pregnancy, as determined by uterine size and confirmed by menstrual history.

It was said that "a well-equipped hospital" offers more protection "to cope with unforeseen difficulties than an office or clinic without such resources. . . . The factor of gestational age is of overriding importance." Thus, it was recommended that abortions in the second trimester and early abortions in the presence of existing medical complications be performed in hospitals as inpatient procedures. For pregnancies in the first trimester, abortion in the hospital with or without overnight stay "is probably the safest practice." An abortion in an extramural facility, however, is an acceptable alternative "provided arrangements exist in advance to admit patients promptly if unforeseen complications develop." Standards for an abortion facility were listed. It was said that at present abortions should be performed by physicians or osteopaths who are licensed to practice and who have "adequate training."

THE POSITION OF THE AMERICAN
BAR ASSOCIATION

At its meeting in February 1972 the ABA House of Delegates approved, 15 with 17 opposing votes, the Uniform Abortion Act that had been drafted and approved the preceding August by the Conference of Commissioners on Uniform State Laws (1972). . . .

Three reasons have been advanced to explain historically the enactment of criminal abortion laws in the nineteenth century and to justify their continued existence.

It has been argued occasionally that these laws were the product of a Victorian social concern to discourage illicit sexual conduct. Texas, however, does not advance this justification in the present case, and it appears that no court or commentator has taken the argument seriously. The appellants and *amici* [friends of the court] contend, moreover, that this is not a proper state purpose at all and suggest that, if it were, the Texas statutes are overbroad in protecting it since the law fails to distinguish between married and unwed mothers.

A second reason is concerned with abortion as a medical procedure. When most criminal abortion laws were first enacted, the procedure was a hazardous one for the woman. This was particularly true prior to the development of antisepsis. Antiseptic techniques, of course, were based on discoveries by Lister, Pasteur, and others first announced in 1867, but were not generally accepted and employed until about the turn of the century. Abortion mortality was high. Even after 1900, and perhaps until as late as the development of antibiotics in the 1940s, standard modern techniques such as dilation and curettage were not nearly so safe as they are today. Thus, it has been argued that a state's real concern in enacting a criminal abortion law was to protect the pregnant woman, that is, to restrain her from submitting to a procedure that placed her life in serious jeopardy.

Modern medical techniques have altered this situation. Appellants and various *amici* refer to medical data indicating that abortion in early pregnancy, that is, prior to the end of the first trimester, although not without its risk, is now relatively safe. Mortality rates for women undergoing early abortions, where the procedure is legal, appear to be as low as or lower than the rates for normal childbirth. Consequently, any interest of the state in protecting the woman from an inherently hazardous procedure, except when it would be equally dangerous for her to forgo it, has largely disappeared. Of course, important state interests in the areas of health and medical standards do remain. . . . The prevalence of high mortality rates at illegal "abortion mills" strengthens, rather than weakens, the state's interest in regulating the conditions under which abortions are performed. Moreover, the risk to the woman increases as her pregnancy continues. Thus, the state retains a definite interest in protecting the woman's own health and safety when an abortion is proposed at a late stage of pregnancy.

The third reason is the state's interest—some phrase it in terms of duty—in protecting prenatal life. Some of the argument for this justification rests on the theory that a new human life is present from the moment of conception. The state's interest and general obligation to protect life then extends, it is argued, to prenatal life. Only when the life of the pregnant mother herself is at stake, balanced against the life she carries within her, should the interest of the embryo or fetus not prevail. 20

Logically, of course, a legitimate state interest in this area need not stand or fall on acceptance of the belief that life begins at conception or at some other point prior to live birth. In assessing the state's interest, recognition may be given to the less rigid claim that as long as at least *potential* life is involved, the state may assert interests beyond the protection of the pregnant woman alone. . . .

The Constitution does not explicitly mention any right of privacy. In a line of decisions, however, going back perhaps as far as *Union Pacific R. Co. v. Botsford*, 141 U.S. 250, 251 (1891), the Court has recognized that a right of personal privacy, or a guarantee of certain areas or zones of privacy, does exist under the Constitution. In varying contexts, the Court or individual Justices have, indeed, found at least the roots of that right in the First Amendment, in the Fourth and Fifth Amendments, in the Ninth Amendment, or in the concept of liberty guaranteed by the first section of the Fourteenth Amendment. These decisions make it clear that only personal rights that can be deemed "fundamental" or "implicit in the concept of ordered liberty" are included in this guarantee of personal privacy. They also make it clear that the right has some extension to activities relating to marriage, procreation, contraception, family relationships, and child rearing and education.

This right of privacy, whether it be founded in the Fourteenth Amendment's concept of personal liberty and restrictions upon state action, as we feel it is, or, as the District Court determined, in the Ninth Amendment's reservation of rights to the people, is broad enough to encompass a woman's decision whether or not to terminate her pregnancy. The detriment that the state would impose upon the pregnant woman by denying this choice altogether is apparent. Specific and direct harm medically diagnosable even in early pregnancy may be involved. Maternity, or additional offspring, may force upon the woman a distressful life and future. Psychological harm may be imminent. Mental and physical health may be taxed by child care. There is also the distress, for all concerned, associated with the unwanted child, and there is the problem of bringing a child into a family already unable, psychologically and otherwise, to care for it. In other cases, as in this one, the additional difficulties and continuing stigma of unwed motherhood may be involved. All these are factors the woman and her responsible physician necessarily will consider in consultation.

On the basis of elements such as these, appellant and some *amici* argue that the woman's right is absolute and that she is entitled to terminate her pregnancy at whatever time, in whatever way, and for whatever reason she alone chooses. With this we do not agree. Appellant's arguments that Texas either has no valid interest at all in regulating the abortion decision, or no interest strong enough to support any limitation upon the woman's sole determination, are unpersuasive. The Court's decisions recognizing a right of privacy also acknowledge that some state regulation in areas

protected by that right is appropriate. As noted above, a state may properly
assert important interests in safeguarding health, in maintaining medical
standards, and in protecting potential life. At some point in pregnancy,
these respective interests become sufficiently compelling to sustain regulation of the factors that govern the abortion decision. The privacy right
involved, therefore, cannot be said to be absolute. In fact, it is not clear to
us that the claim asserted by some *amici* that one has an unlimited right to
do with one's body as one pleases bears a close relationship to the right of
privacy previously articulated in the Court's decisions. . . .

   We, therefore, conclude that the right of personal privacy includes
the abortion decision, but that this right is not unqualified and must be
considered against important state interests in regulation.

   Where certain "fundamental rights" are involved, the Court has held 25
that regulation limiting these rights may be justified only by a "compelling state interest" . . . and that legislative enactments must be narrowly drawn to express only the legitimate state interests at stake. . . .

   In the recent abortion cases, cited above, courts have recognized
these principles. Those striking down state laws have generally scrutinized the state's interests in protecting health and potential life, and
have concluded that neither interest justified broad limitations on the
reasons for which a physician and his pregnant patient might decide
that she should have an abortion in the early stages of pregnancy.
Courts sustaining state laws have held that the state's determinations
to protect health or prenatal life are dominant and constitutionally
justifiable.

A

   The appellee and certain *amici* argue that the fetus is a "person"
within the language and meaning of the Fourteenth Amendment. In
support of this, they outline at length and in detail the well-known facts
of fetal development. If this suggestion of personhood is established, the
appellant's case, of course, collapses, for the fetus' right to life would
then be guaranteed specifically by the Amendment. The appellant conceded as much on reargument. On the other hand, the appellee conceded on reargument that no case could be cited that holds that a fetus is
a person within the meaning of the Fourteenth Amendment.

   The Constitution does not define "person" in so many words. Section
1 of the Fourteenth Amendment contains three references to "person."
The first, in defining "citizens," speaks of "persons born or naturalized in
the United States." The word also appears both in the Due Process Clause
and in the Equal Protection Clause. "Person" is used in other places in the
Constitution. . . . But in nearly all these instances, the use of the word is
such that it has application only postnatally. None indicates, with any
assurance, that it has any possible prenatal application.

This conclusion, however, does not of itself fully answer the contentions raised by Texas, and we pass on to other considerations.

B

The pregnant woman cannot be isolated in her privacy. She carries ³⁰ an embryo and, later, a fetus, if one accepts the medical definitions of the developing young in the human uterus. The situation therefore is inherently different from marital intimacy, or bedroom possession of obscene material, or marriage, or procreation, or education, with which [several decided cases] were respectively concerned. As we have intimated above, it is reasonable and appropriate for a state to decide that at some point in time another interest, that of health of the mother or that of potential human life, becomes significantly involved. The woman's privacy is no longer sole and any right of privacy she possesses must be measured accordingly.

Texas urges that, apart from the Fourteenth Amendment, life begins at conception and is present throughout pregnancy, and that, therefore, the state has a compelling interest in protecting that life from and after conception. We need not resolve the difficult question of when life begins. When those trained in the respective disciplines of medicine, philosophy, and theology are unable to arrive at any consensus, the judiciary, at this point in the development of man's knowledge, is not in a position to speculate as to the answer. . . .

In areas other than criminal abortion, the law has been reluctant to endorse any theory that life, as we recognize it, begins before live birth or to accord legal rights to the unborn except in narrowly defined situations and except when the rights are contingent upon live birth. For example, the traditional rule of tort law denied recovery for prenatal injuries even though the child was born alive. That rule has been changed in almost every jurisdiction. In most states, recovery is said to be permitted only if the fetus was viable, or at least quick, when the injuries were sustained, though few courts have squarely so held. In a recent development, generally opposed by the commentators, some states permit the parents of a stillborn child to maintain an action for wrongful death because of prenatal injuries. Such an action, however, would appear to be one to vindicate the parents' interest and is thus consistent with the view that the fetus, at most, represents only the potentiality of life. Similarly, unborn children have been recognized as acquiring rights or interests by way of inheritance or other devolution of property, and have been represented by guardians *ad litem* [for the purpose of this lawsuit]. Perfection of the interests involved, again, has generally been contingent upon live birth. In short, the unborn have never been recognized in the law as persons in the whole sense.

To summarize and to repeat:

1. A state criminal abortion statute of the current Texas type, that
   excepts from criminality only a *lifesaving* procedure on behalf of
   the mother, without regard to pregnancy stage and without
   recognition of the other interests involved, is violative of the Due
   Process Clause of the Fourteenth Amendment.

   (a) For the stage prior to approximately the end of the first
       trimester, the abortion decision and its effectuation must be
       left to the medical judgment of the pregnant woman's attend-
       ing physician.
   (b) For the stage subsequent to approximately the end of the first
       trimester, the state, in promoting its interest in the health of the
       mother, may, if it chooses, regulate the abortion procedure in
       ways that are reasonably related to maternal health.
   (c) For the stage subsequent to viability, the state in promoting its
       interest in the potentiality of human life may, if it chooses,
       regulate, and even proscribe, abortion except where it is nec-
       essary, in appropriate medical judgment, for the preservation
       of the life or health of the mother.

2. The state may define the term "physician," as it has been
   employed in the preceding paragraphs of this . . . opinion, to mean
   only a physician currently licensed by the state, and may proscribe
   any abortion by a person who is not a physician as so defined. . . .

This holding, we feel, is consistent with the relative weights of the
respective interests involved, with the lessons and examples of medical
and legal history, with the lenity of the common law, and with the
demands of the profound problems of the present day. The decision
leaves the state free to place increasing restrictions on abortion as the
period of pregnancy lengthens, so long as those restrictions are tailored
to the recognized state interests. The decision vindicates the right of
the physician to administer medical treatment according to his professional judgment up to the points where important state interests provide compelling justifications for intervention. Up to those points, the
abortion decision in all its aspects is inherently, and primarily, a medical decision, and basic responsibility for it must rest with the physician.
If an individual practitioner abuses the privilege of exercising proper
medical judgment, the usual remedies, judicial and intra-professional,
are available.

Our conclusion that Article 1196 is unconstitutional means, of 35
course, that the Texas abortion statutes, as a unit, must fall. . . .

Mr. Justice Rehnquist, dissenting.

The Court's opinion brings to the decision of this troubling question
both extensive historical fact and a wealth of legal scholarship. While

the opinion thus commands my respect, I find myself nonetheless in fundamental disagreement with those parts of it that invalidate the Texas statute in question, and therefore dissent.

I

The Court's opinion decides that a state may impose virtually no restriction on the performance of abortions during the first trimester of pregnancy. Our previous decisions indicate that a necessary predicate for such an opinion is a plaintiff who was in her first trimester of pregnancy at some time during the pendency of her lawsuit. While a party may vindicate his own constitutional rights, he may not seek vindication for the rights of others. . . . The Court's statement of facts in this case makes clear, however, that the record in no way indicates the presence of such a plaintiff. We know only that plaintiff Roe at the time of filing her complaint was a pregnant woman; for aught that appears in this record, she may have been in her *last* trimester of pregnancy as of the date the complaint was filed.

Nothing in the Court's opinion indicates that Texas might not constitutionally apply its proscription of abortion as written to a woman in that stage of pregnancy. Nonetheless, the Court uses her complaint against the Texas statute as a fulcrum for deciding that states may impose virtually no restrictions on medical abortions performed during the *first* trimester of pregnancy. In deciding such a hypothetical lawsuit, the Court departs from the longstanding admonition that it should never "formulate a rule of constitutional law broader than is required by the precise facts to which it is to be applied."

II

Even if there were a plaintiff in this case capable of litigating the issue which the Court decides, I would reach a conclusion opposite to that reached by the Court. I have difficulty in concluding, as the Court does, that the right of "privacy" is involved in this case. Texas, by the statute here challenged, bars the performance of a medical abortion by a licensed physician on a plaintiff such as Roe. A transaction resulting in an operation such as this is not "private" in the ordinary usage of that word. Nor is the "privacy" that the Court finds here even a distant relative of the freedom from searches and seizures protected by the Fourth Amendment to the Constitution, which the Court has referred to as embodying a right to privacy.

If the Court means by the term "privacy" no more than that the claim of a person to be free from unwanted state regulation of consensual transactions may be a form of "liberty" protected by the Fourteenth Amendment, there is no doubt that similar claims have been upheld in our earlier decisions on the basis of that liberty. I agree with the statement of Mr. Justice Stewart in his concurring opinion[1] that the "liberty," against deprivation of which without due process the Fourteenth Amendment protects, embraces more than the rights found in the Bill of Rights. But that liberty is not guaranteed absolutely against deprivation, only against deprivation without due process of law. The test traditionally applied in the area of social and economic legislation is whether or not a law such as that challenged has a rational relation to a valid state objective. . . . The Due Process Clause of the Fourteenth Amendment undoubtedly does place a limit, albeit a broad one, on legislative power to enact laws such as this. If the Texas statute were to prohibit an abortion even where the mother's life is in jeopardy, I have little doubt that such a statute would lack a rational relation to a valid state objective under the test stated in *Williamson, supra.* But the Court's sweeping invalidation of any restrictions on abortion during the first trimester is impossible to justify under that standard, and the conscious weighing of competing factors that the Court's opinion apparently substitutes for the established test is far more appropriate to a legislative judgment than to a judicial one.

The Court eschews the history of the Fourteenth Amendment in its reliance on the "compelling state interest" test. . . . But the Court adds a new wrinkle to this test by transposing it from the legal considerations associated with the Equal Protection Clause of the Fourteenth Amendment to this case arising under the Due Process Clause of the Fourteenth Amendment. Unless I misapprehend the consequences of this transplanting of the "compelling state interest test," the Court's opinion will accomplish the seemingly impossible feat of leaving this area of the law more confused than it found it.

While the Court's opinion quotes from the dissent of Mr. Justice Holmes in *Lochner v. New York,* 198 U.S. 45, 74 (1905), the result it reaches is more closely attuned to the majority opinion of Mr. Justice Peckham in that case. As in *Lochner* and similar cases applying substantive due process standards to economic and social welfare legislation, the adoption of the compelling state interest standard will inevitably require this Court to examine the legislative policies and pass on the wisdom of these policies in the very process of deciding whether a particular state interest put forward may or may not be "compelling." The decision here to break pregnancy into three distinct terms and to outline the permissible restrictions the state may impose in each one, for example, partakes more of judicial legislation than it does of a determination of the intent of the drafters of the Fourteenth Amendment.

The fact that a majority of the states reflecting, after all, the majority sentiment in those states, have had restrictions on abortions for at least a century is a strong indication, it seems to me, that the asserted right to an abortion is not "so rooted in the traditions and conscience of our

---

[1]Omitted here. [Editors' note.]

people as to be ranked as fundamental." . . . Even today, when society's views on abortion are changing, the very existence of the debate is evidence that the "right" to an abortion is not so universally accepted as the appellant would have us believe.

To reach its result, the Court necessarily has had to find within the 45 scope of the Fourteenth Amendment a right that was apparently completely unknown to the drafters of the Amendment. As early as 1821, the first state law dealing directly with abortion was enacted by the Connecticut Legislature. . . . By the time of the adoption of the Fourteenth Amendment in 1868, there were at least thirty-six laws enacted by state or territorial legislatures limiting abortion. While many states have amended or updated their laws, twenty-one of the laws on the books in 1868 remain in effect today. Indeed, the Texas statute struck down today was, as the majority notes, first enacted in 1857 and "has remained substantially unchanged to the present time."

There apparently was no question concerning the validity of this provision or of any of the other state statutes when the Fourteenth Amendment was adopted. The only conclusion possible from this history is that the drafters did not intend to have the Fourteenth Amendment withdraw from the states the power to legislate with respect to this matter.

III

Even if one were to agree that the case that the Court decides were here, and that the enunciation of the substantive constitutional law in the Court's opinion were proper, the actual disposition of the case by the Court is still difficult to justify. The Texas statute is struck down *in toto*, even though the Court apparently concedes that at later periods of pregnancy Texas might impose these selfsame statutory limitations on abortion. My understanding of past practice is that a statute found to be invalid as applied to a particular plaintiff, but not unconstitutional as a whole, is not simply "struck down" but is, instead, declared unconstitutional as applied to the fact situation before the Court. . . .

For all of the foregoing reasons, I respectfully dissent.

TOPICS FOR CRITICAL THINKING AND WRITING

1. Abortion is nowhere mentioned in the federal Bill of Rights. Is that an insurmountable obstacle for both opponents and defenders of a woman's right to abortion who seek constitutional support for their position?

2. What does it mean for a pregnant woman to be "'quick with child'" (para. 8)?

3. Can a person consistently believe that (a) a woman has no right to an abortion, (b) a human embryo or fetus has an inviolable right to life, and (c) a woman may have an abortion if it is necessary to save her own

life? Explain in an essay of 500 words why you think these three propositions are or are not inconsistent.

4. Blackmun cites three reasons to explain the enactment of anti-abortion laws in nineteenth-century America (paras. 17–20). How would you rank these reasons in order of their decreasing relevance today? Write an essay of 500 words in which you state succinctly these reasons and your evaluation of them for present policy on abortion.

5. What is a "trimester" in a pregnancy (para. 14)? How, if at all, does this concept relate to the older idea of "quickening"?

6. What is a "state interest" (paras. 19–20), and why is there any such interest concerning human pregnancy and abortion?

7. Suppose someone argued that Blackmun's opinion is hopelessly confused because the issue is not the *privacy* of the pregnant woman but her *autonomy*—that is, her capacity and right to make fundamental decisions about her own life as she sees fit. Write a 250-word opinion for this case in which you defend or attack Roe's autonomy as the fundamental basis for her decision whether to abort.

8. Do you agree with the Supreme Court that a woman's right to abort a pregnancy is not an "absolute" right (paras. 23–24)? Do you agree with the Court's reasons for this conclusion? Explain.

9. Blackmun is unwilling to "endorse any theory that life . . . begins before live birth" (para. 32). Do you share his refusal? Why, or why not?

10. Do you think the unborn human fetus is a "person" in any sense of that term (see paras. 27–28)? How about a month-old human embryo? Suppose we grant that an embryo and a fetus are *alive* (that is, neither dead nor inert) and *human* (that is, not animal or vegetable or inhuman). What do you think needs to be added to establish the personhood of the living but unborn human offspring? Or do you think it is impossible that a human embryo or fetus could be a person? Explain.

11. Rehnquist, in a dissenting opinion, argues that an abortion is "not `private' in the ordinary usage of that word" (para. 40). What is his reason for this view? Do you agree or not? Explain.

12. Rehnquist remarks that the complex position on abortion taken by the majority of the Court (see especially para. 33) "is far more appropriate to a legislative judgment than to a judicial one" (para. 41). Why does he say this, do you think? Do you agree or not? Explain.

A Psychologist's View: Rogerian Argument

Real communication occurs . . . when we listen with understanding.
—CARL ROGERS

The first duty of a wise advocate is to convince his opponents that he understands their arguments, and sympathizes with their just feelings.
—SAMUEL TAYLOR COLERIDGE

ROGERIAN ARGUMENT: AN INTRODUCTION

Carl R. Rogers (1902–1987), perhaps best known for his book entitled *On Becoming a Person* (1961), was a psychotherapist, not a teacher of writing. This short essay by Rogers has, however, exerted much influence on instructors who teach argument. Written in the 1950s, this essay reflects the political climate of the cold war between the United States and the Soviet Union, which dominated headlines for more than forty years (1947–1989). Several of Rogers's examples of bias and frustrated communication allude to the tensions of that era.

On the surface, many arguments seem to show *A* arguing with *B*, presumably seeking to change *B*'s mind; but *A*'s argument is really directed not to *B* but to *C*. This attempt to persuade a nonparticipant is evident in the courtroom, where neither the prosecutor (*A*) nor the defense lawyer (*B*) is really trying to convince the opponent. Rather, both are trying to convince a third party, the jury (*C*). Prosecutors do not care whether they convince defense lawyers; they don't even mind infuriating defense lawyers because their only real goal is to convince the jury. Similarly, the writer of a letter to a newspaper, taking issue with an editorial, does not expect to change the paper's policy. Rather, the writer hopes to convince a third party, the reader of the newspaper.

But suppose *A* really does want to bring *B* around to *A*'s point of view. Suppose Mary really wants to persuade the teacher to allow her little lamb to stay in the classroom. Rogers points out that when we engage in an argument, if we feel our integrity or our identity is threatened, we will stiffen our position. (The teacher may feel that his or her dignity is compromised by the presence of the lamb and will scarcely attend to Mary's argument.) The sense of threat may be so great that we are unable to consider the alternative views being offered, and we therefore remain unpersuaded. Threatened, we may defend ourselves rather than our argument, and little communication takes place. Of course, a third party might say that we or our opponent presented the more convincing case, but we, and perhaps the opponent, have scarcely listened to each other, and so the two of us remain apart.

Rogers suggests, therefore, that a writer who wishes to communicate with someone (as opposed to convincing a third party) needs to reduce the threat. In a sense, the participants in the argument need to become partners rather than adversaries. Rogers writes, "Mutual communication tends to be pointed toward solving a problem rather than toward attacking a person or group." Thus, an essay on whether schools should test students for use of drugs, need not—and probably should not—see the issue as black or white, *either/or*. Such an essay might indicate that testing is undesirable because it may have bad effects, *but in some circumstances* it may be acceptable. This qualification does not mean that one must compromise. Thus, the essayist might argue that the potential danger to liberty is so great that no circumstances justify testing students for drugs. But even such an essayist should recognize the merit (however limited) of the opposition and should grant that the position being advanced itself entails great difficulties and dangers.

A writer who wishes to reduce the psychological threat to the opposition and thus facilitate the partnership in the study of some issue can do several things:

- One can show sympathetic understanding of the opposing argument,
- One can recognize what is valid in it, and
- One can recognize and demonstrate that those who take the other side are nonetheless persons of goodwill.

Advocates of Rogerian argument are likely to contrast it with Aristotelian argument, saying that the style of argument associated with Aristotle (384–322 B.C., Greek philosopher and rhetorician)

- Is adversarial, seeking to refute other views; and
- Sees the listener as wrong, someone who now must be overwhelmed by evidence.

In contrast to the confrontational Aristotelian style, which allegedly seeks to present an airtight case that compels belief, Rogerian argument (it is said)

- Is nonconfrontational, collegial, and friendly;
- Respects other views and allows for plural truths; and
- Seeks to achieve some degree of assent rather than convince utterly.

Thus a writer who takes Rogers seriously will, usually, in the first part of an argumentative essay

1. State the problem,
2. Give the opponent's position, and
3. Grant whatever validity the writer finds in that position — for instance, will recognize the circumstances in which the position would indeed be acceptable.

Next, the writer will, if possible,

4. Attempt to show how the opposing position will be improved if the writer's own position is accepted.

Sometimes, of course, the differing positions may be so far apart that no reconciliation can be proposed, in which case the writer will probably seek to show how the problem can best be solved by adopting the writer's own position. We have discussed these matters in Chapter 6, but not from the point of view of a psychotherapist, and so we reprint Rogers's essay here.

Carl R. Rogers

Communication: Its Blocking and Its Facilitation

It may seem curious that a person whose whole professional effort is devoted to psychotherapy should be interested in problems of communication. What relationship is there between providing therapeutic help to individuals with emotional maladjustments and the concern of this conference with obstacles to communication? Actually the relationship is very close indeed. The whole task of psychotherapy is the task of dealing with a failure in communication. The emotionally maladjusted person, the "neurotic," is in difficulty first because communication within himself has broken down, and second because as a result of this his communication with others has been damaged. If this sounds somewhat strange, then let me put it in other terms. In the "neurotic" individual, parts of himself which have been termed unconscious, or repressed, or denied to awareness, become blocked off so that they no longer communicate themselves to the conscious or managing part of himself. As long as this is true, there are distortions in the way he communicates himself to others, and so he suffers both within himself, and in his interpersonal relations. The task of psychotherapy is to help the person achieve, through a special relationship with a therapist, good communication within himself. Once this is achieved he can communicate more freely and more effectively with others. We may say then that psychotherapy is good communication, within and between men.

We may also turn that statement around and it will still be true. Good communication, free communication, within or between men, is always therapeutic.

It is, then, from a background of experience with communication in counseling and psychotherapy that I want to present here two ideas. I wish to state what I believe is one of the major factors in blocking or impeding communication, and then I wish to present what in our experience has proven to be a very important way to improving or facilitating communication.

I would like to propose, as an hypothesis for consideration, that the major barrier to mutual interpersonal communication is our very natural tendency to judge, to evaluate, to approve or disapprove, the statement of the person, or the other group. Let me illustrate my meaning with some very simple examples. As you leave the meeting tonight, one of the statements you are likely to hear is, "I didn't like that man's talk." Now what do you respond? Almost invariably your reply will be either approval or disapproval of the attitude expressed. Either you respond, "I didn't either. I thought it was terrible," or else you tend to reply, "Oh, I thought it was really good." In other words, your primary reaction is to evaluate what has just been said to you, to evaluate it from *your* point of view, your own frame of reference.

Or take another example. Suppose I say with some feeling, "I think the Republicans are behaving in ways that show a lot of good sound sense these days," what is the response that arises in your mind as you listen? The overwhelming likelihood is that it will be evaluative. You will find yourself agreeing, or disagreeing, or making some judgment about me such as "He must be a conservative," or "He seems solid in his thinking." Or let us take an illustration from the international scene. Russia says vehemently, "The treaty with Japan is a war plot on the part of the United States." We rise as one person to say "That's a lie!"

This last illustration brings in another element connected with my 5 hypothesis. Although the tendency to make evaluations is common in almost all interchange of language, it is very much heightened in those situations where feelings and emotions are deeply involved. So the stronger our feelings, the more likely it is that there will be no mutual element in the communication. There will be just two ideas, two feelings, two judgments, missing each other in psychological space. I'm sure you recognize this from your own experience. When you have not been emotionally involved yourself, and have listened to a heated discussion, you often go away thinking, "Well, they actually weren't talking about the same thing." And they were not. Each was making a judgment, an evaluation, from his own frame of reference. There was really nothing which could be called communication in any genuine sense. This tendency to react to any emotionally meaningful statement by forming an evaluation of it from our own point of view, is, I repeat, the major barrier to interpersonal communication.

But is there any way of solving this problem, of avoiding this barrier? I feel that we are making exciting progress toward this goal and I would like to present it as simply as I can. Real communication occurs, and this evaluative tendency is avoided, when we listen with understanding. What does that mean? It means *to see the expressed idea and attitude from the other person's point of view, to sense how it feels to him, to achieve his frame of reference in regard to the thing he is talking about.*

Stated so briefly, this may sound absurdly simple, but it is not. It is an approach which we have found extremely potent in the field of psychotherapy. It is the most effective agent we know for altering the basic personality structure of an individual, and improving his relationships and his communications with others. If I can listen to what he can tell me, if I can understand how it seems to him, if I can see its personal meaning for him, if I can sense the emotional flavor which it has for him, then I will be releasing potent forces of change in him. If I can really understand how he hates his father, or hates the university, or hates communists—if I can catch the flavor of his fear of insanity, or his fear of atom bombs, or of Russia—it will be of the greatest help to him in altering those very hatreds and fears, and in establishing realistic and harmonious relationships with the very people and situations toward which he has felt hatred and fear. We know from our research that such empathic understanding—understanding *with* a person, not *about* him—is such an effective approach that it can bring about major changes in personality.

Some of you may be feeling that you listen well to people, and that you have never seen such results. The chances are very great indeed that your listening has not been of the type I have described. Fortunately I can suggest a little laboratory experiment which you can try to test the quality of your understanding. The next time you get into an argument with your wife, or your friend, or with a small group of friends, just stop the discussion for a moment and for an experiment, institute this rule. "Each person can speak up for himself only *after* he has first restated the ideas and feelings of the previous speaker accurately, and to that speaker's satisfaction." You see what this would mean. It would simply mean that before presenting your own point of view, it would be necessary for you to really achieve the other speaker's frame of reference—to understand his thoughts and feelings so well that you could summarize them for him. Sounds simple, doesn't it? But if you try it you will discover it one of the most difficult things you have ever tried to do. However, once you have been able to see the other's point of view, your own comments will have to be drastically revised. You will also find the emotion going out of the discussion, the differences being reduced, and those differences which remain being of a rational and understandable sort.

Can you imagine what this kind of an approach would mean if it were projected into larger areas? What would happen to a labor-management dispute if it was conducted in such a way that labor, without necessarily agreeing, could accurately state management's point of view in a way that management could accept; and management, without approving labor's stand, could state labor's case in a way that labor agreed was accurate? It would mean that real communication was established, and one could practically guarantee that some reasonable solution would be reached.

If then this way of approach is an effective avenue to good communi-   10
cation and good relationships, as I am quite sure you will agree if you try the experiment I have mentioned, why is it not more widely tried and used? I will try to list the difficulties which keep it from being utilized.

In the first place it takes courage, a quality which is not too widespread. I am indebted to Dr. S. I. Hayakawa, the semanticist, for pointing out that to carry on psychotherapy in this fashion is to take a very real risk, and that courage is required. If you really understand another person in this way, if you are willing to enter his private world and see the way life appears to him, without any attempt to make evaluative judgments, you run the risk of being changed yourself. You might see it his way, you might find yourself influenced in your attitudes or your personality. This risk of being changed is one of the most frightening prospects most of us can face. If I enter, as fully as I am able, into the private world of a neurotic or psychotic individual, isn't there a risk that I might become lost in that world? Most of us are afraid to take that risk. Or if we had a Russian communist speaker here tonight, or Senator Joe McCarthy, how many of us would dare to try to see the world from each of these points of view? The great majority of us could not *listen;* we would find ourselves compelled to *evaluate,* because listening would seem too dangerous. So the first requirement is courage, and we do not always have it.

But there is a second obstacle. It is just when emotions are strongest that it is most difficult to achieve the frame of reference of the other person or group. Yet it is the time the attitude is most needed, if communication is to be established. We have not found this to be an insuperable obstacle in our experience in psychotherapy. A third party, who is able to lay aside his own feelings and evaluations, can assist greatly by listening with understanding to each person or group and clarifying the views and attitudes each holds. We have found this very effective in small groups in which contradictory or antagonistic attitudes exist. When the parties to a dispute realize that they are being understood, that someone sees how the situation seems to them, the statements grow less exaggerated and less defensive, and it is no longer necessary to maintain the attitude, "I am 100 percent right and you are 100 percent wrong." The influence of such an understanding catalyst in the group permits the members to come closer and closer to the objective truth involved in the relationship. In this way mutual communication is established and some type of agreement becomes much more possible. So we may say that though heightened emotions make it much more difficult to understand *with* an opponent, our experience makes it clear that a neutral, understanding, catalyst type of leader or therapist can overcome this obstacle in a small group.

This last phrase, however, suggests another obstacle to utilizing the approach I have described. Thus far all our experience has been with small face-to-face groups — groups exhibiting industrial tensions, religious tensions, racial tensions, and therapy groups in which many personal tensions are present. In these small groups our experience, confirmed by a limited amount of research, shows that this basic approach leads to improved communication, to greater acceptance of others and by others, and to attitudes which are more positive and more problem-solving in nature. There is a decrease in defensiveness, in exaggerated statements, in evaluative and critical behavior. But these findings are from small groups. What about trying to achieve understanding between larger groups that are geographically remote? Or between face-to-face groups who are not speaking for themselves, but simply as representatives of others, like the delegates at Kaesong?[1] Frankly we do not know the answers to these questions. I believe the situation might be put this way. As social scientists we have a tentative test-tube solution of the problem of breakdown in communication. But to confirm the validity of this test-tube solution, and to adapt it to the enormous problems of communication breakdown between classes, groups, and nations, would involve additional funds, much more research, and creative thinking of a high order.

Even with our present limited knowledge we can see some steps which might be taken, even in large groups, to increase the amount of listening *with*, and to decrease the amount of evaluation *about*. To be imaginative for a moment, let us suppose that a therapeutically oriented international group went to the Russian leaders and said, "We want to achieve a genuine understanding of your views and even more important, of your attitudes and feelings, toward the United States. We will summarize and resummarize the views and feelings if necessary, until you agree that our description represents the situation as it seems to you." Then suppose they did the same thing with the leaders in our own country. If they then gave the widest possible distribution to these two views, with the feelings clearly described but not expressed in name-calling, might not the effect be very great? It would not guarantee the type of understanding I have been describing, but it would make it much more possible. We can understand the feelings of a person who hates us much more readily when his attitudes are accurately described to us by a neutral third party, than we can when he is shaking his fist at us.

But even to describe such a first step is to suggest another obstacle to this approach of understanding. Our civilization does not yet have enough faith in the social sciences to utilize their findings. The opposite is true of the physical sciences. During the war[2] when a test-tube solution was

15

---

[1] **the delegates at Kaesong** Representatives of North and South Korea met at the border town of Kaesong to arrange terms for an armistice to hostilities during the Korean War (1950–1953). [All notes are the editors'.]
[2] **the war** World War II.

found to the problem of synthetic rubber, millions of dollars and an army of talent was turned loose on the problem of using that finding. If synthetic rubber could be made in milligrams, it could and would be made in the thousands of tons. And it was. But in the social science realm, if a way is found of facilitating communication and mutual understanding in small groups, there is no guarantee that the finding will be utilized. It may be a generation or more before the money and the brains will be turned loose to exploit that finding.

In closing, I would like to summarize this small-scale solution to the problem of barriers in communication, and to point out certain of its characteristics.

I have said that our research and experience to date would make it appear that breakdowns in communication, and the evaluative tendency which is the major barrier to communication, can be avoided. The solution is provided by creating a situation in which each of the different parties come to understand the other from the *other's* point of view. This has been achieved, in practice, even when feelings run high, by the influence of a person who is willing to understand each point of view empathically, and who thus acts as a catalyst to precipitate further understanding.

This procedure has important characteristics. It can be initiated by one party, without waiting for the other to be ready. It can even be initiated by a neutral third person, providing he can gain a minimum of cooperation from one of the parties.

This procedure can deal with the insincerities, the defensive exaggerations, the lies, the "false fronts" which characterize almost every failure in communication. These defensive distortions drop away with astonishing speed as people find that the only intent is to understand, not judge.

This approach leads steadily and rapidly toward the discovery of the   20 truth, toward a realistic appraisal of the objective barriers to communication. The dropping of some defensiveness by one party leads to further dropping of defensiveness by the other party, and truth is thus approached.

This procedure gradually achieves mutual communication. Mutual communication tends to be pointed toward solving a problem rather than toward attacking a person or group. It leads to a situation in which I see how the problem appears to you, as well as to me, and you see how it appears to me, as well as to you. Thus accurately and realistically defined, the problem is almost certain to yield to intelligent attack, or if it is in part insoluble, it will be comfortably accepted as such.

This then appears to be a test-tube solution to the breakdown of communication as it occurs in small groups. Can we take this small-scale answer, investigate it further, refine it; develop it and apply it to the tragic and well-nigh fatal failures of communication which threaten the very existence of our modern world? It seems to me that this is a possibility and a challenge which we should explore.

✓ A CHECKLIST FOR ANALYZING ROGERIAN ARGUMENT

☐ Have I stated the problem and indicated that a dialogue is possible?

☐ Have I stated at least one other point of view in a way that would satisfy its proponents?

☐ Have I been courteous to those who hold views other than mine?

☐ Have I enlarged my own understanding to the extent that I can grant validity, at least in some circumstances, to at least some aspects of other positions?

☐ Have I stated my position and indicated the contexts in which I believe it is valid?

☐ Have I pointed out the ground that we share?

☐ Have I shown how other positions will be strengthened by accepting some aspects of my position?

See the companion Web site **bedfordstmartins.com/barnetbedau** for links related to Rogerian argument.

Edward O. Wilson

Edward O. Wilson, born in in Birmingham, Alabama, in 1929, is a professor of evolutionary biology at Harvard University. A distinguished writer as well as a researcher and teacher, Wilson has twice won the Pulitzer Prize for General Non-Fiction.

Letter to a Southern Baptist Minister

Dear Pastor:

We have not met, yet I feel I know you well enough to call you friend. First of all, we grew up in the same faith. As a boy I too answered the altar call; I went under the water. Although I no longer belong to that faith, I am confident that if we met and spoke privately of our deepest beliefs, it would be in a spirit of mutual respect and good will. I know we share many precepts of moral behavior. Perhaps it also matters that we are both Americans and, insofar as it might still affect civility and good manners, we are both Southerners.

I write to you now for your counsel and help. Of course, in doing so, I see no way to avoid the fundamental differences in our respective worldviews. You are a literalist interpreter of Christian Holy Scripture. You reject the conclusion of science that mankind evolved from lower forms. You believe that each person's soul is immortal, making this planet a way station to a second, eternal life. Salvation is assured those who are redeemed in Christ.

I am a secular humanist. I think existence is what we make of it as individuals. There is no guarantee of life after death, and heaven and hell are what we create for ourselves, on this planet. There is no other home. Humanity originated here by evolution from lower forms over millions of years. And yes, I will speak plain, our ancestors were apelike animals. The human species has adapted physically and mentally to life on Earth and no place else. Ethics is the code of behavior we share on the basis of reason, law, honor, and an inborn sense of decency, even as some ascribe it to God's will.

For you, the glory of an unseen divinity; for me, the glory of the universe revealed at last. For you, the belief in God made flesh to save mankind; for me, the belief in Promethean fire seized to set men free. You have found your final truth; I am still searching. I may be wrong, you may be wrong. We may both be partly right.

Does this difference in worldview separate us in all things? It does 5 not. You and I and every other human being strive for the same imperatives of security, freedom of choice, personal dignity, and a cause to believe in that is larger than ourselves.

Let us see, then, if we can, and you are willing, to meet on the near side of metaphysics in order to deal with the real world we share. I put it this way because you have the power to help solve a great problem about which I care deeply. I hope you have the same concern. I suggest that we set aside our differences in order to save the Creation. The defense of living Nature is a universal value. It doesn't rise from, nor does it promote, any religious or ideological dogma. Rather, it serves without discrimination the interests of all humanity.

Pastor, we need your help. The Creation—living Nature—is in deep trouble. Scientists estimate that if habitat conversion and other destructive human activities continue at their present rates, half the species of plants and animals on Earth could be either gone or at least fated for early extinction by the end of the century. A full quarter will drop to this level during the next half century as a result of climate change alone. The ongoing extinction rate is calculated in the most conservative estimates to be about a hundred times above that prevailing before humans appeared on Earth, and it is expected to rise to at least a thousand times greater or more in the next few decades. If this rise continues unabated, the cost to humanity, in wealth, environmental security, and quality of life, will be catastrophic.

Surely we can agree that each species, however inconspicuous and humble it may seem to us at this moment, is a masterpiece of biology, and well worth saving. Each species possesses a unique combination of genetic traits that fits it more or less precisely to a particular part of the environment. Prudence alone dictates that we act quickly to prevent the extinction of species and, with it, the pauperization of Earth's ecosystems—hence of the Creation.

You may well ask at this point, Why me? Because religion and science are the two most powerful forces in the world today, including especially the United States. If religion and science could be united on the common ground of biological conservation, the problem would soon be solved. If there is any moral precept shared by people of all beliefs, it is that we owe ourselves and future generations a beautiful, rich, and healthful environment.

I am puzzled that so many religious leaders, who spiritually repre- 10 sent a large majority of people around the world, have hesitated to make protection of the Creation an important part of their magisterium. Do they believe that human-centered ethics and preparation for the afterlife are the only things that matter? Even more perplexing is the widespread conviction among Christians that the Second Coming is imminent, and that therefore the condition of the planet is of little consequence. Sixty percent of Americans, according to a 2004 poll, believe that the prophecies of the book of Revelation are accurate. Many of these, numbering in the millions, think the End of Time will occur within the life span of those now living. Jesus will return to Earth, and those redeemed by Christian faith will be transported bodily to heaven, while those left behind will struggle through severe hard times and, when they die, suffer eternal damnation. The condemned will remain in hell, like those already consigned in the generations before them, for a trillion trillion years, enough for the universe to expand to its own, entropic death, time enough for countless universes like it afterward to be born, expand, and likewise die away. And that is just the beginning of how long condemned souls will suffer in hell—all for a mistake they made in choice of religion during the infinitesimally small time they inhabited Earth.

For those who believe this form of Christianity, the fate of 10 million other life forms indeed does not matter. This and other similar doctrines are not gospels of hope and compassion. They are gospels of cruelty and despair. They were not born of the heart of Christianity. Pastor, tell me I am wrong!

However you will respond, let me here venture an alternative ethic. The great challenge of the twenty-first century is to raise people everywhere to a decent standard of living while preserving as much of the rest of life as possible. Science has provided this part of the argument for the ethic: the more we learn about the biosphere, the more complex and beautiful it turns out to be. Knowledge of it is a magic well: the more you draw from it, the more there is to draw. Earth, and especially the razor-thin film of life enveloping it, is our home, our wellspring, our physical and much of our spiritual sustenance.

I know that science and environmentalism are linked in the minds of many with evolution, Darwin, and secularism. Let me postpone disentangling all this (I will come back to it later) and stress again: to protect the beauty of Earth and of its prodigious variety of life forms should be a common goal, regardless of differences in our metaphysical beliefs.

To make the point in good gospel manner, let me tell the story of a young man, newly trained for the ministry, and so fixed in his Christian faith that he referred all questions of morality to readings from the Bible. When he visited the cathedral-like Atlantic rainforest of Brazil, he saw the manifest hand of God and in his notebook wrote, "It is not possible to give an adequate idea of the higher feelings of wonder, admiration, and devotion which fill and elevate the mind."

That was Charles Darwin in 1832, early into the voyage of HMS 15 *Beagle*, before he had given any thought to evolution.

And here is Darwin, concluding *On the Origin of Species* in 1859, having first abandoned Christian dogma and then, with his newfound intellectual freedom, formulated the theory of evolution by natural selection: "There is grandeur in this view of life, with its several powers, having been originally breathed into a few forms or into one; and that, whilst this planet has gone cycling on according to the fixed law of gravity, from so simple a beginning endless forms most beautiful and most wonderful have been, and are being, evolved."

Darwin's reverence for life remained the same as he crossed the seismic divide that divided his spiritual life. And so it can be for the divide that today separates scientific humanism from mainstream religion. And separates you and me.

You are well prepared to present the theological and moral arguments for saving the Creation. I am heartened by the movement growing within Christian denominations to support global conservation. The stream of thought has arisen from many sources, from evangelical to unitarian. Today it is but a rivulet. Tomorrow it will be a flood.

I already know much of the religious argument on behalf of the Creation, and would like to learn more. I will now lay before you and others who may wish to hear it the scientific argument. You will not agree with all that I say about the origins of life — science and religion do not easily mix in such matters — but I like to think that in this one life-and-death issue we have a common purpose.

TOPICS FOR CRITICAL THINKING AND WRITING

1. Wilson claims to be a "secular humanist" (para. 3). How would you define that term? Are you a secular humanist? Why, or why not?

2. What does Wilson mean by "metaphysics" (para. 6)? Which if any of his views qualify as metaphysical?

3. Wilson obviously seeks to present his views in a fashion that makes them as palatable as possible. Do you think he succeeds in this endeavor? Write an essay of 500 words arguing for or against his achievement in this regard.

13

A Literary Critic's View: Arguing about Literature

Literary criticism [is] a reasoned account of the feeling produced upon the critic by the book he is reading.

—D. H. LAWRENCE

A writer is someone for whom writing is more difficult than it is for other people.

—THOMAS MANN

You can never draw the line between aesthetic criticism and social criticism . . . You start with literary criticism, and however rigorous an aesthete you may be, you are over the frontier into something else sooner or later. The best you can do is to accept these conditions and know what you are doing when you are doing it.

—T. S. ELIOT

Nothing is as easy as it looks.

—MURPHY'S LAW #23

Everything is what it is and not another thing.

—BISHOP JOSEPH BUTLER

You might think that literature—fiction, poetry (including songs), drama—is meant only to be enjoyed, not to be argued about. Yet literature is constantly the subject of argumentative writing—not all of it by teachers of English. For instance, if you glance at the current issue of *Time* or *Newsweek*, you probably will find a review of a play suggesting that the play is worth seeing or is not worth seeing. Or in the same magazine you may find an article reporting that a senator or member of Congress argued that the National Endowment for the Humanities wasted its grant money by funding research on such-and-such an author or that the National Endowment for the Arts insulted taxpayers by making an award to a writer who defamed the American family.

Probably most writing about literature, whether done by college students, their professors, journalists, members of Congress, or whomever, is devoted to interpreting, judging (evaluating), and theorizing. Let's look at each of these, drawing our examples chiefly from comments about Shakespeare's *Macbeth*.

INTERPRETING

Interpreting is a matter of setting forth the *meaning* or the meanings of a work. For some readers, a work has *a* meaning, the one intended by the writer, which we may or may not perceive. For most critics today, however, a work has *many* meanings—for instance, the meaning it had for the writer, the meanings it has accumulated over time, and the meanings it has for each of today's readers. Take *Macbeth*, a play about a Scottish king, written soon after a Scot—James VI of Scotland—had been installed as James I, King of England. The play must have meant something special to the king—we know that it was presented at court—and something a little different to the ordinary English citizen. And surely it means something different to us. For instance, few if any people today believe in the divine right of kings, although James I certainly did; and few if any people today believe in malignant witches, although witches play an important role in the tragedy. What *we* see in the play must be rather different from what Shakespeare's audience saw in it.

Many interpretations of *Macbeth* have been offered. Let's take two fairly simple and clearly opposed views:

1. Macbeth is a villain who, by murdering his lawful king, offends God's rule, so he is overthrown by God's earthly instruments, Malcolm and Macduff. Macbeth is justly punished; the reader or spectator rejoices in his defeat.

One can offer a good deal of evidence—and if one is taking this position in an essay, of course one must *argue* it—by giving supporting reasons rather than merely assert the position.

Here is a second view.

2. Macbeth is a hero-villain, a man who commits terrible crimes but who never completely loses the reader's sympathy; although he is justly punished, the reader believes that with the death of Macbeth the world has become a smaller place.

Again, one *must* offer evidence in an essay that presents this thesis or indeed presents any interpretation. For instance, one might offer as evidence the fact that the survivors, especially Macduff and Malcolm, have not interested us nearly as much as Macbeth has. One might argue, too, that although Macbeth's villainy is undeniable, his conscience never deserts him—here one would point to specific passages and would offer some brief quotations. Macbeth's pained awareness of what he has done, it can be argued, enables the reader to sympathize with him continually.

Or consider an interpretation of Lady Macbeth. Is she simply evil through and through, or are there mitigating reasons for her actions? Might one argue, perhaps in a feminist interpretation, that despite her intelligence and courage she had no outlet for expression except through her husband? To make this argument, the writer might want to go beyond the text of the play, offering as evidence Elizabethan comments about the proper role of women.

JUDGING (OR EVALUATING)

Literary criticism is also concerned with such questions as these: Is *Macbeth* a great tragedy? Is *Macbeth* a greater tragedy than *Romeo and Juliet*? The writer offers an opinion about the worth of the literary work, but the opinion must be supported by an argument, expressed in sentences that offer supporting evidence.

Let's pause for a moment to think about evaluation in general. When we say "This is a great play," are we in effect saying only "I like this play"? That is, are we merely *expressing* our taste rather than *asserting* anything about something out there—something independent of our tastes and feelings? (The next few paragraphs will not answer this question, but they may start you thinking about your own answer.) Consider these three sentences:

1. It's raining outside.
2. I like vanilla.
3. This is a really good book.

If you are indoors and you say that it is raining outside, a hearer may ask for verification. Why do you say what you say? "Because," you reply, "I'm looking out the window." Or "Because Jane just came in, and she is drenched." Or "Because I just heard a weather report." If, on the other hand, you say that you like vanilla, it's almost unthinkable that anyone would ask you why. No one expects you to justify—to support, to give a reason for—an expression of taste.

Now consider the third statement, "This is a really good book." It is entirely reasonable, we think, for someone to ask you *why* you say that. And you reply, "Well, the characters are realistic, and the plot held my interest," or "It really gave me an insight into what life among the rich [or the poor] must be like," or some such thing.

That is, statement 3 at least seems to be stating a fact, and it seems to be something we can discuss, even argue about, in a way that we cannot argue about a personal preference for vanilla. Almost everyone would agree that when we offer an aesthetic judgment we ought to be able to give reasons for it. At the very least, we might say, we hope to show *why* we evaluate the work as we do, and to suggest that if our readers try to see it from our point of view they may then accept our evaluation.

Evaluations are always based on assumptions, although these assumptions may be unstated, and in fact the writer may even be unaware of them. Some of these assumptions play the role of criteria; they control the sort of evidence the writer believes is relevant to the evaluation. What sorts of assumptions may underlie value judgments? We will mention a few, merely as examples. Other assumptions are possible, and all of these assumptions can themselves become topics of dispute:

1. A good work of art, although fictional, says something about real life.
2. A good work of art is complex yet unified.
3. A good work of art sets forth a wholesome view of life.
4. A good work of art is original.
5. A good work of art deals with an important subject.

Let's look briefly at these views, one by one.

1. *A good work of art, although fictional, says something about real life.* If you hold the view that literature is connected to life and believe that human beings behave in fairly consistent ways—that is, that each of us has an enduring "character"—you probably will judge as inferior a work in which the figures behave inconsistently or seem not to be adequately motivated. (The point must be made, however, that different literary forms or genres are governed by different rules. For instance, consistency of character is usually expected in tragedy but not in melodrama or in comedy, where last-minute reformations may be welcome and greeted with applause. The novelist Henry James said, "You will not write a good novel unless you possess the sense of reality." He is probably right—but does his view hold for the writer of farces?) In the case of *Macbeth* you might well find that the characters are consistent: Although the play begins by showing Macbeth as a loyal defender of King Duncan, Macbeth's later treachery is understandable, given the temptation and the pressure. Similarly, Lady Macbeth's descent into madness, although it may come as a surprise, may strike you as entirely plausible: At the beginning of the play she is confident that she can become an accomplice to a murder, but she has overestimated herself (or, we might say, she has underestimated her own humanity, the power of her guilty conscience, which drives her to insanity).

2. *A good work of art is complex yet unified.* If Macbeth is only a "tyrant" (Macduff's word) or a "butcher" (Malcolm's word), he is a unified character but he may be too simple and too uninteresting a character to be the subject of a great play. But, one argument holds, Macbeth in fact is a complex character, not simply a villain but a hero-villain, and the play as a whole is complex. *Macbeth* is a good work of art, one might argue, partly because it shows us so many aspects of life (courage, fear, loyalty, treachery, for a start) through a richly varied language (the diction

ranges from a grand passage in which Macbeth says that his bloody hands will "incarnadine," or make red, "the multitudinous seas" to colloquial passages such as the drunken porter's "Knock, knock"). The play shows us the heroic Macbeth tragically destroying his own life, and it shows us the comic porter making coarse jokes about deceit and damnation, jokes that (although the porter doesn't know it) connect with Macbeth's crimes.

3. *A good work of art sets forth a wholesome view of life.* The idea that a work should be judged partly or largely on the moral view that it contains is widely held by the general public. (It has also been held by esteemed philosophers, notably Plato.) Thus, a story that demeans women—perhaps one that takes a casual view of rape—would be given a low rating and so would a play that treats a mass murderer as a hero.

Implicit in this approach is what is called an *instrumentalist* view—the idea that a work of art is an instrument, a means, to some higher value. Thus, many people hold that reading great works of literature makes us better—or at least does not make us worse. In this view, a work that is pornographic or in some other way thought to be immoral will be given a low value. At the time we are writing this chapter, a law requires the National Endowment for the Arts to take into account standards of decency when making awards.

Moral judgments, it should be noted, do not come only from the conservative right; the liberal left has been quick to detect political incorrectness. In fact, except for those people who subscribe to the now unfashionable view that a work of art is an independent aesthetic object with little or no connection to the real world—something like a pretty floral arrangement or a wordless melody—most people judge works of literature largely by their content, by what the works seem to say about life.

- Marxist critics, for instance, have customarily held that literature should make the reader aware of the political realities of life.

- Feminist critics are likely to hold that literature should make us aware of gender relationships—for example, aware of patriarchal power and of female accomplishments.

4. *A good work of art is original.* This assumption puts special value on new techniques and new subject matter. Thus, the *first* playwright who introduces a new subject (say, AIDS) gets extra credit, so to speak. Or to return to Shakespeare, one sign of his genius, it is held, is that he was so highly varied; none of his tragedies seems merely to duplicate another, each is a world of its own, a new kind of achievement. Compare, for instance, *Romeo and Juliet*, with its two youthful and innocent heroes, with *Macbeth*, with its deeply guilty hero. Both plays are tragedies, but we can hardly imagine two more different plays—even if a reader perversely argues that the young lovers are guilty of impetuosity and of disobeying appropriate authorities.

5. *A good work of art deals with an important subject.* Here we are concerned with theme: Great works, in this view, must deal with great themes. Love, death, patriotism, and God, say, are great themes; a work that deals with these may achieve a height, an excellence, that, say, a work describing a dog scratching for fleas may not achieve. (Of course, if the reader feels that the dog is a symbol of humanity plagued by invisible enemies, then the poem about the dog may reach the heights, but then, too, it is *not* a poem about a dog and fleas: It is really a poem about humanity and the invisible.)

The point: In writing an evaluation you must let your reader know *why* you value the work as you do. Obviously, it is not enough just to keep saying that *this* work is great whereas *that* work is not so great; the reader wants to know *why* you offer the judgments that you do, which means that you

- Must set forth your criteria and then
- Offer evidence that is in accord with them.

THEORIZING

Some literary criticism is concerned with such theoretical questions as these:

✓ A CHECKLIST FOR AN ARGUMENT ABOUT LITERATURE

☐ Is my imagined reader like a typical classmate of mine, someone who is not a specialist in literature but who is open-minded and interested in hearing my point of view about a work?

☐ Is the essay supported with evidence, usually from the text itself but conceivably from other sources (such as a statement by the author, a statement by a person regarded as an authority, or perhaps the evidence of comparable works)?

☐ Is the essay inclusive? Does it take into account all relevant details (which is not to say that it includes everything the writer knows about the work—for instance, that it was made into a film or that the author died poor)?

☐ Is the essay focused? Does the thesis stay steadily before the reader?

☐ Does the essay use quotations, but as evidence, not as padding? Whenever possible, does it abridge or summarize long quotations?

☐ Are all sources fully acknowledged? (For the form of documentation, see Chapter 7.)

What is tragedy? Can the hero be a villain? How does tragedy differ from melodrama?

Why do tragedies—works showing good or at least interesting people destroyed—give us pleasure?

Does a work of art—a play or a novel, say, a made-up world with imagined characters—offer anything that can be called "truth"? Does an experience of a work of art affect our character?

Does a work of art have meaning in itself, or is the meaning simply whatever anyone wishes to say it is? Does *Macbeth* tell us anything about life, or is it just an invented story?

And, yet again, one hopes that anyone asserting a thesis concerned with any of these topics will offer evidence—will, indeed, *argue* rather than merely assert.

EXAMPLES:
Two Students Interpret Robert Frost's "Mending Wall"

Let's consider two competing interpretations of a poem, Robert Frost's "Mending Wall." We say "competing" because these interpretations clash head-on. Differing interpretations need not be incompatible, of course. For instance, a historical interpretation of *Macbeth*, arguing that an understanding of the context of English-Scottish politics around 1605 helps us to appreciate the play, need not be incompatible with a psycho-analytic interpretation that tells us that Macbeth's murder of King Duncan is rooted in an Oedipus complex, the king being a father figure. Different approaches thus can illuminate different aspects of the work, just as they can emphasize or subordinate different elements in the plot or characters portrayed. But, again, in the next few pages we will deal with mutually incompatible interpretations of the meaning of Frost's poem—of what Frost's poem is about.

After reading the poem and the two interpretations written by students, spend a few minutes thinking about the questions that we raise after the second interpretation.

Robert Frost

Robert Frost (1874–1963) studied for part of one term at Dartmouth College in New Hampshire, then did odd jobs (including teaching), and from 1897 to 1899 was enrolled as a special student at Harvard. He then farmed in New Hampshire,

published a few poems in newspapers, did some more teaching, and in 1912 left
for England, where he hoped to achieve success as a writer. By 1915 he was
known in England, and he returned to the United States. By the time of his death
he was the nation's unofficial poet laureate. "Mending Wall" was first published
in 1914.

Mending Wall

Something there is that doesn't love a wall,
That sends the frozen-ground-swell under it,
And spills the upper boulders in the sun;
And makes gaps even two can pass abreast.
The work of hunters is another thing: 5
I have come after them and made repair
Where they have left not one stone on a stone,
But they would have the rabbit out of hiding,
To please the yelping dogs. The gaps I mean,
No one has seen them made or heard them made,   10
But at spring mending-time we find them there.
I let my neighbor know beyond the hill;
And on a day we meet to walk the line
And set the wall between us once again.
We keep the wall between us as we go.   15
To each the boulders that have fallen to each.
And some are loaves and some so nearly balls
We have to use a spell to make them balance:
"Stay where you are until our backs are turned!"
We wear our fingers rough with handling them.   20
Oh, just another kind of outdoor game,
One on a side. It comes to little more:
There where it is we do not need the wall:
He is all pine and I am apple orchard.
My apple trees will never get across   25
And eat the cones under his pines, I tell him.
He only says, "Good fences make good neighbors."
Spring is the mischief in me, and I wonder
If I could put a notion in his head:
"*Why* do they make good neighbors? Isn't it   30
Where there are cows? But here there are no cows.
Before I built a wall I'd ask to know
What I was walling in or walling out,
And to whom I was like to give offense.
Something there is that doesn't love a wall,   35
That wants it down." I could say "Elves" to him,
But it's not elves exactly, and I'd rather
He said it for himself. I see him there

Bringing a stone grasped firmly by the top
In each hand, like an old-stone savage armed.   40
He moves in darkness as it seems to me,
Not of woods only and the shade of trees.
He will not go behind his father's saying,
And he likes having thought of it so well
He says again, "Good fences make good neighbors."   45

Jonathan Deutsch

Professor Walton

English 102

5 March 2009

The Deluded Speaker in Frost's "Mending Wall"

Our discussions of "Mending Wall" in high school showed that most people think Frost is saying that walls between people are a bad thing and that we should not try to separate ourselves from each other unnecessarily. Perhaps the wall, in this view, is a symbol for race prejudice or religious differences, and Frost is suggesting that these differences are minor and that they should not keep us apart. In this common view, the neighbor's words, "Good fences make good neighbors" (lines 27 and 45) show that the neighbor is shortsighted. I disagree with this view, but first I want to present the evidence that might be offered for it, so that we can then see whether it really is substantial.

First of all, someone might claim that in lines 23 to 26 Frost offers a good argument against walls:

There where it is we do not need the wall:

He is all pine and I am apple orchard.

My apple trees will never get across

And eat the cones under his pines, I tell him.

The neighbor does not offer a valid reply to this argument; in fact, he doesn't offer any argument at all but simply says, "Good fences make good neighbors."

Another piece of evidence supposedly showing that the neighbor is wrong, it is said, is found in Frost's description of him as "an old-stone savage" and someone who "moves in darkness" (40, 41). And a third piece of evidence is said to be that the neighbor "will not go behind his father's saying" (43), but he merely repeats the saying.

Deutsch 2

There is, however, another way of looking at the poem. As I see it, the speaker is a very snide and condescending person. He is confident that he knows it all and that his neighbor is an ignorant savage; he is even willing to tease his supposedly ignorant neighbor. For instance, the speaker admits to "the mischief in me" (28), and he is confident that he could tell the truth to the neighbor but arrogantly thinks that it would be a more effective form of teaching if the neighbor "said it for himself" (38).

The speaker is not only unpleasantly mischievous and condescending toward his neighbor, but he is also shallow, for he does not see the great wisdom that there is in proverbs. The *American Heritage Dictionary of the English Language*, Third Edition, defines a proverb as "A short, pithy saying in frequent and widespread use that expresses a basic truth." Frost, or at least the man who speaks this poem, does not seem to realize that proverbs express truths. He just dismisses them, and he thinks the neighbor is wrong not to "go behind his father's saying" (43). But there is a great deal of wisdom in the sayings of our fathers. For instance, in the Bible (in the Old Testament) there is a whole book of proverbs, filled with wise sayings such as "Reprove not a scorner, lest he hate thee: rebuke a wise man, and he will love thee" (9:8); "He that trusteth in his riches shall fall" (11:28); "The way of a fool is right in his own eyes" (12:15; this might be said of the speaker of "Mending Wall"); "A soft answer turneth away wrath" (15:1); and (to cut short what could be a list many pages long), "Whoso diggeth a pit shall fall therein" (26:27).

The speaker is confident that walls are unnecessary and probably bad, but he doesn't realize that even where there are no cattle, walls serve the valuable purpose of clearly marking out our territory. They help us to preserve our independence and our individuality. Walls — man-made structures — are a sign of civilization. A wall more or less says, "*This* is mine, but I respect *that* as yours."

Frost's speaker is so confident of his shallow view that he makes fun of his neighbor for repeating that "Good fences make good neighbors" (27, 45). But he himself repeats his own saying, "Something there is that doesn't love a wall" (1, 35). And at least the neighbor has age-old tradition on his side, since the proverb is the saying of his father. On the other hand, the speaker has only his own opinion, and he can't even say what the "something" is.

It may be that Frost meant for us to laugh at the neighbor and to take the side of the speaker, but I think it is much more likely that he meant for us to see that the speaker is mean-spirited (or at least given to unpleasant teasing), too self-confident, foolishly dismissing the wisdom of the old times, and entirely unaware that he has these unpleasant characteristics.

Felicia Alonso

Professor Walton

English 102

5 March 2009

The Debate in Robert Frost's "Mending Wall"

I think the first thing to say about Frost's "Mending Wall" is this: The poem is not about a debate over whether good fences do or do not make good neighbors. It is about two debaters: One of the debaters is on the side of vitality, and the other is on the side of an unchanging, fixed—dead, we might say—tradition.

How can we characterize the speaker? For one thing, he is neighborly. Interestingly, it is *he,* and not the neighbor, who initiates the repairing of the wall: "I let my neighbor know beyond the hill" (line 12). This seems strange, since the speaker doesn't see any point in this wall, whereas the neighbor is all in favor of walls. Can we explain this apparent contradiction? Yes; the speaker is a good neighbor, willing to do his share of the work and willing (perhaps in order not to upset his neighbor) to maintain an old tradition even though he doesn't see its importance. It may not be important, he thinks, but it is really rather pleasant, "another kind of outdoor game" (21). In fact, sometimes he even repairs fences on his own, after hunters have destroyed them.

Second, we can say that the speaker is on the side of nature. "Something there is that doesn't love a wall," he says (1, 35), and of course, the "something" is nature itself. Nature "sends the frozen-ground-swell" under the wall and "spills the upper boulders in the sun; / And makes gaps even two can pass abreast" (2–4). Notice that nature itself makes the gaps and that "two can pass abreast"—that is, people can walk together in a companionable way. It is hard to imagine the neighbor walking side by side with anyone.

Third, we can say that the speaker has a sense of humor. When he thinks of trying to get his neighbor interested in the issue, he admits that "the mischief" is in him (28), and he amusingly attributes his playfulness to a natural force, the spring. He playfully toys with the obviously preposterous idea of suggesting to his neighbor that elves caused the stones to fall, but he stops short of making this amusing suggestion to his very serious neighbor. Still, the mere thought assures us that he has a playful, genial nature, and the idea also again implies that not only the speaker but also some sort of mysterious natural force dislikes walls.

Finally, though, of course, he thinks he is right and that his neighbor is mistaken, he at least is cautious in his view. He does not call his neighbor "an old-stone savage" (40); rather, he uses a simile ("like") and then adds that this is only his opinion, so the opinion is softened quite a bit. Here is the description of the neighbor, with underlining added to clarify my point. The neighbor is . . .

> *like* an old-stone savage armed. / He moves
>
> in darkness *as it seems to me* . . . (40–41)

Of course, the only things we know about the neighbor are those things that the speaker chooses to tell us, so it is not surprising that the speaker comes out ahead. He comes out ahead not because he is right about walls (real or symbolic) and his neighbor is wrong — that's an issue that is not settled in the poem. He comes out ahead because he is a more interesting figure, someone who is neighborly, thoughtful, playful. Yes, maybe he seems to us to feel superior to his neighbor, but we can be certain that he doesn't cause his neighbor any embarrassment. Take the very end of the poem. The speaker tells us that the neighbor

> . . . will not go behind his father's saying,
>
> And he likes having thought of it so well
>
> He says again, "Good fences make good neighbors."

Alonso 3

The speaker is telling *us* that the neighbor is utterly unoriginal and that the neighbor confuses *remembering* something with *thinking*. But the speaker doesn't get into an argument; he doesn't rudely challenge his neighbor and demand reasons, which might force the neighbor to see that he can't think for himself. And in fact we probably like the neighbor just as he is, and we don't want him to change his mind. The words that ring in our ears are not the speaker's but the neighbor's: "Good fences make good neighbors." The speaker of the poem is a good neighbor. After all, one can hardly be more neighborly than to let the neighbor have the last word.

TOPICS FOR CRITICAL THINKING AND WRITING

1. State the thesis of each essay. Do you believe the theses are sufficiently clear and appear sufficiently early in the essays?

2. Consider the evidence that each essay offers by way of supporting its thesis. Do you find some of the evidence unconvincing? Explain.

3. Putting aside the question of which interpretation you prefer, comment on the organization of each essay. Is the organization clear? Do you want to propose some other pattern that you think might be more effective?

4. Consult the Checklist for Peer Review on page 255, and offer comments on one of the two essays. Or: If you were the instructor in the course in which these two essays were submitted, what might be your final comments on each of them? Or: Write an analysis (250–500 words) of the strengths and weaknesses of either essay.

EXERCISES: READING A POEM AND A STORY

Andrew Marvell

Andrew Marvell (1621–1678), born in Hull, England, and educated at Trinity College, Cambridge, was traveling in Europe when the civil war between the royalists and the puritans broke out in England in 1642. The puritans were victorious and established the Commonwealth (the monarchy was restored later, in 1660), and Marvell became a tutor to the daughter of the victorious Lord-General. In 1657 he became an assistant to the blind poet John Milton, who held the title of Latin Secretary (Latin was the language of international diplomacy). In 1659 Marvell was elected to represent Hull in Parliament. As a man of letters, during his lifetime he was known chiefly for some satiric prose and poetry; most of the writings for which he is now esteemed were published posthumously. The following poem was first published in 1681.

To His Coy Mistress°

Had we but world enough, and time,
This coyness,° Lady, were no crime.
We would sit down, and think which way
To walk, and pass our long love's day.
Thou by the Indian Ganges' side   5
Shouldst rubies find; I by the tide
Of Humber° would complain. I would
Love you ten years before the Flood,
And you should, if you please, refuse

Mistress Beloved woman.
coyness Reluctance.
Humber An estuary at Hull, Marvell's birthplace.

Till the Conversion of the Jews.°   10
My vegetable° love should grow
Vaster than empires and more slow;
An hundred years should go to praise
Thine eyes, and on thy forehead gaze;
Two hundred to adore each breast,   15
But thirty thousand to the rest;
An age at least to every part,
And the last age should show your heart.
For, Lady, you deserve this state,°
Nor would I love at lower rate.   20
    But at my back I always hear
Time's wingèd chariot hurrying near;
And yonder all before us lie
Deserts of vast eternity.
Thy beauty shall no more be found,   25
Nor, in thy marble vault, shall sound
My echoing song; then worms shall try°
That long-preserved virginity,
And your quaint° honour turn to dust,
And into ashes all my lust: 30
The grave's a fine and private place,
But none, I think, do there embrace.
    Now therefore, while the youthful hue
Sits on thy skin like morning dew,
And while thy willing soul transpires   35
At every pore with instant fires,
Now let us sport us while we may,
And now, like amorous birds of prey,
Rather at once our time devour
Than languish in his slow-chapt° power.   40
Let us roll all our strength and all
Our sweetness up into one ball,
And tear our pleasures with rough strife
Thorough° the iron gates of life:
Thus, though we cannot make our sun   45
Stand still,° yet we will make him run.

Conversion of the Jews Something that would take place in the remote future, at the
end of history.
vegetable Vegetative or growing.
state Ceremonious treatment.
try Test.
quaint Fastidious or finicky, with a pun on a coarse word defined in an Elizabethan dictionary as "a woman's privities."
slow-chapt Slow-jawed.
Thorough Through.
make our sun stand still An allusion to Joshua, the ancient Hebrew who, according to
the Book of Joshua (10.12–13), made the sun stand still.

TOPICS FOR CRITICAL THINKING AND WRITING

1. The motif that life is short and that we should seize the day (Latin: *Vita brevis carpe diem*) is old. Marvell's poem, in fact, probably has its ultimate source in a classical text called *The Greek Anthology*, a collection of about six thousand short Greek poems composed between the first century B.C. and the tenth century A.D. One poem goes thus, in a fairly literal translation:

   > You spare your maidenhead, and to what profit? For when you come to Hades you will not find your lover, girl. Among the living are the delights of Venus, but, maiden, we shall lie in the underworld mere bones and dust.

   If you find Marvell's poem more impressive, offer reasons for your belief.

2. A student, working from the translation just given, produced this rhyming version:

   > You keep your virginity, but to what end?
   > Below, in Hades, you won't find your friend.
   > On earth we enjoy Venus' sighs and moans;
   > Buried below, we are senseless bones.

   What do you think of this version? Why? Prepare your own version — your instructor may divide the class into groups of four, and each group can come up with a collaborative version — and then compare it with other versions, giving reasons for your preferences.

3. Marvell's poem takes the form of a syllogism (see pp. 82–84). It can be divided into three parts:

   a. "Had we" (that is, "If we had") (line 1), a supposition, or suppositional premise;
   b. "But at my back" (line 21), a refutation;
   c. "Now therefore" (line 33), a deduction.

   Look closely at the poem and develop the argument using these three parts, devoting a few sentences to each part.

4. A student wrote of this poem:

   > As a Christian I can't accept the lover's statement that "yonder all before us lie / Deserts of vast eternity" (lines 23–24). The poem may contain beautiful lines, and it may offer clever reasoning, but the reasoning is based on what my religion tells me is wrong. I not only cannot accept the idea of the poem, but I also cannot enjoy the poem, since it presents a false view of reality.

   What assumptions is this student making about a reader's response to a work of literature? Do you agree or disagree? Why?

5. Here are three additional comments by students. For each, list the writer's assumptions, and then evaluate each comment. You may agree or disagree, in whole or in part, with any comment, but give your reasons.

   a. The poem is definitely clever, and that is part of what is wrong with it. It is a blatant attempt at seduction. The man seems to think he is smarter than the woman he is speaking to, and he "proves" that she should go to bed with him. Since we don't hear her side of the argument, Marvell implies that she has nothing to say and that his argument is sound. What the poet doesn't seem to understand is that there is such a thing as virtue, and a woman need not sacrifice virtue just because death is inevitable.

b. On the surface, "To His Coy Mistress" is an attempt to persuade a woman to go to bed with the speaker, but the poem is really less about sex than it is about the terrifying shortness of life.

c. This is not a love poem. The speaker admits that his impulse is "lust" (line 30), and he makes fun of the girl's conception of honor and virginity. If we enjoy this poem at all, our enjoyment must be in the hope that this would-be date-rapist is unsuccessful.

6. Read the poem several times slowly, perhaps even aloud. Do certain lines seem especially moving, especially memorable? If so, which ones? Give reasons for your belief.

7. In *On Deconstruction* (1982), a study of contemporary literary theory, Jonathan Culler remarks that feminist criticism has often stressed "reading as a woman." This concept, Culler says, affirms the "continuity between women's experience of social and familial structures and their experiences as readers." Do you agree with his suggestion that men and women often interpret literary works differently? Consider Marvell's poem in particular: Identify and discuss phrases and images in it to which men and women readers might (or might not) respond very differently.

8. A small point, but perhaps one of some interest. In the original text, line 34 ends with *glew*, not with *dew*. Most editors assume that the printer made an error, and—looking for a word to rhyme with *hue*—they replace *glew* with *dew*. Another possible emendation is *lew*, an archaic word meaning "warmth." But the original reading has been defended, as a variant of the word *glow*. Your preference? Your reasons?

Kate Chopin

Kate Chopin (1851–1904) was born in St. Louis and named Katherine O'Flaherty. At the age of nineteen she married a cotton broker in New Orleans, Oscar Chopin (the name is pronounced something like "show pan"), who was descended from the early French settlers in Louisiana. After her husband's death in 1883, Kate Chopin turned to writing fiction. The following story was first published in 1894.

The Story of an Hour

Knowing that Mrs. Mallard was afflicted with a heart trouble, great care was taken to break to her as gently as possible the news of her husband's death.

It was her sister Josephine who told her, in broken sentences, veiled hints that revealed in half concealing. Her husband's friend Richards was there, too, near her. It was he who had been in the newspaper office when intelligence of the railroad disaster was received, with Brently Mallard's name leading the list of "killed." He had only taken the time to assure himself of its truth by a second telegram, and had hastened to forestall any less careful, less tender friend in bearing the sad message.

She did not hear the story as many women have heard the same, with a paralyzed inability to accept its significance. She wept at once, with sudden, wild abandonment, in her sister's arms. When the storm of grief had spent itself she went away to her room alone. She would have no one follow her.

There stood, facing the open window, a comfortable, roomy armchair. Into this she sank, pressed down by a physical exhaustion that haunted her body and seemed to reach into her soul.

She could see in the open square before her house the tops of trees 5 that were all aquiver with the new spring life. The delicious breath of rain was in the air. In the street below a peddler was crying his wares. The notes of a distant song which some one was singing reached her faintly, and countless sparrows were twittering in the eaves.

There were patches of blue sky showing here and there through the clouds that had met and piled one above the other in the west facing her window.

She sat with her head thrown back upon the cushion of the chair, quite motionless, except when a sob came up into her throat and shook her, as a child who has cried itself to sleep continues to sob in its dreams.

She was young, with a fair, calm face, whose lines bespoke repression and even a certain strength. But now there was a dull stare in her eyes, whose gaze was fixed away off yonder on one of those patches of blue sky. It was not a glance of reflection, but rather indicated a suspension of intelligent thought.

There was something coming to her and she was waiting for it, fearfully. What was it? She did not know; it was too subtle and elusive to name. But she felt it, creeping out of the sky, reaching toward her through the sounds, the scents, the color that filled the air.

Now her bosom rose and fell tumultuously. She was beginning to 10 recognize this thing that was approaching to possess her, and she was striving to beat it back with her will—as powerless as her two white slender hands would have been.

When she abandoned herself a little whispered word escaped her slightly parted lips. She said it over and over under her breath: "Free, free, free!" The vacant stare and the look of terror that had followed it went from her eyes. They stayed keen and bright. Her pulses beat fast, and the coursing blood warmed and relaxed every inch of her body.

She did not stop to ask if it were not a monstrous joy that held her. A clear and exalted perception enabled her to dismiss the suggestion as trivial.

She knew that she would weep again when she saw the kind, tender hands folded in death; the face that had never looked save with love upon her, fixed and gray and dead. But she saw beyond that bitter moment a long procession of years to come that would belong to her absolutely. And she opened and spread her arms out to them in welcome.

There would be no one to live for her during those coming years; she would live for herself. There would be no powerful will bending her in that blind persistence with which men and women believe they have a right to impose a private will upon a fellow creature. A kind intention or a cruel intention made the act seem no less a crime as she looked upon it in that brief moment of illumination.

And yet she had loved him — sometimes. Often she had not. What   15 did it matter! What could love, the unsolved mystery, count for in face of this possession of self-assertion which she suddenly recognized as the strongest impulse of her being.

"Free! Body and soul free!" she kept whispering.

Josephine was kneeling before the closed door with her lips to the keyhole, imploring for admission. "Louise, open the door! I beg; open the door — you will make yourself ill. What are you doing, Louise? For heaven's sake open the door."

"Go away. I am not making myself ill." No; she was drinking in a very elixir of life through that open window.

Her fancy was running riot along those days ahead of her. Spring days, and summer days, and all sorts of days that would be her own. She breathed a quick prayer that life might be long. It was only yesterday she had thought with a shudder that life might be long.

She arose at length and opened the door to her sister's importuni-   20 ties. There was a feverish triumph in her eyes, and she carried herself unwittingly like a goddess of Victory. She clasped her sister's waist, and together they descended the stairs. Richards stood waiting for them at the bottom.

Some one was opening the front door with a latchkey. It was Brently Mallard who entered, a little travel-stained, composedly carrying his grip-sack and umbrella. He had been far from the scene of accident, and did not even know there had been one. He stood amazed at Josephine's piercing cry; at Richards' quick motion to screen him from the view of his wife.

But Richards was too late.

When the doctors came they said she had died of heart disease — of joy that kills.

TOPICS FOR CRITICAL THINKING AND WRITING

Read the following assertions, and consider whether you agree or disagree, and why. For each assertion, draft a paragraph with your arguments.

1. The railroad accident is a symbol of the destructiveness of the industrial revolution.

2. The story claims that women rejoice in the deaths of their husbands.

3. Mrs. Mallard's death at the end is a just punishment for the joy she takes in her husband's death.

4. The story is rich in irony. Some examples: (1) The other characters think she is grieving, but she is rejoicing; (2) she prays for a long life, but she dies almost immediately; (3) the doctors say she died of "the joy that kills," but they think her joy was seeing her husband alive.

5. The story is excellent because it has a surprise ending.

THINKING ABOUT THE EFFECTS OF LITERATURE

Works of art are artifacts — things constructed, made up, fashioned, just like chairs and houses and automobiles. In analyzing works of literature it is therefore customary to keep one's eye on the complex, constructed object and not simply tell the reader how one feels about it. Instead of reporting their feelings, critics usually analyze the relationships between the parts and the relationship of the parts to the whole.

For instance, in talking about literature we can examine the relationship of plot to character, of one character to another, or of one stanza in a poem to the next. Still, although we may try to engage in this sort of analysis as dispassionately as possible, we all know that inevitably

- We are not only examining something out there,
- But are also examining our own responses.

Why? Because literature has an effect on us. Indeed, it probably has several kinds of effects, ranging from short-range emotional responses ("I really enjoyed this," "I burst out laughing," "It revolted me") to long-range effects ("I have always tried to live up to a line in *Hamlet*, 'This above all, to thine own self be true'"). Let's first look at, very briefly, immediate emotional responses.

Analysis usually begins with a response: "This is marvelous," or "What a bore," and we then go on to try to account for our response. A friend mentions a book or a film to us, and we say, "I couldn't stay with it for five minutes." The friend expresses surprise, and we then go on to explain, giving reasons (to the friend and also to ourselves) why we couldn't stay with it. Perhaps the book seemed too remote from life, or perhaps, on the other hand, it seemed to be nothing more than a transcript of the boring talk that we can overhear on a bus or in an elevator.

In such discussions, when we draw on our responses, as we must, the work may disappear; we find ourselves talking about ourselves. Let's take two extreme examples: "I can't abide *Huckleberry Finn*. How am I expected to enjoy a so-called masterpiece that has a character in it called 'Nigger Jim?'" Or: "T. S. Eliot's anti-Semitism is too much for me to take. Don't talk to me about Eliot's skill with meter, when he has such lines as 'Rachel, *née* Rabinovitch / Tears at the grapes with murderous paws.'"

Although everyone agrees that literature can evoke this sort of strong emotional response, not everyone agrees on how much value we should put on our personal experience. Several of the Topics for Critical Thinking and Writing below invite you to reflect on this issue.

What about the *consequences of the effects* of literature? Does literature shape our character and therefore influence our behavior? It is generally believed that it does have an effect. One hears, for example, that literature (like travel) is broadening, that it makes us aware of, and tolerant of, kinds of behavior that differ from our own and from what we see around us. One of the chief arguments against pornography, for instance, is that it desensitizes us, makes us too tolerant of abusive relationships, relationships in which people (usually men) use other people (usually women) as mere things or instruments for pleasure. (A contrary view should be mentioned: Some people argue that pornography provides a relatively harmless outlet for fantasies that otherwise might be given release in the real world. In this view, pornography acts as a sort of safety valve.)

Discussions of the effects of literature that get into the popular press almost always involve pornography, but other topics are also the subjects of controversy. For instance, in recent decades parents and educators have been much concerned with fairy tales. Does the violence in some fairy tales ("Little Red Riding Hood," "The Three Little Pigs") have a bad effect on children? Do some of the stories teach the wrong lessons, implying that women should be passive, men active ("Sleeping Beauty," for instance, in which the sleeping woman is brought to life by the action of the handsome prince)? The Greek philosopher Plato (427–347 B.C.) strongly believed that the literature we hear or read shapes our later behavior, and since most of the ancient Greek traditional stories (notably Homer's *Odyssey* and *Iliad*) celebrate acts of love and war rather than of justice, he prohibited the reading of such material in his ideal society. (We reprint a relevant passage from Plato on page 491.)

TOPICS FOR CRITICAL THINKING AND WRITING

1. If you have responded strongly (favorably or unfavorably) to some aspect of the social content of a literary work—for instance, its depiction of women or of a particular minority group—in an essay of 250 to 500 words analyze the response, and try to determine whether you are talking chiefly about yourself or the work. (Two works widely regarded as literary masterpieces but nonetheless often banned from classrooms are Shakespeare's *The Merchant of Venice* and Mark Twain's *Huckleberry Finn*. If you have read either of these, you may want to write about it and your response.) Can we really see literary value—*really* see it—in a work that deeply offends us?

2. Most people believe that literature influences life—that in some perhaps mysterious way it helps to shape character. Certainly anyone who

believes that some works should be censored, or at least should be made unavailable to minors, assumes that they can have a bad influence, so why not assume that other works can have a good influence?

Read the following brief claims about literature, then choose one and write a 250-word essay offering support or taking issue with it.

The pen is mightier than the sword. — EDWARD BULWER LYTTON

The writer isn't made in a vacuum. Writers are witnesses. The reason we need writers is because we need witnesses to this terrifying century. — E. L. DOCTOROW

When we read of human beings behaving in certain ways, with the approval of the author, who gives his benedictions to this behavior by his attitude towards the result of the behavior arranged by himself, we can be influenced towards behaving in the same way. — T. S. ELIOT

Poetry makes nothing happen. — W. H. AUDEN

Literature is *without proofs*. By which it must be understood that it cannot prove, not only *what* it says, but even that it is worth the trouble of saying it. — ROLAND BARTHES

Of course the illusion of art is to make one believe that great literature is very close to life, but exactly the opposite is true. Life is amorphous, literature is formal. — FRANÇOISE SAGAN

3. At least since the time of Plato (see the piece directly following) some thoughtful people have wanted to ban certain works of literature because they allegedly stimulate the wrong sorts of pleasure or cause us to take pleasure in the wrong sorts of things. Consider, by way of comparison, bullfighting and cockfighting. Of course, they cause pain to the animals, but branding animals also causes pain and is not banned. Bullfighting and cockfighting probably are banned in the United States largely because most of us believe that people should not take pleasure in these activities. Now to return to literature: Should some kinds of writing be prohibited because they offer the wrong sorts of pleasure?

Plato

Plato (427–347 B.C.), an Athenian aristocrat by birth, was the student of one great philosopher (Socrates) and the teacher of another (Aristotle). His legacy of more than two dozen dialogues—imaginary discussions between Socrates and one or more other speakers, usually young Athenians—has been of such influence that the whole of Western philosophy can be characterized, A. N. Whitehead wrote, as "a series of footnotes to Plato." Plato's interests encompassed the full range of topics in philosophy: ethics, politics, logic, metaphysics, epistemology, aesthetics, psychology, and education.

This selection from Plato's Republic, *one of his best-known and longest dialogues, is about the education suitable for the rulers of an ideal society. The*

Republic *begins, typically, with an investigation into the nature of justice. Socrates (who speaks for Plato) convincingly explains to Glaucon that we cannot reasonably expect to achieve a just society unless we devote careful attention to the moral education of the young men who are scheduled in later life to become the rulers. (Here as elsewhere, Plato's elitism and aristocratic bias shows itself; as readers of* The Republic *soon learn, Plato is no admirer of democracy or of a classless society.) Plato cares as much about what the educational curriculum should exclude as what it should include. His special target was the common practice in his day of using for pedagogy the Homeric tales and other stories about the gods. He readily embraces the principle of censorship, as the excerpt explains, because he thinks it is a necessary means to achieve the ideal society.*

"The Greater Part of the Stories Current Today We Shall Have to Reject"

"What kind of education shall we give them then? We shall find it difficult to improve on the time-honored distinction between the physical training we give to the body and the education we give to the mind and character."

"True."

"And we shall begin by educating mind and character, shall we not?"

"Of course."

"In this education you would include stories, would you not?"   5

"Yes."

"These are of two kinds, true stories and fiction.[1] Our education must use both, and start with fiction."

"I don't know what you mean."

"But you know that we begin by telling children stories. These are, in general, fiction, though they contain some truth. And we tell children stories before we start them on physical training."

"That is so."   10

"That is what I meant by saying that we must start to educate the mind before training the body."

"You are right," he said.

"And the first step, as you know, is always what matters most, particularly when we are dealing with those who are young and tender. That is the time when they are easily molded and when any impression we choose to make leaves a permanent mark."

"That is certainly true."

---

[1]The Greek word *pseudos* and its corresponding verb meant not only "fiction"—stories, tales—but also "what is not true" and so, in suitable contexts, "lies": and this ambiguity should be borne in mind. [Editors' note: All footnotes are by the translator, but some have been omitted.]

"Shall we therefore readily allow our children to listen to any 15
stories made up by anyone, and to form opinions that are for the most
part the opposite of those we think they should have when they
grow up?"

"We certainly shall not."

"Then it seems that our first business is to supervise the production
of stories, and choose only those we think suitable, and reject the rest.
We shall persuade mothers and nurses to tell our chosen stories to their
children, and by means of them to mold their minds and characters
which are more important than their bodies. The greater part of the stories current today we shall have to reject."

"Which are you thinking of?"

"We can take some of the major legends as typical. For all, whether
major or minor, should be cast in the same mold and have the same
effect. Do you agree?"

"Yes: but I'm not sure which you refer to as major."   20

"The stories in Homer and Hesiod and the poets. For it is the poets
who have always made up fictions and stories to tell to men."

"What sort of stories do you mean and what fault do you find in
them?"

"The worst fault possible," I replied, "especially if the fiction is an
ugly one."

"And what is that?"

"Misrepresenting the nature of gods and heroes, like a portrait 25
painter whose portraits bear no resemblance to their originals."

"That is a fault which certainly deserves censure. But give me more
details."

"Well, on the most important of subjects, there is first and foremost the foul story about Ouranos[2] and the things Hesiod says he did, and
the revenge Cronos took on him. While the story of what Cronos did, and
what he suffered at the hands of his son, is not fit as it is to be lightly
repeated to the young and foolish, even if it were true; it would be best to
say nothing about it, or if it must be told, tell it to a select few under oath
of secrecy, at a rite which required, to restrict it still further, the sacrifice
not of a mere pig but of something large and difficult to get."

"These certainly are awkward stories."

"And they shall not be repeated in our state, Adeimantus," I said.
"Nor shall any young audience be told that anyone who commits horrible crimes, or punishes his father unmercifully, is doing nothing out of
the ordinary but merely what the first and greatest of the gods have
done before."

"I entirely agree," said Adeimantus, "that these stories are unsuitable." 30

---

[2]**Ouranos** The sky, the original supreme god. Ouranos was castrated by his son Cronos to
separate him from Gaia (mother earth). Cronos was in turn deposed by Zeus in a struggle
in which Zeus was helped by the Titans.

"Nor can we permit stories of wars and plots and battles among the gods; they are quite untrue, and if we want our prospective guardians to believe that quarrelsomeness is one of the worst of evils, we must certainly not let them be told the story of the Battle of the Giants or embroider it on robes, or tell them other tales about many and various quarrels between gods and heroes and their friends and relations. On the contrary, if we are to persuade them that no citizen has ever quarreled with any other, because it is sinful, our old men and women must tell children stories with this end in view from the first, and we must compel our poets to tell them similar stories when they grow up. But we can admit to our state no stories about Hera being tied up by her son, or Hephaestus being flung out of Heaven by his father for trying to help his mother when she was getting a beating, nor any of Homer's Battles of the Gods, whether their intention is allegorical or not. Children cannot distinguish between what is allegory and what isn't, and opinions formed at that age are usually difficult to eradicate or change; we should therefore surely regard it as of the utmost importance that the first stories they hear shall aim at encouraging the highest excellence of character."

"Your case is a good one," he agreed, "but if someone wanted details, and asked what stories we were thinking of, what should we say?"

To which I replied, "My dear Adeimantus, you and I are not engaged on writing stories but on founding a state. And the founders of a state, though they must know the type of story the poet must produce, and reject any that do not conform to that type, need not write them themselves."

"True: but what are the lines on which our poets must work when they deal with the gods?"

"Roughly as follows," I said. "God must surely always be represented 35 as he really is, whether the poet is writing epic, lyric, or tragedy."

"He must."

"And in reality of course god is good, and he must be so described."

"Certainly."

"But nothing good is harmful, is it?"[3]

"I think not."   40

"Then can anything that is not harmful do harm?"

"No."

"And can what does no harm do evil?"

"No again."

"And can what does no evil be the cause of any evil?"   45

"How could it?"

---

[3]The reader of the following passage should bear the following ambiguities in mind: (1) the Greek word for good (*agathos*) can mean (a) morally good, (b) beneficial or advantageous; (2) the Greek word for evil (*kakos*) can also mean harm or injury; (3) the adverb of *agathos* (*eu*—the well) can imply either morally right or prosperous. The word translated "cause of" could equally well be rendered "responsible for."

"Well then; is the good beneficial?"

"Yes."

"So it must be the cause of well-being."

"Yes."   50

"So the good is not the cause of everything, but only of states of well-being and not of evil."

"Most certainly," he agreed.

"Then god, being good, cannot be responsible for everything, as is commonly said, but only for a small part of human life, for the greater part of which he has no responsibility. For we have a far smaller share of good than of evil, and while god must be held to be the sole cause of good, we must look for some factors other than god as cause of the evil."

"I think that's very true," he said.

"So we cannot allow Homer or any other poet to make such a stupid   55 mistake about the gods, as when he says that

> Zeus has two jars standing on the floor of his palace, full of fates, good
> in one and evil in the other

and that the man to whom Zeus allots a mixture of both has 'varying fortunes sometimes good and sometimes bad,' while the man to whom he allots unmixed evil is `chased by ravening despair over the face of the earth.'[4] Nor can we allow references to Zeus as `dispenser of good and evil.' And we cannot approve if it is said that Athene and Zeus prompted the breach of solemn treaty and oath by Pandarus, or that the strife and contentions of the gods were due to Themis and Zeus. Nor again can we let our children hear from Aeschylus that

> God implants a fault in man, when he wishes to destroy a house utterly.

No: We must forbid anyone who writes a play about the sufferings of Niobe (the subject of the play from which these last lines are quoted), or the house of Pelops, or the Trojan war, or any similar topic, to say they are acts of god; or if he does he must produce the sort of interpretation we are now demanding, and say that god's acts were good and just, and that the sufferers were benefited by being punished. What the poet must not be allowed to say is that those who were punished were made wretched through god's action. He may refer to the wicked as wretched because they needed punishment, provided he makes it clear that in punishing them god did them good. But if a state is to be run on the right lines, every possible step must be taken to prevent anyone, young or old, either saying or being told, whether in poetry or prose, that god,

---

[4]Quotations from Homer are generally taken from the translations by Dr. Rieu in the Penguin series. At times (as here) the version quoted by Plato differs slightly from the accepted text.

being good, can cause harm or evil to any man. To say so would be sinful, inexpedient, and inconsistent."

"I should approve of a law for this purpose and you have my vote for it," he said.

"Then of our laws laying down the principles which those who write or speak about the gods must follow, one would be this: *God is the cause, not of all things, but only of good.*"

"I am quite content with that," he said.

TOPICS FOR CRITICAL THINKING AND WRITING

1. In the beginning of the dialogue Plato says that adults recite fictions to very young children and that these fictions help to mold character. Think of some stories that you heard or read when young, such as "Snow White and the Seven Dwarfs" or "Ali Baba and the Forty Thieves." Try to think of a story that, in the final analysis, is not in accord with what you consider to be proper morality, such as a story in which a person triumphs through trickery or a story in which evil actions—perhaps murders—are set forth without unfavorable comment. (Was it naughty of Jack to kill the giant?) On reflection, do you think children should not be told such stories? Why, or why not? Or think of the early film westerns, in which, on the whole, the Indians (except for an occasional Uncle Tonto) are depicted as bad guys and the whites (except for an occasional coward or rustler) are depicted as good guys. Many people who now have gray hair enjoyed such films in their childhood. Are you prepared to say that such films are not damaging? Or on the other hand, are you prepared to say they are damaging and should be prohibited?

2. It is often objected that censorship of reading matter and of television programs available to children underrates their ability to think for themselves and to discount the dangerous, obscene, and tawdry. Do you agree with this objection? Does Plato?

3. Plato says that allowing poets to say what they please about the gods in his ideal state would be "inconsistent." Explain what he means by this criticism, and then explain why you agree or disagree with it.

4. Do you believe that parents should censor the "fiction" their children encounter (literature, films, pictures, music) but that the community should not censor the "fiction" of adults? Write an essay of 500 words on one of these topics: "Censorship and Rock Lyrics"; "X-rated Films"; "Ethnic Jokes." (These topics are broadly worded; you can narrow one and offer whatever thesis you wish.)

5. Were you taught that any of the founding fathers ever acted disreputably, or that any American hero had any serious moral flaw? Or that America ever acted immorally in its dealings with other nations? Do you think it appropriate for children to hear such things?

THINKING ABOUT GOVERNMENT
FUNDING FOR THE ARTS

Our government supports the arts, including writers, by giving grants to numerous institutions. On the other hand, the amount that the government contributes is extremely small when compared to the amounts given to the arts by most European governments. Consider the following questions.

1. Should taxpayers' dollars be used to support the arts? Why, or why not?
2. What possible public benefit can come from supporting the arts? Can one argue that we should support the arts for the same reasons that we support the public schools, that is, to have a civilized society?
3. If dollars are given to the arts, should the political content of the works be taken into account, or only the aesthetic merit? Can we separate content from aesthetic merit? (The best way to approach this issue probably is to begin by thinking of a strongly political work.)
4. Is it censorship not to award public funds to writers whose work is not approved of, or is it simply a matter of refusing to reward them with taxpayers' dollars?
5. Should decisions about grants to writers be made chiefly by government officials or chiefly by experts in the field? Why?

14

A Debater's View: Individual Oral Presentations and Debate

He who knows only his own side of the case knows little of that.
—JOHN STUART MILL

A philosopher who is not taking part in discussions is like a boxer who never goes into the ring.
—LUDWIG WITTGENSTEIN

Freedom is hammered out on the anvil of dissension, dissent, and debate.
—HUBERT HUMPHREY

INDIVIDUAL ORAL PRESENTATIONS

Forensic comes from a Latin word *foris,* meaning "out of doors," which also produced the word *forum,* an open space in front of a public building. In the language of rhetoricians, the place where one delivers a speech to an audience is the forum—whether it is a classroom, a court of law, or the steps of the Lincoln Memorial.

Your instructor may ask you to make an oral presentation (in this case the forum is the classroom), and if your instructor doesn't make such a demand, later life almost certainly will: You will find that at a job interview you will be expected to talk persuasively about what good qualities or experience you can bring to the place of employment. When you have a job you will sometimes have to summarize a report orally or orally argue a case—for instance, that your colleagues should do something they may be hesitant to do.

The goal of your classroom talk is to persuade the audience to share your view, or, if you can't get them to agree completely, to get them to see that at least there is something to be said for this view— that it is a position a reasonable person can hold.

Elsewhere in this book we have said that the subjects of persuasive writing are usually

- Matters of fact (for instance, statistics show that the death penalty does—or does not—deter crime), or
- Matters of value (abortion is—or is not—immoral), or
- Matters of policy (government should—or should not—give money to faith-based institutions).

TWO RULES FOR SPEAKERS:
- *In preparing your oral presentation, keep your thesis in mind.* You may be giving counterarguments, examples, definitions, and so forth, but make sure that your thesis is always evident to your audience.
- *Keep your audience in mind.* Inevitably you will have to make assumptions about what the audience does and does not know about your topic. Do not overestimate their knowledge, and do not underestimate their intelligence.

Whatever your subject, when you draft and revise your talk, make certain that a thesis statement underlies the whole (for instance, "Proposition 2 is a bad idea because. . . .")

The text of an oral presentation ought not to be identical with the text of a written presentation. Both must have a clear **organization,** but oral presentations usually require that the organization be made a bit more obvious, with abundant **signposts** such as "Before I talk about X," "When I discussed Y, I didn't mention such-and-such because I wanted to concentrate on a single instance, but now is the time to consider Y," and so on. You will also have to repeat a bit more than you would in a written presentation. After all, a reader can turn back to check a sentence or a statistic but an auditor cannot, so rather than saying (as one might in a printed text), "When we think further about Smith's comment, we realize. . . ," you will repeat what Smith said before you go on to analyze the statement.

You will want to think carefully about the **organization** of your talk. We've already stressed the need to develop essays with clear thesis statement and logical supporting points. Oral presentations are no different, but remember that when you are speaking in public, a clear organization will always help alleviate anxiety and reassure you. Thus, you can deliver a powerful message without getting tripped up yourself. We suggest you try the following:

- Outline your draft in advance in order to make sure that it has clear organization.

- Inform your audience at the start what the organization of your presentation will be. Early in the talk you probably should say something along these lines, though not in so abbreviated a form:

  > "In talking about *A*, I'll have to define a few terms, *B* and *C*, and I will also have to talk about two positions that differ from mine, *D* and *E*. I'll then try to show why *A* is the best policy to pursue, clearly better than *D* and *E*."

- So that your listeners can easily follow you, be sure to use transitions such as "Furthermore," "Therefore," "Although it is often said," and "It may be objected that," so that your listeners can easily follow your train of thought. Sometimes you may even remind the listeners what the previous stages were, with such a comment as "We have now seen three approaches to the problem of . . . "

After thinking about helping your audience to follow your speech, you might want to consider how much help you'll need delivering it. Depending on your comfort level with the topic and your argument, you might decide to

- Deliver a memorized talk without notes,
- Read the talk from a text,
- Speak from an outline, perhaps with quotations and statistics written down.

Each of these methods has its strengths and its weaknesses. A memorized talk allows for plenty of eye-contact with the audience but unless you are a superb actor it is almost surely going to seem a bit mechanical. A talk that you read from a text will indeed let you say to an audience exactly what you want to say (with the best possible wording), but reading a text inevitably establishes some distance between you and the audience, even if you occasionally glance up from your pages. If you talk from a mere outline, almost surely some of your sentences will turn out to be a bit awkward—though a tiny bit of awkwardness may help to convey sincerity and may therefore be a plus.

Whatever the form of delivery, try to convey the impression that you are conversing with your audience, not talking down to them—even though if you are on a platform you will be literally talking down.

You may want to use **audiovisual aids** in your presentation. These can range from such low-tech materials as handouts, blackboards, and whiteboards to high-tech PowerPoint presentations. Each has its advantages and its disadvantages. For instance, if you distribute handouts when the talk begins, the audience may start thumbing through them even while you are making your opening comments. And although PowerPoint can be a highly useful aid, some speakers make too much use of it simply because it is available. It happens that the day before writing this discussion the author witnessed a PowerPoint presentation, which began with the speaker projecting on the screen the date, the speaker's name, and the name of the university at which the talk was being delivered. Well, most of us knew the date, and we all knew the speaker's name and the name of the university where we were. It seemed like overkill. The truth is, the talk simply did not need any images at all, and we ended up wondering why the speaker bothered with PowerPoint.

For a delightful parody of this sort of talk, consider the parody "The Gettysburg Powerpoint Presentation" (http://norvig.com/Gettysburg/). It begins thus:

> **And now please welcome President Abraham Lincoln.**
> Good morning. Just a second while I get this connection to work. Do I press this button here? Function-F7? No, that's not right. Hmmm. Maybe I'll have to reboot. Hold on a minute. Um, my name is Abe Lincoln and I'm your president. While we're waiting, I want to thank Judge David Wills, chairman of the committee supervising the dedication of the Gettysburg cemetery. It's great to be here, Dave, and you and the committee are doing a great job. Gee, sometimes this new **technology** does have glitches, but **we couldn't live without it, could we?** Oh—is it ready? OK, here we go.

The lesson? Yes, use audiovisual material if it will help you to present your material, but do not use it if it adds nothing or if you have not mastered the technology.

✓ A CHECKLIST FOR AN ORAL PRESENTATION

Keep the following in mind, whether you are evaluating someone else's talk, or preparing your own.

Delivery

☐ Voice loud enough, but not too loud.

☐ Appropriate degree of speed—neither hurried nor drawn out.

☐ Dress and attitude toward audience appropriate.

☐ Gestures and eye contact appropriate.

☐ Language clear, e.g. technical words adequately explained.

☐ Visual aids, if any, appropriate and effectively used.

Content

☐ Thesis clear, and kept in view.

☐ Argument steadily advanced, with helpful transitions.

☐ Thesis supported by evidence.

☐ Light-weight material, e.g. bits of humor, relevant and genuinely engaging.

One final point: If you do use visual material, *make certain that any words on the the images are large enough to be legible to your audience:* A graph with tiny words will not impress your audience, even if you read the words aloud.

THE AUDIENCE

It is not merely because topics are complicated that we cannot agree that one side is reasonable and right and the other side irrational and wrong. The truth is, we are swayed not only by reason (*logos*) but also by appeals to the emotions (*pathos*) and by the character of the speaker (*ethos*). We can combine these last two things and put it this way: Sometimes we are inclined to agree with *X* rather than with *Y* because *X* strikes us as a more appealing person (perhaps more open-minded, more intelligent, better informed, more humane, and less cold). *X* is the sort of person we want to have as a friend. We disagree with *Y*—or at least we are unwilling to associate ourselves with *Y*—because *Y* is, well, *Y* just isn't the sort of person we want to agree with. *Y*'s statistics don't sound right, or *Y* seems like a bully; for some reason, we just don't have confidence in *Y*. Confidence is easily lost: Alas, even a mispronunciation will diminish the audience's confidence in *Y*. As Peter de Vries said, "You can't be happy with someone who pronounces both *d*'s in Wednesday."

Earlier in the book we talked about the importance of **tone** and of the writer's **persona.** And we have made the point that the writer's tone will depend partly on the audience. A person who is writing for a conservative journal whose readership is almost entirely conservatives can adopt a highly satiric manner in talking about liberals and will meet with much approval. But if this conservative writer is writing in a liberal journal and hopes to get at least a sympathetic hearing, he or she will have to avoid satire and wisecracks and will have to present himself or herself as a person of goodwill who is open-minded and eager to address the issue seriously.

The **language** that you use—the degree to which it is formal as opposed to colloquial, and the degree to which it is technical as opposed to general—will also depend on the audience. Speaking a bit broadly, in oral argument speak politely but not formally. You do *not* want to be one of those people who "talk like a book." But you also don't want to be overly colloquial. Choose a middle course, probably a notch below the style you would use if you were handing in a written paper. For instance, in an oral presentation you might say, "We'll consider this point in a minute or two," whereas in a written paper you probably will write "We will consider this point shortly."

Technical language is entirely appropriate *if* your audience is familiar with it. If you are arguing before members of Amnesty International about the use of torture—we include essays in this book that support the use of torture to prevent a disaster like that of

September 11—you can assume certain kinds of specialized knowledge. You can, for instance, breezily speak of the DRC and of KPCS, and your hearers will know what you are talking about because Amnesty International has been active with issues concerning the Democratic Republic of Congo and the Kimberley Process Certification Scheme. On the other hand, if you are arguing the same case before a general public, you will have to explain these abbreviations, and you may even have to explain what Amnesty International is.

If you are arguing before your classmates, you probably have a pretty good idea of what you can assume they know and what you can assume they do not know.

DELIVERY

Your audience will in some measure determine not only your tone but also the way you appear when you give the speech. Part of the delivery is the speaker's **appearance.** The medium is part of the message. The president can appear in jeans when he chats about his reelection plans, but he wears a suit and a tie when he delivers the State of the Union address. Just as we wear one kind of **clothing** when we play tennis, another when we attend classes, and yet another when we go for a job interview, an effective speaker dresses appropriately. A lawyer arguing before the Supreme Court wears a dark suit or dress, and if the lawyer is male he wears a necktie. The same lawyer, arguing at a local meeting, speaking as a community resident who objects to a proposal to allow a porno store to open near a school, may well dress informally, maybe in jeans, to show that he or she is not at all stuffy but still feels that a porno store goes too far.

Your appearance when you speak is not merely a matter of your clothing; it includes your **facial expressions,** your **posture,** your **gestures,** your general demeanor. All that we can say here is that you should avoid those bodily motions—swaying, thumping the table, putting on and taking off eyeglasses, craning your neck, smirking—that are so distracting that they cause the audience to concentrate on the distraction rather than on the argument. ("That's the third time he straightened his necktie. I wonder how many more times he will—oops, that's the fourth!"). Most of us are not aware of our annoying habits; if you are lucky, a friend, when urged, will tell you about them. You may lose a friend, but you will gain some good advice.

You probably can't do much about your **voice**—it may be high-pitched, or it may be gravelly—but you can make sure that you speak loudly enough for the audience to hear you, slowly enough for it to understand you, and clearly enough for it to understand you.

We have some advice about **quotations.** First, if possible, use an effective quotation or two, partly because—we will be frank—the quotations probably are more impressively worded than anything you can come up with on your own. A quotation may be the chief thing that your audience comes away with: "Hey, yes, I liked that: 'War is too important to be left to the generals'" or "When it comes down to it, I agree with that Frenchman who said 'If we are to abolish the death penalty, I should like to see the first step taken by the murderers'" or "You know, I think it was all summed up in that line by Margaret Mead, something like, 'No one would remember the Good Samaritan if he'd had only good intentions. He had money as well.' Yes, that's pretty convincing. Morality isn't enough. You need money." You didn't invent the words that you quote, but you did bring them to the attention of your listeners, and your listeners will be grateful to you.

A second bit of advice about quotations: When you quote, do *not* begin by saying "quote," and do not end by saying "end quote" (or as we once heard a speaker endlessly say, quotation after quotation, "unquote") and do not hook the air with your fingers. How do you make it clear that you are quoting, and how do you make it clear that you have finished quoting? Begin with a clear lead-in ("In *Major Barbara* George Bernard Shaw touches on this issue, when Barbara says, . . ."), slightly pause, and then slightly change (for instance, elevate) your voice. When you have finished quoting—again a slight pause and a return to your normal voice—be sure to use words that clearly indicate the quotation is finished, such as "Shaw here says what everyone thinks," or "Shaw's comment is witty but short-sighted," or "Barbara's point, then, is . . ."

Our third and last piece of advice concerning quotations is this: If the quotation is only a phrase or a brief sentence, you can memorize it and can be confident that you will remember it, but if it is longer than a sentence, write it on a sheet in your notes or on a four- by six-inch card in print large enough for you to read easily. You have chosen these words because they are effectively put, so you don't want to misquote them or even hesitate in delivering them.

THE TALK

As for the talk itself, well, we have been touching on it in our discussion of such matters as the speaker's relation to the audience, the speaker's need to provide signposts, and the use of quotations. All of our comments in earlier chapters about developing a written argument are relevant also to oral arguments, but here we should merely emphasize that because the talk is oral and the audience cannot look back to an earlier page to remind itself of some point, the speaker may have to repeat and summarize a bit more than is usual in a written essay.

Remember, too, that a reader can *see* when the essay ends—there is blank space at the end of the page—but a listener depends on aural cues.

Nothing is more embarrassing—and less effective as argument—than a speaker who seems (to the audience) to suddenly stop and sit down. In short, give your hearers ample clues that you are ending (post such signs as "Finally" or "Last" or "Let me end by saying"), and be sure to end with a strong sentence. It probably won't be as good as the end of the Gettysburg address ("government of the people, by the people, for the people, shall not perish from the earth"), nor will it be as good as the end of Martin Luther King's "I Have a Dream" speech ("Free at last! Free at last! Thank God Almighty, we are free at last!"), but those are the models to emulate.

FORMAL DEBATES

It would be nice if all arguments ended with everyone, participants and spectators, agreeing that the facts are clear, that one presentation is more reasonable than the other, and therefore that one side is right and the other side is wrong. But in life, most issues are complicated. High school students may earnestly debate—this is a real topic in a national debate—

Resolved: That education has failed its mission in the United States,

but it takes only a moment of reflection to see that neither the affirmative nor the negative can be true. Yes, education has failed its mission in many ways, but, No, it has succeeded in many ways. Its job now is (in the words of Samuel Beckett) to try again: "Fail. Fail again. Fail better."

Debates of this sort, conducted before a judge and guided by strict rules concerning "Constructive Speeches," "Rebuttal Speeches," and "Cross-Examinations" are not attempts to get at the truth; like lawsuits, they are attempts to win a case. Each speaker seeks not to persuade the opponent but only to convince the judge. Although most of this section is devoted not to forensics in the strictest sense but more generally to the presentation of oral arguments, we begin with the standard format.

STANDARD DEBATE FORMAT

Formal debates occur within a structure that governs the number of speeches, the order of the speeches, and the maximum time for each speech. The format may vary from place to place, but there is always a structure. In most debates, a formal resolution states the reason for the debate ("Resolved: That capital punishment be abolished in juvenile cases"). The affirmative team supports the resolution; the negative team denies its legitimacy. The basic structure has three parts:

- *The constructive phase*, in which the debaters construct their cases and develop their arguments (usually for ten minutes);

- *The rebuttal,* in which debaters present their responses and also present their final summary (usually for five minutes); and

- *The preparation,* in which the debater prepares for presenting the next speech. (During the preparation—a sort of time-out—the debater is not addressing the opponent or audience. The total time allotted to a team is usually six or eight minutes, which the individual debaters divide as they wish.)

We give, very briefly, the usual structure of each part, though it should be mentioned that another common format calls for a cross-examination of the First Affirmative Construction by the Second Negative, a cross-examination of the First Negative Construction by the First Affirmative, a cross-examination of the Second Affirmative by the First Negative, and a cross-examination of the Second Negative by the Second Affirmative:

First Affirmative Constructive Speech: Serves as introduction, giving summary overview, definitions, criteria for resolution, major claims and evidence, statement, and intention to support the resolution.

First Negative Constructive Speech: Responds by introducing the basic position, challenges the definitions and criteria, suggests the line of attack, emphasizes that the burden of proof lies with the affirmative, rejects the resolution as unnecessary or dangerous, and supports the status quo.

Second Affirmative Constructive: Rebuilds the affirmative case; refutes chief attacks, especially concerning definitions, criteria, and rationale (philosophic framework); and further develops the affirmative case.

✓ A CHECKLIST FOR PREPARING FOR A DEBATE

☐ Have I done adequate preparation in research?

☐ Are my notes legible, with accurate quotations and impressive sources?

☐ Am I prepared to take good notes during the debate?

☐ Is my proposition clearly stated?

☐ Do I have adequate evidence to support the thesis (main point)?

☐ Do I have backup points in mind?

☐ Have I given thought to issues opponents may raise?

☐ Does the opening properly address the instructor, the audience, the opponents? (Remember, you are addressing an audience, not merely the opponents.)

☐ Are my visual aids focused on major points?

☐ Is my demeanor professional, and is my dress appropriate?

Second Negative Constructive: Completes the negative case, if possible advances it by rebuilding portions of the first negative construction, and contrasts the entire negative case with the entire affirmative case.

First Negative Rebuttal: Attacks the opponents' arguments and defends the negative constructive arguments (but a rebuttal may *not* introduce new constructive arguments).

First Affirmative Rebuttal: Usually responds first to the second negative construction and then to the first negative rebuttal.

Second Negative Rebuttal: Constitutes final speech for the negative, summarizing the case and explaining to the judge why the negative should be declared the winner.

Second Affirmative Rebuttal: Summarizes the debate, responds to issues pressed by the second negative rebuttal, and suggests to the judge that the affirmative team should win.

PART FOUR

CURRENT ISSUES: OCCASIONS for DEBATE

DEBATES AS AN AID TO THINKING

Throughout this book we emphasize critical thinking, which—to put the matter briefly—means thinking analytically not only about the ideas of others but also about one's *own* ideas. As we often say in these pages, *you* are your first reader, and you should be a demanding one. You have ideas, but you want to think further about them, to improve them— partly so that you can share them with others but also so that you will live a thoughtful, useful, satisfying life.

This means, as we say elsewhere in the book, that you have (or at least try to have) an open mind, a mind that welcomes comments on your own ideas. You are, we hope, ready to grant that someone whose views differ from yours may indeed have something to teach you. When you have heard other views, of course you will not always embrace them, but sometimes you may find merit in some aspects of them, and you will to some degree reshape your own views. (We discuss the importance of trying to find shared ground and trying to move onward and upward from there in Chapter 12, A Psychologist's View: Rogerian Argument.)

Much of the difficulty in improving our ideas lies in our tendency to think in an either/or pattern. To put the point in academic terms, we incline toward *binary* (Latin, "two by two") or *dichotomous* (Greek, "divided into two") thinking. We often think in terms of contrasts: life and death, good and evil, right and left, up and down, on and off, white and black, boys and girls, men and women (men are from Mars, women from Venus), yes and no, freedom and tyranny. We understand what something is partly by thinking of what it is not: "He is liberal, she is conservative." In Gilbert and Sullivan's *Iolanthe*, one of the characters sees things this way:

> I am an intellectual chap,
> And think of things that would astonish you.
> I often think it is comical
> How nature always does contrive
> That every boy and every gal,
> That's born into the world alive,
> Is either a little Liberal,
> Or else a little Conservative.

We have our liberals and conservatives too, our Democrats and Republicans, and we talk about fate and free will, day and night, and so on. But we also know that there are imperceptible gradations. We know that there are conservative Democrats and liberal Republicans, and we know that although day differs from night, we cannot say at any given moment, "We have just now gone from day to night." True, there are times when gradations are irrelevant: In the polling booth, when we vote for a political candidate or for a particular bill, we must decide between X and Y. At that stage it is either/or, not both/and or "Well, let's think further about this." But in much of life we are finding our way, acting provision-ally—decisively at the moment, yes, but later we may modify our ideas in the light of further thinking, thinking that often is stimulated by the spoken or written thoughts of someone who holds a different view. Elsewhere we quote Virginia Woolf on the topic of writing about complex issues, but the comment is worth repeating:

> When a subject is highly controversial . . . one cannot hope to tell the truth. One can only show how one came to hold whatever opinion one does hold. One can only give one's audience the chance of drawing their own conclusions as they observe the limitations, the prejudices, the idiosyncrasies of the speaker.

What we are getting at is this: The debates in the next six chapters present sharply opposed views, usually of an either/or, day/night sort. Each essay sets forth a point of view, often with the implication that on this particular issue there are only two points of view—the writer's view and the wrong view. Some of the writers in these debates, convinced that only one view makes sense, evidently are not interested in hearing other opinions; they are out to convince, indeed to conquer.

The very word *debate* (from Latin *battere*, "to fight," "to battle") implies a combative atmosphere, a contest in which there will be a winner and a loser. And indeed the language used to describe a debate is often militant. Debaters *aim* their arguments, *destroy* the arguments of their *opponents* by *rebutting* (from Old French, *boter*, "to butt") and *refuting* (from Latin *futare*, "to beat") them.

We urge you, however, to read these arguments not in order to decide who is right and who is wrong but in order to think about the issues. In short, although the debates may be reductive, stating only two sides and supporting only one, think critically about both sides of any given argument, and allow the essays to enrich your own ideas about the topics. Above all, use the cut and thrust of debate as a device to explore the controversy, not as a weapon to force the other side into submission.

See, too, what you can learn about *writing* from these essays—about ways of organizing thoughts, about ways of presenting evidence, and especially about ways of establishing a voice, a *tone* that the reader takes as a representation of the sort of person you are. Remember, as E. B. White said, "No author long remains incognito." Authors reveal their personalities—belligerent, witty, thoughtful, courteous, whatever. If an author here turns you off, let's say by using heavy sarcasm or by an obvious unwillingness to face contrary evidence, well, there is a lesson for you as a writer.

In reading essays debating a given issue, keep in mind the questions given on page 103, "A Checklist for Analyzing an Argument." They are listed again below, with a few additional points of special relevance to debates.

✓ A CHECKLIST FOR ANALYZING A DEBATE

Have I asked myself the following questions?
- [ ] What is the writer's thesis?
  - [ ] What claim is asserted?
  - [ ] What assumptions are made?
  - [ ] Are key terms defined satisfactorily?
- [ ] What support is offered on behalf of the claim?
  - [ ] Are examples relevant and convincing?
  - [ ] Are statistics relevant, accurate, and convincing?
  - [ ] Are the authorities appropriate?
  - [ ] Is the logic—deductive and inductive—valid?
  - [ ] If there is an appeal to emotion, is this appeal acceptable?
- [ ] Does the writer seem fair?
  - [ ] Are counterarguments considered?
  - [ ] Is there any evidence of dishonesty?

Have I asked myself the following additional questions?
- [ ] Do the disputants differ in
  - [ ] assumptions?
  - [ ] interpretations of relevant facts?
  - [ ] selection of and emphasis on these facts?
  - [ ] definitions of key terms?
  - [ ] values and norms?
  - [ ] goals?
- [ ] What common ground do the disputants share?
- [ ] Which disputant seems to me to have the better overall argument? Why?

15

The Equal Rights Amendment: Is It Still Needed?

Idella Moore

Idella Moore is the founder and the Executive Officer of 4ERA, an organization dedicated to supporting the Equal Rights Amendment. This essay appeared in CQ Researcher *on March 14, 2008, as did the one by Phyllis Schlafly that follows.*

Yes, the ERA Is Still Needed

We still need the Equal Rights Amendment (ERA) because sex discrimination is still a problem in our country. Like race or religious discrimination, gender discrimination is intended to render its victims economically, socially, legally, and politically disadvantaged. But unlike racism and religious intolerance—whose practice against certain groups is localized within countries or regions—sex discrimination is universal. Why, then, in our court system are race and religious discrimination considered more serious offenses?

Today, American women—of all races and religions—are still fighting to achieve equal opportunity, pay, status, and recognition in all realms of our society. At this moment, the largest class-action lawsuit in the history of this country is being argued on behalf of 1.6 million women who were discriminated against purely because of their gender. If the ERA had been ratified back in the 1970s, by now these types of lawsuits would be extinct.

We still need the ERA because ratification of the amendment will elevate "sex" to, in legal terms, a so-called suspect class. A suspect class has the advantage in discrimination cases. Gender, as yet, is not afforded that advantage. As we've seen with race, suspect class status increased the chance of favorable outcomes in discrimination cases. This, in turn, served as a deterrent. Consequently, in our society racism is now socially unacceptable. Sex discrimination, however, is not.

We still need the ERA because the continuing struggle for legal equality for women should be seen as a shameful and embarrassing condition of our society. Yet today lawmakers—sworn to represent all their constituents—proudly voice their objections to granting legal equality to women and without any fear of consequences to their political careers. How different our reactions would be if they were espousing racism.

The Equal Rights Amendment will perfect our Constitution by ₅ explicitly guaranteeing that the privileges, laws, and responsibilities it contains apply equally to men and women. As it stands today the Constitution is sometimes interpreted that way, but women, as a universally and historically disadvantaged group, cannot rely on such interpretations. We have seen these "interpretations" vary and change, often due to the whims of the political climate. Therefore, without the ERA any gains women make will always be tenuous.

I see the Equal Rights Amendment, too, as a pledge to ourselves and posterity that we recognize that sexism exists and that we as a country are determined to continue perfecting our democracy by proudly and unequivocally guaranteeing that one's gender will no longer be a detriment to achieving the American dream.

TOPICS FOR CRITICAL THINKING AND WRITING

1. What is the difference, if any, between sex discrimination and gender discrimination?

2. What is a "suspect class"? On what grounds should women be regarded as such a class?

3. In her opening paragraph Moore says that "sex discrimination is still a problem in our country." Does your experience confirm this assertion? Explain.

4. Moore ends her first paragraph with a question. What is your answer to her question?

5. Would the fifth paragraph be improved if Moore gave an example or two of the "interpretations" she has in mind? Why, or why not?

6. Evaluate the final paragraph as a concluding paragraph.

ANALYZING A VISUAL: THE EQUAL RIGHTS AMENDMENT

TOPICS FOR CRITICAL THINKING AND WRITING

1. This photo shows two political buttons worn to support the original ERA in the 1970s. At that time, women reportedly made 59 cents for every dollar a man made. Knowing that, how effective do you think

these buttons are at conveying a political message? Are they powerful? Too oversimplified? Write your analysis in 250 words.

2. How do you think the messages on the buttons might need to be altered to convey the need for an Equal Rights Amendment today? Write a couple of paragraphs in which you argue what the most important issues pertaining to women's rights are right now.

3. Imagine that you want to create a button to express a political opinion that you hold. How might you design it to convey your point as simply as these buttons do? Write 250 words in which you describe your design and how it supports your point of view. If you are artistic, try providing a sketch as well.

Phyllis Schlafly

Phyllis Schlafly, born in 1924, is a conservative political activist and a constitutional attorney. She is also president of the Eagle Forum. Her best-known book is Choice, Not an Echo *(1964). The following essay was paired with the preceding one in* CQ Researcher *on March 14, 2008.*

No, the ERA Is Not Needed

The Equal Rights Amendment (ERA) was fiercely debated across America for ten years (1972–1982) and was rejected. ERA has been reintroduced into the current Congress under a slightly different name, but it's the same old amendment with the same bad effects.

The principal reason ERA failed is that although it was marketed as a benefit to women, its advocates were never able to prove it would provide · any benefit whatsoever to women. ERA would put "sex" (not women) in the Constitution and just make all our laws sex-neutral.

ERA advocates used their massive access to a friendly media to suggest that ERA would raise women's wages. But ERA would have no effect on wages because our employment laws are already sex-neutral. The equal-pay-for-equal-work law was passed in 1963, and the Equal Employment Opportunity Act—with all its enforcement mechanisms—was passed in 1972.

Supreme Court Justice Ruth Bader Ginsburg's book *Sex Bias in the U.S. Code* spells out the changes ERA would require, and it proves ERA would take away benefits from women. For example, the book states that the "equality principle" would eliminate the concept of "dependent women." This would deprive wives and widows of their Social Security dependent-wife benefits, on which millions of mothers and grandmothers depend.

Looking at the experience of states that have put ERA language into 5 their constitutions, we see that ERA would most probably require taxpayer funding of abortions. The feminists aggressively litigate this issue. Their most prominent victory was in the New Mexico Supreme Court, which accepted the notion that since only women undergo abortions, the denial of taxpayer funding is sex discrimination.

ERA would also give the courts the power to legalize same-sex marriages. Courts in four states have ruled that the ERA's ban on gender discrimination requires marriage licenses to be given to same-sex couples. In Maryland and Washington, those decisions were overturned by a higher court by only a one-vote margin. The ERA would empower the judges to rule either way.

If all laws are made sex-neutral, the military draft-registration law would have to include women. We don't have a draft today, but we do have registration, and those who fail to register immediately lose their college grants and loans and will never be able to get a federal job.

TOPICS FOR CRITICAL THINKING AND WRITING

1. Consult available sources to learn why the ERA failed adoption. Do you agree with Schlafly's explanation? Explain.

2. What does Schlafly think would be the legal results of adopting the ERA?

3. Moore thinks that sex inequality is legally permissible. Would Schlafly agree? Do you?

4. In her fourth paragraph Schlafly cites Justice Ginsburg in support of her argument. Why is Justice Ginsburg a better choice than, say, Justice Antonin Scalia or Justice Clarence Thomas?

5. In her sixth paragraph Schlafly introduces the issue of same-sex marriage. Do you think she was wise to bring up this issue? Why, or why not?

6. Putting aside your own position on the issue, which essay do you think is more effective as an example of persuasive writing? Why?

16

Genetic Modification of Human Beings: Is It Acceptable?

Ronald M. Green

Ronald M. Green teaches in the Religion Department at Dartmouth College, where he is the director of the Ethics Institute. He is the author of several books, including Babies by Design: The Ethics of Genetic Choice *(2007). This article was posted online at washingtonpost.com on April 1, 2008.*

Building Baby from the Genes Up

The two British couples no doubt thought that their appeal for medical help in conceiving a child was entirely reasonable. Over several generations, many female members of their families had died of breast cancer. One or both spouses in each couple had probably inherited the genetic mutations for the disease, and they wanted to use in-vitro fertilization and preimplantation genetic diagnosis (PGD) to select only the healthy embryos for implantation. Their goal was to eradicate breast cancer from their family lines once and for all.

In the United States, this combination of reproductive and genetic medicine—what one scientist has dubbed "reprogenetics"—remains largely unregulated, but Britain has a formal agency, the Human Fertilization and Embryology Authority (HFEA), that must approve all requests for PGD. In July 2007, after considerable deliberation, the HFEA approved the procedure for both families. The concern was not about the use of PGD to avoid genetic disease, since embryo screening for serious disorders is commonplace now on both sides of the Atlantic. What troubled the HFEA was the fact that an embryo carrying the cancer mutation could go on to live for forty or fifty years before ever developing cancer, and there was a chance it might never develop. Did this warrant selecting and discarding embryos? To its critics, the HFEA, in approving this request, crossed a bright line separating legitimate medical genetics from the quest for "the perfect baby."

Like it or not, that decision is a sign of things to come—and not necessarily a bad sign. Since the completion of the Human Genome Project in 2003, our understanding of the genetic bases of human disease and non-disease traits has been growing almost exponentially. The National Institutes of Health has initiated a quest for the "$1,000 genome," a ten-year program to develop machines that could identify all the genetic letters in anyone's genome at low cost (it took more than $3 billion to sequence the first human genome). With this technology, which some believe may be just four or five years away, we could not only scan an individual's—or embryo's—genome, we could also rapidly compare thousands of people and pinpoint those DNA sequences or combinations that underlie the variations that contribute to our biological differences.

With knowledge comes power. If we understand the genetic causes of obesity, for example, we can intervene by means of embryo selection to produce a child with a reduced genetic likelihood of getting fat. Eventually, without discarding embryos at all, we could use gene-targeting techniques to tweak fetal DNA sequences. No child would have to face a lifetime of dieting or experience the health and cosmetic problems associated with obesity. The same is true for cognitive problems such as dyslexia. Geneticists have already identified some of the mutations that contribute to this disorder. Why should a child struggle with reading difficulties when we could alter the genes responsible for the problem?

Many people are horrified at the thought of such uses of genetics, 5 seeing echoes of the 1997 science-fiction film *Gattaca*, which depicted a world where parents choose their children's traits. Human weakness has been eliminated through genetic engineering, and the few parents who opt for a "natural" conception run the risk of producing offspring— "invalids" or "degenerates"—who become members of a despised under-class. Gattaca's world is clean and efficient, but its eugenic obsessions have all but extinguished human love and compassion.

These fears aren't limited to fiction. Over the past few years, many bioethicists have spoken out against genetic manipulations. The critics tend to voice at least four major concerns. First, they worry about the effect of genetic selection on parenting. Will our ability to choose our children's biological inheritance lead parents to replace unconditional love with a consumerist mentality that seeks perfection?

Second, they ask whether gene manipulations will diminish our freedom by making us creatures of our genes or our parents' whims. In his book *Enough*, the techno-critic Bill McKibben asks: If I am a world-class runner, but my parents inserted the "Sweatworks2010 GenePack" in my genome, can I really feel pride in my accomplishments? Worse, if I refuse to use my costly genetic endowments, will I face relentless pressure to live up to my parents' expectations?

Third, many critics fear that reproductive genetics will widen our social divisions as the affluent "buy" more competitive abilities for their offspring. Will we eventually see "speciation," the emergence of two or more human populations so different that they no longer even breed with one another? Will we re-create the horrors of eugenics that led, in Europe, Asia, and the United States, to the sterilization of tens of thousands of people declared to be "unfit" and that in Nazi Germany paved the way for the Holocaust?

Finally, some worry about the religious implications of this technology. Does it amount to a forbidden and prideful "playing God"?

To many, the answers to these questions are clear. Not long ago, 10 when I asked a large class at Dartmouth Medical School whether they thought that we should move in the direction of human genetic engineering, more than 80 percent said no. This squares with public opinion polls that show a similar degree of opposition. Nevertheless, "babies by design" are probably in our future — but I think that the critics' concerns may be less troublesome than they first appear.

Will critical scrutiny replace parental love? Not likely. Even today, parents who hope for a healthy child but have one born with disabilities tend to love that child ferociously. The very intensity of parental love is the best protection against its erosion by genetic technologies. Will a child somehow feel less free because parents have helped select his or her traits? The fact is that a child is already remarkably influenced by the genes she inherits. The difference is that we haven't taken control of the process. Yet.

Knowing more about our genes may actually increase our freedom by helping us understand the biological obstacles — and opportunities — we have to work with. Take the case of Tiger Woods. His father, Earl, is said to have handed him a golf club when he was still in the playpen. Earl probably also gave Tiger the genes for some of the traits that help make him a champion golfer. Genes and upbringing worked together to inspire excellence. Does Tiger feel less free because of his inherited abilities? Did he feel pressured by his parents? I doubt it. Of course, his story could have gone the other way, with overbearing parents forcing a child into their mold. But the problem in that case wouldn't be genetics, but bad parenting.

Granted, the social effects of reproductive genetics are worrisome. The risks of producing a "genobility," genetic overlords ruling a vast genetic underclass, are real. But genetics could also become a tool for reducing the class divide. Will we see the day when perhaps all youngsters are genetically vaccinated against dyslexia? And how might this contribute to everyone's social betterment?

As for the question of intruding on God's domain, the answer is less clear than the critics believe. The use of genetic medicine to cure or prevent disease is widely accepted by religious traditions, even those that oppose discarding embryos. Speaking in 1982 at the Pontifical Academy of Sciences, Pope John Paul II observed that modern biological research "can ameliorate the condition of those who are affected by chromosomic diseases," and he lauded this as helping to cure "the smallest and weakest of human beings . . . during their intrauterine life or in the period immediately after birth." For Catholicism and some other traditions, it is one thing to cure disease, but another to create children who are faster runners, longer-lived, or smarter.

But why should we think that the human genome is a once-and-   15
for-all-finished, untamperable product? All of the biblically derived faiths permit human beings to improve on nature using technology, from agriculture to aviation. Why not improve our genome? I have no doubt that most people considering these questions for the first time are certain that human genetic improvement is a bad idea, but I'd like to shake up that certainty.

Genomic science is racing toward a future in which foreseeable improvements include reduced susceptibility to a host of diseases, increased life span, better cognitive functioning, and maybe even cosmetic enhancements such as whiter, straighter teeth. Yes, genetic orthodontics may be in our future. The challenge is to see that we don't also unleash the demons of discrimination and oppression. Although I acknowledge the risks, I believe that we can and will incorporate gene technology into the ongoing human adventure.

Topics for Critical Thinking and Writing

1. By the end of the second paragraph did you think that the British are probably right to be cautious, to require approval for all requests for PGD? Explain your position.

2. The fourth paragraph talks, by way of example, about avoiding obesity and "cognitive problems." At this stage in your reading of the essay, did you find yourself saying "Great, let's go for it," or were you thinking, "Wait a minute"? Why?

3. Do the fifth and sixth paragraphs pretty much set forth your response? If not, what *is* your response?

4. Does Bill McKibben's view, mentioned in the seventh paragraph, represent your view? If not, what would you say to McKibben?

5. If you are a believer in any of "the biblically derived faiths," does the comment in paragraph 15 allay whatever doubts you may have had about the acceptability of human genetic improvement? Explain.

6. In his final paragraph Green says, "I acknowledge the risks." Are you satisfied that he does acknowledge them adequately? Explain.

ANALYZING A VISUAL: GENETIC MODIFICATION OF HUMAN BEINGS

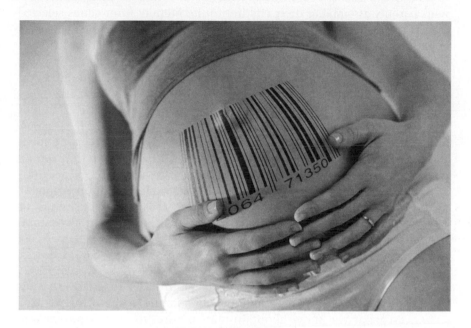

TOPICS FOR CRITICAL THINKING AND WRITING

1. What does this photograph seem to say about human genetic modification? Why do you think the photographer included a bar code in this image? In a couple of paragraphs, please evaluate this photo's effectiveness.

2. Do you agree with this photograph's point of view? In 250 words, write up a description of a photograph that might work as a rebuttal to this one.

Richard Hayes

Born in 1945, Richard Hayes is executive director of the Center for Genetics and Society, an organization that describes itself as "working to encourage responsible uses and effective society governance of the new human genetic and reproductive technologies. . . . The Center supports benign and beneficent medical applications of the new human genetic and reproductive technologies, and opposes those applications that objectify and commodify human life and threaten to divide human society."

This essay is reprinted from the Washington Post *on April 15, 2008.*

Genetically Modified Humans? No Thanks

In an essay in Sunday's Outlook section, Dartmouth ethics professor Ronald Green asks us to consider a neoeugenic future of "designer babies," with parents assembling their children quite literally from genes selected from a catalogue. Distancing himself from the compulsory, state-sponsored eugenics that darkened the first half of the last century, Green instead celebrates the advent of a libertarian, consumer-driven eugenics motivated by the free play of human desire, technology, and markets. He argues that this vision of the human future is desirable and very likely inevitable.

To put it mildly: I disagree. Granted, new human genetic technologies have real potential to help prevent or cure many terrible diseases, and I support research directed towards that end. But these same technologies also have the potential for real harm. If misapplied, they would exacerbate existing inequalities and reinforce existing modes of discrimination. If more widely abused, they could undermine the foundations of civil and human rights. In the worst case, they could undermine our experience of being part of a single human community with a common human future.

Once we begin genetically modifying our children, where do we stop? If it's acceptable to modify one gene, why not two, or twenty or two hundred? At what point do children become artifacts designed to someone's specifications rather than members of a family to be nurtured?

Given what we know about human nature, the development and commercial marketing of human genetic modification would likely spark a techno-eugenic rat-race. Even parents opposed to manipulating their children's genes would feel compelled to participate in this race, lest their offspring be left behind.

Green proposes that eugenic technologies could be used to reduce 5 "the class divide." But nowhere in his essay does he suggest how such a proposal might ever be made practicable in the real world.

The danger of genetic misuse is equally threatening at the international level. What happens when some rogue country announces an ambitious program to "improve the genetic stock" of its citizens? In a world still barely able to contain the forces of nationalism, ethnocentrism, and militarism, the last thing we need to worry about is a high-tech eugenic arms race.

In his essay, Green doesn't distinguish clearly between different uses of genetic technology—and the distinctions are critical. It's one thing to enable a couple to avoid passing on a devastating genetic condition, such as Tay-Sachs. But it's a different thing altogether to create children with a host of "enhanced" athletic, cosmetic, and cognitive traits that could be passed to their own children, who in turn could further genetically modify their children, who in turn . . . you get the picture. It's this second use of gene technology (the technical term is "heritable genetic enhancement") that Green most fervently wants us to embrace.

In this position, Green is well outside the growing national and international consensus on the proper use of human genetic science and technology. To his credit, he acknowledges that 80 percent of the medical school students he surveyed said they were against such forms of human genetic engineering, and that public opinion polls show equally dramatic opposition. He could have noted, as well, that nearly forty countries—including Brazil, Canada, France, Germany, India, Japan, and South Africa—have adopted socially responsible policies regulating the new human genetic technologies. They allow genetic research (including stem cell research) for medical applications, but prohibit its use for heritable genetic modification and reproductive human cloning.

In the face of this consensus, Green blithely announces his confidence that humanity "can and will" incorporate heritable genetic enhancement into the "ongoing human adventure."

Well, it's certainly possible. Our desires for good looks, good brains, 10 wealth and long lives, for ourselves and for our children, are strong and enduring. If the gene-tech entrepreneurs are able to convince us that we can satisfy these desires by buying into genetic modification, perhaps we'll bite. Green certainly seems eager to encourage us to do so.

But he would be wise to listen to what medical students, the great majority of Americans, and the international community appear to be saying: We want all these things, yes, and genetic technology might help us attain them, but we don't want to run the huge risks to the human community and the human future that would come with altering the genetic basis of our common human nature.

TOPICS FOR CRITICAL THINKING AND WRITING

1. Do you believe that in his first paragraph Hayes fairly summarizes Green's essay? If your answer is no, what are your objections?

2. Does the prospect raised in paragraph 6 frighten you? Why, or why not?

3. In his final paragraph Hayes speaks of "huge risks." What are these risks? Are you willing to take them? Why, or why not?

17

Obesity: Who Is Responsible for Our Weight?

Radley Balko

Radley Balko (b. 1975), a graduate of Indiana University with a degree in journalism, is a policy analyst with the Cato Institute, a conservative think tank. On his Web site Balko characterizes himself as a libertarian—that is, someone who believes that individual rights should be maximized, the role of government minimized. Libertarians believe that individuals should be free to do whatever they wish with their property and their persons, so long as they do not infringe on the liberty of others. Most libertarians probably believe, for instance, that individuals should be free not to use seat belts in cars and free not to wear helmets while riding motorcycles.

We reprint Balko's contribution to a debate originally published in Time *magazine in June 2004, paired with an opposing view by Kelly Brownell and Marion Nestle.*

Are You Responsible for Your Own Weight? Pro

Nutrition activists are agitating for a panoply of initiatives that would bring the government between you and your waistline. President Bush earmarked $125 million in his budget for the encouragement of healthy lifestyles. State legislatures and school boards have begun banning snacks and soda from school campuses and vending machines. Several state legislators and Oakland, California, Mayor Jerry Brown, among others, have called for a "fat tax" on high-calorie foods. Congress is considering menu-labeling legislation that would force chain restaurants to list fat, sodium, and calories for each item.

That is precisely the wrong way to fight obesity. Instead of intervening in the array of food options available to Americans, our government ought to be working to foster a personal sense of responsibility for our health and well-being.

We're doing just the opposite. For decades, America's health-care system has been migrating toward nationalized medicine. We have a law that requires some Americans to pay for other Americans' medicine, and several states bar health insurers from charging lower premiums to people who stay fit. That removes the financial incentive for making healthy decisions. Worse, socialized health care makes us troublingly tolerant of government trespasses on our personal freedom. If my neighbor's heart attack shows up on my tax bill, I'm more likely to support state regulation of what he eats — restrictions on what grocery stores can put on their shelves, for example, or what McDonald's can put between its sesame-seed buns.

The best way to combat the public-health threat of obesity is to remove obesity from the realm of "public health." It's difficult to think of a matter more private and less public than what we choose to put in our bodies. Give Americans moral, financial, and personal responsibility for their own health, and obesity is no longer a public matter but a private one — with all the costs, concerns, and worries of being overweight borne only by those people who are actually overweight.

Let each of us take full responsibility for our diet and lifestyle. We're 5 likely to make better decisions when someone else isn't paying for the consequences.

TOPICS FOR CRITICAL THINKING AND WRITING

1. Evaluate Balko's first two paragraphs as opening paragraphs in an argument.

2. Balko says disapprovingly, "We have a law that requires some Americans to pay for other Americans' medicine" (para. 3). Suppose someone replied, "Well, yes, that's the American way. For instance, childless people pay school taxes — that is, they pay for the education of other Americans' children." How might Balko reply? (As the biographical note mentions, Balko is a libertarian. You may want to consult a search engine to find some discussions of libertarianism.) How might you reply?

3. In a sentence, summarize Balko's thesis. Do you agree or disagree with this thesis? Explain.

ANALYZING A VISUAL: OBESITY

TOPICS FOR CRITICAL THINKING AND WRITING

1. Would the image be more interesting or less interesting if it were not cropped at the top? Why?

2. Would it be more interesting or less interesting if it showed only the woman, not the woman with two small children? Why?

3. Putting aside the issue of obesity, what do you think of using the image of the U.S. flag on clothing? Is such a use more or less reprehensible than burning the flag as a political protest?

Kelly Brownell and Marion Nestle

The following essay was paired with the preceding essay in a debate in Time *magazine in June 2004. Kelly Brownell, a professor of psychology at Yale University, specializes in the prevention and treatment of eating disorders. His most recent book, with colleagues, is* Weight Bias: Nature, Consequences, and Remedies *(2005). Marion Nestle, a professor at New York University, specializes in food politics. Her most recent book is* What to Eat *(2006).*

Are You Responsible for Your Own Weight? Con

The food industry, like any other, must grow to stay in business. One way it does so is by promoting unhealthy foods, particularly to children. Each year kids see more than 10,000 food ads on TV alone, almost all for items like soft drinks, fast foods, and sugared cereals. In the same year that the government spent $2 million on its main nutrition-education program, McDonald's spent $500 million on its We Love to See You Smile campaign. It can be no surprise that teenagers consume nearly twice as much soda as milk (the reverse was true twenty years ago) and that 25 percent of all vegetables eaten in the U.S. are French fries.

To counter criticism, the food industry and pro-business groups use a public relations script focused on personal responsibility. The script has three elements: 1) if people are overweight, it is their own fault; 2) industry responds to consumer demand but does not create it; and 3) insisting that industry change—say, by not marketing to children or requiring restaurants to reveal calories—is an attack on freedom.

Why quarrel with the personal-responsibility argument?

First, it's wrong. The prevalence of obesity increases year after year. Were people less responsible in 2002 than in 2001? Obesity is a global problem. Is irresponsibility an epidemic around the world?

Second, it ignores biology. Humans are hardwired, as a survival 5 strategy, to like foods high in sugar, fat, and calories.

Third, the argument is not helpful. Imploring people to eat better and exercise more has been the default approach to obesity for years. That is a failed experiment.

Fourth, personal responsibility is a trap. The argument is startlingly similar to the tobacco industry's efforts to stave off legislative and regulatory interventions. The nation tolerated personal-responsibility arguments from Big Tobacco for decades, with disastrous results.

Governments collude with industry when they shift attention from conditions promoting poor diets to the individuals who consume them. Government should be doing everything it can to create conditions that lead to healthy eating, support parents in raising healthy children, and make decisions in the interests of public health rather than private profit.

TOPICS FOR CRITICAL THINKING AND WRITING

1. Evaluate the opening paragraph as an opening paragraph for an argument.

2. In the first sentence of the second paragraph, the authors speak of "a public relations script." How might the food industry rewrite this phrase?

3. In the next-to-last paragraph, the authors say that the food industry's "argument is startlingly similar to the tobacco industry's efforts to stave off legislative and regulatory interventions." Why do you suppose the authors bring the tobacco industry into the argument? Is this comparison appropriate? Explain.

4. Evaluate the final paragraph as the final paragraph of the argument.

5. Are there arguments against government intervention to reduce obesity that these authors ignore or refute ineffectively? If so, what are they?

6. The authors give four arguments in favor of government intervention with our food intake. Which do you think is the strongest, and why? Which is the weakest, and why?

7. Suppose someone argued that if "humans are hardwired . . . to like foods high in sugar, fat, and calories" (para. 5), it's a waste of time trying to reduce intake of such foods—our human nature's hardwiring is against such a policy. What response would you offer?

For topical links related to the obesity controversy, see the companion Web site: **bedfordstmartins.com/barnetbedau.**

18

Racial Profiling: Should Airports Use It to Screen Passengers?

Clifford S. Fishman

Clifford S. Fishman, a lawyer and a professor of law at the Catholic University of America, has written several books, some for lawyers, some for lay readers. We reprint an essay written in 2001 for CQ Researcher; *it was paired with the next essay that we reprint here as well.*

Yes, Racial Profiling Is Sometimes Acceptable

Airport and airline security in this country—or more accurately, the lack of it—has been an open scandal for decades. On September 11, we paid the price.

Now it is proposed that airport security personnel should "profile" airline passengers from Moslem and Middle Eastern countries for special scrutiny.

To target an entire ethnic group, the overwhelming majority of whom are good, decent, innocent people because of the crimes committed by a tiny handful of them is immoral, in most instances illegal, and violates fundamental American values." = rights"

Nevertheless, in the aftermath of September 11, airport security officials are temporarily justified in doing so, for three reasons.

First, because since 1999, the perpetrators of every terrorist act committed or attempted by foreigners within the United States—the World Trade Center car bomb, September 11, and several unsuccessful conspiracies in between—have been from the Middle East, Algeria, or Pakistan.

Second, September 11 taught us that failing to prevent terrorists from boarding an airliner can cost thousands of lives and significantly disrupt our way of life.

Third, because we do not yet have in place the resources or personnel to properly scrutinize every individual who boards and every package loaded onto a plane, it would be irresponsible not to focus most of our attention on people who fit the "profile" of those most likely to attempt another September 11.

This justification is temporary, for two reasons: Permanently profiling any group violates our ideals and values. And the next group of hijackers might not fit the profile. They might be from Somalia or Indonesia (where allegedly there are Al Qaeda cells in each country). Or they could be members of Aum Shinrikyo, the Japanese sect that a few years ago released a deadly chemical in the Tokyo subway.

Or they might be "all-American guys" like Timothy McVeigh and Terry Nichols, who blew up the federal building in Oklahoma City. Until adequate security resources are put in place to properly screen everyone, we can only hope that security personnel who "profile" Middle Easterners will act professionally and courteously. Inevitably, though, thousands of innocent, decent people will be singled out unfairly, and many will be harassed and humiliated—and that is an outrage, even though it is temporarily necessary.

Let us pray that those who are singled out or mistreated will have 10 the grace to understand, and to forgive us for the wrongs that will be done to them.

TOPICS FOR CRITICAL THINKING AND WRITING

1. Define racial profiling.

2. What—if any—American "ideals and values" does screening violate?

3. What is the function of Fishman's opening paragraph? Of his third paragraph?

4. In paragraphs 5, 6, and 7 Fishman gives three reasons that in his view justify—temporarily—an "immoral" action. Are the three reasons of equal weight, in your opinion? If not, which do you find the most important, and why?

5. Are any or all of the three reasons valid today?

6. In the final paragraph, exactly what is the meaning of "grace"? How effective, in your view, is this concluding paragraph?

ANALYZING A VISUAL: AIRPORT SECURITY

Topics for Critical Thinking and Writing

1. This political cartoon takes a wry look at airport security procedures, chiefly the forced removal of passengers' shoes during the security screening process. How do you interpret this cartoon? Write 250 words in which you analyze the point the cartoonist is trying to make using details from the cartoon to support your analysis.

2. Do you find that this cartoon makes a convincing argument? In 250 words, explain why this cartoon is or isn't effective.

Jean AbiNader

Jean AbiNader is a founding board member of the Arab American Institute and the deputy director of the Moroccan American Center. He has also served as an adjunct professor at Georgetown University. The following essay, when it first appeared, was paired with the preceding essay in CQ Researcher.

No, Racial Profiling Is Unacceptable

In poll after poll taken after September 11, Arab Americans indicated their overwhelming desire to cooperate with the authorities to improve airline security. This desire to cooperate, however, does not justify the rude and abusive behavior by airline crews, ground personnel, and security staff.

Many of the improvements in procedures and technology can be implemented in a nondiscriminatory fashion. Recommendations ranging from baggage matching to better equipment and training for security personnel can be applied to all passengers equally, thus ensuring greater security without the need to single out passengers because of perceived ethnic origin, or other characteristics such as clothes or accents.

There is a continuing need for airlines to restate their policies against racial profiling, especially to inform and advise passengers and crew that federal and state statutes do not permit "vigilantism," particularly if the person in question has passed the common screening procedures for all passengers. Perhaps a variation of the "passenger bill of rights" regarding profiling needs to be included in the materials available to passengers in their seat pockets.

Finally, racial profiling presents more complications than solutions. Based on testimony by security officials, profiling does not make a measurable difference in the prevention of crimes, although it is helpful in investigating criminal activities once there has been a crime. This is not to suggest that law enforcement officials should be passive because of ethnic or racial considerations. Rather, it requires that great caution be exercised if racial or ethnic factors are to be included as one of a number of variants that may warrant that a security person investigate further.

Basing security procedures solely on racial or ethnic characteristics 5 leads to discriminatory behaviors by the officials involved and reinforces stereotypes that damage the government's ability to reach out and coordinate its efforts with the affected communities.

We recommend that the government work diligently to improve its screening of all travelers and their belongings. Equally applied procedures and reminders that racial profiling is unhelpful can also be useful in reducing the potential for disruptive behavior by passengers intent on independently assuming the role of air police.

Efforts should also be made to hire more Arab Americans and American Muslims. Qualified and trained Arab Americans can be resources to the security services and to the airlines by validating nondiscriminatory practices and helping to deal with passengers from Arab and Muslim countries who may feel overwhelmed by enhanced security procedures.

TOPICS FOR CRITICAL THINKING AND WRITING

1. In the first paragraph AbiNader refers to "poll after poll." How convincing is this assertion? Why?

2. In paragraph 3 AbiNader speaks of "vigilantism." Exactly what is "vigilantism"? Do you think racial profiling is an example? Why, or why not?

3. Would AbiNader favor racial profiling if it could be conducted without racial or class bias? Your evidence either way?

4. Do you think the concluding paragraph is effective? Why, or why not?

19

Romantic Relationships Between Faculty and Students: Should Colleges Prohibit Them?

Paul R. Abramson

Paul R. Abramson, a professor of psychology at the University of California, Los Angeles, is the author of several books, including Romance in the Ivory Tower: The Rights and Liberty of Conscience *(2007). This article first appeared in the* Boston Globe *on September 30, 2007.*

The Right to Romance: Why Universities Shouldn't Prohibit Relations Between Teachers and Students

To understand how twisted the sexual politics of university life have become, consider the movie *Legally Blonde*. Elle Woods, played by Reese Witherspoon, is a fashion-design student who ends up, almost accidentally, at Harvard Law School. At one point in the movie, her professor (played by Victor Garber) invites her into his office, asks her "how far [she] will go" for an important summer job, and—you can see where this is going—puts his hand on her leg.

The incident nearly causes Elle to leave law school, but she grits her teeth and perseveres. Eventually, after winning a not-guilty verdict in a murder case, she falls in love with Emmett (played by Luke Wilson), her attractive young cocounsel who was also a teaching assistant in one of her classes. At the end of the film, before the credits roll, the audience is told: "Emmett and Elle dated for the past two years. Emmett is proposing to Elle tonight." The audience, of course, is thrilled.

But under the rules that increasingly hold sway on many university campuses, both relationships—sleazy sexual harassment and true love by consenting adults—are prohibited.

Over the last decade, there has been a dramatic shift in how universities handle romantic relationships between teachers and students. Sparked in part by fears of expensive sexual harassment lawsuits, colleges have widely banned such relationships, adopting strict rules on dating among students, professors, and even teaching assistants. These rules ignore the rights and liberties of students and professors alike, and treat both as if they were children. They also represent an assault on one of the most fundamental rights of conscience: the right to choose our relationships.

If universities—whose existence is built on the value of freedom of 5 expression—were attacking the freedom of religion, or the freedom of speech, there would be a great outcry. But this is a topic that touches on sex, and so it seems difficult to have a reasonable, dispassionate debate on the merits.

There are clearly dangers in allowing romantic relations between teachers and students. Academia can be a fiercely competitive environment, so romance between professors and students invariably creates a risk of favoritism. And the power difference between professors and students raises the possibility that a young student could be coerced—or just charmed—into a relationship with an older teacher. However, if there are straightforward ways of mitigating the potential for damage, like strict conflict-of-interest rules, then the outright bans in place at many universities are an unnecessary affront.

The U.S. Constitution, of course, does not explicitly recognize a "right to romance," but the basis for the right runs deep. Freedom of the mind was an essential concept for the Founders. They sought to protect the rights of conscience, which encompass the rights to think, choose, and judge freely. This is the constitutional bedrock that supports our religious rights, and more generally, our right to make our own intimate choices. The choices we make about love are no less critical to our identity than the choices we make about God and religion. Absent some clear harm, the government should not be in the business of dictating our romantic choices; this is one of the many reasons that laws against marriage between races, or for gay couples, are outrageous. And it certainly shouldn't fall within the power of a quasi-governmental institution such as a university or corporation to rule our private lives.

Yet universities have been increasingly assuming this power. In the late 1990s, these rules started to become more common. In 1998, for example, Yale University passed a ban on consensual romantic relations between students and professors (and others in teaching roles) who supervise them, or could in the future. Offenders would receive disciplinary action. In 2002 the American Association of University Professors concluded that consensual sexual relationships between professors and students are "fraught with difficulties," and suggested that schools address the problem. Some universities, notably Harvard, have opted for a more nuanced position, recommending that professors refrain from a sexual relationship with a student whom they are "officially" grading. But more common are rules, like Yale's, that ban all relationships between professors and students they supervise or could potentially supervise.

There are, undoubtedly, real dangers in professors playing favorites or exploiting their power, but the important question is whether there are more reasonable ways to deal with the issue.

Universities have clear rules about sexual harassment, and these 10 rules should be strictly enforced. Sexual harassment is a coercive and hostile assault upon the integrity and autonomy of another person. It is potentially illegal and always immoral. Many of the worst situations people imagine fall indisputably under the heading of harassment, and are already prohibited and punishable.

Clearly, there is a power differential between professor and student. A professor's position and experience can be both persuasive and attractive. But with one exception (the relationship between psychotherapist and client), people are not generally precluded from romance because of social power gaps. There are no laws stating that judges and senators, billionaires and rock stars, can date only people of comparable influence. The difference in psychotherapy is that it is a nonreciprocal relationship from the start (the client unburdens, but the therapist never does) and the process of transference, whereby the client projects needs and desires on the therapist, is an essential part of therapy. Sex between a therapist and client is thus an abuse of transference, which is not a factor in the faculty-student relationship.

A ban on romantic relations also fails to accord autonomy to students who are legal adults, old enough to vote or to join the Army. Furthermore, although Hollywood is fond of portraying the aging professor and young coed falling in love (*The Wonder Boys* comes to mind), in the real world it is usually people of comparable ages and interests who find each other and start to date—a young professor and a Ph.D. student, for instance, or a graduate student and a college senior. This is no less true on a college campus than in any other environment.

Favoritism is a more pressing concern, but there are solutions. Judges, for example, must disqualify themselves in cases in which a personal bias exists (for example, a former partnership with an attorney on the case). Medical researchers must disclose all sources of funding, particularly from drug manufacturers whose products they are evaluating.

A professor who is romantically involved with a student faces the same problem, and similar procedures should be used: recusal, disclosure, and third-party evaluations. If a student falls in love, he or she should switch classes or professors. If that is not feasible, the professor should assign someone else (another professor, a teaching assistant) to do the grading. These options are not perfect, but they are reasonable, and have been adopted as the standard in other professions.

Despite the high-minded rhetoric of universities, there is a more 15 mundane reason driving these new rules: They save money. In sexual harassment lawsuits, the aggrieved party usually sues the deep-pocketed university as well as the alleged perpetrator. A blanket prohibition on romantic relations gives the university a stronger defense. It is not a coincidence that both Yale and the University of California system adopted their new consensual-romance rules after embarrassing, and presumably expensive, lawsuits.

In any case, the burden should fall on universities to prove that their rules, which abridge a fundamental right, are absolutely necessary. The Ninth Amendment is clear: "The enumeration in the Constitution, of certain rights, shall not be construed to deny or disparage others retained by the people." The choice of one's romantic partner is no less essential to the formation of the self, no less a matter of the integrity of our private sphere, than well-protected First Amendment rights such as religion and speech.

For many students and professors, the university represents virtually their entire social world. This is where they are likely to meet people, and romance is occasionally the result. If we let universities prohibit consenting adults from falling in love, what will be next? Our ultimate freedom lies in our power to make choices, and a university prohibition that suppresses choice tramples the very nature of freedom itself.

Topics for Critical Thinking and Writing

1. What is recusal (para. 15) and in what circumstances does Abramson favor it? Do you concur? Explain your view.

2. What is the "burden" to which Abramson refers (para. 17) and why does he think it should fall on the college or university and not on either the student or faculty member involved? Do you agree? Why, or why not?

3. Abramson draws an analogy between "well-protected First Amendment rights such as religion and speech" (para. 17) and "the right to romance" (para. 17). Is this a good (persuasive, pertinent) analogy? Why, or why not? Can you think of a different and better analogy? Explain.

4. Putting aside your own position on this issue, evaluate Abramson's final paragraph as a concluding paragraph. Do you think it is an effective way of wrapping up his argument? Why, or why not?

5. Has Abramson on the whole convinced you? Or do you have reservations? If you have reservations, what are they?

6. Find out if your college has a code governing romantic relations between teachers and students. If it does, does the code prohibit relations between teachers and graduate students as well as teachers and undergraduates. Does it prohibit relations between graduate teaching assistants and undergraduates? Do any or all of the prohibitions seem appropriate to you?

7. Can it be reasonably argued (see especially para. 6) that all prohibitions of this sort infantalize students—treat them like children—and are contrary to the assumptions that a college should make about its students?

8. Can it be reasonably argued that a ban on "consensual relationships" is reasonable because in fact there cannot be a "consensual relation" between a teacher and a student? Consensual relationships are (in this view) made between equals, but a teacher-student relationship is not equal, it is asymmetrical.

ANALYZING A VISUAL: ROMANTIC RELATIONSHIPS BETWEEN FACULTY AND STUDENTS

"I got ten dollars for my birthday, Miss Kellerman — what time do you get off work?"

TOPIC FOR CRITICAL THINKING AND WRITING

While this cartoon is intended to be humorous, are you able to find a more serious message imbedded in it? Why, or why not? Does the cartoon say anything profound about student-teacher relationships, or is it merely intended to be enjoyed as a joke? Defend your point of view in a couple of paragraphs, using details from the cartoon to support your argument.

Duke University

Duke University, like many other institutions in recent years, formally adopted a policy concerning romantic relationships between students and teachers. This policy was drawn up by a committee that included students, faculty, staff, and administrators.

Duke University Policy on Consensual Relationships

DEFINITIONS

For purposes of this policy, the terms "Duke University," "employee," "supervisor," "faculty," "student," and "consensual relationships" are defined as follows:

Duke University Duke University and related entities, including Duke University Medical Center and Health Systems.

Employee Anyone employed by Duke University as faculty or staff, full-time or part-time.

Supervisor Anyone who oversees, directs, or evaluates the work of others, including, but not limited to, managers, administrators, coaches, directors, physicians, deans, chairs, advisors, housestaff, and teaching assistants, as well as faculty members in their roles as instructors, as supervisors of their staff, and as participants in decisions affecting the careers of other faculty members.

Faculty All those charged with academic instruction, including all ranks recognized as faculty under the bylaws of Duke University and its Medical Center and Health Systems, teaching assistants, academic advisors, coaches, and others who have a role in educating, supervising, or advising students as part of the programs of Duke University and its various schools.

Students All those enrolled full-time or part-time in any program of 5 Duke University and its various schools.

Consensual relationships Dating and sexual relationships willingly undertaken by the parties.

Note Non-consensual situations are covered under the University's policy on Sexual Harassment, marital relationships under the Nepotism policy.

POLICY REGARDING FACULTY–STUDENT CONSENSUAL RELATIONSHIPS

No faculty member should enter into a consensual relationship with a student actually under that faculty member's authority. Situations of authority include, but are not limited to, teaching, formal mentoring, supervision of research, and employment of a student as a research or teaching assistant; and exercising substantial responsibility for grades, honors, or degrees; and considering disciplinary action involving the student.

No faculty member should accept authority over a student with whom he or she has or has had a consensual relationship without agreement with the appropriate dean. Specifically, the faculty member should not, absent such agreement, allow the student to enroll for credit in a course which the faculty member is teaching or supervising; direct the student's independent study, thesis, or dissertation; employ the student as a teaching or research assistant; participate in decisions pertaining to a student's grades, honors, degrees; or consider disciplinary action involving the student.

Students and faculty alike should be aware that entering into a consensual relationship will limit the faculty member's ability to teach and mentor, direct work, employ, and promote the career of a student involved with him or her in a consensual relationship, and that the relationship should be disclosed in any letter of recommendation the faculty member may write on the student's behalf. Furthermore, should the faculty member be the only supervisor available in a particular area of study or research, the student may be compelled to avoid or change the special area of his or her study or research.

If nevertheless a consensual relationship exists or develops between a 10 faculty member and a student involving any situation of authority, that situation of authority must be terminated. Termination includes, but is not limited to, the student withdrawing from a course taught by the faculty member; transfer of the student to another course or section, or assumption of the position of authority by a qualified alternative faculty member or teaching assistant; the student selecting or being assigned to another academic advisor and/or thesis or dissertation advisor; and changing the supervision of the student's teaching or research assistantship. In order for these changes to be made and ratified appropriately, the faculty must disclose the consensual relationship to his or her superior, normally the chair, division head, or dean, and reach an agreement for remediation. In case of failure to reach agreement, the supervisor shall terminate the situation of authority.

TOPICS FOR THINKING AND WRITING

1. As you read over the definitions in the Duke policy statement (paras. 1–7), do you find that you have questions or objections to any of them? Do you think that they reasonably cover all types of roles and relationships addressed later in the policy? Why do you think this section is included?

2. Would you agree with all the restrictions the Duke policy imposes on consensual relationships? Why or why not?

3. Do you think that the term "consensual relationships" as used in the Duke statement is euphemistic? If you don't think it is, what would it take in your judgment to make it euphemistic?

20

Single-Sex Classrooms: Do They Offer Advantages?

Rosalind C. Barnett and Caryl Rivers

Rosalind C. Barnett of Brandeis University and Caryl Rivers of Boston University are authors of Same Difference: How Gender Myths Are Hurting Our Relationships, Our Children, and Our Jobs *(2004). This article appeared in the* Boston Globe *on November 23, 2008.*

Differences Should Not Drive a Curriculum

School Superintendent Carol R. Johnson plans to create two single-sex public schools: a Young Women's Leadership Academy and a Young Men's Public Service Academy to help prepare boys for careers as police officers, firefighters, and emergency medical technicians.

But Johnson's school reorganization is supposed to cut costs, and single-sex public classrooms are both expensive and unproven. Research shows that gender is a minor factor in a public school's success or failure.

Advocacy groups claim there are major gender differences between boys and girls, that they think, see, and hear differently and process information differently. But this science has been roundly debunked. Peer-reviewed research consistently finds that differences in cognitive abilities between boys and girls are trivial. While the media gravitate to any study that shows even the slightest difference in the brains of boys and girls, they misinterpret the meaning of such findings. A study by some of the nation's most influential researchers, including Diane F. Halpern, Camilla P. Benbow, David C. Geary, Ruben C. Gur, Janet Shibley Hyde, and Morton Ann Gernsbacher, focused on this issue in *Science* in 2007.

The scientists warn: Finding sex differences in brain structures and functions does not suggest these are the sole cause of observed cognitive differences between males and females. Because the brain reflects learning and experiences, sex differences can be influenced by culture and social expectations.

Unfortunately, some teachers are leaping on the brain-differences 5 bandwagon. A teacher in South Carolina has girls study science by analyzing cosmetics. Some teachers give boys books about combat instead of the classics because of boys' supposed verbal weaknesses.

The *Science* authors also debunk the comment by former Harvard University president Lawrence Summers that girls are inherently inferior to boys in math and science. They call this idea simplistic and point to the fact that girls are catching up to boys in most areas.

The single-sex classroom is appealing thanks to the success of high-performing private schools. But those schools do well not because of gender, but because they have motivated students, excellent teachers, and involved parents, and because the students often come from affluent homes. When California tried an experiment with public single-sex schools in the '90s, independent evaluators found that they failed to improve student performance, probably because they didn't have extensive resources.

Can single-sex classrooms be good classrooms? Sure, if they have the resources. But such classrooms are expensive to set up and maintain, because federal law requires schools to ensure that the same resources are available for both sexes. And often, segregated classes fall prey to popular but unscientific ideas about how the sexes differ in abilities.

Why opt for the single-sex classrooms in public schools, when we know what really works? Michael Jonas points out in *Commonwealth* magazine what works in the state's poor but high-performing schools: longer school days, intensive tutoring, giving schools wide latitude over teacher hiring, and setting high expectations for all students.

Wouldn't Boston be better off and save money by admitting both 10 boys and girls to leadership and public service academies? As men and women increasingly work side by side in the labor force, does separating them by sex in public school make much sense?

TOPICS FOR CRITICAL THINKING AND WRITING

1. In their second paragraph Barnett and Rivers raise the issue of expense. Yes, cost is a factor, but should it be large factor? That is, if it were agreed that single-sex schools are notably more effective than coed schools, shouldn't we raise the money to support single-sex schools?

2. In their third paragraph the authors say that the idea of "major gender differences between boys and girls" has been "roundly debunked." Did you know that? Or are you skeptical? On what evidence is your view based?

3. In paragraph 7 the authors grant that single-sex schools can be highly effective. Do you think the authors give these schools enough credit— or too much credit? Explain.

4. In the last two paragraphs the authors offer, very briefly of course because the essay is short, their view of the answer to single-sex schools. What is your view?

ANALYZING A VISUAL: SINGLE-SEX CLASSROOMS

TOPICS FOR CRITICAL THINKING AND WRITING

1. How many possible ways can you interpret this image? In your opinion, does it seem like a standard classroom scene? What elements of this image lead you this conclusion? In a couple of paragraphs, see how many interpretations for this photograph you can come up with.

2. What is your opinion on the debate over single-sex classrooms? In 250 words or so, write a defense of your position using this photograph as evidence. Then, write another 250 words in which you take the opposite position and, again, use the same photograph to support a different point of view. Which argument do you think is stronger? How does the image contribute to each argument?

Sally Reed

Sally Reed is director of communications at the National Coalition of Girls' Schools. This article appeared in the Boston Globe *and was paired with the preceding one by Barnett and Rivers in the* Boston Globe *on November 23, 2008.*

Girls and Boys Thrive in Separate Classrooms

There can be no question anymore: Evidence over decades demonstrates that single-sex education is a valid and compelling option.

In 2001, the U.S. Department of Education acted on independent findings to sanction single-sex education as a good choice for some students. Here at the National Coalition of Girls' Schools, we are thrilled that our commitment to providing a single-sex choice within both public and private schools has sparked lively debate in Massachusetts.

Certainly, girls and boys should have the chance to attend single-sex schools whose environments are tailored to their developmental and cognitive needs, offering rich opportunities for both to shine in ways that coeducation, with all its possibilities, has not.

We draw on research from studies conducted two and three decades ago. In the 1990s, an important national study of secondary schools and colleges made "The Case for Single-Sex Schools" by showing that "single-sex schools for females provide a greater opportunity for educational attainment as measured by standardized tests, curriculum and course placement, leadership behavior, number of years of formal education, and occupational achievement."

In other words, girls thrive when their learning style is valued. They 5 are more engaged, more willing to persevere, and enjoy greater satisfaction and success in the classroom, on the playing field, and in the lab. Not to mention at the computer and in front of the class.

Some think that girls' schools leave young women ill-equipped to compete against their male counterparts. Competing with boys is not the point. Girls' schools see their graduates standing side-by-side with men of high achievement. An independent study by the Goodman Research Group, commissioned by the National Coalition of Girls' Schools in 2005, found that more than 80 percent of the 4,200 girls' school graduates surveyed said they were better prepared than their coed school peers to succeed in college.

Others may argue that single-sex educational settings are unnatural, passé, and counterintuitive. That makes sense from a limited perspective. It made sense, too, that the sun revolved around the earth, until Copernicus proved otherwise. We now have evidence from the more than 450 schools (154 public and 300 independent) offering same-sex education around the country. Girls and boys in such settings are more expressive, creative, and adventurous in their learning. Liberated from gender stereotyping, more girls pursue studies (and later careers) in math, science, and technology; with less to prove, boys tend to collaborate rather than clobber one another, and to get more involved in art, music, and drama.

At a time when we are conscious of the need to prepare succeeding generations to take active, innovative roles in a complex world, these reports have particular power. We have graduated into a world that demands competence and courage from all children. To remain competitive as a nation we need as many young women as men stepping into careers in engineering, information technology, math, and science. We cannot afford to lag behind developing nations. Single-gender classrooms and schools have a well-known track record for fostering such choices.

How can we turn a blind eye, knowing what we do about the benefits of single-sex classrooms? Boston has always been the hub of the educational universe in America. It's time to think progressively, and, to borrow a phrase from Thoreau, advance confidently in the direction of our dreams.

Topics for critical Thinking and Writing

1. The first paragraph is authoritative — "There can be no question anymore" — a dangerous way to begin, unless indeed one can offer convincing evidence. Does the rest of Reed's essay live up to this beginning? Explain.

2. In paragraph 5 Reed speaks of the "learning style" of girls, and she goes on to say that girls "are more engaged, more willing to persevere, and enjoy greater satisfaction and success in the classroom, on the playing field, and in the lab." Do your observations confirm these assertions? And, if so, why do you think this is the case? Biology? Culture?

3. In paragraph 6 Reed cites a study in which 80% of the graduates of girls' school said they were "better prepared than their coed school peers to succeed in college." Two points: (1) Isn't it probable that a majority of the graduates of any special kind of school — let's say a religious school, or a military academy — are likely to think they are better prepared than graduates of other schools, simply because they have (so to speak) an investment in that sort of education? And (2) most girls' school are private schools, not public schools, which is to say that the schools are selective, and the students (as a group) probably *are* better, academically, even before they enter the school. Or do you see things differently?

4. Reed cites statistics; Barnett and Rivers do not. Do you think Reed's use of statistics gives her essay a solidity, an authority, that their essay lacks? Explain.

5. What specific aspects of coeducation might diminish a girl's ability to achieve her best? A tendency by boys to monopolize the discussion? A fear of bullying? A fear of outshining boys intellectually and therefore being regarded — by boys — as socially undesirable? Something else? What aspects of a coeducational school might diminish a boy's ability? Would the presence of girls trigger a male desire to show off to girls, which might take the form of disruptive behavior? Or are these conjectures the results of stereotypical thinking?

PART FIVE

CURRENT ISSUES: CASEBOOKS

21

A College Education: What Is Its Purpose?

Stanley Fish

Stanley Fish, born in 1938, taught at both Johns Hopkins University and Duke University before his tenure as dean of the College of Liberal Arts and Sciences at the University of Illinois, Chicago. He is the Davidson-Kahn Distinguished University Professor of Humanities and a professor of law at Florida International University. He is also one of the most influential literary critics in the United States. Among his books are Self-Consuming Artifacts *(1972) and* Is There a Text in This Class? *(1980). This essay and the letters of response following it were published in the* New York Times *in 2004.*

Why We Built the Ivory Tower

After nearly five decades in academia, and five and a half years as a dean at a public university, I exit with a three-part piece of wisdom for those who work in higher education: Do your job; don't try to do someone else's job, as you are unlikely to be qualified; and don't let anyone else do your job. In other words, don't confuse your academic obligations with the obligation to save the world; that's not your job as an academic; and don't surrender your academic obligations to the agenda of any non-academic constituency—parents, legislators, trustees, or donors. In short, don't cross the boundary between academic work and partisan advocacy, whether the advocacy is yours or someone else's.

Marx famously said that our job is not to interpret the world, but to change it. In the academy, however, it is exactly the reverse: Our job is not to change the world, but to interpret it. While academic labors might in some instances play a role in real-world politics—if, say, the Supreme Court cites your book on the way to a decision—it should not be the design or aim of academics to play that role.

While academics in general will agree that a university should not dance to the tune of external constituencies, they will most likely resist the injunction to police the boundary between academic work and political work. They will resist because they simply don't believe in the boundary—they believe that all activities are inherently political, and an injunction to avoid politics is meaningless and futile.

Now there is some truth to that, but it is not a truth that goes very far. And it certainly doesn't go where those who proclaim it would want it to go. It is true that no form of work—including even the work of, say, natural science—stands apart from the political, social, and economic concerns that underlie the structures and practices of a society. This does not mean, however, that there is no difference between academic labors and partisan labors, or that there is no difference between, for example, analyzing the history of welfare reform—a history that would necessarily include opinions pro and con—and urging students to go out and work for welfare reform or for its reversal.

Analyzing welfare reform in an academic context is a political action 5 in the sense that any conclusion a scholar might reach will be one another scholar might dispute. (That, after all, is what political means: subject to dispute.) But such a dispute between scholars will not be political in the everyday sense of the word, because each side will represent different academic approaches, not different partisan agendas.

My point is not that academics should refrain from being political in an absolute sense—that is impossible—but that they should engage in politics appropriate to the enterprise they signed onto. And that means arguing about (and voting on) things like curriculum, department leadership, the direction of research, the content and manner of teaching, establishing standards—everything that is relevant to the responsibilities we take on when we accept a paycheck. These responsibilities include meeting classes, keeping up in the discipline, assigning and correcting papers, opening up new areas of scholarship, and so on.

This is a long list, but there are many in academia who would add to it the larger (or so they would say) tasks of "forming character" and "fashioning citizens." A few years ago the presidents of nearly 500 universities issued a declaration on the "Civic Responsibility of Higher Education." It called for colleges and universities to take responsibility for helping students "realize the values and skills of our democratic society."

Derek Bok, the former president of Harvard and one of the forces behind the declaration, has urged his colleagues to "consider civic responsibility as an explicit and important aim of college education." In January, some 1,300 administrators met in Washington under the auspices of the Association of American Colleges and Universities to take up this topic: "What practices provide students with the knowledge and commitments to be socially responsible citizens?" That's not a bad question, but the answers to it should not be the content of a college or university course.

No doubt, the practices of responsible citizenship and moral behavior should be encouraged in our young adults—but it's not the business of the university to do so, except when the morality in question is the morality that penalizes cheating, plagiarizing, and shoddy teaching, and the desired citizenship is defined not by the demands of democracy, but by the demands of the academy.

This is so not because these practices are political, but because they are the political tasks that belong properly to other institutions. Universities could engage in moral and civic education only by deciding in advance which of the competing views of morality and citizenship is the right one, and then devoting academic resources and energy to the task of realizing it. But that task would deform (by replacing) the true task of academic work: the search for truth and the dissemination of it through teaching. 10

The idea that universities should be in the business of forming character and fashioning citizens is often supported by the claim that academic work should not be hermetically sealed or kept separate from the realm of values. But the search for truth is its own value, and fidelity to it mandates the accompanying values of responsibility in pedagogy and scholarship.

Performing academic work responsibly and at the highest level is a job big enough for any scholar and for any institution. And, as I look around, it does not seem to me that we academics do that job so well that we can now take it upon ourselves to do everyone else's job too. We should look to the practices in our own shop, narrowly conceived, before we set out to alter the entire world by forming moral character, or fashioning democratic citizens, or combating globalization, or embracing globalization, or anything else.

One would like to think that even the exaggerated sense of virtue that is so much a part of the academic mentality has its limits. If we aim low and stick to the tasks we are paid to perform, we might actually get something done.

TOPICS FOR CRITICAL THINKING AND WRITING

1. In a paragraph explain and evaluate the title of Fish's essay.

2. Do you think Fish is relatively indifferent to whether and how his students develop their moral "characters," or is his position rather that this issue deserves to be addressed outside the university? Explain.

3. Fish thinks that it is absurd for academics to add to their proper duties the challenge of "do[ing] everyone else's job too" (para. 12). Is he attacking a straw man (see p. 374)? Explain in an essay of 250 words.

4. Suppose someone were to challenge Fish's dismissal of the famous Marxist epigram that he paraphrases (see para. 2), by arguing that both he and Marx missed the point. Professors *are* in the business of changing the world — and they do it by the ways in which they interpret what the world presents to them. How would you evaluate this reply?

5. Basing your response on the style and content of this essay, would you like to take a course with Professor Fish? Why, or why not?

6. Read Dave Eggers's "Serve or Fail" (p. 794), and then imagine what Eggers might say about Fish's essay. In an essay of 250 words set forth your imagined response.

*"I've finally decided
to go to college. All you lose is four years."*

David Brooks

David Brooks, born in Toronto in 1961, grew up in New York City and then did his undergraduate work at the University of Chicago, where he regarded himself as a liberal. By 1983, however, he had become a conservative. Brooks has pub-lished widely—for instance, in the Weekly Standard, *the* Wall Street Journal, *and* Newsweek. *He now writes regularly for the* New York Times, *in which the following essay first appeared in November 2004.*

Brooks's essay may at first seem to be a review of a recent novel by Tom Wolfe titled I Am Charlotte Simmons, *but, as you will see, it moves toward a discussion of college mores. We follow the essay with several letters that address the issue of college education.*

"Moral Suicide," À la Wolfe

It's easy to write a negative review of a Tom Wolfe novel; hundreds of people do it every few years. First, out of the thousands of sociological details Wolfe gets right, you pick out some he gets wrong (thus establishing your superior hipness). You mention that he obsesses over the superficial details of life while you ignore his moral intent (thus hinting at your own superior depth). Then you graciously allow that many of Wolfe's scenes are hilarious, while lamenting that his characters are not fully developed. Then you call it a day.

But since Wolfe takes risks in his novels to describe the moral climate of the age, it seems only fair that we at least take the chance his books offer to debate the more serious things he's trying to get at.

His latest, *I Am Charlotte Simmons*, is about a young woman who leaves Sparta, a small town in North Carolina, and enters an elite university. She finds all the rules of life there are dissolved: the rules of courtship, the rules of decorum, and polite conversation.

The social rules have dissolved because the morality that used to undergird them dissolved long ago. Wolfe sprinkles his book with observations about how the word "immoral" now seems obsolete, about how sophisticated people now reject the idea of absolute evil, about a hyper-materialistic neuroscience professor who can use the word "soul" only when it is in quotation marks.

Wolfe describes a society in which we still have vague notions about 5 good and bad, virtue and vice, but the moral substructure that fits all those concepts together has been washed away. Everybody is left swirling about in a chaotic rush of desire and action, without a coherent code to make sense of it all.

Charlotte, like other Wolfe-ian heroes, is caught in a maelstrom. All these anarchic social patterns are blowing about her and engulfing her — the mixed-up world of hookups, coed bathrooms, and white suburban frat boys trying to act gangsta.

Within the Hobbesian war for status, Charlotte lacks some solid spot to plant her feet and get her bearings. She is unable to step outside her immediate circumstances and judge her life according to some set of firm criteria.

All her life she has been a mannequin who racks up accomplishments. In a culture that prizes young people for how they can perform certain tasks, she has been adored, at least by adults, and given prizes, scholarships, and expectations.

Honed to excel in academic settings, she's unprepared to face the moral tests thrown up by her sexuality and the sheer formlessness of her new life. She has never really even thought about the question of who she is and how she should actually live, because what she's really addicted to is the admiration she gets when she achieves what others expect her to achieve. When moral judgment and courage are called for, she's unprepared.

So she goes off in the middle of the book and commits what Wolfe 10 calls an act of "moral suicide." Something inside her lets her know that she has committed a great wrong, and she's left alone and depressed with no one and nothing to guide her.

I don't agree with all of Wolfe's depiction of campus life. He overestimates the lingering self-confidence and prestige of the prep school elite. He undervalues the independence of collegiate women, and underplays the great yearning to do good that surges out of most college students. Life on campus isn't really as nasty as Wolfe describes it. Most students are responsible and prudential and thus not as ribald as Wolfe makes them out to be.

But he's located one of the paradoxes of the age. Highly educated young people are tutored, taught, and monitored in all aspects of their lives, except the most important, which is character building. When it comes to this, most universities leave them alone. And they find themselves in a world of unprecedented ambiguity, where it's not clear if you're going out with the person you're having sex with, where it's not clear if anything can be said to be absolutely true.

In other words, we have constructed this great apparatus to fill their minds—with thousands of Ph.D.'s ready to serve. But when it comes to courage, which is the pre-eminent virtue since without it nothing else lasts, we often leave them with the gnawing sense that they really should develop it, though God knows how.

TOPICS FOR CRITICAL THINKING AND WRITING

1. In paragraph 4 Brooks says that "the word 'immoral' now seems obsolete." Do you agree that the word is out of fashion? Your evidence?

2. What does Brooks think Wolfe means (para. 10) by "moral suicide"?

3. In paragraph 11 Brooks says that in Wolfe's novel, college life is "nasty" and "ribald." Your view?

4. In his twelfth paragraph Brooks says that "young people are tutored, taught, and monitored in all aspects of their lives, except the most important, which is character building. When it comes to this, most universities leave them alone." *How* might a college or university teach character building? By requiring certain courses in ethics? By very strictly enforcing rules about plagiarism? By expelling any underage student found guilty of possessing alcohol? Or perhaps simply by urging students to observe the highly moral character of all the members of the faculty? Or what?

5. Does your college experience so far confirm or disconfirm the criticisms Brooks makes (paras. 11–12) of Wolfe?

6. According to Brooks (and Wolfe?), courage is "the pre-eminent virtue" (para. 13). Where does this leave honesty? Fairness? Do you agree? Explain in an essay of 400 words.

Letters of Response by Scott Bradley, Barry Oshry, Paul W. Cutrone, and Rebecca Chopp

To the Editor:

I find it odd that even as universities are excelling at teaching academics, David Brooks calls it a paradox that they are not teaching "moral judgment" and "courage."

As a recent college graduate, I am thankful that my university did not try to act as my parent and respected me as an adult.

Traits like "moral judgment" and "courage" must be developed and fostered by parents.

I would imagine that most universities, short of leaning on religious teachings, would wonder how to develop such traits in already developed adults.

From my own experience, I can attest that when parents expose their children to other cultures, teach them early to be open-minded with different people, and fully discuss with them choices that they will face, including sexuality, those children will not have problems with "moral judgment" and "courage."

SCOTT BRADLEY
Cambridge, Mass., November 16, 2004

To the Editor:

David Brooks uses Tom Wolfe's latest novel to link moral collapse in our society with the conservatives' favorite obsession, sexuality, as if sexual looseness reflected the core moral failing of our society.

Sex is far down the list of moral failures in a society that maims and murders innocent women and children to save them; that destroys ancient cities to liberate them; that launches a righteous war based on lies; and in which greed and corruption in high places are rampant.

It is time to face the real moral failings of this society.

BARRY OSHRY
Boston, November 16, 2004

To the Editor:

David Brooks charges that universities don't develop character.

When I attended an elite secular liberal college, the required curriculum included the Western tradition's great philosophers and writers — Plato, Aristotle, Thomas Moore, and Thomas Aquinas — as well as sections of the Old and New Testaments.

We drew our moral lessons from these works and from our knowledge of the lives their authors led. We did not need the overlay of some half-baked morality course dreamed up by the university to please neo-conservative demagogues.

PAUL W. CUTRONE
Garden City, N.Y., November 16, 2004

To the Editor:

David Brooks is right to point out that character-building is fundamental to education in the 21st century, but contrary to his suggestion, most universities do not leave character-building alone.

Many colleges and universities are working to provide a culture for students to strengthen their character and to hold one another accountable.

At Colgate, we are building on the traditions of a core curriculum by combining it with residential programs that focus on civic education, moral reflection, and leadership development.

Some may think that it is not the place of higher education to encourage these values, but college students need to develop the courage to help others and to build common good if they are to become strong, moral leaders in their communities and professions.

Colleges and universities must be thinking about and educating for character if we are to meet the needs of the students of today.

REBECCA CHOPP
President, Colgate University
Hamilton, N.Y., November 16, 2004

TOPICS FOR CRITICAL THINKING AND WRITING

1. Do you agree with Bradley that teaching "moral judgment" is the business of parents, not of colleges? Explain.

2. Oshry speaks of "the conservatives' favorite obsession, sexuality." He goes on to say that "sex is far down the list of moral failures" in our society. Your view?

3. Cutrone, praising a Great Books course, says, "We drew our moral lessons from these works and from our knowledge of the lives their authors led." Think of an author whose work you admire. Research his or her biography, and then meditate on whether the author's life provides you with any sort of guidance or morals for living your own life.

4. Chopp speaks of a required "core curriculum," and she says that colleges should offer programs that "focus on civil education, moral reflection, and leadership development." Look through your college catalog and see if you can find three or four courses that fit this description. Which one or two would you most like to take? Then invent a course with a focus of this sort. Specify the readings that you would assign.

Patrick Allitt

Patrick Allitt, a professor of American history at Emory University, is the author of I'm a Teacher, You're a Student: A Semester in the University Classroom *(2005). We reprint an essay that first appeared in 2006 in the* Chronicle of Higher Education, *a weekly publication read chiefly by college teachers and administrators. Letters of response to this article follow.*

Should Undergraduates Specialize?

I was a college freshman thirty-two years ago, in 1974. My daughter, Frances, is about to become a college freshman this fall. I went to the University of Oxford in England. She's going to Emory University in America, and her experience is going to be completely different. There are some obvious outward contrasts. I was a shabby pseudo-hippie with a tangle of crazy hair and no decent clothes. She's well dressed, groomed, and presentable. I had a fountain pen and a record player. She has a computer and an iPod.

The ideas and justifications surrounding these two college adventures differ sharply. I was a product of the British meritocratic system which, after World War II, had nationalized higher education. The governing idea was that intelligent people were a national asset and that the nation was investing wisely by educating them, no matter their social origins.

Every student's tuition was paid in full, and every student was given, in addition, a grant to cover living expenses, board, and lodging. Only very wealthy Britons had to pay more than a token sum toward their children's college education. My three years at Oxford cost my parents a total of about $400. In those days, however, only a very small minority of British kids went to any kind of college. Most dropped out of school on the day of their sixteenth birthday, breathed a great sigh of relief, and never thought about education again.

The only criterion for British university admission then was academic. Oxford and Cambridge held their own entrance exams, interviewed students who wrote good answers, and chose the best of the interviewees. My class at Hertford College, Oxford, consisted of ninety students, all of them academic achievers.

Right from the start, each of us studied, or "read," only one discipline; mine was history. Half my friends read in other academic disciplines: physics, biochemistry, English, French, and so on. The other half read in vocational disciplines like medicine, law, and engineering. Central to the entire system was early specialization. Even the broadest curriculum choice, PPE (Philosophy, Politics, and Economics), consisted of just three elements.

Learning was organized through the tutorial system. Every week I and one other student met our tutor. He had assigned a paper the previous week, and we had spent the time reading widely in the relevant literature. One of us read his paper aloud to begin the tutorial, then the tutor rubbished it and told us, in blistering detail, what we should have written, and how we should have interpreted the readings. The tutors didn't show any delicate concern for our feelings.

Frances, by contrast, is entering a decentralized system. Here the assumption is that the person who gets the education is going to be its chief beneficiary and that, accordingly, she should bear the cost. As a member of the great American middle class, she belongs to a generation whose parents have been fretting about the cost of higher education from the moment they beheld their newborns. Paying your way through Emory or its sisters in the American college big leagues is almost certain to cost more than $150,000. It's also a system in which half or more of her generation of eighteen-year-olds enroll in some kind of postsecondary institution; she'll be one of literally millions of freshmen this fall.

Criteria for admission are diverse. Doing well in high school is still a terrific idea, and, bless her heart, Frances has. But ever since seventh grade her teachers and counselors have nudged her to perform community service, play music and competitive sports, act, publish poems, edit magazines, do internships in hospitals, and in a dozen other ways be extracurricular to give her an edge in college applications. Being a legacy or (as in her case) the child of a professor certainly helps.

She will study the liberal arts. In practice that means a couple of science classes, a bit of math, a language, a social-science-methods course, a spot of history, some "health" (such as "Principles of Physical Education," which is the Emory meaning of PPE), something in the performing arts, and then the nine or ten courses of a typical major. None of those courses will be vocational, but ideally they'll make her a well-rounded individual—mature, informed, and tolerant.

She will take classes containing from six to one hundred students. Occasionally she'll have to write a paper, but she'll rarely have to read one aloud to her teacher. She'll be in discussion groups with professors and teaching assistants, all of whom have been trained in sensitivity and diversity. Counselors, tutors, and an array of considerate "campus life" helpers will surround her. After four years, she'll probably have to select a graduate school to pursue her vocation, buckling down there to more years of toil.

How do the two systems compare in the eyes of someone who has seen plenty of each? The great virtue of the British system, particularly the early specialization, was that it enabled us to learn one discipline really well, to become far more deeply engaged with it than was possible for our American counterparts. It gave a marvelous opportunity to students who already knew where they were going to pursue their ambitions without distraction. As an undergraduate, I was already studying historical theory and the philosophy of history, which here is deferred to graduate school.

Its great and equal drawback was that it forced some students to choose too soon, before they were ready. An old girlfriend thought she wanted to be a psychologist but decided after a year that it had been a terrible idea, and had to petition to switch into French, which detained her at college a year longer than the rest of us. The system assumed freshmen were grown-ups who knew their own minds. Anyone familiar with a crowd of seventeen- and eighteen-year-olds knows that assumption is not always dependable.

The great virtue of the American system is its breadth. How impressed I was, as a TA at Berkeley, to have undergraduates in my very first history discussion group mention a relevant insight from Freud that they had picked up in "Psych," or refer to Laffer Curves that they'd studied in "Econ." They made me feel a trifle narrow and parochial.

Then they handed in their papers and wrote their finals, and my feelings of inadequacy disappeared. The great American drawbacks revealed themselves: The students' writing was awful, and their knowledge utterly superficial. Their breadth was the breadth of rivers an inch deep. The experience also drove home to me the truth, verified hundreds of times since, that the study of history is simply far too difficult for most students.

There are pros and cons to both systems. Surely it's possible, now, to combine the merits of each rather than putting up with their weaknesses. I think more American colleges should offer the chance to specialize right from the outset to those students who want it. Bright young physicists who want only to study physics should be free to do so, without laboring through courses in art history that seem to them a waste of valuable time. 15

In the same way, students who already have a clear vocational objective at the age of eighteen should be able to pursue it at top schools. My own experience showed that most law and medical students at Oxford *wanted* to get busy in preparation for the careers they had chosen, and were glad to be able to do so. (Incidentally, it didn't make them philistines; they enjoyed literature and read widely in other disciplines, just as I read plenty of great novels and a little science, even though I didn't take classes in those areas.)

At the same time, the vast American system can maintain the liberal-arts option for those who prefer it and don't yet have a clear sense of direction. Students with the right frame of mind thrive on studying diverse subjects until they're ready, sometimes at age twenty or older, to make a stronger commitment. But let's get rid of the idea that liberal arts is for everyone. America's commitment to equality and to universal education is noble and invigorating. But it shouldn't mean that one size fits all.

Topics for Critical Thinking and Writing

1. In paragraph 6 Allitt says that his tutor "rubbished" his papers, and that "the tutors didn't show any delicate concern for our feelings." Was this

system barbaric, or can something be said for it? In your response, you may want to draw on your personal experience.

2. Do you agree that in college "bright young physicists who want only to study physics should be free to do so" (para. 15)? Explain.

3. Do you wish you were having a college education like the one that Allitt had at Oxford? Explain why or why not in an essay of 250–500 words.

4. In general, would you prefer a system of narrow specialization in higher education or a system that affords great breadth? Explain in 250–500 words.

5. Do you think that Allitt's attempt to join together the best of the Oxford and the American systems (paras. 15–17) is a good idea, or do you think not? Give your reasons in 250–500 words.

Letters of Response by Carol Geary Schneider and Ellis M. West

To the Editor:

Patrick Allitt is right to question whether common frameworks guiding American undergraduate education have outlived their usefulness ("Should Undergraduates Specialize?," *The Chronicle Review,* June 16). The alternatives he proposes, however—specialization for those who know what they want to study and liberal arts for the less focused—are both decidedly inadequate for today's students.

In a volatile, globally interdependent, and fast-changing world, everyone will need more liberal education, not less. But we need a new approach to the design of undergraduate liberal education, a design that takes full account of the needs of an innovation-fueled economy and an increasingly complex and globally interconnected society.

Today's college students should not be presented with a false choice between either vocational preparation or liberal-arts education defined as nonvocational personal development. It is time to embrace a far more purposeful approach to college that sets clear expectations for all students, cultivates the achievement of a set of essential skills and capacities, and enables every student to place his or her interests—including career aspirations—in the broader context of a complex and fast-changing world.

Students certainly should have every opportunity to pursue their interests in depth, and this pursuit can begin as early as the first year of college. But while doing so, they should also be working to develop strong intellectual and practical skills that can be transferred to new settings when the students or their fields move, as they surely will, in new and unexpected directions. Students should develop the ability to communicate clearly; to think through the ethical, civic, and intercultural issues relevant to their interests; and to locate those interests in a wide-ranging understanding of the world in which they live.

To prepare students well both for productive work and responsible 5 citizenship in a complex world, we need a new vision for liberal education that emphasizes inquiry and integration and transferability of learning, rather than narrow depth or shallow breadth.

CAROL GEARY SCHNEIDER
President, Association of American Colleges and Universities
Washington, D.C., August 4, 2006

To the Editor:

Breadth or depth? Patrick Allitt, using the British system as a model, makes a case for allowing some college students—those "who already have a clear vocational objective at the age of eighteen"—to start studying their chosen vocation, like law or medicine, at the beginning of their time in college. They would also be excused from having to take general-education courses such as "art history that seem to them a waste of valuable time." The traditional liberal-arts option—a breadth of courses—would be available to (but presumably not required of) only those students "who prefer it and don't yet have a clear sense of [vocational] direction."

Allitt's case, however, is fundamentally flawed because it is based on a false assumption—that the primary, if not sole, purpose of higher education is to train students in and for a particular vocation. If that were its purpose, then of course early specialization would make sense. . . . Allitt overlooks at least two other purposes of education that in America have been more important than vocational training and that have justified a broad, liberal-arts education.

The first of these purposes is to enable students to get their act together. In other words, a liberal-arts education has traditionally provided students an opportunity to decide what kind of persons they want to be—not just what kind of work they want to do. It forces them to confront the "big questions," as the Teagle Foundation likes to phrase it (see W. Robert Connor's "The Right Time and Place for Big Questions," *The Chronicle Review*, June 9), questions having to do with the purpose or meaning of their lives, including the moral values to which they should adhere.

The second traditional purpose of a liberal-arts education is closely related to the first—to prepare students to be good citizens in a free and democratic society. At a minimum, this means teaching them to be concerned about the public good, to respect the dignity and worth of all persons, and to be informed about our political system and public issues.

Other purposes of a liberal-arts education, such as cultivating a love 5 of beauty, could also be mentioned. In short, as Aristotle argued centuries ago, because humans are spiritual, moral, political, and aesthetic beings, not just producers of goods and services, they should be encouraged, if not required, to study subjects that will help to make them genuinely happy.

Granted, more and more liberal-arts colleges seem to be less and less committed to those goals. Fewer courses are required for a degree; general-education requirements seem to be justified only to give as many departments as possible a piece of the action; and faculty members are concerned mainly with their own disciplines and areas of research and not with the overall education of their students. De facto specialization seems to be the name of the game.

Given this reality, perhaps Allitt can be excused for overlooking the traditional purposes of a higher education. I can only hope that Emory University, where his daughter will be a first-year student in the fall and which is one of my alma maters, has not forsaken these purposes.

ELLIS M. WEST
Professor of Political Science, University of Richmond
Richmond, Va., August 4, 2006

TOPICS FOR CRITICAL THINKING AND WRITING

1. Schneider asserts (para. 4) that while students are pursuing their "interests in depth . . . they should also be working to develop strong intellectual and practical skills that can be transferred to new settings when the students or their fields move. . . . Students should develop the ability to communicate clearly; to think through the ethical, civic, and intercultural issues relevant to their interests; and to locate those interests in a wide-ranging understanding of the world in which they live." Do you think that at least to some degree you are engaged in such a program? If not, why not? Do you perhaps think Schneider's program is overly ambitious? Explain.

2. West says (para. 3) that one purpose of education in America "is to enable students to get their act together. In other words, a liberal-arts education has traditionally provided students an opportunity to decide what kind of persons they want to be." Are you taking courses partly "to get your act together"? Explain.

3. West says (para. 5) that a second purpose of a liberal-arts education is rooted in the fact that we are "spiritual, moral, political, and aesthetic beings." Students should therefore "study subjects that will help to make them genuinely happy." Your view of West's assumptions?

Marty Nemko

Marty Nemko, a career counselor, columnist, and radio host based in Oakland, California, has been an education consultant to numerous college presidents. He is the author of four books, including The All-in-One College Guide: A Consumer Activist's Guide to Choosing a College *(2004). We reprint an essay that originally appeared in the* Chronicle of Higher Education *in 2008.*

America's Most Overrated Product:
The Bachelor's Degree

Among my saddest moments as a career counselor is when I hear a story like this: "I wasn't a good student in high school, but I wanted to prove that I can get a college diploma. I'd be the first one in my family to do it. But it's been five years and $80,000, and I still have forty-five credits to go."

I have a hard time telling such people the killer statistic: Among high-school students who graduated in the bottom 40 percent of their classes, and whose first institutions were four-year colleges, two-thirds had not earned diplomas eight and a half years later. That figure is from a study cited by Clifford Adelman, a former research analyst at the U.S. Department of Education and now a senior research associate at the Institute for Higher Education Policy. Yet four-year colleges admit and take money from hundreds of thousands of such students each year!

Even worse, most of those college dropouts leave the campus having learned little of value, and with a mountain of debt and devastated self-esteem from their unsuccessful struggles. Perhaps worst of all, even those who do manage to graduate too rarely end up in careers that require a college education. So it's not surprising that when you hop into a cab or walk into a restaurant, you're likely to meet workers who spent years and their family's life savings on college, only to end up with a job they could have done as a high-school dropout.

Such students are not aberrations. Today, amazingly, a majority of the students whom colleges admit are grossly underprepared. Only 23 percent of the 1.3 million high-school graduates of 2007 who took the ACT examination were ready for college-level work in the core subjects of English, math, reading, and science.

Perhaps more surprising, even those high-school students who are 5 fully qualified to attend college are increasingly unlikely to derive enough benefit to justify the often six-figure cost and four to six years (or more) it takes to graduate. Research suggests that more than 40 percent of freshmen at four-year institutions do not graduate in six years. Colleges trumpet the statistic that, over their lifetimes, college graduates earn more than nongraduates, but that's terribly misleading. You could lock the collegebound in a closet for four years, and they'd still go on to earn more than the pool of non-collegebound—they're brighter, more motivated, and have better family connections.

Also, the past advantage of college graduates in the job market is eroding. Ever more students attend college at the same time as ever more employers are automating and sending offshore ever more professional jobs, and hiring part-time workers. Many college graduates are forced to take some very nonprofessional positions, such as driving a truck or tending bar.

How much do students at four-year institutions actually learn?

Colleges are quick to argue that a college education is more about enlightenment than employment. That may be the biggest deception of all. Often there is a Grand Canyon of difference between the reality and what higher-education institutions, especially research ones, tout in their viewbooks and on their Web sites. Colleges and universities are businesses, and students are a cost item, while research is a profit center. As a result, many institutions tend to educate students in the cheapest way possible: large lecture classes, with necessary small classes staffed by rock-bottom-cost graduate students. At many colleges, only a small percentage of the typical student's classroom hours will have been spent with fewer than thirty students taught by a professor, according to student-questionnaire data I used for my book. *How to Get an Ivy League Education at a State University*. When students at 115 institutions were asked what percentage of their class time had been spent in classes of fewer than thirty students, the average response was 28 percent.

That's not to say that professor-taught classes are so worthwhile. The more prestigious the institution, the more likely that faculty members are hired and promoted much more for their research than for their teaching. Professors who bring in big research dollars are almost always rewarded more highly than a fine teacher who doesn't bring in the research bucks. Ernest L. Boyer, the late president of the Carnegie Foundation for the Advancement of Teaching, used to say that winning the campus teaching award was the kiss of death when it came to tenure. So, no surprise, in the latest annual national survey of freshmen conducted by the Higher Education Research Institute at the University of California at Los Angeles, 44.6 percent said they were not satisfied with the quality of instruction they received. Imagine if that many people were dissatisfied with a brand of car: It would quickly go off the market. Colleges should be held to a much higher standard, as a higher education costs so much more, requires years of time, and has so much potential impact on your life. Meanwhile, 43.5 percent of freshmen also reported "frequently" feeling bored in class, the survey found.

College students may be dissatisfied with instruction, but, despite 10 that, do they learn? A 2006 study supported by the Pew Charitable Trusts found that 50 percent of college seniors scored below "proficient" levels on a test that required them to do such basic tasks as understand the arguments of newspaper editorials or compare credit-card offers. Almost 20 percent of seniors had only basic quantitative skills. The students could not estimate if their car had enough gas to get to the gas station.

Unbelievably, according to the Spellings Report, which was released in 2006 by a federal commission that examined the future of American higher education, things are getting even worse: "Over the past decade, literacy among college graduates has actually declined. . . . According to the most recent National Assessment of Adult Literacy, for instance, the percentage of college graduates deemed proficient in prose literacy has actually declined from 40 to 31 percent in the past decade. . . . Employers report repeatedly that many new graduates they hire are not prepared to work, lacking the critical thinking, writing, and problem-solving skills needed in today's workplaces."

What must be done to improve undergraduate education?

Colleges should be held at least as accountable as tire companies are. When some Firestone tires were believed to be defective, government investigations, combined with news-media scrutiny, led to higher tire-safety standards. Yet year after year, colleges and universities turn out millions of defective products: students who drop out or graduate with far too little benefit for the time and money spent. Not only do colleges escape punishment, but they are rewarded with taxpayer-financed student grants and loans, which allow them to raise their tuitions even more.

I ask colleges to do no more than tire manufacturers are required to do. To be government-approved, all tires must have—prominently molded into the sidewall—some crucial information, including ratings of tread life, temperature resistance, and traction compared with national benchmarks.

Going significantly beyond the recommendations in the Spellings 15 report, I believe that colleges should be required to prominently report the following data on their Web sites and in recruitment materials:

- Value added. A national test, which could be developed by the major testing companies, should measure skills important for responsible citizenship and career success. Some of the test should be in career contexts: the ability to draft a persuasive memo, analyze an employer's financial report, or use online research tools to develop content for a report.

- Just as the No Child Left Behind Act mandates strict accountability of elementary and secondary schools, all colleges should be required to administer the value-added test I propose to all entering freshmen and to students about to graduate, and to report the mean value added, broken out by precollege SAT scores, race, and gender. That would strongly encourage institutions to improve their undergraduate education and to admit only students likely to derive enough benefit to justify the time, tuition, and opportunity costs. Societal bonus: Employers could request that job applicants submit the test results, leading to more-valid hiring decisions.

- The average cash, loan, and work-study financial aid for varying levels of family income and assets, broken out by race and gender. And because some colleges use the drug-dealer scam—give the first dose cheap and then jack up the price—they should be required to provide the average not just for the first year, but for each year.

- Retention data: the percentage of students returning for a second year, broken out by SAT score, race, and gender.

- Safety data: the percentage of an institution's students who have been robbed or assaulted on or near the campus.

- The four-, five-, and six-year graduation rates, broken out by SAT score, race, and gender. That would allow institutions to better document such trends as the plummeting percentage of male graduates in recent years.

- Employment data for graduates: the percentage of graduates who, within six months of graduation, are in graduate school, unemployed, or employed in a job requiring college-level skills, along with salary data.

- Results of the most recent student-satisfaction survey, to be conducted by the institutions themselves.

- The most recent accreditation report. The college could include the executive summary only in its printed recruitment material, but it would have to post the full report on its Web site.

- Being required to conspicuously provide this information to prospective students and parents would exert long-overdue pressure on colleges to improve the quality of undergraduate education. What should parents and guardians of prospective students do?

- If your child's high-school grades and test scores are in the bottom half for his class, resist the attempts of four-year colleges to woo him. Colleges make money whether or not a student learns, whether or not she graduates, and whether or not he finds good employment. Let the buyer beware. Consider an associate-degree program at a community college, or such nondegree options as apprenticeship programs (see http://www.khake.com), shorter career-preparation programs at community colleges, the military, and on-the-job training, especially at the elbow of a successful small-business owner.

- If your student is in the top half of her high-school class and is motivated to attend college for reasons other than going to parties and being able to say she went to college, have her apply to perhaps a dozen colleges. Colleges vary less than you might think (at least on factors you can readily discern in the absence of the accountability requirements I advocate above), yet financial-aid awards can vary wildly. It's often wise to choose the college that requires you to pay the least cash and take out the smallest loan. College is among the few products that don't necessarily give you what you pay for—price does not indicate quality.

- If your child is one of the rare breed who knows what he wants to do and isn't unduly attracted to academics or to the *Animal House* environment that characterizes many college-living arrangements, then take solace in the fact that countless other people have successfully taken the noncollege road less traveled. Some examples: Maya Angelou, David Ben-Gurion, Richard Branson, Coco Chanel, Walter Cronkite, Michael Dell, Walt Disney, Thomas

Edison, Henry Ford, Bill Gates, Alex Haley, Ernest Hemingway, Wolfgang Puck, John D. Rockefeller Sr., Ted Turner, Frank Lloyd Wright, and nine U.S. presidents, from Washington to Truman.

College is a wise choice for far fewer people than are currently encouraged to consider it. It's crucial that they evenhandedly weigh the pros and cons of college versus the aforementioned alternatives. The quality of their lives may depend on that choice.

Topics for Critical Thinking and Writing

1. According to Nemko, "colleges and universities are businesses" (para. 8). What evidence does he cite to support this claim? What confirming or disconfirming evidence has your experience at college offered?

2. How important is it at your college that (para. 9) the faculty "are hired and promoted much more for their research than for their teaching?" Interview one or two of your current instructors for their view on this issue and summarize what you learn in a paragraph or two.

3. Suppose someone argued that a college education is *not* a business because it is a four-year game of increasing difficulty. How might such an argument be developed? Attacked?

4. What are some of the "opportunity costs" of higher education (second item in para. 15)?

5. Nemko cites thirteen things that ought to be done to improve the quality of a college education (para. 15). How many of these do you agree would result in improvements? Which (if any) of his items would you drop? Can you think of a couple to add?

6. Research Project for Extra Credit: Who are the seven U.S. presidents Nemko does *not* name (last item in his bulleted list) who did not attend college? How successful were they as presidents?

Charles Murray

Born in 1943, Charles Murray is a scholar at the American Enterprise Institute and the author, most recently, of Real Education: Four Simple Truths for Bringing America's Schools Back to Reality *(2008). This essay and the letters of response following it were published in the* New York Times *in 2008.*

Should the Obama Generation Drop Out?

Barack Obama has two attractive ideas for improving post-secondary education—expanding the use of community colleges and tuition tax credits—but he needs to hitch them to a broader platform. As president, Mr. Obama should use his bully pulpit to undermine the bachelor's degree as a job qualification. Here's a suggested battle cry, to be repeated in every speech on the subject: "It's what you can do that should count when you apply for a job, not where you learned to do it."

The residential college leading to a bachelor's degree at the end of four years works fine for the children of parents who have plenty of money. It works fine for top students from all backgrounds who are drawn toward academics. But most eighteen-year-olds are not from families with plenty of money, not top students, and not drawn toward academics. They want to learn how to get a satisfying job that also pays well. That almost always means education beyond high school, but it need not mean four years on a campus, nor cost a small fortune. It need not mean getting a bachelor's degree.

I am not discounting the merits of a liberal education. Students at every level should be encouraged to explore subjects that will not be part of their vocation. It would be even better if more colleges required a rigorous core curriculum for students who seek a traditional bachelor's degree. My beef is not with liberal education, but with the use of the degree as a job qualification.

For most of the nation's youths, making the bachelor's degree a job qualification means demanding a credential that is beyond their reach. It is a truth that politicians and educators cannot bring themselves to say out loud: A large majority of young people do not have the intellectual ability to do genuine college-level work.

If you doubt it, go back and look through your old college textbooks, 5 and then do a little homework on the reading ability of high school seniors. About 10 percent to 20 percent of all eighteen-year-olds can absorb the material in your old liberal arts textbooks. For engineering and the hard sciences, the percentage is probably not as high as 10.

No improvements in primary and secondary education will do more than tweak those percentages. The core disciplines taught at a true college level are tough, requiring high levels of linguistic and logical-mathematical ability. Those abilities are no more malleable than athletic or musical talent.

You think I'm too pessimistic? Too elitist? Readers who graduated with honors in English literature or Renaissance history should ask themselves if they could have gotten a B.S. in physics, no matter how hard they tried. (I wouldn't have survived freshman year.) Except for the freakishly gifted, all of us are too dumb to get through college in many majors.

But I'm not thinking just about students who are not smart enough to deal with college-level material. Many young people who have the intellectual ability to succeed in rigorous liberal arts courses don't want to. For these students, the distribution requirements of the college degree do not open up new horizons. They are bothersome time-wasters.

A century ago, these students would happily have gone to work after high school. Now they know they need to acquire additional skills, but they want to treat college as vocational training, not as a leisurely journey to well-roundedness.

As more and more students who cannot get or don't want a liberal 10 education have appeared on campuses, colleges have adapted by expanding the range of courses and adding vocationally oriented majors. That's appropriate. What's not appropriate is keeping the bachelor's degree as the measure of job preparedness, as the minimal requirement to get your foot in the door for vast numbers of jobs that don't really require a B.A. or B.S.

Discarding the bachelor's degree as a job qualification would not be difficult. The solution is to substitute certification tests, which would provide evidence that the applicant has acquired the skills the employer needs.

Certification tests can take many forms. For some jobs, a multiple-choice test might be appropriate. But there's no reason to limit certifications to academic tests. For centuries, the crafts have used work samples to certify journeymen and master craftsmen. Today, many computer programmers without college degrees get jobs by presenting examples of their work. With a little imagination, almost any corporation can come up with analogous work samples.

The benefits of discarding the bachelor's degree as a job qualification would be huge for both employers and job applicants. Certifications would tell employers far more about their applicants' qualifications than a B.A. does, and hundreds of thousands of young people would be able to get what they want from post-secondary education without having to twist themselves into knots to comply with the rituals of getting a bachelor's degree.

Certification tests would not eliminate the role of innate ability — the most gifted applicants would still have an edge — but they would strip away much of the unwarranted halo effect that goes with a degree from a prestigious university. They would put everyone under the same spotlight.

Discrediting the bachelor's degree is within reach because so many 15 employers already sense that it has become education's Wizard of Oz. All we need is someone willing to yank the curtain aside. Barack Obama is ideally positioned to do it. He just needs to say it over and over: "It's what you can do that should count when you apply for a job, not where you learned to do it."

TOPICS FOR CRITICAL THINKING AND WRITING

1. What does the term "bully pulpit" mean? What does Murray mean by calling President Obama's office a "bully pulpit" (para. 1)?

2. What do you think is the appropriate criterion for deciding whether a job warrants requiring that an applicant has either a B.A. or a B.S. degree?

3. What do you think accounts for the fact that a B.A. or a B.S. degree has become a sine qua non for so many jobs?

4. Explain Murray's reference to the Wizard of Oz (para. 15).

Letters of Response by Charles Axilbund, Jacques Jimenez, Jeff Adler, Lillian Hoodes, Larry Hoffner, Sandra Sherman, and Michel Dedina

To the Editor:

In "Should the Obama Generation Drop Out?" (Op-Ed, Dec. 28), Charles Murray argues that we should have more vocational schools and stop using a college degree as a requirement for jobs.

These "reforms" would institute a class system in the United States on a par with that of Victorian England.

Under these proposals, bachelor's degrees would be restricted to the rich, regardless of qualifications, and the lucky few among the common people who possessed exceptional intellectual endowments. As for the rest, they would receive sufficient training to fill jobs with limited potential for upward mobility.

Mr. Murray's proposals would actually intensify the importance of a prestigious degree—necessary as it would be for entry into the highest occupational echelons.

This might be acceptable if eligibility for these degrees were based on   5 merit alone. But under Mr. Murray's proposals, the rich would have unlimited access, while those less well off would have to compete for limited, subsidized spots in expensive institutions. If this is not a recipe for a closed, permanent upper class, I do not know what is.

CHARLES AXILBUND
Los Angeles, Dec. 28, 2008

To the Editor:

Charles Murray needs to recognize that the liberal arts degree, at its best, validates its holder as one who has skills needed for some of our biggest jobs.

A good half of the liberal arts curriculum is about thinking analogically. The degree says this person has studied "humane letters" and so knows his or her way around a metaphor: how it opens up vistas, alters viewpoints, both frees and constrains thought, and affects decisions.

No one should try to motivate a work force, lead a corporation, plan military strategies, or run a government who does not know how a metaphor works.

Math and science, the other half of the liberal arts curriculum, develop skills that are scarce, yet needed, in our society. They are all about knowing a fact from a factoid, reasoning from data to underlying patterns and practical implications, all while feeding careful observation through the strainer of valid logic.

The liberal arts degree says, or should say, here's someone who has 5 skills we deeply, powerfully, urgently need.

JACQUES JIMENEZ
Stamford, Conn., Dec. 28, 2008

To the Editor:

Devaluing the bachelor's degree would not help students who earn it or those who don't go to college. A bachelor's degree may indeed serve as a foot in the door for a recent graduate, but that's all it does. That graduate still has to show that he or she can do the job.

The degree tells an employer that an applicant had the ability and perseverance to accomplish something.

Charles Murray suggests that instead of degrees, we use "certification tests, which would provide evidence that the applicant has acquired the skills the employer needs." This would amount to a postcollege SAT, when the precollege SAT has enough problems.

An employer takes a chance on any applicant, even one with a degree. There already are two-year colleges and technical training schools for people who can't or won't earn a four-year degree.

The responsible thing to do is to make sure that all students who 5 have the ability to earn a degree aren't prevented from doing so by the cost.

JEFF ADLER
Livingston, N.J., Dec. 28, 2008

To the Editor:

I recently graduated with a bachelor's degree in history and am now in law school, hoping to earn the degree that will lead to a paycheck. Though this will eventually pay my mortgage, my liberal arts education will be what sustains me emotionally, intellectually, and in my relationships with other human beings.

To say that young Americans are, for the most part, "not smart enough to deal with college-level material" and that we must scratch the bachelor's degree from our list of must-haves is to treat a symptom rather than the cause.

Employers must ask that their employees relate to one another and to the world around them; a broad, liberal education helps students to arrive at the point at which that kind of sympathy is possible.

Make college affordable, make it accessible, make it free, make it a requirement for employment. Don't accept defeat.

LILLIAN HOODES
Chicago, Dec. 28, 2008

To the Editor:

Charles Murray's notion of discarding or de-emphasizing academic degrees as a job qualification in lieu of skills or "What you know" makes perfect sense. But let's not stop with postsecondary education.

A greater emphasis on specific job skills in traditional high school education is needed.

Language and mathematics will remain the pillars of our liberal academic institutions, but we also need carpenters, plumbers, electricians, machinists, and more. Our schools should emphasize job skills for those not suited to traditional academic education.

LARRY HOFFNER
New York, Dec. 28, 2008

The writer is a high school teacher.

To the Editor:

Finally, someone dared to say what every college professor knows in her heart: half the students in her classroom shouldn't be there and don't want to be there.

We have created this B.A.-B.S. grail for millions of students who would be far better educated if they could focus on something that they want to learn.

For twelve years, I was a professor of English at the flagship campus of a big state university. My students were majoring in computers, nursing, landscape design, and kinesiology. They didn't care about "Beowulf" or John Milton. The university wanted them there, however, because more four-year graduates meant more money from the legislature. Now we can no longer tolerate such waste.

We should redesign college curriculums so tthat students can study something useful, get a job, and help redevelop the economy.

Rather than dumbing down "hard" courses, so that everyone picks 5 up a smattering of knowledge they will never use, universities should offer challenging courses in students' majors. If that major takes three instead of four years to complete, that's fine. The goal is to become productive without wasting time or money.

SANDRA SHERMAN
New York, Dec 28, 2008

The writer is assistant director of the Intellectual Property Law Institute, Fordham Law School.

To the Editor:

Students who have battled for a bachelor's degree will have learned a valuable skill. It is unlikely that most of them will practice only one trade throughout their career. They will have to learn a range of skills that were unheard of when they were students.

Charles Murray should bless them for having learned how to learn. If they are thus armed, our economy will have a chance.

MICHEL DEDINA
San Francisco, Dec.28, 2008

TOPICS FOR CRITICAL THINKING AND WRITING

1. Do you think Murray would be troubled by Charles Axilbund's claim that Murray's proposal is "a recipe for a closed, permanent upper class"? Explain.

2. What is the significance of Jimenez's distinction between a "factoid" and a "fact"? What *is* the difference? Compare them and give examples.

3. Take one of the letters that seems to you to be especially wrong-headed, and draft a response to that letter-writer.

Louis Menand

Louis Menand, born in Syracuse, New York, in 1952, and educated at Pomona College and Columbia University, is a professor of English and American litera- ture at Harvard University. The author of numerous books, including The Future of Academic Freedom *(1996), Menand also writes regularly for* The New Yorker. *We reprint a portion of a talk that he originally delivered at a sym- posium held at Rollins College in Florida and published in* Education *and* Democracy, *edited by Robert Orrill (1997).*

Re-imagining Liberal Education

. . . It is, in most American colleges, impossible to take a course on the law (apart from an occasional legal history course), because knowl- edge of the law is the preserve of people who go to law school. Yet a knowledge of the law is one of the keys to understanding the political and economic system in which Americans live. Many college students, similarly, never take a class in business, or even in economics. Most take no classes in architecture, education, or engineering, unless they are in a special, and usually segregated, architecture, education, or engineering program. Few students who do not intend to become specialists take courses in subjects touching on health or technology. These are all mat- ters adults have to deal with throughout life, but people who have attended college generally have no more sophisticated an understanding of them than people who have attended only high school.

The suggestion that an understanding of matters of immense practical importance, such as law, business, technology, and health, should have a more central place in the college curriculum smacks of vocationalism, and it is customary to think that nothing could sound more illiberal than that. But the purpose of education is to empower people, to help them acquire some measure of control over their own lives. Some of this empowerment consists of learning how to think critically, how to communicate clearly, how to pose theoretical questions about practical issues. But some of it also must consist in knowing about the way the world works. Critical theory doesn't empower people. Self-esteem doesn't empower people. Knowledge empowers people. You can't dictate what people will do with it, but you can at least give them access to it. That an exposure to the way the world works can be presented in an appropriately high-level curricular setting can be seen in innovative programs underway at a number of private and public colleges. Bradford College, for example, a private college in Massachusetts, offers what it calls a "practical liberal arts" curriculum, in which students combine general education (nonspecialized study) with a "comprehensive" (that is, cross-disciplinary) major and a "practical" (that is, vocationally oriented) minor. Students do internships (called "practical learning experiences") in their junior year. And they are assessed, in part, through portfolios, rather than through individual papers for individual classes. The Bradford program is not vocational. It offers a general education in areas such as "Wellness" and "The Nature of Work" because it presumes that these are matters all college graduates should know something about.

The Bradford model manages to incorporate into its general education curriculum a good deal of exposure to scientific knowledge and methods. One of the drawbacks of the Core Model is that it either omits science completely, or presents it in the form of "culture," as some of the "classic texts." For Dewey,[1] the scientific method was the type for all learning and inquiry. One need not go quite that distance to concede that science and technology do require formal education for nonspecialists to understand, and that most liberal arts colleges do little or nothing to ensure that students receive it in any programmatic way. The modern research university arose in response to the preeminence of scientific approaches to knowledge. The problem of how to put the humanities in proper institutional relation to the sciences has persisted since the turn of the century. The solution has been for scholarship in the humanities to be practiced on a more or less scientific, or positivistic, model (dissertations that constitute "original contributions to knowledge," peer review, and the like), while undergraduate instruction in literature and philosophy stresses moral issues and "human values." It is a divide, between fact and value, that inheres in both prevailing models of liberal education today; and one merit of imagining a fresh model is that it might make this division less antagonistic, an accomplishment that was the aim of nearly everything Dewey wrote.

---

[1]**Dewey** John Dewey (1859–1952), philosopher of education. [Editors' note.]

Innovations similar to Bradford's—particularly out-of-the-classroom, or "service," experience and cross-disciplinary teaching—are becoming standard elsewhere. Twelve Pennsylvania colleges calling themselves the Commonwealth Partnership now advise new Ph.D.s that they must have interests that extend beyond their disciplines, be able to teach "communication skills," be socially involved, and teach by personal example. Candidates for jobs at Evergreen State College in Washington, a public institution, are required to complete a questionnaire about their views on pedagogy and other matters. Professors today have to be able to teach basic skills courses and a much wider range of much-less-specialized courses than they once did. . . .

Let us suppose that the undergraduate curriculum were transformed 5 in a way that eliminated the proto-professional major and that replaced the "culture"-based core requirements with general courses in law, business, government, the arts, and technology—that did not abandon exposure to literature and philosophy, which everyone should have, but that did abandon the idea that literature and philosophy are the mandatory bases for specialized knowledge. What would happen to liberal education? How could it be re-imagined in a way that would enable colleges to produce students who were well rounded, who had cultural breadth and moral imagination, and who knew how to think critically? How would it help students develop the capacity to display curiosity, sympathy, a sense of principle, and independence of mind?

The Deweyan answer to questions like these would be that you cannot teach people a virtue by requiring them to read books about it. You can only teach a virtue by calling upon people to exercise it. Virtue is not an innate property of character; it is an attribute of behavior. People learn, Dewey insisted, socially. They learn, as every progressive nursery school director will tell you, by doing. Dewey believed that the classroom was a laboratory in which to experiment with the business of participating in the associated life. American higher education provides almost no formal structure, almost no self-conscious design, for imagining pedagogy in this spirit. But the only way to develop curiosity, sympathy, principle, and independence of mind is to practice being curious, sympathetic, principled, and independent. For those of us who are teachers, it isn't what we teach that instills virtue; it's how we teach. We are the books our students read most closely. The most important influence on their liberalism is our liberalism.

TOPICS FOR CRITICAL THINKING AND WRITING

1. In his second paragraph Menand says, "The purpose of education is to empower people, to help them acquire some measure of control over their own lives." Write your own sentence, beginning, "The purpose of education is . . ."

2. In paragraph 4 Menand says that "candidates for jobs at Evergreen State College in Washington, a public institution, are required to complete a questionnaire about their views on pedagogy." Suppose two questions were these: "In your view, what is the purpose of teaching?" "What do you hope your students will get out of your course in —————?" Now imagine that you are a candidate for a job at Evergreen, teaching any course you wish. Answer each of the two questions, devoting a paragraph or two to each.

3. What is "vocationalism" (para. 2), and what role do you think it ought to play in higher education? What role, if any, does it play for the students in your college?

4. William Cory, a schoolmaster in nineteenth-century England, wrote:

> You go to a great school not for knowledge so much as for arts and habits; for the habit of attention, for the art of expression, for the art of assuming at a moment's notice a new intellectual posture, for the art of entering quickly into another person's thought, for the habit of submitting to censure and refutation, for the art of indicating assent or dissent in graduated terms, for the habit of regarding minute points of accuracy, for the habit of working out what is possible in a given time, for taste, for discrimination, for mental courage and mental soberness. Above all, you go to a great school for self-knowledge.

What do you think of this view? In an essay of about 500 words indicate "assent or dissent in graduated terms."

For topical links related to the purpose of a college education, see the companion Web site: **bedfordstmartins.com/barnetbedau**.

22

The Death Penalty:
Is It Ever Justified?

Edward I. Koch

Edward I. Koch (b. 1924), long active in Democratic politics, was mayor of New York from 1978 to 1989. This essay first appeared in The New Republic *on April 15, 1985.*

Death and Justice: How Capital Punishment Affirms Life

Last December a man named Robert Lee Willie, who had been convicted of raping and murdering an eighteen-year-old woman, was executed in the Louisiana state prison. In a statement issued several minutes before his death, Mr. Willie said: "Killing people is wrong. . . . It makes no difference whether it's citizens, countries, or governments. Killing is wrong." Two weeks later in South Carolina, an admitted killer named Joseph Carl Shaw was put to death for murdering two teenagers. In an appeal to the governor for clemency, Mr. Shaw wrote: "Killing was wrong when I did it. Killing is wrong when you do it. I hope you have the courage and moral strength to stop the killing."

It is a curiosity of modern life that we find ourselves being lectured on morality by cold-blooded killers. Mr. Willie previously had been convicted of aggravated rape, aggravated kidnapping, and the murders of a Louisiana deputy and a man from Missouri. Mr. Shaw committed another murder a week before the two for which he was executed, and admitted mutilating the body of the fourteen-year-old girl he killed. I can't help wondering what prompted these murderers to speak out against killing as they entered the deathhouse door. Did their newfound reverence for life stem from the realization that they were about to lose their own?

Life is indeed precious, and I believe the death penalty helps to affirm this fact. Had the death penalty been a real possibility in the minds of these murderers, they might well have stayed their hand. They might have shown moral awareness before their victims died, and not after. Consider the tragic death of Rosa Velez, who happened to be home when a man named Luis Vera burglarized her apartment in Brooklyn. "Yeah, I shot her," Vera admitted. "She knew me, and I knew I wouldn't go to the chair."

During my twenty-two years in public service, I have heard the pros and cons of capital punishment expressed with special intensity. As a district leader, councilman, congressman, and mayor, I have represented constituencies generally thought of as liberal. Because I support the death penalty for heinous crimes of murder, I have sometimes been the subject of emotional and outraged attacks by voters who find my position reprehensible or worse. I have listened to their ideas. I have weighed their objections carefully. I still support the death penalty. The reasons I maintain my position can be best understood by examining the arguments most frequently heard in opposition.

1. The death penalty is "barbaric." Sometimes opponents of capital punishment horrify with tales of lingering death on the gallows, of faulty electric chairs, or of agony in the gas chamber. Partly in response to such protests, several states such as North Carolina and Texas switched to execution by lethal injection. The condemned person is put to death painlessly, without ropes, voltage, bullets, or gas. Did this answer the objections of death penalty opponents? Of course not. On June 22, 1984, the *New York Times* published an editorial that sarcastically attacked the new "hygienic" method of death by injection, and stated that "execution can never be made humane through science." So it's not the method that really troubles opponents. It's the death itself they consider barbaric.

Admittedly, capital punishment is not a pleasant topic. However, one does not have to like the death penalty in order to support it any more than one must like radical surgery, radiation, or chemotherapy in order to find necessary these attempts at curing cancer. Ultimately we may learn how to cure cancer with a simple pill. Unfortunately, that day has not yet arrived. Today we are faced with the choice of letting the cancer spread or trying to cure it with the methods available, methods that one day will almost certainly be considered barbaric. But to give up and do nothing would be far more barbaric and would certainly delay the discovery of an eventual cure. The analogy between cancer and murder is imperfect, because murder is not the "disease" we are trying to cure. The disease is injustice. We may not like the death penalty, but it must be available to punish crimes of cold-blooded murder, cases in which any other form of punishment would be inadequate and, therefore, unjust. If we create a society in which injustice is not tolerated, incidents of murder — the most flagrant form of injustice — will diminish.

2. No other major democracy uses the death penalty. No other major democracy—in fact, few other countries of any description—are plagued by a murder rate such as that in the United States. Fewer and fewer Americans can remember the days when unlocked doors were the norm and murder was a rare and terrible offense. In America the murder rate climbed 122 percent between 1963 and 1980. During that same period, the murder rate in New York City increased by almost 400 percent, and the statistics are even worse in many other cities. A study at M.I.T. showed that based on 1970 homicide rates a person who lived in a large American city ran a greater risk of being murdered than an American soldier in World War II ran of being killed in combat. It is not surprising that the laws of each country differ according to differing conditions and traditions. If other countries had our murder problem, the cry for capital punishment would be just as loud as it is here. And I dare say that any other major democracy where 75 percent of the people supported the death penalty would soon enact it into law.

3. An innocent person might be executed by mistake. Consider the work of Hugo Adam Bedau, one of the most implacable foes of capital punishment in this country. According to Mr. Bedau, it is "false sentimentality to argue that the death penalty should be abolished because of the abstract possibility that an innocent person might be executed." He cites a study of the seven thousand executions in this country from 1892 to 1971, and concludes that the record fails to show that such cases occur. The main point, however, is this. If government functioned only when the possibility of error didn't exist, government wouldn't function at all. Human life deserves special protection, and one of the best ways to guarantee that protection is to assure that convicted murderers do not kill again. Only the death penalty can accomplish this end. In a recent case in New Jersey, a man named Richard Biegenwald was freed from prison after serving eighteen years for murder; since his release he has been convicted of committing four murders. A prisoner named Lemuel Smith, who, while serving four life sentences for murder (plus two life sentences for kidnapping and robbery) in New York's Green Haven Prison, lured a woman corrections officer into the chaplain's office and strangled her. He then mutilated and dismembered her body. An additional life sentence for Smith is meaningless. Because New York has no death penalty statute, Smith has effectively been given a license to kill.

But the problem of multiple murder is not confined to the nation's penitentiaries. In 1981, ninety-one police officers were killed in the line of duty in this country. Seven percent of those arrested in the cases that have been solved had a previous arrest for murder. In New York City in 1976 and 1977, eighty-five persons arrested for homicide had a previous arrest for murder. Six of these individuals had two previous arrests for murder, and one had four previous murder arrests. During those two years the New York police were arresting for murder persons with a previous arrest for murder on the average of one every eight and a half days. This is not surprising when we learn that in 1975, for example, the median time served in Massachusetts for homicide was less than two and a half years. In 1976 a study sponsored by the Twentieth Century Fund found that the average time served in the United States for first-degree murder is ten years. The median time served may be considerably lower.

4. Capital punishment cheapens the value of human life. 10 On the contrary, it can be easily demonstrated that the death penalty strengthens the value of human life. If the penalty for rape were lowered, clearly it would signal a lessened regard for the victim's suffering, humiliation, and personal integrity. It would cheapen their horrible experience, and expose them to an increased danger of recurrence. When we lower the penalty for murder, it signals a lessened regard for the value of the victim's life. Some critics of capital punishment, such as columnist Jimmy Breslin, have suggested that a life sentence is actually a harsher penalty for murder than death. This is sophistic nonsense. A few killers may decide not to appeal a death sentence, but the overwhelming majority make every effort to stay alive. It is by exacting the highest penalty for the taking of human life that we affirm the highest value of human life.

5. The death penalty is applied in a discriminatory manner. This factor no longer seems to be the problem it once was. The appeals process for a condemned prisoner is lengthy and painstaking. Every effort is made to see that the verdict and sentence were fairly arrived at. However, assertions of discrimination are not an argument for ending the death penalty but for extending it. It is not justice to exclude everyone from the penalty of the law if a few are found to be so favored. Justice requires that the law be applied equally to all.

6. Thou Shalt Not Kill. The Bible is our greatest source of moral inspiration. Opponents of the death penalty frequently cite the sixth of the Ten Commandments in an attempt to prove that capital punishment is divinely proscribed. In the original Hebrew, however, the Sixth Commandment reads "Thou Shalt Not Commit Murder," and the Torah specifies capital punishment for a variety of offenses. The biblical viewpoint has been upheld by philosophers throughout history. The greatest thinkers of the nineteenth century—Kant, Locke, Hobbes, Rousseau, Montesquieu, and Mill—agreed that natural law properly authorizes the sovereign to take life in order to vindicate justice. Only Jeremy Bentham was ambivalent. Washington, Jefferson, and Franklin endorsed it. Abraham Lincoln authorized executions for deserters in wartime. Alexis de Tocqueville, who expressed profound respect for American institutions, believed that the death penalty was indispensable to the support of social order. The United States Constitution, widely admired as one of the seminal achievements in the history of humanity, condemns cruel and inhuman punishment, but does not condemn capital punishment.

7. The death penalty is state-sanctioned murder. This is the defense with which Messrs. Willie and Shaw hoped to soften the resolve of those who sentenced them to death. By saying in effect, "You're no better than I am," the murderer seeks to bring his accusers down to his own level. It is also a popular argument among opponents of capital punishment, but a transparently false one. Simply put, the state has rights that the private individual does not. In a democracy, those rights are given to the state by the electorate. The execution of a lawfully condemned killer is no more an act of murder than is legal imprisonment an act of kidnapping. If an individual forces a neighbor to pay him money under threat of punishment, it's called extortion. If the state does it, it's called taxation. Rights and responsibilities surrendered by the individual are what give the state its power to govern. This contract is the foundation of civilization itself.

Everyone wants his or her rights, and will defend them jealously. Not everyone, however, wants responsibilities, especially the painful responsibilities that come with law enforcement. Twenty-one years ago a woman named Kitty Genovese was assaulted and murdered on a street in New York. Dozens of neighbors heard her cries for help but did nothing to assist her. They didn't even call the police. In such a climate the criminal understandably grows bolder. In the presence of moral cowardice, he lectures us on our supposed failings and tries to equate his crimes with our quest for justice.

The death of anyone—even a convicted killer—diminishes us all.   15
But we are diminished even more by a justice system that fails to function. It is an illusion to let ourselves believe that doing away with capital punishment removes the murderer's deed from our conscience. The rights of society are paramount. When we protect guilty lives, we give up innocent lives in exchange. When opponents of capital punishment say to the state, "I will not let you kill in my name," they are also saying to murderers: "You can kill in your *own* name as long as I have an excuse for not getting involved."

It is hard to imagine anything worse than being murdered while neighbors do nothing. But something worse exists. When those same neighbors shrink back from justly punishing the murderer, the victim dies twice.

TOPICS FOR CRITICAL THINKING AND WRITING

1. In paragraph 6 Koch draws an analogy between cancer and murder and observes that imperfect as today's cures for cancer are, "to give up and

do nothing would be far more barbaric." What is the relevance of this comment in the context of the analogy and the dispute over the death penalty?

2. In paragraph 8 Koch describes a convicted but unexecuted recidivist murderer as someone who "has effectively been given a license to kill." But a license to kill, as in a deer-hunter's license, entitles the holder to engage in lawful killing. (Think of the fictional hero James Bond—Agent 007—who, we are told, had a "license to kill.") What is the difference between having a license and "effectively" having one? How might the opponent of the death penalty reply to Koch's position here?

3. Koch distinguishes between the "median time" served by persons convicted of murder but not sentenced to death and the "average time" they serve, and he adds that the former "may be considerably lower" than the latter (para. 9). Explain the difference between a "median" and an "average" (review the section on statistics, p. 88). Is knowing one of these statistics more important for certain purposes than the other? Why?

4. Koch identifies seven arguments against the death penalty, and he rejects them all. Which of the seven arguments seems to you to be the strongest objection to the death penalty? Which the weakest? Why? Does Koch effectively refute the strongest argument? Can you think of any argument(s) against the death penalty that he neglects?

5. Koch says he supports the death penalty "for heinous crimes of murder" (para. 4). Does he imply that all murders are heinous crimes or only some? If the latter, what criteria seem to you to be the appropriate ones to distinguish the heinous murders from the rest? Why these criteria?

6. Koch asserts that the death penalty "strengthens the value of human life" (para. 10). Yet opponents of the death penalty often claim the reverse, arguing that capital punishment undermines the idea that human life is precious. Write an essay of 500 words in which you explain what it means to assert that life is precious and why one of the two positions—support for or opposition to the death penalty—best supports (or is consistent with) this principle.

David Bruck

David Bruck (b. 1949) graduated from Harvard College and received his law degree from the University of South Carolina. His practice is devoted almost entirely to the defense of persons charged with a capital crime, through the South Carolina Office of Appellate Defense. The essay reprinted here originally appeared on May 20, 1985, in The New Republic *as a response to the essay by Edward I. Koch (p. 575).*

The Death Penalty

Mayor Ed Koch contends that the death penalty "affirms life." By failing to execute murderers, he says, we "signal a lessened regard for the value of the victim's life." Koch suggests that people who oppose the death penalty are like Kitty Genovese's neighbors, who heard her cries for help but did nothing while an attacker stabbed her to death.

This is the standard "moral" defense of death as punishment: Even if executions don't deter violent crime any more effectively than imprisonment, they are still required as the only means we have of doing justice in response to the worst of crimes.

Until recently, this "moral" argument had to be considered in the abstract, since no one was being executed in the United States. But the death penalty is back now, at least in the southern states, where every one of the more than thirty executions carried out over the last two years has taken place. Those of us who live in those states are getting to see the difference between the death penalty in theory, and what happens when you actually try to use it.

South Carolina resumed executing prisoners in January with the electrocution of Joseph Carl Shaw. Shaw was condemned to death for helping to murder two teenagers while he was serving as a military policeman at Fort Jackson, South Carolina. His crime, propelled by mental illness and PCP, was one of terrible brutality. It is Shaw's last words ("Killing was wrong when I did it. It is wrong when you do it. . . .") that so outraged Mayor Koch: He finds it "a curiosity of modern life that we are being lectured on morality by cold-blooded killers." And so it is.

But it was not "modern life" that brought this curiosity into being. It 5 was capital punishment. The electric chair was J. C. Shaw's platform. (The mayor mistakenly writes that Shaw's statement came in the form of a plea to the governor for clemency: Actually Shaw made it only seconds before his death, as he waited, shaved and strapped into the chair, for the switch to be thrown.) It was the chair that provided Shaw with celebrity and an opportunity to lecture us on right and wrong. What made this weird moral reversal even worse is that J. C. Shaw faced his own death with undeniable dignity and courage. And while Shaw died, the TV crews recorded another "curiosity" of the death penalty—the crowd gathered outside the death-house to cheer on the executioner. Whoops of elation greeted the announcement of Shaw's death. Waiting at the penitentiary gates for the appearance of the hearse bearing Shaw's remains, one demonstrator started yelling, "Where's the beef?"

For those who had to see the execution of J. C. Shaw, it wasn't easy to keep in mind that the purpose of the whole spectacle was to affirm life. It will be harder still when Florida executes a cop-killer named Alvin Ford. Ford has lost his mind during his years of death-row confinement, and now spends his days trembling, rocking back and forth, and muttering unintelligible prayers. This has led to litigation over whether Ford meets a centuries-old legal standard for mental competency. Since the Middle Ages, the Anglo-American legal system has generally prohibited the execution of anyone who is too mentally ill to understand what is about to be done to him and why. If Florida wins its case, it will have earned the right to electrocute Ford in his present condition. If it loses, he will not be executed until the state has first nursed him back to some semblance of mental health.[1]

We can at least be thankful that this demoralizing spectacle involves a prisoner who is actually guilty of murder. But this may not always be so. The ordeal of Lenell Jeter—the young black engineer who recently served more than a year of a life sentence for a Texas armed robbery that he didn't commit—should remind us that the system is quite capable of making the very worst sort of mistake. That Jeter was eventually cleared is a fluke. If the robbery had occurred at 7 P.M. rather than 3 P.M., he'd have had no alibi, and would still be in prison today. And if someone had been killed in that robbery, Jeter probably would have been sentenced to death. We'd have seen the usual execution-day interviews with state officials and the victim's relatives, all complaining that Jeter's appeals took too long. And Jeter's last words from the gurney would have taken their place among the growing literature of death-house oration that so irritates the mayor.

Koch quotes Hugo Adam Bedau, a prominent abolitionist, to the effect that the record fails to establish that innocent defendants have been executed in the past. But this doesn't mean, as Koch implies, that it hasn't happened. All Bedau was saying was that doubts concerning executed prisoners' guilt are almost never resolved. Bedau is at work now on an effort to determine how many wrongful death sentences may have been imposed: His list of murder convictions since 1900 in which the state eventually *admitted* error is some four hundred cases long. Of course, very few of these cases involved actual executions: The mistakes that Bedau documents were uncovered precisely because the prisoner was alive and able to fight for his vindication. The cases where someone is executed are the very cases in which we're least likely to learn that we got the wrong man.

I don't claim that executions of entirely innocent people will occur very often. But they will occur. And other sorts of mistakes already have. Roosevelt Green was executed in Georgia two days before J. C. Shaw. Green and an accomplice kidnapped a young woman. Green swore that his companion shot her to death after Green had left, and that he knew nothing about the murder. Green's claim was supported by a statement that his accomplice made to a witness after the crime. The jury never resolved whether Green was telling the truth, and when he tried to take

---

[1]Florida lost its case to execute Ford. On June 26, 1986, the U.S. Supreme Court ruled that the execution of an insane person violates the Eighth Amendment, which forbids cruel and unusual punishments. Therefore, convicted murderers cannot be executed if they have become so insane that they do not know that they are about to be executed and do not understand the reason for their sentence. If Ford regains his sanity, however, he can be executed. [Editors' note.]

a polygraph examination a few days before his scheduled execution, the state of Georgia refused to allow the examiner into the prison. As the pressure for symbolic retribution mounts, the courts, like the public, are losing patience with such details. Green was electrocuted on January 9, while members of the Ku Klux Klan rallied outside the prison.

Then there is another sort of arbitrariness that happens all the 10 time. Last October, Louisiana executed a man named Ernest Knighton. Knighton had killed a gas station owner during a robbery. Like any murder, this was a terrible crime. But it was not premeditated, and is the sort of crime that very rarely results in a death sentence. Why was Knighton electrocuted when almost everyone else who committed the same offense was not? Was it because he was black? Was it because his victim and all twelve members of the jury that sentenced him were white? Was it because Knighton's court-appointed lawyer presented no evidence on his behalf at his sentencing hearing? Or maybe there's no reason except bad luck. One thing is clear: Ernest Knighton was picked out to die the way a fisherman takes a cricket out of a bait jar. No one cares which cricket gets impaled on the hook.

Not every prisoner executed recently was chosen that randomly. But many were. And having selected these men so casually, so blindly, the death penalty system asks us to accept that the purpose of killing each of them is to affirm the sanctity of human life.

The death penalty states are also learning that the death penalty is easier to advocate than it is to administer. In Florida, where executions have become almost routine, the governor reports that nearly a third of his time is spent reviewing the clemency requests of condemned prisoners. The Florida Supreme Court is hopelessly backlogged with death cases. Some have taken five years to decide, and the rest of the Court's work waits in line behind the death appeals. Florida's death row currently holds more than 230 prisoners. State officials are reportedly considering building a special "death prison" devoted entirely to the isolation and electrocution of the condemned. The state is also considering the creation of a special public defender unit that will do nothing else but handle death penalty appeals. The death penalty, in short, is spawning death agencies.

And what is Florida getting for all of this? The state went through almost all of 1983 without executing anyone: Its rate of intentional homicide declined by 17 percent. Last year Florida executed eight people—the most of any state, and the sixth highest total for any year since Florida started electrocuting people back in 1924. Elsewhere in the United States last year, the homicide rate continued to decline. But in Florida, it actually rose by 5.1 percent.

But these are just the tiresome facts. The electric chair has been a centerpiece of each of Koch's recent political campaigns, and he knows better than anyone how little the facts have to do with the public's support for capital punishment. What really fuels the death penalty is the justifiable frustration and rage of people who see that the government is not coping with violent crime. So what if the death penalty doesn't work? At least it gives us the satisfaction of knowing that we got one or two of the sons of bitches.

Perhaps we want retribution on the flesh and bone of a handful of convicted murderers so badly that we're willing to close our eyes to all of the demoralization and danger that come with it. A lot of politicians think so, and they may be right. But if they are, then let's at least look honestly at what we're doing. This lottery of death both comes from and encourages an attitude toward human life that is not reverent, but reckless.

And that is why the mayor is dead wrong when he confuses such fury with justice. He suggests that we trivialize murder unless we kill murderers. By that logic, we also trivialize rape unless we sodomize rapists. The sin of Kitty Genovese's neighbors wasn't that they failed to stab her attacker to death. Justice does demand that murderers be punished. And common sense demands that society be protected from them. But neither justice nor self-preservation demands that we kill men whom we have already imprisoned.

The electric chair in which J. C. Shaw died earlier this year was built in 1912 at the suggestion of South Carolina's governor at the time, Cole Blease. Governor Blease's other criminal justice initiative was an impassioned crusade in favor of lynch law. Any lesser response, the governor insisted, trivialized the loathsome crimes of interracial rape and murder. In 1912, a lot of people agreed with Governor Blease that a proper regard for justice required both lynching and the electric chair. Eventually we are going to learn that justice requires neither.

TOPICS FOR CRITICAL THINKING AND WRITING

1. After three introductory paragraphs, Bruck devotes two paragraphs to Shaw's execution. In a sentence or two, state the point he is making in his discussion of this execution. Then in another sentence or two (or three), indicate the degree to which this point refutes Edward I. Koch's argument (p. 575).

2. In paragraph 7, Bruck refers to the case of Lenell Jeter, an innocent man who was condemned to a life sentence. Evaluate this point as a piece of evidence used to support an argument against the death penalty.

3. In paragraph 8, Bruck says that "the state eventually *admitted* error" in some four hundred cases. He goes on: "Of course, very few of these cases involved actual executions." How few is "very few"? Why do you suppose Bruck doesn't specify the number? If it is only, say, two, in your opinion does that affect Bruck's point?

4. Discussing the case of Roosevelt Green (para. 9), Bruck points out that Green offered to take a polygraph test but "the state of Georgia refused to allow the examiner into the prison." In a paragraph evaluate the state's position on this matter.

5. In paragraph 13 Bruck points out that although "last year" (1984) the state executed eight people, the homicide rate in Florida rose 5.1 percent, whereas elsewhere in the United States the homicide rate declined. What do you make of these figures? What do you think Koch would make of them?

6. In his next-to-last paragraph Bruck says that Koch "suggests that we trivialize murder unless we kill murderers. By that logic, we also trivialize rape unless we sodomize rapists." Do you agree that this statement brings out the absurdity of Koch's thinking?

7. Evaluate Bruck's final paragraph (a) as a concluding paragraph and (b) as a piece of argumentation.

8. Bruck, writing early in 1985, stresses that all the "more than thirty" executions in the nation "in the last two years" have taken place in the South (para. 3). Why does he think this figure points to a vulnerability in Koch's argument? Would Bruck's argument here be spoiled if some executions were to occur outside of the South? (By the way, where exactly have most of the recent executions in the nation occurred?)

9. Bruck argues that the present death-penalty system—in practice even if not in theory—utterly fails to "affirm the sanctity of human life" (para. 11). Do you think Bruck would, or should, concede that at least in theory it is possible for a death-penalty system to be no more offensive to the value of human life than, say, a system of imprisonment is offensive to the value of human liberty or a system of fines is offensive to the value of human property?

10. Can Bruck be criticized for implying that cases like those he cites— Shaw, Ford, Green, and Knightson, in particular—are the rule rather than the exception? Does either Bruck or Koch cite any evidence to help settle this question?

11. Write a paragraph explaining which of these events seems to you to be the more unseemly: a condemned prisoner, on the threshold of execution, lecturing the rest of us on the immorality of killing; or the crowd that bursts into cheers outside a prison when it learns that a scheduled execution has been carried out.

OLIPHANT © 1971 UNIVERSAL PRESS SYNDICATE. Reprinted with permission. All rights reserved.

George Ryan

George Ryan, born in 1934 in Maquoketa, Iowa, was active in Republican politics and served as the thirty-fourth governor of Illinois from 1998 to 2003. Because his term was marked by charges of corruption—specifically, that he took bribes and awarded contracts and licenses to friends—he chose not to run for reelection in 2002. In September 2006 he was convicted of all charges concerning racketeering and fraud, and sentenced to six-and-a-half years in federal prison. He has said that he will appeal.

A few days before he left office Governor Ryan commuted the sentences of all death row inmates in Illinois. We reprint a speech in which he announces the commutation and gives his reasons.

Speech Announcing Commutation of All Illinois Prisoners' Death Sentences

Four years ago I was sworn in as the thirty-ninth governor of Illinois. That was just four short years ago—that's when I was a firm believer in the American system of justice and the death penalty. I believed that the ultimate penalty for the taking of a life was administrated in a just and fair manner.

Today—three days before I end my term as governor, I stand before you to explain my frustrations and deep concerns about both the administration and the penalty of death. It is fitting that we are gathered here today at Northwestern University with the students, teachers, lawyers, and investigators who first shed light on the sorrowful condition of Illinois' death penalty system. Professors Larry Marshall, Dave Protess, and their students along with investigators Paul Ciolino have gone above the call. They freed the falsely accused Ford Heights Four, they saved Anthony Porter's life, they fought for Rolando Cruz and Alex Hernandez. They devoted time and effort on behalf of Aaron Patterson, a young man who lost fifteen years of his youth sitting among the condemned, and Leroy Orange, who lost seventeen of the best years of his life on death row.

It is also proper that we are together with dedicated people like Andrea Lyon who has labored on the front lines trying capital cases for many years and who is now devoting her passion to creating an innocence center at DePaul University. You saved Madison Hobley's life. Together they spared the lives and secured the freedom of 17 men — men who were wrongfully convicted and rotting in the condemned units of our state prisons. What you have achieved is of the highest calling — thank you!

Yes, it is right that I am here with you, where, in a manner of speaking, my journey from staunch supporter of capital punishment to reformer all began. But I must tell you — since the beginning of our journey — my thoughts and feelings about the death penalty have changed many, many times. I realize that over the course of my reviews I had said that I would not do blanket commutation. I have also said it was an option that was there and I would consider all options. During my time in public office I have always reserved my right to change my mind if I believed it to be in the best public interest, whether it be about taxes, abortions, or the death penalty. But I must confess that the debate with myself has been the toughest concerning the death penalty. I suppose the reason the death penalty has been the toughest is because it is so final — the only public policy that determines who lives and who dies. In addition it is the only issue that attracts most of the legal minds across the country. I have received more advice on this issue than any other policy issue I have dealt with in my thirty-five years of public service. I have kept an open mind on both sides of the issues of commutation for life or death.

I have read, listened to, and discussed the issue with the families of the victims as well as the families of the condemned. I know that my decision will be just that — my decision — based on all the facts I could gather over the past three years. I may never be comfortable with my final decision, but I will know in my heart that I did my very best to do the right thing. 5

Having said that I want to share a story with you:

I grew up in Kankakee which even today is still a small midwestern town, a place where people tend to know each other. Steve Small was a neighbor. I watched him grow up. He would babysit my young children — which was not for the faint of heart since Lura Lynn and I had six children, five of them under the age of three. He was a bright young man who helped run the family business. He got married and he and his wife had three children of their own. Lura Lynn was especially close to him and his family. We took comfort in knowing he was there for us and we for him. One September midnight he received a call at his home. There had been a break-in at the nearby house he was renovating. But as he left his house, he was seized at gunpoint by kidnappers. His captors buried him alive in a shallow hole. He suffocated to death before police could find him. His killer led investigators to where Steve's body was buried. The killer, Danny Edward, was also from my hometown. He now sits on death row. I also know his family. I share this story with you so that you know I do not come to this as a neophyte without having experienced a small bit of the bitter pill the survivors of murder must swallow.

My responsibilities and obligations are more than my neighbors and my family. I represent all the people of Illinois—like it or not. The decision I make about our criminal justice system is felt not only here, but the world over.

The other day, I received a call from former South African President Nelson Mandela who reminded me that the United States sets the example for justice and fairness for the rest of the world. Today the United States is not in league with most of our major allies: Europe, Canada, Mexico, most of South and Central America. These countries rejected the death penalty. We are partners in death with several third world countries. Even Russia has called a moratorium. The death penalty has been abolished in twelve states. In none of these states has the homicide rate increased. In Illinois last year we had about one thousand murders; only 2 percent of that one thousand were sentenced to death. Where is the fairness and equality in that? The death penalty in Illinois is not imposed fairly or uniformly because of the absence of standards for the 102 Illinois state's attorneys, who must decide whether to request the death sentence. Should geography be a factor in determining who gets the death sentence? I don't think so, but in Illinois it makes a difference. You are five times more likely to get a death sentence for first-degree murder in the rural area of Illinois than you are in Cook County. Where is the justice and fairness in that—where is the proportionality?

The Most Reverend Desmond Tutu wrote to me this week stating 10 that "to take a life when a life has been lost is revenge, it is not justice." He says justice allows for mercy, clemency, and compassion. These virtues are not weakness.

"In fact the most glaring weakness is that no matter how efficient and fair the death penalty may seem in theory, in actual practice it is primarily inflicted upon the weak, the poor, the ignorant and against racial minorities." That was a quote from former California Governor Pat Brown. He wrote that in his book—*Public Justice, Private Mercy.* He wrote that nearly fifty years ago—nothing has changed in nearly fifty years.

I never intended to be an activist on this issue. I watched in surprise as freed death row inmate Anthony Porter was released from jail. A free man, he ran into the arms of Northwestern University Professor Dave Protess, who poured his heart and soul into proving Porter's innocence with his journalism students.

He was forty-eight hours away from being wheeled into the execution chamber where the state would kill him.

It would all be so antiseptic and most of us would not have even paused, except that Anthony Porter was innocent of the double murder for which he had been condemned to die. After Mr. Porter's case there was the report by *Chicago Tribune* reporters Steve Mills and Ken Armstrong documenting the systemic failures of our capital punishment system. Half of the nearly three hundred capital cases in Illinois had been reversed for a new trial or resentencing.

Nearly half!   15

Thirty-three of the death row inmates were represented at trial by an attorney who was later disbarred or at some point suspended from practicing law.

Of the more than 160 death row inmates, 35 were African American defendants who had been convicted or condemned to die by all-white juries.

More than two-thirds of the inmates on death row were African American.

Forty-six inmates were convicted on the basis of testimony from jailhouse informants.

I can recall looking at these cases and the information from the   20
Mills/Armstrong series and asking my staff: How does that happen? How in God's name does that happen? I'm not a lawyer, so somebody explain it to me.

But no one could. Not to this day.

Then over the next few months, there were three more exonerated men, freed because their sentence hinged on a jailhouse informant or new DNA technology proved beyond a shadow of doubt their innocence.

We then had the dubious distinction of exonerating more men than we had executed. Thirteen men found innocent, twelve executed.

As I reported yesterday, there is not a doubt in my mind that the number of innocent men freed from our Death Row stands at seventeen, with the pardons of Aaron Patterson, Madison Hobley, Stanley Howard, and Leroy Orange.

That is an absolute embarrassment. Seventeen exonerated death row   25
inmates is nothing short of a catastrophic failure. But the thirteen, now seventeen men, is just the beginning of our sad arithmetic in prosecuting murder cases. During the time we have had capital punishment in Illinois, there were at least thirty-three other people wrongly convicted on murder charges and exonerated. Since we reinstated the death penalty there are

also ninety-three people—ninety-three—where our criminal justice system imposed the most severe sanction and later rescinded the sentence or even released them from custody because they were innocent.

How many more cases of wrongful conviction have to occur before we can all agree that the system is broken?

Throughout this process, I have heard many different points of view expressed. I have had the opportunity to review all of the cases involving the inmates on death row. I have conducted private group meetings, one in Springfield and one in Chicago, with the surviving family members of homicide victims. Everyone in the room who wanted to speak had the opportunity to do so. Some wanted to express their grief, others wanted to express their anger. I took it all in.

My commission and my staff had been reviewing each and every case for three years. But I redoubled my effort to review each case personally in order to respond to the concerns of prosecutors and victims' families. This individual review also naturally resulted in a collective examination of our entire death penalty system.

I also had a meeting with a group of people who are less often heard from, and who are not as popular with the media. The family members of death row inmates have a special challenge to face. I spent an afternoon with those family members at a Catholic church here in Chicago. At that meeting, I heard a different kind of pain expressed. Many of these families live with the twin pain of knowing not only that, in some cases, their family member may have been responsible for inflicting a terrible trauma on another family, but also the pain of knowing that society has called for another killing. These parents, siblings, and children are not to blame for the crime committed, yet these innocents stand to have their loved ones killed by the state. As Mr. Mandela told me, they are also branded and scarred for life because of the awful crime committed by their family member.

Others were even more tormented by the fact that their loved one 30 was another victim, that they were truly innocent of the crime for which they were sentenced to die.

It was at this meeting that I looked into the face of Claude Lee, the father of Eric Lee, who was convicted of killing Kankakee police officer Anthony Samfay a few years ago. It was a traumatic moment, once again, for my hometown. A brave officer, part of that thin blue line that protects each of us, was struck down by wanton violence. If you will kill a police officer, you have absolutely no respect for the laws of man or God.

I've known the Lee family for a number of years. There does not appear to be much question that Eric was guilty of killing the officer. However, I can say now after our review, there is also not much question that Eric is seriously ill, with a history of treatment for mental illness going back a number of years.

The crime he committed was a terrible one—killing a police officer. Society demands that the highest penalty be paid.

But I had to ask myself—could I send another man's son to death under the deeply flawed system of capital punishment we have in Illinois? A troubled young man, with a history of mental illness? Could I rely on the system of justice we have in Illinois not to make another horrible mistake? Could I rely on a fair sentencing?

In the United States the overwhelming majority of those executed 35 are psychotic, alcoholic, drug addicted, or mentally unstable. They frequently are raised in an impoverished and abusive environment.

Seldom are people with money or prestige convicted of capital offenses, even more seldom are they executed.

To quote Governor Brown again—he said, "society has both the right and the moral duty to protect itself against its enemies. This natural and prehistoric axiom has never successfully been refuted. If by ordered death, society is really protected and our homes and institutions guarded, then even the most extreme of all penalties can be justified. Beyond its honor and incredibility, it has neither protected the innocent nor deterred the killers. Publicly sanctioned killing has cheapened human life and dignity without the redeeming grace which comes from justice metered out swiftly, evenly, humanely."

At stake throughout the clemency process was whether some, all, or none of these inmates on death row would have their sentences commuted from death to life without the possibility of parole. One of the things discussed with family members was that life without parole was seen as a life filled with perks and benefits.

Some inmates on death row don't want a sentence of life without parole. Danny Edwards wrote me and told me not to do him any favors because he didn't want to face a prospect of a life in prison without parole. They will be confined in a cell that is about 5-feet-by-12 feet, usually double-bunked. Our prisons have no air conditioning, except at our supermax facility where inmates are kept in their cell twenty-three hours a day. In summer months, temperatures in these prisons exceed one hundred degrees. It is a stark and dreary existence. They can think about their crimes. Life without parole has even, at times, been described by prosecutors as a fate worse than death. Yesterday, I mentioned a lawsuit in Livingston County where a judge ruled the state corrections department cannot force-feed two corrections inmates who are on a hunger strike. The judge ruled that suicide by hunger strike was not an irrational action by the inmates, given what their future holds.

Earlier this year, the U.S. Supreme Court held that it is unconstitu- 40 tional and cruel and unusual punishment to execute the mentally retarded. It is now the law of the land. How many people have we already executed who were mentally retarded and are now dead and buried? Although we now know that they have been killed by the state unconstitutionally and illegally. Is that fair? Is that right?

This court decision was last spring. The General Assembly failed to pass any measure defining what constitutes mental retardation. We are a rudderless ship because they failed to act. This is even after the Illinois Supreme Court also told lawmakers that it is their job and it must be done.

I started with this issue concerned about innocence. But once I studied, once I pondered what had become of our justice system, I came to care above all about fairness. Fairness is fundamental to the American system of justice and our way of life.

The facts I have seen in reviewing each and every one of these cases raised questions not only about the innocence of people on death row, but about the fairness of the death penalty system as a whole.

If the system was making so many errors in determining whether someone was guilty in the first place, how fairly and accurately was it determining which guilty defendants deserved to live and which deserved to die? What effect was race having? What effect was poverty having?

And in almost every one of the exonerated seventeen, we not only   45
have breakdowns in the system with police, prosecutors, and judges, we have terrible cases of shabby defense lawyers. There is just no way to sugarcoat it. There are defense attorneys that did not consult with their clients, did not investigate the case, and were completely unqualified to handle complex death penalty cases. They often didn't put much effort into fighting a death sentence. If your life is on the line, your lawyer ought to be fighting for you. As I have said before, there is more than enough blame to go around.

I had more questions.

In Illinois, I have learned, we have 102 decision makers. Each of them is politically elected, each beholden to the demands of their community and, in some cases, to the media or especially vocal victims' families. In cases that have the attention of the media and the public, are decisions to seek the death penalty more likely to occur? What standards are these prosecutors using? Some people have assailed my power to commute sentences, a power that literally hundreds of legal scholars from across the country have defended. But prosecutors in Illinois have the ultimate commutation power, a power that is exercised every day. They decide who will be subject to the death penalty, who will get a plea deal, or even who may get a complete pass on prosecution. By what objective standards do they make these decisions? We do not know, they are not public. There were more than one thousand murders last year in Illinois. There is no doubt that all murders are horrific and cruel. Yet, less than 2 percent of those murder defendants will receive the death penalty. That means more than 98 percent of victims' families do not get, and will not receive, whatever satisfaction can be derived from the execution of the murderer.

Moreover, if you look at the cases, as I have done—both individually and collectively—a killing with the same circumstances might get forty years in one county and death in another county. I have also seen co-defendants who are equally or even more culpable get sentenced to a term of years, while another less culpable defendant ends up on death row.

In my case-by-case review, I found three people that fell into this category: Mario Flores, Montell Johnson, and William Franklin. Today I have commuted their sentences to a term of forty years to bring their sentences into line with their co-defendants and to reflect the other extraordinary circumstances of these cases.

Supreme Court Justice Potter Stewart has said that the imposition of 50 the death penalty on defendants in this country is as freakish and arbitrary as who gets hit by a bolt of lightning. For years the criminal justice system defended and upheld the imposition of the death penalty for the seventeen exonerated inmates from Illinois' death row. Yet when the real killers are charged, prosecutors have often sought sentences of less than death. In the Ford Heights Four case, Verneal Jimerson and Dennis Williams fought the death sentences imposed upon them for eighteen years before they were exonerated. Later, Cook County prosecutors sought life in prison for two of the real killers and a sentence of eighty years for a third.

What made the murder for which the Ford Heights Four were sentenced to die less heinous and worthy of the death penalty twenty years later with a new set of defendants?

We have come very close to having our state Supreme Court rule our death penalty statute—the one that I helped enact in 1977— unconstitutional. Former state Supreme Court Justice Seymour Simon wrote to me that it was only happenstance that our statute was not struck down by the state's high court. When he joined the bench in 1980, three other justices had already said Illinois' death penalty was unconstitutional. But they got cold feet when a case came along to revisit the question. One judge wrote that he wanted to wait and see if the Supreme Court of the United States would rule on the constitutionality of the new Illinois law. Another said precedent required him to follow the old state Supreme Court ruling with which he disagreed.

Even a pharmacist knows that doesn't make sense. We wouldn't have a death penalty today, and we all wouldn't be struggling with this issue, if those votes had been different. How arbitrary. Several years after we enacted our death penalty statute, Girvies Davis was executed. Justice Simon writes that he was executed because of this unconstitutional aspect of the Illinois law—the wide latitude that each Illinois state's attorney has to determine what cases qualify for the death penalty. One state's attorney waived his request for the death sentence when Davis' first sentencing was sent back to the trial court for a new sentencing hearing. The prosecutor was going to seek a life sentence. But in the interim, a new state's attorney took office and changed directions. He once again sought and secured a death sentence. Davis was executed.

How fair is that?

After the flaws in our system were exposed, the Supreme Court of 55 Illinois began to reform its rules and improve the trial of capital cases. It changed the rule to require that state's attorneys give advance notice to defendants that they plan to seek the death penalty to require notice before trial instead of after conviction. The Supreme Court also enacted new discovery rules designed to prevent trials by ambush and to allow for better investigation of cases from the beginning. But shouldn't that mean if you were tried or sentenced before the rules changed, you ought to get a new trial or sentencing with the new safeguards of the rules? This issue has divided our Supreme Court, some saying yes, a majority saying no. These justices have a lifetime of experience with the criminal justice system and it concerns me that these great minds so strenuously differ on an issue of such importance, especially where life or death hangs in the balance.

What are we to make of the studies that showed that more than 50 percent of Illinois jurors could not understand the confusing and obscure sentencing instructions that were being used? What effect did that problem have on the trustworthiness of death sentences? A review of the cases shows that often even the lawyers and judges are confused about the instructions—let alone the jurors sitting in judgment. Cases still come before the Supreme Court with arguments about whether the jury instructions were proper.

I spent a good deal of time reviewing these death row cases. My staff, many of whom are lawyers, spent busy days and many sleepless nights answering my questions, providing me with information, giving me advice. It became clear to me that whatever decision I made, I would be criticized. It also became clear to me that it was impossible to make reliable choices about whether our capital punishment system had really done its job.

As I came closer to my decision, I knew that I was going to have to face the question of whether I believed so completely in the choice I wanted to make that I could face the prospect of even commuting the death sentence of Daniel Edwards—the man who had killed a close family friend of mine. I discussed it with my wife, Lura Lynn, who has stood by me all these years. She was angry and disappointed at my decision, like many of the families of other victims will be. I was struck by the anger of the families of murder victims. To a family they talked about closure. They pleaded with me to allow the state to kill an inmate in its name to provide the families with closure. But is that the purpose of capital punishment? Is it to soothe the families? And is that truly what the families experience?

I cannot imagine losing a family member to murder. Nor can I imagine spending every waking day for twenty years with a single-minded focus to execute the killer. The system of death in Illinois is so unsure that it is not unusual for cases to take twenty years before they are resolved. And thank God. If it had moved any faster, then Anthony Porter, the Ford Heights Four, Ronald Jones, Madison Hobley, and the other innocent men we've exonerated might be dead and buried. But it is cruel and unusual punishment for family members to go through this pain, this legal limbo for twenty years. Perhaps it would be less cruel if we sentenced the killers to Tamms (Correctional Center) to life, and used our resources to better serve victims.

My heart ached when I heard one grandmother who lost children in 60 an arson fire. She said she could not afford proper grave markers for her grandchildren who died. Why can't the state help families provide a proper burial?

Another crime victim came to our family meetings. He believes an inmate sent to death row for another crime also shot and paralyzed him. The inmate, he says, gets free health care while the victim is struggling to pay his substantial medical bills and, as a result, he has forgone getting proper medical care to alleviate the physical pain he endures.

What kind of victim's services are we providing? Are all of our resources geared toward providing this notion of closure by execution instead of tending to the physical and social service needs of victim families? And what kind of values are we instilling in these wounded families and in the young people? As Gandhi said, an eye for an eye only leaves the whole world blind. President Lincoln often talked of binding up wounds as he sought to preserve the Union. "We are not enemies, but friends. We must not be enemies. Though passion may have strained, it must not break our bonds of affection."

I have had to consider not only the horrible nature of the crimes that put men on death row in the first place, the terrible suffering of the surviving family members of the victims, the despair of the family members of the inmates, but I have also had to watch in frustration as members of the Illinois General Assembly failed to pass even one substantive death penalty reform. Not one. They couldn't even agree on one. How much more evidence is needed before the General Assembly will take its responsibility in this area seriously?

The fact is that the failure of the General Assembly to act is merely a symptom of the larger problem. Many people express the desire to have capital punishment. Few, however, seem prepared to address the tough questions that arise when the system fails. It is easier and more comfortable for politicians to be tough on crime and support the death penalty. It wins votes. But when it comes to admitting that we have a problem, most run for cover. Prosecutors across our state continue to deny that our death penalty system is broken—or they say if there is a problem, it is really a small one and we can fix it somehow. It is difficult to see how the system can be fixed when not a single one of the reforms proposed by my capital punishment commission has been adopted. Even the reforms the prosecutors agree with haven't been adopted.

So when will the system be fixed? How much more risk can we 65 afford? Will we actually have to execute an innocent person before the tragedy that is our capital punishment system in Illinois is really understood? This summer, a United States District Court judge held the federal death penalty was unconstitutional and noted that with the number of recent exonerations based on DNA and new scientific technology we undoubtedly executed innocent people before this technology emerged.

As I prepare to leave office, I had to ask myself whether I could really live with the prospect of knowing that I had the opportunity to act, but that I failed to do so because I might be criticized. Could I take the chance that our capital punishment system might be reformed, that wrongful convictions might not occur, that enterprising journalism students might free more men from death row? A system that's so fragile that it depends on young journalism students is seriously flawed.

"There is no honorable way to kill, no gentle way to destroy. There is nothing good in war. Except its ending." That's what Abraham Lincoln said about the bloody war between the states. It was a war fought to end the sorriest chapter in American history—the institution of slavery. While we are not in a civil war now, we are facing what is shaping up to be one of the great civil rights struggles of our time. Stephen Bright of the Southern Center for Human Rights has taken the position that the death penalty is being sought with increasing frequency in some states against the poor and minorities.

Our own study showed that juries were more likely to sentence to death if the victim were white than if the victim were black—three-and-a-half times more likely to be exact. We are not alone. Just this month Maryland released a study of [its] death penalty system and racial disparities exist there too.

This week, Mamie Till Mobley died. Her son Emmett was lynched in Mississippi in the 1950s. She was a strong advocate for civil rights and reconciliation. In fact just three weeks ago, she was the keynote speaker at the Murder Victims' Families for Reconciliation event in Chicago. This group, many of whom I've met, opposes the death penalty even though their family members have been lost to senseless killing. Mamie's strength and grace not only ignited the civil rights movement—including inspiring Rosa Parks to refuse to go to the back of the bus—but inspired murder victims' families until her dying day.

Is our system fair to all? Is justice blind? These are important human rights issues.   70

Another issue that came up in my individual, case-by-case review was the issue of international law. The Vienna Convention protects U.S. citizens abroad and foreign nationals in the United States. It provides that if you are arrested, you should be afforded the opportunity to contact your consulate. There are five men on death row who were denied that internationally recognized human right. Mexico's President Vicente Fox contacted me to express his deep concern for the Vienna Convention violations. If we do not uphold international law here, we cannot expect our citizens to be protected outside the United States.

My commission recommended the Supreme Court conduct a proportionality review of our system in Illinois. While our appellate courts perform a case-by-case review of the appellate record, they have not done such a big picture study. Instead, they tinker with a case-by-case review as each appeal lands on their docket.

In 1994, near the end of his distinguished career on the Supreme Court of the United States, Justice Harry Blackmun wrote an influential dissent in the body of law on capital punishment. Twenty years earlier he was part of the court that issued the landmark *Furman* decision. The Court decided that the death penalty statutes in use throughout the country were fraught with severe flaws that rendered them unconstitutional. Quite frankly, they were the same problems we see here in Illinois. To many, it looked like the *Furman* decision meant the end of the death penalty in the United States.

This was not the case. Many states responded to *Furman* by developing and enacting new and improved death penalty statutes. In 1976, four years after it had decided *Furman*, Justice Blackmun joined the majority of the United States Supreme Court in deciding to give the states a chance with these new and improved death penalty statutes. There was great optimism in the air. This was the climate in 1977, when the Illinois Legislature was faced with the momentous decision of whether to reinstate the death penalty in Illinois. I was a member of the General Assembly at that time and when I pushed the green button in favor of reinstating the death penalty in this great state, I did so with the belief that whatever problems had plagued the capital punishment system in the past were now being cured. I am sure that most of my colleagues who voted with me that day shared that view.

But twenty years later, after affirming hundreds of death penalty 75 decisions, Justice Blackmun came to the realization, in the twilight of his distinguished career, that the death penalty remains fraught with arbitrariness, discrimination, caprice, and mistake. He expressed frustration with a twenty-year struggle to develop procedural and substantive safeguards. In a now famous dissent he wrote in 1994, "From this day forward, I no longer shall tinker with the machinery of death."

One of the few disappointments of my legislative and executive career is that the General Assembly failed to work with me to reform our deeply flawed system.

I don't know why legislators could not heed the rising voices of reform. I don't know how many more systemic flaws we needed to uncover before they would be spurred to action.

Three times I proposed reforming the system with a package that would restrict the use of jailhouse snitches, create a statewide panel to determine death eligible cases, and reduce the number of crimes eligible for death. These reforms would not have created a perfect system, but they would have dramatically reduced the chance for error in the administration of the ultimate penalty.

The governor has the constitutional role in our state of acting in the interest of justice and fairness. Our state constitution provides broad power to the governor to issue reprieves, pardons, and commutations. Our Supreme Court has reminded inmates petitioning them that the last resort for relief is the governor.

At times the executive clemency power has perhaps been a crutch 80 for courts to avoid making the kind of major change that I believe our system needs.

Our systemic case-by-case review has found more cases of innocent men wrongfully sentenced to death row. Because our three-year study has found only more questions about the fairness of the sentencing; because of the spectacular failure to reform the system; because we have seen justice delayed for countless death row inmates with potentially meritorious claims; because the Illinois death penalty system is arbitrary and capricious—and therefore immoral—I no longer shall tinker with the machinery of death.

I cannot say it as eloquently [as] Justice Blackmun.

The Legislature couldn't reform it.

Lawmakers won't repeal it.

But I will not stand for it.   85

I must act.

Our capital system is haunted by the demon of error—error in determining guilt, and error in determining who among the guilty deserves to die. Because of all of these reasons today I am commuting the sentences of all death row inmates.

This is a blanket commutation. I realize it will draw ridicule, scorn, and anger from many who oppose this decision. They will say I am usurping the decisions of judges and juries and state legislators. But as I have said, the people of our state have vested in me the power to act in the interest of justice. Even if the exercise of my power becomes my burden I will bear it. Our constitution compels it. I sought this office, and even in my final days of holding it I cannot shrink from the obligations to justice and fairness that it demands.

There have been many nights where my staff and I have been deprived of sleep in order to conduct our exhaustive review of the system. But I can tell you this: I will sleep well knowing I made the right decision.

As I said when I declared the moratorium, it is time for a rational 90 discussion on the death penalty. While our experience in Illinois has indeed sparked a debate, we have fallen short of a rational discussion. Yet if I did not take this action, I feared that there would be no comprehensive and thorough inquiry into the guilt of the individuals on death row or of the fairness of the sentences applied.

To say it plainly one more time—the Illinois capital punishment system is broken. It has taken innocent men to a hair's breadth escape from their unjust execution. Legislatures past have refused to fix it. Our new Legislature and our new governor must act to rid our state of the shame of threatening the innocent with execution and the guilty with unfairness.

In the days ahead, I will pray that we can open our hearts and provide something for victims' families other than the hope of revenge. Lincoln once said: "I have always found that mercy bears richer fruits than strict justice." I can only hope that will be so. God bless you. And God bless the people of Illinois.

TOPICS FOR CRITICAL THINKING AND WRITING

1. State in a series of sentences the main stages in Ryan's "journey from staunch supporter of capital punishment to reformer" (para. 4).

2. What does Ryan mean by "blanket commutation" (para. 4)?

3. Can you think of a way to defend the "fairness and equality" of a death penalty system that sentences only 2 percent of all convicted murderers to death? (See paras. 9, 47.) Explain as briefly but as effectively as you can.

4. Suppose a defender of the death penalty argued that Ryan is expecting perfection in the criminal justice system, and that is wholly unreasonable. How might an opponent of the death penalty reply?

5. What does Ryan mean by "the clemency process" (para. 38)?

6. Can you think of a way to explain why a murderer whose victim is white is more likely to get a death sentence than if the victim is non-white (para. 68), without implying that the criminal justice system is racist? Explain.

7. Suppose someone argued that international human rights law ought to have no bearing on whether the United States ought to keep the death penalty (para. 71). How might an opponent of the death penalty reply, in 250 words?

8. Suppose that a defender of the death penalty in Illinois argued that Governor Ryan exceeded his authority in granting executive clemency for over 150 prisoners (para. 79). How might the governor reply, in 250 words?

9. Suppose one were to argue that Ryan's conviction on changes of racketeering and fraud undermine his arguments concerning the death penalty. How might he reply? How would *you* reply?

Garry Wills

Garry Wills, born in Atlanta in 1934, is the author of numerous books, including Under God: Religion and American Politics *(1990),* Why I Am a Catholic *(2002). In 1993 he was awarded a Pulitzer Prize for general nonfiction for* Lincoln at Gettysburg *(1992). Wills often writes for the* New York Review of Books, *where the following essay originally appeared in 2001.*

The Dramaturgy of Death

1. CAPITAL PUNISHMENT: THE RATIONALES

A slight perusal of the laws by which the measures of vindictive and coercive justice are established will discover so many disproportions between crimes and punishments, such capricious distinctions of guilt, and such confusion of remissness and severity as can scarcely be believed to have been produced by public wisdom, sincerely and calmly studious of public happiness.

—SAMUEL JOHNSON, *Rambler* 114

Nietzsche denied that capital punishment ever arose from a single or consistent theory of its intent or effect. It erupted from a tangle of overlapping yet conflicting urges, which would be fitted out with later rationalizations. The only common denominator he found in the original urges was some form of grievance (he used the French term *ressentiment*).[1] One can expand his own list of such urges:

Killing as exclusion. This occurs when society does not want to admit any responsibility for persons considered outsiders. Abandonment of wounded or captured people one does not want to feed or support is an example, or exposure of unwanted children, or exiling the defenseless (as the blind and old Oedipus was extruded from Thebes), or "outlawing"—leaving people without protection to any predators on them. Outlawing was an English practice continued in our colonies. In fact, Thomas Jefferson, when he revised the laws of Virginia for the new republic, left certain categories of offenders "out of the protection of the laws"—freed slaves who either enter the state or refuse to leave it, a white woman bearing a black child who does not leave the state within a year.[2] These could be killed or mistreated in any way without remedy at law. The ancient Greeks denied offenders recourse to law by the penalty of *atimia* (loss of rights). There were lesser degrees of this, but the full degree of "*atimia* . . . and condemnation to death are interchangeable."[3] Nietzsche calls this "Punishment as the expulsion of a degenerate element . . . as a means of preserving the purity of a race or maintaining a social type."

Killing as cleansing. Outlawing abandons people to possible or probable death but does not directly bring it about. Other forms of extrusion require society's purification by *destruction* of a polluted person. Unless society or its agents effect this purification, the pollution continues to taint them. Lesser pollutions can be robbed of their effect by simply driving away the affected person. But deeper taints are removed only by accompanying the expulsion with something like stoning the polluter to death or throwing him off a cliff. Plato said that the murderer of anyone in his own immediate family was to be killed by judicial officers and magistrate, then "thrown down naked on a designated crossroads outside the city; whereupon every official present must throw his own stone at the head of the corpse, to cleanse the whole city, and finally must take him beyond the land's outer boundaries and cast him out, all rites of burial denied" (*Laws* 873b–c).

Killing as execration. Sometimes the community must thrust away contamination by ritual curses (*arai*), joining the punitive cry of the Furies, who are also called Arai (Aeschylus, *Eumenides* 417). When Prometheus is punished by exposure as the penalty of theft, Brute Force (Bia) tells the technician clamping him to the rock (Hephaistos) that he should curse as well as immobilize him (Aeschylus, *Prometheus* 38, 67–68). Southern lynch mobs stayed to curse with fury their hanged victim from a similar impulse.

Killing to maintain social order. Superiors dramatize their dominance   5 by showing that it is easy for those higher in the social scale to kill those lower, but harder for the lower to kill the higher. Plato's legal code devised a penalty for a slave who kills a free man — public scourging to death before the free man's tomb and family — that had no symmetrical penalty for a free man who kills a slave (*Laws* 872b–c). In Jefferson's legal code, slaves could not testify against whites, but whites could testify against slaves.[4] In parts of this country still, a black killing a white is far more likely to receive a death sentence than a white killing a black. Nietzsche calls this "Punishment as a means of inspiring fear of those who determine and execute the punishment."

Killing to delegitimize a former social order. Revolutionary tribunals execute officials of an overthrown regime. Even without a coup, critics of Athenian democracy claimed that mass juries were too ready to condemn their leaders. When the Turkish general Lala Mustafa Pasha captured Cyprus from the Venetians in 1570, the podestà who had held out against him, Marcantonio Bragadin, was mutilated (nose and ears cut off), dragged around the city walls, dangled from a ship's mast, tied naked to a post, skinned alive, beheaded, and "quartered" (his four limbs cut off). Then his skin, stuffed with straw, was tied to a cow and led through the streets of the Famagusta, before being returned as a victory prize to Constantinople. Venetian rule was pulverized in its representative. Nietzsche calls this "Punishment as a festival, namely as the rape and mockery of a finally defeated enemy."

Killing as posthumous delegitimation. Some inquisitors tried dead men and symbolically executed them.[5] The leaders of the Gowrie Plot that tried to supplant King James VI of Scotland in 1600 were tried posthumously and their corpses were hanged, drawn (eviscerated), and quartered. In 897, Pope Formosus had the corpse of his predecessor, Stephen VI, exhumed, propped up in his papal garb, tried and condemned for usurpation, stripped of his vestments, his head (that had borne the tiara) cut off, along with the three fingers of his right hand used in benediction, and head, fingers, and body then thrown in the Tiber — all to declare Stephen's consecration of bishops and ordination of priests invalid.

Killing as total degradation. The previous three forms of execution punished an offender as a member of a class (lower or higher); but other humiliating deaths are contrived to deprive a person of humanity as such. Public torture before death was one means for this—scourging that makes the offender scream and writhe, losing dignity along with his composure. The Greek punishment for theft was *apotympanismos*, the beating of a naked man clamped down in a crouched position before he was left to die of exposure (it is the punishment given to Prometheus in his play, though he cannot die).[6] The death for traitors in Elizabethan England was an elaborate piece of theater. First the offender was dragged backward on a hurdle to the place of execution—signifying, said the Attorney General Sir Edward Coke, that the man was "not worthy any more to tread upon the face of the earth whereof he was made; also for that he hath been retrograde to nature, therefore is he drawn backward at a horse-tail."[7] Then the man (it was a male punishment) was stripped, hanged, cut down living, castrated, disemboweled, his heart and viscera thrown in boiling water, decapitated, quartered, and his head exposed on Tower Bridge. When Jesuit priests were hanged, drawn, and quartered, their head, members, torso, and clothes were hidden away to prevent the taking of relics.

Killing and posthumous degradation. Refusal of burial led the ancient Greeks to let bodies be exposed for ravaging by dogs and kites (Creon's treatment of Polyneices in Sophocles' *Antigone*). Romans let crucified bodies hang to be pecked at and decompose. Florentines in the Renaissance dangled the corpses of criminals from the high windows of the Bargello till they rotted, and commissioned artists like Andrea del Sarto to depict them there, prolonging the shame after they were gone.[8] Joan of Arc was killed by a slow fire that consumed her clothes and skin, then the flames were raked away, to expose her body as a woman's and to show that no demon had spirited her away. Then intense fire was mounted to burn her down to ashes for scattering in the Seine, to prevent any collection of relics.[9]

Killing by ordeal. In this punishment, the innocent were supposed to 10 be protected if subjected to ordeal by combat, ordeal by fire (walking through it, as Saint Francis is supposed to have done in Egypt), or ordeal by water. The latter was especially reserved for suspected witches, who would sink only if innocent. A less lethal form of this punishment survived in the "ducking stool" for immersing witches. Jefferson's revised code says this: "All attempts to delude the people, or to abuse their understanding by exercise of the pretended [claimed] arts of witchcraft, conjuration, enchantment, or sorcery or by pretended prophecies, shall be punished by ducking and whipping at the discretion of a jury, not exceeding 15 stripes."[10]

Threatened killing as inducement to remorse. Refusal to undergo trial by ordeal could be taken as a confession, leading to a lesser penalty than death. Recanting could have the same effect. Joan of Arc, when first brought out to the stake with its kindling, renounced her voices as "idolatry" (devil worship), and was given life imprisonment. Only when she abjured her recantation was she actually put to the stake. Scaffold repentance could reduce the sentence to less than death—or, at the least, make officials perform a "merciful" (a swifter, not a lingering) execution—e.g., letting a man die in the noose before being cut down for disemboweling. Nietzsche calls this punishment for the "improvement" of the criminal.

Killing as repayment. The *lex talionis*, as it exacts "an eye for an eye," must exact a life for a life. We say, "You're going to *pay* for this." Jefferson followed the logic of his state's *lex talionis*:

> Whosoever shall be guilty of Rape, Polygamy, or Sodomy with man or woman shall be punished, if a man, by castration, if a woman, by cutting thro' the cartilage of her nose a hole of one half inch diameter at the least. . . . Whosoever on purpose and of malice forethought shall maim another, or shall disfigure him, by cutting out or disabling the tongue, slitting or cutting off a nose, lip or ear, branding, or otherwise, shall be maimed or disfigured in like sort: or if that cannot be for want of the same part, then as nearly as may be in some other part of at least equal value and estimation in the opinion of a jury, and moreover shall forfeit one half of his lands and goods to the sufferer.[11]

Taking a life for a life on this principle is called by Nietzsche "Punishment as recompense to the injured party for the harm done."

Killing as repayment-plus. In Athenian law, repayment was of equal value if the crime was unintentional, but of double if it was intentional.[12] On that principle, death has not been reserved only for taking a life, but can be considered an added penalty for crimes like major theft, rape, treasonous speech, and the like.

Killing as victim therapy. The Attic orator Antiphon has the father of a son killed by accident plead that the unintentional killer must be punished; the death leaves the father aggrieved (*epithymion*—much like Nietzsche's *ressentiment*).[13] The grievance, of course, would be even greater if the killing were intentional. Soothing this sense of grievance is now called "giving closure" to the ordeal of victims.

Killing as a form of pedagogy. We say that punishing a man will "teach him a lesson." More important, it may teach others the consequence of crime, deterring anyone who contemplates a similar offense. Kant said that the person should be treated as his own end, not as a means for others' advantage. But the person executed is, by this theory, turned into a teaching instrument for the benefit of others.

2. PUBLIC EXECUTION

Experience of past times gives us little reason to hope that any reformation will be effected by a periodical havoc of our fellow beings.
—SAMUEL JOHNSON, *Rambler* 114

The fourteen types of capital punishment listed do not exhaust all the possible urges expressed in our havocking of others. And as Nietzsche said, they are not neat little separate rationales. They conflict with each other at an intellectual level, but they reinforce each other at the emotional level. They are more powerful for certain people in certain combinations. But they have one thing in common: *they all demand, in logic, maximum display and publicity.* The outlaw's status must be proclaimed for people to act on it. The other effects sought—whether cleansing, order enforcement, delegitimation, humiliation, repayment, therapy, deterrence—can only be achieved if an audience sees what is being done to satisfy, intimidate, soothe, or instruct it.

In fact, various means to dramatize the process, to make its meaning clear, to show the right way to "read" it, were invented. Those going to the scaffold often had their crimes blazoned on their backs. Joan of Arc wore a fool's cap with her four crimes printed on it. A crucified man had his crime posted on the cross. Lesser criminals were branded to sustain the memory of their crime. Ingenious means of execution were invented to express society's horror, anger, power, and the like. Any punishment that fits the crime should be *seen* to fit the crime. Indeed, the only urges that people now commonly admit to—the last four in the above list (repayment of two kinds, "closure," and deterrence)—are closely linked with publicity. The repayment is to *us*, to society as well as to the victims, the therapy is for the victims' contemplation, and an act meant to deter should vividly catch the attention of those who might benefit from it. How can they "learn their lesson" if it is not spelled out for them?

Our unconfessed difficulty is that we have given up whatever logic there was to the death penalty, since we have become unable to embrace most of the practices of the past. We no longer believe in a divine miasma to be purged, or divine guidance to be revealed in survival by ordeal. We have given up the desecration of corpses, killing as a reinforcement of class distinctions, torture, maiming, evisceration, and all the multiple methods used to reduce the criminal to a *corpus vile*. Even Jefferson wavered on the *lex talionis* when it came to blinding an offender (he could go as far as a nose for a nose, but not as far as an eye for an eye). Our Constitution forbids cruel and unusual punishment, and we take that to mean that there will be no gratuitous humiliation of the convict—we do not even put people in the stocks anymore, much less invite the public to see a condemned man being strapped onto a gurney. We want painless executions, so we have recurred to one of the few humane-looking methods of the Greeks—lethal injection (hemlock), though among the many deterrents to becoming a philosopher, Socrates' quiet (and self-chosen) death in his seventies has never ranked very high.

So far from stigmatizing or humiliating the inmate of death row, we now provide him with a long and costly process meant to ascertain guilt, with free legal aid if he cannot afford his own, with counseling and family visits, with reading of his choice and TV, a last meal to his specifications, a last request, religious attendance, guaranteed burial, a swift and nearly painless death. We shut up his last hours from the general public, and act as if this secret rite will deter by some magic of mere occurrence. We treat the killing as a dirty little secret, as if we are ashamed of it. Well, we should be ashamed. Having given up on most of the previous justifications for the death penalty, we cling to a mere vestige of the practice, relying most urgently on one of the least defensible defenses of it.

3. DETERRENCE

The gibbet, indeed, certainly disables those who die upon it from infesting the community; but their death seems not to contribute more to the reformation of their associates than any other method of separation.
— SAMUEL JOHNSON, *Rambler* 114

The bad faith of the process shows in the insistence on using the   20 deterrence argument when it has been discredited by all the most reputable studies. This is an old story. In the eighteenth century, Samuel Johnson, who liked to defend any tradition he could, discovered no deterrent effect following on traditional executions, though they were far more numerous and far more public than they are now (factors, some people think, that add to deterrent effect). In the middle of the twentieth century, Arthur Koestler could refer to a strong scholarly record on the matter:

> This belief in the irreplaceable deterrent value of the death-penalty has been proved to be a superstition by the long and patient inquiries of the Parliamentary Select Committee of 1930 and the Royal Commission on Capital Punishment of 1948; yet it pops up again and again. Like all superstitions, it has the nature of a Jack-in-the-box; however often you hit it over the head with facts and statistics, it will solemnly pop up again, because the hidden spring inside it is the unconscious and irrational power of traditional beliefs.[14]

Present and former presidents of the most prestigious criminological societies, polled in 1995, overwhelmingly said they did not think the death penalty significantly reduces the homicide rate (94 percent), and they knew of no empirical evidence that would support such a claim (94.1 percent).[15] They held (79.2 percent) that execution causes no reduction in crime—a finding confirmed by the fact that states with the death penalty have higher murder rates than those without (the region with the highest number of homicides, the South, accounts for over 80 percent of the nation's executions).[16] Furthermore, countries in Europe that have given up the death penalty have far lower murder rates than does the United States (since those countries *do* have gun control laws).[17] Disbelief in the deterring power of execution is also expressed, though not so overwhelmingly, by police chiefs and sheriffs—not a far-left part of the community—surveyed by Peter D. Hart Research Associates in 1995. They did not think (67 percent) that executions significantly reduce homicides. In fact, New York's former police chief Patrick V. Murphy responded that "the flimsy notion that the death penalty is an effective law enforcement tool is being exposed as mere political puffery."[18]

Expert criminologists said (100 percent, joined in this by 85 percent of the police chiefs) that politicians support the death penalty for symbolic reasons, to show they are tough on crime, though that distracts them (86.6 percent of the criminologists, 56 percent of the police chiefs) from addressing better methods of reducing the homicide rate. The police listed five things that would be more effective in fighting crime, including longer sentences, more police, and gun control. It takes little observation of actual politicians to confirm that politicians support the death penalty for electoral reasons. Now-Senator Dianne Feinstein, who had opposed capital punishment as a very active member of the California parole board, embraced it in 1990 when she ran for governor. When I asked her during that campaign what had made her change her position, she said that she had become convinced that executions do deter other criminals. I said that most studies I had seen denied this, but she told me she had read new and better research, though she could not name it for me. "I'll send it to you," she promised—but she never did. The only empirical evidence that mattered to her was her knowledge of the way Rose Bird had been resoundingly defeated for reelection as the chief justice of the Supreme Court of California because she opposed capital punishment.

When Andrew Young ran for governor of Georgia in 1990, he too abandoned his earlier opposition to the death penalty (though his daughter remained an activist opponent of it, because of its disproportionate rate among blacks—the NAACP Legal Defense Fund discovered that a black's chance of being executed in Georgia was eleven times that of a white). I asked Young if he too had been convinced that executions deter. He said that he had not, but that as mayor of Atlanta he had listened to police tell him that it discouraged them to catch criminals and see them escape execution—"I did it for their morale." (He did it, though, only when he was leaving the mayor's office and addressing a much whiter constituency in his race for governor.)

Other politicians obviously look to the polls, not to policy studies, when taking their stand on executions. Campaigning to become the senator from New York, Hillary Clinton knew how much support the state's former governor, Mario Cuomo, had lost because of his resolute stand against executions. William Weld, while he was still governor of Massachusetts, said that he relied not on studies but on "my gut": "My gut is that . . . capital punishment is deterrent."[19] The deft use of the death penalty issue by Bob Graham as governor of Florida and in his 1986 race for the Senate is studied in a book that Timothy McVeigh is known to have read in prison.[20] In 1984, Graham dismissed scholarly studies on the death penalty by saying, "This is an issue that is inherently beyond what empirical research can validate," making him another gut-truster like Weld.[21] But if we cannot know the deterrent effect, we are certainly killing one man for a hypothetical effect on others that is uncertain.

Actually, the deterrent theory of capital punishment, always weak, is especially flimsy now, when a rash of cases—some involving DNA evidence—has proved that some innocent men are on death row. The evidence of incompetent defenses, faked evidence, and negligent procedures has led to announced or informal moratoria on executions.[22] In Oklahoma alone, where Timothy McVeigh's crime was committed, the evidence in approximately three thousand cases is now tainted by the defective lab work of one technician, Joyce Gilchrist.[23] The execution of the innocent is not a new issue, but widespread public awareness of it is. The British study by the Select Committee on Capital Punishment, cited by Arthur Koestler, found cases of mistaken executions, including "many" reported by the governor of Sing Sing in America.[24]

Some try to separate the problem of killing the *right* person from the question of whether we should execute *any* person at all. But since the principal prop of the death penalty is deterrence theory, that prop is knocked out when uncertainty of guilt enters the national consciousness. Even if we were to grant that executions deter, they may not deter people who think it is a random matter whether the right person is caught. If they might get off while guilty, or be killed while innocent, that fact is not a very stable basis for forswearing a particular homicide. And executing the mentally defective or marginally juvenile, like the disproportionate killing of blacks, cannot much intimidate a would-be murderer who is mentally sound, of mature age, or white.

These considerations join longer-term flaws in the deterrence argument. Juries are readiest to convict people for crimes of passion, sexually charged rape-murders, child-abuse murders, or serial killings. To see these offenders caught will not necessarily affect the person most likely to have the coolness and calculation that deterrence requires. And obviously they do not affect other people in the grip of obsessions, mental instability, or drug- or alcohol-induced frenzy. Plato was against executing those guilty of a crime of passion (*Laws* 867c–d), but our juries reflect more the anger of society than the didactic strategies of deterrence. In doing this, the juries fail to make the calculations that we are told future murderers will make. The whole theory is senseless.

4. "CLOSURE"

[People come] in thousands to the legal massacre and look with carelessness, perhaps with triumph, on the utmost exacerbations of human misery.

— SAMUEL JOHNSON, *Rambler* 114

"Closure" has become a buzzword, not only for discussing the death penalty but for addressing any kind of social discontent. When the unmarried mother of Jesse Jackson's child sued Rev. Jackson, it was not about anything so crass as money, it was to find "closure" for herself and her child.[25] Who can deprive a grieving person of solace? This is the argument Antiphon's prosecutor made when he demanded emotional relief for the loss of his child to an accident. Attorney General John Ashcroft endorsed the argument by arranging for the families of Timothy McVeigh's victims to see him die. This conflicts with the logic of deterrence, since the families are not viewing the event to deter them from becoming mass murderers. If the real point of executions is to act *in terrorem* for other criminals, the Oklahoma families are the least appropriate audience.

Ashcroft's response to the hot pressures of the McVeigh case is just that of Dianne Feinstein or Andrew Young to less emotionally charged instances of capital punishment, where no mass murder is involved. McVeigh, the cold killer revealed in *American Terrorist*, by Lou Michel and Dan Herbeck,[26] triggers all the upsurges of emotion Nietzsche described. We feel that the very existence of a McVeigh is an affront to society, a pollutant of our life, a thing we cannot be clean of without execration. But the politician does not want to be seen ministering to atavistic reactions in their raw state. So he invokes deterrence where it does not apply, or says that humane consideration of the victims' sympathies trumps all other considerations. Seeing the murderer die, we are told, will just help the families to "close a chapter of their lives."

But is this really likely? The aim of emotional healing is to bring inflamed emotions of loss and *ressentiment* back into a manageable relationship with other parts of one's life. Does that happen when, for many years in most cases (six years so far in McVeigh's case), a victim's survivors focus on seeing that someone pays for his or her loss? This tends to reenact the outrage in a person's mind, rather than to transcend it. It prolongs the trauma, delaying and impeding the healing process. When I asked Sister Helen Prejean, the author of *Dead Man Walking*,[27] what she has observed, she said that families are asked by prosecutors to attend the trial of a relative's murderer, but to show no emotion lest they cause a mistrial. "They learn new details of the crime, and with each new turn of the trial and its aftermath the media call them to get a reaction." This is less like healing than like tearing scabs open again and again. Some relatives who want to escape this process are accused by their own of not loving the victim, says Sister Helen: "I have seen families torn apart over the death penalty."

What's more, the sterile, anodyne, and bureaucratic procedures of a modern execution can baffle the desire for revenge encouraged before its performance. Sister Helen recalls a man who said he wished to see more suffering, and who comes with pro-death demonstrators to all later executions. This is hardly one who has found "closure." The eeriness of the

30

closure language was revealed when McVeigh himself, through his lawyer, Rob Nigh, expressed sympathy for the relatives' "disappointment" after his execution was delayed.[28] He is more the manipulator of these grieving people than an offering to them.

Emotional counselors work toward reconciliation with the facts, as religious leaders recommend forgiveness. Many church bodies oppose the death penalty, drawing on rich traditions in the various faiths. Saint Augustine resisted the killing of murderers, even of two men who had murdered one of his own priests, arguing that the fate of souls is in God's hands (Letters 133, 134). It is true that Thomas Aquinas likened the killing of murderers to the amputation of a limb for the good of the whole body, but his fellow Dominican Niceto Blázquez points out how defective this argument is: Thomas was drawing an analogy with the excommunication of sinners from the Church, the body of Christ—but that is a move meant to promote reunion, to rescue a person from the death of his soul, not to impose a death on the body.[29]

Conservative Catholics, who are aghast at fellow believers' willingness to ignore the Pope on matters like contraception, blithely ignore in their turn papal pleas to renounce the death penalty (addressed most recently to the McVeigh case). And I have not seen Bible-quoting fundamentalists refer to the one place in the Gospels where Jesus deals with capital punishment. At John 8:3–11, he interrupts a legal execution (for adultery) and tells the officers of the state that their own sinfulness deprives them of jurisdiction. Jesus himself gives up any jurisdiction for this kind of killing: "Neither do I condemn you." George W. Bush said during the campaign debates of last year that Jesus is his favorite philosopher—though he did not hesitate to endorse the execution of 152 human beings in Texas, where half of the public defenders of accused murderers were sanctioned by the Texas bar for legal misbehavior or incompetence. Mr. Bush clearly needs some deeper consultation with the philosopher of his choice.

NOTES

1. Friedrich Nietzsche, *On the Genealogy of Morals* 2.11–14, translated by Walter Kaufmann, in *Basic Writings of Nietzsche* (Modern Library, 1992), pp. 509–18.
2. *The Papers of Thomas Jefferson*, Vol. 2, edited by Julian P. Boyd (Princeton University Press, 1950), p. 471.
3. A. R. W. Harrison, *The Law of Athens*, Vol. 2: *Procedure* (Oxford University Press, 1971), p. 170.
4. *The Papers of Thomas Jefferson*, Vol. 2, p. 471.
5. Robert Adams, *The Abuses of Punishment* (St. Martin's, 1998), p. 156.
6. For the *apotympanismos* of Prometheus, see Louis Gernet, *The Anthropology of Ancient Greece*, translated by John Hamilton, S.J., and Blaise Nagy (Johns Hopkins University Press, 1968), pp. 242–44. Plato has Protagoras identify Prometheus' crime as, precisely, theft (of fire) at *Protagoras* 322e.
7. Coke quoted in Leon Radzinowicz, *A History of English Criminal Law and Its Administration from 1750*, Vol. 1 (Macmillan, 1948), pp. 221–22.

8. Samuel Y. Edgerton Jr., *Pictures and Punishment: Art and Criminal Prosecution during the Florentine Renaissance* (Cornell University Press, 1985), pp. 112–23.
9. *A Parisian Journal, 1405–1449*, translated by Janet Shirley (Clarendon Press/ Oxford University Press, 1968).
10. *The Papers of Thomas Jefferson*, Vol. 2, p. 502.
11. *The Papers of Thomas Jefferson*, Vol. 2, pp. 497–98.
12. Demosthenes, *Against Meidias* 43.
13. Antiphon, *Tetralogy* 2.1.2.
14. Arthur Koestler, *Reflections on Hanging* (Macmillan, 1957), p. 6.
15. Michael L. Radelet and Ronald L. Akers, "Deterrence and the Death Penalty: The View of the Experts," *Journal of Criminal Law and Criminology* (Fall 1996), p. 14 (sun.soci.niu.edu/~critcrim/dp/dppapers/mike.deterence).
16. See "Facts about Deterrence and the Death Penalty" at the Web site for the Death Penalty Information Center, www.deathpenaltyinfo.org/deter.html.
17. "Facts about Deterrence and the Death Penalty."
18. Radelet and Akers, *Deterrence and the Death Penalty*, p. 5.
19. Radelet and Akers, *Deterrence and the Death Penalty*, p. 2.
20. David Von Drehle, *Among the Lowest of the Dead: The Culture of Death Row* (Times Books, 1995), pp. 13–15, 293, 325–26.
21. Radelet and Akers, *Deterrence and the Death Penalty*, p. 5.
22. Richard C. Dieter, *Innocence and the Death Penalty: The Increasing Danger of Executing the Innocent* (Death Penalty Information Center, www.death penaltyinfo.org/inn.html, 1997).
23. Jim Yardley, "Inquiry Focuses on Scientist Employed by Prosecutors," *New York Times*, May 2, 2001, p. A14.
24. Adams, *The Abuses of Punishment*, p. 170.
25. Don Terry and Monica Davey, "'I'm Not a Blackmailer,' Mother of Jesse Jackson's Child Says," *Chicago Tribune*, May 8, 2001.
26. Regan Books, 2001.
27. Vintage, 1996.
28. Helen Kennedy, "McVeigh Execution," *New York Daily News*, May 12, 2001, p. 3.
29. James J. Megivern, *The Death Penalty: An Historical and Theological Survey* (Paulist Press, 1997), pp. 118–20.

Topics for Critical Thinking and Writing

1. Wills contrasts a reasonable defense of the death penalty with a "rationalization" (para. 1) on its behalf. Explain the difference in 150 words.

2. Of the fourteen ways in which the death penalty has been justified historically, which if any do you think play no role in using the death penalty in the United States today? Which are paramount in their influence?

3. What is lynching, and do you think that society ought to use the death penalty to reduce the likelihood of lynching?

4. Is death in the electric chair a "humiliating" form of capital punishment (para. 8)? Is death by lethal injection? Why, or why not? Why does Wills regard some but not all methods of execution as "degrading"? Explain your answers in an essay of 250–500 words.

5. What if anything is wrong with using the death penalty as a "teaching instrument for the benefit of others" (para. 15)?

6. Do you agree with Wills that all the different forms and versions of the death penalty share one feature: the "demand [for] maximum display and publicity" (para. 16)? In any case, in what ways does the death penalty as used in the United States today fail in this regard?

7. Complete the following sentence: "A given punishment is an effective deterrent if and only if . . ."

8. When people say that "my gut is that . . . capital punishment is deterrent" (para. 23), which of the following do you think they mean? (a) Capital punishment is a deterrent to murder whereas other penalties are not. (b) Capital punishment is a better deterrent than available alternatives. (c) Capital punishment is a better deterrent than available alternatives, although there is no good evidence to support that view. (d) None of the above. (e) All of the above.

9. "Since the principal prop of the death penalty is deterrence theory, that prop is knocked out when uncertainty of guilt enters the national consciousness" (para. 25). Do you agree or not? Explain why or why not in about 250 words.

10. Summarize in no more than 250 words Wills's objections to the idea that executions provide "closure" and that that's a good thing.

11. Write an essay of 500 words in which you examine and evaluate Wills's techniques or strategies as a writer of an argument.

Potter Stewart

After the U.S. Supreme Court decided Furman v. Georgia *in 1972, requiring states either to abolish the death penalty or revise their statutes to avoid the "arbitrariness" to which the Court objected in* Furman, *state legislatures reacted in one of two ways. A few states enacted mandatory death penalties, giving the trial court no alternative to a death sentence once the defendant was convicted. Most states, including Georgia, tightened up their procedures by imposing new requirements on the trial and appellate courts in death penalty cases. In 1976 these new statutes were challenged, and in a series of decisions the Court (by a seven to two majority) settled two crucial questions: (1) The death penalty was not "a per se [as such] violation" of the Eighth Amendment (prohibiting "cruel and unusual punishments") and the Fourteenth Amendment (guaranteeing "equal protection of the laws"), and (2) several kinds of new death penalty statutes were constitutionally unobjectionable. The most important of these cases was* Gregg v. Georgia; *we reprint excerpts from the majority opinion by Associate Justice Potter Stewart (1915–1985). (Justice Stewart had voted against the death penalty in* Furman, *but four years later he switched sides, evidently believing that his objections of 1972 were no longer relevant.) In the following opinion, the citations referring to legal documents have been omitted.*

Gregg v. Georgia

The Georgia statute, as amended after our decision in *Furman v. Georgia,* retains the death penalty for six categories of crime: murder, kidnapping for ransom or where the victim is harmed, armed robbery, rape, treason, and aircraft hijacking. The capital defendant's guilt or innocence is determined in the traditional manner, either by a trial judge or a jury, in the first stage of a bifurcated trial. . . .

After a verdict, finding, or plea of guilty to a capital crime, a presentence hearing is conducted before whoever made the determination of guilt. The sentencing procedures are essentially the same in both bench and jury trials. At the hearing:

> [T]he judge [or jury] shall hear additional evidence in extenuation, mitigation, and aggravation of punishment, including the record of any prior criminal convictions and pleas of guilty or pleas of nolo contendere of the defendant, or the absence of any prior conviction and pleas: Provided, however, that only such evidence in aggravations as the State has made known to the defendant prior to his trial shall be admissible. The judge [or jury] shall also hear argument by the defendant or his counsel and the prosecuting attorney . . . regarding the punishment to be imposed.

The defendant is accorded substantial latitude as to the types of evidence that he may introduce. Evidence considered during the guilt stage may be considered during the sentencing stage without being resubmitted.

In the assessment of the appropriate sentence to be imposed the judge is also required to consider or to include in his instructions to the jury "any mitigating circumstances or aggravating circumstances otherwise authorized by law and any of [ten] statutory aggravating circumstances which may be supported by the evidence. . . ." The scope of the nonstatutory aggravating or mitigating circumstances is not delineated in the statute. Before a convicted defendant may be sentenced to death, however, except in cases of treason or aircraft hijacking, the jury, or the trial judge in cases tried without a jury, must find beyond a reasonable doubt one of the ten aggravating circumstances specified in the statute.[1] The sentence of death may be imposed only if the jury (or judge) finds one of the statutory aggravating circumstances and then elects to impose that sentence. If the verdict is death the jury or judge must specify the aggravating circumstance(s) found. In jury cases, the trial judge is bound by the jury's recommended sentence.

In addition to the conventional appellate process available in all criminal cases, provision is made for special expedited direct review by the Supreme Court of Georgia of the appropriateness of imposing the sentence of death in the particular case. The court is directed to consider "the punishment as well as any errors enumerated by way of appeal," and to determine

1. whether the sentence of death was imposed under the influence of passion, prejudice, or any other arbitrary factor, and
2. whether, in cases other than treason or aircraft hijacking, the evidence supports the jury's or judge's finding of a statutory aggravating circumstance as enumerated in §27.2534.1(b), and

3. whether the sentence of death is excessive or disproportionate to the penalty imposed in similar cases, considering both the crime and the defendant.

If the court affirms a death sentence, it is required to include in its decision reference to similar cases that it has taken into consideration.

... We now consider specifically whether the sentence of death for the crime of murder is a per se violation of the Eighth and Fourteenth Amendments to the Constitution. We note first that history and precedent strongly support a negative answer to this question.

The imposition of the death penalty for the crime of murder has a long history of acceptance both in the United States and in England. The common-law rule imposed a mandatory death sentence on all convicted murderers. And the penalty continued to be used into the twentieth century by most American states, although the breadth of the common-law rule was diminished, initially by narrowing the class of murders to be punished by death and subsequently by widespread adoption of laws expressly granting juries the discretion to recommend mercy.

It is apparent from the text of the Constitution itself that the existence of capital punishment was accepted by the Framers. At the time the Eighth Amendment was ratified, capital punishment was a common sanction in every state. Indeed, the First Congress of the United States enacted legislation providing death as the penalty for specified crimes. The Fifth Amendment, adopted at the same time as the Eighth, contemplated the continued existence of the capital sanction by imposing certain limits on the prosecution of capital cases:

No person shall be held to answer for a capital, or otherwise infamous crime, unless on a presentment or indictment of a Grand Jury ... ; nor shall any person be subject for the same offense to be twice put in jeopardy of life or limb; ... nor be deprived of life, liberty, or property, without due process of law....

And the Fourteenth Amendment, adopted over three-quarters of a century later, similarly contemplates the existence of the capital sanction in providing that no state shall deprive any person of "life, liberty, or property" without due process of law.

Four years ago, the petitioners in *Furman* and its companion cases predicated their argument primarily upon the asserted proposition that standards of decency had evolved to the point where capital punishment no longer could be tolerated. The petitioners in those cases said, in effect, that the evolutionary process had come to an end, and that standards of decency required that the Eighth Amendment be construed finally as prohibiting capital punishment for any crime regardless of its depravity and impact on society. This view was accepted by two Justices. Three other Justices were unwilling to go so far; focusing on the procedures by which convicted defendants were selected for the death penalty rather than on the actual punishment inflicted, they joined in the conclusion that the statutes before the Court were constitutionally invalid.

The petitioners in the capital cases before the Court today renew the "standards of decency" argument, but developments during the four years since *Furman* have undercut substantially the assumptions upon which their argument rested. Despite the continuing debate, dating back to the nineteenth century, over the morality and utility of capital punishment, it is now evident that a large proportion of American society continues to regard it as an appropriate and necessary criminal sanction.

The most marked indication of society's endorsement of the death 10 penalty for murder is the legislative response to *Furman*. The legislatures of at least thirty-five states have enacted new statutes that provide for the death penalty for at least some crimes that result in the death of another person. And the Congress of the United States, in 1974, enacted a statute providing the death penalty for aircraft piracy that results in death. . . .

In the only statewide referendum occurring since *Furman* and brought to our attention, the people of California adopted a constitutional amendment that authorized capital punishment, in effect negating a prior ruling by the Supreme Court of California in *People v. Anderson*, that the death penalty violated the California Constitution.

The jury also is a significant and reliable objective index of contemporary values because it is so directly involved. . . .

It may be true that evolving standards have influenced juries in recent decades to be more discriminating in imposing the sentence of death. But the relative infrequency of jury verdicts imposing the death sentence does not indicate rejection of capital punishment per se. Rather, the reluctance of juries in many cases to impose the sentence may well reflect the humane feeling that this most irrevocable of sanctions should be reserved for a small number of extreme cases. Indeed, the actions of juries in many states since *Furman* are fully compatible with the legislative judgments, reflected in the new statutes, as to the continued utility and necessity of capital punishment in appropriate cases. At the close of 1974 at least 254 persons had been sentenced to death since *Furman*, and by the end of March 1976, more than 460 persons were subject to death sentences. . . .

The death penalty is said to serve two principal social purposes: retribution and deterrence of capital crimes by prospective offenders.

In part, capital punishment is an expression of society's moral out- 15 rage at particularly offensive conduct. This function may be unappealing to many, but it is essential in an ordered society that asks its citizens to rely on legal processes rather than self-help to vindicate their wrongs.

> The instinct for retribution is part of the nature of man, and channeling that instinct in the administration of criminal justice serves an important purpose in promoting the stability of a society governed by law. When people begin to believe that organized society is unwilling or unable to

impose upon criminal offenders the punishment they "deserve," then there are sown the seeds of anarchy—of self-help, vigilante justice, and lynch law. *Furman v. Georgia* (Stewart, J., concurring).

"Retribution is no longer the dominant objective of the criminal law," *Williams v. New York*, but neither is it a forbidden objective nor one inconsistent with our respect for the dignity of men. . . . Indeed, the decision that capital punishment may be the appropriate sanction in extreme cases is an expression of the community's belief that certain crimes are themselves so grievous an affront to humanity that the only adequate response may be the penalty of death.[2]

Statistical attempts to evaluate the worth of the death penalty as a deterrent to crimes by potential offenders have occasioned a great deal of debate. The results simply have been inconclusive. As one opponent of capital punishment has said:

> [A]fter all possible inquiry, including the probing of all possible methods of inquiry, we do not know, and for systematic and easily visible reasons cannot know, what the truth about this "deterrent" effect may be. . . .
> The inescapable flaw is . . . that social conditions in any state are not constant through time, and that social conditions are not the same in any two states. If an effect were observed (and the observed effects, one way or another, are not large) then one could not at all tell whether any of this effect is attributable to the presence or absence of capital punishment. A "scientific"—that is to say, a soundly based—conclusion is simply impossible, and no methodological path out of this tangle suggests itself. C. Black, *Capital Punishment: The Inevitability of Caprice and Mistake* 25–26 (1974).

Although some of the studies suggest that the death penalty may not function as a significantly greater deterrent than lesser penalties, there is no convincing empirical evidence either supporting or refuting this view. We may nevertheless assume safely that there are murderers, such as those who act in passion, for whom the threat of death has little or no deterrent effect. But for many others, the death penalty undoubtedly is a significant deterrent. There are carefully contemplated murders, such as murder for hire, where the possible penalty of death may well enter into the cold calculus that precedes the decision to act.[3] And there are some categories of murder, such as murder by a life prisoner, where other sanctions may not be adequate. . . .

In sum, we cannot say that the judgment of the Georgia legislature that capital punishment may be necessary in some cases is clearly wrong. Considerations of federalism, as well as respect for the ability of a legislature to evaluate, in terms of its particular state, the moral consensus concerning the death penalty and its social utility as a sanction, require us to conclude, in the absence of more convincing evidence, that the infliction of death as a punishment for murder is not without justification and thus is not unconstitutionally severe.

Finally, we must consider whether the punishment of death is disproportionate in relation to the crime for which it is imposed. There is no question that death as a punishment is unique in its severity and irrevocability. But we are concerned here only with the imposition of capital punishment for the crime of murder, and when a life has been taken deliberately by the offender,[4] we cannot say that the punishment is invariably disproportionate to the crime. It is an extreme sanction, suitable to the most extreme of crimes.

We hold that the death penalty is not a form of punishment that 20 may never be imposed, regardless of the circumstances of the offense, regardless of the character of the offender, and regardless of the procedure followed in reaching the decision to impose it. . . .

While some have suggested that standards to guide a capital jury's sentencing deliberations are impossible to formulate, the fact is that such standards have been developed. When the drafters of the Model Penal Code faced this problem, they concluded "that it is within the realm of possibility to point to the main circumstances of aggravation and of mitigation that should be weighed *and weighed against each other* when they are presented in a concrete case" (emphasis in original). While such standards are by necessity somewhat general, they do provide guidance to the sentencing authority and thereby reduce the likelihood that it will impose a sentence that fairly can be called capricious or arbitrary. Where the sentencing authority is required to specify the factors it relied upon in reaching its decision, the further safeguard of meaningful appellate review is available to ensure that death sentences are not imposed capriciously or in a freakish manner.

In summary, the concerns expressed in *Furman* that the penalty of death not be imposed in an arbitrary or capricious manner can be met by a carefully drafted statute that ensures that the sentencing authority is given adequate information and guidance. As a general proposition these concerns are best met by a system that provides for a bifurcated proceeding at which the sentencing authority is apprised of the information relevant to the imposition of sentence and provided with standards to guide its use of the information.

For the reasons expressed in this opinion, we hold that the statutory system under which Gregg was sentenced to death does not violate the Constitution. Accordingly, the judgment of the Georgia Supreme Court is affirmed.

NOTES

1. The statute provides in part:
   (a) The death penalty may be imposed for the offenses of aircraft hijacking or treason, in any case.
   (b) In all cases of other offenses for which the death penalty may be authorized, the judge shall consider, or he shall include in his instructions to the

jury for it to consider, any mitigating circumstances or aggravating circumstances otherwise authorized by law and any of the following statutory aggravating circumstances which may be supported by the evidence:

(1) The offense of murder, rape, armed robbery, or kidnapping was committed by a person with a prior record of conviction for a capital felony, or the offense of murder was committed by a person who has a substantial history of serious assaultive criminal convictions.

(2) The offense of murder, rape, armed robbery, or kidnapping was committed while the offender was engaged in the commission of another capital felony, or aggravated battery, or the offense of murder was committed while the offender was engaged in the commission of burglary or arson in the first degree.

(3) The offender by his act of murder, armed robbery, or kidnapping knowingly created a great risk of death to more than one person in a public place by means of a weapon or device which would normally be hazardous to the lives of more than one person.

(4) The offender committed the offense of murder for himself or another, for the purpose of receiving money or any other thing of monetary value.

(5) The murder of a judicial officer, former judicial officer, district attorney or solicitor or former district attorney or solicitor during or because of the exercise of his official duty.

(6) The offender caused or directed another to commit murder or committed murder as an agent or employee of another person.

(7) The offense of murder, rape, armed robbery, or kidnapping was outrageously or wantonly vile, horrible or inhuman in that it involved torture, depravity of mind, or an aggravated battery to the victim.

(8) The offense of murder was committed against any peace officer, corrections employee or fireman while engaged in the performance of his official duties.

(9) The offense of murder was committed by a person in, or who has escaped from, the lawful custody of a peace officer or place of lawful confinement.

(10) The murder was committed for the purpose of avoiding, interfering with, or preventing a lawful arrest or custody in a place of lawful confinement, of himself or another.

(c) The statutory instructions as determined by the trial judge to be warranted by the evidence shall be given in charge and in writing to the jury for its deliberation. The jury, if its verdict be a recommendation of death, shall designate in writing, signed by the foreman of the jury, the aggravating circumstance or circumstances which it found beyond a reasonable doubt. In non-jury cases the judge shall make such designation. Except in cases of treason or aircraft hijacking, unless at least one of the statutory aggravating circumstances enumerated is so found, the death penalty shall not be imposed.

The Supreme Court of Georgia recently held unconstitutional the portion of the first circumstance encompassing persons who have a "substantial history of serious assaultive criminal convictions" because it did not set "sufficiently 'clear and objective standards.'"

2. Lord Justice Denning, Master of the Rolls of the Court of Appeal in England, spoke to this effect before the British Royal Commission on Capital Punishment:

Punishment is the way in which society expresses its denunciation of wrong-doing: and, in order to maintain respect for law, it is essential that the punishment inflicted for grave crimes should adequately reflect the revulsion felt by the great ma-jority of citizens for them. It is a mistake to consider the objects of punishment as being deterrent or reformative or preventive and nothing else. . . . The truth is that some crimes are so outrageous that society insists on adequate punish-ment, because the wrong-doer deserves it, irrespective of whether it is a deter-rent or not.

A contemporary writer has noted more recently that opposition to capital punishment "has much more appeal when the discussion is merely aca-demic than when the community is confronted with a crime, or a series of crimes, so gross, so heinous, so cold-blooded that anything short of death seems an inadequate response." Raspberry, Death Sentence, *Washington Post,* Mar. 12, 1976, p. A27, cols. 5–6.

3. Other types of calculated murders, apparently occurring with increasing fre-quency, include the use of bombs or other means of indiscriminate killings, the extortion murder of hostages or kidnap victims, and the execution-style killing of witnesses to a crime.

4. We do not address here the question whether the taking of the criminal's life is a proportionate sanction where no victim has been deprived of life—for example, when capital punishment is imposed for rape, kidnapping, or armed robbery that does not result in the death of any human being.

TOPICS FOR CRITICAL THINKING AND WRITING

1. What features of Georgia's new death penalty statute does Justice Stewart point to in arguing that the new statute will prevent the prob-lems found in the old statute?

2. Since the new Georgia statute upheld by the Supreme Court in its *Gregg* decision does nothing to affect the discretion the prosecutor has in deciding whether to seek the death penalty in a murder case, and noth-ing to affect the complete discretion the governor has in deciding whether to extend clemency, can it be argued that despite the new death-penalty statutes like Georgia's, the problems that gave rise to the decision in *Furman* will probably reappear?

3. How important do you think public opinion is in determining what the Bill of Rights means? Does it matter to the meaning of "cruel and unusual punishment" that most Americans profess to favor the death penalty? (Think of parallel cases: Does it matter to the meanings of "due process of law," "the right to bear arms," "an impartial jury"—all pro-tected by the Bill of Rights—what a majority of the public thinks?)

4. In 1976, when the Supreme Court decided *Gregg*, it also decided *Woodson v. North Carolina*. In *Woodson*, the Court held unconstitutional under the Eighth and Fourteenth Amendments a *mandatory* death penalty for anyone convicted of first-degree murder. Do you think North Carolina's statute was a reasonable response to objections to the death penalty at the time of *Furman* based on the alleged arbitrary and discriminatory administration of that penalty? Why, or why not?

5. Stewart mentions the kinds of murder where he thinks the death penalty might be a better deterrent than life imprisonment. What are they? What reasons might be given for or against agreeing with him?

6. A year after *Gregg* was decided, the Supreme Court ruled in *Coker v. Georgia* that the death penalty for rape was unconstitutional under the Eighth and Fourteenth Amendments. Do you think that Stewart's opinion in *Gregg* silently implies that *only* murder is punishable by death? (What about a death penalty for treason? Espionage? Kidnapping for ransom? Large-scale illegal drug trafficking?) In an essay of 500 words, argue either for or against that conclusion.

Harry Blackmun

Harry Blackmun (1908–1999) was born in Nashville, Illinois, and educated at Harvard, where he received his undergraduate and law degrees. He was appointed to the United States Supreme Court in 1970 as a conservative, but when he retired in 1994, he was regarded as a liberal. Blackmun became a national figure in 1973 when he wrote the majority opinion in Roe v. Wade, *a case that (although it placed limits on abortion) asserted that the right to privacy includes "a woman's decision whether or not to terminate her pregnancy." We reprint his dissent from the Supreme Court's order denying review in a Texas death-penalty case,* Callins v. Collins, 510 U.S. 1141 (1994). *In his first sentence, Blackmun says that* Callins *"will be executed by the State of Texas," and though in 1994 Callins received a stay of execution, he, in fact, was executed in 1997.*

Dissenting Opinion in Callins v. Collins

Bruce Edwin Callins will be executed by the State of Texas. . . . Intravenous tubes attached to his arms will carry the instrument of death, a toxic fluid designed specifically for the purpose of killing human beings. The witnesses, standing a few feet away, will behold Callins, no longer a defendant, an appellant, or a petitioner, but a man, strapped to a gurney, and seconds away from extinction.

Within days, or perhaps hours, the memory of Callins will begin to fade. The wheels of justice will churn again, and somewhere, another jury or another judge will have the unenviable task of determining whether some human being is to live or die.

We hope, of course, that the defendant whose life is at risk will be represented by competent counsel, someone who is inspired by the awareness that a less-than-vigorous defense truly could have fatal consequences for the defendant. We hope that the attorney will investigate all aspects of the case, follow all evidentiary and procedural rules, and appear before a judge who is still committed to the protection of defendants' rights even now, as the prospect of meaningful judicial oversight has diminished. In the same vein, we hope that the prosecution, in urging the penalty of death, will have exercised its discretion wisely, free from bias, prejudice, or political motive and will be humbled, rather than emboldened, by the awesome authority conferred by the State.

But even if we can feel confident that these actors will fulfill their roles to the best of their human ability, our collective conscience will remain uneasy. Twenty years have passed since this Court declared that the death penalty must be imposed fairly, and with reasonable consistency or not at all (see *Furman v. Georgia,* 1972), and, despite the effort of the states and courts to devise legal formulas and procedural rules to meet this daunting challenge, the death penalty remains fraught with arbitrariness, discrimination, caprice, and mistake.

This is not to say that the problems with the death penalty today are 5 identical to those that were present twenty years ago. Rather, the problems that were pursued down one hole with procedural rules and verbal formulas have come to the surface somewhere else, just as virulent and pernicious as they were in their original form. Experience has taught us that the constitutional goal of eliminating arbitrariness and discrimination from the administration of death . . . can never be achieved without compromising an equally essential component of fundamental fairness: individualized sentencing. (See *Lockett v. Ohio,* 1978.)

It is tempting, when faced with conflicting constitutional commands, to sacrifice one for the other or to assume that an acceptable balance between them already has been struck. In the context of the death penalty, however, such jurisprudential maneuvers are wholly inappropriate. The death penalty must be imposed "fairly, and with reasonable consistency, or not at all." (*Eddings v. Oklahoma,* 1982).

To be fair, a capital sentencing scheme must treat each person convicted of a capital offense with that "degree of respect due the uniqueness of the individual. . . ." That means affording the sentencer the power and discretion to grant mercy in a particular case, and providing avenues for the consideration of any and all relevant mitigating evidence that would justify a sentence less than death.

Reasonable consistency, on the other hand, requires that the death penalty be inflicted evenhandedly, in accordance with reason and objective standards, rather than by whim, caprice, or prejudice.

Finally, because human error is inevitable and because our criminal justice system is less than perfect, searching appellate review of death sentences and their underlying convictions is a prerequisite to a constitutional death penalty scheme.

On their face, these goals of individual fairness, reasonable consis- 10 tency, and absence of error appear to be attainable: Courts are in the very business of erecting procedural devices from which fair, equitable, and reliable outcomes are presumed to flow. Yet, in the death penalty area, this Court, in my view, has engaged in a futile effort to balance these constitutional demands and now is retreating not only from the *Furman* promise of consistency and rationality but from the requirement of individualized sentencing as well.

Having virtually conceded that both fairness and rationality cannot be achieved in the administration of the death penalty (*McClesky v. Kemp,*

1987), the Court has chosen to deregulate the entire enterprise, replacing, it would seem, substantive constitutional requirements with mere aesthetics and abdicating its statutorily and constitutionally imposed duty to provide meaningful judicial oversight to the administration of death by the states.

From this day forward, I no longer shall tinker with the machinery of death. For more than twenty years I have endeavored—indeed, I have struggled, along with a majority of this Court—to develop procedural and substantive rules that would lend more than the mere appearance of fairness to the death penalty endeavor. . . . Rather than continue to coddle the Court's delusion that the desired level of fairness has been achieved and the need for regulation eviscerated, I feel morally and intellectually obligated simply to concede that the death penalty experiment has failed. It is virtually self-evident to me now that no combination of procedural rules or substantive regulations ever can save the death penalty from its inherent constitutional deficiencies. The basic question—does the system accurately and consistently determine which defendants "deserve" to die?—cannot be answered in the affirmative. . . . The problem is that the inevitability of factual, legal, and moral error gives us a system that we know must wrongly kill some defendants, a system that fails to deliver the fair, consistent and reliable sentences of death required by the Constitution. . . .

There is little doubt now that *Furman*'s essential holding was correct. Although most of the public seems to desire, and the Constitution appears to permit, the penalty of death, it surely is beyond dispute that if the death penalty cannot be administered consistently and rationally, it may not be administered at all. . . .

Delivering on the *Furman* promise, however, has proved to be another matter. *Furman* aspired to eliminate the vestiges of racism and the effects of poverty in capital sentencing; it deplored the "wanton" and "random" infliction of death by a government with constitutionally limited power. *Furman* demanded that the sentencer's discretion be directed and limited by procedural rules and objective standards in order to minimize the risk of arbitrary and capricious sentences of death.

In the years following *Furman,* serious efforts were made to comply 15 with its mandate. State legislatures and appellate courts struggled to provide judges and juries with sensible and objective guidelines for determining who should live and who should die. Some states attempted to define who is "deserving" of the death penalty through the use of carefully chosen adjectives, reserving the death penalty for those who commit crimes that are "especially heinous, atrocious, or cruel," or "wantonly vile, horrible, or inhuman." Other states enacted mandatory death penalty statutes, reading *Furman* as an invitation to eliminate sentencer discretion altogether. . . .

Unfortunately, all this experimentation and ingenuity yielded little of what *Furman* demanded. It soon became apparent that discretion could not be eliminated from capital sentencing without threatening the fundamental fairness due a defendant when life is at stake. Just as contemporary society was no longer tolerant of the random or discriminatory infliction of the penalty of death . . . evolving standards of decency required due consideration of the uniqueness of each individual defendant when imposing society's ultimate penalty.

This development in the American conscience would have presented no constitutional dilemma if fairness to the individual could be achieved without sacrificing the consistency and rationality promised in *Furman*. But over the past two decades, efforts to balance these competing constitutional commands have been to no avail. Experience has shown that the consistency and rationality promised in *Furman* are inversely related to the fairness owed the individual when considering a sentence of death. A step toward consistency is a step away from fairness. . . .

While one might hope that providing the sentencer with as much relevant mitigating evidence as possible will lead to more rational and consistent sentences, experience has taught otherwise. It seems that the decision whether a human being should live or die is so inherently subjective, rife with all of life's understandings, experiences, prejudices, and passions, that it inevitably defies the rationality and consistency required by the Constitution. . . .

The consistency promised in *Furman* and the fairness to the individual demanded in *Lockett* are not only inversely related but irreconcilable in the context of capital punishment. Any statute or procedure that could effectively eliminate arbitrariness from the administration of death would also restrict the sentencer's discretion to such an extent that the sentencer would be unable to give full consideration to the unique characteristics of each defendant and the circumstances of the offense.

By the same token, any statute of procedure that would provide the 20 sentencer with sufficient discretion to consider fully and act upon the unique circumstances of each defendant would "thro(w) open the back door to arbitrary and irrational sentencing." . . .

In my view, the proper course when faced with irreconcilable constitutional commands is not to ignore one or the other, nor to pretend that the dilemma does not exist, but to admit the futility of the effort to harmonize them. This means accepting the fact that the death penalty cannot be administered in accord with our Constitution. . . .

Perhaps one day this Court will develop procedural rules or verbal formulas that actually will provide consistency, fairness, and reliability in a capital-sentencing scheme. I am not optimistic that such a day will come. I am more optimistic, though, that this Court eventually will conclude that the effort to eliminate arbitrariness while preserving fairness "in the infliction of (death) is so plainly doomed to failure that it and the death penalty must be abandoned altogether." (*Godfrey v. Georgia*, 1980. . . .) I may not live to see that day, but I have faith that eventually it will arrive. The path the Court has chosen lessens us all.

Topics for Critical Thinking and Writing

1. Who is the "we" to whom Blackmun refers when he says, "We hope . . ." (para. 3)? We on the U.S. Supreme Court? We who are inclined to support the death penalty? We the people of Texas? We Americans? Or is this merely the so-called editorial "we" and of no substantive significance at all?

2. What does Blackmun mean by contrasting "procedural and substantive rules" of law (para. 12)?

3. Assuming for the sake of argument that Blackmun's criticisms of what he elsewhere called "the machinery of death" are correct, what do you think accounts for the failure of the criminal justice system in death-penalty states over the past generation (since *Furman v. Georgia* was decided in 1972) to operate "fairly, and with reasonable consistency" (para. 6) in accordance with "reason and objective standards" (para. 8)?

4. What does Blackmun mean when he says that "consistency and rationality" in death-penalty cases are "inversely related to the fairness owed the individual" offender (para. 17)?

5. Blackmun claims that the appellate courts (of Texas? of all death-penalty states? of the federal government?) have failed to give "meaningful judicial oversight to the administration of death by the states" (para. 11). After reading Blackmun's opinion, explain in an essay of 500 words what you think such "meaningful oversight" ought to involve.

Helen Prejean

Sister Helen Prejean, born in Baton Rouge in 1939, has been a member of the Order of the Sisters of St. Joseph of Medaille since 1957. In 1993, she achieved international fame with her book Dead Man Walking: An Eyewitness Account of the Death Penalty in the United States, *based on her experiences counseling prisoners on death row in Louisiana prisons. An excerpt is printed here. A film with the same title, starring Susan Sarandon (as Sister Helen) and Sean Penn, was released in 1995. When confronted with the argument that the death penalty is appropriate revenge for society to take on a murderer, Sister Helen said, "I would not want my death avenged — especially by government, which can't be trusted to control its own bureaucrats or collect taxes equitably or fill a pothole, much less decide which of its citizens to kill." The title is the editors'.*

Executions Are Too Costly — Morally

I think of the running debate I engage in with "church" people about the death penalty. "Proof texts" from the Bible usually punctuate these discussions without regard for the cultural context or literary genre of the passages invoked. (Will D. Campbell, a Southern Baptist minister and writer, calls this use of scriptural quotations "biblical quarterbacking.")

It is abundantly clear that the Bible depicts murder as a crime for which death is considered the appropriate punishment, and one is hard-pressed to find a biblical "proof text" in either the Hebrew Testament or the New Testament which unequivocally refutes this. Even Jesus' admonition "Let him without sin cast the first stone," when he was asked the appropriate punishment for an adulteress (John 8:7)—the Mosaic law prescribed death—should be read in its proper context. This passage is an "entrapment" story, which sought to show Jesus' wisdom in besting his adversaries. It is not an ethical pronouncement about capital punishment.

Similarly, the "eye for eye" passage from Exodus, which pro-death penalty advocates are fond of quoting, is rarely cited in its original context, in which it is clearly meant to limit revenge.

The passage, including verse 22, which sets the context reads:

> If, when men come to blows, they hurt a woman who is pregnant
> and she suffers a miscarriage, though she does not die of it, the man
> responsible must pay the compensation demanded of him by the
> woman's master; he shall hand it over after arbitration. But should she
> die, you shall give life for life, eye for eye, tooth for tooth, hand for
> hand, foot for foot, burn for burn, wound for wound, stroke for stroke.
> (Exodus 21:22–25)

In the example given (patently patriarchal: the woman is considered the negotiable property of her male master), it is clear that punishment is to be measured out according to the seriousness of the offense. If the child is lost but not the mother, the punishment is less grave than if both mother and child are lost. *Only* an eye for an eye, *only* a life for a life is the intent of the passage. Restraint was badly needed. It was not uncommon for an offended family or clan to slaughter entire communities in retaliation for an offense against one of their members.

Even granting the call for restraint in this passage, it is nonetheless clear—here and in numerous other instances throughout the Hebrew Bible—that the punishment for murder was death.

But we must remember that such prescriptions of the Mosaic Law were promulgated in a seminomadic culture in which the preservation of a fragile society—without benefit of prisons and other institutions—demanded quick, effective, harsh punishment of offenders. And we should note the numerous other crimes for which the Bible prescribes death as punishment:

contempt of parents (Exodus 21:15, 17; Leviticus 24:17);

trespass upon sacred ground (Exodus 19:12-13; Numbers 1:51; 18:7);

sorcery (Exodus 22:18; Leviticus 20:27);

bestiality (Exodus 22:19; Leviticus 20:15–16);

sacrifice to foreign gods (Exodus 22:20; Deuteronomy 13:1–9);

profaning the sabbath (Exodus 31:14);

adultery (Leviticus 20:10; Deuteronomy 22:22–24);

incest (Leviticus 20:11–13);

homosexuality (Leviticus 20:13);

and prostitution (Leviticus 21:19; Deuteronomy 22:13–21).

And this is by no means a complete list.

But no person with common sense would dream of appropriating such a moral code today, and it is curious that those who so readily invoke the "eye for an eye, life for life" passage are quick to shun other biblical prescriptions which also call for death, arguing that modern societies have evolved over the three thousand or so years since biblical times and no longer consider such exaggerated and archaic punishments appropriate.

Such nuances are lost, of course, in "biblical quarterbacking," and more and more I find myself steering away from such futile discussions. Instead, I try to articulate what I personally believe about Jesus and the ethical thrust he gave to humankind: an impetus toward compassion, a preference for disarming enemies without humiliating and destroying them, and a solidarity with poor and suffering people.

So, what happened to the impetus of love and compassion Jesus set blazing into history?

The first Christians adhered closely to the way of life Jesus had taught. They died in amphitheaters rather than offer homage to worldly emperors. They refused to fight in emperors' wars. But then a tragic diversion happened, which Elaine Pagels has deftly explored in her book *Adam, Eve, and the Serpent:* in 313 c.e. (Common Era) the Emperor Constantine entered the Christian church.

Pagels says, "Christian bishops, once targets for arrest, torture, and execution, now received tax exemptions, gifts from the imperial treasury, prestige, and even influence at court; the churches gained new wealth, power and prominence."

Unfortunately, the exercise of power practiced by Christians in alliance with the Roman Empire—with its unabashed allegiance to the sword—soon bore no resemblance to the purely moral persuasion that Jesus had taught.

In the fifth century, Pagels points out, Augustine provided the theological rationale the church needed to justify the use of violence by church and state governments. Augustine persuaded church authorities that "original sin" so damaged every person's ability to make moral choices that external control by church and state authorities over people's lives was necessary and justified. The "wicked" might be "coerced by the sword" to "protect the innocent," Augustine taught. And thus was legitimated for Christians the authority of secular government to "control" its subjects by coercive and violent means—even punishment by death.

In the latter part of the twentieth century, however, two flares of hope—Mohandas K. Gandhi and Martin Luther King—have demonstrated that Jesus' counsel to practice compassion and tolerance even toward one's enemies can effect social change. Susan Jacoby, analyzing the moral power that Gandhi and King unleashed in their campaigns for social justice, finds a unique form of aggression:

"'If everyone took an eye for an eye,' Gandhi said, 'the whole world would be blind.' But Gandhi did not want to take anyone's eye; he wanted to force the British out of India. . . ."

> Nonviolence and nonaggression are generally regarded as interchangeable concepts—King and Gandhi frequently used them that way—but nonviolence, as employed by Gandhi in India and by King in the American South, might reasonably be viewed as a highly disciplined form of aggression. If one defines aggression in the primary dictionary sense of "attack," nonviolent resistance proved to be the most powerful attack imaginable on the powers King and Gandhi were trying to overturn. The writings of both men are filled with references to love as a powerful force against oppression, and while the two leaders were not using the term "force" in the military sense, they certainly regarded nonviolence as a tactical weapon as well as an expression of high moral principle. The root meaning of Gandhi's concept of *satyagraha* . . . is "holding on to truth" . . . Gandhi also called *satyagraha* the "love force" or "soul force" and explained that he had discovered "in the earliest stages that pursuit of truth did not permit violence being inflicted on one's opponent, but that he must be weaned from error by patience and sympathy. . . . And patience means self-suffering." So the doctrine came to mean vindication of truth, not by the infliction of suffering on the opponent, but on one's self.
>
> King was even more explicit on this point: the purpose of civil disobedience, he explained many times, was to force the defenders of segregation to commit brutal acts in public and thus arouse the conscience of the world on behalf of those wronged by racism. King and Gandhi did not succeed because they changed the hearts and minds of southern sheriffs and British colonial administrators (although they did, in fact, change some minds) but because they *made the price of maintaining control too high for their opponents* [emphasis mine].

That, I believe, is what it's going to take to abolish the death penalty in this country: we must persuade the American people that government killings are too costly for us, not only financially, but—more important—morally.

The death penalty *costs* too much. Allowing our government to kill citizens compromises the deepest moral values upon which this country was conceived: the inviolable dignity of human persons.

I have no doubt that we will one day abolish the death penalty in   20 America. It will come sooner if people like me who know the truth about executions do our work well and educate the public. It will come slowly if we do not. Because, finally, I know that it is not a question of malice or ill will or meanness of spirit that prompts our citizens to support executions. It is, quite simply, that people don't know the truth of what is going on. That is not by accident. The secrecy surrounding executions makes it possible for executions to continue. I am convinced that if executions were made public, the torture and violence would be unmasked, and we would be shamed into abolishing executions. We would be embarrassed at the brutalization of the crowds that would gather to watch a man or woman be killed. And we would be humiliated to know that visitors from other countries — Japan, Russia, Latin America, Europe — were watching us kill our own citizens — we, who take pride in being the flagship of democracy in the world.

Topics for Critical Thinking and Writing

1. Suppose you interpret the "eye for eye" passage from Exodus (paras. 3–6) not as a "call for restraint" but as support for the death penalty. Does that mean no exceptions whatsoever — that everyone who kills another must be sentenced to death and executed? Would that require abandoning the distinction between murder and manslaughter or between first- and second-degree murder?

2. Prejean lists ten different crimes for which the Bible prescribes death as the punishment (para. 7) and says "no person with common sense would dream of appropriating [them] today" (para. 9). Do you agree? In an essay of 500 words, defend or criticize the proposition that the death penalty ought to be confined to the crime of first-degree murder.

3. Do you think that someone who endorses the biblical doctrine of "life for life, eye for eye" (para. 4) is also required by consistency to endorse the death penalty for some or all of the ten nonhomicidal crimes Prejean mentions (para. 7)? Explain.

4. In deciding whether to impose the death penalty for serious crimes, what guidance do you think a secular society, such as ours, ought to accept from the Bible? In an essay of 500 words, defend or criticize this thesis: "Biblical teachings ought to play a central role in deciding how we use the death penalty."

5. Prejean does not propose any alternative to the death penalty. Presumably she would favor some form of imprisonment for crimes involving death. She claims that the death penalty is inconsistent with "the inviolable dignity of human persons" (para. 19). Does consistency require her also to reject flogging? Solitary confinement in prison? Life imprisonment without the possibility of parole? Write a 500-word essay on this theme: "Severe Punishment and the Inviolable Dignity of Human Persons."

6. Prejean thinks that if executions were made public, Americans would soon decide to oppose the death penalty (para. 20). Do you agree? Write a 500-word essay for or against the following proposition: "Executions held in public would soon lead to public rejection of the death penalty."

Alex Kozinski and Sean Gallagher

Alex Kozinski is a judge on the Ninth U.S. Circuit Court of Appeals. Sean Gallagher was his law clerk when the two of them wrote this essay, published in the New York Times *on March 8, 1995.*

For an Honest Death Penalty

It is a staple of American politics that there is very strong support for the death penalty; in opinion polls, roughly 70 percent consistently favor it. Yet the popular will on this issue has been thwarted.

To be sure, we have many capital trials, convictions, and death sentences; we have endless and massively costly appeals; and a few people do get put to death every year. But compared to the number of death sentences, the number of executions is minuscule, and the gap is widening fast.

In 1972, the Supreme Court struck down all existing death penalty statutes and emptied the nation's death rows. Almost immediately states began passing death penalty laws to comply with the Court's reinterpretation of the Eighth Amendment. Since then more than 5,000 men and a handful of women have been given the death sentence; about 2,000 of those sentences have been set aside; fewer than 300 have been carried out.

THE WILL OF THE MAJORITY THWARTED

The reasons are complex, but they boil down to this: The Supreme Court's death penalty case law reflects an uneasy accommodation between the will of the popular majority, who favor capital punishment, and the objections of a much smaller—but ferociously committed—minority, who view it as a barbaric anachronism.

Assuaging death penalty opponents, the Court has devised a number   5 of extraordinary safeguards applicable to capital cases; but responding to complaints that these procedures were used for obstruction and delay, it has also imposed various limitations and exceptions to these safeguards. This pull and tug has resulted in a procedural structure—what Justice Harry A. Blackmun called a "machinery of death"—that is remarkably time-consuming, painfully cumbersome, and extremely expensive.

No one knows precisely how large a slice of our productive resources we force-feed to this behemoth, but we can make some educated guesses. To begin with, while 80 to 90 percent of all criminal cases end in plea bargains, capital cases almost always go to trial, and the trials are vastly more complex than their noncapital counterparts. If the defendant is sentenced to death, the case shuttles between the state and Federal courts for years, sometimes decades.

The Robert Alton Harris case, for example, found its way to the California Supreme Court six times; it was reviewed in Federal district court on five occasions, and each time it was appealed to the Ninth Circuit. The U.S. Supreme Court reviewed the case once on the merits, though on five other occasions it considered and declined Mr. Harris's request for review. Before Mr. Harris was executed in 1992, his case was reviewed by at least thirty judges and justices on more than twenty occasions over thirteen years.

State and local governments pay for the prosecution as well as for the defense team—which consists of at least two lawyers and a battery of investigators and experts; much of this money is spent even if the defendant eventually gets a lesser sentence. California reportedly spends $90 million a year on the death penalty. Once the case gets into Federal court, the United States starts picking up the defense tab and the sums can be daunting. In one recent case, a Federal district court paid defense lawyers more than $400,000, which didn't include the appeal or petition to the Supreme Court. Our own estimate is that death cases, on the average, cost taxpayers about a million dollars more than their noncapital counterparts. With 3,000 or so inmates on death row, to paraphrase Senator Everett Dirksen, pretty soon you get into real money.

Another significant cost is the burden on the courts. More than a quarter of the opinions published by the California Supreme Court from 1987 to 1993 involved death penalty cases. Since capital appeals are mandatory while appeals in other cases are discretionary, much of this burden is borne by other litigants who must vie for a diminished share of that court's attention. Estimating the judicial resources devoted to a capital case in the Federal courts is difficult, but a fair guess would be ten times those in other cases.

Perhaps the most significant cost of the death penalty is the lack of 10 finality. Death cases raise many more issues, and far more complex issues, than other criminal cases; convictions are attacked with more gusto and reviewed with more vigor in the courts. As a result, fully 40 percent of the death sentences imposed since 1972 have been vacated, sometimes five, ten or fifteen years after trial. One worries about the effect on the families of the victims, who have to endure the possibility—often the reality—of retrials, evidentiary hearings and last-minute stays of execution for years after the crime.

What are we getting in return? Even though we devote vast resources to the task, we come nowhere near executing the number of people we put on death row, and probably never will. We sentence about 250 inmates to death every year but have never executed more than forty. Just to keep up with the number of new death row inmates, states would have to sextuple the pace of executions; to eliminate the backlog, there would have to be one execution a day for the next twenty-six years.

This reality moots much of the traditional debate about the death penalty. Death penalty opponents have certainly not won the popular battle: Despite relentless assaults, the public remains firmly committed to capital punishment. Nor have opponents won the moral battle: Most of us continue to believe that those who show utter contempt for human life by committing remorseless, premeditated murder justly forfeit the right to their own life.

Other arguments against the death penalty also fall flat. For example, the fear that an innocent person may be convicted also applies to noncapital cases; no one, after all, can give back the twenty years someone wrongfully spends behind bars. Our system is therefore heavily geared to give the criminal defendant the benefit of the doubt. Wrongfully convicted defendants are rare; wrongfully convicted capital defendants are even rarer. The case where the innocent defendant is saved from the electric chair because the one-armed man shows up and confesses happens only in the movies.

Death penalty opponents are winning the war nevertheless. Unable to stop the majority altogether, they have managed to vastly increase the cost of imposing the death penalty while reducing the rate of executions to a trickle. This trend is not likely to be reversed. Even if we were willing to double or triple the resources we devote to the death penalty, even if we could put all other civil and criminal cases handled by the state and Federal courts on the back burner, it would be to no avail.

The great stumbling block is the lawyers: The jurisprudence of death 15 is so complex, so esoteric, so harrowing, this is the one area where there aren't nearly enough lawyers willing and able to handle all the current cases. In California, for example, almost half the pending death penalty appeals—more than 100—are on hold because the state can't find lawyers to handle them.

We are thus left in a peculiar limbo: We have constructed a machine that is extremely expensive, chokes our legal institutions, visits repeated trauma on victims' families, and ultimately produces nothing like the benefits we would expect from an effective system of capital punishment. This is surely the worst of all worlds.

Only two solutions suggest themselves, one judicial and the other political. The judicial solution would require a wholesale repudiation of the Supreme Court's death penalty jurisprudence. This is unlikely to happen. Over the last quarter-century, the Court has developed a substantial body of case law, consisting of some four score opinions, premised on the proposition that death *is* different and we must exercise extraordinary caution before taking human life. As we learned a few years back in the area of abortion, conservative justices are reluctant to reverse such major constitutional judgments.

A political solution may be no easier to achieve, but it's all we have left. The key to any such solution lies with the majority, precisely those among us who consistently strive for imposition of the death penalty for an ever-widening circle of crimes.

The majority must come to understand that this is a self-defeating tactic. Increasing the number of crimes punishable by death, widening the circumstances under which death may be imposed, obtaining more guilty verdicts and expanding death row populations will do nothing to insure that the very worst members of our society are put to death. The majority must accept that we may be willing and able to carry out thirty, forty, maybe fifty executions a year but that we cannot—will not— carry out one a day, every day, for the foreseeable future.

Once that reality is accepted, a difficult but essential next step is to   20 identify where we want to spend our death penalty resources. Instead of adopting a very expansive list of crimes for which the death penalty is an option, state legislatures should draft narrow statutes that reserve the death penalty for only the most heinous criminals. Everyone on death row is very bad, but even within that depraved group, it's possible to make moral judgments about how deeply someone has stepped down the rungs of Hell. Hitler was worse than Eichmann, though both were unspeakably evil by any standard; John Wayne Gacy, with two dozen or so brutal deaths on his conscience, must be considered worse than John Spenkelink, who killed only once.

Differentiating among depraved killers would force us to do some painful soul-searching about the nature of human evil, but it would have three significant advantages. First, it would mean that in a world of limited resources and in the face of a determined opposition, we will sentence to death only those we intend to execute. Second, it would insure that those who suffer the death penalty are the worst of the very bad—mass murderers, hired killers, airplane bombers, for example. This must be better than loading our death rows with many more than we can possibly execute, and then picking those who will die essentially at random.

Third, a political solution would put the process of accommodating divergent viewpoints back into the political arena, where it belongs. This would mean that the people, through their elected representatives, would reassert meaningful control over the process, rather than letting the courts and chance perform the accommodation on an ad hoc, irrational basis.

It will take a heroic act of will for the majority to initiate a political compromise on this emotionally charged issue. But as with democracy itself, the alternatives are much worse.

Topics for Critical Thinking and Writing

1. The authors, writing in 1995, reported that "roughly 70 percent" of the American public "consistently favor" the death penalty (para. 1). Consult the reference librarian in your college library, and verify whether this is true according to the most recent public-opinion polls (Gallup, Harris, or other polling agencies).

2. The authors say that "compared to the number of death sentences, the number of executions is minuscule" (para. 2). Verify this claim by consulting the most recent issue of *Capital Punishment* (issued by the U.S.

Department of Justice, Bureau of Justice Statistics). Exactly how many death sentences and executions occurred last year?

3. The authors cite the case of Robert Alton Harris and the multiple reviews his conviction and sentence received in the state and federal courts (para. 7). Is the reader supposed to infer from this case that (a) the courts are being manipulated by a convicted murderer who doesn't want to die? (b) the courts give extraordinary attention to capital cases to avoid making an irreversible mistake? or (c) neither of the above?

4. The authors say, "One worries about the effect [of these delays] on the families of the victims" (para. 10). This concern for the victims' families assumes that the defendants are guilty and were proved guilty by fair trials. Is it equally appropriate to worry about the effect on the families of defendants who were not guilty or were not proved guilty by a fair trial?

5. The authors identify three costs associated with the death penalty in this country (paras. 8–10). How would you rank their relative importance? Explain your view in an essay of 250 words.

6. The authors refer to "the benefits we would expect from an effective system of capital punishment" (para. 16), but they never tell us what those benefits are. Write a 500-word essay on this topic: "The (Alleged) Benefits of an Ideal Death-Penalty System."

7. Why do the authors insist that increasing the number of crimes punishable by death or increasing the number of persons sentenced to death "will do nothing to insure that the very worst members of our society are put to death" (para. 19)?

8. What is the "political solution" (para. 22) to the death penalty in our society that the authors favor? Do you agree or disagree with them? Why? Explain your position in an essay of 350 words.

For topical links related to the issue of the death penalty, see the companion Web site: **bedfordstmartins.com/barnetbedau.**

23

Drugs: Should Their Sale and Use Be Legalized?

William J. Bennett

William J. Bennett, born in Brooklyn in 1943, was educated at Williams College, the University of Texas, and Harvard Law School. Today he is most widely known as the author of The Book of Virtues: A Treasury of Great Moral Stories *(1993), but he has also been a public servant, Secretary of Education, and a director of the National Drug Control Policy. In 1989, during his tenure as "drug czar," he delivered at Harvard the address that we reprint. Among his recent publications are* The Broken Hearth: Reversing the Moral Collapse of the American Family *(2001),* Why We Fight: Moral Clarity and the War on Terrorism *(2002), and* A Century Turns: New Hopes, New Fears *(2009).*

Drug Policy and the Intellectuals

. . . The issue I want to address is our national drug policy and the intellectuals. Unfortunately, the issue is a little one-sided. There is a very great deal to say about our national drug policy, but much less to say about the intellectuals—except that by and large, they're against it. Why they should be against it is an interesting question, perhaps more a social-psychological question than a properly intellectual one. But whatever the reasons, I'm sorry to say that on properly intellectual grounds the arguments mustered against our current drug policy by America's intellectuals make for very thin gruel indeed.

I should point out, however, that in the fields of medical and scientific research, there is indeed serious and valuable drug-related work going on. But in the great public policy debate over drugs, the academic and intellectual communities have by and large had little to contribute, and little of that has been genuinely useful or for that matter mentally distinguished.

The field of national drug policy is wide open for serious research and serious thinking on both the theoretical and the practical levels; treatment and prevention; education; law enforcement and the criminal-justice system; the proper role of the federal government versus state and local jurisdictions; international diplomacy and foreign intelligence—these are only a few of the areas in which complex questions of policy and politics need to be addressed and resolved if our national drug strategy is to be successful. But apart from a handful of exceptions—including Mark Moore and Mark Kleiman here at the Kennedy School, and Harvard's own, or ex-own, James Q. Wilson—on most of these issues the country's major ideas factories have not just shut down, they've hardly even tooled up.

It's not that most intellectuals are indifferent to the drug issue, though there may be some of that, too. Rather, they seem complacent and incurious. They've made up their minds, and they don't want to be bothered with further information or analysis, further discussion or debate, especially when it comes from Washington. What I read in the opinion columns of my newspaper or in my monthly magazine or what I hear from the resident intellectual on my favorite television talk show is something like a developing intellectual consensus on the drug question. That consensus holds one or both of these propositions to be self-evident: (a) *that the drug problem in America is absurdly simple, and easily solved;* and (b) *that the drug problem in America is a lost cause.*

As it happens, each of these apparently contradictory propositions is false. As it also happens, both are disputed by the *real* experts on drugs in the United States—and there are many such experts, though not the kind the media like to focus on. And both are disbelieved by the American people, whose experience tells them, emphatically, otherwise.

The consensus has a political dimension, which helps account for its seemingly divergent aspect. In some quarters of the far Right there is a tendency to assert that the drug problem is essentially a problem of the inner city, and therefore that what it calls for, essentially, is quarantine. "If those people want to kill themselves off with drugs, let them kill themselves off with drugs," would be a crude but not too inaccurate way of summarizing this position. But this position has relatively few adherents. On the Left, it is something else, something much more prevalent. There we see whole cadres of social scientists, abetted by whole armies of social workers, who seem to take it as catechism that the problem facing us isn't drugs at all, it's poverty, or racism, or some other equally large and intractable social phenomenon. If we want to eliminate the drug problem, these people say, we must first eliminate the "root causes" of drugs, a hopelessly daunting task at which, however, they also happen to make their living. Twenty-five years ago, no one would have suggested that we must first address the root causes of racism before fighting segregation. We fought it, quite correctly, by passing laws against unacceptable conduct. The causes of racism was an interesting question, but the moral imperative was to end it as soon as possible and by all reasonable means: education, prevention, the media and not least of all, the law. So too with drugs.

What unites these two views of the drug problem from opposite sides of the political spectrum is that the issue, inevitably, is a policy of neglect. To me that is a scandalous position, intellectually as well as morally scandalous. For I believe, along with those I have named as the real experts on drugs, and along with most Americans, that the drug problem is not easy but difficult—very difficult in some respects. But at the same time, and again along with those same experts and with the American people, I believe it is not a lost cause but a solvable one. I will return to this theme, but let me pause here to note one specific issue on which the Left/Right consensus has lately come to rest; a position around which it has been attempting to build national sentiment. That position is legalization.

It is indeed bizarre to see the likes of Anthony Lewis and William F. Buckley lining up on the same side of an issue; but such is the perversity that the so-called legalization debate engenders. To call it a "debate," though, suggests that the arguments in *favor* of drug legalization are rigorous, substantial, and serious. They are not. They are, at bottom, a series of superficial and even disingenuous ideas that more sober minds recognize as a recipe for a public policy disaster. Let me explain.

Most conversations about legalization begin with the notion of "taking the profit out of the drug business." But has anyone bothered to examine carefully how the drug business works? As a recent *New York Times* article vividly described, instances of drug dealers actually earning huge sums of money are relatively rare. There are some who do, of course, but most people in the crack business are the low-level "runners" who do not make much money at all. Many of them work as prostitutes or small-time criminals to supplement their drug earnings. True, a lot of naive kids are lured into the drug world by visions of a life filled with big money and fast cars. That's what they think the good life holds for them. But the reality is far different. Many dealers, in the long run, wind up smoking more crack than they sell. Their business becomes a form of slavery: long hours, dangerous work, small pay, and, as the *Times* pointed out, no health benefits either. In many cases, steady work at McDonald's over time would in fact be a step *up* the income scale for these kids. What does straighten them out, it seems, is not a higher minimum wage, or less stringent laws, but the dawning realization that dealing drugs invariably leads to murder or to prison. And that's exactly why we have drug laws—to make drug use a wholly unattractive choice.

Legalization, on the other hand, removes that incentive to stay away   10
from a life of drugs. Let's be honest—there are some people who are going to smoke crack whether it is legal or illegal. But by keeping it illegal, we maintain the criminal sanctions that persuade most people that the good life cannot be reached by dealing drugs.

The big lie behind every call for legalization is that making drugs legally available would "solve" the drug problem. But has anyone actually thought about what that kind of legalized regime would look like?

Would crack be legal? How about PCP? Or smokable heroin? Or ice? Would they all be stocked at the local convenience store, perhaps just a few blocks from an elementary school? And how much would they cost? If we taxed drugs and made them expensive, we would still have the black market and crime problems that we have today; if we sold them cheap to eliminate the black market cocaine at, say, $10 a gram—then we would succeed in making a daily dose of cocaine well within the allowance budget of most sixth-graders. When pressed, the advocates of legalization like to sound courageous by proposing that we begin by legalizing marijuana. But they have absolutely nothing to say on the tough questions of controlling other, more powerful drugs, and how they would be regulated.

As far as marijuana is concerned, let me say this: I didn't have to become drug czar to be opposed to legalized marijuana. As Secretary of Education I realized that, given the state of American education, the last thing we needed was a policy that made widely available a substance that impairs memory, concentration, and attention span; why in God's name foster the use of a drug that makes you stupid?

Now what would happen if drugs were suddenly made legal? Legalization advocates deny that the amount of drug use would be affected. I would argue that if drugs are easier to obtain, drug use will soar. In fact, we have just undergone a kind of cruel national experiment in which drugs became cheap and widely available: That experiment is called the crack epidemic. When powder cocaine was expensive and hard to get, it was found almost exclusively in the circles of the rich, the famous, or the privileged. Only when cocaine was dumped into the country, and a $3 vial of crack could be bought on street corners did we see cocaine use skyrocket, this time largely among the poor and disadvantaged. The lesson is clear: If you're in favor of drugs being sold in stores like aspirin, you're in favor of boom times for drug users and drug addicts. With legalization, drug use will go up, way up.

When drug use rises, who benefits and who pays? Legalization advocates think that the cost of enforcing drug laws is too great. But the real question—the question they never ask—is what does it cost not to enforce those laws. The price that American society would have to pay for legalized drugs, I submit, would be intolerably high. We would have more drug-related accidents at work, on the highways, and in the airways. We would have even bigger losses in worker productivity. Our hospitals would be filled with drug emergencies. We would have more school kids on dope, and that means more dropouts. More pregnant women would buy legal cocaine, and then deliver tiny, premature infants. I've seen them in hospitals across the country. It's a horrid form of child abuse, and under a legalization scheme, we will have a lot more of it. For those women and those babies, crack has the same effect whether it's legal or not. Now, if you add to that the costs of treatment, social welfare, and insurance, you've got the price of legalization. So I ask you again, who benefits, who pays?

What about crime? To listen to legalization advocates, one might think that street crime would disappear with the repeal of our drug laws. They haven't done their homework. Our best research indicates that most drug criminals were into crime well before they got into drugs. Making drugs legal would just be a way of subsidizing their habit. They would continue to rob and steal to pay for food, for clothes, for entertainment. And they would carry on with their drug trafficking by undercutting the legalized price of drugs and catering to teenagers, who, I assume, would be nominally restricted from buying drugs at the corner store.

All this should be old news to people who understand one clear lesson of prohibition. When we had laws against alcohol, there was less consumption of alcohol, less alcohol-related disease, fewer drunken brawls, and a lot less public drunkenness. And contrary to myth, there is no evidence that Prohibition caused big increases in crime. No one is suggesting that we go back to Prohibition. But at least we should admit that legalized alcohol, which is responsible for some 100,000 deaths a year, is hardly a model for drug policy. As Charles Krauthammer has pointed out, the question is not which is worse, alcohol or drugs. The question is can we accept both legalized alcohol *and* legalized drugs? The answer is no.

So it seems to me that on the merits of their arguments, the legalizers have no case at all. But there is another, crucial point I want to make on this subject, unrelated to costs or benefits. Drug use — especially heavy drug use — destroys human character. It destroys dignity and autonomy, it burns away the sense of responsibility, it subverts productivity, it makes a mockery of virtue. As our Founders would surely recognize, a citizenry that is perpetually in a drug-induced haze doesn't bode well for the future of self-government. Libertarians don't like to hear this, but it is a truth that everyone knows who has seen drug addiction up close. And don't listen to people who say drug users are only hurting themselves: They hurt parents, they destroy families, they ruin friendships. And let me remind this audience, here at a great university, that drugs are a threat to the life of the mind; anyone who values that life should have nothing but contempt for drugs. Learned institutions should regard drugs as the plague.

That's why I find the surrender of many of America's intellectuals to arguments for drug legalization so odd and so scandalous. For the past three months, I have been traveling the country, visiting drug-ridden neighborhoods, seeing treatment and prevention programs in action, talking to teachers, cops, parents, kids. These, it seems, are the real drug experts — they've witnessed the problem firsthand. But unlike some prominent residents of Princeton, Madison, Cambridge, or Palo Alto, they refuse to surrender. They are in the community, reclaiming their neighborhoods, working with police, setting up community activities, getting addicts into treatment, saving their children.

Too many American intellectuals don't know about this and seem not to want to know. Their hostility to the national war on drugs is, I think, partly rooted in a general hostility to law enforcement and criminal justice. That's why they take refuge in pseudosolutions like legalization, which stress only the treatment side of the problem. Whenever discussion turns to the need for more police and stronger penalties, they cry that our constitutional liberties are in jeopardy. Well, yes, they are in jeopardy, but not from drug *policy:* On this score, the guardians of our Constitution can sleep easy. Constitutional liberties are in jeopardy, instead, from drugs themselves, which every day scorch the earth of our common freedom. Yes, sometimes cops go too far, and when they do they should be held accountable. But these excursions from the law are the exception. Meanwhile drug dealers violate our rights every day as a rule, as a norm, as their modus operandi. Why can't our civil libertarians see that?

When we are not being told by critics that law enforcement threat-   20
ens our liberties, we are being told that it won't work. Let me tell you that law enforcement does work and why it must work. Several weeks ago I was in Wichita, Kansas, talking to a teenage boy who was now in his fourth treatment program. Every time he had finished a previous round of treatment, he found himself back on the streets, surrounded by the same cheap dope and tough hustlers who had gotten him started in the first place. He was tempted, he was pressured, and he gave in. Virtually any expert on drug treatment will tell you that, for most people, no therapy in the world can fight temptation on that scale. As long as drugs are found on any street corner, no amount of treatment, no amount of education can finally stand against them. Yes, we need drug treatment and drug education. But drug treatment and drug education need law enforcement. And that's why our strategy calls for a bigger criminal justice system: as a form of drug *prevention.*

To the Americans who are waging the drug war in their own front yards every day, this is nothing new, nothing startling. In the San Jose section of Albuquerque, New Mexico, just two weeks ago, I spoke to Rudy Chavez and Jack Candelarla, and police chief Sam Baca. They had wanted to start a youth center that would keep their kids safe from the depredations of the street. Somehow it never worked—until together they set up a police station right in the heart of drug-dealing territory. Then it worked. Together with the cops, the law-abiding residents cleared the area, and made it safe for them and their children to walk outside their homes. The youth center began to thrive.

Scenes like this are being played out all across the country. I've seen them in Tulsa, Dallas, Tampa, Omaha, Des Moines, Seattle, New York. Americans—many of them poor, black, or Hispanic—have figured out what the armchair critics haven't. Drugs may threaten to destroy their neighborhoods, but *they* refuse to stand by and let it happen. *They* have discovered that it is possible not only to fight back, but to win. In some elite circles, the talk may be only of the sad state of the helpless and the hopeless, but while these circles talk on, the helpless and the hopeless themselves are carrying out a national drug policy. They are fighting back.

When I think of these scenes I'm reminded of what John Jacob, president of the Urban League, said recently: Drugs are destroying more black families than poverty ever did. And I'm thankful that many of these poor families have the courage to fight drugs now, rather than declaring themselves passive victims of root causes.

America's intellectuals — and here I think particularly of liberal intellectuals — have spent much of the last nine years decrying the social programs of two Republican administrations in the name of the defenseless poor. But today, on the one outstanding issue that disproportionately hurts the poor — that is wiping out many of the poor — where are the liberal intellectuals to be found? They are on the editorial and op-ed pages, and in magazines like this month's *Harper's*, telling us with an ignorant sneer that our drug policy won't work. Many universities, too, which have been quick to take on the challenges of sexism, racism, and ethnocentrism, seem content on the drug issue to wag a finger at us, or to point it mindlessly at American society in general. In public policy schools, there is no shortage of arms control scholars. Isn't it time we had more drug control scholars?

The current situation won't do. The failure to get serious about the   25 drug issue is, I think, a failure of civic courage — the kind of courage shown by many who have been among the main victims of the drug scourge. But it betokens as well a betrayal of the self-declared mission of intellectuals as the bearers of society's conscience. There may be reasons for this reluctance, this hostility, this failure. But I would remind you that not all crusades led by the U.S. government, enjoying broad popular support, are brutish, corrupt, and sinister. What is brutish, corrupt, and sinister is the murder and mayhem being committed in our cities' streets. One would think that a little more concern and serious thought would come from those who claim to care so deeply about America's problems.

So I stand here this afternoon with a simple message for America's pundits and academic cynics: Get serious about drug policy. We are grappling with complicated, stubborn policy issues, and I encourage you to join us. Tough work lies ahead, and we need serious minds to focus on how we should use the tools that we have in the most effective way.

I came to this job with realistic expectations. I am not promising a drug-free America by next week, or even by next year. But that doesn't mean that success is out of reach. Success will come — I've seen a lot of it already — in slow, careful steps. Its enemies are timidity, petulance, false expectations. But its three greatest foes remain surrender, despair, and neglect. So, for the sake of their fellow citizens, I invite America's deep thinkers to get with the program, or at the very least, to get in the game.

Topics for Critical Thinking and Writing

1. In paragraph 6, Bennett draws a parallel between racism and drug abuse and suggests that society ought to fight the one (drug abuse) as it successfully fought the other (racism). What do you think of this parallel? Explain.

2. Bennett identifies two propositions on the issue of drug abuse that he believes are accepted by "consensus" thinking in America (para. 4). What are these propositions, and what is Bennett's view of them? How does he try to convince the reader to agree with him?

3. What are Bennett's main objections to solving the problem of drug abuse by legalizing drugs?

4. At the time he gave this lecture, Bennett was a cigarette smoker trying to break the habit. Do you see any inconsistency in his opposing legalized marijuana and tolerating (and even using) legalized tobacco?

5. What measures besides stricter law enforcement does Bennett propose for wide-scale adoption to reduce drug abuse? Why does he object to relying only on such measures?

6. Bennett is known to be (or to have been) a heavy gambler, a high roller. On one occasion he said to the press, "It is true that I have gambled large sums of money. . . . I have done too much gambling, and this is not an example I wish to set." Does his admitted heavy gambling weaken his arguments about drugs?

James Q. Wilson

James Q. Wilson (b. 1931) is the first Senior Fellow at Boston College's Clough Center for the Study of Constitutional Democracy and Distinguished Scholar in its Department of Political Science. He is the author of Thinking about Crime *(1975),* Bureaucracy *(1989), and* Crime: Public Policies for Crime Control *(2002), the coauthor of* Crime and Human Nature *(1985), and the coeditor of* Drugs and Crime *(1990). He has also written widely on culture, government, and politics. The essay that we reprint appeared originally in February 1990 in* Commentary, *a conservative magazine.*

Against the Legalization of Drugs

In 1972, the president appointed me chairman of the National Advisory Council for Drug Abuse Prevention. Created by Congress, the Council was charged with providing guidance on how best to coordinate the national war on drugs. (Yes, we called it a war then, too.) In those days, the drug we were chiefly concerned with was heroin. When I took office, heroin use had been increasing dramatically. Everybody was worried that this increase would continue. Such phrases as "heroin epidemic" were commonplace.

That same year, the eminent economist Milton Friedman published an essay in *Newsweek* in which he called for legalizing heroin. His argument was on two grounds: As a matter of ethics, the government has no right to tell people not to use heroin (or to drink or to commit suicide); as a matter of economics, the prohibition of drug use imposes costs on society that far exceed the benefits. Others, such as the psychoanalyst Thomas Szasz, made the same argument.

We did not take Friedman's advice. (Government commissions rarely do.) I do not recall that we even discussed legalizing heroin, though we did discuss (but did not take action on) legalizing a drug, cocaine, that many people then argued was benign. Our marching orders were to figure out how to win the war on heroin, not to run up the white flag of surrender.

That was 1972. Today, we have the same number of heroin addicts that we had then—half a million, give or take a few thousand. Having that many heroin addicts is no trivial matter; these people deserve our attention. But not having had an increase in that number for over fifteen years is also something that deserves our attention. What happened to the "heroin epidemic" that many people once thought would overwhelm us?

The facts are clear: A more or less stable pool of heroin addicts has   5
been getting older, with relatively few new recruits. In 1976 the average age of heroin users who appeared in hospital emergency rooms was about twenty-seven; ten years later it was thirty-two. More than two-thirds of all heroin users appearing in emergency rooms are now over the age of thirty. Back in the early 1970s, when heroin got onto the national political agenda, the typical heroin addict was much younger, often a teenager. Household surveys show the same thing—the rate of opiate use (which includes heroin) has been flat for the better part of two decades. More fine-grained studies of inner-city neighborhoods confirm this. John Boyle and Ann Brunswick found that the percentage of young blacks in Harlem who use heroin fell from 8 percent in 1970–71 to about 3 percent in 1975–76.

Why did heroin lose its appeal for young people? When the young blacks in Harlem were asked why they stopped, more than half mentioned "trouble with the law" or "high cost" (and high cost is, of course, directly the result of law enforcement). Two-thirds said that heroin hurt their health; nearly all said they had had a bad experience with it. We need not rely, however, simply on what they said. In New York City in 1973–75, the street price of heroin rose dramatically and its purity sharply declined, probably as a result of the heroin shortage caused by the success of the Turkish government in reducing the supply of opium base and of the French government in closing down heroin-processing laboratories located in and around Marseilles. These were short-lived gains for, just as Friedman predicted, alternative sources of supply— mostly in Mexico—quickly emerged. But the three-year heroin shortage interrupted the easy recruitment of new users.

Health and related problems were no doubt part of the reason for the reduced flow of recruits. Over the preceding years, Harlem youth had watched as more and more heroin users died of overdoses, were poisoned by adulterated doses, or acquired hepatitis from dirty needles. The word got around: Heroin can kill you. By 1974 new hepatitis cases and drug-overdose deaths had dropped to a fraction of what they had been in 1970.

Alas, treatment did not seem to explain much of the cessation in drug use. Treatment programs can and do help heroin addicts, but treatment did not explain the drop in the number of *new* users (who by definition had never been in treatment) nor even much of the reduction in the number of experienced users.

No one knows how much of the decline to attribute to personal observation as opposed to high prices or reduced supply. But other evidence suggests strongly that price and supply played a large role. In 1972 the National Advisory Council was especially worried by the prospect that U.S. servicemen returning to this country from Vietnam would bring their heroin habits with them. Fortunately, a brilliant study by Lee Robins of Washington University in St. Louis put that fear to rest. She measured drug use of Vietnam veterans shortly after they had returned home. Though many had used heroin regularly while in Southeast Asia, most gave up the habit when back in the United States. The reason: Here, heroin was less available and sanctions on its use were more pronounced. Of course, if a veteran had been willing to pay enough—which might have meant traveling to another city and would certainly have meant making an illegal contact with a disreputable dealer in a threatening neighborhood in order to acquire a (possibly) dangerous dose—he could have sustained his drug habit. Most veterans were unwilling to pay this price, and so their drug use declined or disappeared.

RELIVING THE PAST

Suppose we had taken Friedman's advice in 1972. What would have   10
happened? We cannot be entirely certain, but at a minimum we would have placed the young heroin addicts (and, above all, the prospective addicts) in a very different position from the one in which they actually found themselves. Heroin would have been legal. Its price would have been reduced by 95 percent (minus whatever we chose to recover in taxes). Now that it could be sold by the same people who make aspirin, its quality would have been assured—no poisons, no adulterants. Sterile hypodermic needles would have been readily available at the neighborhood drugstore, probably at the same counter where the heroin was sold. No need to travel to big cities or unfamiliar neighborhoods—heroin could have been purchased anywhere, perhaps by mail order.

There would no longer have been any financial or medical reason to avoid heroin use. Anybody could have afforded it. We might have tried to prevent children from buying it, but as we have learned from our efforts to prevent minors from buying alcohol and tobacco, young people have a way of penetrating markets theoretically reserved for adults. Returning Vietnam veterans would have discovered that Omaha and Raleigh had been converted into the pharmaceutical equivalent of Saigon.

Under these circumstances, can we doubt for a moment that heroin use would have grown exponentially? Or that a vastly larger supply of new users would have been recruited? Professor Friedman is a Nobel Prize–winning economist whose understanding of market forces is profound. What did he think would happen to consumption under his legalized regime? Here are his words: "Legalizing drugs might increase the number of addicts, but it is not clear that it would. Forbidden fruit is attractive, particularly to the young."

Really? I suppose that we should expect no increase in Porsche sales if we cut the price by 95 percent, no increase in whiskey sales if we cut the price by a comparable amount—because young people only want fast cars and strong liquor when they are "forbidden." Perhaps Friedman's uncharacteristic lapse from the obvious implications of price theory can be explained by a misunderstanding of how drug users are recruited. In his 1972 essay he said that "drug addicts are deliberately made by pushers, who give likely prospects their first few doses free." If drugs were legal it would not pay anybody to produce addicts, because everybody would buy from the cheapest source. But as every drug expert knows, pushers do not produce addicts. Friends or acquaintances do. In fact, pushers are usually reluctant to deal with nonusers because a nonuser could be an undercover cop. Drug use spreads in the same way any fad or fashion spreads: Somebody who is already a user urges his friends to try, or simply shows already-eager friends how to do it.

But we need not rely on speculation, however plausible, that lowered prices and more abundant supplies would have increased heroin usage. Great Britain once followed such a policy and with almost exactly those results. Until the mid-1960s, British physicians were allowed to prescribe heroin to certain classes of addicts. (Possessing these drugs without a doctor's prescription remained a criminal offense.) For many years this policy worked well enough because the addict patients were typically middle-class people who had become dependent on opiate painkillers while undergoing hospital treatment. There was no drug culture. The British system worked for many years, not because it prevented drug abuse but because there was no problem of drug abuse that would test the system.

All that changed in the 1960s. A few unscrupulous doctors began 15 passing out heroin in wholesale amounts. One doctor prescribed almost six hundred thousand heroin tablets—that is, over thirteen pounds—in just one year. A youthful drug culture emerged with a demand for drugs far different from that of the older addicts. As a result, the British government required doctors to refer users to government-run clinics to receive their heroin.

But the shift to clinics did not curtail the growth in heroin use. Throughout the 1960s the number of addicts increased—the late John Kaplan of Stanford estimated by fivefold—in part as a result of the diversion of heroin from clinic patients to new users on the streets. An addict would bargain with the clinic doctor over how big a dose he would receive. The patient wanted as much as he could get, the doctor wanted to give as little as was needed. The patient had an advantage in this conflict because the doctor could not be certain how much was really needed. Many patients would use some of their "maintenance" dose and sell the remaining part to friends, thereby recruiting new addicts. As the clinics learned of this, they began to shift their treatment away from heroin and toward methadone, an addictive drug that, when taken orally, does not produce a "high" but will block the withdrawal pains associated with heroin abstinence.

Whether what happened in England in the 1960s was a miniepidemic or an epidemic depends on whether one looks at numbers or at rates of change. Compared to the United States, the numbers were small. In 1960 there were sixty-eight heroin addicts known to the British government; by 1968 there were two thousand in treatment and many more who refused treatment. (They would refuse in part because they did not want to get methadone at a clinic if they could get heroin on the street.) Richard Hartnoll estimates that the actual number of addicts in England is five times the number officially registered. At a minimum, the number of British addicts increased by thirtyfold in ten years; the actual increase may have been much larger.

In the early 1980s the numbers began to rise again, and this time nobody doubted that a real epidemic was at hand. The increase was estimated to be 40 percent a year. By 1982 there were thought to be twenty thousand heroin users in London alone. Geoffrey Pearson reports that many cities—Glasgow, Liverpool, Manchester, and Sheffield among them—were now experiencing a drug problem that once had been largely confined to London. The problem, again, was supply. The country was being flooded with cheap, high-quality heroin, first from Iran and then from Southeast Asia.

The United States began the 1960s with a much larger number of heroin addicts and probably a bigger at-risk population than was the case in Great Britain. Even though it would be foolhardy to suppose that the British system, if installed here, would have worked the same way or with the same results, it would be equally foolhardy to suppose that a combination of heroin available from leaky clinics and from street dealers who faced only minimal law-enforcement risks would not have produced a much greater increase in heroin use than we actually experienced. My guess is that if we had allowed either doctors or clinics to prescribe heroin, we would have had far worse results than were produced in Britain, if for no other reason than the vastly larger number of addicts with which we began. We would have had to find some way to police thousands (not scores) of physicians and hundreds (not dozens) of clinics. If the British civil service found it difficult to keep heroin in the hands of addicts and out of the hands of recruits when it was dealing with a few hundred people, how well would the American civil service have accomplished the same tasks when dealing with tens of thousands of people?

BACK TO THE FUTURE

Now cocaine, especially in its potent form, crack, is the focus of 20 attention. Now as in 1972 the government is trying to reduce its use. Now as then some people are advocating legalization. Is there any more reason to yield to those arguments today than there was almost two decades ago?[1]

I think not. If we had yielded in 1972 we almost certainly would have had today a permanent population of several million, not several hundred thousand, heroin addicts. If we yield now we will have a far more serious problem with cocaine.

Crack is worse than heroin by almost any measure. Heroin produces a pleasant drowsiness and, if hygienically administered, has only the physical side effects of constipation and sexual impotence. Regular heroin use incapacitates many users, especially poor ones, for any productive work or social responsibility. They will sit nodding on a street corner, helpless but at least harmless. By contrast, regular cocaine use leaves the user neither helpless nor harmless. When smoked (as with crack) or injected, cocaine produces instant, intense, and short-lived euphoria. The experience generates a powerful desire to repeat it. If the drug is readily available, repeat use will occur. Those people who progress to "bingeing" on cocaine become devoted to the drug and its effects to the exclusion of almost all other considerations—job, family, children, sleep, food, even sex. Dr. Frank Gawin at Yale and Dr. Everett Ellinwood at Duke report that a substantial percentage of all high-dose, binge users become uninhibited, impulsive, hypersexual, compulsive, irritable, and hyperactive. Their moods vacillate dramatically, leading at times to violence and homicide.

Women are much more likely to use crack than heroin, and if they are pregnant, the effects on their babies are tragic. Douglas Besharov, who has been following the effects of drugs on infants for twenty years, writes that nothing he learned about heroin prepared him for the devastation of cocaine. Cocaine harms the fetus and can lead to physical deformities or neurological damage. Some crack babies have for all practical

---

[1] I do not here take up the question of marijuana. For a variety of reasons—its widespread use and its lesser tendency to addict—it presents a different problem from cocaine or heroin. For a penetrating analysis, see Mark Kleiman, *Marijuana: Costs of Abuse, Costs of Control* (Greenwood Press, 217 pp.). [Wilson's note.]

purposes suffered a disabling stroke while still in the womb. The long-term consequences of this brain damage are lowered cognitive ability and the onset of mood disorders. Besharov estimates that about thirty thousand to fifty thousand such babies are born every year, about seven thousand in New York City alone. There may be ways to treat such infants, but from everything we now know the treatment will be long, difficult, and expensive. Worse, the mothers who are most likely to produce crack babies are precisely the ones who, because of poverty or temperament, are least able and willing to obtain such treatment. In fact, anecdotal evidence suggests the crack mothers are likely to abuse their infants.

The notion that abusing drugs such as cocaine is a "victimless crime" is not only absurd but dangerous. Even ignoring the fetal drug syndrome, crack-dependent people are, like heroin addicts, individuals who regularly victimize their children by neglect, their spouses by improvidence, their employers by lethargy, and their co-workers by carelessness. Society is not and could never be a collection of autonomous individuals. We all have a stake in ensuring that each of us displays a minimal level of dignity, responsibility, and empathy. We cannot, of course, coerce people into goodness, but we can and should insist that some standards must be met if society itself—on which the very existence of the human personality depends—is to persist. Drawing the line that defines those standards is difficult and contentious, but if crack and heroin use do not fall below it, what does?

The advocates of legalization will respond by suggesting that my 25 picture is overdrawn. Ethan Nadelmann of Princeton argues that the risk of legalization is less than most people suppose. Over twenty million Americans between the ages of eighteen and twenty-five have tried cocaine (according to a government survey), but only a quarter million use it daily. From this Nadelmann concludes that at most 3 percent of all young people who try cocaine develop a problem with it. The implication is clear: Make the drug legal and we only have to worry about 3 percent of our youth.

The implication rests on a logical fallacy and a factual error. The fallacy is this: The percentage of occasional cocaine users who become binge users *when the drug is illegal* (and thus expensive and hard to find) tells us nothing about the percentage who will become dependent when the drug is legal (and thus cheap and abundant). Drs. Gawin and Ellinwood report, in common with several other researchers, that controlled or occasional use of cocaine changes to compulsive and frequent use "when access to the drug increases" or when the user switches from snorting to smoking. More cocaine more potently administered alters, perhaps sharply, the proportion of "controlled" users who become heavy users.

The factual error is this: The federal survey Nadelmann quotes was done in 1985, *before* crack had become common. Thus the probability of becoming dependent on cocaine was derived from the responses of users who snorted the drug. The speed and potency of cocaine's action increases dramatically when it is smoked. We do not yet know how greatly the advent of crack increases the risk of dependency, but all the clinical evidence suggests that the increase is likely to be large.

It is possible that some people will not become heavy users even when the drug is readily available in its most potent form. So far there are no scientific grounds for predicting who will and who will not become dependent. Neither socioeconomic background nor personality traits differentiate between casual and intensive users. Thus, the only way to settle the question of who is correct about the effect of easy availability on drug use, Nadelmann or Gawin and Ellinwood, is to try it and see. But the social experiment is so risky as to be no experiment at all, for if cocaine is legalized and if the rate of its abusive use increases dramatically, there is no way to put the genie back in the bottle, and it is not a kindly genie.

HAVE WE LOST?

Many people who agree that there are risks in legalizing cocaine or heroin still favor it because, they think, we have lost the war on drugs. "Nothing we have done has worked" and the current federal policy is just "more of the same." Whatever the costs of greater drug use, surely they would be less than the costs of our present, failed efforts.

That is exactly what I was told in 1972—and heroin is not quite as 30 bad a drug as cocaine. We did not surrender and we did not lose. We did not win, either. What the nation accomplished then was what most efforts to save people from themselves accomplish: The problem was contained and the number of victims minimized, all at a considerable cost in law enforcement and increased crime. Was the cost worth it? I think so, but others may disagree. What are the lives of would-be addicts worth? I recall some people saying to me then, "Let them kill themselves." I was appalled. Happily, such views did not prevail.

Have we lost today? Not at all. High-rate cocaine use is not commonplace. The National Institute of Drug Abuse (NIDA) reports that less than 5 percent of high-school seniors used cocaine within the last thirty days. Of course this survey misses young people who have dropped out of school and miscounts those who lie on the questionnaire, but even if we inflate the NIDA estimate by some plausible percentage, it is still not much above 5 percent. Medical examiners reported in 1987 that about 1,500 died from cocaine use; hospital emergency rooms reported about 30,000 admissions related to cocaine abuse.

These are not small numbers, but neither are they evidence of a nationwide plague that threatens to engulf us all. Moreover, cities vary greatly in the proportion of people who are involved with cocaine. To get city-level data we need to turn to drug tests carried out on arrested persons, who obviously are more likely to be drug users than the average citizen. The National Institute of Justice, through its Drug Use Forecasting (DUF) project, collects urinalysis data on arrestees in twenty-two cities. As we have already seen, opiate (chiefly heroin) use has been flat or declining in most of these cities over the last decade. Cocaine use has gone up sharply, but with great variation among cities. New York, Philadelphia, and Washington, D.C., all report that two-thirds or more of their arrestees tested positive for cocaine, but in Portland, San Antonio, and Indianapolis the percentage was one-third or less.

In some neighborhoods, of course, matters have reached crisis proportions. Gangs control the streets, shootings terrorize residents, and drug dealing occurs in plain view. The police seem barely able to contain matters. But in these neighborhoods—unlike at Palo Alto cocktail parties—the people are not calling for legalization, they are calling for help. And often not much help has come. Many cities are willing to do almost anything about the drug problem except spend more money on it. The federal government cannot change that; only local voters and politicians can. It is not clear that they will.

It took about ten years to contain heroin. We have had experience with crack for only about three or four years. Each year we spend perhaps $11 billion on law enforcement (and some of that goes to deal with marijuana) and perhaps $2 billion on treatment. Large sums, but not sums that should lead anyone to say, "We just can't afford this anymore."

The illegality of drugs increases crime, partly because some users 35 turn to crime to pay for their habits, partly because some users are stimulated by certain drugs (such as crack or PCP) to act more violently or ruthlessly than they otherwise would, and partly because criminal organizations seeking to control drug supplies use force to manage their markets. These also are serious costs, but no one knows how much they would be reduced if drugs were legalized. Addicts would no longer steal to pay black-market prices for drugs, a real gain. But some, perhaps a great deal, of that gain would be offset by the great increase in the number of addicts. These people, nodding on heroin or living in the delusion-ridden high of cocaine, would hardly be ideal employees. Many would steal simply to support themselves, since snatch-and-grab, opportunistic crime can be managed even by people unable to hold a regular job or plan an elaborate crime. Those British addicts who get their supplies from government clinics are not models of law-abiding decency. Most are in crime, and though their per-capita rate of criminality may be lower thanks to the cheapness of their drugs, the total volume of crime they produce may be quite large. Of course, society could decide to support all unemployable addicts on welfare, but that would mean that gains from lowered rates of crime would have to be offset by large increases in welfare budgets.

Proponents of legalization claim that the costs of having more addicts around would be largely if not entirely offset by having more money available with which to treat and care for them. The money would come from taxes levied on the sale of heroin and cocaine.

To obtain this fiscal dividend, however, legalization's supporters must first solve an economic dilemma. If they want to raise a lot of money to pay for welfare and treatment, the tax rate on the drugs will have to be quite high. Even if they themselves do not want a high rate, the politicians' love of "sin taxes" would probably guarantee that it would be high anyway. But the higher the tax, the higher the price of the drug, and the higher the price the greater the likelihood that addicts will turn to crime to find the money for it and that criminal organizations will be formed to sell tax-free drugs at below-market rates. If we managed to keep taxes (and thus prices) low, we would get that much less money to pay for welfare and treatment and more people could afford to become addicts. There may be an optimal tax rate for drugs that maximizes revenue while minimizing crime, bootlegging, and the recruitment of new addicts, but our experience with alcohol does not suggest that we know how to find it.

THE BENEFITS OF ILLEGALITY

The advocates of legalization find nothing to be said in favor of the current system except, possibly, that it keeps the number of addicts smaller than it would otherwise be. In fact, the benefits are more substantial than that.

First, treatment. All the talk about providing "treatment on demand" implies that there is a demand for treatment. That is not quite right. There are some drug-dependent people who genuinely want treatment and will remain in it if offered; they should receive it. But there are far more who want only short-term help after a bad crash; once stabilized and bathed, they are back on the street again, hustling. And even many of the addicts who enroll in a program honestly wanting help drop out after a short while when they discover that help takes time and commitment. Drug-dependent people have very short time horizons and a weak capacity for commitment. These two groups—those looking for a quick fix and those unable to stick with a long-term fix—are not easily helped. Even if we increase the number of treatment slots—as we should—we would have to do something to make treatment more effective.

One thing that can often make it more effective is compulsion. 40 Douglas Anglin of UCLA, in common with many other researchers, has found that the longer one stays in a treatment program, the better the chances of a reduction in drug dependency. But he, again like most other researchers, has found that dropout rates are high. He has also found, however, that patients who enter treatment under legal compulsion stay in the program longer than those not subject to such pressure. His research on the California civil commitment program, for example, found that heroin users involved with its required drug-testing program had over the long term a lower rate of heroin use than similar addicts who were free of such constraints. If for many addicts compulsion is a useful component of treatment, it is not clear how compulsion could be achieved in a society in which purchasing, possessing, and using the drug were legal. It could be managed, I suppose, but I would not want to have to answer the challenge from the American Civil Liberties Union that it is wrong to compel a person to undergo treatment for consuming a legal commodity.

Next, education. We are now investing substantially in drug-education programs in the schools. Though we do not yet know for certain what will work, there are some promising leads. But I wonder how credible such programs would be if they were aimed at dissuading children from doing something perfectly legal. We could, of course, treat drug education like smoking education: Inhaling crack and inhaling tobacco are both legal, but you should not do it because it is bad for you. That tobacco is bad for you is easily shown; the Surgeon General has seen to that. But what do we say about crack? It is pleasurable, but devoting yourself to so much pleasure is not a good idea (though perfectly legal)? Unlike tobacco, cocaine will not give you cancer or emphysema, but it will lead you to neglect your duties to family, job, and neighborhood? Everybody is doing cocaine, but you should not?

Again, it might be possible under a legalized regime to have effective drug-prevention programs, but their effectiveness would depend heavily, I think, on first having decided that cocaine use, like tobacco use, is purely a matter of practical consequences; no fundamental moral significance attaches to either. But if we believe—as I do—that dependency on certain mind-altering drugs *is* a moral issue and that their illegality rests in part on their immorality, then legalizing them undercuts, if it does not eliminate altogether, the moral message.

That message is at the root of the distinction we now make between nicotine and cocaine. Both are highly addictive; both have harmful physical effects. But we treat the two drugs differently, not simply because nicotine is so widely used as to be beyond the reach of effective prohibition, but because its use does not destroy the user's essential humanity. Tobacco shortens one's life, cocaine debases it. Nicotine alters one's habits, cocaine alters one's soul. The heavy use of crack, unlike the heavy use of tobacco, corrodes those natural sentiments of sympathy and duty that constitute our human nature and make possible our social life. To say, as does Nadelmann, that distinguishing morally between tobacco and cocaine is "little more than a transient prejudice" is close to saying that morality itself is but a prejudice.

THE ALCOHOL PROBLEM

Now we have arrived where many arguments about legalizing drugs begin: Is there any reason to treat heroin and cocaine differently from the way we treat alcohol?

There is no easy answer to that question because, as with so many 45 human problems, one cannot decide simply on the basis either of moral principles or of individual consequences; one has to temper any policy by a commonsense judgment of what is possible. Alcohol, like heroin, cocaine, PCP, and marijuana, is a drug—that is, a mood-altering substance—and consumed to excess it certainly has harmful consequences: auto accidents, barroom fights, bedroom shootings. It is also, for some people, addictive. We cannot confidently compare the addictive powers of these drugs, but the best evidence suggests that crack and heroin are much more addictive than alcohol.

Many people, Nadelmann included, argue that since the health and financial costs of alcohol abuse are so much higher than those of cocaine or heroin abuse, it is hypocritical folly to devote our efforts to preventing cocaine or drug use. But as Mark Kleiman of Harvard has pointed out, this comparison is quite misleading. What Nadelmann is doing is showing that a _legalized_ drug (alcohol) produces greater social harm than _illegal_ ones (cocaine and heroin). But of course. Suppose that in the 1920s we had made heroin and cocaine legal and alcohol illegal. Can anyone doubt that Nadelmann would now be writing that it is folly to continue our ban on alcohol because cocaine and heroin are so much more harmful?

And let there be no doubt about it—widespread heroin and cocaine use are associated with all manner of ills. Thomas Bewley found that the mortality rate of British heroin addicts in 1968 was twenty-eight times as high as the death rate of the same age group of nonaddicts, even though in England at the time an addict could obtain free or low-cost heroin and clean needles from British clinics. Perform the following mental experiment: Suppose we legalized heroin and cocaine in this country. In what proportion of auto fatalities would the state police report that the driver was nodding off on heroin or recklessly driving on a coke high? In what proportion of spouse-assault and child-abuse cases would the local police report that crack was involved? In what proportion of industrial accidents would safety investigators report that the forklift or drill-press operator was in a drug-induced stupor or frenzy? We do not know exactly what the proportion would be, but anyone who asserts that it would not be much higher than it is now would have to believe that these drugs have little appeal except when they are illegal. And that is nonsense.

An advocate of legalization might concede that social harm—perhaps harm equivalent to that already produced by alcohol—would follow from making cocaine and heroin generally available. But at least, he might add, we would have the problem "out in the open" where it could be treated as a matter of "public health." That is well and good, _if_ we knew how to treat—that is, cure—heroin and cocaine abuse. But we do not know how to do it for all the people who would need such help. We are having only limited success in coping with chronic alcoholics. Addictive behavior is immensely difficult to change, and the best methods for changing it—living in drug-free therapeutic communities, becoming faithful members of Alcoholics Anonymous or Narcotics Anonymous—require great personal commitment, a quality that is, alas, in short supply among the very persons—young people, disadvantaged people—who are often most at risk for addiction.

Suppose that today we had, not fifteen million alcohol abusers, but half a million. Suppose that we already knew what we have learned from our long experience with the widespread use of alcohol. Would we make whiskey legal? I do not know, but I suspect there would be a lively debate. The surgeon general would remind us of the risks alcohol poses to pregnant women. The National Highway Traffic Safety Administration would point to the likelihood of more highway fatalities caused by drunk drivers. The Food and Drug Administration might find that there is a nontrivial increase in cancer associated with alcohol consumption. At the same time the police would report great difficulty in keeping illegal whiskey out of our cities, officers being corrupted by bootleggers, and alcohol addicts often resorting to crime to feed their habit. Libertarians, for their part, would argue that every citizen has a right to drink anything he wishes and that drinking is, in any event, a "victimless crime."

However the debate might turn out, the central fact would be that the problem was still, at that point, a small one. The government cannot legislate away the addictive tendencies in all of us, nor can it remove completely even the most dangerous addictive substances. But it can cope with harms when the harms are still manageable. 50

SCIENCE AND ADDICTION

One advantage of containing a problem while it is still containable is that it buys time for science to learn more about it and perhaps to discover a cure. Almost unnoticed in the current debate over legalizing drugs is that basic science has made rapid strides in identifying the underlying neurological processes involved in some forms of addiction. Stimulants such as cocaine and amphetamines alter the way certain brain cells communicate with one another. That alteration is complex and not entirely understood, but in simplified form it involves modifying the way in which a neurotransmitter called dopamine sends signals from one cell to another.

When dopamine crosses the synapse between two cells, it is in effect carrying a message from the first cell to activate the second one. In certain parts of the brain that message is experienced as pleasure. After the message is delivered, the dopamine returns to the first cell. Cocaine apparently blocks this return, or "reuptake," so that the excited cell and others nearby continue to send pleasure messages. When the exaggerated high produced by cocaine-influenced dopamine finally ends, the brain cells may (in ways that are still a matter of dispute) suffer from an extreme lack of dopamine, thereby making the individual unable to experience any pleasure at all. This would explain why cocaine users often feel so depressed after enjoying the drug. Stimulants may also affect the way in which other neurotransmitters, such as serotonin and noradrenaline, operate.

Whatever the exact mechanism may be, once it is identified it becomes possible to use drugs to block either the effect of cocaine or its tendency to produce dependency. There have already been experiments using desipramine, imipramine, bromocriptine, carbamazepine, and other chemicals. There are some promising results.

Tragically, we spend very little on such research, and the agencies funding it have not in the past occupied very influential or visible posts in the federal bureaucracy. If there is one aspect of the "war on drugs" metaphor that I dislike, it is its tendency to focus attention almost exclusively on the troops in the trenches, whether engaged in enforcement or treatment, and away from the research-and-development efforts back on the home front where the war may ultimately be decided.

I believe that the prospects of scientists in controlling addiction will   55
be strongly influenced by the size and character of the problem they face. If the problem is a few hundred thousand chronic, high-dose users of an illegal product, the chances of making a difference at a reasonable cost will be much greater than if the problem is a few million chronic users of legal substances. Once a drug is legal, not only will its use increase but many of those who then use it will prefer the drug to the treatment: They will want the pleasure, whatever the cost to themselves or their families, and they will resist—probably successfully—any effort to wean them away from experiencing the high that comes from inhaling a legal substance.

IF I AM WRONG . . .

No one can know what our society would be like if we changed the law to make access to cocaine, heroin, and PCP easier. I believe, for reasons given, that the result would be a sharp increase in use, a more widespread degradation of the human personality, and a greater rate of accidents and violence.

I may be wrong. If I am, then we will needlessly have incurred heavy costs in law enforcement and some forms of criminality. But if I am right, and the legalizers prevail anyway, then we will have consigned millions of people, hundreds of thousands of infants, and hundreds of neighborhoods to a life of oblivion and disease. To the lives and families destroyed by alcohol we will have added countless more destroyed by cocaine, heroin, PCP, and whatever else a basement scientist can invent.

Human character is formed by society; indeed, human character is inconceivable without society, and good character is less likely in a bad society. Will we, in the name of an abstract doctrine of radical individualism, and with the false comfort of suspect predictions, decide to take the chance that somehow individual decency can survive amid a more general level of degradation?

I think not. The American people are too wise for that, whatever the academic essayists and cocktail-party pundits may say. But if Americans today are less wise than I suppose, then Americans at some future time will look back on us now and wonder, what kind of people were they that they could have done such a thing?

Topics for Critical Thinking and Writing

1. Wilson objects to the idea that using cocaine is a "victimless crime" (para. 24; see also para. 49). A crime is said to be "victimless" when the offender consents to the act and those who do not consent are not harmed. Why does it matter to Wilson, do you think, whether using illegal drugs is a victimless crime?

2. Wilson accuses Ethan Nadelmann, an advocate of legalization, of committing "a logical fallacy and a factual error" (para. 26). What is the fallacy, and what is the error?

3. Wilson raises the question of whether we "won" or "lost" the war on heroin in the 1970s and whether we will do any better with the current war on cocaine (paras. 30–31). What would you regard as convincing evidence that we are winning the war on drugs? Losing it?

4. In his criticism of those who would legalize drugs, Wilson points to what he regards as an inescapable "economic dilemma" (para. 37). What is this dilemma? Do you see any way around it?

5. Economists tell us that we can control the use of a good or service by controlling the cost (thus probably reducing the demand), by ignoring the cost and controlling the supply, or by doing both. In the war on drugs, which of these three economic strategies does Wilson apparently favor, and why?

Milton Friedman

Milton Friedman (1912–2006), winner of a Nobel Prize in economics, was born in Brooklyn, New York. Educated at Rutgers University, the University of Chicago, and Columbia University, Friedman, a leading conservative economist, had considerable influence on economic thought in America through his academic and popular writings. We reprint a piece that appeared in the New York Times *in 1998.*

There's No Justice in the War on Drugs

Twenty-five years ago, President Richard M. Nixon announced a "War on Drugs." I criticized the action on both moral and expediential grounds in my *Newsweek* column of May 1, 1972, "Prohibition and Drugs":

On ethical grounds, do we have the right to use the machinery of government to prevent an individual from becoming an alcoholic or a drug addict? For children, almost everyone would answer at least a qualified yes. But for responsible adults, I, for one, would answer no. Reason with the potential addict, yes. Tell him the consequences, yes. Pray for and with him, yes. But I believe that we have no right to use force, directly or indirectly, to prevent a fellow man from committing suicide, let alone from drinking alcohol or taking drugs.

That basic ethical flaw has inevitably generated specific evils during the past quarter century, just as it did during our earlier attempt at alcohol prohibition.

1. The use of informers. Informers are not needed in crimes like robbery and murder because the victims of those crimes have a strong incentive to report the crime. In the drug trade, the crime consists of a transaction between a willing buyer and willing seller. Neither has any incentive to report a violation of law. On the contrary, it is in the self-interest of both that the crime not be reported. That is why informers are needed. The use of informers and the immense sums of money at stake inevitably generate corruption—as they did during Prohibition. They also lead to violations of the civil rights of innocent people, to the shameful practices of forcible entry and forfeiture of property without due process.

As I wrote in 1972: "Addicts and pushers are not the only ones corrupted. Immense sums are at stake. It is inevitable that some relatively low-paid police and other government officials—and some high-paid ones as well—will succumb to the temptation to pick up easy money."

2. Filling the prisons. In 1970, 200,000 people were in prison. 5 Today, 1.6 million people are. Eight times as many in absolute number, six times as many relative to the increased population. In addition, 2.3 million are on probation and parole. The attempt to prohibit drugs is by far the major source of the horrendous growth in the prison population.

There is no light at the end of that tunnel. How many of our citizens do we want to turn into criminals before we yell "enough"?

3. Disproportionate imprisonment of blacks. Sher Hosonko, at the time Connecticut's director of addiction services, stressed this effect of drug prohibition in a talk given in June 1995:

> Today in this country, we incarcerate 3,109 black men for every
> 100,000 of them in the population. Just to give you an idea of the
> drama in this number, our closest competitor for incarcerating black
> men is South Africa. South Africa—and this is pre–Nelson Mandela and
> under an overt public policy of apartheid—incarcerated 729 black men
> for every 100,000. Figure this out: In the land of the Bill of Rights, we

jail over four times as many black men as the only country in the world that advertised a political policy of apartheid.

4. Destruction of inner cities. Drug prohibition is one of the most important factors that have combined to reduce our inner cities to their present state. The crowded inner cities have a comparative advantage for selling drugs. Though most customers do not live in the inner cities, most sellers do. Young boys and girls view the swaggering, affluent drug dealers as role models. Compared with the returns from a traditional career of study and hard work, returns from dealing drugs are tempting to young and old alike. And many, especially the young, are not dissuaded by the bullets that fly so freely in disputes between competing drug dealers—bullets that fly only because dealing drugs is illegal. Al Capone epitomizes our earlier attempt at Prohibition; the Crips and Bloods epitomize this one.

5. Compounding the harm to users. Prohibition makes drugs exorbitantly expensive and highly uncertain in quality. A user must associate with criminals to get the drugs, and many are driven to become criminals themselves to finance the habit. Needles, which are hard to get, are often shared, with the predictable effect of spreading disease. Finally, an addict who seeks treatment must confess to being a criminal in order to qualify for a treatment program. Alternatively, professionals who treat addicts must become informers or criminals themselves.

6. Undertreatment of chronic pain. The Federal Department of 10 Health and Human Services has issued reports showing that two-thirds of all terminal cancer patients do not receive adequate pain medication, and the numbers are surely higher in nonterminally ill patients. Such serious undertreatment of chronic pain is a direct result of the Drug Enforcement Agency's pressures on physicians who prescribe narcotics.

7. Harming foreign countries. Our drug policy has led to thousands of deaths and enormous loss of wealth in countries like Colombia, Peru, and Mexico, and has undermined the stability of their governments. All because we cannot enforce our laws at home. If we did, there would be no market for imported drugs. There would be no Cali cartel. The foreign countries would not have to suffer the loss of sovereignty involved in letting our "advisers" and troops operate on their soil, search their vessels, and encourage local militaries to shoot down their planes. They could run their own affairs, and we, in turn, could avoid the diversion of military forces from their proper function.

Can any policy, however high-minded, be moral if it leads to widespread corruption, imprisons so many, has so racist an effect, destroys our inner cities, wreaks havoc on misguided and vulnerable individuals, and brings death and destruction to foreign countries?

"Your condition is serious, Mr. Reynolds, but fortunately I recently scored some excellent weed that should alleviate your symptoms."

Topics for Critical Thinking and Writing

1. State in one sentence the thesis of Friedman's essay.

2. Which of the seven reasons Friedman cites in favor of revising our "war on drugs" do you find most convincing? Explain why, in a short essay of 100 words.

3. Friedman distinguishes between "moral and expediential" objections to current drug policy (para. 1). What does he mean by this distinction? Which kind of objection do you think is the most persuasive? Why?

4. If a policy, a practice, or an individual act is unethical or immoral, then it violates some ethical standard or moral norm. What norms or standards does Friedman think that our current drug policy violates?

5. Does Friedman favor a policy on addictive (and currently illegal) drugs that is like our policy on alcohol? Explain in an essay of 250 words how the two policies might differ.

Elliott Currie

Elliott Currie is professor of criminology, law, and society at the University of California, Irvine, and until 2009, vice chair of the Eisenhower Foundation in

Washington, D.C., an organization that supports drug-abuse-prevention programs. We reprint an essay that appeared in the journal Dissent *in 1993; the essay is a slightly revised version of a chapter that first appeared in one of Currie's books,* Reckoning: Drugs, the Cities, and the American Future *(1993).*

Toward a Policy on Drugs

One of the strongest implications of what we now know about the causes of endemic drug abuse is that the criminal-justice system's effect on the drug crisis will inevitably be limited. That shouldn't surprise us in the 1990s; it has, after all, been a central argument of drug research since the 1950s. Today, as the drug problem has worsened, the limits of the law are if anything even clearer. But that does not mean that the justice system has no role to play in a more effective strategy against drugs. Drugs will always be a "law-enforcement problem" in part, and the real job is to define what we want the police and the courts to accomplish.

We will never, for reasons that will shortly become clear, punish our way out of the drug crisis. We can, however, use the criminal-justice system, in small but significant ways, to improve the prospects of drug users who are now caught in an endless loop of court, jail, and street. And we can use law enforcement, in small but significant ways, to help strengthen the ability of drug-ridden communities to defend themselves against violence, fear, and demoralization. Today the criminal-justice system does very little of the first and not enough of the second. But doing these things well will require far-reaching changes in our priorities. Above all, we will have to shift from an approach in which discouraging drug use through punishment and fear takes central place to one that emphasizes three very different principles: the reintegration of drug abusers into productive life, the reduction of harm, and the promotion of community safety.

This is a tall order, but, as we shall see, something similar is being practiced in many countries that suffer far less convulsing drug problems than we do. Their experience suggests that a different and more humane criminal-justice response to drugs is both possible and practical. Today, there is much debate about the role of the justice system in a rational drug policy—but for the most part, the debate is between those who would intensify the effort to control drugs through the courts and prisons and those who want to take drugs out of the orbit of the justice system altogether. I do not think that either approach takes sufficient account of the social realities of drug abuse; and both, consequently, exaggerate the role of regulatory policies in determining the shape and seriousness of the problem. But those are not the only alternatives. In between, there is a range of more promising strategies—what some Europeans call a "third way"—that is more attuned to those realities and more compatible with our democratic values.

One response to the failure of the drug war has been to call for more of what we've already done—even harsher sentences, still more money for jails and prisons—on the grounds that we have simply not provided enough resources to fight the war effectively. That position is shared by the Bush administration and many Democrats in Congress as well. But the strategy of upping the ante cannot work; and even to attempt it on a large scale would dramatically increase the social costs that an overreliance on punishment has already brought. We've seen that the effort to contain the drug problem through force and fear has already distorted our justice system in fundamental ways and caused a rippling of secondary costs throughout the society as a whole. Much more of this would alter the character of American society beyond recognition. And it would not solve the drug problem.

Why wouldn't more of the same do the job?   5

To understand why escalating the war on drugs would be unlikely to make much difference—short of efforts on a scale that would cause unprecedented social damage—we need to consider how the criminal-justice system is, in theory, *supposed* to work to reduce drug abuse and drug-related crime. Criminologists distinguish between two mechanisms by which punishment may decrease illegal behavior. One is "incapacitation," an unlovely term that simply means that locking people up will keep them—as long as they are behind bars—from engaging in the behavior we wish to suppress. The other is "deterrence," by which we mean either that people tempted to engage in the behavior will be persuaded otherwise by the threat of punishment ("general deterrence"), or that individuals, once punished, will be less likely to engage in the behavior again ("specific deterrence"). What makes the drug problem so resistant to even very heavy doses of criminalization is that neither mechanism works effectively for most drug offenders—particularly those most heavily involved in the drug subcultures of the street.

The main reason why incapacitation is unworkable as a strategy against drug offenders is that there are so many of them that a serious attempt to put them all—or even just the "hard core"—behind bars is unrealistic, even in the barest fiscal terms. This is obvious if we pause to recall the sheer number of people who use hard drugs in the United States. Consider the estimates of the number of people who have used drugs during the previous year provided annually by the NIDA (National Institute on Drug Abuse) Household Survey—which substantially *understates* the extent of hard-drug use. Even if we exclude the more than 20 million people who used marijuana in the past year, the number of hard-drug users is enormous: the survey estimates over six million cocaine users in 1991 (including over a million who used crack), about 700,000 heroin users, and 5.7 million users of hallucinogens and inhalants. Even if we abandon the aim of imprisoning less serious hard-drug users, thus allowing the most conservative accounting of the costs of incapacitation, the problem remains staggering: by the lowest estimates, there are no fewer than two million hard-core abusers of cocaine and heroin alone.

If we take as a rough approximation that about 25 percent of America's prisoners are behind bars for drug offenses, that gives us roughly 300,000 drug offenders in prison at any given point—and this after several years of a hugely implemented war mainly directed at lower-level dealers and street drug users. We have seen what this flood of offenders has done to the nation's courts and prisons, but what is utterly sobering is that even this massive effort at repression has barely scratched the surface: according to the most optimistic estimate, we may at any point be incarcerating on drug-related charges about one-eighth of the country's hard-core cocaine and heroin abusers. And where drug addiction is truly endemic, the disparity is greater. By 1989 there were roughly 20,000 drug offenders on any given day in New York State's prisons, but there were an estimated 200,000 to 250,000 *heroin* addicts in New York City alone. To be sure, these figures obscure the fact that many prisoners behind bars for *non*drug offenses are also hard-core drug users; but the figures are skewed in the other direction by the large (if unknown) number of active drug dealers who are not themselves addicted.

Thus, though we cannot quantify these proportions with any precision, the basic point should be clear: the pool of *serious* addicts and active dealers is far, far larger than the numbers we now hold in prison—even in the midst of an unprecedented incarceration binge that has made us far and away the world's leader in imprisonment rates.

What would it mean to expand our prison capacity enough to put 10 the *majority* of hard-core users and dealers behind bars for long terms? To triple the number of users and low-level dealers behind bars, even putting two drug offenders to a cell, would require about 300,000 new cells. At a conservative estimate of about $100,000 per cell, that means a $30 billion investment in construction alone. If we then assume an equally conservative estimate of about $25,000 in yearly operating costs per inmate, we add roughly $15 billion a year to our current costs. Yet this would leave the majority of drug dealers and hard-core addicts still on the streets and, of course, would do nothing to prevent new ones from emerging in otherwise unchanged communities to take the place of those behind bars.

It is not entirely clear, moreover, what that huge expenditure would, in fact, accomplish. For if the goal is to prevent the drug dealing and other crimes that addicts commit, the remedy may literally cost more than the disease. Although drug addicts do commit a great deal of crime, most of them are very minor ones, mainly petty theft and small-time drug dealing. This pattern has been best illuminated in the study of Harlem heroin addicts by Bruce Johnson and his co-workers. Most of the street addicts in this study were "primarily thieves and small-scale drug distributors who avoided serious crimes, like robbery, burglary, assault." The average income per nondrug crime among these addicts was $35. Even among the most criminally active group—what these researchers called "robber-dealers"—the annual income from crime amounted on average to only about $21,000, and for the great majority—about 70 percent—of less active addict-criminals, it ranged from $5,000 to $13,000. At the same time, the researchers estimated that the average cost per day of confining one addict in a New York City jail cell was roughly $100, or $37,000 a year. Putting these numbers together, Johnson and his co-workers came to the startling conclusion that it would cost considerably more to lock up all of Harlem's street addicts than to simply let them continue to "take care of business" on the street.

If we cannot expect much from intensified criminalization, would the legalization of hard drugs solve the drug crisis?

No: it would not. To understand why, we need to consider the claims for legalization's effects in the light of what we know about the roots and meanings of endemic drug abuse. First, however, we need to step back in order to sort out exactly what we *mean* by "legalization" — a frustratingly vague and often confused term that means very different things to different interpreters. Many, indeed, who argue most vehemently one way or the other about the merits of legalization are not really clear just what it is they are arguing *about*.

At one end of the spectrum are those who mean by legalization the total deregulation of the production, sale, and use of all drugs — hard and soft. Advocates of this position run the gamut from right-wing economists to some staunch liberals, united behind the principle that government has no business interfering in individuals' choice to ingest whatever substances they desire. Most who subscribe to that general view would add several qualifiers: for example, that drugs (like alcohol) should not be sold to minors, or that drug advertising should be regulated or prohibited, or (less often) that drugs should be sold only in government-run stores, as alcohol is in some states. But these are seen as necessary, if sometimes grudging, exceptions to the general rule that private drug transactions should not be the province of government intervention. For present purposes, I will call this the "free-market" approach to drug control, and describe its central aim as the "deregulation" of the drug market.

Another approach would not go so far as to deregulate the drug 15 trade, but would opt for the controlled dispensation of drugs to addicts who have been certified by a physician, under strict guidelines as to amounts and conditions of use. Something like this "medical model," in varying forms, guided British policy toward heroin after the 1920s. Under the so-called British system, addicts could receive heroin from physicians or clinics — but the private production and distribution of heroin was always subject to strong penalties, as was the use of the drug except in its medical or "pharmaceutical" form. (A small-scale experiment in cocaine prescription is presently being tried in the city of Liverpool.) Since the seventies, the British have largely abandoned prescribing heroin in favor of methadone — a synthetic opiate that blocks the body's craving for heroin but, among other things, produces less of a pleasurable "high" and lasts considerably longer. The practice of dispensing methadone to heroin addicts came into wide use in the United States in the 1960s and remains a major form of treatment. Methadone prescription, of course, does not "legalize" heroin, and the possession or sale of methadone itself is highly illegal outside of the strictly controlled medical relationship.

Still another meaning sometimes given to legalization is what is more accurately called the "decriminalization" of drug *use*. We may continue to define the production and sale of certain drugs as crimes and subject them to heavy penalties, but not punish those who only *use* the drugs (or have small amounts in their possession), or punish them very lightly—with small fines, for example, rather than jail. Something close to this is the practice in Holland, which is often wrongly perceived as a country that has legalized drugs. Though drug use remains technically illegal, Dutch policy is to focus most law-enforcement resources on sales, especially on larger traffickers, while dealing with users mainly through treatment programs and other social services, rather than the police and courts.

Another aspect of Dutch policy illustrates a further possible meaning of legalization: we may selectively decriminalize *some* drugs, in some amounts, and not others. The Dutch, in practice—though not in law—have tolerated both sale and use of small amounts of marijuana and hashish, but not heroin or cocaine. A German court has recently ruled that possession of small amounts of hashish and marijuana is not a crime, and, indeed, marijuana possession has largely been decriminalized in some American states, though usually as a matter of practical policy rather than legislation.

Let me make my own view clear. I think much would be gained if we followed the example of some European countries and moved toward decriminalization of the drug user. I also think there is a strong argument for treating marijuana differently from the harder drugs, and that there is room for careful experiment with strictly controlled medical prescription for some addicts. For reasons that will become clear, decriminalization is not a panacea; it will not end the drug crisis, but it could substantially decrease the irrationality and inhumanity of our present punitive war on drugs.

The free-market approach, on the other hand, is another matter entirely. Some variant of that approach is more prominent in drug-policy debates in the United States than in other developed societies, probably because it meshes with a strongly individualistic and antigovernment political culture. Indeed, the degree to which the debate over drug policy has been dominated by the clash between fervent drug "warriors" and equally ardent free-market advocates is a peculiarly American phenomenon. Much of that clash is about philosophical principles, and addressing those issues in detail would take more space than we have. My aim here is simply to examine the empirical claims of the free-market perspective in the light of what we know about the social context of drug abuse. Here the free-market view fails to convince. It greatly exaggerates the benefits of deregulation while simultaneously underestimating the potential costs.

There is no question that the criminalization of drugs produces nega- 20 tive secondary consequences—especially in the unusually punitive form that criminalization has taken in the United States. Nor is there much question that this argues for a root-and-branch rethinking of our current punitive strategy—to which we'll return later in this essay—especially our approach to drug *users*.

But proponents of full-scale deregulation of hard drugs also tend to gloss over the very real primary costs of drug abuse—particularly on the American level—and to exaggerate the degree to which the multiple pathologies surrounding drug use in America are simply an unintended result of a "prohibitionist" regulatory policy. No country now legalizes the sale of hard drugs. Yet no other country has anything resembling the American drug problem. That alone should tell us that more than prohibition is involved in shaping the magnitude and severity of our drug crisis. But there is more technical evidence as well. It confirms that much (though, of course, not all) of the harm caused by endemic drug abuse is intrinsic to the impact of hard drugs themselves (and the street cultures in which drug abuse is embedded) within the context of a glaringly unequal, depriving, and deteriorating society. And it affirms that we will not substantially reduce that harm without attacking the social roots of the extraordinary demand for hard drugs in the United States. Just as we cannot punish our way out of the drug crisis, neither will we escape its grim toll by deregulating the drug market.

The most important argument for a free-market approach has traditionally been that it would reduce or eliminate the crime and violence now inextricably entwined with addiction to drugs and with the drug trade. In this view it is precisely the illegality of drug use that is responsible for drug-related crime—which, in turn, is seen as by far the largest part of the overall problem of urban violence. Criminal sanctions against drugs, as one observer insists, "cause the bulk of murders and property crime in major urban areas." Because criminalization makes drugs far more costly than they would otherwise be, addicts are forced to commit crimes in order to gain enough income to afford their habits. Moreover, they are forced to seek out actively criminal people in order to obtain their drugs, which exposes them to even more destructive criminal influences. At the same time, the fact that the drug trade is illegal means both that it is hugely profitable and that the inevitable conflicts and disputes over "turf" or between dealers and users cannot be resolved or moderated by legal mechanisms, and hence are usually resolved by violence.

For all of these reasons, it is argued, outlawing drugs has the unintended, but inevitable, effect of causing a flood of crime and urban violence that would not exist otherwise and sucking young people, especially, into a bloody drug trade. If we legalize the sale and use of hard drugs, the roots of drug-related violence would be severed, and much of the larger crisis of criminal violence in the cities would disappear.

But the evidence suggests that although this view contains an element of truth, it is far too simplistic—and that it relies on stereotypical assumptions about the relationship between drugs and crime that have been called into serious question since the classic drug research of the 1950s. In particular, the widely held notion that most of the crime committed by addicts can be explained by their need for money to buy illegal drugs does not fit well with the evidence.

In its popular form, the drugs-cause-crime argument is implicitly 25 based on the assumption that addict crime is caused by pharmacological compulsion—as a recent British study puts it, on a kind of "enslavement" model in which the uncontrollable craving for drugs forces an otherwise law-abiding citizen to engage in crime for gain. As we've seen, however, a key finding of most of the research into the meaning of drug use and the growth of drug subcultures since the 1950s has been that the purely pharmacological craving for drugs is by no means the most important motive for drug use. Nor is it clear that those cravings are typically so uncontrollable that addicts are in any meaningful sense "driven" to crime to satisfy them.

On the surface, there is much to suggest a strong link between crime and the imperatives of addiction. The studies of addict crime by John Ball and Douglas Anglin and their colleagues show not only that the most heavily addicted commit huge numbers of crimes, but also that their crime rates seem to increase when their heroin use increases and to fall when it declines. Thus, for example, heroin addicts in Ball's study in Baltimore had an average of 255 "crime days" per year when they were actively addicted, versus about 65 when they were not. In general, the level of property crime appears in these studies to go up simultaneously with increasing intensity of drug use. One explanation, and perhaps the most common one, is that the increased need for money to buy drugs drives addicts into more crime.

But a closer look shows that things are considerably more complicated. To begin with, it is a recurrent finding that most people who both abuse drugs and commit crimes began committing the crimes *before* they began using drugs—meaning that their need for drugs cannot have caused their initial criminal involvement (though it may have accelerated it later). George Vaillant's follow-up study of addicts and alcoholics found, for example, that, unlike alcoholics, heroin addicts had typically been involved in delinquency and crime well before they began their career of substance abuse. While alcoholics seemed to become involved in crime as a *result* of their abuse of alcohol, more than half of the heroin addicts (versus just 5 percent of the alcoholics) "were known to have been delinquent *before* drug abuse." A federal survey of drug use among prison inmates in 1986, similarly, found that three-fifths of those who had ever used a "major drug" regularly—that is, heroin, cocaine, methadone, PCP, or LSD—had not done so until after their first arrest.

Other studies have found that for many addicts, drug use and crime seem to have begun more or less *independently* without one clearly causing the other. This was the finding, for example, in Charles Faupel and Carl Klockars's study of hard-core heroin addicts in Wilmington, Delaware. "All of our respondents," they note, "reported some criminal activity prior to their first use of heroin." Moreover, "perhaps most importantly, virtually all of our respondents reported that they believed that their criminal and drug careers began independently of one another, although both careers became intimately interconnected as each evolved."

More recent research shows that the drugs-crime relationship may be even more complex than this suggests. It is not only that crime may precede drug use, especially heavy or addictive use, or that both may emerge more or less independently; it is also likely that there are several *different* kinds of drugs-crime connections among different types of drug users. David Nurco of the University of Maryland and his colleagues, for example, studying heroin addicts in Baltimore and New York City, found that nine different kinds of addicts could be distinguished by the type and severity of their crimes. Like earlier researchers, they found that most addicts committed large numbers of crimes—mainly drug dealing and small-scale property crime, notably shoplifting, burglary, and fencing. Others were involved in illegal gambling and what the researchers called "deception crimes"—including forgery and con games—and a relatively small percentage had engaged in violent crime. On the whole, addicts heavily involved in one type of crime were not likely to be involved in others; as the researchers put it, they tended to be either "dealers or stealers," but rarely both. About 6 percent of the addicts, moreover, were "uninvolved"—they did not commit crimes either while addicted or before, or during periods of nonaddiction interspersed in the course of their longer addiction careers.

The most troubling group of addicts—what the researchers called "violent generalists"—were only about 7 percent of the total sample, but they were extremely active—and very dangerous; they accounted for over half of all the violent crimes committed by the entire sample. Moreover, revealingly, the violent generalists were very active in serious crime *before* they became addicted to narcotics as well as during periods of nonaddiction thereafter—again demonstrating that the violence was not dependent on their addiction itself. Nurco and his colleagues measured the addicts' criminal activity by what they called "crime days" per year. Addicts were asked how many days they had committed each of several types of crime; since on any given day they might have committed more than one type of crime, the resulting figure could add up to more than the number of days in the year. The violent generalists averaged an astonishing 900 crime days a year over the course of their

30

careers. The rates were highest during periods when they were heavily addicted to drugs. But even *before* they were addicted, they averaged 573 crime days, and 491 after their addiction had ended. Indeed, the most active group of violent generalists engaged in more crime *prior* to addiction than any other group did *while* addicted. And they continued to commit crimes—often violent ones—long after they had ceased to be addicted to narcotics.

None of this is to deny that serious addiction to heroin or other illegal drugs can accelerate the level of crime among participants in the drug culture, or stimulate crime even in some users who are otherwise not criminal. Higher levels of drug use *do* go hand in hand with increased crime, especially property crime. Certainly, many addicts mug, steal, or sell their bodies for drugs. The point is that—as the early drug researchers discovered in the 1950s—both crime and drug abuse tend to be spawned by the same set of unfavorable social circumstances, and they interact with one another in much more complex ways than the simple addiction-leads-to-crime view proposes. Simply providing drugs more easily to people enmeshed in the drug cultures of the cities is not likely to cut the deep social roots of addict crime.

If we take the harms of drug abuse seriously, and I think we must, we cannot avoid being deeply concerned about anything that would significantly increase the availability of hard drugs within the American social context; and no one seriously doubts that legalization would indeed increase availability, and probably lower prices for many drugs. In turn, increased availability—as we know from the experience with alcohol—typically leads to increased consumption, and with it increased social and public-health costs. A growing body of research, for example, shows that most alcohol-related health problems, including deaths from cirrhosis and other diseases, were far lower during Prohibition than afterward, when per capita alcohol consumption rose dramatically (by about 75 percent, for example, between 1950 and 1980). It is difficult to imagine why a similar rise in consumption—and in the associated public-health problems—would not follow the full-scale legalization of cocaine, heroin, methamphetamine, and PCP (not to mention the array of as yet undiscovered "designer" drugs that a legalized corporate drug industry would be certain to develop).

If consumption increased, it would almost certainly increase most among the strata already most vulnerable to hard-drug use—thus exacerbating the social stratification of the drug crisis. It is among the poor and near-poor that offsetting measures like education and drug treatment are least effective and where the countervailing social supports and opportunities are least strong. We would expect, therefore, that a free-market policy applied to hard drugs would produce the same results it has created with the *legal* killer drugs, tobacco and alcohol—namely, a widening disparity in use between the better-off and the disadvantaged.

And that disparity is already stunning. According to a recent study by Colin McCord and Howard Freeman of Harlem Hospital, between 1979 and 1981 — that is, *before* the crack epidemic of the eighties — Harlem blacks were 283 times as likely to die of drug dependency as whites in the general population. Drug deaths, combined with deaths from cirrhosis, alcoholism, cardiovascular disease, and homicide, helped to give black men in Harlem a shorter life expectancy than men in Bangladesh. This is the social reality that the rather abstract calls for the legalization of hard-drug sales tend to ignore.

TOPICS FOR CRITICAL THINKING AND WRITING

1. Currie claims that "drugs will always be a 'law-enforcement problem'" (para. 1). Why do you think he believes this? Is the evidence he offers adequate to support this troubling judgment?

2. Currie mentions what he regards as "small but significant ways" (para. 2) to reduce the place of drugs in our lives. What are they? Why do you think he doesn't mention (a) curbing the manufacture of illegal addictive drugs, (b) vigorously reducing imports of illegal addictive drugs into the United States, and (c) aggressively educating the public on the harm that illegal addictive drugs cause their users?

3. Why does Currie think that "escalating the war on drugs," with its reliance on "incapacitation" and "deterrence," is doomed to ineffectiveness (para. 6)? Are you persuaded? Explain.

4. Currie eventually states his own views (para. 18). Do you think the essay would have been more effective if he had stated his views in his opening paragraph? Why, or why not?

5. Currie stresses the uniqueness of the drug problem in the United States. What do you think explains "the magnitude and severity of our drug crisis" (para. 21)? Farmers in other countries produce more illegal addictive drugs than ours do. Other countries have graver problems of poverty than we do. Gross manifest disparities between rich and poor are not unique to the United States. So what's the explanation? Does Currie tell us?

6. Why does Currie reject the drugs-cause-crime argument (para. 24)?

For topical links related to the discussion of the legalization of drugs, see the companion Web site: **bedfordstmartins.com/barnetbedau.**

24

Going Green: What Must Be Done?

Daniel Goleman and Gregory Norris

Daniel Goleman, a science journalist, is the author of several books, including Ecological Intelligence: How Knowing the Hidden Impacts of What We Buy Can Change Everything *(2009). He often writes for the* New York Times. *Gregory Norris, a lecturer at the Harvard School of Public Health, is developing* Earthstar, *an open-source software system that conducts life cycle assessments. This essay appeared in the* New York Times *on April 19, 2009*

How Green Was My Bottle

Earth Day is this Wednesday, and all things "green" will be celebrated. But it's worth asking: How environmentally friendly are "green" products, really? Consider, for example, this paragon of eco-virtue: the stainless steel water bottle that lets us hydrate without discarding endless plastic bottles. Using a method called life cycle assessment, we have evaluated the environmental and health impact of a stainless steel thermos—from the extraction and processing of its ingredients, to its manufacture, distribution, use, and final disposal. There were some surprises. What we think of as "green" turns out to be less so (and, yes, sometimes more so) than we assume.

Extraction Processing. Producing stainless steel requires a global supply chain involving more than 1,400 steps, each with its own impact on the environment. For example, the mining of chromium ore, an essential component of stainless steel, can expose workers to a heightened risk of cancer. Next, the ores have to be processed to extract useful metal. This usually involves energy-intensive heating, a process that not only requires enormous amounts of fossil fuel but also releases greenhouse gases, carcinogens, particulates, and toxic material into the air, water, and soil.

Manufacture. Making stainless steel—which requires the processing of nickel and chromium ores—results in about 10 times more pollution than regular steel. But if the steel mills use recycled iron, instead of newly mined pig iron, the environmental and health impact can be reduced by 10 percent to 15 percent. In addition, simple innovations like a lighter single-wall design—rather than the double walls typically found in insulated bottles—can reduce the ecological impact by about 35 percent.

Distribution. The bottle's journey from factory to distribution center to you uses up oil and energy and results in particulates, greenhouse gases, and other emissions. The good news: Shipping the bottle from a factory in Asia in a tightly packed cargo container, plus a few hundred miles by truck, adds only 1 percent to 5 percent to the environmental burden. The bad: The heating, cooling, lighting, and ventilation of the store where you buy the bottle could have nearly as much of a negative effect on the environment as producing the bottle itself.

Use. Obviously, one danger of any reusable water bottle is bacteria   5 buildup, so you have to keep it clean. If you wash your stainless steel water bottle in a dishwasher that uses a half-liter of electrically heated water, 50 to 100 washes can result in the same amount of pollution that was caused by making the bottle in the first place. Washing it in cold water still demands electricity to pump the water and chemicals to treat it—but the impact is tiny by comparison.

Disposal. Steel lasts forever, so disposal probably comes the day you lose the top. Try to ensure that the discarded bottle finds its way to a steel recycler—not just to a landfill, where it could sit for centuries. By recycling stainless steel, you return not only steel but also nickel and chromium alloys to the production chain, reducing the need to mine and process more of these essential ingredients. These benefits are well worth the impact of transporting the steel back to the mill for recycling.

SO, IS STAINLESS STEEL REALLY BETTER THAN PLASTIC?

One stainless steel bottle is obviously much worse than one plastic bottle. Producing that 300-gram stainless steel bottle requires seven times as much fossil fuel, releases 14 times more greenhouse gases, demands the extraction of hundreds of times more metal resources, and causes hundreds of times more toxic risk to people and ecosystems than making a 32-gram plastic bottle. If you're planning to take only one drink in your life, buy plastic.

But chances are buying that stainless steel bottle will prevent you from using and then throwing away countless plastic bottles. And think of the harm done to the environment by making more and more plastic— the electricity needed to form polyethylene terephthalate resin into

bottles, the fossils fuels burned to produce this electricity, the energy used and emissions released from mining the coal and converting crude oil to fuel, and on and on. What it comes down to is this: If your stainless steel bottle takes the place of 50 plastic bottles, the climate is better off, and if it gets used 500 times, it beats plastic in all the environment-impact categories studied in a life cycle assessment.

It's important to keep in mind that the twenty-first century has inherited from the twentieth (and sometimes the nineteenth) manufacturing processes and industrial chemicals that were developed when no one knew—or cared that much—about environmental damage. But even though climate change demands urgent ecological action, this crisis also offers vast entrepreneurial opportunities; we need to re-invent everything with an eye to protecting the planet.

Then again, some old solutions we shouldn't discount. Before stain- 10 less steel thermoses, before bottled water, we already had an eco-friendly method of getting water: drinking fountains.

TOPICS FOR CRITICAL THINKING AND WRITING

1. In one sentence, state the author's thesis—or explain why you think they have no thesis.

2. The authors identify six variables to use in assessing the ecological impact of a product (paras. 2–6). Are these variables independent? Which of these six do you think is the most harmful or costly? The least harmful or

costly? Or is the interplay of these variables so complex that it is impossible to respond to this matter in a nonarbitrary/subjective manner?

3. The authors cite no sources to support the many empirical claims they advance. Does this weaken your confidence in their conclusions? Why, or why not?

4. Do you use a stainless steel water bottle? If so, do you plan to continue using it? Why, or why not? And if you lose the top, will you buy another stainless steel bottle? Why, or why not?

Craig D. Rose

Craig D. Rose, a San Diego based journalist, writes about business and energy. We reprint here a piece that originally appeared in a liberal weekly magazine, The Nation, *on February 16, 2009.*

Here Comes the Sun

As the Obama administration and Congress search for worthy infrastructure projects to fund as part of the stimulus and economic-recovery package, there is a growing consensus in support of major investment in the renewal and greening of America's electricity grid. Texas oilman T. Boone Pickens's plan for a huge new grid to tap wind energy across the Plains States has attracted the most attention, but the grandest aspiration is for a "national backbone grid," a coast-to-coast project tapping renewable energy sources that would cost hundreds of billions of dollars.

Big electric-transmission projects have developed a potent support base that includes large utility companies as well as many environmentalists, who argue that all means must be pursued to save the planet by reducing the burning of fossil fuels. The presumption is that big new transmission projects are required to reach America's vast renewable resources, from the strong, steady winds of the Midwest to the relentless sun of the Southwestern deserts.

Although massive expansion of the electric grid threatens to despoil the last of America's undeveloped places, some environmentalists mistakenly believe the urgency of dealing with climate change leaves no alternative to large, remotely sited renewable electric-generation facilities and the transmission lines they need to get power to consumers. In fact, there is an alternative: "distributed generation," or smaller solar technology installations on rooftops and near existing transmission lines, or even scaled-down wind farms sited closer to consumers.

To be sure, the romance of a renewable national grid is classic American thinking: A big problem requires a big solution. But the distributed generation approach (DG in energy lingo) is emerging from advances in solar technology and detailed studies of alternatives to big power-line projects. Consider what happened when Minnesota regulators looked carefully last year at the CapX 2020 project, a proposed cluster of new power lines costing up to $1.7 billion. A key purpose of the lines was to link Minnesota with proposed wind farms in the Dakotas. This is just the type of project favored by Pickens and other supporters of big electric transmission. But after examination the regulators found that Minnesota could develop many small 10–40 megawatt wind farms within the state totaling 600 megawatts—equivalent to a modern power plant—without any new transmission.

"We call it the '600 megawatts for nothing' study," said Mike 5 Michaud, an engineer and consultant who formerly worked with the state regulatory staff. "There was no denying there were twenty spots on the existing grid [where] you could put generation for no cost at all." Michaud added that there is no guarantee the $1.7 billion transmission project would be restricted to clean power—it might in some cases be used to transport power from coal-burning plants.

The DG strategy is particularly applicable to rooftop solar power. It taps existing transmission infrastructure and thus saves the huge cost of building new lines while avoiding the controversy of running power lines through communities. DG also provides the security of dispersed generating resources, so a power failure in one area is far less likely to cause the massive blackouts that can result from the outage of a single unit in the big, centralized power system we have now.

Clean distributed resources in the form of wind, biomass, and solar are far more available than is generally known. A November study by the Institute for Local Self-Reliance (ILSR), a thirty-five-year-old group focused on community development, may have been the first to examine the potential for DG on a national scale. The study found that half the states could be energy self-sufficient by harnessing renewables within their borders, and most states can satisfy a considerable fraction of their own energy needs this way.

What's more, encouraging local ownership of distributed resources would solidify local support for the projects and increase the economic benefits because much more of the spending—and the jobs created—would stay in the community. This is precisely why big utility companies fear advances in rooftop solar technology: It could make every building owner a power generator and leave utilities with long-term prospects similar to those of Detroit automakers or the newspaper industry. "The big utility companies are looking at the future, and they're getting freaked out," said Tyson Slocum, director of Public Citizen's energy program.

Certain areas of the country do have superior renewable resources, such as solar in Nevada and wind in North Dakota. But when the cost of transmission to move that electricity is included—along with the loss of up to 15 percent of the power from moving it long distances—home-grown electricity proves superior. The ILSR study asserts, for example, that if Ohio's electricity came from North Dakota wind farms 1,000 miles away, the cost of constructing lines to transport that power and the losses during transmission would surpass the lower cost of production, resulting in consumer costs 15 percent higher than those from locally generated power.

A similar conclusion was reached by many who studied the Sunrise 10 Powerlink, a planned $2 billion transmission line to move electricity from desert projects 150 miles east of San Diego to the urban area. Proposed by San Diego Gas & Electric, Sunrise won approval in December from the California Public Utilities Commission (CPUC) only after regulators ignored the recommendation of the administrative law judges who oversaw a three-year review. Those judges recommended rejection, concluding that it would be cheaper and better for the environment if SDG&E developed renewable and other projects closer to home.

Despite SDG&E's assertions to the contrary, the judges found that the utility could meet California's strict 20 percent renewable energy standard by the end of next year without the long-distance power line. Only after Governor Arnold Schwarzenegger suddenly created a 33 percent renewable requirement by 2020 — one that project opponents never had the opportunity to consider in relation to Sunrise — could regulators find cover for approval. The one vote against: CPUC commissioner Dian Grueneich, who was assigned to oversee the Sunrise case. In a scathing dissent, Grueneich noted that regulators were approving a project ostensibly to develop renewable energy but failed to guarantee that it would do so. In other words, after all the money spent on Sunrise, it could wind up carrying mostly dirty electricity. This contradiction was highlighted when SDG&E — which had insisted the line would be used largely for green power — characterized as unacceptable a requirement that the line carry a fixed percentage of green power. In fact, current federal transmission rules prohibit restricting any transmission project to green energy only, a policy the Obama administration should reconsider if it wants to encourage renewable energy.

A broad community coalition has arisen to oppose the Sunrise project; its legal challenge will likely be based on the CPUC's failure to respect the voluminous factual record established in the case. Among its leaders is Bill Powers, a fifty-two-year-old engineer who has worked on licensing power plants. Powers believes that advances in solar technology — in particular, declining costs that are poised to fall even faster this year — should make development of rooftop solar a top priority. Powers wrote a study that found that the $2 billion SDG&E will spend just to access desert renewable energy could be spent building 1,300 megawatts of photovoltaics (PV) in San Diego — with nearly no cost for transmission lines. And researchers — among them, SDG&E itself — have concluded that San Diego has the potential for some 5,000 megawatts of rooftop photovoltaics, or about enough at peak production to power the entire city on a hot day. "The trump card of urban PV is that there is no lengthy environmental review required and no land requirements," said Powers. "PV goes on rooftops and over parking lots. What is going to slow the plans for big, remote solar and wind projects is what is slowing the Sunrise proposal—citizen opposition. The concept of building remote renewable in most cases is the promotion of investor-owned utilities and their holding companies, who want as much high return on investment transmission projects as possible."

To be sure, many environmentalists insist that saving the planet will require DG *and* remotely located projects. And to some extent, the push for a bigger grid piggybacks on the reasonable call for modernizing the nation's badly decayed grid. President Obama apparently sees upgrades and a major expansion of the grid as a single package, with his call for "a bigger, better, smarter grid" along with "more than 3,000 miles of new or modernized transmission lines." In the practical world, dollars translate into priorities, and money spent on major grid expansion is money unavailable for cheaper and more environmentally friendly DG projects. Case in point: while SDG&E could spend $2 billion for its transmission project, it proposes to spend just $250 million over five years for urban solar projects.

The irony is that SDG&E's parent company, Sempra Energy, has reached what has long been considered a historic milestone in solar energy. Using thin-film photovoltaic panels from First Solar, a fast-growing supplier, Sempra's recently completed 10-megawatt generating plant outside Las Vegas can produce electricity at rates comparable to or below those of fossil fuel fired plants, according to Mark Bachman, a research analyst with Pacific Crest Securities. The use of thin-film technology will be revolutionary, says Powers, and California regulators apparently agree. In a recent study by the CPUC, analysts concluded that DG—in particular, small 20-megawatt installations of thin-film photovoltaics—could satisfy most of California's aggressive target for renewable energy at competitive cost and without new transmission lines. The study emphasized that it was only a test case, based on expected cost reductions for thin-film. But those lower costs have already arrived, Powers noted. "That's what Sempra used to make its breakthrough," he said.

And the breakthrough may well be more than Sempra's. If Sempra   15 and First Solar have crossed the threshold for producing electricity at parity—equal to or less than plants that burn coal or natural gas—it should prompt a drastic recalculation of how we generate power.

Let's call it electricity's wireless future.

TOPICS FOR CRITICAL THINKING AND WRITING

1. What does Rose mean (para. 9) by "homegrown electricity," and why does he think it is preferable to the alternative?

2. Do you get the impression that Rose is optimistic about the future of solar power, wind power, and other forms of clean energy—or is his jury still out on this major issue?

3. Do you get the impression that Rose has a favorite form of clean energy? If so, what is it and why does he favor it?

4. What does Rose mean (para. 16) by "electricity's wireless future"?

5. Not until the fourth paragraph does Rose clearly express doubts about the desirability of huge projects, but the earlier paragraphs do contain some hints of his reservations. Point out words or phrases in the first three paragraphs that allow a careful reader to announce that Rose will not go on to support the proposals he discusses those paragraphs. Do you think his strategy is effective, or do you think he should have stated his own position earlier? Please explain your view.

Aldo Leopold

Aldo Leopold was born in 1887 in Burlington, Iowa, and died in 1948, about a year before the publication of his collection of essays, A Sand County Almanac. *We print the most famous part of this book. Leopold, a forester and an ecologist, worked for eighteen years for the United Sates Forest Service and later taught game management at the University of Wisconsin, Madison.*

Thinking Like a Mountain

A deep chesty bawl echoes from rimrock to rimrock, rolls down the mountain, and fades into the far blackness of the night. It is an outburst of wild defiant sorrow, and of contempt for all the adversities of the world.

Every living thing (and perhaps many a dead one as well) pays heed to that call. To the deer it is a reminder of the way of all flesh, to the pine a forecast of midnight scuffles and of blood upon the snow, to the coyote a promise of gleanings to come, to the cowman a threat of red ink at the bank, to the hunter a challenge of fang against bullet. Yet behind these obvious and immediate hopes and fears there lies a deeper meaning, known only to the mountain itself. Only the mountain has lived long enough to listen objectively to the howl of a wolf.

Those unable to decipher the hidden meaning know nevertheless that it is there, for it is felt in all wolf country, and distinguishes that country from all other land. It tingles in the spine of all who hear wolves by night, or who scan their tracks by day. Even without sight or sound of wolf, it is implicit in a hundred small events: the midnight whinny of a pack horse, the rattle of rolling rocks, the bound of a fleeing deer, the way shadows lie under the spruces. Only the ineducable tyro can fail to sense the presence or absence of wolves, or the fact that mountains have a secret opinion about them.

My own conviction on this score dates from the day I saw a wolf die. We were eating lunch on a high rimrock, at the foot of which a turbulent river elbowed its way. We saw what we thought was a doe fording the torrent, her breast awash in white water. When she climbed the bank toward us and shook out her tail, we realized our error: It was a wolf. A half-dozen others, evidently grown pups, sprang from the willows and all joined in a welcoming melee of wagging tails and playful maulings. What was literally a pile of wolves writhed and tumbled in the center of an open flat at the foot of our rimrock.

In those days we had never heard of passing up a chance to kill a   5 wolf. In a second we were pumping lead into the pack, but with more excitement than accuracy: How to aim a steep downhill shot is always confusing. When our rifles were empty, the old wolf was down, and a pup was dragging a leg into impassable slide-rocks.

We reached the old wolf in time to watch a fierce green fire dying in her eyes. I realized then, and have known ever since, that there was something new to me in those eyes—something known only to her and to the mountain. I was young then, and full of trigger-itch; I thought that because fewer wolves meant more deer, that no wolves would mean hunters' paradise. But after seeing the green fire die, I sensed that neither the wolf nor the mountain agreed with such a view.

Since then I have lived to see state after state extirpate its wolves. I have watched the face of many a newly wolfless mountain, and seen the south-facing slopes wrinkle with a maze of new deer trails. I have seen every edible bush and seedling browsed, first to anaemic desuetude, and then to death. I have seen every edible tree defoliated to the height of a saddlehorn. Such a mountain looks as if someone had given God a new pruning shears, and forbidden Him all other exercise. In the end the starved bones of the hoped-for deer herd, dead of its own too-much, bleach with the bones of the dead sage, or molder under the high-lined junipers.

I now suspect that just as a deer herd lives in mortal fear of its wolves, so does a mountain live in mortal fear of its deer. And perhaps with better cause, for while a buck pulled down by wolves can be replaced in two or three years, a range pulled down by too many deer may fail of replacement in as many decades.

So also with cows. The cowman who cleans his range of wolves does not realize that he is taking over the wolf's job of trimming the herd to fit the range. He has not learned to think like a mountain. Hence we have dustbowls, and rivers washing the future into the sea.

We all strive for safety, prosperity, comfort, long life, and dullness.   10 The deer strives with his supple legs, the cowman with trap and poison, the statesman with pen, the most of us with machines, votes, and dollars, but it all comes to the same thing: peace in our time. A measure of success in this is all well enough, and perhaps is a requisite to objective thinking, but too much safety seems to yield only danger in the long run. Perhaps this is behind Thoreau's dictum: In wildness is the salvation of the world. Perhaps this is the hidden meaning in the howl of the wolf, long known among mountains, but seldom perceived among men.

Topics for Critical Thinking and Writing

1. Is Leopold confessing how naive he was in hunting the wolf and her pups (paras. 4–6)? Is he implying that hunting wolves ought to cease? What do you think?

2. "[F]ewer wolves meant more deer" (para. 6) — or so Leopold once thought. But he changed his mind. Why? What do you believe and why?

3. This brief essay is probably the most reprinted portion of Leopold's *A Sand County Almanac*. Whether or not you are impressed by the piece, how do you account for its popularity?

Paul Bloom

Paul Bloom (b. 1963), a professor of psychology at Yale, is the author of numerous books, the most recent of which is Descartes' Baby: How the Science of Child Development Explains What Makes Us Human *(2004). The essay reprinted here appeared in the* New York Times Magazine *on April 19, 2009.*

Natural Happiness

Why should we care about nature? Should we care about it for its own sake — or for our sake because it happens to make us happy or healthy? These might not seem like the brightest questions. Few people need convincing that the destruction of rain forests, the mass extinction of species, and the melting of the ice sheets in Greenland would all be very bad things. Do we really need to list the reasons?

We do. After all, in many regards our species has already kissed nature goodbye, and we are better off for it. Technology has come to be more diverse than the biosphere. In 1867, Karl Marx observed that there were 500 types of hammer made in Birmingham, England. In 1988, Donald Norman, a cognitive scientist at the University of California, San Diego, suggested that the average American encounters 20,000 different kinds of artifacts in everyday life, which would be more than the number of animals and plants that we can distinguish. And right now, there are about 1.5 million identified species on Earth — impressive, but nothing compared to the more than 7 million United States patents.

This is mostly good news. No sane person would give up antibiotics and anesthesia, farming, and the written word. Our constructed environments shield us from heat and cold and protect us from predators. We have access to food and drink and drugs that have been devised to stimulate our nervous systems in magnificent ways. We sleep in soft beds and have immediate access to virtual experiences from pornography to classical symphonies. If a family of hunter-gatherers were dropped into this life, they would think of it as a literal heaven.

Or maybe not. There is a considerable mismatch between the world in which our minds evolved and our current existence. Our species has spent almost all of its existence on the African savanna. While there is debate over the details, we know for sure that our minds were not adapted to cope with a world of billions of people. The life of a modern city dweller, surrounded by strangers, is an evolutionary novelty. Thousands of years ago, there was no television or Internet, no McDonald's, birth-control pills, Viagra, plastic surgery, alarm clocks, artificial lighting, or paternity tests. Instead, there was plenty of nature. We lived surrounded by trees and water and animals and sky.

This history has left its mark on our minds. Children are irrepressible taxonomizers, placing the world of distinct individuals into categories based on their appearance, their patterns of movement, and their presumed deeper natures, and some psychologists have argued that the hard-wired capacity to organize and structure the world is specially adapted to nature: We are natural-born zoologists and botanists. We may also have evolved to get pleasure from certain aspects of the natural world. About twenty-five years ago, the Harvard biologist E. O. Wilson popularized the "biophilia" hypothesis: the idea that our evolutionary history has blessed us with an innate affinity for living things. We thrive in the presence of nature and suffer in its absence.

Our hunger for the natural is everywhere. It is reflected in art: The philosopher Denis Dutton, in his book *The Art Instinct*, suggests that popular taste in landscape painting has been shaped by preferences that evolved for the African savanna. The appeal of the natural is also reflected in where we most want to live. People like to be close to oceans, mountains, and trees. Even in the most urban environments, it is reflected in real estate prices: If you want a view of the trees of Central Park, it'll cost you. Office buildings have atriums and plants; we give flowers to the sick and the beloved and return home to watch Animal Planet and the Discovery Channel. We keep pets, which are a weird combination of constructed things (cats and dogs were bred for human companionship), surrogate people, and conduits to the natural world. And many of us seek to escape our manufactured environments whenever we can—to hike, camp, canoe, or hunt.

Wilson emphasizes the spiritual and moral benefits of an attachment to nature, warning that we "descend farther from heaven's air if we forget how much the natural world means to us." But there are more tangible benefits as well. Many studies show that even a limited dose of nature, like a chance to look at the outside world through a window, is good for your health. Hospitalized patients heal more quickly; prisoners get sick less often. Being in the wild reduces stress; spending time with a pet enhances the lives of everyone from autistic children to Alzheimer's patients. The author Richard Louv argues that modern children suffer from "nature-deficit disorder" because they have been shut out from the physical and psychic benefits of unstructured physical contact with the natural world.

So the preservation of the natural world should be important to us. But how important? The psychologist Philip Tetlock has pointed out that many people talk about the environment as a "sacred value," protected from utilitarian trade-offs—when the *Exxon Valdez* spilled nearly 11 million gallons of crude oil, 80 percent of the respondents in one poll said that we should pursue greater environmental protection "regardless of cost." But he also points to the need to balance environmental concerns with social and political and personal priorities. (Few of these respondents would be willing to hand over their pensions for a more efficient cleanup of the Alaskan shoreline.) And even if we did value nature above everything else, we would still have to decide which aspects of nature we care about the most. You can see this in the debate over the creation of giant wind farms in the ocean or on hillsides. Proponents are enthusiastic about the cheap, green energy; critics worry about the loss of natural beauty and the yearly filleting of thousands of songbirds and ducks.

In the end, an indiscriminate biophilia makes little sense. Natural selection shaped the human brain to be drawn toward aspects of nature that enhance our survival and reproduction, like verdant landscapes and docile creatures. There is no payoff to getting the warm fuzzies in the presence of rats, snakes, mosquitoes, cockroaches, herpes simplex, and the rabies virus. Some of the natural world is appealing, some of it is terrifying, and some of it grosses us out. Modern people don't want to be dropped naked into a swamp. We want to tour Yosemite with our water bottles and G.P.S. devices. The natural world is a source of happiness and fulfillment, but only when prescribed in the right doses.

You might think that technology could provide a simulacrum of nature with all the bad parts scrubbed out. But attempts to do so have turned out to be interesting failures. There is a fortune to be made, for instance, by building a robot that children would respond to as if it were an animal. There have been many attempts, but they don't evoke anywhere near the same responses as puppies, kittens, or even hamsters. They are toys, not companions. Or consider a recent study by the University of Washington psychologist Peter H. Kahn Jr. and his colleagues. They put fifty-inch high-definition televisions in the windowless offices of faculty and staff members to provide a live view of a natural scene. People liked this, but in another study that measured heart-rate recovery from stress, the HDTVs were shown to be worthless, no better than staring at a blank wall. What did help with stress was giving people an actual plate-glass window looking out upon actual greenery.

All of this provides a different sort of argument for the preservation of nature. Put aside for the moment practical considerations like the need for clean air and water, and ignore as well spiritual worries about the sanctity of Mother Earth or religious claims that we are the stewards of creation. Look at it from the coldblooded standpoint of the enhancement of the happiness of our everyday lives. Real natural habitats provide significant sources of pleasure for modern humans. We intuitively grasp this, and this knowledge underlies the anxiety that we feel about nature's loss. It might be that one day we will be able to replace the experience of nature with *Star Trek* holodecks and robotic animals. But until then, this basic fact about human pleasure is an excellent argument for keeping the real thing.

TOPICS FOR CRITICAL THINKING AND WRITING

1. Bloom's first sentence is "Why should we care about nature?" In a sentence or two (or three at the very most) summarize Bloom's answer to his question. Next, in a sentence (or two at the most) state Bloom's thesis. Third, in a paragraph offer your response, perhaps confirming his view but with some bit of personal experience, or perhaps indicating why you differ.

2. In paragraph 11 Bloom suggests that we dismiss, at least for the moment, "spiritual worries about the sanctity of Mother Earth." Does the term "sanctity of Mother Earth" mean much, or can it easily be dismissed? Explain.

3. Another essay in this book, Peter Cave's "Should We Save the Jerboa?" (p. 26), examines issues close to Bloom's. Imagine a meeting of these two professors and write the short dialogue they might have—perhaps one in which each speaks a dozen sentences.

4. Almost certainly you have enjoyed a day at the beach or at a lake, a hike in the woods, or a stroll in a city park, or some comparable experience, but can you confidently say that the experience was any more important to you than, say, seeing a good movie, playing a sport, reading a book, or chatting with a friend in a noisy cafeteria? How significant has the direct experience of nature been in your life? Respond in an essay of about 500 words, in which you argue—don't merely narrate—that, given your experience, Bloom is or is not on to something important.

Bill McKibben

Bill McKibben, born in California in 1960 and educated at Harvard, became a staff writer for The New Yorker, *and then became a freelance writer, publishing in numerous magazines including the* New York Review of Books, Rolling Stone, *and* The New Republic. *Among his many books are* The End of Nature *(1989),* The Age of Missing Information *(1992),* A Year of Living Strenuously *(2000), and* Fight Global Warming Now *(2007). This essay appeared in* These Times *in April 2001.*

Now Or Never

When global warming first emerged as a potential crisis in the late '80s, one academic analyst called it "the public policy problem from hell." The years since have only proven him more astute—fifteen years into our understanding of climate change, we have yet to figure out how we're going to tackle it. And environmentalists are just as clueless as anyone else: Do we need to work on lifestyles or on lobbying, on politics or on photovoltaics? And is there a difference? How well we handle global warming will determine what kind of century we inhabit— and indeed what kind of planet we leave behind to everyone and everything that follows us down into geologic time. It is *the* environmental question, the one that cuts closest to home and also floats off most easily into the abstract. So far it has been the ultimate "can't get there from here" problem, but the time has come to draw a roadmap—one that may help us deal with the handful of other issues on the list of real, world-shattering problems.

The first thing to know about global warming is this: The science is sound. In 1988, when scientists first testified before Congress about the potential for rapid and destabilizing climate change, they were still describing a hypothesis. It went like this: Every time human beings burn coal, gas, oil, wood, or any other carbon-based fuel, they emit large quantities of carbon dioxide. (A car emits its own weight in carbon annually if you drive it the average American distance.) This carbon dioxide accumulates in the atmosphere. It's not a normal pollutant—it doesn't poison you, or change the color of the sunset. But it does have one interesting property: Its molecular structure traps heat near the surface of the planet that would otherwise radiate back out to space. It acts like the panes of glass on a greenhouse.

The hypothesis was that we were putting enough carbon dioxide into the atmosphere to make a difference. The doubters said no—that the earth would compensate for any extra carbon by forming extra clouds and cooling the planet, or through some other feedback mechanism. And so, as scientists will, they went at it. For five years—lavishly funded by governments that wanted to fund research instead of making politically unpopular changes—scientists produced paper after paper. They studied glacial cores and tree rings and old pollen sediments in lake beds to understand past climates; they took temperature measurements on the surface and from space; they refined their computer models and ran them backward in time to see if they worked. By 1995 they had reached a conclusion. That year the Intergovernmental Panel on Climate Change (IPCC), a group of all the world's climatologists assembled under the auspices of the United Nations, announced that human beings were indeed heating up the planet.

The scientists kept up the pace of their research for the next five years, and in the past five months have published a series of massive updates to their findings. These results are uniformly grimmer than even five years before. They include:

- The prediction that humans will likely heat the planet 4 to 6 degrees Fahrenheit in this century, twice as much as earlier forecast, taking global temperatures to a level not seen in millions of years, and never before in human history.

- The worst-case possibility that we will raise the temperature by as much as 11 degrees Fahrenheit, a true science-fiction scenario that no one had seriously envisaged before.
- The near certainty that these temperature increases will lead to rises in sea level of at least a couple of feet.
- The well-documented fear that disease will spread quickly as vectors like mosquitoes expand their range to places that used to be too cool for their survival.

But it isn't just the scientists who are hard at work on this issue. 5 For the past five years, it's almost as if the planet itself has been peer-reviewing their work. We've had the warmest years on record—including 1998, which was warmer than any year for which records exist. And those hot years have shown what even small changes in temperature—barely a degree Fahrenheit averaged globally—can do to the earth's systems.

Consider hydrology, for instance. Warm air holds more water vapor than cold air, so there is an increase in evaporation in dry areas, and hence more drought—something that has been documented on every continent. Once that water is in the atmosphere, it's going to come down somewhere—and indeed we have seen the most dramatic flooding ever recorded in recent years. In 1998, 300 million humans, one in twenty of us, had to leave their homes for a week, a month, a year, forever because of rising waters.

Or look at the planet's cryosphere, its frozen places. Every alpine glacier is in retreat; the snows of Kilimanjaro will have vanished by 2015; and the Arctic ice cap is thinning fast—data collected by U.S. and Soviet nuclear submarines show that it is almost half gone compared with just four decades ago.

In other words, human beings are changing the planet more fundamentally in the course of a couple of decades than in all the time since we climbed down from the trees and began making clever use of our opposable thumbs. There's never been anything like this.

Yet to judge from the political response, this issue ranks well below, say, the estate tax as a cause for alarm and worry. In 1988, there was enough public outcry that George Bush the Elder promised to combat "the greenhouse effect with the White House effect." In 1992, Bill Clinton promised that Americans would emit no more carbon dioxide by 2000 than they had in 1990—and that his administration would do the work of starting to turn around our ocean liner of an economy, laying the foundation for the transition to a world of renewable energy.

That didn't happen, of course. Fixated on the economy, Clinton and 10 Gore presided over a decade when Americans, who already emitted a quarter of the world's carbon dioxide, actually managed to increase their total output by 12 percent. Now we have a president who seems unsure whether global warming is real, and far more concerned with increasing power production than with worrying about trifles like the collapse of the globe's terrestrial systems. In November, the hope of global controls on carbon dioxide production essentially collapsed at an international conference in the Hague, when the United States refused to make even modest concessions on its use of fossil fuels, and the rest of the world finally walked away from the table in disgust.

In the face of all this, what is an environmentalist to do? The normal answer, when you're mounting a campaign, is to look for self-interest, to scare people by saying what will happen to us if we don't do something: All the birds will die, the canyon will disappear beneath a reservoir, we will choke to death on smog.

But in the case of global warming, those kind of answers don't exactly do the trick, at least in the timeframe we're discussing. At this latitude, climate change will creep up on us. Severe storms have already grown more frequent and more damaging. The seasons are less steady in their progression. Some agriculture is less reliable. But face it: Our economy is so enormous that it handles those kinds of changes in stride. Economists who work on this stuff talk about how it will shave a percentage or two off GNP over the next few decades—not enough to notice in the kind of generalized economic boom they describe. And most of us live lives so divorced from the natural world that we hardly notice the changes anyway. Hotter? Turn up the air conditioning. Stormier? Well, an enormous percentage of Americans commute from remote-controlled garage to office parking garage—they may have gone the last year without getting good and wet in a rainstorm. By the time the magnitude of the change is truly in our faces, it will be too late to do much about it: There's such a lag time with carbon dioxide in the atmosphere that we need to be making the switch to solar and wind and hydrogen right about now. Yesterday, in fact.

So maybe we should think of global warming in a different way—as the great moral crisis of our moment, the equivalent in our time of the civil rights movement of the '60s.

Why a moral question? In the first place, because we've never figured out a more effective way to screw the marginalized and poor of this planet. Having taken their dignity, their resources, and their freedom under a variety of other schemes, we now are taking the very physical stability on which they depend for the most bottom-line of existences.

Our economy can absorb these changes for a while, but for a moment 15 consider Bangladesh. A river delta that houses 130 million souls in an area the size of Wisconsin, Bangladesh actually manages food self-sufficiency most years. But in 1998, the sea level in the Bay of Bengal was higher than normal, just the sort of thing we can expect to become more frequent and severe. The waters sweeping down the Ganges and the

Brahmaputra from the Himalayas could not drain easily into the ocean—they backed up across the country, forcing most of its inhabitants to spend three months in thigh-deep water. The fall rice crop didn't get planted. We've seen this same kind of disaster in the last few years in Mozambique or Honduras or Venezuela or any of a dozen other wretched spots.

And a moral crisis, too, if you place any value on the rest of creation. Coral reef researchers indicate that these spectacularly intricate ecosystems are also spectacularly vulnerable—rising water temperatures will likely bleach them to extinction by mid-century. In the Arctic, polar bears are 20 percent scrawnier than they were a decade ago: As pack ice melts, so does the opportunity for hunting seals. All in all, this century seems poised to see extinctions at a rate not observed since the last big asteroid slammed into the planet. But this time the asteroid is us.

A moral question, finally, if you think we owe any debt to the future. No one ever has figured out a more thorough-going way to strip-mine the present and degrade what comes after. Forget the seventh generation—we're talking 70th generation, and 700th. All the people that will ever be related to you. Ever. No generation yet to come will ever forget us—we are the ones present at the moment when the temperature starts to spike, and so far we have not reacted. If it had been done to us, we would loathe the generation that did it, precisely as we will one day be loathed.

But trying to make a moral campaign is no easy task. In most moral crises, there is a villain—some person or class or institution that must be overcome. Once they're identified, the battle can commence. But you can't really get angry at carbon dioxide, and the people responsible for its production are, well, us. So perhaps we need some symbols to get us started, some places to sharpen the debate and rally ourselves to action. There are plenty to choose from: our taste for ever bigger houses and the heating and cooling bills that come with them; our penchant for jumping on airplanes at the drop of a hat; and so on. But if you wanted one glaring example of our lack of balance, you could do worse than point the finger at sport utility vehicles.

SUVs are more than mere symbol. They are a major part of the problem—one reason we emit so much more carbon dioxide now than we did a decade ago is because our fleet of cars and trucks actually has gotten steadily less fuel efficient for the past ten years. If you switched today from the average American car to a big SUV, and drove it for just one year, the difference in carbon dioxide that you produced would be the equivalent of opening your refrigerator door and then forgetting to close it for six years. SUVs essentially are machines for burning fossil fuel that just happen to also move you and your stuff around.

But what makes them such a perfect symbol is the brute fact that 20 they are simply unnecessary. Go to the parking lot of the nearest suburban supermarket and look around: The only conclusion you can draw is that to reach the grocery, people must drive through three or four raging rivers and up the side of a trackless canyon. These are semi-military machines (some, like the Hummer, are not semi at all), Brinks trucks on a slight diet. They don't keep their occupants safer, they do wreck whatever they plow into—they are the perfect metaphor for a heedless, supersized society. And a gullible one, which has been sold on these vast vehicles partly by the promise that they somehow allow us to commune with nature.

That's why we need a much broader politics than the White House-lobbying that's occupied the big enviros for the past decade, or the mass-market mailing that has been their stock in trade for the past quarter century. We need to take all the brilliant and energetic strategies of local grassroots groups fighting dumps and cleaning up rivers, and we need to make those tactics national and international. So that's why some pastors are starting to talk with their congregations about what car they're going to buy, and why some college seniors are passing around petitions pledging to stay away from the Ford Explorers and Excursions and Extraneouses, and why some few auto dealers have begun to notice informational picketers outside on Saturday mornings urging their customers to think about gas mileage when they go inside.

The point is not that by themselves such actions—any individual actions—will make any real dent in the production of carbon dioxide pouring into our atmosphere. Even if you got 10 percent of Americans really committed to changing energy use, their solar homes wouldn't make much of a dent in our national totals. But 10 percent would be enough to change the politics of the issue, to insure the passage of the laws that would cause us all to shift our habits. And so we need to begin to take an issue that is now the province of technicians and turn it into a political issue—just as bus boycotts began to take the issue of race and make it public, forcing the system to respond. That response is likely to be ugly—there are huge companies with a lot to lose, and many people so tied in to their current ways of life that advocating change smacks of subversion. But this has to become a political issue—and fast. The only way that may happen, short of a hideous drought or monster flood, is if it becomes a personal issue first.

TOPICS FOR CRITICAL THINKING AND WRITING

1. Suppose scientists could convince us that exactly one of the four most troubling consequences of global warming could be prevented within the next decade. Which of the four that McKibben identifies (para. 4) would you choose to end and why?

2. McKibben states that we should think of global warming as "the great moral crisis" (para. 13) of our time. What reasons does he give? What makes a crisis a moral crisis? What other kinds of crises are there?

3. Explain why McKibben claims that the SUV is both a "symbol" and a "problem" (para. 18) of what is wrong with our current distribution of material resources.

4. What persona does McKibben convey in this essay? Thoughtful? Belligerent? Hysterical? Concerned but eccentric? Support your answer with evidence.

5. McKibben often varies the length of his sentences, sometimes surprisingly. For instance, in the first paragraph the first sentence contains twenty-four words, the second twenty-nine words, the third twenty-four, but the fourth—a question—contains only five words. What effect does he gain? Take another passage in this essay where there is a sharp contrast and explain the effect.

6. Now that you have read McKibben's essay and have considered his argument, do you plan to change your behavior in any way? Explain.

Edward Abbey

Edward Abbey (1927–1989) was born in Indiana, Pennsylvania. He was educated at the University of New Mexico, where he earned a master's degree. His thesis was titled "Anarchism and the Morality of Violence." A vigorous advocate on behalf of environmental issues, he wrote a novel, The Monkey Wrench Gang *(1975), in which some ecoterrorists destroy property belonging to road builders and other companies that endanger the desert by seeking to "develop" it. The book is said to have inspired radical environmentalists, persons who engage in unlawful activities—including terrorism—in the defense of the environment. (Abbey's response: "The most common form of terrorism in the U.S.A. is that carried on by bulldozers and chain saws.")*

Even before Abbey wrote The Monkey Wrench Gang, *his reputation had been established with* Desert Solitaire *(1968), a nonfictional account of his experiences as a park ranger at Arches National Monument (now a national park) in Utah. In accordance with his dying wish ("I want my body to help fertilize the growth of a cactus or cliff rose or sagebrush or tree"), he is buried in the Cabeza Prieta Desert in Arizona.*

This essay is excepted from One Life at a Time, Please *(1988).*

Eco-Defense

If a stranger batters your door down with an axe, threatens your family and yourself with deadly weapons, and proceeds to loot your home of whatever he wants, he is committing what is universally recognized—by law and morality—as a crime. In such a situation the householder has both the right and the obligation to defend himself, his family, and his property by whatever means are necessary. This right and this obligation is universally recognized, justified, and praised by all civilized human communities. Self-defense against attack is one of the basic laws not only of human society but of life itself, not only of human life but of all life.

The American wilderness, what little remains, is now undergoing exactly such an assault. With bulldozer, earth mover, chainsaw, and dynamite, the international timber, mining, and beef industries are invading our public lands—property of all Americans—bashing their way into our forests, mountains, and rangelands and looting them for everything they can get away with. This for the sake of short-term profits in the corporate sector and multimillion-dollar annual salaries for the three-piece-suited gangsters (M.B.A.—Harvard, Yale, University of Tokyo, et alia) who control and manage these bandit enterprises. Cheered on, naturally, by *Time, Newsweek,* and the *Wall Street Journal,* actively encouraged, inevitably, by those jellyfish government agencies that are supposed to *protect* the public lands, and as always aided and abetted in every way possible by the compliant politicians of our Western states, such as Babbitt, DeConcini, Goldwater, McCain, Hatch, Garn, Simms, Hansen, Andrus, Wallop, Domenici and Co. Inc.—who would sell the graves of their mothers if there's a quick buck in the deal, over or under the table, what do they care?

Representative government in the United States has broken down. Our legislators do not represent the public, the voters, or even those who voted for them but rather the commercial-industrial interests that finance their political campaigns and control the organs of communication—the TV, the newspapers, the billboards, the radio. Politics is a game for the rich only. Representative government in the U.S.A. represents money, not people, and therefore has forfeited our allegiance and moral support. We owe it nothing but the taxation it extorts from us under threats of seizure of property, imprisonment, or in some cases already, when resisted, a violent death by gunfire.

Such is the nature and structure of the industrial megamachine (in Lewis Mumford's term) which is now attacking the American wilderness. That wilderness is our ancestral home, the primordial homeland of all living creatures including the human, and the present final dwelling place of such noble beings as the grizzly bear, the mountain lion, the eagle and the condor, the moose and the elk and the pronghorn antelope, the redwood tree, the yellow pine, the bristlecone pine, and yes, why not say it?—the streams, waterfalls, rivers, the very bedrock itself of our hills, canyons, deserts, mountains. For many of us, perhaps for most of us, the wilderness is more our home than the little stucco boxes, wallboard apartments, plywood trailer-houses, and cinderblock condominiums in which the majority are now confined by the poverty of an overcrowded industrial culture.

And if the wilderness is our true home, and if it is threatened with 5 invasion, pillage, and destruction—as it certainly is—then we have the right to defend that home, as we would our private quarters, by whatever means are necessary. (An Englishman's home is his castle; the American's home is his favorite forest, river, fishing stream, her favorite mountain or desert canyon, his favorite swamp or woods or lake.) We have the right to resist and we have the obligation; not to defend that which we love would be dishonorable. The majority of the American people have demonstrated on every possible occasion that they support the ideal of wilderness preservation; even our politicians are forced by popular opinion to *pretend* to support the idea; as they have learned, a vote against wilderness is a vote against their own reelection. We are justified then in defending our homes—our private home and our public home—not only by common law and common morality but also by common belief. We are the majority; they—the powerful—are in the minority.

How best defend our homes? Well, that is a matter of the strategy, tactics, and technique, which eco-defense is all about.

What is eco-defense? Eco-defense means fighting back. Eco-defense means sabotage. Eco-defense is risky but sporting; unauthorized but fun; illegal but ethically imperative. Next time you enter a public forest scheduled for chainsaw massacre by some timber corporation and its flunkies in the U.S. Forest Service, carry a hammer and a few pounds of sixty-penny nails in your creel, saddlebag, game bag, backpack, or picnic basket. Spike those trees; you won't hurt them; they'll be grateful for the protection; and you may save the forest. Loggers hate nails. My Aunt Emma back in West Virginia has been enjoying this pleasant exercise for years. She swears by it. It's good for the trees, it's good for the woods, and it's good for the human soul. Spread the word.

TOPICS FOR CRITICAL THINKING AND WRITING

1. Abbey's opening paragraph speaks of a stranger battering down the reader's door, threatening the family, and so on. His second paragraph begins, "The American wilderness, what little remains of it, is now undergoing exactly such an assault." Really? "Exactly such an assault"? Do you find Abbey's analogy appropriate, helpful, convincing—or do you think he weakens his case by overstating it? Explain.

2. Abbey lists ten "compliant politicians" who, he says, would "sell the graves of their mothers" (para. 2) if the price were right. Choose two or three from the list and investigate their voting records in Congress. What does your investigation tell you about the legitimacy of Abbey's scorn?

3. Who is or was Lewis Mumford (para. 4)? Why does Abbey cite him?

4. Abbey, in a somewhat cute manner, writes "yes, why not say it?" (para. 4), followed by a list of seven items in the physical environment. Why the cute comment? Does it advance his argument or not? Explain.

5. How do these seven items compare with the ten "noble beings" (also para. 4) that precede the list of seven? What others might belong on either of these lists?

6. Evaluate the final paragraph as a piece of writing (Is it effective?) and as a piece of advice (Is it good advice?). Support your responses with reasons.

25

Immigration: What Is to Be Done?

David Cole

David Cole (b. 1958), a professor at Georgetown University Law Center, is a volunteer staff attorney for the Center for Constitutional Rights. This essay originally appeared in The Nation *on October 17, 1994.*

Five Myths about Immigration

For a brief period in the mid-nineteenth century, a new political movement captured the passions of the American public. Fittingly labeled the "Know-Nothings," their unifying theme was nativism. They liked to call themselves "Native Americans," although they had no sympathy for people we call Native Americans today. And they pinned every problem in American society on immigrants. As one Know-Nothing wrote in 1856: "Four-fifths of the beggary and three-fifths of the crime spring from our foreign population; more than half the public charities, more than half the prisons and almshouses, more than half the police and the cost of administering criminal justice are for foreigners."

At the time, the greatest influx of immigrants was from Ireland, where the potato famine had struck, and Germany, which was in political and economic turmoil. Anti-alien and anti-Catholic sentiments were the order of the day, especially in New York and Massachusetts, which received the brunt of the wave of immigrants, many of whom were dirt-poor and uneducated. Politicians were quick to exploit the sentiment: There's nothing like a scapegoat to forge an alliance.

I am especially sensitive to this history: My forebears were among those dirt-poor Irish Catholics who arrived in the 1860s. Fortunately for them, and me, the Know-Nothing movement fizzled within fifteen years. But its pilot light kept burning, and is turned up whenever the American public begins to feel vulnerable and in need of an enemy.

Although they go by different names today, the Know-Nothings have returned. As in the 1850s, the movement is strongest where immigrants are most concentrated: California and Florida. The objects of prejudice are of course no longer Irish Catholics and Germans; 140 years later, "they" have become "us." The new "they" — because it seems "we" must always have a "they" — are Latin Americans (most recently, Cubans), Haitians, and Arab Americans, among others.

But just as in the 1850s, passion, misinformation and shortsighted 5 fear often substitute for reason, fairness, and human dignity in today's immigration debates. In the interest of advancing beyond know-nothingism, let's look at five current myths that distort public debate and government policy relating to immigrants.

America is being overrun with immigrants. In one sense, of course, this is true, but in that sense it has been true since Christopher Columbus arrived. Except for the real Native Americans, we are a nation of immigrants.

It is not true, however, that the first-generation immigrant share of our population is growing. As of 1990, foreign-born people made up only 8 percent of the population, as compared with a figure of about 15 percent from 1870 to 1920. Between 70 and 80 percent of those who immigrate every year are refugees or immediate relatives of U.S. citizens.

Much of the anti-immigrant fervor is directed against the undocumented, but they make up only 13 percent of all immigrants residing in the United States, and only 1 percent of the American population. Contrary to popular belief, most such aliens do not cross the border illegally but enter legally and remain after their student or visitor visa expires. Thus, building a wall at the border, no matter how high, will not solve the problem.

Immigrants take jobs from U.S. citizens. There is virtually no evidence to support this view, probably the most widespread misunderstanding about immigrants. As documented by a 1994 A.C.L.U. Immigrants' Rights Project report, numerous studies have found that immigrants actually *create* more jobs than they fill. The jobs immigrants take are of course easier to see, but immigrants are often highly productive, run their own businesses, and employ both immigrants and citizens. One study found that Mexican immigration to Los Angeles County between 1970 and 1980 was responsible for 78,000 new jobs. Governor Mario Cuomo reports that immigrants own more than 40,000 companies in New York, which provide thousands of jobs and $3.5 billion to the state's economy every year.

Immigrants are a drain on society's resources. This claim fuels many of the 10 recent efforts to cut off government benefits to immigrants. However, most studies have found that immigrants are a net benefit to the economy because, as a 1994 Urban Institute report concludes, "immigrants generate significantly more in taxes paid than they cost in services received." The Council of Economic Advisers similarly found in 1986 that "immigrants have a favorable effect on the overall standard of living."

Anti-immigrant advocates often cite studies purportedly showing the contrary, but these generally focus only on taxes and services at the local or state level. What they fail to explain is that because most taxes go to the federal government, such studies would also show a net loss when applied to U.S. citizens. At most, such figures suggest that some redistribution of federal and state monies may be appropriate; they say nothing unique about the costs of immigrants.

Some subgroups of immigrants plainly impose a net cost in the short run, principally those who have most recently arrived and have not yet "made it." California, for example, bears substantial costs for its disproportionately large undocumented population, largely because it has on average the poorest and least educated immigrants. But that has been true of every wave of immigrants that has ever reached our shores; it was as true of the Irish in the 1850s, for example, as it is of Salvadorans today. From a long-term perspective, the economic advantages of immigration are undeniable.

Some have suggested that we might save money and diminish incentives to immigrate illegally if we denied undocumented aliens public services. In fact, undocumented immigrants are already ineligible for most social programs, with the exception of education for schoolchildren, which is constitutionally required, and benefits directly related to health and safety, such as emergency medical care and nutritional assistance to poor women, infants, and children. To deny such basic care to people in need, apart from being inhumanly callous, would probably cost us more in the long run by exacerbating health problems that we would eventually have to address.

Aliens refuse to assimilate, and are depriving us of our cultural and political unity. This claim has been made about every new group of immigrants to arrive on U.S. shores. Supreme Court Justice Stephen Field wrote in 1884 that the Chinese "have remained among us a separate people, retaining their original peculiarities of dress, manners, habits, and modes of living, which are as marked as their complexion and language." Five years later, he upheld the racially based exclusion of Chinese immigrants. Similar claims have been made over different periods of our history about Catholics, Jews, Italians, Eastern Europeans, and Latin Americans.

In most instances, such claims are simply not true; "American culture" has been created, defined, and revised by persons who for the most part are descended from immigrants once seen as anti-assimilationist. Descendants of the Irish Catholics, for example, a group once decried as separatist and alien, have become presidents, senators, and representatives (and all of these in one family, in the case of the Kennedys). Our society exerts tremendous pressure to conform, and cultural separatism rarely survives a generation. But more important, even if this claim were true, is this a legitimate rationale for limiting immigration in a society built on the values of pluralism and tolerance?

Noncitizen immigrants are not entitled to constitutional rights. Our government has long declined to treat immigrants as full human beings, and nowhere is that more clear than in the realm of constitutional rights. Although the Constitution literally extends the fundamental protections in the Bill of Rights to all people, limiting to citizens only the right to vote and run for federal office, the federal government acts as if this were not the case.

In 1893 the executive branch successfully defended a statute that required Chinese laborers to establish their prior residence here by the testimony of "at least one credible white witness." The Supreme Court ruled that this law was constitutional because it was reasonable for Congress to presume that nonwhite witnesses could not be trusted.

The federal government is not much more enlightened today. In a pending case I'm handling in the Court of Appeals for the Ninth Circuit, the Clinton Administration has argued that permanent resident aliens lawfully living here should be extended no more First Amendment rights than aliens applying for first-time admission from abroad—that is, none. Under this view, students at a public university who are citizens may express themselves freely, but students who are not citizens can be deported for saying exactly what their classmates are constitutionally entitled to say.

Growing up, I was always taught that we will be judged by how we treat others. If we are collectively judged by how we have treated immigrants—those who would appear today to be "other" but will in a generation be "us"—we are not in very good shape.

TOPICS FOR CRITICAL THINKING AND WRITING

1. What are the "five current myths" (para. 5) about immigration that Cole identifies? Why does he describe them as "myths" (rather than errors, mistakes, or falsehoods)?

2. In an encyclopedia or other reference work in your college library, look up the "Know-Nothings" (para. 1). What, if anything, of interest do you learn about this movement that is not mentioned by Cole in his opening paragraphs (1–4)?

3. Cole attempts to show how insignificant the immigrant population really is (in paras. 7 and 13) because it involves such a small fraction (8 percent in 1990) of the total population. Suppose someone said to him, "That's all very well, but 8 percent of the population is still 20 million people—far more than the 15 percent of the population during the years from 1870 to 1920." How might he reply?

4. Suppose Cole is right that most illegal immigration results from overstaying visitor and student visas (para. 8). Why not pass laws prohibiting foreign students from studying here, since so many abuse the privilege? Why not pass other laws forbidding foreign visitors?

5. Cole cites a study (para. 9) showing that "Mexican immigration to Los Angeles County between 1970 and 1980 was responsible for 78,000

new jobs." Suppose it were also true that this immigration was responsible for 78,000 other Mexican immigrants who joined criminal gangs or were otherwise not legally employed. How might Cole respond?

6. Cole admits (para. 12) that in California, the large population of undocumented immigrants imposes "substantial costs" on taxpayers. Does Cole offer any remedy for this problem? Should the federal government bear some or all of these extra costs that fall on California?

7. Cole thinks that "cultural separatism" among immigrants "rarely survives a generation" (para. 15). His evidence? Look at the Irish Catholics. But suppose someone argued that this is weak evidence: Because today's immigrants are not Europeans, but are Asian and Hispanic, they will never assimilate to the degree that European immigrants did — their race, culture, religion, language, and the trend toward "multiculturalism" all block the way. How might Cole reply?

8. Do you think that immigrants who are not citizens and not applying for citizenship ought to be allowed to vote in state and local elections (the Constitution forbids them to vote in federal elections, as Cole points out in para. 16)? Why, or why not? How about illegal immigrants?

Barry R. Chiswick

Barry R. Chiswick holds a Ph.D. in economics from Columbia University. A specialist in the labor market, Chiswick is head of the economics department at the University of Illinois at Chicago. We reprint an essay that originally appeared in the New York Times *in June 2006.*

The Worker Next Door

It is often said that the American economy needs low-skilled foreign workers to do the jobs that American workers will not do. These foreign workers might be new immigrants, illegal aliens, or, in the current debate, temporary or guest workers. But if low-skilled foreign workers were not here, would lettuce not be picked, groceries not bagged, hotel sheets not changed, and lawns not mowed? Would restaurants use disposable plates and utensils?

On the face of it, this assertion seems implausible. Immigrants and low-skilled foreign workers in general are highly concentrated in a few states. The "big six" are California, Florida, Illinois, New Jersey, New York, and Texas. Even within those states, immigrants and low-skilled foreign workers are concentrated in a few metropolitan areas — while there are many in New York City and Chicago, relatively few are in upstate New York or downstate Illinois.

Yet even in areas with few immigrants, grass is cut, groceries are bagged, and hotel sheets are changed. Indeed, a large majority of low-skilled workers are native to the United States. A look at the 2000 census is instructive: among males age twenty-five to sixty-four years employed that year, of those with less than a high school diploma, 64 percent were born in the United States and 36 percent were foreign born.

Other Americans nominally graduated from high school but did not learn a trade or acquire the literacy, numeracy, or decision-making skills needed for higher earnings. Still others suffer from a physical or emotional ailment that limits their labor productivity. And some low-skilled jobs are performed by high school or college students, housewives, or the retired who wish to work part time. Put simply, there are no low-skilled jobs that American workers would not and do not do.

Over the past two decades the number of low-skilled workers in the 5 United States has increased because of immigration, both legal and illegal. This increase in low-skilled workers has contributed to the stagnation of wages for all such workers. The proposed "earned legalization" (amnesty) and guest worker programs would allow still more low-skilled workers into the country, further lowering their collective wages.

True, the prices of the goods and services that these new immigrants produce are reduced for the rich and poor alike. But the net effect of this dynamic is a decline in the purchasing power of low-skilled families and a rise in the purchasing power of high-income families—a significant factor behind the increase in income inequality that has been of considerable public concern over the past two decades.

In short, the continued increase in the flow of unskilled workers into the United States is the economic and moral equivalent of a regressive tax.

If the number of low-skilled foreign workers were to fall, wages would increase. Low-skilled American workers and their families would benefit, and society as a whole would gain from a reduction in income inequality.

Employers facing higher labor costs for low-skilled workers would raise their prices, and to some extent they would change the way they operate their businesses. A farmer who grows winter iceberg lettuce in Yuma County, Arizona, was asked on the ABC program *Nightline* in April what he would do if it were more difficult to find the low-skilled hand harvesters who work on his farm, many of whom are undocumented workers. He replied that he would mechanize the harvest. Such technology exists, but it is not used because of the abundance of low-wage laborers. In their absence, mechanical harvesters—and the higher-skilled (and higher wage) workers to operate them—would replace low-skilled, low-wage workers.

But, you might ask, who would mow the lawns in suburbia? The 10 higher wages would attract more lower-skilled American workers (including teenagers) to these jobs. Facing higher costs, some homeowners would switch to grass species that grow more slowly, to alternative ground cover, or to flagstones. Others would simply mow every other week, or every ten days, instead of weekly. And some would combine one or more of these strategies to offset rising labor costs.

Few of us change our sheets and towels at home every day. Hotels and motels could reduce the frequency of changing sheets and towels from every day to, say, every third day for continuing guests, perhaps offering a price discount to guests who accept this arrangement.

Less frequent lawn mowing and washing of hotel sheets and towels would reduce air, noise, and water pollution in the bargain.

With the higher cost of low-skilled labor, we would import more of some goods, in particular table-quality fruits and vegetables for home consumption (as distinct from industrial use) and lower-priced off-the-rack clothing. But it makes no sense to import people to produce goods in the United States for which we lack a comparative advantage—that is, goods that other countries can produce more efficiently.

The point is that with a decline in low-skilled foreign workers, life would go on. The genius of the American people is their ingenuity, and the genius of the American economy is its flexibility. And throughout our nation's history, this flexibility, the finding of alternative ways of doing things, has been a prime engine of economic growth and change.

Topics for Critical Thinking and Writing

1. Reread Chiswick's first paragraph, and try to remember the effect it had on you when you first read it. Did you think, "Hey, he is right; of course the lettuce would get picked, the groceries would be bagged, and the hotel sheets would be changed"? Or did you think, "Where is this guy going?" Or what? Evaluate Chiswick's first paragraph as the opening of an argument.

2. What is the program known as "earned legalization" (para. 5)?

3. In paragraph 6 Chiswick says that although cheap labor reduces the price of goods and services for the poor as well as for the rich, "the net effect . . . is a decline in the purchasing power of low-skilled families." Are you convinced? Why, or why not?

4. What is a "regressive tax" (para. 7)?

5. Why does Chiswick think (para. 8) wages would increase if the number of low-skilled foreign workers declined? Are you convinced by his argument? Why, or why not?

6. Suppose someone replied to Chiswick, saying, in effect, "You are right, but the fact is this. We have some 12 million Mexicans living here who entered illegally. America is big enough, and rich enough, and great-spirited enough to welcome them, and in fact America will probably be the gainer." What would you say?

7. Analyze and evaluate Chiswick's essay as an example of persuasive writing. What devices does he use, and how effectively does he use them?

"Well, they look pretty undocumented to me."

John Tierney

John Tierney, born in 1953, has written for the New York Times *since 1990, where he is now a regular columnist. He is the coauthor of a comic novel,* God Is My Broker *(1998), and the author of* The Best-Case Scenario Handbook *(2002), which tells you how to cope with such likely things as an ATM that keeps disgorging money. We reprint one of his columns written for the* New York Times *in April 2006.*

Ángels in America

Ángel Espinoza doesn't understand why Republicans on Capitol Hill are determined to deport Mexicans like him. I don't get it, either. He makes me think of my Irish grandfather.

They both left farms and went to the South Side of Chicago, arriving with relatively little education. My grandfather took a job in the stock-yards and lived in an Irish boarding house nearby. Espinoza started as a dishwasher and lived with his brother in a Mexican neighborhood.

Like my grandfather, who became a streetcar motorman and then a police officer, Espinoza moved on to better-paying jobs and a better home of his own. Like my grandfather, Espinoza married an American-born descendant of immigrants from his native country.

But whereas my grandfather became a citizen, Espinoza couldn't even become a legal resident. Once he married an American, he applied, but was rejected because he'd once been caught at the border and sent home with an order to stay out. Violating that order made him ineligible for a green card and eligible for deportation.

"I had to tell my four-year-old daughter that one day I might not 5 come home," he said. "I work hard and pay taxes and don't want any welfare. Why deport me?"

The official answer, of course, is that he violated the law. My grandfather didn't. But my grandfather didn't have to. There weren't quotas on Europeans or most other immigrants in 1911, even though, relative to the population, there were more immigrants arriving and living here than there are today. If America could absorb my grandfather, why keep out Espinoza?

It's been argued that Mexicans are different from past immigrants because they're closer to home and less likely to assimilate. Compared with other immigrants today, they're less educated, and their children are more likely to get poor grades and drop out of school. Therefore, the argument goes, Mexicans are in danger of becoming an underclass living in linguistically isolated ghettos.

Those concerns sound reasonable in theory. But if you look at studies of immigrants, you find that the typical story is much more like Espinoza's. He dropped out of school at age sixteen in southern Mexico, when his family needed money for medical bills. He paid a coyote to sneak him across the border and went to the Mexican neighborhood of Pilsen in Chicago, a metropolitan area that is now home to the second-largest Mexican population in the nation.

Espinoza started off making less than $4 an hour as a dishwasher in a restaurant that flouted the minimum-wage law. But he became a cook and worked up to $15 an hour. He switched to driving a street-cleaning truck, a job that now pays him $17 an hour, minus taxes and Social Security.

By age twenty-four, he and his wife, Anita, had saved enough to buy 10 a house for about $200,000 in Villa Park, a suburb where most people don't speak Spanish. Now twenty-seven, Espinoza's still working on his English (we spoke in Spanish), but his daughter is already speaking English at her preschool.

There's nothing unusual about his progress. More than half of the Mexican immigrants in Chicago own their own homes, and many are moving to the suburbs. No matter where they live, their children learn English.

You can hear this on the sidewalks and school corridors in Mexican neighborhoods like Pilsen, where most teenagers speak to one another in English. A national survey by the Pew Hispanic Center found that nearly all second-generation Latinos are either bilingual or English-dominant, and by the next generation 80 percent are English-dominant and virtually none speak just Spanish.

Yesterday, the Senate seemed close to a deal letting most immigrants become legal residents. But it fell apart when Republicans fought to add restrictions, including some that could prevent an immigrant with Espinoza's history from qualifying.

Bobby Rush, a Democratic representative from Chicago, is trying to pass protections for the Espinozas and other families in danger of being separated. The issue has galvanized other Chicago public officials and immigrant advocates, who are planning to take the families to Washington to press their case.

I'd like to see Republicans on Capitol Hill explain to Espinoza why 15 he's less deserving than their immigrant ancestors, but that's probably too much to expect. Espinoza has a simpler wish: "I would like them to tell my American daughter why her father can't stay with her."

Topics for Critical Thinking and Writing

1. Evaluate the effectiveness of Tierney's use of Ángel Espinoza in this essay. What does Tierney gain by introducing us to Espinoza?

2. In paragraph 4 Tierney explains why Espinoza is not eligible for a green card. If you could change the system, would you change the provision that makes him ineligible? Why, or why not?

3. Tierney ends his sixth paragraph with a question. What answer would you give to this question?

4. Who or what is a "coyote" (para. 8)?

5. In paragraph 8 Tierney refers to "studies of immigrants," but he does not cite any. Do you assume that there are such studies? Do you also assume, perhaps, that other studies may come to different conclusions? Do you believe that "studies" of this sort are highly relevant to the issue of whether or not immigration laws concerning Mexicans should or should not be revised. Explain.

6. Tierney ends his essay by saying that he would like to hear Republicans on Capitol Hill explain why Espinoza is less deserving than their ancestors. What do you think a Republican on Capitol Hill might say? What would *you* say?

7. Tierney implies that there are only bad reasons for excluding Latino immigrants from citizenship. Do you agree? Explain.

Victor Davis Hanson

Victor Davis Hanson, born in 1953 in Fowler, California, did his undergraduate work at the University of California at Santa Cruz and his Ph.D. work at Stanford University. A specialist in military history, he has taught classics at California State

University at Fresno. A noted conservative, Hanson is a senior fellow at the Hoover Institution. You can read many of his publications by entering his name in a search engine. This piece first appeared at realclearpolitics.com on May 25, 2006.

Our Brave New World of Immigration

In the dark of these rural spring mornings, I see full vans of Mexican laborers speeding by my farmhouse on their way to the western side of California's San Joaquin Valley to do the backbreaking work of weeding cotton, thinning tree fruit, and picking strawberries.

In the other direction, even earlier morning crews drive into town — industrious roofers, cement layers, and framers heading to a nearby new housing tract. While most of us are still asleep, thousands of these hard-working young men and women in the American Southwest rise with the sun to provide the sort of unmatched labor at the sort of wages that their eager employers insist they cannot find among citizens.

But just when one thinks that illegal immigration is an efficient win-win way of providing excellent workers to needy businesses, there are also daily warnings that there is something terribly wrong with a system predicated on a cynical violation of the law.

Three days ago, as I watched the daily early-morning caravan go by, I heard a horrendous explosion. Not far from my home, one of these vans had crossed the white line down the middle of the road and hit a pickup truck head-on. Perhaps the van had blown a bald tire. Perhaps the driver was intoxicated. Or perhaps he had no experience driving an overloaded minivan at high speed in the dark of early morning.

We will probably never know — since the driver ran away from the 5 carnage of the accident. That often happens when an illegal alien who survives an accident has no insurance or driver's license. But he did leave in his wake his three dead passengers. Eight more people were injured. Both cars were totaled. Traffic was rerouted around the wreckage for hours.

Ambulances, fire trucks, and patrol cars lined the nearby intersection. That accident alone must have imparted untold suffering for dozens of family members, as well as cost the state thousands of dollars.

Such mayhem is no longer an uncommon occurrence here. I have had four cars slam into our roadside property, with the drivers running off, leaving behind damaged vines and trees, and wrecked cars with phony licenses and no record of insurance. I have been broadsided by an undocumented driver, who ran a stop sign and then tried to run from our collision.

These are the inevitable but usually unmentioned symptoms of illegal immigration. After all, the unexpected can often happen when tens of thousands of young males from Mexico arrive in a strange country, mostly alone, without English or legality — an estimated 60 percent of them without a high-school degree and most obligated to send nearly half of their hard-won checks back to kin in Mexico.

Many Americans—perhaps out of understandable and well-meant empathy for the dispossessed who toil so hard for so little—support this present open system of non-borders. But I find nothing liberal about it.

Zealots may chant *¡Sí, se puede!* all they want. And the libertarian 10 right may dress up the need for cheap labor as a desire to remain globally competitive. But neither can disguise a cynicism about illegal immigration, one that serves to prop up a venal Mexican government, undercut the wages of our own poor, and create a new apartheid of millions of aliens in our shadows.

We have entered a new world of immigration without precedent. This current crisis is unlike the great waves of nineteenth-century immigration that brought thousands of Irish, Eastern Europeans, and Asians to the United States. Most immigrants in the past came legally. Few could return easily across an ocean to home. Arrivals from, say, Ireland or China could not embrace the myth that our borders had crossed them rather than vice versa.

Today, almost a third of all foreign-born persons in the United States are here illegally, making up 3 to 4 percent of the American population. It is estimated that the United States is home to 11 or 12 million illegal aliens, whose constantly refreshed numbers ensure there is always a perpetual class of unassimilated recent illegal arrivals. Indeed almost one-tenth of Mexico's population currently lives here illegally!

But the real problem is that we, the hosts, are also different from our predecessors. Today we ask too little of too many of our immigrants. We apparently don't care whether they come legally or learn English—or how they fare when they're not at work. Nor do we ask all of them to accept the brutal bargain of an American melting pot that rapidly absorbs the culture of an immigrant in exchange for the benefits of citizenship.

Instead, we are happy enough that most labor vans of hardworking helots stay on the road in the early-morning hours, out of sight and out of mind. Sometimes, though, they tragically do not.

Topics for Critical Thinking and Writing

1. Speakers and writers who take care to present themselves as decent, trustworthy people are concerned with what the Greeks called *ethos*, character. What impression do you get of Hanson's character from the first two paragraphs? If you had to guess—basing your guess only on the first two paragraphs—where Hanson stood on immigration, what would you say? Why?

2. What do you make of Hanson's title?

3. The third paragraph begins "But," a clear transition indicating that we will be going in a different direction. What other words in the third paragraph indicate what the writer's position will be?

4. What does Hanson mean in paragraph 3 when he calls the labor market in the San Joaquin Valley "a system predicated on a cynical violation of the law"? Do you agree with that description? Explain.

5. In his eleventh paragraph Hanson speaks of "the myth that our borders had crossed [the immigrants from Mexico]" rather than vice versa. What does he mean by this? Do you agree that it is a myth? Explain.

6. What are the differences between current immigration from Mexico and historic immigration from Europe a century ago (see para. 11)?

7. How does Hanson know that "almost a third of all foreign-born persons in the United States are here illegally" (para. 12)? Could it be that, from a sample of arrested immigrants, 30 percent or so turn out to be illegal? Is such a method of calculation persuasive? Explain.

8. In his next-to-last paragraph Hanson says, "We apparently don't care whether [immigrants] come legally or learn English." Do you agree with this assertion? On what evidence do you base your response?

9. Evaluate Hanson's final paragraph. Given his earlier paragraphs, does the paragraph make an effective ending? Explain.

Cardinal Roger Mahony

Roger Mahony, born in 1936 in Hollywood, California, was ordained a priest in 1962. In 1975 Governor Jerry Brown appointed Mahony as the first chair of the California Agricultural Labor Relations Board, where he worked to resolve disputes between the United Farm Workers and the growers. In 1980 Mahony was appointed bishop, in 1985 archbishop, and in 1991 cardinal. He has made controversial statements, sometimes disturbing liberals and sometimes disturbing conservatives. This following op-ed selection was originally published in the New York Times *in March 2006.*

Called by God to Help

I've received a lot of criticism for stating last month that I would instruct the priests of my archdiocese to disobey a proposed law that would subject them, as well as other church and humanitarian workers, to criminal penalties. The proposed Border Protection, Antiterrorism, and Illegal Immigration Control bill, which was approved by the House of Representatives in December and is expected to be taken up by the Senate next week, would among other things subject to five years in prison anyone who "assists" an undocumented immigrant "to remain in the United States."

Some supporters of the bill have even accused the church of encouraging illegal immigration and meddling in politics. But I stand by my statement. Part of the mission of the Roman Catholic Church is to help people in need. It is our Gospel mandate, in which Christ instructs us to clothe the naked, feed the poor, and welcome the stranger. Indeed, the Catholic Church, through Catholic Charities agencies around the country, is one of the largest nonprofit providers of social services in the nation, serving both citizens and immigrants.

Providing humanitarian assistance to those in need should not be made a crime, as the House bill decrees. As written, the proposed law is so broad that it would criminalize even minor acts of mercy like offering a meal or administering first aid.

Current law does not require social service agencies to obtain evidence of legal status before rendering aid, nor should it. Denying aid to a fellow human being violates a law with a higher authority than Congress—the law of God.

That does not mean that the Catholic Church encourages or supports 5 illegal immigration. Every day in our parishes, social service programs, hospitals, and schools, we witness the baleful consequences of illegal immigration. Families are separated, workers are exploited, and migrants are left by smugglers to die in the desert. Illegal immigration serves neither the migrant nor the common good.

What the church supports is an overhaul of the immigration system so that legal status and legal channels for migration replace illegal status and illegal immigration. Creating legal structures for migration protects not only those who migrate but also our nation, by giving the government the ability to better identify who is in the country as well as to control who enters it.

Only comprehensive reform of the immigration system, embodied in the principles of another proposal in Congress, the Secure America and Orderly Immigration bill, will help solve our current immigration crisis.

Enforcement-only proposals like the Border Protection act take the country in the opposite direction. Increasing penalties, building more detention centers, and erecting walls along our border with Mexico, as the act provides, will not solve the problem.

The legislation will not deter migrants who are desperate to survive and support their families from seeking jobs in the United States. It will only drive them further into the shadows, encourage the creation of more elaborate smuggling networks and cause hardship and suffering. I hope that the Senate will not take the same enforcement-only road as the House.

The unspoken truth of the immigration debate is that at the same 10 time our nation benefits economically from the presence of undocumented workers, we turn a blind eye when they are exploited by employers. They work in industries that are vital to our economy yet they have little legal protection and no opportunity to contribute fully to our nation.

While we gladly accept their taxes and sweat, we do not acknowledge or uphold their basic labor rights. At the same time, we scapegoat them for our social ills and label them as security threats and criminals to justify the passage of anti-immigrant bills.

This situation affects the dignity of millions of our fellow human beings and makes immigration, ultimately, a moral and ethical issue.

That is why the church is compelled to take a stand against harmful legislation and to work toward positive change.

It is my hope that our elected officials will understand this and enact immigration reform that respects our common humanity and reflects the values—fairness, compassion, and opportunity—upon which our nation, a nation of immigrants, was built.

Topics for Critical Thinking and Writing

1. Would it matter to Cardinal Mahony's position if the legislation he mentions in paragraph 1 proposed a mandatory rather than a discretionary prison term for violators? Why, or why not?

2. Do you agree with the author that the proposed law is overly broad (para. 3)? How does he argue for such a conclusion? How might you argue for or against it?

3. What's the difference between supporting "humanitarian assistance" to all comers (para. 3) and not "encourag[ing]" or "support[ing] illegal immigration" (para. 5)? Is the distinction an important one? Explain.

4. Does Cardinal Mahony just favor breaking the law (if law it becomes), penalizing those who "assist" undocumented immigrants to remain in the United States? Or does he favor civil disobedience on this issue? What's the difference, in any case?

5. Suppose someone accused the cardinal of exaggerating the threat; no sensible prosecutor or district attorney is going to seek a conviction of someone for "administering first aid" (para. 3) to an illegal immigrant. How might he reply?

6. What are the main features of the Secure America and Orderly Immigration bill (para. 7)? What would it do (if enacted into law) to cure the problem of illegal immigration? Can you think of some other measures that, if enacted into law, might help solve this problem?

7. Do you think it is unfair to tax the earnings of undocumented workers and at the same time refuse to provide them with basic human rights (para. 11)? Explain why or why not in an essay of 250 words.

For topical links related to the issue of immigration, see the companion Web site: **bedfordstmartins.com/barnetbedau.**

26

Sexual Harassment: Is There Any Doubt about What It Is?

Tufts University

Many colleges and universities have drawn up statements of policy concerning sexual harassment. The following statement is fairly typical in that it seeks to define sexual harassment, to suggest ways of stopping it (these range from informal discussion to a formal grievance procedure), and to indicate resources that can provide help.

Sexual Harassment

POLICY STATEMENT

Sexual harassment violates the dignity of individuals. It is a form of discrimination that violates federal and state laws and is prohibited at Tufts University. Tufts is committed to providing an education and work environment that is free from sexual harassment. The University works to prevent and address sexual harassment through educational programs, training, and complaint resolution. Tufts encourages all members of the University community to report any concerns or complaints of sexual harassment.

Managers, supervisors, and other agents of the University are required to respond promptly and appropriately to allegations of sexual harassment that are brought to their attention.

Identifying Sexual Harassment

1. **What is sexual harassment?**
   Sexual harassment is a form of sex discrimination. It includes unwelcome sexual advances, requests for sexual favors, and other physical or verbal conduct of a sexual nature or conduct directed at a person because of his or her gender when:

   • Submission to such conduct is made either explicitly or implicitly a term and condition of an individual's academic status or employment; or

- Submission to, or rejection of, such conduct by an individual is used as a basis for academic decisions or
- employment decisions; or
- Such conduct, whether verbal or
- physical, has the purpose or effect of unreasonably interfering with the individual's academic or work performance or
- of creating an intimidating, hostile, or
- offensive environment in which to work or to learn.

2. **What are my rights under this policy?**
   You have the right to work, learn, and live in an environment free from sexual harassment.
3. **Who could be involved in an incident of sexual harassment?**
   Sexual harassment can occur between any individuals associated with the University, whether between people of different sexes or the same sex. Sexual harassment can occur between people of unequal power or between peers. Examples of who could be involved in a sexual harassment allegation could include, but are not limited to, any combination of the following: supervisor and subordinate, faculty and staff, coworkers, student and professor, student and staff, student and student, contractor or vendor and staff.

   A victim does not have to be the direct recipient of the conduct but could be anyone affected by the conduct.
4. **What actions constitute sexual harassment?**

The following are some examples of conduct, particularly when unwel- 5
come, which may constitute sexual harassment:

- Direct proposition of a sexual nature and/or subtle pressure for sexual activity that is unwanted and unreasonably interferes with a person's work or academic environment
- gender harassment, including sexist statements and behavior that convey insulting, degrading, or sexist attitudes
- persistent and unwanted requests for dates, unwelcome and inappropriate letters, telephone calls, email, or other communications or gifts
- direct or implied threats that submission to sexual advances will be a condition of employment, work status, promotion, grades, or letters of recommendation
- subtle or overt pressure for sexual favors
- unwanted physical contact such as touching, hugging, brushing against a person's body, impeding or blocking movements
- sexually explicit statements, questions, jokes, or anecdotes regardless of the means of communication (oral, written, email, text messages, etc.)

- the display of inappropriate sexually oriented materials in a location where others can view them
- sexual assault, attempted rape, or rape. (Please see section on sexual assault)

5. Where does sexual harassment occur?
Sexual harassment does not restrict itself to the workplace nor does it have to take place on University property. Sexual harassment could occur at any University sponsored program or activity regardless of location. For example, sexual harassment could occur out of state, such as at a conference, off site project, or an externship.

6. What can I do if I feel I have been sexually harassed?
- If you feel comfortable enough, you may talk with the person, inform him or her of the unwelcome behavior and ask that the behavior stop. Document the incident and the steps taken to resolve it.
- Staff/faculty: You may report it to any supervisor or manager; Student: You may report it to any university faculty member or university administrator.

RIGHTS AND RESPONSIBILITIES

As a member of the Tufts community you have the right to work, learn, and live in an environment free from sexual harassment. All members are responsible for reporting incidents of possible sexual harassment. Managers, supervisors, and other agents of the University are required to respond promptly and appropriately to allegations of sexual harassment that are brought to their attention.

Duty to Report. Managers, supervisors, faculty and other agents of the University have a duty to report any known or alleged incidents of sexual harassment to the OEO.

Duty to Cooperate. Faculty, staff, student employees, and students must cooperate with University investigations into sexual harassment. Refusal to cooperate with an investigation may result in disciplinary action.

Freedom from Retaliation. Any member of the University community has the right to raise concerns about or complaints of, sexual harassment without fear of reprisal. It is unlawful and it is a violation of University policy to retaliate against an individual for filing a complaint of sexual harassment or for cooperating in a sexual harassment investigation. Any person who retaliates against an individual reporting sexual

10

harassment, filing a sexual harassment complaint, or participating in a sexual harassment investigation is subject to disciplinary action up to and including expulsion or termination by the University.

Confidentiality. The University recognizes the importance of confidentiality and understands that some individuals filing complaints or involved in an investigation may want their identity to remain confidential. In some instances, the alleged harasser can be spoken to without the Complainant being identified. In other cases, issues of confidentiality must be balanced against the University's need to investigate and take appropriate action. The University will respect the privacy and confidentiality of individuals involved in a sexual harassment investigation to the fullest extent possible.

Consequences of Sexual Harassment. Sexual harassment affects the victim of harassment. The student or employee may suffer a diminished ability to work and study, which may have a lasting career impact or a loss of confidence in the University's ability to provide a comfortable and safe environment for work and learning. A student's educational goals may also be significantly affected if the student decides to avoid certain courses, change his or her area of study, or transfer to another institution.

In addition, sexual harassment impacts the University and the department(s) involved. The University and the department(s) may experience an atmosphere of fear, intimidation, declining work productivity and office morale.

A person found responsible for sexual harassment may face:

- student disciplinary action
- letter of reprimand
- denial of promotion
- demotion
- suspension
- termination

Sexual Assault Cases. Students who are survivors of sexual 15 assault are highly encouraged to contact University police. Reporting an assault to University police does not require filing criminal charges; however, it does allow the University to assist and support the survivor. Sexual assault is an egregious form of sexual harassment and it is a crime. The University takes all incidents seriously. The University supports the right of the survivor of a sexual assault to decide how best to utilize various university, community, private, and public support systems designated to address crimes of sexual assault.

TOPICS FOR CRITICAL THINKING AND WRITING

1. Where, if at all, would you draw the line between harmless, inoffensive flirtation and sexual harassment?

2. For an act to qualify as sexual harassment, is it, or should it be, necessary that the aggressor persist in behavior the victim doesn't want after the victim has said "Stop!"? What position does the Tufts policy take on this issue?

3. Evaluate the list of actions that constitute sexual harassment. Does it seem comprehensive to you? In your opinion, does each do a good enough job defining expectations for student, faculty, and staff behavior? Can you identify any gaps or gray areas in this list?

4. Why do you think Tufts University includes the section titled "Rights and Responsibilities"? How does this section contribute to the policy as a whole?

5. If your school has a comparable statement of policy, study it closely, partly by comparing it with the Tufts policy. Then (assuming that your school's statement does not in every respect satisfy you), set forth (with supporting reasons) the revisions you would make in it.

Ellen Goodman

Ellen Goodman (b. 1941), was educated at Radcliffe College and worked as a reporter for Newsweek *and the* Detroit Free Press. *Since 1976 she has written for the* Boston Globe, *and since 1972 her column has been nationally syndicated. In 1980 she was the recipient of the Pulitzer Prize for Distinguished Commentary. The essay that we reprint appeared in the* Boston Globe *in October 1991. (For another essay by Goodman, see p. 726.)*

The Reasonable Woman Standard

Since the volatile mix of sex and harassment exploded under the Capitol dome, it hasn't just been senators scurrying for cover. The case of the professor and judge has left a gender gap that looks more like a crater.[1]

We have discovered that men and women see this issue differently. Stop the presses. Sweetheart, get me rewrite.

On the *Today* show, Bryant Gumbel asks something about a man's right to have a pinup on the wall and Katie Couric says what she thinks

---

[1]Professor Anita Hill, of the University of Oklahoma Law School, accused Clarence Thomas of sexually harassing her while he was her supervisor. The accusations were made before the Senate Judiciary Committee in hearings to confirm Thomas's appointment to a seat on the U.S. Supreme Court. During the televised hearings, several senators were widely regarded as having treated Hill badly. [Editors' note.]

of that. On the normally sober *MacNeil/Lehrer* hour the usual panel of legal experts doesn't break down between left and right but between male and female.

On a hundred radio talk shows, women are sharing experiences and men are asking for proof. In ten thousand offices, the order of the day is the nervous joke. One boss asks his secretary if he can still say "good morning," or is that sexual harassment. Heh, heh. The women aren't laughing.

Okay boys and girls, back to your corners. Can we talk? Can we hear?   5

The good news is that women have stopped rolling their eyes at each other and started speaking out. The bad news is that we may each assume the other gender not only doesn't understand but can't understand. "They don't get it" becomes "they can't get it."

Let's start with the fact that sexual harassment is a concept as new as date rape. Date rape, that should-be oxymoron, assumes a different perspective on the part of the man and the woman. His date, her rape. Sexual harassment comes with some of the same assumptions. What he labels sexual, she labels harassment.

This produces what many men tend to darkly call a "murky" area of the law. Murky, however, is a step in the right direction. When everything was clear, it was clearly biased. The old single standard was [a] male standard. The only options a working woman had were to grin, bear it, or quit.

Sexual harassment rules are based on the point of view of the victim, nearly always a woman. The rules ask, not just whether she has been physically assaulted, but whether the environment in which she works is intimidating or coercive. Whether she feels harassed. It says that her feelings matter.

This, of course, raises all sorts of hackles about women's *feelings*,   10
women's *sensitivity.* How can you judge the sensitivity level of every single woman you work with? What's a poor man to do?

But the law isn't psychiatry. It doesn't adapt to individual sensitivity levels. There is a standard emerging by which the courts can judge these cases and by which people can judge them as well. It's called "the reasonable woman standard." How would a reasonable woman interpret this? How would a reasonable woman behave?

This is not an entirely new idea, although perhaps the law's belief in the reasonableness of women is. There has long been a "reasonable man" in the law not to mention a "reasonable pilot," a "reasonable innkeeper," a "reasonable train operator."

Now the law is admitting that a reasonable woman may see these situations differently than a man. That truth—available in your senator's mailbag—is also apparent in research. We tend to see sexualized situations from our own gender's perspective. Kim Lane Scheppele, a political science and law professor at the University of Michigan, summarizes the miscues this way: "Men see the sex first and miss the coercion. Women see the coercion and miss the sex."

Does that mean that we are genetically doomed to our double vision? Scheppele is quick to say no. Our justice system rests on the belief that one person can get in another's head, walk in her shoes, see things from another perspective. And so does our hope for change.

If a jury of car drivers can understand how a "reasonable pilot" 15 would see one situation, a jury of men can see how a reasonable woman would see another event. The crucial ingredient is empathy.

Check it out in the office tomorrow. He's coming on, she's backing off, he keeps coming. Read the body language. There's a *Playboy* calendar on the wall and a PMS joke in the boardroom and the boss is just being friendly. How would a reasonable woman feel?

At this moment, when the air is crackling with hostility and consciousness-raising has the hair sticking up on the back of many necks, guess what? Men can "get it." Reasonable men.

TOPICS FOR CRITICAL THINKING AND WRITING

1. Goodman is a journalist, which means in part that her writing is lively. Point to two or three sentences that you would not normally find in a textbook, and evaluate them. (Example: "Okay boys and girls, back to your corners," para. 5.) Are the sentences you have selected effective? Why, or why not?

2. Why does Goodman describe date rape as a "should-be oxymoron" (para. 7)?

3. In paragraphs 11 and 12 Goodman speaks of "the reasonable woman standard." In recent years several cases have come to the courts in which women have said that they are harassed by posters of nude women in the workplace. Such posters have been said to create an "intimidating, hostile, or offensive environment." (a) What do you think Goodman's opinion of these cases would be? (b) Imagine that you are a member of the jury deciding such a case. What is your verdict? Why?

4. According to Goodman's account of the law (paras. 8–13), the criterion for sexual harassment is whether the "reasonable woman" would regard the "environment" in which she works (or studies) as "intimidating" or "coercive," thus causing her to "feel harassed." In a 500-word essay describe three hypothetical cases, one of which you believe clearly involves sexual harassment, a second that clearly does not, and a third that is a borderline case.

5. Given what Goodman says about sexual harassment, can men be victims of sexual harassment? Why, or why not?

Ellen Frankel Paul

Ellen Frankel Paul is deputy director of the Social Philosophy and Policy Center and professor of political science at Bowling Green State University. Among the many books that she has written, edited, or coedited are Equity and Gender *(1989),* Self-Interest *(1997),* The Right to Privacy *(2000),* Morality and Politics *(2004),* Personal Identity *(2005), and* Justice and Global Politics *(2006). The essay that we reprint here was originally published in* Society *in 1991.*

Bared Buttocks and Federal Cases

Women in American society are victims of sexual harassment in alarming proportions. Sexual harassment is an inevitable corollary to class exploitation; as capitalists exploit workers, so do males in positions of authority exploit their female subordinates. Male professors, supervisors, and apartment managers in ever increasing numbers take advantage of the financial dependence and vulnerability of women to extract sexual concessions.

These are the assertions that commonly begin discussions of sexual harassment. For reasons that will be adumbrated below, dissent from the prevailing view is long overdue. Three recent episodes will serve to frame this disagreement.

Valerie Craig, an employee of Y & Y Snacks, Inc., joined several coworkers and her supervisor for drinks after work one day in July of 1978. Her supervisor drove her home and proposed that they become more intimately acquainted. She refused his invitation for sexual relations, whereupon he said that he would "get even" with her. Ten days after the incident she was fired from her job. She soon filed a complaint of sexual harassment with the Equal Employment Opportunity Commission (EEOC), and the case wound its way through the courts. Craig prevailed, the company was held liable for damages, and she received back pay, reinstatement, and an order prohibiting Y & Y from taking reprisals against her in the future.

Carol Zabowicz, one of only two female forklift operators in a West Bend Company warehouse, charged that her coworkers over a four-year period 1978–1982 sexually harassed her by such acts as: asking her whether she was wearing a bra; two of the men exposing their buttocks between ten and twenty times; a male coworker grabbing his crotch and making obscene suggestions or growling; subjecting her to offensive and abusive language; and exhibiting obscene drawings with her initials on them. Zabowicz began to show symptoms of physical and psychological stress, necessitating several medical leaves, and she filed a sexual harassment complaint with the EEOC. The district court judge remarked that "the sustained, malicious, and brutal harassment meted out . . . was more than merely unreasonable;

it was malevolent and outrageous." The company knew of the harassment and took corrective action only after the employee filed a complaint with the EEOC. The company, was, therefore, held liable, and Zabowicz was awarded back pay for the period of her medical absence, and a judgment that her rights were violated under the Civil Rights Act of 1964.

On September 17, 1990, Lisa Olson, a sports reporter for the *Boston Herald*, charged five football players of the just-defeated New England Patriots with sexual harassment for making sexually suggestive and offensive remarks to her when she entered their locker room to conduct a post-game interview. The incident amounted to nothing short of "mind rape," according to Olson. After vociferous lamentations in the media, the National Football League fined the team and its players $25,000 each. The National Organization for Women called for a boycott of Remington electric shavers because the owner of the company, Victor Kiam, also own[ed] the Patriots and allegedly displayed insufficient sensitivity at the time when the episode occurred.

All these incidents are indisputably disturbing. In an ideal world—one needless to say far different from the one that we inhabit or are ever likely to inhabit—women would not be subjected to such treatment in the course of their work. Women, and men as well, would be accorded respect by coworkers and supervisors, their feelings would be taken into account, and their dignity would be left intact. For women to expect reverential treatment in the workplace is utopian, yet they should not have to tolerate outrageous, offensive sexual overtures and threats as they go about earning a living.

One question that needs to be pondered is: What kinds of undesired sexual behavior should women be protected against by law? That is, what kind of actions are deemed so outrageous and violate a woman's rights to such extent that the law should intervene, and what actions should be considered inconveniences of life, to be morally condemned but not adjudicated? A subsidiary question concerns the type of legal remedy appropriate for the wrongs that do require redress. Before directly addressing these questions, it might be useful to diffuse some of the hyperbole adhering to the sexual harassment issue.

Surveys are one source of this hyperbole. If their results are accepted at face value, they lead to the conclusion that women are disproportionately victims of legions of sexual harassers. A poll by the Albuquerque *Tribune* found that nearly 80 percent of the respondents reported that they or someone they knew had been victims of sexual harassment. The Merit Systems Protection Board determined that 42 percent of the women (and 14 percent of men) working for the federal government had experienced some form of unwanted sexual attention between 1985 and 1987, with unwanted "sexual teasing" identified as the most prevalent form. A Defense Department survey found that 64 percent of women in the military (and 17 percent of the men) suffered "uninvited and unwanted sexual attention" within the previous year. The United Methodist Church established that 77 percent of its clergywomen experienced incidents of sexual harassment, with 41 percent of these naming a pastor or colleague as the perpetrator, and 31 percent mentioning church social functions as the setting.

A few caveats concerning polls in general, and these sorts of polls in particular, are worth considering. Pollsters looking for a particular social ill tend to find it, usually in gargantuan proportions. (What fate would lie in store for a pollster who concluded that child abuse, or wife beating, or mistreatment of the elderly had dwindled to the point of negligibility!) Sexual harassment is a notoriously ill-defined and almost infinitely expandable concept, including everything from rape to unwelcome neck massaging, discomfiture upon witnessing sexual overtures directed at others, yelling at and blowing smoke in the ears of female subordinates, and displays of pornographic pictures in the workplace. Defining sexual harassment, as the United Methodists did, as "any sexually related behavior that is unwelcome, offensive or which fails to respect the rights of others," the concept is broad enough to include everything from "unsolicited suggestive looks or leers [or] pressures for dates" to "actual sexual assaults or rapes." Categorizing everything from rape to "looks" as sexual harassment makes us all victims, a state of affairs satisfying to radical feminists, but not very useful for distinguishing serious injuries from the merely trivial.

Yet, even if the surveys exaggerate the extent of sexual harassment, however defined, what they do reflect is a great deal of tension between the sexes. As women in ever increasing numbers entered the workplace in the last two decades, as the women's movement challenged alleged male hegemony and exploitation with ever greater intemperance, and as women entered previously all-male preserves from the board rooms to the coal pits, it is lamentable, but should not be surprising, that this tension sometimes takes sexual form. Not that sexual harassment on the job, in the university, and in other settings is a trivial or insignificant matter, but a sense of proportion needs to be restored and, even more importantly, distinctions need to be made. In other words, sexual harassment must be deideologized. Statements that paint nearly all women as victims and all men and their patriarchal, capitalist system as perpetrators, are ideological fantasy. Ideology blurs the distinction between being injured—being a genuine victim—and merely being offended. An example is this statement by Catharine A. MacKinnon, a law professor and feminist activist: 10

> Sexual harassment perpetuates the interlocked structure by which women have been kept sexually in thrall to men and at the bottom of the labor market. Two forces of American society converge: men's control over women's sexuality and capital's control over employees' work lives. Women historically have been required to exchange sexual services for material survival, in one form or another. Prostitution and

marriage as well as sexual harassment in different ways institutionalize this arrangement.

Such hyperbole needs to be diffused and distinctions need to be drawn. Rape, a nonconsensual invasion of a person's body, is a crime clear and simple. It is a violation of the right to the physical integrity of the body (the right to life, as John Locke or Thomas Jefferson would have put it). Criminal law should and does prohibit rape. Whether it is useful to call rape "sexual harassment" is doubtful, for it makes the latter concept overly broad while trivializing the former.

Intimidation in the workplace of the kind that befell Valerie Craig — that is, extortion of sexual favors by a supervisor from a subordinate by threatening to penalize, fire, or fail to reward — is what the courts term *quid pro quo*[1] sexual harassment. Since the mid-1970s, the federal courts have treated this type of sexual harassment as a form of sex discrimination in employment proscribed under Title VII of the Civil Rights Act of 1964. A plaintiff who prevails against an employer may receive such equitable remedies as reinstatement and back pay, and the court can order the company to prepare and disseminate a policy against sexual harassment. Current law places principal liability on the company, not the harassing supervisor, even when higher management is unaware of the harassment and, thus, cannot take any steps to prevent it.

Quid pro quo sexual harassment is morally objectionable and analogous to extortion: The harasser extorts property (i.e., use of the woman's body) through the leverage of fear for her job. The victim of such behavior should have legal recourse, but serious reservations can be held about rectifying these injustices through the blunt instrument of Title VII: In egregious cases the victim is left less than whole (for back pay will not compensate her for ancillary losses), and no prospects for punitive damages are offered to deter would-be harassers. Even more distressing about Title VII is the fact that the primary target of litigation is not the actual harasser, but rather the employer. This places a double burden on a company. The employer is swindled by the supervisor because he spent his time pursuing sexual gratification and thereby impairing the efficiency of the workplace by mismanaging his subordinates, and the employer must endure lengthy and expensive litigation, pay damages, and suffer loss to its reputation. It would be fairer to both the company and the victim to treat sexual harassment as a tort — that is, as a private wrong or injury for which the court can assess damages. Employers should be held vicariously liable only when they know of an employee's behavior and do not try to redress it.

As for the workplace harassment endured by Carol Zabowicz — the bared buttocks, obscene portraits, etc. — that too should be legally redressable. Presently, such incidents also fall under the umbrella of

---

[1]*quid pro quo* This for that, or one thing in return for another (Latin). [Editors' note.]

Title VII, and are termed hostile environment sexual harassment, a category accepted later than *quid pro quo* and with some judicial reluctance. The main problem with this category is that it has proven too elastic: cases have reached the courts based on everything from off-color jokes to unwanted, persistent sexual advances by coworkers. A new tort of sexual harassment would handle these cases better. Only instances above a certain threshold of egregiousness or outrageousness would be actionable. In other words, the behavior that the plaintiff found offensive would also have to be offensive to the proverbial "reasonable man" of the tort law. That is, the behavior would have to be objectively injurious rather than merely subjectively offensive. The defendant would be the actual harasser not the company, unless it knew about the problem and failed to act. Victims of scatological jokes, leers, unwanted offers of dates, and other sexual annoyances would no longer have their day in court.

A distinction must be restored between morally offensive behavior 15 and behavior that causes serious harm. Only the latter should fall under the jurisdiction of criminal or tort law. Do we really want legislators and judges delving into our most intimate private lives, deciding when a look is a leer, and when a leer is a Civil Rights Act offense? Do we really want courts deciding, as one recently did, whether a school principal's disparaging remarks about a female school district administrator was sexual harassment and, hence, a breach of Title VII, or merely the act of a spurned and vengeful lover? Do we want judges settling disputes such as the one that arose at a car dealership after a female employee turned down a male coworker's offer of a date and his colleagues retaliated by calling her offensive names and embarrassing her in front of customers? Or another case in which a female shipyard worker complained of an "offensive working environment" because of the prevalence of pornographic material on the docks? Do we want the state to prevent or compensate us for any behavior that someone might find offensive? Should people have a legally enforceable right not to be offended by others? At some point, the price for such protection is the loss of both liberty and privacy rights.

Workplaces are breeding grounds of envy, personal grudges, infatuation, and jilted loves, and beneath a fairly high threshold of outrageousness, these travails should be either suffered in silence, complained of to higher management, or left behind as one seeks other employment. No one, female or male, can expect to enjoy a working environment that is perfectly stress-free, or to be treated always and by everyone with kindness and respect. To the extent that sympathetic judges have encouraged women to seek monetary compensation for slights and annoyances, they have not done them a great service. Women need to develop a thick skin in order to survive and prosper in the workforce. It is patronizing to think that they need to be recompensed by male judges for seeing a few pornographic pictures on a wall. By their efforts to extend sexual harassment charges to even the most trivial behavior, the radical feminists send a message that women are not resilient enough to ignore the run-of-the-mill, churlish provocation from male coworkers. It is difficult to imagine a suit by a longshoreman complaining of mental stress due to the display of nude male centerfolds by female coworkers. Women cannot expect to have it both ways: equality where convenient, but special dispensations when the going gets rough. Equality has its price and that price may include unwelcome sexual advances, irritating and even intimidating sexual jests, and lewd and obnoxious colleagues.

Egregious acts — sexual harassment per se — must be legally redressable. Lesser but not trivial offenses, whether at the workplace or in other more social settings, should be considered moral lapses for which the offending party receives opprobrium, disciplinary warnings, or penalties, depending on the setting and the severity. Trivial offenses, dirty jokes, sexual overtures, and sexual innuendoes do make many women feel intensely discomfited, but, unless they become outrageous through persistence or content, these too should be taken as part of life's annoyances. The perpetrators should be either endured, ignored, rebuked, or avoided, as circumstances and personal inclination dictate. Whether Lisa Olson's experience in the locker room of the New England Patriots falls into the second or third category is debatable. The media circus triggered by the incident was certainly out of proportion to the event.

As the presence of women on road gangs, construction crews, and oil rigs becomes a fact of life, the animosities and tensions of this transition period are likely to abate gradually. Meanwhile, women should "lighten up," and even dispense a few risqué barbs of their own, a sure way of taking the fun out of it for offensive male bores.

TOPICS FOR CRITICAL THINKING AND WRITING

1. Reread the first paragraph, trying *not* to bring to it your knowledge of what Paul says in the rest of the essay. What was your response? Then, in light of what you know about the entire essay, explain Paul's strategy in beginning this way.

2. Paul occasionally uses a word that probably is not part of everyone's vocabulary, such as "adumbrated" (para. 2), "adjudicated" (7), "hegemony" (10), "deideologized" (10), and "ancillary" (13). What is your response? Is the essay needlessly obscure? Are some words not part of everyday speech but appropriate here? Explain.

3. How, if at all, does Paul define *sexual harassment* (see especially paras. 9–10)? How would you define it? Consider what is common to the three cases of sexual harassment with which Paul opens her essay (paras. 3–5).

4. Paul asserts that women ought to be prepared to encounter a certain amount of inappropriate behavior in the workplace. Are you satisfied with the reasons she gives? Explain.

5. Paul thinks Title VII places an unfair burden on employers whose employees are guilty of sexual harassment because the employer may not know about the employee's misbehavior (paras. 12–13). Suppose one argues that employers ought to know about such harassment and ought to take steps to prevent it. How might Paul reply?

6. Paul distinguishes between "offensive behavior" and harm (para. 15) and the behavior that causes each. Can you think of cases of sexual harassment (actual or hypothetical) in which the distinction is blurred? If so, explain.

7. If you have read Ellen Goodman's "The Reasonable Woman Standard" (p. 708), compare Goodman's views with Paul's. On what significant points do they disagree?

"I'd like you to keep your ears open, make sure our office is safe from any charges of sexual harassment. Thanks, babe."

Sarah J. McCarthy

As Sarah J. McCarthy indicates in this essay, she is the owner of a small restaurant. The essay originally appeared in the December 9, 1991, issue of Forbes, *a magazine that reports on business and financial issues.*

Cultural Fascism

On the same day that Ted Kennedy asked forgiveness for his personal "shortcomings," he advocated slapping lottery-size punitive damages on small-business owners who may be guilty of excessive flirting or whose employees may be guilty of talking dirty. Senator Kennedy expressed regrets that the new civil rights bill caps punitive damages for sexual harassment as high as $300,000 (depending on company size), and he promises to push for increases next year. Note that the senators have voted to exempt themselves from punitive damages.

I am the owner of a small restaurant/bar that employs approximately twenty young males whose role models range from Axl Rose to John Belushi. They work hard in a high-stress, fast-paced job in a hot kitchen and at times they are guilty of colorful language. They have also been overheard telling Pee-Wee Herman jokes and listening to obnoxious rock lyrics. They have discussed pornography and they have flirted with waitresses. One chef/manager has asked out a pretty blonde waitress probably a hundred times in three years. She seems to enjoy the game, but always says no. Everyone calls everyone else "Honey"—it's a ritual, a way of softening what sound like barked orders: "I need the medium-rare shish kebab *now*!"

"Honey" doesn't mean the same thing here as it does in women's studies departments or at the EEOC.[1] The auto body shop down the street has pinups. Perhaps under the vigilant eyes of the feminist political correctness gestapo we can reshape our employees' behavior so they act more like nerds from the Yale women's studies department. The gestapo will not lack for potential informers seeking punitive damages and instant riches.

With the Civil Rights Bill of 1991 we are witnessing the most organized and systematic assault on free speech and privacy since the McCarthy era. The vagueness of the sexual harassment law, combined with our current litigation explosion, is a frightening prospect for small businesses. We are now financially responsible for sexually offensive verbal behavior, even if we don't know it is occurring, under a law that provides no guidelines to define "offensive" and "harassment." This is a cultural fascism unmatched since the Chinese communists outlawed hand-holding, decorative clothing, and premarital sex.

This law is detrimental even to the women it professes to help. I am   5 a feminist, but the law has made me fearful of hiring women. If one of our cooks or managers—or my husband or sons—offends someone, it could cost us $100,000 in punitive damages and legal expenses. There will be no insurance fund or stockholders or taxpayers to pick up the tab.

When I was a feminist activist in the 1970s, we knew the dangers of a pedestal—it was said to be as confining as any other small place. As we were revolted and outraged by the woman-hatred in violent pornography, we reminded each other that education, not laws, was the solution to our problems. In Women against Sexist Violence in Pornography and Media, in Pittsburgh, we were well aware of the dangers of encroaching on the First Amendment. Free speech was, perhaps more than anything else, what made our country grow into a land of enlightenment and diversity. The lesbians among us were aware that the same laws used to censor pornography could be used against them if their sexual expressions were deemed offensive.

We admired powerful women writers such as Marge Piercy and poets like Robin Morgan who swooped in from nowhere, writing break-your-chains poems about women swinging from crystal chandeliers like monkeys on vines and defecating in punch bowls. Are we allowed to talk about these poems in the current American workplace?

The lawyers—the prim women and men who went to the politically correct law schools—believe with sophomoric arrogance that the solution to all the world's problems is tort litigation. We now have eternally complicated questions of sexual politics judged by the shifting standards of the reasonable prude.

---

[1]**EEOC** Equal Employment Opportunity Commission. [Editors' note.]

To the leadership of the women's movement: You do women a dis-service. You ladies—and I use that term intentionally—have trivialized the women's movement. You have made us ladies again. You have not considered the unintended effects of your sexual harassment law. You are saying that too many things men say and do with each other are too rough-and-tumble for us. Wielding the power of your $300,000 lawsuits, you are frightening managers into hiring men over women. I know that I am so frightened. You have installed a double pane of glass on the glass ceiling with the help of your white knight and protector, Senator Kennedy.

You and your allies tried to lynch Clarence Thomas. You alienate 10 your natural allies. Men and women who wanted to work shoulder to shoulder with you are now looking over their shoulders. You have made women into china dolls that if broken come with a $300,000 price tag. The games, intrigue, nuances, and fun of flirting have been made into criminal activity.

We women are not as delicate and powerless as you think. We do not want victim status in the workplace. Don't try to foist it on us.

TOPICS FOR CRITICAL THINKING AND WRITING

1. Reread McCarthy's opening paragraph. What is her point? How effec-tive do you think this paragraph is as the opening of an argumentative essay?

2. In her third paragraph McCarthy speaks of "the feminist political cor-rectness gestapo." What does she mean by this phrase, and why does she use it?

3. In paragraph 8 McCarthy refers to "tort litigation." Explain the phrase.

4. In her second paragraph McCarthy suggests that in "a high-stress, fast-paced" environment with young (and presumably not highly educated) males, "colorful language," dirty jokes, and "obnoxious rock lyrics" are to be expected. Would you agree that a woman who takes a job in such an environment cannot reasonably complain that this sort of behavior constitutes sexual harassment? Explain.

5. How do you think McCarthy would define sexual harassment? That is, how according to her views should we complete the following sentence: "Person *A* sexually harasses person *B* if and only if . . ."?

6. Read the essay by Ellen Goodman (p. 708), and explain in a brief essay of 100 words where she and McCarthy differ. With whom do you agree? Why?

For topical links related to the issue of sexual harassment, see the companion Web site: **bedfordstmartins.com/barnetbedau.**

27

Marriage: What Is Its Future?

Thomas B. Stoddard

Thomas B. Stoddard (1948–1997) was executive director of the Lambda Legal Defense and Education Fund, a gay rights organization. In 1995 New York University School of Law established a fellowship in Stoddard's name, honoring him for his work on behalf of gay and lesbian rights. This article is from the op-ed section of the New York Times, *March 4, 1988.*

Gay Marriages: Make Them Legal

"In sickness and in health, 'til death do us part." With those familiar words, millions of people each year are married, a public affirmation of a private bond that both society and the newlyweds hope will endure. Yet for nearly four years, Karen Thompson was denied the company of the one person to whom she had pledged lifelong devotion. Her partner is a woman, Sharon Kowalski, and their home state of Minnesota, like every other jurisdiction in the United States, refuses to permit two individuals of the same sex to marry.

Karen Thompson and Sharon Kowalski are spouses in every respect except the legal. They exchanged vows and rings; they lived together until November 13, 1983—when Ms. Kowalski was severely injured when her car was struck by a drunk driver. She lost the capacity to walk or to speak more than several words at a time, and needed constant care.

Ms. Thompson sought a court ruling granting her guardianship over her partner, but Ms. Kowalski's parents opposed the petition and obtained sole guardianship. They moved Ms. Kowalski to a nursing home three-hundred miles away from Ms. Thompson and forbade all visits between the two women. Last month, as part of a reevaluation of Ms. Kowalski's mental competency, Ms. Thompson was permitted to visit her partner again. But the prolonged injustice and anguish inflicted on both women hold a moral for everyone.

Marriage, the Supreme Court declared in 1967, is "one of the basic civil rights of man" (and, presumably, of woman as well). The freedom to marry, said the Court, is "essential to the orderly pursuit of happiness."

Marriage is not just a symbolic state. It can be the key to survival, 5 emotional and financial. Marriage triggers a universe of rights, privileges, and presumptions. A married person can share in a spouse's estate even when there is no will. She is typically entitled to the group insurance and pension programs offered by the spouse's employer, and she enjoys tax advantages. She cannot be compelled to testify against her spouse in legal proceedings.

The decision whether or not to marry belongs properly to individuals — not the government. Yet at present, all fifty states deny that choice to millions of gay and lesbian Americans. While marriage has historically required a male partner and a female partner, history alone cannot sanctify injustice. If tradition were the only measure, most states would still limit matrimony to partners of the same race.

As recently as 1967, before the Supreme Court declared miscegenation statutes unconstitutional, sixteen states still prohibited marriages between a white person and a black person. When all the excuses were stripped away, it was clear that the only purpose of those laws was, in the words of the Supreme Court, "to maintain white supremacy."

Those who argue against reforming the marriage statutes because they believe that same-sex marriage would be "antifamily" overlook the obvious: Marriage creates families and promotes social stability. In an increasingly loveless world, those who wish to commit themselves to a relationship founded upon devotion should be encouraged, not scorned. Government has no legitimate interest in how that love is expressed.

And it can no longer be argued — if it ever could — that marriage is fundamentally a procreative unit. Otherwise, states would forbid marriage between those who, by reason of age or infertility, cannot have children, as well as those who elect not to.

As the case of Sharon Kowalski and Karen Thompson demonstrates, 10 sanctimonious illusions lead directly to the suffering of others. Denied the right to marry, these two women are left subject to the whims and prejudices of others, and of the law.

Depriving millions of gay American adults the marriages of their choice, and the rights that flow from marriage, denies equal protection of the law. They, their families and friends, together with fair-minded people everywhere, should demand an end to this monstrous injustice.

TOPICS FOR CRITICAL THINKING AND WRITING

1. Study the essay as an example of ways to argue. What sorts of arguments does Stoddard offer? He does not offer statistics or cite authorities, but what *does* he do in an effort to convince the reader?

2. Stoddard draws an analogy between laws that used to prohibit marriage between persons of different races and laws that still prohibit marriage

between persons of the same sex. Evaluate this analogy in an essay of 100 words.

3. Stoddard cites Karen Thompson and Sharon Kowalski (para. 2). Presumably he could have found, if he had wished, a comparable example using two men rather than two women. Do you think the effect of his essay would be better, worse, or the same if his example used men rather than women? Why?

4. Do you find adequate Stoddard's response to the charge that "same sex marriage would be 'antifamily'" (para. 8)? Why, or why not?

5. One widespread assumption is that the family exists to produce children. Stoddard mentions this, but he does not mention that although gay couples cannot produce children, they can (where legally permitted to do so) adopt and rear children and thus fulfill a social need. One partner can even be the natural parent. Do you think he was wise to omit this argument in behalf of same-sex marriages? Why?

6. Think about what principal claims one might make to contradict Stoddard's claims, and then write a 500-word essay defending this proposition: "Lawful marriage should be limited to heterosexual couples." Or if you believe that gay marriages should be legitimized, write an essay offering additional support to Stoddard's essay.

7. Stoddard's whole purpose is to break down the prejudice against same-sex marriages, and he seems to take for granted the appropriateness of monogamy. Yet one might argue against Stoddard that if society opened the door to same sex marriages, it would be hard to keep the door closed to polygamy or polyandry. Write a 500-word essay exploring this question.

8. Would Stoddard's argument require him to allow marriage between a brother and a sister? A parent and a child? A human being and an animal? Why, or why not?

9. On November 18, 2003, the Massachusetts Supreme Judicial Court (the highest court in the state) ruled 4–3 that the state's constitution gives gay couples the right to marry. The majority opinion held that the state "failed to identify any constitutionally adequate reason for denying civil marriage to same-sex couples." Many legislators and many citizens throughout the country who oppose this decision—including some people who favor "civil unions" for those gays who want recognition of their status—have vowed that they will work for an amendment to the United States Constitution that would limit marriage to the union of a male and a female. In an essay of 500 words indicate why you do or do not favor amending the nation's Constitution so that "marriage" is limited to heterosexual couples.

Lisa Schiffren

Lisa Schiffren was a speechwriter for former Vice President Dan Quayle. We reprint an essay that originally was published in the New York Times *on March 23, 1996.*

Gay Marriage, an Oxymoron

As study after study and victim after victim testify to the social dev-astation of the sexual revolution, easy divorce, and out-of-wedlock motherhood, marriage is fashionable again. And parenthood has trans-formed many baby boomers into advocates of bourgeois norms.

Indeed, we have come so far that the surprise issue of the political season is whether homosexual "marriage" should be legalized. The Hawaii courts will likely rule that gay marriage is legal, and other states will be required to accept those marriages as valid.

Considering what a momentous change this would be—a radical redefinition of society's most fundamental institution—there has been almost no real debate. This is because the premise is unimaginable to many, and the forces of political correctness have descended on the dis-cussion, raising the cost of opposition. But one may feel the same affec-tion for one's homosexual friends and relatives as for any other and be genuinely pleased for the happiness they derive from relationships while opposing gay marriage for principled reasons.

"Same-sex marriage" is inherently incompatible with our culture's understanding of the institution. Marriage is essentially a lifelong com-pact between a man and woman committed to sexual exclusivity and the creation and nurture of offspring. For most Americans, the marital union—as distinguished from other sexual relationships and legal and economic partnerships—is imbued with an aspect of holiness. Though many of us are uncomfortable using religious language to discuss social and political issues, Judeo-Christian morality informs our view of fam-ily life.

Though it is not polite to mention it, what the Judeo-Christian tradi-tion has to say about homosexual unions could not be clearer. In a diverse, open society such as ours, tolerance of homosexuality is a neces-sity. But for many, its practice depends on a trick of cognitive dissonance that allows people to believe in the Judeo-Christian moral order while accepting, often with genuine regard, the different lives of homosexual acquaintances. That is why, though homosexuals may believe that they are merely seeking a small expansion of the definition of marriage, the majority of Americans perceive this change as a radical deconstruction of the institution.

Some make the conservative argument that making marriage a civil right will bring stability, an end to promiscuity, and a sense of fairness to gay men and women. But they miss the point. Society cares about stabil-ity in heterosexual unions because it is critical for raising healthy chil-dren and transmitting the values that are the basis of our culture.

Whether homosexual relationships endure is of little concern to society. That is also true of most childless marriages, harsh as it is to say. Society has wisely chosen not to differentiate between marriages, because it would require meddling into the motives and desires of everyone who applies for a license.

In traditional marriage, the tie that really binds for life is shared responsibility for the children. (A small fraction of gay couples may choose to raise children together, but such children are offspring of one partner and an outside contributor.) What will keep gay marriages together when individuals tire of each other?

Similarly, the argument that legal marriage will check promiscuity by gay males raises the question of how a "piece of paper" will do what the threat of AIDS has not. Lesbians seem to have little problem with monogamy or the rest of what constitutes "domestication," despite the absence of official status.

Finally, there is the so-called fairness argument. The government 10 gives tax benefits, inheritance rights, and employee benefits only to the married. Again, these financial benefits exist to help couples raise children. Tax reform is an effective way to remove distinctions among earners.

If the American people are interested in a radical experiment with same-sex marriages, then subjecting it to the political process is the right route. For a court in Hawaii to assume that it has the power to radically redefine marriage is a stunning abuse of power. To present homosexual marriage as a fait accompli, without national debate, is a serious political error. A society struggling to recover from thirty years of weakened norms and broken families is not likely to respond gently to having an institution central to most people's lives altered.

TOPICS FOR CRITICAL THINKING AND WRITING

1. What is an oxymoron, and why does Schiffren think the phrases *gay marriage* and *same-sex marriage* are oxymorons?

2. In paragraph 3 Schiffren refers to "political correctness." How would you define that term? So defined, do you think political correctness is sometimes objectionable? Always objectionable? Sometimes justifiable? Always justifiable?

3. Schiffren defines marriage in paragraph 4 in such a way that a man and woman who marry with no intention of having children are deviant. She does not imply, however, that such marriages should be prohibited by law or otherwise nullified. Does consistency require her to grant that while same-sex marriages are no doubt deviant—in the sense of atypical or relatively rare—they are nonetheless legitimate?

4. Schiffren refers to "cognitive dissonance" (para. 5). What does she mean by this term, and how does she think it plays a role in our society's prevailing attitude toward homosexuality?

5. Schiffren says (para. 7), "Whether homosexual relationships endure is of little concern to society" because such relationships do not involve nurturing children. By the same token, does society have little concern for heterosexual marriages to endure when there are no children involved? Or do you think that there are other considerations that make stable intimate relations between consenting adults important to society?

6. List the reasons for same-sex marriage unions that Schiffren mentions. Which, if any, do you think are significant? Can you think of any reasons that she fails to mention?

7. In her final paragraph, Schiffren deplores the federal court in Hawaii that ratified same-sex marriage. Is it the process or the result of this decision to which she mostly objects? Do you agree with her objection? Go to your college library, find out the current status of this issue in the courts, and write a 500-word paper on the Hawaiian same-sex marriage law, how it became law, and what it provides.

8. If gay marriage is recognized as legal, are we necessarily on a slippery slope (see p. 372) that will bring us to recognition of polygamy or polyandry (perhaps heterosexual, but perhaps a marriage of a bisexual to a man and also to a woman) and incest. Why, or why not?

9. Schiffren was not replying directly to Thomas B. Stoddard (p. 721), but she probably knew his arguments. Does he make any points that you wish she had faced? If so, what are they? If she were asked to comment on these points by Stoddard, what do you think her responses would be?

10. How would you characterize Schiffren's tone? Haughty? Earnest? Smart-alecky? (You need not come up with a one-word answer; you might say, "She is chiefly *X* but also sometimes *Y*.") Do you think her tone will help her to persuade people to accept her views?

Ellen Goodman

Ellen Goodman (b. 1941) was educated at Radcliffe College and worked as a reporter for Newsweek *from 1963 to 1965. Since then she has been a columnist and an associate editor for the* Boston Globe. *In 1980 she won a Pulitzer Prize for Distinguished Commentary. We reprint one of her columns from the* Globe *for August 4, 2006.*

Goodman is writing about the decision of the Washington State Supreme Court, which on July 26, 2006, in Andersen v. King County, *ruled 5–4 against gay marriage. Justice Barbara Madsen, writing for the majority, argued that the state's 1998 prohibition against state recognition of gay marriages "bears a reasonable relationship to legitimate state interests." Madsen wrote that the state legislature "was entitled to believe that limiting marriage to opposite-sex couples furthers procreation, essential to survival of the human race, and furthers the well-being of children by encouraging families where children are reared in homes headed by the children's biological parents."*

In a dissent, Justice Mary Fairhurst called the majority opinion "blatant discrimination." Fairhurst's chief argument, as we understand it, is that, admittedly, the state has an interest in furthering procreation and in the well-being of children, but denying *marriage to same-sex couples in no way furthers the right that opposite-sex couples already enjoy.*

Backward Logic in the Courts

Now I got it. After hours spent poring over Washington [S]tate's Supreme Court decision upholding the ban on same-sex marriage, I've finally figured it out. The court wasn't just ruling against same-sex marriage. It was ruling in favor of "procreationist marriage."

This is the heart of the opinion written by Justice Barbara Madsen: "Limiting marriage to opposite-sex couples furthers procreation, essential to survival of the human race, and furthers the well-being of children by encouraging families where children are reared in homes headed by the children's biological parents." In short, the state's wedding bells are ringing for procreators.

Well if that's true, isn't it time for the legislatures in Washington and in New York, which issued a similar ruling against same-sex marriage this summer, to follow their own logic? If marriage is for procreation, shouldn't they refuse to wed anyone past menopause? Shouldn't they withhold a license, let alone blessings and benefits, from anyone who is infertile? What about those who choose to be childless? Nothing borrowed or blue for them. Indeed the state could offer young couples licenses with sunset clauses. After five years they have to put up (kids) or split up.

Of course the states' other interest is in families "headed by the children's biological parents." Why then give licenses to the couples who are raising 1.5 million adopted children? We can ban those blended families like, say, the Brady Bunch. And surely we should release partners from their vows upon delivery of their offspring to the nearest college campus.

This is where the courts' reasoning leads us, and I use the word "rea-   5
soning" loosely. If anything, these two decisions are proof that the courts and the country are running out of reasons for treating straight and gay citizens differently.

Since the landmark Supreme Court ruling in *Lawrence v. Texas* in 2003, gay sex is no longer a crime. Today, if some straight couples cannot or do not procreate, some gay couples do, using all the old and new technologies. Gays aren't banned from fertility clinics. They aren't the slam-dunk losers in divorce custody fights. Even Arkansas has just ruled that gay couples can become foster parents. And New York and Washington, the very states now refusing to let gays marry, have supported gay adoption.

Against this evolving backdrop, the courts had to reach pretty far to find some explanation for banning gay marriage other than old-fashioned discrimination. Even so—as Justice Mary Fairhurst wrote in her Washington dissent—neither court actually explained why "giving same-sex couples the same right that opposite-sex couples enjoy [would] injure the state's interest in procreation and healthy child rearing." After all, as Chief Judge Judith Kaye of New York wrote in her dissent, "There are enough marriage licenses to go around. . . . No one rationally decides to have children because gays and lesbians are excluded from marriage."

I am a citizen of Massachusetts where gay people have been getting married for two years without the sky falling. (The ceiling on the Big Dig has fallen, but that's another story.) The furor over the decision here produced a national backlash that has scared a lot of judges straight. The current decisions reek of that anxiety.

These judges seem ready to bow to any legislation on this hot-button subject that isn't certifiably nuts. For example, the American Academy of Pediatrics reports that: "There is ample evidence to show that children raised by same-gender parents fare as well as those raised by heterosexual parents." The Washington court still determined that "the legislature was entitled to believe" the opposite. The legislature's *entitlement* overruled gay entitlement to marry.

Columbia Law School's Suzanne Goldberg says, "It's hard to believe   10 that intelligent judges believe what they are writing. The idea that exclusion of same-sex couples from marriage could be justified by the way an egg and sperm might meet is illogical."

The backlash against gay marriage has produced strong passions and weak arguments. It's no longer enough to state in court that marriage has always been for straight couples, ergo it should be only for straight couples. This time the courts ended up arguing on procreationist grounds, pretty shaky legal terrain.

"It is the exclusive and permanent commitment of the marriage partners to one another, not the begetting of children, that is the sine qua non of civil marriage," wrote Chief Justice Margaret Marshall in the Massachusetts decision that extended marital rights to gays and brought conservative wrath down on her head.

Marshall has been demonized as an "activist judge"—a label pinned on the author of any ruling you dislike. Now, in an anxious attempt to put their courts into neutral, judges in Washington and New York have thrown logic into reverse.

TOPICS FOR CRITICAL THINKING AND WRITING

1. Can you think of any reasons why "'giving same-sex couples the same right that opposite-sex couples enjoy [would] injure the state's interest in procreation . . .'" (para. 7)? If so, what are those reasons?

2. To support her case, Goodman in paragraph 9 quotes the American Academy of Pediatrics. Do you give much weight to this testimony, or

do you think, "Well, I don't know what this outfit is, so why should I accept the quotation as significant evidence?" Explain.

3. In paragraph 10 Goodman quotes a Columbia Law School professor. Are you impressed by the quotation? Explain.

4. In paragraph 12 Goodman quotes Chief Justice Margaret Marshall. To what extent do you agree with the quotation? Explain.

5. Evaluate Goodman's final two paragraphs as concluding paragraphs for her argument.

Jeff Jacoby

Jeff Jacoby, born in 1925 in present-day Slovakia, received his bachelor's degree from George Washington University and a law degree from Boston University School of Law. Since 1994 he has been a columnist for the Boston Globe, *which first published the following essay on May 2, 2007.*

Lawful Incest May Be on Its Way

When the BBC invited me onto one of its talk shows recently to talk about the day's hot topic—legalizing adult incest—I thought of Rick Santorum.

Back in 2003, as the Supreme Court was preparing to rule in *Lawrence v. Texas*, a case challenging the constitutionality of laws criminalizing homosexual sodomy, then-Senator Santorum caught holy hell for warning out that if the law were struck down, there would be no avoiding the slippery slope.

"If the Supreme Court says you have the right to consensual sex within your home," he told a reporter, "then you have the right to bigamy, you have the right to polygamy, you have the right to incest, you have the right to adultery. You have the right to anything."

It was a common-sensical observation, though you wouldn't have known it from the nail-spitting it triggered in some quarters. When the justices, voting 6-3, did in fact declare it unconstitutional for any state to punish consensual gay sex, the dissenters echoed Santorum's point. "State laws against bigamy, same-sex marriage, adult incest, prostitution, masturbation, adultery, fornication, bestiality, and obscenity are . . . called into question by today's decision," Justice Antonin Scalia wrote for the minority. Now, *Time* magazine acknowledges: "It turns out the critics were right."

Time's attention, like the BBC's, has been caught by the legal battles 5 underway to decriminalize incest between consenting adults. An article last month by *Time* reporter Michael Lindenberger titled "Should Incest Be Legal?" highlights the case of Paul Lowe, an Ohio man convicted of incest for having sex with his twenty-two-year-old stepdaughter. Lowe has appealed his conviction to the Supreme Court, making *Lawrence* the basis of his argument. In *Lawrence*, the court had ruled that people "are entitled to respect for their private lives" and that under the Fourteenth Amendment, "the state cannot demean their existence or control their destiny by making their private sexual conduct a crime." If that was true for the adult homosexual behavior in *Lawrence*, why not for the adult incestuous behavior in the Ohio case?

The BBC program focused on the case of Patrick and Susan Stubing, a German brother and sister who live as a couple and have had four children together. Incest is a criminal offense in Germany, and Patrick has already spent more than two years in prison for having sex with his sister. The two of them are asking Germany's highest court to abolish the law that makes incest illegal.

"We've done nothing wrong," Patrick told the BBC. "We are like normal lovers. We want to have a family." They dismiss the conventional argument that incest should be banned because the children of close relatives have a higher risk of genetic defects. After all, they point out, other couples with known genetic risks aren't punished for having sex. In any event, Patrick has had himself sterilized so that he cannot father any more children.

Some years back, I'd written about a similar case in Wisconsin—that of Allen and Patricia Muth, a brother and sister who fell in love as adults, had several children together, and were prosecuted, convicted, and imprisoned as a result. Following the Supreme Court's decision in *Lawrence*, they appealed their conviction and lost in the Seventh Circuit Court of Appeals. Lowe will probably lose too.

But the next Lowe or Muth to come along, or the one after that, may not lose. In *Lawrence*, it is worth remembering, the Supreme Court didn't just invalidate all state laws making homosexual sodomy a crime. It also overruled its own decision just seventeen years earlier (*Bowers v. Hardwick*, 1986) *upholding* such laws. If the court meant what it said in *Lawrence*—that states are barred from "making . . . private sexual conduct a crime"—it will not take that long for laws criminalizing incest to go by the board as well. Impossible? That's what they used to say about normalizing homosexuality and legalizing same-sex marriage.

In Germany, the Green Party is openly supporting the Stubings in their bid to decriminalize incest. According to the BBC, incest is no longer a criminal offense in Belgium, Holland, and France. Sweden already permits half-siblings to marry. 10

Your reaction to the prospect of lawful incest may be "Ugh, gross." But personal repugnance is no replacement for moral standards. For more than three thousand years, a code of conduct stretching back to Sinai has kept incest unconditionally beyond the pale. If sexual morality is jettisoned as a legitimate basis for legislation, personal opinion and cultural fashion are all that will remain. "Should Incest Be Legal?" *Time* asks. Expect more and more people to answer yes.

Topics for Critical Thinking and Writing

1. What is sodomy and why has it traditionally been against the law?

2. Do you think there is a slippery slope from consensual sex in one's home to the "right to [do] anything" (para. 3), including adultery and (as Jacoby's next paragraph says) masturbation? Are these activities illegal? Should they be illegal? Why, or why not? Explain your answer.

3. How would you respond to the challenge Jacoby issues at the end of paragraph 5?

4. If incest is illegal chiefly because of genetic risks, is Patrick Stubing's solution—he had himself sterilized—an adequate response? Why, or why not? A related matter: How impressed are you by the fact that in Belgium, Holland, France, and Sweden half-siblings may marry? Explain.

5. Do you think Jacoby is neutral as to whether homosexuality and incest ought to be "normalized" (para. 9)? What evidence either way can you cite?

6. Is "personal repugnance" (para. 11) a good guide to moral issues? Explain.

MARRIAGE: A PORTFOLIO OF CARTOONS

*"My mom has a new boyfriend, my dad has a new
girlfriend, and all I got was a new therapist."*

*"Well, now that the kids have grown up and left
I guess I'll be shoving along, too."*

"We want to register a domestic partnership."

"Gays and lesbians getting married—haven't they suffered enough?"

"There's nothing wrong with <u>our</u> marriage, but the spectre of gay marriage has hopelessly eroded the institution."

Diane Medved

Diane Medved was born in 1951 in Los Angeles and educated (B.A., M.A., and Ph.D.) at the University of California, Los Angeles. She is a licensed clinical therapist and the author of Children, To Have or Have Not? *(1982),* First Comes Love: Deciding Whether or Not to Get Married *(1983) and* The Case against Divorce *(1989), in which the material that we reprint here was first published. She was also co-author, with former Vice President Dan Quayle, of* The American Family: Discovering the Values That Make Us Strong *(1996) and with Michael Medved, of* Saving Childhood: Protecting Our Children from the National Assault on Innocence *(1998).*

The Case against Divorce

I have to start with a confession: This isn't the book I set out to write.

I planned to write something consistent with my previous professional experience—helping people with decision making. In ten years as a psychologist, I've run scores of workshops that specialized in weighing the pros and cons of major life choices. I've even published books on two of life's major turning points: whether or not to have a child and whether or not to get married. When I conceptualized this book on divorce, it was in that mold—a guide to help people decide if separation is appropriate.

I based this concept on some firmly held assumptions and beliefs. For example, I started this project believing that people who suffer over an extended period in unhappy marriages ought to get out. In my private practice, I'd seen plenty of struggling couples, and in every case, I anguished along with them when they described manipulation, lack of attention, or emotional dissatisfaction. I knew from their stories, as well as from my own experience, the heart-wrenching desperation that precedes separating and the liberation that leaving represents. I originally thought that staying together in turmoil was ultimately more traumatic than simply making the break.

I was convinced that recent no-fault divorce laws were a praiseworthy step toward simplifying a legally, psychologically, and emotionally punishing process. I thought that striking down taboos about divorce was another part of the ongoing enlightenment of the women's, civil rights, and human potential movements of the last twenty-five years. I had learned early in my graduate school training that crisis fosters growth, and therefore I assumed that the jolt of divorce almost always brings beneficial psychological change.

To my utter befuddlement, the extensive research I conducted for 5 this book brought me to one inescapable and irrefutable conclusion: I had been wrong. The statistics and anecdotes I gathered forced me to scuttle my well-prepared plans. I had to face the fact that writing a "morally neutral" book showing divorce to be just another option—a life choice no better or worse than staying married—would be irreparably damaging to the audience I wanted to help.

The change came as I shifted my focus from still-married couples in conflict, who made up the bulk of my practice, to now-single individuals who had already received their decrees.

I asked questions—and got some predictable answers: Are you glad you divorced? Yes. Do you regret getting your divorce? No. I was pleased that the responses to these two questions confirmed my original thinking.

But then I plumbed beneath the surface: What kind of contact do you have with your ex-spouse? How has the divorce affected your children? What kinds of experiences have you had in the dating world since your divorce? How has your style of living changed?

"Oh, everything's fine, fine," the respondents at first insisted. Everyone was without a doubt stronger and more hearty than ever.

But my questions kept coming. And the truth was difficult to avoid. Often in a rush of tears, they described the suffering and anguish they had endured—nights of fantasies about the husband or wife who left them; days of guilt after abandoning a once-devoted mate. They talked about the nuts-and-bolts of daily life, of uprooting, of shifting to an apartment and splitting possessions, of balancing parental duties with now-pressing work demands. They spoke of changing relationships with their children, who moved from innocent babes to confidants to arbitrators and sometimes to scapegoats.

And they mourned a part of themselves never to be recaptured. The part they had once invested in a marital or family unit was now destroyed. Wearily, they told of the transformation of the optimism and enthusiasm they had devoted to the now-crushed marriage to bitterness, skepticism, and self-preservation. "Never again," echoed my respondents. "Never again will I combine my income with another's." "Never again will I trust my spouse away overnight." "Never again will I believe someone when he says 'I'll take care of you.'"

I didn't want to hear it. I wanted to hear that they got past their divorces and emerged better for it. And while the women and men I spoke to were more sure of themselves and capable of living independently, I also heard that they had gained this self-reliance out of painful necessity, not out of free choice.

For given a choice, they preferred to be married. Everyone said he or she wanted to find somebody new. Many women were panic-stricken, afraid they would not find the "right" man before their childbearing years were lost. Others had become so jaded that they lamented the sobering truth that they were unlikely to find another mate at all. With their newfound strength, they all said they would survive; all said they were perfectly content with themselves and the lives they'd recently reconstructed. Still, there was regret. "Looking back now, do you think that you could have made it work with you first husband?" I asked.

"Well, he was crazy," they'd begin. "He was a slob. He was unromantic. He only thought of himself and his career. But knowing what I know now . . . yes, I probably could have made it work."

I was aghast. But the more I heard these or similar words, and the 15 more I read from the library, the more I was forced to concede that the ruinous stories of my divorced clients and interviewees were true. Divorce was catastrophic—but not in the commonly acceptable terms of a simple year or two thrown away. I found that the mere contemplation of divorce—the acceptance of it as an imminent option (rather than dedication to working on a wounded marriage) is debilitating. The process of evaluating the injuries—of cajoling and pleading and threatening—is emotionally exhausting. The physical act of packing a bag and moving out is traumatic. And from there the trauma escalates.

Quite simply, I discovered in my research that the process and aftermath of divorce is so pervasively disastrous—to body, mind, and spirit—that in an overwhelming number of cases, the "cure" that it brings is surely worse than marriage's "disease."

Of course, there are exceptions. There are times when divorce is clearly the only recourse. When physical or mental abuse exists. When emotional cruelty or neglect becomes intolerable. When one partner adamantly refuses to stay in the marriage or withdraws to the point where in reality you're alone.

I used to think that the range of situations when divorce is appropriate encompassed quite a bit more than that. But when I look at the balance of the bad and the good that divorced individuals endure, my only possible conclusion is that people could be spared enormous suffering if they scotched their permissive acceptance of divorce and viewed marriage as a serious, lifelong commitment, a bond not to be entered into—or wriggled out of—lightly.

The old wedding vows read "for better or for worse . . . until death do us part." They now commonly intone, "through good times and bad . . . as long as our love shall last." Until recently, I nodded at the "improvement"; now I soberly acknowledge the wisdom in the message of the past.

TOO LATE FOR MARLEEN

The grim stories of crippled couples whom I interviewed for this 20 book got me thinking about the permanent distrust, anguish, and bitterness divorce brings. But the catalyst coalescing these thoughts was a simple workaday lunch with a friend I've known for about eight years. Marleen Gaines, a school district administrator, is a handsome woman of forty who wears sophisticated silks, renews season tickets to the symphony, and stays sharp on the decisions of the courts, cabinet, and city council. When a mutual friend originally introduced us, I instantly clicked into Marleen's quick wit, upbeat attitude, and direct, self-confident zest. But as we sat down to salads at a café near my office, her usual sunny veneer gave way to a depressing monotone of desolation.

Three years ago, Marleen startled her friends by suddenly walking out of her nine-year marriage. At the time she left him, her husband Bob, now forty-two, seemed unbearably boring, uneducated, and unmotivated to achieve. Marleen wanted more of a dynamo, a brilliant intellectual she could admire, successful in his career. She met lots of these stimulating men at the office, and casual flirtations suggested to her that once she was free to pursue them, she would have plenty of opportunities for a more satisfying marriage.

But after three years single, she has found only frustration—and the humiliating realization that at her age, she is considered witty and glib but not especially desirable. There were a couple of flings with married men and an unrequited crush on her self-absorbed boss, who encouraged her attention merely to further inflate his swollen ego. She fell in love with a coworker, who treasured her company so much he told her every excruciating detail of his romantic exploits and eventual engagement. Meanwhile, her three closest friends remarried one by one and had stylishly late-in-life babies.

Now alone in a rambling house in San Bernardino with only her three dogs for companionship, she yearns for the simple warmth of Bob's presence. Though he was a college dropout and works now as a supermarket manager, Bob had his virtues. Always gentle and good-natured, he doted on Marleen and provided consistent encouragement. He may not have been the go-getter she desired, but he had an intuitive intelligence and a good, steady income to maintain their comfortable lifestyle.

It took all this time for Marleen to realize her mistake. At first, Bob had begged her to return; rebuked, he rebounded into one, then another serious relationship. He now lives with a woman who's pushing for marriage, and he's grown quite fond of her two teenage sons. When they speak every few weeks, Bob confesses to Marleen that his current companion "can be a pain" and swears that Marleen is the only woman he's ever "really" loved. Now Marleen has asked for a reconciliation, but weak-willed Bob is too dominated in his new world to leave, and Marleen, realizing that "possession is nine-tenths of the law," has resigned herself to the fact that he's not coming back.

DIVORCES ARE FOREVER

Sitting in the restaurant trying to console my friend, I was struck by 25 the frequency with which I've heard stories similar to hers—not only in my workshops and clinical psychology practice, but increasingly in everyday social chatter. It's a well-known U.S. Census Bureau statistic that half of all marriages fail; equally well-publicized is how both men and women suffer financially as a result. Sociologist Leonore Weitzman found that women's standard of living declines by a whopping 73 percent in the first year after divorce, and those who are mothers are further saddled with additional child care and logistics chores.

While everyone laments the immediate trauma of "going through a divorce," more discomfiting is the alarming news of its lingering emotional and psychological effects. Research by the California Children of Divorce Project headed by Judith Wallerstein, for example, shows an especially dismal future for women forty and over—even ten years after the divorce. Half of the women studied at that distant point could be diagnosed as "clinically depressed," and all were moderately or severely lonely, despite the fact that 50 percent of them had initiated the divorce themselves. Exacerbating their malaise might be alarming new statistics on their chances of finding another husband—chances *Newsweek* magazine (June 1986) claims are so low that these women face a greater likelihood of being struck by a terrorist!

Uncovering these facts during the preparation of this book only made me determined to probe reactions to divorce further. I jotted down some ideas and then developed an informal questionnaire that I distributed to an unscientific but diverse sample of two hundred people who had been separated or divorced. The results brought home undeniably that the effects of divorce last a lifetime. And they are in actuality far worse than we care to confront.

Everyone has some understanding of the pain of divorce. And yet, in these days of disposable marriage, at one time or another every married person contemplates separation. It may be in the heat of an argument, or during a fantasy about a more perfect mate. It may appear amid recurrent minor irritations, or it may come as the cumulative result of larger problems stored away for years. Everyone in the throes of a flirtation or affair considers the possibility of chucking the safe and boring for the exciting and glamorous. And people on the cusp of new success are tempted to leave reminders of the less glorious past and begin anew.

Clashing with this casual attitude toward divorce is America's reclaiming of traditional values. Religion has gained renewed respectability. Women who cried "career first" are now honoring their maternal instincts and realizing they may not be able to "have it all." Conservative politics have recently attracted many of yesterday's liberals. And college students, once esoterically majoring in philosophy and sociology, are taking the most direct routes to their MBAs.

Personal lives are more conservative as well, due to the sheer terror 30 provoked by the specter of AIDS. People are practicing "safe sex" not only with frank conversation prior to intimacy and with the use of condoms, but through definite changes in outlook toward recreational sex. A 1987 bestseller, taken seriously enough to be the subject of a day's discussion on the Oprah Winfrey television talk show and a return appearance by the author, advocated sexual abstinence before marriage. In addition, a representative national survey of twelve hundred college students undertaken by *Glamour* magazine revealed that "the AIDS epidemic is a serious damper on sexual activity: about half of all college students say the threat of AIDS has caused them to change their sexual habits."

The AIDS scare and the broader shift toward conservative attitudes, however, seem distant to couples in the throes of conjugal combat. In the midst of a shouting match, a gloriously portrayed single life and freedom from the oppression of a particular spouse call much more loudly.

Unfortunately, veterans of divorce like my friend Marleen, who yearn for families and secure, permanent relationships, now see that they have been sadly duped by those compelling myths, which suggest that divorce "can open up new horizons," that the dating scene is exciting, and that bright, attractive people will always find new partners with whom to share their lives.

It's finally time to renounce—openly and clearly—these self-serving platitudes about independence and fulfillment and look at the reality of divorce. We act too frequently as if every infirm marriage deserves to die, based simply upon the emotional report of one distressed partner. Rather than viewing a separation first with alarm, we're full of sympathy for a divorcing friend, and we offer understanding of the temporary insanity involved in severing old ties.

Still influenced by the "do your own thing" era, we don't act constructively. We don't take the husband (or wife) by the shoulders and shake him. We don't shout in his ear that he might be making a disastrous mistake. Even if we care immensely about him, we feel it's too intrusively "judgmental" to do more than step back and say, "Okay, if that's what you want," and close our eyes to the consequences. My research suggests that this is more cruelty than friendship.

EVEN WINNERS PAY THE PRICE

Some people who know me well ask how I could take this position, having been divorced and then happily remarried myself. It is partially because I have faced divorce that I can speak with some authority. It is true that I am one of the very lucky few who entered the chancy world of potential happiness or permanent pain and was ultimately given a break. But there are so many others—just as bright, just as desirable or more so— who bitterly ask why their "best years" must be spent alone. Even though I found a satisfying relationship, I am still paying the price of my divorce.

It is difficult for me to discuss something as personal as my own divorce, partially because I now invest so much in the new life I have created. I also don't like writing about my divorce because I am embarrassed and ashamed, and those feelings are painful to express. 35

Though my ex-husband and I were constitutionally quite different, we were nevertheless also the same in many ways, or at least had grown that way over the years. And because we shared our adolescence and formative adult period, we had a bond I found excruciating to discard. Unfortunately, like almost all of the divorced couples I have seen and researched, we cannot manage that ridiculous myth of being "just friends." So in becoming divorced, I severed an important extension of myself, negating a crucial and memorable chunk of my history and development. It is an enormous loss.

I am humiliated and mortified at failing in a relationship others at one time held exemplary. My divorce clashes with the self-image I work earnestly to cultivate: that I am triumphant in my endeavors, that the things I attempt are not only worthwhile but likely to succeed. By divorcing, I have proven myself inept—at least once—in perhaps the most crucial arena, one which by profession is my stock-in-trade—the ability to analyze choices and proceed wisely.

My divorce would have been bad enough were I able to keep my downfall a secret, like the dieter who sneaks a bag of cookies while driving on the anonymous freeway. But I am embarrassed further because of the public discredit and the possibility that former admirers now view me as diminished. Whether or not my associates really do see my character as smirched, or whether they are truly forgiving, is not as relevant as the fact that I *feel* I am now less worthy of their regard.

For those who do go on to build a second life, the future, built more on hope than confidence, may falter. Only about half of those I interviewed who remarried stayed with the second spouse or reported conjugal satisfaction; many found themselves reeling from their first marriages years later and admitted repeating the same mistakes.

The book *Crazy Time* by Abigail Trafford describes the weeks and   40 months after separation, when typically people replay those crushing moments over and over in their minds. The one who is rejected remembers the years together in measured fragments, dissecting every retort, every misplaced movement, for signs of failure or symbols of flawed passion.

The one who leaves in search of something better is so wracked by guilt and remorse that he can do nothing more than look ahead, shielding himself from the overwhelming self-loathing and embarrassment of looking at his past. Like Pharaoh, who refused the Jews' pleas for freedom even when confronted by the convincing pressure of the ten plagues, a spouse who negates his marriage must harden his heart against it. He must bury all the love that still exists for his partner, even if he realizes that it is love shaped by gratitude rather than attraction. The safe and cozy, welcoming home that the estranged partner once provided must be temporarily barred from consciousness. Years of striving together for the success of the other, for the enhancement of the unit, must be eliminated from the mind.

No one ever emerges from a divorce unscathed—he or she is inevitably permanently harmed.

That the divorced end up even more unhappy is not their fault. They're told by innumerable subtle and direct messages that they ought to be "mad as hell and unwilling to take it anymore," to paraphrase the inciteful slogan of the movie *Network*. They're encouraged by magazines sold at checkout stands to dissect their relationships. They're led by business-seeking shrinks to believe they can't possibly be fulfilled unless they're undergoing turmoil and instigating change.

I've read more than fifty books off my local public library shelves that comfort and cheer on those involved in divorce. These volumes take you step-by-step through the court procedure and tell you what stages of distress your "normal" child will endure. These books ease you like silk into the singles game and tout your "new freedom" as if it, rather than marriage, is the ultimate means toward fulfillment.

I write this book as a counterbalance, to shake a few shoulders, with hopes that I might spare some children helplessness and some partners pain. I want to expose the forces that strive to hide the damage of divorce. Too many people think "If only I could be out of this marriage . . ." and conclude that sentence with their own private miracles. To repeat: It's not their fault; they're victims of propaganda. But the lure lets them down, for after they buy it they inevitably remain the same people, with the same problem-solving skills, values, and styles of relating to another. And so they can't help but choose and shape new relationships into duplications of their spoiled romance. How can they be expected to see that divorce is, with very few exceptions, the wrong way to improve their lives?

And so this book is for everyone who is now focusing on some infuriating characteristic of their mate and thinking, "I can't take this much longer." It is for those who have already packed and moved out, either physically or emotionally, who look ahead and therefore can't see that their brightest path lies behind them. It is for those who have been hurt, whose wounds are so painful that they simply want to run away, and for others who see signs and want to prevent a breakup before the repairs become too overwhelming.

Perhaps you or someone you know has uttered something similar to one or more of these lines:

"Our fights are getting so fierce, the good times don't seem worth the
   arguments anymore."
"Sure I love him. But I know I could do better."
"I've found the love of my life—I have to get out of my marriage
   because I just can't end this affair and give up such a good thing."
"I've been smothered in this marriage too long—I need to go off on my
   own and prove myself."
"I don't respect or admire her anymore."
"He's been bugging me for a long time. I've just stuck it out for the sake
   of the children."

When any of these statements are used long after the fact—years beyond a final decree—there's nothing to be done. But in many other cases, it may not be too late. I've found that none of these sentiments automatically signals an irreparable tear in the basic fiber of a marriage. If you hear someone for whom you have any feeling at all hinting at separation, instead of tacitly endorsing the move, instantly protest. Nearly every marriage has something worth preserving, something that can be restored. Revitalizing a relationship brings triumph and ongoing reward; and as you'll see, avoiding divorce spares those concerned from the greatest trauma of their lives.

THE CASE AGAINST DIVORCE

Of course, nobody *wants* to get divorced. Or does he? Joseph Epstein, in *Divorced in America*, recognizes the respectability of divorce: "In some circles, not to have gone through a divorce seems more exceptional than having gone through one; here living out one's days within the confines of a single marriage might even be thought to show an insufficiency of imagination, evidence that one is possibly a bit callow emotionally."

God forbid we appear emotionally callow! How dare we assume that   50
those in the same dreary marriage they claim to have treasured for years could have gotten a lot out of it! The unspoken popular wisdom declares that only by undergoing this rite of psychological passage can anyone mature. I've heard the tales of postdivorce development: people who finally find themselves; who finally learn to be self-sufficient; who finally achieve independence. It is true that after divorce women especially, and men to some extent, report emotional growth. But they won't admit that they might have blossomed even more had they gathered the gumption to stick with and heal the marriage.

Of course, it's useless to speculate about what might have been accomplished in any particular relationship. But some things we *do* know—and these comprise the major arguments in the case against divorce:

1. *Divorce hurts you.* Divorce brings out selfishness, hostility, and vindictiveness. It ruins your idealism about marriage. It leaves emotional scars from which you can never be free. It costs a bunch of money—and significantly reduces your standard of living.
2. *Divorce hurts those around you.* It devastates your children for at least two years and probably for life. It hurts your family by splitting it in two; both family and friends are compelled to take sides. It forces you to be hardened against people you once loved. It rips the fabric of our society, each divorce providing another example of marriage devalued.
3. *The single life isn't what it's cracked up to be.* Ask anyone—the "swinging singles" life is full of frustration, rejection, and disappointment. The Mr. and Ms. Right you assume waits for you may be only a futile fantasy. Even a successful affair that bridges you from one marriage to another often becomes merely a second failure.
4. *Staying married is better for you.* You don't have to disrupt your life for two to seven years; instead, solving marital problems provides a sense of teamwork and stands as a concrete accomplishment that enhances problem-solving skills in the larger world. Marriage is statistically proven to be the best status for your health, divorce the worst. Marriage gives you something to show for your time on earth—children (usually) and a bond built on continuity and history.

I don't expect that everyone will agree with what I've found. It's largely a matter of values and also one of semantics. For example, I write that a family is worth preserving, and therefore it is worth compromising your goals or habits to save your marriage. Others holding different values might say that no marriage is worth burying your "true self" by dashing the goals you truly desire or stifling your personal inclinations. Obviously, it's not so easy to make a marriage work. But few achievements are as major or lasting.

TOPICS FOR CRITICAL THINKING AND WRITING

1. Medved opens her essay with two short, blunt sentences. Do you think this is an effective opening? Explain why, or why not, in a paragraph.

2. Medved insists that her approval of divorce was "wrong" (para. 5). In her newfound wisdom, does she reject all or only some of the assumptions with which she began her research for her book? And what, exactly, were these assumptions?

3. Invite some of your divorced relatives or close friends to share with you their views about their divorces. Do their experiences confirm or disconfirm Medved's (paras. 10–11, and later)? Was divorce for them "catastrophic," as Medved says it was for most of her clients (para. 15)?

4. Suppose a critic of Medved alleged that most of the examples of ruinous divorce she cites are the stories that women tell, not men, and therefore she gives a distorted picture of the after-life of divorce. What would your response be?

5. Medved lists four "major arguments" against divorce (para. 51). Yet she concedes that many cases of divorce—including her own (paras. 34–38)—do not suffer these consequences. How should you tell whether the divorce you are contemplating (for the sake of the argument) will be one of many ruinous ones or one of the few others?

6. If you oppose divorce, put aside your own personal feelings and in 250 words set forth the strongest case you can imagine *in favor of* divorce.

Wendy Kaminer

Wendy Kaminer (b. 1949) graduated from Smith College in 1971. A lawyer and an author, Kaminer is especially known for her defense of First Amendment freedoms. Her defense of free speech includes opposition to efforts to censor pornography. At thefreeforall.net Kaminer blogs on civil liberties.

Why Is Polygamy Illegal?

Opponents of gay rights often warn that legalizing same-sex marriage would inexorably lead to legalizing polygamy. Maybe it would, and maybe it should. Denying gay couples the right to marry violates state constitutional guarantees of equality, as the California and Massachusetts high courts have rightly ruled. (The Supreme Court of California also held that the right to marry is fundamental.) Surely Mormons have the same rights to equal treatment under law—and of course, they have a substantial First Amendment claim to engage in multiple marriages according to the dictates of their faith.

So why is polygamy illegal? Why don't Mormons have the right to enter into multiple marriages sanctified by their church, if not the state? There's a short answer to this question but not a very good one: polygamy is illegal and unprotected by the Constitution because the Supreme Court doesn't like it. Over one hundred years ago, the Court held in *Reynolds v. U.S.* that polygamy was "an offence against society." The *Reynolds* decision upheld the criminal conviction of a man accused of taking a second wife in the belief that he had a religious duty to practice polygamy, a duty he would violate at risk of damnation. The Court compared polygamy to murders sanctified by religious belief, such as human sacrifice or the burning of women on their husbands' funeral pyres.

Even in Victorian America, this comparison made little sense. (Most Victorian women, I suspect, would have chosen polygamous marriages over death by burning.) Today the Court's analogy is as anachronistic as a ban on adultery. After all, what's the difference between an adulterer and a polygamist? And if it's not illegal for a married man to support a girlfriend or two and father children out of wedlock with them, how can it be illegal for him to bind himself to them according to the laws of his church? Why is a practicing Mormon with two wives a criminal while Staten Island Congressman Vito Fosella, recently embarrassed by the discovery of his second family, is simply a punchline? What's the moral and practical difference between a man who maintains multiple families without the approval of any church and a man who maintains multiple families with his church's approval?

Nontheists who favor civil unions for everyone—taking the state out of the business of approving or disapproving religious matrimonial rites— should be especially supportive of the First Amendment right to engage in polygamous marriages sanctified by any faith. Whether or not polygamy should be legalized so that people in polygamous marriages enjoy equal rights and entitlements (like Social Security benefits), it should at least be decriminalized. Why should we care about other people's private religious ceremonies? How dare we criminalize them?

"Polygamy encourages child abuse," people say, citing instances 5 involving the marriage of older men to underage girls. Assuming for the sake of argument that this is true, it still doesn't justify categorical prohibitions on polygamy. Alcohol consumption may encourage sexual violence; it's often blamed for date rape. Should we prohibit its use, as members of the Women's Christian Temperance Union demanded over one hundred years ago? Or should we prosecute alcohol-fueled violence whenever we find it?

We rightly prohibit violence, not drunkenness, even though some drunks are violent; we should prohibit child abuse, not polygamy, even though some polygamists are abusers. To do otherwise is to court worse abuses than we seek to prevent, as the raid on the Search for Zion compound in Texas this past April demonstrated. On the basis of one anonymous phone call (that later appeared to be a hoax), Texas authorities forcibly removed more than 460 children from their parents without evidence of actual abuse in each case. Parents and children were ordered to undergo DNA testing (Who knows how long the state will maintain the DNA database, or to what uses it will be put?), and the children were summarily consigned to the notorious Texas foster-care system. They were subsequently reunited with their parents on order of Texas courts, which rightly held that the state had acted unlawfully, but who knows how much damage was done?

It's hard to explain the relative complacency or cautiousness that initially greeted this extraordinary abuse of power, except with reference to religious bigotry or squeamishness about polygamy. Members of the Search for Zion sect tried taking their case to the public—some attorneys defended their rights, and the American Civil Liberties Union eventually expressed more than cautious concern for them—but predictably, the national conversation generally reflected little sympathy for the civil liberties of people involved in a religious group far outside the mainstream. Imagine the reaction had the state instead invaded a community of Christian Scientists and removed all their children after receiving an anonymous tip that one child had been harmed by the refusal of his or her parents to provide medical care.

The Search for Zion case is different, some reply, because polygamy is illegal. Exactly. Polygamy's illegality doesn't make the state's actions less abusive—imagine the reaction if the state summarily removed all the children from a commune in which parents were suspected of smoking dope—but it does provide authorities with an argument, however flawed.

Of course, I'm not suggesting that any parent have a religious right to harm their children by denying them medical care, subjecting them to sexual molestation, or otherwise abusing them. I'm simply pointing out that the state should not abuse the power to prosecute people or forcibly remove their children because authorities don't approve of their "lifestyle." Gay men were once routinely suspected of being pedophiles, a suspicion that persists today but with considerably less prevalence and respectability. Indeed, opposition to gay marriage still relies on specious arguments about the harm it poses to children. Some fools still compare homosexuality to bestiality, just as the Supreme Court once compared polygamy to human sacrifice. We progress when we base the extension of rights on reason, not bias or judicial hyperbole.

TOPICS FOR CRITICAL THINKING AND WRITING

1. "If we allow a man or a woman to have more than one spouse, we are on a slippery slope; soon we will have to allow people to marry their cats and dogs." Evaluate the thinking here.

2. In her second paragraph, Kaminer refers to *Reynolds v U. S.* (1878), a case in which the U. S. Supreme Court ruled that a law against polygamy did not violate the Constitution's guarantee of religious freedom. George Reynolds, a member of the Church of Jesus Christ of Later-day Saints, argued that a law enacted by Congress for the territory of Utah prohibiting plural marriage violated his religious duty. The Court ruled that, "Congress was deprived of all legislative power over mere opinion, but was left free to reach actions which were in violation of social duties or subversive of good order." The Court suggested that if Reynolds's argument was accepted, a later petitioner might argue that his religious belief required human sacrifice. In short, the Court asserted that "Laws are made for the government of actions, and while they cannot interfere with mere religious beliefs and opinions, they may with practices." What is your view of this line of thinking?

3. In your view, should polygamy be illegal? If so, Why?

B. Aisha Lemu

B. Aisha Lemu was born in England and became a Muslim while in college. She is Director General of the Islamic Education Trust in Niger State, Nigeria. Reprinted here is part of a talk she gave (and part of the discussion that followed) at the International Islamic Conference held in London.

In Defense of Polygamy

Perhaps the aspect of Islam in respect of women which is most prominent in the Western mind is that of polygamy. Firstly let me clarify that Islam does not impose polygamy as a universal practice. The Prophet himself was a monogamist for the greater part of his married life, from the age of twenty-five when he married Khadija until he was fifty when she died.

One should therefore regard monogamy as the norm and polygamy as the exception.

One may observe that, although it has been abused in some times and some places, polygamy has under certain circumstances a valuable function. In some situations it may be considered as the lesser of two evils, and in other situations it may even be a positively beneficial arrangement.

The most obvious example of this occurs in times of war when there are inevitably large numbers of widows and girls whose fiances and husbands have been killed in the fighting. One has only to recall the figures of the dead in the first and second world wars to be aware that literally millions of women and girls lost their husbands and fiances and were left alone without any income or care or protection for themselves or their children. If it is still maintained that under these circumstances a man may marry only one wife, what options are left to the millions of other women who have no hope of getting a husband? Their choice, bluntly stated, is between a chaste and childless old maidenhood, or becoming somebody's mistress—that is, an unofficial second wife with no legal rights for herself or for her children. Most women would not welcome either of these since most women have always wanted and still do want the security of a legal husband and family.

The compromise therefore is for women under these circumstances 5 to face the fact that if given the alternative many of them would rather share a husband than have none at all. And there is no doubt that it is easier to share a husband when it is an established and publicly recognised practice than when it is carried on secretly along with attempts to deceive the first wife.

And it is no secret that polygamy of a sort is widely carried on in Europe and America. The difference is that while the Western man has no legal obligations to his second, third, or fourth mistresses and their children, the Muslim husband has complete legal obligations towards his second, third, or fourth wife and their children.

There may be other circumstances unrelated to war—individual circumstances, where marriage to more than one wife may be preferable to other available alternatives—for example, where the first wife is chronically sick or disabled. There are of course some husbands who can manage this situation, but no one would deny its potential hazards. A second marriage in some cases could be a solution acceptable to all three parties.

Again there are cases in which a wife is unable to have children, while the husband very much wants them. Under Western laws a man must either accept his wife's childlessness if he can, or if he cannot he must find a means of divorce in order to marry again. This could be avoided in some cases if the parties agreed on a second marriage.

There are other cases where a marriage has not been very successful and the husband loves another woman. This situation is so familiar that it is known as the Eternal Triangle. Under Western laws the husband cannot marry the second woman without divorcing the first one. But the first wife may not wish to be divorced. She may no longer love her husband, but she may still respect him and wish to stay with him for the security of marriage, for herself and their children. Similarly the second woman may not wish to break up the man's first family. There are certain cases such as this where both women could accept a polygamous marriage rather than face divorce on the one hand or an extramarital affair on the other.

I have mentioned some of these examples because to the majority of 10 Westerners polygamy is only thought of in the context of a harem of glamorous young girls, not as a possible solution to some of the problems of Western society itself. I have given some time to it not in order to advocate its indiscriminate use, but in an attempt to show that it is a practice not to be condemned without thinking of its uses and possible benefits in any community.

[A slightly edited version of the discussion that followed Lemu's talk follows on 748.]

DISCUSSION

Question: I would like to ask a question in relation to polygamy. If one concedes the arguments you have given in support of a man having more than one wife in certain circumstances, would the same arguments be extended to the situation of a woman in relation to her husband/husbands? To be more precise, if a woman becomes invalid and sexually incapacitated and because of that the husband is allowed to have a second wife, why should not the same hold good in respect of men? If a husband becomes invalid, would it be permitted for the wife to have a second husband?

B. Aisha Lemu: The instances which I quoted were examples of human circumstances where there is a genuine problem and I mentioned that in the Western world the options are limited. That is, either you stay with it or you obtain divorce, you cannot bring the third alternative of another wife. Now the question of a woman having more than one husband raises a number of other problems. One of them is the question of inheritance. If a woman has more than one husband, there is no certainty of the paternity of the child, and I think this is something which will be very disturbing to men, not to be sure that a certain child is their own, that it might be the child of another husband. Another problem that one could foresee here is that for a woman to look after one husband is, generally speaking, considered to be quite enough trouble (laughter and applause) without bringing upon herself more than one.

Topics for Critical Thinking and Writing

1. If you were to favor lawful polygamy, would you allow no upper limit to the number of spouses in any given marriage? Why, or why not?

2. Make a list of the kinds of circumstances favoring polygamy that Lemu mentions. Which do you find the most persuasive? The least persuasive? Explain in an essay of 350 words.

3. Can an argument be made for polyandry (one wife with several husbands) in the United States? If so, make it, in about 500 words. If not, explain why the system is unsound, immoral, impractical, or whatever, again in about 500 words.

> For topical links related to the future of marriage, see the companion Web site: **bedfordstmartins.com/barnetbedau.**

28

Reproductive Rights: What Are the Limits?

Rush H. Limbaugh III

Rush Limbaugh, born in Cape Girardeau, Missouri in 1951, became a Top 40 deejay in the 1960s before becoming a radio talk show host in Sacramento. In 1988 his show went national. Among his books are The Way Things Ought To Be *(1992), the source of this essay;* The Way Things Aren't *(1995), and* The IRS v. the People *(1999).*

Condoms: The New Diploma

The logic and motivation behind this country's mad dash to distribute free condoms in our public schools is ridiculous and misguided. Worse, the message conveyed by mass condom distribution is a disservice and borders on being lethal. Condom distribution sanctions, even encourages, sexual activity, which in teen years tends to be promiscuous and relegates to secondary status the most important lesson to be taught: abstinence. An analysis of the entire condom distribution logic also provides a glimpse into just what is wrong with public education today.

First things first. Advocates of condom distribution say that kids are going to have sex, that try as we might we can't stop them. Therefore they need protection. Hence, condoms. Well, hold on a minute. Just whose notion is it that "kids are going to do it anyway, you can't stop them"? Why limit the application of that brilliant logic to sexual activity? Let's just admit that kids are going to do drugs and distribute safe, untainted drugs every morning in homeroom. Kids are going to smoke, too, we can't stop them, so let's provide packs of low-tar cigarettes to the students for their after-sex smoke. Kids are going to get guns and shoot them, you can't stop them, so let's make sure that teachers have bullet-proof vests. I mean, come on! If we are really concerned about safe sex, why stop at condoms? Let's convert study halls to Safe Sex Centers where students can go to actually have sex on nice double beds with clean sheets under the watchful and approving eye of the school nurse, who will be on hand to demonstrate, along with the principal, just how to use a condom. Or even better: If kids are going to have sex, let's put disease-free hookers in these Safe Sex Centers. Hey, if safe sex is the objective, why compromise our standards?

There is something else very disturbing about all this. Let's say that Johnnie and Susie are on a date in Johnny's family sedan. Johnny pulls in to his town's designated Teen Parking Location hoping to score a little affection from Susie. They move to the backseat and it isn't long before Johnny, on the verge of bliss, whips out his trusty high school distributed condom and urges Susie not to resist him. She is hesitant, being a nice girl and all, and says she doesn't think the time is right.

"Hey, everything is okay. Nothing will go wrong. Heck, the *school gave me this condom,* they know what they're doing. You'll be fine," coos the artful and suave Johnny.

Aside from what is obviously wrong here, there is something you   5 probably haven't thought of which to me is profound. Not that long ago, school policy, including that on many college campuses, was designed to protect the girls from the natural and instinctive aggressive pursuit of young men. Chaperones, for example, were around to make sure the girls were not in any jeopardy. So much for that thinking now. The schools may just as well endorse and promote these backseat affairs. The kids are going to do it anyway.

Well, here's what's wrong. There have always been consequences to having sex. Always. Now, however, some of these consequences are severe: debilitating venereal diseases and AIDS. You can now die from having sex. It is that simple. If you look, the vast majority of adults in America have made adjustments in their sexual behavior in order to protect themselves from some of the dire consequences floating around out there. For the most part, the sexual revolution of the sixties is over, a miserable failure. Free love and rampant one-night stands are tougher to come by because people are aware of the risks. In short, we have modified our behavior. Now, would someone tell me what is so difficult about sharing this knowledge and experience with kids? The same stakes are involved. Isn't that our responsibility, for crying out loud, to teach them what's best for them? If we adults aren't responding to these new dangers by having condom-protected sex anytime, anywhere, why should such folly be taught to our kids?

Let me try the Magic Johnson example for you who remain unconvinced. Imagine that you are in the Los Angeles Lakers locker room after a game and you and Magic are getting ready to go hit the town. Outside the locker room are a bunch of young women, as there always are, and as Magic had freely admitted there always were, and that you know that the woman Magic is going to pick up and take back to the hotel has AIDS. You approach Magic and say, "Hey, Magic! Hold on! That girl you're going to take back to the hotel with you has AIDS. Here, don't worry about it. Take these condoms, you'll be fine."

Do you think Magic would have sex with that woman? Ask yourself: Would you knowingly have sex with *anyone* who has AIDS with only a condom to protect you from getting the disease? It doesn't take Einstein to answer that question. So, why do you think it's okay to send kids out into the world to do just that? Who is to know who carries the HIV virus, and on the chance your kid runs into someone who does have it, are you confident that a condom will provide all the protection he or she needs?

Doesn't it make sense to be honest with kids and tell them the best thing they can do to avoid AIDS or any of the other undesirable consequences is to abstain from sexual intercourse? It is the best way—in fact, it is the only surefire way—to guard against sexual transmission of AIDS, pregnancy, and venereal diseases. What's so terrible about saying so?

Yet, there are those who steadfastly oppose the teaching of absti- 10 nence, and I think they should be removed from any position of authority where educating children is concerned. In New York, the City Board of Education *narrowly won* (4–3) the passage of a resolution requiring the inclusion of teaching abstinence in the AIDS education program in the spring of 1992. No one was trying to eliminate anything from the program, such as condom distribution or anal sex education (which does occur in New York public school sex education classes). All they wanted was that abstinence also be taught. Yet, the Schools Chancellor, Joseph Fernandez, vigorously fought the idea, saying it would do great damage to their existing program! Well, just how is that? The fact is that abstinence works every time it is tried. As this book went to press, the New York Civil Liberties Union was considering filing a lawsuit to stop this dangerous new addition to the curriculum. Now what in the name of God is going on here? This is tantamount to opposing a drug education program which instructs students not to use drugs because it would not be useful.

The Jacksonville, Florida, school board also decided that abstinence should be the centerpiece of their sexual education curriculum, and the liberals there were also outraged about this. What is so wrong with this? Whose agenda is being denied by teaching abstinence and just what is that agenda?

Jacksonville teachers are telling seventh graders that "the only safe sex is no sex at all." Sex education classes provide some information about birth control and sexually transmitted diseases, but these areas are not the primary focus of the classes. Nancy Corwin, a member of the school board, admits the paradox when she says that the schools send a nonsensical message when they teach kids not to have sex but then give them condoms.

Instead of this twaddle, the Jacksonville school board has decided to teach real safe sex, which is abstinence. However, six families, along with Planned Parenthood and the ACLU, are suing the schools over this program. This bunch of curious citizens says that teaching abstinence puts the children at a greater risk of catching AIDS or other sexually transmitted diseases. Greater risk? !£#$£@! How can that be? What kind of contaminated thinking is this? The suit alleges that the schools are providing a "fear-based program that gives children incomplete, inaccurate, biased, and sectarian information." You want more? Try this: Linda Lanier of Planned Parenthood says, "It's not right to try to trick our students." Trick the students? #£&@£!? If anyone is trying to trick students, it's Planned Parenthood and this band of hedonists who try to tell kids that a condom will protect them from any consequences of sex.

Folks, here you have perhaps the best example of the culture war being waged in our country today. To say that "teaching abstinence is a trick" is absurd. Is Ms. Lanier having sex every night of the week? What adjustments has she made in her sex life because of AIDS? Does she think that a little sheath of latex will be enough to protect her?

This is terribly wrong. The Jacksonville public school system is 15 attempting to teach right from wrong, as opposed to teaching that sex does not have any consequences, which I believe is the selfish agenda these people hold dear. I have stated elsewhere in this book, and I state it again here, that there are many people who wish to go through life guilt-free and engage in behavior they know to be wrong and morally vacant. In order to assuage their guilt they attempt to construct and impose policies which not only allow them to engage in their chosen activities but encourage others to do so as well. There is, after all, strength in numbers.

Promiscuous and self-gratifying, of-the-moment sex is but one of these chosen lifestyles. Abortions on demand and condom distribution are but two of the policies and programs which, as far as these people are concerned, ensure there are no consequences. As one disgusted member of the Jacksonville school board said, "Every yahoo out there has a social program that they want to run through the school system. We are here for academic reasons and we cannot cure the social evils of the world."

The worst of all of this is the lie that condoms really protect against AIDS. The condom failure rate can be as high as 20 percent. Would you get on a plane—or put your children on a plane—if one in five passengers would be killed on the flight? Well, the statistic holds for condoms, folks.

Ah, but there is even more lunacy haunting the sacred halls of academe. According to the *Los Angeles Times*, administrators in the Los Angeles public schools have regretfully acknowledged that the sex education courses undertaken in the early 1970s "might" have a correlation to the rising teen pregnancy rates in their schools which can be traced to the same years. They have devised an enlightened and marvelous new approach to modernize and correct the sex education curriculum. It is called Outercourse. I am not making this up. Outercourse is, in essence, instruction in creative methods of masturbation.

"Hi, class, and welcome to Outercourse 101. I am your instructor, Mr. Reubens, from Florida, and I want to remind you that this is a hands-on course." We will know the graduates of Outercourse 101 in about forty years. They will be the people walking around with seeing-eye dogs.

TOPICS FOR CRITICAL THINKING AND WRITING

1. In his second paragraph Limbaugh attempts to give a reductio ad absurdum of the proposal to distribute condoms in high school. (We discuss reductio on p. 356.) Do you think this tactic of criticism as used here is successful or not? Explain.

2. Limbaugh thinks that distributing condoms in high school will encourage sex among adolescents as well as give premarital sex a stamp of approval by school authorities. Do you agree? Why, or why not?

3. In paragraph 17 Limbaugh says, "The condom failure rate can be as high as 20 percent." What do you take this statement to mean?

4. Limbaugh says that those who favor condom distribution "try to tell kids that a condom will protect them from *any* consequences of sex" (para. 13, emphasis added). Inquire at your campus health office to find out what current medical practice advises about the likelihood of condom failure, resulting in unwanted pregnancy or in acquiring a sexually transmitted disease.

5. Make a list of the *reasons* Limbaugh gives for opposing the distribution of condoms; evaluate those reasons.

6. Limbaugh quotes (para. 16) with evident approval the public school official who complained, "'Every yahoo out there has a social program that they want to run through the school system. We are here for academic reasons. . . .'" Yet elsewhere Limbaugh supports prayer in the public schools. Do you think he is inconsistent or not? Explain.

ANALYZING A VISUAL: SEX EDUCATION

Topics for Critical Thinking and Writing

1. What is SIECUS? (If you don't know, you can easily find out by using a search engine such as Google.)

2. Exactly what are the protesters saying about SIECUS, and how effective is their statement? Judging from what you know about SIECUS (perhaps by reading some of its statements online and some of the statements opposing SIECUS), is the charge on the placard appropriate? Explain.

Anna Quindlen

Anna Quindlen, born in Philadelphia in 1953 and educated at Barnard College in New York City, regularly wrote a column for the New York Times *from 1986 to 1994. In 1992 she won a Pulitzer Prize for commentary, and she now writes a column for* Newsweek. *Quindlen is also a distinguished novelist. We reprint a piece originally written for the* Times *in January 1994.*

A Pyrrhic Victory

Pop quiz: A sixteen-year-old is appropriately treated at a school clinic after he is advised that the reason it feels as if he is going to die when he urinates is because he has a sexually transmitted disease. Told that condoms could have protected him from infection, he asks for some. A nurse tells him to wait while she looks for his name on the list of students whose parents have confidentially requested that their sons and daughters not receive them.

The student replies: (a) "No problem"; (b) "Hmmm—an interesting way to balance the reproductive health of adolescents and the rights of parents"; (c) Nothing. He sidles out of the office and not long afterward gets a whopping case of chlamydia.

Condoms, condoms, condoms. As those who oppose condom distribution in the schools gloated over an appellate court decision that said the program violated parents' rights, Alwyn Cohall, the pediatrician who oversees several school-based clinics in New York, quoted Yogi Berra. "It's déjà vu all over again," said Dr. Cohall, who has to clean up the messes made when sexually active kids don't use condoms. And he wasn't smiling.

Over the last two years the Board of Education has wasted time better spent on instructional issues giving and receiving lectures on latex. The opt-out provision its members are now likely to adopt is the "let me see if you're on the list, dear" scenario outlined above, and if you think it might have a chilling effect on a young man too self-conscious to ask for Trojans in a drugstore, then you get an A in adolescent psychology.

You get extra credit if you figure that being on the list will be scant   5
protection against disease if the young man has sex anyhow. "A victory for parents," some have called the provision. But is it Pyrrhic?

Dr. Cohall, a champion of condom distribution, agrees that it is best if teenagers abstain from sexual activity and talk to their parents about issues of sex, morality, and health. But he also notes that in 1992 his three high school clinics saw around 150 cases of sexually transmitted diseases like condyloma, chlamydia, and the better-known gonorrhea and syphilis.

He has a sixteen-year-old in the hospital right now who got AIDS from her second sexual partner. And he recalls a girl who broke her leg jumping out an apartment window because her mother found her birth control pills, seized her by the throat, and said, according to the kid, "I brought you into the world; I can take you out of it."

Don't you just love those little mother-daughter sex talks?

He also knows that at the heart of the balancing act between keeping kids healthy and keeping parents involved there has always been a covert place in which many opponents of condom distribution really settle. It's called Fantasyland.

You could see that in the response to the rather mild commercials 10 on condom use and abstinence that the Department of Health and Human Services unveiled this week. The general secretary of the National Conference of Catholic Bishops immediately said the ads "promote promiscuity" and the networks should reject them. At the same time ABC said it would not run the spots during its prime-time "family-oriented" programs.

So foolish. ABC's own *Roseanne* has been far more candid about sexuality than any of the new government public-service spots. And what could be a better way to foment conversation with the children of the video age than a television advertisement? Right there in your living room you have a goad to the kind of discussion that opponents of condom distribution have always argued is the purview of parents. And you put the ads on late at night? Do we really want to talk with our kids? Or do we just want to talk about talking to them?

The Board of Education could do a great good if it found ways to truly foster parent-child communication in all things, not just matters sexual. But instead its members argue about condoms. This isn't really about condoms, of course, but about control and the shock of adolescent sexuality and the difficulty parents have communicating with their kids and a deep and understandable yearning for simpler times.

While we yearn and argue, Dr. Cohall visits his sixteen-year-old AIDS patient. Her parents' involvement may someday consist of visiting the cemetery. Imagine how they'd feel if they put her on the no-condom list, then put her in the hospital, then put her in the ground. Some victory.

TOPICS FOR CRITICAL THINKING AND WRITING

1. Exactly what is a Pyrrhic victory?

2. Quindlen offers three possible responses for her sixteen-year-old male student (para. 2). Write a fourth and (if possible) a fifth response.

3. As paragraph 3 indicates, some parents argue that the distribution of condoms violates parents' rights. What parental right is at stake in the dispute over whether high schools should distribute condoms to students who seek them? Or is there no such right, but instead a parental duty involved?

4. Quindlen mentions four sexually transmitted diseases. What are their names, their symptoms, and the cure in each case? (You will probably need to talk to a physician or nurse, or do some library research, to answer this question.)

5. Some people argue that any discussion of condoms, even in a context that advocates abstinence, in effect promotes promiscuity. Do you agree or disagree? Why?

6. Evaluate Quindlen's final paragraph as a piece of persuasive writing.

Ellen Willis

Ellen Willis (b. 1941) was educated at Barnard College and the University of California at Berkeley. She has been a freelance writer since 1966, publishing in such journals as The New Yorker, Rolling Stone, *and the* Village Voice, *where this essay first appeared on July 16, 1985.*

Putting Women Back into the Abortion Debate

Some years ago I attended a New York Institute for the Humanities seminar on the new right. We were a fairly heterogeneous group of liberals and lefties, feminists and gay activists, but on one point nearly all of us agreed: The right-to-life movement was a dangerous antifeminist crusade. At one session I argued that the attack on abortion had significance far beyond itself, that it was the linchpin of the right's social agenda. I got a lot of supporting comments and approving nods. It was too much for Peter Steinfels, a liberal Catholic, author of *The Neoconservatives*, and executive editor of *Commonweal*. Right-to-lifers were not all right-wing fanatics, he protested. "You have to understand," he said plaintively, "that many of us see abortion as a *human life issue*." What I remember best was his air of frustrated isolation. I don't think he came back to the seminar after that.

Things are different now. I often feel isolated when I insist that abortion is, above all, a *feminist issue*. Once people took for granted that abortion was an issue of sexual politics and morality. Now, abortion is most often discussed as a question of "life" in the abstract. Public concern over abortion centers almost exclusively on fetuses; women and their bodies are merely the stage on which the drama of fetal life and death takes place. Debate about abortion—if not its reality—has become sexlessly scholastic. And the people most responsible for this turn of events are, like Peter Steinfels, on the left.

The left wing of the right-to-life movement is a small, seemingly eccentric minority in both "progressive" and antiabortion camps. Yet it has played a critical role in the movement: By arguing that opposition to abortion can be separated from the right's antifeminist program, it has given antiabortion sentiment legitimacy in left-symp and (putatively) profeminist circles. While left antiabortionists are hardly alone in emphasizing fetal life, their innovation has been to claim that a consistent "pro-life" stand involves opposing capital punishment, supporting disarmament, demanding government programs to end poverty, and so on. This is of course a leap the right is neither able nor willing to make. It's been liberals—from Garry Wills to the Catholic bishops—who have supplied the mass media with the idea that prohibiting abortion is part of a "seamless garment" of respect for human life.

Having invented this countercontext for the abortion controversy, left antiabortionists are trying to impose it as the only legitimate context for debate. Those of us who won't accept their terms and persist in seeing opposition to abortion, antifeminism, sexual repression, and religious sectarianism as the real seamless garment have been accused of obscuring the issue with demagoguery. Last year *Commonweal*—perhaps the most important current forum for left antiabortion opinion—ran an editorial demanding that we shape up: "Those who hold that abortion is immoral believe that the biological dividing lines of birth or viability should no more determine whether a developing member of the species is denied or accorded essential rights than should the biological dividing lines of sex or race or disability or old age. This argument is open to challenge. Perhaps the dividing lines are sufficiently different. Pro-choice advocates should state their reasons for believing so. They should meet the argument on its own grounds. . . ."

In other words, the only question we're allowed to debate—or the 5 only one *Commonweal* is willing to entertain—is "Are fetuses the moral equivalent of born human beings?" And I can't meet the argument on its own grounds because I don't agree that this is the key question, whose answer determines whether one supports abortion or opposes it. I don't doubt that fetuses are alive, or that they're biologically human—what else would they be? I do consider the life of a fertilized egg less precious than the well-being of a woman with feelings, self-consciousness, a history, social ties; and I think fetuses get closer to being human in a moral sense as they come closer to birth. But to me these propositions are intuitively self-evident. I wouldn't know how to justify them to a "nonbeliever," nor do I see the point of trying.

I believe the debate has to start in a different place—with the recognition that fertilized eggs develop into infants inside the bodies of women. Pregnancy and birth are active processes in which a woman's body shelters, nourishes, and expels a new life; for nine months she is immersed in the most intimate possible relationship with another being. The growing fetus makes considerable demands on her physical and emotional resources, culminating in the cataclysmic experience of birth. And childbearing has unpredictable consequences; it always entails some risk of injury or death.

For me all this has a new concreteness: I had a baby last year. My much-desired and relatively easy pregnancy was full of what antiabortionists like to call "inconveniences." I was always tired, short of breath; my digestion was never right; for three months I endured a state of hormonal siege; later I had pains in my fingers, swelling feet, numb spots on my legs, the dread hemorrhoids. I had to think about everything I ate. I developed borderline glucose intolerance. I gained fifty pounds and am still overweight; my shape has changed in other ways that may well be permanent. Psychologically, my pregnancy consumed me—though I'd happily bought the seat on the roller coaster, I was still terrified to be so out of control of my normally tractable body. It was all bearable, even interesting—even, at times, transcendent—because I wanted a baby. Birth was painful, exhausting, and wonderful. If I hadn't wanted a baby it would only have been painful and exhausting—or worse. I can hardly imagine what it's like to have your body and mind taken over in this way when you not only don't look forward to the result, but positively dread it. The thought appalls me. So as I see it, the key question is "Can it be moral, under any circumstances, to make a woman bear a child against her will?"

From this vantage point, *Commonweal*'s argument is irrelevant, for in a society that respects the individual, no "member of the species" in *any* stage of development has an "essential right" to make use of someone else's body, let alone in such all-encompassing fashion, without that person's consent. You can't make a case against abortion by applying a general principle about everybody's human rights; you have to show exactly the opposite—that the relationship between fetus and pregnant woman is an exception, one that justifies depriving women of their right to bodily integrity. And in fact all antiabortion ideology rests on the premise—acknowledged or simply assumed—that women's unique capacity to bring life into the world carries with it a unique obligation that women cannot be allowed to "play God" and launch only the lives they welcome.

Yet the alternative to allowing women this power is to make them impotent. Criminalizing abortion doesn't just harm individual women with unwanted pregnancies, it affects all women's sense of themselves. Without control of our fertility we can never envision ourselves as free, for our biology makes us constantly vulnerable. Simply because we are female our physical integrity can be violated, our lives disrupted and transformed, at any time. Our ability to act in the world is hopelessly compromised by our sexual being.

Ah, sex—it does have a way of coming up in these discussions, 10 despite all. When pressed, right-to-lifers of whatever political persuasion invariably point out that pregnancy doesn't happen by itself. The leftists often give patronizing lectures on contraception (though some find only "natural birth control" acceptable), but remain unmoved when reminded that contraceptives fail. Openly or implicitly they argue that people shouldn't have sex unless they're prepared to procreate. (They are quick to profess a single standard—men as well as women should be sexually "responsible." Yes, and the rich as well as the poor should be allowed to sleep under bridges.) Which amounts to saying that if women want to lead heterosexual lives they must give up any claim to self-determination, and that they have no right to sexual pleasure without fear.

Opposing abortion, then, means accepting that women must suffer sexual disempowerment and a radical loss of autonomy relative to men: If fetal life is sacred, the self-denial basic to women's oppression is also basic to the moral order. Opposing abortion means embracing a conservative sexual morality, one that subordinates pleasure to reproduction: If fetal life is sacred, there is no room for the view that sexual passion—or even sexual love—for its own sake is a human need and a human right. Opposing abortion means tolerating the inevitable double standard, by which men may accept or reject sexual restrictions in accordance with their beliefs, while women must bow to them out of fear . . . or defy them at great risk. However much *Commonweal*'s editors and those of like mind want to believe their opposition to abortion is simply about saving lives, the truth is that in the real world they are shoring up a particular sexual culture, whose rules are stacked against women. I have yet to hear any left right-to-lifers take full responsibility for that fact or deal seriously with its political implications.

Unfortunately, their fuzziness has not lessened their appeal—if anything it's done the opposite. In increasing numbers liberals and leftists, while opposing antiabortion laws, have come to view abortion as an "agonizing moral issue" with some justice on both sides, rather than an issue—however emotionally complex—of freedom versus repression, or equality versus hierarchy, that affects their political self-definition. This above-the-battle stance is attractive to leftists who want to be feminist good guys but are uneasy or ambivalent about sexual issues, not to mention those who want to ally with "progressive" factions of the Catholic church on Central America, nuclear disarmament, or populist economics without that sticky abortion question getting in the way.

Such neutrality is a way of avoiding the painful conflict over cultural issues that continually smolders on the left. It can also be a way of coping with the contradictions of personal life at a time when liberation is a dream deferred. To me the fight for abortion has always been the cutting edge of feminism, precisely because it denies that anatomy is destiny, that female biology dictates women's subordinate status. Yet recently I've found it hard to focus on the issue, let alone summon up the militance needed to stop the antiabortion tanks. In part that has to do with second-round weariness—do we really have to go through all these things twice?—in part with my life now.

Since my daughter's birth my feelings about abortion—not as a political demand but as a personal choice—have changed. In this society, the difference between the situation of a childless woman and of a mother is immense; the fear that having a child will dislodge one's tenuous hold on a nontraditional life is excruciating. This terror of being forced into the sea-change of motherhood gave a special edge to my convictions about abortion. Since I've made that plunge voluntarily, with consequences still unfolding, the terror is gone; I might not want another child, for all sorts of reasons, but I will never again feel that my identity is at stake. Different battles with the culture absorb my energy now. Besides, since I've experienced the primal, sensual passion of caring for an infant, there will always be part of me that does want another. If I had an abortion today, it would be with conflict and sadness unknown to me when I had an abortion a decade ago. And the antiabortionists' imagery of dead babies hits me with new force. Do many women—left, feminist women—have such feelings? Is this the sort of "ambivalence about abortion" that in the present atmosphere slides so easily into self-flagellating guilt?

Some left antiabortionists, mainly pacifists—Juli Loesch, Mary   15 Meehan, and other "feminists for life"; Jim Wallis and various writers for Wallis's radical evangelical journal *Sojourners*—have tried to square their position with concern for women. They blame the prevalence of abortion on oppressive conditions—economic injustice, lack of child care and other social supports for mothers, the devaluation of childrearing, men's exploitative sexual behavior and refusal to take equal responsibility for children. They disagree on whether to criminalize abortion now (since murder is intolerable no matter what the cause) or to build a long-term moral consensus (since stopping abortion requires a general social transformation), but they all regard abortion as a desperate solution to desperate problems, and the women who resort to it as more sinned against than sinning.

This analysis grasps an essential feminist truth: that in a male-supremacist society no choice a woman makes is genuinely free or entirely in her interest. Certainly many women have had abortions they didn't want or wouldn't have wanted if they had any plausible means of caring for a child; and countless others wouldn't have gotten pregnant in the first place were it not for inadequate contraception, sexual confusion and guilt, male pressure, and other stigmata of female powerlessness. Yet forcing a woman to bear a child she doesn't want can only add injury to insult, while refusing to go through with such a pregnancy can be a woman's first step toward taking hold of her life. And many women who have abortions are "victims" only of ordinary human miscalculation, technological failure, or the vagaries of passion, all bound to exist in any society, however utopian. There will always be women who, at any given moment, want sex but don't want a child; some of these women will get pregnant; some of them will have abortions. Behind the victim theory of abortion is the implicit belief that women are always ready to be mothers, if only conditions are right, and that sex for pleasure rather than procreation is not only "irresponsible" (i.e., bad) but something men impose on women, never something women actively seek. Ironically, left right-to-lifers see abortion as always coerced (it's "exploitation" and "violence against women"), yet regard motherhood—which for most women throughout history has been inescapable, and is still our most socially approved role—as a positive choice. The analogy to the feminist antipornography movement goes beyond borrowed rhetoric: the antiporners, too, see active female lust as surrender to male domination and traditionally feminine sexual attitudes as expressions of women's true nature.

This Orwellian version of feminism, which glorifies "female values" and dismisses women's struggles for freedom—particularly sexual freedom—as a male plot, has become all too familiar in recent years. But its use in the abortion debate has been especially muddleheaded. Somehow we're supposed to leap from an oppressive patriarchal society to the egalitarian one that will supposedly make abortion obsolete without ever allowing women to see themselves as people entitled to control their reproductive function rather than be controlled by it. How women who have no power in this most personal of areas can effectively fight for power in the larger society is left to our imagination. A "New Zealand feminist" quoted by Mary Meehan in a 1980 article in *The Progressive* says, "Accepting short-term solutions like abortion only delays the implementation of real reforms like decent maternity and paternity leaves, job protection, high-quality child care, community responsibility for dependent people of all ages, and recognition of the economic contribution of childminders"—as if these causes were progressing nicely before legal abortion came along. On the contrary, the fight for reproductive freedom is the foundation of all the others, which is why antifeminists resist it so fiercely.

As "pro-life" pacifists have been particularly concerned with refuting charges of misogyny, the liberal Catholics at *Commonweal* are most exercised by the claim that antiabortion laws violate religious freedom. The editorial quoted above hurled another challenge at the proabortion forces:

> It is time, finally, for the pro-choice advocates and editorial writers to abandon, once and for all, the argument that abortion is a religious "doctrine" of a single or several churches being imposed on those of other persuasions in violation of the First Amendment. . . . Catholics and their bishops are accused of imposing their "doctrine" on abortion, but not their "doctrine" on the needs of the poor, or their "doctrine" on the arms race, or their "doctrine" on human rights in Central America. . . .
> The briefest investigation into Catholic teaching would show that the church's case against abortion is utterly unlike, say, its belief in the Real Presence, known with the eyes of faith alone, or its insistence on a Sunday obligation, applicable only to the faithful. The church's moral teaching on abortion . . . is for the most part like its teaching on racism,

warfare, and capital punishment, based on ordinary reasoning common to believers and nonbelievers. . . .

This is one more example of right-to-lifers' tendency to ignore the sexual ideology underlying their stand. Interesting, isn't it, how the editorial neglects to mention that the church's moral teaching on abortion jibes neatly with its teaching on birth control, sex, divorce, and the role of women. The traditional, patriarchal sexual morality common to these teachings is explicitly religious, and its chief defenders in modern times have been the more conservative churches. The Catholic and evangelical Christian churches are the backbone of the organized right-to-life movement and—a few Nathansons and Hentoffs notwithstanding— have provided most of the movement's activists and spokespeople.

Furthermore, the Catholic hierarchy has made opposition to abor-   20
tion a litmus test of loyalty to the church in a way it has done with no other political issue—witness Archbishop O'Connor's harassment of Geraldine Ferraro during her vice-presidential campaign. It's unthinkable that a Catholic bishop would publicly excoriate a Catholic officeholder or candidate for taking a hawkish position on the arms race or Central America or capital punishment. Nor do I notice anyone trying to read William F. Buckley out of the church for his views on welfare. The fact is there is no accepted Catholic "doctrine" on these matters comparable to the church's absolutist condemnation of abortion. While differing attitudes toward war, racism, and poverty cut across religious and secular lines, the sexual values that mandate opposition to abortion are the bedrock of the traditional religious world view, and the source of the most bitter conflict with secular and religious modernists. When churches devote their considerable political power, organizational resources, and money to translating those values into law, I call that imposing their religious beliefs on me—whether or not they're technically violating the First Amendment.

Statistical studies have repeatedly shown that people's views on abortion are best predicted by their opinions on sex and "family" issues, not on "life" issues like nuclear weapons or the death penalty. That's not because we're inconsistent but because we comprehend what's really at stake in the abortion fight. It's the antiabortion left that refuses to face the contradiction in its own position: you can't be wholeheartedly for "life"—or for such progressive aspirations as freedom, democracy, equality—and condone the subjugation of women. The seamless garment is full of holes.

TOPICS FOR CRITICAL THINKING AND WRITING

1. What does Willis mean when she insists, in her second paragraph, that "abortion is . . . a *feminist issue*"? Whether or not you agree, write a

paragraph explaining her point. You may want to begin simply by saying, "When Ellen Willis says abortion is a *'feminist issue,'* she means . . ."

2. After describing the physical and psychological difficulties of pregnancy, Willis says (para. 8) that

> in a society that respects the individual, no "member of the species" in *any* stage of development has an "essential right" to make use of someone else's body, let alone in such all-encompassing fashion, without that person's consent. You can't make a case against abortion by applying a general principle about everybody's human rights; you have to show exactly the opposite — that the relationship between fetus and pregnant woman is an exception, one that justifies depriving women of their right to bodily integrity.

Do you accept all of Willis's declarations? Any of them? Why, or why not? And (another topic) consider the expression, "without that person's consent." Suppose a woman takes no precautions against becoming pregnant — possibly she even wants to become pregnant — but at a late stage in pregnancy decides she does not wish to bear a child. Can she withdraw her "consent" at any time during her pregnancy?

3. In the previous question we asked you to consider Willis's expression "without that person's consent." Here is a related problem: The relationship between fetus and pregnant woman is different from all other relationships, but is it relevant to point out that women are not alone in having their bodies possessed, so to speak, by others? In time of war, men — but not women — are drafted; the interruption of their normal career causes considerable hardship. At the very least, a draftee is required to give up months or even years of his life and to live in circumstances that severely interfere with his privacy and his autonomy. And of course he may in fact be required to risk — and lose — his life.

4. Do you think (in contrast to Willis) that persons who are opposed to capital punishment and to increased military spending — persons who are, so to speak, "pro-life" — must, if they are to be consistent, also oppose abortion? Why, or why not?

Randall A. Terry

Randall A. Terry (b. 1959) is the founder of the antiabortion organization Operation Rescue. This essay originally appeared in the Boston Globe, *January 9, 1995.*

The Abortion Clinic Shootings: Why?

As the nation heard with sorrow the news of the deplorable shooting spree at abortion facilities in Brookline,[1] the question is asked: Why? Why this sudden rise of violence in this arena?

[1] On December 30, 1994, a gunman opened fire at two abortion facilities in Brookline, Massachusetts, wounding several people, two of them fatally. [Editors' note.]

I have been intricately involved in the antiabortion movement for more than a decade. I have led thousands of people in peaceful antiabortion activism via Operation Rescue. Hence, I enjoy a perspective few have. So I submit these answers to the question "Why?"

Enemies of the babies and the antiabortion movement will argue that the conviction that abortion is murder, and the call to take nonviolent direct action to save children from death, inevitably leads to the use of lethal force. This argument is ludicrous—unless one is prepared to argue that Gandhi's nonviolent civil disobedience in India during the 1930s led to the murder of British officials; or that Dr. Martin Luther King's nonviolent civil disobedience led to the violent actions that accompanied the civil rights movement in the United States during the 1960s.

So why, then, this recent violent outburst? Law enforcement officials need look no further than *Roe v. Wade;* abortion providers need look no further than their own instruments of death; and Congress and the president need look no further than the Freedom of Access to Clinic Entrances Act to understand the roots of the shootings.

The Supreme Court's attempt to overthrow Law (capital "L") in order 5 to legalize and legitimize murder has led to the inevitable—a disregard of or contempt for law. I say the court's attempt, for the court can no more overturn Law and legalize murder than it can overturn the law of gravity. God's immutable commandment "Thou shalt not murder" has forever made murder illegal. The court's lawlessness is breeding lawlessness. The court cannot betray the foundation of law and civilization—the Ten Commandments—and then expect a people to act "lawful" and "civilized."

Let us look at the abortion industry itself. Abortion is murder. And just as segregation and the accompanying violence possess the seeds for further violence, likewise it appears that the Law of sowing and reaping is being visited upon the abortion industry. A society cannot expect to tear 35 million innocent babies from their mothers' wombs without reaping horrifying consequences. Was it perhaps inevitable that the violent abortion industry should itself reap a portion of what it has so flagrantly and callously sown?

Now to Congress and the judiciary. Similar to the civil rights activists, antiabortion activists have often been brutalized at the hands of police and then subjected to vulgar injustices in sundry courts of law. Add to this the Freedom of Access to Clinic Entrances Act, which turns peaceful antiabortion activists into federal felons and perhaps one can understand the frustration and anger that is growing in Americans.

The abortion industry can partly blame itself for the recent shootings. It clamored for harsh treatment of peaceful antiabortion activists, and it usually got it. Now it has to deal with an emerging violent fringe. John F. Kennedy stated, "Those who make peaceful revolution impossible will make violent revolution inevitable." One would think the pro-choice crowd would belatedly heed the late president's warning, but they haven't. They're urging an all too political Justice Department to launch a witch hunt into the lives of peaceful antiabortion activists and leaders. Make no mistake—what the pro-choice people want is to pressure law enforcement and the courts to intimidate anyone who condemns abortion as murder. Their recent public relations scam is to blame all antiabortion people for the shootings. And they will not be content until they have crushed all dissent against abortion. We must not allow them to cause us to cower in silence.

To those who support the recent shootings or herald John Salvi as a hero, I ask you: Has God authorized one person to be policeman, judge, jury, and executioner? Is it logical to leap from nonviolent life-saving activities to lethal force? Read your history! Remember the principles of Calvin, Knox, and Cromwell concerning lower magistrates. Are you likening John Salvi and Co. to Knox or Cromwell? Are you calling for revolution? Please consider these questions before calling someone who walks into a clinic and starts randomly shooting people a hero.

So what can be done to curtail this trend? First, the Freedom of 10 Access to Clinic Entrances Act should be repealed immediately. This oppressive law is an outrage. The crushing weight of the federal government punishing peaceful protesters is the kind of thing we would expect in Communist China against political dissidents.

Second, the courts must stop abusing antiabortion activists. We must be accorded the same tolerance and leniency that every politically correct protester receives nationwide, i.e., small fines, two days in jail, charges dismissed, etc.

Finally, and this is most urgent, child killing must be brought to an immediate end. Whether the Supreme Court declares the personhood and inalienable right to life of preborn children or the Constitution is amended or the president signs an emancipation proclamation for children or Congress outlaws abortion outright, we must bring a swift end to the murder of innocent children.

Topics for Critical Thinking and Writing

1. In his third paragraph, Terry draws a parallel between Operation Rescue and the nonviolent civil disobedience campaigns in India led by Gandhi and in the United States led by Martin Luther King Jr. Is the analogy a good one? Why, or why not?

2. Does Terry think that the Supreme Court's decision in *Roe v. Wade* (upholding a woman's right to have an abortion) *causes* violent disruption of abortion clinics? Or that it *justifies* that violence? If so, spell out the details of this causation or justification. If not, what does he mean when he says in paragraph 4 that "law enforcement officials need look no further than *Roe v. Wade*"?

3. Why does Terry think that "abortion is murder" (see paras. 5–6)?

4. In paragraph 8 Terry cites a remark of President Kennedy: "'Those who make peaceful revolution impossible will make violent revolution inevitable.'" Evaluate the aptness of this quotation as an explanation of violent disruption of medical services at an abortion clinic.

5. What is the purpose and the effect of Terry's choice of these words in paragraph 8: a "public relations scam," "crushed all dissent," "cower in silence"?

6. In the library, find some information about the Freedom of Access to Clinic Entrances Act (mentioned by Terry in paras. 7 and 10). Do you think its repeal, which Terry advocates, would help reduce violence at abortion clinics? Why, or why not? Why do you think this law was enacted by Congress in the first place?

7. Terry describes abortion as "child killing" (para. 12). Do you think that is a fair description? Why, or why not?

8. At the end of his essay (paras. 10–12), Terry proposes three things government ought to do to end the trend toward violence in the antiabortion movement. Do you think pro-choice advocates can accept any of these policies? Why, or why not?

9. Terry asserts that "preborn children" have an "inalienable right to life" (para. 12). What does "inalienable" mean? Suppose a pregnant woman would die because of medical complications if she carried her unborn child to birth. Do you think Terry would favor the mother dying because we must respect the "inalienable right to life" of the unborn? Does the mother, too, have such a right? How do you think he ought to resolve this conflict of rights, and why?

Kathleen Nolan

Kathleen Nolan is a visiting associate for medicine at the Hastings Center, a nonpartisan and nonprofit bioethics research institute. It publishes the Hastings Center Report *and* Bioethics Forum, *a free Web site concerned with bioethical issues.*

In the following selection from the Hastings Center Report, *Nolan summarizes an ethical issue, and then two writers offer opposed comments.*

Live Sperm, Dead Bodies

Bill K., a twenty-two-year-old man engaged to be married in four months, has just been diagnosed as brain-dead after a car accident. His father arrives and agrees to mulitple organ donations to be coordinated by a local organ procurement agency. Bill's father also makes an unusual request: Can sperm be obtained and frozen for later use? Bill's fiancée is unavailable for consultation, but the father believes that she may be interested in conceiving Bill's child, so that "a part of him can live on." Sperm have been successfully harvested in similar circumstances in a few cases. Bill was his father's only son, and the father states that even if the financée is not interested in using the sperm, he would welcome the donation so that the family line could be continued in at least that fashion. Assuming that adequate technical means are available, should the sperm be retrieved?

Cappy Miles Rothman

Dr. Rothman, a urologist in private practice in Los Angeles, runs Chryobank, the nation's largest sperm bank.

Commentary

Not only do technical means exist for post-mortem sperm recovery, but compelling ethical reasons as well. As a physician, my primary motivation is to relieve pain and suffering. Eleven years ago I harvested sperm from a young man who had sustained fatal head injuries. While the deceased was unmarried and without a fiancée, this man's father was consoled by knowing that viable sperm were stored. When I recovered sperm from another young man who had died of a gunshot wound, his parents followed me to the sperm bank and were comforted when they saw motile sperm from their son. Preserving "part of the deceased" let them identify with their lost son, and allowed the possibility of continuation of the patrilineal heritage. To bestow such consolation at a time of grief and tragedy is clearly part of my role as a healer.

Thousands of children have been born from sperm stored for many years and some have been conceived after the death of their fathers. The most publicized case occured in France when the National Sperm Bank refused to release sperm to a woman whose husband had recently died. Public opinion in her favor was so strong as to compel the release of the sperm to her. Such instances provide for individual rights, pose no harm to society, and allow for freedom of choice on an issue that, while unusual, is important to them.

Clearly there is a growing demand for information on post-mortem sperm recovery. National medical conferences, lay publications, radio, and television have all covered this issue. More and more instances occur where a wife requests recovery and storage of sperm from her recently deceased spouse.

At present, no legislation exists to restrict or regulate sperm retrieval. To date, no children have been born from sperm stored after such recovery, but the possibility exists; recent advances have enabled men with vas obstruction to have children by aspirating epididymal sperm. Such valuable and available technology should not be unnecessarily restricted. If parents can legally release their son's organs for transplantation, why should they not be able to store his sperm? And if a man can store sperm prior to an anticipated death, why shouldn't the wife of a man who dies an untimely death have the same opportunity?

Certainly situations could complicate what might seem a fairly straight-forward issue. If Bill's fiancée, for example, objects to the use of his sperm, should his father or parents retain rights to its use with another woman? What would be the rights of the offspring with regard to property and position? Who will establish informed consent for the woman who will carry this child and also have a genetic interest? (Perhaps Bill has genetic abnormalities that his fiancée is unaware of and that are not apparent during harvesting and storage . . .) Who controls release of the stored sperm and for which purposes?

I can envision circumstances under which I would decline to retrieve sperm from the deceased—when there is clearly a conflict of interest between survivors as to the use of the sperm or when there are questions regarding the intent of the deceased to father children. But deciding whose rights prevail is not my role, lessening grief and offering alternatives remain my priorities.

Sperm harvesting requires immediate action to recover viable and motile sperm. At present, sperm recovery has been successfully performed because such immediate action can be taken based on the "best judgement" of the physician. If an ethics committee review were necessary for each procedure, would the sperm still be viable? If the committee ruled "yes," and the delay prevented successful retrieval, who would be liable? Unless a clearly adverse situation exists, recovery should proceed at once to enable well-considered decisions later.

Judith Wilson Ross

Judith Wilson Ross, author of several studies of medical ethics is associate director of the UCLA Medical Center's program in medical ethics.

Commentary

Is Bill, dead, simply bits and pieces that can be used to fulfill others' rational desires? Surely not. Sperm harvesting should not be permitted because persons should participate in a decision to beget a child and because children should be assured a relationship with their genetic parents based upon each parent's acceptance of the child's future existence.

The parallel implied by Mr. K.'s request is that, as he is legally and morally empowered to donate his dead son's heart, liver, etc., to save the life of another person in need, so also is he entitled to donate his dead son's sperm. Organ donation by proxy does not provide an appropriate parallel to "sperm harvesting," however. First, there is a great shortage of donated organs, but there is no shortage of donated sperm. While taking organs from those who have not consented in advance is justified by the recipient's great need, there is no comparable need in this case. Second, organ donation involves an existing person in need; sperm donation creates the possibility of a new person who would otherwise not exist. If we permit surrogates to consent to organ removal because society has a commitment to help identified individuals with life-threatening or debilitating illnesses, no such individuals exist in this case. Sperm harvesting creates new needs rather than fulfilling existing ones.

We might try to justify the sperm removal by speculating that Bill would want this done if he could be asked. However, in the absence of any indication that he has such wishes (a desire to become a parent when he was alive would not be sufficient) or that most people would have such a preference, this line of argument is not convincing.

Suppose Bill had not been killed in the car accident but had suffered significant brain injury resulting in permanent and severe mental incapacity. Though alive, he would not be able to experience parenthood in any meaningful way. He would not be able to express personal preferences. Under these circumstances, Mr. K., as Bill's guardian, might be able to donate Bill's kidney, but only if the donation would benefit Bill in some distinct manner. (Suppose it was his cousin who needed the kidney and she was Bill's caretaker.) It is difficult to see, however, how Bill could benefit in any comparable way from sperm harvesting. Indeed, such harvesting would constitute the use of Bill purely as a means to his father's or fiancée's desires. This would be morally unacceptable.

Does the fact that Bill is dead, rather than alive but lacking self-consciousness, make it acceptable to use him (or his body parts) in this way? 5

Because in our culture procreation represents a more direct kind of personal continuity than does organ donation, the fact that Bill is dead, rather than alive but unaware, should make no difference. Mr. K.'s desire to continue Bill through sperm harvesting appears to reduce Bill to his body parts. If Bill had said that, in the event of his sudden death, he wanted sperm harvested and made available to his fiancée or a sperm bank, such a wish could be honored (though it would not be obligatory), for it would represent Bill's desire to be a father, even if he could not fully realize that role. In the absence of such wishes, it is difficult to see how the proposed use of Bill's sperm would foster any central cultural values, in particular those of personal identity or of parent-child connection.

Parenthood, both in terms of *being* a parent and of *having* a parent, is integral to personal identity. Parenthood offers to child and adult a sense of continuity, of belonging, and of identification, resting as it does on the acknowledgment of the parent-child relationship. As parents, in intending or accepting a pregnancy, further define and discover themselves in acknowledging their relationship with the child-that-is-to-be (even if they do not accept the relationship), so the child-that-is begins to understand its own self through that parental acknowledgment and connection. Because this society places so much value on the individual's understanding and development of self, it behooves us to support every person's having that sense of continuity, belonging, and identification through acknowledged relationships. We can achieve this goal by keeping decisions to beget a child as closely connected as possible to those who are the parents-to-be. We acknowledge this value in our unwillingness to let procreation decisions be made for minors by parents, for mentally disabled individuals by conservators, or for women by doctors.

Clearly, in the face of this sudden and tragic death, Mr. K. has a psychological need to extend Bill's life. But there are many ways of dealing with that need other than setting in motion the mechanistic manufacture of a child who cannot be acknowledged by the genetic father (and who can thus have no beneficial relationship with the memory of that father). If a decision to harvest the sperm represents Mr. K.'s desire to extend his own genetic line, then perhaps he should investigate the possibility of donating his own sperm — an act that would reach his goal more directly and with greater genetic integrity.

Topics for Critical Thinking and Writing

1. We learn from Nolan's headnote that Bill's father hopes that Bill's fiancée will use the sperm, but we also learn that the father would gladly donate the sperm to some other woman "so that the family line could be continued." Do you draw a line between these two uses? Why, or why not?

2 Cappy Miles Rothman speaks "as a physician," which, he says, means that he speaks as someone whose "primary motivation is to relieve pain and suffering." Do you think this biographical point significantly contributes to his argument? Please explain.

3. Judith Wilson Ross, in her third sentence, forcefully gives her reasons against harvesting sperm. Evaluate Ross's first three sentences. Are they effective? Why, or why not?

4. In her fourth paragraph Ross introduces a hypothetical: "Suppose Bill had not been killed . . . ." Does Ross thereby convince you of the soundness of her position? Why, or why not?

5. At the end of her fourth paragraph Ross asks two questions. They amount to shifting the burden of proof to those who would prohibit or at least closely regulate sperm donation. Choose one of Ross's questions and write an essay of 250 words explaining your answer.

29

Service: A Duty? A Benefit? Or Both, or Perhaps Neither?

Barack Obama

President Obama (born in 1961) delivered the commencement address at Wesleyan University in Connecticut in the spring of 2008 while he was a candidate for the presidency. As he explains in the speech, he was substituting for Senator Edward Kennedy, who had recently undergone surgery.

Commencement Address

Thank you, President Roth, for that generous introduction, and congratulations on your first year at the helm of Wesleyan. Congratulations also to the class of 2008, and thank you for allowing me to be a part of your graduation.

I have the distinct honor today of pinch-hitting for one of my personal heroes and a hero to this country, Senator Edward Kennedy. Teddy wanted to be here very much, but as you know, he's had a very long week and is taking some much-needed rest. He called me up a few days ago and I said that I'd be happy to be his stand-in, even if there was no way I could fill his shoes.

I did, however, get the chance to glance at the speech he planned on delivering today, and I'd like to start by passing along a message from him: "To all those praying for my return to good health, I offer my heartfelt thanks. And to any who'd rather have a different result, I say, don't get your hopes up just yet!"

So we know that Ted Kennedy's legendary sense of humor is as strong as ever, and I have no doubt that his equally legendary fighting spirit will carry him through this latest challenge. He is our friend, he is our champion, and we hope and pray for his return to good health.

The topic of his speech today was common for a commencement, 5 but one that nobody could discuss with more authority or inspiration than Ted Kennedy. And that is the topic of service to one's country—a cause that is synonymous with his family's name and their legacy.

I was born the year that his brother John called a generation of Americans to ask their country what they could do. And I came of age at a time when they did it. They were the Peace Corps volunteers who won a generation of goodwill toward America at a time when America's ideals were challenged. They were the teenagers and college students, not much older than you, who watched the Civil Rights Movement unfold on their television sets; who saw the dogs and the fire hoses and the footage of marchers beaten within an inch or their lives; who knew it was probably smarter and safer to stay at home, but still decided to take those Freedom Rides down South—who still decided to march. And because they did, they changed the world.

I bring this up because today, you are about to enter a world that makes it easy to get caught up in the notion that there are actually two different stories at work in our lives.

The first is the story of our everyday cares and concerns—the responsibilities we have to our jobs and our families—the bustle and busyness of what happens in our own life. And the second is the story of what happens in the life of our country—of what happens in the wider world. It's the story you see when you catch a glimpse of the day's headlines or turn on the news at night—a story of big challenges like war and recession; hunger and climate change; injustice and inequality. It's a story that can sometimes seem distant and separate from our own—a destiny to be shaped by forces beyond our control.

And yet, the history of this nation tells us this isn't so. It tells us that we are a people whose destiny has never been written for us, but by us—by generations of men and women, young and old, who have always believed that their story and the American story are not separate, but shared. And for more than two centuries, they have served this country in ways that have forever enriched both.

I say this to you as someone who couldn't be standing here today if 10 not for the service of others, and wouldn't be standing here today if not for the purpose that service gave my own life.

You see, I spent much of my childhood adrift. My father left my mother and I when I was two. When my mother remarried, I lived in Indonesia for a time, but was mostly raised in Hawaii by her and my grandparents from Kansas. My teenage years were filled with more than the usual dose of adolescent rebellion, and I'll admit that I didn't always take myself or my studies very seriously. I realize that none of you can probably relate to this, but there were many times when I wasn't sure where I was going, or what I would do.

But during my first two years of college, perhaps because the values my mother had taught me—hard work, honesty, empathy—had resurfaced after a long hibernation; or perhaps because of the example of wonderful teachers and lasting friends, I began to notice a world beyond myself. I became active in the movement to oppose the apartheid regime of South Africa. I began following the debates in this country about poverty and health care. So that by the time I graduated from college, I was possessed with a crazy idea—that I would work at a grassroots level to bring about change.

I wrote letters to every organization in the country I could think of. And one day, a small group of churches on the South Side of Chicago offered me a job to come work as a community organizer in neighborhoods that had been devastated by steel plant closings. My mother and grandparents wanted me to go to law school. My friends were applying to jobs on Wall Street. Meanwhile, this organization offered me $12,000 a year plus $2,000 for an old, beat-up car.

And I said yes.

Now, I didn't know a soul in Chicago, and I wasn't sure what this community organizing business was all about. I had always been inspired by stories of the Civil Rights Movement and JFK's call to service, but when I got to the South Side, there were no marches, and no soaring speeches. In the shadow of an empty steel plant, there were just a lot of folks who were struggling. And we didn't get very far at first.

I still remember one of the very first meetings we put together to discuss gang violence with a group of community leaders. We waited and waited for people to show up, and finally, a group of older people walked into the hall. And they sat down. And a little old lady raised her hand and asked, "Is this where the bingo game is?"

It wasn't easy, but eventually, we made progress. Day by day, block by block, we brought the community together, and registered new voters, and set up after-school programs, and fought for new jobs, and helped people live lives with some measure of dignity.

But I also began to realize that I wasn't just helping other people. Through service, I found a community that embraced me; citizenship that was meaningful; the direction I'd been seeking. Through service, I discovered how my own improbable story fit into the larger story of America.

Each of you will have the chance to make your own discovery in the years to come. And I say "chance" because you won't have to take it. There's no community service requirement in the real world; no one forcing you to care. You can take your diploma, walk off this stage, and chase only after the big house and the nice suits and all the other things that our money culture says you should buy. You can choose to narrow your concerns and live your life in a way that tries to keep your story separate from America's.

But I hope you don't. Not because you have an obligation to those who are less fortunate, though you do have that obligation. Not because you have a debt to all those who helped you get here, though you do have that debt.

It's because you have an obligation to yourself. Because our individual salvation depends on collective salvation. Because thinking only about yourself, fulfilling your immediate wants and needs, betrays a poverty of ambition. Because it's only when you hitch your wagon to something larger than yourself that you realize your true potential and discover the role you'll play in writing the next great chapter in America's story.

There are so many ways to serve and so much need at this defining moment in our history. You don't have to be a community organizer or do something crazy like run for president. Right here at Wesleyan, many of you have already volunteered at local schools, contributed to United Way, and even started a program that brings fresh produce to needy families in the area. One hundred and sixty-four graduates of this school have joined the Peace Corps since 2001, and I'm especially proud that two of you are about to leave for my father's homeland of Kenya to bring alternative sources of energy to impoverished areas.

I ask you to seek these opportunities when you leave here, because the future of this country—your future—depends on it. At a time when our security and moral standing depend on winning hearts and minds in the forgotten corners of this world, we need more of you to serve abroad. As president, I intend to grow the Foreign Service, double the Peace Corps over the next few years, and engage the young people of other nations in similar programs, so that we work side by side to take on the common challenges that confront all humanity.

At a time when our ice caps are melting and our oceans are rising, we need you to help lead a green revolution. We still have time to avoid the catastrophic consequences of climate change if we get serious about investing in renewable sources of energy, and if we get a generation of volunteers to work on renewable energy projects, and teach folks about conservation, and help clean up polluted areas; if we send talented engineers and scientists abroad to help developing countries promote clean energy.

At a time when a child in Boston must compete with children in Beijing and Bangalore, we need an army of you to become teachers and principals in schools that this nation cannot afford to give up on. I will pay our educators what they deserve, and give them more support, but I will also ask more of them to be mentors to other teachers, and serve in high-need schools and high-need subject areas like math and science.

At a time when there are children in the city of New Orleans who still spend each night in a lonely trailer, we need more of you to take a weekend or a week off from work, and head down South, and help rebuild. If you can't get the time, volunteer at the local homeless shelter or soup kitchen in your own community. Find an organization that's fighting poverty, or a candidate who promotes policies you believe in, and find a way to help them.

At a time of war, we need you to work for peace. At a time of inequality, we need you to work for opportunity. At a time of so much cynicism and so much doubt, we need you to make us believe again.

Now understand this—believing that change is possible is not the same as being naive. Go into service with your eyes wide open, for change will not come easily. On the big issues that our nation faces, difficult choices await. We'll have to face some hard truths, and some sacrifice will be required—not only from you individually, but from the nation as a whole.

There is no magic bullet to our energy problems, for example; no perfect energy source—so all of us will have to use the energy sources we have more wisely. Deep-rooted poverty will not be reversed overnight, and will require both money and reform at a time when our federal and state budgets are strapped and Washington is skeptical that reform is possible. Transforming our education system will require not only bold government action, but a change in attitudes among parents and students. Bringing an end to the slaughter in Darfur will involve navigating extremely difficult realities on the ground, even for those with the best of intentions.

And so, should you take the path of service, should you choose to   30 take up one of these causes as your own, know that you'll experience frustrations and failures. Even your successes will be marked by imperfections and unintended consequences. I guarantee you, there will certainly be times when friends or family urge you to pursue more sensible endeavors with more tangible rewards. And there will be times when you are tempted to take their advice.

But I hope you'll remember, during those times of doubt and frustration, that there is nothing naive about your impulse to change this world. Because all it takes is one act of service—one blow against injustice—to send forth that tiny ripple of hope that Robert Kennedy spoke of.

You know, Ted Kennedy often tells a story about the fifth anniversary celebration of the Peace Corps. He was there, and he asked one of the young Americans why he had chosen to volunteer. And the man replied, "Because it was the first time someone asked me to do something for my country."

I don't know how many of you have been asked that question, but after today, you have no excuses. I am asking you, and if I should have the honor of serving this nation as president, I will be asking again in the coming years. We may disagree on certain issues and positions, but I believe we can be unified in service to a greater good. I intend to make it a cause of my presidency, and I believe with all my heart that this generation is ready, and eager, and up to the challenge.

We will face our share of cynics and doubters. But we always have. I can still remember a conversation I had with an older man all those years ago just before I left for Chicago. He said, "Barack, I'll give you a bit of advice. Forget this community organizing business and do something that's gonna make you some money. You can't change the world, and people won't appreciate you trying. But you've got a nice voice, so you should think about going into television broadcasting. I'm telling you, you've got a future."

Now, he may have been right about the TV thing, but he was wrong   35 about everything else. For that old man has not seen what I have seen.

He has not seen the faces of ordinary people the first time they clear a vacant lot or build a new playground or force an unresponsive leader to provide services to their community. He has not seen the face of a child brighten because of an inspiring teacher or mentor. He has not seen scores of young people educate their parents on issues like Darfur, or mobilize the conscience of a nation around the challenge of climate change. He has not seen lines of men and women that wrap around schools and churches, that stretch block after block just so they could make their voices heard, many for the very first time.

And that old man who didn't believe the world could change — who didn't think one person could make a difference — well he certainly didn't know much about the life of Joseph Kennedy's youngest son.

It is rare in this country of ours that a person exists who has touched the lives of nearly every single American without many of us even realizing it. And yet, because of Ted Kennedy, millions of children can see a doctor when they get sick. Mothers and fathers can leave work to spend time with their newborns. Working Americans are paid higher wages, and compensated for overtime, and can keep their health insurance when they change jobs. They are protected from discrimination in the workplace, and those who are born with disabilities can still get an education, and health care, and fair treatment on the job. Our schools are stronger and our colleges are filled with more Americans who can afford it. And I have a feeling that Ted Kennedy is not done just yet.

But surely, if one man can achieve so much and make such a difference in the lives of so many, then each of us can do our part. Surely, if his service and his story can forever shape America's story, then our collective service can shape the destiny of this generation. At the very least, his living example calls each of us to try. That is all I ask of you on this joyous day of new beginnings; that is what Senator Kennedy asks of you as well, and that is how we will keep so much needed work going, and the cause of justice everlasting, and the dream alive for generations to come. Thank you so much to the class of 2008, and congratulations on your graduation.

TOPICS FOR CRITICAL THINKING AND WRITING

1. What is the central topic of Obama's address (para. 5)? Does he make a persuasive case for public service? Are there relevant issues he fails to confront? If so, what are they and how do you think they should be handled?

2. In paragraph 11 Obama says, "I realize that none of you can probably relate to this." Given the immediate context — the sentence that precedes the words we have quoted — do you think most of his hearers agreed? Why, or why not?

3. In paragraph 17—a paragraph consisting of two sentences—Obama repeats the word "and" four times. Is the sentence inept, or does Obama have some rhetorical purpose? If so, what is the purpose?

4. In paragraph 20 Obama says that we *do* "have an obligation to those who are less fortunate." Putting aside his specific reason, which he gives in the next sentence, do you agree with this assertion? Why, or why not? Now think about his reason, his assertion that "our individual salvation depends on collective salvation." Does this make sense to you? Explain.

5. The last two paragraphs are a tribute to Ted Kennedy. Do you think they are appropriate and effective? Explain.

6. What sort of persona does Obama project in this speech? Specify certain passages that convey a particular personality, or at least a distinctive tone.

7. Do you know anyone who is a recent immigrant to this country? If so, interview this person and write an essay describing his or her experience adapting to life in the United States.

8. How would you define "green revolution" (para. 24)? Are you and some (all? none?) of your friends or roommates active in this "revolution"? Explain your answer.

9. Conservatives led by former president Ronald Reagan argued that government is the problem, not the solution. Often cited as an exception to this generalization is the case of the G.I. Bill of Rights. Look up its history, and write up your findings in an essay of 350 words. Explain whether or not you agree with Reagan and why.

Peter Levine

Peter Levine (b. 1967) is research director of the Jonathan M. Tisch College of Citizenship and Pubic Service at Tufts University. Among his publications is a book entitled The Future of Democracy: Developing the Next Generation of American Citizens *(2007). This selection appeared in* Philosophy and Public Policy Quarterly, *Summer/Fall 2008.*

The Case for "Service"

On September 11, 2008, both major presidential candidates traveled to New York City, where some of the nation's most prominent corporations and foundations were sponsoring a forum on civilian community service. September 11 is a solemn day, rich with patriotic meanings, when politicians are expected to demonstrate their commitment to essential American values. But they can choose *which* values to emphasize, from military strength to prosperity to civil rights. This year, Barack Obama and John McCain joined such luminaries as Arnold Schwarzenegger and Hillary Clinton to affirm the value of service. More concretely, they endorsed a bill, the Kennedy-Hatch "Serve America Act of 2008" (S.3487), that would dramatically expand federal support for civilian service programs. Given their support and the leadership of Senators Orrin Hatch and Edward Kennedy, the Serve America Act seems destined for passage—although perhaps not for full funding at a time of economic and fiscal crisis.

The bill has many sections and features, but two of its major objectives are to get at least 250,000 Americans involved in federally supported service every year and to institutionalize "service-learning" (the combination of community service with academic study) in school systems and colleges. Kennedy-Hatch would provide significant new funding to programs that recruit economically disadvantaged Americans to participate in service and service-learning, and it would focus volunteers' work on three social objectives: reducing the dropout rate, improving public health, and conserving energy.

In current legislative parlance, "service" refers to a variety of programs funded by the government but often organized by private contractors. To a philosopher who wants to consider whether government-funded service is a good thing, the heterogeneity of these programs—with their diverse purposes, constituents, and methods—poses a challenge. Nevertheless, "service" constitutes a field of practice, with many overlapping networks of alumni and leaders, similar funding sources, frequent meetings and conferences, a common genealogy, and a shared political agenda— currently focused on the passage of Kennedy-Hatch. We ought to be able to say whether supporting such fields of practice is good public policy, and whether it is wise to *shift* such fields by preferring some of their elements over others. Kennedy-Hatch seeks to alter the field of service through the two proposals mentioned above: investing in lower-income volunteers and focusing on three major social purposes. Does an expanded civilian service initiative with these priorities merit government support?

ADDRESSING NATIONAL CHALLENGES

One major argument for service programs is that federally financed volunteers can effectively address public problems. If Kennedy-Hatch becomes law, it will put Congress on record as saying that "focused national service efforts can effectively tackle pressing national challenges, such as improving education for low-income students, increasing energy conservation, and improving the health, well-being, and economic opportunities of the neediest individuals in the Nation."

It remains to be seen whether this proposition is true. AmeriCorps 5 has sometimes tried to estimate its members' impact on the neighborhoods they serve; a 1995–96 evaluation of Learn & Serve America concluded that each hour volunteered by students was worth about $8.76 to their communities. But such a statistic is not especially helpful in assessing a program's ability to address "pressing national challenges." Perhaps a dollar spent on tax credits would have more impact on energy conservation than a dollar spent to recruit volunteers to weatherize homes.

To take another example, consider YouthBuild, a job training program for disadvantaged youth ages sixteen to twenty-four. YouthBuild members learn construction trades by building houses for people in their communities. An evaluation by the Department of Housing and Urban Development found that the program generated relatively few new housing units. On the other hand, 29 percent of participants who entered without having graduated from high school obtained diplomas while they served, and 12 percent pursued higher education afterwards. These figures suggest that the best rationale for supporting YouthBuild is not that it will address the urban housing crisis, but that, through its impact on participants, it will address the dropout problem.

Certainly the organizers of service programs need to pay *some* attention to their impact on communities. When volunteers contribute tangible public goods, such as affordable homes and clean parks, they offset the programs' costs. Besides, volunteers need to have a positive impact to be satisfied and motivated. If National Civilian Community Corps members never planted any trees, they would become cynical and discouraged.

Nevertheless, it is only a hypothesis that community service is an efficient and effective way to address national problems. I hope the hypothesis is true, but we should also consider other rationales for government support of service programs. As the YouthBuild example suggests, one such rationale emphasizes the value of service not for the recipients, but for the volunteers.

INDIVIDUALS AS PUBLIC ASSETS

Service programs regard individuals as potential public assets, as contributors to the common good. This is philosophically appealing because it reflects a basic principle (which we could call Kantian) of respecting other people's moral agency. Kant insisted that all human beings be treated as responsible, as members of the Kingdom of Ends.

Among the various social groups who tend *not* to be treated that way, disadvantaged youth are a leading example. Many schools and other institutions treat teenagers in low-income communities as bundles of problems or risks. Cumulatively, such treatment sends a debilitating message. An alternative approach is supported by the psychological theory known as "positive youth development." This theory tells us that young people are more likely to avoid pitfalls such as crime, unwanted pregnancy, and academic failure when they are given opportunities to contribute their talents to the community. For low-income youth, the need for such opportunities would seem to be especially great.

Positive youth development is consistent with a Kantian view of human agency, but it is also an empirical theory: It holds that society can enhance individuals' welfare by giving them opportunities to serve. This theory may seem romantic, but it has been vindicated in numerous studies. For example, a randomized experiment showed that it was possible to cut the teen pregnancy rate by offering young women service opportunities. Generalizing from other studies, the Kennedy-Hatch bill notes that "high-quality service-learning programs keep students engaged in school and increase the likelihood that they will graduate."

At present, however, the most expansive and rewarding service programs tend to be provided in affluent schools and communities. In a survey of more than two thousand California students, Joseph Kahne and Ellen Middaugh found that service-learning experiences were less common for African American and Latino youth than for white and Asian youth; less common for students whose parents had low education levels; and much less common for students who had low grade-point averages. To its credit, Kennedy-Hatch addresses such inequalities by giving priority to schools and independent programs that offer service-learning opportunities to disadvantaged students.

SERVICE AND CIVIC ENGAGEMENT

We have seen that service has the potential to benefit those who serve as well as those who are served. One rationale for publicly funded service programs emphasizes its potential to foster the participants' civic identity and improve the relationship between citizens and their government.

Richard Stengel made this case for *universal* service in an August 2007 cover story for *Time* magazine. He began by noting that "while confidence in our democracy and our government is near an all-time low, volunteerism and civic participation since the '70s are near all-time highs." To Stengel, the explanation for this paradox seemed obvious: "People, especially young people, think the government and the public sphere are broken, but they feel they can personally make a difference through community service. . . . People see volunteering not as a form of public service but as an antidote for it."

Stengel argued that universal service, undertaken in a patriotic 15 spirit, would reconnect volunteerism to the ideals of public service and a common civic identity. Devoting a year to national service, he wrote, "should become a countrywide rite of passage, the common expectation and widespread experience of virtually every young American." The program he favored would not be "mandatory or compulsory," he explained. But it would "harness the spirit of volunteerism that already exists and make it a permanent part of American culture." It would also lead, presumably, to greater political participation, in the forms of voting, following the news, and running for public office. In Stengel's view, nothing much less ambitious than universal national service could achieve the goal of reconnecting millions of Americans to public life.

But the Serve America Act stops far short of creating a universal service program—and I think its relatively small scale is wise. About 4.5 million Americans are eighteen years old. If they were all to participate in service programs, we would need an enormous new infrastructure. As a point of comparison, there are 18 million students enrolled in all the institutions of higher education in the United States. Thus, universal national service programs would have to serve as many young people as one fourth of all our colleges and universities do. To build valuable new learning opportunities for all those participants would cost billions of dollars and require hundreds of thousands of new full-time, permanent positions for corps leaders and administrators.

It is difficult to provide high-quality learning opportunities through service, and we could do damage by calling on young people—especially disadvantaged young people—to fill menial or make-work positions. Michelle Charles has described inner-city Philadelphians doing a deliberately lackluster job on a service project that was designed by outsiders. The project (temporarily removing graffiti from a wall) sounds pointless, and one might argue that the participants' foot-dragging was a form of civic action that achieved a desirable social outcome: ending a misguided program. I am not suggesting that the Philadelphia project is typical. But as Paul Light recently observed, "[T]oo many charitable organizations do not know how to manage volunteers effectively or recruit new employees. Young Americans want the chance to make a difference and learn new skills, not work in the back office stuffing envelopes." Under Kennedy-Hatch, nonprofits applying for federal grants would have an incentive to develop truly educational and meaningful service opportunities. In addition, the bill creates a new commission to investigate how nonprofits use volunteers.

I would support creating as many service positions as we can that do not displace regular employees and that attract applicants because of their social impact and the opportunities they offer for experiential learning. The right number is hard to predict, but 250,000 sounds like a reasonable estimate. (It translates to about 1 in every 18 eighteen-year olds.) I would want to see AmeriCorps and other federal service programs attracting more applicants than they have places, as evidence that these programs were truly desirable and voluntary. But I hope they would not pick the most academically successful applicants; more important is each candidate's likelihood of benefiting from participation in service.

PUBLIC SERVANTS AND THE REST OF US

The opportunity to engage in the kind of high-quality, rigorously evaluated service envisioned by Kennedy-Hatch has the potential to close what we might think of as an identity gap between citizens and employees of the government. I believe this gap is a major cause of the civic disengagement that Stengel and others bemoan.

Consider the diminishing involvement of parents and other commu- 20 nity members in public education. Belonging to a PTA is about half as common today as it was in 1960, and those parents who are still involved in schools are often asked to provide money or low-skilled labor rather than input on how the schools should be run. In the 1970s, according to the DDB Life Style survey, more than 40 percent of Americans said they worked on community projects, many of which involved education; that percentage is now down to the 20s. There are many explanations for these changes, but surely one reason is the growing monopoly over education by credentialed, professional experts, especially state and district administrators and test-writers.

Elinor Ostrom has shown that in the mid-twentieth century, a substantial proportion of American households had members who served on elected public bodies, such as school boards, at some time in their lives. But consolidation of governments and heavy use of professional managers has reduced such participation to a trivial level. Today, some Americans are in "public service," and the rest are not. Meanwhile, the all-volunteer military, for better *and* for worse, separates civilians from professional warriors in a way that was not true under the draft.

I believe we need to weaken this distinction between public servants and the rest of us—to help people move in and out of public service so that each side learns more about the other. National and community service can be a powerful tool to achieve this goal. It doesn't require universal participation, because the purpose is to generate opportunities for interested individuals to move between the private and public sectors, so that they can learn and contribute in both sectors and create models for others.

Teach for America (TFA) provides a vivid illustration. TFA recruits top graduates from the nation's colleges and universities and places them in public schools—usually low-performing schools—for two years. It differs from federal service programs in that local school authorities employ its teachers directly, but it resembles the Peace Corps and City Year in that it places young people temporarily in full-time public service work. Although many of its recruits have stayed in education (TFA's alumni include many influential school reformers), that was never the program's overriding goal. The idea was that TFA members who left the classroom after two years would become advocates for educational equality. Their experience would motivate them to "continue the struggle" as informed citizens, community activists, school board members, and political leaders.

TFA illustrates another principle as well: the impact of service on volunteers' civic commitments and beliefs is more diverse and unpredictable than the paeans to service typically acknowledge. Many TFA teachers go to work in profoundly dysfunctional school systems—an experience that is hardly likely to strengthen their trust in the public sector. One TFA alumna, Michelle Rhee, has brought controversial corporate efficiency measures to the public schools in Washington, D.C., where she was appointed chancellor in 2007. Traditional liberals, libertarian-leaning conservatives, good-government reformers, efficiency experts, and others will have different *hopes* about what a stint in public service may teach. In my view, we should be willing to learn from the young people who have had that experience.

EXPANDING THE AGENDA

Service has the potential to restore Americans' civic engagement, but 25 it also has limitations. I have already noted the difficulty of providing excellent learning opportunities on a large scale. To make matters worse, federally funded service programs cannot engage in political activities, which narrows the scope of participants' civic action.

The very word "service," moreover, can send a message contrary to the ideal of respecting individual agency that I described above. A recent survey by the National Conference on Citizenship found that, for many people, the word "service" connotes episodic charitable or "helping" behavior. The word can suggest that some people are helpless and therefore need to be served, which is the opposite of the idea that everyone can be a moral agent and a contributor.

We need to find ways to encourage deliberation, problem-solving, the creation of public goods, and other roles for citizens that go beyond service. No one tool will reverse the disengagement of Americans from public life. But several policies, undertaken in a coordinated fashion, could make a substantial difference.

- *Civic education.* There is evidence that teaching young people about civic and political issues increases the odds that they will discuss such issues, join groups, volunteer, and vote later in life. Moreover, the impact of such teaching is enhanced when students engage in community service projects that include research or reflection.

- *Deliberation.* In addition to "serving," citizens should also deliberate, which involves real decision-making. The recent National Conference on Citizenship poll (see graph on page 785) found strong and bipartisan support for a proposal, developed by the nonprofit America*Speaks*, to involve more than one million Americans in a national deliberation on an important public issue. Although it has never been tried, a national deliberation might improve public policy and also provide a valuable model of organized, meaningful public involvement.

- *Influence on local institutions.* A comprehensive reform agenda would include efforts to increase local citizens' influence on everyday public institutions, such as schools, local governments, and police forces. One promising model is the elaborate series of Study Circles that encouraged broad discussion of education in Bridgeport, Conn., and gradually built public support for school reform while raising the level of parental volunteering in the city's schools. In Hampton, Va., youth involvement in boards and committees has improved education and policing in that city.

- *Public service reform.* Finally, a civic engagement agenda would include changing the nature of careers in public service. The

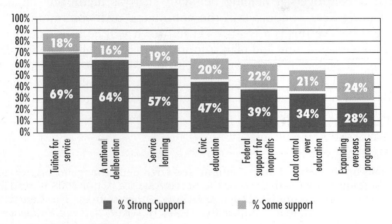

PUBLIC SUPPORT FOR POLICIES TO ENHANCE CIVIC ENGAGEMENT

■ % Strong Support   ■ % Some support

Proposals tested

- Tuition for service: "offering every young person a chance to earn money toward college or advanced training if they complete a full year of national or community service."

- A national deliberation: "involving more than one million Americans in a national discussion of an important public issue and requiring Congress to respond to what the citizens say."

- Service learning: "requiring all high school students to do community service as part of their work for one or more courses."

- Civic education: "requiring high school students to pass a new test on civics or government."

- Federal support for nonprofits: "providing federal money to support non-profit, faith-based, and civic organizations that use volunteers."

- Local control over education: "changing the law so that local citizens must take the lead in setting standards and choosing tests for students in their local schools."

- Expanding overseas programs: "funding and promoting overseas service as a way of improving our relations with other countries."

Source: National Conference on Citizenship survey ("America's Civic Health Index"), Conducted by CIRCLE (the Center for Information & Research on Civic Learning and Engagement), July 2008.

imminent retirement of roughly one million federal employees offers an opportunity to rethink public service so that jobs in the public sector become more rewarding and creative—to flatten hierarchies and promote collaboration, including partnerships between the government and community groups. Paul Light calls on the next administration to "reverse the federal government's well-deserved reputation as a destination of last resort for young Americans. The government's antiquated personnel system must be modernized to reward performance, not time on the job, and give new recruits the career paths to make a difference faster."

It appears, then, that service is the politically easy part of restoring active citizenship in America. With enough money, we can enroll 250,000 Americans in activities that we call "service," most of which will involve uncontroversial helping behavior such as mentoring children and planting trees, conducted in the volunteers' own communities. On balance, I believe this is a worthy cause. But it will be much harder to use volunteers to define and plan solutions to hard problems, to increase public participation in deliberative decision making, or to redesign the civil service. I support Kennedy-Hatch as an element of the reform agenda. But success on these other fronts will be just as critical to strengthening civic engagement in the United States.

SOURCES

For details on the ServiceNation Summit, see www.bethechangeinc.org/service-nation/summit/purpose. The text of the Serve America Act of 2008 is available at www.opencongress.org/bill/110-s3487/show. Other sources: The Center for Human Resources, Brandeis University, *Summary Report, National Evaluation of Learn and Serve America School and Community-Based Programs* (Corporation for National Service, July 1999), p. 24; Maxine V. Mitchell, Davis Jenkins, Dao Nguyen, Alona Lerman, and Marian DeBerry, *Evaluation of the YouthBuild Program* (U.S. Department of Housing and Urban Development, August 2003); Jacquelynne Eccles and Jennifer Appleton Gootman, eds., *Community Programs to Promote Youth Development*, a report of the National Research Council and Institute of Medicine, Board on Children, Youth, and Families, Committee on Community-Level Programs for Youth (National Academies Press, 2002), pp. 181–184; Joseph Kahne and Ellen Middaugh, "Democracy for Some: The Civic Opportunity Gap in High School," CIRCLE Working Paper 59 (February 2008), www.civicyouth.org; Richard Stengel, "A Time to Serve," *Time* (August 7, 2007) (for a link to an online version, see the ServiceNation Web site); Michelle M. Charles, "Giving Back to the Community: African American Inner City Teens and Civic Engagement," CIRCLE Working Paper 38 (August 2005), pp. 15–16, www.civicyouth.org; Paul Light, "Make it Easier to Say Yes to Public Service," *Huffington Post* (Sept. 9, 2008), www.huffingtonpost.com; Robert D. Putnam, *Bowling Alone: The Collapse and Revival of American Community* (Simon & Schuster, 2000), p. 442 (for data on PTA membership); DDB Life Style Survey, www.bowlingalone.com/data.htm (data analyzed by the author); Peter Levine, "Education and the Limits of Technocracy," *Philosophy & Public Policy Quarterly*, vol. 27, no. 3/4 (Summer/Fall 2007), pp. 17–21; Elinor Ostrom, "A Frequently Overlooked Precondition of Democracy: Citizens Knowledgeable about and

Engaged in Collective Action," Workshop in Political Theory and Policy Analysis, 2005; America*Speaks, Millions of Voices: A Blueprint for Engaging the American Public in Policymaking* (September 2004), www.americaspeaks.org; Will Friedman, Alison Kadlec, and Lara Birnbeck, *Transforming Public Life: A Decade of Citizen Engagement in Bridgeport, Ct.*, Public Agenda Foundation Center for Advances in Public Engagement, *Case Studies in Public Agenda* (2007), www.publicagenda.org; Carmen Sirianni, "Youth Civic Engagement: Systems and Culture Change in Hampton, Virginia," CIRCLE Working Paper 31 (April 2005), www.civicyouth.org.

TOPICS FOR CRITICAL THINKING AND WRITING

1. How does Levine propose to define "service"? Can you improve on his definition?

2. Summarize in 100 words the main provisions of the Kennedy-Hatch bill, "Serve America Act of 2008." What is its status today?

3. Would you volunteer for some form of public service? What incentives, if any, would be necessary to get you to volunteer for a year or two of public service? What reasons against volunteering would you respect? Explain in an essay of 250 words.

4. What does it mean to say with the philosopher Immanuel Kant that "all human beings [are to] be treated as members of the Kingdom of Ends" (para. 9)? Are you such a member? Why, or why not?

5. Should public service be universal? Mandatory? Evaluate the reasons advanced by Richard Stengel in paragraph 17.

6. What forms of public service would most attract you? Why those and not others as well?

7. Consider the graph on page 785. Imagine you had to explain it to a classmate. What would you stress and what would you ignore or downplay? Which if any of its findings do you find surprising?

8. Are you impressed with the wealth and variety of sources that Levine relies on in his essay, or are they mainly window dressing? How can you tell which it is?

Andrew J. Bacevich

Andrew Bacevich (b. 1947), author of numerous books about military affairs, is a professor of international relations at Boston University. This article appeared in the Boston Globe *on January 21, 2007.*

The Failure of an All-Volunteer Military

"War is the great auditor of institutions," the British historian Corelli Barnett has observed. In Iraq, the United States has undergone such an audit and been found wanting. The defects of basic U.S. national security institutions stand exposed. Failure to correct those defects will only invite more Iraqs—unnecessary wars that once begun prove unwinnable.

The essential guarantor of U.S. national security is the all-volunteer force. In its heyday—the 1990s—the all-volunteer force underwrote America's claim to global preeminence. Its invincibility taken for granted, the volunteer force seemed a great bargain to boot. Maintaining the world's most powerful military establishment imposed a negligible burden on the average citizen. No wonder Americans viewed the volunteer military as the most successful federal reform program of the postwar era. What was there not to like?

In fact, questions of efficacy or economy did not figure significantly in the decision to create the all-volunteer force. Back in the early 1970s, the object of the exercise had been quite simple: to terminate an increasingly illegitimate reliance on conscription. During the Vietnam War, thanks in no small part to the draft, the armed services had become estranged from American society. The all-volunteer force creation severed relations altogether.

This divorce had large implications. After Vietnam, citizenship no longer included an obligation to contribute to the nation's defense. Military service became a matter of personal preference, devoid of political or moral significance. Although providing for the common defense remained a primary function of government, federal officials no longer possessed the authority to command citizens to bear arms. Henceforth, they could only encourage young Americans to enlist, offering inducements to sweeten the invitation.

Historically, Americans had viewed a "standing army" with suspicion. 5 After Vietnam they embraced the idea. By 1991 they were celebrating it. After Operation Desert Storm—with its illusion of a cheap, easy victory—soldiers like General Colin Powell persuaded themselves that "the people fell in love with us again."

If love, it was a peculiar version, neither possessive nor signifying a desire to be one with the beloved. For the vast majority of Americans, Desert Storm affirmed the wisdom of contracting out national security. Cheering the troops on did not imply any interest in joining their ranks. Especially among the affluent and well-educated, the notion took hold that national defense was something "they" did, just as "they" bused tables, collected trash, and mowed lawns. The stalemated war in Iraq has revealed two problems with this arrangement.

The first is that "we" have forfeited any say in where "they" get sent to fight. When it came to invading Iraq, President Bush paid little attention to what voters of the First District of Massachusetts or the 50th District of California thought. The people had long since forfeited any ownership of the army. Even today, although a clear majority of Americans want the Iraq war shut down, their opposition counts for next to nothing: the will of the commander-in-chief prevails.

The second problem stems from the first. If "they" — the soldiers we contract to defend us — get in trouble, "we" feel little or no obligation to bail them out. All Americans support the troops, yet support does not imply sacrifice. Yellow-ribbon decals displayed on the back of gas-guzzlers will suffice, thank you.

Stipulate for the sake of argument that President Bush is correct in saying that failure in Iraq is not an option. Then why limit the "surge" to a measly 21,500 additional troops? Why not 50,000? With the population of the United States having now surpassed 300 million, why not send 100,000 reinforcements to Iraq?

The question answers itself: There are not an additional 100,000 Americans willing to commit their lives to the cause. Even offering up 21,500 finds the Pentagon scraping the bottom of the barrel, extending the tours of soldiers already in the combat zone while accelerating the deployment of those heading back for a second or third tour of duty.   10

After the Cold War, Americans came to see war as something other than a human enterprise; the secret of military superiority ostensibly lay in the microchip. The truth is that the sinews of military power lie among the people, who legitimate war and sustain it.

For the United States to remain a great military power will require a genuine reconciliation of the military and American society. But this implies the people exercising a greater say in deciding when and where American soldiers fight. And it also implies reviving the tradition of the citizen-soldier so that all share in the burden of national defense.

Topics for Critical Thinking and Writing

1. What is meant by saying (para. 1) that war is "an auditor of institutions"?

2. What does Bacevich mean in his seventh paragraph where he says that "The people had long since forfeited any ownership of the army"?

3. What does it mean (para. 9) to tell us to "stipulate for the sake of argument"?

4. Do you agree that the United States is "a great military power" (para. 12)? What evidence can you supply to support your position?

5. What, according to Bacevich, is required for there to be a "genuine reconciliation of the military and American people" (para. 12)? Do you agree? Do you think such a reconciliation is desirable? Explain your position.

6. What incentive would it take for you to volunteer for the armed services?

7. Does your college have an ROTC program? If not, would you favor creating such a program? If your institution does have an ROTC program, do you favor its presence? Why, or why not?

Anonymous

The following editorial appeared in the New York Times *on November 21, 2006. We follow it with several letters of response.*

Rejecting the Draft

There are many reasons why we are distressed to hear that Representative Charles Rangel of New York plans to reintroduce his annual measure aimed at resurrecting the draft when the Democrats take control of the House in January. We don't favor military conscription in general. And in this particular case, compelling military service won't achieve the things Mr. Rangel says he wants, either.

Mr. Rangel wants to replenish an army that is in critical condition, make the armed services more equitably representative of American society as a whole, and find a way to prevent future presidents from embarking on military misadventures. Those are laudable goals, but not ones the nation can achieve by bringing back the draft.

Even if the draft was a good idea, it would be politically impossible to achieve. Members of Congress are well aware that their constituents oppose it. This White House has never been willing to ask the American public to do anything but accept more tax cuts; it's hardly going to embrace something as difficult and unpopular as military conscription.

But the idea is flawed as well. Because of the dire situation in Iraq, the army is indeed having trouble meeting its yearly quota of eighty thousand recruits. Yet military leaders nevertheless oppose a draft. They believe you don't get a highly skilled army by forcing people to serve against their will, and they are right.

The draft would not demonstrate to young people that everyone 5 must do his or her fair share. It is more likely to convince them that the demand for sacrifice is made mainly on those too poor to avoid it. The volunteer force in Iraq has been a truer cross section of America than the force created under the last draft, which ended in 1973, before the end of the Vietnam War. The wealthy and well-connected could get deferments then or assignments to safe alternatives, and many did. While there are plenty of underprivileged in the current force, at least they are there by their own choosing.

The problem with the draft does not lie in the fact that it requires young people to spend some time contributing to the nation's well-being before they embark on their life careers. We wish the president had called for such sacrifices after September 11, 2001, when so many Americans were aching to contribute.

For those young people who do not feel moved by patriotism or propelled by economics to enlist in the military, there should be other options for national service—like AmeriCorps. These programs need money and attention. Some of the potential candidates for president in

2008 have said the United States should require all young people to devote a year or two to service after high school or college, and that idea should be debated during the upcoming campaign.

But the urgency of the army's current needs requires a different solution. There are many ways for the armed services to meet their recruitment goals outside of general conscription. After all, the army's annual quota of eighty thousand recruits is barely a drop in the ocean of some 60 million Americans between eighteen and thirty-five. Forcing the issue, with a draft, is no solution.

Letters of Response by Richard Roth, Christian Danielsen, Norman Daniels, Samuel Z. Klausner, Per Halvorsen, and Jerry Wallingford

To the Editor:

Re "Rejecting the Draft" (editorial, November 21):

If, as President Bush insists, the Iraq war is the ultimate struggle for civilization, a draft seems like the least our country should ask of its citizenry.

Of course, there won't ever be a draft for this fiasco because while the military, Congress, and to a large extent the mainstream media are championing and enabling this war, the American people are not, especially not the children of the chattering classes.

So Representative Charles B. Rangel is shrewd to call America's bluff. We haven't taken any of the steps that dignify a commitment to war: a declaration of war, universal conscription, the reorientation of the economy and tax increases primarily to support the war effort, and sacrifice as a civic given.

If you can't decide if you're really in a war, then, trust me, you aren't. Despite what you say, drafts are not inherently unjust, but many wars (Vietnam, Iraq) turn out that way. Unjust wars make drafts immoral.

RICHARD ROTH
Seattle, November 21, 2006

To the Editor:

Bravo to Representative Charles B. Rangel for his courage, and shame on you for dismissing a new military draft. If the draft had been in place before the war, we could have avoided this disaster.

The war in Iraq has been waged with entirely too little consequence for the vast majority of Americans who are not connected to the military. Unlike the situation in World War II, there are no war bonds or victory gardens or any sense of shared national sacrifice beyond crass yellow ribbon stickers placed on the back of oil-guzzling automobiles.

The staggering cost might as well be Monopoly money, as we shamefully pass the cost on to our grandchildren by increasing the debt.

As a recent college graduate and a vehement opponent of the war from its inception, I welcome the return of a universal draft to end the practice of going to war with other people's money and other people's children.

CHRISTIAN DANIELSEN
Portland, Ore., November 21, 2006

To the Editor:
Your editorial responds to some of Representative Charles B. Rangel's reasons for calling for the reinstatement of the draft, but not one of the main ones:

Does having a draft make it harder to begin and sustain wars like the one in Iraq?

The strength of the Vietnam antiwar movement was no doubt fed by the threat of being drafted, even if the draft was full of loopholes for the rich and better connected.

Though the public lies about weapons of mass destruction and a Saddam Hussein–terrorist connection might have fooled the public even with a draft, resistance to the war might have materialized in an organized form earlier and with more force if a draft had been in place and the threat of broader sacrifice had been present as a motivator against President Bush's adventurism.

NORMAN DANIELS
Brewster, Mass., November 21, 2006

To the Editor:
Is a draft politically impossible? We have some historical precedents. So to institute one would be difficult but not impossible.

One objection cited in the editorial is that you don't build a highly skilled army by forcing people to serve. But that is an insult to World War II veterans and other vets who fought with intellect and valor.

The wealthy or well connected get deferments? This is a matter of recruitment policy.

Alternative service? O.K. for conscientious objectors, but do not confuse obligation to defend America with obligation to promote social welfare.

I support national conscription as a way of sharing the burden, enjoying social equity, and relieving us of the shame of being defended by the minority "moved by patriotism or propelled by economics."

Right on, Charles Rangel!

SAMUEL Z. KLAUSNER
Philadelphia, November 21, 2006

To the Editor:
While I agree with you that reinstating the draft is not the solution, I also strongly agree with Representative Charles B. Rangel that we should all share some of the burden when the country goes to war.

If our leaders had asked for a greater shared burden before sending us to war in Iraq, we would be more united as a country today through our shared "ownership" of the problem.

Rather than the draft, why not impose a stiff $2-per-gallon gasoline war tax? Such a tax should be structured to end as soon as the war ends and the vast majority of our troops have returned.

Nearly all of us would feel the sting, and would share a desire to find real solutions rather than using the misery for political advantage.

A $2-per-gallon war tax could finance much of the war's cost without saddling future generations with debt, and would force all of us to consider how our enormous consumption of oil contributes to the problem.

PER HALVORSEN
Branford, Conn., November 21, 2006

To the Editor:

Representative Charles B. Rangel's proposal to reinstate the draft is not a military strategy. Rather, it is intended to get the college crowd off its iPods and into the streets to end this illegal and immoral war.

JERRY WALLINGFORD
San Diego, November 21, 2006

TOPICS FOR CRITICAL THINKING AND WRITING

1. What, if any, military alternatives to the draft does the editorial promote?

2. Under what conditions, if any, would you favor the draft?

3. Do you find merit in Halvorsen's idea of imposing a gasoline tax to fund wars? Can you think of some other alternative to the draft that you would favor?

4. Explain what Roth means by claiming that "unjust wars make drafts immoral" and give your reasons for agreeing or disagreeing.

5. What does Roth mean by the "the children of the chattering classes"? Does this include you? Explain your answer.

6. What does Norman Daniels mean when he describes President Bush's war in Iraq as "adventurism"?

7. In April 2009, gasoline sold for about $2.00 a gallon. Was that price a "war tax" of the sort Per Halvorsen has in mind? How could you tell one way or the other? Explain your answer.

8. Is imposing a "war tax" a way of taxing future generations to pay the costs of the war in Iraq? Is it fair to do that? Explain your answer in an essay of 300 words.

Dave Eggers

Dave Eggers (b. 1970), the founder of 826 National, nonprofit learning centers, and the founder and editor of McSweeney's, *an independent publisher, is also an author, most notably of* A Heartbreaking Work of Staggering Genius *(2000),* How We Are Hungry: Stories *(2005), and* What Is the What? The Autobiography of Valentino Achak Deng *(2007). This essay and the letters of response originally appeared in the* New York Times *in 2004.*

Serve or Fail

About now, most recent college graduates, a mere week or two beyond their last final, are giving themselves a nice respite. Maybe they're on a beach, maybe they're on a road trip, maybe they're in their rooms, painting their toenails black with a Q-tip and shoe polish. Does it matter? What's important is that they have some time off.

Do they deserve the time off? Well, yes and no. Yes, because finals week is stressful and sleep-deprived and possibly involves trucker-style stimulants. No, because a good deal of the four years of college is spent playing foosball.

I went to a large state school—the University of Illinois—and during my time there, I became one of the best two or three foosball players in the Land of Lincoln. I learned to pass deftly between my rigid players, to play the corners, to strike the ball like a cobra would strike something a cobra would want to strike. I also mastered the dart game called Cricket, and the billiards contest called Nine-ball. I became expert at whiffle ball, at backyard archery, and at a sport we invented that involved one person tossing roasted chickens from a balcony to a group of us waiting below. We got to eat the parts that didn't land on the patio.

The point is that college is too long—it should be three years—and that even with a full course load and part-time jobs (I had my share) there are many hours in the days and weeks that need killing. And because most of us, as students, saw our hours as in need of killing—as opposed to thinking about giving a few of these hours to our communities in one way or another—colleges should consider instituting a service requirement for graduation.

I volunteered a few times in Urbana-Champaign—at a Y.M.C.A. and 5
at a home for senior citizens—and in both cases it was much too easy to quit. I thought the senior home smelled odd, so I left, and though the Y.M.C.A. was a perfect fit, I could have used nudging to continue—nudging the university might have provided. Just as parents and schools need to foster in young people a "reading habit"—a love of reading that becomes a need, almost an addiction—colleges are best-poised to create in their students a lifelong commitment to volunteering even a few hours a month.

Some colleges, and many high schools, have such a thing in place, and last year Michael R. Veon, a Democratic member of Pennsylvania's House of Representatives, introduced a bill that would require the more than 90,000 students at fourteen state-run universities to perform twenty-five hours of community service annually. That comes out to more than two million volunteer hours a year.

College students are, for the most part, uniquely suited to have time for and to benefit from getting involved and addressing the needs of those around them. Unlike high school students, they're less programmed, less boxed in by family and after-school obligations. They're also more mature, and better able to handle a wide range of tasks. Finally, they're at a stage where exposure to service—and to the people whose lives nonprofit service organizations touch—would have a profound effect on them. Meeting a World War II veteran who needs meals brought to him would be educational for the deliverer of that meal, I would think. A college history major might learn something by tutoring a local middle school class that's studying the Underground Railroad. A connection would be forged; a potential career might be discovered.

A service requirement won't work everywhere. It probably wouldn't be feasible, for example, for community college students, who tend to be transient and who generally have considerable family and work demands. But exempt community colleges and you would still have almost 10 million college students enrolled in four-year colleges in the United States. If you exempted a third of them for various reasons, that would leave more than 6 million able-bodied young people at the ready. Even with a modest ten-hour-a-year requirement (the equivalent of two mornings a year) America would gain 60 million volunteer hours to invigorate the nation's nonprofit organizations, churches, job corps, conservation groups, and college outreach programs.

And with some flexibility, it wouldn't have to be too onerous. Colleges could give credit for service. That is, at the beginning of each year, a student could opt for service, and in return he or she might get credits equal to one class period. Perhaps every twenty-five hours of service could be traded for one class credit, with a maximum of three credits a year. What a student would learn from working in a shelter for the victims of domestic abuse would surely equal or surpass his or her time spent in racquetball class—at my college worth one full unit.

Alternatively, colleges could limit the service requirement to a student's junior year—a time when the students are settled and have more hours and stability in their schedules. Turning the junior year into a year when volunteering figures prominently could also help colleges bridge the chasm that usually stands between the academic world and the one that lies beyond it.

When Gov. Gray Davis of California proposed a service requirement in 1999, an editorial in the *Daily Californian*, the student newspaper at the University of California at Berkeley, opposed the plan: "Forced philanthropy will be as much an oxymoron in action as it is in terms. Who would want to receive community service from someone who is forced to serve? Is forced community service in California not generally reserved for criminals and delinquents?"

First of all, that's putting forth a pretty dim view of the soul of the average student. What, is the unwilling college volunteer going to *throw food* at visitors to the soup kitchen? Volunteering is by nature transformative — reluctant participants become quick converts every day, once they meet those who need their help.

Second, college is largely about fulfilling requirements, isn't it? Students have to complete this much work in the sciences, that much work in the arts. Incoming freshmen accept a tacit contract, submitting to the wisdom of the college's founders and shapers, who decide which experiences are necessary to create a well-rounded scholar, one ready to make a contribution to the world. But while colleges give their students the intellectual tools for life beyond campus, they largely ignore the part about how they might contribute to the world. That is, until the commencement speech, at which time all the "go forth's" and "be helpful's" happen.

But what if such a sentiment happened on the student's first day? What if graduating seniors already knew full well how to balance jobs, studies, family, and volunteer work in the surrounding community? What if campuses were full of under-served high school students meeting with their college tutors? What if the tired and clogged veins of thousands of towns and cities had the energy of millions of college students coursing through them? What if the student who might have become a foosball power — and I say this knowing how much those skills have enhanced my life and those who had the good fortune to have watched me — became instead a lifelong volunteer? That might be pretty good for everybody.

TOPICS FOR CRITICAL THINKING AND WRITING

1. Eggers argues that colleges should consider instituting a service requirement for graduation. How does he support his argument? What kinds of evidence does he offer?

2. Suppose someone objected to Eggers that he presents a confusing picture of what he desires. Is it "volunteering" (para. 12), or is it service, whether volunteered or not? How should Eggers reply?

3. Let's be a bit cynical. When we were in college, physical ed was a required not-for-credit course. The result? Students became quite skillful in evading it. Why wouldn't the same thing happen with a requirement of public service? Give your reasoned view in 250 words.

4. Does Eggers give us any reason to believe that installing a service participation requirement will have a beneficial effect on the problem of

student boredom and mismanagement of spare time—which was the issue with which he opened his essay?

5. If you have read Stanley Fish's essay, "Why We Built the Ivory Tower" (p. 547), in 250–500 words set forth what you think would be Fish's reply to Eggers. If you detect a distinct persona in Fish's essay, try to capture this persona in your essay.

Letters of Response by Dixie Dillon, Sharon S. Epstein, and Patricia R. King

To the Editor:

Dave Eggers has a rather low opinion of college students ("Serve or Fail," Op-Ed, June 13).

As a college senior, I believe that I am a contributing member of the community I live in. Whatever the town-gown troubles may be in Middlebury, the citizens of the town and the students at Middlebury College have helped one another.

I live here. How can Mr. Eggers imagine that I do not work to better my community (though I do not appear in the statistics of structured volunteering, which many students here do)?

By the way, those "intellectual tools" my college experience is providing me do a great deal of good work in our country.

I invite Mr. Eggers to spend a few weeks talking, working, and playing with the students at my college and then to reconsider his plan.

Dixie Dillon
Middlebury, Vt., June 13, 2004

To the Editor:

Dave Eggers's view that colleges should require students to do volunteer work is valuable. But the volunteer work should begin at the elementary school level. The actual volunteer work can be as simple as a group project to make cards for people who are hospitalized or to make food baskets for the poor. In other words, children don't have to be transported to a place to volunteer.

I'd also recommend that parents teach their children volunteering by example. If a parent and a child go together to a place to volunteer, then volunteering becomes a positive and bonding activity learned early in life.

Sharon S. Epstein
Stony Brook, N.Y., June 13, 2004

To the Editor:

Dave Eggers, in proposing a community service requirement for college students, would allow for exemptions. Indeed, I would remind him that like the community college students he mentions, many college students "have considerable family and work demands"; unlike Mr. Eggers, they do not major in social games. All that spare time he talks about does not exist for them.

Many of today's students are not the children of privilege. Believe me, they know how the world works.

PATRICIA R. KING
Tennyson, Ind., June 14, 2004

TOPIC FOR CRITICAL THINKING AND WRITING

Imagine that you are Eggers and that you have seen the three letters of response. Write a letter in which you address all three letter-writers.

30

Testing: What Value Do Tests Have?

Paul Goodman

Paul Goodman (1911–1972) did his undergraduate work at the City College of New York and his graduate work—he held a Ph.D.—at the University of Chicago. He taught in several colleges and universities, where he was highly popular even in the 1960s, a period when students tended to distrust anyone over thirty. Perhaps some of his popularity was due to his often expressed view that students were exploited by a corrupt society. "A Proposal to Abolish Grading" (the title is ours) is an extract from Goodman's Compulsory Miseducation *and the* Community of Scholars *(1966).*

A Proposal to Abolish Grading

Let half a dozen of the prestigious Universities—Chicago, Stanford, the Ivy League—abolish grading, and use testing only and entirely for pedagogic purposes as teachers see fit.

Anyone who knows the frantic temper of the present schools will understand the transvaluation of values that would be effected by this modest innovation. For most of the students, the competitive grade has come to be the essence. The naive teacher points to the beauty of the subject and the ingenuity of the research; the shrewd student asks if he is responsible for that on the final exam.

Let me at once dispose of an objection whose unanimity is quite fascinating. I think that the great majority of professors agree that grading hinders teaching and creates a bad spirit, going as far as cheating and plagiarizing. I have before me the collection of essays, *Examining in Harvard College*, and this is the consensus. It is uniformly asserted, however, that the grading is inevitable; for how else will the graduate schools, the foundations, the corporations *know* whom to accept, reward, hire? How will the talent scouts know whom to tap?

By testing the applicants, of course, according to the specific task-requirements of the inducting institution, just as applicants for the Civil

Service or for licenses in medicine, law, and architecture are tested. Why should Harvard professors do the testing *for* corporations and graduate schools?

The objection is ludicrous. Dean Whitla, of the Harvard Office of Tests, points out that the scholastic-aptitude and achievement tests used for *admission* to Harvard are a super-excellent index for all-around Harvard performance, better than high-school grades or particular Harvard course-grades. Presumably, these college-entrance tests are tailored for what Harvard and similar institutions want. By the same logic, would not an employer do far better to apply his own job-aptitude test rather than to rely on the vagaries of Harvard sectionmen. Indeed, I doubt that many employers bother to look at such grades; they are more likely to be interested merely in the fact of a Harvard diploma, whatever that connotes to them. The grades have most of their weight with the graduate schools—here, as elsewhere, the system runs mainly for its own sake.

It is really necessary to remind our academics of the ancient history of Examination. In the medieval university, the whole point of the gruelling trial of the candidate was whether or not to accept him as a peer. His disputation and lecture for the Master's was just that, a masterpiece to enter the guild. It was not to make comparative evaluations. It was not to weed out and select for an extra-mural licensor or employer. It was certainly not to pit one young fellow against another in an ugly competition. My philosophic impression is that the medievals thought they knew what a good job of work was and that we are competitive because we do not know. But the more status is achieved by largely irrelevant competitive evaluation, the less will we ever know.

(Of course, our American examinations never did have this purely guild orientation, just as our faculties have rarely had absolute autonomy; the examining was to satisfy Overseers, Elders, distant Regents— and they as paternal superiors have always doted on giving grades, rather than accepting peers. But I submit that this set-up itself makes it impossible for the student to *become* a master, to *have* grown up, and to commence on his own. He will always be making A or B for some overseer. And in the present atmosphere, he will always be climbing on his friend's neck.)

Perhaps the chief objectors to abolishing grading would be the students and their parents. The parents should be simply disregarded; their anxiety has done enough damage already. For the students, it seems to me that a primary duty of the university is to deprive them of their props, their dependence on extrinsic valuation and motivation, and to force them to confront the difficult enterprise itself and finally lose themselves in it.

A miserable effect of grading is to nullify the various uses of testing. Testing, for both student and teacher, is a means of structuring, and also of finding out what is blank or wrong and what has been assimilated and can be taken for granted. Review—including high-pressure review—is a means of bringing together the fragments, so that there are flashes of synoptic insight.

There are several good reasons for testing, and kinds of test. But if the aim is to discover weakness, what is the point of down-grading and punishing it, and thereby inviting the student to conceal his weakness, by faking and bulling, if not cheating? The natural conclusion of synthesis is the insight itself, not a grade for having had it. For the important purpose of placement, if one can establish in the student the belief that one is testing *not* to grade and make invidious comparisons but for his own advantage, the student should normally seek his own level, where he is challenged and yet capable, rather than trying to get by. If the student dares to accept himself as he is, a teacher's grade is a crude instrument compared with a student's self-awareness. But it is rare in our universities that students are encouraged to notice objectively their vast confusion. Unlike Socrates, our teachers rely on power-drives rather than shame and ingenuous idealism.

Many students are lazy, so teachers try to goad or threaten them by grading. In the long run this must do more harm than good. Laziness is a character-defense. It may be a way of avoiding learning, in order to protect the conceit that one is already perfect (deeper, the despair that one *never* can). It may be a way of avoiding just the risk of failing and being down-graded. Sometimes it is a way of politely saying, "I won't." But since it is the authoritarian grown-up demands that have created such attitudes in the first place, why repeat the trauma? There comes a time when we must treat people as adult, laziness and all. It is one thing courageously to fire a do-nothing out of your class; it is quite another thing to evaluate him with a lordly F.

Most important of all, it is often obvious that balking in doing the work, especially among bright young people who get to great universities, means exactly what it says: The work does not suit me, not this subject, or not at this time, or not in this school, or not in school altogether. The student might not be bookish; he might be school-tired; perhaps his development ought now to take another direction. Yet unfortunately, if such a student is intelligent and is not sure of himself, he *can* be bullied into passing, and this obscures everything. My hunch is that I am describing a common situation. What a grim waste of young life and teacherly effort! Such a student will retain nothing of what he has "passed" in. Sometimes he must get mononucleosis to tell his story and be believed.

And ironically, the converse is also probably commonly true. A student flunks and is mechanically weeded out, who is really ready and eager to learn in a scholastic setting, but he has not quite caught on. A good teacher can recognize the situation, but the computer wreaks its will.

TOPICS FOR CRITICAL THINKING AND WRITING

1. Consider Goodman's opening paragraph. What is he assuming when he proposes that "prestigious Universities . . . abolish grading"? Do you agree with the assumption? Why, or why not?

2. In paragraph 3, Goodman says that "the great majority of professors agree that grading hinders teaching." What evidence does he offer to support this claim? What arguments might be made that grading assists teaching? Should Goodman have made them and perhaps then shown their weakness?

3. Goodman proposes that business, industry, and government do their own testing (para. 4). Can you think of a sensible reply in defense of the status quo? If so, set it forth in 500 words.

4. Goodman relies on (but never defends) a strong correlation between testing and the competition for grades he thinks is characteristic even of the best colleges. Write a 250-word essay on this topic: "Does Testing Lead to Competition for Grades?"

5. Suppose the faculty of your college voted to continue grading as usual but not to divulge the grades to students, except at graduation and for students who are failing or on the verge of failure. Would such practice mitigate, aggravate, or leave untouched the complaints Goodman voices against grades?

6. As a student, have grades helped you to learn, or have grades hindered you? Drawing on your own experience, argue for or against grades in an essay of 500 words.

7. If you have been a student in an ungraded course, describe the course, and evaluate the experience.

8. Read the essay by Diane Ravitch (p. 806). Where, if at all, does she agree with Goodman about the role of testing in higher education?

Howard Gardner

Howard Gardner, born in 1943 and educated at Harvard, is the John H. and Elisabeth A. Hobbs Professor of Cognition and Education at the Harvard Graduate School of Education. He also holds positions as Adjunct Professor of Psychology at Harvard University and Senior Director of Harvard Project Zero. Among his books are Who Owns Intelligence? *(1999),* Good Work: When Excellence and Ethics Meet *(2001),* Changing Minds: The Art and Science of Changing Our Own and Other People's Minds *(2004), and* Five Minds for the Future *(2007). The following essay, published in the* New York Times *on July 18, 2002, stimulated several readers to send letters to the editor, which we print after the essay.*

Test for Aptitude, Not for Speed

Changes in educational policy invariably evoke strong and contrary reactions. The College Board's announcement this week that it will no longer tell colleges and universities which students have been given extra time to complete the SAT is no exception. Some see this decision, which came as a result of a legal settlement with a student who had a physical disability, as fair and overdue. Others see it as unfairly handicapping those students who do not request or receive such accommodations and say it will deprive admissions officers of pertinent information.

The College Board's decision is right. But I question whether there is any rationale for timing such tests at all.

Underlying the contrasting reactions are two opposing views. The original thinking behind the SAT is that individuals possess varying scholastic aptitudes. The SAT is designed to discover those who've got the intellectual goods and merit a college education.

For the last 50 years, the test has culled those individuals who are skilled in selecting the correct response from four or five choices. The questions sample verbal skills (vocabulary, reading and understanding short passages, analogies) and mathematical ability (basic arithmetic, algebra and geometry). Speed is of the essence; the test-taker should be able to answer about one question a minute. Those who are familiar with these types of questions can answer quickly and are able to shift rapidly from one question type to another are at a distinct advantage. Those who believe the timed format is central to the test resist efforts to give any group of students an exemption.

Those with a contrasting view believe that the point of the test is to   5
see whether a person can ultimately provide a correct answer—from scratch or from multiple choices. Therefore, it students are revealed by screening to have any kind of disability, they ought to be provided with appropriate aid. Those who are blind get a version in braille; those who are myopic get large print; those who have a good reason for needing more time should get it.

But why give a time exemption only to those who can make a case that they need one? Why not let anyone who wants extra time (or, for that matter, braille or large print) have it, no questions asked? My own guess is that most people would not take much extra time, but the decision would be theirs, not that of a screening body.

Nothing of consequence would be lost by getting rid of timed tests by the College Board or, indeed, by universities in general. Few tasks in life—and very few tasks in scholarship—actually depend on being able to read passages or solve math problems rapidly. As a teacher, I want my students to read, write and think well; I don't care how much time they spend on their assignments. For those few jobs where speed is important, timed tests may be useful. But getting into college, or doing satisfactorily once there, is not in that category.

Indeed, by eliminating the timed component, the College Board would signal that background knowledge, seriousness of purpose and effort—not speed and glibness—are the essentials of good scholarship. What matters is not what you have at the starting point, but whether and how well you finish.

And if, the day after tomorrow, students were allowed to bring along dictionaries, or even to have access to the Web, so much the better. Such a change would far more accurately duplicate the conditions under which serious individuals at any level of expertise actually do their work.

Topics for Critical Thinking and Writing

1. In paragraph 7, Gardner says, "Few tasks in life . . . actually depend on being able to read passages or solve math problems rapidly." Of course, few tasks in life—for instance, watching television, putting out the garbage, taking the bus to work, filling cavities—require doing any reading or math at all. Does Gardner have a substantial point? Explain.

2. What can be said in support of Gardner's final paragraph? What can be said against it? Offer the best evidence you can for each view.

Letters of Response by Thomas M. Johnson Jr., Garver Moore, Arnie Lichten, and Janet Rudolph

To the Editor:

Re "Test for Aptitude, Not for Speed," by Howard Gardner (Op-Ed, July 18):

Mr. Gardner is correct that few tasks in life require the completion of math problems under exacting time constraints. However, he ignores the fact that one of the principal rationales for a timed SAT is that it tests the student's ability to perform well under pressure. Such discipline is a valuable predictive indicator of success both in college and life.

Thomas M. Johnson Jr.
Park Ridge, N.J., July 18, 2002

To the Editor:

I write as a student who recently completed the undergraduate collegiate admissions process. In reading "Test for Aptitude, Not for Speed," by Howard Gardner (Op-Ed, July 18), I was struck by the fact that, apparently, a few people aren't quite aware that the "T" in SAT stands for Test.

The whole idea behind this particular test is its standardization. Conditions are held constant so that only a student's brain is responsible for his or her score. If I can get 90 percent of the questions right in 20 minutes at 9 a.m. using my own vocabulary, and it takes the person next to me 93 minutes, a dictionary, a laptop and a textbook, the Educational Testing Service would be doing a grave disservice to report the same score, without any indication of the variables, to colleges.

It's time to wake up and realize that the SAT isn't there to make people feel good.

GARVER MOORE
Atlanta, July 18, 2002

To the Editor:

I wonder if Howard Gardner (Op-Ed, July 18) assigns due dates for his assignments to his students. If he does, shouldn't these students be allowed to take as much time as necessary, rather than submit the assignments on an arbitrary date?

ARNIE LICHTEN
Easton, Pa., July 18, 2002

To the Editor:

After reading Howard Gardner's July 18 Op-Ed article and the July 21 letters in response, I am more convinced than ever of the foolishness of the SAT culture. One letter writer called the test a "valuable predictive indicator of success," another praised its work in standardization, and another pointed to its divisiveness between "haves and have-nots."

I know brilliant writers who can't balance a checkbook, exceptional artists who are unremarkable readers, and exquisite musicians who can't work quickly in the realm of academics. I've known students with 1500's on their SAT's who don't know how to get along with a friend or feel content with their own achievements.

Obviously, much depends on one's definition of success. This much I know: We humans do not fit into standardized boxes, and attempts to do so not only create conflict, but they also demean the skills of those whose abilities are not so easily quantifiable.

JANET RUDOLPH
Woodmere, N.Y., July 21, 2002

TOPICS FOR CRITICAL THINKING AND WRITING

1. Take one of the preceding letters, and set forth the assumption(s) that the writer makes. Do you think all reasonable people would agree with the assumption(s)? If not, why not?

2. Write (but do not mail) a short letter to one of the letter-writers, supporting or modifying the view expressed in the writer's letter.

3. If you were the editor of the newspaper and could print only one of these letters, which one would you print? Why?

Diane Ravitch

Diane Ravitch (b. 1938) has taught history and education at Teachers College, Columbia University, and has served as Assistant Secretary of Education. Her works include Left Back: A Century of Failed School Reforms *(2000), and more recently,* The Death and Life of the Great American School System: How Testing and Choice Are Undermining Education *(2010). The following essay was originally published in* Time *on September 11, 2000.*

In Defense of Testing

No one wants to be tested. We would all like to get a driver's license without answering questions about right of way or showing that we can parallel park a car. Many future lawyers and doctors probably wish they could join their profession without taking an exam.

But tests and standards are a necessary fact of life. They protect us — most of the time — from inept drivers, hazardous products, and shoddy professionals. In schools too, exams play a constructive role. They tell public officials whether new school programs are making a difference and where new investments are likely to pay off. They tell teachers what their students have learned — and have not. They tell parents how their children are doing compared with others their age. They encourage students to exert more effort.

It is important to recall that for most of this century, educators used intelligence tests to decide which children should get a high-quality education. The point of IQ testing was to find out how much children were capable of learning rather than to test what they had actually learned. Based on IQ scores, millions of children were assigned to dumbed-down programs instead of solid courses in science, math, history, literature, and foreign languages.

This history reminds us that tests should be used to improve education, not ration it. Every child should have access to a high-quality education. Students should have full opportunity to learn what will be tested; otherwise their test scores will merely reflect whether they come from an educated family.

In the past few years, we have seen the enormous benefits that flow 5 to disadvantaged students because of the information provided by state tests. Those who fall behind are now getting extra instruction in after-school classes and summer programs. In their efforts to improve student performance, states are increasing teachers' salaries, testing new teachers, and insisting on better teacher education.

Good tests should include a mix of essay, problem-solving, short-answer, and even some multiple-choice questions. On math quizzes, students should be able to show how they arrived at their answer. The tests widely used today often rely too much on multiple-choice questions, which encourage guessing rather than thinking. Also, they frequently ignore the importance of knowledge. Today's history tests, for example, seldom expect the student to know any history—sometimes derided as "mere facts"—but only to be able to read charts, graphs, and cartoons.

Performance in education means the mastery of both knowledge and skills. This is why it is reasonable to test teachers to make sure they know their subject matter, as well as how to teach it to young children. And this is why it is reasonable to assess whether students are ready to advance to the next grade or graduate from high school. To promote students who cannot read or do math is no favor to them. It is like pushing them into a deep pool before they have learned to swim. If students need extra time and help, they should get it, but they won't unless we first carefully assess what they have learned.

TOPICS FOR CRITICAL THINKING AND WRITING

1. Ravitch asserts that "every child should have access to a high-quality education" (para. 4). On what assumptions do you think this assertion rests?

2. State in one sentence the thesis of Ravitch's essay; which of the seven paragraphs in her essay do you rely on?

3. Ravitch (para. 2) claims that tests "encourage students to exert more effort." She does not say to what they devote this extra effort. What do you think?

4. Ravitch claims that "performance in education means the mastery of both knowledge and skills" (para. 7). Explain the difference between knowledge and skills. Are the studies you are taking (or took) in your freshman year in college devoted more to acquiring knowledge or to acquiring skills?

5. Ravitch believes that graduation from high school ought to be based on some standard of performance, even if it means holding back some students so that they cannot graduate with their classmates (para. 7). Can you think of a case from your own experience where an obviously unqualified classmate (a) was promoted with the rest of the class or (b) was held back to repeat a year's work? What is your evaluation of the results from either a or b?

Alfie Kohn

Alfie Kohn, born in 1957, received a bachelor's degree from Brown University and a master's degree from the University of Chicago. He has taught in both high school and college, but he is now an independent scholar—the author of numerous articles and eleven books. We reprint an essay from Kohn's What Does It Mean to Be Well-Educated? *(2004).*

From Degrading to De-grading

You can tell a lot about a teacher's values and personality just by asking how he or she feels about giving grades. Some defend the practice, claiming that grades are necessary to "motivate" students. Many of these teachers actually seem to enjoy keeping intricate records of students' marks. Such teachers periodically warn students that they're "going to have to know this for the test" as a way of compelling them to pay attention or do the assigned readings—and they may even use surprise quizzes for that purpose, keeping their grade books at the ready.

Frankly, we ought to be worried for these teachers' students. In my experience, the most impressive teachers are those who despise the whole process of giving grades. Their aversion, as it turns out, is supported by solid evidence that raises questions about the very idea of traditional grading.

THREE MAIN EFFECTS OF GRADING

Researchers have found three consistent effects of using—and especially, emphasizing the importance of—letter or number grades:

1. Grades tend to reduce students' interest in the learning itself. One of the best-researched findings in the field of motivational psychology is that the more people are rewarded for doing something, the more they tend to lose interest in whatever they had to do to get the reward (Kohn, 1993). Thus, it shouldn't be surprising that when students are told they'll need to know something for a test—or, more generally, that something they're about to do will count for a grade—they are likely to come to view that task (or book or idea) as a chore.

While it's not impossible for a student to be concerned about getting 5 high marks and also to like what he or she is doing, the practical reality is that these two ways of thinking generally pull in opposite directions. Some research has explicitly demonstrated that a "grade orientation" and a "learning orientation" are inversely related (Beck, Rorrer-Woody, and Pierce 1991; Milton, Pollio, and Eison 1986). More strikingly, study after study has found that students—from elementary school to graduate school, and across cultures—demonstrate less interest in learning as a result of being graded (Benware and Deci 1984; Butler 1987; Butler and Nisan 1986; Grolnick and Ryan 1987; Harter and Guzman 1986; Hughes, Sullivan, and Mosley 1985; Kage 1991; Salili et al. 1976). Thus, anyone who wants to see students get hooked on words and numbers and ideas already has reason to look for other ways of assessing and describing their achievement.

2. Grades tend to reduce students' preference for challenging tasks. Students of all ages who have been led to concentrate on getting a good grade are likely to pick the easiest possible assignment if given a choice (Harter 1978; Harter and Guzman 1986; Kage 1991; Milton, Pollio, and Eison 1986). The more pressure to get an A, the less inclination to truly challenge oneself. Thus, students who cut corners may not be lazy so much as rational; they are adapting to an environment where good grades, not intellectual exploration, are what count. They might well say to us, "Hey, you told me the point here is to bring up my GPA, to get on the honor roll. Well, I'm not stupid: The easier the assignment, the more likely that I can give you what you want. So don't blame me when I try to find the easiest thing to do and end up not learning anything."

3. Grades tend to reduce the quality of students' thinking. Given that students may lose interest in what they're learning as a result of grades, it makes sense that they're also apt to think less deeply. One series of studies, for example, found that students given numerical grades were significantly less creative than those who received qualitative feedback but no grades. The more the task required creative thinking, in fact, the worse the performance of students who knew they were going to be graded. Providing students with comments in addition to a grade didn't help: The highest achievement occurred only when comments were given *instead* of numerical scores (Butler 1987; Butler 1988; Butler and Nisan 1986).

In another experiment, students told they would be graded on how well they learned a social studies lesson had more trouble understanding the main point of the text than did students who were told that no grades would be involved. Even on a measure of rote recall, the graded group remembered fewer facts a week later (Grolnick and Ryan 1987). And students who tended to think about current events in terms of what they'd need to know for a grade were less knowledgeable than their peers, even after taking other variables into account (Anderman and Johnston 1998).

MORE REASONS TO JUST SAY NO TO GRADES

The preceding three results should be enough to cause any conscientious educator to rethink the practice of giving students grades. But there's more.

Grades aren't valid, reliable, or objective. A B in English says nothing 10
about what a student can do, what she understands, where she needs

help. Moreover, the basis for that grade is as subjective as the result is uninformative. A teacher can meticulously record scores for one test or assignment after another, eventually calculating averages down to a hundredth of a percentage point, but that doesn't change the arbitrariness of each of these individual marks. Even the score on a math test is largely a reflection of how the test was written: what skills the teacher decided to assess, what kinds of questions happened to be left out, and how many points each section was "worth."

Moreover, research has long been available to confirm what all of us know: Any given assignment may well be given two different grades by two equally qualified teachers. It may even be given two different grades by a single teacher who reads it at two different times (for example, see some of the early research reviewed in Kirschenbaum, Simon, and Napier 1971). In short, what grades offer is spurious precision — a subjective rating masquerading as an objective evaluation.

Grades distort the curriculum. A school's use of letter or number grades may encourage a fact- and skill-based approach to instruction because that sort of learning is easier to score. The tail of assessment thus comes to wag the educational dog.

Grades waste a lot of time that could be spent on learning. Add up all the hours that teachers spend fussing with their grade books. Then factor in the (mostly unpleasant) conversations they have with students and their parents about grades. It's tempting to just roll our eyes when confronted with whining or wheedling, but the real problem rests with the practice of grading itself.

Grades encourage cheating. Again, we can either continue to blame and punish all the students who cheat — or we can look for the structural reasons this keeps happening. Researchers have found that the more students are led to focus on getting good grades, the more likely they are to cheat, even if they themselves regard cheating as wrong (Anderman, Griesinger, and Westerfield 1998; Milton, Pollio, and Eison 1986).

Grades spoil teachers' relationships with students. Consider this lament, 15 which could have been offered by a teacher in your district: "I'm getting tired of running a classroom in which everything we do revolves around grades. I'm tired of being suspicious when students give me compliments, wondering whether or not they are just trying to raise their grade. I'm tired of spending so much time and energy grading your papers, when there are probably a dozen more productive and enjoyable ways for all of us to handle the evaluation of papers. I'm tired of hearing you ask me 'Does this count?' And, heaven knows, I'm certainly tired of all those little arguments and disagreements we get into concerning marks which take so much fun out of the teaching and the learning . . ." (Kirschenbaum, Simon, and Napier 1971, p. 115).

Grades spoil students' relationships with one another. The quality of students' thinking has been shown to depend partly on the extent to which they are permitted to learn cooperatively (Johnson and Johnson 1989;

Kohn 1992). Thus, the ill feelings, suspicion, and resentment generated by grades aren't just disagreeable in their own right; they interfere with learning.

The most destructive form of grading by far is that which is done "on a curve," such that the number of top grades is artificially limited: No matter how well all the students do, not all of them can get an A. Apart from the intrinsic unfairness of this arrangement, its practical effect is to teach students that others are potential obstacles to their own success. The kind of collaboration that can help all students to learn more effectively doesn't stand a chance in such an environment. Sadly, even teachers who don't explicitly grade on a curve may assume, perhaps unconsciously, that the final grades "ought to" come out looking more or less this way: a few very good grades, a few very bad grades, and the majority somewhere in the middle.

The competition that turns schooling into a quest for triumph and ruptures relationships among students doesn't just happen within classrooms, of course. The same effect is witnessed at a schoolwide when kids are not just rated but ranked, sending the message that the point isn't to learn, or even to perform well, but to defeat others. Some students might be motivated to improve their class rank, but that is completely different from being motivated to understand ideas. (Wise educators realize that it doesn't matter how motivated students are; what matters is *how* students are motivated. It is the type of motivation that counts, not the amount.)

EXCUSES AND DISTRACTIONS

Most of us are directly acquainted with at least some of these disturbing consequences of grades, yet we continue to reduce students to letters or numbers on a regular basis. Perhaps we've become inured to these effects and take them for granted. This is the way it's always been, we assume, and the way it has to be. It's rather like people who have spent all their lives in a terribly polluted city and have come to assume that this is just the way air looks—and that it's natural to be coughing all the time.

Oddly, when educators are shown that it doesn't have to be this way, 20 some react with suspicion instead of relief. They want to know why you're making trouble, or they assert that you're exaggerating the negative effects of grades (it's really not so bad—cough, cough), or they dismiss proven alternatives to grading on the grounds that our school could never do what others schools have done.

The practical difficulties of abolishing letter grades are real. But the key question is whether those difficulties are seen as problems to be solved or as excuses for perpetuating the status quo. The logical response to the arguments and data summarized here is to say: "Good heavens! If even half of this is true, then it's imperative we do whatever we can, as soon as we can, to phase out traditional grading." Yet many people begin and end with the problems of implementation, responding to all this evidence by saying, in effect, "Yeah, yeah, yeah, but we'll never get rid of grades because . . ."

It is also striking how many educators never get beyond relatively insignificant questions, such as how many tests to give, or how often to send home grade reports, or what number corresponds to what letter. Some even reserve their outrage for the possibility that too many students are ending up with good grades, a reaction that suggests stinginess with A's is being confused with intellectual rigor.

COMMON OBJECTIONS

Let's consider the most frequently heard responses to the above arguments—which is to say, the most common objections to getting rid of grades.

First, it is said that students expect to receive grades and even seem addicted to them. This is often true; I've taught high school students who reacted to the absence of grades with what I can only describe as existential vertigo. *(Who am I, if not a B+?)* But as more elementary and even some middle schools move to replace grades with more informative (and less destructive) systems of assessment, the damage doesn't begin until students get to high school. Moreover, elementary and middle schools that *haven't* changed their practices often cite the local high school as the reason they must get students used to getting grades regardless of their damaging effects—just as high schools point the finger at colleges.

Even when students arrive in high school already accustomed to 25 grades, already primed to ask teachers, "Do we have to know this?" or "What do I have to do to get an A?," this is a sign that something is very wrong. It's more an indictment of what has happened to them in the past than an argument to keep doing it in the future.

Perhaps because of this training, grades can succeed in getting students to show up on time, hand in their work, and otherwise do what they're told. Many teachers are loath to give up what is essentially an instrument of control. But even to the extent this instrument works (which is not always), we are obliged to reflect on whether mindless compliance is really our goal. The teacher who exclaims, "These kids would blow off my course in a minute if they weren't getting a grade for it!" may be issuing a powerful indictment of his or her course. Who would be more reluctant to give up grades than a teacher who spends the period slapping transparencies on the overhead projector and lecturing endlessly at students about Romantic poets or genetic codes? Without bribes (A's) and threats (F's), students would have no reason to do such assignments. To maintain that this proves something is wrong with the kids—or that grades are simply "necessary"—suggests a willful refusal to examine one's classroom practices and assumptions about teaching and learning.

"If I can't give a child a better reason for studying than a grade on a report card, I ought to lock my desk and go home and stay there." So wrote Dorothy De Zouche, a Missouri teacher, in an article published in February . . . of 1945. But teachers who *can* give a child a better reason for studying don't need grades. Research substantiates this: when the curriculum is engaging—for example, when it involves hands-on, interactive learning activities—students who aren't graded at all perform just as well as those who are graded (Moeller and Reschke 1993).

Another objection: It is sometimes argued that students must be given grades because colleges demand them. One might reply that "high schools have no responsibility to serve colleges by performing the sorting function for them"—particularly if that process undermines learning (Krumboltz and Yeh 1996, p. 325). But in any case the premise of this argument is erroneous: Traditional grades are not mandatory for admission to colleges and universities. (See Addendum.)

MAKING CHANGE

A friend of mine likes to say that people don't resist change—they resist being changed. Even terrific ideas (like moving a school from a grade orientation to a learning orientation) are guaranteed to self-destruct if they are simply forced down people's throats. The first step for an administrator, therefore, is to open up a conversation—to spend perhaps a full year just encouraging people to think and talk about the effects of (and alternatives to) traditional grades. This can happen in individual classes, as teachers facilitate discussions about how students regard grades, as well as in evening meetings with parents, or on a Web site—all with the help of relevant books, articles, speakers, videos, and visits to neighboring schools that are further along in this journey.

The actual process of "de-grading" can be done in stages. For example, a high school might start by freeing ninth-grade classes from grades before doing the same for upperclassmen. (Even a school that never gets beyond the first stage will have done a considerable service, giving students one full year when they can think about what they're learning instead of their GPAs.)

Another route to gradual change is to begin by eliminating only the most pernicious practices, such as grading on a curve or ranking students. Although grades, per se, may continue for a while, at least the message will be sent from the beginning that all students can do well, and that the point is to succeed rather than to beat others.

Anyone who has heard the term *authentic assessment* knows that abolishing grades doesn't mean eliminating the process of gathering information about student performance—and communicating that information to students and parents. Rather, abolishing grades opens up possibilities that are far more meaningful and constructive. These include narratives (written comments), portfolios (carefully chosen collections of students' writings and projects that demonstrate their interests, achievement, and improvement over time), student-led parent-teacher conferences, exhibitions, and other opportunities for students to show what they can do.

Of course, it's harder for a teacher to do these kinds of assessments if he or she has 150 or more students and sees each of them for forty-five to fifty-five minutes a day. But that's not an argument for continuing to use traditional grades; it's an argument for challenging these archaic remnants of a factory-oriented approach to instruction, structural aspects of high schools that are bad news for reasons that go well beyond the issue of assessment. It's an argument for looking into block scheduling, team teaching, interdisciplinary courses—and learning more about schools that have arranged things so each teacher can spend more time with fewer students (e.g., Meier 1995).

Administrators should be prepared to respond to parental concerns, some of them completely reasonable, about the prospect of edging away from grades. "Don't you value excellence?" You bet—and here's the evidence that traditional grading *undermines* excellence. "Are you just trying to spare the self-esteem of students who do poorly?" We are concerned that grades may be making things worse for such students, yes, but the problem isn't just that some kids won't get A's and will have their feelings hurt. The real problem is that almost all kids (including yours) will come to focus on grades and, as a result, their learning will be hurt.

If parents worry that grades are the only window they have into the 35 school, we need to assure them that alternative assessments provide a far better view. But if parents don't seem to care about getting the most useful information or helping their children become more excited learners—if they demand grades for the purpose of documenting how much better their kids are than everyone else's—then we need to engage them in a discussion about whether this is a legitimate goal, and whether schools exist for the purpose of competitive credentialing or for the purpose of helping everyone to learn (Kohn 1998; Labaree 1997). Above all, we need to make sure that objections and concerns about the details don't obscure the main message, which is the demonstrated harm of traditional grading on the quality of students' learning and their interest in exploring ideas.

High school administrators can do a world of good in their districts by actively supporting efforts to eliminate conventional grading in elementary and middle schools. Working with their colleagues in these schools can help pave the way for making such changes at the secondary school level.

IN THE MEANTIME

Finally, there is the question of what classroom teachers can do while grades continue to be required. The short answer is that they should do everything within their power to make grades as invisible as possible for as long as possible. Helping students forget about grades is the single best piece of advice for those who want to create a learning-oriented classroom.

When I was teaching high school, I did a lot of things I now regret. But one policy that still seems sensible to me was saying to students on the first day of class that, while I was compelled to give them a grade at the end of the term, I could not in good conscience ever put a letter or number on anything they did during the term—and I would not do so. I would, however, write a comment—or, better, sit down and talk with them—as often as possible to give them feedback.

At this particular school I frequently faced students who had been prepared for admission to Harvard since their early childhood—a process I have come to call "Preparation H." I knew that my refusal to rate their learning might cause some students to worry about their marks all the more, or to create suspense about what would appear on their final grade reports, which of course would defeat the whole purpose. So I said that anyone who absolutely had to know what grade a given paper would get could come see me and we would figure it out together. An amazing thing happened: As the days went by, fewer and fewer students felt the need to ask me about grades. They began to be more involved with what we were learning, because I had taken responsibility as a teacher to stop pushing grades into their faces, so to speak, whenever they completed an assignment.

What I didn't do very well, however, was to get students involved in 40 devising the criteria for excellence (what makes a math solution elegant, an experiment well designed, an essay persuasive, a story compelling) or in deciding how well their projects met those criteria. I'm afraid I unilaterally set the criteria and evaluated the students' efforts. But I have seen teachers who were more willing to give up control, more committed to helping students participate in assessment and turn that into part of the learning. Teachers who work with their students to design powerful alternatives to letter grades have a replacement ready to go when the school finally abandons traditional grading—and are able to minimize the harm of such grading in the meantime.

ADDENDUM: MUST CONCERNS ABOUT COLLEGE DERAIL HIGH SCHOOL LEARNING?

Here is the good news: College admissions practices are not as rigid and reactionary as many people think. Here is the better news: Even when that process doesn't seem to have its priorities straight, high schools don't have to be dragged down to that level.

Sometimes it is assumed that admissions officers at the best universities are eighty-year-old fuddy-duddies, peering over their spectacles and muttering about "highly irregular" applications. In truth, the people charged with making these decisions are often just a few years out of college themselves, and after making their way through a pile of inter-changeable applications from 3.8-GPA, student-council-vice-president, musically accomplished hopefuls from high-powered traditional subur-ban high schools, they are desperate for something unconventional. Given that the most selective colleges have been to known to accept home-schooled children who have never set foot in a classroom, second-ary schools have more latitude than they sometimes assume. It is not widely known, for example, that at hundreds of colleges and universities don't require applicants to take either the SAT or the ACT.

Admittedly, large state universities are more resistant to unconven-tional applications than are small private colleges simply because of eco-nomics: It takes more time, and therefore more money, for admissions officers to read meaningful application materials than it does for them to glance at a GPA or an SAT score and plug it into a formula. But I have heard of high schools approaching the admissions directors of nearby universities and saying, in effect, "We'd like to improve our school by getting rid of grades. Here's why. Will you work with us to make sure our seniors aren't penalized?" This strategy may well be successful for the simple reason that not many high schools are requesting this at pres-ent and the added inconvenience for admissions offices is likely to be negligible. Of course, if more and more high schools abandon traditional grades, then the universities will have no choice but to adapt. This is a change that high schools will have to initiate rather than waiting for col-leges to signal their readiness.

At the moment, plenty of admissions officers enjoy the convenience of class ranking, apparently because they have confused being better than one's peers with being good at something; they're looking for winners rather than learners. But relatively few colleges actually insist on this practice. When a 1993 survey by the National Association of Secondary School Principals asked eleven hundred admissions officers what would happen if a high school stopped computing class rank, only 0.5 percent said the school's applicants would not be considered for admission, 4.5 percent said it would be a "great handicap," and 14.4 percent said it would be a "handicap" (Levy and Riordan 1994). In other words, it appears that the absence of class ranks would not interfere at all with students' prospects for admission to four out of five colleges.

Even more impressive, some high schools not only refuse to rank 45 their students but refuse to give any sort of letter or number grades. Courses are all taken pass/fail, sometimes with narrative assessments of the students' performance that become part of a college application. I have spoken to representatives of each of the schools listed below, and all assure me that, year after year, their graduates are accepted into large state universities and small, highly selective colleges. *Even the complete absence of high school grades is not a barrier to college admission*, so we don't have that excuse for continuing to subject students to the harm done by traditional grading.

Any school considering the abolition of grades might want to submit a letter with each graduating student's transcript that explains why the school has chosen this course. In the meantime, feel free to contact any of these successful grade-free schools:

Metropolitan Learning Center
2033 NW Glisan
Portland, OR 97209
503/916-5737
www.pps.k12.or.us/schools/
 profiles/?location_id=154

Poughkeepsie Day School
39 New Hackensack Rd.
Poughkeepsie, NY 12603
914/462-7600
www.poughkeepsieday.org

School Without Walls
480 Broadway
Rochester, NY 14607
585/546-6732
www.schoolwithoutwalls.org

Alternative Community School
111 Chestnut St.
Ithaca, NY 14850
607/274-2183
www.icsd.k12.ny.us/acs/info.html

Hawthorne Valley School
330 Route 21C
Ghent, NY 12075
518/672-7092
www.hawthornevalleyschool.org

Malcolm Shabazz City High
School
1601 N. Sherman Ave.
Madison, WI 53704
608/284-2440
www.madison.k12.wi.us/shabazz

Waring School
35 Standley St.
Beverly, MA 01915
978/927-8793
www.waringschool.org

Carolina Friends School
4809 Friends School Rd.
Durham, NC 27705
919/383-6602
www.cfsnc.org

Saint Ann's School
129 Pierrepont St.
Brooklyn Heights, NY 11201
718/522-1660
www.saintanns.k12.ny.us

REFERENCES

Anderman, E. M., T. Griesinger, and G. Westerfield. 1998. "Motivation and Cheating During Early Adolescence." *Journal of Educational Psychology* 90: 84–93.
———, and J. Johnston. 1998. "Television News in the Classroom: What Are Adolescents Learning?" *Journal of Adolescent Research* 13: 73–100.
Beck, H. P., S. Rorrer-Woody, and L. G. Pierce. 1991. "The Relations of Learning and Grade Orientations to Academic Performance." *Teaching of Psychology* 18: 35–37.
Benware, C. A., and E. L. Deci. 1984. "Quality of Learning With an Active Versus Passive Motivational Set." *American Educational Research Journal* 21: 755–65.
Butler, R. 1987. "Task-Involving and Ego-Involving Properties of Evaluation: Effects of Different Feedback Conditions on Motivational Perceptions, Interest, and Performance." *Journal of Educational Psychology* 79: 474–82.

————. 1988. "Enhancing and Undermining Intrinsic Motivation: The Effects of Task-Involving and Ego-Involving Evaluation on Interest and Performance." *British Journal of Educational Psychology* 58: 1–14.

————, and M. Nisan. 1986. "Effects of No Feedback, Task-Related Comments, and Grades on Intrinsic Motivation and Performance." *Journal of Educational Psychology* 78: 210–16.

De Zouche, D. 1945. "'The Wound Is Mortal': Marks, Honors, Unsound Activities." *The Clearing House* 19: 339–44.

Grolnick, W. S., and R. M. Ryan. 1987. "Autonomy in Children's Learning: An Experimental and Individual Difference Investigation." *Journal of Personality and Social Psychology* 52: 890–98.

Harter, S. 1978. "Pleasure Derived from Challenge and the Effects of Receiving Grades on Children's Difficulty Level Choices." *Child Development* 49: 788–99.

————, and M. E. Guzman. 1986. "The Effect of Perceived Cognitive Competence and Anxiety on Children's Problem-Solving Performance, Difficulty Level Choices, and Preference for Challenge." Unpublished manuscript, University of Denver.

Hughes, B., H. J. Sullivan, and M. L. Mosley. 1985. "External Evaluation, Task Difficulty, and Continuing Motivation." *Journal of Educational Research* 78: 210–15.

Johnson, D. W., and R. T. Johnson. *Cooperation and Competition: Theory and Research*. Edina, Minn.: Interaction Book Co.

Kage, M. 1991. "The Effects of Evaluation on Intrinsic Motivation." Paper presented at the meeting of the Japan Association of Educational Psychology, Joetsu, Japan.

Kirschenbaum, H., S. B. Simon, and R. W. Napier. 1971. *Wad-Ja-Get?: The Grading Game in American Education*. New York: Hart.

Kohn, A. 1992. *No Contest: The Case Against Competition*. Rev. ed. Boston: Houghton Mifflin.

————. 1993. *Punished by Rewards: The Trouble with Gold Stars, Incentive Plans, A's, Praise, and Other Bribes*. Boston: Houghton Mifflin.

————. 1998. "Only for *My* Kid: How Privileged Parents Undermine School Reform." *Phi Delta Kappan*, April: 569–77.

Krumboltz, J. D., and C. J. Yeh. 1996. "Competitive Grading Sabotages Good Teaching." *Phi Delta Kappan*, December: 324–26.

Labaree, D. F. 1997. *How to Succeed in School Without Really Learning: The Credentials Race in American Education*. New Haven, Conn.: Yale University Press.

Levy, J., and P. Riordan. 1994. *Rank-in-Class, Grade Point Average, and College Admission*. Reston, Va.: NASSP. (Available as ERIC Document 370988.)

Meier, D. 1995. *The Power of Their Ideas: Lessons for America from a Small School in Harlem*. Boston: Beacon.

Milton, O., H. R. Pollio, and J. A. Eison. 1986. *Making Sense of College Grades*. San Francisco: Jossey-Bass.

Moeller, A. J., and C. Reschke. 1993. "A Second Look at Grading and Classroom Performance: Report of a Research Study." *Modern Language Journal* 77: 163–69.

Salili, F., M. L. Maehr, R. L. Sorensen, and L. J. Fyans, Jr. 1976. "A Further Consideration of the Effects of Evaluation on Motivation." *American Educational Research Journal* 13: 85–102.

TOPICS FOR CRITICAL THINKING AND WRITING

1. Kohn gets to the heart of the matter in his opening sentence. Do you think this opener is effective? Explain your answer.

2. Kohn identifies "three main effects of grading" (paras. 3–7). What are they, and do you agree with him about their importance? Why, or why not?

3. Does what Kohn reports as "one of the best-researched findings in motivational psychology" (para. 4) fit with your experience? Explain.

4. What evidence does Kohn cite to the effect that grades are invalid, unreliable, or subjective (paras. 10–18)?

5. Why do you think that so many courses involve grading on a curve when doing so is — as Kohn insists — "intrinsically unfair" (para. 17)?

6. What is the difference between rating students and ranking them (para. 18)?

7. In paragraph 20 Kohn recognizes that some instructors regard him or other investigators as troublemarkers. Judging from his essay, do you think that if you were a teacher you would welcome a visit? Explain.

8. In paragraph 28 Kohn imagines someone saying that "high schools have no responsibility to serve colleges by performing the sorting function for them." (He amplifies this point in his "addendum", p. 815). Do you agree? Why, or why not?

9. What does Kohn mean when he calls grading an "instrument of control" (para. 26)? Do you agree with him? Why, or why not?

10. Could a course you are now taking be improved by "de-grading" (para. 30) it? Explain how this might be done and what the improvement would be.

11. What does Kohn mean by the prevailing "factory-oriented approach to instruction" (para. 33)?

12. In the first sentence of paragraph 39 Kohn makes a little joke. What is the joke?

our Day
9:00 - circle time
10:00 - art fun
11:00 - snack
12:00 - S.A.T. prep

B. Smaller

Joy Alonso

Joy Alonso, now retired, for many years taught Spanish language and literature in high school, community colleges, and four-year colleges. We reprint a talk that she gave at Tufts University in 2004.

Two Cheers for Examinations

First, I must say that my title is [adapted] from E. M. Forster's collection of essays. I am speaking about an academic topic, to an audience of students and teachers, and I don't want to be accused of plagiarism.

Second, I want to tell a joke, a joke that I believe is highly relevant to our topic, "The Role of Examinations in College Courses." A father visited the college where he had been a student, and where his daughter was now a student. They happened to encounter an instructor who some twenty years earlier had taught the father and who last year had taught the daughter. The father said, sincerely, that he had greatly enjoyed the course and that his daughter had raved to him about the course, but he confessed that he was greatly disappointed in one respect. "The questions on the examination you gave to my daughter's class were exactly the same as the ones you gave to my class twenty years ago." "Ah, yes," the professor explained, "the questions are the same, but we have changed the answers."

A joke, but with a good deal of truth in it. No one can doubt the truth with reference to courses in the sciences. I have heard that a distinguished professor at a medical school begins his lectures by telling his students, "Half of what we are teaching you will, in twenty years, be disproved. The trouble is, we don't know which half." But even in the humanities and in the social sciences it is evident, at least to those who have been teaching the subjects for a couple of decades, that things change, that new knowledge makes us look differently at the works and issues that we studied when we were students.

What are the purposes of examinations? I think most people will agree that examinations have a dual purpose: to test or measure achievement, and to stimulate learning. The first purpose serves the interests of those who want to evaluate the student, perhaps for honors within the college, for admission to a graduate or professional school, or for employment. This purpose, this business of measuring students, may even serve the students themselves or their parents, who are interested in knowing how things seem to be going, where the students stand. I take this last point seriously; many students need reassurance that they are doing just fine. I suppose I should also mention, while speaking about tests as an instrument of measuring, that tests measure the *teachers* too; they measure how well we have taught. But this is not relevant to our topic today, which is the pros and cons of tests in two- and four-year colleges.

The second purpose of a test is to stimulate learning. On the most 5 obvious level, a vocabulary quiz or a quiz on a reading assignment forces the student to do the necessary work before the quiz. The usual metaphor is that such a test is a police measure, a device that forces the student to obey the law, in this case to master (at least to some degree) the assigned work. I don't think this is a bad thing. Yes, it would be better if all students at all times eagerly turned to their studies without any sort of compulsion, but none of us is cut from this sort of cloth. We all have lots of pressures on us, and inevitably we neglect some things— even things that we want to do—unless deadlines are imposed. A quiz tomorrow morning is a sort of deadline, a deadline that makes busy students turn for an hour or two to the assigned reading.

But when I say that tests stimulate learning, I am also thinking of something larger than this. Quizzes tend to test only details—the meanings of certain words, the uses of the subjunctive, the dates of certain events, and so forth. Midterm examinations and especially final examinations help a student to see how details may connect. In studying for examinations, a student begins to see not just the trees but the forest.

The student has perhaps taken a quiz that established whether he or she had read the assigned novel—Who did what to whom?—but not until the student prepares for the final examination does the student achieve an overview, partly by reviewing notes and readings, partly by trying to anticipate examination questions, perhaps by discussing the course with fellow students in a study group, and in any case by thinking about what the course adds up to. And finally, when the student actually faces the questions on the exam and responds thoughtfully to them, he or she is likely to experience a gratifying sense of accomplishment, an intellectual high.

I won't go so far as to say that students like examinations, but I will claim that many students experience a sense of exhilaration when the ordeal is over, when, so to speak, the initiation rite is completed and they justifiably feel that they have achieved something, they know things (at least for the moment) that they hadn't known they knew. They have met the challenge, risen to the occasion, learned (among other things) that they can do pretty well when it comes to the test—and the effort was worthwhile. Perhaps here I should say that in most of my courses, where there were several assigned papers and a midterm examination, I assured students that the final examination would count heavily if they did well, but if their grade on the final was notably lower than the average of their papers and midterm, it would count only as one unit in computing the average. I believe this system encouraged students to take the final seriously, but it protected the very rare student whose final examination was for some unfathomable reason far below his or her earlier work.

Why did I regularly put more emphasis on the final examination than on papers on topics that the students select? I did indeed assign several papers, of varying lengths, in my literature courses, but papers usually are on a relatively limited topic, rarely allowing for more than a comparison of two works. Students can write excellent papers on how the Elizabethans may have regarded the ghost in *Hamlet*, or how a director today might stage the scenes with the ghost, or they might write on, say, Shakespeare's use of prose in *Hamlet*: "Why does Hamlet sometimes speak verse, and sometimes prose?" And does Hamlet's prose differ from other prose in the play? These are worthy topics; students will learn a great deal about the play by working on them—but even the student who in a course in Shakespeare's Tragedies has written three such essays will not achieve an overview of the topic such as is afforded by studying for a final examination.

The title of my talk is "Two Cheers for Examinations." Why not three cheers? Because I know that there are drawbacks to examinations. Examinations can indeed deal with trivia, they can be badly conceived and thus can cause needless anxiety in the students who struggle to make sense out of poorly-written or poorly-focused questions.

Most damaging of all, perhaps, is the fact that professors are human 10 beings and therefore they will sometimes grade examinations unfairly.

Probably very few instructors are knowingly unfair, but an instructor who grades a paper at 8:00 p.m. is not quite the same person when he or she is grading at midnight. My own practice—an effort to guard against the unfairness that may be inherent in reading dozens of papers, one after the other, was to grade the first question on all the papers, then, when I had graded all of the responses to the first question, I turned to the second, and so on, in an effort to make certain that no student had the bad luck of being the first to be graded, when I might be more demanding, and no student had the bad luck to be the last to be graded, when I may have run out of patience. Still, even this system could not insure that I was fair to those papers that were barely legible.

I confess that I often found grading examinations to be a tedious job, but I must also add that the examinations were often a learning experience for me as well as for the students. How and why? In preparing the questions for the examination I had to think about the course as a whole, and I tried to construct questions that would help students to make connections, to go beyond the details of each day's assignment. And in reading the essays, I learned something about my failures, *my* failures, not the students'; some of the responses let me see where I had not been clear, or perhaps even where I had been misleading. On the whole, however, after reading all of the essays I felt pretty good, I felt something of the satisfaction that I hope students felt after they finished writing their examinations. It's been a lot of effort, thought, but it was worth it.

As for me, now that I am retired, well, I am preparing for my Final Examination.

TOPICS FOR CRITICAL THINKING AND WRITING

1. Suppose a critic of Alonso said that the chief effect of examinations is not "to stimulate learning" (para. 5) but to stimulate cramming. How might she reply? How would *you* reply to such a critic of Alonso?

2. Consider what another critic of Alonso might say: Studying for examinations does not promote learning. What it does is create students who have learned how to take examinations. Your reply? Your reasons?

> For topical links related to the issue of testing, see the companion Web site: **bedfordstmartins.com/barnetbedau.**

31

Torture: Is It Ever Justifiable?

Michael Levin

Michael Levin (b. 1943), educated at Michigan State University and Columbia University, has taught philosophy at Columbia and now at City College of the City University of New York. Levin has written numerous papers for professional journals and a book entitled Metaphysics and the Mind-Body Problem *(1979). His most recent book (with Laurence Thomas) is* Sexual Orientation and Human Rights *(1999). The following essay first appeared in the June 7, 1982, issue of* Newsweek.

The Case for Torture

It is generally assumed that torture is impermissible, a throwback to a more brutal age. Enlightened societies reject it outright, and regimes suspected of using it risk the wrath of the United States.

I believe this attitude is unwise. There are situations in which torture is not merely permissible but morally mandatory. Moreover, these situations are moving from the realm of imagination to fact.

Death: Suppose a terrorist has hidden an atomic bomb on Manhattan Island which will detonate at noon on July 4 unless. . . . (here follow the usual demands for money and release of his friends from jail). Suppose, further, that he is caught at 10 A.M. of the fateful day, but — preferring death to failure — won't disclose where the bomb is. What do we do? If we follow due process — wait for his lawyer, arraign him — millions of people will die. If the only way to save those lives is to subject the terrorist to the most excruciating possible pain, what grounds can there be for not doing so? I suggest there are none. In any case, I ask you to face the question with an open mind.

Torturing the terrorist is unconstitutional? Probably. But millions of lives surely outweigh constitutionality. Torture is barbaric? Mass murder is far more barbaric. Indeed, letting millions of innocents die in deference to one who flaunts his guilt is moral cowardice, an unwillingness to dirty one's hands. If *you* caught the terrorist, could you sleep nights knowing that millions died because you couldn't bring yourself to apply the electrodes?

Once you concede that torture is justified in extreme cases, you have 5 admitted that the decision to use torture is a matter of balancing innocent lives against the means needed to save them. You must now face more realistic cases involving more modest numbers. Someone plants a bomb on a jumbo jet. He alone can disarm it, and his demands cannot be met (or if they can, we refuse to set a precedent by yielding to his threats). Surely we can, we must, do anything to the extortionist to save the passengers. How can we tell 300, or 100, or 10 people who never asked to be put in danger, "I'm sorry, you'll have to die in agony, we just couldn't bring ourselves to . . ."

Here are the results of an informal poll about a third, hypothetical, case. Suppose a terrorist group kidnapped a newborn baby from a hospital. I asked four mothers if they would approve of torturing kidnappers if that were necessary to get their own newborns back. All said yes, the most "liberal" adding that she would like to administer it herself.

I am not advocating torture as punishment. Punishment is addressed to deeds irrevocably past. Rather, I am advocating torture as an acceptable measure for preventing future evils. So understood, it is far less objectionable than many extant punishments. Opponents of the death penalty, for example, are forever insisting that executing a murderer will not bring back his victim (as if the purpose of capital punishment were supposed to be resurrection, not deterrence or retribution). But torture, in the cases described, is intended not to bring anyone back but to keep innocents from being dispatched. The most powerful argument against using torture as a punishment or to secure confessions is that such practices disregard the rights of the individual. Well, if the individual is all that important—and he is—it is correspondingly important to protect the rights of individuals threatened by terrorists. If life is so valuable that it must never be taken, the lives of the innocents must be saved even at the price of hurting the one who endangers them.

Better precedents for torture are assassination and pre-emptive attack. No Allied leader would have flinched at assassinating Hitler, had that been possible. (The Allies did assassinate Heydrich.) Americans would be angered to learn that Roosevelt could have had Hitler killed in 1943—thereby shortening the war and saving millions of lives—but refused on moral grounds. Similarly, if nation *A* learns that nation *B* is about to launch an unprovoked attack, *A* has a right to save itself by destroying *B*'s military capability first. In the same way, if the police can by torture save those who would otherwise die at the hands of kidnappers or terrorists, they must.

Idealism: There is an important difference between terrorists and their victims that should mute talk of the terrorists' "rights." The terrorist's victims are at risk unintentionally, not having asked to be endangered. But the terrorist knowingly initiated his actions. Unlike his victims, he volunteered for the risks of his deed. By threatening to kill for profit or idealism, he renounces civilized standards, and he can have no complaint if civilization tries to thwart him by whatever means necessary.

Just as torture is justified only to save lives (not extort confessions or recantations) it is justifiably administered only to those *known* to hold innocent lives in their hands. Ah, but how can the authorities ever be sure they have the right malefactor? Isn't there a danger of error and abuse? Won't We turn into Them? 10

Questions like these are disingenuous in a world in which terrorists proclaim themselves and perform for television. The name of their game is public recognition. After all, you can't very well intimidate a government into releasing your freedom fighters unless you announce that it is your group that has seized its embassy. "Clear guilt" is difficult to define, but when 40 million people see a group of masked gunmen seize an airplane on the evening news, there is not much question about who the perpetrators are. There will be hard cases where the situation is murkier. Nonetheless, a line demarcating the legitimate use of torture can be drawn. Torture only the obviously guilty, and only for the sake of saving innocents, and the line between Us and Them will remain clear.

There is little danger that the Western democracies will lose their way if they choose to inflict pain as one way of preserving order. Paralysis in the face of evil is the greater danger. Some day soon a terrorist will threaten tens of thousands of lives, and torture will be the only way to save them. We had better start thinking about this.

TOPICS FOR CRITICAL THINKING AND WRITING

1. In his first four paragraphs, Levin uses hypothetical cases (these are also commonly called *invented instances*), and he pretty much assumes you agree in these cases that torture is acceptable. (For this presumed agreement, see the first sentence in para. 5.) Do you agree? If not, why?

2. In paragraph 11 Levin asserts that although "there will be hard cases" where the situation is murky, "nonetheless, a line demarcating the legitimate use of torture can be drawn." He then draws the line: "Torture only the obviously guilty, and only for the sake of saving innocents, and the line between Us and Them will remain clear." His essay is built on hypothetical cases. Can you invent a hypothetical case where the line between Us and Them is *not* clear?

3. Levin ends his essay by saying, "Some day soon a terrorist will threaten tens of thousands of lives, and torture will be the only way to save them." Given the fact that he wrote this essay in 1982, can we say that time has refuted this argument?

4. Is it reasonable to reply to Levin that since we never know that the accused both is really guilty and will break under torture, therefore that torture is never justified? Why, or why not?

"All I'm getting out of him is a lot of profanity."

5. Let's look now at some matters of style. Evaluate Levin's title and his first two paragraphs. Notice that the first paragraph ends with a relatively long sentence and the second paragraph begins with a relatively short sentence. What is the effect of this sequence?

6. In paragraph 7, Levin says that "opponents of the death penalty, for example, are forever insisting that executing a murderer will not bring back his victim." Suppose instead of "are forever insisting" he had said "sometimes argue." What would be the difference in tone—the difference in the speaker's voice and therefore in your sense of what sort of person the speaker is? What does Levin gain or lose by writing the sentence as he does?

Charles Krauthammer

Charles Krauthammer was born in New York City in 1950, but he grew up in Montreal, Canada. After graduating from McGill University in 1970, he studied in England at Oxford University, and then returned to the United States, where he entered Harvard Medical School. He graduated from the medical school in 1975, but in 1978 he quit practicing medicine and began a career as a writer. He is now a syndicated conservative columnist. This selection first appeared in the Weekly Standard *in 2005.*

The Truth about Torture

During the last few weeks in Washington the pieties about torture have lain so thick in the air that it has been impossible to have a reasoned discussion. The McCain amendment that would ban "cruel, inhuman, or degrading" treatment of any prisoner by any agent of the United States sailed through the Senate by a vote of 90–9. The Washington establishment remains stunned that nine such retrograde, morally inert persons—let alone senators—could be found in this noble capital.

Now, John McCain has great moral authority on this issue, having heroically borne torture at the hands of the North Vietnamese. McCain has made fine arguments in defense of his position. And McCain is acting out of the deep and honorable conviction that what he is proposing is not only right but is in the best interest of the United States. His position deserves respect. But that does not mean, as seems to be the assumption in Washington today, that a critical analysis of his "no torture, ever" policy is beyond the pale.

Let's begin with a few analytic distinctions. For the purpose of torture and prisoner maltreatment, there are three kinds of war prisoners:

First, there is the ordinary soldier caught on the field of battle. There is no question that he is entitled to humane treatment. Indeed, we have no right to disturb a hair on his head. His detention has but a single purpose: to keep him *hors de combat.* The proof of that proposition is that if there were a better way to keep him off the battlefield that did not require his detention, we would let him go. Indeed, during one year of the Civil War, the two sides did try an alternative. They mutually "paroled" captured enemy soldiers, i.e., released them to return home on the pledge that they would not take up arms again. (The experiment failed for a foreseeable reason: cheating. Grant found that some paroled Confederates had reenlisted.)

Because the only purpose of detention in these circumstances is to   5 prevent the prisoner from becoming a combatant again, he is entitled to all the protections and dignity of an ordinary domestic prisoner—indeed, more privileges, because, unlike the domestic prisoner, he has committed no crime. He merely had the misfortune to enlist on the other side of a legitimate war. He is therefore entitled to many of the privileges enjoyed by an ordinary citizen—the right to send correspondence, to engage in athletic activity and intellectual pursuits, to receive allowances from relatives—except, of course, for the freedom to leave the prison.

Second, there is the captured terrorist. A terrorist is by profession, indeed by definition, an unlawful combatant: He lives outside the laws of war because he does not wear a uniform, he hides among civilians, and he deliberately targets innocents. He is entitled to no protections whatsoever.

People seem to think that the postwar Geneva Conventions were written only to protect detainees. In fact, their deeper purpose was to provide a deterrent to the kind of barbaric treatment of civilians that had become so horribly apparent during the first half of the twentieth century, and in particular, during the Second World War. The idea was to deter the abuse of civilians by promising combatants who treated noncombatants well that they themselves would be treated according to a code of dignity if captured—and, crucially, that they would be denied the protections of that code if they broke the laws of war and abused civilians themselves.

Breaking the laws of war and abusing civilians are what, to understate the matter vastly, terrorists do for a living. They are entitled, therefore, to nothing. Anyone who blows up a car bomb in a market deserves to spend the rest of his life roasting on a spit over an open fire. But we don't do that because we do not descend to the level of our enemy. We don't do that because, unlike him, we are civilized. Even though terrorists are entitled to no humane treatment, we give it to them because it is in our nature as a moral and humane people. And when on rare occasions we fail to do that, as has occurred in several of the fronts of the war on terror, we are duly disgraced.

The norm, however, is how the majority of prisoners at Guantanamo have been treated. We give them three meals a day, superior medical care, and provision to pray five times a day. Our scrupulousness extends even to providing them with their own Korans, which is the only reason alleged abuses of the Koran at Guantanamo ever became an issue. That we should have provided those who kill innocents in the name of Islam with precisely the document that inspires their barbarism is a sign of the absurd lengths to which we often go in extending undeserved humanity to terrorist prisoners.

Third, there is the terrorist with information. Here the issue of torture gets complicated and the easy pieties don't so easily apply. Let's take the textbook case. Ethics 101: A terrorist has planted a nuclear bomb in New York City. It will go off in one hour. A million people will die. You capture the terrorist. He knows where it is. He's not talking.

Question: If you have the slightest belief that hanging this man by 10 his thumbs will get you the information to save a million people, are you permitted to do it?

Now, on most issues regarding torture, I confess tentativeness and uncertainty. But on this issue, there can be no uncertainty: Not only is it permissible to hang this miscreant by his thumbs. It is a moral duty.

Yes, you say, but that's an extreme and very hypothetical case. Well, not as hypothetical as you think. Sure, the (nuclear) scale is hypothetical, but in the age of the car- and suicide-bomber, terrorists are often captured who have just set a car bomb to go off or sent a suicide bomber out to a coffee shop, and you only have minutes to find out where the attack is to take place. This "hypothetical" is common enough that the Israelis have a term for precisely that situation: the ticking time bomb problem.

And even if the example I gave were entirely hypothetical, the conclusion—yes, in this case even torture is permissible—is telling because it establishes the principle: Torture is not always impermissible. However rare the cases, there are circumstances in which, by any rational moral calculus, torture not only would be permissible but would be required (to acquire life-saving information). And once you've established the principle, to paraphrase George Bernard Shaw, all that's left to haggle about is the price. In the case of torture, that means that the argument is not *whether* torture is ever permissible, but *when*—i.e., under what obviously stringent circumstances: how big, how imminent, how preventable the ticking time bomb.

That is why the McCain amendment, which by mandating "torture never" refuses even to recognize the legitimacy of any moral calculus, cannot be right. There must be exceptions. The real argument should be over what constitutes a legitimate exception.

Let's take an example that is far from hypothetical. You capture 15 Khalid Sheikh Mohammed in Pakistan. He not only has already killed innocents, he is deeply involved in the planning for the present and future killing of innocents. He not only was the architect of the 9/11 attack that killed nearly three thousand people in one day, most of them dying a terrible, agonizing, indeed tortured death. But as the top al Qaeda planner and logistical expert he also knows a lot about terror attacks to come. He knows plans, identities, contacts, materials, cell locations, safe houses, cased targets, etc. What do you do with him?

We have recently learned that since 9/11 the United States has maintained a series of "black sites" around the world, secret detention centers where presumably high-level terrorists like Khalid Sheikh Mohammed have been imprisoned. The world is scandalized. Black sites? Secret detention? Jimmy Carter calls this "a profound and radical change in the . . . moral values of our country." The Council of Europe demands an investigation, calling the claims "extremely worrying." Its human rights commissioner declares "such practices" to constitute "a serious human rights violation, and further proof of the crisis of values" that has engulfed the war on terror. The gnashing of teeth and rending of garments has been considerable.

I myself have not gnashed a single tooth. My garments remain entirely unrent. Indeed, I feel reassured. It would be a gross dereliction of duty for any government *not* to keep Khalid Sheikh Mohammed isolated, disoriented, alone, despairing, cold, and sleepless, in some god-forsaken hidden location in order to find out what he knew about plans for future mass murder. What are we supposed to do? Give him a nice cell in a warm Manhattan prison, complete with Miranda rights, a mellifluous lawyer, and his own Web site? Are not those the kinds of courtesies we extended to the 1993 World Trade Center bombers, then congratulated ourselves on how we "brought to justice" those responsible for an attack that barely failed to kill tens of thousands of Americans, only to discover a decade later that we had accomplished nothing — indeed, that some of the disclosures at the trial had helped Osama bin Laden avoid U.S. surveillance?

Have we learned nothing from 9/11? Are we prepared to go back with complete amnesia to the domestic-crime model of dealing with terrorists, which allowed us to sleepwalk through the nineties while al Qaeda incubated and grew and metastasized unmolested until on 9/11 it finished what the first World Trade Center bombers had begun?

Let's assume (and hope) that Khalid Sheikh Mohammed has been kept in one of these black sites, say, a cell somewhere in Romania, held entirely incommunicado and subjected to the kind of "coercive interrogation" that I described above. McCain has been going around praising the Israelis as the model of how to deal with terrorism and prevent terrorist attacks. He does so because in 1999 the Israeli Supreme Court outlawed all torture in the course of interrogation. But in reality, the Israeli case is far more complicated. And the complications reflect precisely the dilemmas regarding all coercive interrogation, the weighing of the lesser of two evils: the undeniable inhumanity of torture versus the abdication of the duty to protect the victims of a potentially preventable mass murder.

In a summary of Israel's policies, Glenn Frankel of the *Washington Post* noted that the 1999 Supreme Court ruling struck down secret guidelines established twelve years earlier that allowed interrogators to use the kind of physical and psychological pressure I described in imagining how KSM might be treated in America's "black sites." 20

"But after the second Palestinian uprising broke out a year later, and especially after a devastating series of suicide bombings of passenger buses, cafes and other civilian targets," writes Frankel, citing human rights lawyers and detainees, "Israel's internal security service, known as the Shin Bet or the Shabak, returned to physical coercion as a standard practice." Not only do the techniques used "command widespread support from the Israeli public," but "Israeli prime ministers and justice ministers with a variety of political views," including the most conciliatory and liberal, have defended these techniques "as a last resort in preventing terrorist attacks."

Which makes McCain's position on torture incoherent. If this kind of coercive interrogation were imposed on any inmate in the American prison system, it would immediately be declared cruel and unusual, and outlawed. How can he oppose these practices, which the Israelis use, and yet hold up Israel as a model for dealing with terrorists? Or does he countenance this kind of interrogation in extreme circumstances — in which case, what is left of his categorical opposition to inhuman treatment of any kind?

But let us push further into even more unpleasant territory, the territory that lies beyond mere coercive interrogation and beyond McCain's self-contradictions. How far are we willing to go?

This "going beyond" need not be cinematic and ghoulish. (Jay Leno once suggested "duct tape" for Khalid Sheikh Mohammed.) Consider, for example, injection with sodium pentathol. (Colloquially known as "truth serum," it is nothing of the sort. It is a barbiturate whose purpose is to sedate. Its effects are much like that of alcohol: disinhibiting the higher brain centers to make someone more likely to disclose information or thoughts that might otherwise be guarded.) Forcible sedation is a clear violation of bodily integrity. In a civilian context it would be considered assault. It is certainly impermissible under any prohibition of cruel, inhuman, or degrading treatment.

Let's posit that during the interrogation of Khalid Sheikh Mohammed, perhaps early on, we got intelligence about an imminent al Qaeda attack. And we had a very good reason to believe he knew about it. And if we knew what he knew, we could stop it. If we thought we could glean a critical piece of information by use of sodium pentathol, would we be permitted to do so?

Less hypothetically, there is waterboarding, a terrifying and deeply shocking torture technique in which the prisoner has his face exposed to water in a way that gives the feeling of drowning. According to CIA sources cited by ABC News, Khalid Sheikh Mohammed "was able to last between two and 2½ minutes before begging to confess." Should we regret having done that? Should we abolish by law that practice, so that it could never be used on the next Khalid Sheikh Mohammed having thus gotten his confession?

And what if he possessed information with less imminent implications? Say we had information about a cell that he had helped found or direct, and that cell was planning some major attack and we needed information about the identity and location of its members. A rational moral calculus might not permit measures as extreme as the nuke-in-Manhattan scenario, but would surely permit measures beyond mere psychological pressure.

Such a determination would not be made with an untroubled conscience. It would be troubled because there is no denying the monstrous evil that is any form of torture. And there is no denying how corrupting it can be to the individuals and society that practice it. But elected leaders, responsible above all for the protection of their citizens, have the obligation to tolerate their own sleepless nights by doing what is necessary—and only what is necessary, nothing more—to get information that could prevent mass murder.

Given the gravity of the decision, if we indeed cross the Rubicon—as we must—we need rules. The problem with the McCain amendment is that once you have gone public with a blanket ban on all forms of coercion, it is going to be very difficult to publicly carve out exceptions. The Bush administration is to be faulted for having attempted such a codification with the kind of secrecy, lack of coherence, and lack of strict enforcement that led us to the McCain reaction.

What to do at this late date? Begin, as McCain does, by banning 30
all forms of coercion or inhuman treatment by anyone serving in the military—an absolute ban on torture by all military personnel everywhere.
We do not want a private somewhere making these fine distinctions
about ticking and slow-fuse time bombs. We don't even want colonels or
generals making them. It would be best for the morale, discipline, and
honor of the Armed Forces for the United States to maintain an absolute
prohibition, both to simplify their task in making decisions and to offer
them whatever reciprocal treatment they might receive from those who
capture them—although I have no illusion that any anti-torture provision will soften the heart of a single jihadist holding a knife to the throat
of a captured American soldier. We would impose this restriction on ourselves for our own reasons of military discipline and military honor.

Outside the military, however, I would propose, contra McCain, a
ban against all forms of torture, coercive interrogation, and inhuman
treatment, except in two contingencies: (1) the ticking time bomb and
(2) the slower-fuse high-level terrorist (such as KSM). Each contingency
would have its own set of rules. In the case of the ticking time bomb, the
rules would be relatively simple: Nothing rationally related to getting
accurate information would be ruled out. The case of the high-value suspect with slow-fuse information is more complicated. The principle
would be that the level of inhumanity of the measures used (moral honesty is essential here—we would be using measures that are by definition inhumane) would be proportional to the need and value of the
information. Interrogators would be constrained to use the least inhumane treatment necessary relative to the magnitude and imminence of
the evil being prevented and the importance of the knowledge being
obtained.

These exceptions to the no-torture rule would not be granted to just
any nonmilitary interrogators, or anyone with CIA credentials. They
would be reserved for highly specialized agents who are experts and
experienced in interrogation, and who are known not to abuse it for the
satisfaction of a kind of sick sadomasochism Lynndie England and her
cohorts indulged in at Abu Ghraib. Nor would they be acting on their
own. They would be required to obtain written permission for such
interrogations from the highest political authorities in the country (cabinet level) or from a quasi-judicial body modeled on the Foreign
Intelligence Surveillance Court (which permits what would ordinarily be
illegal searches and seizures in the war on terror). Or, if the bomb was
truly ticking and there was no time, the interrogators would be allowed
to act on their own, but would require post facto authorization within,
say, twenty-four hours of their interrogation, so that they knew that
whatever they did would be subject to review by others and be justified
only under the most stringent terms.

One of the purposes of these justifications would be to establish that
whatever extreme measures are used are for reasons of nothing but
information. Historically, the torture of prisoners has been done for a

variety of reasons apart from information, most prominently reasons of justice or revenge. We do not do that. We should not do that. Ever. Khalid Sheikh Mohammed, murderer of 2,973 innocents, is surely deserving of the most extreme suffering day and night for the rest of his life. But it is neither our role nor our right to be the agents of that suffering. Vengeance is mine, sayeth the Lord. His, not ours. Torture is a terrible and monstrous thing, as degrading and morally corrupting to those who practice it as any conceivable human activity including its moral twin, capital punishment.

If Khalid Sheikh Mohammed knew nothing, or if we had reached the point where his knowledge had been exhausted, I'd be perfectly prepared to throw him into a nice, comfortable Manhattan cell and give him a trial to determine what would be fit and just punishment. But as long as he had useful information, things would be different.

Very different. And it simply will not do to take refuge in the claim   35 that all of the above discussion is superfluous because torture never works anyway. Would that this were true. Unfortunately, on its face, this is nonsense. Is one to believe that in the entire history of human warfare, no combatant has ever received useful information by the use of pressure, torture, or any other kind of inhuman treatment? It may indeed be true that torture is not a reliable tool. But that is very different from saying that it is *never* useful.

The monstrous thing about torture is that sometimes it does work. In 1994, nineteen-year-old Israeli corporal Nachshon Waxman was kidnapped by Palestinian terrorists. The Israelis captured the driver of the car used in the kidnapping and tortured him in order to find where Waxman was being held. Yitzhak Rabin, prime minister and peacemaker, admitted that they tortured him in a way that went even beyond the '87 guidelines for "coercive interrogation" later struck down by the Israeli Supreme Court as too harsh. The driver talked. His information was accurate. The Israelis found Waxman. "If we'd been so careful to follow the ['87] Landau Commission [which *allowed* coercive interrogation]," explained Rabin, "we would never have found out where Waxman was being held."

In the Waxman case, I would have done precisely what Rabin did. (The fact that Waxman's Palestinian captors killed him during the Israeli rescue raid makes the case doubly tragic, but changes nothing of the moral calculus.) Faced with a similar choice, an American president would have a similar obligation. To do otherwise—to give up the chance to find your soldier lest you sully yourself by authorizing torture of the person who possesses potentially lifesaving information—is a deeply immoral betrayal of a soldier and countryman. Not as cosmically immoral as permitting a city of one's countrymen to perish, as in the Ethics 101 case. But it remains, nonetheless, a case of moral abdication— of a kind rather parallel to that of the principled pacifist. There is much to admire in those who refuse on principle ever to take up arms under any conditions. But that does not make pure pacifism, like no-torture absolutism, any less a form of moral foolishness, tinged with moral vanity. Not reprehensible, only deeply reproachable and supremely impracticable. People who hold such beliefs are deserving of a certain respect. But they are not to be put in positions of authority. One should be grateful for the saintly among us. And one should be vigilant that they not get to make the decisions upon which the lives of others depend.

Which brings us to the greatest irony of all in the torture debate. I have just made what will be characterized as the pro-torture case contra McCain by proposing two major exceptions carved out of any no-torture rule: the ticking time bomb and the slow-fuse high-value terrorist. McCain supposedly is being hailed for defending all that is good and right and just in America by standing foursquare against any inhuman treatment. Or is he?

According to *Newsweek*, in the ticking time bomb case McCain says that the president should disobey the very law that McCain seeks to pass—under the justification that "you do what you have to do. But you take responsibility for it." But if torturing the ticking time bomb suspect is "what you have to do," then why has McCain been going around arguing that such things must never be done?

As for exception number two, the high-level terrorist with slow-fuse information, Stuart Taylor, the superb legal correspondent for *National Journal*, argues that with appropriate legal interpretation, the "cruel, inhuman, or degrading" standard, "though vague, is said by experts to codify . . . the commonsense principle that the toughness of interrogation techniques should be calibrated to the importance and urgency of the information likely to be obtained." That would permit "some very aggressive techniques . . . on that small percentage of detainees who seem especially likely to have potentially life-saving information." Or as Evan Thomas and Michael Hirsh put it in the *Newsweek* report on McCain and torture, the McCain standard would "presumably allow for a sliding scale" of torture or torture-lite or other coercive techniques, thus permitting "for a very small percentage—those High Value Targets like Khalid Sheikh Mohammed—some pretty rough treatment." 40

But if that is the case, then McCain embraces the same exceptions I do, but prefers to pretend he does not. If that is the case, then his much-touted and endlessly repeated absolutism on inhumane treatment is merely for show. If that is the case, then the moral preening and the phony arguments can stop now, and we can all agree that in this real world of astonishingly murderous enemies, in two very circumscribed circumstances, we must all be prepared to torture. Having established that, we can then begin to work together to codify rules of interrogation for the two very unpleasant but very real cases in which we are morally permitted—indeed morally compelled—to do terrible things.

TOPICS FOR CRITICAL THINKING AND WRITING

1. How does Krauthammer define torture? Do you agree with his definition? Explain.

2. Krauthammer would allow torture in two kinds of cases. What objections, if any, do you offer to these exceptions?

3. Do you think Krauthammer would hold that torture was permissible during the American War of Independence for captured British and Hessian soldiers?

4. What are the Geneva Conventions, and does Krauthammer accept or reject them?

5. What is "waterboarding" (para. 26)? Is it a permissible method of torture for Krauthammer?

6. What is "the ticking time bomb problem" (para. 31), and what does Krauthammer think it proves?

7. If Krauthammer thinks torture is such a morally terrible thing to do, why does he make exceptions to its prohibition?

8. How might Krauthammer respond to the objection that once a government opens the door to torture, it proves very difficult, if not impossible, to close it?

Association for the Prevention of Torture

The Association, founded in 1977, describes itself as "an independent non-governmental organization based in Geneva."

Defusing the Ticking Bomb Scenario

Defusing the Ticking Bomb Scenario reaffirms and reinforces the absolute and non-derogable prohibition of torture and all other forms of cruel, inhuman, or degrading treatment or punishment, against challenges based on the so-called ticking bomb scenario.

Torture must be seen for what it is: abhorrent and shameful. Torture is never courageous or honorable. There is good reason why torture, like genocide and slavery, became taboo in the modern era, and taboo it must remain.

WHAT IS THE TICKING BOMB SCENARIO?

The ticking bomb scenario is a hypothetical "thought experiment" that is used to question the absolute prohibition of torture. It can be formulated as follows:

Suppose that a perpetrator of an imminent terrorist attack, that will kill many people, is in the hands of the authorities and that he will disclose the information needed to prevent the attack only if he is tortured. Should he be tortured?

In public discussions, the scenario is often posed as a personal question to someone who is before an audience and says they are against torture. In this context it is often personalized:

> But suppose that you know of an imminent attack that will kill thousands of people and you have the perpetrator. The only way to prevent the attack is to torture him. Would you do it, yes or no?

WHY ARE SO MANY PEOPLE TALKING ABOUT THE SCENARIO?

The ticking bomb scenario operates by manipulating the emotional reactions of the audience. It creates a context of fear and anger. It artificially tilts the circumstances to evoke sympathy or even admiration for the torturer, and hatred or indifference towards the torture victim. Its dramatic nature has made it a favorite plotline for popular television programs and action movies. It creates a powerful mental image that has to some extent captured the imagination of a portion of the global public, meaning that discussion of the scenario has taken on a momentum of its own, beyond its original explicitly legal/political context. This has made its impact a matter of grave concern, not just among human rights organizations and advocates, but among senior members of military institutions as well.[1]

Whatever the reason for its presentation in a given context, the intended effect of the ticking bomb scenario is to create doubt about the wisdom of the absolute prohibition of torture. This doubt, in turn, is usually designed to lead the audience to accept the creation of a legal exception to the prohibition, or at least to accept non-application of the criminal law against torture in particular cases. The true aim of proponents of the ticking bomb argument may be to create a broad exception while seeming to argue for a narrow one. By trying to force torture opponents to concede that torture may be acceptable in at least one extreme case, proponents of the ticking bomb argument hope to undermine the very idea that opposition to torture must be absolute as a matter of principle and practice. As such, the scenario has been given prominence lately by those who seek to end the taboo against torture, to make its application to prisoners suspected of involvement in terrorism seem acceptable, and to provide legal immunity for themselves and others who authorize, tolerate, order, or inflict it.

---

[1]See, for example, the article "Whatever it Takes: The Politics of the Man Behind 24" by Jane Mayer, *The New Yorker* (19 February 2007), describing the deep concerns expressed by U.S. Army Brigadier General Patrick Finnegan, dean of the U.S. Military Academy at West Point, about the toxic effect of the ticking bomb torture plots of the popular TV show 24 on the real-life ethical judgment of the commanders-in-training he teaches.

"NO" TO ANY EXCEPTION TO THE TORTURE PROHIBITION

The stakes raised by the ticking bomb scenario are high: the destruction of the absolute prohibition of torture. The answer must be a correspondingly resolute "NO" to any exception to the prohibition of torture, no matter how narrow the circumstances are claimed to be.

A quick explanation of this absolute "NO" could be as follows:

First, the idea that I, you, or any other average citizen (or for that matter any government agent), with no prior experience or training in torture, could actually succeed in getting information from a terrorist (likely trained or indoctrinated to resist it) is ridiculous.

On the other hand, if you are asking me whether I, you, or anyone else in our society, should become a trained torturer desensitized to the pain and suffering of people under my control, in anticipation of some hypothetical future case, my answer is no. I don't want to become that kind of person and I don't want people like that in my society. Anyway, as intelligence professionals attest, we would stand a much better chance of actually getting life-saving information by using persuasion, trickery, or some other means. So, if my life depended on getting fast, accurate, information, I sure wouldn't want anyone wasting their time on torture.

This is only a quick answer, however. The following sections set out much more detailed arguments, including:

1. Exposing the fallacies in the scenario itself in order to demonstrate its misleading nature by first exposing the hidden assumptions of the scenario and second debunking those assumptions.
2. Reiterating the toxic effect of torture, like its brethren slavery and genocide, on the societies that tolerate it.
3. Revealing the slippery slope towards the more wide-spread use of torture that any supposedly "exceptional" tolerance of torture would set us down.
4. Recalling the absolute and fundamental nature of the legal prohibition of torture.
5. Highlighting the ways in which the ticking bomb scenario manipulates moral and ethical judgment by obscuring the true moral cost of tolerating any act of torture.

ASSUMPTIONS OF THE SCENARIO

The ticking bomb is based on a number of assumptions, some of   10 which may be hidden or only implied when it is first presented. These hidden assumptions should be exposed.

For instance, the ticking bomb scenario typically supposes certainty, or near certainty, as to all of the following:

1. A specific planned attack is known to exist.
2. The attack will happen within a very short time (it is "imminent").

3. The attack will kill a large number of people.
4. The person in custody is a perpetrator of the attack.
5. The person has information that will prevent the attack.
6. Torturing the person will obtain the information in time to prevent the attack.
7. No other means exist that might get the information in time.
8. No other action could be taken to avoid the harm.

The scenario also assumes:

9. The motive of the torturer is to get information, with the genuine intention of saving lives, and nothing more.
10. It is an isolated situation, not often to be repeated.

The proponent of the scenario may adjust these assumptions or otherwise make concessions in response to challenges, in order to make the scenario more realistic. Such maneuvers can be pointed to as evidence that the scenario inevitably leads to a much wider exception to the prohibition of torture than was initially suggested, and ultimately down a disastrously "slippery slope" (described in greater detail below). In any event, the "pure" ticking bomb scenario described by these ten assumptions is the hardest case; if it can be dealt with, more realistic variations (and therefore broader exceptions) should be easier to counter.

DEBUNKING THE ASSUMPTIONS

These assumptions can be challenged to demonstrate that any real-world "exception" to accommodate the ticking bomb scenario would actually be much broader than the artificially narrow situation initially described. In part, this is because in the real world we individually and collectively are always acting on partial information and varying degrees of uncertainty.

Demonstrating the true scope of the "exception" through debunking some or all of the assumptions (as is explained in greater detail below), reveals that what is really being proposed is not a rare exception but a new rule permitting torture, which would take us back to the Dark Ages and the worst totalitarian societies. Ultimately, accepting the "ends justify the means" logic of any "ticking bomb" exception to the prohibition of torture, means adopting the same moral principles as terrorism itself.

Debunking the assumptions also demonstrates how little the idea of 15 the pure ticking bomb scenario contributes to any serious consideration of the problem of torture, or for that matter the problem of terrorism.

The debunking exercise can raise the following points:

Assumption 1: A specific planned attack is known to exist.

Assumption 2: The attack will happen within a very short time (is imminent). As the scenario is being presented, consciously or not, in favor of some sort of legal exception to the prohibition, precision is essential. How "imminent" exactly, then, must an attack be to justify torture? Hours? Days? Months?

On the one hand, to represent some type of ticking bomb scenario, the timing of attack must be far enough in the future that there is a realistic chance of doing something to stop it. On the other hand, if it is so far off in the future that the loss of life can be prevented in some other way (evacuation, for instance) then the supposed "need" for torture simply disappears. Furthermore, the more time until the attack, the greater the chance that humane interrogation methods will produce results.

Assumption 3: The attack will kill a large number of people. 20
Again, given that a legal exception to the prohibition of torture is at stake, precision is required. How many lives must be at risk to justify torture? Ten? A hundred? A thousand? 10,000? 100,000? More? Or less? Is one enough to justify torture?

Assumption 4: The person in custody is a perpetrator of the attack.

Assumption 5: The person has information that will prevent the attack. In the "pure" ticking bomb scenario, the person in custody is someone who is known beyond doubt to be a perpetrator of the attack and possesses information that can prevent it. This is the stuff of TV drama and Hollywood action movies, where the super-villain has a super-ego that compels him to boast and taunt his captors. In reality, the torturers are unlikely to have such a degree of certainty that the person they are holding is a perpetrator or even has relevant information. One of the most insidious things about torture is that, perversely, a person who has no connection to, or knowledge of, the attack is likely to suffer the deepest and longest, having no means to affect his or her fate and no hope of anything but continued torture.

Ultimately, some proponents of a ticking bomb exception to the prohibition of torture may be willing to go further and concede that they would allow torture of someone who ultimately is not involved in any terrorist activity, and who may turn out not to have any relevant information. Of course, the point at which any particular proponent of a ticking bomb exception would draw the line will vary, but any proponent should be pressed to say whether their proposed exception would be flexible enough to allow the torture of:

- a person who the authorities are almost certain is a perpetrator, but who denies it.
- any person who the authorities suspect of any degree of involvement.
- a person not suspected of involvement, but who has relevant information that he or she is for some reason unwilling to divulge.

- a relative who is not involved but may know, for instance, where their family member may be hiding.

- a child who may or may not know some relevant information but does not trust the authorities or has been told not to tell.

- a child who has no relevant information, but whose torture in the presence of the perpetrator is the only thing that can get him to talk.

If the proponent agrees to torture some or all of the broader range of victims described above, this can be highlighted as illustrating how any supposedly narrow ticking bomb exception quickly and naturally grows to drag more and more victims into its clutches.

Assumption 6: Torturing the person will obtain the informa- 25 **tion in time to prevent the attack.** First, the scenario assumes that the information the tortured person gives will be correct and not misinformation designed to send authorities in the wrong direction until the bomb goes off (i.e. wild goose chases). However, short timelines are integral to the scenario, and the scenario also implies that the torture will stop as soon as the interrogator believes he has the information needed to stop the attack (as he would have to do if his motives are genuine). Thus, it seems likely that a perpetrator would be able both to stop the torture and to misdirect authorities long enough for the bomb to go off, in which case torture is not likely to be an effective means of preventing the attack.

Second, it is important to understand that torture is not some sort of magic fix. The types of persons who would plan and execute such an attack are the very ones most likely to have been trained to withstand torture until it is too late anyway. Indeed, professional interrogators have repeatedly emphasised that interrogation can be conducted much more effectively without the use of torture, and that if they thought they had only one opportunity to succeed, they would not choose torture as their "one shot" at success.[2]

Third, even assuming that torture could be effective in such circumstances, the short timelines involved would presumably mean that you would need the "best" torturers to be readily available if you intend to rely on torture to save the day. This in turn assumes that societies facing sophisticated attacks would establish the institutional arrangements to create and maintain a professional class of torturers, and to equip them with continuously-updated torture techniques and equipment. Grave dangers to democracy and to individual freedoms would be posed by an institutionalized professional "torture squad." This more realistic picture

---

[2]See, for example: "Whatever it Takes" (cited above); the 31 July 2006 "Statement on Interrogation Practices" presented to the U.S. Congress by twenty former interrogators; Amnesty International USA's online Q&A session with former interrogator Peter Bauer (www.amnestyusa.org).

of becoming prepared to torture in a ticking bomb scenario is much less palatable than the naive idea that a "heroic Everyman" could spontaneously and on a one-time basis effectively apply torture to a supposed perpetrator, presumably trained to resist such treatment. Further, devoting resources to developing a capacity to torture in this way would only divert resources from developing greater capacity for other means of preventing such an attack.

Assumption 7: No other means exist that might get the information in time. Usually the scenario is based on the premise that the torturer already knows everything about the plot except for one key piece of information that the victim, and maybe only the victim, knows. This of course naturally leads to the question of whether, having all this information, it is really possible that there are no other leads to pursue, including humane methods of interrogation, search warrants, wiretaps, and so on?

Assumption 8: No other action could be taken to avoid the harm. The ticking bomb scenario assumes that no other action can be taken to avoid the harm. This assumption may be worth questioning. In a pure ticking bomb scenario, there must not be enough time or means to evacuate the building, neighborhood, or city under threat, whether because the attack will happen too soon or its target is too imprecisely known.

Assumption 9: Genuine motive of the torturer? Even if the 30
torturer were to begin with the genuine motive only to torture to obtain the specific piece of information, torture corrupts. This is in the nature of torture. For instance, a former U.S. military interrogator in Iraq described how in applying torture to detainees he was affected by the desire for revenge and a "thrilling" feeling associated with provoking fear in others.[3] Proponents of the "ticking bomb" exception insist that the aim of torture is intelligence gathering, not punishment. In the real world, however, motives are not that simple. Anger, a thirst for payback, and the desire "to show who's boss" can all-too-easily take over under extreme circumstances, and it is unrealistic to assume that interrogators' motives will be pure.

Assumption 10: It is an isolated situation. As will be explained in greater detail, it is in the nature of torture that any authorization of torture, whether granted in advance through legal permissions or granted post-facto by non-prosecution or other means, leads inevitably to a "slippery slope" where its use quickly becomes much more widespread.

[3] *Washington Post*, "The Tortured Lives of Interrogators." Monday, June 4, 2007; p. A01.

Especially if contemplation of the ticking bomb scenario were to lead to establishment of a legal exception, we must anticipate a grave proliferation of torture.

Usually the process of debunking shows that not even the *proponent* 30 of an exception can precisely delineate the circumstances in which he or she considers torture to be "justified." Even if the proponent could clearly describe such circumstances in ordinary language, it is even less probable that a legal exception could be crafted whose application is precisely limited to the kind of situation contemplated. Even assuming such precise legal language could be found, it is even more improbable that there could be any agreement on the scope of persons who could lawfully be tortured.

ARGUMENTS IN RESPONSE TO THE SCENARIO AS A WHOLE

Once the assumptions hidden in the ticking bomb scenario have been exposed and challenged, several things should be clear. The scenario's popularity of late is part of a concerted effort to create a legal exception to the prohibition against torture. The lack of precision in defining the scope of the scenario means that any such exception will necessarily be much broader than the "pure" ticking bomb scenario initially suggests.

The next step, therefore, is to set out the reasons why any talk of an exception to the prohibition of torture must be categorically rejected. Some of the arguments in this regard are:

1. Torture, Slavery, Genocide: Destroyers of Humanity
2. Slippery Slope
3. Legal Prohibition
4. Morality and Ethics

1. Torture, Slavery, Genocide: Destroyers of Humanity Among 35 the progressive achievements of humanity over the course of our shared history, one of the most fundamental advances was the recognition around the world that each and every human being is indeed an individual person, as is enshrined for instance in the Universal Declaration of Human Rights. It may seem astonishing to think that there was a time when societies generally considered it respectable, normal, or tolerable for some human beings to view others as little more than animals, to be used as one needed or pleased; and indeed we should celebrate the incomprehensibility of such beliefs to most people today.

Several further realizations followed from this fundamental understanding. Believing in human dignity required that dignity be accorded to every human being. Certain ways of treating others were also recognized as being fundamentally incompatible with their recognition as individual persons, as human beings, and as such never justified.

In order to consolidate this foundation of progressive discovery and recognition of the humanity of one another, practices such as slavery, genocide, and torture were absolutely prohibited by international law. The fundamental incompatibility of any of these practices with the recognition of another person as a human being, means they can never be tolerated without shattering the common edifice of humanity on which human society itself is based. Torture, slavery, genocide: each of these acts always denies not only the dignity but the very humanity of its victims.

Genocide cannot be justified by claiming, perhaps even truthfully, that one will only apply it once, or only if forced to by some kind of extreme emergency. Slavery cannot be justified by claiming it is instituted in the pursuit of a greater good. Just as no one could justify the enslavement of a people as necessary to the survival of another, and no one could justify a genocide even to prevent another larger genocide, anyone who attempts to justify torture in the name of saving lives is assaulting the common humanity of us all. We must treat them with shame and revulsion as we would any proponent of genocide or slavery.

2. The Slippery Slope Any legal exception created to accommodate a ticking bomb scenario would inevitably lead us down a slippery slope, at the bottom of which torture becomes arbitrary and unpunished, or widespread and systematic, or both. The ultimate result of any exception to the prohibition of torture is the erosion of democratic institutions and the destruction of any open, free and just society. At the end of the day, we have much more to lose by creating a legal exception to accommodate some future ticking bomb scenario, than we do by maintaining the absolute prohibition of torture even if that means assuming some hypothetical risk. This is because arguments about the ticking bomb hypothetical are not truly about what we *would* do in some imagined future, it is about the kind of society we want to live in *today* and every day.

If it exists in reality at all, the pure ticking bomb scenario is vanish- 40 ingly rare. It does not correspond to the reality of the vast majority of events, where a plot is foiled before the intended attack becomes imminent, or the attack takes place, but there was no perpetrator in custody immediately beforehand who could have revealed information to avert the attack. Further, since the ticking bomb scenario is often raised in the context of threats represented by organized networks of terrorists, it is worth recognizing that any attack planned by a network is likely to be designed to succeed even if one of their members is taken into custody. This only emphasises how rarely all the improbable assumptions of the pure ticking bomb scenario could coincide. If such situations are so rare, does it make sense to twist our system of international and national laws to accommodate them, even assuming one agreed with the calculus posed by the pure hypothetical (which, for the reasons explained earlier, we do not)?

It is in the nature of law that creating exceptions to deal with largely unknown future risks can undermine the effectiveness of the underlying prohibition in the present. This is in part because the exception must be cast in broad terms to encompass the specific facts of any such theoretical situation should it appear in the real world. Yet, casting the exception so broadly means that it comes to be applied to situations much different from those for which it was originally intended. Legislative bodies are also extremely risk-averse when it comes to public safety, and can be expected over time to gradually increase the scope of any exception, as has been the case with virtually every counter-terrorism measure enacted since 2001. Torture in particular has an extremely corrosive social effect. Law as an institution cannot accommodate any exception to the prohibition of torture without the prohibition itself quickly becoming ineffective. Creating a legal exception to the prohibition of torture can be expected to open the flood gates to much more widespread use of torture in practice.

Further, since it is not realistic to expect near certainty about the various elements of the scenario in any real-world situation, any exception based on the ticking bomb scenario would presumably allow torture to be carried out based on various degrees of suspicion. As the degree of certainty required declines, the likelihood that people who are not involved at all will be tortured based on mistaken identity, or for having been at the "wrong place at the wrong time," increases.

History also shows that any tolerance of torture leads to its proliferation, in respect of other types of "evil" as serious as the "ticking bomb" evil, and in respect of its use for purposes other than obtaining information.

The establishment of a legalised exception in a single state would also cause international proliferation. If states that purport to be world leaders on human rights express their tolerance of torture, even in narrow circumstances, other states will take this as their cue to continue or expand their own use of torture against their own populations, in a much broader range of circumstances than the ticking bomb scenario. It is not hard to see the huge reduction in diplomatic leverage that would result for a state that goes from being a "torture prohibitionist" to simply being a less enthusiastic torturer.

Further, using torture ourselves allows other countries to more easily justifying using torture against our own soldiers and nationals. It is no wonder, then, that many military leaders themselves strongly object to any tolerance of torture among their own forces.

The use or tolerance of torture by a democratic government as a counter-terrorism measure blurs the moral distinctions between such a government and the terrorists, at least in the eyes of populations in third states. It is precisely the terrorists' attempt to justify inhuman acts in the name of some greater good, that forms the basis for criticism of their actions by governments. It also feeds into the claim of terrorists that democratic governments only pretend to live by strong principles, and readily abandon them when it suits them. Finally, torture itself can radicalize both its victims and their sympathizers. All of this only makes it easier for terrorist networks to recruit new members and win the sympathy or support of local populations, which could eventually simply lead to more attacks, presumably feeding the argument for more torture to be used in response.

Every minute that is spent contemplating and planning for the use of torture as a counter-terrorism measure is also a minute not spent on building capacity to use other means to prevent attacks. Over time, focussing on coercive techniques that frequently generate unreliable or useless information distracts resources away from the development and deployment of other more appropriate investigation techniques. Reliance on torture as an investigative technique in some circumstances tends to lead to dependence on torture as a general practice.

Finally, we must recognize that being prepared to use torture, even in exceptional circumstances, implies certain institutional arrangements that seem fundamentally inconsistent with the kind of society most people desire. We can anticipate clandestine interrogation centers staffed with interrogators trained in torture techniques (presumably in some sort of torture academy). On our streets we would walk amongst men and women who have been encouraged to override their natural revulsion at causing pain and suffering to another human being helpless to defend himself. Researchers and entrepreneurs would work to discover and produce ever more horrific torture equipment and techniques. In the past these types of institutional arrangements have been associated with the Nazis, with other fascist states and totalitarian societies and dictatorships. What would it say about our society if we were to adopt the same techniques that were central to theirs? What kind of company do we wish to keep?

3. The Legal Prohibition The absolute prohibition of torture and other cruel, inhuman and degrading treatment or punishment is included in every relevant international treaty and is a norm of general (customary) international law binding on all states. No exception or derogation to the prohibition is permitted in any circumstances, even emergencies.

Torture is a crime under international law for which states have agreed every perpetrator must ultimately be brought to justice no matter where in the world he is found.

Neither ticking bomb-type circumstances nor any other claim to 50 have acted with good motives can ever be a valid basis to exempt a person from criminal responsibility for torture. Necessity, self-defence, and other justification defences are not permitted in any case of torture, no matter how extreme or grave the circumstances.[4] Even in the unlikely circumstances of the ticking bomb scenario, torturers must not be exonerated from legal responsibility for their crimes; otherwise, pleas of "I thought it was necessary" would thereafter rob the law against torture of any real force.

However, a separate question is the specific sentence appropriate to any individual case of torture. From a human rights perspective it is important to make sure that each sentence is individualized to the circumstances of the offence and the convicted person, keeping in mind that all sentences in torture cases must take into account the grave nature of all such acts.[5]

4. Morality and Ethics Expression by the countries of the world of our fundamental shared moral values can be found in the Universal Declaration of Human Rights and other Declarations by the United Nations General Assembly.

The fifth article of the Universal Declaration of Human Rights states that "No one shall be subjected to torture or to cruel, inhuman or degrading treatment or punishment."

This prohibition is reinforced by article two of the UN General Assembly Declaration against Torture, which says:

> Any act of torture or other cruel, inhuman, or degrading treatment or punishment is an offence to human dignity and shall be condemned as a denial of the purposes of the Charter of the United Nations and as a violation of the human rights and fundamental freedoms proclaimed in the Universal Declaration of Human Rights.

Article three of the Declaration against Torture eliminates any doubt that the nations of the world have already long rejected the moral logic of the ticking bomb scenario:

> Exceptional circumstances such as a state of war or a threat of war, internal political instability, or any other public emergency may not be invoked as a justification of torture or other cruel, inhuman, or degrading treatment or punishment.

As was noted earlier, the substance of these Declarations have also become part of international law, and there is no question that any use of torture in a ticking bomb situation is a violation of international law and a crime under international law. However, even leaving aside the question

---

[4]Article 2(2) and (3) of the UN Convention against Torture: "No exceptional circumstances whatsoever, whether a state of war or a threat of war, internal political in stability, or any other public emergency, may be invoked as a justification of torture. An order from a superior officer or a public authority may not be invoked as a justification of torture."
[5]Article 4(2) of the UN Convention against Torture.

of international legality, there are solid moral and ethical grounds for rejecting any act of torture in a ticking bomb situation or any attempt to legalize torture under any circumstances under national law.

It is worth distinguishing the question of what moral response society should take in anticipation of a realistic ticking bomb scenario, from the question of what any individual person would or would not in fact do were they to find themselves in such circumstances. The way in which the ticking bomb scenario is most often posed is designed to blur these lines, and this is one of its most dangerous and insidious effects.

Of course, for many people the answer to the question "what should society morally expect of me" and "what should I morally do" will be the same: Torture is absolutely prohibited as a matter of morals and ethics, and so no torture must be applied or tolerated no matter how great the costs. People may find the basis for an absolute moral prohibition against torture, at both the personal and societal level, in any of a range of sources: the same universal and absolute commitment to human dignity from which the UN human rights declarations emanate; or personal systems of ethics; or religious faith; or military doctrine; or elsewhere.

That any of these sources of moral and ethical belief might lead a person to reject the use of torture in the ticking bomb scenario, in both societal and personal moral terms, should not be surprising given the many aspects that make torture particularly terrible:

- It is among the worst kinds of suffering a person can inflict on another. Many people would rather die than undergo torture.

- The tortured captive is helpless. A person who has no information is entirely unable to affect his or her fate and faces only continued torture.

- The victim's human dignity has been reduced to nothing, his body and mind treated as a mere means.

- The society that tolerates or endorses the act thereby tolerates or endorses one person intentionally depriving another of the totality of his human dignity, degrading the society itself.

- The consequences of torture are often lifelong.

- Torture is intimately associated with the most horrific and oppressive governments that human history has ever known.

- Torture is the concentrated essence of tyranny, one person tyrannizing another — the breaking of a person's will by inflicting pain. Our society cannot tolerate tyranny, it is the opposite of our society.

- Most normal human beings feel an intense physical revulsion in witnessing or even imagining the mutilation or infliction of severe pain on others.

- The torturer himself may be corrupted, psychologically damaged, degraded, and deprived of dignity by the acts, with consequent harm to his family and others around him.

Nor should we be surprised that the personal moral commitment 60 against torture of many people would imply that they accept the risk that many others could lose their lives as a result. While protecting human lives is important, most people believe there is more to human existence than simply preserving individual lives. Indeed, people consciously choose to sacrifice their own lives all the time for the preservation of a way of life. The core international human rights treaties and the laws of war codify the principle that there are some things so morally reprehensible that they cannot be used even when the life of a nation is at stake, and torture is expressly listed among those things.

But one need not believe that as a matter of personal ethics he or she would never use torture even in the pure ticking bomb scenario, in order to reject any attempt to justify torture as morally acceptable at the societal level. The utilitarian calculation that lies within the pure ticking bomb scenario manipulates the moral intuition of audiences by making obvious only some of the consequences of torturing or not torturing, while hiding other consequences that are equally or more grave. When these hidden consequences are brought into the equation, it becomes clearer that creating any exception to the absolute legal and moral rule against torture, would lead to practical and moral consequences that vastly outweigh any theoretical moral "injustice" that could arise from convicting an individual torturer in such circumstances.

For example, the scenario hides from the audience the reality that creating an exception would, as it has in all historical precedents, lead to a proliferation of torture over time. Thus, we must no longer weigh the suffering of one or a few potential perpetrators in any utilitarian calculus, we must add the suffering of these many hundreds or thousands or more other, potentially completely uninvolved, future victims. We must weigh the corrosive effect on society of accepting the risk of torturing individuals who have no connection to terrorism, through cases of mistaken identity such as those that have already come to light in the revelations about international renditions to torture. We must consider the consequences of preparing ourselves to use torture: creating a professional class of torturers, training and equipping them. We must add to the scenario the long-term effect of adopting the methods of terrorists, which would likely include an increase in the number of terrorist attacks, in so far as our use of torture could lead to the expanded recruitment of new members of terrorist networks, or less willingness of foreign populations to cooperate with efforts to prevent future acts of terrorism. For instance, people who otherwise would provide us information about planned attacks may be reluctant to do so if they fear this will lead to further interrogation through torture of themselves or others, or resent our use of torture against others they know or with whom they identify. There are other intangible but grave effects on a society whose government promotes or tolerates the intentional infliction of suffering on those whose bodies it controls: Torture is a poison, and once even a small amount of this poison is injected into the society's lifeblood it will spread and corrupt the flesh until the entire patient is consumed.

Once these factors are added into the equation, the utilitarian balance implicit in the ticking bomb scenario is no longer artificially weighted in favor of torture. Thus, even those who approach the scenario from a utilitarian, rather than an absolute, moral perspective, must morally reject any legalization of any act of torture. In short, the response of society to any attempt to justify torture must always be to insist that torture is never morally justified.

CONCLUSION

We return, then, to where we began. The absolute and non-derogable prohibition of torture and all other forms of cruel, inhuman, and degrading treatment or punishment, must be unwaveringly promoted, not only the face of challenges based on the so-called ticking bomb scenario, but everywhere that torture or talk of torture still lurks.

Torture is of the same species as genocide and slavery. The political and legal projects that have become associated with the ticking bomb scenario must be rejected in precisely the same way we would meet any proposal for the use of genocide or slavery: with condemnation, shame, abhorrence, and a resounding and absolute "NO." 65

ACKNOWLEDGEMENTS

This text was prepared by the Association for the Prevention of Torture (APT) based on consultation with the following individuals and organizations present at a meeting held in Geneva in June 2007:

Amnesty International.
Dr Jean Maria Arrigo, International Intelligence Ethics Association.
Sylvie Bukhari-de Pontual, President, International Federation of Action by Christians for the Abolition of Torture (FIACAT).
Claire Chimelli, Geneva Representative, International Federation of Action by Christians for the Abolition of Torture (FIACAT).
Ralph Crawshaw, former Police Chief Superintendent; Fellow, Essex Human Rights Centre.
Edouard Delaplace, UN & Legal Senior Programme Officer, Association for the Prevention of Torture (APT).
Carla Ferstman, Director, The Redress Trust.
Bernadette Jung, Delegate of International Bureau, International Federation of Action by Christians for the Abolition of Torture (FIACAT).
Anne-Laurence Lacroix, Deputy Director, World Organisation Against Torture (OMCT).
David Luban, University Professor and Professor of Law and Philosophy, Georgetown University Law Center.

Nieves Molina Clemente, Legal Adviser, International Rehabilitation Council for Torture Victims (IRCT).
Matt Pollard, Legal Adviser, Association for the Prevention of Torture (APT).
Eric Prokosch, Board Member, Association for the Prevention of Torture (APT).
Dr Jose Quiroga, Vice-President, International Rehabilitation Council for Torture Victims (IRCT).
Dr Lawrence Rockwood, former military counter-intelligence officer.
Sir Nigel Rodley, Professor of Law and Chair of the Human Rights Centre, University of Essex; Member of UN Human Rights Committee; former UN Special Rapporteur on Torture.
James Ross, Senior Legal Advisor, Human Rights Watch.
Eric Sottas, Director, World Organisation Against Torture (OMCT).
Wilder Tayler, Deputy Secretary General, International Commission of Jurists (ICJ).
Mark Thomson, Secretary General, Association for the Prevention of Torture (APT).
Fernando Delgado, JD Candidate, Harvard Law School.

TOPICS FOR CRITICAL THINKING AND WRITING

1. What is a "non-derogable prohibition" (para. 1)? Should torture be non-derogable? Explain your answer.

2. Why does the "ticking bomb scenario" (paras. 13–14) require—if it does—granting the ten "assumptions" identified by the APT? Or does it?

3. Why does the APT connect the ticking bomb with "torture, slavery, genocide" (paras. 39–42)? Can you think of other modes of treatment that deserve to be added to this list of three, or do you think the list is exhaustive as it stands? Or is it wrong-headed?

4. From a moral point of view (paras. 57–63), what are the worst things involved in the use or threat of torture?

5. What are the practices the APT mentions that are alternatives to torture—that are more effective and less harmful?

6. What is a "torture squad" (para. 27) and why is the APT concerned about creating such an entity?

For topical links related to the discussion of the use of torture, see the companion Web site: **bedfordstmartins.com/barnetbedau.**

PART SIX

ENDURING QUESTIONS: ESSAYS, a STORY, POEMS, and a PLAY

32

What Is the Ideal Society?

Thomas More

The son of a prominent London lawyer, More (1478–1535) served as a page in the household of the Archbishop of Canterbury, went to Oxford University, and then studied law in London. More's charm, brilliance, and gentle manner caused Erasmus, the great Dutch humanist who became his friend during a visit to London, to write to a friend: "Did nature ever create anything kinder, sweeter, or more harmonious than the character of Thomas More?"

More served in Parliament, became a diplomat, and after holding several important positions in the government of Henry VIII, rose to become Lord Chancellor. But when Henry married Anne Boleyn, broke from the Church of Rome, and established himself as head of the Church of England, More refused to subscribe to the Act of Succession and Supremacy. Condemned to death as a traitor, he was executed in 1535, nominally for treason but really because he would not recognize the king rather than the pope as the head of his church. A moment before the ax fell, More displayed a bit of the whimsy for which he was known: When he put his head on the block, he brushed his beard aside, commenting that his beard had done no offense to the king. In 1886 the Roman Catholic Church beatified More, and in 1935, the four-hundredth anniversary of his death, it canonized him as St. Thomas More.

More wrote Utopia *(1514–15) in Latin, the international language of the day. The book's name, however, is Greek for "no place" (*ou topos*), with a pun on "good place" (*eu topos*).* Utopia *owes something to Plato's* Republic *and something to then-popular accounts of voyagers such as Amerigo Vespucci.* Utopia *purports to record an account given by a traveler named Hytholodaeus (Greek for "learned in nonsense"), who allegedly visited Utopia. The work is playful, but it is also serious. In truth, it is hard to know exactly where it is serious and how serious it is. One inevitably wonders, for example, if More the devoted Roman Catholic could really have advocated euthanasia. And could More the persecutor of heretics really have approved of the religious tolerance practiced in Utopia? Is he perhaps in effect saying, "Let's see what reason, unaided by Christian revelation, can tell us about an ideal society"? But if so, is he nevertheless also saying, very strongly, that Christian countries, though blessed with the revelation of Christ's teachings, are far behind these unenlightened pagans?* Utopia *has been widely praised by all sorts of readers—from Roman Catholics to communists—but for all sorts of reasons. The selection presented here is about one-twelfth of the book (in a translation by Paul Turner).*

From *Utopia*

[A DAY IN UTOPIA]

And now for their working conditions. Well, there's one job they all do, irrespective of sex, and that's farming. It's part of every child's education. They learn the principles of agriculture at school, and they're taken for regular outings into the fields near the town, where they not only watch farm work being done, but also do some themselves, as a form of exercise.

Besides farming which, as I say, is everybody's job, each person is taught a special trade of his own. He may be trained to process wool or flax, or he may become a stonemason, a blacksmith, or a carpenter. Those are the only trades that employ any considerable quantity of labor. They have no tailors or dressmakers, since everyone on the island wears the same sort of clothes—except that they vary slightly according to sex and marital status—and the fashion never changes. These clothes are quite pleasant to look at, they allow free movement of the limbs, they're equally suitable for hot and cold weather—and the great thing is, they're all home-made. So everybody learns one of the other trades I mentioned, and by everybody I mean the women as well as the men— though the weaker sex are given the lighter jobs, like spinning and weaving, while the men do the heavier ones.

Most children are brought up to do the same work as their parents, since they tend to have a natural feeling for it. But if a child fancies some other trade, he's adopted into a family that practices it. Of course, great care is taken, not only by the father, but also by the local authorities, to see that the foster father is a decent, respectable type. When you've learned one trade properly, you can, if you like, get permission to learn another—and when you're an expert in both, you can practice whichever you prefer, unless the other one is more essential to the public.

The chief business of the Stywards[1]—in fact, practically their only business—is to see that nobody sits around doing nothing, but that everyone gets on with his job. They don't wear people out, though, by keeping them hard at work from early morning till late at night, like cart horses. That's just slavery—and yet that's what life is like for the working classes nearly everywhere else in the world. In Utopia they have a six-hour working day—three hours in the morning, then lunch—then a two-hour break—then three more hours in the afternoon, followed by supper. They go to bed at 8 P.M., and sleep for eight hours. All the rest of the twenty-four they're free to do what they like—not to waste their

---

[1]**Stywards** In Utopia, each group of thirty households elects a styward; each town has two hundred stywards, who elect the mayor. [All notes are the editors'.]

time in idleness or self-indulgence, but to make good use of it in some congenial activity. Most people spend these free periods on further education, for there are public lectures first thing every morning. Attendance is quite voluntary, except for those picked out for academic training, but men and women of all classes go crowding in to hear them—I mean, different people go to different lectures, just as the spirit moves them. However, there's nothing to stop you from spending this extra time on your trade, if you want to. Lots of people do, if they haven't the capacity for intellectual work, and are much admired for such public-spirited behavior.

After supper they have an hour's recreation, either in the gardens ₅ or in the communal dining-halls, according to the time of year. Some people practice music, others just talk. They've never heard of anything so silly and demoralizing as dice, but they have two games rather like chess. The first is a sort of arithmetical contest, in which certain numbers "take" others. The second is a pitched battle between virtues and vices, which illustrates most ingeniously how vices tend to conflict with one another, but to combine against virtues. It also shows which vices are opposed to which virtues, how much strength vices can muster for a direct assault, what indirect tactics they employ, what help virtues need to overcome vices, what are the best methods of evading their attacks, and what ultimately determines the victory of one side or the other.

But here's a point that requires special attention, or you're liable to get the wrong idea. Since they only work a six-hour day, you may think there must be a shortage of essential goods. On the contrary, those six hours are enough, and more than enough to produce plenty of everything that's needed for a comfortable life. And you'll understand why it is, if you reckon up how large a proportion of the population in other countries is totally unemployed. First you have practically all the women—that gives you nearly 50 percent for a start. And in countries where the women *do* work, the men tend to lounge about instead. Then there are all the priests, and members of so-called religious orders—how much work do they do? Add all the rich, especially the landowners, popularly known as nobles and gentlemen. Include their domestic staffs—I mean those gangs of armed ruffians that I mentioned before. Finally, throw in all the beggars who are perfectly hale and hearty, but pretend to be ill as an excuse for being lazy. When you've counted them up, you'll be surprised to find how few people actually produce what the human race consumes.

And now just think how few of these few people are doing essential work—for where money is the only standard of value, there are bound to be dozens of unnecessary trades carried on, which merely supply luxury goods or entertainment. Why, even if the existing labor force were distributed among the few trades really needed to make life reasonably comfortable, there'd be so much overproduction that prices would fall too low for the workers to earn a living. Whereas, if you took all those

engaged in nonessential trades, and all who are too lazy to work — each
of whom consumes twice as much of the products of other people's labor
as any of the producers themselves — if you put the whole lot of them
on to something useful, you'd soon see how few hours' work a day
would be amply sufficient to supply all the necessities and comforts of
life — to which you might add all real and natural forms of pleasure.

[THE HOUSEHOLD]

But let's get back to their social organization. Each household, as I
said, comes under the authority of the oldest male. Wives are subordinate to their husbands, children to their parents, and younger people
generally to their elders. Every town is divided into four districts of equal
size, each with its own shopping center in the middle of it. There the
products of every household are collected in warehouses, and then distributed according to type among various shops. When the head of a
household needs anything for himself or his family, he just goes to one
of these shops and asks for it. And whatever he asks for, he's allowed to
take away without any sort of payment, either in money or in kind.
After all, why shouldn't he? There's more than enough of everything to
go round, so there's no risk of his asking for more than he needs — for
why should anyone want to start hoarding, when he knows he'll never
have to go short of anything? No living creature is naturally greedy,
except from fear of want — or in the case of human beings, from vanity,
the notion that you're better than people if you can display more superfluous property than they can. But there's no scope for that sort of thing
in Utopia.

[UTOPIAN BELIEFS]

The Utopians fail to understand why anyone should be so fascinated
by the dull gleam of a tiny bit of stone, when he has all the stars in the
sky to look at — or how anyone can be silly enough to think himself better than other people, because his clothes are made of finer woollen
thread than theirs. After all, those fine clothes were once worn by a
sheep, and they never turned it into anything better than a sheep.

Nor can they understand why a totally useless substance like gold 10
should now, all over the world, be considered far more important than
human beings, who gave it such value as it has, purely for their own
convenience. The result is that a man with about as much mental agility
as a lump of lead or a block of wood, a man whose utter stupidity is paralleled only by his immorality, can have lots of good, intelligent people at
his beck and call, just because he happens to possess a large pile of gold
coins. And if by some freak of fortune or trick of the law — two equally
effective methods of turning things upside down — the said coins were
suddenly transferred to the most worthless member of his domestic staff,

you'd soon see the present owner trotting after his money, like an extra piece of currency, and becoming his own servant's servant. But what puzzles and disgusts the Utopians even more is the idiotic way some people have of practically worshipping a rich man, not because they owe him money or are otherwise in his power, but simply because he's rich—although they know perfectly well that he's far too mean to let a single penny come their way, so long as he's alive to stop it.

They get these ideas partly from being brought up under a social system which is directly opposed to that type of nonsense, and partly from their reading and education. Admittedly, no one's allowed to become a full-time student, except for the very few in each town who appear as children to possess unusual gifts, outstanding intelligence, and a special aptitude for academic research. But every child receives a primary education, and most men and women go on educating themselves all their lives during those free periods that I told you about. . . .

In ethics they discuss the same problems as we do. Having distinguished between three types of "good," psychological, physiological, and environmental, they proceed to ask whether the term is strictly applicable to all of them, or only to the first. They also argue about such things as virtue and pleasure. But their chief subject of dispute is the nature of human happiness—on what factor or factors does it depend? Here they seem rather too much inclined to take a hedonistic view, for according to them human happiness consists largely or wholly in pleasure. Surprisingly enough, they defend this self-indulgent doctrine by arguments drawn from religion—a thing normally associated with a more serious view of life, if not with gloomy asceticism. You see, in all their discussions of happiness they invoke certain religious principles to supplement the operations of reason, which they think otherwise ill-equipped to identify true happiness.

The first principle is that every soul is immortal, and was created by a kind God, Who meant it to be happy. The second is that we shall be rewarded or punished in the next world for our good or bad behavior in this one. Although these are religious principles, the Utopians find rational grounds for accepting them. For suppose you didn't accept them? In that case, they say, any fool could tell you what you ought to do. You should go all out for your own pleasure, irrespective of right and wrong. You'd merely have to make sure that minor pleasures didn't interfere with major ones, and avoid the type of pleasure that has painful aftereffects. For what's the sense of struggling to be virtuous, denying yourself the pleasant things of life, and deliberately making yourself uncomfortable, if there's nothing you hope to gain by it? And what *can* you hope to gain by it, if you receive no compensation after death for a thoroughly unpleasant, that is, a thoroughly miserable life?

Not that they identify happiness with every type of pleasure—only with the higher ones. Nor do they identify it with virtue—unless they belong to a quite different school of thought. According to the normal view, happiness is the *summum bonum*[2] toward which we're naturally impelled by virtue—which in their definition means following one's natural impulses, as God meant us to do. But this includes obeying the instinct to be reasonable in our likes and dislikes. And reason also teaches us, first to love and reverence Almighty God, to Whom we owe our existence and our potentiality for happiness, and secondly to get through life as comfortably and cheerfully as we can, and help all other members of our species to do so too.

The fact is, even the sternest ascetic tends to be slightly inconsistent 15 in his condemnation of pleasure. He may sentence *you* to a life of hard labor, inadequate sleep, and general discomfort, but he'll also tell you to do your best to ease the pains and privations of others. He'll regard all such attempts to improve the human situation as laudable acts of humanity—for obviously nothing could be more humane, or more natural for a human being, than to relieve other people's sufferings, put an end to their miseries, and restore their *joie de vivre,* that is, their capacity for pleasure. So why shouldn't it be equally natural to do the same thing for oneself?

Either it's a bad thing to enjoy life, in other words, to experience pleasure—in which case you shouldn't help anyone to do it, but should try to save the whole human race from such a frightful fate—or else, if it's good for other people, and you're not only allowed, but positively obliged to make it possible for them, why shouldn't charity begin at home? After all, you've a duty to yourself as well as to your neighbor, and, if Nature says you must be kind to others, she can't turn round the next moment and say you must be cruel to yourself. The Utopians therefore regard the enjoyment of life—that is, pleasure—as the natural object of all human efforts, and natural, as they define it, is synonymous with virtuous. However, Nature also wants us to help one another to enjoy life, for the very good reason that no human being has a monopoly of her affections. She's equally anxious for the welfare of every member of the species. So of course she tells us to make quite sure that we don't pursue our own interests at the expense of other people's.

On this principle they think it right to keep one's promises in private life, and also to obey public laws for regulating the distribution of "goods"—by which I mean the raw materials of pleasure—provided such laws have been properly made by a wise ruler, or passed by common consent of a whole population, which has not been subjected to any form of violence or deception. Within these limits they say it's sensible to consult one's own interests, and a moral duty to consult those of the community as well. It's wrong to deprive someone else of a pleasure so that you can enjoy one yourself, but to deprive yourself of a pleasure so that you can add to someone else's enjoyment is an act of humanity

[2]*summum bonum* Latin for "the highest good."

by which you always gain more than you lose. For one thing, such benefits are usually repaid in kind. For another, the mere sense of having
done somebody a kindness, and so earned his affection and goodwill,
produces a spiritual satisfaction which far outweighs the loss of a physical one. And lastly—a belief that comes easily to a religious mind—God
will reward us for such small sacrifices of momentary pleasure, by giving
us an eternity of perfect joy. Thus they argue that, in the final analysis,
pleasure is the ultimate happiness which all human beings have in view,
even when they're acting most virtuously.

Pleasure they define as any state or activity, physical or mental, which
is naturally enjoyable. The operative word is *naturally.* According to them,
we're impelled by reason as well as an instinct to enjoy ourselves in any
natural way which doesn't hurt other people, interfere with greater pleasures, or cause unpleasant aftereffects. But human beings have entered
into an idiotic conspiracy to call some things enjoyable which are naturally nothing of the kind—as though facts were as easily changed as
definitions. Now the Utopians believe that, so far from contributing to
happiness, this type of thing makes happiness impossible—because, once
you get used to it, you lose all capacity for real pleasure, and are merely
obsessed by illusory forms of it. Very often these have nothing pleasant
about them at all—in fact, most of them are thoroughly disagreeable. But
they appeal so strongly to perverted tastes that they come to be reckoned
not only among the major pleasures of life, but even among the chief reasons for living.

In the category of illusory pleasure addicts they include the kind of
person I mentioned before, who thinks himself better than other people
because he's better dressed than they are. Actually he's just as wrong
about his clothes as he is about himself. From a practical point of view,
why is it better to be dressed in fine woollen thread than in coarse? But
he's got it into his head that fine thread is naturally superior, and that
wearing it somehow increases his own value. So he feels entitled to far
more respect than he'd ever dare to hope for, if he were less expensively
dressed, and is most indignant if he fails to get it.

Talking of respect, isn't it equally idiotic to attach such importance to 20
a lot of empty gestures which do nobody any good? For what real pleasure can you get out of the sight of a bared head or a bent knee? Will it
cure the rheumatism in your own knee, or make you any less weak in
the head? Of course, the great believers in this type of artificial pleasure
are those who pride themselves on their "nobility." Nowadays that
merely means that they happen to belong to a family which has been
rich for several generations, preferably in landed property. And yet they
feel every bit as "noble" even if they've failed to inherit any of the said
property, or if they have inherited it and then frittered it all away.

Then there's another type of person I mentioned before, who has a
passion for jewels, and feels practically superhuman if he manages to get
hold of a rare one, especially if it's a kind that's considered particularly

precious in his country and period—for the value of such things varies according to where and when you live. But he's so terrified of being taken in by appearances that he refuses to buy any jewel until he's stripped off all the gold and inspected it in the nude. And even then he won't buy it without a solemn assurance and a written guarantee from the jeweler that the stone is genuine. But my dear sir, why shouldn't a fake give you just as much pleasure, if you can't, with your own eyes, distinguish it from a real one? It makes no difference to you whether it's genuine or not—any more than it would to a blind man!

And now, what about those people who accumulate superfluous wealth, for no better purpose than to enjoy looking at it? Is their pleasure a real one, or merely a form of delusion? The opposite type of psychopath buries his gold, so that he'll never be able to use it, and may never even see it again. In fact, he deliberately loses it in his anxiety not to lose it—for what can you call it but lost, when it's put back into the earth, where it's no good to him, or probably to anyone else? And yet he's tremendously happy when he's got it stowed away. Now, apparently, he can stop worrying. But suppose the money is stolen, and ten years later he dies without ever knowing it has gone. Then for a whole ten years he has managed to survive his loss, and during that period what difference has it made to him whether the money was there or not? It was just as little use to him either way.

Among stupid pleasures they include not only gambling—a form of idiocy that they've heard about but never practiced—but also hunting and hawking. What on earth is the fun, they ask, of throwing dice onto a table? Besides, you've done it so often that, even if there was some fun in it at first, you must surely be sick of it by now. How can you possibly enjoy listening to anything so disagreeable as the barking and howling of dogs? And why is it more amusing to watch a dog chasing a hare than to watch one dog chasing another? In each case the essential activity is running—if running is what amuses you. But if it's really the thought of being in at the death, and seeing an animal torn to pieces before your eyes, wouldn't pity be a more appropriate reaction to the sight of a weak, timid, harmless little creature like a hare being devoured by something so much stronger and fiercer?

So the Utopians consider hunting below the dignity of free men, and leave it entirely to butchers, who are, as I told you, slaves. In their view hunting is the vilest department of butchery, compared with which all the others are relatively useful and honorable. An ordinary butcher slaughters livestock far more sparingly, and only because he has to, whereas a hunter kills and mutilates poor little creatures purely for his own amusement. They say you won't find that type of blood lust even among animals, unless they're particularly savage by nature, or have become so by constantly being used for this cruel sport.

There are hundreds of things like that, which are generally regarded 25 as pleasures, but everyone in Utopia is quite convinced that they've got nothing to do with real pleasure, because there's nothing naturally enjoyable about them. Nor is this conviction at all shaken by the argument that most people do actually enjoy them, which would seem to indicate an appreciable pleasure content. They say this is a purely subjective reaction caused by bad habits, which can make a person prefer unpleasant things to pleasant ones, just as pregnant women sometimes lose their sense of taste, and find suet or turpentine more delicious than honey. But however much one's judgment may be impaired by habit or ill health, the nature of pleasure, as of everything else, remains unchanged.

Real pleasures they divide into two categories, mental and physical. Mental pleasures include the satisfaction that one gets from understanding something, or from contemplating truth. They also include the memory of a well-spent life, and the confident expectation of good things to come. Physical pleasures are subdivided into two types. First there are those which fill the whole organism with a conscious sense of enjoyment. This may be the result of replacing physical substances which have been burnt up by the natural heat of the body, as when we eat or drink. Or else it may be caused by the discharge of some excess, as in excretion, sexual intercourse, or any relief of irritation by rubbing or scratching. However, there are also pleasures which satisfy no organic need, and relieve no previous discomfort. They merely act, in a mysterious but quite unmistakable way, directly on our senses, and monopolize their reactions. Such is the pleasure of music.

Their second type of physical pleasure arises from the calm and regular functioning of the body—that is, from a state of health undisturbed by any minor ailments. In the absence of mental discomfort, this gives one a good feeling, even without the help of external pleasures. Of course, it's less ostentatious, and forces itself less violently on one's attention than the cruder delights of eating and drinking, but even so it's often considered the greatest pleasure in life. Practically everyone in Utopia would agree that it's a very important one, because it's the basis of all the others. It's enough by itself to make you enjoy life, and unless you have it, no other pleasure is possible. However, mere freedom from pain, without positive health, they would call not pleasure but anesthesia.

Some thinkers used to maintain that a uniformly tranquil state of health couldn't properly be termed a pleasure since its presence could only be detected by contrast with its opposite—oh yes, they went very thoroughly into the whole question. But that theory was exploded long ago, and nowadays nearly everybody subscribes to the view that health is most definitely a pleasure. The argument goes like this—illness involves pain, which is the direct opposite of pleasure, and illness is the direct opposite of health, therefore health involves pleasure. They don't think it matters whether you say that illness *is* or merely *involves* pain. Either way it comes to the same thing. Similarly, whether health *is* a pleasure, or merely *produces* pleasure as inevitably as fire produces heat, it's equally logical to assume that where you have an uninterrupted state of health you cannot fail to have pleasure.

Besides, they say, when we eat something, what really happens is this. Our failing health starts fighting off the attacks of hunger, using the food as an ally. Gradually it begins to prevail, and, in this very process of winning back its normal strength, experiences the sense of enjoyment which we find so refreshing. Now, if health enjoys the actual battle, why shouldn't it also enjoy the victory? Or are we to suppose that when it has finally managed to regain its former vigor—the one thing that it has been fighting for all this time—it promptly falls into a coma, and fails to notice or take advantage of its success? As for the idea that one isn't conscious of health except through its opposite, they say that's quite untrue. Everyone's perfectly aware of feeling well, unless he's asleep or actually feeling ill. Even the most insensitive and apathetic sort of person will admit that it's delightful to be healthy—and what is delight, but a synonym for pleasure?

They're particularly fond of mental pleasures, which they consider of 30 primary importance, and attribute mostly to good behavior and a clear conscience. Their favorite physical pleasure is health. Of course, they believe in enjoying food, drink, and so forth, but purely in the interests of health, for they don't regard such things as very pleasant in themselves—only as methods of resisting the stealthy onset of disease. A sensible person, they say, prefers keeping well to taking medicine, and would rather feel cheerful than have people trying to comfort him. On the same principle it's better not to need this type of pleasure than to become addicted to it. For, if you think that sort of thing will make you happy, you'll have to admit that your idea of perfect felicity would be a life consisting entirely of hunger, thirst, itching, eating, drinking, rubbing, and scratching—which would obviously be most unpleasant as well as quite disgusting. Undoubtedly these pleasures should come right at the bottom of the list, because they're so impure. For instance, the pleasure of eating is invariably diluted with the pain of hunger, and not in equal proportions either—for the pain is both more intense and more prolonged. It starts before the pleasure, and doesn't stop until the pleasure has stopped too.

So they don't think much of pleasures like that, except insofar as they're necessary. But they enjoy them all the same, and feel most grateful to Mother Nature for encouraging her children to do things that have to be done so often, by making them so attractive. For just think how dreary life would be, if those chronic ailments, hunger and thirst, could only be cured by foul-tasting medicines, like the rarer types of disease!

They attach great value to special natural gifts such as beauty, strength, and agility. They're also keen on the pleasures of sight, hearing, and smell, which are peculiar to human beings—for no other species admires the beauty of the world, enjoys any sort of scent, except as a method of locating food, or can tell the difference between a harmony and a discord. They say these things give a sort of relish to life.

However, in all such matters they observe the rule that minor pleasures mustn't interfere with major ones, and that pleasure mustn't cause pain—which they think is bound to happen, if the pleasure is immoral. But they'd never dream of despising their own beauty, overtaxing their strength, converting their agility into inertia, ruining their physique by going without food, damaging their health, or spurning any other of Nature's gifts, unless they were doing it for the benefit of other people or of society, in the hope of receiving some greater pleasure from God in return. For they think it's quite absurd to torment oneself in the name of an unreal virtue, which does nobody any good, or in order to steel oneself against disasters which may never occur. They say such behavior is merely self-destructive, and shows a most ungrateful attitude toward Nature—as if one refused all her favors, because one couldn't bear the thought of being indebted to her for anything.

Well, that's their ethical theory, and short of some divine revelation, they doubt if the human mind is capable of devising a better one. We've no time to discuss whether it's right or wrong—nor is it really necessary, for all I undertook was to describe their way of life, not to defend it.

[TREATMENT OF THE DYING]

As I told you, when people are ill, they're looked after most sympa- 35 thetically, and given everything in the way of medicine or special food that could possibly assist their recovery. In the case of permanent invalids, the nurses try to make them feel better by sitting and talking to them, and do all they can to relieve their symptoms. But if, besides being incurable, the disease also causes constant excruciating pain, some priests and government officials visit the person concerned, and say something like this:

"Let's face it, you'll never be able to live a normal life. You're just a nuisance to other people and a burden to yourself—in fact you're really leading a sort of posthumous existence. So why go on feeding germs? Since your life's a misery to you, why hesitate to die? You're imprisoned in a torture chamber—why don't you break out and escape to a better world? Or say the word, and we'll arrange for your release. It's only common sense to cut your losses. It's also an act of piety to take the advice of a priest, because he speaks for God."

If the patient finds these arguments convincing, he either starves himself to death, or is given a soporific and put painlessly out of his misery. But this is strictly voluntary, and, if he prefers to stay alive, everyone will go on treating him as kindly as ever.

[THE SUMMING UP]

Well, that's the most accurate account I can give you of the Utopian Republic. To my mind, it's not only the best country in the world, but the only one that has any right to call itself a republic. Elsewhere, people are always talking about the public interest, but all they really care about is private property. In Utopia, where's there's no private property, people take their duty to the public seriously. And both attitudes are perfectly reasonable. In other "republics" practically everyone knows that, if he doesn't look out for himself, he'll starve to death, however prosperous his country may be. He's therefore compelled to give his own interests priority over those of the public; that is, of other people. But in Utopia, where everything's under public ownership, no one has any fear of going short, as long as the public storehouses are full. Everyone gets a fair share, so there are never any poor men or beggars. Nobody owns anything, but everyone is rich—for what greater wealth can there be than cheerfulness, peace of mind, and freedom from anxiety? Instead of being worried about his food supply, upset by the plaintive demands of his wife, afraid of poverty for his son, and baffled by the problem of finding a dowry for his daughter, the Utopian can feel absolutely sure that he, his wife, his children, his grandchildren, his great-grandchildren, his great-great-grandchildren, and as long a line of descendants as the proudest peer could wish to look forward to, will always have enough to eat and enough to make them happy. There's also the further point that those who are too old to work are just as well provided for as those who are still working.

Now, will anyone venture to compare these fair arrangements in Utopia with the so-called justice of other countries?—in which I'm damned if I can see the slightest trace of justice or fairness. For what sort of justice do you call this? People like aristocrats, goldsmiths, or money-lenders, who either do no work at all, or do work that's really not essential, are rewarded for their laziness or their unnecessary activities by a splendid life of luxury. But laborers, coachmen, carpenters, and farmhands, who never stop working like cart horses, at jobs so essential that, if they *did* stop working, they'd bring any country to a standstill within twelve months—what happens to them? They get so little to eat, and have such a wretched time, that they'd be almost better off if they *were* cart horses. Then at least, they wouldn't work quite such long hours, their food wouldn't be very much worse, they'd enjoy it more, and they'd have no fears for the future. As it is, they're not only ground down by unrewarding toil in the present, but also worried to death by the prospect of a poverty-stricken old age—since their daily wages aren't enough to support them for one day, let alone leave anything over to be saved up when they're old.

Can you see any fairness or gratitude in a social system which lav- 40
ishes such great rewards on so-called noblemen, goldsmiths, and people like that, who are either totally unproductive or merely employed in producing luxury goods or entertainment, but makes no such kind provision for farmhands, coal heavers, laborers, carters, or carpenters, without whom society couldn't exist at all? And the climax of ingratitude comes when they're old and ill and completely destitute. Having taken

advantage of them throughout the best years of their lives, society now forgets all the sleepless hours they've spent in its service, and repays them for all the vital work they've done, by letting them die in misery. What's more, the wretched earnings of the poor are daily whittled away by the rich, not only through private dishonesty, but through public legislation. As if it weren't unjust enough already that the man who contributes most to society should get the least in return, they make it even worse, and then arrange for injustice to be legally described as justice.

In fact, when I consider any social system that prevails in the modern world, I can't, so help me God, see it as anything but a conspiracy of the rich to advance their own interests under the pretext of organizing society. They think up all sorts of tricks and dodges, first for keeping safe their ill-gotten gains, and then for exploiting the poor by buying their labor as cheaply as possible. Once the rich have decided that these tricks and dodges shall be officially recognized by society—which includes the poor as well as the rich—they acquire the force of law. Thus an unscrupulous minority is led by its insatiable greed to monopolize what would have been enough to supply the needs of the whole population. And yet how much happier even these people would be in Utopia! There, with the simultaneous abolition of money and the passion for money, how many other social problems have been solved, how many crimes eradicated! For obviously the end of money means the end of all those types of criminal behavior which daily punishments are powerless to check: fraud, theft, burglary, brawls, riots, disputes, rebellion, murder, treason, and black magic. And the moment money goes, you can also say goodbye to fear, tension, anxiety, overwork, and sleepless nights. Why, even poverty itself, the one problem that has always seemed to need money for its solution, would promptly disappear if money ceased to exist.

Let me try to make this point clearer. Just think back to one of the years when the harvest was bad, and thousands of people died of starvation. Well, I bet if you'd inspected every rich man's barn at the end of that lean period you'd have found enough corn to have saved all the lives that were lost through malnutrition and disease, and prevented anyone from suffering any ill effects whatever from the meanness of the weather and the soil. Everyone could so easily get enough to eat, if it weren't for that blessed nuisance, money. There you have a brilliant invention which was designed to make food more readily available. Actually it's the only thing that makes it unobtainable.

I'm sure that even the rich are well aware of all this, and realize how much better it would be to have everything one needed, than lots of things one didn't need—to be evacuated altogether from the danger area, than to dig oneself in behind a barricade of enormous wealth. And I've no doubt that either self-interest, or the authority of our Savior Christ—Who was far too wise not to know what was best for us, and far too kind to recommend anything else—would have led the whole world to adopt the Utopian system long ago, if it weren't for that beastly root of all evils, pride. For pride's criterion of prosperity is not what you've got yourself, but what other people haven't got. Pride would refuse to set foot in paradise, if she thought there'd be no underprivileged classes there to gloat over and order about—nobody whose misery could serve as a foil to her own happiness, or whose poverty she could make harder to bear, by flaunting her own riches. Pride, like a hellish serpent gliding through human hearts—or shall we say, like a sucking-fish that clings to the ship of state?—is always dragging us back, and obstructing our progress toward a better way of life.

But as this fault is too deeply ingrained in human nature to be easily eradicated, I'm glad that at least one country has managed to develop a system which I'd like to see universally adopted. The Utopian way of life provides not only the happiest basis for a civilized community, but also one which, in all human probability, will last forever. They've eliminated the root causes of ambition, political conflict, and everything like that. There's therefore no danger of internal dissension, the one thing that has destroyed so many impregnable towns. And as long as there's unity and sound administration at home, no matter how envious neighboring kings may feel, they'll never be able to shake, let alone to shatter, the power of Utopia. They've tried to do so often enough in the past, but have always been beaten back.

TOPICS FOR CRITICAL THINKING AND WRITING

1. More, writing early in the sixteenth century, was living in a primarily agricultural society. Laborers were needed on farms, but might More have had any other reason for insisting (para. 1) that all people should do some farming and that farming should be "part of every child's education"? Do you think everyone should put in some time as a farmer? Why, or why not?

2. More indicates that in the England of his day many people loafed or engaged in unnecessary work (producing luxury goods, for one thing), putting an enormous burden on those who engaged in useful work. Is this condition, or any part of it, true of our society? Explain.

3. The Utopians cannot understand why the people of other nations value gems, gold, and fine clothes. If you value any of these, can you offer an explanation?

4. What arguments can you offer against the Utopians' treatment of persons who are incurably ill and in pain?

5. Take three or four paragraphs to summarize More's report of the Utopians' idea of pleasure.

6. More's Utopians cannot understand why anyone takes pleasure in gambling or in hunting. If either activity gives you pleasure, in an essay of 500 words explain why, and offer an argument on behalf of your view.

7. As More makes clear in the part we entitle "The Summing Up," in Utopia there is no private property. In a sentence or two summarize the reasons he gives for this principle, and then in a paragraph evaluate them.

Niccolò Machiavelli

Niccolò Machiavelli (1469–1527) was born in Florence at a time when Italy was divided into five major states: Venice, Milan, Florence, the Papal States, and Naples. Although these states often had belligerent relations with one another as well as with lesser Italian states, under the Medici family in Florence they achieved a precarious balance of power. In 1494, however, Lorenzo de' Medici, who had ruled from 1469 to 1492, died, and two years later Lorenzo's successor was exiled when the French army arrived in Florence. Italy became a field where Spain, France, and Germany competed for power. From 1498 to 1512 Machiavelli held a high post in the diplomatic service of the Florentine Republic, but when the French army reappeared and the Florentines in desperation recalled the Medici, Machiavelli lost his post, was imprisoned, tortured, and then exiled. Banished from Florence, he nevertheless lived in comfort on a small estate nearby, writing his major works and hoping to obtain an office from the Medici. In later years he was employed in a few minor diplomatic missions, but even after the collapse and expulsion of the Medici in 1527 and the restoration of the republic, he did not regain his old position of importance. He died shortly after the restoration.

Our selection comes from The Prince, *which Machiavelli wrote in 1513 during his banishment hoping that it would interest the Medici and thus restore him to favor; but the book was not published until 1532, five years after his death. In this book of twenty-six short chapters, Machiavelli begins by examining different kinds of states, but the work's enduring power resides in the discussions (in Chapters 15–18, reprinted here) of qualities necessary to a prince—that is, a head of state. Any such examination obviously is based in part on assumptions about the nature of the citizens of the realm.*

This selection was taken from a translation edited by Peter Bondanella and Mark Musa.

From *The Prince*

ON THOSE THINGS FOR WHICH MEN, AND PARTICULARLY PRINCES, ARE PRAISED OR BLAMED

Now there remains to be examined what should be the methods and procedures of a prince in dealing with his subjects and friends. And because I know that many have written about this, I am afraid that by writing about it again I shall be thought of as presumptuous, since in discussing this material I depart radically from the procedures of others. But since my intention is to write something useful for anyone who understands it, it seemed more suitable to me to search after the effectual truth of the matter rather than its imagined one. And many writers have imagined for themselves republics and principalities that have never been seen nor known to exist in reality; for there is such a gap between how one lives and how one ought to live that anyone who abandons what is done for what ought to be done learns his ruin rather than his preservation: for a man who wishes to make a vocation of being good at all times will come to ruin among so many who are not good. Hence it is necessary for a prince who wishes to maintain his position to learn how not to be good, and to use this knowledge or not to use it according to necessity.

Leaving aside, therefore, the imagined things concerning a prince, and taking into account those that are true, I say that all men, when they are spoken of, and particularly princes, since they are placed on a higher level, are judged by some of these qualities which bring them either blame or praise. And this is why one is considered generous, another miserly (to use a Tuscan word, since "avaricious" in our language is still used to mean one who wishes to acquire by means of theft; we call "miserly" one who excessively avoids using what he has); one is considered a giver, the other rapacious; one cruel, another merciful; one treacherous, another faithful; one effeminate and cowardly, another bold and courageous; one humane, another haughty; one lascivious, another chaste; one trustworthy, another cunning; one harsh, another lenient; one serious, another frivolous; one religious, another unbelieving; and the like. And I know that everyone will admit that it would be a very praiseworthy thing to find in a prince, of the qualities mentioned above, those that are held to be good; but since it is neither possible to have them nor to observe them all completely, because human nature does not permit it, a prince must be prudent enough to know how to escape the bad reputation of those vices that would lose the state for him, and must protect himself from those that will not lose it for him, if this is possible; but if he cannot, he need not concern himself unduly if he ignores these less serious vices. And, moreover, he need not worry about incurring the bad reputation of those vices without which it would be difficult to hold his state; since, carefully taking everything into account, one will discover that something which appears to be a virtue, if pursued, will end in his destruction; while some other thing which seems to be a vice, if pursued, will result in his safety and his well-being.

ON GENEROSITY AND MISERLINESS

Beginning, therefore, with the first of the above-mentioned qualities, I say that it would be good to be considered generous; nevertheless, generosity used in such a manner as to give you a reputation for it will harm you; because if it is employed virtuously and as one should employ it, it will not be recognized and you will not avoid the reproach of its opposite. And so, if a prince wants to maintain his reputation for generosity among men, it is necessary for him not to neglect any possible means of lavish display; in so doing such a prince will always use up all his resources and he will be obliged, eventually, if he wishes to maintain his reputation for generosity, to burden the people with excessive taxes and to do everything possible to raise funds. This will begin to make him hateful to his subjects, and, becoming impoverished, he will not be much esteemed by anyone; so that, as a consequence of his generosity, having offended many and rewarded few, he will feel the effects of any slight unrest and will be ruined at the first sign of danger; recognizing this and wishing to alter his policies, he immediately runs the risk of being reproached as a miser.

A prince, therefore, unable to use this virtue of generosity in a manner which will not harm himself if he is known for it, should, if he is wise, not worry about being called a miser; for with time he will come to be considered more generous once it is evident that, as a result of his parsimony, his income is sufficient, he can defend himself from anyone who makes war against him, and he can undertake enterprises without overburdening his people, so that he comes to be generous with all those from whom he takes nothing, who are countless, and miserly with all those to whom he gives nothing, who are few. In our times we have not seen great deeds accomplished except by those who were considered miserly; all others were done away with. Pope Julius II, although he made use of his reputation for generosity in order to gain the papacy, then decided not to maintain it in order to be able to wage war; the present King of France has waged many wars without imposing extra taxes on his subjects, only because his habitual parsimony has provided for the additional expenditures; the present King of Spain, if he had been considered generous, would not have engaged in nor won so many campaigns.

Therefore, in order not to have to rob his subjects, to be able to defend himself, not to become poor and contemptible, and not to be forced to become rapacious, a prince must consider it of little importance if he incurs the name of miser, for this is one of those vices that permits him to rule. And if someone were to say: Caesar with his generosity came to rule the empire, and many others, because they were generous and known to be so, achieved very high positions; I reply: You are either already a prince or you are on the way to becoming one; in the first instance such generosity is damaging; in the second it is very necessary to be thought generous. And Caesar was one of those who wanted to gain the principality of Rome; but if, after obtaining this, he had lived and had not moderated his expenditures, he would have destroyed that empire. And if someone were to reply: There have existed many princes who have accomplished great deeds with their armies who have been reputed to be generous; I answer you: A prince either spends his own money and that of his subjects or that of others; in the first case he must be economical; in the second he must not restrain any part of his generosity. And for that prince who goes out with his soldiers and lives by looting, sacking, and ransoms, who controls the property of others, such generosity is necessary; otherwise he would not be followed by his troops. And with what does not belong to you or to your subjects you can be a more liberal giver, as were Cyrus, Caesar, and Alexander; for spending the wealth of others does not lessen your reputation but adds to it; only the spending of your own is what harms you. And there is nothing that uses itself up faster than generosity, for as you employ it you lose the means of employing it, and you become either poor or despised or, in order to escape poverty, rapacious and hated. And above all other things a prince must guard himself against being despised and hated; and generosity leads you to both one and the other. So it is wiser to live with the reputation of a miser, which produces reproach without hatred, than to be forced to incur the reputation of rapacity, which produces reproach along with hatred, because you want to be considered as generous.

ON CRUELTY AND MERCY AND WHETHER IT IS BETTER TO BE LOVED THAN TO BE FEARED OR THE CONTRARY

Proceeding to the other qualities mentioned above, I say that every prince must desire to be considered merciful and not cruel; nevertheless, he must take care not to misuse this mercy. Cesare Borgia[1] was considered cruel; nonetheless, his cruelty had brought order to Romagna, united it, restored it to peace and obedience. If we examine this carefully, we shall see that he was more merciful than the Florentine people, who, in order to avoid being considered cruel, allowed the destruction of Pistoia.[2] Therefore, a prince must not worry about the reproach of cruelty when it is a matter of keeping his subjects united and loyal; for with a very few examples of cruelty he will be more compassionate than those who, out of excessive mercy, permit disorders to continue, from which arise murders and plundering; for these usually harm the community at large, while the executions that come from the prince harm one individual in particular. And the new prince, above all other princes,

---

[1]**Cesare Borgia** The son of Pope Alexander VI, Cesare Borgia (1476–1507) was ruthlessly opportunistic. Encouraged by his father, in 1499 and 1500 he subdued the cities of Romagna, the region including Ferrara and Ravenna. [All notes are the editors' unless otherwise specified.]

[2]**Pistoia** A town near Florence; Machiavelli suggests that the Florentines failed to treat dissenting leaders with sufficient severity.

cannot escape the reputation of being called cruel, since new states are full of dangers. And Virgil, through Dido, states: "My difficult condition and the newness of my rule make me act in such a manner, and to set guards over my land on all sides."[3]

Nevertheless, a prince must be cautious in believing and in acting, nor should he be afraid of his own shadow; and he should proceed in such a manner, tempered by prudence and humanity, so that too much trust may not render him imprudent nor too much distrust render him intolerable.

From this arises an argument: whether it is better to be loved than to be feared, or the contrary. I reply that one should like to be both one and the other; but since it is difficult to join them together, it is much safer to be feared than to be loved when one of the two must be lacking. For one can generally say this about men: that they are ungrateful, fickle, simulators and deceivers, avoiders of danger, greedy for gain; and while you work for their good they are completely yours, offering you their blood, their property, their lives, and their sons, as I said earlier, when danger is far away; but when it comes nearer to you they turn away. And that prince who bases his power entirely in their words, finding himself stripped of other preparations, comes to ruin; for friendships that are acquired by a price and not by greatness and nobility of character are purchased but are not owned, and at the proper moment they cannot be spent. And men are less hesitant about harming someone who makes himself loved than one who makes himself feared because love is held together by a chain of obligation which, since men are a sorry lot, is broken on every occasion in which their own self-interest is concerned; but fear is held together by a dread of punishment which will never abandon you.

A prince must nevertheless make himself feared in such a manner that he will avoid hatred, even if he does not acquire love; since to be feared and not to be hated can very well be combined; and this will always be so when he keeps his hands off the property and the women of his citizens and his subjects. And if he must take someone's life, he should do so when there is proper justification and manifest cause; but, above all, he should avoid the property of others; for men forget more quickly the death of their father than the loss of their patrimony. Moreover, the reasons for seizing their property are never lacking; and he who begins to live by stealing always finds a reason for taking what belongs to others; on the contrary, reasons for taking a life are rarer and disappear sooner.

But when the prince is with his armies and has under his command 10 a multitude of troops, then it is absolutely necessary that he not worry about being considered cruel; for without that reputation he will never

---

[3]In *Aeneid* I, 563–64, **Virgil** (70–19 B.C.) puts this line into the mouth of **Dido,** the queen of Carthage.

keep an army united or prepared for any combat. Among the praise-worthy deeds of Hannibal[4] is counted this: that, having a very large army, made up of all kinds of men, which he commanded in foreign lands, there never arose the slightest dissension, neither among themselves nor against their prince, both during his good and his bad fortune. This could not have arisen from anything other than his inhuman cruelty, which, along with his many other abilities, made him always respected and terri-fying in the eyes of his soldiers; and without that, to attain the same effect, his other abilities would not have sufficed. And the writers of his-tory, having considered this matter very little, on the one hand admire these deeds of his and on the other condemn the main cause of them.

And that it be true that his other abilities would not have been suf-ficient can be seen from the example of Scipio,[5] a most extraordinary man not only in his time but in all recorded history, whose armies in Spain rebelled against him; this came about from nothing other than his excessive compassion, which gave to his soldiers more liberty than military discipline allowed. For this he was censured in the senate by Fabius Maximus, who called him the corruptor of the Roman militia. The Locrians, having been ruined by one of Scipio's officers, were not avenged by him, nor was the arrogance of that officer corrected, all because of his tolerant nature; so that someone in the senate who tried to apologize for him said that there were many men who knew how not to err better than they knew how to correct errors. Such a nature would have, in time, damaged Scipio's fame and glory if he had maintained it during the empire; but, living under the control of the senate, this harm-ful characteristic of his not only concealed itself but brought him fame.

I conclude, therefore, returning to the problem of being feared and loved, that since men love at their own pleasure and fear at the pleasure of the prince, a wise prince should build his foundation upon that which belongs to him, not upon that which belongs to others: He must strive only to avoid hatred, as has been said.

HOW A PRINCE SHOULD KEEP HIS WORD

How praiseworthy it is for a prince to keep his word and to live by integrity and not by deceit everyone knows; nevertheless, one sees from the experience of our times that the princes who have accomplished great deeds are those who have cared little for keeping their promises and who have known how to manipulate the minds of men by shrewd-ness; and in the end they have surpassed those who laid their founda-tions upon honesty.

[4]**Hannibal** The Carthaginian general (247–183 B.C.) whose crossing of the Alps with ele-phants and full baggage train is one of the great feats of military history.
[5]**Scipio** Publius Cornelius Scipio Africanus the Elder (235–183 B.C.), the conqueror of Hannibal in the Punic Wars. The mutiny of which Machiavelli speaks took place in 206 B.C.

You must, therefore, know that there are two means of fighting: one according to the laws, the other with force; the first way is proper to man, the second to beasts; but because the first, in many cases, is not sufficient, it becomes necessary to have recourse to the second. Therefore, a prince must know how to use wisely the natures of the beast and the man. This policy was taught to princes allegorically by the ancient writers, who described how Achilles and many other ancient princes were given to Chiron[6] the Centaur to be raised and taught under his discipline. This can only mean that, having a half-beast and half-man as a teacher, a prince must know how to employ the nature of the one and the other; and the one without the other cannot endure.

Since, then, a prince must know how to make good use of the nature   15
of the beast, he should choose from among the beasts the fox and the lion; for the lion cannot defend itself from traps and the fox cannot protect itself from wolves. It is therefore necessary to be a fox in order to recognize the traps and a lion in order to frighten the wolves. Those who play only the part of the lion do not understand matters. A wise ruler, therefore, cannot and should not keep his word when such an observance of faith would be to his disadvantage and when the reasons which made him promise are removed. And if men were all good, this rule would not be good; but since men are a sorry lot and will not keep their promises to you, you likewise need not keep yours to them. A prince never lacks legitimate reasons to break his promises. Of this one could cite an endless number of modern examples to show how many pacts, how many promises have been made null and void because of the infidelity of princes; and he who has known best how to use the fox has come to a better end. But it is necessary to know how to disguise this nature well and to be a great hypocrite and a liar: and men are so simpleminded and so controlled by their present necessities that one who deceives will always find another who will allow himself to be deceived.

I do not wish to remain silent about one of these recent instances. Alexander VI[7] did nothing else, he thought about nothing else, except to deceive men, and he always found the occasion to do this. And there never was a man who had more forcefulness in his oaths, who affirmed a thing with more promises, and who honored his word less; nevertheless, his tricks always succeeded perfectly since he was well acquainted with this aspect of the world.

Therefore, it is not necessary for a prince to have all of the above-mentioned qualities, but it is very necessary for him to appear to have them. Furthermore, I shall be so bold as to assert this; that having them and practicing them at all times is harmful; and appearing to have them

---

[6]**Chiron** (Kī'ron) A centaur (half man, half horse) who was said in classical mythology to have been the teacher not only of Achilles but also of Theseus, Jason, Hercules, and other heroes.
[7]**Alexander VI** Pope from 1492 to 1503; father of Cesare Borgia.

useful; for instance, to seem merciful, faithful, humane, forthright, religious, and to be so; but his mind should be disposed in such a way that
should it become necessary not to be so, he will be able and know how
to change to the contrary. And it is essential to understand this: that a
prince, and especially a new prince, cannot observe all those things by
which men are considered good, for in order to maintain the state he is
often obliged to act against his promise, against charity, against humanity, and against religion. And therefore, it is necessary that he have a
mind ready to turn itself according to the way the winds of Fortune and
the changeability of affairs require him; and, as I said above, as long as it
is possible, he should not stray from the good, but he should know how
to enter into evil when necessity commands.

A prince, therefore, must be very careful never to let anything slip
from his lips which is not full of the five qualities mentioned above: He
should appear, upon seeing and hearing him, to be all mercy, all faithful-
ness, all integrity, all kindness, all religion. And there is nothing more
necessary than to seem to possess this last quality. And men in general
judge more by their eyes than their hands; for everyone can see but few
can feel. Everyone sees what you seem to be, few perceive what you are,
and those few do not dare to contradict the opinion of the many who
have the majesty of the state to defend them; and in the actions of all
men, and especially of princes, where there is no impartial arbiter, one
must consider the final result.[8] Let a prince therefore act to seize and to
maintain the state; his methods will always be judged honorable and will
be praised by all; for ordinary people are always deceived by appearances
and by the outcome of a thing; and in the world there is nothing but
ordinary people; and there is no room for the few, while the many have
a place to lean on. A certain prince of the present day, whom I shall
refrain from naming, preaches nothing but peace and faith, and to both
one and the other he is entirely opposed; and both, if he had put them
into practice, would have cost him many times over either his reputation
or his state.

TOPICS FOR CRITICAL THINKING AND WRITING

1. In the opening paragraph, Machiavelli claims that a ruler who wishes
   to keep in power must "learn how not to be good" — that is, must
   know where and when to ignore the demands of conventional morality. In the rest of the excerpt, does he give any convincing evidence to
   support this claim? Can you think of any recent political event in
   which a political leader violated the requirements of morality, as
   Machiavelli advises?

---

[8]The Italian original, *si guarda al fine*, has often been mistranslated as "the ends justify the
means," something Machiavelli never wrote. [Translators' note.]

2. Machiavelli says in paragraph 1 that "a man who wishes to make a vocation of being good at all times will come to ruin among so many who are not good." (By the way, the passage is ambiguous. "At all times" is, in the original, a squinting modifier. It may look backward to "being good" or forward to "will come to ruin," but Machiavelli probably means, "A man who at all times wishes to make a vocation of being good will come to ruin among so many who are not good.") Is this view realistic or cynical? (What is the difference between these two?) Assume for the moment that the view is realistic. Does it follow that society requires a ruler who must act according to the principles Machiavelli sets forth?

3. In his second paragraph Machiavelli claims that it is impossible for a ruler to exhibit *all* the conventional virtues (trustworthiness, liberality, and so on). Why does he make this claim? Do you agree with it?

4. In paragraph 4 Machiavelli cites as examples Pope Julius II, the King of France, the King of Spain, and other rulers. Is he using these examples to illustrate his generalizations or to provide evidence for them? If you think he is using them to provide evidence, how convincing do you find the evidence? (Consider: Could Machiavelli be arguing from a biased sample?)

5. In paragraphs 6 to 10 Machiavelli argues that it is sometimes necessary for a ruler to be cruel, and so he praises Cesare Borgia and Hannibal. What in human nature, according to Machiavelli, explains this need to have recourse to cruelty? (By the way, how do you think *cruelty* should be defined here?)

6. Machiavelli says that Cesare Borgia's cruelty brought peace to Romagna and that, on the other hand, the Florentines who sought to avoid being cruel in fact brought pain to Pistoia. Can you think of recent episodes supporting the view that cruelty can be beneficial to society? If so, restate Machiavelli's position, using these examples from recent history. Then go on to write two paragraphs, arguing on behalf of your two examples. Or if you believe that Machiavelli's point here is fundamentally wrong, explain why, again using current examples.

7. In *The Prince*, Machiavelli is writing about how to be a successful ruler. He explicitly says he is dealing with things as they are, not things as they should be. Do you think that in fact one can write usefully about statecraft without considering ethics? Explain. Or you may want to think about it in this way: The study of politics is often called *political science*. Machiavelli can be seen as a sort of scientist, objectively analyzing the nature of governing — without offering any moral judgments. In an essay of 500 words, argue for or against the view that the study of politics is rightly called *political science*.

8. In paragraph 18 Machiavelli declares that "one must consider the final result." Taking account of the context, do you think the meaning is that (a) any end, goal, or purpose of anyone justifies using any means to reach it or (b) the end of governing the state, nation, or country justifies using any means to achieve it? Or do you think Machiavelli means both? Something else entirely?

9. In 500 words, argue that an important contemporary political figure does or does not act according to Machiavelli's principles.

10. If you have read the selection from Thomas More's *Utopia* (p. 855), write an essay of 500 words on one of these two topics: (a) why More's book is or is not wiser than Machiavelli's or (b) why one of the books is more interesting than the other.

11. More and Machiavelli wrote their books at almost exactly the same time. Write a dialogue of two or three double-spaced typed pages in which the two men argue about the nature of the state. (During the argument, they will have to reveal their assumptions about the nature of human beings and the role of government.)

Thomas Jefferson

Thomas Jefferson (1743–1826) was a congressman, the governor of Virginia, the first secretary of state, and the president of the United States, but he said he wished to be remembered for only three things: drafting the Declaration of Independence, writing the Virginia Statute for Religious Freedom, and founding the University of Virginia. All three were efforts to promote freedom.

Jefferson was born in Virginia and educated at William and Mary College in Williamsburg, Virginia. After graduating he studied law, was admitted to the bar, and in 1769 was elected to the Virginia House of Burgesses, his first political office. In 1776 he went to Philadelphia as a delegate to the second Continental Congress, where he was elected to a committee of five to write the Declaration of Independence. Jefferson drafted the document, which was then subjected to some changes by the other members of the committee and by the Congress. Although he was unhappy with the changes (especially with the deletion of a passage against slavery), his claim to have written the Declaration is just.

The Declaration of Independence

When in the course of human events, it becomes necessary for one people to dissolve the political bands which have connected them with another, and to assume among the Powers of the earth, the separate and equal station to which the Laws of Nature and of Nature's God entitle them, a decent respect to the opinions of mankind requires that they should declare the causes which impel them to the separation.

We hold these truths to be self-evident, that all men are created equal, that they are endowed by their Creator with certain unalienable Rights, that among these are Life, Liberty and the pursuit of Happiness.

That to secure these rights, Governments are instituted among Men, deriving their just powers from the consent of the governed.

That whenever any Form of Government becomes destructive of these ends, it is the Right of the People to alter or to abolish it, and to institute a new Government, laying its foundation on such principles and organizing its powers in such form, as to them shall seem most likely to effect their Safety and Happiness. Prudence, indeed, will dictate that Governments long established should not be changed for light and transient causes; and accordingly all experience hath shown that mankind are more disposed to suffer, while evils are sufferable, than to right themselves by abolishing the forms to which they are accustomed. But when a long train of abuses and usurpations pursuing invariably the same Object evinces a design to reduce them under absolute Despotism, it is their right, it is their duty, to throw off such government, and to provide new Guards for their future security.

Such has been the patient sufferance of these Colonies; and such is   5
now the necessity which constrains them to alter their former Systems of Government. The history of the present King of Great Britain is a history of repeated injuries and usurpations, all having in direct object the establishment of an absolute Tyranny over these States. To prove this, let Facts be submitted to a candid world.

He has refused his Assent to Laws, the most wholesome and necessary for the public good.

He has forbidden his Governors to pass Laws of immediate and pressing importance, unless suspended in their operation till his Assent should be obtained; and when so suspended, he has utterly neglected to attend to them.

He has refused to pass over Laws for the accommodation of large districts of people, unless those people would relinquish the right of Representation in the Legislature, a right inestimable to them and formidable to tyrants only.

He has called together legislative bodies at places unusual, uncomfortable, and distant from the depository of their Public Records, for the sole purpose of fatiguing them into compliance with his measures.

He has dissolved Representative Houses repeatedly, for opposing   10
with manly firmness his invasions on the rights of the people.

He has refused for a long time, after such dissolutions, to cause others to be elected; whereby the Legislative Powers, incapable of Annihilation, have returned to the People at large for their exercise; the State remaining in the mean time exposed to all the dangers of invasion from without, and convulsions within.

He has endeavored to prevent the population of these States, for that purpose obstructing the Laws of Naturalization of Foreigners; refusing to pass others to encourage their migration hither, and raising the conditions of new Appropriations of Lands.

He has obstructed the Administration of Justice, by refusing his Assent to Laws for establishing Judiciary Powers.

He has made Judges dependent on his Will alone, for the tenure of their offices, and the amount and payment of their salaries.

He has erected a multitude of New Offices, and sent hither swarms   15
of Officers to harass our People, and eat out their substance.

He has kept among us, in time of peace, Standing Armies without the consent of our Legislature.

He has affected to render the Military independent of and superior to the Civil Power.

He has combined with others to subject us to jurisdictions foreign to our constitution, and unacknowledged by our laws; giving his Assent to their acts of pretended Legislation:

For quartering large bodies of armed troops among us:

For protecting them, by a mock Trial, from Punishment for any   20
Murders which they should commit on the Inhabitants of these States:

For cutting off our Trade with all parts of the world:

For imposing Taxes on us without our Consent:

For depriving us in many cases, of the benefits of Trial by Jury:

For transporting us beyond Seas to be tried for pretended offenses:

For abolishing the free System of English Laws in a Neighbouring   25
Province, establishing therein an Arbitrary government, and enlarging its boundaries so as to render it at once an example and fit instrument for introducing the same absolute rule into these Colonies:

For taking away our Charters, abolishing our most valuable Laws, and altering fundamentally the Forms of our Governments.

For suspending our own Legislatures, and declaring themselves invested with Power to legislate for us in all cases whatsoever.

He has abdicated Government here, by declaring us out of his Protection and waging War against us.

He has plundered our seas, ravaged our Coasts, burnt our towns and destroyed the Lives of our people.

He is at this time transporting large Armies of foreign Mercenaries to   30
compleat the works of death, desolation and tyranny, already begun with circumstances of Cruelty & perfidy scarcely paralleled in the most barbarous ages, and totally unworthy the Head of a civilized nation.

He has constrained our fellow Citizens taken Captive on the high Seas to bear Arms against their Country, to become the executioners of their friends and Brethren, or to fall themselves by their Hands.

He has excited domestic insurrections amongst us, and has endeavored to bring on the inhabitants of our frontiers, the merciless Indian Savages, whose known rule of warfare is an undistinguished destruction of all ages, sexes and conditions.

In every stage of these Oppressions We Have Petitioned for Redress in the most humble terms: Our repeated petitions have been answered only by repeated injury. A Prince, whose character is thus marked by every act which may define a Tyrant, is unfit to be the ruler of a free People.

Nor have We been wanting in attention to our British brethren. We have warned them from time to time of attempts by their legislature to extend an unwarrantable jurisdiction over us. We have reminded them of the circumstances of our emigration and settlement here. We have appealed to their native justice and magnanimity and we have conjured them by the ties of our common kindred to disavow these usurpations, which would inevitably interrupt our connections and correspondence. They too have been deaf to the voice of justice and of consanguinity. We must, therefore, acquiesce in the necessity, which denounces our Separation, and hold them, as we hold the rest of mankind, Enemies in War, in Peace Friends.

We, therefore, the Representatives of the United States of America, 35 in General Congress, Assembled, appealing to the Supreme Judge of the world of the rectitude of our intentions, do, in the Name, and by Authority of the good People of these Colonies, solemnly publish and declare, That these United Colonies are, and of Right ought to be, Free and Independent States; that they are Absolved from all Allegiance to the British Crown, and that all political connection between them and the State of Great Britain, is and ought to be totally dissolved; and that as Free and Independent States, they have full power to levy War, conclude Peace, contract Alliances, establish Commerce, and so all the other Acts and Things which Independent States may of right do. And for the support of this Declaration, with a firm reliance on the protection of Divine Providence, we mutually pledge to each other our lives, our Fortunes and our sacred Honor.

Topics for Critical Thinking and Writing

1. According to the first paragraph, for what audience was the Declaration written? What other audiences do you think the document was (in one way or another) addressed to?

2. The Declaration states that it is intended to "prove" that the acts of the government of George III had as their "direct object the establishment of an absolute Tyranny" in the American colonies (para. 5). Write an essay of 500 to 750 words showing whether the evidence offered in the Declaration "proves" this claim to your satisfaction. (You will, of course, want to define *absolute tyranny*.) If you think further evidence is needed to "prove" the colonists' point, indicate what this evidence might be.

3. Paying special attention to the paragraphs beginning "That whenever any Form of Government" (para. 4), "In every stage" (para. 33), and "Nor have We been wanting" (para. 34), in a sentence or two set forth the image of themselves that the colonists seek to convey.

4. In the Declaration of Independence it is argued that the colonists are entitled to certain things and that under certain conditions they may behave in a certain way. Make explicit the syllogism that Jefferson is arguing.

5. What evidence does Jefferson offer to support his major premise? His minor premise?

6. In paragraph 2 the Declaration cites "certain unalienable Rights" and mentions three: "Life, Liberty and the pursuit of Happiness." What is an unalienable right? If someone has an unalienable (or inalienable) right, does that imply that he or she also has certain duties? If so, what are these duties? John Locke, a century earlier (1690), asserted that all men have a natural right to "life, liberty, and property." Do you think the decision to drop "property" and substitute "pursuit of Happiness" improved Locke's claim? Explain.

7. The Declaration ends thus: "We mutually pledge to each other our lives, our Fortunes and our sacred Honor." Is it surprising that honor is put in the final, climactic position? Is this a better ending than "our Fortunes, our sacred Honor, and our lives," or than "our sacred Honor, our lives, and our Fortunes?" Why?

8. King George III has asked you to reply, on his behalf, to the colonists, in 500 to 750 words. Write his reply. (Caution: A good reply will probably require you to do some reading about the period.)

9. Write a declaration of your own, setting forth in 500 to 750 words why some group is entitled to independence. You may want to argue that adolescents should not be compelled to attend school, that animals should not be confined in zoos, or that persons who use drugs should be able to buy them legally. Begin with a premise, then set forth facts illustrating the unfairness of the present condition, and conclude by stating what the new condition will mean to society.

Elizabeth Cady Stanton

Elizabeth Cady Stanton (1815–1902), a lawyer's daughter and journalist's wife, proposed in 1848 a convention to address the "social, civil, and religious condition and rights of women." Responding to Stanton's call, women and men from all over the Northeast traveled to the Woman's Rights Convention held in the village of Seneca Falls, New York. Her Declaration, adopted by the Convention—but only after vigorous debate and some amendments by others—became the platform for the women's rights movement in this country.

Declaration of Sentiments and Resolutions

When, in the course of human events, it becomes necessary for one portion of the family of man to assume among the people of the earth a position different from that which they have hitherto occupied, but one to which the laws of nature and of nature's God entitle them, a decent respect to the opinions of mankind requires that they should declare the causes that impel them to such a course.

We hold these truths to be self-evident: that all men and women are created equal; that they are endowed by their Creator with certain inalienable rights; that among these are life, liberty and the pursuit of happiness; that to secure these rights governments are instituted, deriving their just powers from the consent of the governed. Whenever any form of government becomes destructive of these ends, it is the right of those who suffer from it to refuse allegiance to it, and to insist upon the institution of a new government, laying its foundation on such principles, and organizing its powers in such form, as to them shall seem most likely to effect their safety and happiness. Prudence, indeed, will dictate that governments long established should not be changed for light and transient causes; and accordingly all experience hath shown that mankind are more disposed to suffer, while evils are sufferable, than to right themselves by abolishing the forms to which they were accustomed. But when a long train of abuses and usurpations, pursuing invariably the same object, evinces a design to reduce them under absolute despotism, it is their duty to throw off such government, and to provide new guards for their future security. Such has been the patient sufferance of the women under this government, and such is now the necessity which constrains them to demand the equal station to which they are entitled.

The history of mankind is a history of repeated injuries and usurpations on the part of man toward woman, having in direct object the establishment of an absolute tyranny over her. To prove this, let facts be submitted to a candid world.

He has never permitted her to exercise her inalienable right to the elective franchise.

He has compelled her to submit to laws, in the formation of which 5 she had no voice.

He has withheld from her rights which are given to the most ignorant and degraded men—both natives and foreigners.

Having deprived her of this first right of a citizen, the elective franchise, thereby leaving her without representation in the halls of legislation, he has oppressed her on all sides.

He has made her, if married, in the eye of the law, civilly dead.

He has taken from her all right in property, even to the wages she earns.

He has made her, morally, an irresponsible being, as she can commit 10 many crimes with impunity, provided they be done in the presence of her husband. In the covenant of marriage, she is compelled to promise obedience to her husband, he becoming to all intents and purposes, her master—the law giving him power to deprive her of her liberty, and to administer chastisement.

He has so framed the laws of divorce, as to what shall be the proper causes, and in case of separation, to whom the guardianship of the children shall be given, as to be wholly regardless of the happiness of women—the law, in all cases, going upon a false supposition of the supremacy of man, and giving all power into his hands.

After depriving her of all rights as a married woman, if single, and the owner of property, he has taxed her to support a government which recognizes her only when her property can be made profitable to it.

He has monopolized nearly all the profitable employments, and from those she is permitted to follow, she receives but a scanty remuneration. He closes against her all the avenues to wealth and distinction which he considers most honorable to himself. As a teacher of theology, medicine, or law, she is not known.

He has denied her the facilities for obtaining a thorough education, all colleges being closed against her.

He allows her in Church, as well as State, but a subordinate position, 15 claiming Apostolic authority for her exclusion from the ministry, and, with some exceptions, from any public participation in the affairs of the Church.

He has created a false public sentiment by giving to the world a different code of morals for men and women, by which moral delinquencies which exclude women from society, are not only tolerated, but deemed of little account in man.

He has usurped the prerogative of Jehovah himself, claiming it as his right to assign for her a sphere of action, when that belongs to her conscience and to her God.

He has endeavored, in every way that he could, to destroy her confidence in her own powers, to lessen her self-respect, and to make her willing to lead a dependent and abject life.

Now, in view of this entire disfranchisement of one-half the people of this country, their social and religious degradation—in view of the unjust laws above mentioned, and because women do feel themselves aggrieved, oppressed, and fraudulently deprived of their most sacred rights, we insist that they have immediate admission to all the rights and privileges which belong to them as citizens of the United States.

In entering upon the great work before us, we anticipate no small 20 amount of misconception, misrepresentation, and ridicule; but we shall use every instrumentality within our power to effect our object. We shall employ agents, circulate tracts, petition the State and National legislatures, and endeavor to enlist the pulpit and the press in our behalf. We hope this Convention will be followed by a series of Conventions embracing every part of the country.

[The following resolutions were discussed by Lucretia Mott, Thomas and Mary Ann McClintock, Amy Post, Catharine A. F. Stebbins, and others, and were adopted:]

Whereas, The great precept of nature is conceded to be, that "man shall pursue his own true and substantial happiness." Blackstone in his Commentaries remarks, that this law of Nature being coeval with mankind, and dictated by God himself, is of course superior in obligation to any other. It is binding over all the globe, in all countries, and at all times; no human laws are of any validity if contrary to this, and such of them as are valid, derive all their force, and all their validity, and all their authority, mediately and immediately, from this original; therefore,

Resolved, That such laws as conflict, in any way, with the true and substantial happiness of woman, are contrary to the great precept of nature and of no validity, for this is "superior in obligation to any other."

Resolved, That all laws which prevent woman from occupying such a station in society as her conscience shall dictate, or which place her in a position inferior to that of man, are contrary to the great precept of nature, and therefore of no force or authority.

Resolved, That woman is man's equal—was intended to be so by the Creator, and the highest good of the race demands that she should be recognized as such.

Resolved, That the women of this country ought to be enlightened in   25 regard to the laws under which thcy livc, that thcy may no longer publish their degradation by declaring themselves satisfied with their present position, nor their ignorance, by asserting that they have all the rights they want.

Resolved, That inasmuch as man, while claiming for himself intellectual superiority, does accord to woman moral superiority, it is preeminently his duty to encourage her to speak and teach, as she has an opportunity, in all religious assemblies.

Resolved, That the same amount of virtue, delicacy, and refinement of behavior that is required of woman in the social state, should also be required of man, and the same transgressions should be visited with equal severity on both man and woman.

Resolved, That the objection of indelicacy and impropriety, which is so often brought against woman when she addresses a public audience, comes with a very ill-grace from those who encourage, by their attendance, her appearance on the stage, in the concert, or in feats of the circus.

Resolved, That woman has too long rested satisfied in the circumscribed limits which corrupt customs and a perverted application of the Scriptures have marked out for her, and that it is time she should move in the enlarged sphere which her great Creator has assigned her.

Resolved, That it is the duty of the women of this country to secure to   30 themselves their sacred right to the elective franchise.

Resolved, That the equality of human rights results necessarily from the fact of the identity of the race in capabilities and responsibilities.

Resolved, therefore, That, being invested by the Creator with the same capabilities, and the same consciousness of responsibility for their exercise, it is demonstrably the right and duty of woman, equally with man, to promote every righteous cause by every righteous means; and especially in regard to the great subjects of morals and religion, it is self-evidently her right to participate with her brother in teaching them, both in private and in public, by writing and by speaking, by any instrumentalities proper to be used, and in any assemblies proper to be held; and this being a self-evident truth growing out of the divinely implanted principles of human nature, any custom or authority adverse to it, whether modern or wearing the hoary sanction of antiquity, is to be regarded as a self-evident falsehood, and at war with mankind.

[At the last session Lucretia Mott offered and spoke to the following resolution:]

Resolved, That the speedy success of our cause depends upon the zealous and untiring efforts of both men and women, for the overthrow of the monopoly of the pulpit, and for the securing to woman an equal participation with men in the various trades, professions, and commerce.

Topics for Critical Thinking and Writing

1. Stanton echoes the Declaration of Independence because she wishes to associate her ideas and the movement she supports with a document and a movement that her readers esteem. And she must have believed that if readers esteem the Declaration of Independence, they must grant the justice of her goals. Does her strategy work, or does it backfire by making her essay seem strained?

2. When Stanton insists that women have an "inalienable right to the elective franchise" (para. 4), what does she mean by "inalienable"?

3. Stanton complains that men have made married women, "in the eye of the law, civilly dead" (para. 8). What does she mean by "civilly dead"? How is it possible for a person to be biologically alive and yet civilly dead?

4. Stanton objects that women are "not known" as teachers of "theology, medicine, or law" (para. 13). Is this still true today? Do some research in your library, and then write three 100-word biographical sketches, one each on well-known woman professors of theology, medicine, and law.

5. How might you go about proving (rather than merely asserting) that, as paragraph 24 says, "woman is man's equal—was intended to be so by the Creator"?

6. The Declaration claims that women have "the same capabilities" as men (para. 32). Yet in 1848 Stanton and the others at Seneca Falls knew, or should have known, that history recorded no example of a woman philosopher comparable to Plato or Kant, a composer comparable to Beethoven or Chopin, a scientist comparable to Galileo or Newton, or a mathematician comparable to Euclid or Descartes. Do these facts contradict the Declaration's claim? If not, why not? How else but by different intellectual capabilities do you think such facts can be explained?

7. Stanton's Declaration is over 155 years old. Have all of the issues she raised been satisfactorily resolved? If not, which ones remain?

8. In our society, children have very few rights. For instance, a child cannot decide to drop out of elementary school or high school, and a child cannot decide to leave his or her parents to reside with some other fam-

ily that he or she finds more compatible. Whatever your view of children's rights, compose the best Declaration of the Rights of Children that you can.

Martin Luther King Jr.

Martin Luther King Jr. (1929–1968) was born in Atlanta and educated at Morehouse College, Crozer Theological Seminary, and Boston University. In 1954 he was called to serve as a Baptist minister in Montgomery, Alabama. During the next two years he achieved national fame when, using a policy of nonviolent resistance, he successfully led the boycott against segregated bus lines in Montgomery. He then organized the Southern Christian Leadership Conference, which furthered civil rights, first in the South and then nationwide. In 1964 he was awarded the Nobel Peace Prize. Four years later he was assassinated in Memphis, Tennessee, while supporting striking garbage workers.

The speech presented here was delivered from the steps of the Lincoln Memorial, in Washington, D.C., in 1963, the hundredth anniversary of the Emancipation Proclamation. King's immediate audience consisted of more than two hundred thousand people who had come to demonstrate for civil rights.

I Have a Dream

I am happy to join with you today in what will go down in history as the greatest demonstration for freedom in the history of our nation.

Five score years ago, a great American, in whose symbolic shadow we stand today, signed the Emancipation Proclamation. This momentous decree came as a great beacon light of hope to millions of Negro slaves who had been seared in the flames of withering injustice. It came as a joyous daybreak to end the long night of their captivity. But one hundred years later, the Negro still is not free. One hundred years later, the life of the Negro is still sadly crippled by the manacles of segregation and the chains of discrimination. One hundred years later, the Negro lives on a lonely island of poverty in the midst of a vast ocean of material prosperity. One hundred years later, the Negro is still anguished in the corners of American society and finds himself in exile in his own land. And so we have come here today to dramatize a shameful condition.

In a sense we have come to our nation's capital to cash a check. When the architects of our republic wrote the magnificent words of the Constitution and the Declaration of Independence, they were signing a promissory note to which every American was to fall heir. This note was the promise that all men—yes, black men as well as white men—would be guaranteed the inalienable rights of life, liberty, and the pursuit of happiness.

It is obvious today that America has defaulted on this promissory note insofar as her citizens of color are concerned. Instead of honoring this sacred obligation, America has given the Negro people a bad check, a check which has come back marked "insufficient funds." But we refuse to believe that the bank of justice is bankrupt. We refuse to believe that there are insufficient funds in the great vaults of opportunity of this nation; and so we have come to cash this check, a check that will give us upon demand the riches of freedom and the security of justice.

We have also come to this hallowed spot to remind America of the 5 fierce urgency of *now*. This is no time to engage in the luxury of cooling off or to take the tranquilizing drug of gradualism. *Now* is the time to make real promises of democracy. *Now* is the time to rise from the dark and desolate valley of segregation to the sunlit path of racial justice. *Now* is the time to lift our nation from the quicksands of racial injustice to the solid rock of brotherhood. *Now* is the time to make justice a reality for all of God's children.

It would be fatal for the nation to overlook the urgency of the moment. This sweltering summer of the Negro's legitimate discontent will not pass until there is an invigorating autumn of freedom and equality. Nineteen sixty-three is not an end, but a beginning. And those who hope that the Negro needed to blow off steam and will now be content will have a rude awakening if the nation returns to business as usual. There will be neither rest nor tranquility in America until the Negro is granted his citizenship rights. The whirlwinds of revolt will continue to shake the foundations of our nation until the bright day of justice emerges.

But there is something that I must say to my people who stand on the warm threshold which leads into the palace of justice. In the process of gaining our rightful place, we must not be guilty of wrongful deeds. Let us not seek to satisfy our thirst for freedom by drinking from the cup of bitterness and hatred. We must forever conduct our struggle on the high plane of dignity and discipline. We must not allow our creative protest to degenerate into physical violence. Again and again we must rise to the majestic heights of meeting physical force with soul force. And the marvelous new militancy which has engulfed the Negro community must not lead us to a distrust of all white people; for many of our white brothers, as evidenced by their presence here today, have come to realize that their destiny is tied up with our destiny, and they have come to realize that their freedom is inextricably bound to our freedom.

We cannot walk alone. And as we walk we must make the pledge that we shall always march ahead. We cannot turn back. There are those who are asking the devotees of civil rights, "When will you be satisfied?" We can never be satisfied as long as the Negro is the victim of the unspeakable horrors of police brutality. We can never be satisfied as long as our bodies, heavy with the fatigue of travel, cannot gain lodging in the motels of the highways and the hotels of the cities. We cannot be satisfied as long as the Negro's basic mobility is from a smaller ghetto to a larger one. We can never be satisfied as long as our children are stripped of their selfhood and robbed of their dignity by signs stating "For Whites Only." We cannot be satisfied as long as the Negro in Mississippi cannot vote and a Negro in New York believes he has nothing for which to vote. No, no, we are not satisfied, and we will not be satisfied until justice rolls down like waters and righteousness like a mighty stream.[1]

I am not unmindful that some of you have come here out of great trials and tribulations. Some of you have come fresh from narrow jail cells. Some of you have come from areas where your quest for freedom left you battered by the storms of persecution and staggered by the winds of police brutality. You have been the veterans of creative suffering. Continue to work with the faith that unearned suffering is redemptive.

Go back to Mississippi, and go back to Alabama. Go back to South 10 Carolina. Go back to Georgia. Go back to Louisiana. Go back to the slums and ghettos of our Northern cities, knowing that somehow this situation can and will be changed. Let us not wallow in the valley of despair.

I say to you today, my friends, even though we face the difficulties of today and tomorrow, I still have a dream. It is a dream deeply rooted in the American dream. I have a dream that one day this nation will rise up and live out the true meaning of its creed: "We hold these truths to be self-evident, that all men are created equal." I have a dream that one day, on the red hills of Georgia, sons of former slaves and the sons of former slave owners will be able to sit down together at the table of brotherhood. I have a dream that one day even the state of Mississippi, a state sweltering with the heat of injustice, sweltering with the heat of oppression, will be transformed into an oasis of freedom and justice. I have a dream that my four little children will one day live in a nation where they will not be judged by the color of their skin, but by the content of their character.

I have a dream today. I have a dream that one day down in Alabama—with its vicious racists, with its governor's lips dripping with the words of interposition and nullification—one day right there in Alabama, little black boys and black girls will be able to join hands with little white boys and white girls as sisters and brothers.

I have a dream today. I have a dream that one day every valley shall be exalted and every hill and mountain shall be made low, the rough places will be made plain and the crooked places will be made straight, and the glory of the Lord shall be revealed, and all flesh shall see it together.[2]

This is our hope. This is the faith that I go back to the South with. And with this faith we will be able to hew out of the mountain of despair a stone of hope. With this faith we will be able to transform the jangling discords of our nation into a beautiful symphony of brotherhood. With

[1]**justice . . . stream** A quotation from the Hebrew Bible: Amos 5:24. [All notes are the editors'.]
[2]**every valley . . . see it together** Another quotation from the Hebrew Bible: Isaiah 40:4–5.

this faith we will be able to work together, to play together, to struggle together, to go to jail together, to stand up for freedom together, knowing that we will be free one day.

And this will be the day—this will be the day when all of God's chil- 15
dren will be able to sing with new meaning:

> My country, 'tis of thee,
> Sweet land of liberty,
>   Of thee I sing;
> Land where my fathers died,
> Land of the Pilgrim's pride,
> From every mountainside
>   Let freedom ring.

And if America is to be a great nation, this must become true.

And so let freedom ring from the prodigious hilltops of New Hampshire. Let freedom ring from the mighty mountains of New York. Let freedom ring from the heightening Alleghenies of Pennsylvania. Let freedom ring from the snow-capped Rockies of Colorado. Let freedom ring from the curvaceous slopes of California.

But not only that. Let freedom ring from Stone Mountain of Georgia. Let freedom ring from Lookout Mountain of Tennessee. Let freedom ring from every hill and molehill of Mississippi. "From every mountainside let freedom ring."

And when this happens—when we allow freedom to ring, when we let it ring from every village and every hamlet, from every state and every city—we will be able to speed up that day when all of God's children, Black men and white men, Jews and Gentiles, Protestants and Catholics, will be able to join hands and sing in the words of the old Negro spiritual: "Free at last! Free at last! Thank God Almighty. We are free at last!"

TOPICS FOR CRITICAL THINKING AND WRITING

1. Analyze the rhetoric—the oratorical art—of the second paragraph. What, for instance, is gained by saying "five score years ago" instead of "a hundred years ago"? By metaphorically calling the Emancipation Proclamation "a great beacon light of hope"? By saying that "Negro slaves . . . had been seared in the flames of withering injustice"? And what of the metaphors "daybreak" and "the long night of . . . captivity"?

2. Do the first two paragraphs make an effective opening? Why?

3. In the third and fourth paragraphs King uses the metaphor of a bad check. Rewrite the third paragraph *without* using any of King's metaphors, and then in a paragraph evaluate the differences between King's version and yours.

4. King's highly metaphoric speech appeals to emotions. But it also offers *reasons*. What reasons, for instance, does King give to support his belief

that African Americans should not resort to physical violence in their struggle against segregation and discrimination?

5. When King delivered the speech, his audience at the Lincoln Memorial was primarily African American. Do you think that the speech is also addressed to other Americans? Explain.

6. The speech can be divided into three parts: paragraphs 1 through 6; paragraphs 7 ("But there is") through 10; and paragraph 11 ("I say to you today, my friends") to the end. Summarize each of these three parts in a sentence or two so that the basic organization is evident.

7. King says (para. 11) that his dream is "deeply rooted in the American dream." First, what is the American dream, as King seems to understand it? Second, how does King establish his point — that is, what evidence does he use to convince us — that his dream is the American dream? (On this second issue, one might start by pointing out that in the second paragraph King refers to the Emancipation Proclamation. What other relevant documents does he refer to?)

8. King delivered his speech in 1963, more than forty years ago. In an essay of 500 words, argue that the speech still is — or is not — relevant. Or write an essay of 500 words in which you state what you take to be the "American dream," and argue that it now is or is not readily available to African Americans.

W. H. Auden

Wystan Hugh Auden (1907–1973) was born in York, England, and educated at Oxford University. In the 1930s his witty left-wing poetry earned him wide acclaim as the leading poet of his generation. In 1939 he came to the United States, becoming a citizen in 1946 but returning to England for his last years. Much of Auden's poetry is characterized by a combination of colloquial diction and technical dexterity. The poem reprinted here was originally published in 1940.

The Unknown Citizen

(To JS/07/M/378
This Marble Monument
Is Erected by the State)

He was found by the Bureau of Statistics to be
One against whom there was no official complaint,
And all the reports on his conduct agree
That, in the modern sense of an old-fashioned word, he was a saint,
For in everything he did he served the Greater Community.   5
Except for the War till the day he retired
He worked in a factory and never got fired,
But satisfied his employers, Fudge Motors Inc.
Yet he wasn't a scab or odd in his views,

For his Union reports that he paid his dues,   10
(Our report on his Union shows it was sound)
And our Social Psychology workers found
That he was popular with his mates and liked a drink.
The Press are convinced that he bought a paper every day
And that his reactions to advertisements were normal in every way.   15
Policies taken out in his name prove that he was fully insured,
And his Health-card shows he was once in hospital but left it cured.
Both Producers Research and High-Grade Living declare
He was fully sensible to the advantages of the Installment Plan
And had everything necessary to the Modern Man,   20
A phonograph, radio, a car and a frigidaire.
Our researches into Public Opinion are content
That he held the proper opinions for the time of year;
When there was peace, he was for peace; when there was war, he went.
He was married and added five children to the population,   25
Which our Eugenist says was the right number for a parent of his
    generation,
And our teachers report that he never interfered with their education.
Was he free? Was he happy? The question is absurd:
Had anything been wrong, we should certainly have heard.

TOPICS FOR CRITICAL THINKING AND WRITING

1. Who is the narrator in Auden's poem, and on what sort of occasion is he speaking? How do you know?

2. France, Great Britain, and the United States all have monuments to "The Unknown" (formerly "The Unknown Soldier"). How is Auden's proposed monument like and unlike these war memorials?

3. The poem ends by asking "Was he free? Was he happy?" and the questions are dismissed summarily. Is that because the answers are so obvious? What answers (obvious or subtle) do you think the poem offers to these questions?

4. Evaluate the poem, making clear the reasons behind your evaluation. (On literary evaluations, see p. 469.)

5. If you have read the selection from Thomas More's *Utopia* (p. 855), write an essay of 500 to 750 words—in More's voice—setting forth More's response to Auden's poem.

Langston Hughes

Langston Hughes (1902–1967), an African American writer, was born in Joplin, Missouri, but after his parents divorced, he lived with his grandmother in Lawrence, Kansas, then in Cleveland, and then for fifteen months in Mexico with his father. He returned to the United States in 1921 and spent a year at Columbia University, served as a merchant seaman, and worked in a Paris nightclub, where he showed some of his poems to Dr. Alain Locke, a strong advocate of African American literature. Encouraged by Locke, when Hughes returned to the United States, he studied at the University of Pennsylvania and Lincoln University, where he earned a bachelor's degree. He continued to write, publishing fiction, plays, essays, and biographies; he also founded theaters, gave public readings, and was, in short, a highly visible presence. Esquire *magazine first published an abridged version of "Let America Be America Again" in 1936.*

Let America Be America Again

Let America be America again.
Let it be the dream it used to be.
Let it be the pioneer on the plain
Seeking a home where he himself is free.

(America never was America to me.)   5

Let America be the dream the dreamers dreamed—
Let it be that great strong land of love
Where never kings connive nor tyrants scheme
That any man be crushed by one above.

(It never was America to me.)   10

O, let my land be a land where Liberty
Is crowned with no false patriotic wreath,
But opportunity is real, and life is free,
Equality is in the air we breathe.

(There's never been equality for me,   15
Nor freedom in this "homeland of the free.")

Say, who are you that mumbles in the dark?
And who are you that draws your veil across the stars?

I am the poor white, fooled and pushed apart,
I am the Negro bearing slavery's scars.   20
I am the red man driven from the land,
I am the immigrant clutching the hope I seek—
And finding only the same old stupid plan
Of dog eat dog, of mighty crush the weak.

I am the young man, full of strength and hope,   25
Tangled in that ancient endless chain
Of profit, power, gain, of grab the land!
Of grab the gold! Of grab the ways of satisfying need!
Of work the men! Of take the pay!
Of owning everything for one's own greed!   30

I am the farmer, bondsman to the soil.
I am the worker sold to the machine.

I am the Negro, servant to you all.
I am the people, humble, hungry, mean—
Hungry yet today despite the dream.   35
Beaten yet today—O, Pioneers!
I am the man who never got ahead,
The poorest worker bartered through the years.

Yet I'm the one who dreamt our basic dream
In that Old World while still a serf of kings,   40
Who dreamt a dream so strong, so brave, so true,
That even yet its mighty daring sings
In every brick and stone, in every furrow turned
That's made America the land it has become.
O, I'm the man who sailed those early seas   45
In search of what I meant to be my home—
For I'm the one who left dark Ireland's shore,
And Poland's plain, and England's grassy lea,
And torn from Black Africa's strand I came
To build a "homeland of the free."   50

The free?

Who said the free? Not me?
Surely not me? The millions on relief today?
The millions shot down when we strike?
The millions who have nothing for our pay?   55
For all the dreams we've dreamed
And all the songs we've sung
And all the hopes we've held
And all the flags we've hung,
The millions who have nothing for our pay—   60
Except the dream that's almost dead today.

O, let America be America again—
The land that never has been yet—
And yet must be—the land where *every* man is free.
The land that's mine—the poor man's, Indian's, Negro's, ME—   65
Who made America,
Whose sweat and blood, whose faith and pain,
Whose hand at the foundry, whose plow in the rain,
Must bring back our mighty dream again.

Sure, call me any ugly name you choose—   70
The steel of freedom does not stain.
From those who live like leeches on the people's lives,
We must take back our land again,
America!

O, yes,   75
I say it plain,
America never was America to me,

And yet I swear this oath—
America will be!

Out of the rack and ruin of our gangster death,   80
The rape and rot of graft, and stealth, and lies,
We, the people, must redeem
The land, the mines, the plants, the rivers.
The mountains and the endless plain—
All, all the stretch of these great green states—   85
And make America again!

Topics for Critical Thinking and Writing

1. Hughes says in line 1, "Let America be America again," but do you suppose that America ever was what he seems to assume that it once was? For instance, might not his "pioneer" (line 3) have been sexist and racist? Or is it evident that contemporary society is morally inferior to early American society?

2. In line 24 Hughes speaks of a system "of dog eat dog," where the "mighty crush the weak," and in line 27 he speaks of a system of "profit, power, gain, of grab the land." Do you believe that this charge can be lodged today against our system of capitalism? Explain.

3. When *Esquire* magazine bought the poem, it bought only the first fifty lines. Why do you suppose the magazine declined to publish the remainder? Because the latter part is less good as poetry? Because it is too radical? In an essay of 500 words compare the two versions (lines 1–50 and 1–86), and indicate which version you would publish if you were an editor today and why.

Ursula K. Le Guin

Ursula K. Le Guin was born in 1929 in Berkeley, California, the daughter of a distinguished mother (Theodora Kroeber, a folklorist) and father (Alfred L. Kroeber, an anthropologist). After graduating from Radcliffe College, she earned a master's degree at Columbia University; in 1952 she held a Fulbright Fellowship for study in Paris, where she met and married Charles Le Guin, a historian. She began writing in earnest while bringing up three children. Although her work is most widely known to buffs of science fiction, because it usually has larger moral or political dimensions, it interests many other readers who normally do not care for sci-fi.

Le Guin has said that she was prompted to write the following story by a remark she encountered in William James's "The Moral Philosopher and the Moral Life." James suggests there that if millions of people could be "kept permanently happy on the one simple condition that a certain lost soul on the far-off edge of things should lead a life of lonely torment," our moral sense "would make us immediately feel" it would be "hideous" to accept such a bargain. This story first appeared in New Dimensions 3 *(1973).*

The Ones Who Walk Away from Omelas

With a clamor of bells that set the swallows soaring, the Festival of Summer came to the city Omelas, bright-towered by the sea. The rigging of the boats in harbor sparkled with flags. In the streets between houses with red roofs and painted walls, between old moss-grown gardens and under avenues of trees, past great parks and public buildings, processions moved. Some were decorous: old people in long stiff robes of mauve and gray, grave master workmen, quiet, merry women carrying their babies and chatting as they walked. In other streets the music beat faster, a shimmering of gong and tambourine, and the people went dancing, the procession was a dance. Children dodged in and out, their high calls rising like the swallows' crossing flights over the music and the singing. All the processions wound towards the north side of the city, where on the great water-meadow called the Green Fields boys and girls, naked in the bright air, with mudstained feet and ankles and long, lithe arms, exercised their restive horses before the race. The horses wore no gear at all but a halter without bit. Their manes were braided with streamers of silver, gold, and green. They flared their nostrils and pranced and boasted to one another; they were vastly excited, the horse being the only animal who has adopted our ceremonies as his own. Far off to the north and west the mountains stood up half encircling Omelas on her bay. The air of morning was so clear that the snow still crowning the Eighteen Peaks burned with white-gold fire across the miles of sunlit air, under the dark blue of the sky. There was just enough wind to make the banners that marked the racecourse snap and flutter now and then. In the silence of the broad green meadows one could hear the music winding through the city streets, farther and nearer and ever approaching, a cheerful faint sweetness of the air that from time to time trembled and gathered together and broke out into the great joyous clanging of the bells.

Joyous! How is one to tell about joy? How describe the citizens of Omelas?

They were not simple folk, you see, though they were happy. But we do not say the words of cheer much any more. All smiles have become archaic. Given a description such as this one tends to make certain assumptions. Given a description such as this one tends to look next for the King, mounted on a splendid stallion and surrounded by his noble knights, or perhaps in a golden litter borne by great-muscled slaves. But there was no king. They did not use swords, or keep slaves. They were not barbarians. I do not know the rules and laws of their society, but I suspect that they were singularly few. As they did without monarchy and slavery, so they also got on without the stock exchange, the advertisement, the secret police, and the bomb. Yet I repeat that these were not simple folk, not dulcet shepherds, noble savages, bland utopians. They were not less complex than us. The trouble is that we have a bad habit, encouraged by pedants and sophisticates, of considering happiness as something rather stupid. Only pain is intellectual, only evil interesting. This is the treason of the artist: a refusal to admit the banality of evil and the terrible boredom of pain. If you can't lick 'em, join 'em. If it hurts, repeat it. But to praise despair is to condemn delight, to embrace violence is to lose hold of everything else. We have almost lost hold, we can no longer describe a happy man, nor make any celebration of joy. How can I tell you about the people of Omelas? They were not naïve and happy children — though their children were, in fact, happy. They were mature, intelligent, passionate adults whose lives were not wretched. O miracle! But I wish I could describe it better. I wish I could convince you. Omelas sounds in my words like a city in a fairy tale, long ago and far away, once upon a time. Perhaps it would be best if you imagined it as your own fancy bids, assuming it will rise to the occasion, for certainly I cannot suit you all. For instance, how about technology? I think that there would be no cars or helicopters in and above the streets; this follows from the fact that the people of Omelas are happy people. Happiness is based on a just discrimination of what is necessary, what is neither necessary nor destructive, and what is destructive. In the middle category, however — that of the unnecessary but undestructive, that of comfort, luxury, exuberance, etc. — they could perfectly well have central heating, subway trains, washing machines, and all kinds of marvelous devices not yet invented here, floating light-sources, fuelless power, a cure for the common cold. Or they could have none of that: it doesn't matter. As you like it. I incline to think that people from towns up and down the coast have been coming in to Omelas during the last days before the Festival on very fast little trains and double-decked trams, and that the train station of Omelas is actually the handsomest building in town, though plainer than the magnificent Farmers' Market. But even granted trains, I fear that Omelas so far strikes some of you as goody-goody. Smiles, bells, parades, horses, bleh. If so, please add an orgy. If an orgy would help, don't hesitate. Let us not, however, have temples from which issue beautiful nude priests and priestesses already half in ecstasy and ready to copulate with any man or woman, lover or stranger, who desires union with the deep godhead of the blood, although that was my first idea. But really it would be better not to have any temples in Omelas — at least, not manned temples. Religion yes, clergy no. Surely the beautiful nudes can just wander about, offering themselves like divine soufflés to the hunger of the needy and the rapture of the flesh. Let them join the processions. Let tambourines be struck above the copulations, and the glory of desire be proclaimed upon the gongs, and (a not unimportant point) let the offspring of these delightful rituals be beloved and looked after by all. One thing I know there is none of in Omelas is guilt. But what else should there be? I thought that first there were no drugs, but that is puritanical. For those who like it, the faint insistent sweetness of *drooz* may perfume the ways of the city, *drooz* which first brings a great lightness and brilliance to the mind and limbs, and then after some hours a dreamy languor, and wonderful visions at last of the very arcana and inmost secrets of the Universe, as well as exciting the pleasure of sex beyond all belief; and it is not habit-forming. For more modest tastes I think there ought to be beer. What else, what else belongs in the joyous city? The sense of victory, surely, the celebration of courage. But as we did without clergy, let us do without soldiers. The joy built upon successful slaughter is not the right kind of joy; it will not do; it is fearful and it is trivial. A boundless and generous contentment, a magnanimous triumph felt not against some outer enemy but in communion with the finest and fairest in the souls of all men everywhere and the splendor of the world's summer: this is what swells the hearts of the people of Omelas, and the victory they celebrate is that of life. I really don't think many of them need to take *drooz*.

Most of the processions have reached the Green Fields by now. A marvelous smell of cooking goes forth from the red and blue tents of the provisioners. The faces of small children are amiably sticky; in the benign grey beard of a man a couple of crumbs of rich pastry are entangled. The youths and girls have mounted their horses and are beginning to group around the starting line of the course. An old woman, small, fat, and laughing, is passing out flowers from a basket, and tall young men wear her flowers in their shining hair. A child of nine or ten sits at the edge of the crowd, alone, playing on a wooden flute. People pause to listen, and they smile, but they do not speak to him, for he never ceases playing and never sees them, his dark eyes wholly rapt in the sweet, thin magic of the tune.

He finishes, and slowly lowers his hands holding the wooden flute.   5

As if that little private silence were the signal, all at once a trumpet sounds from the pavilion near the starting line: imperious, melancholy, piercing. The horses rear on their slender legs, and some of them neigh in answer. Sober-faced, the young riders stroke the horses' necks and soothe them, whispering, "Quiet, quiet, there my beauty, my hope. . . ." They begin to form in rank along the starting line. The crowds along the racecourse are like a field of grass and flowers in the wind. The Festival of Summer has begun.

Do you believe? Do you accept the festival, the city, the joy? No? Then let me describe one more thing.

In a basement under one of the beautiful public buildings of Omelas, or perhaps in the cellar of one of its spacious private homes, there is a room. It has one locked door, and no window. A little light seeps in dustily between cracks in the boards, secondhand from a cobwebbed window somewhere across the cellar. In one corner of the little room a couple of mops, with stiff, clotted, foul-smelling heads, stand near a rusty bucket. The floor is dirt, a little damp to the touch, as cellar dirt usually is. The room is about three paces long and two wide: a mere broom closet or disused tool room. In the room a child is sitting. It could be a boy or a girl. It looks about six, but actually is nearly ten. It is feeble-minded. Perhaps it was born defective, or perhaps it has become imbecile through fear, malnutrition, and neglect. It picks its nose and occasionally fumbles vaguely with its toes or genitals, as it sits hunched in the corner farthest from the bucket and the two mops. It is afraid of the mops. It finds them horrible. It shuts its eyes, but it knows the mops are still standing there; and the door is locked; and nobody will come. The door is always locked; and nobody ever comes, except that sometimes—the child has no understanding of time or interval—sometimes the door rattles terribly and opens, and a person, or several people, are there. One of them may come in and kick the child to make it stand up. The others never come close, but peer in at it with frightened, disgusted eyes. The food bowl and the water jug are hastily filled, the door is locked, the eyes disappear. The people at the door never say anything, but the child, who has not always lived in the tool room, and can remember sunlight and its mother's voice, sometimes speaks. "I will be good," it says. "Please let me out. I will be good!" They never answer. The child used to scream for help at night, and cry a good deal, but now it only makes a kind of whining, "eh-haa, eh-haa," and it speaks less and less often. It is so thin there are no calves to its legs; its belly protrudes; it lives on a half-bowl of corn meal and grease a day. It is naked. Its buttocks and thighs are a mass of festered sores, as it sits in its own excrement continually.

They all know it is there, all the people of Omelas. Some of them have come to see it, others are content merely to know it is there. They all know that it has to be there. Some of them understand why, and some do not, but they all understand that their happiness, the beauty of their city, the tenderness of their friendships, the health of their children, the wisdom of their scholars, the skill of their makers, even the abundance of their harvest and the kindly weathers of their skies, depend wholly on this child's abominable misery.

This is usually explained to children when they are between eight   10 and twelve, whenever they seem capable of understanding; and most of those who come to see the child are young people, though often enough an adult comes, or comes back, to see the child. No matter how well the matter has been explained to them, these young spectators are always shocked and sickened at the sight. They feel disgust, which they had thought themselves superior to. They feel anger, outrage, impotence, despite all the explanations. They would like to do something for the child. But there is nothing they can do. If the child were brought up into the sunlight out of that vile place, if it were cleaned and fed and comforted, that would be a good thing, indeed; but if it were done, in that day and hour all the prosperity and beauty and delight of Omelas would

wither and be destroyed. Those are the terms. To exchange all the goodness and grace of every life in Omelas for that single, small improvement: to throw away the happiness of thousands for the chance of the
happiness of one: that would be to let guilt within the walls indeed.

The terms are strict and absolute; there may not even be a kind word
spoken to the child.

Often the young people go home in tears, or in a tearless rage,
when they have seen the child and faced this terrible paradox. They
may brood over it for weeks or years. But as time goes on they begin to
realize that even if the child could be released, it would not get much
good of its freedom: a little vague pleasure of warmth and food, no
doubt, but little more. It is too degraded and imbecile to know any real
joy. It has been afraid too long ever to be free of fear. Its habits are too
uncouth for it to respond to humane treatment. Indeed, after so long it
would probably be wretched without walls about it to protect it, and
darkness for its eyes, and its own excrement to sit in. Their tears at the
bitter injustice dry when they begin to perceive the terrible justice of
reality, and to accept it. Yet it is their tears and anger, the trying of their
generosity and the acceptance of their helplessness, which are perhaps
the true source of the splendor of their lives. Theirs is no vapid, irresponsible happiness. They know that they, like the child, are not free.
They know compassion. It is the existence of the child, and their knowledge of its existence, that makes possible the nobility of their architecture, the poignancy of their music, the profundity of their science. It is
because of the child that they are so gentle with children. They know
that if the wretched one were not there snivelling in the dark, the other
one, the flute-player, could make no joyful music as the young riders
line up in their beauty for the race in the sunlight of the first morning
of summer.

Now do you believe in them? Are they not more credible? But there
is one more thing to tell, and this is quite incredible.

At times one of the adolescent girls or boys who go to see the child
does not go home to weep or rage, does not, in fact, go home at all.
Sometimes also a man or woman much older falls silent for a day or two,
and then leaves home. These people go out into the street, and walk
down the street alone. They keep walking, and walk straight out of the
city of Omelas, through the beautiful gates. They keep walking across
the farmlands of Omelas. Each one goes alone, youth or girl, man or
woman. Night falls; the traveler must pass down village streets, between
the houses with yellow-lit windows, and on out into the darkness of the
fields. Each alone, they go west or north, towards the mountains. They
go on. They leave Omelas, they walk ahead into the darkness, and they
do not come back. The place they go towards is a place even less imag-
inable to most of us than the city of happiness. I cannot describe it at all.
It is possible that it does not exist. But they seem to know where they
are going, the ones who walk away from Omelas.

TOPICS FOR CRITICAL THINKING AND WRITING

1. Summarize the point of the story—not the plot, but what the story adds up to, what the author is getting at. Next, set forth what you would probably do (and why) if you were born in Omelas.

2. Consider the narrator's assertion that happiness "is based on a just discrimination of what is necessary" (para. 3).

3. Do you think the story implies a criticism of contemporary American society? Explain.

33

How Free Is the Will of the Individual within Society?

THOUGHTS ABOUT FREE WILL

All theory is against the freedom of the will; all experience for it.
—Samuel Johnson

Free will is doing gladly and freely that which one must do.
—Carl G. Jung

The will is never free—it is always attached to an object, a purpose.
It is simply the engine in the car—it can't steer.
—Joyce Cary

A man may be a pessimistic determinist before lunch and an optimistic believer in the will's freedom after it.
—Aldous Huxley

Fatalism, whose solving word in all crises of behavior is all striving is vain, will never reign supreme, for the impulse to take life strivingly is indestructible in the race. Moral creeds which speak to that impulse will be widely successful in spite of inconsistency, vagueness, and shadowy determination of expectancy. Man needs a rule for his will, and will invent one if one be not given him.
—William James

Man is a masterpiece of creation if for no other reason than that, all the weight of evidence for determinism notwithstanding, he believes he has free will.
—Georg C. Lichtenberg

We human beings do have some genuine freedom of choice and therefore some effective control over our own destinies. I am not a determinist. But I also believe that the decisive choice is seldom the latest choice in the series. More often than not, it will turn out to be some choice made relatively far back in the past.
—Arnold Toynbee

We are responsible human beings, not blind automatons; persons, not puppets. By endowing us with freedom, God relinquished a measure of his own sovereignty and imposed certain limitations upon himself. If his children are free, they must do his will by a voluntary choice.

—Martin Luther King Jr.

Life is a card game. You play the hand that is dealt to you.

—Proverbial

We must believe in free will. We have no choice.

—Isaac Bashevis Singer

Topics for Critical Thinking and Writing

1. If any one of these passages especially appeals to you, make it the thesis of an essay of about 500 words.

2. Take two of these passages—perhaps one that you especially like and one that you think is wrong-headed—and write a dialogue of about 500 words in which the two authors converse. They may each try to convince the other, or they may find that to some degree they share views and they may then work out a statement that both can accept. If you do take the position that one writer is on the correct track but the other is utterly mistaken, try to be fair to the view that you think is mistaken. (As an experiment in critical thinking, imagine that you accept it, and make the best case for it that you possibly can.)

Plato

Plato (427–347 B.C.), an Athenian aristocrat by birth, was the student of one great philosopher (Socrates) and the teacher of another (Aristotle). His legacy of more than two dozen dialogues—imaginary discussions between Socrates and one or more other speakers, usually young Athenians—has been of such influence that the whole of Western philosophy can be characterized, A. N. Whitehead wrote, as "a series of footnotes to Plato." Plato's interests encompassed the full range of topics in philosophy: ethics, politics, logic, metaphysics, epistemology, aesthetics, psychology, and education.

The selection reprinted here, Crito, is the third of four dialogues telling the story of the final days of Socrates (469–399 B.C.). The first in the sequence, Euthyphro, portrays Socrates in his typical role, questioning someone about his beliefs (in this case, the young aristocrat, Euthyphro). The discussion is focused on the nature of piety, but the conversation breaks off before a final answer is reached—perhaps none is possible—because Socrates is on his way to stand trial before the Athenian assembly. He has been charged with "preaching false gods" (heresy) and "corrupting the youth" by causing them to doubt or disregard the wisdom of their elders. (How faithful to any actual event or discussion Euthyphro and Plato's other Socratic dialogues really are, scholars cannot say with assurance.)

In Apology, the second dialogue in the sequence, Plato (who remains entirely in the background, as he does in all the dialogues) recounts Socrates' public reply to the charges against him. During the speech, Socrates explains his life, reminding his fellow citizens that if he is (as the oracle had pronounced) "the wisest of men," then it is only because he knows that he doesn't know what others believe or pretend they do know. The dialogue ends with Socrates being found guilty and duly sentenced to death.

The third in the series is Crito, *but we will postpone comment on it for a moment and glance at the fourth dialogue,* Phaedo, *in which Plato portrays Socrates' final philosophical discussion. The topic, appropriately, is whether the soul is immortal. It ends with Socrates, in the company of his closest friends, bidding them a last farewell and drinking the fatal cup of hemlock.*

Crito, *the whole text of which is reprinted here, is the debate provoked by Crito, an old friend and admirer of Socrates. He visits Socrates in prison and urges him to escape while he still has the chance. After all, Crito argues, the guilty verdict was wrong and unfair, few Athenians really want to have Socrates put to death, his family and friends will be distraught, and so forth. Socrates will not have it. He patiently but firmly examines each of Crito's arguments and explains why it would be wrong to follow his advice.*

Plato's Crito *thus ranks with Sophocles' tragedy* Antigone *as one of the first explorations in Western literature of the perennial theme of our responsibility for obeying laws that challenge our conscientious moral convictions.* Antigone *concludes that she must disobey the law of Creon, tyrant of Thebes; Socrates concludes that he must obey the law of democratic Athens. In* Crito, *we have not only a superb illustration of Socratic dialogue and argument but also a portrait of a virtuous thinker at the end of a long life, reflecting on its course and on the moral principles that have guided him. We see Socrates living an "examined life," the only life he thought was worth living.*

This translation is by Hugh Tredennick.

Crito

(**SCENE:** *A room in the State prison at Athens in the year 399 B.C. The time is half an hour before dawn, and the room would be almost dark but for the light of a little oil lamp. There is a pallet bed against the back wall. At the head of it a small table supports the lamp; near the foot of it Crito is sitting patiently on a stool. He is an old man, kindly, practical, simple-minded; at present he is suffering from acute emotional strain. On the bed lies Socrates asleep. He stirs, yawns, opens his eyes, and sees Crito.*)

SOCRATES: Here already, Crito? Surely it is still early?

CRITO: Indeed it is.

SOCRATES: About what time?

CRITO: Just before dawn.

SOCRATES: I wonder that the warder paid any attention to you.   5

CRITO: He is used to me now, Socrates, because I come here so often; besides, he is under some small obligation to me.

SOCRATES: Have you only just come, or have you been here for long?

CRITO: Fairly long.

SOCRATES: Then why didn't you wake me at once, instead of sitting by my bed so quietly?

CRITO: I wouldn't dream of such a thing, Socrates. I only wish I were not   10
    so sleepless and depressed myself. I have been wondering at you,
    because I saw how comfortably you were sleeping; and I deliberately
    didn't wake you because I wanted you to go on being as comfortable
    as you could. I have often felt before in the course of my life how
    fortunate you are in your disposition, but I feel it more than ever
    now in your present misfortune when I see how easily and placidly
    you put up with it.

SOCRATES: Well, really, Crito, it would be hardly suitable for a man of my
    age to resent having to die.

CRITO: Other people just as old as you are get involved in these misfor-
    tunes, Socrates, but their age doesn't keep them from resenting it
    when they find themselves in your position.

SOCRATES: Quite true. But tell me, why have you come so early?

CRITO: Because I bring bad news, Socrates; not so bad from your point of
    view, I suppose, but it will be very hard to bear for me and your
    other friends, and I think that I shall find it hardest of all.

SOCRATES: Why, what is this news? Has the boat come in from Delos—the   15
    boat which ends my reprieve when it arrives?[1]

CRITO: It hasn't actually come in yet, but I expect that it will be here
    today, judging from the report of some people who have just arrived
    from Sunium and left it there. It's quite clear from their account that
    it will be here today; and so by tomorrow, Socrates, you will have
    to—to end your life.

SOCRATES: Well, Crito, I hope that it may be for the best; if the gods will it
    so, so be it. All the same, I don't think it will arrive today.

CRITO: What makes you think that?

SOCRATES: I will try to explain. I think I am right in saying that I have to
    die on the day after the boat arrives?

CRITO: That's what the authorities say, at any rate.   20

SOCRATES: Then I don't think it will arrive on this day that is just begin-
    ning, but on the day after. I am going by a dream that I had in the
    night, only a little while ago. It looks as though you were right not
    to wake me up.

CRITO: Why, what was the dream about?

SOCRATES: I thought I saw a gloriously beautiful woman dressed in white
    robes, who came up to me and addressed me in these words: "Socrates,
    to the pleasant land of Phthia on the third day thou shalt come."

CRITO: Your dream makes no sense, Socrates.

SOCRATES: To my mind, Crito, it is perfectly clear.   25

---

[1]**Delos . . . arrives** Ordinarily execution was carried out immediately after sentencing, but
the day before Socrates' trial was the first day of an annual ceremony that involved sending a ship to Delos. When the ship was absent—in this case for about a month—executions could not be performed. As Crito goes on to say, Socrates could easily escape, and
indeed he could have left the country before being tried. [All notes are the editors'.]

CRITO: Too clear, apparently. But look here, Socrates, it is still not too late to take my advice and escape. Your death means a double calamity for me. I shall not only lose a friend whom I can never possibly replace, but besides a great many people who don't know you and me very well will be sure to think that I let you down, because I could have saved you if I had been willing to spend the money; and what could be more contemptible than to get a name for thinking more of money than of your friends? Most people will never believe that it was you who refused to leave this place although we tried our hardest to persuade you.

SOCRATES: But my dear Crito, why should we pay so much attention to what "most people" think? The really reasonable people, who have more claim to be considered, will believe that the facts are exactly as they are.

CRITO: You can see for yourself, Socrates, that one has to think of popular opinion as well. Your present position is quite enough to show that the capacity of ordinary people for causing trouble is not confined to petty annoyances, but has hardly any limits if you once get a bad name with them.

SOCRATES: I only wish that ordinary people *had* unlimited capacity for doing harm; then they might have an unlimited power for doing good; which would be a splendid thing, if it were so. Actually they have neither. They cannot make a man wise or stupid; they simply act at random.

CRITO: Have it that way if you like; but tell me this, Socrates. I hope that you aren't worrying about the possible effects on me and the rest of your friends, and thinking that if you escape we shall have trouble with informers for having helped you to get away, and have to forfeit all our property or pay an enormous fine, or even incur some further punishment? If any idea like that is troubling you, you can dismiss it altogether. We are quite entitled to run that risk in saving you, and even worse, if necessary. Take my advice, and be reasonable. 30

SOCRATES: All that you say is very much in my mind, Crito, and a great deal more besides.

CRITO: Very well, then, don't let it distress you. I know some people who are willing to rescue you from here and get you out of the country for quite a moderate sum. And then surely you realize how cheap these informers are to buy off; we shan't need much money to settle them; and I think you've got enough of my money for yourself already. And then even supposing that in your anxiety for my safety you feel that you oughtn't to spend my money, there are these foreign gentlemen staying in Athens who are quite willing to spend theirs. One of them, Simmias of Thebes, has actually brought the money with him for this very purpose; and Cebes and a number of others are quite ready to do the same. So as I say, you mustn't let any fears on these grounds make you slacken your efforts to escape;

and you mustn't feel any misgivings about what you said at your trial, that you wouldn't know what to do with yourself if you left this country. Wherever you go, there are plenty of places where you will find a welcome; and if you choose to go to Thessaly, I have friends there who will make much of you and give you complete protection, so that no one in Thessaly can interfere with you.

Besides, Socrates, I don't even feel that it is right for you to try to do what you are doing, throwing away your life when you might save it. You are doing your best to treat yourself in exactly the same way as your enemies would, or rather did, when they wanted to ruin you. What is more, it seems to me that you are letting your sons down too. You have it in your power to finish their bringing up and education, and instead of that you are proposing to go off and desert them, and so far as you are concerned they will have to take their chance. And what sort of chance are they likely to get? The sort of thing that usually happens to orphans when they lose their parents. Either one ought not to have children at all, or one ought to see their upbringing and education through to the end. It strikes me that you are taking the line of least resistance, whereas you ought to make the choice of a good man and a brave one, considering that you profess to have made goodness your object all through life. Really, I am ashamed, both on your account and on ours your friends'; it will look as though we had played something like a coward's part all through this affair of yours. First, there was the way you came into court when it was quite unnecessary—that was the first act; than there was the conduct of the defense—that was the second; and finally, to complete the farce, we get this situation, which makes it appear that we have let you slip out of our hands through some lack of courage and enterprise on our part, because we didn't save you, and you didn't save yourself, when it would have been quite possible and practicable, if we had been any use at all.

There, Socrates; if you aren't careful, besides the suffering there will be all this disgrace for you and us to bear. Come, make up your mind. Really it's too late for that now; you ought to have it made up already. There is no alternative; the whole thing must be carried through during this coming night. If we lose any more time, it can't be done, it will be too late. I appeal to you, Socrates, on every ground; take my advice and please don't be unreasonable!

SOCRATES: My dear Crito, I appreciate your warm feelings very much— 35 that is, assuming that they have some justification; if not, the stronger they are, the harder they will be to deal with. Very well, then; we must consider whether we ought to follow your advice or not. You know that this is not a new idea of mine; it has always been my nature never to accept advice from any of my friends unless reflection shows that it is the best course that reason offers. I cannot abandon the principles which I used to hold in the past simply because this accident has happened to me; they seem to me to be much as they were, and I respect and regard the same principles now as before. So unless we can find better principles on this occasion, you can be quite sure that I shall not agree with you; not even if the power of the people conjures up fresh hordes of bogies to terrify our childish minds, by subjecting us to chains and executions and confiscations of our property.

Well, then, how can we consider the question most reasonably? Suppose that we begin by reverting to this view which you hold about people's opinions. Was it always right to argue that some opinions should be taken seriously but not others? Or was it always wrong? Perhaps it was right before the question of my death arose, but now we can see clearly that it was a mistaken persistence in a point of view which was really irresponsible nonsense. I should like very much to inquire into this problem, Crito, with your help, and to see whether the argument will appear in any different light to me now that I am in this position, or whether it will remain the same; and whether we shall dismiss it or accept it.

Serious thinkers, I believe, have always held some such view as the one which I mentioned just now: that some of the opinions which people entertain should be respected, and others should not. Now I ask you, Crito, don't you think that this is a sound principle?—You are safe from the prospect of dying tomorrow, in all human probability; and you are not likely to have your judgment upset by this impending calamity. Consider, then; don't you think that this is a sound enough principle, that one should not regard all the opinions that people hold, but only some and not others? What do you say? Isn't that a fair statement?

CRITO: Yes, it is.

SOCRATES: In other words, one should regard the good ones and not the bad?

CRITO: Yes.   40

SOCRATES: The opinions of the wise being good, and the opinions of the foolish bad?

CRITO: Naturally.

SOCRATES: To pass on, then: What do you think of the sort of illustration that I used to employ? When a man is in training, and taking it seriously, does he pay attention to all praise and criticism and opinion indiscriminately, or only when it comes from the one qualified person, the actual doctor or trainer?

CRITO: Only when it comes from the one qualified person.

SOCRATES: Then he should be afraid of the criticism and welcome the praise   45 of the one qualified person, but not those of the general public.

CRITO: Obviously.

SOCRATES: So he ought to regulate his actions and exercises and eating and drinking by the judgment of his instructor, who has expert knowledge, rather than by the opinions of the rest of the public.

CRITO: Yes, that is so.

SOCRATES: Very well. Now if he disobeys the one man and disregards his opinion and commendations, and pays attention to the advice of the many who have no expert knowledge, surely he will suffer some bad effect?

CRITO: Certainly.   50

SOCRATES: And what is this bad effect? Where is it produced?—I mean, in what part of the disobedient person?

CRITO: His body, obviously; that is what suffers.

SOCRATES: Very good. Well now, tell me, Crito—we don't want to go through all the examples one by one—does this apply as a general rule, and above all to the sort of actions which we are trying to decide about: just and unjust, honorable and dishonorable, good and bad? Ought we to be guided and intimidated by the opinion of the many or by that of the one—assuming that there is someone with expert knowledge? Is it true that we ought to respect and fear this person more than all the rest put together; and that if we do not follow his guidance we shall spoil and mutilate that part of us which, as we used to say, is improved by right conduct and destroyed by wrong? Or is this all nonsense?

CRITO: No, I think it is true, Socrates.

SOCRATES: Then consider the next step. There is a part of us which is   55 improved by healthy actions and ruined by unhealthy ones. If we spoil it by taking the advice of nonexperts, will life be worth living when this part is once ruined? The part I mean is the body; do you accept this?

CRITO: Yes.

SOCRATES: Well, is life worth living with a body which is worn out and ruined by health?

CRITO: Certainly not.

SOCRATES: What about the part of us which is mutilated by wrong actions and benefited by right ones? Is life worth living with this part ruined? Or do we believe that this part of us, whatever it may be, in which right and wrong operate, is of less importance than the body?

CRITO: Certainly not.   60

SOCRATES: It is really more precious?

CRITO: Much more.

SOCRATES: In that case, my dear fellow, what we ought to consider is not so much what people in general will say about us but how we stand with the expert in right and wrong, the one authority, who represents the actual truth. So in the first place your proposition is not correct when you say that we should consider popular opinion in questions of what is right and honorable and good, or the opposite. Of course one might object "All the same, the people have the power to put us to death."

CRITO: No doubt about that! Quite true, Socrates; it is a possible objection.

SOCRATES: But so far as I can see, my dear fellow, the argument which we 65
have just been through is quite unaffected by it. At the same time I
should like you to consider whether we are still satisfied on this
point: that the really important thing is not to live, but to live well.

CRITO: Why, yes.

SOCRATES: And that to live well means the same thing as to live honorably
or rightly?

CRITO: Yes.

SOCRATES: Then in the light of this agreement we must consider whether
or not it is right for me to try to get away without an official discharge. If it turns out to be right, we must make the attempt; if not,
we must let it drop. As for the considerations you raise about
expense and reputation and bringing up children, I am afraid, Crito,
that they represent the reflections of the ordinary public, who put
people to death, and would bring them back to life if they could,
with equal indifference to reason. Our real duty, I fancy, since the
argument leads that way, is to consider one question only, the one
which we raised just now: Shall we be acting rightly in paying
money and showing gratitude to these people who are going to rescue
me, and in escaping or arranging the escape ourselves, or shall we
really be acting wrongly in doing all this? If it becomes clear that such
conduct is wrong, I cannot help thinking that the question whether
we are sure to die, or to suffer any other ill effect for that matter, if we
stand our ground and take no action, ought not to weigh with us at all
in comparison with the risk of doing what is wrong.

CRITO: I agree with what you say, Socrates; but I wish you would consider 70
what we ought to *do*.

SOCRATES: Let us look at it together, my dear fellow; and if you can challenge any of my arguments, do so and I will listen to you; but if you
can't, be a good fellow and stop telling me over and over again that I
ought to leave this place without official permission. I am very anxious to obtain your approval before I adopt the course which I have
in mind; I don't want to act against your convictions. Now give your
attention to the starting point of this inquiry—I hope that you will
be satisfied with my way of stating it—and try to answer my questions to the best of your judgment.

CRITO: Well, I will try.

SOCRATES: Do we say that one must never willingly do wrong, or does it
depend upon circumstance? Is it true, as we have often agreed
before, that there is no sense in which wrongdoing is good or honorable? Or have we jettisoned all our former convictions in these last
few days? Can you and I at our age, Crito, have spent all these years
in serious discussions without realizing that we were no better than
a pair of children? Surely the truth is just what we have always said.
Whatever the popular view is, and whether the alternative is pleas-
anter than the present one or even harder to bear, the fact remains

that to do wrong is in every sense bad and dishonorable for the person who does it. Is that our view, or not?

CRITO: Yes, it is.

SOCRATES: Then in no circumstances must one do wrong.   75

CRITO: No.

SOCRATES: In that case one must not even do wrong when one is wronged, which most people regard as the natural course.

CRITO: Apparently not.

SOCRATES: Tell me another thing, Crito: Ought one to do injuries or not?

CRITO: Surely not, Socrates.   80

SOCRATES: And tell me: Is it right to do an injury in retaliation, as most people believe, or not?

CRITO: No, never.

SOCRATES: Because, I suppose, there is no difference between injuring people and wronging them.

CRITO: Exactly.

SOCRATES: So one ought not to return a wrong or an injury to any person, 85 whatever the provocation is. Now be careful, Crito, that in making these single admissions you do not end by admitting something contrary to your real beliefs. I know that there are and always will be few people who think like this; and consequently between those who do think so and those who do not there can be no agreement on principle; they must always feel contempt when they observe one another's decisions. I want even you to consider very carefully whether you share my views and agree with me, and whether we can proceed with our discussion from the established hypothesis that it is never right to do a wrong or return a wrong or defend one's self against injury by retaliation; or whether you dissociate yourself from any share in this view as a basis for discussion. I have held it for a long time, and still hold it; but if you have formed any other opinion, say so and tell me what it is. If, on the other hand, you stand by what we have said, listen to my next point.

CRITO: Yes, I stand by it and agree with you. Go on.

SOCRATES: Well, here is my next point, or rather question. Ought one to fulfill all one's agreements, provided that they are right, or break them?

CRITO: One ought to fulfill them.

SOCRATES: Then consider the logical consequence. If we leave this place without first persuading the State to let us go, are we or are we not doing an injury, and doing it in a quarter where it is least justifiable? Are we or are we not abiding by our just agreements?

CRITO: I can't answer your question, Socrates; I am not clear in my mind. 90

SOCRATES: Look at it in this way. Suppose that while we were preparing to run away from here (or however one should describe it) the Laws and Constitution of Athens were to come and confront us and ask this question: "Now, Socrates, what are you proposing to do? Can you deny that by this act which you are contemplating you intend, so far as you have the power, to destroy us, the Laws, and the whole State as well? Do you imagine that a city can continue to exist and not be turned upside down, if the legal judgments which are pronounced in it have no force but are nullified and destroyed by private persons?"—how shall we answer this question, Crito, and others of the same kind? There is much that could be said, especially by a professional advocate, to protest against the invalidation of this law which enacts that judgments once pronounced shall be binding. Shall we say "Yes, I do intend to destroy the laws, because the State wronged me by passing a faulty judgment at my trial"? Is this to be our answer, or what?

CRITO: What you have just said, by all means, Socrates.

SOCRATES: Then what supposing the Laws say, "Was there provision for this in the agreement between you and us, Socrates? Or did you undertake to abide by whatever judgments the State pronounced?" If we expressed surprise at such language, they would probably say: "Never mind our language, Socrates, but answer our questions; after all, you are accustomed to the method of question and answer. Come now, what charge do you bring against us and the State, that you are trying to destroy us? Did we not give you life in the first place? Was it not through us that your father married your mother and begot you? Tell us, have you any complaint against those of us Laws that deal with marriage?" "No, none," I should say. "Well, have you any against the laws which deal with children's upbringing and education, such as you had yourself? Are you not grateful to those of us Laws which were instituted for this end, for requiring your father to give you a cultural and physical education?" "Yes," I should say. "Very good. Then since you have been born and brought up and educated, can you deny, in the first place, that you were our child and servant, both you and your ancestors? And if this is so, do you imagine that what is right for us is equally right for you, and that whatever we try to do to you, you are justified in retaliating? You did not have equality of rights with your father, or your employer (supposing that you had had one), to enable you to retaliate; you were not allowed to answer back when you were scolded or to hit back when you were beaten, or to do a great many other things of the same kind. Do you expect to have such license against your country and its laws that if we try to put you to death in the belief that it is right to do so, you on your part will try your hardest to destroy your country and us its Laws in return? And will you, the true devotee of goodness, claim that you are justified in doing so? Are you so wise as to have forgotten that compared with your mother and father and all the rest of your ancestors your country is something far more precious, more venerable, more sacred, and held in greater honor both among gods and among all reasonable men? Do you not realize that you are even more bound to respect and placate the anger of your country than your father's anger? That if you cannot persuade your country you must do whatever it orders, and patiently submit to any punishment that it imposes, whether it be flogging or imprisonment? And if it leads you out to war, to be wounded or killed, you must comply, and it is right that you should do so; you must not give way or retreat or abandon your position. Both in war and in the law courts and everywhere else you must do whatever your city and your country commands, or else persuade it in accordance with universal justice; but violence is a sin even against your parents, and it is a far greater sin against your country" — What shall we say to this, Crito? — that what the Laws say is true, or not?

CRITO: Yes, I think so.

SOCRATES: "Consider, then, Socrates," the Laws would probably continue, 95 "whether it is also true for us to say that what you are now trying to do to us is not right. Although we have brought you into the world and reared you and educated you, and given you and all your fellow citizens a share in all the good things at our disposal, nevertheless by the very fact of granting our permission we openly proclaim this principle: that any Athenian, on attaining to manhood and seeing for himself the political organization of the State and us its Laws, is permitted, if he is not satisfied with us, to take his property and go away wherever he likes. If any of you chooses to go to one of our colonies, supposing that he should not be satisfied with us and the State, or to emigrate to any other country, not one of us Laws hinders or prevents him from going away wherever he likes, without any loss of property. On the other hand, if any one of you stands his ground when he can see how we administer justice and the rest of our public organization, we hold that by so doing he has in fact undertaken to do anything that we tell him; and we maintain that anyone who disobeys is guilty of doing wrong on three separate counts: first because we are his parents, and secondly because we are his guardians; and thirdly because, after promising obedience, he is neither obeying us nor persuading us to change our decision if we are at fault in any way; and although all our orders are in the form of proposals, not of savage commands, and we give him the choice of either persuading us or doing what we say, he is actually doing neither. These are the charges, Socrates, to which we say that you will be liable if you do what you are contemplating; and you will not be the least culpable of your fellow countrymen, but one of the most guilty." If I said "Why do you say that?" they would no doubt pounce upon me with perfect justice and point out that there are very few people in Athens who have entered into this agreement with them as explicitly as I have. They would say "Socrates, we have substantial evidence that you are satisfied with us and with the State. You would not have been so exceptionally reluctant to cross the borders of your country if you had not been exceptionally attached to it. You have never left the city to attend a festival or for any other purpose, except on some military expedition; you have never traveled abroad as other people do, and you have never felt the impulse to acquaint yourself with another country or constitution; you have been content with us and with our city. You have definitely chosen us, and undertaken to observe us in all your activities as a citizen; and as the crowning proof that you are satisfied with our city, you have begotten children in it. Furthermore, even at the time of your trial you could have proposed the penalty of banishment, if you had chosen to do so; that is, you could have done then with the sanction of the State what you are now trying to do without it. But whereas at that time you made a noble show of indifference if you had to die, and in fact preferred death, as you said, to banishment, now you show no respect for your earlier professions, and no regard for us, the Laws, whom you are trying to destroy; you are behaving like the lowest type of menial, trying to run away in spite of the contracts and undertakings by which you agreed to live as a member of our State. Now first answer this question: Are we or are we not speaking the truth when we say that you have undertaken, in deed if not in word, to live your life as a citizen in obedience to us?" What are we to say to that, Crito? Are we not bound to admit it?

CRITO: We cannot help it, Socrates.

SOCRATES: "It is a fact, then," they would say, "that you are breaking covenants and undertakings made with us, although you made them under no compulsion or misunderstanding, and were not compelled to decide in a limited time; you had seventy years in which you could have left the country, if you were not satisfied with us or felt that the agreements were unfair. You did not choose Sparta or Crete—your favorite models of good government—or any other Greek or foreign state; you could not have absented yourself from the city less if you had been lame or blind or decrepit in some other way. It is quite obvious that you stand by yourself above all other Athenians in your affection for this city and for us its Laws;—who would care for a city without laws? And now, after all this, are you not going to stand by your agreement? Yes, you are, Socrates, if you will take our advice; and then you will at least escape being laughed at for leaving the city.

"We invite you to consider what good you will do to yourself or your friends if you commit this breach of faith and stain your conscience. It is fairly obvious that the risk of being banished and either losing their citizenship or having their property confiscated will extend to your friends as well. As for yourself, if you go to one of the neighboring states, such as Thebes or Megara, which are both well governed, you will enter them as an enemy to their constitution[2] and all good patriots will eye you with suspicion as a destroyer of law and order. Incidentally you will confirm the opinion of the jurors who tried you that they gave a correct verdict; a destroyer of laws might very well be supposed to have a destructive influence upon young and foolish human beings. Do you intend, then, to avoid well governed states and the higher forms of human society? And if you do, will life be worth living? Or will you approach these people and have the impudence to converse with them? What arguments will you use, Socrates? The same which you used here, that goodness and integrity, institutions and laws, are the most precious possessions of mankind? Do you not think that Socrates and everything about him will appear in a disreputable light? You certainly ought to think so. But perhaps you will retire from this part of the world and go to Crito's friends in Thessaly? That is the home of indiscipline and laxity, and no doubt they would enjoy hearing the amusing story of how you managed to run away from prison by arraying yourself in some costume or putting on a shepherd's smock or some other conventional runaway's disguise, and altering your personal appearance. And will no one comment on the fact that an old man of your age, probably with only a short time left to live, should dare to cling so greedily to life, at the price of violating the most stringent laws? Perhaps not, if you avoid irritating anyone. Otherwise, Socrates, you will hear a good many humiliating comments. So you will live as the toady and slave of all the populace, literally 'roistering in Thessaly,' as though you had left this country for Thessaly to attend a banquet there; and where will your discussions about goodness and uprightness be then, we should like to know? But of course you want to live for your children's sake, so that you may be able to bring them up and educate them. Indeed! by first taking them off to Thessaly and making foreigners of them, so that they may have that additional enjoyment? Or if that is not your intention, supposing that they are brought up here with you still alive, will they be better cared for and educated without you, because of course your friends will look after them? Will they look after your children if you go away to Thessaly, and not if you go away to the next world? Surely if those who profess to be your friends are worth anything, you must believe that they would care for them.

"No, Socrates; be advised by us your guardians, and do not think more of your children or of your life or of anything else than you think of what is right; so that when you enter the next world you may have all this to plead in your defense before the authorities there. It seems clear that if you do this thing, neither you nor any of your friends will be the better for it or be more upright or have a

---

[2]**as an enemy to their constitution** As a lawbreaker.

cleaner conscience here in this world, nor will it be better for you when you reach the next. As it is, you will leave this place, when you do, as the victim of a wrong done not by us, the Laws, but by your fellow men. But if you leave in that dishonorable way, returning wrong for wrong and evil for evil, breaking your agreements and covenants with us, and injuring those whom you least ought to injure—yourself, your friends, your country, and us—then you will have to face our anger in your lifetime, and in that place beyond when the laws of the other world know that you have tried, so far as you could, to destroy even us their brothers, they will not receive you with a kindly welcome. Do not take Crito's advice, but follow ours."

That, my dear friend Crito, I do assure you, is what I seem to   100
hear them saying, just as a mystic seems to hear the strains of music; and the sound of their arguments rings so loudly in my head that I cannot hear the other side. I warn you that, as my opinion stands at present, it will be useless to urge a different view. However, if you think that you will do any good by it, say what you like.

CRITO: No, Socrates, I have nothing to say.

SOCRATES: Then give it up, Crito, and let us follow this course, since God points out the way.

TOPICS FOR CRITICAL THINKING AND WRITING

1. State as precisely as you can all the arguments Crito uses to try to convince Socrates that he ought to escape. Which of these arguments seems to you to be the best? The worst? Why?

2. Socrates says to Crito, "I cannot abandon the principles which I used to hold in the past simply because this accident [the misfortune of being convicted by the Athenian assembly and then sentenced to death] has happened to me" (para. 35). Does this remark strike you as self-righteous? Stubborn? Smug? Stupid? Explain.

3. Socrates declares that "serious thinkers" have always held the view that "some of the opinions which people entertain should be respected, and others should not" (para. 37). There are two main alternatives to this principle: (a) One should respect *all* the opinions that others hold, and (b) one should respect *none* of the opinions of others. Socrates attacks (a) but he ignores (b). What are his objections to (a)? Do you find them convincing? Can you think of any convincing arguments against (b)?

4. As Socrates shows in his reply to Crito, he seems ready to believe (para. 63) that there are "expert[s] in right and wrong"—that is, persons with expert opinion or even authoritative knowledge on matters of right and wrong conduct—and that their advice should be sought and followed. Do you agree? Consider the thesis that there are no such experts, and write a 500-word essay defending or attacking it.

5. Socrates, as he comments to Crito, believes that "it is never right to do a wrong or return a wrong or defend one's self against injury by retaliation" (para. 85). He does not offer any argument for this thesis in the dialogue (although he does elsewhere). It was a very strange doctrine in his day, and even now it is not generally accepted. Write a 1,000-word essay defending or attacking this thesis.

6. Socrates seems to argue that (a) no one ought to do wrong, (b) it would injure the state for someone in Socrates' position to escape, and (c) this act would break a "just agreement" between the citizen and his state; therefore, (d) no one in Socrates' position should escape. Do you think this argument is valid? If not, what further assumptions would be needed to make it valid? Do you think the argument is sound (that is, both valid and true in all its premises)? If not, explain. If you had to attack premise (b) or (c), which do you think is the more vulnerable, and why?

7. In the imaginary speech by the Laws of Athens to Socrates, especially in paragraph 93, the Laws convey a picture of the supremacy of the state over the individual—and Socrates seems to assent to this picture. Do you? Why, or why not?

8. The Laws (para. 95) claim that if Socrates were to escape, he would be "guilty of doing wrong on three separate counts." What are they? Do you agree with all or any? Why, or why not? Read the essay by Martin Luther King Jr., "Letter from Birmingham Jail" (p. 932), and decide how King would have responded to the judgment of the Laws of Athens.

9. At the end of their peroration (para. 99), the Laws of Athens say to Socrates: Take your punishment as prescribed, and at your death "you will leave this place . . . as the victim of a wrong done not by us, the Laws, but by your fellow men." To what wrong do the Laws allude? Do you agree that it is men and not laws who perpetrated this wrong? If you were in Socrates' position, would it matter to you if you were being wronged not by laws but only by men? Explain.

10. Compose a letter from Socrates to Martin Luther King Jr. in which Socrates responds to King's "Letter from Birmingham Jail" (p. 932).

George Orwell

George Orwell was the pen name adopted by Eric Blair (1903–1950), an Englishman born in India. Orwell was educated at Eton, in England, but in 1921 he went back to the East and served for five years as a police officer in Burma (now Myanmar). Disillusioned with colonial imperialism, he returned to Europe, doing odd jobs while writing novels and stories. In 1936 he fought in the Spanish Civil War on the side of the Republicans, an experience he reported in Homage to Catalonia *(1938). His last years were spent writing in England. His best-known work probably is the satiric allegory* 1984 *(1949), showing a totalitarian state in which the citizens are perpetually under the eye of Big Brother. The following essay is from* Shooting an Elephant and Other Essays *(1950).*

Shooting an Elephant

In Moulmein, in Lower Burma, I was hated by large numbers of people—the only time in my life that I have been important enough for this to happen to me. I was sub-divisional police officer of the town, and in an aimless, petty kind of way anti-European feeling was very bitter. No one had the guts to raise a riot, but if a European woman went through the bazaars alone somebody would probably spit betel juice over her dress. As a police officer I was an obvious target and was baited whenever it seemed safe to do so. When a nimble Burman tripped me up on the football field and the referee (another Burman) looked the other way, the crowd yelled with hideous laughter. This happened more than once. In the end the sneering yellow faces of young men that met me everywhere, the insults hooted after me when I was at a safe distance, got badly on my nerves. The young Buddhist priests were the worst of all. There were several thousands of them in the town and none of them seemed to have anything to do except stand on street corners and jeer at Europeans.

All this was perplexing and upsetting. For at that time I had already made up my mind that imperialism was an evil thing and the sooner I chucked up my job and got out of it the better. Theoretically—and secretly, of course—I was all for the Burmese and all against their oppressors, the British. As for the job I was doing, I hated it more bitterly than I can perhaps make clear. In a job like that you see the dirty work of Empire at close quarters. The wretched prisoners huddling in the stinking cages of the lock-ups, the grey, cowed faces of the long-term convicts, the scarred buttocks of the men who had been flogged with bamboos—all these oppressed me with an intolerable sense of guilt. But I could get nothing into perspective. I was young and ill-educated and I had had to think out my problems in the utter silence that is imposed on every Englishman in the East. I did not even know that the British Empire is dying, still less did I know that it is a great deal better than the younger empires that are going to supplant it. All I knew was that I was stuck between my hatred of the empire I served and my rage against the evil-spirited little beasts who tried to make my job impossible. With one part of my mind I thought of the British Raj[1] as an unbreakable tyranny, as something clamped down, in *saecula saeculorum,*[2] upon the will of prostrate peoples; with another part I thought that the greatest joy in the world would be to drive a bayonet into a Buddhist priest's guts. Feelings like these are the normal by-products of imperialism; ask any Anglo-Indian official, if you can catch him off duty.

One day something happened which in a roundabout way was enlightening. It was a tiny incident in itself, but it gave me a better

---

[1]**British Raj** British imperial government in India and Burma. [All notes are the editors'.]
[2]**in *saecula saeculorum*** Forever (Latin). A term used in Christian liturgy.

glimpse than I had had before of the real nature of imperialism—the real motives for which despotic governments act. Early one morning the sub-inspector at a police station the other end of the town rang me up on the 'phone and said that an elephant was ravaging the bazaar. Would I please come and do something about it? I did not know what I could do, but I wanted to see what was happening and I got on to a pony and started out. I took my rifle, an old .44 Winchester and much too small to kill an elephant, but I thought the noise might be useful *in terrorem*.[3] Various Burmans stopped me on the way and told me about the elephant's doings. It was not, of course, a wild elephant, but a tame one which had gone "must."[4] It had been chained up, as tame elephants always are when their attack of "must" is due, but on the previous night it had broken its chain and escaped. Its mahout, the only person who could manage it when it was in that state, had set out in pursuit, but had taken the wrong direction and was now twelve hours' journey away, and in the morning the elephant had suddenly reappeared in the town. The Burmese population had no weapons and were quite helpless against it. It had already destroyed somebody's bamboo hut, killed a cow and raided some fruit-stalls and devoured the stock; also it had met the municipal rubbish van and, when the driver jumped out and took to his heels, had turned the van over and inflicted violences upon it.

The Burmese sub-inspector and some Indian constables were waiting for me in the quarter where the elephant had been seen. It was a very poor quarter, a labyrinth of squalid bamboo huts, thatched with palm-leaf, winding all over a steep hillside. I remember that it was a cloudy, stuffy morning at the beginning of the rains. We began questioning the people as to where the elephant had gone and, as usual, failed to get any definite information. That is invariably the case in the East; a story always sounds clear enough at a distance, but the nearer you get to the scene of events the vaguer it becomes. Some of the people said that the elephant had gone in one direction, some said that he had gone in another, some professed not even to have heard of any elephant. I had almost made up my mind that the whole story was a pack of lies, when we heard yells a little distance away. There was a loud, scandalized cry of "Go away, child! Go away this instant!" and an old woman with a switch in her hand came round the corner of a hut, violently shooing away a crowd of naked children. Some more women followed, clicking their tongues and exclaiming; evidently there was something that the children ought not to have seen. I rounded the hut and saw a man's dead body sprawling in the mud. He was an Indian, a black Dravidian coolie, almost naked, and he could not have been dead many minutes. The people said that the elephant had come suddenly upon him round the corner of the hut, caught him with its trunk, put its foot on his back

---

[3]*in terrorem* As a warning.
[4]"must" Into sexual heat.

and ground him into the earth. This was the rainy season and the ground was soft, and his face had scored a trench a foot deep and a couple of yards long. He was lying on his belly with arms crucified and head sharply twisted to one side. His face was coated with mud, the eyes wide open, the teeth bared and grinning with an expression of unendurable agony. (Never tell me, by the way, that the dead look peaceful. Most of the corpses I have seen looked devilish.) The friction of the great beast's foot had stripped the skin from his back as neatly as one skins a rabbit. As soon as I saw the dead man I sent an orderly to a friend's house nearby to borrow an elephant rifle. I had already sent back the pony, not wanting it to go mad with fright and throw me if it smelt the elephant.

The orderly came back in a few minutes with a rifle and five cartridges, and meanwhile some Burmans had arrived and told us that the elephant was in the paddy fields below, only a few hundred yards away. As I started forward practically the whole population of the quarter flocked out of the houses and followed me. They had seen the rifle and were all shouting excitedly that I was going to shoot the elephant. They had not shown much interest in the elephant when he was merely ravaging their homes, but it was different now that he was going to be shot. It was a bit of fun to them, as it would be to an English crowd; besides they wanted the meat. It made me vaguely uneasy. I had no intention of shooting the elephant — I had merely sent for the rifle to defend myself if necessary — and it is always unnerving to have a crowd following you. I marched down the hill, looking and feeling a fool, with the rifle over my shoulder and an ever-growing army of people jostling at my heels. At the bottom, when you got away from the huts, there was a metalled road and beyond that a miry waste of paddy fields a thousand yards across, not yet ploughed but soggy from the first rains and dotted with coarse grass. The elephant was standing eight yards from the road, his left side towards us. He took not the slightest notice of the crowd's approach. He was tearing up bunches of grass, beating them against his knees to clean them and stuffing them into his mouth.

I had halted on the road. As soon as I saw the elephant I knew with perfect certainty that I ought not to shoot him. It is a serious matter to shoot a working elephant — it is comparable to destroying a huge and costly piece of machinery — and obviously one ought not to do it if it can possibly be avoided. And at that distance, peacefully eating, the elephant looked no more dangerous than a cow. I thought then and I think now that his attack of "must" was already passing off; in which case he would merely wander harmlessly about until the mahout came back and caught him. Moreover, I did not in the least want to shoot him. I decided that I would watch him for a little while to make sure that he did not turn savage again, and then go home.

But at that moment I glanced round at the crowd that had followed me. It was an immense crowd, two thousand at the least and growing every minute. It blocked the road for a long distance on either side. I looked at the sea of yellow faces above the garish clothes—faces all happy and excited over this bit of fun, all certain that the elephant was going to be shot. They were watching me as they would watch a conjurer about to perform a trick. They did not like me, but with the magical rifle in my hands I was momentarily worth watching. And suddenly I realized that I should have to shoot the elephant after all. The people expected it of me and I had got to do it; I could feel their two thousand wills pressing me forward, irresistibly. And it was at this moment, as I stood there with the rifle in my hands, that I first grasped the hollowness, the futility of the white man's dominion in the East. Here was I, the white man with his gun, standing in front of the unarmed native crowd—seemingly the leading actor of the piece; but in reality I was only an absurd puppet pushed to and fro by the will of those yellow faces behind. I perceived in this moment that when the white man turns tyrant it is his own freedom that he destroys. He becomes a sort of hollow, posing dummy, the conventionalized figure of a sahib. For it is the condition of his rule that he shall spend his life in trying to impress the "natives," and so in every crisis he has got to do what the "natives" expect of him. He wears a mask, and his face grows to fit it. I had got to shoot the elephant. I had committed myself to doing it when I sent for the rifle. A sahib has got to act like a sahib; he has got to appear resolute, to know his own mind and do definite things. To come all that way, rifle in hand, with two thousand people marching at my heels, and then to trail feebly away, having done nothing—no, that was impossible. The crowd would laugh at me. And my whole life, every white man's life in the East, was one long struggle not to be laughed at.

But I did not want to shoot the elephant. I watched him beating his bunch of grass against his knees, with that preoccupied grandmotherly air that elephants have. It seemed to me that it would be murder to shoot him. At that age I was not squeamish about killing animals, but I had never shot an elephant and never wanted to. (Somehow it always seems worse to kill a *large* animal.) Besides, there was the beast's owner to be considered. Alive, the elephant was worth at least a hundred pounds; dead, he would only be worth the value of his tusks, five pounds, possibly. But I had got to act quickly. I turned to some experienced-looking Burmans who had been there when we arrived, and asked them how the elephant had been behaving. They all said the same thing; he took no notice of you if you left him alone, but he might charge if you went too close to him.

It was perfectly clear to me what I ought to do. I ought to walk up to within, say, twenty-five yards of the elephant and test his behavior. If he charged, I could shoot; if he took no notice of me, it would be safe to leave him until the mahout came back. But also I knew that I was going to do no such thing. I was a poor shot with a rifle and the ground was soft mud into which one would sink at every step. If the elephant charged and I missed him, I should have about as much chance as a toad under a steam-roller. But even then I was not thinking particularly of my own skin, only of the watchful yellow faces behind. For at that moment, with the crowd watching me, I was not afraid in the ordinary sense, as I would have been if I had been alone. A white man mustn't be frightened in front of "natives"; and so, in general, he isn't frightened. The sole thought in my mind was that if anything went wrong those two thousand Burmans would see me pursued, caught, trampled on and reduced to a grinning corpse like that Indian up the hill. And if that happened it was quite probable that some of them would laugh. That would never do. There was only one alternative. I shoved the cartridges into the magazine and lay down on the road to get a better aim.

The crowd grew very still, and a deep, low, happy sigh, as of people 10 who see the theatre curtain go up at last, breathed from innumerable throats. They were going to have their bit of fun after all. The rifle was a beautiful German thing with cross-hair sights. I did not then know that in shooting an elephant one would shoot to cut an imaginary bar running from ear-hole to ear-hole. I ought, therefore, as the elephant was sideways on, to have aimed straight at his ear-hole; actually I aimed several inches in front of this, thinking the brain would be further forward.

When I pulled the trigger I did not hear the bang or feel the kick— one never does when a shot goes home—but I heard the devilish roar of glee that went up from the crowd. In that instant, in too short a time, one would have thought, even for the bullet to get there, a mysterious, terrible change had come over the elephant. He neither stirred nor fell, but every line of his body had altered. He looked suddenly stricken, shrunken, immensely old, as though the frightful impact of the bullet had paralyzed him without knocking him down. At last, after what seemed a long time—it might have been five seconds, I dare say— he sagged flabbily to his knees. His mouth slobbered. An enormous senility seemed to have settled upon him. One could have imagined him thousands of years old. I fired again into the same spot. At the second shot he did not collapse but climbed with desperate slowness to his feet and stood weakly upright, with legs sagging and head dropping. I fired a third time. That was the shot that did for him. You could see the agony of it jolt his whole body and knock the last remnant of strength from his legs. But in falling he seemed for a moment to rise, for as his hind legs collapsed beneath him he seemed to tower upward like a huge rock toppling, his trunk reaching skywards like a tree. He trumpeted, for the first and only time. And then down he came, his belly towards me, with a crash that seemed to shake the ground even where I lay.

I got up. The Burmans were already racing past me across the mud. It was obvious that the elephant would never rise again, but he was not dead. He was breathing very rhythmically with long rattling gasps, his great mound of a side painfully rising and falling. His mouth was wide open—I could see far down into caverns of pale pink throat. I waited a long time for him to die, but his breathing did not weaken. Finally I fired my two remaining shots into the spot where I thought his heart must be. The thick blood welled out of him like red velvet, but still he did not die. His body did not even jerk when the shots hit him, the tortured breathing continued without a pause. He was dying, very slowly and in great agony, but in some world remote from me where not even a bullet could damage him further. I felt that I had got to put an end to that dreadful noise. It seemed dreadful to see the great beast lying there, powerless to move and yet powerless to die, and not even to be able to finish him. I sent back for my small rifle and poured shot after shot into his heart and down his throat. They seemed to make no impression. The tortured gasps continued as steadily as the ticking of a clock.

In the end I could not stand it any longer and went away. I heard later that it took him half an hour to die. Burmans were bringing dahs[5] and baskets even before I left, and I was told they had stripped his body almost to the bones by the afternoon.

Afterwards, of course, there were endless discussions about the shooting of the elephant. The owner was furious, but he was only an Indian and could do nothing. Besides, legally I had done the right thing, for a mad elephant has to be killed, like a mad dog, if its owner fails to control it. Among the Europeans opinion was divided. The older men said I was right, the younger men said it was a damn shame to shoot an elephant for killing a coolie, because an elephant was worth more than any damn Coringhee coolie. And afterwards I was very glad that the coolie had been killed; it put me legally in the right and it gave me a sufficient pretext for shooting the elephant. I often wondered whether any of the others grasped that I had done it solely to avoid looking a fool.

Topics for Critical Thinking and Writing

1. Did Orwell shoot the elephant of his own free will? Or did he shoot the elephant because he *had* to shoot it? What does he say about this? Do you find his judgment convincing or not? Write a 500-word essay explaining your answer.

2. Was Orwell justified in shooting the elephant? Did he do the right thing in killing it? In the aftermath, did he think he did the right thing? Do you? Write a 500-word essay explaining your answers.

3. Orwell says that "as soon as I saw the elephant I knew with perfect certainty that I ought not to shoot him" (para. 6). How could he claim to "know" this, when moments later he did shoot the elephant?

4. Orwell says in passing, "Somehow it always seems worse to kill a *large* animal" (para. 8). Explain why you think Orwell says this and whether you agree.

[5]**dahs** Large knives.

5. A biographer who did research on Orwell in Burma reported that he could find no supporting documentation, either in the local newspapers or in the files of the police, that this episode ever occurred. Suppose that Orwell made it up. If so, is your response different? Explain.

6. If, pressured by circumstances, you have ever acted against what you might think is your reason or your nature, report the experience, and give your present evaluation of your behavior.

Walter T. Stace

Walter T. Stace (1886–1967), a professor of philosophy at Princeton University for many years, was the author of several books, including Religion and the Modern Mind *(1952), from which this selection is taken. The title is the editors'.*

Is Determinism Inconsistent with Free Will?

The second great problem which the rise of scientific naturalism has created for the modern mind concerns the foundations of morality. The old religious foundations have largely crumbled away, and it may well be thought that the edifice built upon them by generations of men is in danger of collapse. A total collapse of moral behavior is, as I pointed out before, very unlikely. For a society in which this occurred could not survive. Nevertheless the danger to moral standards inherent in the virtual disappearance of their old religious foundations is not illusory.

I shall first discuss the problem of free will, for it is certain that if there is no free will there can be no morality. Morality is concerned with what men ought and ought not to do. But if a man has no freedom to choose what he will do, if whatever he does is done under compulsion, then it does not make sense to tell him that he ought not to have done what he did and that he ought to do something different. All moral precepts would in such case be meaningless. Also if he acts always under compulsion, how can he be held morally responsible for his actions? How can he, for example, be punished for what he could not help doing?

It is to be observed that those learned professors of philosophy or psychology who deny the existence of free will do so only in their professional moments and in their studies and lecture rooms. For when it comes to doing anything practical, even of the most trivial kind, they invariably behave as if they and others were free. They inquire from you at dinner whether you will choose this dish or that dish. They will ask a child why he told a lie, and will punish him for not having chosen the way of truthfulness. All of which is inconsistent with a disbelief in free will. This should cause us to suspect that the problem is not a real one; and this, I believe, is the case. The dispute is merely verbal, and is due to nothing but a confusion about the meanings of words. It is what is now fashionably called a semantic problem.

How does a verbal dispute arise? Let us consider a case which, although it is absurd in the sense that no one would ever make the mistake which is involved in it, yet illustrates the principle which we shall have to use in the solution of the problem. Suppose that someone believed that the word "man" means a certain sort of five-legged animal; in short that "five-legged animal" is the correct *definition* of man. He might then look around the world, and rightly observing that there are no five-legged animals in it, he might proceed to deny the existence of men. This preposterous conclusion would have been reached because he was using an incorrect definition of "man." All you would have to do to show him his mistake would be to give him the correct definition; or at least to show him that his definition was wrong. Both the problem and its solution would, of course, be entirely verbal. The problem of free will, and its solution, I shall maintain, is verbal in exactly the same way. The problem has been created by the fact that learned men, especially philosophers, have assumed an incorrect definition of free *will*, and then finding that there is nothing in the world which answers to their definition, have denied its existence. As far as logic is concerned, their conclusion is just as absurd as that of the man who denies the existence of men. The only difference is that the mistake in the latter case is obvious and crude, while the mistake which the deniers of free will have made is rather subtle and difficult to detect.

Throughout the modern period, until quite recently, it was assumed, 5 both by the philosophers who denied free will and by those who defended it, that *determinism is inconsistent with free will*. If a man's actions were wholly determined by chains of causes stretching back into the remote past, so that they could be predicted beforehand by a mind which knew all the causes, it was assumed that they could not in that case be free. This implies that a certain definition of actions done from free will was assumed, namely that they are actions *not* wholly determined by causes or predictable beforehand. Let us shorten this by saying that free will was defined as meaning indeterminism. This is the incorrect definition which has led to the denial of free will. As soon as we see what the true definition is we shall find that the question whether the world is deterministic, as Newtonian science implied, or in a measure indeterministic, as current physics teaches, is wholly irrelevant to the problem.

Of course there is a sense in which one can define a word arbitrarily in any way one pleases. But a definition may nevertheless be called correct or incorrect. It is correct if it accords with a *common usage* of the word

defined. It is incorrect if it does not. And if you give an incorrect definition, absurd and untrue results are likely to follow. For instance, there is
nothing to prevent you from arbitrarily defining a man as a five-legged
animal, but this is incorrect in the sense that it does not accord with the
ordinary meaning of the word. Also it has the absurd result of leading to
a denial of the existence of men. This shows that *common usage is the criterion for deciding whether a definition is correct or not.* And this is the principle
which I shall apply to free will. I shall show that indeterminism is not
what is meant by the phrase "free will" *as it is commonly used.* And I shall
attempt to discover the correct definition by inquiring how the phrase is
used in ordinary conversation.

Here are a few samples of how the phrase might be used in ordinary
conversation. It will be noticed that they include cases in which the
question whether a man acted with free will is asked in order to determine whether he was morally and legally responsible for his acts.

JONES: I once went without food for a week.
SMITH: Did you do that of your own free will?
JONES: No. I did it because I was lost in a desert and could find no food.

But suppose that the man who had fasted was Mahatma Gandhi.
The conversation might then have gone:

GANDHI: I once fasted for a week.
SMITH: Did you do that of your own free will?
GANDHI: Yes. I did it because I wanted to compel the British Government
     to give India its independence.

Take another case. Suppose that I had stolen some bread, but that I
was as truthful as George Washington. Then, if I were charged with the
crime in court, some exchange of the following sort might take place:

JUDGE: Did you steal the bread of your own free will?
STACE: Yes. I stole it because I was hungry.

Or in different circumstances the conversation might run: 10

JUDGE: Did you steal of your own free will?
STACE: No. I stole because my employer threatened to beat me if I did
     not.

At a recent murder trial in Trenton some of the accused had signed
confessions, but afterwards asserted that they had done so under police
duress. The following exchange might have occurred:

JUDGE: Did you sign this confession of your own free will?
PRISONER: No. I signed it because the police beat me up.

Now suppose that a philosopher had been a member of the jury. We
could imagine this conversation taking place in the jury room.

FOREMAN OF THE JURY: The prisoner says he signed the confession because he was beaten, and not of his own free will.

PHILOSOPHER: This is quite irrelevant to the case. There is no such thing as free will.

FOREMAN: Do you mean to say that it makes no difference whether he signed because his conscience made him want to tell the truth or because he was beaten?

PHILOSOPHER: None at all. Whether he was caused to sign by a beating or by some desire of his own—the desire to tell the truth, for example— in either case his signing was causally determined, and therefore in neither case did he act of his own free will. Since there is no such thing as free will, the question whether he signed of his own free will ought not to be discussed by us.

The foreman and the rest of the jury would rightly conclude that the philosopher must be making some mistake. What sort of a mistake could it be? There is only one possible answer. The philosopher must be using the phrase "free will" in some peculiar way of his own which is not the way in which men usually use it when they wish to determine a question of moral responsibility. That is, he must be using an incorrect definition of it as implying action not determined by causes.

Suppose a man left his office at noon, and were questioned about it. Then we might hear this:

JONES: Did you go out of your own free will?
SMITH: Yes. I went out to get my lunch.

But we might hear: 15

JONES: Did you leave your office of your own free will?
SMITH: No. I was forcibly removed by the police.

We have now collected a number of cases of actions which, in the ordinary usage of the English language, would be called cases in which people have acted of their own free will. We should also say in all these cases that they *chose* to act as they did. We should also say that they could have acted otherwise, if they had chosen. For instance, Mahatma Gandhi was not compelled to fast; he chose to do so. He could have eaten if he had wanted to. When Smith went out to get his lunch, he chose to do so. He could have stayed and done some more work, if he had wanted to. We have also collected a number of cases of the opposite kind. They are cases in which men were not able to exercise their free will. They had no choice. They were compelled to do as they did. The man in the desert did not fast of his own free will. He had no choice in the matter. He was compelled to fast because there was nothing for him to eat. And so with the other cases. It ought to be quite easy, by an inspection of these cases, to tell what we ordinarily mean when we say that a man did or did not exercise free will. We ought therefore to be able to extract from them the proper definition of the term. Let us put the cases in a table:

Free Acts	Unfree Acts
Gandhi fasting because he wanted to free India.	The man fasting in the desert because there was no food.
Stealing bread because one is hungry.	Stealing because one's employer threatened to beat one.
Signing a confession because one wanted to tell the truth.	Signing because the police beat one.
Leaving the office because one wanted one's lunch.	Leaving because forcibly removed.

It is obvious that to find the correct definition of free acts we must discover what characteristic is common to all the acts in the left-hand column, and is, at the same time, absent from all the acts in the right-hand column. This characteristic which all free acts have, and which no unfree acts have, will be the defining characteristic of free will.

Is being uncaused, or not being determined by causes, the characteristic of which we are in search? It cannot be, because although it is true that all the acts in the right-hand column have causes, such as the beating by the police or the absence of food in the desert, so also do the acts in the left-hand column. Mr. Gandhi's fasting was caused by his desire to free India, the man leaving his office by his hunger, and so on. Moreover there is no reason to doubt that these causes of the free acts were in turn caused by prior conditions, and that these were again the results of causes, and so on back indefinitely into the past. Any physiologist can tell us the causes of hunger. What caused Mr. Gandhi's tremendously powerful desire to free India is no doubt more difficult to discover. But it must have had causes. Some of them may have lain in peculiarities of his glands or brain, others in his past experiences, others in his heredity, others in his education. Defenders of free will have usually tended to deny such facts. But to do so is plainly a case of special pleading, which is unsupported by any scrap of evidence. The only reasonable view is that all human actions, both those which are freely done and those which are not, are either wholly determined by causes, or at least as much determined as other events in nature. It may be true, as the physicists tell us, that nature is not as deterministic as was once thought. But whatever degree of determinism prevails in the world, human actions appear to be as much determined as anything else. And if this is so, it cannot be the case that what distinguishes actions freely chosen from those which are not free is that the latter are determined by causes while the former are not. Therefore, being uncaused or being undetermined by causes must be an incorrect definition of free will.

What, then, is the difference between acts which are freely done and those which are not? What is the characteristic which is present to all the acts in the left-hand column and absent from all those in the right-hand column? It is not obvious that, although both sets of actions have causes, the causes of those in the left-hand column are *of a different kind* from the causes of those in the right-hand column? The free acts are all caused by desires, or motives, or by some sort of internal psychological states of the agent's mind. The unfree acts, on the other hand, are all caused by physical forces or physical conditions, outside the agent. Police arrest means physical force exerted from the outside; the absence of food in the desert is a physical condition of the outside world. We may therefore frame the following rough definitions. *Acts freely done are those whose immediate causes are psychological states in the agent. Acts not freely done are those whose immediate causes are states of affairs external to the agent.*

It is plain that if we define free will in this way, then free will cer-   20
tainly exists, and the philosopher's denial of its existence is seen to be what it is—nonsense. For it is obvious that all those actions of men which we should ordinarily attribute to the exercise of their free will, or of which we should say that they freely chose to do them, are in fact actions which have been caused by their own desires, wishes, thoughts, emotions, impulses, or other psychological states.

In applying our definition we shall find that it usually works well, but that there are some puzzling cases which it does not seem exactly to fit. These puzzles can always be solved by paying careful attention to the ways in which words are used, and remembering that they are not always used consistently. I have space for only one example. Suppose that a thug threatens to shoot you unless you give him your wallet, and suppose that you do so. Do you, in giving him your wallet, do so of your own free will or not? If we apply our definition, we find that you acted freely, since the immediate cause of the action was not an actual outside force but the fear of death, which is a psychological cause. Most people, however, would say that you did not act of your own free will but under compulsion. Does this show that our definition is wrong? I do not think so. Aristotle, who gave a solution of the problem of free will substantially the same as ours (though he did not use the term "free will") admitted that there are what he called "mixed" or borderline cases in which it is difficult to know whether we ought to call the acts free or compelled. In the case under discussion, though no actual force was used, the gun at your forehead so nearly approximated to actual force that we tend to say the case was one of compulsion. It is a borderline case.

Here is what may seem like another kind of puzzle. According to our view an action may be free though it could have been predicted beforehand with certainty. But suppose you told a lie, and it was certain beforehand that you would tell it. How could one then say, "You could have told the truth"? The answer is that it is perfectly true that you could have told the truth *if* you had wanted to. In fact you would have done so, for in that case the causes producing your action, namely your desires, would have been different, and would therefore have produced different effects. It is a delusion that predictability and free will are incompatible.

This agrees with common sense. For if, knowing your character, I predict that you will act honorably, no one would say when you do act honorably, that this shows you did not do so of your own free will.

Since free will is a condition of moral responsibility, we must be sure that our theory of free will gives a sufficient basis for it. To be held morally responsible for one's actions means that one may be justly punished or rewarded, blamed or praised, for them. But it is not just to punish a man for what he cannot help doing. How can it be just to punish him for an action which it was certain beforehand that he would do? We have not attempted to decide whether, as a matter of fact, all events, including human actions, are completely determined. For that question is irrelevant to the problem of free will. But if we assume for the purposes of argument that complete determinism is true, but that we are nevertheless free, it may then be asked whether such a deterministic free will is compatible with moral responsibility. For it may seem unjust to punish a man for an action which it could have been predicted with certainty beforehand that he would do.

But that determinism is incompatible with moral responsibility is as much a delusion as that it is incompatible with free will. You do not excuse a man for doing a wrong act because, knowing his character, you felt certain beforehand that he would do it. Nor do you deprive a man of a reward or prize because, knowing his goodness or his capabilities, you felt certain beforehand that he would win it.

Volumes have been written on the justification of punishment. But so far as it affects the question of free will, the essential principles involved are quite simple. The punishment of a man for doing a wrong act is justified, either on the ground that it will correct his own character, or that it will deter other people from doing similar acts. The instrument of punishment has been in the past, and no doubt still is, often unwisely used; so that it may often have done more harm than good. But that is not relevant to our present problem. Punishment, if and when it is justified, is justified only on one or both of the grounds just mentioned. The question then is how, if we assume determinism, punishment can correct character or deter people from evil actions.

Suppose that your child develops a habit of telling lies. You give him a mild beating. Why? Because you believe that his personality is such that the usual motives for telling the truth do not cause him to do so. You therefore supply the missing cause, or motive, in the shape of pain and the fear of future pain if he repeats his untruthful behavior. And you hope that a few treatments of this kind will condition him to the habit of truth-telling, so that he will come to tell the truth without the infliction of pain. You assume that his actions are determined by causes, but that the usual causes of truth-telling do not in him produce their usual effects. You therefore supply him with an artificially injected motive, pain and fear, which you think will in the future cause him to speak truthfully.

The principle is exactly the same where you hope, by punishing one man, to deter others from wrong actions. You believe that the fear of punishment will cause those who might otherwise do evil to do well.

We act on the same principle with nonhuman, and even with inanimate, things, if they do not behave in the way we think they ought to behave. The rose bushes in the garden produce only small and poor blooms, whereas we want large and rich ones. We supply a cause which will produce large blooms, namely fertilizer. Our automobile does not go properly. We supply a cause which will make it go better, namely oil in the works. The punishment for the man, the fertilizer for the plant, and the oil for the car are all justified by the same principle and in the same way. The only difference is that different kinds of things require different kinds of causes to make them do what they should. Pain may be the appropriate remedy to apply, in certain cases, to human beings, and oil to the machine. It is, of course, of no use to inject motor oil into the boy or to beat the machine.

Thus we see that moral responsibility is not only consistent with determinism, but requires it. The assumption on which punishment is based is that human behavior is causally determined. If pain could not be a cause of truth-telling there would be no justification at all for punishing lies. If human actions and volitions were uncaused, it would be useless either to punish or reward, or indeed to do anything else to correct people's bad behavior. For nothing that you could do would in any way influence them. Thus moral responsibility would entirely disappear. If there were no determinism of human beings at all, their actions would be completely unpredictable and capricious, and therefore irresponsible. And this is in itself a strong argument against the common view of philosophers that free will means being undetermined by causes.

TOPICS FOR CRITICAL THINKING AND WRITING

1. Stace asserts that "if there is no free will there can be no morality" (para. 2). What is his reasoning (see para. 23)? Do you agree?

2. "The dispute is merely verbal," Stace proclaims in paragraph 3. What "dispute"? Why "merely verbal"? What would Stace say to someone who insists that the existence or nonexistence of free will is a question of *fact*?

3. What is *determinism* (para. 5)? Why does Stace seem to think that philosophers are strongly inclined to believe in it?

4. Stace claims that he will show that "indeterminism is not what is meant by . . . 'free will' *as it is commonly used*" (para. 6). What is his argument? What does he think *free will* means as the term is "commonly used"? Are you convinced? Why, or why not? Write a 500-word paper answering these questions.

5. Stace insists that "all human actions . . . are . . . at least as much deter-mined as other events in nature" (para. 18). How might one argue against this?

6. Complete the following definition so that it captures Stace's view: "When Smith did *X*, he acted freely if and only if . . ."

7. Stace mentions some "puzzling cases" (para. 21) that do not quite fit, he admits, his analysis of free will. Give an example of such a case, and explain why it is puzzling.

8. Why does Stace conclude in paragraph 22 that "it is a delusion that predictability and free will are incompatible"? Do you agree? Why, or why not?

9. It seems paradoxical to assert, as Stace does in his last paragraph, that "moral responsibility is not only consistent with determinism, but requires it." Explain Stace's view here in no more than 250 words.

Martin Luther King Jr.

Martin Luther King Jr. (1929–1968) was born in Atlanta and educated at Morehouse College, Crozer Theological Seminary, and Boston University. In 1954 he was called to serve as a Baptist minister in Montgomery, Alabama. During the next two years he achieved national fame when, using a policy of nonviolent resistance, he successfully led the boycott against segregated bus lines in Montgomery. He then organized the Southern Christian Leadership Conference, which furthered civil rights, first in the South and then nationwide. In 1964 he was awarded the Nobel Peace Prize. Four years later he was assassi-nated in Memphis, Tennessee, while supporting striking garbage workers.

In 1963 King was arrested in Birmingham, Alabama, for participating in a march for which no parade permit had been issued by city officials. In jail he wrote a response to a letter that eight local clergymen had published in a newspaper.

Note: Their letter, titled "A Call for Unity," is printed here, followed by King's response.

A CALL FOR UNITY

April 12, 1963

We the undersigned clergymen are among those who, in January, issued "An Appeal for Law and Order and Common Sense," in dealing with racial problems in Alabama. We expressed understanding that honest convictions in racial matters could properly be pursued in the courts, but urged that decisions of those courts should in the meantime be peacefully obeyed.

Since that time there had been some evidence of increased fore-bearance and a willingness to face facts. Responsible citizens have undertaken to work on various problems which cause racial friction and unrest. In Birmingham, recent public events have given indication that we all have opportunity for a new constructive and realistic approach to racial problems.

However, we are now confronted by a series of demonstrations by some of our Negro citizens, directed and led in part by outsiders. We recognize the natural impatience of people who feel that their hopes are slow in being realized. But we are convinced that these demonstrations are unwise and untimely.

We agree rather with certain local Negro leadership which has called for honest and open negotiation of racial issues in our area. And we believe this kind of facing of issues can best be accomplished by citizens of our own metropolitan area, white and Negro, meeting with their knowledge and experience of the local situation. All of us need to face that responsibility and find proper channels for its accomplishment.

Just as we formerly pointed out that "hatred and violence have no 5 sanction in our religious and political traditions," we also point out that such actions as incite to hatred and violence, however technically peaceful those actions may be, have not contributed to the resolution of our local problems. We do not believe that these days of new hope are days when extreme measures are justified in Birmingham.

We commend the community as a whole, and the local news media and law enforcement officials in particular, on the calm manner in which these demonstrations have been handled. We urge the public to continue to show restraint should the demonstrations continue, and the law enforcement officials to remain calm and continue to protect our city from violence.

We further strongly urge our own Negro community to withdraw support from these demonstrations, and to unite locally in working peacefully for a better Birmingham. When rights are consistently denied, a cause should be pressed in the courts and in negotiations among local leaders, and not in the streets. We appeal to both our white and Negro citizenry to observe the principles of law and order and common sense.

> C.C.J. Carpenter, D.D., L.L.D., Bishop of Alabama; Joseph A. Durick, D.D., Auxiliary Bishop, Diocese of Mobile-Birmingham; Rabbi Milton L. Grafman, Temple Emanu-El, Birmingham, Alabama; Bishop Paul Hardin, Bishop of the Alabama-West Florida Conference of the Methodist Church; Bishop Nolan B. Harmon, Bishop of the North Alabama Conference of the Methodist Church; George M. Murray, D.D., L.L.D., Bishop Coadjutor, Episcopal Diocese of Alabama; Edward V. Ramage, Moderator, Synod of the Alabama Presbyterian Church in the United States; Earl Stallings, Pastor, First Baptist Church, Birmingham, Alabama.

Letter from Birmingham Jail

April 16, 1963

My Dear Fellow Clergymen:

While confined here in the Birmingham city jail, I came across your recent statement calling my present activities "unwise and untimely."[1] Seldom do I pause to answer criticism of my work and ideas. If I sought to answer all the criticisms that cross my desk, my secretaries would have little time for anything other than such correspondence in the course of the day, and I would have no time for constructive work. But since I feel that you are men of genuine good will and that your criticisms are sincerely set forth, I want to try to answer your statement in what I hope will be patient and reasonable terms.

I think I should indicate why I am here in Birmingham, since you have been influenced by the view which argues against "outsiders coming in." I have the honor of serving as president of the Southern Christian Leadership Conference, an organization operating in every southern state, with headquarters in Atlanta, Georgia. We have some eighty-five affiliated organizations across the South, and one of them is the Alabama Christian Movement for Human Rights. Frequently we share staff, educational, and financial resources with our affiliates. Several months ago the affiliate here in Birmingham asked us to be on call to engage in a nonviolent direct-action program if such were deemed necessary. We readily consented, and when the hour came we lived up to our promise. So I, along with several members of my staff, am here because I was invited here. I am here because I have organizational ties here.

But more basically, I am in Birmingham because injustice is here. Just as the prophets of the eighth century B.C. left their villages and carried their "thus saith the Lord" far beyond the boundaries of their home towns, and just as the Apostle Paul left his village of Tarsus and carried the gospel of Jesus Christ to the far corners of the Greco-Roman world, so am I compelled to carry the gospel of freedom beyond my own home town. Like Paul, I must constantly respond to the Macedonian call for aid.

Moreover, I am cognizant of the interrelatedness of all communities and states. I cannot sit idly by in Atlanta and not be concerned about what happens in Birmingham. Injustice anywhere is a threat to justice

---

[1]This response to a published statement by eight fellow clergymen from Alabama (Bishop C.C.J. Carpenter, Bishop Joseph A. Durick, Rabbi Milton L. Grafman, Bishop Paul Hardin, Bishop Nolan B. Harmon, the Reverend George M. Murray, the Reverend Edward V. Ramage, and the Reverend Earl Stallings) was composed under somewhat constricting circumstances. Begun on the margins of the newspaper in which the statement appeared while I was in jail, the letter was continued on scraps of writing paper supplied by a friendly Negro trusty, and concluded on a pad my attorneys were eventually permitted to leave me. Although the text remains in substance unaltered, I have indulged in the author's prerogative of polishing it for publication. [King's note.]

everywhere. We are caught in an inescapable network of mutuality; tied in a single garment of destiny. Whatever affects one directly, affects all indirectly. Never again can we afford to live with the narrow, provincial "outside agitator" idea. Anyone who lives inside the United States can never be considered an outsider anywhere within its bounds.

You deplore the demonstrations taking place in Birmingham. But your statement, I am sorry to say, fails to express a similar concern for the conditions that brought about the demonstrations. I am sure that none of you would want to rest content with the superficial kind of social analysis that deals merely with effects and does not grapple with underlying causes. It is unfortunate that demonstrations are taking place in Birmingham, but it is even more unfortunate that the city's white power structure left the Negro community with no alternative.

In any nonviolent campaign there are four basic steps: collection of the facts to determine whether injustices exist; negotiation; self-purification; and direct action. We have gone through all these steps in Birmingham. There can be no gainsaying the fact that racial injustice engulfs this community. Birmingham is probably the most thoroughly segregated city in the United States. Its ugly record of brutality is widely known. Negroes have experienced grossly unjust treatment in the courts. There have been more unsolved bombings of Negro homes and churches in Birmingham than in any other city in the nation. These are the hard, brutal facts of the case. On the basis of these conditions, Negro leaders sought to negotiate with the city fathers. But the latter consistently refused to engage in good-faith negotiation.

Then, last September, came the opportunity to talk with leaders of Birmingham's economic community. In the course of the negotiations, certain promises were made by the merchants—for example, to remove the stores' humiliating racial signs. On the basis of these promises, the Reverend Fred Shuttleworth and the leaders of the Alabama Christian Movement for Human Rights agreed to a moratorium on all demonstrations. As the weeks and months went by, we realized that we were the victims of a broken promise. A few signs, briefly removed, returned; the others remained.

As in so many past experiences, our hopes had been blasted, and the shadow of deep disappointment settled upon us. We had no alternative except to prepare for direct action, whereby we would present our very bodies as a means of laying our case before the conscience of the local and the national community. Mindful of the difficulties involved, we decided to undertake a process of self-purification. We began a series of workshops on nonviolence, and we repeatedly asked ourselves: "Are you able to accept blows without retaliating?" "Are you able to endure the ordeal of jail?" We decided to schedule our direct-action program for the Easter season, realizing that except for Christmas, this is the main shopping period of the year. Knowing that a strong economic-withdrawal program would be the by-product of direct action, we felt that this would be the best time to bring pressure to bear on the merchants for the needed change.

Then it occurred to us that Birmingham's mayoralty election was coming up in March, and we speedily decided to postpone action until after election day. When we discovered that the Commissioner of Public Safety, Eugene "Bull" Connor, had piled up enough votes to be in the run-off, we decided again to postpone action until the day after the run-off so that the demonstrations could not be used to cloud the issues. Like many others, we waited to see Mr. Connor defeated, and to this end we endured postponement after postponement. Having aided in this community need, we felt that our direct-action program could be delayed no longer.

You may well ask: "Why direct action? Why sit-ins, marches, and so forth? Isn't negotiation a better path?" You are quite right in calling for negotiation. Indeed, this is the very purpose of direct action. Nonviolent direct action seeks to create such a crisis and foster such a tension that a community which has constantly refused to negotiate is forced to confront the issue. It seeks so to dramatize the issue that it can no longer be ignored. My citing the creation of tension as part of the work of the nonviolent-resister may sound rather shocking. But I must confess that I am not afraid of the word "tension." I have earnestly opposed violent tension, but there is a type of constructive, nonviolent tension which is necessary for growth. Just as Socrates felt that it was necessary to create a tension in the mind so that individuals could rise from the bondage of myths and half-truths to the unfettered realm of creative analysis and objective appraisal, so must we see the need for nonviolent gadflies to create the kind of tension in society that will help men rise from the dark depths of prejudice and racism to the majestic heights of understanding and brotherhood.

The purpose of our direct-action program is to create a situation so crisis-packed that it will inevitably open the door to negotiation. I therefore concur with you in your call for negotiation. Too long has our beloved Southland been bogged down in a tragic effort to live in monologue rather than dialogue.

One of the basic points in your statement is that the action that I and my associates have taken in Birmingham is untimely. Some have asked: "Why didn't you give the new city administration time to act?" The only answer that I can give to this query is that the new Birmingham administration must be prodded about as much as the outgoing one, before it will act. We are sadly mistaken if we feel that the election of Albert Boutwell as mayor will bring the millennium to Birmingham. While Mr. Boutwell is a much more gentle person than Mr. Connor, they are both segregationists, dedicated to maintenance of the status quo. I have hope that Mr. Boutwell will be reasonable enough to see the futility of massive resistance to desegregation. But he will not see this without pressure from devotees of civil rights. My friends, I must say to you that we have not made a single gain in civil rights without determined legal and nonviolent pressure. Lamentably, it is an historical fact that privileged groups seldom give up their privileges voluntarily. Individuals may see the moral light and voluntarily give up their unjust posture; but as Reinhold Niebuhr[2] has reminded us, groups tend to be more immoral than individuals.

We know through painful experience that freedom is never voluntarily given by the oppressor; it must be demanded by the oppressed. Frankly, I have yet to engage in a direct-action campaign that was "well timed" in the view of those who have not suffered unduly from the disease of segregation. For years now I have heard the word "Wait!" It rings in the ear of every Negro with piercing familiarity. This "Wait" has almost always meant "Never." We must come to see, with one of our distinguished jurists, that "justice too long delayed is justice denied."[3]

We have waited for more than 340 years for our constitutional and God-given rights. The nations of Asia and Africa are moving with jetlike speed toward gaining political independence, but we still creep at horse-and-buggy pace toward gaining a cup of coffee at a lunch counter. Perhaps it is easy for those who have never felt the stinging darts of segregation to say, "Wait." But when you have seen vicious mobs lynch your mothers and fathers at will and drown your sisters and brothers at whim; when you have seen hate-filled policemen curse, kick, and even kill your black brothers and sisters; when you see the vast majority of your twenty million Negro brothers smothering in an airtight cage of poverty in the midst of an affluent society; when you suddenly find your tongue twisted and your speech stammering as you seek to explain to your six-year-old daughter why she can't go to the public amusement park that has just been advertised on television, and see tears welling up in her eyes when she is told that Funtown is closed to colored children, and see ominous clouds of inferiority beginning to form in her little mental sky, and see her beginning to distort her personality by developing an unconscious bitterness toward white people; when you have to concoct an answer for a five-year-old son who is asking: "Daddy, why do white people treat colored people so mean?"; when you take a cross-country drive and find it necessary to sleep night after night in the uncomfortable corners of your automobile because no motel will accept you; when you are humiliated day in and day out by nagging signs reading "white" and "colored"; when your first name becomes "nigger," your middle name becomes "boy" (however old you are) and your last name becomes "John," and your wife and mother are never given the respected

[2]**Reinhold Niebuhr** Niebuhr (1892–1971) was a minister, political activist, author, and professor of applied Christianity at Union Theological Seminary. [All notes are the editors' unless otherwise specified.]
[3]**Justice ... denied** A quotation attributed to William E. Gladstone (1809–1898), British statesman and prime minister.

title "Mrs."; when you are harried by day and haunted by night by the fact that you are a Negro, living constantly at tiptoe stance, never quite knowing what to expect next, and are plagued with inner fears and outer resentments; when you are forever fighting a degenerating sense of "nobodiness"—then you will understand why we find it difficult to wait. There comes a time when the cup of endurance runs over, and men are no longer willing to be plunged into the abyss of despair. I hope, sirs, you can understand our legitimate and unavoidable impatience.

You express a great deal of anxiety over our willingness to break 15 laws. This is certainly a legitimate concern. Since we so diligently urge people to obey the Supreme Court's decision of 1954 outlawing segregation in the public schools, at first glance it may seem rather paradoxical for us consciously to break laws. One may well ask: "How can you advocate breaking some laws and obeying others?" The answer lies in the fact that there are two types of laws: just and unjust. I would be the first to advocate obeying just laws. One has not only a legal but a moral responsibility to obey just laws. Conversely, one has a moral responsibility to disobey unjust laws. I would agree with St. Augustine that "an unjust law is no law at all."

Now, what is the difference between the two? How does one determine whether a law is just or unjust? A just law is a man-made code that squares with the moral law or the law of God. An unjust law is a code that is out of harmony with the moral law. To put it in the terms of St. Thomas Aquinas: An unjust law is a human law that is not rooted in eternal law and natural law. Any law that uplifts human personality is just. Any law that degrades human personality is unjust. All segregation statutes are unjust because segregation distorts the soul and damages the personality. It gives the segregator a false sense of superiority and the segregated a false sense of inferiority. Segregation, to use the terminology of the Jewish philosopher Martin Buber, substitutes an "I-it" relationship for an "I-thou" relationship and ends up relegating persons to the status of things. Hence segregation is not only politically, economically, and sociologically unsound, it is morally wrong and sinful. Paul Tillich[4] has said that sin is separation. Is not segregation an existential expression of man's tragic separation, his awful estrangement, his terrible sinfulness? Thus it is that I can urge men to obey the 1954 decision of the Supreme Court, for it is morally right; and I can urge them to disobey segregation ordinances, for they are morally wrong.

Let us consider a more concrete example of just and unjust laws. An unjust law is a code that a numerical or power majority group compels a minority group to obey but does not make binding on itself. This is *difference*

---

[4]**Paul Tillich** Tillich (1886–1965), born in Germany, taught theology at several German universities, but in 1933 he was dismissed from his post at the University of Frankfurt because of his opposition to the Nazi regime. At the invitation of Reinhold Niebuhr, he came to the United States and taught at Union Theological Seminary.

made legal. By the same token, a just law is a code that a majority compels a minority to follow and that it is willing to follow itself. This is *sameness* made legal.

Let me give another explanation. A law is unjust if it is inflicted on a minority that, as a result of being denied the right to vote, had no part in enacting or devising the law. Who can say that the legislature of Alabama which set up that state's segregation laws was democratically elected? Throughout Alabama all sorts of devious methods are used to prevent Negroes from becoming registered voters, and there are some counties in which, even though Negroes constitute a majority of the population, not a single Negro is registered. Can any law enacted under such circumstances be considered democratically structured?

Sometimes a law is just on its face and unjust in its application. For instance, I have been arrested on a charge of parading without a permit. Now, there is nothing wrong in having an ordinance which requires a permit for a parade. But such an ordinance becomes unjust when it is used to maintain segregation and to deny citizens the First Amendment privilege of peaceful assembly and protest.

I hope you are able to see the distinction I am trying to point out. In 20 no sense do I advocate evading or defying the law, as would the rabid segregationist. That would lead to anarchy. One who breaks an unjust law must do so openly, lovingly, and with a willingness to accept the penalty. I submit that an individual who breaks a law that conscience tells him is unjust, and who willingly accepts the penalty of imprisonment in order to arouse the conscience of the community over its injustice, is in reality expressing the highest respect for law.

Of course, there is nothing new about this kind of civil disobedience. It was evidenced sublimely in the refusal of Shadrach, Meshach, and Abednego to obey the laws of Nebuchadnezzar, on the ground that a higher moral law was at stake. It was practiced superbly by the early Christians, who were willing to face hungry lions and the excruciating pain of chopping blocks rather than submit to certain unjust laws of the Roman Empire. To a degree, academic freedom is a reality today because Socrates practiced civil disobedience. In our own nation, the Boston Tea Party represented a massive act of civil disobedience.

We should never forget that everything Adolf Hitler did in Germany was "legal" and everything the Hungarian freedom fighters did in Hungary was "illegal." It was "illegal" to aid and comfort a Jew in Hitler's Germany. Even so, I am sure that, had I lived in Germany at the time, I would have aided and comforted my Jewish brothers. If today I lived in a Communist country where certain principles dear to the Christian faith are suppressed, I would openly advocate disobeying that country's anti-religious laws.

I must make two honest confessions to you, my Christian and Jewish brothers. First, I must confess that over the past few years I have been gravely disappointed with the white moderate. I have almost reached the regrettable conclusion that the Negro's great stumbling block in his stride toward freedom is not the White Citizen's Counciler or the Ku Klux Klanner, but the white moderate, who is more devoted to "order" than to justice; who prefers a negative peace which is the absence of tension to a positive peace which is the presence of justice; who constantly says: "I agree with you in the goal you seek, but I cannot agree with your methods or direct action"; who paternalistically believes he can set the timetable for another man's freedom; who lives by a mythical concept of time and who constantly advises the Negro to wait for a "more convenient season." Shallow understanding from people of good will is more frustrating than absolute misunderstanding from people of ill will. Lukewarm acceptance is much more bewildering than outright rejection.

I had hoped that the white moderate would understand that law and order exist for the purpose of establishing justice and that when they fail in this purpose they become the dangerously structured dams that block the flow of social progress. I had hoped that the white moderate would understand that the present tension in the South is a necessary phase of the transition from an obnoxious negative peace, in which the Negro passively accepted his unjust plight, to a substantive and positive peace, in which all men will respect the dignity and worth of human personality. Actually, we who engage in nonviolent direct action are not the creators of tension. We merely bring to the surface the hidden tension that is already alive. We bring it out in the open, where it can be seen and dealt with. Like a boil that can never be cured so long as it is covered up but must be opened with all its ugliness to the natural medicines of air and light, injustice must be exposed, with all the tension its exposure creates, to the light of human conscience and the air of national opinion before it can be cured.

In your statement you assert that our actions, even though peaceful, 25 must be condemned because they precipitate violence. But is this a logical assertion? Isn't this like condemning a robbed man because his possession of money precipitated the evil act of robbery? Isn't this like condemning Socrates because his unswerving commitment to truth and his philosophical inquiries precipitated the act by the misguided populace in which they made him drink hemlock? Isn't this like condemning Jesus because his unique God-consciousness and never-ceasing devotion to God's will precipitated the evil act of crucifixion? We must come to see that, as the federal courts have consistently affirmed, it is wrong to urge an individual to cease his efforts to gain his basic constitutional rights because the quest may precipitate violence. Society must protect the robbed and punish the robber.

I had also hoped that the white moderate would reject the myth concerning time in relation to the struggle for freedom. I have just received a letter from a white brother in Texas. He writes: "All Christians know that the colored people will receive equal rights eventually, but it is possible that you are in too great a religious hurry. It has taken Christianity almost two thousand years to accomplish what it has. The teachings of Christ take time to come to earth." Such an attitude stems from a tragic misconception of time, from the strangely irrational notion that there is something in the very flow of time that will inevitably cure all ills. Actually, time itself is neutral; it can be used either destructively or constructively. More and more I feel that the people of ill will have used time much more effectively than have the people of good will. We will have to repent in this generation not merely for the hateful words and actions of the bad people but for the appalling silence of the good people. Human progress never rolls in on wheels of inevitability; it comes through the tireless efforts of men willing to be co-workers with God, and without this hard work, time itself becomes an ally of the forces of social stagnation. We must use time creatively, in the knowledge that the time is always ripe to do right. Now is the time to make real the promise of democracy and transform our pending national elegy into a creative psalm of brotherhood. Now is the time to lift our national policy from the quicksand of racial injustice to the solid rock of human dignity.

You speak of our activity in Birmingham as extreme. At first I was rather disappointed that fellow clergymen would see my nonviolent efforts as those of an extremist. I began thinking about the fact that I stand in the middle of two opposing forces in the Negro community. One is a force of complacency, made up in part of Negroes who, as a result of long years of oppression, are so drained of self-respect and a sense of "somebodiness" that they have adjusted to segregation; and in part of a few middle-class Negroes who, because of a degree of academic and economic security and because in some ways they profit by segregation, have become insensitive to the problems of the masses. The other force is one of bitterness and hatred, and it comes perilously close to advocating violence. It is expressed in the various black nationalist groups that are springing up across the nation, the largest and best-known being Elijah Muhammad's Muslim movement. Nourished by the Negro's frustration over the continued existence of racial discrimination, this movement is made up of people who have lost faith in America, who have absolutely repudiated Christianity, and who have concluded that the white man is an incorrigible "devil."

I have tried to stand between these two forces, saying that we need emulate neither the "do-nothingism" of the complacent nor the hatred and despair of the black nationalist. For there is the more excellent way of love and nonviolent protest. I am grateful to God that, through the influence of the Negro church, the way of nonviolence became an integral part of our struggle.

If this philosophy had not emerged, by now many streets of the South should, I am convinced, be flowing with blood. And I am further convinced that if our white brothers dismiss as "rabble-rousers" and "outside agitators" those of us who employ nonviolent direct action, and if they refuse to support our nonviolent efforts, millions of Negroes will, out of frustration and despair, seek solace and security in black-nationalist ideologies—a development that would inevitably lead to a frightening racial nightmare.

Oppressed people cannot remain oppressed forever. The yearning 30 for freedom eventually manifests itself, and that is what has happened to the American Negro. Something within has reminded him of his birthright of freedom, and something without has reminded him that it can be gained. Consciously or unconsciously, he has been caught up by the *Zeitgeist*,[5] and with his black brothers of Africa and his brown and yellow brothers of Asia, South America, and the Caribbean, the United States Negro is moving with a sense of great urgency toward the promised land of racial justice. If one recognizes this vital urge that has engulfed the Negro community, one should readily understand why public demonstrations are taking place. The Negro has many pent-up resentments and latent frustrations, and he must release them. So let him march; let him make prayer pilgrimages to the city hall; let him go on freedom rides—and try to understand why he must do so. If his repressed emotions are not released in nonviolent ways, they will seek expression through violence; this is not a threat but a fact of history. So I have not said to my people: "Get rid of your discontent." Rather, I have tried to say that this normal and healthy discontent can be channeled into the creative outlet of nonviolent direct action. And now this approach is being termed extremist.

But though I was initially disappointed at being categorized as an extremist, as I continued to think about the matter I gradually gained a measure of satisfaction from the label. Was not Jesus an extremist for love: "Love your enemies, bless them that curse you, do good to them that hate you, and pray for them which despitefully use you, and persecute you." Was not Amos an extremist for justice: "Let justice roll down like waters and righteousness like an ever-flowing stream." Was not Paul an extremist for the Christian gospel: "I bear in my body the marks of the Lord Jesus." Was not Martin Luther an extremist: "Here I stand; I cannot do otherwise, so help me God." And John Bunyan: "I will stay in jail to the end of my days before I make a butchery of my conscience." And Abraham Lincoln: "This nation cannot survive half slave and half free." And Thomas Jefferson: "We hold these truths to be self-evident, that all men are created equal...." So the question is not whether we will be extremists, but what kind of extremists we will be. Will we be extremists for hate or for love? Will we be extremists for the preservation of injustice or for the extension of justice? In that dramatic scene on Calvary's hill three men were crucified. We must never forget that all three were crucified for the same crime—the crime of extremism. Two were extremists for immorality, and thus fell below their environment.

[5]***Zeitgeist*** Spirit of the age (German).

The other, Jesus Christ, was an extremist for love, truth, and goodness, and thereby rose above his environment. Perhaps the South, the nation, and the world are in dire need of creative extremists.

I had hoped that the white moderate would see this need. Perhaps I was too optimistic; perhaps I expected too much. I suppose I should have realized that few members of the oppressor race can understand the deep groans and passionate yearnings of the oppressed race, and still fewer have the vision to see that injustice must be rooted out by strong, persistent, and determined action. I am thankful, however, that some of our white brothers in the South have grasped the meaning of this social revolution and committed themselves to it. They are still all too few in quantity, but they are big in quality. Some—such as Ralph McGill, Lillian Smith, Harry Golden, James McBride Dabbs, Ann Braden, and Sarah Patton Boyle—have written about our struggle in eloquent and prophetic terms. Others have marched with us down nameless streets of the South. They have languished in filthy, roach-infested jails, suffering the abuse and brutality of policemen who view them as "dirty nigger-lovers." Unlike so many of their moderate brothers and sisters, they have recognized the urgency of the moment and sensed the need for powerful "action" antidotes to combat the disease of segregation.

Let me take note of my other major disappointment. I have been so greatly disappointed with the white church and its leadership. Of course, there are some notable exceptions. I am not unmindful of the fact that each of you has taken some significant stands on this issue. I commend you, Reverend Stallings, for your Christian stand on this past Sunday, in welcoming Negroes to your worship service on a nonsegregated basis. I commend the Catholic leaders of this state for integrating Spring Hill College several years ago.

But despite these notable exceptions, I must honestly reiterate that I have been disappointed with the church. I do not say this as one of those negative critics who can always find something wrong with the church. I say this as a minister of the gospel, who loves the church; who was nurtured in its bosom; who has been sustained by its spiritual blessings and who will remain true to it as long as the cord of life shall lengthen.

When I was suddenly catapulted into the leadership of the bus 35 protest in Montgomery, Alabama, a few years ago, I felt we would be supported by the white church. I felt that the white ministers, priests, and rabbis of the South would be among our strongest allies. Instead, some have been outright opponents, refusing to understand the freedom movement and misrepresenting its leaders; all too many others have been more cautious than courageous and have remained silent behind the anesthetizing security of stained-glass windows.

In spite of my shattered dreams, I came to Birmingham with the hope that the white religious leadership of this community would see the justice of our cause and, with deep moral concern, would serve as the channel through which our just grievances could reach the power structure. I had hoped that each of you would understand. But again I have been disappointed.

I have heard numerous southern religious leaders admonish their worshipers to comply with a desegregation decision because it is the law, but I have longed to hear white ministers declare: "Follow this decree because integration is morally right and because the Negro is your brother." In the midst of blatant injustices inflicted upon the Negro, I have watched white churchmen stand on the sideline and mouth pious irrelevancies and sanctimonious trivialities. In the midst of a mighty struggle to rid our nation of racial and economic injustice, I have heard many ministers say: "Those are social issues, with which the gospel has no real concern." And I have watched many churches commit themselves to a completely otherworldly religion which makes a strange, unbiblical distinction between body and soul, between the sacred and the secular.

I have traveled the length and breadth of Alabama, Mississippi, and all the other southern states. On sweltering summer days and crisp autumn mornings I have looked at the South's beautiful churches with their lofty spires pointing heavenward. I have beheld the impressive outlines of her massive religious-education buildings. Over and over I have found myself saying: "What kind of people worship here? Who is their God? Where were their voices when the lips of Governor Barnett dripped with words of interposition and nullification? Where were they when Governor Wallace gave a clarion call for defiance and hatred? Where were their voices of support when bruised and weary Negro men and women decided to rise from the dark dungeons of complacency to the bright hills of creative protest?"

Yes, these questions are still in my mind. In deep disappointment I have wept over the laxity of the church. But be assured that my tears have been tears of love. There can be no deep disappointment where there is not deep love. Yes, I love the church. How could I do otherwise? I am in the rather unique position of being the son, the grandson, and the great-grandson of preachers. Yes, I see the church as the body of Christ. But, Oh! How we have blemished and scarred that body through social neglect and through fear of being nonconformists.

There was a time when the church was very powerful—in the time 40 when the early Christians rejoiced at being deemed worthy to suffer for what they believed. In those days the church was not merely a thermometer that recorded the ideas and principles of popular opinion; it was a thermostat that transformed the mores of society. Whenever the early Christians entered a town, the people in power became disturbed and immediately sought to convict the Christians for being "disturbers of the peace" and "outside agitators." But the Christians pressed on, in the conviction that they were "a colony of heaven," called to obey God rather than man. Small in number, they were big in commitment. They were too God-intoxicated to be "astronomically intimidated." By their effort and example they brought an end to such ancient evils as infanticide and gladiatorial contests.

Things are different now. So often the contemporary church is a weak, ineffectual voice with an uncertain sound. So often it is an archdefender of the status quo. Far from being disturbed by the presence of the church, the power structure of the average community is consoled by the church's silent—and often even vocal—sanction of things as they are.

But the judgment of God is upon the church as never before. If today's church does not recapture the sacrificial spirit of the early church, it will lose its authenticity, forfeit the loyalty of millions, and be dismissed as an irrelevant social club with no meaning for the twentieth century. Every day I meet young people whose disappointment with the church has turned into outright disgust.

Perhaps I have once again been too optimistic. Is organized religion too inextricably bound to the status quo to save our nation and the world? Perhaps I must turn my faith to the inner spiritual church, the church within the church, as the true *ekklesia*[6] and the hope of the world. But again I am thankful to God that some noble souls from the ranks of organized religion have broken loose from the paralyzing chains of conformity and joined us as active partners in the struggle for freedom. They have left their secure congregations and walked the streets of Albany, Georgia, with us. They have gone down the highways of the South on tortuous rides for freedom. Yes, they have gone to jail with us. Some have been dismissed from their churches, have lost the support of their bishops and fellow ministers. But they have acted in the faith that right defeated is stronger than evil triumphant. Their witness has been the spiritual salt that has preserved the true meaning of the gospel in these troubled times. They have carved a tunnel of hope through the dark mountain of disappointment.

I hope the church as a whole will meet the challenge of this decisive hour. But even if the church does not come to the aid of justice, I have no despair about the future. I have no fear about the outcome of our struggle in Birmingham, even if our motives are at present misunderstood. We will reach the goal of freedom in Birmingham and all over the nation, because the goal of America is freedom. Abused and scorned though we may be, our destiny is tied up with America's destiny. Before the pilgrims landed at Plymouth, we were here. Before the pen of Jefferson etched the majestic words of the Declaration of Independence across the pages of history, we were here. For more than two centuries our forebears labored in this country without wages; they made cotton king; they built the homes of their masters while suffering gross injustice and shameful humiliation—and yet out of a bottomless vitality they continue to thrive and develop. If the inexpressible cruelties of slavery could not stop us, the opposition we

[6]*ekklesia* A gathering or assembly of citizens (Greek).

now face will surely fail. We will win our freedom because the sacred heritage of our nation and the eternal will of God are embodied in our echoing demands.

Before closing I feel impelled to mention one other point in your 45 statement that has troubled me profoundly. You warmly commended the Birmingham police force for keeping "order" and "preventing violence." I doubt that you would have so warmly commended the police force if you had seen its dogs sinking their teeth into unarmed, nonviolent Negroes. I doubt that you would so quickly commend the policemen if you were to observe their ugly and inhumane treatment of Negroes here in the city jail; if you were to watch them push and curse old Negro women and young Negro girls; if you were to see them slap and kick old Negro men and young boys; if you were to observe them, as they did on two occasions, refuse to give us food because we wanted to sing our grace together. I cannot join you in your praise of the Birmingham police department.

It is true that the police have exercised a degree of discipline in handling the demonstrators. In this sense they have conducted themselves rather "nonviolently" in public. But for what purpose? To preserve the evil system of segregation. Over the past few years I have consistently preached that nonviolence demands that the means we use must be as pure as the ends we seek. I have tried to make clear that it is wrong to use immoral means to attain moral ends. But now I must affirm that it is just as wrong, or perhaps even more so, to use moral means to preserve immoral ends. Perhaps Mr. Connor and his policemen have been rather nonviolent in public, as was Chief Pritchett in Albany, Georgia, but they used the moral means of nonviolence to maintain the immoral end of racial injustice. As T. S. Eliot has said: "The last temptation is the greatest treason: To do the right deed for the wrong reason."

I wish you had commended the Negro sit-inners and demonstrators of Birmingham for their sublime courage, their willingness to suffer, and their amazing discipline in the midst of great provocation. One day the South will recognize its real heroes. They will be the James Merediths, with the noble sense of purpose that enables them to face jeering and hostile mobs, and with the agonizing loneliness that characterizes the life of the pioneer. They will be old, oppressed, battered Negro women, symbolized in a seventy-two-year-old woman in Montgomery, Alabama, who rose up with a sense of dignity and with her people decided not to ride segregated buses, and who responded with ungrammatical profundity to one who inquired about her weariness: "My feets is tired, but my soul is at rest." They will be the young high school and college students, the young ministers of the gospel and a host of their elders, courageously and nonviolently sitting in at lunch counters and willingly going to jail for conscience's sake. One day the South will know that when these disinherited children of God sat down at lunch counters, they were in reality standing up for what is best in the American dream and for the most sacred values in our Judaeo-Christian heritage, thereby bringing our nation back to those great wells of democracy which were dug deep by the founding fathers in their formulation of the Constitution and the Declaration of Independence.

Never before have I written so long a letter. I'm afraid it is much too long to take your precious time. I can assure you that it would have been much shorter if I had been writing from a comfortable desk, but what else can one do when he is alone in a narrow jail cell, other than write long letters, think long thoughts, and pray long prayers?

If I have said anything in this letter that overstates the truth and indicates an unreasonable impatience, I beg you to forgive me. If I have said anything that understates the truth and indicates my having a patience that allows me to settle for anything less than brotherhood, I beg God to forgive me.

I hope this letter finds you strong in the faith. I also hope that cir- 50 cumstances will soon make it possible for me to meet each of you, not as an integrationist or a civil-rights leader but as a fellow clergyman and a Christian brother. Let us all hope that the dark clouds of racial prejudice will soon pass away and the deep fog of misunderstanding will be lifted from our fear-drenched communities, and in some not too distant tomorrow the radiant stars of love and brotherhood will shine over our great nation with all their scintillating beauty.

Yours for the cause of Peace and Brotherhood,
Martin Luther King Jr.

TOPICS FOR CRITICAL THINKING AND WRITING

1. In his first five paragraphs of the "Letter," how does King assure his audience that he is not a meddlesome intruder but a man of good will?

2. In paragraph 3 King refers to Hebrew prophets and to the Apostle Paul and later (para. 10) to Socrates. What is the point of these references?

3. In paragraph 11 what does King mean when he says that "our beloved Southland" has long tried to "live in monologue rather than dialogue"?

4. King begins paragraph 23 with "I must make two honest confessions to you, my Christian and Jewish brothers." What would have been gained or lost if he had used this paragraph as his opening?

5. King's last three paragraphs do not advance his argument. What do they do?

6. Why does King advocate breaking unjust laws "openly, lovingly" (para. 20)? What does he mean by these words? What other motives or attitudes do these words rule out?

7. Construct two definitions of *civil disobedience,* and explain whether and to what extent it is easier (or harder) to justify civil disobedience, depending on how you have defined the expression.

8. If you feel that you wish to respond to King's letter on some point, write a letter nominally addressed to King. You may, if you wish, adopt the persona of one of the eight clergymen whom King initially addressed.

9. King writes (para. 46) that "nonviolence demands that the means we use must be as pure as the ends we seek." How do you think King would evaluate the following acts: (a) occupying a college administration building to protest the administration's unsatisfactory response to a racial incident on campus or its failure to hire minority persons as staff and faculty; (b) occupying an abortion clinic to protest abortion? Set down your answer in an essay of 500 words.

10. Compose a letter from King in which he responds to Plato's "Crito" (p. 903).

Stanley Milgram

Stanley Milgram (1933–1984) taught at Yale and Harvard Universities and at the Graduate Center, City University of New York. In 1963, while at Yale, he devised an experiment that tested the willingness of people to submit to the authority of an experimenter even if it meant they would violate their conscience by inflicting pain on another person during the course of the experiment. He published his research on conformity in a book, Obedience to Authority *(1974), which was nominated for the National Book Award.*

The Perils of Obedience

Obedience is as basic an element in the structure of social life as one can point to. Some system of authority is a requirement of all communal living, and it is only the person dwelling in isolation who is not forced to respond, with defiance or submission, to the commands of others. For many people, obedience is a deeply ingrained behavior tendency, indeed a potent impulse overriding training in ethics, sympathy, and moral conduct.

The dilemma inherent in submission to authority is ancient, as old as the story of Abraham, and the question of whether one should obey when commands conflict with conscience has been argued by Plato, dramatized in *Antigone*, and treated to philosophic analysis in almost every historical epoch. Conservative philosophers argue that the very fabric of society is threatened by disobedience, while humanists stress the primacy of the individual conscience.

The legal and philosophic aspects of obedience are of enormous import, but they say very little about how most people behave in concrete situations. I set up a simple experiment at Yale University to test how much pain an ordinary citizen would inflict on another person simply because he was ordered to by an experimental scientist. Stark authority was pitted against the subjects' strongest moral imperatives against hurting others, and, with the subjects' ears ringing with the screams of the victims, authority won more often than not. The extreme willingness of adults to go to almost any lengths on the command of an authority constitutes the chief finding of the study and the fact most urgently demanding explanation.

In the basic experimental design, two people come to a psychology laboratory to take part in a study of memory and learning. One of them is designated as a "teacher" and the other a "learner." The experimenter explains that the study is concerned with the effects of punishment on learning. The learner is conducted into a room, seated in a kind of miniature electric chair; his arms are strapped to prevent excessive movement, and an electrode is attached to his wrist. He is told that he will be read lists of simple word pairs, and that he will then be tested on his ability to remember the second word of a pair when he hears the first one again. Whenever he makes an error, he will receive electric shocks of increasing intensity.

The real focus of the experiment is the teacher. After watching the 5 learner being strapped into place, he is seated before an impressive shock generator. The instrument panel consists of thirty lever switches set in a horizontal line. Each switch is clearly labeled with a voltage designation ranging from 15 to 450 volts. The following designations are clearly indicated for groups of four switches, going from left to right: Slight Shock, Moderate Shock, Strong Shock, Very Strong Shock, Intense Shock, Extreme Intensity Shock, Danger: Severe Shock. (Two switches after this last designation are simply marked XXX.)

When a switch is depressed, a pilot light corresponding to each switch is illuminated in bright red; an electric buzzing is heard; a blue light, labeled "voltage energizer," flashes; the dial on the voltage meter swings to the right; and various relay clicks sound off.

The upper left-hand corner of the generator is labeled SHOCK GEN-ERATOR, TYPE ZLB, DYSON INSTRUMENT COMPANY, WALTHAM, MASS. OUTPUT 15 VOLTS — 450 VOLTS.

Each subject is given a sample 45-volt shock from the generator before his run as teacher, and the jolt strengthens his belief in the authenticity of the machine.

The teacher is a genuinely naïve subject who has come to the laboratory for the experiment. The learner, or victim, is actually an actor who receives no shock at all. The point of the experiment is to see how far a person will proceed in a concrete and measurable situation in which he is ordered to inflict increasing pain on a protesting victim.

Conflict arises when the man receiving the shock begins to show 10 that he is experiencing discomfort. At 75 volts, he grunts; at 120 volts, he complains loudly; at 150, he demands to be released from the experiment. As the voltage increases, his protests become more vehement and emotional. At 285 volts, his response can be described only as an agonized scream. Soon thereafter, he makes no sound at all.

For the teacher, the situation quickly becomes one of gripping tension. It is not a game for him; conflict is intense and obvious. The manifest suffering of the learner presses him to quit; but each time he hesitates to administer a shock, the experimenter orders him to continue. To extricate himself from this plight, the subject must make a clear break with authority.

The subject, Gretchen Brandt, is an attractive thirty-one-year-old medical technician who works at the Yale Medical School. She had emigrated from Germany five years before.[1]

On several occasions when the learner complains, she [Brandt] turns to the experimenter coolly and inquires, "Shall I continue?" She promptly returns to her task when the experimenter asks her to do so. At the administration of 210 volts, she turns to the experimenter, remarking firmly, "Well, I'm sorry, I don't think we should continue."

EXPERIMENTER: The experiment requires that you go on until he has learned all the word pairs correctly.

BRANDT: He has a heart condition, I'm sorry. He told you that before.   15

EXPERIMENTER: The shocks may be painful but they are not dangerous.

BRANDT: Well, I'm sorry, I think when shocks continue like this, they *are* dangerous. You ask him if he wants to get out. It's his free will.

EXPERIMENTER: It is absolutely essential that we continue. . . .

BRANDT: I'd like you to ask him. We came here of our free will. If he wants to continue I'll go ahead. He told you he had a heart condition. I'm sorry. I don't want to be responsible for anything happening to him. I wouldn't like it for me either.

EXPERIMENTER: You have no other choice.   20

BRANDT: I think we are here on our own free will. I don't want to be responsible if anything happens to him. Please understand that.

She refuses to go further and the experiment is terminated.

The woman is firm and resolute throughout. She indicates in the interview that she was in no way tense or nervous, and this corresponds to her controlled appearance during the experiment. She feels that the last shock she administered to the learner was extremely painful and reiterates that she "did not want to be responsible for any harm to him."

The woman's straightforward, courteous behavior in the experiment, lack of tension, and total control of her own action seem to make disobedience a simple and rational deed. Her behavior is the very embodiment of what I envisioned would be true for almost all subjects.

---

[1]Names of subjects described in this piece have been changed. [Milgram's note.]

AN UNEXPECTED OUTCOME

Before the experiments, I sought predictions about the outcome from 25 various kinds of people—psychiatrists, college sophomores, middle-class adults, graduate students, and faculty in the behavioral sciences. With remarkable similarity, they predicted that virtually all subjects would refuse to obey the experimenter. The psychiatrists, specifically, predicted that most subjects would not go beyond 150 volts, when the victim makes his first explicit demand to be freed. They expected that only 4 percent would reach 300 volts, and that only a pathological fringe of about one in a thousand would administer the highest shock on the board.

These predictions were unequivocally wrong. Of the forty subjects in the first experiment, twenty-five obeyed the orders of the experimenter to the end, punishing the victim until they reached the most potent shock available on the generator. After 450 volts were administered three times, the experimenter called a halt to the session. Many obedient subjects then heaved sighs of relief, mopped their brows, rubbed their fingers over their eyes, or nervously fumbled cigarettes. Others displayed only minimal signs of tension from beginning to end.

When the very first experiments were carried out, Yale undergraduates were used as subjects, and about 60 percent of them were fully obedient. A colleague of mine immediately dismissed these findings as having no relevance to "ordinary" people, asserting that Yale undergraduates are a highly aggressive, competitive bunch who step on each other's necks on the slightest provocation. He assured me that when "ordinary" people were tested, the results would be quite different. As we moved from the pilot studies to the regular experimental series, people drawn from every stratum of New Haven life came to be employed in the experiment: professionals, white-collar workers, unemployed persons, and industrial workers. *The experiment's total outcome was the same as we had observed among the students.*

Moreover, when the experiments were repeated in Princeton, Munich, Rome, South Africa, and Australia, the level of obedience was invariably somewhat *higher* than found in the investigation reported in this article. Thus one scientist in Munich found 85 percent of his subjects obedient.

Fred Prozi's reactions, if more dramatic than most, illuminate the conflicts experienced by others in less visible form. About fifty years old and unemployed at the time of the experiment, he has a good-natured, if slightly dissolute, appearance, and he strikes people as a rather ordinary fellow. He begins the session calmly but becomes tense as it proceeds. After delivering the 180-volt shock, he pivots around in his chair and, shaking his head, addresses the experimenter in agitated tones:

PROZI: I can't stand it. I'm not going to kill that man in there. You 30 hear him hollering?

EXPERIMENTER: As I told you before, the shocks may be painful, but . . .

PROZI: But he's hollering. He can't stand it. What's going to happen to him?

EXPERIMENTER (his voice is patient, matter-of-fact): The experiment requires that you continue, Teacher.

PROZI: Aaah, but, unh, I'm not going to get that man sick in there— know what I mean?

EXPERIMENTER: Whether the learner likes it or not, we must go on, 35 through all the word pairs.

PROZI: I refuse to take the responsibility. He's in there hollering!

EXPERIMENTER: It's absolutely essential that you continue, Prozi.

PROZI (indicating the unused questions): There's too many left here, I mean, Jeez, if he gets them wrong, there's too many of them left. I mean, who's going to take the responsibility if anything happens to that gentleman?

EXPERIMENTER: I'm responsible for anything that happens to him. Continue, please.

PROZI: All right. (Consults list of words.) The next one's "Slow— 40 walk, truck, dance, music." Answer, please. (A buzzing sound indicates the learner has signaled his answer.) Wrong. A hundred and ninety-five volts. "Dance." (Zzumph!)

LEARNER (yelling): Let me out of here! My heart's bothering me! (Teacher looks at experimenter.)

EXPERIMENTER: Continue, please.

LEARNER (screaming): Let me out of here! You have no right to keep me here! Let me out of here, my heart's bothering me, let me out!

PROZI (shakes head, pats the table nervously): You see, he's hollering. Hear that? Gee, I don't know.

EXPERIMENTER: The experiment requires . . .   45

PROZI (interrupting): I know it does, sir, but I mean—hunh! He don't know what he's getting in for. He's up to 195 volts! (Experiment continues, through 210 volts, 225 volts, 240 volts, 255 volts, 270 volts, at which point Prozi, with evident relief, runs out of word-pair questions.)

EXPERIMENTER: You'll have to go back to the beginning of that page and go through them again until he's learned them all correctly.

PROZI: Aw, no. I'm not going to kill that man. You mean I've got to keep going up with the scale? No sir. He's hollering in there. I'm not going to give him 450 volts.

EXPERIMENTER: The experiment requires that you go on.

LEARNER: Ohhh. I absolutely refuse to answer any more. (Shouting 50 urgently now.) Let me out of here! You can't hold me here! Get me out. Get-me-out-of-here!

EXPERIMENTER: Continue. The next word is "Green," please.

PROZI: "Green — grass, hat, ink, apple." (Nothing happens. No answering buzz. Just gloomy silence.)

PROZI: I don't think he is going to answer.

EXPERIMENTER: If the learner doesn't answer in a reasonable time, about four or five seconds, consider the answer wrong. And follow the same procedures you have been doing for wrong answers. Say, "Wrong," tell him the number of volts, give him the punishment, read him the correct answer. Continue, please.

PROZI: "Green — grass, hat, ink, apple." Answer, please. (More silence. 55 Subject just sits there.)

EXPERIMENTER: Go on with the procedure, please.

PROZI: Three hundred and fifteen volts. The answer is "ink." (Zzumph!)

LEARNER: Ohh. Ooohh.

PROZI (relieved to hear response): Next one . . .

LEARNER: I absolutely refuse to answer.   60

PROZI: You got to. You get a shock if you don't answer. (Experiment continues with learner refusing to answer, and, finally, failing even to grunt or groan. At 375 volts, the subject stands up.)

PROZI: I think something's happened to that fellow in there. I don't get no answer. He was hollering at less voltage. Can't you check in and see if he's all right, please?

EXPERIMENTER (with same detached calm): Not once we've started. Please continue, Teacher.

PROZI (sits down, sighs deeply): "Cool — day, shade, water, paint." Answer, please. Are you all right in there? Are you all right?

EXPERIMENTER: Please continue, Teacher. Continue, please. (Subject 65 pushes lever. Zzumph!)

PROZI (swiveling around in his chair): Something's happened to that man in there. (Swiveling back.) Next one. "Low — dollar, necklace, moon, paint." (Turning around again.) Something's happened to that man in there. You better check in on him, sir. He won't answer or nothing.

EXPERIMENTER: Continue. Go on, please.

PROZI: You accept all responsibility?

EXPERIMENTER: The responsibility is mine. Correct. Please go on. (Subject returns to his list, starts running through words as rapidly as he can read them, works through to 450 volts.)

PROZI: That's that.   70

EXPERIMENTER: Continue using the 450 switch for each wrong answer. Continue, please.

PROZI: But I don't get anything!

EXPERIMENTER: Please continue. The next word is "white."

PROZI: Don't you think you should look in on him, please?

EXPERIMENTER: Not once we've started the experiment.   75

PROZI: What if he's dead in there? (Gestures toward the room with the electric chair.) I mean, he told me he can't stand the shock, sir. I don't mean to be rude, but I think you should look in on him. All you have to do is look in on him. All you have to do is look in the door. I don't get no answer, no noise. Something might have happened to the gentleman in there, sir.

EXPERIMENTER: We must continue. Go on, please.

PROZI: You mean keep giving him what? Four-hundred-fifty volts, what he's got now?

EXPERIMENTER: That's correct. Continue. The next word is "white."

PROZI (now at a furious pace): "White — cloud, horse, rock, house." 80 Answer, please. The answer is "horse." Four hundred and fifty volts. (Zzumph!) Next word, "Bag — paint, music, clown, girl." The answer is "paint." Four hundred and fifty volts. (Zzumph!) Next word is "Short — sentence, movie . . ."

EXPERIMENTER: Excuse me, Teacher. We'll have to discontinue the experiment.

PECULIAR REACTIONS

Morris Braverman, another subject, is a thirty-nine-year-old social worker. He looks older than his years because of his bald head and serious demeanor. His brow is furrowed, as if all the world's burdens were carried on his face. He appears intelligent and concerned.

When the learner refuses to answer and the experimenter instructs Braverman to treat the absence of an answer as equivalent to a wrong answer, he takes his instruction to heart. Before administering 300 volts he asserts officiously to the victim, "Mr. Wallace, your silence has to be considered as a wrong answer." Then he administers the shock. He offers half-heartedly to change places with the learner, then asks the experimenter, "Do I have to follow these instructions literally?" He is satisfied with the experimenter's answer that he does. His very refined and authoritative manner of speaking is increasingly broken up by wheezing laughter.

The experimenter's notes on Mr. Braverman at the last few shocks are:

- Almost breaking up now each time gives shock. Rubbing face to hide laughter.
- Squinting, trying to hide face with hand, still laughing.
- Cannot control his laughter at this point no matter what he does.
- Clenching fist, pushing it onto table.

In an interview after the session, Mr. Braverman summarizes the 85 experiment with impressive fluency and intelligence. He feels the experiment may have been designed also to "test the effects on the teacher of being in an essentially sadistic role, as well as the reactions of a student to a learning situation that was authoritative and punitive." When asked how painful the last few shocks administered to the learner were, he indicates that the most extreme category on the scale is not adequate (it read EXTREMELY PAINFUL) and places his mark at the edge of the scale with an arrow carrying it beyond the scale.

It is almost impossible to convey the greatly relaxed, sedate quality of his conversation in the interview. In the most relaxed terms, he speaks about his severe inner tension.

EXPERIMENTER: At what point were you most tense or nervous?
MR. BRAVERMAN: Well, when he first began to cry out in pain, and I realized this was hurting him. This got worse when he just blocked and refused to answer. There was I. I'm a nice person, I think, hurting somebody, and caught up in what seemed a mad situation . . . and in the interest of science, one goes through with it.

When the interviewer pursues the general question of tension, Mr. Braverman spontaneously mentions his laughter.

"My reactions were awfully peculiar. I don't know if you were 90 watching me, but my reactions were giggly, and trying to stifle laughter. This isn't the way I usually am. This was a sheer reaction to a totally impossible situation. And my reaction was to the situation of having to hurt somebody. And being totally helpless and caught up in a set of circumstances where I just couldn't deviate and I couldn't try to help. This is what got me."

Mr. Braverman, like all subjects, was told the actual nature and purpose of the experiment, and a year later he affirmed in a questionnaire that he had learned something of personal importance: "What appalled me was that I could possess this capacity for obedience and compliance to a central idea, i.e., the value of a memory experiment, even after it became clear that continued adherence to this value was at the expense of violation of another value, i.e., don't hurt someone who is helpless and not hurting you. As my wife said, 'You can call yourself Eichmann.' I hope I deal more effectively with any future conflicts of values I encounter."

THE ETIQUETTE OF SUBMISSION

One theoretical interpretation of this behavior holds that all people harbor deeply aggressive instincts continually pressing for expression, and that the experiment provides institutional justification for the release of these impulses. According to this view, if a person is placed in a situation in which he has complete power over another individual, whom he may punish as much as he likes, all that is sadistic and bestial in man comes to the fore. The impulse to shock the victim is seen to flow from the potent aggressive tendencies, which are part of the motivational life of the individual, and the experiment, because it provides social legitimacy, simply opens the door to their expression.

It becomes vital, therefore, to compare the subject's performance when he is under orders and when he is allowed to choose the shock level.

The procedure was identical to our standard experiment, except that the teacher was told that he was free to select any shock level on any of the trials. (The experimenter took pains to point out that the teacher could use the highest levels on the generator, the lowest, any in between, or any combination of levels.) Each subject proceeded for thirty critical trials. The learner's protests were coordinated to standard shock levels, his first grunt coming at 75 volts, his first vehement protest at 150 volts.

The average shock used during the thirty critical trials was less than 95 60 volts—lower than the point at which the victim showed the first signs of discomfort. Three of the forty subjects did not go beyond the very lowest level on the board, twenty-eight went no higher than 75 volts, and thirty-eight did not go beyond the first loud protest at 150 volts. Two subjects provided the exception, administering up to 325 and 450 volts, but the overall result was that the great majority of people delivered very low, usually painless, shocks when the choice was explicitly up to them.

This condition of the experiment undermines another commonly offered explanation of the subjects' behavior—that those who shocked the victim at the most severe levels came only from the sadistic fringe of society. If one considers that almost two-thirds of the participants fall into the category of "obedient" subjects, and that they represented ordinary people drawn from working, managerial, and professional classes, the argument becomes very shaky. Indeed, it is highly reminiscent of the issue that arose in connection with Hannah Arendt's 1963 book, *Eichmann in Jerusalem*. Arendt contended that the prosecution's effort to depict Eichmann as a sadistic monster was fundamentally wrong, that he came closer to being an uninspired bureaucrat who simply sat at his desk and did his job. For asserting her views, Arendt became the object of considerable scorn, even calumny. Somehow, it was felt that the monstrous deeds carried out by Eichmann required a brutal, twisted personality, evil incarnate. After witnessing hundreds of ordinary persons submit to the authority in our own experiments, I must conclude that Arendt's conception of the banality of evil comes closer to the truth than one might dare imagine. The ordinary person who shocked the victim did so out of a sense of obligation—an impression of his duties as a subject—and not from any peculiarly aggressive tendencies.

This is, perhaps, the most fundamental lesson of our study: Ordinary people, simply doing their jobs, and without any particular hostility on their part, can become agents in a terrible destructive process. Moreover, even when the destructive effects of their work become patently clear, and they are asked to carry out actions incompatible with fundamental standards of morality, relatively few people have the resources needed to resist authority.

Many of the people were in some sense against what they did to the learner, and many protested even while they obeyed. Some were totally convinced of the wrongness of their actions but could not bring themselves to make an open break with authority. They often derived satisfaction from their thoughts and felt that—within themselves, at least—they had been on the side of the angels. They tried to reduce strain by obeying the experimenter but "only slightly," encouraging the learner, touching the generator switches gingerly. When interviewed, such a subject would stress that he had "asserted my humanity" by administering the briefest shock possible. Handling the conflict in this manner was easier than defiance.

The situation is constructed so that there is no way the subject can stop shocking the learner without violating the experimenter's definitions of his own competence. The subject fears that he will appear arrogant, untoward, and rude if he breaks off. Although these inhibiting emotions appear small in scope alongside the violence being done to the learner, they suffuse the mind and feelings of the subject who is miserable at the prospect of having to repudiate the authority to his face. (When the experiment was altered so that the experimenter gave his instructions by telephone instead of in person, only a third as many people were fully obedient through 450 volts.) It is a curious thing that a measure of compassion on the part of the subject—an unwillingness to "hurt" the experimenter's feelings—is part of those binding forces inhibiting his disobedience. The withdrawal of such deference may be as painful to the subject as to the authority he defies.

DUTY WITHOUT CONFLICT

The subjects do not derive satisfaction from inflicting pain, but they 100 often like the feeling they get from pleasing the experimenter. They are proud of doing a good job, obeying the experimenter under difficult circumstances. While the subjects administered only mild shocks on their own initiative, one experimental variation showed that, under orders, 30 percent of them were willing to deliver 450 volts even when they had to forcibly push the learner's hand down on the electrode.

Bruno Batta is a thirty-seven-year-old welder who took part in the variation requiring the use of force. He was born in New Haven, his parents in Italy. He has a rough-hewn face that conveys a conspicuous lack of alertness. He has some difficulty in mastering the experimental procedure and needs to be corrected by the experimenter several times. He shows appreciation for the help and willingness to do what is required. After the 150-volt level, Batta has to force the learner's hand down on the shock plate, since the learner himself refuses to touch it.

When the learner first complains, Mr. Batta pays no attention to him. His face remains impassive, as if to dissociate himself from the learner's disruptive behavior. When the experimenter instructs him to force the learner's hand down, he adopts a rigid, mechanical procedure. He tests the generator switch. When it fails to function, he immediately forces the learner's hand onto the shock plate. All the while he maintains the same rigid mask. The learner, seated alongside him, begs him to stop, but with robotic impassivity he continues the procedure.

What is extraordinary is his apparent total indifference to the learner; he hardly takes cognizance of him as a human being. Meanwhile, he relates to the experimenter in a submissive and courteous fashion.

At the 330-volt level, the learner refuses not only to touch the shock plate but also to provide any answers. Annoyed, Batta turns to him, and chastises him: "You better answer and get it over with. We can't stay here all night." These are the only words he directs to the learner in the course of an hour. Never again does he speak to him. The scene is brutal and depressing, his hard, impassive face showing total indifference as he subdues the screaming learner and gives him shocks. He seems to derive no pleasure from the act itself, only quiet satisfaction at doing his job properly.

When he administers 450 volts, he turns to the experimenter and asks, "Where do we go from here, Professor?" His tone is deferential and expresses his willingness to be a cooperative subject, in contrast to the learner's obstinacy. 105

At the end of the session he tells the experimenter how honored he has been to help him, and in a moment of contrition, remarks, "Sir, sorry it couldn't have been a full experiment."

He has done his honest best. It is only the deficient behavior of the learner that has denied the experimenter full satisfaction.

The essence of obedience is that a person comes to view himself as the instrument for carrying out another person's wishes, and he therefore no longer regards himself as responsible for his actions. Once this critical shift of viewpoint has occurred, all of the essential features of obedience follow. The most far-reaching consequence is that the person feels responsible *to* the authority directing him but feels no responsibility *for* the content of the actions that the authority prescribes. Morality does not disappear—it acquires a radically different focus: The subordinate person feels shame or pride depending on how adequately he has performed the actions called for by authority.

Language provides numerous terms to pinpoint this type of morality: *Loyalty, duty, discipline* all are terms heavily saturated with moral meaning and refer to the degree to which a person fulfills his obligations to authority. They refer not to the "goodness" of the person per se but to the adequacy with which a subordinate fulfills his socially defined role. The most frequent defense of the individual who has performed a heinous act under command of authority is that he has simply done his duty. In asserting this defense, the individual is not introducing an alibi concocted for the moment but is reporting honestly on the psychological attitude induced by submission to authority.

For a person to feel responsible for his actions, he must sense that the behavior has flowed from "the self." In the situation we have studied, 110 subjects have precisely the opposite view of their actions—namely, they see them as originating in the motives of some other person. Subjects in the experiment frequently said, "If it were up to me, I would not have administered shocks to the learner."

Once authority has been isolated as the cause of the subject's behavior, it is legitimate to inquire into the necessary elements of authority and how it must be perceived in order to gain his compliance. We conducted some investigations into the kinds of changes that would cause the experimenter to lose his power and to be disobeyed by the subject. Some of the variations revealed that

- *The experimenter's physical presence has a marked impact on his authority.* As cited earlier, obedience dropped off sharply when orders were given by telephone. The experimenter could often induce a disobedient subject to go on by returning to the laboratory.

- *Conflicting authority severely paralyzes action.* When two experimenters of equal status, both seated at the command desk, gave incompatible orders, no shocks were delivered past the point of their disagreement.

- *The rebellious action of others severely undermines authority.* In one variation, three teachers (two actors and a real subject) administered a test and shocks. When the two actors disobeyed the experimenter and refused to go beyond a certain shock level, thirty-six of forty subjects joined their disobedient peers and refused as well.

Although the experimenter's authority was fragile in some respects, it is also true that he had almost none of the tools used in ordinary command structures. For example, the experimenter did not threaten the subjects with punishment—such as loss of income, community ostracism, or jail—for failure to obey. Neither could he offer incentives. Indeed, we should expect the experimenter's authority to be much less than that of someone like a general, since the experimenter has no power to enforce his imperatives, and since participation in a psychological experiment scarcely evokes the sense of urgency and dedication found in warfare. Despite these limitations, he still managed to command a dismaying degree of obedience.

I will cite one final variation of the experiment that depicts a dilemma that is more common in everyday life. The subject was not ordered to pull the lever that shocked the victim, but merely to perform a subsidiary task (administering the word-pair test) while another person administered the shock. In this situation, thirty-seven of forty adults continued to the highest level on the shock generator. Predictably, they excused their behavior by saying that the responsibility belonged to the man who actually pulled the switch. This may illustrate a dangerously typical arrangement in a complex society: It is easy to ignore responsibility when one is only an intermediate link in a chain of action.

The problem of obedience is not wholly psychological. The form and shape of society and the way it is developing have much to do with it. There was a time, perhaps, when people were able to give a fully human response to any situation because they were fully absorbed in it as human beings. But as soon as there was a division of labor things changed. Beyond a certain point, the breaking up of society into people carrying out narrow and very special jobs takes away from the human quality of work and life. A person does not get to see the whole situation but only a small part of it, and is thus unable to act without some kind of overall direction. He yields to authority but in doing so is alienated from his own actions.

Even Eichmann was sickened when he toured the concentration 115 camps, but he had only to sit at a desk and shuffle papers. At the same time the man in the camp who actually dropped Cyclon-b into the gas chambers was able to justify *his* behavior on the ground that he was only following orders from above. Thus there is a fragmentation of the total human act; no one is confronted with the consequences of his decision to carry out the evil act. The person who assumes responsibility has evaporated. Perhaps this is the most common characteristic of socially organized evil in modern society.

Topics for Critical Thinking and Writing

1. Milgram says that "the dilemma inherent in submission to authority is ancient, as old as the story of Abraham" (para. 2). What is the story of Abraham to which he refers? And what is the "dilemma inherent in submission"? (Review the section on dilemmas, p. 355.)

2. Describe the Milgram experiments in an essay of 150 words. In a sentence, what conclusion does Milgram himself draw from the experiments?

3. Read the essay by Walter T. Stace (p. 924), and decide whether he would regard the dialogue between the experimenter and Brandt (paras. 14–21) as a good example of people acting of their own "free will." Is the experimenter correct when he tells her "You have no other choice" (para. 20)?

4. Milgram explains that prior to the experiment he asked various people to predict the results; these predictions were "unequivocally wrong" (para. 26). Explain, if you can, why these groups predicted a very different outcome from what actually happened.

5. Did the experimenter ever threaten the subjects in the experiments? Use coercion? What is your evidence, one way or the other?

6. Milgram eventually offers "one theoretical interpretation" of the behavior of the experimenters (para. 92). What is that interpretation? Do you think it is plausible?

7. What, according to Milgram (para. 108), is "the essence of obedience"? Does an obedient person, in this sense of the term, cease to act of his own free will? Explain why or why not in an essay of 250 words.

8. Suppose someone were to criticize Milgram for his experiments, arguing that they were unethical because they were based fundamentally on deceiving the subjects about what they were really doing. How might Milgram reply?

Peter Cave

Peter Cave teaches philosophy at the Open University and City University of London. He is the author of Can a Robot be Human?: 33 Perplexing Philosophy Puzzles *(2007) and* What's Wrong with Eating People?: 33 More Perplexing Philosophy Puzzles *(2008). We reprint an essay from the second book. (For another essay by Cave, see p. 26.)*

Man or Sheep?

Thomas Hobbes, a key political philosopher of the seventeenth century, wrote that man's life was "solitary, poor, nasty, brutish, and short." The obvious reply is, 'It could have been worse, Thomas; it could have been solitary, poor, nasty, brutish—and long."

Hobbes was describing life before the existence of a state, government, and law. Humans are competitive. They lack reason to trust each other, unless there is a powerful authority that sets laws and punishes law-breakers. In a state of nature, individuals would be in constant conflict or, at least, always on their guard, insecure, and ready for battle. The state of nature, of life pre-government, is a state of war. With the state of nature so horrible, human beings would obviously want to get out, into something better. According to Hobbes, they would come together and agree on a sovereign, an absolute authority, to represent and rule over them, giving them security and opportunity to lead reasonable lives.

There are many puzzles, not least why individuals in the state of nature would risk trusting each other to keep to any agreement. Let us, though, not worry about how government arises. Here we are, living within a state. Let us assume we have a government democratically elected. However, whatever the degree of democracy, laws are imposed that restrict what we may do. We may disapprove of some laws because of some moral or religious principles; we may disapprove of other laws simply because they prevent us from getting what we want. The general concern becomes: By what authority does any government rightfully rule over us?

WHY SHOULD WE OBEY THE STATE AND ITS LAWS?

We may answer in practical terms. We obey the law because we are scared of the consequences of disobedience, not wanting to risk fines and imprisonment. The rational thing to do, given the aim of getting on with our lives as best we can, is to obey. When asked whether man or mouse, some of us tend to squeak and take the cheese. Even more so may most of us squeak, when the tentacles of the law and the long arm of the police take hold. We mice may, indeed, be more akin to sheep, sheepishly following each other in our general obedience. Our puzzle though is what, if anything, makes obeying the law the *right* thing to do — even if we could get away with disobeying.

Many of us benefit because of the state's existence: We are defended 5 from others, receive state education, health services, in return for paying taxes. We are better off with law than without. So, we are obligated, in return, to obey the laws that confer those benefits. One immediate objection is that this justification for lawful obedience fails to work for those who overall do not benefit. A significant number do very badly, sleeping rough, being denied state benefits, and being avoided by those better off. Why should they obey? Also, some at society's top may argue that they contribute more than they receive — probably forgetting that they secured the more because of society's stability and protection of gross inequalities often inherited.

Even when overall we do benefit from the state's existence, it does not follow that we are under any obligation to the benefactor. Did we ever sign up, agreeing that we would accept benefits in return for obeying the law? If someone buys us a drink, without our asking, are we under an obligation to buy one in return?

Reference to 'signing up' casts us along another line, a line orientated towards the 'social contract.' What justifies the state and our obedience is that we consented to the set-up. Some philosophers, John Locke and arguably Hobbes, believed that historically some individuals made contracts to be governed by an authority acting in their interests, leading to our societies. Of course, there is no reason to believe in such historical events; but, even if they occurred, whatever relevance do they have for us today? We were not around hundreds of years ago, engaged in any contractual deals.

The response to that last thought is to spot features of our current lives that may indicate consent. We make use of the state's services; we travel freely on the King's highway, notes Locke — well, today the Queen's highway. This shows that we tacitly consent to the state — or does it? Just because we remain in this country, using its facilities, it does not follow that we consent: After all, what other options are available? Can most people afford to go elsewhere? Would other countries, with acceptable laws, permit entry? It is as if we find ourselves on a ship in the middle of the ocean, with the captain making the point that we are free to leave.

Rationality is often wheeled out, to come to the rescue. True, we were not involved in any original social contract; true, our remaining within our society fails to establish consent. But suppose we were rational, not yet in a society, and needing to create society's laws. Suppose, too, we were ignorant of our sex, race, abilities, and the position we probably would reach in society, be it through chance or talent. In such an original position, behind a veil of ignorance, where everything is fair between us, our thinking, even though we remain as individuals, would not be distorted by a distinctive self-interest differing from the self-interest of others. Rather, our common rationality and interests should lead us to see and accept what would be fair laws, benefits, and rights for all. Behind the veil of ignorance, it would seem rational to consent to a society that permitted basic freedoms, did not discriminate between individuals on irrelevant grounds, and provided welfare benefits for when things go badly. After all, behind the veil of ignorance, we have no idea whether we may end up belonging to minority groups or hitting on hard times. If our current society possesses the features it would be rational to consent to behind the veil, then our obedience today is justified by this hypothetical consent, by what is seen as a hypothetical contract.

The response, by way of jibe, is that hypothetical contracts are not 10 worth the paper they are not written upon. Hypothetical consent is not consent. The jibe, though, misses the point. Justifications can rightly involve hypotheticals. Why did you battle with the man, yanking him from the cliff's path, despite his protests? "Because, had he been sober, he would have consented to the yanking, to save him from risking a fatal fall."

The resort to the veil of ignorance, to rationality, and the hypothetical, though, raises its own puzzles. Quite what does rationality involve behind such a veil? Is it rational, for example, to place liberty higher than greater welfare benefits requiring higher levels of taxation?

Whatever justifications are offered for general obedience to the state, sometimes we morally ought to disobey. Had only many, many consulted their conscience instead of the law, various atrocities, instituted by governments, could have been avoided. Had only many, many been aware of their humanity rather than going along with the mice and the sheep . . .

Mind you, that is so easy for me to say and you to read as, in all likelihood, we sit reasonably well off, looking at this book, not having to stand up and be counted—and also not scraping a living in desperate circumstances. We are cocooned, indeed, from millions of dispossessed in the world for whom life is certainly nasty, brutish, and short.

TOPICS FOR CRITICAL THINKING AND WRITING

1. Name five things or services (e.g., paved sidewalks, the police) that you did not create or establish but from which you benefit (para. 6).

2. Why is the "social contract" so called (paras. 6–8)?

3. Did the voyagers on the *Mayflower* (1620) create a social contract among themselves? How can you tell?

4. Is the following proposition—"We are not morally obligated by the deeds of our predecessors"—true? Why, or why not? Explain your answer.

5. What counts as a free, voluntary compact to obey some laws? What would you have to do to show that you (no longer) consent to be governed by the government under which you live?

Thomas Hardy

Thomas Hardy (1840–1928) was born in Dorset, England, the son of a stonemason. Despite great obstacles, he studied the classics and architecture, and in 1862 he moved to London to study and practice as an architect. Ill health forced him to return to Dorset, where he continued to work as an architect and to write. Best known for his novels, Hardy ceased writing fiction after the hostile reception of Jude the Obscure *in 1896 and turned to writing lyric poetry. We print a poem of 1902.*

The Man He Killed

"Had he and I but met
By some old ancient inn,
We should have sat us down to wet
Right many a nipperkin°!

"But ranged an infantry,   5
And staring face to face,
I shot at him as he at me,
And killed him in his place.

"I shot him dead because—
Because he was my foe,   10
Just so: my foe of course he was;
That's clear enough; although

"He thought he'd 'list, perhaps,
Off-hand like—just as I—
Was out of work—had sold his traps°—   15
No other reason why.

"Yes; quaint and curious war is!
You shoot a fellow down
You'd treat if met where any bar is,
Or help to half-a-crown."   20

4 nipperkin Cup.   **15 traps** Personal belongings. [Both notes are the editors'.]

Topics for Critical Thinking and Writing

1. Hardy published this poem in 1902, at the conclusion of the Boer War (1899–1902, also called the South African War), a war between the Boers (Dutch) and the British for possession of part of Africa. The speaker of the poem is an English veteran of the war. Do you think such a poem might just as well have been written by an English (or American) soldier in World War II? Explain.

2. Characterize the speaker. What sort of man does he seem to be? Pay special attention to the punctuation in the third and fourth stanzas — what do the pauses indicated by the dashes, the colons, and the semi-colon tell us about him? — and pay special attention to the final stanza, in which he speaks of war as "quaint and curious" (line 17). Do you think that Hardy too would speak of war this way? Why, or why not? Can you imagine an American soldier in the Vietnam War speaking of the war as "quaint and curious"? Explain.

T. S. Eliot

Thomas Stearns Eliot (1888–1965) was born into a New England family that had moved to St. Louis. He attended a preparatory school in Massachusetts, graduated from Harvard University, and then continued his studies in literature in France, Germany, and England. In 1914 he began working for Lloyds Bank in London, and three years later he published his first book of poems, which included "Prufrock." In 1925 he joined a publishing firm, and in 1927 he became a British citizen and a member of the Church of England. In 1948 he received the Nobel Prize for Literature.

The Love Song of J. Alfred Prufrock

> *S'io credesse che mia risposta fosse*
> *A persona che mai tornasse al mondo,*
> *Questa fiamma staria senza più scosse.*
> *Ma perciocchè giammai di questo fondo*
> *Non torno vivo alcun, s' i' odo il vero,*
> *Senza tema d'infamia ti rispondo.*°

Let us go then, you and I,
When the evening is spread out against the sky
Like a patient etherised upon a table;

S'io . . . rispondo The Italian epigraph that begins the poem is a quotation from Dante's *Divine Comedy* (1321). In this passage, a damned soul in hell who had sought absolution before committing a crime addresses Dante, thinking that his words will never reach the earth. He says: "If I thought that my answer were to someone who could ever return to the world, this flame would be still, without further motion. But because no one has ever returned alive from this depth, if what I hear is true, without fear of shame I answer you." [All notes are the editors'.]

Let us go, through certain half-deserted streets,
The muttering retreats   5
Of restless nights in one-night cheap hotels
And sawdust restaurants with oyster-shells:
Streets that follow like a tedious argument
Of insidious intent
To lead you to an overwhelming question . . .   10
Oh, do not ask, "What is it?"
Let us go and make our visit.

In the room the women come and go
Talking of Michelangelo.

The yellow fog that rubs its back upon the window-panes,   15
The yellow smoke that rubs its muzzle on the window-panes
Licked its tongue into the corners of the evening,
Lingered upon the pools that stand in drains,
Let fall upon its back the soot that falls from chimneys,
Slipped by the terrace, made a sudden leap,   20
And seeing that it was a soft October night,
Curled once about the house, and fell asleep.

And indeed there will be time
For the yellow smoke that slides along the street,
Rubbing its back upon the window-panes;   25
There will be time, there will be time
To prepare a face to meet the faces that you meet;
There will be time to murder and create,
And time for all the works and days° of hands
That lift and drop a question on your plate;   30
Time for you and time for me,
And time yet for a hundred indecisions,
And for a hundred visions and revisions,
Before the taking of a toast and tea.

In the room the women come and go   35
Talking of Michelangelo
And indeed there will be time
To wonder, "Do I dare?" and, "Do I dare?"
Time to turn back and descend the stair,
With a bald spot in the middle of my hair—   40
[They will say: "How his hair is growing thin!"]
My morning coat, my collar mounting firmly to the chin,
My necktie rich and modest, but asserted by a simple pin—
[They will say: "But how his arms and legs are thin!"]

29 works and days The title of a poem on farm life by Hesiod (Greek, eighth century B.C.).

Do I dare   45
Disturb the universe?
In a minute there is time
For decisions and revisions which a minute will reverse.

For I have known them all already, known them all:—
Have known the evenings, mornings, afternoons,   50
I have measured out my life with coffee spoons;
I know the voices dying with a dying fall°
Beneath the music from a farther room.
            So how should I presume?

And I have known the eyes already, known them all—   55
The eyes that fix you in a formulated phrase,
And when I am formulated, sprawling on a pin,
When I am pinned and wriggling on the wall,
Then how should I begin
To spit out all the butt-ends of my days and ways?   60
            And how should I presume?

And I have known the arms already, known them all—
Arms that are braceleted and white and bare
[But in the lamplight, downed with light brown hair!]
Is it perfume from a dress   65
That makes me so digress?
Arms that lie along a table, or wrap about a shawl.
            And should I then presume?
            And how should I begin?

                        . . . . .

Shall I say, I have gone at dusk through narrow streets   70
And watched the smoke that rises from the pipes
Of lonely men in shirt-sleeves, leaning out of windows? . . .

I should have been a pair of ragged claws
Scuttling across the floors of silent seas.

                        . . . . .

And the afternoon, the evening, sleeps so peacefully!   75
Smoothed by long fingers,
Asleep . . . tired . . . or it malingers,
Stretched on the floor, here beside you and me.
Should I, after tea and cakes and ices,
Have the strength to force the moment to its crisis?   80
But though I have wept and fasted, wept and prayed,
Though I have seen my head [grown slightly bald]
            brought in upon a platter,°

---

52 dying fall Echoes Shakespeare's *Twelfth Night* 1.1.4.   **82 head . . . platter** Alludes to
John the Baptist, whose head was delivered on a platter to Salome.

I am no prophet—and here's no great matter;
I have seen the moment of my greatness flicker,
And I have seen the eternal Footman hold my coat, and
     snicker,   85
And in short, I was afraid.

And would it have been worth it, after all,
After the cups, the marmalade, the tea,
Among the porcelain, among some talk of you and me,
Would it have been worth while,   90
To have bitten off the matter with a smile,
To have squeezed the universe into a ball
To roll° it toward some overwhelming question,
To say: "I am Lazarus,° come from the dead,
Come back to tell you all, I shall tell you all"—   95
If one, settling a pillow by her head,
       Should say: "That is not what I meant at all.
       That is not it, at all."

And would it have been worth it, after all,
Would it have been worth while,   100
After the sunsets and the dooryards and the sprinkled streets,
After the novels, after the teacups, after the skirts
       that trail along the floor—
And this, and so much more?—
It is impossible to say just what I mean!
But as if a magic lantern threw the nerves in patterns
       on a screen: 105
Would it have been worth while
If one, settling a pillow or throwing off a shawl,
And turning toward the window, should say:
       "That is not it at all,
       That is not what I meant, at all."   110

           · · · · ·

No! I am not Prince Hamlet,° nor was meant to be;
Am an attendant lord, one that will do
To swell a progress, start a scene or two,
Advise the prince; no doubt, an easy tool,
Deferential, glad to be of use,   115
Politic, cautious, and meticulous;

92–93 ball to roll Echoes Andrew Marvell's "To His Coy Mistress," lines 41–42 (see p. 482).
94 Lazarus Mentioned in the New Testament: John 11; Lazarus rises from the dead at the command of Jesus.
111 Prince Hamlet The next few lines allude to lesser figures in Shakespeare's tragedy, specifically to Polonius, a self-satisfied fatuous courtier.

Full of high sentence,° but a bit obtuse;
At times, indeed, almost ridiculous—
Almost, at times, the Fool.

I grow old . . . I grow old . . .   120
I shall wear the bottoms of my trousers rolled.

Shall I part my hair behind? Do I dare to eat a peach?
I shall wear white flannel trousers, and walk upon the beach.
I have heard the mermaids singing, each to each.
I do not think that they will sing to me.   125

I have seen them riding seaward on the waves
Combing the white hair of the waves blown back
When the wind blows the water white and black.

We have lingered in the chambers of the sea
By sea-girls wreathed with seaweed red and brown   130
Till human voices wake us, and we drown.

TOPICS FOR CRITICAL THINKING AND WRITING

1. One of the most famous images of the poem compares the evening to "a patient etherised upon a table" (lines 2–3). Does the image also suggest that individuals—for instance, Prufrock—may not be fully conscious and therefore are not responsible for their actions or their inactions?

2. Are lines 57 to 60 meant to evoke the reader's pity for the speaker? If not, what (if any) response are these lines intended to evoke?

3. The speaker admits he is "At times, indeed, . . . / Almost . . . the Fool" (lines 118–19). Where, if at all, in the poem do we see him not at all as a fool?

4. Do you take the poem to be a criticism of an individual, a society, neither, or both? Why?

5. Evaluate this critical judgment, offering evidence to support your view: "The poem is obscure: It begins in Italian, and it includes references that most readers can't know. It is not at all uplifting. In fact, in so far as it is comprehensible, it is depressing. These are not the characteristics of a great poem."

6. The poem is chiefly concerned with the thoughts of a man, J. Alfred Prufrock. Do you think it therefore is of more interest to men than to women? Explain.

7. The speaker describes the streets he walks as "follow[ing] like a tedious argument" (line 8). Is the simile apt? When do you think an argument becomes tedious?

---

117 full of high sentence Full of thoughtful sayings; comes from Chaucer's description of the Oxford student in *The Canterbury Tales.*

Susan Glaspell

Susan Glaspell (1882–1948) was born in Davenport, Iowa, and educated at Drake University in Des Moines. In 1903 she married George Cram Cook and, with Cook and other writers, actors, and artists, in 1915 founded the Provincetown Players, a group that remained vital until 1929. Glaspell wrote Trifles *(1916) for the Provincetown Players, but she also wrote stories, novels, and a biography of her husband. In 1931 she won the Pulitzer Prize for* Alison's House, *a play about the family of a deceased poet who in some ways resembles Emily Dickinson.*

Trifles

(**SCENE:** *The kitchen in the now abandoned farmhouse of John Wright, a gloomy kitchen, and left without having been put in order—unwashed pans under the sink, a loaf of bread outside the breadbox, a dish towel on the table—other signs of incompleted work. At the rear the outer door opens, and the Sheriff comes in, followed by the County Attorney and Hale. The Sheriff and Hale are men in middle life, the County Attorney is a young man; all are much bundled up and go at once to the stove. They are followed by the two women—the Sheriff's Wife first; she is a slight wiry woman, a thin nervous face. Mrs. Hale is larger and would ordinarily be called more comfortable looking, but she is disturbed now and looks fearfully about as she enters. The women have come in slowly and stand close together near the door.*)

COUNTY ATTORNEY *(rubbing his hands).* This feels good. Come up to the fire, ladies.

MRS. PETERS *(after taking a step forward).* I'm not—cold.

SHERIFF *(unbuttoning his overcoat and stepping away from the stove as if to the beginning of official business).* Now, Mr. Hale, before we move things about, you explain to Mr. Henderson just what you saw when you came here yesterday morning.

COUNTY ATTORNEY. By the way, has anything been moved? Are things just as you left them yesterday?

SHERIFF *(looking about).* It's just the same. When it dropped below zero last 5 night, I thought I'd better send Frank out this morning to make a fire for us—no use getting pneumonia with a big case on; but I told him not to touch anything except the stove—and you know Frank.

COUNTY ATTORNEY. Somebody should have been left here yesterday.

SHERIFF. Oh—yesterday. When I had to send Frank to Morris Center for that man who went crazy—I want you to know I had my hands full yesterday. I knew you could get back from Omaha by today, and as long as I went over everything here myself—

COUNTY ATTORNEY. Well, Mr. Hale, tell just what happened when you came here yesterday morning.

HALE. Harry and I had started to town with a load of potatoes. We came along the road from my place; and as I got here, I said, "I'm going to see if I can't get John Wright to go in with me on a party telephone." I spoke to Wright about it once before, and he put me off, saying folks talked too much anyway, and all he asked was peace and quiet—I guess you know about how much he talked himself; but I thought maybe if I went to the house and talked about it before his wife, though I said to Harry that I didn't know as what his wife wanted made much difference to John—

COUNTY ATTORNEY. Let's talk about that later, Mr. Hale. I do want to talk   10
about that, but tell now just what happened when you got to the house.

HALE. I didn't hear or see anything; I knocked at the door, and still it was all quiet inside. I knew they must be up, it was past eight o'clock. So I knocked again, and I thought I heard somebody say, "Come in." I wasn't sure, I'm not sure yet, but I opened the door—this door *(indicating the door by which the two women are still standing),* and there in that rocker—*(pointing to it)* sat Mrs. Wright. *(They all look at the rocker.)*

COUNTY ATTORNEY. What—was she doing?

HALE. She was rockin' back and forth. She had her apron in her hand and was kind of—pleating it.

COUNTY ATTORNEY. And how did she—look?

HALE. Well, she looked queer.   15

COUNTY ATTORNEY. How do you mean—queer?

HALE. Well, as if she didn't know what she was going to do next. And kind of done up.

COUNTY ATTORNEY. How did she seem to feel about your coming?

HALE. Why, I don't think she minded—one way or other. She didn't pay much attention. I said, "How do, Mrs. Wright, it's cold, ain't it?" And she said, "Is it?"—and went on kind of pleating at her apron. Well, I was surprised; she didn't ask me to come up to the stove, or to set down, but just sat there, not even looking at me, so I said, "I want to see John." And then she—laughed. I guess you would call it a laugh. I thought of Harry and the team outside, so I said a little sharp: "Can't I see John?" "No," she says, kind o' dull like. "Ain't he home?" says I. "Yes," says she, "he's home." "Then why can't I see him?" I asked her, out of patience. "'Cause he's dead," says she. *"Dead?"* says I. She just nodded her head, not getting a bit excited, but rockin' back and forth. "Why—where is he?" says I, not knowing what to say. She just pointed upstairs—like that *(himself pointing to the room above).* I got up, with the idea of going up there. I walked from there to here—then I says, "Why, what did he die of?" "He died of a rope around his neck," says she, and just went on pleatin' at her apron. Well, I went out and called Harry. I thought I might—need help. We went upstairs, and there he was lyin'—

COUNTY ATTORNEY. I think I'd rather have you go into that upstairs, where   20
you can point it all out. Just go on now with the rest of the story.

HALE. Well, my first thought was to get that rope off. I looked . . . *(Stops, his face twitches.)* . . . but Harry, he went up to him, and he said, "No, he's dead all right, and we'd better not touch anything." So we went back downstairs. She was still sitting that same way. "Has anybody been notified?" I asked. "No," says she, unconcerned. "Who did this, Mrs. Wright?" said Harry. He said it businesslike—and she stopped pleatin' of her apron. "I don't know," she says. "You don't *know*?" says Harry. "No," says she. "Weren't you sleepin' in the bed with him?" says Harry. "Yes," says she, "but I was on the inside." "Somebody slipped a rope round his neck and strangled him, and you didn't wake up?" says Harry. "I didn't wake up," she said after him. We must 'a looked as if we didn't see how that could be, for after a minute she said, "I sleep sound." Harry was going to ask her more questions, but I said maybe we ought to let her tell her story first to the coroner, or the sheriff, so Harry went fast as he could to Rivers' place, where there's a telephone.

COUNTY ATTORNEY. And what did Mrs. Wright do when she knew that you had gone for the coroner?

HALE. She moved from that chair to this over here . . . *(Pointing to a small chair in the corner.)* . . . and just sat there with her hands held together and looking down. I got a feeling that I ought to make some conversation, so I said I had come in to see if John wanted to put in a telephone, and at that she started to laugh, and then she stopped and looked at me—scared. *(The County Attorney, who has had his notebook out, makes a note.)* I dunno, maybe it wasn't scared. I wouldn't like to say it was. Soon Harry got back, and then Dr. Lloyd came, and you, Mr. Peters, and so I guess that's all I know that you don't.

COUNTY ATTORNEY *(looking around)*. I guess we'll go upstairs first—and then out to the barn and around there. *(To the Sheriff.)* You're convinced that there was nothing important here—nothing that would point to any motive?

SHERIFF. Nothing here but kitchen things. *(The County Attorney, after again* 25 *looking around the kitchen, opens the door of a cupboard closet. He gets up on a chair and looks on a shelf. Pulls his hand away, sticky.)*

COUNTY ATTORNEY. Here's a nice mess. *(The women draw nearer.)*

MRS. PETERS *(to the other woman)*. Oh, her fruit; it did freeze. *(To the Lawyer.)* She worried about that when it turned so cold. She said the fire'd go out and her jars would break.

SHERIFF. Well, can you beat the woman! Held for murder and worryin' about her preserves.

COUNTY ATTORNEY. I guess before we're through she may have something more serious than preserves to worry about.

HALE. Well, women are used to worrying over trifles. *(The two women move* 30 *a little closer together.)*

COUNTY ATTORNEY *(with the gallantry of a young politician)*. And yet, for all their worries, what would we do without the ladies? *(The women do not unbend. He goes to the sink, takes a dipperful of water from the pail and, pouring it into a basin, washes his hands. Starts to wipe them on the roller towel, turns it for a cleaner place.)* Dirty towels! *(Kicks his foot against the pans under the sink.)* Not much of a housekeeper, would you say, ladies?

MRS. HALE *(stiffly).* There's a great deal of work to be done on a farm.

COUNTY ATTORNEY. To be sure. And yet . . . *(With a little bow to her.)* . . . I know there are some Dickson county farmhouses which do not have such roller towels. *(He gives it a pull to expose its full length again.)*

MRS. HALE. Those towels get dirty awful quick. Men's hands aren't always as clean as they might be.

COUNTY ATTORNEY. Ah, loyal to your sex. I see. But you and Mrs. Wright 35 were neighbors. I suppose you were friends, too.

MRS. HALE *(shaking her head).* I've not seen much of her of late years. I've not been in this house — it's more than a year.

COUNTY ATTORNEY. And why was that? You didn't like her?

MRS. HALE. I liked her all well enough. Farmers' wives have their hands full, Mr. Henderson. And then —

COUNTY ATTORNEY. Yes — ?

MRS. HALE *(looking about).* It never seemed a very cheerful place. 40

COUNTY ATTORNEY. No — it's not cheerful. I shouldn't say she had the home-making instinct.

MRS. HALE. Well, I don't know as Wright had, either.

COUNTY ATTORNEY. You mean they didn't get on very well?

MRS. HALE. No, I don't mean anything. But I don't think a place'd be any cheerfuller for John Wright's being in it.

COUNTY ATTORNEY. I'd like to talk more of that a little later. I want to get the 45 lay of things upstairs now. *(He goes to the left, where three steps lead to a stair door.)*

SHERIFF. I suppose anything Mrs. Peters does'll be all right. She was to take in some clothes for her, you know, and a few little things. We left in such a hurry yesterday.

COUNTY ATTORNEY. Yes, but I would like to see what you take, Mrs. Peters, and keep an eye out for anything that might be of use to us.

MRS. PETERS. Yes, Mr. Henderson. *(The women listen to the men's steps on the stairs, then look about the kitchen.)*

MRS. HALE. I'd hate to have men coming into my kitchen, snooping around and criticizing. *(She arranges the pans under the sink which the Lawyer had shoved out of place.)*

MRS. PETERS. Of course it's no more than their duty. 50

MRS. HALE. Duty's all right, but I guess that deputy sheriff that came out to make the fire might have got a little of this on. *(Gives the roller towel a pull.)* Wish I'd thought of that sooner. Seems mean to talk about her for not having things slicked up when she had to come away in such a hurry.

MRS. PETERS *(who has gone to a small table in the left rear corner of the room, and lifted one end of a towel that covers a pan).* She had bread set. *(Stands still.)*

MRS. HALE *(eyes fixed on a loaf of bread beside the breadbox, which is on a low shelf at the other side of the room. Moves slowly toward it).* She was going to put this in there. *(Picks up loaf, then abruptly drops it. In a manner of returning to familiar things.)* It's a shame about her fruit. I wonder if it's all gone. *(Gets up on the chair and looks.)* I think there's some here that's all right, Mrs. Peters. Yes—here; *(Holding it toward the window.)* this is cherries, too. *(Looking again.)* I declare I believe that's the only one. *(Gets down, bottle in her hand. Goes to the sink and wipes it off on the outside.)* She'll feel awful bad after all her hard work in the hot weather. I remember the afternoon I put up my cherries last summer. *(She puts the bottle on the big kitchen table, center of the room. With a sigh, is about to sit down in the rocking chair. Before she is seated realizes what chair it is; with a slow look at it, steps back. The chair, which she has touched, rocks back and forth.)*

MRS. PETERS. Well, I must get those things from the front room closet. *(She goes to the door at the right, but after looking into the other room steps back.)* You coming with me, Mrs. Hale? You could help me carry them. *(They go into the other room; reappear, Mrs. Peters carrying a dress and skirt, Mrs. Hale following with a pair of shoes.)*

MRS. PETERS. My, it's cold in there. *(She puts the cloth on the big table, and hur-* 55
ries to the stove.)

MRS. HALE *(examining the skirt).* Wright was close. I think maybe that's why she kept so much to herself. She didn't even belong to the Ladies' Aid. I suppose she felt she couldn't do her part, and then you don't enjoy things when you feel shabby. She used to wear pretty clothes and be lively, when she was Minnie Foster, one of the town girls singing in the choir. But that—oh, that was thirty years ago. This all you was to take in?

MRS. PETERS. She said she wanted an apron. Funny thing to want, for there isn't much to get you dirty in jail, goodness knows. But I suppose just to make her feel more natural. She said they was in the top drawer in this cupboard. Yes, here. And then her little shawl that always hung behind the door. *(Opens stair door and looks.)* Yes, here it is. *(Quickly shuts door leading upstairs.)*

MRS. HALE *(abruptly moving toward her).* Mrs. Peters?

MRS. PETERS. Yes, Mrs. Hale?

MRS. HALE. Do you think she did it?   60

MRS. PETERS *(in a frightened voice).* Oh, I don't know.

MRS. HALE. Well, I don't think she did. Asking for an apron and her little shawl. Worrying about her fruit.

MRS. PETERS *(starts to speak, glances up, where footsteps are heard in the room above. In a low voice).* Mr. Peters says it looks bad for her. Mr. Henderson is awful sarcastic in speech, and he'll make fun of her sayin' she didn't wake up.

MRS. HALE. Well, I guess John Wright didn't wake when they was slipping that rope under his neck.

MRS. PETERS. No, it's strange. It must have been done awful crafty and still. 65
They say it was such a—funny way to kill a man, rigging it all up
like that.

MRS. HALE. That's just what Mr. Hale said. There was a gun in the house.
He says that's what he can't understand.

MRS. PETERS. Mr. Henderson said coming out that what was needed for the
case was a motive; something to show anger or—sudden feeling.

MRS. HALE *(who is standing by the table)*. Well, I don't see any signs of anger
around here. *(She puts her hand on the dish towel which lies on the table,
stands looking down at the table, one half of which is clean, the other half
messy.)* It's wiped here. *(Makes a move as if to finish work, then turns and
looks at loaf of bread outside the breadbox. Drops towel. In that voice of coming back to familiar things.)* Wonder how they are finding things
upstairs? I hope she had it a little more red-up there. You know, it
seems kind of *sneaking.* Locking her up in town and then coming out
here and trying to get her own house to turn against her!

MRS. PETERS. But, Mrs. Hale, the law is the law.

MRS. HALE. I s'pose 'tis. *(Unbuttoning her coat.)* Better loosen up your things, 70
Mrs. Peters. You won't feel them when you go out. *(Mrs. Peters takes
off her fur tippet, goes to hang it on hook at the back of room, stands looking
at the under part of the small corner table.)*

MRS. PETERS. She was piecing a quilt. *(She brings the large sewing basket, and
they look at the bright pieces.)*

MRS. HALE. It's log cabin pattern. Pretty, isn't it? I wonder if she was goin'
to quilt or just knot it? *(Footsteps have been heard coming down the stairs.
The Sheriff enters, followed by Hale and the County Attorney.)*

SHERIFF. They wonder if she was going to quilt it or just knot it. *(The men
laugh, the women look abashed.)*

COUNTY ATTORNEY *(rubbing his hands over the stove)*. Frank's fire didn't do
much up there, did it? Well, let's go out to the barn and get that
cleared up. *(The men go outside.)*

MRS. HALE *(resentfully)*. I don't know as there's anything so strange, our 75
takin' up our time with little things while we're waiting for them to
get the evidence. *(She sits down at the big table, smoothing out a block
with decision.)* I don't see as it's anything to laugh about.

MRS. PETERS *(apologetically)*. Of course they've got awful important things
on their minds. *(Pulls up a chair and joins Mrs. Hale at the table.)*

MRS. HALE *(examining another block)*. Mrs. Peters, look at this one. Here, this
is the one she was working on, and look at the sewing! All the rest
of it has been so nice and even. And look at this! It's all over the
place! Why, it looks as if she didn't know what she was about! *(After
she has said this, they look at each other, then start to glance back at the door.
After an instant Mrs. Hale has pulled at a knot and ripped the sewing.)*

MRS. PETERS. Oh, what are you doing, Mrs. Hale?

MRS. HALE *(mildly)*. Just pulling out a stitch or two that's not sewed very
good. *(Threading a needle.)* Bad sewing always made me fidgety.

MRS. PETERS *(nervously).* I don't think we ought to touch things.   80

MRS. HALE. I'll just finish up this end. *(Suddenly stopping and leaning forward.)* Mrs. Peters?

MRS. PETERS. Yes, Mrs. Hale?

MRS. HALE. What do you suppose she was so nervous about?

MRS. PETERS. Oh—I don't know. I don't know as she was nervous. I sometimes sew awful queer when I'm just tired. *(Mrs. Hale starts to say something, looks at Mrs. Peters, then goes on sewing.)* Well, I must get these things wrapped up. They may be through sooner than we think. *(Putting apron and other things together.)* I wonder where I can find a piece of paper, and string.

MRS. HALE. In that cupboard, maybe.   85

MRS. PETERS *(looking in cupboard).* Why, here's a birdcage. *(Holds it up.)* Did she have a bird, Mrs. Hale?

MRS. HALE. Why, I don't know whether she did or not—I've not been here for so long. There was a man around last year selling canaries cheap, but I don't know as she took one; maybe she did. She used to sing real pretty herself.

MRS. PETERS *(glancing around).* Seems funny to think of a bird here. But she must have had one, or why should she have a cage? I wonder what happened to it?

MRS. HALE. I s'pose maybe the cat got it.

MRS. PETERS. No, she didn't have a cat. She's got that feeling some people   90 have about cats—being afraid of them. My cat got in her room, and she was real upset and asked me to take it out.

MRS. HALE. My sister Bessie was like that. Queer, ain't it?

MRS. PETERS *(examining the cage).* Why, look at this door. It's broke. One hinge is pulled apart.

MRS. HALE *(looking, too).* Looks as if someone must have been rough with it.

MRS. PETERS. Why, yes. *(She brings the cage forward and puts it on the table.)*

MRS. HALE. I wish if they're going to find any evidence they'd be about it. I   95 don't like this place.

MRS. PETERS. But I'm awful glad you came with me, Mrs. Hale. It would be lonesome for me sitting here alone.

MRS. HALE. It would, wouldn't it? *(Dropping her sewing.)* But I tell you what I do wish, Mrs. Peters. I wish I had come over sometimes when *she* was here. I—*(Looking around the room.)*—wish I had.

MRS. PETERS. But of course you were awful busy, Mrs. Hale—your house and your children.

MRS. HALE. I could've come. I stayed away because it weren't cheerful— and that's why I ought to have come. I—I've never liked this place. Maybe because it's down in a hollow, and you don't see the road. I dunno what it is, but it's a lonesome place and always was. I wish I had come over to see Minnie Foster sometimes. I can see now— *(Shakes her head.)*

MRS. PETERS. Well, you mustn't reproach yourself, Mrs. Hale. Somehow we 100
    just don't see how it is with other folks until—something comes up.

MRS. HALE. Not having children makes less work—but it makes a quiet
    house, and Wright out to work all day, and no company when he
    did come in. Did you know John Wright, Mrs. Peters?

MRS. PETERS. Not to know him; I've seen him in town. They say he was a
    good man.

MRS. HALE. Yes—good; he didn't drink, and kept his word as well as most,
    I guess, and paid his debts. But he was a hard man, Mrs. Peters. Just
    to pass the time of day with him. *(Shivers.)* Like a raw wind that gets
    to the bone. *(Pauses, her eye falling on the cage.)* I should think she
    would 'a' wanted a bird. But what do you suppose went with it?

MRS. PETERS. I don't know, unless it got sick and died. *(She reaches over and*
    swings the broken door, swings it again; both women watch it.)

MRS. HALE. You weren't raised around here, were you? *(Mrs. Peters shakes* 105
    her head.) You didn't know—her?

MRS. PETERS. Not till they brought her yesterday.

MRS. HALE. She—come to think of it, she was kind of like a bird herself—
    real sweet and pretty, but kind of timid and—fluttery. How—
    she—did—change. *(Silence; then as if struck by a happy thought and*
    relieved to get back to everyday things.) Tell you what, Mrs. Peters, why
    don't you take the quilt in with you? It might take up her mind.

MRS. PETERS. Why, I think that's a real nice idea, Mrs. Hale. There couldn't
    possible be any objection to it, could there? Now, just what would I
    take? I wonder if her patches are in here—and her things. *(They look*
    in the sewing basket.)

MRS. HALE. Here's some red. I expect this has got sewing things in it. *(Brings*
    out a fancy box.) What a pretty box. Looks like something somebody
    would give you. Maybe her scissors are in here. *(Opens box. Suddenly*
    puts her hand to her nose.) Why—*(Mrs. Peters bends nearer, then turns her*
    face away.) There's something wrapped up in this piece of silk.

MRS. PETERS. Why, this isn't her scissors. 110

MRS. HALE *(lifting the silk)*. Oh, Mrs. Peters—it's—*(Mrs. Peters bends closer.)*

MRS. PETERS. It's the bird.

MRS. HALE *(jumping up)*. But, Mrs. Peters—look at it. Its neck! Look at its
    neck! It's all—other side *to*.

MRS. PETERS. Somebody—wrung—its neck. *(Their eyes meet. A look of grow-*
    ing comprehension of horror. Steps are heard outside. Mrs. Hale slips box
    under quilt pieces, and sinks into her chair. Enter Sheriff and County
    Attorney, Mrs. Peters rises.)

COUNTY ATTORNEY *(as one turning from serious things to little pleasantries)*. Well, 115
    ladies, have you decided whether she was going to quilt it or knot it?

MRS. PETERS. We think she was going to—knot it.

COUNTY ATTORNEY. Well, that's interesting, I'm sure. *(Seeing the birdcage.)* Has
    the bird flown?

MRS. HALE *(putting more quilt pieces over the box).* We think the—cat got it.

COUNTY ATTORNEY *(preoccupied).* Is there a cat? *(Mrs. Hale glances in a quick covert way at Mrs. Peters.)*

MRS. PETERS. Well, not now. They're superstitious, you know. They leave.   120

COUNTY ATTORNEY *(to Sheriff Peters, continuing an interrupted conversation).* No sign at all of anyone having come from the outside. Their own rope. Now let's go up again and go over it piece by piece. *(They start upstairs.)* It would have to have been someone who knew just the— *(Mrs. Peters sits down. The two women sit there not looking at one another, but as if peering into something and at the same time holding back. When they talk now, it is the manner of feeling their way over strange ground, as if afraid of what they are saying, but as if they cannot help saying it.)*

MRS. HALE. She liked the bird. She was going to bury it in that pretty box.

MRS. PETERS *(in a whisper).* When I was a girl—my kitten—there was a boy took a hatchet, and before my eyes—and before I could get there—*(Covers her face an instant.)* If they hadn't held me back, I would have—*(Catches herself, looks upstairs where steps are heard, falters weakly.)*—hurt him.

MRS. HALE *(with a slow look around her).* I wonder how it would seem never to have had any children around. *(Pause.)* No, Wright wouldn't like the bird—a thing that sang. She used to sing. He killed that, too.

MRS. PETERS *(moving uneasily).* We don't know who killed the bird.   125

MRS. HALE. I knew John Wright.

MRS. PETERS. It was an awful thing was done in this house that night, Mrs. Hale. Killing a man while he slept, slipping a rope around his neck that choked the life out of him.

MRS. HALE. His neck. Choked the life out of him. *(Her hand goes out and rests on the birdcage.)*

MRS. PETERS *(with a rising voice).* We don't know who killed him. We don't know.

MRS. HALE *(her own feeling not interrupted).* If there'd been years and years   130 of nothing, then a bird to sing to you, it would be awful—still, after the bird was still.

MRS. PETERS *(something within her speaking).* I know what stillness is. When we homesteaded in Dakota, and my first baby died—after he was two years old, and me with no other then—

MRS. HALE *(moving).* How soon do you suppose they'll be through, looking for evidence?

MRS. PETERS. I know what stillness is. *(Pulling herself back.)* The law has got to punish crime, Mrs. Hale.

MRS. HALE *(not as if answering that).* I wish you'd seen Minnie Foster when she wore a white dress with blue ribbons and stood up there in the choir and sang. *(A look around the room.)* Oh, I *wish* I'd come over here once in a while! That was a crime! That was a crime! Who's going to punish that?

MRS. PETERS *(looking upstairs).* We mustn't—take on.   135

MRS. HALE. I might have known she needed help! I know how things can be—for women. I tell you, it's queer, Mrs. Peters. We live close together and we live far apart. We all go through the same things— it's all just a different kind of the same thing. *(Brushes her eyes, noticing the bottle of fruit, reaches out for it.)* If I was you, I wouldn't tell her her fruit was gone. Tell her it *ain't.* Tell her it's all right. Take this in to prove it to her. She—she may never know whether it was broke or not.

MRS. PETERS *(takes the bottle, looks about for something to wrap it in; takes petticoat from the clothes brought from the other room, very nervously begins winding this around the bottle. In a false voice).* My, it's a good thing the men couldn't hear us. Wouldn't they just laugh! Getting all stirred up over a little thing like a—dead canary. As if that could have anything to do with—with—wouldn't they *laugh! (The men are heard coming downstairs.)*

MRS. HALE *(under her breath).* Maybe they would—maybe they wouldn't.

COUNTY ATTORNEY. No, Peters, it's all perfectly clear except a reason for doing it. But you know juries when it comes to women. If there was some definite thing. Something to show—something to make a story about—a thing that would connect up with this strange way of doing it. *(The women's eyes meet for an instant. Enter Hale from outer door.)*

HALE. Well, I've got the team around. Pretty cold out there.   140

COUNTY ATTORNEY. I'm going to stay here a while by myself. *(To the Sheriff.)* You can send Frank out for me, can't you? I want to go over everything. I'm not satisfied that we can't do better.

SHERIFF. Do you want to see what Mrs. Peters is going to take in? *(The Lawyer goes to the table, picks up the apron, laughs.)*

COUNTY ATTORNEY. Oh, I guess they're not very dangerous things the ladies have picked up. *(Moves a few things about, disturbing the quilt pieces which cover the box. Steps back.)* No, Mrs. Peters doesn't need supervising. For that matter, a sheriff's wife is married to the law. Ever think of it that way, Mrs. Peters?

MRS. PETERS. Not—just that way.

SHERIFF *(chuckling).* Married to the law. *(Moves toward the other room.)* I just   145 want you to come in here a minute, George. We ought to take a look at these windows.

COUNTY ATTORNEY *(scoffingly).* Oh, windows!

SHERIFF. We'll be right out, Mr. Hale. *(Hale goes outside. The Sheriff follows the County Attorney into the other room. Then Mrs. Hale rises, hands tight together, looking intensely at Mrs. Peters, whose eyes take a slow turn, finally meeting Mrs. Hale's. A moment Mrs. Hale holds her, then her own eyes point the way to where the box is concealed. Suddenly Mrs. Peters throws back quilt pieces and tries to put the box in the bag she is carrying. It is too big. She opens box, starts to take the bird out, cannot touch it, goes to pieces, stands there helpless. Sound of a knob turning in the other room. Mrs. Hale snatches the box and puts it in the pocket of her big coat. Enter County Attorney and Sheriff.)*

COUNTY ATTORNEY *(facetiously).* Well, Henry, at least we found out that she was not going to quilt it. She was going to—what is it you call it, ladies?

MRS. HALE *(her hand against her pocket).* We call it—knot it, Mr. Henderson.

TOPICS FOR CRITICAL THINKING AND WRITING

1. The dead canary in the box isn't evidence that Mrs. Wright has killed her husband. So what is the point of the dead canary in the play?

2. Do you think the play is immoral? Explain.

3. Assume that Minnie is indicted for murder and that you are asked to serve as Minnie's defense lawyer. If you somehow know that the evidence of the canary has been suppressed, would you accept the case? Why, or why not? (It is unlawful for *prosecutors* to suppress evidence, but it is not unlawful for defense lawyers to withhold incriminating evidence that they are aware of.)

4. Assume that you have accepted Minnie's case. In 500 words set forth the defense you will offer for her. (Take any position that you wish. You may, for example, argue that she committed justifiable homicide or that—on the basis of her behavior as reported by Mr. Hale—she is innocent by reason of insanity.)

5. Assume that Minnie has been found guilty. Compose the speech she might give before being sentenced.

6. "*Trifles* is badly dated. It cannot speak to today's audience." In an essay of 500 words evaluate this view: Offer an argument supporting or rejecting it, or take a middle position.

Mitsuye Yamada

Mitsuye Yamada, the daughter of Japanese immigrants to the United States, was born in Japan in 1923, during her mother's return visit to her native land. Yamada was raised in Seattle, but in 1942 she and her family were incarcerated and then relocated to a camp in Idaho, when Executive Order 9066 (signed by President Franklin D. Roosevelt that year) gave military authorities the right to remove any and all persons from "military areas." In 1954 she became an American citizen. A professor of English at Cypress Junior College in San Luis Obispo, California, Yamada is the author of poems and stories; she retired in 1989.

Yamada's poem concerns the compliant response to Executive Order 9066, which brought about the incarceration and relocation of the entire Japanese and Japanese American population on the Pacific coast—about 120,000 people. More than two-thirds of the people moved were native-born citizens of the United States. (The 158,000 Japanese residents of the Territory of Hawaii were not affected.) There was virtually no protest at the time, but in recent years the order has been widely regarded as an outrageous infringement on liberty, and some younger Japanese Americans cannot fathom why their parents and grandparents complied with it. This poem first appeared in Camp Notes and Other Poems *in 1976.*

To the Lady

The one in San Francisco who asked:
Why did the Japanese Americans let
the government put them in
those camps without protest?

Come to think of it I   5
    should've run off to Canada
    should've hijacked a plane to Algeria
    should've pulled myself up from my
    bra straps
    and kicked'm in the groin   10
    should've bombed a bank
    should've tried self-immolation
    should've holed myself up in a
    woodframe house
    and let you watch me   15
    burn up on the six o'clock news
    should've run howling down the street
    naked and assaulted you at breakfast
    by AP wirephoto
    should've screamed bloody murder   20
    like Kitty Genovese°

    Then
YOU would've
    come to my aid in shining armor
    laid yourself across the railroad track   25
    marched on Washington
    tattooed a Star of David on your arm
    written six million enraged
    letters to Congress
    But we didn't draw the line   30
    anywhere
    law and order Executive Order 9066
    social order moral order internal order
    YOU let'm
    I let'm   35
    All are punished.

21 Kitty Genovese In 1964 Kitty Genovese of Kew Gardens, New York, was stabbed to death when she left her car and walked toward her home. Thirty-eight persons heard her screams, but no one came to her assistance. [Editors' note.]

Topics for Critical Thinking and Writing

1. Has the lady's question (lines 2–4) ever crossed your mind? If so, what answers did you think of?

2. What, in effect, is the speaker really saying in lines 5 to 21? And in lines 22 to 29?

3. What possible arguments can you offer for and against the removal of Japanese Americans in 1942?

4. Do you think the survivors of the relocation are entitled to some sort of redress? Why, or why not? If you think they merit compensation, what should the compensation be?

34

What Is Happiness?

THOUGHTS ABOUT HAPPINESS, ANCIENT AND MODERN

Here are some brief comments about happiness, from ancient times to the present. Read them, think about them, and then write on one of the two topics that appear after the last quotation.

> Happiness is prosperity combined with virtue.
> —Aristotle (384–322 B.C.)

> Pleasure is the beginning and the end of living happily. . . . It is impossible to live pleasurably without living wisely, well, and justly, and impossible to live wisely, well, and justly without living pleasurably.
> —Epicurus (341–270 B.C.)

> Very little is needed to make a happy life.
> —Marcus Aurelius (121–180)

> Society can only be happy and free in proportion as it is virtuous.
> —Mary Wollstonecraft Shelley (1759–1797)

> The supreme happiness of life is the conviction that we are loved.
> —Victor Hugo (1802–1885)

> Ask yourself whether you are happy, and you cease to be so.
> —John Stuart Mill (1806–1873)

> A lifetime of happiness! No man alive could bear it: it would be hell on earth.
> —George Bernard Shaw (1856–1950)

> We have no more right to consume happiness without producing it than to consume wealth without producing it.
> —George Bernard Shaw (1856–1950)

> If only we'd stop trying to be happy, we could have a pretty good time.
> —Edith Wharton (1862–1937)

Happiness makes up in height for what it lacks in length.
— Robert Frost (1874–1963)

Point me out the happy man and I will point you out either egotism, selfishness, evil—or else an absolute ignorance.
— Graham Greene (1904–1991)

Those who are unhappy have no need for anything in this world but people capable of giving them their attention.
— Simone Weil (1909–1943)

Happiness is always a by-product. It is probably a matter of temperament, and for anything I know it may be glandular. But it is not something that can be demanded from life, and if you are not happy you had better stop worrying about it and see what treasures you can pluck from your own brand of unhappiness.
— Robertson Davies (1913–1995)

TOPICS FOR CRITICAL THINKING AND WRITING

1. If any one of these passages especially appeals to you, make it the thesis of an essay of about 500 words.

2. Take two of these passages—perhaps one that you especially like and one that you think is wrong-headed—and write a dialogue of about 500 words in which the two authors converse. They may each try to convince the other, or they may find that to some degree they share views and they may then work out a statement that both can accept. If you do take the position that one writer is on the correct track but the other is utterly mistaken, try to be fair to the view that you think is mistaken. (As an experiment in critical thinking, imagine that you accept it, and make the best case for it that you possibly can.)

Daniel Gilbert

Daniel Gilbert (b. 1957) a professor of psychology of Harvard, is the author of Stumbling on Happiness *(2006)—a best seller that won the Royal Society Prize ($20,000) for Science Books. Hearing of the award, Gilbert said, "There are very few countries, including my own, the United States, where a somewhat cheeky book about happiness could win a science prize—but the British invented intellectual humor and have always understood that enlightenment and entertainment are natural friends."*

A high school dropout, Gilbert was nineteen when he visited a community college, intending to take a writing course but enrolling instead in the only course still open—a psychology course.

We reprint here an essay that appeared in Time *a few days before Father's Day in June 2006.*

Does Fatherhood Make You Happy?

Sonora Smart Dodd was listening to a sermon on self-sacrifice when she decided that her father, a widower who had raised six children, deserved his very own national holiday. Almost a century later, people all over the world spend the third Sunday in June honoring their fathers with ritual offerings of aftershave and neckties, which leads millions of fathers to have precisely the same thought at precisely the same moment: "My children," they think in unison, "make me happy."

Could all those dads be wrong?

Studies reveal that most married couples start out happy and then become progressively less satisfied over the course of their lives, becoming especially disconsolate when their children are in diapers and in adolescence, and returning to their initial levels of happiness only after their children have had the decency to grow up and go away. When the popular press invented a malady called "empty-nest syndrome," it failed to mention that its primary symptom is a marked increase in smiling.

Psychologists have measured how people feel as they go about their daily activities, and have found that people are less happy when they are interacting with their children than when they are eating, exercising, shopping, or watching television. Indeed, an act of parenting makes most people about as happy as an act of housework. Economists have modeled the impact of many variables on people's overall happiness and have consistently found that children have only a small impact. A small negative impact.

Those findings are hard to swallow because they fly in the face of 5 our most compelling intuitions. We love our children! We talk about them to anyone who will listen, show their photographs to anyone who will look, and hide our refrigerators behind vast collages of their drawings, notes, pictures, and report cards. We feel confident that we are happy with our kids, about our kids, for our kids, and because of our kids — so why is our personal experience at odds with the scientific data?

Three reasons.

First, when something makes us happy we are willing to pay a lot for it, which is why the worst Belgian chocolate is more expensive than the best Belgian tofu. But that process can work in reverse: When we pay a lot for something, we assume it makes us happy, which is why we swear to the wonders of bottled water and Armani socks. The compulsion to care for our children was long ago written into our DNA, so we toil and sweat, lose sleep and hair, play nurse, housekeeper, chauffeur, and cook, and we do all that because nature just won't have it any other way. Given the high price we pay, it isn't surprising that we rationalize those costs and conclude that our children must be repaying us with happiness.

Second, if the Red Sox and the Yankees were scoreless until Manny Ramirez hit a grand slam in the bottom of the ninth, you can be sure that Boston fans would remember it as the best game of the season. Memories are dominated by their most powerful—and not their most typical—instances. Just as a glorious game-winning homer can erase our memory of eight and a half dull innings, the sublime moment when our three-year-old looks up from the mess she is making with her mashed potatoes and says, "I wub you, Daddy," can erase eight hours of no, not yet, not now, and stop asking. Children may not make us happy very often, but when they do, that happiness is both transcendent and amnesic.

Third, although most of us think of heroin as a source of human misery, shooting heroin doesn't actually make people feel miserable. It makes them feel really, really good—so good, in fact, that it crowds out every other source of pleasure. Family, friends, work, play, food, sex— none can compete with the narcotic experience; hence all fall by the wayside. The analogy to children is all too clear. Even if their company were an unremitting pleasure, the fact that they require so much company means that other sources of pleasure will all but disappear. Movies, theater, parties, travel—those are just a few of the English nouns that parents of young children quickly forget how to pronounce. We believe our children are our greatest joy, and we're absolutely right. When you have one joy, it's bound to be the greatest.

Our children give us many things, but an increase in our average 10 daily happiness is probably not among them. Rather than deny that fact, we should celebrate it. Our ability to love beyond all measure those who try our patience and weary our bones is at once our most noble and most human quality. The fact that children don't always make us happy—and that we're happy to have them nonetheless—is the fact for which Sonora Smart Dodd was so grateful. She thought we would all do well to remember it, every third Sunday in June.

TOPICS FOR CRITICAL THINKING AND WRITING

1. How would you define the "empty nest syndrome" (paras. 3–4)?

2. Do you believe the "studies" that Gilbert mentions in his third paragraph? Why, or why not? Similarly, do you believe the "psychologists" of the fourth paragraph? Explain.

3. What does Gilbert mean when he describes the happiness that children cause their parents as "transcendent" (para. 8)? Are there other, non-transcendent, kinds of happiness that parents experience?

4. Let's assume that even if you do not fully accept Gilbert's view about fatherhood and happiness, you are willing to grant that it is just possible that there may be something to what he says. Are you willing to take the next step and say that what he says of fatherhood—he was writing on Father's Day—may also be true of motherhood? Explain.

5. What do you think Gilbert's chief purpose is in this essay? To inform? To persuade? To entertain? Something else? Support your answer with evidence.

6. You may have been told that you should not write paragraphs consisting of only a sentence or two, but Gilbert's essay includes two such paragraphs, 2 and 6. Should Gilbert have revised these paragraphs? Or does their brevity serve a purpose? Explain.

Henry David Thoreau

Henry David Thoreau (1817–1862) was born in Concord, Massachusetts, where he spent most of his life ("I have travelled a good deal in Concord"). He taught and lectured, but chiefly he observed, thought, and wrote. From July 5, 1847, to September 6, 1847, he lived near Concord in a cabin at Walden Pond, an experience recorded in Walden *(1854).*

"As for Clothing" (editors' title) comes from Walden, *Chapter 1. "We do not Ride on the Railroad; It Rides upon Us" (also the editors' title) is from Chapter 2.*

Selections from *Walden*

[AS FOR CLOTHING]

As for Clothing, to come at once to the practical part of the question, perhaps we are led oftener by the love of novelty and a regard for the opinions of men, in procuring it, than by a true utility. Let him who has work to do recollect that the object of clothing is, first, to retain the vital heat, and secondly, in this state of society, to cover nakedness, and he may judge how much of any necessary or important work may be accomplished without adding to his wardrobe. Kings and queens who wear a suit but once, though made by some tailor or dressmaker to their majesties, cannot know the comfort of wearing a suit that fits. They are no better than wooden horses to hang the clean clothes on. Every day our garments become more assimilated to ourselves, receiving the impress of the wearer's character, until we hesitate to lay them aside, without such delay and medical appliances and some such solemnity even as our bodies. No man ever stood the lower in my estimation for having a patch in his clothes; yet I am sure that there is greater anxiety, commonly, to have fashionable, or at least clean and unpatched clothes, than to have a sound conscience. But even if the rent is not mended, perhaps the worst vice betrayed is improvidence. I sometimes try my acquaintances by such tests as these,—Who could wear a patch, or two extra seams only, over the knee? Most have as if they believed that their prospects for life would be ruined if they should do it. It would be easier for them to hobble to town with a broken leg than with a broken pantaloon. Often if an accident happens to a gentleman's legs, they can be mended; but if a similar accident happens to the legs of his pantaloons, there is no help for it; for he considers, not what is truly respectable, but what is respected. We know but few men, a great many coats and breeches. Dress a scarecrow in your last shift, you standing shiftless by, who would not soonest salute the scarecrow? Passing a cornfield the other day, close by a hat and coat on a stake, I recognized the owner of the farm. He was only a little more weather-beaten than when I saw him last. I have heard of a dog that barked at every stranger who approached his master's premises with clothes on, but was easily quieted by a naked thief. It is an interesting question how far men would retain their relative rank if they were divested of their clothes. Could you, in such a case, tell surely of any company of civilized men which belonged to the most respected class? When Madam Pfeiffer,[1] in her adventurous travels round the world, from east to west, had got so near home as Asiatic Russia, she says that she felt the necessity of wearing other than a traveling dress, when she went to meet the authorities, for she "was now in a civilized country, where . . . people are judged of by their clothes." Even in our democratic New England towns the accidental possession of wealth, and its manifestation in dress and equipage alone, obtain for the possessor almost universal respect. But they who yield such respect, numerous as they are, are so far heathen, and need to have a missionary sent to them. Beside, clothes introduced sewing, a kind of work which you may call endless; a woman's dress, at least, is never done.

A man who has at length found something to do will not need to get a new suit to do it in; for him the old will do, that has lain dusty in the garret for an indeterminate period. Old shoes will serve a hero longer than they have served his valet—if a hero even has a valet—bare feet are older than shoes, and he can make them do. Only they who go to soirées and legislative halls must have new coats, coats to change as often as the man changes in them. But if my jacket and trousers, my hat and shoes, are fit to worship God in, they will do; will they not? Who ever saw his old clothes—his old coat, actually worn out, resolved into its primitive elements, so that it was not a deed of charity to bestow it on some poor boy, by him perchance to be bestowed on some poorer still, or shall we say richer, who could do with less? I say, beware of all enterprises that require new clothes, and not rather a new wearer of clothes. If there is not a new man, how can the new clothes be made to fit? If you have any enterprise before you, try it in your old clothes. All men want, not something to *do with*, but something to *do*, or rather something to *be*. Perhaps we should never procure a new suit, however ragged or dirty the old, until we have so conducted, so enterprised or sailed in some way, that we feel like new men in the old, and that to retain it would be like keeping new wine in old bottles. Our moulting season, like that of the fowls must be a crisis in our lives. The loon retires

[1]**Madame Pfeiffer** Ida Pfeiffer (1797–1858), author of travel books. (All notes are the editors'.)

to solitary ponds to spend it. Thus also the snake casts its slough, and the caterpillar its wormy coat, by an internal industry and expansion; for clothes are but our outmost cuticle and mortal coil. Otherwise we shall be found sailing under false colors, and be inevitably cashiered at last by our own opinion, as well as that of mankind.

We don garment after garment, as if we grew like exogenous plants by addition without. Our outside and often thin and fanciful clothes are our epidermis, or false skin, which partakes not of our life, and may be stripped off here and there without fatal injury; our thicker garments, constantly worn, are our cellular integument, or cortex; but our shirts are our liber,[2] or true bark, which cannot be removed without girdling and so destroying the man. I believe that all races at some seasons wear something equivalent to the shirt. It is desirable that a man be clad so simply that he can lay his hands on himself in the dark, and that he live in all respects so compactly and preparedly, that, if an enemy take the town, he can, like the old philosopher, walk out the gate empty-handed without anxiety. While one thick garment is, for most purposes, as good as three thin ones, and cheap clothing can be obtained at prices really to suit customers; while a thick coat can be bought for five dollars, which will last as many years, thick pantaloons for two dollars, cowhide boots for a dollar and a half a pair, a summer hat for a quarter of a dollar, and a winter cap for sixty-two and a half cents, or a better be made at home at a nominal cost, where is he so poor that, clad in such a suit, *of his own earning*, there will not be found wise men to do him reverence?

When I ask for a garment of a particular form, my tailoress tells me gravely, "They do not make them so now," not emphasizing the "They" at all, as if she quoted an authority as impersonal as the Fates, and I find it difficult to get made what I want, simply because she cannot believe that I mean what I say, that I am so rash. When I hear this oracular sentence, I am for a moment absorbed in thought, emphasizing to myself each word separately that I may come at the meaning of it, that I may find out by what degree of consanguinity *They* are related to *me*, and what authority they may have in an affair which affects me so nearly; and finally, I am inclined to answer her with equal mystery, and without any more emphasis of the "they" — "It is true, they did not make them so recently, but they do now." Of what use this measuring of me if she does not measure my character, but only the breadth of my shoulders, as it were a peg to hang the coat on? We worship not the Graces, nor the Parcæ, but Fashion. She spins and weaves and cuts with full authority. The head monkey at Paris puts on a traveller's cap, and all the monkeys in America do the same. I sometimes despair of getting anything quite simple and honest done in this world by the help of men. They would have to be passed through a powerful press first, to squeeze their old notions out of them, so that they would not soon get upon their legs

[2]**liber** Inner bark of a tree.

again; and then there would be some one in the company with a maggot in his head, hatched from an egg deposited there nobody knows when, for not even fire kills these things, and you would have lost your labor. Nevertheless, we will not forget that some Egyptian wheat was handed down to us by a mummy.

On the whole, I think that it cannot be maintained that dressing has   5 in this or any country risen to the dignity of an art. At present men make shift to wear what they can get. Like shipwrecked sailors, they put on what they can find on the beach, and at a little distance, whether of space or time, laugh at each other's masquerade. Every generation laughs at the old fashions, but follows religiously the new. We are amused at beholding the costume of Henry VIII, or Queen Elizabeth, as much as if it was that of the King and Queen of the Cannibal Islands. All costume off a man is pitiful or grotesque. It is only the serious eye peering from and the sincere life passed within it which restrain laughter and consecrate the costume of any people. Let Harlequin be taken with a fit of the colic and his trappings will have to serve that mood too. When the soldier is hit by a cannon ball rags are as becoming as purple.

The childish and savage taste of men and women for new patterns keeps how many shaking and squinting through kaleidoscopes that they may discover the particular figure which this generation requires today. The manufacturers have learned that this taste is merely whimsical. Of two patterns which differ only by a few threads more or less of a particular color, the one will be sold readily, the other lie on the shelf, though it frequently happens that after the lapse of a season the latter becomes the most fashionable. Comparatively, tattooing is not the hideous custom which it is called. It is not barbarous merely because the printing is skin-deep and unalterable.

I cannot believe that our factory system is the best mode by which men may get clothing. The condition of the operatives is becoming every day more like that of the English; and it cannot be wondered at, since, as far as I have heard or observed, the principal object is, not that mankind may be well and honestly clad, but, unquestionably, that the corporations may be enriched. In the long run men hit only what they aim at. Therefore, though they should fail immediately, they had better aim at something high.

[WE DO NOT RIDE ON THE RAILROAD; IT RIDES UPON US]

Still we live meanly, like ants; though the fable tells us that we were long ago changed into men; like pygmies we fight with cranes; it is error upon error, and clout upon clout, and our best virtue has for its occasion a superfluous and evitable wretchedness. Our life is frittered away by detail. An honest man has hardly need to count more than his ten fingers, or in extreme cases he may add his ten toes, and lump the rest. Simplicity, simplicity, simplicity! I say, let your affairs be as two or three, and not a hundred or a thousand; instead of a million count half a dozen, and keep your accounts on your thumb nail. In the midst of this chopping sea of civilized life, such are the clouds and storms and quicksands and thousand-and-one items to be allowed for, that a man has to live, if he would not founder and go to the bottom and not make his port at all, by dead reckoning, and he must be a great calculator indeed who succeeds. Simplify, simplify. Instead of three meals a day, if it be necessary eat but one; instead of a hundred dishes, five; and reduce other things in proportion. Our life is like a German Confederacy, made up of petty states, with its boundary forever fluctuating, so that even a German cannot tell you how it is bounded at any moment. The nation itself, with all its so-called internal improvements, which, by the way are all external and superficial, is just such an unwieldy and overgrown establishment, cluttered with furniture and tripped up by its own traps, ruined by luxury and heedless expense, by want of calculation and a worthy aim, as the million households in the land; and the only cure for it as for them is in a rigid economy, a stern and more than Spartan simplicity of life and elevation of purpose. It lives too fast. Men think that it is essential that the *Nation* have commerce, and export ice, and talk through a telegraph, and ride thirty miles an hour, without a doubt, whether *they* do or not; but whether we should live like baboons or like men, is a little uncertain. If we do not get out sleepers,[3] and forge rails, and devote days and nights to the work, but go to tinkering upon our *lives* to improve *them*, who will build railroads? And if railroads are not built, how shall we get to heaven in season? But if we stay at home and mind our business, who will want railroads? We do not ride on the railroad; it rides upon us. Did you ever think what those sleepers are that underlie the railroad? Each one is a man, an Irishman, or a Yankee man. The rails are laid on them, and they are covered with sand, and the cars run smoothly over them. They are sound sleepers, I assure you. And every few years a new lot is laid down and run over; so that, if some have the pleasure of riding on a rail, others have the misfortune to be ridden upon. And when they run over a man that is walking in his sleep, a supernumerary sleeper in the wrong position, and wake him up, they suddenly stop the cars, and make a hue and cry about it, as if this were an exception. I am glad to know that it takes a gang of men for every five miles to keep the sleepers down and level in their beds as it is, for this is a sign that they may sometime get up again.

Topics for Critical Thinking and Writing

1. What, according to Thoreau, are the legitimate functions of clothing? What other functions does he reject, or fail to consider?

---

[3]**sleepers** The woody ties beneath railroad rails.

992   34 / WHAT IS HAPPINESS?

2. Many of Thoreau's sentences mean both what they say literally and something more; often, like proverbs, they express abstract or general truths in concrete, homely language. How might these sentences be interpreted?

   a. We know but few men, a great many coats and breeches.
   b. Dress a scarecrow in your last shift, you standing shiftless by, who would not soonest salute the scarecrow?
   c. If you have any enterprise before you, try it in your old clothes.
   d. Every generation laughs at the old fashions, but follows religiously the new.
   e. When the soldier is hit by a cannon ball rags are as becoming as purple.

3. We have just quoted some of Thoreau's epigrammatic sentences. Is this style effective or not? Explain.

4. Notice that Thoreau writes in long paragraph. (The first of them runs to more than 450 words — the length of many respectable essays. Can such long paragraphs do their job effectively? What is the job of a paragraph? Or is there no one such job?

5. Toward the end of paragraph 2 we meet the cliché "new wine in old bottles." Do you think his sentence is effective? Why, or why not? Was this expression a cliché already in Thoreau's day? Complete the following definition: "A word or phrase is a cliché if and only if . . . ."

6. In paragraph 7, Thoreau criticizes the factory system. Is the criticism mild or severe? Explain. Point out some of the earlier passages in which he touches on the relation of clothes to a faulty economic system.

7. In paragraph 8, Thoreau asserts that "Our life is frittered away by detail." First, is it possible to argue that "Yes, our life is frittered away by detail, but, perhaps oddly, attention to detail — studying for examinations, grading papers, walking the dog — is largely responsible for human happiness"? Explain.

Darrin M. McMahon

Darrin M. McMahon was educated at the University of California, Berkeley, where he received his Ph.D. in 1997. The author of Happiness: A History *(2006), he has taught at Columbia University, Yale University, and New York University.*

In Pursuit of Unhappiness

"Happy New Year!" We seldom think of those words as an order. But in some respects that is what they are.

Doesn't every American want to be happy? And don't most Americans yearn, deep down, to be happy all of the time? The right laid out in our nation's Declaration of Independence — to pursue happiness to our hearts content—is nowhere on better display than in the rites of the holiday season. With glad tidings and good cheer, we seek to bring one year to its natural happy conclusion, while preparing to usher in a happy new year and many happy returns.

Like the cycle of the seasons, our emphasis on mirth may seem timeless, as though human beings have always made merry from beginning to end. But in fact this preoccupation with perpetual happiness is relatively recent. As Thomas Carlyle observed in 1843, "'Happiness our being's end and aim' is at bottom, if we will count well, not yet two centuries old in the world."

Carlyle's arithmetic was essentially sound, for changes in both religious and secular culture since the seventeenth century made "happiness," in the form of pleasure or good feeling, not only morally acceptable but commendable in and of itself. While many discounted religious notions that consigned life in this world to misery and sin, others discovered signs of God's providence in earthly satisfaction. The result was at once to weaken and transpose the ideal of heavenly felicity, in effect bringing it to earth. Suffering was not our natural state. Happy was the way we were meant to be.

That shift was monumental, and its implications far reaching. Among   5 other things, it was behind the transformation of the holiday season from a time of pious remembrance into one of unadulterated bliss. Yet the effects were greater than that. As Carlyle complained, "Every pitifulest whipster that walks within a skin has had his head filled with the notion that he is, shall be, or by all human and divine laws ought to be, 'happy.'"

Carlyle was notoriously cranky, but his central insight—that the new doctrine of happiness tended to raise expectations that could never possibly be fulfilled—remains as relevant today as it was in 1843. Despite enjoying far better living standards and more avenues for pleasure than before, human beings are arguably no happier now than they've ever been.

Sociologists like to point out that the percentage of those describing themselves as "happy" or "very happy" has remained virtually unchanged in Europe and the United States since such surveys were first conducted in the 1950's. And yet, this January, like last year and next, the self-help industry will pour forth books promising to make us happier than we are today. The very demand for such books is a strong indication that they aren't working.

Should that be a cause for concern? Some critics say it is. For example, economists like Lord Richard Layard and Daniel Kahneman have argued that the apparent stagnancy of happiness in modern societies should prompt policymakers to shift their priorities from the creation of wealth to the creation of good feelings, from boosting gross national product to increasing gross national happiness.

But before we take such steps, we might do well to reflect on the darker side of holiday cheer: those mysterious blues that are apt to set in while the streamers stream and the corks pop; the little voice that even in the best of souls is sometimes moved to say, "Bah, humbug." As Carlyle put it, "The prophets preach to us, 'Thou shalt be happy; thou shalt love pleasant things.'" But as he well knew, the very commandment tended to undermine its fulfillment, even to make us sad.

Carlyle's sometime friend and long-time rival, the philosopher John   10 Stuart Mill, came to a similar conclusion. His words are all the more worth heeding in that Mill himself was a determined proponent of the greatest happiness for the greatest number. "Ask yourself whether you are happy, and you cease to be so," Mill concluded after recovering from a serious bout of depression. Rather than resign himself to gloom, however, Mill vowed instead to look for happiness in another way.

"Those only are happy," he came to believe, "who have their minds fixed on some object other than their own happiness; on the happiness of others; on the improvement of mankind, even on some art or pursuit, followed not as a means, but as itself an ideal end. Aiming thus at something else, they find happiness by the way." For our own culture, steeped as it is in the relentless pursuit of personal pleasure and endless cheer, that message is worth heeding.

So in these last days of 2005 I say to you, "Don't have a happy new year!" Have dinner with your family or walk in the park with friends. If you're so inclined, put in some good hours at the office or at your favorite charity, temple, or church. Work on your jump shot or your child's model trains. With luck, you'll find happiness by the by. If not, your time won't be wasted. You may even bring a little joy to the world.

Topics for Critical Thinking and Writing

1. Who or what gives us the "order" to be happy—or is the whole idea silly? (See paragraphs 1 and 9.) Explain.

2. What's the difference between happiness and pleasure, or are these two different ways of saying the same thing? Explain.

3. Has McMahon persuaded you to think of happiness in a fresh way? Explain.

4. McMahon's article was originally published on December 29, so it is not surprising that in his second paragraph he says his readers are preparing "to usher in a happy new year." Try to recall how you spent the most recent New Year's Eve. Was it a happy evening? Or was it tinged with melancholy, perhaps even with sorrow as you remembered sad things and hoped that the next year would be happier? If you can't remember New Year's Eve, think of the last year as a whole: Was it predominantly happy or unhappy? Or can't you judge it in such terms? Explain.

5. McMahon says (para. 4) that since the seventeenth century a shift in thinking has occurred: "Suffering [is] not our natural state. Happy was the way we were meant to be." Assume you are speaking to someone who has not read McMahon's essay. How would you explain this point?

6. John Stuart Mill (para. 10) is often described as a hedonist. What do you have to do or believe to be a hedonist? Are you a hedonist? Explain why or why not in 250 words.

7. Are you likely to take the advice McMahon offers in his final paragraph? Explain.

8. Suppose you believed that we (say, American citizens) are happier today than we were three centuries ago. How would you go about arguing for your belief?

Epictetus

Epictetus (pronounced Epic-TEE-tus) was born in Phrygia (now southwestern Turkey) some sixty years after Jesus and died about 135 c.e. His mother was a slave, and he was brought to Rome as a slave. At an uncertain date he was given his freedom, and he went to Nicopolis in northwestern Greece, where he taught philosophy. One of his students, a Roman named Flavius Arrian, recorded the teachings of Epictetus in two books written in Greek, the Discourses *(or* Lectures*) and the* Handbook *(or* Manual, *often known by its Greek title,* Enchiridion*).*

The doctrine that Epictetus taught is stoicism, which can be briefly characterized thus: The goal of life (as other philosophers of the period would agree) is "happiness" or "a flourishing life" (eudaimonia). The way to achieve this condition is to understand the nature of the good. Such things as health, wealth, and rank are not good because they do not always benefit those who possess them. True, such things are "preferred," and sickness, poverty, and low social status are "not preferred," but all of these are "indifferent" when it comes to being good or evil. The only true good is virtue. Yes, wealth can be useful, but it is not good or bad. What is good or bad is the way in which one makes use of what one has. The life that is happy or fruitful (eudaimôn) is the virtuous life. Of course, some things are beyond our power, but we are able to judge whatever comes to us, to see that what is "not preferred"—for instance poverty—is not bad but is morally indifferent (just as wealth is morally indifferent). And we also have the power to adapt ourselves to whatever comes our way. A slightly later contemporary reported that Epictetus said that if one wanted to be free from wrongdoing and wanted to live a peaceful life, then one should endure *and* abstain.

The stoic doctrine of enduring was put in its most uncompromising way by the Victorian poet William Ernest Henley (1849–1903), in a poem called "Invictus" (that is, "unconquered"). The first stanza runs thus:

> Out of the night that covers me,
> Black as the Pit from pole to pole,
> I thank whatever gods may be
> For my unconquerable soul.

And here is the final stanza:

> It matters not how strait the gate,
> How charged with punishment the scroll,
> I am the captain of my fate;
> I am the master of my soul.

From *The Handbook*

Translated by Helena Orozco

1. Some things are in our control, and some are not. Our opinions are within our control, and our choices, our likes and dislikes. In a word, whatever is our own doing. Beyond our control are our bodies, our possessions, reputation, position; in a word, things not our own doings.

Now, the things that are within our control are by nature free, unhindered, unimpeded, but those beyond our control are weak, slavish, hindered, up to others. Keep in mind, then, that if you think things are free that by nature are slavish, and if you think that things that are up to others are yours, you will be hindered, you will suffer, you will complain, you will blame the gods and your fellows. But, on the other hand, if you take as yours only what in fact is yours, and if you see that what belongs to others belongs to others, nobody will compel you, nobody will restrict you; you will blame nobody, and you will do nothing against your will. No one will harm you, you will have no enemies.

5. People are not disturbed by what happens but by the view they take of what happens. For instance, death is not to be feared; if it were to be feared, Socrates would have feared it. The fear consists in our wrong idea of death, our idea that it is to be feared. When, therefore, we are disturbed or feel grief, we should not blame someone else, but our [false] opinion. An uneducated person blames others for his misfortunes; a person just starting his education blames himself; an educated person blames neither others nor himself.

6. Do not take pride in any excellence that is not your own. If a horse could be proud, it might say, "I am handsome," and such a statement might be acceptable. But when you proudly say, "I have a handsome horse," you should understand that you are taking pride in a horse's good. What has the horse's good to do with you? What is yours? Only your reaction to things. When you behave in accordance with nature, you will take pride only in some good that is your own.

7. As when on a voyage, when the ship is at anchor, if you go ashore to get fresh water, you may amuse yourself by picking up a seashell or a vegetable, but keep the ship in mind. Be attentive to the captain's call, and when you hear the call, give up the trifles, or you will be thrown back into the ship like a bound sheep. So it is in life: If instead of a seashell or a vegetable, you are given a wife or child, fine, but when the captain calls, you must abandon these things without a second thought. And if you are old, keep close to the ship lest you are missing when you are called.

9. Sickness impedes the body but not the ability to make choices, unless you choose so. Lameness impedes the leg, but not the ability to

make choices, unless the mind chooses so. Remember this with regard to everything that happens: Happenings are impediments to something else, but not to you.

15. Remember, behave in life as though you are attending a banquet. Is a dish brought to you? Put out your hand and take a moderate share. Does the dish pass you by? Do not grab for it. Has it not yet reached you? Don't yearn for it, but wait until it reaches you. Do this with regard to children, a spouse, position, wealth, and eventually you will be worthy to banquet with the gods. And if you can forgo even the things that are set before you, you are worthy not only to feast with the gods but to rule with them.

17. Remember: You are an actor in a play that you did not write. If the play is short, then it is short; if long, then it is long. If the author has assigned you the part of a poor man, act it well. Do the same if your part is that of a lame man or a ruler or an ordinary citizen. This is yours to do: Act your part well (but picking the part belongs to someone else).

21. Keep in mind death and exile and all other things that appear terrible — especially death — and you will never harbor a low thought nor too eagerly covet anything.

36. At a feast, to choose the largest portion might satisfy your body but would be detrimental to the social nature of the affair. When you dine with another, then, keep in mind not only the value to the body of the dishes set before you, but the value of your behavior to your host and fellow diners.

43. Everything has two handles, one by which it can be carried and one by which it cannot. If your brother acts unjustly, do not take up the affair by the handle of his injustice, for it cannot be carried that way. Rather, take the other handle: He is your brother, he was brought up with you. Taken this way, it can be carried.

TOPICS FOR CRITICAL THINKING AND WRITING

1. Does Epictetus exaggerate the degree to which events in our lives are under our control? Write a 250-word essay explaining your answer.

2. Epictetus advises us not to fear death. What is his argument?

3. Would you agree with Epictetus that "sickness impedes the body but not the ability to make choices" (excerpt 9)? Is he wrong because there is such a thing as mental illness?

4. Choose one from among the eleven paragraphs by Epictetus that best expresses your own view of life — or are you entirely at odds with what Epictetus believes? Explain.

"If I won the lottery, I would go on living as I always did."

(© The New Yorker Collection, 1996, Mischa Richter from cartoonbank.com. All Rights Reserved.)

Bertrand Russell

Bertrand Russell (1872–1970), British mathematician and philosopher, was born in Wales and educated at Trinity College, Cambridge, where he later taught. His pacifist opposition to World War I cost him this teaching appointment and earned him a prison sentence of six months. In 1940 an appointment to teach at the College of the City of New York was withdrawn because of his unorthodox moral views. But he was not always treated shabbily. He won numerous prizes, including a Nobel Prize for Literature in 1950. Much of his work is highly technical, but he also wrote frequently for the general public. We reprint a passage from one of his most widely read books, The Conquest of Happiness *(1930).*

The Happy Life

The happy life is to an extraordinary extent the same as the good life. Professional moralists have made too much of self-denial, and in so doing have put the emphasis in the wrong place. Conscious self-denial leaves a man self-absorbed and vividly aware of what he has sacrificed; in consequence it fails often of its immediate object and almost always of its ultimate purpose. What is needed is not self-denial, but that kind of direction of interest outward which will lead spontaneously and naturally to the same acts that a person absorbed in the pursuit of his own virtue could only perform by means of conscious self-denial. I have written in this book as a hedonist, that is to say, as one who regards happiness as the good, but the acts to be recommended from the point of view of the hedonist are on the whole the same as those to be recommended by the sane moralist. The moralist, however, is too apt, though this is not, of course, universally true, to stress the act rather than the state of mind. The effects of an act upon the agent will be widely different, according to his state of mind at the moment. If you see a child drowning and save it as the result of a direct impulse to bring help, you will emerge none the worse morally. If, on the other hand, you say to yourself, "It is the part of virtue to succor the helpless, and I wish to be a virtuous man, therefore I must save this child," you will be an even worse man afterwards than you were before. What applies in this extreme case, applies in many other instances that are less obvious.

There is another difference, somewhat more subtle, between the attitude towards life that I have been recommending and that which is recommended by the traditional moralists. The traditional moralist, for example, will say that love should be unselfish. In a certain sense he is right, that is to say, it should not be selfish beyond a point, but it should undoubtedly be of such a nature that one's own happiness is bound up in its success. If a man were to invite a lady to marry him on the ground that he ardently desired her happiness and at the same time considered that she would afford him ideal opportunities of self-abnegation, I think it may be doubted whether she would be altogether pleased. Undoubtedly we should desire the happiness of those whom we love, but not as an alternative to our own. In fact the whole antithesis between self and the rest of the world, which is implied in the doctrine of self-denial, disappears as soon as we have any genuine interest in persons or things outside ourselves. Through such interests a man comes to feel himself part of the stream of life, not a hard separate entity like a billiard ball, which can have no relation with other such entities except that of collision. All unhappiness depends upon some kind of disintegration or lack of integration; there is disintegration within the self through lack of coördination between the conscious and the unconscious mind; there is lack of integration between the self and society, where the two are not knit together by the force of objective interests and affections. The happy man is the man who does not suffer from either of these failures of unity, whose personality is neither divided against itself nor pitted against the world. Such a man feels himself a citizen of the universe, enjoying freely the spectacle that it offers and the joys that it affords, untroubled by the thought of death because he feels himself not really separate from those who will come after him. It is in such profound instinctive union with the stream of life that the greatest joy is to be found.

TOPICS FOR CRITICAL THINKING AND WRITING

1. In his first paragraph Russell says, "The happy life is to an extraordinary extent the same as the good life." First of all, how do you suppose Russell knows this? How might one confirm or refute the statement? Second, do you agree with Russell? Explain in detail.

2. In his final paragraph Russell says that it is through their interests that people come to feel they are "part of the stream of life, not a hard separate entity like a billiard ball, which can have no relation with other such entities except that of collision." Does this sentence strike you as (a) effective and (b) probably true? Explain.

3. In the final sentence of the final paragraph, Russell says that happy people feel connected to themselves (do not feel internally divided) and connected to society (do not feel pitted against the world). Describe in some detail a person who seems to you connected to the self and to society. Do you think that person is happy? Explain. Describe two people, one of whom seems to you internally divided, and one of whom seems to you separated from society. Now think about yourself. Do you feel connected to yourself and to the world? If so, are you happy?

The Dalai Lama and Howard C. Cutler

The fourteenth Dalai ("ocean-wide") Lama ("superior person"), Tenzin Gyatso, is the spiritual leader of the Tibetan people but has lived in exile in Dharamsala, India, since 1959, when China invaded Tibet. In 1989 he was awarded the Nobel Peace Prize. In 1982 Howard C. Cutler, a psychiatrist who practices in Phoenix, Arizona, met the Dalai Lama while visiting India to study Tibetan medicine. Cutler and the Dalai Lama had frequent conversations, which Cutler later summarized and submitted to the Dalai Lama for approval. The material was then published in a book they entitled The Art of Happiness *(1998). We give one selection.*

Inner Contentment

Crossing the hotel parking lot on my way to meet with the Dalai Lama one afternoon, I stopped to admire a brand-new Toyota Land Cruiser, the type of car I had been wanting for a long time. Still thinking of that car as I began my session, I asked, "Sometimes it seems that our whole culture, Western culture, is based on material acquisition; we're surrounded, bombarded, with ads for the latest things to buy, the latest car and so on. It's difficult not to be influenced by that. There are so many things we want, things we desire. It never seems to stop. Can you speak a bit about desire?"

"I think there are two kinds of desire," the Dalai Lama replied. "Certain desires are positive. A desire for happiness. It's absolutely right. The desire for peace. The desire for a more harmonious world, a friendlier world. Certain desires are very useful.

"But at some point, desires can become unreasonable. That usually leads to trouble. Now, for example, sometimes I visit supermarkets. I really love to see supermarkets, because I can see so many beautiful things. So, when I look at all these different articles, I develop a feeling of desire, and my initial impulse might be, 'Oh, I want this; I want that.' Then, the second thought that arises, I ask myself, 'Oh, do I really need this?' The answer is usually no. If you follow after that first desire, that initial impulse, then very soon your pockets will empty. However, the other level of desire, based on one's essential needs of food, clothing, and shelter, is something more reasonable.

"Sometimes, whether a desire is excessive or negative depends on the circumstances or society in which you live. For example, if you live in a prosperous society where a car is required to help you manage in your daily life, then of course there's nothing wrong in desiring a car. But if you live in a poor village in India where you can manage quite well without a car but you still desire one, even if you have the money to buy it, it can ultimately bring trouble. It can create an uncomfortable feeling among your neighbors and so on. Or, if you're living in a more prosperous society and have a car but keep wanting more expensive cars, that leads to the same kind of problems."

"But," I argued, "I can't see how wanting or buying a more expen- 5 sive car leads to problems for an individual, as long as he or she can afford it. Having a more expensive car than your neighbors might be a problem for them—they might be jealous and so on—but having a new car would give you, yourself, a feeling of satisfaction and enjoyment."

The Dalai Lama shook his head and replied firmly, "No. . . . Self-satisfaction alone cannot determine if a desire or action is positive or negative. A murderer may have a feeling of satisfaction at the time he is committing the murder, but that doesn't justify the act. All the nonvirtuous actions—lying, stealing, sexual misconduct, and so on—are committed by people who may be feeling a sense of satisfaction at the time. The demarcation between a positive and a negative desire or action is not whether it gives you an immediate feeling of satisfaction but whether it ultimately results in positive or negative consequences. For example, in the case of wanting more expensive possessions, if that is based on a mental attitude that just wants more and more, then eventually you'll reach a limit of what you can get; you'll come up against reality. And when you reach that limit, then you'll lose all hope, sink down into depression, and so on. That's one danger inherent in that type of desire.

"So I think that this kind of excessive desire leads to greed—an exaggerated form of desire, based on overexpectation. And when you reflect upon the excesses of greed, you'll find that it leads an individual to a feeling of frustration, disappointment, a lot of confusion, and a lot of problems. When it comes to dealing with greed, one thing that is quite characteristic is that although it arrives by the desire to obtain something, it is not satisfied by obtaining. Therefore, it becomes sort of limitless, sort of bottomless, and that leads to trouble. One interesting thing about greed is that although the underlying motive is to seek satisfaction, the irony is that even after obtaining the object of your desire, you are still not satisfied. *The true antidote of greed is contentment.* If you have a strong sense of contentment, it doesn't matter whether you obtain the object or not; either way, you are still content."

So, how can we achieve inner contentment? There are two methods. One method is to obtain everything that we want and desire — all the money, houses, and cars; the perfect mate; and the perfect body. The Dalai Lama has already pointed out the disadvantage of this approach; if our wants and desires remain unchecked, sooner or later we will run up against something that we want but can't have. The second, and more reliable, method is not to have what we want but rather to want and appreciate what we have.

The other night, I was watching a television interview with Christopher Reeve, the actor who was thrown from a horse in 1994 and suffered a spinal cord injury that left him completely paralyzed from the neck down, requiring a mechanical ventilator even to breathe. When questioned by the interviewer about how he dealt with the depression resulting from his disability, Reeve revealed that he had experienced a brief period of complete despair while in the intensive care unit of the hospital. He went on to say, however, that these feelings of despair passed relatively quickly, and he now sincerely considered himself to be a "lucky guy." He cited the blessings of a loving wife and children but also spoke gratefully about the rapid advances of modern medicine (which he estimates will find a cure for spinal cord injury within the next decade), stating that if he had been hurt just a few years earlier, he probably would have died from his injuries. While describing the process of adjusting to his paralysis, Reeve said that while his feelings of despair resolved rather quickly, at first he was still troubled by intermittent pangs of jealousy that could be triggered by another's innocent passing remark such as, "I'm just gonna run upstairs and get something." In learning to deal with these feelings, he said, "I realized that the only way to go through life is to look at your assets, to see what you can still do; in my case, fortunately I didn't have any brain injury, so I still have a mind I can use." Focusing on his resources in this manner, Reeve has elected to use his mind to increase awareness and educate the public about spinal cord injury, to help others, and has plans to continue speaking as well as to write and direct films.[1]

TOPICS FOR CRITICAL THINKING AND WRITING

1. In the first paragraph, Cutler says that he had long wanted a Toyota Land Cruiser. Exactly why might a person want such a vehicle? Do you

[1]Christopher Reeve died on October 10, 2004. [Editors' note.]

want a Toyota Land Cruiser? Why, or why not? (By the way, a friend of ours—a professor of philosophy—says, "The key to happiness is the key to the ignition." In your opinion, how much truth is there in this philosophic view?)

2. At the end of paragraph 8, Cutler reports that the Dalai Lama suggests that the best way to achieve inner contentment "is not to have what we want but rather to want and appreciate what we have." In the next (final) paragraph, Cutler cites the example of Christopher Reeve. Drawing on your own experiences—which include your experience of persons whom you know or have heard about—can you offer confirming evidence? Explain.

3. Compare the Dalai Lama's views with those of Epictetus (p. 995). Would you say they are virtually the same? Explain.

C. S. Lewis

Clive Staples Lewis (1898–1963) taught medieval and Renaissance literature at Oxford, his alma mater, and later at Cambridge. He wrote about literature; he wrote fiction and poetry. Lewis became an atheist at age thirteen. He held that view until he was about thirty-one years old. He wrote numerous essays and books on Christianity from the point of view of a believer.

We Have No "Right to Happiness"

"After all," said Clare, "they had a right to happiness."

We were discussing something that once happened in our own neighborhood. Mr. A. had deserted Mrs. A. and got his divorce in order to marry Mrs. B., who had likewise got her divorce in order to marry Mr. A. And there was certainly no doubt that Mr. A. and Mrs. B. were very much in love with one another. If they continued to be in love, and if nothing went wrong with their health or their income, they might reasonably expect to be very happy.

It was equally clear that they were not happy with their old partners. Mrs. B. had adored her husband at the outset. But then he got smashed up in the war. It was thought he had lost his virility, and it was known that he had lost his job. Life with him was no longer what Mrs. B. had bargained for. Poor Mrs. A., too. She had lost her looks—and all her liveliness. It might be true, as some said, that she consumed herself by bearing his children and nursing him through the long illness that overshadowed their earlier married life.

You mustn't, by the way, imagine that A. was the sort of man who nonchalantly threw a wife away like the peel of an orange he'd sucked dry. Her suicide was a terrible shock to him. We all knew this, for he told us so himself. "But what could I do?" he said. "A man has a right to happiness. I had to take my one chance when it came."

I went away thinking about the concept of a "right to happiness."   5

At first this sounds to me as odd as a right to good luck. For I believe—whatever one school of moralists may say—that we depend for a very great deal of our happiness or misery on circumstances outside all human control. A right to happiness doesn't, for me, make much more sense than a right to be six feet tall, or to have a millionaire for your father, or to get good weather whenever you want to have a picnic.

I can understand a right as a freedom guaranteed me by the laws of the society I live in. Thus, I have a right to travel along the public roads because society gives me that freedom; that's what we mean by calling the roads "public." I can also understand a right as a claim guaranteed me by the laws, and correlative to an obligation on someone else's part. If I have a right to receive £100 from you, this is another way of saying that you have a duty to pay me £100. If the laws allow Mr. A. to desert his wife and seduce his neighbor's wife, then, by definition, Mr. A. has a legal right to do so, and we need bring in no talk about "happiness."

But of course that was not what Clare meant. She meant that he had not only a legal but a moral right to act as he did. In other words, Clare is—or would be if she thought it out—a classical moralist after the style of Thomas Aquinas, Grotius, Hooker, and Locke. She believes that behind the laws of the state there is a Natural Law.

I agree with her. I hold this conception to be basic to all civilization. Without it, the actual laws of the state become an absolute, as in Hegel. They cannot be criticized because there is no norm against which they should be judged.

The ancestry of Clare's maxim, "They have a right to happiness," is 10 august. In words that are cherished by all civilized men, but especially by Americans, it has been laid down that one of the rights of man is a right to "the pursuit of happiness." And now we get to the real point.

What did the writers of that august declaration mean?

It is quite certain what they did not mean. They did not mean that man was entitled to pursue happiness by any and every means—including, say, murder, rape, robbery, treason, and fraud. No society could be built on such a basis.

They meant "to pursue happiness by all lawful means"; that is, by all means which the Law of Nature eternally sanctions and which the laws of the nation shall sanction.

Admittedly this seems at first to reduce their maxim to the tautology that men (in pursuit of happiness) have a right to do whatever they have a right to do. But tautologies, seen against their proper historical context, are not always barren tautologies. The declaration is primarily a denial of the political principles which long governed Europe: a challenge flung down to the Austrian and Russian empires, to England before the Reform Bills, to Bourbon France. It demands that whatever means of pursuing happiness are lawful for any should be lawful for all; that "man," not men of some particular caste, class, status, or religion, should be free to use them. In a century when this is being unsaid by nation after nation and party after party, let us not call it a barren tautology.

But the question as to what means are "lawful"—what methods of pursuing happiness are either morally permissible by the Law of Nature or should be declared legally permissible by the legislature of a particular nation—remains exactly where it did. And on that question I disagree with Clare. I don't think it is obvious that people have the unlimited "right to happiness" which she suggests.

For one thing, I believe that Clare, when she says "happiness," means simply and solely "sexual happiness." Partly because women like Clare never use the word "happiness" in any other sense. But also because I never heard Clare talk about the "right" to any other kind. She was rather leftist in her politics, and would have been scandalized if anyone had defended the actions of a ruthless man-eating tycoon on the ground that his happiness consisted in making money and he was pursuing his happiness. She was also a rabid teetotaler; I never heard her excuse an alcoholic because he was happy when he was drunk.

A good many of Clare's friends, and especially her female friends, often felt— I've heard them say so—that their own happiness would be perceptibly increased by boxing her ears. I very much doubt if this would have brought her theory of a right to happiness into play.

Clare, in fact, is doing what the whole western world seems to me to have been doing for the last forty-odd years. When I was a youngster, all the progressive people were saying, "Why all this prudery? Let us treat sex just as we treat all our other impulses." I was simple-minded enough to believe they meant what they said. I have since discovered that they meant exactly the opposite. They meant that sex was to be treated as no other impulse in our nature has ever been treated by civilized people. All the others, we admit, have to be bridled. Absolute obedience to your instinct for self-preservation is what we call cowardice; to your acquisitive impulse, avarice. Even sleep must be resisted if you're a sentry. But every unkindness and breach of faith seems to be condoned provided that the object aimed at is "four bare legs in a bed."

It is like having a morality in which stealing fruit is considered wrong—unless you steal nectarines.

And if you protest against this view you are usually met with chatter about the legitimacy and beauty and sanctity of "sex" and accused of harboring some Puritan prejudice against it as something disreputable or shameful. I deny the charge. Foam-born Venus . . . golden Aphrodite . . . Our Lady of Cyprus . . . I never breathed a word against you. If I object to boys who steal my nectarines, must I be supposed to disapprove of nectarines in general? Or even of boys in general? It might, you know, be stealing that I disapproved of.

The real situation is skillfully concealed by saying that the question of Mr. A.'s "right" to desert his wife is one of "sexual morality." Robbing an orchard is not an offense against some special morality called "fruit morality." It is an offense against honesty. Mr. A.'s action is an offense against good faith (to solemn promises), against gratitude (toward one to whom he was deeply indebted) and against common humanity.

Our sexual impulses are thus being put in a position of preposterous privilege. The sexual motive is taken to condone all sorts of behavior which, if it had any other end in view, would be condemned as merciless, treacherous, and unjust.

Now though I see no good reason for giving sex this privilege, I think I see a strong cause. It is this.

It is part of the nature of a strong erotic passion—as distinct from a transient fit of appetite—that it makes more towering promises than any other emotion. No doubt all our desires make promises, but not so impressively. To be in love involves the almost irresistible conviction that one will go on being in love until one dies, and that possession of the beloved will confer, not merely frequent ecstasies, but settled, fruitful, deep-rooted, lifelong happiness. Hence *all* seems to be at stake. If we miss this chance we shall have lived in vain. At the very thought of such a doom we sink into fathomless depths of self-pity.

Unfortunately these promises are found often to be quite untrue. 25 Every experienced adult knows this to be so as regards all erotic passions (except the one he himself is feeling at the moment). We discount the world-without-end pretensions of our friends' amours easily enough. We know that such things sometimes last—and sometimes don't. And when they do last, this is not because they promised at the outset to do so. When two people achieve lasting happiness, this is not solely because they are great lovers but because they are also—I must put it crudely—good people; controlled, loyal, fairminded, mutually adaptable people.

If we establish a "right to (sexual) happiness" which supersedes all the ordinary rules of behavior, we do so not because of what our passion shows itself to be in experience but because of what it professes to be while we are in the grip of it. Hence, while the bad behavior is real and works miseries and degradations, the happiness which was the object of the behavior turns out again and again to be illusory. Everyone (except Mr. A. and Mrs. B.) knows that Mr. A. in a year or so may have the same reason for deserting his new wife as for deserting his old. He will feel again that all is at stake. He will see himself again as the great lover, and his pity for himself will exclude all pity for the woman.

Two further points remain.

One is this. A society in which conjugal infidelity is tolerated must always be in the long run a society adverse to women. Women, whatever a few male songs and satires may say to the contrary, are more naturally monogamous than men; it is a biological necessity. Where promiscuity prevails, they will therefore always be more often the victims than the culprits. Also, domestic happiness is more necessary to them than to us. And the quality by which they most easily hold a man, their beauty, decreases every year after they have come to maturity, but this does not happen to those qualities of personality—women don't really care twopence about our *looks*—by which we hold women. Thus in the ruthless war of promiscuity women are at a double disadvantage. They play for higher stakes and are also more likely to lose. I have no sympathy with moralists who frown at the increasing crudity of female provocativeness. These signs of desperate competition fill me with pity.

Secondly, though the "right to happiness" is chiefly claimed for the sexual impulse, it seems to me impossible that the matter should stay there. The fatal principle, once allowed in that department, must sooner or later seep through our whole lives. We thus advance toward a state of society in which not only each man but every impulse in each man claims *carte blanche*. And then, though our technological skill may help us survive a little longer, our civilization will have died at heart, and will— one dare not even add "unfortunately"—be swept away.

TOPICS FOR CRITICAL THINKING AND WRITING

1. Having read the entire essay, look back at Lewis's first five paragraphs and point out the ways in which he is not merely recounting an episode but is already conveying his attitude and seeking to persuade his readers.

2. Do you want to argue: If I have a right to happiness, you or someone has a duty to see to it that I'm happy (see para. 7)? Or do you want to argue: No one has a right to happiness because no one has a duty to make anyone happy? Argue one of these positions in 250 words.

3. What's the difference between being happy in a marriage and being content in a marriage? Explain the difference in an essay of 250 words.

4. What is absurd about the idea (para. 6) of having "a right to be six feet tall"? Explain in 100 words or fewer.

5. What, if anything, do the absurd candidates for rights (para. 6) have in common?

6. What's the difference between having a legal right to something and having a moral right to that thing (see paras. 8–9)? Give an example of each.

7. Do you agree with Lewis (paras. 26, 29) that "a right to happiness" really means "a right to sexual happiness"? Why, or why not?

8. Do you agree with Lewis (para. 28) that monogamy is "a biological necessity" for women? Explain, in an essay of 250 words.

Danielle Crittenden

Danielle Crittenden (b. 1963), the founder of The Woman's Quarterly, *has written for numerous publications, including the* New York Times *and the* Wall Street Journal. *We reprint a selection from her book,* What Our

Mothers Didn't Tell Us: Why Happiness Eludes the Modern Woman *(1999). Not all readers agree with her contention that women can be happy only if they will put aside what she sees as misleading feminist ideas.*

About Love

From a feminist view, it would be nice, I suppose—or at the very least handy—if we were able to derive total satisfaction from our solitude, to be entirely self-contained organisms, like earthworms or amoebas, having relations with the opposite sex whenever we felt a need for it but otherwise being entirely contented with our own company. Every woman's apartment could be her Walden Pond. She'd be free of the romantic fuss and interaction that has defined, and given meaning to, human existence since its creation. She could spend her evenings happily ensconced with a book or a rented video, not having to deal with some bozo's desire to watch football or play mindless video games. How children would fit into this vision of autonomy, I'm not sure, but surely they would infringe upon it; perhaps she could simply farm them out. If this seems a rather chilling outcome to the quest for independence, well, it is. If no man is an island, then no woman can be, either. And it's why most human beings fall in love, and continue to take on all the commitments and responsibilities of family life. We *want* the warm body next to us on the sofa in the evenings; we *want* the noise and embrace of family around us; we *want,* at the end of our lives, to look back and see that what we have done amounts to more than a pile of pay stubs, that we have loved and been loved, and brought into this world life that will outlast us.

The quest for autonomy—the need "to be oneself" or, as Wurtzel declares, the intention "to answer only to myself"—is in fact not a brave or noble one; nor is it an indication of strong character. Too often, autonomy is merely the excuse of someone who is so fearful, so weak, that he or she can't bear to take on any of the responsibilities that used to be shouldered by much younger but more robust and mature souls. I'm struck by the number of my single contemporaries—men and women in their early to mid-thirties—who speak of themselves as if they were still twenty years old, just embarking upon their lives and not, as they actually are, already halfway through them. In another era, a thirty-three-year-old man or woman might have already lived through a depression and a world war and had several children. Yet at the suggestion of marriage—or of buying a house or of having a baby—these modern thirtysomethings will exclaim, "But I'm so young!" their crinkled eyes widening at the thought. In the relationships they do have—even "serious" ones—they will take pains to avoid the appearance of anything that smacks of permanent commitment. The strange result is couples who are willing to share *everything* with each other—leases, furniture, cars, weekends, body fluids, holidays with their relatives—just as long as it comes with the right to cancel the relationship *at any moment.*

Unfortunately, postponing marriage and all the responsibilities that go with it does not prolong youth. It only prolongs the illusion of it, and then again only in one's own eyes. The traits that are forgivable in a twenty-year-old—the constant wondering about who you are and what you will be; the readiness to chuck one thing, or person, for another and move on—are less attractive in a thirty-two-year-old. More often what results is a middle-aged person who retains all the irritating self-absorption of an adolescent without gaining any of the redeeming qualities of maturity. Those qualities—wisdom, a sense of duty, the willingness to make sacrifices for others, an acceptance of aging and death—are qualities that spring directly from our relationships and commitments to others.

A woman will not understand what true dependency is until she is cradling her own infant in her arms; nor will she likely achieve the self-confidence she craves until she has withstood, and transcended, the weight of responsibility a family places upon her—a weight that makes all the paperwork and assignments of her in-basket seem feather-light. The same goes for men. We strengthen a muscle by using it, and that is true of the heart and mind, too. By waiting and waiting and waiting to commit to someone, our capacity for love shrinks and withers. This doesn't mean that women or men should marry the first reasonable person to come along, or someone with whom they are not in love. But we should, at a much earlier age than we do now, take a serious attitude toward dating and begin preparing ourselves to settle down. For it's in the act of taking up the roles we've been taught to avoid or postpone— wife, husband, mother, father—that we build our identities, expand our lives, and achieve the fullness of character we desire.

Still, critics may argue that the old way was no better; that the risk of loss women assume by delaying marriage and motherhood overbalances the certain loss we'd suffer by marrying too early. The habit of viewing marriage as a raw deal for women is now so entrenched, even among women who don't call themselves feminists, that I've seen brides who otherwise appear completely happy apologize to their wedding guests for their surrender to convention, as if a part of them still feels there is something embarrassing and weak about an intelligent and ambitious woman consenting to marry. But is this true? Or is it just an alibi we've been handed by the previous generation of women in order to justify the sad, lonely outcomes of so many lives?

What we rarely hear—or perhaps are too fearful to admit—is how *liberating* marriage can actually be. As nerve-racking as making the decision can be, it is also an enormous relief once it is made. The moment we say, "I do," we have answered one of the great, crucial questions of our lives: We now know with whom we'll be spending the rest of our years, who will be the father of our children, who will be our family. That our marriages may not work, that we will have to accommodate ourselves to the habits and personality of someone else—these are, and always have been, the risks of commitment, of love itself. What is important is that our lives have been thrust forward. The negative—that we are no longer able to live entirely for ourselves—is also the positive: *We no longer have to live entirely for ourselves!* We may go on to do any number of interesting things, but we are free of the gnawing wonder of *with whom* we will do them. We have ceased to look down the tunnel, waiting for a train.

The pull between the desire to love and be loved and the desire to be free is an old, fierce one. If the error our grandmothers made was to have surrendered too much of themselves for others, this was perhaps better than not being prepared to surrender anything at all. The fear of losing oneself can, in the end, simply become an excuse for not giving any of oneself away. Generations of women may have had no choice but to commit themselves to marriage early and then to feel imprisoned by their lifelong domesticity. So many of our generation have decided to put it off until it is too late, not foreseeing that lifelong independence can be its own kind of prison, too.

TOPICS FOR CRITICAL THINKING AND WRITING

1. In her second paragraph Crittenden quotes a writer who speaks of "the need 'to be oneself.'" What does "to be oneself" mean? Perhaps begin at the beginning: What is "oneself"? In *Hamlet,* Polonius says to his son,

   > This above all, to thine own self be true,
   > And it must follow, as the night the day,
   > Thou canst not then be false to any man.

   What is the "self" to which one should be true? Notice that in the fourth paragraph Crittenden says that "it's in the act of taking up [certain] roles . . . that we build our identities, expand our lives, and achieve the fullness of character we desire." Does this make sense to you? Explain.

2. In her third paragraph Crittenden talks about "postponing marriage and all the responsibilities that go with it." What responsibilities go with marriage? Might these responsibilities *add* to one's happiness? Explain.

3. In paragraph 6, Crittenden says, "What we rarely hear . . . is how *liberating* marriage can actually be." Consider the married people whom you know best. Does Crittenden's statement apply to some? To most? Does your experience—your familiarity with some married people—tend to offer evidence that confirms or refutes her assertion? Explain.

Judy Brady

Born in San Francisco in 1937, Judy Brady married in 1960 and two years later earned a bachelor's degree in painting at the University of Iowa. Active in the women's movement and in other political causes, she has worked as an author, an editor, and a secretary. The essay reprinted here, written before she and her husband separated, appeared originally in the first issue of Ms. *magazine in 1971.*

I Want a Wife

I belong to that classification of people known as wives. I am A Wife. And, not altogether incidentally, I am a mother.

Not too long ago a male friend of mine appeared on the scene fresh from a recent divorce. He had one child, who is, of course, with his ex-wife. He is looking for another wife. As I thought about him while I was ironing one evening, it suddenly occurred to me that I, too, would like to have a wife. Why do I want a wife?

I would like to go back to school so that I can become economically independent, support myself, and, if need be, support those dependent upon me. I want a wife who will work and send me to school. And while I am going to school I want a wife to take care of my children. I want a wife to keep track of the children's doctor and dentist appointments. And to keep track of mine, too. I want a wife to make sure my children eat properly and are kept clean. I want a wife who will wash the children's clothes and keep them mended. I want a wife who is a good nurturant attendant to my children, who arranges for their schooling, makes sure that they have an adequate social life with their peers, takes them to the park, the zoo, etc. I want a wife who takes care of the children when they are sick, a wife who arranges to be around when the children need special care, because, of course, I cannot miss classes at school. My wife must arrange to lose time at work and not lose the job. It may mean a small cut in my wife's income from time to time, but I guess I can tolerate that. Needless to say, my wife will arrange and pay for the care of the children while my wife is working.

I want a wife who will take care of *my* physical needs. I want a wife who will keep my house clean. A wife who will pick up after my children, a wife who will pick up after me. I want a wife who will keep my clothes clean, ironed, mended, replaced when need be, and who will see to it that my personal things are kept in their proper place so that I can find what I need the minute I need it. I want a wife who cooks the meals, a wife who is a *good* cook. I want a wife who will plan the menus, do the necessary grocery shopping, prepare the meals, serve them pleasantly, and then do the cleaning up while I do my studying. I want a wife who will care for me when I am sick and sympathize with my pain and loss of time from school. I want a wife to go along when our family takes a vacation so that someone can continue to care for me and my children when I need a rest and change of scene.

I want a wife who will not bother me with rambling complaints 5 about a wife's duties. But I want a wife who will listen to me when I feel the need to explain a rather difficult point I have come across in my course of studies. And I want a wife who will type my papers for me when I have written them.

I want a wife who will take care of the details of my social life. When my wife and I are invited out by my friends, I want a wife who will take care of the babysitting arrangements. When I meet people at school that I like and want to entertain, I want a wife who will have the house clean, will prepare a special meal, serve it to me and my friends, and not interrupt when I talk about things that interest me and my friends. I want a wife who will have arranged that the children are fed and ready for bed before my guests arrive so that the children do not bother us. I want a wife who takes care of the needs of my guests so that they feel comfortable, who makes sure that they have an ashtray, that they are passed the hors d'oeuvres, that they are offered a second helping of the food, that their wine glasses are replenished when necessary, that their coffee is served to them as they like it. And I want a wife who knows that sometimes I need a night out by myself.

I want a wife who is sensitive to my sexual needs, a wife who makes love passionately and eagerly when I feel like it, a wife who makes sure that I am satisfied. And, of course, I want a wife who will not demand sexual attention when I am not in the mood for it. I want a wife who assumes the complete responsibility for birth control, because I do not want more children. I want a wife who will remain sexually faithful to me so that I do not have to clutter up my intellectual life with jealousies. And I want a wife who understands that *my* sexual needs may entail more than strict adherence to monogamy. I must, after all, be able to relate to people as fully as possible.

If, by chance, I find another person more suitable as a wife than the wife I already have, I want the liberty to replace my present wife with another one. Naturally, I will expect a fresh, new life; my wife will take the children and be solely responsible for them so that I am left free.

When I am through with school and have a job, I want my wife to quit working and remain at home so that my wife can more fully and completely take care of a wife's duties.

My God, who *wouldn't* want a wife?   10

TOPICS FOR CRITICAL THINKING AND WRITING

1. If one were to summarize Brady's first paragraph, one might say it adds up to "I am a wife and a mother." But analyze it closely. Exactly what does the second sentence add to the first? And what does "not altogether incidentally" add to the third sentence?

2. Brady uses the word *wife* in sentences where one ordinarily would use *she* or *her*. Why? And why does she begin paragraphs 4, 5, 6, and 7 with the same words, "I want a wife"?

3. In her second paragraph Brady says that the child of her divorced male friend "is, of course, with his ex-wife." In the context of the entire essay, what does this sentence mean?

4. Complete the following sentence by offering a definition: "According to Judy Brady, a wife is . . ."

5. Try to state the essential argument of Brady's essay in a simple syllogism. (*Hint:* Start by identifying the thesis or conclusion you think she is trying to establish, and then try to formulate two premises, based on what she has written, that would establish the conclusion.)

6. Drawing on your experience as observer of the world around you (and perhaps as husband, wife, or former spouse), do you think Brady's picture of a wife's role is grossly exaggerated? Or is it (allowing for some serious playfulness) fairly accurate, even though it was written in 1971? If grossly exaggerated, is the essay therefore meaningless? If fairly accurate, what attitudes and practices does it encourage you to support? Explain.

7. Whether or not you agree with Brady's vision of marriage in our society, write an essay (500 words) titled "I Want a Husband," imitating her style and approach. Write the best possible essay, and then decide which of the two essays—yours or hers—makes a fairer comment on current society. Or if you believe Brady is utterly misleading, write an essay titled "I Want a Wife," seeing the matter in a different light.

8. If you feel that you have been pressed into an unappreciated, unreasonable role—built-in babysitter, listening post, or girl (or boy or man or woman) Friday—write an essay of 500 words that will help the reader to see both your plight and the injustice of the system. (*Hint:* A little humor will help to keep your essay from seeming to be a prolonged whine.)

Duke University, Policy on Consensual Relationships. Reprinted by permission of Duke University.

Tufts University, Policy on Sexual Harassment, Medford MA, June 26, 2009. Reprinted by permission of Tufts University. All rights reserved.

Carol Weston, Letter in response to Harlan Coben's New York Times Op-Ed "The Undercover Parent" March 16, 2008. Reprinted by permission of Carol Weston, author of *GirlTalk: All the Stuff Your Sister Never Told You.*

George F. Will, "Being Green at Ben and Jerry's." Originally published in *Newsweek*, May 6, 2002, p. 72. Copyright © George F. Will. Reprinted by permission of the author.

Ellen Willis, " Putting Women Back into the Abortion Debate." First published in *The Village Voice*, July 16, 1985. From *No More Nice Girls* by Ellen Willis. Copyright © 1993 by Ellen Willis. Reprinted by permission.

Garry Wills, "The Dramaturgy of Death." From *The New York Review of Books*, June 21, 2001. Copyright © 2001 NYREV, Inc. Reprinted by permission of *The New York Review of Books*.

Edward O. Wilson, from *The Creation: An Appeal To Save Life On Earth* by Edward O. Wilson. Copyright © 2006 by Edward O. Wilson. Used by permission of W.W. Norton & Company, Inc.

James Q. Wilson, "Just Take Away Their Guns" *New York Times*, Magazine Section, 3/20/1994. Copyright 1994 by the New York Times Co. Reprinted by permission. All rights reserved.

James Q. Wilson, "Against the Legalization of Drugs." *Commentary*, February 1990. Copyright © 1990 by James Q. Wilson. Reprinted by permission.

Mitsuye Yamada, *Camp Notes and Other Poems.* Copyright © 1998 by Mitsuye Yamada. Reprinted by permission of Rutgers University Press.

Art Credits

Airport security, By permission of Gary Markstein and Creators Syndicate, Inc.

"All I'm getting out of him is a lot of profanity" © Frank Cotham/Condé Nast Publications/ www. cartoonbank.com

"Anabolic Steroid Research Report" Web page, Courtesy of National Institute on Drug Abuse

Attention Paid to a Poor Sick Negro, From Josiah Priest, *Biblical Defense of Slavery*

"Bloggers' Legal Guide" screen capture, http://www.eff.org/issues/bloggers/legal

Boy and girl in classroom, © Corbis

Calvin and Hobbes, "I used to hate writing assignments . . ." CALVIN AND HOBBES ©1993 Watterson. Dist. By UNIVERSAL UCLICK. Reprinted by permission. All rights reserved.

Coffins at Dover Air Force Base, Getty Images

"Cyberporn", Reprinted through the courtesy of the Editors of *Time* Magazine © 2009 Time Inc.

Department of Logic, © Robert Mankoff/Condé Nast Publications/www.cartoonbank.com

Diagram of slave ship, The Lundoff Collection

Dorothea Lange, Mother and Two Children, Library of Congress, Prints and Photographs Division, Washington, DC; Mother, Child, and Baby, Library of Congress, Prints and Photographs Division, Washington, DC

Equal Rights Amendment buttons, David J. & Janice L. Frent Collection/Corbis

Execution of Viet Cong prisoner, Saigon, 1968, AP Images/Eddie Adams

"Gays and lesbians getting married . . ." © Michael Shaw/Condé Nast Publications/ www.cartoonbank.com

Home of a Rebel Sharpshooter, Gettysburg, July, 1863 by Alexander Gardner. Courtesy of the Division of Rare & Manuscript Collections, Cornell University Library.

"I got ten dollars for my birthday, Miss Kellerman," © Original Artist/CartoonStock

"I'd like you to keep your ears open . . ." ©1997 Randy Glasbergen

"I've finally decided to go to college . . ." © Mary Petty/Condé Nast Publications/www .cartoonbank.com

"If I won the lottery . . ." © Mischa Richter/Condé Nast Publications/www.cartoonbank.com

"In the Blood" screen capture, www.newyorker.com/The New Yorker; Courtesy of Condé Nast Publications.

Landfill, Walter Bibikow/Getty Images

The Man on the Left, Courtesy: DeVito/Verdi, New York, NY

Index of Authors and Titles

Index of Terms

DIRECTORY TO DOCUMENTATION MODELS IN MLA FORMAT

IN-TEXT OR PARENTHETICAL CITATIONS, 290

LIST OF WORKS CITED, 295

IDEA PROMPTS

Below is an index to the Idea Prompts that appear in the book.
Idea Prompts provide models and strategies for: